# THE PAPERS OF MARTIN LUTHER KING, JR.

*Initiated by*

The King Center

*in association with*

Stanford University

After a request to negotiate with the Albany City Commission on 27 July 1962 was denied, King, Ralph Abernathy, William G. Anderson, and seven others are escorted to jail by Police Chief Laurie Pritchett for disorderly conduct, congregating on the sidewalk, and disobeying a police officer. © Corbis.

# THE PAPERS OF MARTIN LUTHER KING, JR.

VOLUME VII

## To Save the Soul of America

*January 1961–August 1962*

*Senior Editor*

Clayborne Carson

*Volume Editor*

Tenisha Armstrong

UNIVERSITY OF CALIFORNIA PRESS

University of California Press, one of the most distinguished university presses in the United States, enriches lives around the world by advancing scholarship in the humanities, social sciences, and natural sciences. Its activities are supported by the UC Press Foundation and by philanthropic contributions from individuals and institutions. For more information, visit www.ucpress.edu.

University of California Press
Oakland, California

Library of Congress Cataloging-in-Publication Data
King, Martin Luther, Jr., 1929–1968.
  The papers of Martin Luther King, Jr.
    V. 7. To Save the Soul of America, January 1961–August 1962
    Contents: V. 1. Called to serve, January 1929–June 1951—
V. 2. Rediscovering precious values, July 1951–November 1955—
V. 3. Birth of a new age, December 1955–December 1956—
V. 4. Symbol of the movement, January 1957–December 1958—
V. 5. Threshold of a new decade, January 1959–December 1960—
V. 6. Advocate of the social gospel, September 1948–March 1963.
      p.    cm.
  Includes bibliographical references and index.
  ISBN-978-0-520-28269-8 (cloth: alk. paper).
    1. Afro-Americans—Civil rights.   2. Civil rights movements—
United States—History—20th century.   3. King, Martin Luther, Jr., 1929–1968—Archives.   4. United States—Race relations.   I. Carson, Clayborne, 1944–   .  II. Armstrong, Tenisha   III. Title.

E185.97.K5A2   2014
323'092—dc22                                              91-42336

Manufactured in the United States of America

23  22  21  20  19  18  17  16  15  14
10  9  8  7  6  5  4  3  2  1

The paper used in this publication meets the minimum requirements of ANSI/NISO Z39.48-1992 (R 1997) (*Permanence of Paper*).

*The thing that is hurting us most is the continued
existence of segregation and discrimination, and we
think we're rendering a great service to our nation.
For this is not a struggle for ourselves alone;
it is a struggle to save the soul of America.*

MARTIN LUTHER KING, JR.
*23 May 1961*

The editors of the Martin Luther King, Jr., Papers Project wish to acknowledge the generosity of the following major contributors, without whose support this volume would not have been possible.

*Martin Luther King, Jr., Research and Education Institute Founding Endowment Donors*

Ronnie Lott/All Stars Helping Kids
The Mumford Family–Agape Foundation

*Sustaining Contributors*

Ronnie Lott/All Stars Helping Kids
Myra Reinhard Family Foundation/All Stars Helping Kids
National Endowment for the Humanities
National Historical Publications and Records Commission
Stanford University
The Andrew W. Mellon Foundation

*Major Contributors*

Clayborne and Susan Carson
Betty A. Williams Curtis and G. Russell Curtis, Sr.
Do A Little Fund
Fletcher Asset Management, Inc.
Google
The William and Flora Hewlett Foundation
Herbert Kurz
Leonard Merrill Kurz
Lilly Endowment Inc.
Jay and Kimberly Mitchell
The Peninsula Community Foundation
George P. Shultz
Andrea McEvoy Spero and Jason D. Spero
Woodside Summit Group, Inc.

*Patrons*

John and Carolyn Barnes
Bob Ceremsak (Goldman, Sachs & Co.)
Wayne Duckworth

*The Papers of Martin Luther King, Jr.*

CLAYBORNE CARSON,
*Senior Editor*

ADVISORY BOARD

The publishers gratefully acknowledge the many individuals and foundations that have contributed to the publication of the Papers of Martin Luther King, Jr., and the General Endowment Fund of the Associates of the University of California Press for its contribution toward the publication of this volume.

Our special thanks to Maya Angelou, Sukey Garcetti, Maxine Griggs, Mary Jane Hewitt, Franklin Murphy, Joan Palevsky, and Marilyn Solomon for their leadership during the campaign.

*Challenge Grant*

Times Mirror Foundation

*Leadership Grants*

The Ahmanson Foundation
AT&T Foundation

*Partners*

ARCO Foundation
William H. Cosby and Camille O. Cosby
The George Gund Foundation
The Walter and Elise Haas Fund
LEF Foundation
Sally Lilienthal
J. Michael Mahoney
The Andrew W. Mellon Foundation
National Historical Publications and Records Commission
Peter Norton Family Foundation
Joan Palevsky
The Ralph M. Parsons Foundation

CONTENTS

ILLUSTRATIONS

*Photographs*

*Facsimiles*

# ACKNOWLEDGMENTS

The Martin Luther King, Jr., Papers Project continues to rely on the generous contributions of many individuals who are drawn together by a common desire to disseminate the ideas of King and the social justice movements he inspired. The participants in the project's editorial and research activities constitute a uniquely dedicated and talented community. As the project's director, I have appreciated the opportunity to work closely with my colleagues, both staff members and student researchers, and with supporters who contributed funding, historical information, documents, and generous encouragement. In the previous six volumes of this edition, I have described the contributions of many individuals whose association with the Project has been long-term. Thus, I will focus attention on those contributions since the completion of *Volume VI: Advocate of the Social Gospel* that have been of particular significance during the final stages of this volume's preparation.

## *Institutional Support*

The King Papers Project would not be possible without the continuing support of the Martin Luther King, Jr., Estate and the King Center in Atlanta. This cooperative relationship was initiated in 1985 by the King Center's founding president, the late Coretta Scott King, and has been maintained in recent years by the heirs of the King Estate: Martin Luther King III, Dexter King, and Bernice King. We are also grateful for the assistance provided to us by the staff of the King Library and Archive, particularly the Director of Archives, Cynthia Lewis, and her assistant, Elaine Hall.

Since 1997, when the responsibility for the administration of the Project's federal grants was transferred from the King Center to Stanford University, we have benefited more than ever from Stanford's research resources and administrative support. The Project has been very fortunate to count on the enthusiastic backing of President John Hennessy and Provost John Etchemendy. Regarding the Project's ongoing needs, Vice Provost for Undergraduate Education Harry J. Elam, Jr., and Dean of Humanities and Sciences Richard P. Saller have been consistently gracious and supportive. We are also thankful for the encouragement of History Department chair Karen Wigen, and Monica Wheeler, Administrative Services Manager for the History Department. While Stanford's bureaucracy remains a source of mystery, the personnel of the Humanities and Sciences Dean's Office has helped us navigate the maze. In particular, we would like to acknowledge the service of Adam R. Daniel, Ian H. Gotlib, Stephen D. Krasner, Martha Langill, Matt Riley, Aron Rodrigue, and Debra Satz. Regarding personnel matters, we have received vital assistance from Human Resource officers Jennifer St. John, Renee Sombilon, and Amber Washington. Ken Merritt and Ann George, from the Office of the Vice Provost and Dean of Research, have also provided consistent guidance. James V. Henry, Director of Finance, along with his colleague, Financial Management Advisor Megan Gorman, and her predecessors Sue Chau, Susana Ching, Elsie Phillips, and Kristi Schulze, have gone above

Acknowledgments and beyond in their support. Margaret E. Fox, head of Accounting and Department Liaisons, has also assisted greatly. In the Office of Sponsored Research we appreciate the aid of Dora Brown, Teresa Lane, Gary Podesta, Blanca Rubuelta, April-Joy Santos, Esther M. Santos, Dell Sy, Kevin Vermilion, and Jennifer Wang in our never-ending pursuit of additional funding.

We are also deeply grateful for the continuing interest and assistance of the staff at Stanford's Cecil H. Green Library, especially Mary Louise Munill with the interlibrary loan office, whose tireless efforts have helped to locate many obscure regional newspapers and other contemporary documents used in the volume's research. Similarly, the staff at the Robert Crown Law Library, and in particular Rachael G. Samberg and George David Wilson, has been of monumental service in helping locate court documents and verifying court cases and citations.

The King Papers Project has continued to have a supportive relationship with the publisher of our edition, the University of California Press. We have enjoyed working with the all of the staff members involved in the painstaking work of producing our volumes. Those involved with this volume include Director Alison Mudditt, Niels Hooper, Kim Hogeland, Kathleen MacDougall, and Kate Warne. Their enthusiasm and organizational skills in coordinating this effort at UC Press are especially noteworthy.

The involvement of the Project's Advisory Board has declined in recent years, but we continue to appreciate the advice we receive from this extraordinary group of distinguished scholars and former associates of Dr. King. I wish to acknowledge in particular the critical comments regarding Volume VII that we received from David Garrow. His thoughtful criticisms on the manuscript drafts were a valuable addition to the volume. Other scholars who provided suggestions on specific documents and/ or the essay included Raymond Arsenault, Lee Formwalt, Catherine Fosl, Michael Honey, Keith Miller, and Kerry Taylor.

In addition to benefiting from the advice of members of the Advisory Board and other scholars, the Project has also relied on its Stanford University Advisory Committee, which has expanded its role in recent years. Determined efforts on behalf of the Project have been championed by the committee's chair, Harold Boyd, and the following members: Barton J. Bernstein, Vicki Brooks, Capri Silverstri Cafaro, Roy Clay, Greg Crossfield, Karl Cureton, Morris Graves, Julie Anne Henderson, Henry Organ, John Rickford, Betty A. Williams Curtis and Russell Curtis, Alene Smith, and David Tyack.

*Financial Supporters*

The King Papers Project could not have survived without funding from numerous generous donors. Founding donors to this volume include Ronnie Lott/All Stars Helping Kids and the Mumford Family–Agape Foundation.

Sustaining contributors include Ronnie Lott/All Stars Helping Kids, Myra Reinhard Family Foundation/All Stars Helping Kids, the National Endowment for the Humanities (NEH), the National Historical Publications and Records Commission (NHPRC), Stanford University, and the Andrew W. Mellon Foundation. Individuals at these institutions have often demonstrated a concern for the Project far outside the bounds of professional responsibilities. I acknowledge in particular Chairman James Leach and his predecessor Bruce Cole, Deputy Chairman Carole Watson, Program

Analyst Lydia Medici, and Grant Administrators Peter Scott, Alice Hudgins, and Michael Hall of the NEH. NHPRC Executive Director Kathleen Williams, Director of Publications Timothy Connelly, and their colleagues Christine Dunham, Nancy Taylor, Daniel Stokes, and former Executive Director Max Evans have been generous in their assistance to the Project. Donald J. Waters and Paula Muir from the Mellon Foundation have also offered unwavering guidance and support.

Major contributors are Clayborne and Susan Carson, Betty A. Williams Curtis and G. Russell Curtis, Sr., Do A Little Fund, Fletcher Asset Management, Inc., Google, the William and Flora Hewlett Foundation, Herbert Kurz, Leonard Merrill Kurz, Lilly Endowment Inc., Jay and Kimberly Mitchell, the Peninsula Community Foundation, George P. Shultz, Andrea McEvoy Spero and Jason D. Spero, and the Woodside Summit Group, Inc.

Patrons include John and Carolyn Barnes, Bob Ceremsak (Goldman, Sachs & Co.), Wayne Duckworth, Mary McKinney Edmonds, Bonnie Fisher and Boris Dramov, Gwen Gasque, James and Jewelle Taylor Gibbs, Glenn Holsclaw and Donna Hubbard, Heather Jackson, Sur-Mamn Jackson, Earl W. Lawson and Rachel Idowu, Tamara Morales and Albert Frazier, Cordell and Carolyn Olive, Henry Organ, David and Katy Orr, Judith and George Prather, Joan S. Reid, Jim C. Robinson, Robert and Sallie Reid Tasto, Isaiah Washington, L. Tyrone and Kim Willingham, Michelle Yee, and Michelle Yee in memory of Don Main Yee.

Donors consist of Benjamin Ahmad, Althea F. Andersen, Bettina Aptheker, Barbara Armentrout, Darrell and Melanie Armstrong, Avago Technologies, Paul Bodine and Tamami Shirai, Harold and Sarah Boyd, Vicki Brooks, William Brown, Evan J. Charkes and Juli A. Steadman, Andrew Chase, Glenda and Richard Chenier, Marsha and Robert Clark, Thomas and Jane David, John A. Dittmer, Lawrence S. Elswit and Bernice Speiser, Susan Englander, Candace Falk and Lowell Finley, George L. Fisher, George M. and Helene Frederickson, Jesika and Saumil Gandhi, Leonard and Scarlet Gordon, William B. Gould IV, Arjun Gupta, Allan Hammond IV and Linda Darling-Hammond, John and Marthelia Hargrove, R. Steven and Jeanne Hargrove, Jerry M. Harris, Cynthia and Alex Harui, Charles P. Henry, Pete Holloran, Michael Honey, Roslind C. Hooper, Donna Hubbard, Gerald W. Jackson and Myra Woods Jackson, Benjamin and Audrey Kamin, Drue Kataoka, Tetsuya and Barbara Kataoka, Evelyn Kelsey, Amanda Kemp, Ravi Kollipara, Patricia Krueger, Kimberly Lake, Deanna F. Lamb, Steven F. Lawson, Ronald and Shoshana Levy, Stacey Leyton and Pierre Barolette, Meg Lilienthal, Delroy Lindo, Kail Lubarsky, Karen McAlmon, Tag and Joan Mansour, Patricia Margulies, Steven McNichols, Meri H. Mitsuyoshi, Borce and Malissa Nastovski, Lela Garner Noble, Bharathi Nuthi, Robert V. Oakford, Obama Democratic Club of Silicon Valley, M. Brigid O'Farrell and T.J. Glauthier, Keisho and Lauren Okayama, Steven Phillips, Progressive Jewish Alliance, Rhonda Racine, Kevin and Kathryne Gambell Reeves, Jon C. and Carol S. Richards, Joel and Rachel Samoff, Lucille H. Sansing, Silicon Valley Community Foundation, Niel and Nancy Sanchez Smit, Sterling Stuckey, Cheryl Taylor, George Tribble, Ronald and Sheila Troupe, Charles and Margaret Tuggle, David Tyack and Elisabeth Hansot, Wesley Umeda, Sharon Read Veach, Merti Walker, Stewart Walker, Victoria Walker, Gail Wentler, Christopher L. Williams, Constance and Preston Williams, Robert and Vicki Wilkins, Warren Wilson, Rosalind Wolf, and Peter Zeughauser.

Friends of the King Papers Project are comprised of Cecil A. Aird, Vaughn Booker, Jr., John Carter, Katiana Catan, Circle 1 United Church of Los Alamos,

Acknowledgments    Reverend Willie E. Cooper, Marshall Covington, Merritt and Betty Creasy, Caroline Girgis, Jonathan Gluckman, Teresa Goodwin, Hanan Hardy, Kathryn Haysbert, Charles P. Henry, Daniel Hoffman, Mark Jeter, Andrew Matlins, Eric N. McMillan, S. Moran, Laura Murra, Mary Nilsson, Rebecca West Noble, Coleen Patterson, Wazir Peacock, Mansoor Rahman, Ana A. Olivencia Rivera, Lucille Sansing, Deborah A. Scalise, Willy Schaeken, Stephan Somerstein, R. Lasana and Cathy Taylor, Alvira Thompson, Barbara Turner, Bob and Nancy Weeks, Kathleen V. Welder, and Joseph Witcher.

The Scholar-in-Residence Program was graciously supported by sustaining contributor Steven Ungerleider. Major contributors include Citigroup Global Wealth Management Legal Department, Andrew Kurth LLP, Morgan Stanley Smith Barney LLC, Michael Sharp, and Joan and Sanford I. Weill. Patrons of the program include Faye Jamille Boatright, Eduardo Bohoques, Citigroup Smith Barney, Bruce Green, Bonnie L. Greenberg, Bonnie L. Greenberg in memory of Mersh Greenberg, Beth M. James, Malcolm Lee, Raymond McGuire, Alexsander and Susan Stewart, Torrance Area Chamber of Commerce, Twenty-First Century Foundation, and Thurman V. White, Jr. Donors include Herbert Ellis, Jody Klein, Macy's, Alfred J. Puchala, Rivertowns Arts Council, Inc., and Sandra Steinman. Friends of the program are William Aiken, Jr., and Hazel and Dennis Harris.

*Staff Members*

This volume, as with all the volumes of King's papers, has been the result of a long-term collaboration involving student and postgraduate researchers, in which academic credentials counted for less than demonstrated ability and dedication. From its inception, the mission of the King Papers Project has not only been to produce a definitive edition of King's papers but to provide an opportunity for able and dedicated students to acquire research skills and to increase their understanding of the modern African American freedom struggle. As the Project has evolved, a few veteran staff members have provided an essential degree of stability amidst the continual turnover of student researchers and professionals.

This volume could not have been completed without the contribution of associate editor Tenisha Armstrong, who first came to the Project as a Summer Research Fellow. After finishing work on Volume V in 2005, Armstrong assumed responsibility as lead editor for this volume. Over the course of the manuscript's development, Armstrong's dedication to obtaining and presenting the most illustrative documents and tirelessly researching the minutia presented in the introduction, annotations, and footnotes cannot be understated. Her work has surpassed the special research and editorial challenges of the volume, and the manuscript's scholarly prowess is a testament to her efforts.

In turn, Armstrong was supported by a host of talented and dedicated researchers. Dave Beals, Stacey Zwald Costello, David Lai, Madolyn Orr, Sarah Overton, and Alex Marquand-Willse demonstrated a keen eye for details and gladly conquered any task handed to them. Josh Kunz ably managed the Project's records database and assisted greatly on the Calendar of Documents. Although not directly involved in the research or writing of this volume, other staff members also provided essential support. Former managing editor Susan Carson has continued to be a vital and steadfast source of guidance, lending her expertise and advice even after her retirement in 2007. Project Administrator Jane Abbott and Assistant Administrator Regina Covington provided essential administrative support to all staff. Although no longer with the Project, Susan Englander, Jesika Gandhi, and Louis Jackson deserve recognition for their good work and indispensable contributions to the Project.

A special thank you to Anena Otii, who translated Spanish newspaper articles, which allowed us to gain a greater understanding of King's 1962 trip to Puerto Rico, and to Barbara Armentrout, a volunteer, who edited King's audio recordings for this volume. Additional thanks to Alyssa Stalsberg Canelli (Emory University), Karma deGruy (Emory University), and Justin Stoll (Boston University) for their help in obtaining King-related documents from the special collection libraries at their home institutions. Their work greatly augmented our collection of King documents when out-of-state research trips were not feasible.

*Student Researchers*

The King Papers Project is immensely grateful for the many hours of thoughtful, sometimes tedious, work put in by high school, undergraduate, and graduate students over the years. These students, representing many disciplines, brought their methods and perspectives to bear upon the important task of locating King's words in time and place. They plotted his daily movements against the sweep of events in a region too often shadowed by racial violence. With diligence they discovered unknown documents and patiently deciphered recordings of King's voice, sometimes barely audible, to produce some of this volume's most distinctive documents. Their individual and collective contributions are many, as are their number.

Stanford students, working as interns, volunteers, or for academic credit, have contributed much to our work through their deep interest in, and enthusiasm for, the material. Undergraduate and graduate researchers who assisted with Volume VII or whose work was not acknowledged in previous volumes include Coral Abbott, Zaid Adhami, Victoria Asbury, Alicia Barber, Leah Barnes, Lonnie Browne, Michael Cruz, Adhaar Desai, Gayon Douglas, Kevin Dumolga, Aiden Dunn, Eron Eguavoen, Donovan Ervin, Tim Fleming, Jordan Gilchrist, April Gregory, Mariah Haberman, Madeline Hawes, Margaret Hayden, Austin Henderson, Jasmine Hu, Michael Huggins, Luisa Hulsroj, Kyonne Isaac, Aaron Jackson, Sharada Jambulapati, Jessica Knight, David Lai, Elizabeth Lake, Lauren Mathews, Zoe Levitt, Ahmad Lewis, Lisa Brown, James Locus, Betty Luan, Fahad Mahmood, Dagem Mammo, Amanda Mener, Matthew Miller, Jidenna Mobisson, Miguel Molina, Kelsey Moss, Casey Nichols, Bavin Ondieki, Kwadwo Osei-Opare, Brianna Pang, Juliana Partridge, Sam Pressman, Jenna Queenan, Anneliese Rice, Jason Robinson, Alison Root, Lisa Ruskin, Katie Salisbury, Andrew Schneider, Tiana Seymore, Ariel Smith, Lindsey Smith, Christopher Stallworth, Trinity Thompson, Elizabeth Titus, Michael Vang, Claudia Wack, Eric Wilson, Juliana Yanez, and Robert Zimbroff.

Over the years, the Project has benefited from the help of several interns from other colleges and local high schools, including Ari Jones (Spelman College), Laura Mitchell (Menlo-Atherton High School), Rosalyn Reed (Spelman College), and Anthony Sandusky (Vanderbilt University).

## *King Summer Research Fellows*

The Project has also gained immensely from the contributions of graduate and undergraduate students from Stanford who interned as part of the Martin Luther King, Jr., Summer Research Fellowship. The Summer Fellows from 2007 through 2012 are Victoria Asbury, Michael Cruz, Shara Esbenshade, Sunny Huang, David Lai, Ahmad Lewis, James Locus, Ty McCormick, Cole Manley, Kelsey Moss, Bavin Ondieki, Jenna Queenan, Alex Reiger, Andrew Schneider, Lindsey Smith, Alexandra To, and Katrice Williams.

## *Scholar-In-Residence*

Since 2006, Clarence B. Jones, speechwriter and counsel for Martin Luther King, Jr., has offered his unyielding support and assistance to the staff and students of the Project. His intimate knowledge of King and the movement, coupled with lifelong relationships with movement soldiers, has provided staff with an invaluable resource and font of knowledge. His enthusiasm and contributions cannot be measured.

## *Acquisition and Research Assistance*

Volume VII, like the volumes that preceded it, would not have been possible without the King-related documents that have been provided to us by numerous individuals and institutions. The King collections at Boston University, the King Center, and the Woodruff Library at Atlanta University Center have been at the core of our selection. In addition to documents obtained from the King Center and Boston University, and the Woodruff Library at Atlanta University Center, we identified more than 180 manuscript collections with King-related material important for this volume. Institutions, archives, and libraries that assisted us in locating documents for this volume include Albany Civil Rights Movement Museum at Old Mt. Zion Church, American Baptist Historical Society, Amistad Research Center, Antioch College Archives (Antioch College), Archives of the Evangelical Lutheran Church in America, Associated Press/Wide World Photos, Auburn Avenue Research Library on African American Culture and History, Avery Research Center (College of Charleston), Bard College Archives (Bard College), Beloit College Archives (Beloit College), Birmingham Public and Jefferson County Free Library, California State University (Sacramento), Calumet Regional Archives (Indiana University Northwest), Catalina United Methodist Church (Tucson, Ariz.), Center for the Study of Southern Political Culture (Calhoun Community College), Charles E. Young Research Library (University of California, Los Angeles), Chicago History Museum, Columbia Broadcasting System, Columbia University Rare Book and Manuscript Library, Corbis-Bettmann Archives, David M. Rubenstein Rare Book & Manuscript Library (Duke University), Department of Rare Books and Special Collections (Princeton University), Dexter Avenue King Memorial Baptist Church (Montgomery, Ala.), Ebenezer Baptist Church (Atlanta, Ga.), Elmwood Park Public Library (Elmwood Park, Ill.), Film and Television Archive (University of California, Los Angeles), Frank Mt. Pleasant Library of Special Collections and Archives (Chapman University), Franklin D. Roosevelt Presidential Library, G. Robert Vincent Voice Library (Michigan State University), Georgia Department of Archives and History, Hargrett Rare Book and Manuscript Library (University of Georgia), Harvard Law School Library,

International Civil Rights Center & Museum, ITN Source, Jean and Alexander Acknowledgments Heard Library Special Collections and University Archives (Vanderbilt University), John F. Kennedy Presidential Library, Kenan Research Center at the Atlanta History Center, Kheel Center for Labor-Management Documentation and Archives at the M. P. Catherwood Library (Cornell University), Lambeth Palace Library (London, England), Langston Hughes Memorial Library Special Collections and Archives (Lincoln University), Library of Congress, Los Angeles Valley College (Van Nuys, Calif.), Lyndon Baines Johnson Presidential Library, Lynn and Louis Wolfson II Florida Moving Image Archive (Miami-Dade College), Magnum Photos Inc., Magnus Walstrom Library (University of Bridgeport), Manuscript, Archives, and Rare Book Library (Emory University), Marquette University Raynor Memorial Libraries Special Collections and University Archives (Marquette University), McCain Library and Archives (University of Southern Mississippi), Moorland-Spingarn Research Center (Howard University), Morris Library Special Collections Research Center (Southern Illinois University), National Broadcasting Company Inc., National Park Service Museum Resource Center (National Capital Region), Oakwood University Archives at the Eva B. Dykes Library, Oregon Historical Society, Pacific School of Religion (Berkeley, Calif.), Presbyterian Historical Society, Rauner Special Collections Library (Dartmouth College), Richard B. Russell Library for Political Research and Studies (University of Georgia), Richard Nixon Foundation, Robert F. Wagner Labor Archives (New York University), Rockefeller Archive Center, Schomburg Center for Research in Black Culture (The New York Public Library), Seeley G. Mudd Manuscript Library (Princeton University), Southern Baptist Historical Library and Archives, Southern Baptist Theological Seminary Archives and Special Collections, Southern Historical Collection at the Wilson Library (University of North Carolina at Chapel Hill), State Historical Society of Wisconsin, Sumter County Clerk of the Court's Office (Americus, Ga.), Swarthmore College Peace Collection, Syracuse University Special Collections Research Center, Tampa Library Special Collections (University of South Florida), Temple Emanuel Sinai Archives (Worcester, Mass.), The Dirksen Congressional Center, Time Inc., Tougaloo College Archives and Special Collections, United States Department of Justice, United States National Archives and Records Administration, University of Maryland Special Collections & University Archives, University of Pittsburgh Archives Service Center, University of Tours (France), University of Washington Special Collections, Waidner-Spahr Library Archives and Special Collections (Dickinson College), Walter J. Brown Media Archive & Peabody Awards Collection (University of Georgia), Walter P. Reuther Library of Labor and Urban Affairs (Wayne State University), White Rock Baptist Church (Philadelphia, Pa.), William Ready Division of Archives and Research Collections (McMaster University), Woodland Hills Community Church (Woodland Hills, Calif.), Yale University Library Manuscripts and Archives, and Z. Smith Reynolds Library Special Collections and Archives (Wake Forest University).

King's colleagues, acquaintances, and their families have been among the most important sources of King-related documents. Of those whom we were able to contact, many assisted us immeasurably in our research. Some graciously allowed us to make duplicates of the materials in their possession, which until now have not been available, and many kindly consented to interviews in connection with this volume. These individuals include Carolyn Hunt Anderson, William G. Anderson, Lewis Baldwin, Margaret Bates, Charles Black, Julian Bond, Ralph F. Boyd, Gurdon

Brewster, Paul H. Brown, Gordon R. Carey, Barbara Adams Carney, Jini Kilgore Cockroft, Joseph B. Cumming, Jimmy Davis, Dave Dennis, Fred O. Doty, Leslie Dunbar, Christine King Farris, Robert Brank Fulton, William H. Fulton, Sonnie W. Hartford, Esau Jenkins Family, David Johnson, Charles Jones, Clarence B. Jones, I. Logan Kearse II, Walter Kelley, Theodore W. Kheel, Pauline Knight-Ofosu, Bernard LaFayette, James M. Lawson, John Lewis, A. Lincoln James, Clarence Logan, Washington Long, Sam Massell, Les Margolis, Phillip Middleton, Otis Moss, Jr., Teresa Pritchett Owens, John M. Patterson, Charles Person, Dan Pollitt, Dan Pritchett, Lawrence Pritchett, James Purks, Robert L. Render, James Robinson, Tom Roland, Ralph Lord Roy, Donald Secord, Charles Sellers, Mary V. Spraitzer, Loren Stell, Wilda Stephens, Henry Thomas, Barry Tulloss, Solomon Walker, Theresa Ann Walker, Wyatt Tee Walker, Mervyn A. Warren, Brenda Watson, I. Margaret White, Willard A. Williams, Harris Wofford, Carl L. Zelznick, and Jim Zwerg. We continue to utilize the documents provided to us from the churches King pastored: Dexter Avenue King Memorial Baptist Church and Ebenezer Baptist Church.

Individuals who gave permission for publication of their documents or those of relatives include Juanita Abernathy, Maya Angelou, Worth Littlejohn Barbour, James Braden, Gordon R. Carey, Herschelle S. Challenor, Virginia Durr, Victor H. Eskridge, Frank Gregory, Lonnie King, Andrew Levison, Carl L. Manfred, Solomon S. Seay, Jr., Fred Shuttlesworth, Nomatemba Tambo, Gardner Taylor, Elizabeth Chalmers Todrank, John Williams, Mary Ann Smith Wilson, Blanche C. Wood, and Jim Zwerg.

Permissions were obtained with the assistance of Jack Ammerman (School of Theology Library at Boston University), Tina Barbour, Brian Brown, Yvonne Shade Cook, Lynda DeLoach (University of Maryland Special Collections & University Archives), Lolis Elie (Elie, Jones and Associates), Valerie Harris (The Industrial Areas Foundation, University of Illinois), Elliot L. Hoffman (Beldock Levine & Hoffman LLP), C.B. Kackworth, Walter Naegle (Bayard Rustin Fund), Ram Chandra Rahi (Gandhi Smarak Nidhi), Elaine Eason Steele (Rosa and Raymond Parks Institute for Self Development), and Joan Scott Wallace.

Several institutions and individuals assisted the Project on our audiovisual acquisitions and research for the volume: Tewedros Abebe (Moorland-Spingarn Research Center, Howard University), Ruta Abolins (Walter J. Brown Media Archive & Peabody Awards Collection, University of Georgia), Sam Adams (Montgomery City-County Public Library), Margaret Ahmann, Alabama Civil Rights Museum, Cherran Allison (Warren Memorial United Methodist Church, Atlanta, Ga.), Okezie Amalaha (Auburn Avenue Research Library), American Baptist Historical Society, American Jewish Archives, Alan Anderson (Sumter County Historical Trust), Francis Anderson, Laura Anderson (Birmingham Civil Rights Institute), Lena Anderson (White Plains/Greenburgh, New York NAACP), William G. Anderson, Ruth Ash (Merrick Archives, Allegheny College), Associated Press/Wide World Photos, Fred and Vonda Atkinson, Atlanta Time Machine, Jim Auchmutey, Avery Research Center, Jim Baggett (Birmingham Public Library), Melissa Bailey (Morehouse College), Marvin Bargar (Jewish Historical Society of Greater New Haven), Susan Barker (Smith College Archives), Peggy Bates, Lou Benedict (Woodland Hills Community Church, Woodland Hills, Calif.), Tad Bennicoff (Mudd Manuscript Library, Princeton University), Bentley Historical Library, Bethel Baptist Church (Baltimore, Md.), David Blight, Barbara Bollinger (Cedar Crest College), Boston

Public Library, Peggy Boswell (Trinity United Methodist Church, Denver, Colo.), Taylor Branch, Gurdon Brewster, Veronica Burke (Tax Assessor's Office, Jefferson County, Ala.), Randall K. Burkett (Manuscript, Archives, and Rare Books Library, Emory University), Fred Burwell (Beloit College Archives), Calvary Baptist Church (White Plains, N.Y.), William Monroe Campbell (SCLC of Greater Los Angeles), Janet Carleton (Ohio University), Jo-Anne Carr (College of the Holy Cross Archives), Arthur Carter (Second Baptist Church, Detroit, Mich.), Vicki Catozza (Western Reserve Historical Society), Central United Church (Detroit, Mich.), Patrick Chabal, Champaign County Historical Archives (Urbana Free Library), Wesley Chenault (Auburn Avenue Research Library), Wendy Chmielewski (Swarthmore College Peace Collection), Clarendon County Archives, Clark-Atlanta University, U. W. Clemon, Phyllis Cole (Yonkers Public Library), Denise Coleman (Samuel DeWitt Proctor School of Theology, Virginia Union University), Wayne Coleman (Birmingham Civil Rights Institute), College of Charleston, Columbia Broadcasting System News Archives, Columbia University Rare Book and Manuscript Library, Corbis-Bettmann Archives, Coshocton Public Library, Christine Crandall (American Jewish Archives), Paul Crater (Kenan Research Center), Heather Crocetto (National Press Club), Deborah Crowdy, Bernard Crystal (Columbia University Rare Book and Manuscript Library), Jane Danjin (United Auto Workers Solidarity House), Daria D'Arenzio (Amherst College Archives and Special Collections), Margaret R. Dakin (Amherst College Archives and Special Collections), David B. Davis, Don Davis (American Friends Service Committee Archives), Jim Davis, Sally DeBauche (Dolph Briscoe Center for American History, University of Texas), John Paul Deley (University of Washington Special Collections), Michael Desmond (John F. Kennedy Presidential Library), Dougherty County Public Library, Julie Doughtery (Lycoming College Archives), Eugene Downing (New Hope Baptist Church, Denver, Colo.), Michael Dresner (Temple Sha'ary Shalom), Cyd Dyer (Simpson College Archives), Cheryl Eberly (Santa Ana Public Library), Eisenhower Presidential Library and Museum, Eisterhold Foundation, Elmwood Park Public Library, Elmwood Park, Ill., Clyde "Buddy" Farnan, Thomas Featherstone (Walter P. Reuther Library, Wayne State University), Norma Feingold (Temple Emanuel Sinai Archives, Worcester, Mass.), Janet Ferguson (Atlanta Friends Meeting), Ralph Fertig (Chicago Freedom Action Committee), Meredith Firetog (*Stanford Law Review*), Alma Fisher (Tougaloo College Archives and Special Collections), Bill Fleming, Fox Movietone News Clips, Janice Frazier, Earl Fredrick, David Friedman (*Stanford Law Review*), Thomas Fu (*Stanford Law Review*), Karen Fung (Stanford University), Michelle Gachette (Harvard University Archives), Jim Gannon (Transport Workers Union), Willie Gardner, Winafred Gardner, Raven Gaston (Catalina United Methodist Church, Tucson, Ariz.), Trevor Getz (California State University, San Francisco), Phyllis Gilbert (Rauner Special Collections Library, Dartmouth College), Miriam Goldberg, Courtney Goolsby (Thronateeska Heritage Center), Howard Grant (Atlanta Public Schools), Adam Green (Trinity College Library, University of Cambridge), Julian Greene, Jr. (First Baptist Church, Petersburg, Va.), Wilma Brown Griffin (Albany, Georgia, Police Department), H. Council Trenholm State Technical College, Linda Hall (Williams College Archives and Special Collections), Frank Hanawalt, Vera Harris, Valda Harris-Montgomery, Shireen Hassim, Ida Hays (Moorland-Spingarn Research Center, Howard University), Ryan Hendrickson (Howard Gotlieb Archival Research Center, Boston

Acknowledgments    University), Sharon Henneborn (Art Educators of New Jersey), Brenda Hodges-Tiller, Kevin Hogencamp, Hope College (Holland, Mich.), Marian Turner Hopkins, Claudia Horn (Frank Mt. Pleasant Library of Special Collections and Archives, Chapman University), Illinois State Archives, Internal Revenue Service, Petrina Jackson (Cornell University Library Rare and Manuscript Collections Division), Sally Jacobs (State Historical Society of Wisconsin), A.J. Jenkins Photography, David W. Johnson (Waidner-Spahr Library Archives and Special Collections, Dickinson College), Matthew V. Johnson, Nigh Johnson (Robidoux Row Museum), Sean Kareshiro (Stanford Law School), May Kay (West Hunter Street Baptist Church), Warren Knouff, Lou Ellen Kramer (Lynn and Louis Wolfson II Florida Moving Image Archives, Miami-Dade College), Aishwary Kumar (Stanford University), M. Bahati Kuumba (Spelman College), Susan LaCette (Kheel Center, Cornell University), Carla Ledgerwood (Kenan Research Center), William LeFevre (Walter P. Reuther Library, Wayne State University), Lewis and Clark College, Abraham Lincoln Presidential Library, Jim Lindsay, Washington Long, Alfred Lott (City of Albany, Ga.), Cathy Loving (Atlanta Public Schools), Dennis Lowen (Palm Beach County Clerk's Office), Tommie Luke (WDAF-TV, Kansas City, Mo.), Arnetta Mack (SCLC of Greater Los Angeles), Jeffrey Makala (Wesleyan University Special Collections and Archives), Peggy Mapp (West Hunter Street Baptist Church), J. Willard Marriot Library, Thurgood Marshall Law Library (University of Maryland), Carol Maryan-George (National Archives for Black Women's History), Lopez Matthews (Moorland-Spingarn Research Center, Howard University), David G. May (Los Angeles Valley College), Rosalie McCall-Johnson (Montview Boulevard Presbyterian Church, Denver, Colo.), Stephanie McCurry, Clarence Lewis McFadden (Friendship Baptist Church, Los Angeles, Calif.), LaVerne L. McLaughlin (Albany State University), Harry Miller (State Historical Society of Wisconsin), Paul Mogren (J. Willard Marriot Library, University of Utah), Bruce Montgomery (Temple B'nai Jehudah), Morning Star Missionary Baptist Church (Albany, N.Y.), Heather Muir (University of Wisconsin – Eau Clair Special Collections), Kathy Mundale (Robert W. Woodruff Library, Atlanta University), Brenan Murphey (United Auto Workers Solidarity House), Museum of Broadcast Communication, Vanessa Nastro (Adelphi University), National Broadcasting Company News Archives, National Center for the Study of Civil Rights and African-American Culture (Alabama State University), National Student Clearinghouse, New Haven Colony Historical Society, Edwina Nikoi (Schomburg Center for Research in Black Culture), Madelyn P. Nix (Warren Memorial United Methodist Church, Atlanta, Ga.), Sean Noel (Howard Gotlieb Archival Research Center, Boston University), Sara Nyman (Kansas City Public Library), Lisa Oberhofer (Columbia Broadcasting System News Archives), John Oliver (Montgomery, Alabama YMCA), Catherine Oseas (Birmingham Public Library), Maurice Otieno, Vita Paladino (Howard Gotlieb Archival Research Center, Boston University), Gwen Patton (H. Council Trenholm State Technical College), Lawrence Lee Pelletier Library, Lisa Persinger (Z. Smith Reynolds Library, Wake Forest University), Richard W. Peuser (National Archives and Records Administration), Susan Pevar (Langston Hughes Memorial Library, Lincoln University), David Pfeiffer (National Archives and Records Administration), Jennifer Pino (Howard Gotlieb Archival Research Center, Boston University), Stephen Plotkin (John F. Kennedy Presidential Library), Trina Purcell (Denver Public Library), Sarah Quigley (Manuscript, Archives, and Rare Books Library, Emory

University), Miranda Rectenwald (University Archives, Washington University in St. Louis), Robert L. Render, Z. Smith Reynolds Library (Wake Forest University), Barbara Rehkop (University Archives, Washington University in St. Louis), Benjamin Ridgeway (Ebenezer Baptist Church), Emille Mercer Robinson (Holland and Knight), Randy Roeder (Coe College), David Roundtree (University Archives, Washington University in St. Louis), Michael Rush (Beinecke Rare Book & Manuscript Library, Yale University), Saint James AME Church, Katherine Salzmann (Morris Library Special Collections Research Center, Southern Illinois University), Joel Samoff (Stanford University), Robert W. Saunders, Bob Scar (Georgia Department of Archives and History), Kay Schellhase (Pacific School of Religion), Jeffrey D. Schielke, Amy Schindler (State University of New York, Albany), Benjamin Scott (Auburn Avenue Research Library), Stephen S. Selig, Kathy Shoemaker (Manuscript, Archives, and Rare Books Library, Emory University), Benjamin Singleton (Moving Image Research Collection, University of South Carolina), Patrizia Sione (Kheel Center for Labor-Management Documentation and Archives, Cornell University), Paula Skreslet (Virginia Union University Archives and Special Collections), William Smart (SCLC of Greater Los Angeles), Karen Smiga (University of Bridgeport), Geri Soloman (Hofstra University), Southern Baptist Historical Library and Archives, Special Collections (Bryn Mawr College), Spelman College, St. Joseph Illinois Public Library, St. Philip Monumental AME Church (Savannah, Ga.), Anne Stenzel (University Archives and Southern Minnesota Historical Center, Minnesota State University, Mankato), Holly Stephenson (St. Joseph County Historical Society of Michigan), Katherine Stine (University of Chicago Special Collections Research Center), David Stiver (Graduate Theological Union), Syracuse University Special Collections Research Center, Richard J. Taylor (Ohio Council of Churches), Mary Ann Teed (Monterey Peninsula College), Julie Thomas (California State University, Sacramento), Joel Thoreson (Evangelical Lutheran Church of America), Helene Tieger (Bard College Archives), Time Inc., Rebecca Tischler (Birmingham Civil Rights Institute), Rozalyn Todd, Eleanor Toews (Seattle Public Schools), Sonja Tolbert (City Clerk's Office, Albany, Ga.), Trinity College, Timothy Tyson (Duke Divinity School), Jennifer Ulrich (Columbia University Rare Book and Manuscript Library), Union Theological Seminary, United Automobile Workers of America (CIO), University of Alabama (Tuscaloosa), University of Michigan, University of Minnesota, Vanderbilt University Special Collections and University Archives, Barbara Vasquez (Los Angeles City College), Nuño Vidal, Anke Voss-Hubbard (Tate Archives & Special Collections, Illinois Wesleyan University), Scott Warner, Raphael Warnock (Ebenezer Baptist Church), Janet Waters (University of Northern Colorado Archival Services), Eileen Weston (Pacific School of Religion), Karen Weston (University of Wisconsin-Whitewater Research Center), Helene Whitson (San Francisco State University Special Collections), Jocelyn K. Wilk (Columbia University Archives), Amanda Williams (Live Oak Public Libraries), Joyce Williams (Oakwood University Archives), Susan Williams (Highlander Center Library and Resource Center), Wilson Library (University of North Carolina), Janet Woodward (Garfield High School, Seattle, Wash.), Lindsey Wyckoff (Bankstreet College), and Nanci Young (Smith College Archives).

A few individuals have enhanced the work of the Project simply by visiting us and talking about their involvement with or scholarship on the civil rights movement or other movements for social change. Among the Project's distinguished guests

Acknowledgments    and event participants are Aldo Billingslea, Julian Bond, Dorothy Cotton, Connie Curry, the 14th Dalai Lama, Vincent Harding, Bruce Hartford, Mary King, Eric Mann, Bernice Johnson Reagon, Tavis Smiley, Isaiah Washington, Cornell West, and Andrew Young. Additionally, Wyatt Tee and Anne Walker and Andrew Levison spent countless hours assisting with research for this volume.

Certainly there are other individuals and organizations that participated in and contributed to the success of the King Papers Project. Failure to mention them simply reflects the limits of my memory rather than of my gratitude.

CLAYBORNE CARSON
AUGUST 2013

# INTRODUCTION

*And those people who are working to bring into being the dream of democracy*
*are not the agitators. They are not the dangerous people in America. They are*
*not the un-American people. They are people who are doing more for America*
*than anybody that we can point to. And I submit to you that it may well be that*
*the Negro is God's instrument to save the soul of America.*

Martin Luther King, Jr.
2 January 1961

When forty-three-year-old John F. Kennedy took office on 20 January 1961 as the youngest elected American president, Martin Luther King Jr. had just turned thirty-two but had already risen to national prominence as a result of his leadership role in the Montgomery bus boycott that ended four years earlier. Early in 1957 he had become founding president of the Southern Christian Leadership Conference (SCLC) and subsequently was in great demand as a speaker throughout the nation. His understanding of Gandhian principles had deepened as a result of his 1959 trip to India, but, during the following year, college student sit-in protesters, rather than King, became the vanguard of a sustained civil disobedience campaign. Having already weathered a near-fatal stabbing and six arrests, King was uncertain about how best to support the new militancy. Moving to Atlanta to be near SCLC head-quarters and to serve as co-pastor with his father at Ebenezer Baptist Church, he had assumed a wide range of responsibilities. He relied on his wife, Coretta Scott, to take the lead role of raising their two small children with a third due any day. Cautious about initiating major protests, King sought to enhance SCLC's ability to aid local protest movements that he hoped would prod the federal government to support southern civil rights reform. Aware that Kennedy had voted against a key provision of the 1957 civil rights bill while serving in the Senate, King was nonetheless optimistic that the new president would reward the crucial support he received from black voters by backing the civil rights cause.[1]

---

1. The jury amendment would have allowed the attorney general to bypass a jury and issue contempt citations for violations of constitutional rights. When King met in June 1960 with then-senator Kennedy to discuss his civil rights stance, King recalled that the candidate regretted voting against the amendment even after sit-in protests revealed the "injustices and the indignities that Negroes were facing all over the South." King was convinced that Kennedy had an "intellectual" rather than "emotional commitment" to civil rights. King argued that while Kennedy knew that segregation was morally wrong, "he had never really had the personal experience of knowing the deep groans and passionate yearnings

"The new Administration," King wrote in *The Nation* during the initial weeks of Kennedy's presidency, "has the opportunity to be the first in one hundred years of American history to adopt a radically new approach to the question of civil rights." King insisted that the "intolerably slow pace of civil rights is due at least as much to the limits which the federal government has imposed on its own actions as it is to the actions of the segregationist opposition." By eliminating federal support and sponsorship of discrimination, the president would be setting "a clear example for Americans everywhere." King cited historic precedents for the use of federal action in times of crisis and called on Kennedy to redefine federal leadership during his presidency. "It is no exaggeration to say that the President could give segregation its death blow through a stroke of the pen." In King's estimation, executive power had never been fully "exploited"; instead "its use in recent years has been microscopic in scope and timid in conception."[2]

Ignoring King's calls for immediate presidential action, Kennedy decided against proposing new civil rights legislation. After signing Executive Order 10925, establishing the President's Committee on Equal Employment Opportunity, Kennedy acknowledged the usefulness of legislation but argued that his administration had not yet exhausted all means of enforcing laws previously passed by Congress. At a press conference, he asserted that no new laws would be proposed until he felt "that there is a necessity for a congressional action, with a chance of getting that congressional action."[3] Soon afterward, King expressed impatience with the administration during a question-and-answer session at Temple Emanuel in Worcester, Massachusetts. He said that he was "willing to wait a few more days; not many more; but a few more days to see what he's gonna do." King surmised that Kennedy was hesitant to push for civil rights legislation for fear of jeopardizing other legislative proposals before Congress.[4] On 16 March King sent the president "belated congratu-

of the Negroes for freedom because he just didn't know Negroes generally" (King, Interview by Berl Bernhard, 9 March 1964).

2. King, "Equality Now: The President Has the Power," 4 February 1961, pp. 139, 140, 144, 145 in this volume. During a presidential debate with Richard Nixon, Kennedy said that discrimination in federally funded housing could be eliminated by a "stroke of the President's hand" ("Transcript of the Second Nixon-Kennedy Debate on Nation-Wide Television," *New York Times*, 8 October 1960). Kennedy also promised that he would end discrimination in government contracts and ensure compliance of the Supreme Court's mandate to desegregate schools. He asserted that the country had "lost valuable years" because President Dwight D. Eisenhower failed to implement a civil rights plan and thereby show presidential and moral leadership (Kennedy, Remarks at National Conference on Constitutional Rights and American Freedom, 12 October 1960). After the election, King began urging Kennedy to enact the civil rights planks adopted at the 1960 Democratic convention. He told an audience in Chattanooga: "Now we must remind Mr. Kennedy that we helped him to get in the White House. We must remind Mr. Kennedy that we are expecting him to use the whole weight of his office to remove the ugly weight of segregation from the shoulders of our nation." King argued that in the past the federal government had exclusively relied on the judicial branch to deal with the civil rights issue, while the legislative and executive branches have been "hypocritical, apathetic, and silent." King added, "we must remind Mr. Kennedy that when he gets the pen in his hand, we expect him to write a little bit and give some orders" (King, "The Negro and the American Dream," Address delivered at Memorial Auditorium, 30 December 1960).

3. *Public Papers of the Presidents of the United States: John F. Kennedy, 1961* (Washington, D.C.: U.S. Government Printing Office, 1962), pp. 156–157.

4. King, Question and answer period at Temple Emanuel, 12 March 1961; see also King, The Question

lations" and offered him "support and prayers" as he led the nation "through the difficult yet challenging days ahead." Acknowledging Kennedy's busy schedule, King requested a White House meeting, explaining that "a brief discussion on the present status of the civil rights struggle may prove to be mutually beneficial."[5]

While King waited for a response from Kennedy, the administration partially fulfilled a campaign promise by asking a federal court to add the U.S. Department of Justice as a plaintiff in the Prince Edward County, Virginia, school desegregation case.[6] King sent Attorney General Robert F. Kennedy a telegram applauding the Justice Department's "forthrightness and courage in a sincere attempt to solve many of the crises that face our Southland" and promised to support the attorney general's efforts "to bring our country closer to the fulfillment of its ideals of equal opportunities for all."[7] Soon after receiving King's praise, Kennedy gave his first formal address as attorney general at the University of Georgia Law School and called for compliance with federal court orders regarding civil rights. "We know that if one man's rights are denied, the rights of all are endangered. In our country the courts have a most important role in safeguarding these rights." He insisted that court decisions "must be followed and respected" and "if we disagree with a court decision and, thereafter, irresponsibly assail the court and defy its rulings, we challenge the foundations of our society."[8]

As King pressed the Kennedy administration to support civil rights reform, he also recognized that his 1960 tax evasion trial had been a major distraction from his effort to increase SCLC's effectiveness.[9] During the winter and spring of 1961, his speaking invitations brought in contributions for the group's depleted coffers. A celebrity gala in January at New York's Carnegie Hall netted over $20,000, and a direct mail appeal brought in $30,000 more by May.[10] Even as SCLC built its national

---

of Progress in the Area of Race Relations, Address delivered at Temple Emanuel, 12 March 1961. King later recalled the president seemed "committed" to civil rights but was "not quite sure that he had a mandate from the people" because of his "very small margin of victory in the election" (King, Interview by Bernhard, 9 March 1964).

5. King to Kennedy, 16 March 1961, p. 175 in this volume. Although King was invited to Kennedy's inauguration, he did not attend. For a facsimile of the invitation, see p. 129 in this volume. Kennedy was slow to respond to King's request for a meeting, which did not take place until October 1961 (see King, Press Conference after Meeting with John F. Kennedy, 16 October 1961, pp. 308–311 in this volume).

6. In June 1961 the Justice Department's petition was denied (*Eva Allen et al. v. County School Board of Prince Edward County, Va., etc., et al.*, 28 F.R.D. 358 [1961]). The Prince Edward County school desegregation case was one of five cases consolidated into the Supreme Court's 1954 *Brown* decision, which outlawed segregation in public schools (*Brown et al. v. Board of Education of Topeka et al.*, 347 U.S. 483). Five years after the *Brown* decision, Prince Edward County school board officials closed the county's public schools rather than obey a federal court order to desegregate.

7. King and Wyatt Tee Walker to Kennedy, 28 April 1961.

8. "Text of Attorney General Kennedy's Civil Rights Speech at University of Georgia," *New York Times*, 7 May 1961. SCLC's executive board expressed its "sincere appreciation for the Attorney General Robert Kennedy and his forthright leadership he is giving the enforcement arm of the Federal Government" (SCLC, Press release, "King and SCLC meet in Montgomery," 12 May 1961).

9. For more on King's tax evasion case, see Introduction, in *The Papers of Martin Luther King, Jr.*, vol. 5: *Threshold of a New Decade*, ed. Clayborne Carson, Tenisha Armstrong, Susan Carson, Adrienne Clay, Kieran Taylor (Berkeley: University of California Press, 2005), pp. 24–26, 30–31.

10. King to Sammy Davis, Jr., 28 March 1961, pp. 188–189 in this volume; Ralph Abernathy, "Report of the treasurer," 1 November 1960–30 April 1961.

donor network, however, King's concern with fundraising limited his ability to build his group's local programs.

The challenge King faced from the Congress of Racial Equality (CORE) and college students affiliated with the Student Nonviolent Coordinating Committee (SNCC) would become increasingly evident during 1961 and 1962. Protesters eager to practice civil disobedience not only prodded the Kennedy administration to speed the pace of civil rights reform but also put pressure on King to overcome his reluctance to engage in militant direct action. On 31 January, the eve of the first anniversary of the lunch counter sit-in in Greensboro, North Carolina, a small group of protesters affiliated with CORE launched a "jail-in" campaign in Rock Hill, South Carolina.[11] When CORE requested assistance from other civil rights groups, SNCC sent four students to Rock Hill to be arrested and join those in jail. In a letter to the students, King praised them for their willingness to remain jailed rather than accept bail, but he did not become involved.[12]

While the Rock Hill protesters were in jail, the Atlanta students resumed the demonstrations they had started a year earlier. King had been jailed for participating in the previous fall's student-led sit-ins in Atlanta, but this time he played only a supportive role.[13]

He also appeared in a Fulton County courtroom on 15 February for the arraignment of a group of protesting ministers, including his former Morehouse and Crozer classmate Walter McCall, who had been arrested for joining the sit-in demonstrations.[14] At a rally that evening, King praised the efforts of the students and ministers to defy unjust laws and called upon African Americans to reject token integration. Soon afterward he left Atlanta for a two-week vacation in the Bahamas.[15]

Upon his return to Atlanta, King mediated conflicts between increasingly impatient student activists and older black leaders. When black attorney A. T. Walden, acting on behalf of the Student-Adult Liaison Committee, negotiated an agreement with downtown Atlanta merchants to end the protests in return for desegregation of downtown stores and a promise to desegregate public schools the following fall, some students objected. White leaders praised the agreement, and several prominent African American leaders, including King's father, signed it.[16]

11. Thomas Walter Gaither, "Jailed-In," April 1961.

12. King to Diane Nash and Charles Sherrod, 17 February 1961, pp. 167–168 in this volume.

13. After his October arrest at Rich's department store, King was convicted of violating the conditions of his probation stemming from a May 1960 traffic violation and sentenced to four months in Georgia's state prison at Reidsville (see Introduction in *Papers* 5:36–40). Student sit-in leaders later suspended demonstrations for thirty days while Atlanta officials promised to try and secure the release of jailed protesters. After negotiations collapsed, however, the students resumed the boycott of downtown stores ("Atlanta Negroes Suspend Sit-Ins," *New York Times*, 23 October 1960; John Britton, "Demonstrations Are Resumed Here after Truce of 30 Days," *Atlanta Daily World*, 26 November 1960).

14. Keeler McCartney, "8 Ministers Seized in Sit-In, Vow to Remain in Fulton Jail," *Atlanta Constitution*, 16 February 1961.

15. Charles Moore, "Negroes Here Plan Huge Rally at Jail," *Atlanta Constitution*, 16 February 1961. Lonnie C. King and Mary Ann Smith, two members of the Atlanta Committee on Appeal for Human Rights, wrote King on 25 February thanking him for his "eloquent" address: "You have been an inspiration to all of us" (p. 169 in this volume).

16. The merchants also agreed to rehire black employees who had been laid off (Bruce Galphin, "Negroes Agree to End Sit-Ins," *Atlanta Constitution*, 8 March 1961; SCLC, *Newsletter* 1, no. 1, May 1961).

During a 10 March mass meeting at Warren Memorial Methodist Church, some
students charged that the adult leaders had sold them out.[17] King watched as students shouted down his father's attempt to defend the agreement and then pleaded for calm and unity between both groups. "No greater tragedy could befall the Negro in Atlanta now than to be infected with the cancerous disease of disunity," King argued.[18] Addressing those who believed that the adult leadership had sold out by accepting the agreement, King said:

> If I had been on that committee that met Monday afternoon, I wouldn't mind anybody saying, Martin Luther King, Jr., you made a mistake. I wouldn't mind anybody saying, Martin Luther King, Jr., you should have thought it over a little longer. I wouldn't have minded anybody saying to me, Martin Luther King, Jr., maybe we made a tactical blunder. But I would have been terribly hurt if anybody said to me, Martin Luther King, Jr., you sold us out! . . . I would have been hurt by that.[19]

King's pleas did not repair the rupture between impatient youthful activists and older leaders favoring a more gradualist approach to desegregation.

As he dealt with this growing youth-led militancy, King also struggled to respond to the request of white SCLC supporter Anne Braden that he initiate a clemency petition on behalf of her husband.[20] Carl Braden had recently lost his appeal to the U.S. Supreme Court of his one-year prison sentence for refusing to answer the House Un-American Activities Committee's (HUAC) questions about his alleged communist ties.[21] Although the Bradens had been longtime associates of King, he knew that involvement in this controversial issue would make him vulnerable to red-baiting, especially from segregationists who demonized any civil rights advocacy

17. Lionel Newsom and William Gorden, "A Stormy Rally in Atlanta," *Today's Speech* 11, no. 2 (April 1963): 18–21; Trezzvant W. Anderson, "Repudiate Boycott 'Settlement': 'You Sold Us Out,' Cry Angry Atlanta 'Sit-Ins,'" *Pittsburgh Courier*, 18 March 1961. In a later interview, Lonnie C. King, chairman of the Atlanta Committee on Appeal for Human Rights, said that although he had wanted immediate desegregation of downtown businesses he was "browbeat" by the adult leadership into signing the agreement (Lonnie C. King, Interview by John H. Britton, 29 August 1967).

18. "King Pleads to Students: Atlanta Accord Followed by Dispute," *New York Amsterdam News*, 25 March 1961. Before King, Jr. addressed the meeting, Daddy King explained his position: "By your saying I've sold out bothers me very little. I keep my record up and my business is to keep any of that from being true. . . . If you want the little place I have you can have it. I'm tired, as tired as I can be. . . Now God bless you, and let's keep working together for the good of all of us" (Newsom and Gorden, "A Stormy Rally in Atlanta").

19. Newsom and Gorden, "A Stormy Rally in Atlanta." According to Lonnie C. King, King, Jr. "made the greatest speech" he had ever made with "tears were in his eyes" after seeing "his daddy being castigated by those people" (King, Interview by Britton, 29 August 1967).

20. Braden went to Atlanta to ask King personally to initiate a petition on behalf of her husband (Anne Braden, *The Wall Between* [Knoxville: University of Tennessee Press, 1999], pp. 325–326; see also Braden to King, 5 March 1961).

21. *Braden v. United States*, 365 U.S. 431 (1961); "Witness Balked in Inquiry on Reds," *New York Times*, 31 July 1958; "A Year for Contempt," *New York Times*, 3 February 1959. Created in 1938, the House Un-American Activities Committee investigated the threat of subversive activities by organizations, private citizens, and public employees suspected of having communist sympathies.

as communistic.[22] Anne Braden sought to convince King to act by citing Supreme Court justice Hugo Black's warning in his dissenting opinion that "the power to interrogate everyone who is called a Communist" would allow all legislative committees "to subpoena all persons anywhere who take a public stand for or against segregation."[23] After King failed to respond to her request, Braden reluctantly decided to move ahead without him. King finally phoned her to indicate that he would support the petition, but only if other black leaders also agreed to sign it. "Anne," he said, "I've been praying about this thing all night. I want you to put my name on that petition."[24]

Anne Braden made revisions to the petition in consultation with King and then secured sponsorship from sixteen others, including Fred Shuttlesworth, Ralph Abernathy, and C.K. Steele.[25] A day after Braden surrendered to U.S. marshals in Atlanta, King told a reporter with the *Atlanta Journal* that the case against Carl revealed the resurgence of McCarthyism, insisting that Carl was being punished for his "integration activities." King also made clear that the clemency petition circulating for Carl was not a defense of communism, but a response to the anticommunist crusade intended to silence those calling for civil rights: "We see the rise of McCarthyism in the South again because all other weapons of the segregationists have failed."[26] This same sentiment was echoed in an SCLC press release that announced the "unanimous agreement" of the organization's executive board to support Carl Braden.[27]

22. Anne Braden had met King at Highlander's 1957 anniversary celebration on 2 September 1957 (see Braden to King, 14 October 1958, in *The Papers of Martin Luther King, Jr.,* vol. 4: *Symbol of the Movement, January 1957–December 1958,* ed. Clayborne Carson, Susan Carson, Adrienne Clay, Virginia Shadron, Kieran Taylor [Berkeley and Los Angeles: University of California Press, 2000], pp. 510–511). Following his address at Highlander, King was denounced in billboards in the South for being at a "Communist Training School." The billboards featured a photograph of King sitting near a reporter for a Communist Party newspaper (see King, "A Look to the Future," Address Delivered at Highlander Folk School's Twenty-fifth Anniversary Meeting, 2 September 1957, in *Papers* 4:269–276).

23. Braden to King, 5 March 1961. Black, an Alabama native, also wrote in his dissent that the decision against Braden "may well strip the Negro of the aid of many of the white people who have been willing to speak on his behalf" (*Braden v. United States,* 365 U.S. 431).

24. Braden, *The Wall Between,* pp. 325–326; see also Braden to James A. Dombrowski, 20 April 1961. In her autobiography, Braden wrote: "There was absolutely no personal advantage for him in his unwavering support of us; it could only bring him trouble and criticism—which it did" (Braden, *The Wall Between,* p. 326). After receiving word that King would sign the petition, Braden sent him a letter: "I know that we have agreed that it is not so much a personal thing for Carl as a weapon to keep the witch hunters from damaging the integration movement, but since I'm personally involved I can't help having a certain sense of appreciation. But more important than that, I admire your courage" (Braden to King, 14 March 1961).

25. Braden to Wood, 27 March 1961. The petition was circulated on 22 April 1961. Additional signees included both black and white Southerners: William B. Abbot, Sarah-Patton Boyle, Carl P. Brannin, James McBride Dabbs, W.W. Finlator, Clarence Jordan, James M. Lawson, Edgar A. Love, Dorcas Ruthenburg, Charles Eubank Tucker, Wyatt Tee Walker, Aubrey W. Williams, and Marion A. Wright (Petition for clemency for Carl Braden, 22 April 1961).

26. Douglas Kiker, "King Sees 'McCarthyism' in 2 U.S. Contempt Sentences," *Atlanta Journal,* 2 May 1961. A day before Braden's surrender on 1 May, King and his wife, Coretta, attended a reception in Atlanta to honor Carl Braden and Frank Wilkinson, who also refused to answer questions before HUAC and was sentenced to a year in jail. For a photograph taken at the reception, see p. 97 in this volume.

27. SCLC, Press release, "King and SCLC meet in Montgomery."

As King came to the defense of Carl Braden, he realized that SCLC's effectiveness was also being threatened by legal attacks against four executive board members who had been sued for libel after signing a 1960 *New York Times* advertisement published by the Committee to Defend Martin Luther King and the Struggle for Freedom in the South.[28] A court had ordered Ralph Abernathy, S.S. Seay, Joseph Lowery, and Fred Shuttlesworth to pay two Alabama officials $500,000 each in damages, and by early 1961 the plaintiffs were seeking to force payment of the judgments.[29] On 8 May King met in New York with the newly formed Lawyers Advisory Committee, a group of eighteen lawyers seeking to raise funds in response to the legal judgments against the four SCLC leaders. King warned that "if these judgments are not reversed, victims of injustice dare not express opposition to their oppressors." He also contended that this kind of "misuse" of the legal system is a "new and potent weapon in the arsenal of the segregationists" that "not only deprives the victim of his economic security, but it undermines his confidence in law."[30]

Following a two-day SCLC board meeting in Montgomery, King and Wyatt Tee Walker returned to Atlanta to meet with participants of the Freedom Rides campaign, organized by CORE to test compliance with the 1960 U.S. Supreme Court ruling outlawing segregation in waiting rooms, restaurants, and restrooms in transportation terminals.[31] The interracial group of thirteen volunteers left Washington, D.C., on 4 May intending to arrive in New Orleans on 17 May, the seventh anniversary of the *Brown* decision.[32] Their first week on the road was mostly uneventful, except for a skirmish in Rock Hill, South Carolina.[33] By the time the group arrived in Atlanta on 13 May to meet with King, the campaign had drawn little national

---

28. According to an SCLC treasurer's report, the Emergency Defense fund balance by the end of April 1961 was $775.42 (Abernathy, "Report of the treasurer"). For more on the libel suits and a facsimile of the advertisement, see Introduction in *Papers* 5:25–26, 382.

29. In two of the five libel cases, the plaintiffs were awarded a combined total of $1 million in damages. Although the ministers appealed the verdicts, the plaintiffs immediately began taking possession of the defendants' personal and real property. Some of the defendants' wages were garnished and their land and cars auctioned ("Background, The Alabama Libel Suits," 8 May 1961; "Car Is Impounded as Libel Payment," *New York Times*, 4 February 1961). In a 9 April 1961 letter to Stanley Levison, King's advisor, Seay pleaded for a loan of $500: "As a result of these suits my credit has been completely nullified here in the community. I am the pastor of a small church, but my main income is from a farm that I operate." In June 1961 federal district court judge Frank M. Johnson ruled that the ministers had been wrongly named as codefendants with the *New York Times* since they had no knowledge that their names were being used in the ad. Johnson's ruling absolved the ministers in two of the three remaining cases ("U.S. Court Keeps Times Libel Suits," *New York Times*, 27 June 1961).

30. King, Statement at Lawyers Advisory Committee Meeting, 8 May 1961, pp. 219, 220 in this volume. The Committee was founded by Theodore W. Kheel, former president of the National Urban League and an arbitrator in labor disputes.

31. SCLC, Press release, "King and SCLC Meet in Montgomery"; *Boynton v. Virginia*, 364 U.S. 454 (1960).

32. Elsie Carper, "Pilgrimage Off on Racial Test," *Washington Post*, 5 May 1961. The group planned to make stops in Virginia, North Carolina, South Carolina, Georgia, Alabama, Mississippi, and Louisiana.

33. SNCC, *The Student Voice* 2, nos. 4 & 5, April–May 1961.

publicity. At Paschal's, a popular black-owned restaurant, King listened as the riders recounted their experiences integrating bus terminals in the Deep South, and later he expressed pride in being a member of CORE's national advisory committee. According to CORE national director James Farmer, the freedom riders were "heartened" by their interaction with King, "the man who had become, without question, the symbol of the civil rights movement in America."[34] Although King supported the freedom riders' objectives, he nonetheless harbored doubts about whether they would accomplish their mission, telling *Jet* reporter Simeon Booker, who was one of two journalists riding the buses, that he had "gotten word you won't reach Birmingham. They're going to waylay you."[35]

On 14 May, both groups of freedom riders left Atlanta for Birmingham, while King preached a Mother's Day sermon at Ebenezer Baptist Church.[36] Later that afternoon, the freedom riders in the first bus encountered trouble when a mob awaited them upon their arrival at the Greyhound bus terminal in Anniston, Alabama. With no police in sight, segregationists slashed the tires and smashed windows on the bus. When police finally arrived, no arrests were immediately made, and the group was allowed to continue on to Birmingham with local Klansmen following closely behind. Six miles outside of Anniston when the bus was forced to pull over because of a flat tire, a member of the pursuing mob hurled a firebomb through one of the bus windows, filling the bus with dense smoke and forcing riders off the bus. Despite the threat of mob violence, the freedom riders got off the bus shortly before it burst into flames. Some of the riders were taken to the hospital, while others were driven to Birmingham in cars dispatched by the Reverend Fred Shuttlesworth, president of the Alabama Christian Movement for Human Rights.[37]

The second contingent of riders met a similar fate upon their arrival at the Trailways bus terminal in Birmingham. With Birmingham police conspicuously absent upon the riders' arrival, segregationists assaulted several freedom riders including James Peck, who was left lying unconscious on the ground outside the terminal. Others were beaten as they tried to enter the segregated waiting room.[38]

34. James Farmer, *Lay Bare the Heart: An Autobiography of the Civil Rights Movement* (New York: Plume, 1985), p. 200. CORE field director Gordon R. Carey asked King to attend a rally in support of the freedom riders at Atlanta's Warren Memorial Methodist Church on 13 May and to arrange for a private dinner with them that evening. The rally was later canceled (Carey to King, 8 May 1961, pp. 217–218 in this volume). Farmer recalled that he expected King to pick up the dinner check at the "not inexpensive" restaurant. "I finally reached slowly for it, certain King would beat me to the punch," but King "made no move, so to my surprise I found myself picking up the tab" (Farmer, *Lay Bare the Heart,* p. 200).

35. Simeon Booker and Carol McCabe Booker, *Shocking the Conscience: A Reporter's Account of the Civil Rights Movement* (Jackson: University Press of Mississippi, 2013), p. 189.

36. King's sermon at Ebenezer was "Crisis in the Modern Family" (Ebenezer Baptist Church, Press release, "'Crisis in the Modern Family,' Dr. King Jr.'s topic at Ebenezer," 13 May 1961).

37. "One Vehicle Is Set Afire at Anniston," *Birmingham Post-Herald,* 15 May 1961; James Peck, *Freedom Ride* (New York: Grove Press, 1962), pp. 96–97.

38. Jerry McCloy, "Attackers Here Use Lead Pipes against Victims," *Birmingham Post-Herald,* 15 May 1961; Peck, *Freedom Ride,* pp. 97–98; "Ambushers Burn Bus, Riot Hits Birmingham," *Montgomery Advertiser,* 15 May 1961. Peck was an original participant in CORE's 1947 Journey of Reconciliation. Prior to their arrival in Birmingham, riders on the Trailways bus also made a brief stop at the Greyhound bus station in Anniston, where, unbeknownst to them, their fellow riders had been attacked an hour earlier. Local thugs boarded the bus and beat several of the riders, forcing them to sit at the rear of the bus.

The next day, Greyhound bus drivers refused to continue the trip.[39] In order to remain on schedule, the group decided to fly from Birmingham to New Orleans, where local CORE members feted the group's heroic efforts.[40] Although the decision to fly to New Orleans effectively marked the end of the initial Freedom Ride, members of the Nashville Christian Leadership Council and SNCC vowed to continue the campaign.[41]

Incensed by the violence in Anniston and Birmingham, King, Fred Shuttlesworth, and Wyatt Tee Walker sent a telegram to Alabama governor John Patterson protesting the brutal treatment of the freedom riders: "Once again Alabama has shamed our nation. The disgraceful and unprovoked violence at Anniston and Birmingham inflicted upon interstate passengers and the failure of law enforcement officials to give adequate protection reeks of Hitlerism."[42] SCLC sent an equally blunt telegram to the attorney general: "It is inconceivable that American citizens peacefully travelling under interstate law cannot be protected from segregationist terrorism and mob violence." The telegram complained that the violence in Alabama mocked the Fourteenth Amendment's guarantee of "equal protection under law" and urged "immediate steps be taken to end the tyranny in Alabama and other states to fully safeguard American citizens from racist brutality."[43]

Spurred by Nashville student activist Diane Nash a new group of ten volunteers left Nashville for Birmingham on 17 May, hoping to resume the Freedom Rides. Upon their arrival in Birmingham, Public Safety commissioner Eugene "Bull" Connor arrested them, holding the group in "protective custody" overnight before driving

---

Throughout the two-hour ride to Birmingham, segregationists occupied the front part of the bus (Peck, *Freedom Ride*, pp. 97–98).

39.  "'Freedom Riders' Fly to N.O. after Bomb Reports Delay Trip before Takeoff," *Birmingham Post-Herald,* 16 May 1961. On 15 May 1961, Robert Kennedy placed a call to George E. Cruit, superintendent of Birmingham's Greyhound bus station, asking if anything could be done to "get this bus down to Montgomery." Cruit insisted that no regular drivers were willing to take the assignment for fear of their safety. Kennedy suggested getting a "driver of one of the colored buses" or even "some Negro school bus driver" to take them to Montgomery. Cruit steadfastly insisted that "amateurs can't handle" $45,000 buses. Frustrated by Cruit's insistence that no driver could be found, Kennedy warned that he was "going to be very much upset if this group does not get to continue their trip" since "they are entitled to transportation provided by Greyhound and we are looking for you to get them on their way." Despite his pleas, no driver was found to take the riders to Montgomery (Transcript, Phone conversation between Robert F. Kennedy and George E. Cruit, 15 May 1961; "Bi-Racial Group Cancels Bus Trip," *New York Times,* 16 May 1961).

40.  Peck, *Freedom Ride*, p. 101. Just before the freedom riders were scheduled to fly from Birmingham, a telephoned bomb threat prompted all passengers to get off the plane, and the freedom riders waited several hours at the airport before departing for New Orleans ("Bi-Racial Group Cancels Bus Trip," 16 May 1961).

41.  Howard Zinn, *SNCC: The New Abolitionists* (Boston: Beacon Press, 1964), pp. 44–45.

42.  The telegram, which was reproduced in an SCLC press release, also called upon the governor to uphold the Constitution and "to begin giving responsible moral leadership to your state before America completely loses her prestige in the world community" (SCLC, Press release, "Freedom riders attacked in Alabama," 15 May 1961).

43.  SCLC, Press release, "Freedom riders attacked in Alabama." In a statement released by CORE, James Farmer said that if mobs can "terrorize American citizens who are peacefully and legally traveling interstate, then existing Federal Laws are not adequate and additional civil rights legislation must be given top priority" (CORE, "Statement by CORE National Director, James Farmer," 16 May 1961).

several of them to the Alabama-Tennessee border and ordering them out of the car.[44] The Nashville contingent was able to catch a ride back to Birmingham's Greyhound bus station, but, once again, bus drivers refused to take them on to Montgomery.[45]

Behind the scenes Justice Department and White House officials sought an agreement that would allow for continued protests without further violence. Robert Kennedy sent his assistant, John Seigenthaler, to Alabama to secure a pledge from Governor John M. Patterson to protect the riders.[46] When a recalcitrant Patterson repeatedly refused, Floyd Mann, Alabama's director of public safety, assured Seigenthaler that the riders would arrive in Montgomery unharmed. Patterson finally capitulated, asserting that he had "the will, the force, the men, and the equipment to give full protection to everyone in Alabama."[47] On 20 May, the riders boarded a Greyhound bus and were escorted to the city limits by Birmingham police, who turned the bus over to the Alabama Highway Patrol for the remainder of the ride to the state capital.[48] The riders expected that Montgomery police would assume responsibility for their safety once they arrived at the Montgomery bus station, but no one was there to shield them from a mob wielding clubs, sticks, and metal pipes. SNCC activists John Lewis, Jim Zwerg, and William Barbee were badly beaten, as was Seigenthaler, who was knocked unconscious trying to come to the aid of a white female rider.[49]

Several attempts by Robert Kennedy to reach Patterson for an explanation went unanswered. Irritated by Patterson's flagrant snub, the attorney general, on orders from the president, deployed federal marshals to Alabama and obtained a federal injunction preventing the Ku Klux Klan and other white supremacists from harassing the riders and interfering with interstate travel.[50] Responding to the violence in Montgomery, the president issued a statement pleading with state and local officials

---

44. "Police Jail 10 'Mixed' Riders for 'Protection' in Bus Delay," *Birmingham Post-Herald*, 18 May 1961. A newspaper quoted Connor as saying he drove the students back to Tennessee for their own protection. When Connor dropped the students off, he reportedly said: "There is the Tennessee line. Cross it and save this state and yourself a lot of trouble." One student replied: "We'll see you back in Birmingham about noon" ("Crowd at Bus Station," *New York Times*, 20 May 1961).

45. Peck, *Freedom Ride*, p. 106.

46. Robert F. Kennedy and Burke Marshall, Interview by Anthony Lewis, 4 December 1964.

47. Burke Marshall, Interview by Louis F. Oberdorfer, 29 May 1964; "'Protection Assured': Patterson, JFK Aide Talk Here," *Montgomery Advertiser*, 20 May 1961.

48. Marshall, Interview by Oberdorfer.

49. Marshall, Interview by Oberdorfer; "Freedom Riders Attacked by Whites in Montgomery," *New York Times*, 21 May 1961; Don Martin, "U.S. Official Is Knocked Unconscious," *Washington Post*, 21 May 1961.

50. "Text of Telegram from Robert Kennedy," *Montgomery Advertiser*, 21 May 1961. In a telegram to Patterson that was released to the public, Robert Kennedy blamed the violence against Seigenthaler and the demonstrators on the governor's failure to enforce the law. Kennedy also argued that while he "strongly" believed that law enforcement should be left to local authorities, his futile attempts to discuss with Patterson how he planned to protect the demonstrations going forward left him no alternative but to call in federal marshals ("Text of Telegram from Robert Kennedy," 21 May 1961). Kennedy acknowledged that his decision to send marshals to Alabama was done "with great reluctance" (Robert F. Kennedy, Summary of telephone conversation with John Malcolm Patterson, 20 May 1961). Following his conversation with Kennedy, Patterson announced that the federal government had no "legal or constitutional right" to send federal marshals into Alabama and that the Kennedy administration had encouraged "busloads of incident-hunting 'students'" to violate our state laws." He also postulated that the federal government's failure to stop "outside agitators" from "invading Alabama" made his efforts

to "exercise their lawful authority to prevent any further outbreaks of violence," while also requesting that the protesters refrain from actions that would provoke further violence.[51]

Canceling a scheduled appearance at Dartmouth College, King flew to Montgomery on 21 May to lead a mass meeting in support of the freedom riders at Abernathy's First Baptist Church.[52] Black residents began filling the pews several hours before the rally began at First Baptist Church, and more than a thousand residents eventually gathered inside. As the meeting got underway, a crowd of angry whites brandishing weapons and yelling racial epithets was growing outside. With only the federal marshals to restrain them, some members of the mob began vandalizing and burning automobiles.[53]

When King stepped to the pulpit, he expressed concern about the "ugly mob outside," but cautioned black residents against becoming "panicky."[54] In King's draft of the remarks he planned to deliver, he charged that "responsibility for the hideous action in Alabama last week must be placed at the doorsteps of the Governor of this State." Governor Patterson's "consistent preaching of defiance of the law, his vitriolic public pronouncements, and his irresponsible actions," King said, "created the atmosphere in which violence could thrive."[55] King also maintained that the federal government's refusal to act amounted to condoning such behavior: "Unless the Federal Government acts forthrightly in the South to assure every citizen his constitutional rights, we will be plunged into a dark abyss of chaos. The federal government must not stand idly by while blood thirsty mobs beat non-violent students with impunity."[56]

Throughout the evening King remained in communication with Robert Kennedy, calling the attorney general several times by phone to inquire about the federal government's plans to resolve the situation.[57] As the mob surrounding the church overwhelmed the outnumbered federal marshals, the attorney general tried to assure King that national guardsmen reinforcements were on the way, but the civil rights leader pressed Kennedy for a more forceful response.[58] After a harrowing eight

---

to enforce the law more difficult ("Riot Incidents May Cloud Patterson, JFK Relations," *Montgomery Advertiser*, 22 May 1961).

51. *Public Papers of the Presidents: John F. Kennedy, 1961*, p. 391.

52. "Dr. King Cancels Visits at College, Returns to South for Race Crisis; Tension Increases in Montgomery," *The Dartmouth*, 22 May 1961; "Graham Asks Negro Group Stay Overnight in Church," *Montgomery Advertiser*, 22 May 1961.

53. "Angry Mob Quits Church before Cloud of Tear Gas," *Montgomery Advertiser*, 22 May 1961.

54. "Graham Asks Negro Group Stay Overnight in Church," 22 May 1961; King, Statement Delivered at Freedom Riders Rally at First Baptist Church, 21 May 1961, p. 232 in this volume.

55. King, Address at Freedom Riders Rally at First Baptist Church, 21 May 1961, p. 229 in this volume. Several days after the rioting, Patterson contended that the federal government was responsible for the mayhem: "They caused that rioting by bringing King to Montgomery. There were about sixty marshals on hand. They escorted him to the church. It looked like the President of the United States" (Claude Sitton, "Bi-Racial Riders Decide to Go On," *New York Times*, 24 May 1961).

56. King, Address at Freedom Riders Rally, 21 May 1961, p. 229 in this volume.

57. "Negroes Leave Church after Long Stay," *Montgomery Advertiser*, 23 May 1961.

58. "Angry Mob Quits Church before Cloud of Tear Gas," 22 May 1961. Attempting to regain his power from federal authorities, Patterson declared Montgomery under martial law, sending in guardsmen to do whatever necessary to restore peace ("Montgomery under Martial Law; Troops Called after New Riot; Marshals and Police Fight Mob," *New York Times*, 22 May 1961).

hours for those trapped inside the church, federal marshals used tear gas to disperse the mob and Alabama national guardsmen evacuated the church and escorted those inside to their homes.[59]

Over the course of the next two days, King, Farmer, and other SCLC officials met with student protesters, who urged King to join their planned Freedom Rides into Mississippi. Fearing that any new arrests would be a violation of the probation he received after his arrest in Atlanta the previous year, King declined.[60] King's decision disappointed and angered some students, who mocked King's comparison of himself to Christ and noted that they were also on probation. But King did not budge, insisting, "I think I should pick the time and place of my Golgotha." The students walked out of the meeting in protest.[61]

On 23 May King joined James Farmer, Ralph Abernathy, and John Lewis at a press conference in Abernathy's home that sought to clarify the overall mission of the Freedom Rides while also affirming that the rides would continue from Montgomery to Jackson, Mississippi. "The students have made it crystal clear that the ride will take place with or without federal protection," King asserted.[62] Asked about the possibility that someone could be severely injured or killed during the campaign, he responded: "We would not like to see anyone die. . . . but the philosophy of the non-violence involves the spirit of willingness to die for a cause. We are willing to face anything—even if it is death."[63] King's appearance at the press conference prompted some leaders and activists to praise him. Labor leader A. Philip Randolph pledged his "unstinting aid," while educator Septima Clark commended King for not merely making a statement, but going "into the thickest fight as a real symbol of courage to the grass roots people." Clark told King that she "could not sit on this mountain top and not let you know how much taller you have grown in my estimation."[64]

As the students readied themselves for the next leg of the Freedom Ride on 24 May, King stood outside the Montgomery bus terminal, shaking hands with some of the riders and wishing them a safe journey to Mississippi. Under protection by police and the National Guard, the first group of freedom riders was en route to Mississippi when the attorney general issued a press release reiterating that federal

59. "Angry Mob Quits Church before Cloud of Tear Gas," 22 May 1961; "Negroes Leave Church after Long Stay," 23 May 1961.

60. Samuel Hoskins, "Fear New Ala. Riot Outbreak," *Chicago Daily Defender*, 24 May 1961; John Lewis and Michael D'Orso, *Walking with the Wind: A Memoir of the Movement* (New York: Harcourt Brace, 1998), p. 163. In May 1960 King received a traffic violation for driving with an invalid license. Later that year, he pled guilty and was fined $25 in addition to receiving a year of probation (see note 187, Introduction in *Papers* 5:37).

61. James Farmer, Interview by Taylor Branch, 18 November 1983; see also "A Disappointing King" in *The Crusader* 2, no. 31 (5 June 1961). According to John Lewis's autobiography, after that meeting the students jeeringly began referring to King as "De Lawd" (Lewis and D'Orso, *Walking with the Wind*, p. 164).

62. King, Press Conference Announcing the Continuation of the Freedom Rides, 23 May 1961, p. 235 in this volume.

63. "'Freedom Riders' Sight Miss. As Next Target," *Los Angeles Times*, 24 May 1961.

64. A. Philip Randolph to King, 23 May 1961; Clark to King, 23 May 1961, p. 233 in this volume. King also received telegrams of support from couples Ruby Dee and Ossie Davis and Sidney and Juanita Poitier (Dee and Davis to King, 25 May 1961, pp. 237–238 in this volume; Sidney and Juanita Poitier to King and Freedom Riders, 25 May 1961).

marshals would not be on hand to protect them and that Alabama and Mississippi officials intended to maintain law and order.[65] The attorney general explained that the administration's obligation was "to protect interstate travelers and maintain law and order only when local authorities are unable or unwilling to do so." Kennedy also voiced his concern that the domestic turmoil associated with the rides would undermine the nation during the president's June 1961 meeting in Vienna with Soviet Premier Nikita Khrushchev: "Whatever we do in the United States at this time, which brings or causes discredit on our Country, can be harmful to his mission."[66]

Unlike their previous bus rides, the trip to Mississippi was peaceful and uneventful, but once the riders arrived in Jackson, local police promptly arrested them.[67] Robert Kennedy had received assurance from Mississippi governor Ross Barnett that the mayhem and rioting in Alabama would not happen in his state.[68] Kennedy also called for a halt to the Freedom Rides, suggesting in a phone call to King that freedom riders jailed in Mississippi could be released in exchange for a "cooling-off period" that would allow for the "present state of confusion and danger" to pass and an "atmosphere of reason and normalcy" to be restored.[69] When King insisted that the freedom riders would remain in jail as a "matter of conscience and morality," Kennedy responded: "That is not going to have the slightest effect on what the government is going to do in this field or any other. The fact that they stay in jail is not going to have the slightest effect on me." King warned: "Perhaps it would help if students came down here by the hundreds—by the hundreds of thousands." Kennedy did not appreciate what he perceived to be a threat by King: "The country belongs to you as much as to me. You can determine what's best just as well as I can, but don't make statements that sound like a threat. That's not the way to deal with us." While King stood firm in his conviction that the riders must stay jailed, he tried to salvage the conversation by telling the attorney general: "It's difficult to understand the position of oppressed people. Ours is a way out—creative, moral and nonviolent. It

---

65. "'Freedom Riders' Exit Under Eyes of Guard, Police," *Montgomery Advertiser*, 25 May 1961.

66. U.S. Department of Justice, Statement, Robert F. Kennedy on protection of freedom riders, 24 May 1961. In a 19 July 1961 press conference, the president was asked to give his views on the Freedom Rides: "I think the Attorney General has made it clear that we believe that everyone who travels, for whatever reason they travel, should enjoy the full constitutional protection given to them by the law and by the Constitution. They should be able to move freely in interstate commerce. . . . In my judgment, there's no question of the legal rights of the freedom travelers—Freedom Riders, to move in interstate commerce. And those rights, whether we agree with those who travel, whether we agree with the purpose for which they travel, those rights stand, providing they are exercised in a peaceful way" (*Public Papers of the Presidents: John F. Kennedy, 1961*, p. 517).

67. "27 Arrested in Mississippi As Rides Continued," *Birmingham World*, 27 May 1961.

68. Transcript, Phone conversation between Robert F. Kennedy and Ross R. Barnett, 23 May 1961. In a later interview Kennedy said his "primary interest" was that the riders "weren't beaten up," and he conceded that he knew the riders were going to be arrested, but "I didn't have any control over it" (Kennedy and Marshall, Interview by Lewis, 4 December 1964).

69. "Attorney General's Pleas," *New York Times*, 25 May 1961. In a 1964 interview, Kennedy recalled being criticized for calling for a "cooling-off" period: "I thought that people were going to get killed, and they had made their point. What was the purpose of continuing with it?" (Kennedy and Marshall, Interview by Lewis, 4 December 1964). In a 10 September 1961 article in the *New York Times Magazine*, King criticized those who advocated for "cooling-off" periods (see King, "The Time for Freedom Has Come," pp. 275, 276–277 in this volume).

is not tied to black supremacy or Communism, but to the plight of the oppressed. It can save the soul of America. You must understand that we've made no gains without pressure and I hope that pressure will always be moral, legal and peaceful." After Kennedy repeated his offer to have the protesters released, King firmly replied: "They'll stay."[70]

From his Atlanta office the following day, King told *New York Times* reporter Claude Sitton that the arrests in Mississippi were a minor setback and that the rides would resume "in full force" in a few days. As he had said in his conversation with Robert Kennedy the previous evening, King defended the freedom riders and their tactics: "These are the pioneers who are making the way possible for people of all areas to ride buses unmolested by segregation as well as to use the facilities of the bus terminals without being segregated."[71]

With no clear end in sight for the Freedom Rides, CORE, SCLC, SNCC, and Nashville Christian Leadership Council formed the Freedom Ride Coordinating Committee, an independent organization.[72] During a 26 May meeting, the new organization agreed that the rides would last until "interstate travel can be enjoyed throughout the nation by all citizens." The immediate objective was fourfold: coordinate the bus rides, intensify demonstrations to bring segregation in interstate travel to the forefront of the nation's conscience, convince the attorney general to order the Interstate Commerce Commission (ICC) to uphold the Supreme Court decisions in *Morgan* and *Boynton,* and fill the Montgomery and Jackson jails to "keep a sharp image of the issues before the public." To get the Freedom Ride Coordinating Committee up and running, SCLC and CORE each pledged $1,000, and Wyatt Tee Walker was appointed to administer the funds.[73]

Three days after the Committee's founding, Robert Kennedy petitioned the ICC to issue regulations banning segregation in interstate travel and the ICC complied

---

70. Edwin Guthman, *We Band of Brothers* (New York: Harper & Row, 1971), pp. 154–155.

71. Also in the interview with Sitton, King argued that the continuation of the Freedom Rides was necessary: "I can conceive of no great social change or progress without some individuals who are willing to take the blows and who are temporarily misunderstood" (Sitton, "Dr. King Refuses to End Bus Test," *New York Times,* 26 May 1961).

72. In a 24 May press release, SCLC announced that King had authorized the launch of the Committee to organize the continuation of the Freedom Rides. King pledged SCLC's full cooperation and "entire resources" until interstate travel facilities were fully integrated: "It must be made clear to the nation, and the south in particular, that American citizens will not be restrained in the practice of their legal, moral and Constitutional privileges." And despite government officials who refuse to "recognize that racial segregation has no place in the fabric of our democracy," King insisted, they are "fighting a lost cause" (James R. Wood, Press release, Freedom Ride Coordinating Committee formed, 24 May 1961). The committee consisted of Gordon Carey of CORE, Ed King of SNCC, Diane Nash of the Nashville Christian Leadership Council, and Wyatt Tee Walker of SCLC. Although the founding documents indicated that the committee would not have a chairman, and each member would function equally in the organization, Walker was later quoted as saying that the students would handle most of the work: "They are the ones serving as the shock troops and we've got to go along" (James R. Wood, Report on meeting of the Freedom Ride Coordinating Committee, 26 May 1961; Claude Sitton, "Group Maps Plans on Freedom Rides," *New York Times,* 1 June 1961).

73. Wood, Report on meeting of the Freedom Ride Coordinating Committee; *Morgan v. Virginia,* 328 U.S. 373 (1946). Since October 1959 King had been lobbying the ICC to end discriminatory practices against black interstate travelers (King to Kenneth H. Tuggle, 19 October 1959, in *Papers* 5:309–310; see also King, Recommendations to the SCLC Executive Committee, 30 September 1959, in *Papers* 5:295–297).

a few months later.[74] Although King would rather have had a second Emancipation Proclamation ending all forms of segregation, he was pleased with the success of the Freedom Rides and the pressure that the attorney general placed on the ICC. King told an audience at Lincoln University in June:

> We think of the Freedom Rides. Think of the fact that more than sixty-five people are now in jail in Jackson, Mississippi. What has this done, we say? These people have been beaten. They've suffered. Let us realize that it has brought to the attention of this nation the indignities and the injustices which Negro people still confront in interstate travel. So it has had an educational value. But not only that—signs have come down from bus stations in Montgomery, Alabama. They've never been down before. Not only that—the attorney general of this nation has called on ICC to come out with new regulations making it palpably clear that segregation in interstate travel is illegal and unconstitutional.[75]

Although King never joined a freedom ride, many people thought of him as the leader of the campaign. King's reluctance to ride the buses irked some of his critics, especially Robert F. Williams, head of the Monroe, North Carolina branch of the NAACP, who sent the SCLC president a telegram: "No sincere leader asks his followers to make sacrifices that he himself will not endure. You are a phony." Williams insisted that if King lacked the courage to ride the buses, he should remove himself "from the vanguard," for "now is the time for true leaders to take to the field of battle."[76] Despite Williams's criticism, King insisted that although CORE had originated the Freedom Rides, the "central involvement since May 17th organizational wise has been SCLC oriented."[77] King's declining popularity among militant activists was gradually becoming evident to outside observers. A *Time* magazine article published in early 1962 suggested that students who had once idolized King were turning against him, charging that he was "status seeking" and "more interested in making speeches across the U.S. than in head-on action."[78]

---

74. Kennedy, "Petition for rule making," 29 May 1961; ICC, Resolution MC–C–3358, "Discrimination in operations of interstate motor carriers of passengers," 22 September 1961. Harris Wofford, special assistant to the president, forwarded a copy of Kennedy's petition to King (Wofford to King, 6 June 1961). In a fundraising letter to an SCLC supporter, King called the ICC ruling a "remarkable victory which in no small way is attributable to the way in which the Freedom Rides dramatized the travel [*conditions?*] in our nation for persons of color." He also wrote of likely attempts to circumvent the ICC ruling, saying that money would be needed to sponsor activities to test the ICC ruling when it comes into effect on 1 November (King to Russell Buckner, 25 October 1961; see also King, Christ Lives in the World, Address delivered at the American Lutheran Church Luther League Convention, 16 August 1961; King to Evelyn Spraitzar, 29 December 1961, pp. 357–358 in this volume).

75. King, "The American Dream," Address delivered at Lincoln University Commencement, 6 June 1961.

76. Williams to King, 31 May 1961, pp. 241, 242 in this volume. Williams had clashed with King in 1959 over the role of nonviolence in the movement. For more on King's relationship with Williams, see Introduction in *Papers* 5:17–18.

77. King to J. Raymond Henderson, 6 June 1961, p. 248 in this volume.

78. "Confused Crusade," *Time*, 12 January 1962. While in London in October 1961, King appeared on John Freeman's "Face to Face," where he was asked to respond to criticism that he lacked "fire" and that he was "not really keen on challenging" segregation "except on the margins." King responded: "I don't know if I lack fire. I do feel that at times I am rather soft, and maybe a little gentle, but on the other hand,

Behind the scenes, the Kennedy administration sought to steer the civil rights movement away from protest by encouraging private donors, such as the Field and Taconic Foundations, to provide financial support for nonpartisan voter registration efforts.[79] King, however, did not view such efforts as inconsistent with protest activities. In 1957 SCLC had launched its own Crusade for Citizenship campaign, although few black voters were registered as a result.[80]

Plans for the new voter registration program got underway at a meeting called by the Taconic Foundation in July 1961.[81] Representatives from six leading civil rights organizations—SCLC, NAACP, CORE, SNCC, National Student Association (NSA), and the National Urban League—gathered in New York to discuss each agency's existing voter registration programs and how they could be augmented by the Taconic Foundation and other philanthropic groups.[82] The meeting was harmonious and all agreed that the Southern Regional Council (SRC) would administer and coordinate the new Voter Education Project (VEP). In the following months, the leaders of the major civil rights organizations continued to meet to discuss a variety of issues, including how to address the apathy of potential black voters, the feat of organizing several national organizations, and program finances.[83] Despite the obstacles, the SRC urged the organizations to press on, and by November 1961 the SRC submitted a two-year grant proposal for $500,000 in seed money to the Taconic Foundation to be distributed among the six civil rights organizations based on an evaluation of each group's program.[84]

---

I have strongly advocated direct action. I have made it clear that I believe this is one of the most potent weapons available to oppressed people in their struggle for freedom and human dignity. So that I don't consider this a marginal approach. I consider this as an approach going to the very depths. I have participated in sit-ins myself. I have been arrested as a result of my participating in sit-ins with the students at lunch counters. I served as one of the coordinators of the Freedom Rides so that I don't think it is true to say that I am not in accord with these particular methods. I believe in them, and I have advocated them and participated in them" (King, Interview by John Freeman on "Face to Face," 29 October 1961).

79. King to Leslie Dunbar, 19 January 1962, pp. 368–369 in this volume; Harris Wofford, *Of Kennedys & Kings: Making Sense of the Sixties* (New York: Farrar, Straus, Giroux, 1980), pp. 158–159.

80. Introduction in *Papers* 4:23–25.

81. Agenda and outline for meeting discussing voter registration, 28 July 1961.

82. Representatives of the six groups included King and Wyatt Tee Walker of SCLC; Roy Wilkins, Thurgood Marshall, and Robert Carter of the NAACP; James Farmer of CORE; Charles McDew and Marion Barry of SNCC; Timothy Jenkins of NSA; and Lester Granger and Whitney Young of the National Urban League. Also at the meeting were Burke Marshall, assistant attorney general; Harris Wofford, assistant to President Kennedy; Stephen Currier, cofounder of the Taconic Foundation; Lloyd K. Garrison, trustee of the Taconic Foundation; Jane Lee Eddy, executive secretary of the Taconic Foundation; Harold Fleming, executive vice president of the Potomac Institute; Justine Wise Polier, executive board member of the Field Foundation; Vernon Eagle, executive director of the New World Foundation; Leslie Dunbar, executive director of the Southern Regional Council (SRC); and John H. Wheeler, chairman of the executive committee of the SRC (Leslie Dunbar, Memo to the members of the Executive Committee, 31 July 1961).

83. Dunbar, Memo to members of the Executive Committee; SRC, Memo for discussion regarding Voter Education Project, 23 August 1961; and Dunbar to Farmer, Wilkins, Young, Walker, McDew, and Jenkins, 13 September 1961.

84. Dunbar to Stephen R. Currier, 10 November 1961. Roy Wilkins, executive secretary of the NAACP, was not pleased with SRC's plans to distribute funds. He insisted that the money be given to established and proven voter registration programs, commenting that "it would, we think, be a disservice to the objectives

Seeking to take advantage of the financial resources and social networks of its constituent black churches, SCLC proposed increased voter registration efforts in various geographic locations throughout the South. While maintaining respect for the work of the NAACP, SCLC suggested working in Alabama where the NAACP had been banned in 1956.[85] SCLC would hire five field secretaries to coordinate efforts to increase the number of African American registered voters in the South over the next two years.[86]

King would eventually follow through on the idea of building a grassroots voter registration program, but during the fall of 1961 he found it difficult to avoid controversies. For example, King continued to be involved in Carl Braden's legal battles. On 17 August 1961 a delegation led by SCLC treasurer Ralph Abernathy met with presidential assistants Harris Wofford and Lee C. White at the White House to present the petition in support of Carl Braden's clemency signed by King and nearly 2,000 other "high stature" individuals.[87] No immediate action resulted from the delegation's appeal to the White House, and in September Anne Braden turned to both King and Walker for advice on whether or not her husband should accept parole. Walker rejected the idea, voicing concern that this would damage not only Braden's reputation but also his prospects for overturning his sentence entirely. King, however, questioned whether accepting parole would prohibit Carl Braden from continuing his work in the freedom struggle. "This, I think, would be too great a compromise," King said. "It would be exchanging one kind of prison for another kind. There might be no bars, but it would be telling him he could not do the thing his life is committed to."[88]

After the parole board declined Braden's parole, King continued to support Anne Braden's efforts to win her husband's release from prison, including accepting her invitation to participate in a documentary about HUAC.[89] A few weeks after agree-

and confusing to the public if the NAACP's cooperative joint listing with other groups, some of which thus far have little more than good intentions to offer, should be taken to imply equality as regards their relative importance and potential in the work to be done" (Wilkins to Dunbar, 17 October 1961).

85. SCLC, "Southwide Voter Registration Prospectus," 1961. In June 1956 Alabama attorney general John Patterson obtained a court order banning most NAACP activities in Alabama after the organization refused to hand over their membership lists. SCLC's prospectus to the SRC expressed great respect and admiration for the work of the NAACP. It vowed to work jointly and cooperatively with the NAACP and would only accept responsibilities for locals upon their mutual agreement (SCLC, "Southwide Voter Registration Prospectus").

86. SCLC, "Southwide Voter Registration Prospectus"; see also Southern Regional Council, Press release, Voter Education Project to study voter registration in the South, 29 March 1962.

87. Carl Braden Clemency Appeal Committee, Press release, "Statement by Dr. Ralph D. Abernathy, spokesman for the committee," 17 August 1961; Carl Braden Clemency Appeal Committee, Press release, Committee presents clemency appeal petition to John F. Kennedy, 17 August 1961.

88. Anne Braden to Carl Braden, 14 September 1961.

89. Anne Braden, Memo to advisors in Carl Braden clemency case, 9 October 1961. On behalf of the documentary's producer Robert Cohen and advisor Bertram Edises, Braden asked King to participate in the film (Braden to King, 31 October 1961).

ing to appear in the film, however, King was dismayed to learn from Braden that the film's advisor, Bertram Edises, was a former member of the Communist Party. Although Anne Braden tried to assuage King's concern about red-baiting—"I think you are far above any such attack and absolutely invulnerable"—King withdrew from the project.[90] Writing on King's behalf, Wyatt Tee Walker explained to the documentary's producer Robert Cohen that Edises's prior political affiliation would tarnish King's reputation and "create more problems than we have time to deal with as it relates to the major work of Dr. King."[91]

After distancing himself from the film, King's attention was again diverted after becoming mired in controversy within the National Baptist Convention (NBC), the nation's largest black Baptist organization. Events within the National Baptist Convention proved to be even more tumultuous than relationships among civil rights leaders. Smoldering disagreements led to a rupture within the Convention over differences regarding the lines of authority within the group as well as its approach to civil rights. The Convention's president J. H. Jackson had long resisted the efforts of King and other ministers to involve the group more directly in direct action protests and had successfully dodged previous challenges to his leadership.[92] When Gardner Taylor, a minister from New York who was allied with King, mounted a challenge to Jackson's presidency at the 1960 convention, the gathering ended with both Taylor and Jackson declaring victory.[93] Despite subsequent efforts to find a compromise, King was pessimistic that Jackson would work in the spirit of cooperation: "I have not had a chance to talk with Dr. Jackson, and while I am somewhat doubtful about his willingness to work out the problem in a mutually agreeable manner, I do think that we must continue to urge him to do this."[94]

During the annual meeting of the National Sunday School and Baptist Training Union (BTU) Congress in June 1961, King, who had been vice president of the congress since September 1958, praised the Freedom Rides and the religious underpinning of the campaign, urging African Americans to continue to test segregated transportation facilities. Jackson then publicly denounced civil disobedience, insisting that the jailing of black people did little to arouse the conscience of segregationists and that integration should come through lawful appeals to the courts and the federal government.[95]

An ominous tone pervaded the 1961 NBC convention in Kansas City, Missouri, after opposing factions set up separate registration booths.[96] During the opening session on 6 September, Taylor and his supporters rushed the platform to take con-

90. King to Braden, 7 November 1961; Braden to King, 24 November 1961, p. 329 in this volume; and Walker to Robert Carl Cohen, 30 January 1962.

91. Walker to Cohen, 30 January 1962.

92. See Introductions in *Papers* 4:17–18 and 5:34.

93. See Introduction in *Papers* 5:34.

94. King to H. Grady Neal, 11 January 1961. Grady had sent King copies of the letters he had sent to Jackson and Taylor (Neal to Jackson, 7 December 1960; Neal to Taylor, 15 December 1960).

95. "Two Negro Baptist Leaders Disagree on Freedom Riders," *St. Louis Dispatch,* 22 June 1961; Introduction in *Papers* 4:18.

96. Kenneth C. Field, "Say Baptist 'Fireworks' Shape Up in Kansas City," *Chicago Daily Defender,* 6 September 1961.

trol of the convention, but were blocked by Jackson devotees. The attempt ignited a physical confrontation in which sixty-four-year-old Arthur Wright, a minister from Detroit who supported Jackson, fell four feet from the podium and suffered a fatal head injury.[97]

Wright's death was followed by mounting negative publicity for the convention and a floor vote monitored by the Jackson County Circuit Court. Taylor eventually conceded the presidency to Jackson on 8 September.[98] As one of his first official acts after his reelection, Jackson relieved King of his duties as vice president of the BTU.[99] Upon hearing the news, King acknowledged that as president Jackson had the right to surround himself with people sympathetic to his views.[100]

King's ouster came as no surprise to many as Jackson had long felt threatened by King's rising prominence. Jackson's motives for removing King were so transparent that Reverend Charles Butler warned King that Jackson's actions were "a strategic move to counteract your possible rivalry to his office and to mar your hard and gloriously won international prestige."[101] Disappointed over his removal, King later confided in O. Clay Maxwell, president of the BTU, that he did not want to risk his own reputation by taking further action against Jackson. He did not, however, rule out a protest led by other delegates, reasoning that "Dr. Jackson will continue his un-Christian, unethical and dictatorial tactics as long as no-one openly opposes him."[102]

Angered by the rancorous challenge to his presidency, Jackson escalated simmering hostility with King by laying responsibility for Wright's death at King's feet, accusing King of having "masterminded" the invasion of the convention.[103] On 10

97. Lucille Bluford, "I Saw It When It Happened . . . ," *New York Amsterdam News*, 16 September 1961; "Minister Hurt in Church Brawl Dies of Injuries after Surgery," *Washington Post*, 8 September 1961.

98. "Mayor Begs Battling Preachers to 'Go Home!'," *New York Amsterdam News*, 16 September 1961.

99. "Dr. King Ousted from S.S. Congress Position," *Kansas City Call*, 22 September 1961. In addition to King, C.C. Adams, a minister from Philadelphia and a Taylor supporter, was also dismissed from his post as secretary of the Foreign Mission board. King was replaced by Jackson stalwart E.C. Estell and Adams was succeeded by William H. Harvey ("Dr. King Ousted from S.S. Congress Position," 22 September 1961). In his memoirs, Jackson claimed that it was not he that initiated King's removal, but that it was Reverend Julian Taylor who moved to oust King. Taylor asserted that King "has used his influence and his technique to disrupt, confuse and disorganize our Convention and has done little or nothing to strengthen the fellowship between the Congress and the Convention, or to aid the Congress in its educational objectives. The truth is, we have his name but have not had his constructive support. The National Baptist Convention does not need Dr. King's name without Dr. King's loyalty" (Jackson, *A Story of Christian Activism: The History of the National Baptist Convention, U.S.A., Inc.* [Nashville: Townsend Press, 1980], p. 484).

100. "Dr. King Ousted from S.S. Congress Position," 22 September 1961.

101. Butler to King, 15 September 1961. In 1957, King, Sr. had tried to quell Jackson's fears that King, Jr. was seeking to unseat him as president (see Introduction in *Papers* 4:18). J. Pius Barbour, King's mentor while at Crozer, urged King to contest his removal as vice president of the BTU (Barbour to King, 14 September 1961, pp. 282–283 in this volume). In addition, a group of ministers and lay leaders sent O. Clay Maxwell, president of the National Sunday School and BTU Congress, a letter protesting Jackson's "undemocratic removal" of King from office (Baptist Pastors and Lay Leaders of the National Baptist Convention of the United States of America to Maxwell, 9 October 1961).

102. King to Maxwell, 20 December 1961, p. 353 in this volume.

103. "Church Conclave Violence Blamed on Martin King," *Birmingham News*, 10 September 1961. At a 9 September press conference Jackson said: "This disregard for Convention officers and the pushing of folks off platforms was a result of an election campaign so vicious it produced violence" (Wallace H. Terry, "Baptist Leader Charges Dr. King Sparked 'Invasion' of Rival Forces," *Washington Post*, 10

September, an enraged King sent a telegram to Jackson demanding an immediate retraction for the "libelous and injurious" charges, which not only stood to tarnish his public image but also potentially to damage the freedom struggle.[104] In his response to King, Jackson denied making the defamatory statement, instead pointing to several instances in which the press misquoted him.[105] In a press release sent to King, Jackson maintained that his statement was intended to credit King for work in the nonviolent movement and for being the "master-mind behind the protest techniques" of the sit-ins and Freedom Rides.[106] King did not accept Jackson's apology and retraction but, nevertheless, he declined to sue the NBC president for libel.[107]

In the days following Jackson's statement, the dispute continued. More than thirty Baptist leaders sent a telegram to Jackson condemning his accusations against King. "Whatever may be our differences within the denomination," the ministers wrote, "this uncalled for and provoked attack (credited to you) upon one of the greatest men of our time, will only serve the purposes of the segregationist forces in America who are determined to suppress the Negro community all over the nation."[108]

King seemed eager to put the situation behind him, but Jackson further polarized the NBC by renewing his attacks against King and Taylor while delivering the eulogy at Wright's funeral. Jackson's eulogy was punctuated by thinly veiled references implicating King and Taylor for Wright's death: "Our denomination is full of men who have diplomas hanging on the wall, who have the cloth on but not the God in. A man who is going to preach Christ will have to know him, you can't be one thing at your church, and another thing at the convention. You've got to be a Christian in town and out of town."[109]

---

September 1961). Jackson's accusation against King ran in several newspapers ("Calls Dr. King 'Master Mind' of Fatal Riot," *Chicago Tribune,* 10 September 1961; "Dr. King Is Accused in Baptist Dispute," *New York Times,* 10 September 1961).

104. In his defense, King maintained that he was not in the auditorium when the *mêlée* occurred and that he had never taken part in any strategy sessions aimed at supplanting Jackson as president (King to Jackson, 10 September 1961, pp. 278–279 in this volume).

105. Jackson to King, 12 September 1961, pp. 281–282 in this volume.

106. Jackson elaborated: "I did not blame any individual, but placed the responsibility directly on two groups. I do not believe the press was malicious in this, I believe that they misunderstood. I have not in the past, and I do not now intend to inflict any injury on any person in the public press. I know what it means to be so victimized, for I have suffered so much of this in the past ten years" (Jackson, "Statement by Dr. J. H. Jackson, President National Baptist Convention of the United States of America," 10 September 1961).

107. Eddie L. Madison, Press release, "Dr. Martin Luther King says he will not sue Dr. Jackson for alleged statement that he masterminded convention violence 'at this time,'" 20 September 1961.

108. The telegram was signed by several religious leaders, including Benjamin E. Mays, Ralph Abernathy, Samuel W. Williams, Fred L. Shuttlesworth, Kelly Miller Smith, Gardner C. Taylor, and Sandy Ray (SCLC, Press release, "Religious leaders protest alleged attack on Dr. Martin Luther King, Jr.," 12 September 1961). For more on the reaction to Jackson's accusations against King, see King to Erma Jewell Hughes, 19 September 1961, pp. 285–286 in this volume. Jackson had his supporters as well. Not everyone felt that King was an innocent bystander, including Robert E. L. Hardmond, an NBC member and minister from New York. Hardmond confided to Jackson that he had heard King say "slanderous and malicious" things about Jackson, including that Jackson was to blame for Wright's death (Hardmond to Jackson, 26 September 1961).

109. Chester Higgins, "Wright Funeral an Uproar," *Pittsburgh Courier,* 23 September 1961. Following
Jackson's eulogy of Wright, the Trade Union Leadership Council released a statement condemning

Despite the debacle in Kansas City, Taylor and King called for unification within the NBC. "What ever is wrong with the convention," King said, "cannot be corrected by a split."[110] Efforts to keep the Convention intact became more difficult when a group of ministers led by L. Venchael Booth called for a meeting in November to discuss the schism.[111] From the outset some pastors lobbied Booth to get King more involved with the new organization, later called the Progressive National Baptist Convention (PNBC). King, however, did not attend the founding meeting in November 1961 and later expressed concern that Booth's unilateral decision to form the PNBC "greatly weakened the potential effectiveness of the new Convention."[112] Although King's involvement and leadership of the PNBC had been assumed by other black ministers, he did not immediately join the group because he did not want to exacerbate the division between black Baptists.[113]

∿∿∿∿∿

To add to his already busy schedule, King began coteaching a course in philosophy with Samuel W. Williams at Morehouse College in late September 1961.[114] In his first and only teaching position, King relished the opportunity to be in the classroom given his desire to pursue an academic post after finishing his qualifying examinations at Boston University in 1952. He had received previous job offers, including one from Shaw University in Raleigh, North Carolina.[115]

King was well versed in philosophy having taken courses on the subject while a student at Morehouse, Crozer Theological Seminary, and Boston University, where he wrote his doctoral dissertation on Paul Tillich's and Henry Nelson Weiman's

---

Jackson's renewed attack against King and called for a unified black community: "So that there will be no doubt we want to make it emphatically clear that we feel that the 'freedom movement,' with all of its acknowledged imperfections, and Dr. Martin Luther King are two of the best things that have happened to America in many a year" (Ernest Dillard, Press release, Telegram to J. H. Jackson, 23 September 1961).

110. "New Split Threatens Baptists; Jackson Denies Rapping Dr. King," *Jet,* 28 September 1961.

111. See note 5, King to T.Y. Rogers, 8 March 1962, p. 424 in this volume.

112. King to Rogers, 8 March 1962, p. 424 in this volume; J.C. Austin to L. Venchael Booth, 26 September 1961, and "Organizational Meeting of the Progressive National Baptist Convention," 14–15 November 1961, in William D. Booth, *A Call to Greatness* (Lawrenceville: Brunswick Publishing, 2001), pp. 90–91, 181; and J. Raymond Henderson to Booth, 13 October 1961.

113. In addition to its membership in the NBC, Ebenezer Baptist Church voted to affiliate with the predominately white American Baptist Convention (King to William H. Rhoades, 26 January 1962, pp. 374–376 in this volume). King had expressed interest in joining the American Baptist Convention before his 1959 trip to India (King to Reuben E. Nelson, 23 March 1959, in *Papers* 5:157–158). King spoke at the ABC's 1962 annual meeting (King, "The Mission to the Social Frontiers," Address at the American Baptist Convention, 24 May 1962). Ebenezer joined the PNBC in 1963.

114. Mays to King, 3 August 1961. In a 20 July 1961 letter Morehouse College president Benjamin E. Mays offered King $1,500 to teach the course during the 1961–1962 academic year. King agreed to Mays's offer on 1 August (see p. 258 in this volume).

115. Crozer president Sankey L. Blanton recommended King for a position as dean of the school of religion at Shaw University (Introduction in *The Papers of Martin Luther King, Jr.,* vol. 2: *Rediscovering Precious Values, July 1951–November 1955,* ed. Clayborne Carson, Ralph E. Luker, Penny A. Russell, Peter Holloran (Berkeley and Los Angeles: University of California Press, 1994), p. 28.

philosophies of God.[116] Nine students from both Morehouse and its female counterpart, Spelman, enrolled in the course, which met on Tuesdays and was designed as a broad introduction to social philosophy using the ideas of Plato, Aristotle, Hobbes, Rousseau, and Locke among others.[117] King's lecture notes showed similarities to a synthesis of many introductory-level philosophy texts, including those by Will Durant, William Kelley Wright, and A. C. McGiffert.[118]

In an effort to honor his commitment to Morehouse, King frequently canceled or rescheduled events and fundraising opportunities.[119] Although his enthusiasm for teaching led him to entertain the idea of extending his tenure at Morehouse, his increasing responsibilities in the civil rights movement caused him to decline Mays's invitation to return for the following academic year. In a note to Mays, King thanked him for the privilege to teach at Morehouse, and although he did not attend as many classes as he had hoped, King found the experience rewarding: "It gave me an opportunity to spend a few quiet hours with some of the great thinkers of the ages." King further expressed his hope that he might be able to "return to such a challenging responsibility sometime in the future," and admitted his deep-seated passion for scholarship: "I certainly have my moments of intellectual nostalgia—moments when I long to leave the arena of endless activity, and spend creative moments in the world of ideas."[120]

Also, in September, efforts to move forward with plans to transfer the Citizenship Education Program from Highlander Folk School to SCLC received a huge boost when Andrew Young, formerly the associate director of the Department of Youth Work at the National Council of the Churches of Christ, joined the SCLC staff and was tapped to direct the program.[121] Modeled after the citizenship schools founded on Johns Island, South Carolina, in 1956, SCLC's pilot program, which began in February 1961, taught local people the fundamentals of reading, writing, and civil engagement, including how to register to vote.[122] The Field Foundation awarded SCLC and Highlander a $26,000 grant to initiate the program's expansion; however,

116. See Introduction in *The Papers of Martin Luther King, Jr.*, vol. 1: *Called to Serve, January 1929–June 1951*, ed. Clayborne Carson, Ralph E. Luker, Penny A. Russell, Louis R. Harlan (Berkeley and Los Angeles: University of California Press, 1992), pp. 40, 48, and *Papers* 2:18; King, "A Comparison of the Conceptions of God in the Thinking of Paul Tillich and Henry Nelson Wieman," 15 April 1955, in *Papers* 2:339–544).

117. Mays to King, 1 August 1961; King, "Outline of Lecture in Social Philosophy," 3 October 1961, pp. 288–291 in this volume. The students enrolled in the course were Barbara J. Adams, Benjamin D. Berry, Charles A. Black, Julian Bond, Amos C. Brown, Graham F. Prindle, Mary N. Worthy, and Willie J. Wright (Morehouse College, Class roll, Seminar in Social Philosophy, 27 January 1962).

118. King, "Outline of Lecture in Social Philosophy," 3 October 1961, and King, Notes, Seminar in Social Philosophy, 3 October 1961–23 January 1962, pp. 288–291 and 291–304 in this volume, respectively.

119. For example, see King to Robert Brank Fulton, 7 November 1961; King to Allan Knight Chalmers, 22 January 1962.

120. King to Mays, 6 September 1962.

121. Young to King, 11 September 1961, pp. 279–281 in this volume. Young's staff consisted of Septima Clark, educational director, and Dorothy Cotton, educational consultant.

122. Memo, "Leadership Training Program and Citizenship Schools," December 1960–January 1961, pp. 136–138 in this volume. The program also taught the philosophy of nonviolence, civil disobedience, direct action, and leadership skills (James R. Wood, Press release, "SCLC starts leadership training program," 14 February 1961). SCLC tested the program with several affiliate organizations with the goal of training 240 teachers to establish satellite citizenship schools throughout the South (Wood to Edward Stovall, 3 February 1961).

with Highlander's tax-exempt charter in limbo, the Field Foundation insisted that another organization be in charge of administering the funds.[123] The American Missionary Association agreed to dispense the funding and made the Dorchester Center in Midway, Georgia, available to house the workshops.[124] Several months into the program, King wrote Maxwell Hahn, executive vice president of the Field Foundation, touting the program's success. As of early February, SCLC had trained one hundred people to start citizenship schools in their home towns, and King felt privileged to "observe the students as their horizons were broadened by the kind of practical information which is so desperately needed by these people who have been so long deprived the opportunities to learn and grow as responsible citizens."[125]

SCLC's venture into voter education was complicated by its association with the red-tainted Highlander Folk School. In an article published in the *New York Times*, James R. Wood, public relations director of SCLC, was quoted as saying: "We find no reason not to cooperate with any organization that is interested in the development of full citizenship for Americans which cannot be proved to have conducted itself in a manner which is not American or patriotic."[126] Consumed with its own legal problems, Highlander's role in the program was eventually reduced, and under Young's directorship, the Citizenship Education Program was restructured and expanded Southwide.[127]

On 1 November 1961 student activists throughout the South began to test compliance with the ICC ruling to desegregate interstate transportation facilities.[128] In his hometown of Atlanta, King played a supportive role after four SNCC activists were arrested for trespassing at the Trailways bus station. King sent a telegram requesting that Atlanta mayor William Hartsfield "use the great influence of your office to resolve the four arrests made in violation of the new ICC ruling."[129]

When students in Albany, Georgia, staged a similar protest at the Trailways bus terminal they set in motion a series of demonstrations that eventually involved King.[130] To coordinate the demonstrations, local black leaders formed the Albany

---

123. Minutes, Citizenship Education Committee meeting, 8 June 1961. Highlander was closed in late 1961 after the state of Tennessee revoked its charter on falsified charges that the school was being run for profit and did not fulfill its nonprofit requirements.

124. Aimee Horton, "Citizenship School Committee meeting," 12 July 1961.

125. King to Hahn, 6 February 1962.

126. Claude Sitton, "2 Groups in South Training Negroes," *New York Times*, 23 February 1961.

127. Horton to Young, 12 October 1961; Young, Memo to SCLC, Citizenship School Committee, American Missionary Association, Field Foundation, December 1961.

128. Claude Sitton, "I.C.C. Travel Rule Is Defied in South," *New York Times*, 2 November 1961.

129. King to Hartsfield, 1 November 1961, p. 320 in this volume. The SNCC students were arrested after trespassing at Jake's Fine Foods, a privately owned restaurant located at the bus station ("Four Arrested in ICC Ruling Test," *Atlanta Daily World*, 2 November 1961). King also sent a telegram to Everett Hutchinson, chairman of the ICC, demanding swift action to rectify the violation of the ICC's ruling (King and Walker to Hutchinson, 1 November 1961).

130. Vic Smith, "Bus Mix Hearing Proceeds," *Albany Herald*, 27 November 1961. In October 1961 SNCC field secretaries Charles Sherrod and Cordell Reagan went to Albany to help spur a protest movement (Zinn, *SNCC: The New Abolitionists*, pp. 123–124).

Movement, a coalition of SNCC, NAACP, and other organizations. William G. Anderson, a local doctor and a former classmate of Ralph Abernathy's at Alabama State, was elected president of the new organization, with Slater King, realtor, as vice president. The principal goals of the movement were varied, including the desegregation of downtown businesses, transportation terminals, libraries, parks, hospitals, and city buses, as well as ending police brutality and expanding employment opportunities for blacks.[131]

Tensions in Albany escalated quickly and by 12 December nearly 500 protesters had been arrested and city officials refused to negotiate.[132] Overwhelmed by the mass arrests and with no foreseeable way to get protesters out of jail, Anderson phoned SCLC headquarters to plead for the organization's help.[133] Anderson hoped that King's fame would rally local participation, and, most importantly, spur fundraising efforts. According to Anderson, King was sensitive about encroaching on the movement and gave numerous excuses why he should not come to Albany, including his prior commitments and fear that local leaders would feel displaced by his presence. Unbeknownst to King, when Anderson broached the idea of bringing in King and SCLC, some civil rights activists were less than enthusiastic. King begrudgingly agreed to go to the small southwest Georgia town to make an address and immediately return to Atlanta.[134]

On the evening of his arrival on 15 December nearly a thousand people flocked to hear King at rallies held at Mt. Zion Baptist Church and Shiloh Baptist Church. King was greeted with thunderous and prolonged ovations.[135] "You are saying as you assemble here tonight and as you continue to move on in your movement that you are willing to struggle, to suffer, to sacrifice, and even die if necessary," King told the crowd.[136] As the rally came to a close, Anderson rose to give the benediction and

---

131. Zinn, *SNCC: The New Abolitionists*, pp. 127–128; Albany Movement, "Minutes," Meeting of the Albany Movement, 17 November 1961.

132. SNCC, Press release, "Latest from Albany," 13 December 1961; Norma L. Anderson and William G. Anderson, *Autobiographies of a Black Couple of the Greatest Generation* (n.p.: privately printed, 2004), pp. 195–196. On 13 December the Albany City Commission announced: "At this point, it is the feeling of the city commission that there is no area of possible agreement" (Claude Sitton, "202 More Negroes Seized in Georgia," *New York Times*, 14 December 1961).

133. The jail facilities in Albany were inadequate to accommodate the mass arrests, but Albany police chief Laurie Pritchett used surrounding jails within a seventy-mile radius to house protesters (Pritchett, Interview by James Reston, 23 April 1976; SNCC, "Latest from Albany").

134. Anderson and Anderson, *Autobiographies of a Black Couple of the Greatest Generation*, pp. 195–197. In his autobiography Ralph Abernathy similarly recalled tension between the organizations: "When we got to Albany we discovered the black community—and more particularly, the black demonstrators—hopelessly divided. All of the organizations participating in the campaign had agreed to merge their identity into one group, to be called the 'Albany Movement,' and to be governed by a steering committee. But by the time we arrived, any unity they may have achieved had already collapsed. Everyone had a different strategy. Everyone wanted to be in charge. Everyone was mad at everyone else. And as soon as we arrived in town, everyone was mad at us" (Abernathy, *And the Walls Came Tumbling Down* [New York: Harper & Row, 1989], p. 206).

135. Also addressing the rallies were Abernathy, Wyatt Tee Walker, SCLC executive director, and Ruby Hurley, field secretary of the NAACP (Bruce Galphin, "Albany Balks at Truce Price; Rev. King Rallies Negroes," *Atlanta Constitution*, 16 December 1961).

136. See King, Address Delivered at Albany Movement Mass Meeting at Mt. Zion Baptist Church, 15 December 1961, p. 343 in this volume.

called for a mass march to take place the following day: "Be here at 7 o'clock in the morning. Eat a good breakfast. Wear warm clothes and wear your walking shoes."[137]

Albany mayor Asa Kelley reacted to King's arrival by notifying Albany Movement leaders that he had nullified all previous agreements because King was "encouraging the violations of valid ordinances and statutes and that you have requested continued demonstrations and unlawful parades." He charged that by inviting King they were "not acting in good faith and until you can do so we can give no response to your demand."[138] Having been accused of causing the breakdown of negotiations between Albany city officials and Albany Movement leaders, King decided he would have to remain in Albany: "I had just intended to give an address," King told reporters, "but seeing that negotiations were broken between Negro and white, I felt I had to join the pilgrimage."[139]

On 16 December King joined Abernathy, Anderson, and over 260 others to march from Shiloh Baptist Church to Albany City Hall for a prayer vigil. When the demonstrators reached city hall, Albany police chief Laurie Pritchett arrested them.[140] As King waited to be booked into jail, he began preaching to the demonstrators: "They have no respect for humans. They have no respect for justice. They have no respect for man."[141] King and several others were secretly transferred and booked into the Sumter County Jail in Americus, Georgia.[142] There he told a reporter that if convicted he would not accept bond and fully expected to be behind bars through Christmas, adding: "I hope thousands will join me."[143] Wyatt Tee Walker called for a "blackout" of Christmas celebrations while King remained jailed. "Tell the children that we are postponing Christmas," he announced. "We don't want a single Christmas tree lit. We want no Christmas toys bought downtown. We want to turn downtown Albany into a ghost town."[144]

---

137. Galphin, "Albany Balks at Truce Price," 16 December 1961.

138. Kelley added: "Under no circumstances will the City Commission of Albany act under threat or duress" (Kelley to William G. Anderson and Marion S. Page, 16 December 1961).

139. Bill Shipp, "U.S. Pilgrimage Is Urged As Albany Negroes Call Halt," *Atlanta Constitution,* 18 December 1961.

140. The protesters were charged with parading without a permit, congregating on a sidewalk, and obstructing traffic. By 16 December the total number of arrests in Albany exceeded 700 (Claude Sitton, "Dr. King among 265 Negroes Seized in March on Albany, Ga., City Hall," *New York Times,* 17 December 1961). Laurie Pritchett (1926–2000), born in Griffin, Georgia, attended Auburn University and South Georgia College on athletic scholarships before graduating from the National Academy of the Federal Bureau of Investigation and the Southern Police Institute at the University of Louisville. In 1959 Pritchett became Albany's police chief. As head of the department, Pritchett hired the town's first black policemen. After leaving Albany, he became police chief in High Point, North Carolina, and was credited with keeping the peace following King's assassination in 1968. In 1975, Pritchett left the High Point Police Department amid controversy.

141. James Gillespy, "King, Marchers to Courthouse Steps, Jailed," *Atlanta Daily World,* 17 December 1961.

142. Facsimile of Sumter County Jail ledger, 16 December 1961, p. 347 in this volume. After hearing that King had been transferred to the jail in Americus, FBI officials contacted local authorities and were told that King was moved for his protection and to prevent any further demonstrations (C.L. McGowan to Alex Rosen, 17 December 1961, Bureau File 157-6-2-229).

143. David Miller, "Non-Violence: Police Chief and Minister," *New York Herald Tribune,* 18 December 1961.

144. "Integration: 'Albany Movement,'" *Newsweek,* 25 December 1961.

While King and Anderson prepared themselves for a long jail stay, Abernathy posted $200 bond on 16 December and returned to Atlanta. In a press conference from his church the following day, Abernathy tried to mobilize support for King and the others by calling for a nonviolent pilgrimage to Albany. "This is the greatest mass movement which has taken place since the Montgomery bus protest," Abernathy asserted. He also beckoned supporters to contact the president, Albany mayor Asa Kelley, and Georgia governor S. Ernest Vandiver to demand the release of hundreds jailed during demonstrations.[145] That evening, Abernathy sent a telegram to King, expressing concern for his welfare and professing that "I should not be here but I should be with you and with the hundreds of sons and daughters of slaves who have the courage to say to the sons and daughters of former slave holders that this is a new day and we want our freedom now."[146] Writing on behalf of the imprisoned King and Anderson, Abernathy sent a telegram to Kennedy reiterating King's call for the president to issue a second Emancipation Proclamation.[147]

Within days, the White House and Justice Department were flooded with telegrams, one of which called the federal government's reluctance to intervene "shocking and deplorable."[148] King advisor Stanley Levison sent a telegram to Attorney General Kennedy requesting that federal marshals be sent to Albany: "Local authority is flouting law and consequently action from your department is an imperative."[149] As Anderson had hoped, King's arrest attracted the national media attention that the Albany Movement had been lacking. Responding to the extensive press coverage, Albany government officials agreed that if mass protests against white merchants were halted for the next thirty days, the city would comply with the ICC ruling, local demonstrators would be released on bail, and the Albany Movement would be given the opportunity to present their demands to the city commission. The agreement paved the way for King's release from jail.[150] Although King was reportedly "less than

---

145. SCLC, Press release, "Abernathy issues call for nation-wide protest at Albany, Ga.," 17 December 1961.

146. Abernathy to King, 17 December 1961, p. 346 in this volume.

147. King, Anderson, and Abernathy to John F. Kennedy, 17 December 1961, pp. 349–350 in this volume. For King's earlier calls for a second Emancipation Proclamation see King, "Equality Now," 4 February 1961, King, Press Release, Statement Calling for Executive Order Declaring Segregation Illegal, 5 June 1961, King, Press Conference after Meeting with John F. Kennedy, 16 October 1961, and King, Abernathy, and Anderson to John F. Kennedy, 17 December 1961, pp. 139–150, 243–245, 308–311, and 349–350 in this volume, respectively.

148. L. Joseph Overton to Robert F. Kennedy, 18 December 1961, Department File 144–101–19M–9. According to an FBI memorandum, Nelson A. Rockefeller called Attorney General Robert F. Kennedy to express concern for King's safety. Kennedy reportedly told Burke Marshall that the Justice Department should do everything possible to ensure King's safety (C.L. McGowan to Alex Rosen, 17 December 1961, Bureau File 157–6–2–229).

149. Levison to Kennedy, 18 December 1961, Department File 144–101–19M–9.

150. In addition, the city commission also agreed to reduce the bonds for freedom riders from outside the Albany community and those local riders facing state charges ("Dr. King Is Freed," *New York Times*, 19 December 1961). Reports coming from the jails describing the intolerable conditions may have ignited a sense of urgency to the negotiations on the part of the Albany Movement leaders. Slater King, vice president of the Albany Movement, had suffered injuries as a result of being shoved by a jailer into the bars of his jail cell (Galphin, "Albany Balks at Truce Price," 16 December 1961; see also Shipp, "U.S. Pilgrimage Is Urged As Albany Negroes Call Halt," 18 December 1961). King commented that for the most part he was treated well but resented being called "boy" by guards. "I have never been called Reverend or Doctor or Mister in this jail," King said, adding that "I am the pastor of a church with 4,000

satisfied" with the concessions, he was determined not "to stand in the way of meaningful negotiations." He allowed Anderson to post his bond.[151]

King left for Atlanta the evening of 18 December, but not before telling a crowd gathered at Shiloh Baptist that he could leave Albany knowing his goal had been achieved: "The bus terminal and train station in Albany, Ga., are thoroughly integrated."[152] Despite King's positive assessment, he left amid reports of a rift between the Albany Movement and SCLC. Marion Page, the Albany Movement treasurer who was acting as chair while Anderson was jailed, denounced Walker for suggesting that SCLC was in charge of the movement. "This is an Albany movement," Page said. "We will accept help if we need it. As of now, we don't need help."[153] A *New York Times* article published the day King was released speculated that competition between SNCC and SCLC for "financial support and power" was fueling the internal conflicts, which would have "important implications for the future of the civil rights movement throughout the South."[154] Hoping to quell further rumors, King explained that "if there was an indication of division, it grew out of a breakdown of communications. The unity is far greater than our inevitable points of disagreement."[155]

Albany police chief Laurie Pritchett bragged to reporters that the Albany Movement was the "first time in the history of the Negro non-violent movement that non-violence has been met with non-violence."[156] Pritchett's police avoided the kind

---

members" (Shipp, "U.S. Pilgrimage Is Urged As Albany Negroes Call Halt," 18 December 1961; David Miller, "Non-Violence: Police Chief and Minister," 18 December 1961). King later recalled that Sumter County sheriff Fred Chappell was the "meanest man in the world" ("Rev. King Meets 'Meanest Man in World' in Jail," *Jet*, 4 January 1962).

151. "Dr. King Is Freed," 19 December 1961. An article in *Time* magazine argued that King lost support from some students after "meekly" posting bond despite promising to remain in jail indefinitely ("Confused Crusade," 12 January 1962). In response to the *Time* article, Stanley Levison sent a letter in defense of King to the magazine's editor (Levison to the Editor of *Time* Magazine, 11 January 1962, pp. 363–365 in this volume). King later admitted that his decision to leave jail was a mistake: "Looking back over it, I'm sorry I was bailed out. I didn't understand at the time what was happening. We thought that the victory had been won. When we got out, we discovered it was all a hoax. We had lost a real opportunity to redo Albany, and we lost an initiative that we never regained" ("Man of the Year," *Time*, 3 January 1964).

152. Bill Shipp, "Albany, Negroes Seal Peace; Prisoners to Go Free on Bail," *Atlanta Constitution*, 19 December 1961.

153. "Delay Trials of 730 Integrationists in Albany, Ga.; Parley Under Way," *Chicago Daily Defender*, 19 December 1961; Claude Sitton, "Negro Groups Split on Georgia Protests," *New York Times*, 18 December 1961.

154. Sitton, "Negro Groups Split on Georgia Protests," 18 December 1961. A day after King's release from jail, a fundraising letter under his signature was sent to supporters directing contributions to SCLC rather than the Albany Movement: "The Southern Christian Leadership Conference, which I have the pleasure of leading, is giving full moral and financial support to the Albany Movement and the noble efforts of this community to realize justice, equal rights and an end to second-class citizenship" (King to Friend, 19 December 1961). In a special article published in the *Times*, Sitton argued that the differences in the protest movement were centered on methods rather than goals and the rivalry between the organizations stemmed from fundraising. He cautioned of the perils of competition in the field: "The danger is that in the heat of competition some second-ranking leaders may subordinate a community's welfare to their organization's interest. Conflicting advice from two or more groups causes confusion and impotence at best. Carried to the extreme, it could have tragic consequences" (Sitton, "Rivalries Beset Integration Campaigns," *New York Times*, 24 December 1961).

155. "Dr. King Is Freed," 19 December 1961.

156. David Miller, "A Loss for Dr. King—New Negro Roundup: They Yield," *New York Herald Tribune*, 19 December 1961. Pritchett claimed that he had been preparing for demonstrations, and had studied

of brutal force that would attract press attention and sympathy for the demonstrators.[157] Pritchett's tactics stymied King's effectiveness and succeeded in getting him to leave Albany. Soon after King left, the City Commission reneged on its agreement to meet face-to-face with Albany Movement officials.[158] A journalist with the *New York Herald Tribune* praised Pritchett for displaying a "standard of professional achievement that would be difficult to emulate in a situation so made-to-order for violence" and claimed that King had suffered "one of the most stunning defeats of his career," leaving the Albany Movement "considerably weaker than before."[159] Despite leaving without any tangible gains, King told Herbert Eaton, his successor at Dexter Avenue Baptist Church, that although "we did not achieve all that we had anticipated in the Albany situation, I think it was a real victory for the Negro community."[160]

ဢဢ၀ဢ၀ဢ၀ဢ

Hoping to refocus and reorganize in 1962, King met with SCLC board and staff members in February to hammer out the details of an ambitious grassroots organizing campaign.[161] At their annual meeting the previous fall, SCLC leaders had decided to launch new voter registration efforts.[162] With the expectation that the Justice Department and liberal philanthropic foundations would support voter registration efforts, King developed a grassroots organizing campaign called the People to People tour. Designed to expand SCLC's presence in Deep South states with strong segregationist resistance to black voting, the goal of the tour, according to Wyatt Tee Walker, was "to take the message of Freedom to our people in the cotton fields, and at the crossroads and country stores, in the churches and the schools."[163] While seeking to avoid competing with the voting rights efforts of the NAACP and CORE, King expressed determination "to do even more in the area of direct action that we have done in the past."[164] He urged his colleagues to recruit volunteers for a "Freedom Corps" comprised of voter registration workers and activists trained for a

---

the situations in Montgomery, Little Rock, and Birmingham. While professing to be a staunch segregationist, Pritchett admitted that he believed total integration would be achieved one day: "It might not be in my lifetime or in my children's, but it will come. As the laws change to meet the times, I will support the law" (David Miller, "Non-Violence: Police Chief and Minister," 18 December 1961).

157. Although Pritchett was adamant that his officers refrained from violence against demonstrations, he could not guarantee the safety of those jailed outside his jurisdiction (Howard Zinn, "Albany: Special report of Southern Regional Council," 8 January 1962).

158. Miller, "A Loss for Dr. King," 19 December 1961.

159. Miller, "Non-Violence: Police Chief and Minister," 18 December 1961; Miller, "A Loss for Dr. King," 19 December 1961.

160. King to Eaton, 21 December 1961, p. 355 in this volume.

161. SCLC, Agenda, "Southwide meeting of SCLC state and local leaders," 2 February 1962; SCLC, Memo to Affiliate heads, 3 February 1962.

162. "Southern Negroes Map a Voter Drive," *New York Times*, 30 September 1961; Walker, "Report of the director," 28 September 1961; and Introduction in *Papers* 4:22–25.

163. Walker, "Report of the director," October 1961–September 1962; see also King, Notes on Recruitment of Volunteers, 7 February–9 February 1962, pp. 381–384 in this volume.

164. Walker, "Report of the director," 28 September 1961; SCLC, "Minutes of annual board meeting, Southern Christian Leadership Conference," 27 September 1961.

"Nonviolent Army" to be "ready on a stand-by basis for any specific attack on segregation." The People to People tours would begin in the Mississippi Delta—"the symbol of hard-core resistance to desegregation"—and then venture into Virginia, South Carolina, and Louisiana.[165] In each state, SCLC planned "door knocking" campaigns to "stimulate the Negroes' interest in their right to vote" with the goal of doubling the number of black registered voters in the South over a two-year period.[166]

SCLC's three-day visit to the Mississippi Delta began on 7 February and included stops in six towns. SCLC staffer James M. Lawson conducted nonviolence workshops in Cleveland, Laurel, Tougaloo, and Jackson before King arrived for a crowded schedule of speeches and face-to-face "fireside chats" intended "to determine the most pressing problems affecting the Negro people of the Deep South."[167] He appeared at a rally for Clarksdale minister Theodore Trammell, who was seeking to become the first black congressman from Mississippi since the Reconstruction era.[168] Despite his general policy of nonpartisanship, King assured an overflow audience at Clarksdale's First Baptist Church that if black residents registered and voted "in spite of the resistance and the conniving methods of Southern registrars and county sheriffs, we can change the entire political structure of the state of Mississippi."[169] By the end of the tour, King had participated in more than a dozen events. Writing about his experiences in "People in Action," the biweekly column he recently had begun publishing in the *New York Amsterdam News,* King noted the effects of intimidation, economic exploitation, and police brutality on the lives of African Americans in the Mississippi Delta. "As we rode along the dusty roads of the Delta country," he recounted, "our riding companions cited unbelievable cases of police brutality and incidents of Negroes being brutally murdered by white mobs, which never became known to the outside world. In spite of this, there is a ray of hope."[170]

---

165.  SCLC, Press release, Martin Luther King, Jr. to begin People to People program, 1 February 1962; SCLC, Press release, "Dr. King and staff head for delta country of Mississippi," 6 February 1962.

166.  "Southern Negroes Map a Voter Drive," 30 September 1961.

167.  SCLC, Press release, "Dr. King and staff head for delta country of Mississippi." An editorial in the *Clarksdale Press Register* questioned King's motives for coming to Mississippi, declaring that he and "local agitators" were trying to foment disunity between blacks and whites: "The leaders, both local and imported, of these perpetually-meeting organizations seem to thrive on agitation. They contribute very little if anything to their community" ("Time for Questions," *Clarksdale Press Register,* 6 February 1962).

168.  SCLC, Press release, "Dr. King and staff head for delta country of Mississippi"; SCLC, *Newsletter* 1, no. 5, March 1962; see also King, "People in Action: Pathos and Hope," 3 March 1962, pp. 419–421 in this volume. At one event in Sherard, the only person to show up was a man who walked thirteen miles to meet King. He explained that others wanted to come but feared retaliation and eviction from their land (SCLC, *Newsletter,* March 1962).

169.  "Rev. King Tells Mississippians They Could Have 5 Congressmen," *New York Amsterdam News,* 24 February 1962. King's appearance at Trammell's rally precipitated pressure from Baltimore minister I. Logan Kearse, who had asked King to support his bid for a congressional district seat in Maryland (Kearse to King, 25 September 1961; King to Kearse, 2 November 1961, pp. 321–322 in this volume). Despite Kearse's persistence, King reiterated his nonpartisan policy, maintaining that he did not know the Trammell rally was political (Kearse to King, 6 April 1962; King to Kearse, 11 April 1962).

170.  King, "Pathos and Hope," 3 March 1962, p. 420 in this volume. An SCLC representative estimated that King made "personal contact" with over five thousand people in the Coahoma County region alone (SCLC, Press release, "King says Mississippi can elect five Negro congressmen," 8 February 1962). For King's inaugural column in the *New York Amsterdam News,* see King, "People in Action: Turning Point of Civil Rights," 3 February 1962, pp. 377–379 in this volume.

Even as King sought to expand SCLC's reach into the rural Deep South, he could not ignore other matters that demanded his time and attention. Soon after returning to Atlanta, King delivered a sermon at West Hunter Baptist Church at the installation service for his friend Ralph Abernathy.[171] Then he traveled to Puerto Rico to fulfill a commitment he had made in 1958 to the trip's sponsors, Inter-American University and the Puerto Rico chapter of the Fellowship of Reconciliation (FOR).[172] In four days, King made a television appearance and delivered seven speeches before spending an additional eight days resting on the island.[173] According to FOR chairman Lillian Pope, King left a lasting impression on Puerto Ricans, challenging many listeners to "give serious consideration for the first time to the merits of non-violent direct action as a technique and as a philosophy."[174]

King returned from Puerto Rico to stand trial with Abernathy in Albany for their December 1961 arrests.[175] Lawyers Donald Hollowell and C. B. King represented the two civil rights leaders, who had not traveled to Albany since being released from jail on 18 December. Spectators packed the small courtroom for King's trial, the first of the cases resulting from the mass arrests of the previous year. The prosecution called only one witness—Albany police chief Laurie Pritchett, who testified that King and the others were arrested for parading without a permit and obstructing traffic. King's lawyers requested a dismissal of the charges, arguing that the Albany city code provided no criteria for what constituted a parade and that the permit section of the code violated their client's Fourteenth Amendment rights. Recorder's Court judge A. N. Durden denied the motion, and the defense opened its case by calling King to the stand. King testified that the march from Shiloh Baptist Church to downtown Albany was "strictly nonviolent and purely peaceful." He denied reports that the group obstructed traffic or violated any traffic laws. "Our main interest was to negotiate with city officials," King testified. Judge Durden recessed the proceedings and announced that he would not issue a verdict for at least sixty

---

171. King, A Knock at Midnight, Sermon Delivered at the Installation Service of Ralph Abernathy at West Hunter Baptist Church, 11 February 1962, pp. 385–394 in this volume. After the death of the church's previous pastor, A. Franklin Fisher, King had declined to become a candidate to fill the vacancy but suggested Abernathy instead (King to Samuel L. Spear, 16 December 1960, in *Papers* 5:581–582). In February 1961, King wrote a letter recommending Abernathy for the pastorship at West Hunter Baptist Church: "As a community leader, he has few equals. His character is above repute and his dedication to the Christian ministry unquestioned" (King to J. R. Butts, 8 February 1961, p. 154 in this volume).

172. Press release, "Martin Luther King to visit Puerto Rico," 22 January 1962; Robert Brank Fulton to King, 18 October 1958. King had initially agreed to come to Puerto Rico in February 1961, but he canceled because of prior SCLC commitments and the impending arrival of his second son, Dexter Scott, who was born on 30 January (King to Fulton, 5 October 1960).

173. See King, Interview by Inter-American University Students and Faculty, 14 February 1962, pp. 399–410 in this volume. While in Puerto Rico, King would learn from his assistant Dora McDonald of intra-staff tensions at SCLC headquarters. Wyatt Tee Walker had become infuriated when Gould Maynard, SCLC's new public relations director, had given every woman in the office a rose for Valentine's Day, a gesture that Walker felt made him "look bad." McDonald observed: "Wyatt will never reach his full potential because he is so very childish and narrow" (McDonald to King, 15 February 1962).

174. Pope to King, 4 March 1962.

175. The trial was originally set for 20 February, but King was still in Puerto Rico, and the trial was postponed another week ("City Slates Trial of Negroes," *Albany Herald*, 15 February 1962; Vic Smith, "Decision on King Due in Sixty Days," *Albany Herald*, 27 February 1962).

days.[176] Standing in front of the Albany courthouse at the end of the proceedings, King said, "I think at many points the City of Albany, or certainly those who are seeking to prosecute us, are making a tragic mistake because they are standing against the tide of history which is rolling toward a democratic social order."[177]

While awaiting the Albany verdict, King continued to pressure President Kennedy to issue a second Emancipation Proclamation.[178] It had been four months since King met with President Kennedy at the White House on 16 October to discuss comprehensive civil rights reforms, and although King told reporters that his visit was "fruitful" and that the president "listened very sympathetically" to his concerns, he remained frustrated at Kennedy's failure to make any firm guarantees.[179] King's disappointment in Kennedy's unwillingness to make good on some of his campaign promises was evident in his second article published in *The Nation* since February 1961.[180] The title of King's article, "Fumbling on the New Frontier," was a slight to Kennedy's domestic and foreign programs agenda, which he had defined upon accepting the Democratic nomination for president at the Party's 1960 convention. Kennedy saw the "The New Frontier" as a set of challenges—"science and space"; "peace and war"; "ignorance and prejudice"; and "poverty and surplus"—that he would address in his first term as president.[181] While King praised some elements of Kennedy's civil rights record, he criticized Kennedy's refusal to sign an executive order ending discrimination in housing.[182]

Looking back on Kennedy's first year in office, King characterized the Kennedy administration's approach to civil rights as "cautious" and criticized the lack of moral urgency by the president to commit to full integration. According to King, Kennedy lacked the leadership needed to grapple with the enormity of the civil rights problem. "The year passed and the President fumbled," King wrote.[183] While King's initial hopes hinged on Kennedy's campaign promises to use executive orders to end segregation and discrimination, by 1962 King's expectations were shattered

---

176. Smith, "Decision on King Due in Sixty Days," 27 February 1962.

177. King, Statement at Albany, Ga. courthouse, 27 February 1962.

178. King, "Fumbling on the New Frontier," 3 March 1962, pp. 412–419 in this volume; King, "An Appeal to the Honorable John F. Kennedy, President of the United States for National Rededication to the Principles of the Emancipation Proclamation and for an Executive Order," 17 May 1962.

179. King, Press Conference after Meeting with John F. Kennedy, 16 October 1961, and photograph of King at the press conference, pp. 308 and 99 in this volume, respectively.

180. King, "Fumbling on the New Frontier," 3 March 1962, pp. 412–419 in this volume. For King's previous article published in *The Nation*, see King, "Equality Now," 4 February 1961, pp. 139–150 in this volume.

181. Kennedy, "The New Frontier," Address at the Democratic National Convention, 15 July 1960.

182. In his article, King highlighted some of the administration's achievements, including the increase in civil rights cases and investigations of disenfranchised voters; more African Americans in key government positions than any other previous administration; and the signing of an executive order establishing the President's Committee on Equal Employment Opportunity (King, "Fumbling on the New Frontier," 3 March 1962, pp. 412–419 in this volume). Although a draft of the executive order banning housing discrimination was ready for Kennedy's signature in late November 1961, he reportedly did not sign it for fear of losing Southern votes for his other proposed initiatives (Peter Braestrup, "Order to Ban Bias in Housing Ready," *New York Times*, 27 November 1961; "Discrimination Order on Housing Is Delayed," *New York Times*, 28 December 1961).

183. King, "Fumbling on the New Frontier," 3 March 1962, p. 416 in this volume.

when the administration shifted its plan from executive orders to "consensus" leadership for fear of alienating key Southern congressmen.[184] Citing the moral courage it took Abraham Lincoln to sign the Emancipation Proclamation in the face of slave owners, King described a similar dilemma for Kennedy. The president, King wrote, "may well be compelled to make an equally fateful decision—one which, if correct, could be found a century later to have made the nation greater and the man more memorable." Using the examples of the sit-ins, Freedom Rides, and voter registration efforts as evidence that the nation's people are ready for "bold leadership in civil rights" despite the "absence of sustained, strong, national leadership," King argued that Kennedy still has an opportunity to stop civil rights from being used as a "political football," but only if he "abandons the traditional piecemeal approach" to desegregation in favor of a constructive long-term plan.[185]

On 9 April, a month after the publication of *The Nation* article, King met in Washington, D.C., with Attorney General Robert F. Kennedy and Burke Marshall, head of the Justice Department's Civil Rights Division.[186] At a press conference before the meeting, King voiced criticisms of President Kennedy's civil rights record, but acknowledged that the Kennedy administration was far more progressive than its predecessors. King declared that civil rights reform still required "forthright, vigorous leadership."[187] During his meeting with Kennedy and Marshall, King presented evidence of voting rights violations and called upon the Justice Department to provide greater protection for black voters. Kennedy assured him that the Justice Department would take measures to protect voter registration workers and investigate racial discrimination in the voting process.[188] After King's meeting with the attorney general he met with Vice President Lyndon B. Johnson, who had been appointed head of the newly established President's Committee on Equal Employment Opportunity. Johnson assured King that the executive order barring discrimination against qualified employees seeking work with the federal government or with companies under government contracts would be "vigorously enforced."[189]

184. King, "Fumbling on the New Frontier," 3 March 1962, p. 416 in this volume. In one of his articles published in his biweekly column in the *New York Amsterdam News*, King indicted President Kennedy for failing to strengthen the proposed Manpower Development and Training bill, which allowed for a three-year program to retrain unemployed workers replaced by automation. Although Kennedy signed the bill on 15 March 1962, King felt that it did little to put the 4.5 million unemployed back to work (King, "People in Action: Nothing Changing Unless," 28 April 1962, pp. 449–451 in this volume).

185. King, "Fumbling on the New Frontier," 3 March 1962, pp. 417, 418 in this volume.

186. Wallace Terry, "JFK's Action on Civil Rights Lagging, Says Negro Leader," *Washington Post*, 10 April 1962. King was accompanied by Walker, Shuttlesworth, and C.O. Simpkins, a minister from Shreveport, Louisiana, whose home was bombed because of his voter registration activities (SCLC, Press release, "Attorney General promises immediate aid in voting complaints," 25 April 1962).

187. Terry, "JFK's Action on Civil Rights Lagging," 10 April 1962.

188. "Dr. King, Aides Offer Proof of Voting Bias," *Pittsburgh Courier*, 21 April 1962; SCLC, Press release, "Attorney General promises immediate aid in voting complaints."

189. Terry, "JFK's Action on Civil Rights Lagging," 10 April 1962. In a 13 April letter to King, Johnson said he had investigated discrimination in federal employment in Atlanta, a topic they likely discussed at their meeting in Washington, and found that the situation needed to be improved. He vowed to keep King apprised of the progress (Johnson to King, 13 April 1962, pp. 435–437 in this volume). In the press conference prior to his meetings with Kennedy, Marshall, and Johnson, King applauded the president for signing executive order 10925 banning discrimination in federal hiring on 6 March 1961 (Terry, "JFK's Action on Civil Rights Lagging," 10 April 1962).

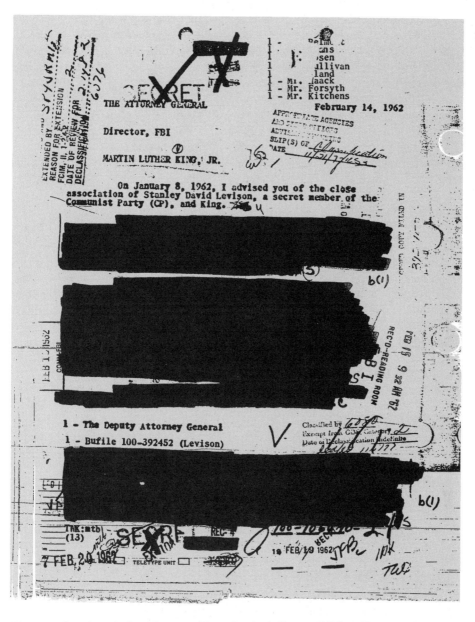

As King sought to press the Justice Department to move more forthrightly on civil rights issues, the Federal Bureau of Investigation (FBI), under the direction of J. Edgar Hoover, was paying closer attention to King and several of his associates.[190] Hoover had warned the Kennedys of King's relationship with Stanley Levison, who the bureau believed was a secret member of the Communist Party USA (CPUSA).[191] A month after reminding attorney general Robert F. Kennedy of Levison's alleged Party membership, a wiretap was placed on Levison's office phone.[192] Ensuing FBI memorandums showed that Levison discussed several issues with King such as King's decision to publicly call for the nomination of William Hastie to the Supreme Court and the hiring of Jack O'Dell, also a former member of the CPUSA, as King's administrative assistant.[193]

⤜⤛⤚⤙⤘⤗

On 27 March 1962 King traveled to Virginia for the second leg of SCLC's People to People tour. Escorted by SCLC representatives and clergymen from all over the Fourth Congressional District, he started by going door to door in Petersburg encouraging voter registration and recruiting participants in the Freedom Corps. As part of operation "Door Knock," King and a team of thirty-five others canvassed the Blandford district of Petersburg.[194] Later that evening, King spoke before an estimated crowd of over 2,400 packed into the auditorium at Lynchburg's E.C. Glass High School.[195]

---

190. In his February 1962 article published in *The Nation*, King criticized discriminatory practices in federal agencies, including the FBI: "If, for instance, the law-enforcement personnel in the FBI were integrated, many persons who now defy federal law might come under restraints from which they are presently free" (King, "Equality Now," 4 February 1961, pp. 145–146 in this volume). A few days later, FBI deputy director Cartha D. DeLoach received a memorandum from agent M.A. Jones summarizing King's criticisms of the bureau with the recommendation to not respond because King "would only welcome any controversy or resulting publicity that might ensue." At the bottom of the memo, Hoover wrote: "I concur" (Jones to DeLoach, 7 February 1961, Bureau File 100–106670).

191. J. Edgar Hoover to Robert F. Kennedy, 14 February 1962, Bureau File 100–106670; see also Wofford, *Of Kennedys & Kings*, pp. 215–216. King met Levison soon after the end of the Montgomery bus boycott. For more on King's early relationship with Levison, see Introduction, and Rustin to King, 23 December 1956, in *Papers* 3:32 and 491–494, respectively.

192. Special Agent in Charge, New York, N.Y., to J. Edgar Hoover, 20 March 1962, Bureau File 100–392452–147.

193. An FBI memorandum described a phone call between Wyatt Tee Walker and Levison about King's strategy to pressure the president to nominate Hastie as a Supreme Court justice following the resignation of Charles Whittaker in 1962 (Special Agent in Charge, New York, N.Y., to J. Edgar Hoover, 30 March 1962, Bureau File 100–106670–33). King sent a telegram to Kennedy on 30 March 1962, requesting that the president fill the vacancy on the court with either Hastie or Thurgood Marshall (pp. 428–429 in this volume). A 21 June 1962 memorandum indicated that Levison and King talked about hiring O'Dell. King allegedly said it did not "matter what a man was, if he could stand up now and say he is not connected, then as far as I am concerned, he is eligible to work for me" (FBI, Report on Martin Luther King, Jr., 21 June 1962, Bureau File 100–106670–80).

194. SCLC, Press release, "Martin Luther King, Jr., moves into Virginia," 30 March 1962. King was accompanied by Walker, Abernathy, Cotton, and SCLC field secretaries Bernard Lee and Herbert Coulton (SCLC, "SCLC People to People tour," *Newsletter* 1, no. 6, April 1962).

195. SCLC, *Newsletter*, April 1962; King, "The American Dream," Address delivered at E.C. Glass High School, 27 March 1962.

At the mass meeting sponsored by the local SCLC affiliate, King urged Lynchburg residents to find strength in nonviolent direct action and to use the ballot against Southern Dixiecrats and Republicans who joined together to "defeat almost every liberal move in the area of civil rights." Moments before taking his seat, King warned that "before the struggle is won, before the victory is won, some will have to suffer." But despite the suffering, King expressed confidence that "we shall overcome."[196]

Following King's address, Abernathy made an appeal for Freedom Corps volunteers, and for a brief moment, no one moved until eleven-year-old Chuck Moran, a white boy from Charlottesville, Virginia, came forward and extended his hand to King, saying: "I want to help you in this struggle."[197] The next day, King and his entourage detoured to Prince Edward County, where public schools had been closed since 1959 to avoid court-ordered desegregation.[198] King encouraged an audience assembled at First Baptist Church to "stand fast for what you believe in and some day people everywhere will thank you for your part in bringing about peace and freedom." Promising SCLC's full support, King pledged to return to Prince Edward County, telling the more than one hundred black school children in the audience: "When I come back I will see you sitting in integrated schools."[199]

Although voter registration dominated the tour agenda, Milton Reid, president of the SCLC affiliate in Virginia, and King led a march in Hopewell, protesting the contempt trial of Reverend Curtis W. Harris, president of the Hopewell Improvement Association. Harris had earlier been indicted for refusing to disclose the names of civil rights activists to the Committee on Offenses Against the Administration of Justice.[200] By the end of the tour, Wyatt Tee Walker observed that

---

196. King, "The American Dream," 27 March 1962.

197. Walker, "Fifty-three Hours with Martin Luther King Jr.," 27 March–29 March 1962. Like an "electric current," 118 people followed Moran's lead and volunteered to participate in SCLC's Nonviolent Army (see Walker, "Fifty-three Hours with Martin Luther King Jr."). For a photograph of King and Chuck Moran, see p. 100 in this volume.

198. SCLC, *Newsletter*, April 1962.

199. "King in Prince Edward Sees Schools Restored," *Washington Post*, 29 March 1962. In an essay written by Wyatt Tee Walker about the Virginia tour, he marveled at how many people local leader Reverend L. Francis Griffin was able to get at the church to see King: "This was a farm community. How could he have a church full on Wednesday. These people have to be in the fields. It was mid-morning. But they [were?] there! They wanted to see and hear this internationally known leader who was hop-scotching around the South, off the beaten paths, bringing hope and lifting the morale of the plain and simple people of the land. You could see it in their eyes and written all over their faces. 'Martin Luther King Jr. is really here in Prince Edward County, Virginia'" (Walker, "Fifty-three Hours with Martin Luther King Jr.").

200. SCLC, Press release, "Martin Luther King, Jr., moves into Virginia." Endorsing the protest march, King said: "The strongest resource that is possessed by those of us desiring to see an America free of racism, is our strength of numbers. Whenever a fighter for freedom, such as Reverend Harris, is under attack, every available person ought to witness with his person two fundamental concepts: His opposition to the persecution of those who believe segregation is an intolerable evil, and his unqualified support of those whose lives are a living embodiment of the necessity of striving toward freedom" (SCLC, *Newsletter*, April 1962). King also attended Harris's trial. Harris was found guilty of contempt but was not fined or sentenced. Harris's attorney, Len Holt, wrote that King's presence "was a substantial factor" in the victory (Holt to King, 3 April 1962).

King appeared worn down by the pace, but King reassured him: "Oh, I'm doing all right. I think I can make it." [201]

In mid-April King traveled to South Carolina for the third leg of the tour where he visited Charleston, Clarendon County, and Claflin College in Orangeburg. According to SCLC, the South Carolina tour secured 332 additional volunteers for the voter registration campaign and nonviolent army. At a meeting at St. Matthew's Baptist Church in Charleston, King reiterated: "We can help the South, cure its problems by registering and voting, and electing to office men of goodwill who will act in the Legislature in the spirit of the Constitution and insure equitable treatment for all Americans."[202] Looking back at the last two tours through Virginia and South Carolina, King estimated that SCLC had recruited more than a thousand Freedom Corps volunteers. "I did not realize that this tour would turn out to be so inspiring to me and serve in a way to have such an impact," King told SCLC board members at their annual meeting. "We will continue these tours until we have covered every southern state."[203]

Heading into the summer of 1962, King once again had to respond to persistent rumors about tensions between SCLC and other civil rights groups, namely the NAACP. In early May, John H. McCray, a columnist for the *Pittsburgh Courier*, published an article asserting that SCLC was attempting to take over NAACP territory in the Deep South. He quoted an anonymous NAACP member as saying that "SCLC and CORE either ramrodded or joined in on a great many sit-ins, sent hundreds of youths into activities costing money in bail and fines, and then ducked out and left NAACP to foot the bills."[204] King expressed concern about the negative press to Chicago lawyer Chauncey Eskridge, who used his connections at the *Courier* to rein in McCray and arranged to have another journalist write a series of positive articles about King and SCLC.[205] "Disunity in the civil rights movement is becoming a favorite topic for a certain number of newspapers and magazines," King acknowledged when he spoke at the NAACP's fifty-third annual convention in early July. Defining disunity as "alienation" and the "severing of parts," King maintained that the movement was not suffering from disunity as much as a difference of opinion and interests. "Let us stay together," he admonished, "remembering that we are all moving down the same road. It may be a three-lane road, with some emphasizing the way

---

201. Walker, "Fifty-three Hours with Martin Luther King, Jr." As Walker lay awake in his hotel room at the conclusion of the tour, he called over to Bernard Lee and said: "You know, fifty seven hours with Martin Luther King Jr. could kill a man." Lee responded: "Yeah, you ain't kidding" (Walker, "Fifty-three Hours with Martin Luther King, Jr."). For more on King's People to People tour in Virginia, see King, "People in Action: Virginia's Black Belt," 14 April 1962, pp. 437–440 in this volume).

202. SCLC, Press release, "Martin Luther King signs up 332 volunteers in South Carolina," 19 April 1962.

203. SCLC, Minutes, SCLC board meeting, 15 May 1962. For more on the tour through South Carolina, see King, "People in Action: Unknown Heroes," 12 May 1962, pp. 454–457 in this volume. During early summer, SCLC undertook a one-day People to People tour of Louisiana. On 8 June SCLC staffers Wyatt Tee Walker and Harry Blake were arrested in Shreveport on charges of criminal anarchy. After being given a lunacy test they were released the following day (King, "People in Action: New Harassment," 23 June 1962, pp. 486–488 in this volume).

204. McCray, "Need for Changing," *Pittsburgh Courier*, 5 May 1962.

205. Eskridge to King, 22 May 1962, pp. 464–465 in this volume.

of litigation and mobilizing forces for meaningful legislation and others emphasiz-  Introduction
ing the way of nonviolent direct action and others moving through research and
education."[206]

After a busy start to the New Year, the SCLC executive board regrouped over the
course of two days in Chattanooga, Tennessee, in mid-May 1962.[207] With fewer than
half of the thirty-one board members in attendance, King set the tone of the meeting by acknowledging that the organization had faced challenges over the past year:
"There is a good deal that we could have done but did not do."[208] On 16 May, the
second day of the board meeting, the group had a lengthy discussion regarding
how affiliate organizations would relate to SCLC and then added three new members to the executive board, including Virgil Wood, president of the Lynchburg
Improvement Association; John Lewis of SNCC; and Hosea Williams, president of
the Chatham County Crusade for Voters. SCLC historian L.D. Reddick observed
that adding Lewis might help to lessen the resentment felt by some SNCC members
toward SCLC.[209]

The following day, King was the keynote speaker at the founding of the Gandhi
Society for Human Rights, a tax-exempt organization providing legal and financial
support to the civil right movement.[210] The new organization was cofounded by
Theodore Kheel, who had a year earlier established the Lawyers Advisory Committee
(LAC), to assist SCLC with legal support. Kheel teamed up with Harry Wachtel, who
had volunteered to help SCLC out of the financial rut caused by the lawsuits against
the four ministers being sued for libel.[211] Speaking at the Sheraton-Carlton Hotel in
Washington, D.C., King began by noting that the occasion coincided with several
triumphs in the civil rights struggle, most notably the eighth anniversary of the
*Brown v. Board of Education* decision and that SCLC had decided to use the historic

206. King, Address Delivered at the "Freedom Fund Dinner" at the Fifty-third Annual Convention of
the NAACP, 5 July 1962, pp. 504, 505 in this volume.
207. SCLC, Minutes, SCLC board meeting, 15 May 1962; Minutes, SCLC board meeting, 16 May 1962.
208. SCLC, Minutes, SCLC board meeting, 15 May 1962.
209. SCLC, Minutes, SCLC board meeting, 16 May 1962.
210. King, Address at the Formation of the Gandhi Society for Human Rights, 17 May 1962, pp. 457–
462 in this volume.
211. Although Kheel had founded the LAC in May 1961 to help with the libel suits, the organization
was defunct by December 1961, and Kheel collaborated with Wachtel to establish a more permanent
organization (King to Kheel, 11 December 1961; King to Wachtel, 12 February 1962, pp. 397–398 in this
volume). In a meeting with King advisor Clarence B. Jones, Wachtel expressed interest in helping SCLC
raise funds to pay for future legal actions against the movement and its participants. King was pleased
to hear of Wachtel's offer, and in a 7 November 1961 letter to Wachtel, he outlined two areas of pressing
concern for SCLC: the need for stellar legal representation for the libel cases and a memorandum of law
to be sent to President Kennedy in support of an executive order ending segregation (see pp. 325–327
in this volume). The Society's executive board had twenty-five members, including Kheel, Wachtel,
Mordecai Johnson, Joseph Curran, and Benjamin E. Mays. King would act as honorary chairman of the
Society, while Clarence B. Jones would serve as acting executive director ("Gandhi Society for Rights
Formed; King Presents Document to JFK," *Atlanta Daily World,* 20 May 1962).

occasion to deliver a 130-page document urging President John F. Kennedy to sign an Emancipation Proclamation banning racial discrimination.[212] In a press conference following the luncheon, King clarified that the new organization would "not be an action organization, nor will it be a membership organization"; instead it would provide legal assistance to civil rights activists and "supplement what is being done by the NAACP and CORE and the Southern Christian Leadership Conference in the realm of direct action."[213] The Society's board of directors worked through the summer to draft the organization's mission, using Gandhi's fundamental principle of "Satyagraha, or 'truth force'" as a guide.[214]

King's enthusiasm for the Gandhi Society was tempered when critics derided it as a "departure" from orthodox Christianity. One critic called it "a new crucifixion when Gandhi displaces Christ as the source of power and motivation for those who call themselves Christian."[215] An editorial appearing in the *Christian Century,* a prominent religious magazine, charged that the name of the new group suggested that it was seeking spiritual guidance from Gandhi rather than from Christ.[216] Responding in a five-page letter, King, editor-at-large of the *Christian Century,* questioned the assumption that the Gandhi Society was a "turn away from the church," explaining that "one's commitment to Jesus Christ as Lord and Savior, however, should not mean that one cannot be inspired by another great personality that enters the stage of history." He scolded *Christian Century* editor Harold Fey for attacking the organization without fully understanding its nature and purpose. "It is fallacious to think of the Gandhi Society as an attempt to deify Gandhi or establish a cult around his name. It seems only natural for this new foundation to take the name of Gandhi since he, more than anyone in the modern world, lifted the method of non-violence to a powerful level of socio-political action."[217] In a postscript to his letter, King said that he was not writing the letter for publication, but, after Fey apologized to King, he received permission to publish excerpts of King's letter.[218]

---

212. King, Address at the Formation of the Gandhi Society, 17 May 1962, pp. 458–460 in this volume; King, "An Appeal to the Honorable John F. Kennedy, President of the United States for National Rededication to the Principles of the Emancipation Proclamation and for an Executive Order"; and "Gandhi Society for Rights Formed; King Presents Document to JFK," 20 May 1962.

213. King, Excerpts, Press conference on the formation of the Gandhi Society for Human Rights and the appeal for a second Emancipation Proclamation, 17 May 1962.

214. Clarence B. Jones, Memo, "The formation of the Gandhi Society for Human Rights, Inc.," 20 June 1962.

215. Episcopal Society for Cultural and Racial Unity, Press release, John Burnett Morris statement on disappointment in religious divergence, 29 May 1962. Victor Riesel of the *Los Angeles Times* wrote: "It is my guess that the image of Gandhi soon will overshadow the more direct Freedom Riders" ("Spirit of Gandhi May Replace the Freedom Riders in New Race Drive," *Los Angeles Times,* 27 April 1962).

216. "A Gandhi Society?," *Christian Century,* 79 (13 June 1962): 735–736.

217. King to Fey, 27 June 1962, p. 491 in this volume.

218. King to Fey, 27 June 1962, p. 493 in this volume; Fey to King, 6 July 1962; Dora E. McDonald to Fey, 16 July 1962; and "Gandhi Society Explained," *Christian Century,* 79 (1 August 1962): 929–930.

The second week in July, King and Abernathy returned to Recorder's Court in Albany to hear the verdict from their trial in February.[219] Standing before the judge on 10 July, they were found guilty and ordered to either pay a $178 fine or serve forty-five days in jail. Choosing the jail sentence, King and Abernathy called the verdict a "mortal wound in the body of justice" and announced that they would serve the sentence to demonstrate that "it is better to go to jail with dignity and self respect than to pay an unjust fine and cooperate with evil and immorality." In preparation for their jail stay, King and Abernathy staged a twenty-four-hour fast.[220]

In jail, King kept a diary and wrote an article for his biweekly column in the *New York Amsterdam News*.[221] In the column, he reiterated his determination to serve his sentence, and explained the difference between practicing civil disobedience and using the law to enforce racial injustice. King noted that a person's decision to break an unjust law and willingly pay the penalty evidences the highest respect for the law and "transforms the jail into a haven of liberty and freedom." In contrast, King argued, the segregationist practices "uncivil disobedience" because "he breaks, circumvents, flouts, and evades the law" and "is unwilling to pay the penalty."[222]

In a show of solidarity with King and Abernathy, demonstrations continued. An afternoon march on 11 July resulted in the arrest of about fifty protesters. In his diary, King wrote that as they approached the jail he could hear them singing freedom songs, which was "naturally" a "big lift to us."[223] In addition to visits from family and close friends, King also received letters of support, including one from Birmingham leader Fred Shuttlesworth, who encouraged King to "win this battle for our country" for "there can be no retreat." Ever ready to join the battle, Shuttlesworth offered his assistance, affirming "you have only to call."[224] Albany officials sought to counter the publicity surrounding King's arrest by surreptitiously arranging for someone to pay his fine. On 12 July after serving only two days of their forty-five-day sentence, King and Abernathy were released. Police chief Laurie Pritchett announced that an anonymous, "tall, well-dressed Negro" paid their bond.[225]

A crowd of 1,500 gathered at Shiloh Baptist Church to welcome King after his

---

219.  C. B. King to King, 5 July 1962. The trial stemmed from King and Abernathy's 16 December 1961 arrest after leading more than 260 demonstrators on a march to City Hall (see Ralph Abernathy to King, 17 December 1961, pp. 346–348 in this volume).

220.  Press Release, King and Abernathy Choose Jail Time over Fine, 10 July 1962, p. 510 in this volume.

221.  King, Albany Jail Diary from 10 July–11 July 1962, pp. 511–516 in this volume; King, "People in Action: A Message from Jail," 14 July 1962.

222.  King, "A Message from Jail."

223.  King, Albany Jail Diary from 10 July–11 July 1962, p. 516 in this volume.

224.  Shuttlesworth to King, 20 July 1962. In a letter to Georgia governor S. Ernest Vandiver, Jewish writer Harry Golden urged him to personally rethink the arrest of King and Abernathy, arguing that "this might be an opportunity for the great state of Georgia to strike a final blow against this evil." He went on to say: "The human story remains supreme over all technological and scientific wonders, because the greatest of all wonders is human kindness" (Golden to Vandiver, 11 July 1962).

225.  Bill Shipp, "Freed by Mystery Fine Donor, Rev. King Meets Police Chief," *Atlanta Constitution*, 13 July 1962. William G. Anderson later fingered B. C. Gardner, a law partner of Asa Kelley, as the person who paid the fines (Anderson and Anderson, *Autobiographies of a Black Couple of the Greatest Generation*, p. 220).

release. King registered his disappointment at the "subtle and conniving methods" Albany officials used to get him and Abernathy out of jail. His frustration gave way to optimism when he announced that negotiations with Police Chief Laurie Pritchett had resulted in concessions on three of the five Albany Movement demands: enforcement of the ICC ruling desegregating interstate travel and facilities, desegregating city buses if and when routes resumed, and returning bond money for the more than 700 people arrested. The next day, Pritchett told reporters that he had not agreed to any of the Albany Movement's demands.[226]

The breakdown in communication hardened King's resolve to remain in Albany until demands were met.[227] On 15 July, Albany Movement leaders submitted a manifesto to city officials outlining their grievances, which included compliance with the ICC ruling, desegregation of public facilities, and fair and speedy trials or a dismissal of charges for those arrested the previous December. They reaffirmed their commitment to nonviolence and their willingness to accept help from SCLC and other civil rights organizations.[228] In addition, they sent a telegram to city officials expressing their disappointment at the "long record of broken promises and bad faith agreements" and requested a "special meeting" with the commission no later than 17 July to discuss their grievances. Responding to the Albany Movement, Albany mayor Asa Kelley flatly refused to negotiate: "It is the decision of the Commission not to deal with law violators."[229] Upon hearing the news, King met with Albany Movement leaders to plan their "counter move against the city commission" and according to a newspaper account, King said, "When we finish this thing, the City Commission will want to talk to me."[230] In a mass meeting at Shiloh Baptist Church that evening, King called for renewed demonstrations.[231]

King then left Albany to fulfill a previous commitment to speak at the National Press Club on 19 July in Washington. The first African American to address the club, King called for immediate and complete desegregation, citing Albany as proof of the unyielding determination of black Americans to achieve full citizenship. He warned that the "issue is not whether segregation and discrimination will be eliminated, but how they will pass from the American scene."[232] Afterward King canceled an appearance at a Jackie Robinson testimonial dinner, choosing

226. King, Address Delivered at Mass Meeting at Shiloh Baptist Church, 12 July 1962, pp. 518, 520 in this volume; Shipp, "Freed by Mystery Fine Donor, Rev. King Meets Police Chief," 13 July 1962; and Claude Sitton, "Dr. King Is Freed against His Will," *New York Times*, 13 July 1962.

227. King, Address Delivered at Albany Movement Mass Meeting at Shiloh Baptist Church, 16 July 1962, pp. 522–525 in this volume.

228. Albany Movement, "Albany Manifesto," 15 July 1962, pp. 521–522 in this volume.

229. Vic Smith, "'No Deal,' City Informs Negro Violators of Law," *Albany Herald*, 16 July 1962. In a 17 July telegram, Albany Movement officials urged the mayor and city commission to reconsider their decision not to negotiate (Anderson, King, Abernathy, and Slater King to Albany City Commission and Asa D. Kelley, 17 July 1962, pp. 525–526 in this volume).

230. Bill Shipp, "Turn Albany Upside Down by Non-Violence, King Asks," *Atlanta Constitution*, 17 July 1962.

231. King, Address Delivered at Albany Movement Mass Meeting at Shiloh Baptist Church, 16 July 1962, pp. 522–525 in this volume.

232. King, Address Delivered at the National Press Club and Question and Answer Period, 19 July 1962, p. 528 in this volume.

instead to return immediately to Albany, where he announced plans to march to city hall.[233]

A few hours before the demonstration was to begin, a federal court issued an injunction forbidding future marches. Albany Movement president W. G. Anderson and other leaders agreed to honor the order until the issue could be resolved in a higher court. However, in a joint statement, King and Anderson scoffed at Albany city officials' "illusions that the legitimate aspirations of the Negro community for freedom and human dignity can be snuffed out by a series of evasions and legal maneuvers."[234] With the understanding that the order applied only to leaders and not the entire African American community, 160 Albany residents marched toward city hall, following Williams Springs Baptist Church pastor Samuel B. Wells, on 21 July.[235]

As the protest continued, King, Abernathy, Anderson, and Wyatt Tee Walker met with Chief Pritchett on 23 July. King reportedly offered to leave Albany if the city commission would agree to meet with the Albany Movement leadership. Pritchett declined King's offer, claiming he could not speak for the city commission.[236] That afternoon, the pregnant wife of Slater King, Marion, was attacked by a white police officer when she went to the Mitchell County Jail in Camilla, Georgia, to visit protesters arrested during earlier demonstrations. As she approached the jail carrying her three-year-old daughter, the officer told her to leave, but she did not move quickly enough before he began shoving her and struck her across the face with enough force to knock her out.[237]

With racial tensions in Albany reaching a flashpoint, Albany Movement lawyers filed two class action lawsuits against the City of Albany and its officials asking the court to end segregation in public facilities and to prevent interference with citizens' right to protest.[238] They also appeared in an Atlanta courtroom to argue for a withdrawal of the temporary restraining order prohibiting demonstrations by movement leaders. On 24 July, Fifth Circuit Court of Appeals judge Elbert P. Tuttle vacated the order, ruling that the "trial court had no jurisdiction to enter this order at all."[239]

---

233. King to Jackie Robinson Testimonial Dinner, 20 July 1962, and King, Address Delivered at Albany Movement Mass Meeting at Third Kiokee Baptist Church, 20 July 1962, pp. 544–545 and 541–544 in this volume, respectively. In place of King, Wyatt Tee Walker delivered King's prepared remarks (King, Address at Jackie Robinson Hall of Fame Dinner, 20 July 1962; "It Was Jackie Robinson's Week," *New York Amsterdam News*, 28 July 1962).

234. Joint statement of Martin Luther King, Jr. and William G. Anderson, 22 July 1962; see also King, Press Conference Regarding Albany Injunction, 22 July 1962, pp. 545–546 in this volume.

235. Claude Sitton, "Negroes Defy Ban, March in Georgia," *New York Times*, 22 July 1962.

236. Special Agent in Charge, Atlanta, Ga., to J. Edgar Hoover, 23 July 1962, Bureau File 157–6–2–453.

237. Marion King, Statement on beating at Mitchell County Jail, 23 July 1962. Four months after the attack, Marion King delivered a stillborn child, whose death was attributed to her attack (Slater King to John F. Kennedy, 26 December 1962). King had complained to Robert Kennedy about the "inhumane treatment and unhealthy conditions" at the Mitchell County Jail (King and Anderson to Kennedy, 23 July 1962, p. 547 in this volume).

238. *W. G. Anderson et al., v. Asa D. Kelly et al.*, 32 F.R.D. 355 (M.D. Ga. 1963); *W. G. Anderson et al., v. City of Albany et al.*, 321 F.2d 649 (5th Cir. 1963). For more on the lawsuits, see note 1, King, Anderson, and Slater King to Albany City Commission and Asa D. Kelley, 24 July 1962, p. 548 in this volume.

239. Claude Sitton, "Albany, Ga., Police Break Up Protest by 2,000 Negroes," *New York Times*, 25 July 1962. Before appealing to Tuttle, Albany Movement lawyers asked U.S. District Court judge W. A. Bootle

Immediately upon hearing the verdict, King along with Anderson and Slater King, implored the city commission to sit down "as brothers" to discuss "ways and means to grant citizenship rights that can no longer be postponed."[240] Praising the "sober and sound decision on the part of Judge Tuttle to preserve basic constitutional rights," King acknowledged in a mass meeting later that day that the racial hostility in Albany was "not tension merely between black people and white people," but between "justice and injustice." He concluded by urging his audience to keep the "weapon of nonviolence" at the forefront of the movement.[241]

King's rousing address was followed by an impromptu march by 300 protesters to Albany city hall. The march attracted a crowd of approximately 2,000 onlookers, some of whom hurled rocks and bottles at police, prompting a *mêlée* that resulted in injuries to two law enforcement officers and the arrest of forty others.[242] Although no movement leaders had participated in the march, King and Anderson called for a day of penance to demonstrate the movement's commitment to nonviolence.[243] King, Abernathy, and SNCC representatives Charles Jones and Charles Sherrod walked the streets of Harlem, Albany's African American district, on 25–26 July, encouraging nonviolence. In addition to several street corner meetings, the group visited a shoe shine parlor, a drugstore, a dry cleaners, and Dick's Pool Room, where King showed off his pool skills and warned customers that any violent outbursts would "defeat all of our efforts." Abernathy also addressed the pool hall patrons, explaining that the meaning of nonviolence was not "an appeal to you to slacken up in the struggle, or to stop resisting this evil system of segregation," for "nonviolence is the way for the strong, and not for the weak. It takes a strong man to be a nonviolent man."[244]

Resuming demonstrations on 27 July, King, Anderson, Abernathy, Slater King, Albany Movement chaplain Benjamin Gay, and five women led a prayer vigil in front of city hall. After Pritchett announced that everyone was under arrest, King asked Abernathy to lead the group in prayer.[245] A statement released by the Albany Movement explained that the demonstration was "a final effort to soften the hearts of the City Commission of Albany." Asserting that appeals to reason and nonviolent protests had proved futile, the statement affirmed that the black community of

---

of Macon, Georgia, to intervene in the case, but he refused (Vic Smith, "Negroes Rebutted by Judge Bootle," *Albany Herald*, 23 July 1962).

240. King, Anderson, and Slater King to Albany City Commission and Asa D. Kelley, 24 July 1962, p. 548 in this volume.

241. King, Anderson, and Slater King to Albany City Commission and Asa D. Kelley, 24 July 1962, and King, Address Delivered at Albany Movement Mass Meeting, 24 July 1962, pp. 548 and 552 in this volume, respectively.

242. King, Address Delivered at Albany Movement Mass Meeting, 24 July 1962, pp. 549–553 in this volume; see also Claude Sitton, "Dr. King Sets a Day of Penance After Violence in Albany, Ga.," *New York Times*, 26 July 1962; Vic Smith, "Uneasy Calm Prevails Here As M.L. King Cries 'Penance,'" *Albany Herald*, 25 July 1962; and "Albany Demonstrations Halted for a 24 Hour Penance Period," *Atlanta Daily World*, 26 July 1962.

243. King, Press Conference Denouncing Violence in Albany, 25 July 1962, pp. 553–555 in this volume.

244. Laurie Pritchett, Bill Manley, and J. Ed. Friend, Statement of police officers concerning activities of Martin Luther King, Jr., 25 July 1962; Statement on Nonviolence at Pool Hall, 26 July 1962, pp. 556, 558 in this volume.

245. Abernathy and King, Prayer vigil and arrests at Albany City Hall, 27 July 1962; see also King, Albany Jail Diary from 27 July–31 July 1962, pp. 558–566 in this volume.

Albany under the auspices of the Albany Movement and guidance of the SCLC did "not seek victory, only reconciliation." The statement concluded, "If the beloved community is to be established in Albany, we must begin by talking together."[246]

After Walker called for nationwide support, sympathizers sent telegrams to local and federal officials, mobilized prayer vigils, and wore black armbands symbolizing "murdered justice" in Albany.[247] Prayer vigils were held in cities all over the country. From Fresno, California, to New York City, New York, leaders vowed to continue the vigils until the federal government took action to resolve the situation in Albany. In the nation's capital, over one hundred clergy traveled to the White House and presented officials with petitions signed by 5,000, requesting immediate government intervention.[248] Supporters also inundated the president with telegrams calling for federal intervention.[249] One of the support letters King received came from Montgomery Improvement Association board member Irene West, who thanked King and Abernathy for their "kindness, patient understanding and dedicated service . . . to the nation" and predicted that "Good will soon triumph over wrong."[250]

Prior to being jailed, King had agreed to appear on "Meet the Press" on 29 July. Although he described his incarceration in Albany as his worst jail experience, King refused to post bond and asked Anderson to secure bail and substitute for him on the television show.[251] Despite the grim conditions, King was encouraged by the outpouring of support and was also heartened when President Kennedy told reporters: "The United States Government is involved in sitting down at Geneva with the Soviet Union. I can't understand why the government of Albany, City Council of Albany, cannot do the same for American citizens."[252] In a telegram sent from jail, King thanked Kennedy for his statement. "Rev. Abernathy and I earnestly hope you

---

246. King and Abernathy, Press release, "Why our prayer vigil," 27 July 1962.

247. Walker to Friend of Freedom, 27 July 1962.

248. SCLC, Press release, "Nation-wide prayer vigils support Albany," 1 August 1962.

249. On 30 July 1962, the president and the attorney general received telegrams from SCLC special project director Roy C. Bell, Connecticut governor John Dempsey, CORE executive director James Farmer, Brotherhood of Sleeping Car Porters president A. Philip Randolph, Montgomery Improvement Association president S.S. Seay, and NAACP executive secretary Roy Wilkins, who wrote: "The time-honored rights of assembly and of petition of regress of grievances have been denied and a community of 22,000 citizens is being repressed in ruthless fashion. This curtailment of free speech and assembly violates the constitutional rights of Doctor King and the others who languish in crowded jails in nearby counties. Practically on the eve of the one hundredth anniversary of the drafting of the Emancipation Proclamation, the United States of America is witnessing in Albany, Georgia, the flouting not only of that document, but of the bill of rights to our constitution. This is a peril to all Americans and well warrants the attention of the president of all the people" (Wilkins to John F. Kennedy, 30 July 1962; see also Bell to John F. Kennedy and Robert F. Kennedy, 30 July 1962; Dempsey to John F. Kennedy, 30 July 1962; Farmer to John F. Kennedy, 30 July 1962; Randolph to John F. Kennedy, 30 July 1962; and Seay to Robert F. Kennedy, 30 July 1962).

250. West to King and Abernathy, 1 August 1962. King also received letters from Kelly Miller Smith, cofounder of the Nashville Christian Leadership Council; Harold Fey, editor of the *Christian Century*; and S.S. Seay, president of the MIA (Smith to King, 2 August 1962; Fey to King, 7 August 1962; and Seay to King, 1 August 1962, pp. 566–567 in this volume).

251. Betty Cole to King, 23 July 1962; see also King, Albany Jail Diary from 27 July–31 July 1962, pp. 559–560, 561 in this volume; and Anderson, Interview on "Meet the Press," 29 July 1962.

252. *Public Papers of the Presidents of the United States: John F. Kennedy, 1962* (Washington, D.C.: U.S. Government Printing Office, 1963), pp. 592–593.

will continue to use the great moral influence of your office to help this crucial situation," he asserted. "There is no need for another Little Rock here."[253] In addition, he released a statement to the press rebutting Mayor Asa Kelley's contention that the city commission would not negotiate with "outsiders." King, who had never insisted on being part of the negotiating team, called this an "excuse and another evasive scheme to maintain the system of segregation."[254]

As with his confinement in early July, King chronicled his jail experiences in a diary that was later published by *Jet* magazine.[255] He described the daily arrival of new arrestees and the flow of his visitors, including colleagues and family. Complaining of the heat and overall exhaustion, King described feeling so ill that Anderson had to provide medical treatment.[256] Despite the conditions, King completed three sermons for his forthcoming book, *Strength to Love,* including "A Tender Heart and a Tough Mind," "Love in Action," and "Loving Your Enemies." He attempted to maintain a positive attitude, but King's entries also expressed despair and frustration.[257]

While still being held on local charges, King testified in the civil case brought by Albany mayor Asa D. Kelley and other officials to prevent the Albany Movement from engaging in further protest. Taking the stand on 8 August, King recounted his involvement in the Albany Movement since December 1961 and explained his philosophy of nonviolence and civil disobedience.[258] The Albany Movement's defense was bolstered when the U.S. Department of Justice filed an amicus curiae brief, arguing that the Supreme Court and lower federal courts have "repeatedly held that racial segregation in facilities operated by or under control of the State or its officials is illegal under the United States Constitution and under Federal law." As a solution to the pending litigation, the Justice Department suggested that if Albany officials followed the law "there would be no demonstrations and no need for litigation and bitterness."[259] Despite federal intervention in the case, Judge J. Robert Elliott adjourned proceedings without pronouncing judgment.[260] Two days later, King was in court

253.  King to John F. Kennedy, 2 August 1962, p. 567 in this volume; see also William G. Anderson to John F. Kennedy, 2 August 1962.

254. King, Statement on stand of John F. Kennedy on negotiations in Albany, Ga., 1 August 1962.

255.  See King, Albany Jail Diary from 27 July–31 July 1962, Albany Jail Diary from 1 August–7 August 1962, and Albany Jail Diary from 8 August–10 August 1962, pp. 558–566, 568–569, 589–590 this volume, respectively.

256.  King, Albany Jail Diary from 27 July–31 July 1962, and King, Albany Jail Diary from 1 August–7 August 1962, pp. 558–566 and 568–569 in this volume, respectively.

257.  King, Albany Jail Diary from 27 July–31 July 1962, and King, Albany Jail Diary from 8 August–10 August 1962, pp. 558–566 and 589–590 in this volume, respectively. King later wrote in the preface to *Strength to Love,* that he penned "Shattered Dreams," "Love in Action," and "Loving Your Enemies" while jailed in Albany (King, *Strength to Love* [New York: Harper & Row, 1963], p. ix).

258.  For King's testimony, see Testimony in *Asa D. Kelly et al., v. M.S. Page et al.*, 8 August 1962, pp. 570–587 in this volume.

259.  Jimmy Robinson, "Racial Situation Simmers as U.S. Intervenes in City," *Albany Herald*, 9 August 1962. King said U.S. intervention in the case "further vindicates the position of the Albany Movement in its insistence on the right of citizens to peacefully demonstrate (Robinson, "Racial Situation Simmers," 9 August 1962).

260.  In 1963 Elliott denied both parties' requests for permanent injunctions, but the case was later appealed (see note 6, Testimony in *Asa D. Kelly et al., v. M.S. Page et al.*, 8 August 1962, pp. 570–571 in this volume).

again. This time in Albany Recorder's Court to answer charges stemming from his 27 July arrest. Testifying before a desegregated courtroom, King and his associates were found guilty, fined $200 each, and given a sixty-day suspended sentence. Before freeing the leaders, Judge Addie Durden admonished them to refrain from further demonstrations or be subject to re-arrest. Although expecting a harsher sentence, King was not surprised by the verdict, calling it "unjust," but agreed to temporarily leave Albany to give the commission a chance to enter into "good-faith" negotiations with the Albany Movement.[261]

King returned to Atlanta the following day in time to preach at Ebenezer on Sunday.[262] On the same day he left Albany, officials closed public parks and libraries after an interracial group tried to integrate them.[263] A disappointed King told a reporter that the "present action of the city commission can lead to the most explosive racial situation in the United States today" and he vowed to "regroup our forces and renew mass nonviolent demonstrations in order to keep this issue before the conscience of Albany and the nation."[264] Arriving back in Albany on 13 August, King addressed a cheering crowd at Mt. Zion Baptist Church. He warned the city commission that the turmoil in Albany will not abate until the commission is "willing to sit down and face reality." They must recognize, King said, that "segregation is on its deathbed in Albany, and the only thing uncertain about it is how costly the City Commission will make the funeral."[265]

A few days after King returned to Albany, the Shady Grove Baptist Church in nearby Leesburg that had been used as a voter registration center was bombed. King, who had endured the bombing of his own home in January 1956, reacted with outrage: "All property is significant, but this is a church of God. And when men will do this, when men will seek to destroy the church of God, they have degenerated to a tragic level of inhumanity and sin and evil."[266] While visiting the ruins, King pledged $500 to begin the rebuilding process, declaring that the bombing of the church "illustrates the ends to which the white racist community in the South will go to discourage Negroes from voting. This strikes at the very heart of our more prized freedoms—freedoms of speech and the right to vote. We cannot be leaders of the free world with Negro churches being bombed in the Deep South."[267]

In the evening, a delegation of Albany Movement leaders, headed by William G. Anderson, met in closed session for the first time with Mayor Asa D. Kelley and the

261. Hedrick Smith, "Dr. King Set Free after Conviction," *New York Times*, 11 August 1962; Milton L. Carr, "Dr. King, 3 Others Get Suspended Terms," *Atlanta Daily World*, 11 August 1962.

262. King's sermon was "God in Albany" ("Dr. King, Jr., to Fill Pulpit at Ebenezer Sunday," *Atlanta Daily World*, 11 August 1962).

263. Hedrick Smith, "Albany, Ga., Closes Parks and Libraries to Balk Integration," *New York Times*, 12 August 1962.

264. "Albany Police Lock City Parks, Library," *Nashville Tennessean*, 12 August 1962.

265. Hedrick Smith, "Dr. King Speaks to 1,000 in Albany," *New York Times*, 14 August 1962.

266. King, Statement Delivered at Bombed Church, 15 August 1962, p. 591 in this volume. For more on the bombing of King's home, see Joe Azbell, "Blast Rocks Residence of Bus Boycott Leader," 31 January 1956, in *The Papers of Martin Luther King, Jr.*, vol. 3: *Birth of a New Age, December 1955–December 1956*, ed. Clayborne Carson, Stewart Burns, Susan Carson, Peter Holloran, Dana L. H. Powell (Berkeley: University of California Press, 1997), pp. 114–115.

267. SCLC, Press release, "SCLC pledges special fund to rebuild dynamited church," 15 August 1962.

entire city commission. Marion Page, executive secretary of the Albany Movement, read a three-page petition reiterating the movement's demands. Once again, Kelley steadfastly refused to discuss or implement any of the requests: "It strikes me that every area covered tonight now rests with the Federal courts where it should be and where it should have been months ago." King, who was not a member of the negotiating team, said the city commission's refusal to talk demonstrated that they hold "the Negro citizen of this community in utter contempt."[268]

With the movement at a nine-month stalemate, King inconspicuously boarded a plane for Atlanta on 16 August. When a reporter asked Andrew J. Young why King left Albany, he refused to say, but disclosed that the civil rights leader would "definitely be back." As to whether or not demonstrations in Albany would continue, Young replied: "Not at this moment."[269] From Atlanta, King called for an interracial, interfaith pilgrimage of Northern religious leaders to come to southwest Georgia and "stand with the people of Albany as they strive for freedom." Seventy-five men and women representing many denominations and geographic locations answered King's call and were arrested on 27 August.[270] Arriving back in Albany to greet the religious leaders, King commended those arrested for recognizing "that justice and morality know no limits of geography and that Albany is but a symptom of the cancerous sore of segregation within our American democracy."[271] Police Chief Laurie Pritchett accused the clergy of coming to "aid and abet the law violators of this city" and urged them to instead "clear your own city of sin and of lawlessness before you come here to try and convert us."[272] Unable to overcome the obstinacy of Albany's white leaders, King, his SCLC colleagues, and Albany Movement leaders were forced to recognize that months of struggle had produced few tangible gains and racial tensions remained high.

Although the Albany protests had attracted national attention, appeals to the Kennedy administration did not result in sustained and concrete action. When city officials remained intransigent, King once again pleaded for Kennedy's help. In a 31 August 1962 telegram, King urged the president to invite members of the Albany City Commission to Washington for mediated discussion on the Albany situation.[273] Attorney General Robert Kennedy's reply reiterated the federal government's policy

268. "Albany, Ga., Hears Negro Pleas But Refuses to Take Any Action," *New York Times*, 16 August 1962.

269. "Martin Luther Leaves Albany," *Albany Herald*, 16 August 1962. Although King pledged to remain involved in the Albany struggle, he would split his time between Albany and Atlanta (Hedrick Smith, "Georgians Balk Albany Movement for Civil Rights," *New York Times*, 18 August 1962).

270. King to Friend of Freedom, 22 August 1962; King to Ralph Lord Roy, 22 August 1962, pp. 603–604 in this volume.

271. King, Press statement concerning the arrest of ministers in Albany, Ga., 28 August 1962.

272. Pritchett, Statement on arrest of clergy in Albany, Ga., 28 August 1962. King's nemesis J. H. Jackson called the ministers hypocrites for leaving Chicago to "fight segregation" in Albany. "You wouldn't need to leave Chicago to fight segregation," Jackson was quoted as saying ("Negro Baptist Chief Assails Racial Battles," *Los Angeles Times*, 5 September 1962). In response, Anderson called Jackson a "disgrace, not only to the Negro people, but to the human race. He's a Mississippi boy who's been away so long that he has no idea what the Negro in the Deep South is up against" (Albany Movement, Press release, "Albany Movement leader blasts National Baptist prexy on movement," 13 September 1962).

273. King to John F. Kennedy, 31 August 1962, pp. 605–607 in this volume.

to uphold the "constitutional rights of all Americans . . . against state or other official discriminations or segregation on the basis of race color or creed." He also reminded King of the president's earlier statement urging officials to negotiate with Albany Movement leaders and that the federal courts are now in the process of hearings to determine the constitutionality of segregated public facilities in Albany and the right to citizens to protest segregation. "The Department of Justice," Kennedy said, "will continue to take all appropriate steps within its power to uphold and enforce the law of the land."[274]

A year and a half after he had expressed guarded optimism about the prospects for civil rights reform during Kennedy's presidency, King had seen only a slight shift in the administration's civil rights policies. President Kennedy had ignored King's repeated appeals for a second Emancipation Proclamation that would eliminate statutory segregation through an executive order. His meetings with Kennedy had secured promises of support for voting rights efforts, but SCLC's People to People campaign and Citizenship Schools produced only gradual gains; major obstacles to black voting rights persisted. The newly created Gandhi Society for Human Rights had not yet demonstrated that it could provide effective legal assistance and ongoing financial support for SCLC. Much had been accomplished during 1961 and 1962, but SCLC had played mainly a supportive role in the Freedom Rides and the Albany protests, the most visible indications that black discontent with the pace of civil rights reform could become a powerful force for change.

As Wyatt Tee Walker reflected on SCLC efforts during 1961 and 1962, he admitted that in the "crucial testing ground" of Albany a "decisive victory has not come," but he nonetheless concluded that the organization had achieved significant gains. "The system of segregation was also on trial, and we were able to demonstrate to the world through the flesh and blood of the Albany, Georgia, situation, the complete moral indefensibility of the segregation system." The Albany campaign had achieved "the psychological freeing of the Negro mind and spirit." In assessing SCLC's future, he recalled King's description of SCLC "as a 'sleeping giant' in the social transition of the South" and concluded that the organization "totaled more successes than failures." Walker repeated the metaphor he had used at SCLC's annual gathering in September 1961: "There is (still) more of the road before us than there is behind us, and that road we have traveled has at times been most tortuous."[275] King, however, saw the importance of the Albany Movement in a broader context: "If you had not

---

274. Robert F. Kennedy to King, 2 September 1962. Earlier King told a reporter that President Kennedy would need to take real steps toward ending segregation if he wanted to maintain black support: "Mr. Kennedy will have to do a great deal to implement his campaign promises in order to hold the support he received from Negro voters in the last election." When asked if blacks would switch their support to Nelson Rockefeller if he became the Republican Party candidate for president, King said: "Rockefeller certainly has taken a stand and if he continues and if he implements this (desegregation) in our state, then we will be greatly impressed" (William Hannah, "Albany Jails 50 Ministers from North," *Atlanta Constitution*, 29 August 1962). In August 1962, Rockefeller made a $5,000 donation to SCLC to help the "cause" (Vic Smith, "Race Mix Pastors Converge on City," *Albany Herald*, 27 August 1962). For details on King's relationship with Rockefeller, see King to Rockefeller, 9 August 1961, pp. 260–261 in this volume.

275. Walker, "Report of the director," October 1961–September 1962; see also Walker, "Report of the director," 28 September 1961.

had a movement like this, thousands of Negroes would be walking around with their heads buried. The victory of the Albany Movement has already been won. Thousands of Negroes have won a new sense of dignity and self-respect."[276]

At the end of August, King offered his own more hopeful assessment of SCLC's prospects when he wrote to his brother, Birmingham minister A. D. King. King wrote that the coming year "calls for a real mobilization of our civil rights forces in the State of Alabama. We want to help you to help Alabama. Through our reciprocal efforts, we can bring a new day in the Deep South and your state."[277]

---

276. Smith, "Georgians Balk Albany Movement for Civil Rights," 18 August 1962.
277. King to Alfred Daniel King, 30 August 1962, p. 605 in this volume.

1961

| | |
|---|---|
| Jan | *Ebony* publishes King's article "What Happened to Hell?" |
| 1 Jan | King preaches "How Big Is Your God?" at Ebenezer Baptist Church in Atlanta. |
| 2 Jan | At the Savannah, Georgia, Municipal Auditorium King delivers "The Negro and the American Dream" at a rally for the Emancipation Proclamation Association. |
| 12 Jan | In Sioux Falls, South Dakota, King attends a reception held in his honor at First Baptist Church and later speaks before the Knife and Fork Club at the Sheraton-Cataract Hotel. |
| 13 Jan | On the first day of his three-day speaking tour in Los Angeles, King gives a press conference at the Ambassador Hotel. |
| 14 Jan | At Zion Hill Baptist Church in Los Angeles, King delivers the keynote address at the founding meeting of the Western Christian Leadership Conference (WCLC). Following the address, King attends a reception in his honor at the Wilfandel Club. |
| 15 Jan | King preaches "Three Dimensions of a Complete Life" at the morning worship services at Woodland Hills Community Church in Woodland Hills, California. In the evening, he delivers "The Future of Integration" at Canoga Park High School. |
| 16 Jan | In St. Louis, King attends a meeting of the Executive Committee of the National Sunday School and Baptist Training Union (BTU) Congress at the Baptist Educational Center to plan the Congress's annual meeting. Following the meeting, King and the other members of the executive committee have lunch at Memorial Baptist Church. Those attending the meeting, including King, board a plane for Hot Springs, Arkansas. |
| 17–19 Jan | King is in Hot Springs at the National Baptist Hotel and Bath House where National Baptist Convention (NBC) officials headed by J. H. Jackson vote to recognize as independent a competing group of NBC members headed by Gardner C. Taylor and to assume the mortgages of African American farmers in two Tennessee counties facing foreclosure because they registered to vote. |
| 20 Jan | King flies from Atlanta to Chicago. |

| | |
|---|---|
| 21 Jan | King attends the Public Review Advisory Commission meeting of the United Packinghouse, Food and Allied Workers of America at the Palmer House hotel in Chicago. Afterward, he flies back to Atlanta. |
| 27 Jan | At New York's Carnegie Hall, King is the guest of honor at a Southern Christian Leadership Conference (SCLC) fundraiser and celebrity gala organized by Harry Belafonte and A. Philip Randolph. |
| 28 Jan | King flies from New York to Chicago. |
| 29 Jan | In Chicago, King preaches at the morning worship service at Pilgrim Missionary Baptist Church. Later that evening, King delivers "The Man Who Was a Fool" at Orchestra Hall for the Chicago Sunday Evening Club. The address is broadcast on radio station WIND. |
| 30 Jan | King flies from Chicago to Atlanta, canceling an appearance in Philadelphia at an Americans for Democratic Action (ADA) Roosevelt Day dinner to be with his wife, Coretta, who has given birth to Dexter Scott, the couple's third child. Once in Atlanta, King addresses the ADA over the phone. |
| 31 Jan | In Salt Lake City, King delivers "The Future of Integration" at the University of Utah. |
| 1 Feb | King arrives in New York. |
| 2 Feb | In New York, King receives the 1961 Distinguished Award at an ADA Roosevelt Day dinner. He is also a guest on "Mike Wallace Interviews," which airs on WNTA-TV the following week. |
| 3 Feb | Still in New York, King meets with Stephen Courier of the Taconic Foundation. At the home of Dorothy Norman, an activist and philanthropist from New York, King meets Eleanor Roosevelt and others, to raise funds and talk informally about nonviolence. |
| 4 Feb | King remains in New York. *The Nation* magazine publishes an article by King entitled "Equality Now: The President Has the Power." |
| 5 Feb | King travels from New York to Washington, D.C. and then flies home to Atlanta. |
| 7 Feb | At Columbia Theological Seminary in Decatur, Georgia, King addresses the Interseminary Movement. Part one of King's interview with Wallace airs. |
| 8 Feb | Part two of King's interview with Wallace airs. |
| 9 Feb | In New York King speaks at Newark State College as part of the M. Ernest Townsend Memorial Lecture Series. |
| 10 Feb | At New York University (NYU), King lunches at the Stevenson Faculty Club, then speaks on "The Future of Integration" at the Hall of Fame Playhouse at the University Heights campus of NYU before flying back to Atlanta. |
| 14 Feb | Upon his arrival at Illinois Wesleyan University in Bloomington, King is interviewed by reporters. Later that evening he delivers "Facing the Challenge of a New Age" at the Religious Emphasis Banquet, followed by a public question and answer session. |

| | |
|---|---|
| 15 Feb | In Atlanta, King sits in a Fulton County courtroom to lend moral support to ministers arrested during a sit-in. Later that day, before an overflow crowd, King speaks at a mass meeting at Warren Memorial Methodist Church to garner support for students and ministers involved in the Atlanta sit-ins. |
| 17 Feb | King flies from Atlanta to Washington, D.C., where he delivers an address at Metropolitan Baptist Church to the Negro American Labor Council's Workshop and Institute on Race Bias in Trade Unions, Industry and Government. |
| 18 Feb | King is en route to the Bahamas. |
| 19–26 Feb | King is in Nassau, Bahamas, for vacation with Gardner Taylor and Chauncey Eskridge. |
| 26 Feb | At Chicago's Shoreland Hotel, King speaks to the Eighth Annual Brotherhood Week dinner of the Chicago Conference for Brotherhood. |
| 28 Feb | King flies from Chicago to Atlanta. |
| 5 Mar | King delivers "Why Dives Went to Hell" at Ebenezer. |
| 6 Mar | King preaches "The Man Who Was a Fool" at Central Methodist Church as part of the Detroit Council of Churches Noon-Day Lenten Service series, followed by a question and answer period and luncheon. He later gives the keynote address following a dinner meeting sponsored by the cultural committee of Detroit's Second Baptist Church. |
| 7 Mar | At Detroit's Central Methodist Church, King preaches "Loving Your Enemies" at the Noon-Day Lenten Service. |
| 8–9 Mar | King attends an emergency SCLC Administrative Committee meeting at Ebenezer to discuss programming and the *New York Times Co. v. Sullivan* (1964) libel case. |
| 10 Mar | At a mass meeting at Warren Memorial Methodist Church in Atlanta, King urges unity among groups seeking to end segregation in Atlanta stores and lunch counters. |
| 12 Mar | In Worcester, Massachusetts, King delivers "The Question of Progress in the Area of Race Relations" at the Temple Emanuel Community Forum series. His address and the question and answer period that followed are broadcast on radio station WTAG the next evening. |
| 13 Mar | At the University of Bridgeport in Connecticut, King receives a humanitarian award, delivers "The American Dream" for the annual Frank Jacoby Lecture, and answers questions from the audience. Afterward, he travels to New York. |
| 14 Mar | King is in New York. |
| 15 Mar | In Kansas City, Missouri, King speaks at a dinner hosted by the Temple Brotherhood of Congregation B'nai Jehudah. He also conducts an interview with WDAF-TV. |
| 16 Mar | King flies from Kansas City to Atlanta. |

19 Mar    King preaches at Ebenezer on the observance of the church's seventy-fourth anniversary. At Jacksonville, Florida's Mt. Ararat Baptist Church, he delivers "This is a Great Time to Be Alive" at an event sponsored by the Duval County Citizens Benefit Corporation and the Interdenominational Ministerial Alliance.

20 Mar    In Atlanta, King attends the opening session of a seminar series presented by the Atlanta Meeting of the Religious Society of Friends.

22 Mar    King is interviewed in his office at Ebenezer by Lester Margolies, a graduate student at Southern Illinois University.

23 Mar    King begins a four-day tour of the West Coast with a press conference at the San Francisco International Airport.

24 Mar    Under the auspices of Monterey Peninsula College's faculty Spiritual and Moral Subcommittee, King discusses the moral and spiritual aspects of integration with a student assembly. Following the discussion he holds a press conference in the student union and lunches with Talcott and Margaret Bates, local civil rights activists. That evening King dines with the college faculty before delivering a free public lecture at the college on "The Power of Nonviolence" and answering questions from the audience. In the late evening he gives a short address at Friendship Baptist Church in Seaside, California.

25 Mar    In the morning, King visits Easter Hill Methodist Church in Richmond, California, where he speaks to ministers involved in WCLC about the role of clergy in the civil rights movement.

26 Mar    King preaches at Progressive Baptist Church in Berkeley, California. Later he delivers an address to an overflow crowd at a mass meeting at the Oakland Auditorium in Oakland, California.

27–30 Mar    King and Coretta Scott King are in Miami.

2 Apr    King delivers "The Easter Faith" at Ebenezer. King's contribution to a collection of essays on the topic "What Is the World's Greatest Need?" appears in the *New York Times Magazine*.

5 Apr    In Atlanta, King receives a phone call from Attorney General Robert F. Kennedy.

7 Apr    Following the Georgia Court of Appeals' decision that King's sentence of twelve months' probation for a traffic violation he received in 1960 was excessive, he appears in DeKalb County Superior Court and receives a reduced sentence of six months' probation.

9 Apr    King preaches "The Meaning of Freedom" at Ebenezer.

10 Apr    King flies to Philadelphia.

11 Apr    At Dickinson College in Carlisle, Pennsylvania, King delivers "The Dimensions of a Complete Life" at the campus's Allison Church. Following his sermon, King attends a luncheon with college faculty at the James Wilson Hotel.

12 Apr    King arrives in New York for a three-day fundraising trip.

14 Apr    In Ithaca, New York, King delivers "The Future of Integration" at a fundraising event held at Cornell University's Bailey Hall, sponsored

by the Ithaca Freedom Walk and the Cornell Committee Against Segregation.

15 Apr  King is in New York City.

16 Apr  At Smith College in Northampton, Massachusetts, King delivers "The Dimensions of a Complete Life" at the Helen Hills Hills Chapel morning worship services. Following the service, King attends a lunch reception and leads a discussion for the Smith community at the Cushing House. In Williamstown, Massachusetts, King attends a dinner meeting of the Williams College Chapel Association and speaks on "The Strategy of Southern Sit-ins." Afterward King delivers "The Three Dimensions of a Complete Man" at Williams College's Thompson Memorial Chapel. Before an overflow audience in Jessup Hall on campus, King attends a question and answer session on the civil rights movement. King spends the night at the college's Faculty House.

17 Apr  In Massachusetts, King speaks in Johnson Chapel at Amherst College. Later that night, he flies from Hartford, Connecticut, to Chicago.

18 Apr  King leaves Chicago for Louisville, Kentucky.

19 Apr  King preaches "The Church on the Frontier of Racial Tension" as part of the Julius B. Gay Lecture series at the morning chapel service at Southern Baptist Theological Seminary in Louisville, Kentucky. Following his speech, King meets with an overflow noontime class on Christian Ethics in the chapel, and attends a luncheon with the seminary faculty. At the invitation of Louisville mayor Bruce Hoblitzell, King is a guest of a community committee studying the city's integration problems. Concluding his day, King speaks at a mass meeting before student activists at Quinn Chapel AME Church.

21 Apr  In Washington, D.C., King meets with Attorney General Robert F. Kennedy. King flies to New York.

22 Apr  King is in New York for conferences regarding the *New York Times v. Sullivan* (1964) libel suit. He flies back to Atlanta.

23 Apr  King preaches "The Prodigal Son" at Ebenezer.

24–26 Apr  At Ebenezer, King attends a training class on Church Methods sponsored by the Atlanta Baptist Education Center.

27 Apr  King speaks at the 25th Anniversary Dinner of the International Union, United Automobile, Aircraft and Agricultural Implement Workers of America (UAW) at Cobo Hall in Detroit, Michigan.

30 Apr  At the United Liberal Church in Atlanta, King and Coretta Scott King attend a reception by the Southern Conference Education Fund in honor of Carl Braden and Frank Wilkinson, who are about to enter prison for refusing to answer the questions of the House Un-American Activities Committee.

3 May — King flies to New York to consult with officials from the UAW regarding a voter registration campaign.

5 May — King speaks at a luncheon meeting of the All Citizens Voter Registration Drive at the Butler Street YMCA in Atlanta and holds a conference call with students of Professor James A. Burkhart at Stephens College in Columbia, Missouri.

6 May — King is in Atlanta.

7 May — King preaches "The Other Prodigal Son" at Ebenezer.

8 May — King travels to New York to confer with lawyers on the *New York Times v. Sullivan* (1964) libel suit, and speaks at the founding meeting of the Lawyers Advisory Committee on the same subject. In the evening, he travels to East Orange, New Jersey, to lecture on "The Impact of Religion on Community Living in the United States" and answer audience questions at Temple Sharey Tefilo as part of their series on "The Impact of Religion on American Life."

9 May — King flies from New York to Atlanta and then to Montgomery.

10 May — Before the start of the two-day SCLC Executive Board meeting in Montgomery, King meets with the Administrative Committee during lunch at the Regal Café. Later that afternoon, the executive board meets at Abernathy's First Baptist Church to discuss the *New York Times v. Sullivan* (1964) libel suit. In the evening, King leads a mass meeting at Holt Street Baptist Church.

11 May — King and other members of SCLC's executive board meet in closed session to discuss strategy and tactics for gaining full citizenship for African Americans. The board passes resolutions in support of Carl Braden, the U.S. Department of Justice's suit to reopen public schools in Prince Edward County, and in opposition to the treatment of African American protestors by Mississippi police forces.

13 May — King eats dinner with Congress of Racial Equality's (CORE's) freedom riders as they pass through Atlanta.

14 May — King preaches "Crisis in the Modern Family" at Sunday morning services at Ebenezer.

15 May — King is in Atlanta.

18 May — In Greensboro, North Carolina, King addresses the local branch of the National Association for the Advancement of Colored People (NAACP) at the War Memorial Auditorium. He spends the evening with Dr. Samuel DeWitt Proctor, president of North Carolina A&T College.

19–20 May — King is in Chicago.

21 May — King travels from New York, intending to fly to Hanover, New Hampshire, but departs without appearing at scheduled Dartmouth College events, after learning of violent attacks on freedom riders in Montgomery, Alabama, the day before. In Montgomery, King speaks to an estimated 1,000 people at an evening rally sponsored by the

Montgomery Improvement Association at Abernathy's First Baptist
Church. Due to a violent mob gathered outside, King and others are
forced to spend the night inside the church. King speaks to Attorney
General Robert F. Kennedy by phone as the crisis at First Baptist
unfolds.

22 May    In the early morning, a few hours after speaking by phone with
Robert F. Kennedy, King and others are escorted from First Baptist
Church by Alabama national guardsmen, and King is taken to the
home of Dr. Richard Harris. That evening King meets with James
Farmer and the freedom riders at the local YMCA. The meeting
continues at the home of Dr. Richard Harris where the freedom
riders and Dr. King are staying. The freedom riders ask King to join
them on the bus to Jackson, Mississippi, but he declines.

23 May    Into the early morning hours, King continues meeting with freedom
riders to discuss the future of the campaign. At a press conference in
Abernathy's house in Montgomery, King, Abernathy, James Farmer,
and John Lewis announce the rides will continue on to Jackson,
Mississippi, despite threats of danger.

24 May    In the morning King holds a prayer meeting with the freedom riders,
then sees off the first bus of riders at the Montgomery bus station as
they leave for Jackson a little after nine. At Abernathy's home, King
meets with a group of freedom riders led by Yale University chaplain
William Sloane Coffin and speaks with Robert F. Kennedy and Burke
Marshall by telephone. The *Los Angeles Mirror* publishes a letter to the
editor from King, thanking journalist Bill Kiley for his thoughtful
coverage of the civil rights movement. King returns to Atlanta.

25 May    King has a phone interview and asserts that the Freedom Rides will
resume on 29 or 30 May.

26 May    At Ebenezer King convenes a meeting of representatives from SCLC,
CORE, Student Nonviolent Coordinating Committee (SNCC),
Nashville Christian Leadership Council, and the National Student
Association (NSA). The group discusses the future of the Freedom
Rides and creates a Freedom Ride Coordinating Committee.

28 May    King preaches the Sunday morning service at Ebenezer.

29 May    King flies to Montgomery.

31 May    Before returning to Atlanta, King testifies at a hearing in Montgomery
on whether to grant the federal government's request for an injunction to prevent factions of the Ku Klux Klan and Montgomery police
officials from interfering with interstate bus travel.

2 June    King is in Atlanta for a strategy meeting to discuss whether to appeal
an injunction granted against the freedom riders.

3 June    King leaves Atlanta on a fundraising tour.

4 June    King is hosted by Dr. Charles F. Petitjean in Bridgeport, Connecticut,
where he receives an honorary Doctor of Laws (L.L.D.) degree at

the University of Bridgeport's commencement exercises. King and the other award recipients are recognized at a luncheon before the exercises and a reception afterward.

5 June King holds a press conference at the Sheraton-Atlantic Hotel in New York, at which he urges President Kennedy to issue a second Emancipation Proclamation making racial segregation illegal by executive order. Later that evening, King speaks to an overflow crowd at Mount Olivet Baptist Church along with Reverends Abernathy, Wyatt Tee Walker, S.S. Seay, and George Lawrence.

6 June At the commencement exercises at Lincoln University in Pennsylvania, King delivers "The American Dream" and receives an honorary doctor of laws. In the evening King speaks at an SCLC fundraising event at Concord Baptist Church in Brooklyn, New York.

8 June King speaks at Calvary Baptist Church, in Jamaica, New York.

9 June King speaks before the Negro Affairs Committee of District 65 in Astor Place in New York.

11 June King delivers "Mastering Our Fears" at Ebenezer.

13 June King gives testimony by deposition at the federal courthouse in the Middle District of Alabama, Montgomery, in the case of *Parks v. New York Times Co.*, 308 F.2d 474 (1962).

14 June King speaks at a voter registration rally sponsored by the Alabama State Coordinating Association for Registration and Voting at Birmingham's Sixteenth Street Baptist Church.

15 June King attends a dinner meeting at the home of New York lawyer Theodore Kheel.

16 June King arrives in Albany, New York, on Governor Nelson Rockefeller's private plane, and is his guest at a large reception and small private dinner at the Sheraton-Ten Eyck Hotel. He then appears at a fundraising rally at Wilborn Temple First Church of God in Christ under the auspices of the New York State Empire Baptist Convention.

17 June King arrives in Los Angeles for an afternoon of press interviews, including an exclusive interview with the *Los Angeles Times*, a taping of the "Los Angeles Report," and an appearance with commentator Tom Duggan.

18 June In Los Angeles, King preaches at The People's Independent Church of Christ for their Men's Day Sunday. King's interview with the "Los Angeles Report" airs at eleven A.M. on channel two. That afternoon he participates in a "Freedom Riders Rally" at the Los Angeles Sports Arena, sponsored by WCLC. Among the estimated 26,000 people in attendance were California's Governor Edmund Brown and Lieutenant Governor Glenn Anderson.

21 June After missing his flight, King arrives a day late to the National Sunday School and BTU Congress convention held at the Kiel Auditorium

in St. Louis, Missouri. He is a guest on Parker Wheatley's "Eye on St. Louis."

23 June    Still in St. Louis, King delivers "The American Dream" at a rally sponsored by the National Sunday School and BTU Congress. He is later interviewed at the Sheraton-Jefferson Hotel where he speaks out in support of the Freedom Rides.

25 June    King preaches at St. Louis's Central Baptist Church. He then flies to Indianapolis.

26 June    In Indianapolis, King visits Marion Stuart, the owner of a local trucking company, and his wife, Cordie King Stuart, a model for *Ebony* magazine. Accompanied by Abernathy, King addresses a packed audience at a membership drive on behalf of the NAACP at Mount Zion Hill Baptist Church.

27 June    In Jackson, Mississippi, King meets with the Freedom Riders Coordinating Committee and visits Wyatt Tee Walker, who was in the Hinds County Jail along with his wife, for participating in a freedom ride.

30 June    King flies to Norfolk, Virginia, and speaks at a mass rally for the Virginia Christian Leadership Conference at the Municipal Auditorium.

1 July    King flies to Atlanta.

2 July    King delivers "Our Christian Witness" at Ebenezer.

5 July    At the AME Minister's Institute at Flipper Temple AME Church in Atlanta, King delivers "Paul's Letter to American Christians."

6 July    In Jackson, Mississippi, King speaks at an evening mass meeting sponsored by the newly formed Jackson SNCC, where he advocates nonviolent methods for ending segregation.

7 July    King returns to Atlanta.

9 July    King speaks at Forbes Field in Pittsburgh, at the second annual Freedom Jubliee.

10 July    In Philadelphia King attends the 52nd Annual Convention of the NAACP.

11 July    King flies to Washington, D.C., and meets with Attorney General Robert F. Kennedy regarding voter registration. He then boards a plane for New York.

12 July    King attends a fundraising dinner at the New York home of Mrs. Von Rutledge Gordon.

13 July    King delivers "The American Dream" at Syracuse University's 10th Annual All-University Summer Sessions Reception and Dinner. The address, which was advertised as "Facing the Challenge of a New Age," was later broadcast on the University radio station, WAER.

14 July    King briefly travels to Philadelphia, where his father is in the Methodist-Episcopal Hospital following a car accident. King then flies to Hartford, Connecticut, and speaks at a rally sponsored by the

Hartford Interdenominational Alliance at Bushnell Memorial Hall. At the rally, King receives the keys to the city from Hartford mayor Dominick DeLucco.

15 July    King flies from New York to Baltimore to address a SNCC conference at the Masonic Lodge, and attends its business sessions. He then catches a flight to Atlanta.

20 July    At Tougaloo Christian College outside of Jackson, Mississippi, King attends a conference of interracial clergy in support of the Freedom Rides. King then spends the night in Philadelphia, where his father is still hospitalized after a car accident.

23 July    King preaches "The Motive for Being Good" at Ebenezer. In San Francisco, King speaks at a rally at the Cow Palace sponsored by WCLC.

24 July    King stays in San Francisco.

25 July    King delivers "The Future of Integration" at Wisconsin State College in Whitewater, Wisconsin.

26 July    King is in Chicago.

28 July    In New York, King meets with the Taconic Foundation regarding voting rights. That evening he attends the Committee for Better Human Relations' salute to SCLC and the freedom riders at the Waldorf Astoria Hotel.

29 July    King speaks about race relations to a conference of foreign students at Ebenezer.

30 July    King preaches at Ebenezer.

31 July    King flies from Atlanta to Martha's Vineyard.

1–4 Aug    King is in Martha's Vineyard working on the manuscript for *Strength to Love*.

5 Aug    King is in Atlanta.

6 Aug    King delivers "Paul's Letter to the American Christians" at Ebenezer's morning service. He also preaches the evening service.

10 Aug    At Ward AME Church in Los Angeles, King speaks at a Bon Voyage Banquet for Dr. L. Sylvester Odom, who will attend the World Council of Methodism in Norway.

12 Aug    King is in New York.

13 Aug    King delivers "Paul's Letter to American Christians" at the Riverside Church in New York. That evening, he preaches at a rally at Bright Hope Baptist Church in Philadelphia, and spends the night in New York.

14 Aug    King is in New York.

16 Aug    In Miami Beach, Florida, King participates in a panel discussion and speaks on the topic "Christ Lives in the World" at the first international convention of the Luther League of the American Lutheran Church at the Miami Beach Convention Hall.

| | |
|---|---|
| 20 Aug | King delivers "Man's Sin and God's Grace" at Ebenezer. At the home of Lorimer D. Milton, King attends a meeting for Atlanta mayoral candidate Ivan Allen. |
| 21 Aug | King is in Martha's Vineyard. |
| 22 Aug | King flies to New York. |
| 23 Aug | At the Taconic Foundation in New York, King meets with Stephen Currier to discuss voter registration. |
| 25 Aug | King is in New York. |
| 30–31 Aug | King is in Martha's Vineyard. |
| Sept 1961– May 1962 | King coteaches Social Philosophy at Morehouse College with Reverend Samuel Williams. The upper level course was designed to consider problems of social thought, justice, property rights, natural and divine law, the state and the individual, and nonviolent action. |
| 1 Sept | King flies from Martha's Vineyard to New York. |
| 2 Sept | King flies from New York to give the invocation at the funeral services of John Wesley Dobbs, Grand Master of the Georgia Prince Hall Masons, at Big Bethel AME Church in Atlanta. |
| 3 Sept | King delivers "The Meaning of Christ's Temptation" at Ebenezer's morning services, and also presides over evening services. |
| 5–9 Sept | With his wife, Coretta, King attends the NBC in Kansas City, Missouri. |
| 10 Sept | King preaches the morning and evening worship services at Ebenezer. *New York Times Magazine* publishes King's article "The Time for Freedom Has Come." |
| 11 Sept | King delivers the invocation at the funeral of Samuel Garrett Sellers, a local funeral parlor director, at West Hunter Baptist Church in Atlanta. |
| 14 Sept | At Atlanta University, King speaks to a group of twenty-five African students participating in the United Negro College Fund Orientation to American Life and Education Program. |
| 17 Sept | King delivers "Where God Is Found" at the morning worship service at Ebenezer. He also presides at the evening worship service. |
| 24 Sept | King attends the Men's Day celebration at Ebenezer. Dr. Mordecai Johnson, president emeritus of Howard University in Washington, D.C., is the guest speaker. |
| 25 Sept | In New York, King speaks at a meeting of Local 1199 of the Drug and Hospital Employees Union at the Hotel Diplomat, then flies back to Atlanta. |
| 26 Sept | King travels to Nashville. |
| 27 Sept | At Nashville's First Baptist Church, King convenes a morning meeting of the SCLC Executive Committee followed by an SCLC annual board meeting in the afternoon. In the evening, King presents scholarships to ten Freedom Ride participants during a "Tribute to |

|          | the Freedom Riders" that included the Chad Mitchell Trio, comedian George Kirby, and Miriam Makeba. |
|----------|---|
| 28 Sept  | In the morning, King formally opens SCLC's annual meeting at Clark Memorial Methodist Church. Later, he delivers an address at a rally at the War Memorial Auditorium. |
| 29 Sept  | On the last day of SCLC's annual meeting, King is reelected president. He returns to Atlanta. |
| Oct      | King's article "Crisis and the Church" appears in *Council Quarterly*. |
| 1 Oct    | At Ebenezer King delivers "Making Life Worth Living" at morning worship and later presides over the evening worship. |
| 4 Oct    | King arrives in New York and stays at the Hotel Roosevelt. |
| 5 Oct    | In New York, King addresses a morning session at the Eleventh Constitutional Convention of the Transport Workers Union of America at the Hotel Roosevelt. He then returns to Atlanta. |
| 8 Oct    | King delivers "Paul's Letter to American Christians" as guest minister for New Calvary Baptist Church's Annual Men's Day in Detroit. |
| 9 Oct    | In Schenectady, New York, King delivers "The Future of Integration" at the Freedom Forum at Linton High School, followed by a question and answer session. |
| 10 Oct   | King remains in New York. |
| 12 Oct   | King speaks on "Non-Violence, Civil Disobedience and the Future of the Negro" and answers audience questions at the Atlanta University Center's monthly town meeting. |
| 15 Oct   | At Ebenezer, King delivers the morning sermon, "Dealing with an Inferiority Complex." In the evening, he delivers "The Wind of Change Is Blowing" before the Winston-Salem, North Carolina, branch of the NAACP at Goler Metropolitan AME Zion Church. |
| 16 Oct   | In Washington, D.C., King meets with Attorney General Robert F. Kennedy and later discusses with President John F. Kennedy his ideas for ending segregation in federally funded housing and a second Emancipation Proclamation declaring all segregation illegal. Following the meetings, King gives a press conference outside the White House. |
| 17 Oct   | King is back in Atlanta. |
| 18 Oct   | At Atlanta's Butler Street YMCA's Hungry Club, King speaks on the subject of "The Changing South: The Redefining of Human Relations." The first fifteen minutes of the event are broadcast on radio station WERD. |
| 20 Oct   | King delivers "Facing the Challenge of a New Age" to a crowd of more than a thousand people at the Temple Mishkan Israel in Hamden, Connecticut. |
| 21 Oct   | King takes a train to Philadelphia for the start of a four-day visit to the city. Upon arriving at the station, he is escorted by motorcade to |

Fellowship House. Afterward he holds a press conference and tours the city.

22 Oct    King delivers "Paul's Letter to American Christians" at the Sunday morning sermon at Philadelphia's White Rock Baptist Church in celebration of their sixty-third anniversary. In the evening, he addresses a crowd of over 500 people at the Fellowship House.

23 Oct    King attends a reception at Philadelphia's city hall. He then visits three playgrounds where he speaks to adults and children. In the evening King dines with civic leaders at Fellowship House.

24 Oct    In Philadelphia, King meets with senior and junior high school Fellowship Clubs at an event sponsored by Fellowship House in the afternoon. That evening he gives a press conference, then presides over and gives the main address at a mass meeting at Philadelphia's Academy of Music, where he is presented with a resolution from the City Council. King then returns to Atlanta.

27 Oct    King flies to New York to attend a reception in his honor at the Men's Faculty Club before delivering the keynote address at Columbia University, at an event sponsored by the Columbia OWL. He then departs for London, England.

28 Oct    King arrives in London. His portrait is drawn by artist Felix Topolski at his studio.

29 Oct    In London, King delivers the "Three Dimensions of a Complete Life," at Bloomsbury Central Baptist Church. In the evening, he is interviewed live by John Freeman, editor of the *New Statesman*, on the British Broadcasting Corporation's program "Face to Face." King is also interviewed by Bill Grundy for the Granada TV network program "Protest," for a later broadcast.

30 Oct    At London's Central Hall King speaks at a Christian Action meeting, where he is heckled with shouts of "keep Britain white" and "go back to your own country." He later attends a reception sponsored by the Afro Asian West Indian Community at Africa Unity House.

31 Oct    King departs London for New York.

3 Nov    King and Coretta Scott King attend the symphony in Atlanta; on the program are "La Gazza Ladra" by Gioacchino Rossini, "Symphony 1" by Serge Prokofieff, "Violoncello Concerto" by Luigi Boccherini, "A Night On Bald Mountain" by Modeste Moussorgky, and "Concerto for Violoncello and Orchestra" by Charles-Camille Saint-Saëns.

5 Nov    At Ebenezer, King delivers "Dealing with Fear and Anxiety" at the morning service. He later attends a homecoming dinner before speaking at a special afternoon service.

6 Nov    Accompanied by his wife, Coretta, King participates in the afternoon session of the Fellowship of the Concerned, sponsored by the Southern Regional Council at Clark College in Atlanta. In the

evening, at Montgomery's Bethel Baptist Church, King delivers remarks at a celebration for Ralph D. Abernathy sponsored by the MIA.

7 Nov   King flies from Atlanta to Chicago, and spends most of his seven-hour layover at the Morrison Hotel.

8 Nov   King arrives in Portland, Oregon, in the early morning hours. He holds a morning press conference at the Multnomah Hotel before speaking to the student body at Portland State College. In the afternoon, he delivers "The Future of Integration" at Lewis and Clark College and is interviewed by a panel for a television program to broadcast on KOAP-TV the next day. King has dinner with the boards of the local Urban League, B'nai B'rith, and NAACP at the Multnomah Hotel, then delivers "Facing the Challenge of a New Age" at the Urban League's Equal Opportunity Day program in the Civic Auditorium. Afterward, he attends a reception sponsored by the Albina Ministerial Association at the home of Rev. O.B. Williams, then departs for Seattle.

9 Nov   At Meany Hall on the University of Washington campus, King delivers an address on "Segregation and Civil Liberties: Implications for Students." Afterward, he attends a luncheon in his honor and answers questions from faculty. In the evening, he speaks at the Temple De Hirsch's lecture series in the synagogue's sanctuary.

10 Nov   King delivers "The American Dream" to the student body of Seattle's Garfield High School followed by a luncheon sponsored by the Civic Unity Committee at the Windsor Hotel where he is greeted by Mayor Gordon S. Slinton and Washington governor Albert D. Rosellini. In the evening, King speaks at the third annual lecture of the Brotherhood of Mount Zion Baptist Church at the Eagles Auditorium. The event is followed by a reception at nearby Plymouth Congregational Church.

11 Nov   King departs Seattle for Minneapolis.

12 Nov   In Mankato, Minnesota, as part of the Wesley Foundation at Mankato State College's Third Annual Lectureship, King delivers two morning sermons, both entitled "The Good Neighbor," at Centenary Methodist Church, and in the evening delivers "Facing the Challenge of a New Age" at Mankato High School.

19 Nov   At Ebenezer, King delivers the morning sermon on the "Secrets of Married Happiness." In Tampa, Florida, King is interviewed while being transported from the Tampa International Airport to the Fort Homer Hesterly Armory for an event sponsored by the Florida State Conference of Branches of the NAACP. King's address was delayed by a bomb scare.

23 Nov   King is in Atlanta.

24 Nov   In Indianapolis, King speaks before a crowd of more than one thousand at a fundraising rally at the Murat Temple. Hours before

King's address, a bomb threat was made, prompting Indianapolis police to guard King.

25 Nov   King is in Cleveland, Ohio.

26 Nov   In Cleveland, King delivers "The Three Dimensions of a Complete Life," at two morning services at Antioch Baptist Church on behalf of the church's Laymen's Fellowship. Later King is interviewed and answers questions from the public live on "Open Circuit."

27 Nov   King returns to Atlanta and attends a Georgia Council on Human Relations dinner at The Progressive Club. There he introduces Carl T. Rowan, the principal speaker.

30 Nov–   King is in Mercy-Douglass Hospital in Philadelphia for tests to
2 Dec   determine whether he would need surgery to remove scar tissue around the stab wound he received in 1958. He is given a clean bill of health.

3 Dec   King delivers "The Secret of Adjustment" at Ebenezer's morning service and also presides over evening services.

4 Dec   In his Atlanta office, King meets with Teamster leaders from all over the country to acquaint them with the conditions involving discrimination against black unionists in the South.

7 Dec   In Los Angeles King delivers "The Future of Integration" at Los Angeles Valley College as part of their Athenaeum Series and Bill of Rights Week.

8 Dec   Before a crowd of more than 1,800 King speaks at the Santa Monica Civic Auditorium at an event sponsored by Calvary Baptist Church and the Santa Monica Business and Professional Men's Council. There he receives an official greeting by Mayor Thomas McCarthy.

10 Dec   At Chapman College in Orange, California, King receives a standing ovation for his address on "Non-Violence and Racial Justice" during the college's Artist Lecture Series.

11 Dec   In Miami Beach, Florida, King delivers the keynote address before 1,000 delegates to the American Federation of Labor and Congress of Industrial Organization's (AFL-CIO) Fourth Constitutional Convention at the Americana Hotel. He urges an end to racial discrimination in trade unions.

14 Dec   Following protests from groups who successfully prevented King's scheduled appearance at New Orleans Municipal Auditorium, King speaks at Union Bethel AME Church under the auspices of the Consumer's League of Greater New Orleans.

15 Dec   At the invitation of W. G. Anderson, president of the Albany Movement, King arrives in Albany, Georgia, to spur fundraising efforts for the movement. Later King speaks to packed audiences at Shiloh and Mt. Zion Baptist Churches.

16 Dec   After addressing a group of protesters at Shiloh Baptist Church, King, Anderson, Abernathy, and more than two hundred marchers file out

of the church and march toward Albany 's city hall to pray. They are stopped short of their goal when Albany police chief Laurie Pritchett orders the arrest of all the demonstrators for parading without a permit, obstructing traffic, and blocking sidewalks. King, Abernathy, and Anderson are held at city hall and later transferred to Sumter County Jail in Americus, Georgia.

17 Dec     King is in Sumter County Jail in Americus, Georgia, and announces to visiting reporter David Miller that he will refuse bond and remain in jail through Christmas if necessary.

18 Dec     In the morning, King and Anderson are transferred from Sumter County Jail in Americus, Georgia, to a coat closet in Albany's city hall, where they spend most of the day. After several hours of closed-door negotiations between C. B. King and Donald Hollowell and local city officials, the Albany Movement agrees to temporarily halt demonstrations in exchange for the immediate release of employed tax-paying adult protestors on bond by their own signatures, and the release of unemployed adult protestors on bond upon the signature of a financially responsible local citizen. At an afternoon court hearing, Anderson posts $400 security bonds for himself and King. Before leaving for Atlanta, King speaks at a mass meeting at Shiloh Baptist Church.

19 Dec     King is in Atlanta. The *Nashville Tennessean* publishes King's response to an editorial accusing him of advocating Communism and Black Nationalism as solutions for discrimination.

23 Dec     In New York, King attends the 100th performance of the Broadway hit "Purlie Victorious," written by Ossie Davis and starring Davis and his wife, Ruby Dee. King celebrates with the couple backstage.

24 Dec     King preaches on "God's Love" at Ebenezer.

25 Dec     King spends Christmas surrounded by his extended family at his home in Atlanta.

27 Dec     In Atlanta, King speaks to a reporter with the *New York Amsterdam News* about his stay in the Americus jail and SCLC's plans for the upcoming year.

31 Dec     King delivers "Remaining Awake through the Revolution" at United Liberal Church of Atlanta.

## 1962

4–5 Jan     In Atlanta King convenes an informal SCLC meeting to discuss future plans for the People to People tours and voter registration.

7 Jan     King preaches "The Ultimate Triumph of Goodness" during morning worship service at Ebenezer.

12 Jan     In Wellesley, Massachusetts, King delivers "The Future of Integration" to a large audience in Alumnae Hall at Wellesley

College. His address is followed by a question and answer period. King spends the night in New York.

14 Jan  In New Haven, Connecticut, King delivers "The Dimensions of a Complete Life" at Sunday morning services in Yale University's Battell Chapel and then answers questions at a coffee hour. That evening King preaches to a capacity audience at Wesleyan University's Memorial Chapel in Middletown, Connecticut. Afterward he speaks at a rally sponsored by the Wesleyan Committee on Civil Rights.

15 Jan  At a fundraising rally sponsored by the Bridgeport-Stratford branch of the NAACP and the Interdenominational Ministerial Alliance of Greater Bridgeport, King calls for voter registration and a second Emancipation Proclamation during a speech at Central High School in Bridgeport, Connecticut.

16 Jan  *Look* magazine publishes King's contribution to "I Predict: Twenty-five Farseeing People Tell What They Hope, Fear and Imagine for 1987."

19–20 Jan  King travels to Midway, Georgia, to attend a Citizenship School training session at the Dorchester Center.

20 Jan  Following dinner at Top of the Mart in Atlanta, King and Coretta Scott King spend the evening in discussion with Leslie Dunbar, Dan Pollitt, Sam Cook, and their wives as well as G. W. Foster and several Morehouse University students.

21 Jan  King preaches "Transformed Nonconformists" during morning worship service at Ebenezer. Later that day, the AME Church's Laymen's Organization presents King and SCLC with a check during a program at Big Bethel AME Church in Atlanta.

27 Jan  King flies to Columbus, Ohio.

28 Jan  King speaks for the Annual Youth Day at Mt. Olivet Baptist Church in Columbus, Ohio.

29 Jan  In Columbus, Ohio, King addresses the Ohio Council of Churches' Ohio Pastors Convention.

1 Feb  At the Lotus Club in New York, King attends a luncheon meeting of attorneys hosted by Theodore Kheel to discuss the *New York Times v. Sullivan* (1964) libel case. He then meets with Harry Wachtel and discusses the possibility of establishing a new foundation dedicated to citizenship education and legal aid for the movement.

2 Feb  King flies to Atlanta and meets with SCLC state and local leaders to discuss SCLC's People to People tour, voter registration, nonviolent workshops, citizenship schools, and the second Emancipation Proclamation.

3 Feb  King's first article, "Turning Point of Civil Rights," of his biweekly column "People in Action" is published in the *New York Amsterdam News*.

4 Feb  King preaches "The Worth of Man" at Ebenezer's morning worship service.

6 Feb  King leaves Atlanta for his first People to People tour in Mississippi.

7 Feb   In Clarksdale, Mississippi, King meets with local clergy. He then visits Higgins High School, Coahoma Junior College, Chapel Hill Baptist Church, and Immaculate Conception Catholic School. In the evening, he attends a mass meeting at the Centennial Baptist Church, where Wyatt Tee Walker is the featured speaker.

8 Feb   King travels to Jonestown, Coahoma, Sherard, and Mound Bayou, Mississippi, speaking to local residents about voter registration. Later that evening, he speaks at a political rally for congressional candidate Theodore Trammell at First Baptist Church in Clarksdale, Mississippi.

9 Feb   At Tougaloo College outside of Jackson, King concludes the People to People tour by leading a chapel service before attending a series of nonviolent workshops led by James Lawson.

11 Feb   In the afternoon King delivers A Knock at Midnight at Abernathy's installation service at West Hunter Baptist Church in Atlanta.

12 Feb   In the morning, King meets in Atlanta with leaders from Huntsville, Alabama, to discuss SCLC involvement in their local sit-in movement. Later that day King speaks at a meeting of the Alabama Christian Movement for Human Rights at Sixteenth Street Baptist Church in Birmingham.

13 Feb   King flies to San Juan, Puerto Rico, and holds a press conference at Green Island Airport where he is greeted by Christian Action Party president José Luis Feliú Pesquera. That evening he tapes an interview for the Puerto Rican show "Pico a Pico."

14 Feb   In the morning King travels to San Germán, Puerto Rico, where he delivers "The Future of Integration" to upperclassmen at Inter-American University. In the afternoon he delivers "Remaining Awake Through a Great Revolution" at the University of Puerto Rico's Mayagüez campus followed by a return to Inter-American University where he delivers "Non-violence and Racial Justice" to faculty.

15 Feb   King delivers "Stride Toward Freedom" to a morning assembly of freshman at Inter-American University. He later returns to San Juan, where he meets with musician Pablo Casals before attending a dinner with Fellowship of Reconciliation (FOR) members at Union Church. King stays the night in the guest quarters of the Evangelical Seminary of Puerto Rico. King's appearance on "Pico a Pico" airs.

16 Feb   King addresses the Evangelical Seminary of Puerto Rico on "Non-Violence and Racial Justice." Later, he delivers "The Future of Integration" and "The Challenge of a New Age" at the San Juan campus of the University of Puerto Rico.

17 Feb   The *New York Amsterdam News* publishes King's article "The President's Record" in his "People in Action" column.

17–24 Feb   King vacations in San Juan, Puerto Rico.

27 Feb    King and Ralph Abernathy return to Albany, Georgia, to stand trial in Recorder's Court on charges resulting from arrests during the 16 December 1961 protests there. A verdict is postponed for sixty days to allow time for King's defense team to present additional legal arguments. He returns to Atlanta.

3 Mar     King's article "Pathos and Hope" appears in his column in the *New York Amsterdam News*. *The Nation* publishes his article "Fumbling on the New Frontier."

4 Mar     After preaching at Ebenezer, King meets with Jerome Davis, who is writing a book on modern world leaders.

5 Mar     In Montgomery, Alabama, King attends the MIA's installation of officers. He also meets with Moreland Griffith Smith about the situation in Montgomery.

8 Mar     King attends a Birmingham banquet and rally held in the L. R. Gaston Auditorium to honor Reverends Fred Shuttlesworth and J. S. Phifer, who had recently been jailed for protesting segregated bus seating.

9 Mar     In the evening, King dines at the University of Texas at Austin, and speaks to a capacity audience on "Civil Liberties and Social Action" at an event sponsored by the Texas Union Speakers Committee and the University Religious Council. Afterward King attends a reception with faculty and students.

11 Mar    In Tucson, Arizona, King preaches "Paul's Letter to the American Christians" at the morning service at Catalina Methodist Church. That afternoon, he attends a Press Club Forum and then delivers "Stride Toward Freedom" at Catalina Methodist's Sunday Evening Forum in the University of Arizona Auditorium. Afterward, the local NAACP hosts a reception for King.

12 Mar    King leaves Tucson, Arizona, in the early morning hours.

13 Mar    King spends the night in New York en route to Montreal, Canada.

14 Mar    In Montreal, King delivers an evening address on "The Future of Integration" at the Temple Emanu-El Brotherhood Forum.

15 Mar    King travels to Toronto and attends a luncheon hosted by the Social Action Committee of Holy Blossom Temple. He then speaks to capacity crowd on "Non-Violence and Racial Justice" as part of the Holy Blossom Temple's Brotherhood Forum Series.

18 Mar    King delivers "Facing Life's Inescapables" at the morning worship service at Ebenezer. In Birmingham, King delivers "Not to Conquer, but to Excel" at the installation service of his brother, A. D. King, at First Baptist Church.

19 Mar    In Huntsville, Alabama, King lunches with local clergy, meets informally with college and youth groups, and speaks at a banquet at First Baptist Church. In the evening, he speaks at a city-wide mass meeting

in the Oakwood College Gymnasium, sponsored by the Community Service Committee.

20 Mar    After his afternoon class at Morehouse College, King travels to Seabury House in Greenwich, Connecticut, arriving late for the first day of a two-day meeting of the Joint Consultative Council. The meeting, organized by Allan Knight Chalmers, is also attended by Walker and the heads of other civil rights organizations, and is intended to address problems of interorganizational cooperation within the movement.

21 Mar    King attends the second day of the Joint Consultative Council conference, which adjourns after lunch.

23 Mar    Arriving in Cincinnati, Ohio, King holds a press conference at the Netherland Hilton Hotel before meeting informally with local clergy at Zion Baptist Church. At the hotel, King is the principal speaker at a testimonial banquet honoring the birthday of Fred Shuttlesworth, sponsored by the Pastors Aid Club of Revelation Baptist Church.

25 Mar    At the morning worship service at Ebenezer, King delivers "The Unpardonable Sin" and later presides over the vesper service at Morris Brown College in Atlanta, Georgia.

27–29 Mar    King embarks on a second People to People tour across Virginia with Abernathy, Walker, Dorothy Cotton, Bernard Lee, and Herbert Coulton.

27 Mar    Upon landing at the Byrd Airport in Richmond, Virginia, King holds a morning press conference and then attends a luncheon at Zion Baptist Church in Petersburg before canvassing door to door discussing voter registration with residents. Later that evening, King travels to Lynchburg where he addresses a crowd of over 2,400 supporters at rally at E. C. Glass High School.

28 Mar    In Prince Edward County, Virginia, where public schools were closed in an attempt to prevent school integration, King meets informally with residents and children at First Baptist Church in Farmville. At in the invitation of the Inter-Fraternal Council, he delivers "The Tragedy of Sleeping Through a Revolution" at Virginia State College. Afterward, King travels to Hopewell, where he meets with sit-in protesters before heading to Mount Level, Virginia, to talk to residents at a local church. In the evening, he makes a brief stop in Rocky Branch and ends the day at a public meeting at First Baptist Church in Petersburg.

29 Mar    Back in Hopewell, King attends the contempt trial of Curtis Harris, who was arrested for refusing to answer questions about his integration activities before the Virginia Legislative Committee on Offenses against the Administration of Justice. Later that day he travels to Wisconsin State College in Eau Claire, where he delivers "Stride Toward Freedom."

30 Mar   King delivers "The Future of Integration" at the Second Annual Jonas Rosenfield Lecture at the University of Wisconsin, Madison. The lecture, sponsored by the Union Forum Committee, is followed by a question and answer session.

31 Mar   King's article "Most Abused Man in Nation" is published in his biweekly column in the *New York Amsterdam News*.

1 Apr   King delivers "Great, But . . . " at morning services at Ebenezer.

2 Apr   At Tabernacle Baptist Church in Augusta, Georgia, King addresses a rally of 3,000 as part of a week of protests aimed at integrating the Masters Golf Tournament.

5 Apr   King holds a press conference at the SCLC office in Atlanta to announce the expansion of the organization's voter registration program and the success of the People to People tours.

7 Apr   King flies to Washington, D.C., where he is greeted by labor leader Theodore Brown.

8 Apr   King delivers "Remaining Awake Through a Revolution" at Howard University's All University Religious Service in Cramton Auditorium. After the service he lunches with Evans Crawford, dean of the campus chapel.

9 Apr   Still in Washington, D.C., King gives a morning press conference and attends a luncheon meeting of clergy to discuss a local SCLC affiliate at Metropolitan Baptist Church. In the afternoon King meets Attorney General Robert F. Kennedy and Assistant Attorney General Burke Marshall about discrimination in voter registration. Afterward, he meets with Vice President Lyndon B. Johnson and discusses equal employment opportunities. That evening, King speaks at a rally at Metropolitan Baptist Church.

12 Apr   King begins his third People to People tour by addressing a luncheon at St. Matthew's Baptist Church in Charleston, South Carolina, on the theme "Our nation has a date with destiny. . . . " He spends the afternoon canvassing for voters in Charleston and Mt. Pleasant before speaking at an evening rally at Emmanuel AME Church.

13 Apr   On the second day of his tour to South Carolina, King attends informal meetings in Manning, Ellerlee, and Roseville, and addresses students at Clafin College in Orangeburg. He ends the day speaking at a rally at Trinity Methodist Church, also in Orangeburg.

14 Apr   King officiates at funeral services for Hillman Hanley at Ebenezer. His article "Virginia's Black Belt" is published in his *New York Amsterdam News* column.

15 Apr   At Ebenezer, King gives an opening prayer before Wyatt Tee Walker preaches the Palm Sunday sermon. He travels to Chicago to speak before the Chicago Sunday Evening Club. King's address "Remaining Awake Through a Great Revolution" is televised on WTTW.

| | |
|---|---|
| 16 Apr | In Colorado for the Denver Area Council of Churches of Christ's Holy Week services, King delivers "The Dimensions of a Complete Life" at First Baptist Church. |
| 17 Apr | King tapes an interview on Max Goldberg's "On the Spot" television program. He speaks again on behalf of the Denver Area Council of Churches, delivering "Love in Action" at Trinity Methodist Church. At Central Presbyterian Church, King holds an informal question and answer session followed by delivering "Loving Your Enemies" at Park Methodist Church. |
| 18 Apr | In his third address for the Denver Area Council of Churches Holy Week services, King delivers "The Man Who Was a Fool" at Trinity Methodist Church, and in the evening he delivers "Remember Who You Are" at Augustana Lutheran Church. |
| 19 Apr | King visits Denver's New Hope Baptist Church. |
| 22 Apr | King delivers "The Meaning of Easter" at Ebenezer. |
| 23 Apr | King meets with Harry Wachtel in Atlanta. |
| 27 Apr | King speaks at a SCLC fundraising event at Akron University's Memorial Hall in Akron, Ohio. |
| 28 Apr | King's article "Nothing Changing Unless" is published in his column in the *New York Amsterdam News*. |
| 29 Apr | In Princeton, New Jersey, King delivers "Remaining Awake Through a Revolution" at the Princeton University Chapel as part of the university's Student Christian Association's seventh Biennial Religious Conference. After the service, King lunches at the home of Carl D. Reimers, assistant dean of the Chapel. |
| 30 Apr | At Irvine Auditorium in Philadelphia, King is honored along with Major League Baseball Hall of Famer Jackie Robinson, CORE president James Farmer, and others at the President's First Award Night of the Baptist Minister's Conference of Philadelphia. |
| 2 May | King speaks at Emory University in Atlanta before flying to Chicago to speak at SCLC's benefit dinner starring Dick Gregory and Mahalia Jackson. |
| 4 May | At Newark, New Jersey's Mosque Theater, King addresses an audience of 2,500 as the keynote speaker at a rally sponsored by the city's Baptist Ministers Conference and Interdenominational Ministerial Alliance of Newark and Vicinity. |
| 6 May | King delivers "Lord, Is It I?" at Ebenezer's morning service. He also preaches the evening sermon. |
| 8 May | King flies to New York. |
| 10 May | In New York, King meets with Stanley Levison and Clarence Jones. At Salem Methodist Church in New York City, King receives the Frederick A. Cullen Achievement Award from the church's Young Adult Fellowship. |

| | |
|---|---|
| 11 May | King travels to Nashville, where he addresses a mass meeting sponsored by the Nashville Christian Leadership Council at the Fisk University gymnasium. |
| 12 May | King's article "Unknown Heroes" is published in his column in the *New York Amsterdam News.* |
| 15 May | King attends SCLC's board meeting in Chattanooga, Tennessee, at New Monumental Baptist Church. In the evening he addresses an audience of 1,200 at a mass meeting at Memorial Auditorium. |
| 16 May | King attends the morning business sessions and the closing session of SCLC's board meeting in Chattanooga. |
| 17 May | At the Sheraton-Carlton Hotel in Washington, D.C., King addresses the founding meeting of the Gandhi Society for Human Rights, followed by a press conference. In the evening, he speaks at the Annual Dinner Conference of the Allied Real Estate Board on Long Island, New York. |
| 18 May | In New York, King meets with SCLC supporter Ada Murray to accept her donation. |
| 20 May | King's interview with Paul Niven is broadcast on CBS-TV's "Washington Conversation" program. |
| 21 May | King addresses the United Packinghouse, Food and Allied Workers' Thirteenth Constitutional International Convention at the Pick-Nicollet Hotel in Minneapolis, Minnesota. |
| 22 May | King delivers the Call to Worship at Ebenezer's 75th Diamond Jubilee Anniversary service. |
| 23 May | At Dartmouth College in Hanover, New Hampshire, King delivers "Towards Freedom" as part of the Dartmouth College Lecture Series. Afterward King visits the home of Professor Gene Lyons. |
| 24 May | King gives a press conference before delivering "The Mission to the Social Frontier" at the national meeting of the American Baptist Convention in Philadelphia. Earlier in the week, King's Ebenezer Baptist Church and Abernathy's West Hunter Baptist Church became members of the predominately white organization. King dines with D. T. Niles. |
| 26 May | The *New York Amsterdam News* publishes King's article "Literacy Bill Dies" in his biweekly column. |
| 27 May | King attends Ebenezer's seventy-fifth anniversary celebration. Gardner C. Taylor is the guest preacher. |
| 28 May | King arrives at O'Hare International Airport in Chicago in company with evangelist Billy Graham. Approximately a hundred people representing several organizations meet at the Jackson Park YMCA to hear King report on his work with SCLC and to plan a mass meeting to be held in Chicago in the fall. In the evening King speaks at Johnson Products Company's annual banquet at the Sheraton-Blackstone Hotel. |

| 29 May | King leaves Chicago and returns to Atlanta. |
| 3 June | King delivers "The Perfect Faith" at the morning service at Ebenezer. Later in the day, King and Coretta Scott King host New York minister Thomas Kilgore, who preaches the evening sermon at Ebenezer. |
| 5 June | In New York City, King receives a Better Race Relations Award and $500 from the Hotel and Club Employees Union Local 6. |
| 6 June | King travels from New York to Atlanta with Harry Belafonte and others. They are denied service at the King's Inn restaurant, and that afternoon they host a press conference calling for the restaurant to desegregate. Later that evening, King attends an SCLC benefit concert featuring Belafonte and Miriam Makeba at Atlanta's Municipal Auditorium. |
| 8 June | As part of SCLC's People to People tour, King addresses a voter registration rally at Little Union Baptist Church in Shreveport, Louisiana. |
| 9 June | King publishes "Can We Ever Repay Them?" in his weekly column in the *New York Amsterdam News*. |
| 10 June | King preaches on "False Gods We Worship" at Ebenezer. |
| 11 June | King meets with Stanley Levison in New York City. In the evening, he speaks to a crowd of 1,500 at a Freedom Rally sponsored by the Interdenominational Ministerial Alliance at Memorial Auditorium in Gary, Indiana. |
| 12 June | King speaks about the evils of war, economic injustice, and racial injustice at a public reception during the 93rd Annual Grand Communication of the Georgia Prince Hall Grand Lodge Free and Accepted Masons at St. Philip AME Church in Savannah, Georgia. |
| 13 June | In the afternoon King meets in Atlanta with attendees of the Westminster Fellowship Leadership School of the University of Georgia's Westminster House. At Antioch East Baptist Church, he speaks on the theme "Our Baptist Witness Through Stewardship in an Emerging Age of Freedom" at the Youth Rally for Freedom as part of the 58th Annual Session of the Atlanta Baptist District Sunday School and BTU Congress. |
| 15 June | King speaks with the *Washington Post* regarding criticisms of the Gandhi Society for Human Rights before flying from Atlanta to Los Angeles. Upon his arrival at Los Angeles International Airport, King holds a press conference before flying to San Diego. Later that night, he speaks on "The Powers Greater Than Violence" at a meeting at San Diego's Calvary Baptist Church. |
| 16 June | In Los Angeles, King speaks in support of efforts to recall City Councilman Joe Hollingsworth at a breakfast held at McCarty Memorial Church. He dines with city leaders at the Statler-Hilton Hotel at a luncheon hosted by the Southern California-Nevada Council of Churches. In the evening, King speaks on "Powers Greater |

Than Violence" to a public meeting hosted by the American Friends
Service Committee and WCLC at Westminster Presbyterian Church
in Pasadena, California.

17 June  King preaches the morning sermon at Los Angeles's Ward AME
Church. His afternoon is packed with events at Tabernacle of
Faith Baptist Church, Connor-Johnson Funeral Home, the Bovard
Auditorium on the University of Southern California campus, and
Zion Hill Baptist Church.

19 June  King flies from Los Angeles to Denver, where he makes a statement
about the progress of desegregation.

20 June  At Denver's New Hope Baptist Church, King speaks at an evening
rally.

21 June  King flies to Atlanta.

23 June  King receives an honorary Doctor of Civil Laws degree during the
commencement ceremony at Bard College in Annandale-on-Hudson,
New York. Before the ceremony, King and other honorees attend
a luncheon hosted by college president Reamer Kline. As part of
King's biweekly column, the *New York Amsterdam News* publishes "New
Harassment."

24 June  King addresses the Most Worshipful Prince Hall Grand Lodge of
Maryland at the organization's semi-annual St. John's Day Religious
Service at the Masonic Temple in Baltimore.

26 June  King delivers "The Theology of Freedom" at a morning session of the
48th Annual Hampton Institute Ministers Conference in Hampton,
Virginia.

27 June  Still at the Hampton Institute conference, King delivers "The Church
in An Age of Revolution."

28 June  In an afternoon session of the Hampton Institute's conference, King
delivers "Non-Violence and Social Change." He then speaks at a
fundraising rally at First Baptist Church in Newport News, Virginia.

29 June  King attends an informal board meeting of the Gandhi Society for
Human Rights at the Dorset hotel in New York.

30 June  King speaks at the annual CORE conference at the Hampton House
in Miami, Florida.

1 July  King preaches the morning worship service at Ebenezer.

5 July  King speaks at the Freedom Fund dinner held at Morehouse College
during the fifty-third annual NAACP Convention.

7 July  The *New York Amsterdam News* publishes King's article "The Wind of
Change" in his column.

8 July  King preaches at Ebenezer.

10 July  Accompanied by their wives, King and Abernathy fly to Albany,
Georgia, to appear in court for sentencing related to their 16
December arrest. Both men are sentenced to either pay a $178 fine or

serve forty-five days in jail. They elect to fulfill the jail sentence, and do a day-long fast.

11 July    King and Abernathy end their fast and remain in the Albany jail. They are visited by C. K. Steele, Andrew Young, and Henry Elkins.

12 July    In the early morning, Albany police chief Laurie Pritchett informs King and Abernathy that their fines had been paid by an "unidentified 'tall, well-dressed Negro'" and requires them to leave the jail involuntarily. Following their release, they hold a press conference at Shiloh Baptist Church. Later that day, King, Abernathy, W. G. Anderson, and C. B. King meet with Pritchett to renew negotiations. At a mass meeting that night, King announces a potential agreement between the Albany Movement and city officials.

13 July    King and other Albany Movement leaders meet with Pritchett and Albany city manager Stephen Roos in the afternoon. At a mass meeting that evening King promises to stay in Albany until demands are met.

14 July    After speaking at an evening rally in Albany at Mt. Zion Baptist Church, King drives back to Atlanta with Abernathy, Walker, and Andrew Young. The *New York Amsterdam News* publishes King's article "A Message from Jail," which he wrote while detained in the Albany jail.

15 July    King preaches the morning service at Ebenezer. He later gives a press conference with Ralph Abernathy at West Hunter Baptist Church.

16 July    King returns to Albany and meets with local ministers in the afternoon to discuss a strategy for dealing with city officials and goes to Mitchell County Jail in Camilla, Georgia, to visit protesters arrested on 11 July. In the evening, he addresses mass meetings at Mt. Zion and Shiloh Baptist Churches.

17 July    King addresses two groups of teenaged volunteers in Albany.

18 July    King travels to Washington, D.C., and that night he reviews potential questions that may be asked during the National Press Club luncheon the next day.

19 July    King speaks at the National Press Club Luncheon. King, the first African American speaker in the Club's history, discusses the merits of nonviolence and answers questions from the audience. He then travels to New York.

20 July    King cancels planned visits to New York and Hartford, Connecticut, to return to Albany, Georgia. In the evening, King announces plans to march on city hall to a mass meeting of 1,200 at Third Kiokee Baptist Church.

21 July    Judge J. Robert Elliott of the U.S. District Court of Columbus, Georgia, issues a temporary restraining order preventing King and other named activists from engaging in public protests in Albany. In the afternoon, King and others voluntarily receive the injunction at

city hall before meeting privately with Police Chief Laurie Pritchett.
Late that day, King holds an impromptu press conference and
appears at a mass meeting at Shiloh Baptist Church.

22 July    At a press conference held in W. G. Anderson's backyard, King speaks
out against the recent restraining order prohibiting movement leaders from participating in demonstrations in the city. In the evening,
King attends a rally at Mt. Zion Baptist Church before meeting with
SNCC representatives in Slater King's backyard to discuss his decision
to obey the federal restraining order.

23 July    King, Abernathy, Walker, and Anderson meet with police chief
Laurie Pritchett at city hall. In the evening King addresses a large
rally at Mt. Zion Baptist Church in Albany, and announces that he
had earlier called Burke Marshall to request an investigation into
the treatment of jailed protesters and the beating of Slater King's
pregnant wife by policemen earlier in the day. He later travels to
Atlanta.

24 July    King attends a morning hearing before Chief Judge Elbert Tuttle
of the Fifth Circuit Court of Appeals in Atlanta, challenging the
temporary restraining order issued by Judge Elliott a few days
earlier. Judge Tuttle vacates Elliott's temporary restraining order
against demonstrations in Albany, Georgia. King returns to Albany
with Coretta Scott King, Anderson, Abernathy, and Charles Jones.
The group proceeds directly to a meeting with police chief Laurie
Pritchett at city hall. Following the meeting, King visits protesters in
the Albany city jail and takes a brief respite at Elliot Funeral Home.
That evening, King speaks at mass meetings at Mt. Zion and Shiloh
Baptist Churches.

25 July    After violence erupted in Albany the previous night, King holds a
press conference calling for a "Day of Penance" at Anderson's home.
King, Abernathy, Charles Jones, and others tour Harlem district
bars and pool halls, urging nonviolence. Later that evening, he
speaks at a mass meeting and urges marches to resume the following day.

26 July    King continues urging nonviolence in bars and pool halls in the
Harlem District of Albany. He calls Albany mayor Asa Kelley to seek a
meeting between city officials and Albany Movement leaders.

27 July    King, Abernathy, Anderson, Slater King, Reverend Benjamin
Gay, and five female protesters appear outside city hall to request
negotiations with the Albany City Commission and to pray. After
several warnings, Chief Pritchett arrests them for disorderly conduct,
congregating on the sidewalk, and disobeying a police officer. In the
evening Lawrence Spivak, host of the television show *Meet the Press*,
calls King collect to request that he post bond so that he can appear

| | |
|---|---|
| | on the show on 29 July. King and Abernathy elect to remain in jail, while Anderson posts bond to appear on the show in King's place. |
| 27 July–10 Aug | King is in jail in Albany, Georgia. |
| 28 July | Coretta Scott King and Wyatt Tee Walker visit King in jail. Pritchett informs King that C. B. King was assaulted by Dougherty County sheriff D. C. Campbell. King tells Walker to contact the Justice Department. |
| 30 July | King attends the first session of a hearing in federal district court before Judge Elliott on whether to dismiss the City of Albany's temporary injunction barring further protests. He gives a brief press conference, telling the press he will abide by the injunction but appeal it. King goes back to his jail cell. |
| 31 July | King appears at the continued federal court hearing before Judge Elliott. Later he is visited in jail by Congressman William Fitts Ryan (D-NY), his father, Martin Luther King, Sr., and J. A. Middleton, president of the Atlanta chapter of SCLC. |
| 1 Aug | For a second time, Daddy King and Middleton visit King, Jr. in jail. |
| 2 Aug | Dora McDonald, King's secretary, visits him in Albany jail. King issues a statement from his jail cell praising President Kennedy's support for a resolution in Albany. |
| 3 Aug | During a break in the hearing before Judge Elliott, King speaks with a reporter about the segregationist opposition in Albany and the importance of the Albany Movement. |
| 4 Aug | In this week's column, the *New York Amsterdam News* publishes "Hall of Famer," King's tribute to Jackie Robinson. |
| 5 Aug | Coretta Scott King brings Yolanda, Martin III, and Dexter to visit King in the jail. *New York Times Magazine* publishes King's "The Case Against Tokenism." |
| 6 Aug | In the morning, Coretta Scott King visits King in jail. King spends the rest of the day answering letters, reading, and writing. |
| 7 Aug | King attends the continued federal court hearing before Judge Elliott. |
| 8 Aug | King testifies during the closing session of the federal hearing before Judge Elliott. Anderson treats King in his jail cell for exhaustion. |
| 10 Aug | King testifies on his own behalf in Recorder's Court in Albany before Judge A. N. Durden on charges stemming from his 27 July arrest. King and Abernathy are found guilty and given suspended sentences of sixty days in jail and $200 fines. King is released from jail and later announces at a news conference that he will travel to Atlanta for weekend church obligations, but return to Albany the following week. |
| 11 Aug | Before returning to Atlanta, King criticizes the Albany City Commission's decision to decline to meet with Albany Movement representatives. |
| 12 Aug | King preaches on "God in Albany" at morning services at Ebenezer. |

13 Aug    Upon his return to Albany, King speaks at a mass meeting at Mt. Zion where he vows to stay in Albany until it is integrated. "Why Non-Violence Will Win in Albany," the first installment in a three-article series by King, appears in the *Chicago Daily Defender*.

14 Aug    In Albany, King speaks to a session of voter registration canvassers and tells the press of plans to integrate Albany's junior high and high schools. King's article "New Negro Battling for Rights in Albany" appears in the *Chicago Daily Defender*.

15 Aug    In the morning, King travels to Lee County, Georgia, to lead a prayer meeting and view the destruction caused by the fire-bombing of Shady Grove Baptist Church. In the evening he returns to the ruins of the church to lead a prayer meeting before traveling back to Albany to speak at a mass meeting at Shiloh Baptist Church. The *Chicago Daily Defender* publishes King's article "U.S. Help Needed in Rights Fight."

16 Aug    King returns to Atlanta.

18 Aug    King's article "Why It's Albany" appears in the *New York Amsterdam News*.

19 Aug    At Ebenezer, King delivers "Love Your Enemies."

23 Aug    *Jet* publishes King's diary from his second stint in jail from 27 July through 10 August.

24 Aug    King delivers the eulogy for jazz organist Cleveland Lyons at Ebenezer.

27 Aug    King returns to Albany to coordinate a march of clergy and speaks at a mass meeting at Shiloh Baptist Church in the evening.

28 Aug    King addresses a group of clergy in an Albany church shortly before they march to city hall to stage a mass prayer meeting. Following the arrest of seventy-five of the clergy during the demonstration, King holds a press conference. In the evening King speaks at a rally at Third Kiokee Baptist Church, then returns to Atlanta.

30 Aug    King visits clergy in jail in Albany.

The central goal of the Martin Luther King, Jr., Papers Project is to produce an authoritative, multivolume edition of King's works. These chronologically arranged volumes contain accurate, annotated transcriptions of King's most important sermons, speeches, correspondence, published writings, unpublished manuscripts, and other papers.

We assign highest priority to King's writings, public statements, and publications, although such materials are not included when they repeat significant portions of the text of other documents from the period. When one of King's addresses or sermons is available in different versions, we prefer recordings rather than printed or published transcripts, complete versions rather than excerpts, and versions that have greater rather than lesser public impact. We also include correspondence containing significant information about King's thought or activities and incoming letters illuminating his relationships with or impact on others. We generally exclude office-generated replies, mass mailings, and unsolicited incoming letters, except in the few instances when such letters are of exceptional interest or provoked a personal reply from King.

For this volume we have examined nearly seven thousand King-related documents and recordings from more than 280 archives and individuals and selected those that are the most biographically or historically significant to King's life, thought, and leadership. We have selected for inclusion some documents that do not fit within the previously mentioned categories when they provide vital information regarding King's attitudes, activities, associations, and leadership. This category includes newspaper articles quoting King speeches or sermons for which the entire text is not available; recorded or transcribed interviews; and press releases or statements issued by King or jointly with others.

This volume also contains other sections designed to provide information useful to lay and scholarly readers alike. The Chronology lists King's significant activities for the period. The Introduction is a narrative essay based on the documentary records assembled by the King Papers Project. It is intended to place King's papers in a historical context rather than to substitute for a thorough biographical or historical treatment of King's activities from January 1961 to August 1962. Finally, to assist scholars and others seeking further information regarding King-related primary documents, this volume includes a Calendar of Documents that provides full citations for items referred to in annotations. It also lists a selection of other significant King-related documents. King Papers Project descriptions of archival collections related to King are available in an electronic database of the Research Libraries Information Network (RLIN).

Documents are introduced by a title, date, and place of origin. Existing titles are used, when available, and are designated by quotation marks. When necessary in titles, we have corrected errors or irregularities in punctuation, capitalization, and spelling, and we have standardized names; these corrected titles are not designated by quotation marks. In addition, descriptive titles that appear on the document are similarly designated with quotation marks (e.g., "Outline of Lecture in Social Philosophy"). For untitled items, we have created descriptive titles reflecting content (e.g., Address at Freedom Riders Rally at First Baptist Church). Speech or sermon titles indicate the occasion of the address. In King's correspondence, the title contains the author or recipient (e.g., To Carl Braden), leaving King's participation implied. When the date was not specified in the document but has been determined through research, it is rendered in italics and enclosed in square brackets. When a specific date could not be determined through research, we have provided a range date. Documents are placed in the volume where they will provide the strongest narrative continuity. In some instances, the dateline of published documents is dropped when the date of delivery is indicated in the document's title and the actual publication date is given in the document's source line. If the place of origin appears on the document, it is included; if not and it could be determined through research, it is provided for King-authored documents only. (A more detailed explanation of procedures for assigning titles, dates, and other cataloging information appears at the end of the volume in the Calendar of Documents.)

Annotations are intended to enhance readers' understanding of documents. Headnotes preceding documents explain the context of their creation; in the case of longer documents a brief summary may be offered. Headnotes and editorial footnotes also identify individuals, organizations, events, literary quotations, biblical allusions, and other references in the document, as well as relevant correspondence or related documents. Biographical sketches describe the background and relationship to King of individuals who corresponded with him or are mentioned prominently in documents. We have not included such sketches for individuals described in previous volumes, nor have we annotated theological ideas and persons likely to be discussed in standard reference works. Editorial footnotes, on occasion, refer to alternative accounts of events and to variations among versions (e.g., sentences altered or added by King when he modified an address for a different occasion). Marginal notes on the document, particularly those written by King, are also noted. Annotations may contain implicit or abbreviated references to documents (e.g., "King replied on 12 June 1961"); full bibliographic information for such documents can be found in the Calendar of Documents.

The source note following each document provides information on the characteristics of the original document and its provenance. Codes are used to describe the document's format, type, version, and form of signature. The code "TLS," for example, identifies the document as a typed letter with a signature. The location of the original or source document is described next, using standard abbreviations from *USMARC Code List for Organizations*. (See List of Abbreviations for all codes used.) Since the publication of Volume I in 1992, some archival collections have been moved from their original repositories, and archival coding standards have changed; therefore, the King Papers Project has updated the archival codes accordingly. Although

# To Carl Braden ———————————— Title

9 February 1962 — Date
Atlanta, Ga. — Place of origin

*King welcomes Braden home following his 1 February release from* ————— Headnote
*prison after serving a nine-month sentence for refusing to testify before*
*HUAC in 1958. SCLC executive director Wyatt Tee Walker read King's*
*letter at a Southern Conference Educational Fund (SCEF) reception in*
*Braden's honor on 9 February.*[1] *Braden's wife, Anne, replied, expressing*
*her appreciation "for the beautiful message that you sent to Carl."*[2]

Mr. Carl Braden
C/O Hotel Biltmore
New York, New York

Dear Carl:

    I am forwarding this message by our mutual friend, Wyatt Tee Walker.
You cannot imagine how good it is to say to you, "Welcome Home".
    The days you have spent away from your family and friends have not
been spent in vain. They have become a part of the catalogue of sacrifices — Document
by which freedom is earned.
    All of us are indebted to you. It is a debt that can never be repaid. Our
dedication and determination has been fired by the example of your selflessness. Democracy has a better chance of being realized here in America
because of you.

My continued good wishes,
[*signed*] Martin
Martin Luther King Jr., President
Southern Christian Leadership Conference

    Physical
    description
———————————————————————— codes
TLS. CAABP-WHi: Box 11.
———————————————————————— Document's
    archival code

———————

    1. King had just begun his People to People tour in Mississippi and was unable to attend — Editorial footnote
the event.
    2. Braden to King, 19 February 1962. King's letter was reprinted in the March 1962 SCEF — Brief reference;
newsletter *The Southern Patriot*.     full citation in
    Calendar of
    Documents

this causes discrepancies between volumes, it provides the most accurate list of archival collections accessed by the Project at the time of publication. For example, some of the documents previously contained in the CSKC, CSKCH, and MLKJP-GAMK: Vault collections were transferred in 2006 to Morehouse College in Atlanta. The documents included in the Morehouse College acquisition are now identified as RWWL.

*Transcription Practices*

Transcriptions are intended to reproduce the documents accurately, adhering to the exact wording and punctuation of the original. In general, errors in spelling, punctuation, and grammar, which may offer important insights into the author's state of mind and conditions under which a document was composed, have been neither corrected nor indicated by *sic*. Capitalization, boldface, underscores, subscripts, abbreviations, hyphenation, strikeouts, ellipses, and symbols are likewise replicated.

This rule has certain exceptions, however. Single-letter emendations by the author have been silently incorporated, and typographical errors, such as malformed and superimposed characters, have been corrected. In published documents, spelling and grammatical errors have been retained unless an earlier draft revealed the author's intention. Moreover, some formatting practices such as outlining, underlining, paragraph indentation, and spacing between words or lines of text have been regularized to maintain consistency within the edition (e.g., continuous rather than discontinuous underscoring). Dashes, which appeared in several styles in the original manuscripts, have been regularized. The overall appearance of the source document (e.g., line breaks, pagination, vertical and horizontal spacing, end-of-line hyphenation) has not been replicated, and some features that could not be readily reproduced, such as letterheads and typographic variations, are described in annotations (in a few cases, visually interesting documents such as advertisements or postcards have been reproduced as facsimiles). The internal address, salutation, and complimentary closing of a letter have been reproduced left-aligned, regardless of the original format. Insertions in the text by the author (usually handwritten) are indicated by curly braces ({ }) and placed as precisely as possible within the text. Telegrams are rendered using small capital letters.

Editorial explanations are rendered in italics and enclosed by square brackets. Conjectural renderings of text are set in italic type followed by a question mark and placed within brackets: e.g., [*There's?*]. Instances of illegible text are indicated: e.g., [*strikeout illegible*] or [*word illegible*]. If the strikeout was by someone other than the author, it has not been replicated, but is described in a footnote. If part of a document is lost, the condition is described: e.g., [*remainder missing*]. In some instances, long documents may be excerpted to highlight passages that were most significant with respect to King. Editorial deletions to eliminate repetitive or extraneous segments are explained by an editorial comment or are indicated by ellipses: [ . . . ]. Signatures that are identical with the typed name are reproduced as follows:

Sincerely,

[*signed*]

Martin Luther King, Jr.

The King Papers Project's transcriptions of audio recordings are intended to replicate, to the extent possible, King's public statements as they were delivered, excluding only those utterings that do not convey significant meaning (e.g., unintentional stutters and pause words, such as "uh"). Certain sharply stressed phrases are rendered in italics to indicate the speaker's emphasis and non-English words are italicized as well. When available, King's written text is used to clarify ambiguous phrases and as a guide to delineating sentences, paragraphs, and punctuation. In cases where the written text is not available, we have supplied punctuation for clarity. Transcriptions also attempt to convey some of the quality of the speech event, particularly the interplay between speaker and audience. When practical, audience responses to King's orations are enclosed in parentheses and placed appropriately within King's text. Editorial descriptions of audience participation are enclosed in square brackets. The first instance of a verbal audience response to a speech is indicated as follows: e.g., [*Audience:*] (*Preach*). Subsequent audience interjections are enclosed, as is appropriate, in brackets or parenthesis: e.g., [*applause*] or (*Lord help him*). Multiple audience responses are indicated in order of occurrence, separated with commas: e.g., (*Tell it, Don't stop*). In addition, transcriptions occasionally suggest the loudness or duration of audience responses: e.g., [*sustained applause*]. In cases where a recording or its transcription is incomplete or unintelligible, that status is indicated within the text proper: e.g., [*gap in tape*] or [*words inaudible*].

# ABBREVIATIONS

*Collections and Repositories*

| | |
|---|---|
| ABHSR-GaAaBHS | American Baptist Historical Society Records, American Baptist Historical Society, Atlanta, Ga. |
| ACA-OYesA | Antioch College Archives, Antioch College, Yellow Springs, Ohio |
| ACCP-MdU | Office of the President, The George Meany Memorial AFL-CIO Archive, Special Collections & University Archives, University of Maryland Libraries, Silver Spring, Md. |
| ACLUR-NjP-SC | American Civil Liberties Union Records, Department of Rare Books and Special Collections, Princeton University Library, Princeton University, Princeton, N.J. |
| ACOA-ARC | American Committee on Africa Records, Amistad Research Center, New Orleans, La. |
| ACRMtZ | Albany Civil Rights Movement Museum at Old Mt. Zion Church, Albany, Ga. |
| ADAR-WHi | Americans for Democratic Action Records, State Historical Society of Wisconsin, Madison, Wis. |
| AEJ | A. E. Jenkins Collection (in private hands) |
| AFF-WBB | Alumni and Faculty Files, Beloit College Archives, Beloit, Wis. |
| AJC-ICHi | Archibald James Carey Collection, Chicago History Museum, Chicago, Ill. |
| AJYP-GA | Andrew J. Young Papers, Atlanta Public Library, Auburn Avenue Research Center, Atlanta, Ga. |
| AlHvCFS | Center for the Study of Southern Political Culture, Calhoun Community College, Huntsville, Ala. |
| AMR-GAMK | Albany Movement Records, Martin Luther King, Jr., Center for Nonviolent Social Change, Inc., Atlanta, Ga. |
| APRP-DLC | A. Philip Randolph Papers, Manuscript Division, Library of Congress, Washington, D.C. |
| ASRC-RWWL | Southern Regional Council Papers, Atlanta University Center, Robert W. Woodruff Library Archives and Special Collections, Atlanta, Ga. |
| AzTCM | Catalina United Methodist Church, Tuscon, Ariz. |

| | |
|---|---|
| BAA-CSt-KPP | The Boffard Audio Collection: University of Tours, France, Martin Luther King, Jr. Papers Project, Stanford University, Stanford, Calif. |
| BMPP-MBJFK | Burke Marshall Personal Papers, John F. Kennedy Presidential Library, Boston, Mass. |
| BRP-DLC | Bayard Rustin Papers, Manuscript Division, Library of Congress, Washington, D.C. |
| BTC | Barry Tulloss Collection (in private hands) |
| BWOF-AB | Birmingham World Office Files, Birmingham Public and Jefferson County Free Library, Birmingham, Ala. |
| CAABP-WHi | Carl and Anne Braden Papers, State Historical Society of Wisconsin, Madison, Wis. |
| CABP-ICHi | Claude A. Barnett Papers, Chicago History Museum, Chicago, Ill. |
| CBGP-WHi | Carlton Benjamin Goodlett Papers, State Historical Society of Wisconsin, Madison, Wis. |
| CBPaC | Pacific School of Religion, Berkeley, Calif. |
| CBSNA-NNCBS | CBS News Archives, Columbia Broadcasting System, Inc., New York, N.Y. |
| CCCSU | Clayborne Carson Collection (in private hands) |
| CCDP-DHU-MS | Charles C. Diggs Papers, Howard University, Moorland-Spingarn Research Center, Washington, D.C. |
| CCFA-ICarbS | Christian Century Foundation Archives, Special Collections Research Center, Morris Library, Southern Illinois University, Carbondale, Ill. |
| CHAC | Carolyn Hunt Anderson Collection (in private hands) |
| CJMSR-WHi | Committee to Secure Justice for Morton Sobell Records, State Historical Society of Wisconsin, Madison, Wis. |
| CKFC | Christine King Farris Collection (in private hands) |
| CLU-FT | University of California, Los Angeles, Film and Television Archive, Los Angeles, Calif. |
| COREP-A-GAMK | Papers of the Congress of Racial Equality: Addendum, 1944–1968, Martin Luther King, Jr., Center for Nonviolent Social Change, Inc., Atlanta, Ga. |
| CORER-WHi | Congress of Racial Equality Records, State Historical Society of Wisconsin, Madison, Wis. |
| CRA-InU-N | Calumet Regional Archives, Indiana University Northwest, Gary, Ind. |
| CRC-NN-Sc | Civil Rights Collection, 1962–1969, Catherine Clarke Series, Manuscripts, Archives and Rare Books Division, Schomburg Center for Research in Black Culture, The New York Public Library, New York, N.Y. |

| | | |
|---|---|---|
| CRDPad-DJ | Public Accommodations and Demonstrations, Albany, Georgia, United States Department of Justice, Washington, D.C. | |
| CRLHRC-IcarbS | Cyril Robinson Labor History Research Collection, 1959–2011, Special Collections Research Center, Morris Library, Southern Illinois University, Carbondale, Ill. | |
| CSKC | Coretta Scott King Collection (in private hands) | |
| CSKCH | Coretta Scott King Home Study Collection (in private hands) | |
| CSS | California State University, Sacramento, Calif. | |
| CVnL | Los Angeles Valley College, Van Nuys, Calif. | |
| DABCC | Dexter Avenue King Memorial Baptist Church Collection (in private hands) | |
| DJG-GEU-S | David J. Garrow Collection, Manuscript, Archives, and Rare Book Library, Emory University, Atlanta, Ga. | |
| DPC | Dan Pollitt Collection (in private hands) | |
| DSEC | Donald E. Secord Collection (in private hands) | |
| EBCR | Ebenezer Baptist Church, Miscellaneous Records (in private hands) | |
| EJBC-NN-Sc | Ella J. Baker Papers, Manuscripts, Archives and Rare Books Division, Schomburg Center for Research in Black Culture, The New York Public Library, New York, N.Y. | |
| EMDP-IPekDC | Everett McKinley Dirksen Papers, The Dirksen Congressional Center, Pekin, Ill. | |
| ERP-NHyF | Ana Eleanor Roosevelt Papers, Franklin D. Roosevelt Presidential Library, Hyde Park, N.Y. | |
| FBIDG-NN-Sc | David Garrow Federal Bureau of Investigation Collection, Manuscripts, Archives and Rare Books Division, Schomburg Center for Research in Black Culture, The New York Public Library, New York, N.Y. | |
| FFPP-GEU-S | Frances F. Pauley Papers, Manuscript, Archives, and Rare Book Library, Emory University, Atlanta, Ga. | |
| FMIA-FlMiMLW | Lynn and Louis Wolfson II Florida Moving Image Archive, Miami-Dade College, Miami, Fla. | |
| FMPL-SCA-CorC | Frank Mt. Pleasant Library of Special Collections and Archives, Leatherby Libraries, Chapman University, Orange, Calif. | |
| FODC | Fred O. Doty Collection (in private hands) | |
| FORR-PSC-P | Fellowship of Reconciliation Records, 1943–1973, Swarthmore College Peace Collection, Swarthmore, Pa. | |
| GBC | Gurdon Brewster Collection (in private hands) | |
| GCC-NhD | Papers of Grenville Clark, Rauner Special Collections Library, Dartmouth College, Hanover, N.H. | |

| | | |
|---|---|---|
| GDL-G-Ar | Georgia Department of Law, Record group 9, Georgia Department of Archives and History, Morrow, Ga. |
| GEpNASR | United States National Archives and Records Administration, National Archives at Atlanta, Morrow, Ga. |
| GI-NNTI | Getty Images, Time Inc., New York, N.Y. |
| GIDC-NhD | Great Issues (Dartmouth College), Rauner Special Collections Library, Dartmouth College, Hanover, N.H. |
| GRCC-ICRCM | Gordon R. Carey Collection, International Civil Rights Center & Museum, Greensboro, N.C. |
| GRVVL-MiEM | G. Robert Vincent Voice Library, Michigan State University Libraries, Michigan State University, East Lansing, Mich. |
| HETC-GU | Herman E. Talmadge Collection, Richard B. Russell Library for Political Research and Studies, University of Georgia Libraries, Athens, Ga. |
| HG-GAMK | Hazel Gregory Papers, 1955–1965, Martin Luther King, Jr., Center for Nonviolent Social Change, Inc., Atlanta, Ga. |
| HHBP-NcWsW | Henlee Hulix Barnette Papers, MS474, Special Collections and Archives, Z. Smith Reynolds Library, Wake Forest University, Winston-Salem, N.C. |
| HRECR-WHi | Highlander Research and Education Center Records, State Historical Society of Wisconsin, Madison, Wis. |
| HZP-WHi | Howard Zinn Papers, 1956–1970, State Historical Society of Wisconsin, Madison, Wis. |
| ICEL | Archives of the Evangelical Lutheran Church in America, Chicago, Ill. |
| ICHi | Chicago History Museum, Chicago, Ill. |
| IElwp | Elmwood Park Public Library, Elmwood Park, Ill. |
| JaRP-DLC | Jackie Robinson Papers, Manuscript Division, Library of Congress, Washington, D.C. |
| JBMP-NcD | J. B. Matthews Papers, Duke University, David M. Rubenstein Rare Book & Manuscript Library, Durham, N.C. |
| JDGP-SBHLA | James David Grey Papers, Southern Baptist Historical Library and Archives, Nashville, Tenn. |
| JFKCAMP-MBJFK | John F. Kennedy Pre-Presidential Papers, Presidential Campaign Files, 1960, John F. Kennedy Presidential Library, Boston, Mass. |
| JFKOH-MBJFK | John F. Kennedy Library Oral History Program, John F. Kennedy Presidential Library, Boston, Mass. |

| | |
|---|---|
| JFKPOF-MBJFK | John F. Kennedy Presidential Papers, President's Office Files, John F. Kennedy Presidential Library, Boston, Mass. |
| JFKWHCNF-MBJFK | John F. Kennedy Presidential Papers, White House Central Name Files, John F. Kennedy Presidential Library, Boston, Mass. |
| JFKWHCSF-MBJFK | John F. Kennedy Presidential Papers, White House Central Subject Files, John F. Kennedy Presidential Library, Boston, Mass. |
| JFKWHSFHW-MBJFK | White House Staff Files: Harris Wofford, John F. Kennedy Presidential Library, Boston, Mass. |
| JTWP-AB | James T. Waggoner Papers, Birmingham Public and Jefferson County Free Library, Birmingham, Ala. |
| JWBC-DcWaMMB | Jeanetta Welch Brown Collection, National Park Service Museum Resource Center, National Capital Region, National Archives for Black Women's History, Landover, Md. |
| JWD-ARC | John Wesley Dobbs Family Papers, Amistad Research Center, New Orleans, La. |
| JWWP-DHU-MS | Julius Waties Waring Papers, Howard University, Moorland-Spingarn Research Center, Washington, D.C. |
| KLMDA-NNCorI | Kheel Center for Labor-Management Documentation & Archives, M. P. Catherwood Library, Cornell University, Ithaca, N.Y. |
| KyLoS | Archives and Special Collections, Southern Baptist Theological Seminary, Louisville, Ky. |
| LBJOH-TxAuLBJ | Oral History Collection, Lyndon Baines Johnson Presidential Library, Austin, Texas |
| LBRP-WRDA-OHMa | Bertrand Russell Papers, William Ready Division of Archives and Research Collections, McMaster University Library, Hamilton, Canada |
| LDRP-NN-Sc | Lawrence Dunbar Reddick Papers, Manuscripts, Archives and Rare Books Division, Schomburg Center for Research in Black Culture, The New York Public Library, New York, N.Y. |
| LewBP | Lewis V. Baldwin Papers (in private hands) |
| LJCC-UK-LoLPL | Lewis John Collins Collection, Lambeth Palace Library, London SE1 7JU, United Kingdom |
| LKGP-MH-L | Lloyd K. Garrison Papers, Harvard Law School Library, Harvard University, Cambridge, Mass. |
| LSP-GU-HR | Lillian Eugenia Smith Papers, MS 1283a, Hargrett Rare Book and Manuscript Library, University of Georgia Libraries, Athens, Ga. |

| | |
|---|---|
| LVBP-DHU-MS | Reverend L. Venchael Booth Papers, Howard University, Moorland-Spingarn Research Center, Washington, D.C. |
| MAWC | Mervyn A. Warren Collection (in private hands) |
| MCMLK-RWWL | Morehouse College Martin Luther King, Jr. Collection, Atlanta University Center, Robert W. Woodruff Library Archives and Special Collections, Atlanta, Ga. |
| MJMCRC-MsHaU | Michael J. Miller Civil Rights Collection, Special Collections, McCain Library and Archives, University of Southern Mississippi, Hattiesburg, Miss. |
| MLKEC | Martin Luther King, Jr. Estate Collection (in private hands) |
| MLKJP-GAMK | Martin Luther King, Jr. Papers, 1954–1968, Martin Luther King, Jr., Center for Nonviolent Social Change, Inc., Atlanta, Ga. |
| MLKP-MBU | Martin Luther King, Jr. Papers, 1954–1968, Boston University, Boston, Mass. |
| MMFR | Montgomery to Memphis Film Research Files (in private hands) |
| MWallP-NSyU | Mike Wallace Papers, Special Collections Research Center, Syracuse University Libraries, Syracuse University, Syracuse, N.Y. |
| MWL-CtBU | Magnus Walstrom Library, University of Bridgeport, Bridgeport, Conn. |
| NAACPP-DLC | National Association for the Advancement of Colored People Collection, Manuscript Division, Library of Congress, Washington, D.C. |
| NAnB | Bard College Archives, Annandale-on-Hudson, N.Y. |
| NARGR-NNttR | Nelson A. Rockefeller Gubernatorial Records, Rockefeller Family Archive, Rockefeller Archive Center, Sleepy Hollow, N.Y. |
| NBCNA-NNNBC | National Broadcasting Company News Archives, National Broadcasting Company, Inc., General Library, New York, N.Y. |
| NCCIJR-WMM | National Catholic Conference for Interracial Justice Records Collection, Special Collections & University Archives, Raynor Memorial Libraries, Marquette University, Milwaukee, Wis. |
| NCCR-PPPrHi | National Council of the Churches of Christ in the United States of America Records, Presbyterian Historical Society, Philadelphia, Pa. |
| NNAPWW | AP/Wide World Photos, New York, N.Y. |
| NNMAGPC | Magnum Photos, Inc. Collection, New York, N.Y. |

| | | |
|---|---|---|
| NNU-LA | New York University, Robert F. Wagner Labor Archives, New York, N.Y. | Abbreviations |
| NyNyFMN | Fox Movietone News Clips, ITN Source, New York, N.Y. | |
| OUA-AHO | Oakwood University Archives, Eva B. Dykes Library, Oakwood University, Huntsville, Ala. | |
| PHBC | Paul H. Brown Collection (in private hands) | |
| PLPC-DHU-MS | Percival Leroy Prattis Collection, Howard University, Moorland-Spingarn Research Center, Washington, D.C. | |
| PMC-OrHi | Politics Miscellaneous Collection, Oregon Historical Society, Portland, Or. | |
| PP-WHi | *Progressive*, Inc. Records, State Historical Society of Wisconsin, Madison, Wis. | |
| PPRN-CYlRMN | Pre-Presidential Papers of Richard M. Nixon, Special Files, PPS 320, Richard Nixon Foundation, Yorba Linda, Calif. | |
| RBC | Ralph F. Boyd Collection (in private hands) | |
| RBFP | Robert Brank Fulton Papers (in private hands) | |
| RBOH-DHU-MS | Ralph J. Bunche Oral History Collection, Howard University, Moorland-Spingarn Research Center, Washington, D.C. | |
| RFBI-DNA | Records of the Federal Bureau of Investigation, United States National Archives and Records Service, National Archives Library, Washington, D.C. | |
| RFKAG-MBJFK | Robert F. Kennedy, Attorney General Papers, John F. Kennedy Presidential Library, Boston, Mass. | |
| RJBP-NN-Sc | Ralph J. Bunche Papers, Manuscripts, Archives and Rare Books Division, Schomburg Center for Research in Black Culture, The New York Public Library, New York, N.Y. | |
| RJBPC-CLU-AR | Ralph J. Bunche Collection (2051), University of California, Los Angeles, Charles E. Young Research Library, Special Collections, Los Angeles, Calif. | |
| RLRP | Robert L. Render Papers (in private hands) | |
| RPP-NN-Sc | Richard Parrish Papers (Additions), 1959–1976, Manuscripts, Archives and Rare Books Division, Schomburg Center for Research in Black Culture, The New York Public Library, New York, N.Y. | |
| RWSP-FTS | Robert W. and Helen S. Saunders Papers, Special Collections Department, Tampa Library, University of South Florida, Tampa, Fla. | |
| SAVFC-WHi | Social Action Vertical File, State Historical Society of Wisconsin, Madison, Wis. | |
| SBHLA | Southern Baptist Historical Library and Archives, Nashville, Tenn. | |

| | |
|---|---|
| THSR-WaU-AR | Temple de Hirsch Sinai Records, ACCP. #2370–018, University of Washington Libraries, Special Collections, Seattle, Wash. |
| TWKC | Theodore W. Kheel Collection (in private hands) |
| TWUP | Transport Workers Union Papers (in private hands) |
| UERR-PPiU-IS | United Electrical, Radio, and Machine Workers of America (UE) Records, Archives Service Center, University of Pittsburgh, Pittsburgh, Pa. |
| UPIR-NNBETT | UPI and Reuters Photo Collection, Corbis-Bettman Archives, New York, N.Y. |
| UPWR-WHi | United Packinghouse, Food and Allied Workers Records, State Historical Society of Wisconsin, Madison, Wis. |
| USDCAlb-GEpNASR | Civil Cases, U.S. District Court for the Middle District of Georgia (Albany), United States National Archives and Records Administration, National Archives at Atlanta, Morrow, Ga. |
| USIA-MBJFK | U.S. Information Agency Records, John F. Kennedy Presidential Library, Boston, Mass. |
| WAC | William G. Anderson Collection (in private hands) |
| WALB-TV-GU | WALB-TV Newsfilm Collection, Walter J. Brown Media Archive & Peabody Awards Collection, University of Georgia Libraries, Athens, Ga. |
| WAWP | Willard A. Williams Papers (in private hands) |
| WGAC-GAMK | William G. Anderson Collection, Martin Luther King, Jr., Center for Nonviolent Social Change, Inc., Atlanta, Ga. |
| WHCCR | Woodland Hills Community Church Records (in private hands) |
| WHDP-WHi | William Hammatt Davis Papers, State Historical Society of Wisconsin, Madison, Wis. |
| WPRC-MiDW-AL | UAW President's Office: Walter P. Reuther Collection, Wayne State University, Walter P. Reuther Library of Labor and Urban Affairs, Detroit, Mich. |
| WRBC | White Rock Baptist Church, Philadelphia, Pa. (in private hands) |
| WSB-TV-GU | WSB-TV Newsfilm Collection, Walter J. Brown Media Archive & Peabody Awards Collection, University of Georgia Libraries, Athens, Ga. |
| WSCC-CtY | William Sloane Coffin, Jr. Papers (MS 1665), Manuscripts and Archives, Yale University Library, New Haven, Conn. |
| WTWP | Wyatt Tee Walker Papers (in private hands) |
| WYP-NNC | Whitney M. Young Papers, Rare Book and Manuscript Library, Columbia University, New York, N.Y. |

The following symbols are used to describe the original documents:

*Format*

| | |
|---|---|
| A | Autograph (author's hand) |
| H | Handwritten (other than author's hand) |
| P | Printed |
| T | Typed |

*Type*

| | |
|---|---|
| At | Audio tape |
| Aw | Art work |
| D | Document |
| F | Film |
| Fm | Form |
| L | Letter or memo |
| Ph | Photo |
| Ta | Audio transcript |
| Tv | Video transcript |
| Vt | Video tape |
| W | Wire or telegram |

*Version*

| | |
|---|---|
| c | Copy |
| d | Draft |
| f | Fragment |

*Signature*

| | |
|---|---|
| I | Initialed |
| S | Signed |
| Sr | Signed with representation of author |

# Photographs

At Morehouse College on 30 April 1961, King attends a reception for Carl Braden and Frank Wilkinson, who will begin serving a one-year prison sentence for contempt after refusing to answer questions before the House Un-American Activities Committee. From left to right: James A. Dombrowski, Carl Braden, Anne Braden, Frank Wilkinson, King, and Coretta Scott King. Courtesy of Wisconsin Historical Society.

King, Ralph Abernathy, and hundreds of supporters of the Freedom Rides, wait inside Abernathy's First Baptist Church in Montgomery while the Alabama National Guard and federal marshals subdue a violent mob surrounding the sanctuary. Although the rally began on the evening of 21 May, those trapped inside were not escorted home until the morning of 22 May 1961. Courtesy of Paul Schutzer/Time & Life Pictures/Getty Images.

Following violent attacks against freedom riders in Alabama, King, CORE national director James Farmer, SCLC executive director Wyatt Tee Walker, SCLC treasurer Ralph Abernathy, and freedom rider John Lewis hold a press conference announcing the continuation of the Freedom Rides at Abernathy's home on 23 May 1961. Courtesy of Bruce Davidson/Magnum Photos.

After freedom riders decide to continue the rides from Montgomery, Alabama, to Jackson, Mississippi, King attends a strategy session with participants on 23 May 1961 at the home of Montgomery pharmacist Richard H. Harris. From left to right: Len Holt, David Dennis, Edward B. King, B. Elton Cox, Bernard LaFayette, Matthew Walker, Dion Diamond, King, Ernest Patton, and Henry Thomas. Courtesy of Lee Lockwood/Time & Life Images/Getty Images.

In his office at
Ebenezer Baptist
Church, King
meets with Gurdon
Brewster, an intern
at the church during
the summer of 1961.
Courtesy of Gurdon
Brewster.

King talks to report-
ers following his 16
October 1961 meeting
with President John F.
Kennedy at the White
House. Courtesy
of AP/Wide World
Photos.

On 16 December 1961 Albany police chief Laurie Pritchett arrests King and Albany Movement president William G. Anderson for parading without a permit, obstructing traffic, and congregating on sidewalks. © Corbis.

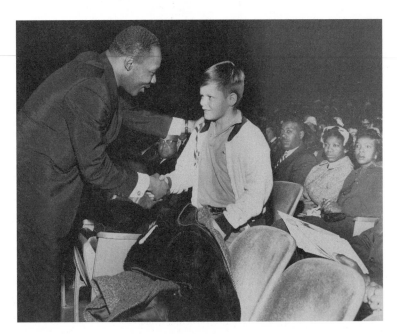

During SCLC's 1962 People to People tour, King stops at E. C. Glass High School in Lynchburg, Virginia, on 27 March 1962, where he meets eleven-year-old Chuck Moran, who was the first to answer King's call for volunteers. Courtesy of Wyatt Tee Walker.

On 12 July 1962 King and Ralph Abernathy talk to reporters following their release from Albany Jail after an unidentified black man paid their fines. Courtesy of AP/Wide World Photos.

King recounts his disappointment in his unexpected release from jail on 12 July 1962 to a packed audience at Albany's Mt. Zion Baptist Church. Courtesy of AP/Wide World Photos.

At his home in Albany, William G. Anderson poses with King and Ralph Abernathy on 12 July 1962.  Courtesy of William G. Anderson.

On 20 July 1962, with his wife by his side, King confers with William G. Anderson at a mass meeting at Albany's Third Kiokee Baptist Church. Courtesy of AP/ Wide World Photos.

King, Ralph Abernathy, and William G. Anderson are bombarded by reporters following a 21 July 1962 meeting with Albany police chief Laurie Pritchett. Earlier in the day, King and other local leaders were served with an injunction prohibiting any further demonstrations in Albany. Courtesy of Donald Uhrbrock/Time & Life Images/Getty Images.

King leaves the federal courthouse in Atlanta with his attorneys Constance Baker Motley and William M. Kunstler after a federal appeals judge vacated an injunction against demonstrations in Albany on 24 July 1962. © Corbis.

King speaks at a mass meeting at Mt. Zion Baptist Church in Albany on 24 July 1962. Courtesy of AP/Wide World Photos.

At a 25 July 1962 press conference in the backyard of William G. Anderson's home in Albany, King calls for a day of penance following the outbreak of violence at a march the day before. Wyatt Tee Walker stands near the fence. Courtesy of AP/Wide World Photos.

As part of the day of penance, King and Ralph Abernathy visit a pool hall in the Harlem district of Albany, appealing to the patrons to adhere to nonviolence. © Corbis.

Following his release from the Albany jail on 10 August 1962, King attends a mass meeting at Mt. Zion Baptist Church. From left to right: Slater King, Charles Sherrod, Norma L. Anderson, Lois Steele, William G. Anderson, King, Coretta Scott King, and Ralph Abernathy. Courtesy of William G. Anderson.

Bernard Scott Lee, Wyatt Tee Walker, unidentified man, Ralph Abernathy, and James Bevel join King at the ruins of Shady Grove Baptist Church in Leesburg, Georgia, on 15 August 1962. The church was bombed in retaliation for its participation in the local voter registration campaign. Later that evening, King returned to the ruins, telling a group: "When men will seek to destroy the church of God, they have degenerated to a tragic level of inhumanity and sin and evil." Courtesy of the Martin Luther King, Jr., Center for Nonviolent Social Change, Inc.

At a mass meeting at Mt. Zion Baptist Church on 27 August 1962, King welcomes Northern religious leaders who came to Albany at his behest to aid desegregation efforts. The following day, seventy-five clergy and lay leaders were arrested while leading a prayer vigil. Courtesy AP/Wide World Photos.

# The Papers

# "The Negro and the American Dream,"
## Emancipation Day Address Delivered
## at Municipal Auditorium

[*2 January 1961*]
Savannah, Ga.

*In the spring of 1960, African Americans in Savannah, Georgia, began a boycott of the white downtown merchants to protest their segregationist practices.[1] Speaking before a capacity crowd in honor of the ninety-eighth anniversary of the Emancipation Proclamation, King calls on protesters to remain nonviolent as they continue their "program of economic withdrawal."[2] He compares the black struggle for equality with that of Jews, who have "proven that inner determination can often break through the outer shackles of circumstance." Challenging America to hold true to its ideals, King maintains that black Americans do not want to "upset the social structure" or "dominate the nation politically," but simply "want to be free." King concludes that one day "all of God's children, black men and white men, Jews and Gentiles, Catholics and Protestants, will be able to join hands and sing with meaning, 'Free at last, free at last, thank God almighty, we are free at last.'"[3] The following transcript is taken from an audio recording.*

Mr. Chairman, and to all of the distinguished platform guests, ladies and gentlemen.[4] I would like first to say how very delighted and happy I am to be here today,

---

1. On 16 March 1960, Savannah students requested service at over five different lunch counters in local stores without success. This led to a fifteen-month boycott of the stores, with over approximately one hundred protesters arrested and an estimated five stores declaring bankruptcy. In July 1961, local citizens agreed to desegregate the lunch counters in exchange for ending the boycott ("Lunch Bias Protests Hit in Savannah," *Atlanta Daily World*, 17 March 1960; "Savannah Lowers Lunch Counter Racial Barriers after 15-Month Protest," *Atlanta Daily World*, 9 July 1961).

2. Emancipation Association, Program, "Emancipation Celebration," 2 January 1961; "King Asks Non-Violent Integration," *Savannah News*, 3 January 1961. Three days earlier King made a similar address in Chattanooga, Tennessee ("The Negro and the American Dream," Address delivered at Memorial Auditorium, 30 December 1960). Abraham Lincoln signed the Emancipation Proclamation on 22 September 1862; it went into effect on 1 January 1863.

3. In April 1957, King used a similar refrain when he addressed a freedom rally in St. Louis ("A Realistic Look at the Question of Progress in the Area of Race Relations," 10 April 1957, in *The Papers of Martin Luther King, Jr.*, vol. 4: *Symbol of the Movement, January 1957–December 1958*, ed. Clayborne Carson, Susan Carson, Adrienne Clay, Virginia Shadron, Kieran Taylor [Berkeley and Los Angeles: University of California Press, 2000], p. 179).

4. F.D. Jaudon (1899–1972), pastor of Saint Philip Monumental AME Church, was president of the Emancipation Association Committee.

to be in this community. And I want to express my personal appreciation to the Emancipation [*words inaudible*] Reverend Stell for his very kind and generous introduction.[5] And one day I hope I will be able to live up to all of the wonderful things he said about me. It's good to see all of you and to somehow reaffirm and renew friendships and fellowships with men that I have known from [*word inaudible*] for years. I shouldn't say, of course, for many, many years because I'm not that old, but of course a few years [*laughter*]. I see here many of my colleagues in the ministry that I have known and worked with throughout various [*words inaudible*] organizations across the country. And it is a real pleasure and privilege to be here with all of my good friends. To be in the home of my good friend Reverend Curtis Jackson and his lovely wife is also a great pleasure.[6]

And I tell you it's a real inspiration to come to Savannah, because I have kept up with you and your activities. Let's hope they only last a few months. And certainly you have made us proud. [*word inaudible*] to a real degree you have inspired the people of Atlanta. And it is commendable that you have stuck together so long and that you have remained united for the great cause. Your program of economic withdrawal is something that needs to be mentioned and needs to be duplicated in many, many places. And I can only say to you, "Keep up the good work and stay together and continue the struggle."

Now, I know sometimes it seems to be a long, hard struggle, and you wonder when things will open as you desire. It's something like going down a long, dark, and desolate corridor, and you constantly seek an exit sign. And it seems that it doesn't come. But never forget that all of our dreams must come through a persistent and consistent struggle. I'm reminded of Montgomery, Alabama, for instance, when we were struggling to break down the shackles and the great [*word inaudible*] from the shackles that cause segregation. And then at that moment we wondered how long. You know, we walked that city 381 days. And I'm here to say to you, this afternoon, that after 381 days, after the Negro citizens of Montgomery were willing to substitute tired feet for tired souls, and after they were willing to walk the streets of that city for all of those months, the buses of Montgomery, Alabama, were finally integrated, and today Negro citizens can ride anywhere on the buses that they want to. [*applause*]

And so don't give up, but keep going. And I cannot pass on without saying just a word concerning this great student movement which has engulfed our Southland. To my mind, this is one of the great, if not the greatest, development that has taken place in the struggle for civil rights in our United States. These students have felt the palpitation of purpose. They have taken our deep groans and passionate yearnings for freedom and filtered them in their own souls and fashioned them into a creative protest which is an effort known all over our nation. For all of these months they have moved in a uniquely meaningful order, imparting light and heat to distant satellites. And as a result of their nonviolent, peaceful struggle, they have been able to inte-

5. L. Scott Stell (1911–1985) was a minister at Bethlehem Baptist Church in Savannah and vice president of the Emancipation Association Committee.

6. Curtis J. Jackson (1922–2005), a graduate of Morehouse College, was pastor of Antioch Baptist Church in Atlanta from 1951–1957 before moving to Savannah. King refers to Jackson's wife, Marion Briggs Jackson.

grate lunch counters in more than a hundred and twelve cities. It is no overstatement to say that this is revolutionary, and I'm convinced that when the history books are written in future generations, they will have to look back and call this student movement one of the most significant epics of our day. [*applause*]

So I know you will continue to support the student movement and you will continue to support the movement that is taking place in this community. And I could not come here also without saying a word concerning the great work that has been done by the National Association for the Advancement of Colored People under the leadership of my good friend Mr. Law and Mr. Williams in this community.[7] [*applause*] There can be no gainsaying of the fact that he is one of the most dedicated and one of the most resourceful leaders that we have in the South today. [*applause*]

Now, this is the day that we pause to celebrate a great event in our history. We think of the Emancipation Proclamation, one of the great and significant documents in our nation. And as we pause on this day to think of emancipation, I would like to use as a subject from which to speak "The Negro and the American dream."

My friends, whether you realize it or not, America is essentially a dream—a dream yet unfulfilled but nevertheless a dream—a great dream. It is a dream of a land where men of all races, of all colors and all creeds will be able to live together as brothers. The substance of the dream is expressed in these sublime words, words [*lifted to?*] cosmic proportions: "All men are created equal. They are endowed by their Creator with certain inalienable rights. Among these are life, liberty, and the pursuit of happiness." This is the dream.

And at the very center of this dream we notice an amazing universalism, for it does not say "some men are created equal," but it says "all men [*Audience:*] (*Yes, Yes*) are created equal." [*applause*] (*That's right*) It doesn't say "all white men," but it says "all men," which includes black men. [*applause*] It does not say "all the Gentiles," but it says "all men," which includes Jews. (*Yes*) [*applause*] Not even says "all Protestants," but it says "all men," which includes Catholics. (*Yes*) [*applause*]

But there is something else that you notice at the center of that dream, something that ultimately distinguishes democracy from any system of government which makes the state an end within itself. It affirms that there are certain basic rights (*Yes*) that are neither confirmed by nor derived from the state. In order to discover where they came from, we must go back behind the dim mists of eternity. They are God's gifts. (*Preach, Preach, Preach*) [*applause*]

Very seldom, if ever, in the history of the world has a socio-political document expressed in more eloquent, profound, and unequivocal language the dignity and the worth of human personality. For this dream reminds us that every man (*Yes, every man*) is the heir of a legacy of dignity. (*Yes*) It's a great dream.

Ever since our founding fathers dreamed this dream—to use a big word that the psychologists use—America has been something of a schizophrenic personality tragically divided against itself. (*Yes*) On the one hand, she has proudly professed the principles of democracy. And on the other hand she has sadly practiced the

---

7. King refers to W. W. Law (1923–2002), president of the Savannah chapter of the NAACP from 1950–1976, and Hosea Williams (1926–2000), vice president of the Savannah NAACP and president of the Chatham County Crusade for Voters. Williams later became a member of the SCLC executive board.

very opposite of those principles. Slavery and segregation have always been strange paradoxes in a nation founded on the principle that all men are created equal. [*applause*] (*That's right*) More than ever before, America is challenged to bring the ideals and principles of this dream into full realization. My friends, the shape of the world today does not permit America the luxury of an anemic democracy. The price that America must pay for the continued oppression of the Negro is the price of its own destruction. (*Yes*)

We look over the world, we see new nations coming into being, and they are watching. (*Yes*) In 1957 when Mrs. King and I journeyed over Africa to attend the independence celebration of the new nation of Ghana, there were only seven independent nations in the whole of Africa.[8] And just last month I went back to Africa. I went to Nigeria to attend the independence, I mean the inauguration of the new governor-general of Nigeria, Governor-General Azikiwe.[9] As I got off the plane in Africa I thought of the fact that today there are twenty-seven independent countries in Africa.[10] Within less than three years, more than eighteen countries have received their independence in Africa. (*Yeah*)

They are looking over here. The wind of change is blowing all about, all through Africa and Asia. They want to know what we are doing about democracy, and they are making it clear that racism and colonialism must go. (*Yes*) I tell you that the hour is late. The crop of destiny is peeking out. We must act now before it's too late. It is trite but nevertheless profoundly true that if America is to remain a first-class nation, she can no longer have second-class citizens. (*That's right*) [*sustained applause*]

So, there is the need today people of goodwill all over this nation to rise up, seek to fulfill the great dream of America. If we fail to do it at this hour, we may well lose our moral, our political stature in the world. And those people who are working to bring into being the dream of democracy are not the agitators. They are not the dangerous people in America. They are not the un-American people. (*Well*) They are people who are doing more for America than anybody that we can point to. And I submit to you that it may well be that the Negro is God's instrument (*Yeah*) to save the soul of America. [*applause*]

So many forces are working in our nation to scar the dream, and we are challenged to bring this dream into its full realization. Now, what are some of things that we must do as a people to remind our nation over and over again that it must bring this dream into reality? First, my friends, we must continue, courageously, to challenge the system of segregation. (*Yes*) Segregation is still the Negro's burden and America's shame.

---

8. As of 1957 the following nations in Africa were independent: Liberia, South Africa, Egypt, Libya, Ethiopia, Sudan, Morocco, Tunisia, and Ghana. For more on King's trip to Ghana, see Introduction in *Papers* 4:7–10.

9. King was in Lagos from 14–18 November 1960 to attend the inauguration of Nnamdi Azikiwe, who served as governor-general from 1960–1963 and as president of the Republic of Nigeria from 1963–1966 (see Azikiwe to King, 26 October 1960, in *The Papers of Martin Luther King, Jr.*, vol. 5: *Threshold of a New Decade, January 1959–December 1960*, ed. Clayborne Carson, Tenisha Armstrong, Susan Carson, Adrienne Clay, Kieran Taylor (Berkeley and Los Angeles: University of California Press, 2005), pp. 533–534).

10. As of 1960 the following nations in Africa were independent: Cameroon, Togo, Senegal, Mali, Madagascar, Zaire, Somalia, Benin, Niger, Burkina Faso, Cote d'Ivoire, Chad, Central African Republic, Congo, Gabon, Nigeria, and Mauritania.

(*Yes*) [*applause*] Therefore, we must not rest until segregation is removed from every area of our nation's life. Segregation—whether at lunch counters, whether in public schools, whether in public parks, or whether in the Christian church—is a cancerous disease which must be removed from the body politic before our democratic health can be realized. (*Yes*) [*applause*] Yes, segregation is nothing but a new form of slavery covered up with certain niceties of complexity. [*gap in tape*] [*applause*] We must make it palpably clear that we cannot settle for all of the delaying tactics and the gradualism that has engulfed our Southland. For gradualism is little more than an escapism and a do-nothingism which ends up in stand-stillism. [*applause*]

On May seventeenth 1954, the Supreme Court of our nation rendered a great decision.[11] That decision said, in substance, that the old Plessy doctrine of 1896 must go, that separate facilities are inherently unequal, and that to segregate a child on the basis of his race is to deny that child equal protection of the law.[12] That was six years ago. You know that today only six percent of the Negro children of the South and the border states are attending integrated schools. And most of these are in the border states, in the District of Columbia, in Kentucky and Missouri, in West Virginia. And we see, my friends, that six percent—actually, when you see what it means—it means that we have integrated on the basis of one percent a year. Now, if you keep on following that, that means that you have ninety-four percent of the Negro children of the South still attending segregated schools. And if we keep on moving at the pace we are moving now, it would take *ninety-four* more years to get there. [*applause*] I submit to America that we don't have that long. (*No, No*) I submit at this hour that we must get up and move now. (*Move now*) Somehow, we must come to see that this is what is right, and this is what must be.

In our own state of Georgia, in Atlanta, the schools are to be integrated next September. The governor, the legislature are saying that they are not going to comply with this, and they are threatening to close the schools.[13] [*word inaudible*] we must make it clear in all good conscience that no threat of closing schools will cause us for one moment to cease in our determination to have our Constitutional rights in the state of Georgia. [*sustained applause*]

I know it's hard sometimes for at least the schoolteachers to face this realistically. But I say it with as firm a point of view as I can say that we must make it clear that the rush to erect beautiful school buildings for Negroes to maintain segregation will not satisfy us. [*sustained applause*] Somehow, we must get it over that we will never sell our birthright of freedom for a mess of separate but equal. [*applause*] We are engaged in a destiny-making moment in history not for ourselves alone but to save the soul of America. And in order to do that we must continue courageously to challenge the system of segregation.

There is a second thing that we must do, my friends, which is just as important as

---

11. King refers to *Brown v. Board of Education of Topeka*, 347 U.S. 483 (1954).

12. King refers to *Plessy v. Ferguson*, 163 U.S. 537 (1896).

13. In June 1959, Judge Frank Hooper ruled in *Calhoun v. Members of Board of Education, City of Atlanta*, 188 F. Supp. 401 (N.D. Ga. 1959) that Atlanta must desegregate its schools by September 1960, though the deadline was later extended to September 1961. In response, the state legislature and Georgia governor S. Ernest Vandiver threatened to shut down the public schools rather than comply with the court order ("Georgia Is Easing Pupil Segregation," *New York Times*, 28 January 1961).

the first. We must make full and constructive use of the freedom we already possess. We must not use our oppression as an excuse for laziness. (*No*) History has proven that inner determination can often break through the outer shackles of circumstance. Someone mentioned the Jews earlier, and I think we have a great example here. For years, Jews have been forced to walk through the long and desolate night of oppression. This did not keep them from rising up from the dense cloud-filled nights of affliction to new and blazing stars of inspiration.

So, being a Jew did not keep [*George Frideric*] Handel from lifting his visions of high heaven and merging with the inspiration to leave for unfolding generations the [*broad?*] thunders and the gentle sighings of a great *Messiah*. (*Yes*)

Being a Jew did not keep [*Albert*] Einstein from challenging an axiom and using his genius-packed mind to leave for the lofty insights of science a theory of relativity.

Being Jews did not keep Isaiah and Jeremiah, Amos and Hosea from rising up amid religious idolatry and unjust power structures (*That's right*) to declare the eternal word of God and the never-ceasing necessity of being obedient to His will. (*Yes*)

And I say this afternoon that being a Negro should not keep us from making a contribution, continual contribution, to the life of this nation. (*Yes*) We already have numerous and inspiring examples of Negroes who have proven that human nature cannot be catalogued (*No*), that we need not wait until the day of full emancipation the day we make a creative contribution. From an old slave's cabin in Virginia fields, Booker T. Washington rose up to the stature of one of America's greatest leaders. He lived of course in Alabama, and darkness fled. From the red hills of Gordon County, Georgia, and iron foundry of Chattanooga, Tennessee, Roland Hayes rose up to be one of the best singers of the world and carried his melodious voice to the palace of King George V and the mansion of the Queen Mother of Spain. From a poverty-stricken area of Philadelphia, Pennsylvania, Marian Anderson rose up to be the world's greatest contralto (*Yeah*) so that Toscanini could declare that a voice like this comes only once in a century. And Sibelius of Finland had to cry out, "My roof is too low for such a voice."[14] [*applause*]

[*word inaudible*] oppressive circumstances George Washington Carver rose up and carved for himself an impenetrable niche in the halls of time. Yes, there was a star in the sky of female leadership (*Yes*): Mary McLeod Bethune reached up and grabbed it and allowed it to shine. [*applause*] There is a star in the diplomatic sky: Ralph Bunche, the grandson of a slave preacher, reached up and grabbed it and allowed it to shine with all of its beautiful outpour of light. There is a star in the athletic sky: Then came Joe Louis with his educated fists (*Yes*) [*applause*], Jesse Owens with his fleet and dashing feet, Jackie Robinson with his powerful bat and his calm spirit, and all of these [*words inaudible*] who proved to us that we need not wait until the day of full emancipation before we make a contribution.[15] [*applause*]

---

14. Booker T. Washington (1856–1915) founded the Tuskegee Institute. Roland Hayes (1887–1977) was a well-known lyric tenor. Marian Anderson (1897–1993) was an internationally acclaimed opera singer. Arturo Toscanini (1867–1957) was an Italian conductor who led the New York Philharmonic-Symphony Orchestra. Jean Sibelius (1865–1957) was a Finnish composer.

15. George Washington Carver (1864?–1943) was a scientist particularly famed for his agricultural research. Mary McLeod Bethune (1875–1955) was a pioneering educator who founded the National Council of Negro Women. Ralph J. Bunche (1904–1971) was a United Nations diplomat who in 1950

Now, in the eyes they have justified a conviction of the poet,

Fleecy locks and black complexion (*Yes*)
Cannot [*halt nature's claim?*];
Skin may differ, but affection
Dwells in black and white the same.
Were I so tall to, I could reach the pole
Or could grasp the ocean at its span,
I must be measured by my soul. (*Yes*)
The mind is the standard of the man.[16] [*applause*]

And now to help America realize its dream, we must do another thing. We must make a determined effort to achieve the ballot. (*All right*) I am convinced more than ever before that one of the most decisive steps that the Negro can take at this hour is that short walk to the voting booth. [*applause*] Now, in many communities and many counties and rural areas, in many instances we know that there are problems against our resistance, and many conniving methods are being used to keep Negroes from registering. We must also remember that we as Negroes don't register as much as we should in places where we have no difficulties. The only barrier are our own [*applause*]. Now I urge you today in Savannah, I urge our fellow voters of Georgia, all over the South, all over the United States to go out with a determined effort to achieve the ballot. I urge every church in this community to establish a social and political action committee and make it a part of this 1961 church program to have every member in that church registered before the end of this year.[17] [*applause*] There are five million eligible Negro voters in the South, and we only have 1,300,000 registered. We have a long, long way to go.

And we've got to get up and go, because I tell you the politicians listen to votes [*laughter*], and when they know that they have their ballot in your hand (*Yes*), they will talk with you in a nice manner [*words inaudible*] was before. [*We've?*] learned this reality more than ever before in this election: the power of the vote. Mr. Kennedy is President of the United States today because of the Negro vote. [*applause*] My friends, a few days ago we must not hesitate to remind Mr. Kennedy that the Negro vote

---

became the first African American to win the Nobel Peace Prize. Joe Louis (1914–1981) held the world heavyweight championship from 1937 to 1949. Jesse Owens (1913–1980) was a track and field star who won four gold medals in the 1936 Berlin Summer Olympics. Jackie Robinson (1919–1972) was the first African American to play modern major league baseball.

16. For the first four lines, cf. "The Negro's Complaint" (1788) by William Cowper. For the remaining lines, cf. "False Greatness," *Horae Lyricae* (1706) by Isaac Watts.

17. King established a Social and Political Action Committee at Dexter Avenue Baptist Church in 1954 and one at Ebenezer Baptist Church in 1960. Members of both churches were required to be registered voters (King, "Recommendations to the Dexter Avenue Baptist Church for the Fiscal Year 1954–1955," 5 September 1954, in *The Papers of Martin Luther King, Jr.*, vol. 2: *Rediscovering Precious Values, July 1951–November 1955*, ed. Clayborne Carson, Ralph E. Luker, Penny A. Russell, Peter Holloran [Berkeley and Los Angeles: University of California Press, 2005], p. 290; King, Sr., and King, Jr., "Recommendations to the Ebenezer Baptist Church for the Fiscal Year 1960–1961," February–March 1960, in *Papers* 5:379).

helped get him elected, and we expect him to do something to remove the weight of segregation from our shoulders.[18] [*applause*]

Another thing that people who are seeking to bring this dream into being must do, another thing they must realize is this: that in order to gain freedom there must be a willingness to suffer and sacrifice. Freedom is not free. It must be brought forth with the highest height of pain and sacrifice. And I think there are too many among us who want the fruits of integration but who are not willing to go through the sacrifice necessary to challenge the roots of segregation. [*applause*]

And I just think of what many men and women in other nations have had to go through to gain their freedom. Last year Mrs. King and I journeyed over that great country known as India.[19] Spent several weeks there with the people, the wonderful people, of that very country. We hardly met a single person who had not been to jail during the independence struggle. Never forget that Mohandas K. Gandhi spent twelve years of his life in jail. Never forget that the man who is the head of the second most populous nation in the world today, Jawaharlal Nehru, spent fourteen years of his life in jail. (*That's right*) Never forget that Prime Minister [*Kwame*] Nkrumah was elected prime minister of the Gold Coast while he was in jail.

And here we are afraid even to stand up and be counted for what we believe. [*applause*] Unless we come to see this, we will postpone our freedom almost too long. We must get this over to every section of the Negro community. We must rise above our fears now; there is nothing to be afraid of. (*No*) If you believe, and you know that the cause for which you stand is right, you will never have to face anything—you'll face it with a humble smile on your face (*Yes*) 'cause you know that all of the eternity stands with you; the angels stand by. (*Yes*) And you know that, because you know that you're right. This cause in which we are engaged is a righteous cause. (*Yes*) So let us get up and fight the fight.

That could mean going down in our pockets, giving big money for freedom. We waste too much money on frivolities and other things. Now it's time to give it for freedom. Any Negro who is not a member of the National Association for the Advancement of Colored People should be ashamed of himself. [*applause*]

All I am saying is that we will not gain our freedom on a silver platter. It will not be handed out like that. We must suffer and sacrifice for it. And this means that those who have had the good fortune of getting education and the good fortune

---

18. At a December 1960 rally in observance of the Emancipation Proclamation, King called on president-elect Kennedy to sign an executive order outlawing segregation: "It is pretty conclusive now that the Negro played a decisive role in electing the president of the United States and maybe for the first time we came to see the power of the ballot and what the ballot can do. Now we must remind Mr. Kennedy that we helped him to get in the White House. We must remind Mr. Kennedy that we are expecting him to use the whole weight of his office to remove the ugly weight of segregation from the shoulders of our nation" (King, "The Negro and the American Dream," Address delivered at the Memorial Auditorium, 30 December 1960). For more on King's calls for a second Emancipation Proclamation, see King, "Equality Now: The President Has the Power," 4 February 1961, King, Press Release, Statement Calling for Executive Order Declaring Segregation Illegal, 5 June 1961, King, Press Conference after Meeting with John F. Kennedy, 16 October 1961, and King, Abernathy, and Anderson to John F. Kennedy, 17 December 1961, pp. 139–150, 243–245, 308–311, and 349–350, respectively.

19. For more on King's 1959 trip to India, see Introduction in *Papers* 5:2–12.

of accumulating a little money must get in this struggle. Too often the middle class, the Negro middle class, stood aside with the sort of philosophy, "I've got mine, so it doesn't matter what happens." [*applause*] No one individual in the Negro or white race will be free until we are all free. [*applause*]

So, we must get together, and we must remind our white brothers, because some-times they don't know, but we must remind them that these few Uncle Toms who sell their souls do not speak for the Negro. [*applause*] All I'm saying to you is that we must go out now and remind America that, that we want to be free. (*Yes*) We are not [*word inaudible*] making excessive demands; we just want to be free. This must be our message for the new year and the years ahead: we want to be free. We are not seeking to upset the social structure of the nation; we simply want to be free. We are not seek-ing to dominate the nation politically; we just want to be free. We are not dangerous rabble-rousers, or professional agitators; we simply want to be free.

So now, we must say to America, "America, we've been loyal to you. (*Yes*) We haven't produced traitors, America; we've been loyal to you in every situation. (*Yes*) America, we have not turned to some sort of ideology to solve our problems." There have been those who have said that our movement came into being or was inspired by Communism, but we must remind those who would say it, even if it's a former president of the United States, that it is an insult to our intelligence (*Yes*) to tell us that a man is standing on our neck.[20] Mr. Khrushchev has to come over from Russia to remind us all.[21] [*applause*]

Oh yes, America, Communism is not our way of life. We reject its metaphysical basis; we reject its message; we reject its totalitarianism. (*Yes*)

But America, we're simply saying now, "We want to be free." (*That's right*) [*applause*] Yes, America we've been with you when your security was threatened. Your security, America—our sons sailed the bloody seas of two world wars. Your security, America—our sons died in the trenches of France, in the foxholes of Germany, on the beachheads of Italy, on the islands of Japan. (*Yes*) Now America, we are simply saying, "We want to be free." [*applause*] This must be our message. (*Yes*) We stand to save the souls of our nation.

There is another final thing that we must do. We must be committed to a method that is consistent with the noble end that we seek. (*Yes*) We must be sure that our method is nonviolent to the core. (*Yes*) There are three ways that oppressed people deal with their oppression. One way is to just sit down and accept it. This has hap-pened through history. Some people resign themselves to the fate of oppression and they feel that that's the way to deal with it. They become conditioned to it; they adjust to it. And [*then they are just like this man?*] who was playing his guitar in Atlanta—he

---

20. After former president Harry S. Truman claimed in a news conference in Ithaca, New York, that the student sit-in movement was engineered by Communists, King responded: "the sit-ins were not inspired by Communism. They were inspired by the passionate yearning and the timeless longing for freedom and human dignity on the part of a people who have for years been trampled over by the iron feet of oppression" (King to Harry S. Truman, 19 April 1960, in *Papers* 5:438).

21. In a speech before the General Assembly of the United Nations in New York the previous September, Khrushchev questioned having the U.N. headquartered in a country where representatives from African and Asian countries were subject to discrimination ("Text of Premier Khrushchev's Speech Before the United Nations General Assembly," *New York Times*, 24 September 1960).

was just playing and started singing, "Been down so long that down don't bother me."[22] [*applause*]

That is the way. We will now have to respect [*for?*] ourselves, or our white brothers will not respect us if we [*hand back?*] this power to sit down and do nothing. (*That's right*) Noncooperation with evil is as a much a moral obligation as is cooperation with good.[23] Don't let anybody fool you: we're not trying to free ourselves alone. (*No*) If we cease to stand up, be counted, we are not our brother's keeper. We're seeking to free the white man. Why, I tell you the system of segregation puts him in more slavery than it puts the Negro. [*applause*] Anybody who's a slave there, anybody who's a slave to prejudice, anybody who's a slave to fear—and many white people are, who really believe in integration but they're afraid to say it. We're seeking to free these people. (*Yes sir*) So I say to you that it isn't moral to sit down because at that point we refuse to be our brother's keeper. (*Yes*)

Now, the other way that people use so often is to rise up against the oppressor with a rolling hatred and physical violence. They've lived with the problem and dealt with it, and they feel that the only way they can deal with it is somehow hate the opponent and arm themselves so that they can use violence against the opponent. (*Well*) But I submit to you that this isn't the way. Violence often brings about temporary victory, but it never brings about permanent peace. (*No*) It ends up creating many more social problems than it solves. There is still a voice crying through the vista of time, saying to every potential recruit to put up your sword. (*Yes*) History is replete with the bleak bones of nations. History is crowded with the records of communities that failed to follow this command. (*Yes*)

So I must remind you that there is another way. You need not sit down and do nothing. You need not rise up with arms. There is another way (*Yes*), a way as old as the insights of Jesus of Nazareth (*Yes*) and as modern as the techniques of Mohandas K. Gandhi, a way as old as Jesus looking into the faces of men and women of this generation saying, "Love them. (*Yeah*) Bless them that curse you. Pray for them that spitefully use you."[24] (*Yes*) There is another way (*Yes*), a way as old as Jesus saying, "Do unto others as you would have them do unto you."[25] There is another way (*Yes*), a way as old as Jesus saying, "Turn the other cheek."[26] (*Yes*) We realize that turning the other cheek didn't always mean that you would get along all right in terms of the physical structure. It may mean that you'll get scarred up. It may mean that your house will get bombed. It may mean you get shot at. You may get stabbed in the process, but Jesus would say, in substance, that it is better to go through life with a scarred-up body than a scarred-up soul.[27] [*applause*]

---

22. Blues singer Ishman Bracey's 1928 recording of "Trouble Hearted Blues" included the following lyric: "Down so long, down don't worry me." Billie Holiday's 1954 recording of "Stormy Blues" had similar lyrics: "I've been down so long that down don't worry me."

23. Cf. M. K. Gandhi, *Satyagraha* (Ahmadabad: Navajivan Publishing House, 1951), p. 165: "Non-co-operation with evil is as much a duty as co-operation with good"; see also Gandhi, "The Poet's Anxiety," *Young India*, 1 June 1921.

24. Cf. Matthew 5:44.

25. Cf. Matthew 7:12.

26. Cf. Matthew 5:39.

27. Cf. Matthew 16:26. King's home was bombed on 30 January 1956, and he was stabbed on 20 September 1958 by a mentally deranged woman while signing copies of *Stride Toward Freedom* in a Harlem department store. For more on the bombing and King's stabbing, see Introduction in *The Papers of*

There is another way. (*Another way, Yes*) God grant that as we move on in our nation

nation (*Well*), God grant that we speak to remind America and our white brothers that this system is evil and that we want to be as brothers. God grant that we will use the proper method. (*Yes*) It will lead us to the point that we will not only achieve freedom for ourselves, but we will somehow change the structure of society. (*Yes*) It will give us the proper attitude in the process. I am convinced, my friends, that the problem we face down here in Georgia and all over the South is not only tension between black men and white men. (*No*) That isn't it. It is the tension between justice and injustice (*Yes*), between the forces of light and the forces of darkness. (*Well*)

So, our aim must never be to defeat or humiliate the white man, but to win his friendship and understanding. (*Yes*) Now, sometimes we have to boycott him, and that's necessary. Sometimes, we must boycott these stores, and we have to do it to remind them that just as they respect our dollar, they must respect our friendship. [*applause*] But even if we boycott, we do it with a loving spirit, because we somehow know that a boycott is not an end within itself (*No*), merely a means to awaken a sense of shame with the opponent, within the opponent. But the end is reconciliation.

The end is the creation of the beloved community. (*Yes*) This is why I have to disagree with those who've gotten weary along the way in our race, who are now saying we must adopt a policy of black supremacy.[28] (*Well*) I say to you this afternoon if this becomes our philosophy, it becomes a dangerous one, for black supremacy is as dangerous as white supremacy. (*Yes*) [*applause*] God is not interested [*applause*], God is not interested merely in the freedom of black men and brown men and yellow men. God is interested in the freedom of the whole human race (*Yes*) and the creation of a society where all men live together as brothers, and every man will respect the dignity and the worth of human personality. This is what God wants. (*Yes, Yes*)

So, our aim must not be to rise from a position of disadvantage to one of advantage [*while subverting justice?*] but to achieve democracy for everybody. (*Yes*) I believe that if we will follow this method, we will help America bring the dream into being. (*Yes*)

Now, some of you are asking now, I know, "How long will it take, brother King? [*laughter*] We are tired. We are weary along the way. It's been another long time." For years and years, our forefathers had to live amid the bondage and the tragedy of slavery. Then we've been inflicted with segregation, and he still wonders, "How long do I have to wait before the dream comes into being?" Somebody's crying out this afternoon, "How long shall prejudice blind the visions of men, darken their understanding, drive bright-eyed wisdom from her sacred throne? How long will the rich dominate the poor and the strong trample over the weak?" Somebody's asking, "When will wounded justice, lying prostrate on the streets of our cities, be lifted from this dust of shame to reign supreme among the children of men." Somebody else is asking, "When will the radiant star of hope be plunged against the nocturnal bosom of this lonely life, plucked from weary souls the manacles of fear and the

---

*Martin Luther King, Jr.*, vol 3: *Birth of a New Age, December 1955–December 1956*, ed. Clayborne Carson, Susan Carson, Stewart Burns, Peter Holloran, Dana L. H. Powell (Berkeley and Los Angeles: University of California Press, 1997), pp. 10–11, and *Papers* 4:34–35.

28. King may be referring to the Nation of Islam, a black separatist organization founded by Elijah Muhammad.

chains of death?"[29] How long (*Yes, How long, How long*) will truth be crucified and justice dead?

I come to my conclusion by saying to you: "Not long." I can't give you an exact date, but not long. (*Not long*) Go back, if you don't believe me, to the sands of Egypt. (*Yes*) Watch the Pharaohs as they hold God's children in the clutches of their political power. Not long after that, watch the Red Sea as it opens, watch the children of God move on out of Egypt. Go back if you will. (*Preach*) Watch Caesar as he occupies the palace (*Yes*) and Christ as he occupies the throne (*Yes*), but not long after that, that same Christ rises up to split history into AD and BC (*Yes*) so that even the life of Caesar must be dated by his name. (*Yes*) How long? Not long. (*Not long*) [*applause*]

So, children, don't get weary.[30] There is something in this universe that justifies Carlyle in saying, "No lie can live forever."[31] (*Yeah*) There is something right here in the course of cosmos that justifies William Cullen Bryant in saying, "Truth crushed to earth will rise again."[32] And there is something right here in this universe which justifies James Russell Lowell in saying, "Truth forever on the scaffold, Wrong forever on the throne,—/Yet that scaffold sways the future, and, behind the dim unknown/Standeth God within the shadows, keeping watch above his own."[33] (*Yes*) So, down in Montgomery, Alabama, we can walk and never get weary. (*Yes*) [*applause*]

So, this is our hope. Let us work together, pray together, picket together, boycott together, keeping on the struggling (*Yes*) so that America will be truly America. (*Yes*) Then we can sing the new meanings of song [*everywhere?*]: "My country, 'tis of thee (*Yes*), Sweet land of liberty, Of thee I sing; Yes, land where my fathers died (*Yes*), Land of the Pilgrims' pride (*Yes*), From every mountain-side (*Yes*), Let freedom ring."

And that must become literally true. [*laughter*] Freedom must ring from every mountainside if America's dream is to be real. (*Yes*) So, let it ring from the prodigious hilltops of New Hampshire (*Yes*), and let it ring from the mighty Alleghenies of Pennsylvania. (*Yes*) Let it ring from the snow-capped Rockies of Colorado. Let it ring from the curvaceous slopes of California. But not only that. If freedom is to be real, democracy is to be real, if the American dream is to be real, freedom must ring from every mountainside. So let it ring from Lookout Mountain in Tennessee. (*Yes*) Let it ring from every mountain and hill in Alabama. Let it ring from every hill

29. J.H. Jackson, "The Last Frontier of Democracy," 1957, in *The Story of The National Baptists*, Owen D. Pelt and Ralph Lee Smith (New York: Vantage Press, 1960), pp. 232–233: "How long must prejudice blind the minds of men, darken understanding, and drive bright-eyed wisdom from her sacred throne? O Spirit of Freedom how long must there be continued man's inhumanity to man, the domination of the strong over the weak, and the conquest of the poor by the rich, and the slaughter of the innocent by the guilty. And when will wounded Justice, now prostrate in the streets of cities, be lifted from the dust of shame to reign supreme among the children of men? Spirit of Freedom, child of destiny, and daughter of love, hold high your torch of hope in this dark hour of despair, and push your guiding star out upon the nocturnal bosom of this gloomy night, and pluck from weary souls the chains of fear and the manacles of death, and open wide the prison house of cursed discrimination and let God's people go."

30. Cf. Galatians 6:9.

31. King paraphrases Thomas Carlyle, *The French Revolution* (1837), vol. 1, book 6, chap. 3: "No lie you can speak or act but it will come, after longer or shorter circulation, like a bill drawn on Nature's Reality, and be presented there for payments—with the answer, No effects."

32. Cf. William Cullen Bryant, "The Battlefield" (1839), stanza 9.

33. Cf. James Russell Lowell, "The Present Crisis" (1844), stanza 8.

and molehill in Mississippi. (*Yes*) Let it ring from Stone Mountain in Georgia. From all the mountainsides, let freedom ring. And when that happens, all of God's children—black men and white men (*Yes*), Jews and Gentiles, Catholics and Protestants (*Well*)—will be able to join hands and sing with meaning, "Free at last! Free at last! Thank God almighty. We are free at last!"[34] [*sustained applause*]

At. MLKEC: B-24.

34. King's language mirrors that of Archibald J. Carey, a Chicago preacher and civil rights activist, who on 8 July 1952, addressed the Republican National Convention using similar language: "That's exactly what we mean—from every mountain side, let freedom ring. Not only from the Green Mountains and the White Mountains of Vermont and New Hampshire; not only from the Catskills of New York; but from the Ozarks in Arkansas, from the Stone Mountain in Georgia, from the Great Smokies of Tennessee and from the Blue Ridge Mountains of Virginia—Not only for the minorities of the United States, but for the persecuted of Europe, for the rejected of Asia, for the disfranchised of South Africa and for the disinherited of all the earth—may the Republican Party, under God, from every mountain side, LET FREEDOM RING!" (Carey, Address delivered to the Republican National Convention, 8 July 1952).

# From Saul David Alinsky

3 January 1961
Chicago, Ill.

*During a television program titled "Housing Decision," Chicago community organizer Alinsky included King among supporters of a quota system as a strategy for integrating neighborhoods.[1] In response to letters from concerned viewers, King denied ever having made such a statement, and called the quota idea "morally wrong and legally indefensible."[2] In this letter to King, Alinsky attributes King's quote to a December 1959 article in the* Chicago Daily News *and admits that it never occurred to him that the statement could have been misconstrued.[3]*

1. Saul David Alinsky (1909–1972), born in Chicago, Illinois, earned a B.A. in sociology in 1930 from the University of Chicago. While working in Chicago for the Congress of Industrial Organizations during the Great Depression, Alinsky became a community organizer in the Back of the Yards neighborhood. He formed the Back of the Yards Neighborhood Council in 1939, and the Industrial Areas Foundation in 1940. He published a handbook on neighborhood organizing, *Reveille for Radicals,* in 1946. In 1961 he founded the Temporary Woodlawn Organization to promote integration on Chicago's Southside.

2. Harold Edward Fey to King, 30 November 1960; King to Fey, 21 December 1960.

3. The newspaper quoted King as saying that quota systems were "all right as . . . an attempt to set an example in a community to prove that integration can work. This is not the ultimate aim. By setting it (integration) forth before people, they'll be able to see it work" ("Sets 10-Year Target for Desegregation," *Chicago Daily News,* 16 December 1959).

3 Jan
1961

Dr. Martin Luther King, Jr.
Ebenezer Baptist Church
407 Auburn Avenue, N.E.
Atlanta, Georgia

Dear Dr. King:

The attached copy of my letter to Mr. John H. Wagner is self-explanatory.[4] I deeply regret the way this matter was brought to your attention. If Mr. Wagner had contacted me prior to writing you he would have been given these facts which would have provided you with a specific situation for comment. I too have been involved in similar situations and know how much more helpful and fairer it is to be presented the facts. As you will note from my letter to Mr. Wagner I point out my gratitude to you for insisting that he contact me and that I write you on the background of the statement.

The program was part of your television presentation of that particular evening.[5] In Chicago and I understand on the West Coast the network went in for a regional discussion of race issues pertaining to that particular area. My major function seemed to involve an attack on the Chicago Real Estate Board for what I consider to be segregational practices and my insistence on the initiation and carrying through of integration practices in our residential living.

You more than anyone else will appreciate the difference between the cool comfortable climate on the mountain-top where one can indulge in self-satisfied, safe, militant denunciations of the evils of segregation as over against the heat of the valleys with all of the irrationalities of human motivations when one attempts to implement and really do something about integration. I repeat that I know no one who could understand these differences more than yourself. For years I stood on the mountain-tops with many of my liberal friends indulging in righteous anger against the inequities of discrimination and segregation and suffered few if any inconveniences. It was not until I and my organization descended into the valleys of implementation on this issue that I suddenly felt the full violence and anger of every racist Negro hating group in Chicago. It was not until then that I found my family as well as myself being physically threatened. A sample of the kind of correspondence which I am graced with is also enclosed. This came on the heels of the television speech which is the subject of discussion.

The attached will indicate why I made the statement about you and the quota system which I did along the lines described in the copy of the letter to Mr. Wagner. Since without one single exception every known area of integrated residential housing in the north from the Milgram projects to the Spring Hill Gardens in Pittsburgh

---

4. Alinsky to Wagner, 3 January 1961. King also received a letter from Wagner, assistant secretary of the National Lutheran Council, who watched the program and asked King to explain "on what basis you would accept 'quota integration!'" (Wagner to King, 7 December 1960). Responding to Wagner's letter, King denied ever making the "proposal in private or public," and suggested that perhaps he had been "misquoted in the press" (King to Wagner, 15 December 1960).

5. In Chicago, Alinsky's appearance on the "Housing Decision" was preceded by King's appearance on "The Nation's Future" (Debate with James J. Kilpatrick, 26 November 1960, in *Papers* 5:556–564).

to the Mount Royal community in Baltimore to the Palo Alto, California interracial
housing experiment utilize the quota as the opening wedge in securing and settling
an integration residential pattern (obviously once the whites have become accustomed to living with their Negro neighbors and getting to know Negroes as human
beings and not as faceless racial symbols then the quota idea is dismissed)—and
since the honor roll of those (both Negro and white) who have fought for equal
rights though the years and include many of our most distinguished Americans realize that there is no alternative at this time to the quota procedure (a procedure which
incidentally is viciously opposed by every racist group) it never occurred to me that
there might possibly have been anything out of line as far as the interview reported
with you by the <u>Chicago Daily News</u> on December 16, 1959.[6] On the contrary I felt
that it was courageous for you to take the position since so many of those I know in
the field (and the kind for whom I am sure that you would have the same feelings
about that I have) have assured me of their private commitment to this procedure
but felt that it was not yet time for them to make a public commitment to this effect.
I trust that I am not imposing by also attaching a copy of my testimony before the
United States Civil Rights Commission, a photostat of the kind of reaction which it
received in this city (which served one good function of ending a newspaper taboo of
any discussion on the issue except in the most indirect and vague terms) and also an
article by Mr. Oscar Cohen, "The Case for Benign Quotas in Housing," published in
the spring issue, 1960 of <u>Phylon</u>.[7] This article is regarded as the most perceptive and
best balanced analysis of the subject to this date. I am sure you know it and also know
that it is widely accepted as a most delineating analysis of the issue.

Our mutual friend, Ralph Helstein, informs me that you will be in Chicago on
the 21st of this month and he hopes to make it possible for us to meet at that time.
Needless to say I am eagerly looking forward to this opportunity of getting to know
you and to be able to personnally express my deep admiration for all that you have
done and what you represent. I would appreciate hearing from you before then.[8]

---

6. Alinsky refers to several privately owned integrated housing programs throughout the United
States that utilize the racial quota system. In 1954, Morris Milgram, the former national secretary of the
Workers Defense League, created Concord Park, the country's first private interracial housing project
in Philadelphia. Completed in 1959, the Spring Hill Gardens included 209 apartment units divided into
nineteen sections; the plan was to place two or three black families in each section. In Baltimore, the
Mount Royal Improvement Association opened its membership to blacks in 1954 and set an informal
quota at 12–15 percent black. In Palo Alto in 1948, two groups partnered to buy a small tract with space
for twenty-four homes. The home buyership was open to equal parts white, black, and Asian families. In
order to maintain the multiracial composition, the buyers agreed to sell their homes to people of their
own race.

7. In 1959 Alinsky spoke in favor of a housing quota system before the United States Commission
on Civil Rights (U.S. Commission on Civil Rights, *Hearings before the United States Commission on Civil
Rights, 1959* [Washington, D.C.: U.S. Government Printing Office, 1959], pp. 769–781). In Cohen's article,
Alinsky was again quoted in favor of housing quotas (Oscar Cohen, "The Case for Benign Quotas in
Housing," *Phylon* 21, no. 1 [1960]: 20–29).

8. Helstein was president of the United Packinghouse Workers of America (UPWA). King went to
Chicago in late January for the Public Review Advisory Committee meeting of the UPWA but he did not
have time to meet with Alinksy (James R. Wood to Alinksy, 24 January 1961).

Sincerely yours,

[*signed*]

Saul D. Alinsky

SDA:cmf

Enclosures

TLS. MLKP-MBU.

# To Gordon R. Carey

10 January 1961
[*Atlanta, Ga.*]

*King responds to a 31 October 1960 letter from Congress of Racial Equality*
*(CORE) field director Gordon R. Carey, who heard that King was "not pleased*
*with some of the recent activities and/or attitudes of CORE."[1] In his reply, King*
*admits that there were issues; however, he sees "no basis for conflict between CORE*
*and SCLC."*

Mr. Gordon R. Carey
459 West 44th Street
New York 36, New York

Dear Gordon:

I have just realized that I have not answered your letter of October 31. For some strange reason the letter was misplaced and left in the file of answered mail. It was just two days ago that I came across it again. I can assure you that this was not done though sheer negligence but as a result of the human errors that occur in an office receiving a flood of mail.

I regret that time will not permit me to write a long letter in answer to some of the questions you raise. It may be possible for us to talk these things over when I am in New York again. Suffice it to say, I am still intensely interested in the work of CORE and will support it wherever it is humanly possible. There are some minor things that I have been concerned about, but I think they have been cleared up now. I have

---

1. While speaking with CORE executive secretary James R. Robinson at CORE's Action Institute in Miami in August 1960, King expressed frustrations with "organizational interrelationships" (Robinson to King, 7 September 1960). In his letter to King, Carey advised that King should "feel free" to criticize the organization directly given his position on CORE's advisory committee. Gordon Ray Carey (1932– ), born in Grand Rapids, Michigan, began working with CORE in 1953. After serving a year in prison as a conscientious objector during the Korean War, Carey became CORE's vice chairman in 1956 and subsequently worked with CORE in various capacities. In 1970 he began working with Floyd B. McKissick, a former national director of CORE, on Soul City, a federally funded black community in North Carolina.

never felt that my dissatisfaction with some developments in CORE were of major 10 Jan proportions so I could well leave the matter where it is and say that I see no basis 1961 for conflict between CORE and SCLC. I think we can work together very well and indeed we must.

Just a few days ago I had a most rewarding discussion with Charles Oldham, Gladys Harrington and Val Coleman.[2] I believe we came up with some good ideas concerning coordination and possible points of cooperation. I am sure that they will share some of the ideas we discussed with you and other staff members.

I will call you when I am in New York and may be we can take a few minutes to discuss some of the things that concern me a great deal. I am sure that the new administration will find some of these matters of value.[3]

Very sincerely yours,
[*signed*]
Martin

MLK.m

TLS. GRCC-ICRCM.

---

2. Oldham, Harrington, and Coleman were all CORE staff members. Oldham was the national chairman, Harrington was a regional representative, and Coleman was a public relations specialist.

3. King refers to the appointment of James Farmer, who was elected national director of CORE at the end of 1960.

# From Elizabeth Knight

10 January 1961
Atlanta, Ga.

*Knight, the founder of the Atlanta-based singing group Gladys Knight and The Pips, requests King's assistance in securing a performance for her sixteen-year-old daughter, Gladys, at president-elect John F. Kennedy's inaugural ball.[1] James R. Wood, SCLC's public relations director, replied that King did "not have any*

---

1. Elizabeth Woods Knight (1917–1997), born in East Point, Georgia, was a member of Mount Moriah Baptist Church and also a member of the Wings Over Jordan gospel choir in Atlanta. In 1953, she helped form the singing group The Pips, which included her daughter, Gladys, and other members of the extended family. Knight was also a member of the Atlanta branch of the NAACP. Gladys Knight (1944– ), born in Atlanta, Georgia, began her singing career at age four, appearing with several Atlanta-based choirs. In 1961, Gladys Knight and The Pips recorded their first album. During the 1960s, she sang at fundraisers for the Atlanta student movement. Throughout her career, Knight earned numerous awards, including four Grammy's, an honorary degree from Morris Brown College, and the NAACP Image Award.

*direct relationship" with the inaugural committee, "and therefore could not be
instrumental in influencing decisions it makes."[2]*

Dr. Martin Luther King, Jr.
413 Auburn Avenue, N.E.
Atlanta, Georgia

Dear Dr. King:

There has been a question in my mind. Since you have had dealings in so many fields. I feel you are the logical person with whom I should consult.

Previously, Artists as Marion Anderson, Mahalia Jackson, and others, have performed for various presidents. My daughter, Gladys Knight, who is now sixteen years old, mentioned casually that it would be wonderful if she were able to sing at the inaugural ball of President-Elect John F. Kennedy.[3]

Of course Gladys is of no great fame, but when seven years old, she won the championship of the Ted Mack Original Amateur Hour.[4] Since then, she has appeared at the Madison Square Garden, New York City, before 50,000 people, The Comodore Hotel, New York City, The Colliseum, Detroit, Michigan, and she has appeared on radio and television. She is the leader of the Youth For Christ Choir at Mt. Moriah Baptist Church where Dr. R.J. [*Julian*] Smith, Jr. is pastor.

I wonder if this appearance could be possible, and if the arrangements could be made through you? If not, to whom should I go to inquire or negotiate?

If you should need any futher information, please contact me at the above address or call me at Ja 1–1241. I would like to have an appointment with you at your convenience.

Thank you very much.

Very truly yours,
[*signed*] Elizabeth Knight

ALS. MLKP-MBU.

---

2. Wood further suggested that Knight contact the committee directly, and warned that it might be too late to make changes to the program (Wood to Knight, 17 January 1961). Although King was invited to the inauguration, he did not attend.

3. Anderson, an internationally acclaimed opera singer, performed for Franklin D. Roosevelt during the visit of Great Britain's King George and Queen Elizabeth in 1939 and sang the national anthem at the inaugurations of Dwight D. Eisenhower in 1953 and John F. Kennedy in 1961. Jackson, a well-renowned gospel singer, sang at a birthday party for Eisenhower in 1959 and at Kennedy's inaugural ball.

4. In 1952 Knight won the national grand prize and $2,000 on The Original Amateur Hour, a variety show hosted by Ted Mack.

The Inaugural Committee

requests the honor of your presence

to attend and participate in the Inauguration of

John Fitzgerald Kennedy

as President of the United States of America

and

Lyndon Baines Johnson

as Vice President of the United States of America

on Friday, the twentieth of January

one thousand nine hundred and sixty-one

in the City of Washington

Edward H. Foley

Chairman

Although King was invited to attend the 20 January 1961 presidential inauguration of John F. Kennedy and Lyndon B. Johnson, he did not attend. Courtesy of the Martin Luther King, Jr., Center for Nonviolent Social Change, Inc.

# To Milton A. Reid

12 January 1961
*[Atlanta, Ga.]*

*Since June of 1959, Prince Edward County, Virginia, officials had kept their
public schools closed to avoid desegregation. In a 10 January 1961 letter to King,
Reid, president of the Virginia Christian Leadership Conference (VCLC) discussed
his organization's plans for a sit-in in Congress to draw national attention to the
closed schools.[1] Reid asked King if SCLC would join other national organizations
in sponsoring the event.[2] In his reply below, King notes that VCLC's plans
violate SCLC bylaws, adding that some organizations might take "offense" to
being contacted by a "'unit' of our organization."[3] Despite King's concerns,
Reid received permission from SCLC to coordinate the demonstration, but it was
eventually canceled.[4]*

Dr. Milton A. Reid
Virginia Christian Leadership Conference
236 Harrison Street
Petersburg, Virginia

---

1. The Prince Edward schools were among the five districts consolidated into the 1954 *Brown v.
Board of Education* (347 U.S. 483) case. Prince Edward County's board of supervisors closed the county's
public schools rather than obey a federal court order to desegregate them. The proposed sit-in was one
of VCLC's first large-scale activities. The demonstration, which was planned for 17 May 1961, the seventh
anniversary of the *Brown* decision, was to include 500 black and white students from Prince Edward
County ("Whites Expected to Shun Edward Public Schools," *Washington Post*, 8 September 1964; Milton
A. Reid, "President's report," May 1961). Milton Annias Reid (1930–2010), born in Chesapeake, Virginia,
received his B.A. (1955) and M.Div. (1958) from Virginia Union University. He later completed doctoral
studies at Boston University School of Theology (1980). He served as pastor of First Baptist Church in
Petersburg, Virginia, from 1957 to 1966. In November 1960, Reid helped establish VCLC and became
its president until his resignation in late 1962. Reid participated in planning Pilgrimages of Prayer for
Public Schools held in Prince Edward County (1961) and in Richmond (1962). He remained an active
member of SCLC through his work against segregation in Danville, Virginia, in 1963.
2. In addition to SCLC, Reid invited sponsorship from the American Friends Service Committee
(AFSC), CORE, NAACP, American Federation of Labor and Congress of Industrial Organizations
(AFL-CIO), National Beauticians Association, and the National Council of Negro Women (Reid to King,
10 January 1961).
3. In his reply to King, Reid apologized to the SCLC president for this "national embarrassment"
and suggested that an SCLC orientation would make clear the function of state conferences in relation
to the national organization (Reid to King, 25 January 1961). Referring to himself as "your lowness," Reid
also sent a formal apology addressed to "Your Highness," Wyatt Tee Walker, executive director of SCLC,
expressing his willingness to work with SCLC and making clear that VCLC would act under the authority
of the national organization (Reid to Walker, 25 January 1961).
4. In a confidential memo to all participating organizations, Walker wrote that SCLC could not fully
sponsor the demonstrations due to budgetary considerations and since this was a "Virginia situation," it
was "logical" for VCLC to coordinate it (Walker, Memo to Participating Agencies, 1961). VCLC canceled
the demonstration after U.S. Attorney General Robert F. Kennedy announced on 26 April that the U.S.
Justice Department would become a plaintiff in the Prince Edward County school desegregation case
(Reid, "President's report"). Almost three years later, residents of Prince Edward County were still trying

Dear Dr. Reid:

Thank you so very much for your letter of January 10. I am pleased to know that our Virginia Conference is really "moving."

As you probably know, Wyatt and I had given some serious thought and concern to the Prince Edward situation (along with some other areas) prior to the organizational meeting of VCLC in November. It was our thinking then, as it is now, that, if the people of Prince Edward were willing, and our Virginia affiliates were willing, SCLC would sponsor this project with VCLC serving as the co-ordinating agency on the local scene.

My grave concern at this moment is that we function according to the demands of our organizational structure. I refer you to the section on <u>Administrative Function</u> of the "General Program" of SCLC adopted by the National Board in Shreveport, October 11, 1960. It determines that " . . . The State Conference will act as liason with the national office in the execution of national program, state program, and the distribution of publicity. . . . " The fund-raising of the State Conference is limited to funds necessary to maintain the State Conference office, e.g. supplies, stationary, etc.

I do not feel it would be proper for a State unit of SCLC to make this kind of proposal for sponsorship to national organizations. Some of them might take offense that they are being contacted by a "unit" of our organization.

I am leaving today for an extended speaking tour in the Far West. I will have Wyatt get in touch with you immediately to work out some suggestions as to how we might best proceed. I trust his judgment very strongly in matters like these.

Let me say in closing how very proud I am that you are doing such a great work for the Southern Christian Leadership Conference. My prayers shall follow you.

Very truly yours,
Martin Luther King, Jr.

MLK.m

CC: Mr. Wyatt Tee Walker
208 Auburn Avenue, N.E.
Atlanta 3, Georgia

TLc. MLKP-MBU.

---

to settle disputes in the courts over whether or not the state was required to allocate funds toward public education. In 1964 the U.S. Supreme Court ruled in *Griffin v. Prince Edward School Board*, 377 U.S. 218, that Prince Edward County had to reopen its public schools on an integrated basis, and a few white children joined an estimated 1,400 black children when the schools reopened in September 1964 ("Virginia Negroes Return to School: Public Education Resumes in County after 5 years," *New York Times*, 9 September 1964).

# To Adam Clayton Powell

28 January 1961
[*Atlanta, Ga.*]

*In the summer of 1960, Congressman Powell urged King to call off planned*
*demonstrations at the national political conventions, fearing that the disruptions*
*would jeopardize his nomination as chairman of the House Committee on*
*Education and Labor. In this letter, King congratulates Powell as he assumes*
*the chairmanship, but expresses regret that he is unable to attend a 29 January*
*celebration in Powell's honor.*[1]

Adam Clayton Powell
Abysinnian Baptist Church
West 138th Street
New York

The Honorable 1Adam Clayton Powell:

I extend my sincere and harty congratulations on the occasion of this great tribute to the one clear voice that has sounded the accent of freedom for the past two and a half decades throughout the nation. Your unswerving dedication and loyalty without compromise to the civil rights struggle of the Negro people has been an inspiration to all Americans. I regret very deeply that I cannot be with you on this momentous occasion due to a long standing commitment in Chicago.[2] My very best wishes for this memorable night and for the promise for the days that are ahead.

Very sincerely yours,
MLKJr

TWc. MLKP-MBU.

---

1. Nat Hentoff, "Adam Clayton Powell: What Price, Principle?," *Village Voice,* 14 July 1960. Powell threatened that should the protests take place he would allege that King and Bayard Rustin were having a sexual relationship (see Introduction in *Papers* 5:31–32). In a 19 December 1960 letter, Angier Biddle Duke, chairman of the sponsoring committee for the Powell tribute, invited King to serve as honorary co-chairman of the committee, which King accepted (King to John Young, 27 December 1960).

2. On 29 January, King addressed the Chicago Sunday Evening Club (Chicago Sunday Evening Club, Program, "Chicago Sunday Evening Club," 29 January 1961).

# To Aurelia Sheller

30 January 1961
[*Atlanta, Ga.*]

*After hearing reports of King's contribution to John F. Kennedy's narrow victory
over Richard Nixon in the 1960 presidential election, Sheller, a homemaker
from Mineral Ridge, Ohio, suggested that King had been manipulated by the
Kennedy family and the Vatican.[1] As he had done several times before, King
denied endorsing either presidential candidate, claiming that the "price that one
has to pay for being in public life is that of being misquoted, misrepresented and
misunderstood."[2] King closes by thanking Sheller for her thoughtful remarks about
his work and acknowledging that he struggles "all the time to make the ideals of
freedom and justice a reality and I constantly pray that my motives will be pure
and my means moral in the process."*

Mrs. Frank Skeller
R. R. Box 282
Mineral Ridge, Ohio

Dear Mrs. Skeller:

I am in receipt of your letter concerning the presidential election, my arrest, and
the general political implications. I am very sorry that you got the impression that I
supported Senator Kennedy in the campaign. The fact is that I made it palpably clear
in a press conference immediately after my release from psison that I would endorse
neither candidate. I took this position in order to maintain a non-partisan posture
which I have followed all along. I said in that press conference that it was necessary
for me to take a non-partisan position in order to be able to look objectively at both
parties at all times.

---

1. Sheller called King a "wonderful spiritual leader" and argued that King was "great, and accomplished more" for blacks when he was "going it alone" (Sheller to King, 27 December 1960). While taking part in a sit-in on 19 October 1960, King, who was on probation for a previous traffic violation, was
arrested and sentenced to four months at Georgia State Prison at Reidsville. Then-presidential candidate
John F. Kennedy phoned Coretta Scott King to express his concern for King's jailing, while Robert F.
Kennedy called Georgia governor S. Ernest Vandiver and DeKalb County judge J. Oscar Mitchell to
secure King's release. The Kennedy campaign immediately began outreach in black communities all
over the country, contrasting Kennedy's concern for King with Nixon's silence. The press speculated that
the "King episode" may have accounted for the senator's slim margin of victory (Anthony Lewis, "Negro
Vote Held Vital to Kennedy: Dramatic Shift in South—Senator Widens Margins Scored by Stevenson,"
*New York Times*, 27 November 1960). For more on King's arrest and its impact on the 1960 presidential
election, see Introduction in *Papers* 5:36–40. Aurelia Sheller (1921–2006), born in Mineral Ridge, Ohio,
graduated from high school in 1939. She worked as a beautician and in a factory before becoming a
homemaker.
2. After King's release from Reidsville, he told reporters that he owed a great deal of gratitude to
Senator Kennedy but refused to endorse him (King, Interview after Release from Georgia State Prison
at Reidsville, 27 October 1960, and King, Statement on Presidential Endorsement, 1 November 1960, in
*Papers* 5:535–536 and 537, 540, respectively).

133

As you well know, the price that one has to pay for being in public life is that of being misquoted, misrepresented and misunderstood. I have tried to condition muself to this inevitable situation. It is possible that you read that my father switched his vote from Nixon to Kennedy after the telephone call.[3] This was quite true and again my father has a right to make his own individual decisions and this is not to be represented as the decision of Martin Luther King, Jr.

I am deeply grateful to you for your kind words concerning my work. I can only say that I am struggling all the time to make the ideals of freedom and justice a reality and I constantly pray that my motives will be pure and my means moral in the process.

Enclosed is the press release which was given at the press conference immediately after my arrest.

Sincerely yours
Martin Luther King, Jr.

Km
Encls
Dictated by Dr King but signed in his absence.

TLc. MLKP-MBU.

---

3. King, Sr. had planned to vote for Richard Nixon given John F. Kennedy's Catholic faith. After Kennedy made the call to Coretta, King, Sr. reportedly announced his support for Kennedy at a mass meeting celebrating his son's release: "I've got all my votes, and I've got a suitcase, and I'm going to take them up there and dump them in his lap" (Margaret Shannon and Douglas Kiker, "Out on Bond, King to Name Choice," *Atlanta Journal*, 28 October 1960).

# From Maya Angelou

31 January 1961
London, England

*Angelou, the former northern regional coordinator of SCLC's New York office, writes King and Wyatt Tee Walker a belated resignation letter.[1] She tells King of her recent marriage and writes that although she intends to dedicate her "life and my energy to the cause of Human Liberation" her inability to discuss issues regarding SCLC with Walker has left her "thwarted." In closing, Angelou wishes*

---

1. Maya Angelou (1928–2014) was born Marguerite Johnson in St. Louis, Missouri. After a brief marriage to Tosh Angelos in 1950, she moved to New York City to study dance and was cast in a production of "Porgy and Bess." In 1960, Angelou heard King speak in Harlem and pledged to help SCLC raise funds by staging a revue, "Cabaret for Freedom," and that summer she became northerner coordinator of SCLC's New York office after Bayard Rustin's resignation. Later in the year she resigned from SCLC

*SCLC "unlimited strides" in the new year. On 1 March 1961 King thanked*
*Angelou for her service.*[2]

31 Jan
1961

Rev. King & Rev. Walker

Dear Sirs:

I extend to you my heartiest wishes for a prosperous and progressive year and a profound apology for the tardiness of this letter.

It has been my intention to dedicate my life and my energy to the cause of Human Liberation. In the New York office of the Southern Christian Leadership Conference, I found myself at once on the road I had chosen to take and at the same time thwarted in that undertaking. Several times I asked the Rev. Walker for an audience to discuss certain matters that had been mentioned to me by people who work with to some degree or for the S.C.L.C.. I suppose the were brought to me precisely because I was the only Negro with the New York office that could be reached easily. Unfortuanately I was unable to meet with Rev. Walker in conference and as far as I know the problems still go begging. Though I am no longer with the Organization I am sure the people (Negro) who are in the office now would be more than pleased to discuss with any official from the Atlanta office the situations that exist in the north.

I would also like to inform you that I was married on Jan. 1st, to the South African freedom fighter who was the first Black man to escape from the Union of South Africa.[3] He is stationed in the Cairo office of the South Africa United Front but we will be coming back to New York when the U.N. resumes for that session so I hope during the time we are in New York City you will find business there that I might have the pleasure again of seeing and talking with you.

Again, I wish to you, the Organization and the cause a year of unlimited strides and I join with millions of black people the world over in saying 'You are our leader'.

Sincerely,
[*signed*] Maya Make
Maya Angelou Make

THLS. MLKP-MBU.

---

and moved to Cairo with her son and new husband Vusimuzi Make. After her second marriage ended in divorce, Angelou taught at the University of Ghana for several years before moving back to the United States in 1966. Her first autobiography, *I Know Why the Caged Bird Sings*, was published in 1970. Angelou went on to write four other volumes of her autobiography, publish several books of poetry, and appear on Broadway and in films.

2. At the top of Angelou's letter, King handwrote an instruction to SCLC public relations director James R. Wood: "Tell her how good it is to hear from her and I hope to see her when she is in the states again."

3. Vusimuzi Make, a representative of the Pan Africanist Congress, was exiled to Sibasa in the Transvaal for his political activities, but managed to obtain fake documentation and escape to Rhodesia. There he made contact with leaders who helped him escape to Nairobi, Kenya. When he met Angelou, Make was in New York to petition the United Nations against apartheid in South Africa.

# Memo, "Leadership Training Program
## and Citizenship Schools"

*[December 1960–January 1961]*
*[Atlanta, Ga.]*

*At the Southern Christian Leadership Conference's (SCLC) annual meeting in
October 1960, executive director Wyatt Tee Walker suggested that SCLC create a
Citizenship Education program, similar to the one that had been at Tennessee's
Highlander Folk School since 1956.[1] Soon after the meeting, King and Highlander
director Myles Horton agreed that SCLC would take over the citizenship program
in February 1961 due to the fact that Highlander's charter had been revoked.[2]
The following memo, likely intended for SCLC affiliate organizations, outlines the
structure of the new program and invites participants to trainings beginning in
March 1961.[3]*

To:
From: Southern Christian Leadership Conference National Office
Subject: Leadership Training Program and Citizenship Schools

A.  A study has been completed that documents the need for the training of new
leadership in the south to implement the program of the Southern Christian
Leadership Conference adopted at Shreveport, Louisiana in October, 1960. In
order that the Negro in all walks of life may achieve and enjoy the full benefits of
citizenship it has been found necessary that full understanding through training be
placed at his disposal. The use of the ballot effectively requires a systematic knowledge of politics. To safeguard civil rights necessitates understanding government
and those who control it. To protect and improve jobs, wages, working conditions,
business opportunities, the use of borrowed money demands an understanding of

---

1. Dorothy Cotton, "Minutes of annual board meeting," 11 October 1960. In 1956 one of the first
Citizenship Schools was conducted on Johns Island, South Carolina, by educator Septima Clark, her
cousin beautician Bernice Robinson, and activist Esau Jenkins. That same year, Clark began working at
Highlander as director of workshops and began teaching citizenship classes. For more information on
Jenkins and the Citizenship Schools, see note 1, King, "People in Action: Unknown Heroes," 12 May 1962,
p. 454 in this volume.

2. Under scrutiny for its affiliations with the civil rights and labor movements as well as with
Communists and their sympathizers, Highlander's charter was revoked by the State of Tennessee by 1960
for a host of reasons, including the unlawful sale of alcohol. After working its way through the local and
state courts, Highlander's appeal was refused by the U.S. Supreme Court in October 1961. Anticipating the
outcome, Horton had chartered a new organization in August to seamlessly continue operating the adult
education programs as the Highlander Research and Education Center, based in Knoxville, Tennessee.
According to a *New York Times* article, some worried that King's alliance with Highlander would jeopardize
SCLC's prestige among Southern white liberals and moderates. Responding to the concerns, Jim Wood,
SCLC public relations director, said: "We find no reason not to cooperate with any organization that is inter-
ested in the development of full citizenship for Americans which cannot be proved to have conducted itself
in a manner which is not American or patriotic" (Claude Sitton, "2 Groups in South Training Negroes," *New
York Times*, 23 February 1961; "Highlander School Plans New Center," *New York Times*, 10 October 1961).

3. SCLC, Minutes, "First quarterly meeting of Administrative Committee," 8 March–9 March 1961.

the economics of living. To protect civil, public and private rights, a knowledge of Jan 1961
common and statutory law is required. To break down the barriers of segregation,
to destroy the institutions of prejudice, to successfully apply mass direct action
through picketing and boycotting a knowledge of these techniques is desirable.
To effect the social change by protest necessary to achieve full citizenship a full
understanding of nonviolence and its application must be learned.

B.   Through Myles Horton and Septima Clark, professional educators, a method
to train individuals for these purposes was developed and tested for a period
exceeding five years. This program was designed to equip persons for citizenship
starting with the teaching of reading and writing in order to become registered
to vote. The addition and inclusion of other areas of training took place as the
need presented itself. The complete success of this training method developed
in the Sea Islands of South Carolina and Huntsville, Alabama projects has met
fully and successfully the objectives and requirements.[4] It is the good fortune of
the Southern Christian Leadership Conference to have been offered the use of
this educational program in the development of its activities in social action.

C.   SCLC has accepted the invitation to use this educational plan and considers its
unique advantage is in filling the need for developing new leadership as teachers
and supervisors and providing the broad educational base for the population at
large through the establishment of Citizenship Schools conducted by these new
leaders throughout the South.

LEADERSHIP TRAINING PROGRAM

D.   At Highlander Folk School, Monteagle, Tennessee, there is provided a training
facility which affords comfortable living quarters, excellent food and ample
classroom space. There is a fresh water lake and beautiful scenic views from the
mountain top on which the school is located. Here will be provided an interracial
living and learning experience. It will be the duty of the teacher, who will have
learned the methods of teaching, the subject matter to be taught and how to set
up and operate these Citizenship Schools to return to his locality and extablish
a Citizenship School. Admission will be open to all. The training of teachers will
include use of simplified methods, visual aids, proper materials to use and how to
order them in proper quantities. Participants will be taught how to operate tape
recorders, record players, film and slide projectors, etc.

Demonstrations of actual teaching situations will enable the teacher-trainee to
solve real problems. Available are refresher courses which the teacher may attend
for advanced training. Here problems encountered by the new teacher may be
brought for discussion and analysis leading to solution.

CITIZENSHIP SCHOOL

For the training of adults in equipping them for the role of full citizenship.
Reference: see attached report (Citizenship Training School Program)[5]

---

4.  By December 1960 Highlander set up test schools and experimental teacher training workshops
in Huntsville, Alabama, and Savannah, Georgia.

5.  SCLC, "Citizenship school training program," December 1960–January 1961.

The responsibility of the affiliate is to direct and control the operation of the Citizenship School so that it will properly implement the program of the Southern Christian Leadership Conference in the manner outlined above. (See: paragraphs A, B, and C)

The affiliate will recruit teachers and supervisors as outlined on page six (6) of report: Citizenship Training School Program.[6]

## COSTS OF TRAINING PROGRAM

Scholarships are available from Highlander to cover tuition, room and board while in training. This amounts to $8.00 per day. The cost of operating the local Citizenship School is $35.00 per month per class when classes meet eight (8) times per month.

The Southern Christian Leadership Conference is negotiating with philanthropic foundations to provide funds for most of the educational program.[7] Meetings are now in progress and there is every indication that sharp reductions in the cost to the affiliate of training leaders and operating schools will take place. However, it is necessary that this training program be established and operating in order that investors may observe the program in operation.

The breadth and scope of this program, its construction and design, its purpose and intent will make possible for your organization and the Southern Christian Leadership Conference to strike at the heart of the problems standing in the way of the Negro becoming an American in the true sense. This program with your cooperation will represent the greatest single contribution to the establishment of the great Democratic ideal of this century.

We urge your cooperation in the creation of new leaders and more informed citizens in our struggle for freedom and equality. Please direct all correspondence to Mrs. Dorothy F. Cotton, our newly appointed Educational Consultant.[8]

Yours very truly,
[*signed*] M. L. King Jr.
Martin Luther King, Jr.,
President

MLK: dc

TLS. SCLCR-GAMK: Box 136.

---

6. Highlander Folk School, "Training leaders for citizenship schools," 1961.

7. SCLC was later given a grant of $26,500 by the Field Foundation to begin the Leadership Training Program (Maxwell Hahn to Charles Miles Jones, 28 April 1961).

8. Cotton was promoted to educational consultant in December 1960 (James R. Wood to Septima Poinsette Clark, 23 December 1960). In September 1961, Andrew Young became administrator of SCLC's Citizenship Education Program (see Young to King, 11 September 1961, pp. 279–281 in this volume).

# "Equality Now: The President Has the Power"

4 February 1961
New York, N.Y.

*Just days before the presidential election of 1960, Carey McWilliams, editor of* The
Nation, *asked King to write an article replying to the question "What would you
have this Administration do?"[1] In his article, King calls for the president to push
for civil rights legislation, throw his support behind the movement, use the power
of executive orders to enforce integration in federally sponsored activities, and
appoint a Secretary of Integration. Claiming that the "federal government is the
nation's highest investor in segregation," King writes that "when our government
determines to ally itself with those of its citizens who are crusading for their
freedom within our borders, and lends the might of its resources creatively and
unhesitatingly to the struggle, the blight of discrimination will begin rapidly to
fade." King later acknowledged that his ideas "relied a great deal" on a study by
University of North Carolina, Chapel Hill, law professor Daniel H. Pollitt.[2]*

The new Administration has the opportunity to be the first in one hundred years
of American history to adopt a radically new approach to the question of civil rights.
It must begin, however, with the firm conviction that the principle is no longer in
doubt. The day is past for tolerating vicious and inhuman opposition on a subject
which determines the lives of 20,000,000 Americans. We are no longer discussing
the wisdom of democracy over monarchism—and we would not permit hoodlum
royalists to terrorize the streets of our major cities or the legislative halls of our states.
We must decide that in a new era, there must be new thinking. If we fail to make this
positive decision, an awakening world will conclude that we have become a fossil
nation, morally and politically; and no floods of refrigerators, automobiles or color
TV sets will rejuvenate our image.[3]

The second element in a new approach is the recognition by the federal govern-

---

1. McWilliams to King, 3 November 1960. King's article was republished in a four-part series in the
Baltimore *Afro-American* ("What's Behind the Freedom Rides," 17 June 1961; "What the President Can
Do," 1 July 1961; "With a Simple Stroke of a Pen," 8 July 1961; "Why Not Have a Secretary of Integration?,"
15 July 1961). Senator Abraham J. Multer (D-NY) inserted King's speech in the *Congressional Record* (U.S.
Congress, Senate, *Congressional Record*, 87th Cong., 1st sess., 1961, Vol. 107, pt. 21, A3007–A3009).

2. Pollitt, "The president's powers in areas of race relations: An exploration," 27 November 1960.
King sent Pollitt a copy of this article (King to Pollitt, 15 February 1961). The Southern Regional Council
(SRC) had commissioned Pollitt to prepare recommendations for the Kennedy Administration (Leslie
Dunbar to Charles H. Slayman, 16 December 1960; SRC, "The federal executive and civil rights," January
1961). Atlanta Urban League executive director R.A. Thompson, who had read the Pollitt report, also
noted the similarities between the documents and wrote to King, "I sincerely regret that you omitted
reference to Pollitt's study" in your article (Thompson to King, 27 February 1961).

3. King indirectly references the July 1959 "Kitchen Debate" between U.S. Vice President Richard
M. Nixon and Soviet Premier Nikita Khrushchev at the U.S. Trade and Cultural Fair in Moscow's
Sokolniki Park. While standing in front of a model kitchen, the two leaders debated the merits of communism, capitalism, and the quality of each country's new innovations and technology, such as washing
machines, televisions, and refrigerators.

ment that it has sufficient power at its disposal to guide us through the changes ahead. The intolerably slow pace of civil rights is due at least as much to the limits which the federal government has imposed on its own actions as it is to the actions of the segregationist opposition.

If we examine the total of all judicial, executive and legislative acts of the past three decades and balance them against the sum needed to achieve fundamental change, two startling conclusions are inescapable. The first is the hopeless inadequacy of measures adopted—pitifully insufficient in scope and limited in conception. The second conclusion is even more disturbing. Federal action has been not only inadequate; viewed as a whole, it has also been self-nullifying. In 1954, the Supreme Court declared school segregation to be unconstitutional.[4] Yet, since then federal executive agencies and vast federal legislative programs have given millions of dollars yearly to educational institutions which continue to violate the Supreme Court decision.

Further, the federal government collects taxes from all citizens, Negro and white, which it is Constitutionally obligated to use for the benefit of all; yet, billions of these tax dollars have gone to support housing programs and hospital and airport construction in which discrimination is an open and notorious practice. Private firms which either totally exclude Negroes from the work force, or place them in discriminatory status, receive billions of dollars annually in government contracts. The federal government permits elections and seats representatives in its legislative chambers in disregard of the fact that millions of Negro citizens have no vote. It directly employs millions in its various agencies and departments; yet its employment practices, especially in Southern states, are rife with discrimination.

These illustrations can be multiplied many times. The shocking fact is that while the government moves sluggishly, and in patchwork fashion, to achieve equal rights for all citizens, in the daily conduct of its own massive economic and social activities it participates directly and indirectly in the denial of these rights. We must face the tragic fact that the federal government is the nation's highest investor in segregation.

Therefore, a primary goal of a well-meaning Administration should be a thorough examination of its own operations and the development of a rigorous program to wipe out immediately every vestige of federal support and sponsorship of discrimination. Such a program would serve not only to attack the problem centrally, where results can be produced, but collaterally to educate and influence the whole American populace, especially in the Deep South of massive resistance. It would also be the first step in the evolution of federal leadership to guide the entire nation to its new democratic goals.

There is impressive precedent in recent history for massive governmental mobilization to create new conditions. As a consequence of economic crisis in the early thirties, the federal government, under the leadership of President Kennedy's party, undertook to change fundamental economic relationships. Every person in the nation was affected. In a bewilderingly brief period, wages were regulated at new levels, unemployment insurance created, relief agencies set up, public works planned and executed. Regulatory legislation covering banking, the stock market

---

4. King refers to *Brown v. Board of Education of Topeka* (1954).

and money market was immediately enacted. Laws protecting trade-union organiza- 4 Feb
tion were brought into being and administrative agencies to interpret and enforce 1961
the labor laws were created.[5] Along with this broad assault on the depression went
an educational campaign to facilitate the changes in public psychology requisite to
the acceptance of such formidable alternatives to old thought patterns. The nation
which five years earlier viewed federal intervention on any level as collectivism or
socialism, in amazingly swift transition, supported [*the?*] new role of government as
appropriate and justified.

These breathtaking, fundamental changes took place because a leadership
emerged that was both determined and bold, that rejected inhibitions imposed by
old traditions and habits. It utilized all agencies and organs of government in a massive drive to change a situation which imperiled the very existence of our society.

Viewed in this light, an Administration with good will, sincerely desirous of eliminating discrimination from American life, could accomplish its goal by mobilizing
the immense resources of the organs of government and throwing them into every
area where the problem appears. There are at least three vital areas in which the
President can work to bring about effective solutions.

First, there is the legislative area. The President could take the offensive, despite
Southern opposition, by fighting for a really far-reaching legislative program. With
resolute Presidential leadership, a majority in both houses could be persuaded to
pass meaningful laws. A determined majority-party leadership possesses the means
to carry the reluctant along—and to hasten the end of the political careers, or the
privileges, of those who prove unyielding. The influence the President can exert
upon Congress when, with crusading zeal, he summons support from the nation has
been demonstrated more than once in the past.

An example of an area in which a vigorous President could significantly influence
Congress is that of voter registration. The Civil Rights Commission has revealed that
"many Negro American citizens find it difficult, and often impossible, to vote."[6] It
went on to assert that these voting denials are accomplished through the creation of
legal impediments, administrative obstacles and the fear of economic reprisal and
physical harm.[7] A truly decisive President would work passionately and unrelent-

---

5. Among other provisions, President Franklin D. Roosevelt's New Deal legislation mandated a
minimum wage and forty-hour workweek in the 1936 Walsh-Healey Public Contracts Act and the 1938
Fair Labor Standards Act. Regarding economic regulation, Congress approved creation of the Federal
Deposit Insurance Corporation and the Securities Exchange Commission in the 1933 Banking Act and
the 1934 Securities Exchange Act, respectively. In 1935 Congress passed the National Labor Relations
Act, also known as the Wagner Act, which guaranteed the right of unions to organize, and authorized
a National Labor Relations Board to adjudicate labor disputes between management and workers.
Congress also created unemployment insurance in the form of the 1935 Social Security Act, and estab-
lished various relief agencies including the Civil Works Administration, the Federal Emergency Relief
Administration, and the Works Progress Administration.

6. U.S. Commission on Civil Rights, *Report of the United States Commission on Civil Rights 1959*
(Washington, D.C.: U.S. Government Printing Office, 1959), p. 134. Pollitt also used this quote in his
report ("The president's powers").

7. Pollitt, "The president's powers": "'This is accomplished,' states the report, 'through the creation
of legal impediments, administrative obstacles, and positive discouragement engendered by fears of
economic reprisal and physical harm.'"

The new Administration has the opportunity to be the first in 100 years of American History to adopt a radically new approach to the question of Civil Rights. It must begin, however, with the firmly fixed conviction that the question is settled. The day is past for tolerating vicious and inhuman opposition on a subject which determines the lives of 20,000,000 Americans. We are not still discussing the wisdom of democracy over monarchism and we would not permit hoodlum royalists to terrorize or dominate streets of major cities or their legislative halls. We must decide that in a new era, there must be new thinking. If we fail to make this positive decision, an awakening world will conclude that we have become a fossil nation, morally and politically, and no floods of refrigerators, automobiles or color television sets will rejuvenate our image.

The second element in a new approach is the recognition by the Federal Government that Federal power is enormous and

First two pages from handwritten draft of "Equality Now: The President Has the Power." Courtesy of the Howard Gotlieb Archival Research Center, Boston University.

~~amply~~ sufficient to guide us through
the changes ahead. If we would
search for the key problem in the
intolerably slow progress in civil
rights, we will find that the self-
imposed limits in the case of bold,
creative Federal action constitute barriers
as difficult as those erected by the
opposition.

If we examine the sum total
of all Judicial, Executive and Legislative
facts of the past three decades and
balance them against the ~~sum~~ sum
needed to achieve fundamental change,
two startling conclusions are inescapable.
The first is the hopeless inadequacy
of measures adopted — pitifully
insufficient in scope and limited in
conception. The second conclusion is
even more disturbing. Federal action in
a positive direction is diluted, diminished
and in many instances cancelled out by
Federal action in a negative direction.
The federal ~~power~~ power is
viewed as a whole, self-nullifying.
In 1954 the Judiciary declared f

ingly to change these shameful conditions. He would take such a creative general proposal as that made by the Civil Rights Commission of 1959 on Federal Registrars to insure the right to vote, and would campaign "on the Hill" and across the nation until Congress acted. He would also have the courage to insist that, in compliance with the Fourteenth Amendment, a state's representation in Congress be reduced in proportion to the number of citizens denied the right to vote because of race [see "Forgotten Remedy for the Voteless Negro," by Thomas I. Emerson and Arthur E. Bonfield, *The Nation*, January 21].[8]

This approach would help us eliminate the defeatist psychology engendered by the alliance of Dixiecrats and Northern reactionaries in Congress. The same alliance, existing in even greater strength, failed in the past to stop legislation that altered patterns just as deeply imbedded in American mores as racial discrimination. It is leadership and determination that counts—and these have been lacking of recent years.

A second area in which the President can make a significant contribution toward the elimination of racial discrimination is that of moral persuasion. The President is the embodiment of the democratic personality of the nation, both domestically and internationally. His own personal conduct influences and educates. If he were to make it known that he would not participate in any activities in which segregation exists, he would set a clear example for Americans everywhere, of every age, on a simple, easily understood level.

The calling of White House conferences of Negro and white leaders could be extremely useful. The President could serve the great purpose of opening the channels of communication between the races. Many white Southerners who, for various reasons, fear to meet with Negro leaders in their own communities would participate unhesitatingly in a biracial conference called by the President.

It is appropriate to note here that, even in the hard core South, a small but growing number of whites are breaking with the old order. These people believe in the morality as well as the Constitutionality of integration. Their still, small voices often go unheard amid the louder shouts of defiance, but they are active in the field. They often face problems of ostracism and isolation as a result of their stand. Their isolation and difficulties would be lessened if they were among the invitees to the White House to participate in a conference on desegregation.

No effort to list the President's opportunities to use the prestige of his office to further civil rights could be adequate; from fireside chats to appearances at major events, the list is endless.[9] All that is needed at the outset is a firm resolve to make the Presidency a weapon for this democratic objective; the opportunities would then arise by themselves.

But beyond the legislative area and the employment of Presidential prestige, a

---

8. In the 21 January 1961 edition of *The Nation*, Yale University professor Thomas Irwin Emerson and graduate student Arthur Earl Bonfield argued that political leader had tried to enforce Section 2 of the Fourteenth Amendment, which allows for reduction of representation in proportion to those denied the right to vote (*The Nation* 192, no. 3 [21 January 1961]: 55–59).

9. From 1933 to 1944, President Franklin D. Roosevelt delivered a series of radio addresses, known as Fireside Chats, in an effort to keep the American people abreast of political and economic issues confronting the nation.

weapon of overwhelming significance lies in the Executive itself. It is no exaggeration to say that the President could give segregation its death blow through a stroke of the pen.[10] The power inherent in Executive orders has never been exploited; its use in recent years has been microscopic in scope and timid in conception.

Historically, the Executive has promulgated orders of extraordinary range and significance. The Emancipation Proclamation was an Executive order.[11] The integration of the Armed Forces grew out of President Truman's Executive Order 8891.[12] Executive orders could require the immediate end to all discrimination in any housing accommodations financed with federal aid.[13] Executive orders could prohibit any contractor dealing with any federal agency from practicing discrimination in employment by requiring (a) cancellation of existing contracts, (b) and/or barring violators from bidding, (c) and/or calling in of government loans of federal funds extended to violators, (d) and/or requiring renegotiation of payment to exact financial penalties where violations appear after performance of a contract. With such effective penalties, enforcement of fair employment practices would become self-imposed by those enjoying billions of dollars in contracts with federal agencies.[14]

An Executive order could also bring an immediate end to the discriminatory employment policies of federal agencies and departments. It is no secret that, despite statutes to the contrary, Negroes are almost totally excluded from skilled, clerical and supervisory jobs in the federal government. A recent report of the President's Committee on Government Employment states: "That there is discrimination in federal employment is unquestionably true."[15] A basic reason for this is that there have never been any sanctions imposed for violations of the law. In a real sense, a President can eliminate discrimination in federal employment, just as it was eliminated in the military services, by setting up adequately staffed committees with authority to punish those who violate official government policy from the inside.[16]

We can easily see how an end to discriminatory practices in federal agencies would have tremendous value in changing attitudes and behavior patterns. If, for instance, the law-enforcement personnel in the FBI were integrated, many persons who now defy federal law might come under restraints from which they are presently

---

10. During the second presidential debate with Richard M. Nixon, Kennedy said that "equality of opportunity in the field of housing" could be done "by a stroke of the President's hand" ("Transcript of the Second Nixon-Kennedy Debate on Nation-Wide Television," *New York Times*, 8 October 1960).

11. Abraham Lincoln signed the Emancipation Proclamation on 22 September 1862, and it went into effect on 1 January 1863.

12. Harry S. Truman issued Executive Order 9981 on 26 July 1948.

13. On 20 November 1962, President Kennedy signed Executive Order 11063 banning discrimination in federally funded housing.

14. Pollitt's report outlined five ways the president could end discrimination in government contracts: disqualification from future contracting, termination of contract, liquidated damages, injunctive relief, and certificate of compliance. Pollitt cited a committee organized by President Harry Truman as the original source of these recommendations (Pollitt, "The president's powers").

15. Pollitt, "The president's powers." U.S. President's Committee on Government Employment Policy, *Third Report of the President's Committee on Government Employment Policy* (Washington, D.C.: U.S. Government Printing Office, 1959), p. 17.

16. Cf. Pollitt, "The president's powers."

free.[17] If other law-enforcement agencies under the Treasury Department, such as the Internal Revenue Service, the Bureau of Narcotics, the Alcohol Tax Unit, the Secret Service and Customs had an adequate number of field agents, investigators and administrators who were Negro, there would be a greater respect for Negroes as well as the assurance that prejudicial behavior in these agencies toward citizens would cease.

Another area in which an Executive order can bring an end to a considerable amount of discrimination is that of health and hospitalization. Under the Hill-Burton Act, the federal government grants funds to the states for the construction of hospitals.[18] Since this program began in 1948, more than $100 million a year has gone to the states in direct aid. The government also makes grants to the states for mental health, maternal and child-care services, and for programs designed to control tuberculosis, cancer and heart disease.[19] In spite of this sizable federal support, it is a known fact that most of the federally financed and approved health and hospitalization programs in the South are operated on a segregated basis. In many instances, the Southern Negroes are denied access to them altogether.[20]

The President could wipe out these shameful conditions almost overnight by simply ordering his Secretary of Health, Education and Welfare not to approve grants to states whose plans authorize segregation or denial of service on the basis of race.[21] This type of sanction would bring even the most recalcitrant Southerners into line.

There is hardly any area in which Executive leadership is needed more than in housing. Here the Negro confronts the most tragic expression of discrimination; he is consigned to ghettos and overcrowded conditions. And here the North is as guilty as the South.

Unfortunately, the federal government has participated directly and indirectly in the perpetuation of housing discrimination. Through the Federal Housing Administration (FHA), the Public Housing Administration (PHA), Urban Renewal Administration (URA), and the Veterans Administration Loan Program, the federal government makes possible most of the building programs in the United States. Since its creation in 1934, the FHA alone has insured more than $33 billion in mortgages involving millions of homes. As a result of PHA programs, more than two

---

17. On 7 February 1961, FBI Special Agent M.A. Jones wrote the Bureau's Deputy Director Cartha DeLoach about King's criticisms of the organization in his article published in *The Nation*. Jones recommended that the Bureau ignore King's comments because the civil rights leader would "welcome any controversy or resulting publicity that might ensue." FBI director J. Edgar Hoover handwrote "I concur" at the end of the memo.

18. Cf. Pollitt, "The president's powers." In 1946, the Hospital Survey and Construction Act (Hill-Burton), sponsored by Senators Lister Hill and Harold Burton, was passed to renovate hospitals and reduce medical fees for people who could not pay for health care.

19. Cf. Pollitt, "The president's powers."

20. Cf. Pollitt, "The president's powers."

21. Cf. Pollitt, "The president's powers." Abraham Ribicoff was the Secretary of Health, Education and Welfare from January 1961 to July 1962. An SRC report charged that no work had been done by 1961 to enforce desegregation in hospitals funded by Hill-Burton (SRC, "Executive support of civil rights," 13 March 1962). In 1963, in *G.C. Simkins et al., v. Moses H. Cone Memorial Hospital*, 323 F.2d 959, the Fourth Circuit Court of Appeals ruled that the "separate but equal" clause in Hill-Burton was unconstitutional because it discriminated against individuals on the basis of race.

million people presently live in more than 2,000 low-rent housing projects in forty-four states and the District of Columbia. The URA, which was established in 1954 to help cities eliminate slum and blighted areas, has approved projects in more than 877 localities. The GI Bill of Rights authorizes the Veterans Administration to make loans outright to veterans for the construction of homes. This program has become so extensive that there have been years in which 30 per cent of all new urban dwelling units were built with the help of VA loan guarantees.[22]

While most of these housing programs have anti-discrimination clauses, they have done little to end segregated housing. [*It?*] is a known fact that FHA continues to finance private developers who openly proclaim that none of their homes will be sold to Negroes.[23] The Urban Renewal program has, in many instances, served to accentuate, even to initiate, segregated neighborhoods. (Since a large percentage of the people to be relocated are Negroes, they are more than likely to be relocated in segregated areas.)[24]

A President seriously concerned about this problem could direct the Housing Administrator to require all participants in federal housing programs to agree to a policy of "open occupancy." Such a policy could be enforced by (a) making it mandatory for all violators to be excluded from future participation in federally financed housing programs and (b) by including a provision in each contract giving the government the right to declare the entire mortgage debt due and payable upon breach of the agreement.[25]

These are merely illustrations of acts possible of multiplication in many other fields.

Executive policy could reshape the practices and programs of other agencies and departments whose activities affect the welfare of millions. The Department of Health, Education and Welfare could be directed to coordinate its resources to give special aid in those areas of the country where assistance might change local attitudes. The department could give valuable assistance to local school boards without any additional legislative enactments.

The Department of Agriculture—which doubtless considers civil-rights issues as remote from its purview—could fruitfully reappraise its present operations with a view to taking certain steps that require no new legislative powers. The department could be of tremendous assistance to Negro farmers who are now denied credit simply because of their desire to exercise their citizenship rights. To wipe out this kind of

22. Pollitt cites the same facts in his report ("The president's powers").

23. Cf. Pollitt, "The president's powers." In New Jersey, the FHA continued in 1958 to insure builder William Levitt's development, despite his stated intention to enforce segregation and despite being approached by several African American prospective buyers. Although the FHA affirmed in 1950 that it would extend benefits to people regardless of race, color, creed, or national origin, the U.S. Commission on Civil Rights estimated that less than two percent of FHA funds made after that promise went to build homes for African Americans. Witnesses testified at the 1960 Commission on Civil Rights hearings that FHA-approved lenders and builders refused to sell homes to nonwhites in Detroit and Los Angeles (*1961 U.S. Commission on Civil Rights Report, Book 4: Housing* [Washington D.C.: U.S. Government Printing Office, 1961], pp. 31, 63–64).

24. Cf. Pollitt, "The president's powers."

25. Cf. Pollitt, "The president's powers."

discrimination would be to transform the lives of hundreds of thousands of Negroes on the land. A department zealous to implement democratic ideals might become a source of security and help to struggling farmers rather than a symbol of hostility and discrimination on the federal level.[26]

A Justice Department that is imbued with a will to create justice has vast potential. The employment of powerful court orders, enforced by sizable numbers of federal marshals, would restrain lawless elements now operating with inexcusable license. It should be remembered that in early American history it was the federal marshal who restored law in frontier communities when local authority broke down.

In the opinion of many authorities Executive power, operating through the Attorney General, opens many hitherto untried avenues for Executive action in the field of school desegregation. There are existing laws under which the Attorney General could go into court and become a force in the current school struggles.[27] Atrophy is not alone a medical phenomenon; it has its counterpart in social and political life. Long years of ignoring this area of law and Executive power have led, indeed, to atrophy; nothing is done, nothing is studied, though new situations arise constantly where existing laws could reasonably be utilized.

Space will not permit a spelling out of all the measures by which every federal body could contribute to the enforcement of civil rights. This is the task of a master plan. Nor is it necessary to detail a legislative program, nor to list still unused powers inherent in the Judiciary. Justices J. Skelley Wright and W. A. Bootle in Louisiana and Georgia respectively have given examples of the ability of a single Federal District Judge to handle the unconstitutional maneuverings of state legislatures.[28]

The purpose of this review is to emphasize that a recognition of the potentials of federal power is a primary necessity if the fight for full racial equality is to be won. With it, however, must go another indispensable factor—the recognition by the government of its moral obligation to solve the problem.

A recent visit to India revealed to me the vast opportunities open to a government determined to end discrimination.[29] When it confronted the problem of centuries-old discrimination against the "untouchables," India began its thinking at a point that we have not yet reached. Probing its moral responsibilities, it concluded that the

---

26. In August 1961, the Leadership Conference on Civil Rights, an organization composed of civil rights leaders, issued a report criticizing the informal practice requiring black farmers to have unofficial approval of a "white citizen of substance" to obtain funding from the Farmers Home Administration (FHA), a program run by the Department of Agriculture (Report on discrimination by the federal government, 29 August 1961).

27. Pollitt's report specified three recommendations: withhold financial support, exercise moral leadership, and have the Justice Department intervene in court cases regarding school integration. According to the report, the attorney general could appoint "any officer of the Department of Justice to 'attend to the interests of the United States in any suit pending in any' court, federal or state" ("The president's powers").

28. Wright, a judge for the U.S. District Court, Eastern District of Louisiana, ruled to admit black students to Louisiana State University, mandated desegregation in public accommodations in Louisiana, and in 1960 ordered the New Orleans public schools desegregated. In January 1961, Bootle ordered the University of Georgia to admit black students Charlayne Hunter and Hamilton Holmes.

29. King toured India in February and March 1959. For more on King's trip to India, see Introduction in *Papers* 5:2–12.

country must atone for the immense injustices imposed upon the untouchables. It therefore made provision not alone for equality, but for special treatment to enable the victims of discrimination to leap the gap from backwardness to competence. Thus, millions of rupees are set aside each year to provide scholarships, financial grants and special employment opportunities for the untouchables. To the argument that this is a new form of discrimination inflicted upon the majority population, the Indian people respond by saying that this is their way of atoning for the injustices and indignities heaped in the past upon their 70 million untouchable brothers.

Although discrimination has not yet been eliminated in India, the atmosphere there differs sharply from that in our country. In India, it is a crime punishable by imprisonment to practice discrimination against an untouchable. But even without this coercion, so successfully has the government made the issue a matter of moral and ethical responsibility that no government figure or political leader on any level would dare defend discriminatory practices. One could wish that we here in the United States had reached this level of morality.[30]

To coordinate the widespread activities on the civil rights front, the President should appoint a Secretary of Integration. The appointee should be of the highest qualifications, free from partisan political obligations, imbued with the conviction that the government of the most powerful nation on earth cannot lack the capacity to accomplish the rapid and complete solution to the problem of racial equality.[31]

These proposals for federal action do not obviate the necessity for the people themselves to act, of course. An Administration of good faith can be strengthened immeasurably by determined popular action. This is the great value of the non-violent direct-action movement that has engulfed the South. On the one hand, it gives large numbers of people a method of securing moral ends through moral means. On the other hand, it gives support and stimulation to all those agencies which have the power to bring about meaningful change. Thousands of courageous students, sitting peacefully at lunch counters, can do more to arouse the Administration to positive action than all of the verbal and written commentaries on governmental laxity put together.

When our government determines to ally itself with those of its citizens who are crusading for their freedom within our borders, and lends the might of its resources creatively and unhesitatingly to the struggle, the blight of discrimination will begin rapidly to fade.

History has thrust upon the present Administration an indescribably important destiny—to complete a process of democratization which our nation has taken far too long to develop, but which is our most powerful weapon for earning world

---

30. In an *Ebony* magazine article about his trip to India King applauded Indian leaders for placing "their moral power" behind anti-discrimination laws: "But in the United States some of our highest officials decline to render a moral judgment on segregation and some from the South publicly boast of their determination to maintain segregation. This would be unthinkable in India" (King, "My Trip to the Land of Gandhi," July 1959, in *Papers* 5:236).

31. Percival Prattis, executive editor of the *Pittsburgh Courier*, disagreed with King's suggestion that Kennedy should appoint a Secretary of Integration, arguing that such a position would have much to gain in promoting segregation as it would integration (Prattis to King, 17 February 1961; King to Prattis, 26 April 1961, pp. 208–209 in this volume).

respect and emulation. How we deal with this crucial problem of racial discrimination will determine our moral health as individuals, our political health as a nation,
our prestige as a leader of the free world. I can think of few better words for the
guidance of the new Administration than those which concluded the 1946 report of
the President's Commission on Civil Rights: "The United States is not so strong, the
final triumph of the democratic ideal not so inevitable that we can ignore what the
world thinks of us or our record."[32] These words are even more apt today than on
the day they were written.

PD. *The Nation* 192, no. 5 (4 February 1961): 91–95.

---

32. President's Committee on Civil Rights, *To Secure These Rights: The Report of the President's Committee
on Civil Rights* (Washington, D.C.: U.S. Government Printing Office, 1947), p. 148.

# To Nathan Paul Feinsinger

6 February 1961
[*Atlanta, Ga.*]

*In 1958 Anthony Stephens, a former vice president of the United Packinghouse
Workers of America (UPWA), charged that the union had fallen under communist
influence. The following year, King joined the Public Review Advisory Committee
created by the union to investigate the charges.[1] In this letter to the chairman
of the commission, King approves of a draft report of the investigation.[2] "There
were probably some Communist influences in UPWA in the 40s and maybe in the
early 50s," King wrote, however, the union is now "following a road of honest
Democratic trade unionism." Feinsinger attached the letter below to his final
report.[3]*

---

1. Ralph Helstein to King, 8 July 1959. The commission included church, labor, and academic leaders (UPWA, "Report of Public Review Advisory Commission of United Packinghouse, Food, and Allied
Workers of America, AFL-CIO," 15 February 1961).

2. The UPWA Executive Board appointed a subcommittee of UPWA officials to investigate the
charges of Communist membership in the union (Russell R. Lasley, Frank Schultz, Glenn Chinander,
George Thomas, and Dave Hart, "Report of the subcommittee of the international executive board,"
6 May 1960). After investigating twenty-four members of the union, the subcommittee found no basis
for Stephens's claims of communist infiltration and declared the UPWA in full compliance with the
requirements of the AFL-CIO's Ethical Practices Code. Nathan Paul Feinsinger (1902–1983), was born
in Brooklyn, New York, received a J.D. in 1928 from the University of Michigan, and had a forty-four year
career as a professor of law at the University of Wisconsin. While at the university, Feinsinger founded the
Center for Teaching and Research in Dispute Settlement. He served on the War Labor Relations Board
(1942–1945) and the Wage Stabilization Board (1951–1952).

3. UPWA, "Report of Public Review Advisory Commission of United Packinghouse, Food, and
Allied Workers of America, AFL-CIO."

Professor Nathan P. Feinsinger          6 Feb
University of Wisconsin                 1961
Madison, Wisconsin

Dear Professor Feinsinger:

First, let me apologize for being somewhat tardy in writing you concerning my reaction to the draft of the report of the Public Review Advisory Commission. A series of long standing speaking commitments, plus the excitement accompanying the birth of our third child a few days ago, kept me out of the office well nigh ten days.[4] This accounts for the delay.

I have read the report very scrutinizingly and I think it is so well done and so thoroughly states the issues involved that there is very little, if anything, that I can suggest in terms of expansion or deletion.

I was very impressed with the sincerity and good faith of the Sub-committee. Their honest and forthright answers to our questions convinced me that they went about their job with a maximum of good faith and intelligence. Therefore, I think we are on solid ground in accepting the Sub-committee's report.

I have tried to study this whole issue with as much objectivity as humanly possible. As I have read the various documents and thought through the various facets of the problem, I have reached two conclusions. First, I feel that there were probably some Communist influences in UPWA in the 40's and maybe in the early 50's. I feel, as you do, that the union should have taken a more vigorous and forthright stand against Communism after it was accused of such influences. This would have made it palpably clear that their endorsement of the AFL-CIO Codes of Ethical Practices was more than a perfunctory gesture. On the other hand, I am convinced that UPWA has gone a long, long way in solving this internal problem and that it is now following a road of honest Democratic trade unionism. While you have rightly stated that we are not trying the accuser, I cannot help but feel that Mr. Stevens' actions were consciously or unconsciously motivated by something much deeper than a desire to expose alleged Comminism in the union.[5]

I say all of this to say that I am in complete agreement with the report you have drafted for the Commission. I can only hope that our acceptance of the Sub-committee's report and the accompanying constructive criticism will serve to help a union that has had its problems and growing pains realize its great potential and continue to move in line with the noble principles of trade unionism.

Very sincerely yours,
Martin Luther King, Jr.

Km

TLc. MLKP-MBU.

---

4. On 30 January, Coretta Scott King gave birth to the couple's third child, Dexter Scott.

5. After trying to usurp control of the UPWA from president Ralph Helstein, Stephens was fired from the union and later accused the union of being overrun by communists (Leslie F. Orear, Interview by Cyril Robinson, 31 March 1995).

# From Bayard Rustin

6 February 1961
New York, N.Y.

*In May 1960, writer James Baldwin shadowed King for an article he was writing
for* Harper's Magazine.[1] *Following the publication of the article in February
1961, Rustin, King's longtime advisor, objects to Baldwin's portrayal of his
resignation from SCLC.[2] In a 6 March reply to Rustin, King wrote that he had
thought about responding to Baldwin's article, but decided that it would be "better
coming from you."*[3]

Dear Martin,

You have no doubt seen James Baldwin's article on you in Harper's Magazine.
I was distressed with his comment on me and my relation to you.

I have therefore, today, sent Harpers Magazine a copy of the enclosed letter.[4]
I tried to handle it simply. I presume Jim Lawson will write a similar letter.[5]

Hope all goes well with you and the hard job you have to do.

Sincerely,
[*signed*] Bayard

AHLS. MLKP-MBU.

---

1. Baldwin to King, 26 May 1960, in *Papers* 5:460–461.

2. In the article, Baldwin wrote that King lost "moral credit" when he allowed pressure from Congressman Adam Clayton Powell to force Rustin's resignation from SCLC ("The Dangerous Road Before Martin Luther King," *Harper's Magazine*, February 1961, p. 42).

3. King to Rustin, 6 March 1961. King later wrote Baldwin thanking him for the "many kind things you said about me and my work in the article," and made no mention of the Rustin controversy (see King to Baldwin, 26 September 1961, pp. 286–287 in this volume).

4. In the letter, Rustin explained that he had resigned from SCLC because Powell "suggested that I am an obstacle to his giving full, enthusiastic support to Dr. King" (Rustin to the Editor of *Harper's Magazine*, 6 February 1961).

5. In his article, Baldwin also questioned the exclusion of James M. Lawson from SCLC: "It would seem, certainly, that so able, outspoken, and energetic a man might prove of great value to this organization: why, then, is he not a part of it?" (Baldwin, "The Dangerous Road," p. 42). Responding to a query to King about Lawson's relationship to SCLC, James R. Wood emphatically stated that Lawson had been a member of SCLC since October 1960. "Very often opinion articles create concepts which are more personal to the writer than factually correct," Wood wrote. He further elaborated that "Mr. Lawson is a personal friend of Dr. King. This friendship has existed for a very long time" (June Megill to King, 1 March 1961; Wood to June Megill, 27 March 1961).

# To J. R. Butts

8 February 1961
Atlanta, Ga.

*King writes the chairman of the board of deacons of West Hunter Baptist Church*
*in Atlanta to recommend his friend Ralph Abernathy as a replacement for the*
*church's recently deceased pastor, A. Franklin Fisher.[1] Fearing that Abernathy*
*would accept a call from a northern church, King admits that his recommendation*
*is for selfish reasons: "I just don't think we can afford to lose Ralph Abernathy*
*from the south at this momentous period of our history." King urged other*
*ministers to recommend Abernathy as well.[2] Abernathy accepted the call to West*
*Hunter in August 1961.[3]*

Mr. J. R. Butts
152 Raymond Street, S.W.
Atlanta,
Georgia

Dear Mr. Butts:

Since the passing of your pastor and my good friend and coworker, The Rev.
A. Franklin Fisher, you and West Hunter Baptist Church have been greatly in my
thoughts. It is always a serious and sacred thing to call a pastor to a church. I know
that you and the Board are now going through the process of selecting a man that
will give West Hunter the leadership that its great heritage deserves.[4]

If it is not being too presumptuous, I would like to recommend a man to you who
is superbly equipped to give West Hunter a unique pastorate and leadership. I refer
to The Rev. Ralph David Abernathy, pastor of the First Baptist Church, Montgomery,

---

1. Albert Franklin Fisher was the pastor of West Hunter Baptist Church from 1948 until his death
in November 1960. Upon Fisher's death, a West Hunter parishioner wrote King asking if he might be
interested in filling the vacancy. King declined the offer, but recommended Ralph Abernathy as a suit-
able replacement (King to Samuel L. Spear, 16 December 1960, in *Papers* 5:581–582). Joseph Roney Butts
(1886–1969) was born in McDuffie County, Georgia. He worked for the Atlanta Board of Education.
Butts joined West Hunter Baptist Church in 1914 and served as a deacon, a trustee, and chairman of
the board of deacons. As deacon, Butts was instrumental to West Hunter's efforts to build a new church
during the 1950s. Abernathy officiated at Butts's funeral in February 1969.

2. King solicited letters of recommendation from A.A. Banks, pastor of Second Baptist Church in
Detroit; J. Raymond Henderson, pastor of Second Baptist Church in Los Angeles; Gardner C. Taylor,
pastor of Concord Baptist Church of Christ in Brooklyn; and O. Clay Maxwell, pastor of Mount Olivet
Baptist Church in New York (King to Banks, 10 February 1961; King to Henderson, 15 February 1961; King
to Taylor, 16 February 1961; King to Maxwell, 9 February 1961).

3. On 11 February 1962 King preached at Abernathy's installation service at West Hunter (see pp.
385–394 in this volume).

4. According to Abernathy's 1989 autobiography, the church also considered giving the pastorate to
Wyatt Tee Walker, who had been filling in since Fisher's death (*And the Walls Came Tumbling Down* [New
York: Harper & Row], pp. 197–198).

Alabama.[5] Very seldom do I go to the point of giving anyone an absolute and an unqualified recommendation. But I can do this for him because I am absolutely convinced that he is one of the most capable men in our nation today. As a preacher he is powerful profound, and dynamic. As a pastor, he has proved to be exceptionally efficient. As a community leader, he has few equals. His character is above repute and his dedication to the Christian ministry unquestioned. Because of his leadership in the Montgomery community he is one of the best loved ministers in the United States today. For all of these reasons I think Ralph Abernathy could bring to your church something that could hardly be matched by anyone else. I have always felt that West Hunter has potentialities for one of the truly great churches of our nation. I am sure that a man like Ralph Abernathy could bring these vast potentialities into actuality. He would have a unique appeal to all classes of people. He has great ability to move the masses and he also greatly appeals to the so-called intelligentsia. I am convinced that a man of his stature, his organizational ability, and his tremendous preaching ability would double the membership of West Hunter in a short period.

Briefly, let me give you a biographical sketch of Rev. Abernathy's life. He was born in Demopolis, Alabama thirty four years ago.[6] He holds an A.B. degree from Alabama State College, and M.A. from Atlanta University. He has an honorary degree from Allen University; has pastored at the First Baptist Church of Demopolis, Alabama; taught at Alabama State College for three years, and is presently pastor of the historic First Baptist Church of Montgomery. He is married and has three children (two girls and a boy).[7]

I hope you will find it possible to invite him to preach at West Hunter.[8] While I cannot definitely say that he would accept a call, I do believe that he would give it serious consideration.[9] I must admit that I have something of a selfish reason for wanting West Hunter to consider him. I happen to know that two churches in the north are presently interested in calling him, and I am afraid that he may accept one of them if he is not called to a church in the south very soon. I just don't think we can afford to lose Ralph Abernathy from the south at this momentous period of our history.

Again let me say that you are very much in my thought and prayers as you embark upon this sacred responsibility of calling a pastor. If I can be of any assistance to you, please feel free to call on me.

Sincerely yours,
Martin Luther King, Jr.

Km

TLc. SCLCR-GAMK: Box 1.

---

5. Abernathy had been pastor of First Baptist Church since 1952.

6. Abernathy was born in Linden, Alabama, on 11 March 1926.

7. King refers to Abernathy's wife, Juanita, and his children, Juandalynn, Donzaleigh, and Ralph David III.

8. Abernathy preached at West Hunter in early May 1961 ("Rev. Abernathy to Preach at West Hunter," *Atlanta Daily World*, 6 May 1961).

9. In his autobiography, Abernathy recalled initially not being interested in leaving Montgomery or his congregation at First Baptist Church (*And the Walls*, p. 193).

# To Robert Clifton Weaver

13 February 1961
[*Atlanta, Ga.*]

*Sending a copy of his* Nation *article "Equality Now," King congratulates Weaver on his appointment and confirmation to head the Housing and Home Finance Agency (HHFA).*[1] *The appointment elevated Weaver to the highest federal post ever held by an African American.*[2] *Weaver thanked King on 21 February 1961, saying that he found the article "most interesting."*

Dr. Robert K. Weaver, Administrator
Housing and Home Finance Agency
1626 K Street, N W.
Washington 25, D.C.

Dear Dr. Weaver:

Enclosed is a re-print of an article which I wrote over the Christmas holidays. I thought you may be interested in reading it. I was amazed to discover, after careful research, the powerful things that the President can do in the area of civil rights through Executive Orders. I hope that through the necessary pressure and persuasion we will be able to bring many of these possibilities into full realization under the new administration. I tried to bring some of these things out in the article.

May I take this way to congratulate you for being appointed and confirmed to serve in the highest post than any Negro has ever held in the federal government. I am convinced that Mr. Kennedy could not have found a better man for the job any-

---

1. See King, "Equality Now," 4 February 1961, pp. 139–150 in this volume. King also sent copies to Whitney Young, Roy Wilkins, Thurgood Marshall, and Harris Wofford, whom he asked for suggestions "on how I can best get this to President Kennedy so that he will actually read it" (King to Young, King to Wilkins, King to Marshall, and King to Wofford, all dated 13 February 1961). Although Weaver faced opposition from members of the Senate Banking Currency Committee, who disagreed with his views on integration and believed he had associated with subversive organizations, he was confirmed on 8 February and was sworn in three days later. Robert Clifton Weaver (1907–1997) was born in Washington, D.C., and earned a B.S. (1929) and an M.A. (1931) in economics from Harvard University. After graduation, Weaver taught economics at North Carolina A&T College for one year, and in 1932 returned to Harvard to complete his Ph.D. (1934) in economics. In 1933 Weaver began his political career as advisor to Secretary of the Interior Harold L. Ickes. As a member of the Federal Council of Negro Affairs (also known as the "Black Cabinet") in Franklin D. Roosevelt's administration, Weaver had by then become one of the most influential African Americans in government. In 1960 he chaired the board of directors of the NAACP. In 1966 President Lyndon B. Johnson nominated Weaver to lead the Department of Housing and Urban Development (HUD), a position he held until 1969. Weaver subsequently taught at Hunter College, Columbia Teachers' College, and New York University.

2. Kennedy had also planned to nominate Weaver to head the new Department of Urban Affairs, which would have made Weaver the first African American cabinet member, but Congress voted against creating the department (Weaver, Interview by Daniel P. Moynihan, 6 May 1964; "Congress Shelves Kennedy Plan to Form Cabinet-Level Urban Affairs Department," *Wall Street Journal*, 8 September 1961; see also King, Statement to *Newsweek* Magazine, 26 February 1962, p. 411 in this volume).

where in the country. I know that we will see many new and creative developments in the area of housing under your leadership. If I can ever be of any assistance to you at any point, please feel free to call on me. I would like to stop in to chat with you a few minutes when I am in Washington in the very near future.

Sincerely yours,
Martin Luther King, Jr.

Km

TLc. MLKP-MBU.

## "Self-Portrait of a Symbol: Martin Luther King"

13 February 1961
New York, N.Y.

*On 7–8 February, King appeared on "The Mike Wallace Interviews" on WNTA-TV. Wallace had interviewed King in 1958 for a column he wrote for the* New York Post.[1] *During his appearances King clarifies his views regarding the distinction between just and unjust laws. He also denies organizational conflict between NAACP and SCLC. Responding to Wallace's comparison of King with Jesus, Henry David Thoreau, and Gandhi, he says: "Their ideas were greater, and I feel that I am dependent upon them, and I've been greatly inspired by them and influenced by them." He also discusses his increasing comfort with his role as a symbol in the civil rights movement: "I'm bent on doing what I think is right, and I think this is a great cause and I'm caught up in it and I get a great internal satisfaction as a result of this." The transcripts of the interviews were published in the* New York Post *over the course of three days.*[2]

WALLACE: Our guest is the leader of a new movement in the American Negro's struggle for dignity and equality. In the words of one reporter: "The new gospel of the American Negro is rooted in the theology of desegregation. Its major prophets are Christ, Thoreau, Gandhi and Martin Luther King."[3]

We'll talk with Martin Luther King about this new gospel, about the sit-ins in the South, and we'll ask him to explain what he calls "the tragic fact that the federal government is the nation's highest investor in segregation."[4]

Dr. King, a recent article in Harper's magazine talking about the struggle now

---

1. Wallace (1918–2012) rose to prominence in 1957 for his show "Night Beat." For Wallace's 1958 interview with King, see King, Interview by Mike Wallace, 25 June 1958, in *Papers* 4:431–441.

2. The transcripts were also published in the Baltimore *Afro-American* on 4–18 March 1961.

3. Wallace quotes from Louis E. Lomax, "The Negro Revolt against 'The Negro Leaders,'" *Harper's Magazine,* June 1960, p. 42.

4. See King, "Equality Now," 4 February 1961, p. 140 in this volume.

going on within the ranks of the American Negro had this to say: "For nearly a century a small ruling class has served as spokesman and has planned the strategy for all American Negroes." And it goes on: "Now it is being overwhelmed by an upsurge of aggressive young people who feel that the NAACP is far too conservative and slow-moving."[5] So my question to you is, how serious is this struggle within the ranks of the American Negro?

KING: Well, I don't think the present problem—the present revolt—is against the NAACP as such. I think the revolt is against the snail-like pace of the implementation of the Supreme Court decision on desegregation in 1954. Now, the NAACP isn't responsible for this, but it's often accused, because it is the organization that has worked through the channel of legalism to achieve citizenship rights for Negroes. But I don't think it is valid to say that it is the NAACP that is bringing about, or rather using, the delaying methods—the delaying tactics. It is rather the forces at work in the South that are seeking to delay and nullify the decision.

WALLACE: The New York Times has said something a little bit different from that. They say, "There has been some conflict between the NAACP and the Southern Christian Leadership Conference," which is the group that you've organized. And then the Times goes on to say this: "Roy Wilkins, executive secretary of the NAACP, and King have sought to hold it" [i.e., the conflict] to a minimum, "but some of the more ambitious men in the SCLC have made no secret of their scorn for the NAACP, calling it the Black Bourgeoise Club, and worse."[6] And you know that there is a joke in Harlem to the effect that the NAACP is the "National Association of *Certain* People."[7] So what really is at the core of this conflict?

### No Official Conflict

KING: I don't think there's any conflict. Certainly this isn't the official policy of SCLC or the NAACP. As in any organization, you may have individuals who have their points of view, but as far as the organization itself taking a stand against the NAACP, or the NAACP taking a stand against the SCLC, this isn't true and we have worked together very cooperatively on various projects. In the other registration drive, in the various pilgrimages that we have had to Washington, and in so many other areas so that there isn't any conflict on the basis of the official policy of either organization.

WALLACE: Well, then what is the conflict between individuals in the two groups? Is it a question of direct action on the part of SCLC versus more legal action on the part of NAACP?

---

5. In his *Harper's Magazine* article, Lomax argued that the sit-in protests demonstrated impatience among African Americans with traditional top-down leadership and that organizations would have to accept "being servants rather than catalysts" to survive (Lomax, "The Negro Revolt," p. 48).

6. Claude Sitton, "Dr. King, Symbol of the Segregation Struggle," *New York Times Magazine*, 22 January 1961. At the SCLC-sponsored founding conference of the Student Nonviolent Coordinating Committee (SNCC) in April 1960, James M. Lawson reportedly criticized the NAACP for being "too conservative" and stated that its magazine, *The Crisis*, was for the "black bourgeois club" (Sitton, "Negro Criticizes N.A.A.C.P. Tactics," *New York Times*, 17 April 1960; Roy Wilkins to King, 27 April 1960, in *Papers* 5:444–446).

7. During the 1910s and 1920s African American writer Hubert Harrison and activist Marcus Garvey referred to the NAACP as the "National Association for the Advancement of Certain People."

KING: Well, this is a matter of emphasis here. SCLC is committed to non-violent action as an approach to the problem. The NAACP has worked mainly in the area of legal strategy and has achieved excellence in this area. But this is not to say the NAACP has ignored the other approaches. The NAACP has worked in the area of non-violent direct action also.[8]

WALLACE: Also, they're late to the game. Wasn't the NAACP's hand forced to a certain extent by the activities particularly of certain of the Negro young people of the South?

KING: Well, I don't know about that. I'm certain they could answer that a little better than I can, but I would simply say that the NAACP has supported the sit-in movement. They have supported it financially, helping the students in the court cases that they faced, and I don't think there has been any negative statement concerning the sit-ins from the officials of the National Association.[9]

WALLACE: So you, Martin Luther King, are perfectly satisfied with the progress that is being made by the NAACP?

KING: Oh, I think the NAACP has done more than any other organization to achieve citizenship rights for Negro people in the U.S. and I would say that our organization does not seek to substitute for the NAACP but to supplement the noble work that has been done. And I think we can work together in a very cooperative and creative manner. There need be no conflict.

WALLACE: All right, sir, let's move to something else. We've been hearing for a long time that the Supreme Court decision to desegregate the public schools is the law of the land. The NAACP has been trying to impress this upon the segregationists in the South. Now you come along and have said in defense of your methods from time to time, and I think I quote you accurately, "When conscience tells someone that a law is unjust, then I think a righteous man has no alternative but to conscientiously disobey that law."[10] Is there no conflict here?

KING: Well, not for me. I think when we deal with this question, we must face the fact that there are two types of laws—what I call just laws and unjust laws. Now, what is a just law and what is an unjust law? I would say that an unjust; first on the moral plane, is a law that serves to degrade the human personality—a law that stands against that which is morally right, what I call the moral laws of the universe.

### On What's Just and Unjust

Now, this would only appeal to those persons who are religious or who have a philosophical bent. So I would say there are other things that we must say would constitute an immoral or unjust law. I would say that a law is unjust where the majority enforces a code on the minority which is not binding on itself. Also, a law which

---

8. In the summer of 1958, members of the NAACP youth councils in Wichita, Kansas, and Oklahoma City, Oklahoma, initiated sit-in demonstrations which led to the desegregation of several local and statewide lunch counters and drugstores.

9. At its 1960 annual convention, the NAACP passed a resolution backing the lunch counter sit-in, promising "moral, financial, legal, consultant, and participatory" aid to demonstrators (Farnsworth Fowle, "N.A.A.C.P. Upholds Students' Sit-Ins," *New York Times*, 26 June 1960).

10. Sitton, "Dr. King, Symbol of the Segregation Struggle."

comes into being which all the people had no part in bringing into being, in creating or enacting. This is true in the South where many Negroes don't vote. So I would use all these arguments for the basis of an unjust law.

On the other hand, a just law is a law in which we have respect for the dignity of the human personality, from the moral point of view, and on the other hand, a law in which all the people had the right to participate by voting and a law in which the majority enforces a code that the minority will have to follow, but the majority itself follows.

Now, this is a sameness made legal, where on the other hand you have difference made legal. So I would say when we find an unjust law, on the basis of all these points that I've brought out, a moral individual has no alternative but to take a stand against that law—to protest it, not to evade it, not to defy it. I'm against defiance of the law, seeking to evade it, but I mean to openly disobey that unjust law and willingly accept the penalty in order to arouse the conscience of the community so that it will ultimately be altered.

WALLACE: Would you and the NAACP agree, sir, that the Southern whites, if they feel that a law is unjust, have the same right or duty to consciously disobey that law?

### Opposes Defiance of Law

KING: Well, I would say on that question, if they actually feel that these laws are unjust—say the laws calling for integration of the schools—if they actually feel this, on the basis of conscience, and if they can also prove to themselves that this is something that the majority is forcing on them, and the majority is not following it itself, then I'd say they would have a right.

But they can't prove that. Number one, I would doubt very seriously if most of these people deep down within think it's right morally. On the other hand, I think they rationalize sometimes and try to convince themselves it's right. But on the other hand, the majority, the people of the nation, accept this, and not only do they accept it, they follow it. So I think they are wrong in disobeying it. But if they, on the basis of conscience after all of this, decide to disobey it, I think they should certainly do it peacefully and non-violently, and this is what they are not doing. They are seeking to evade the law. They are seeking to defy the law. And I think this is wrong, and I think these persons should be condemned morally and legally for doing this.

PD. *New York Post*, 13 February 1961.

14 February 1961
New York, N.Y.

WALLACE: Dr. King, do you feel that there is no feeling among some Negro leaders that the methods of sit-ins and economic boycotts, which you and your group employ—that there's no feeling that they have perhaps alienated many Southern moderates who were formerly more sympathetic to your cause?

KING: Well, I am sure there are some Negroes who feel this. I don't think it's a majority opinion. I think there are some few.

WALLACE: Some older, more conservative groups, perhaps?

KING: Well, there are some few, yes. But I don't think this would be the majority. I think the vast majority of Negroes and Negro leaders feel that they are good.

WALLACE: Is there some small minority, too, who feel that you're not moving fast enough?

KING: Well, I'm sure there are.

## Moving Too Fast?

WALLACE: For example, did you share the concern of some Negro leaders over the mass wade-ins in which Negro bathers hit public, but segregated, beaches last summer.[11] One Negro leader said, "We must keep moving all right, but this is too fast. Half-naked bathers raised the sexual fears that are at the bottom of the whole racial question in the South."[12] Did you feel that that was moving too fast?

KING: Well, I think we have to work in many areas simultaneously and I think as we know we are in a period of social transition and whenever we find ourselves in such a period, various methods will be used, and I would not condemn the wade-in approach. Maybe some things are more important right now, if you put a sort of hierarchy here and say that this should be at the top and other things following. But I would not say, of course, that the wade-in should be thrown out altogether.

WALLACE: In the current issue of The Nation magazine, Dr. King, you say, "The intolerably slow pace of civil rights is due at least as much to the limits which the federal government has imposed on its own action as it is to the action of the segregationist opposition," and then you add this: "We must face the tragic fact that the federal government is the nation's highest investor in segregation."[13] What did you mean by that?

KING: The federal government has done more. I mean it places more money in segregated situations than anything in the nation.

## Bias Examples Cited

WALLACE: For instance?

KING: Most of the housing in the U.S. would fall somewhere under the federal government, either FHA, PHA, urban renewal or veterans' loans. Now, it is a known fact that in many of these housing situations, many of these agencies have received money from the federal government. We find outright discrimination. Levittown [N.J.], for instance, is a situation where they boasted that they would not allow Negroes to live, and many of the houses were built with FHA loans.[14]

These are common situations. Not only housing, airports are constructed every day, every week and every month in the South—with federal funds, and yet many of them have segregated facilities. Hospitals are constructed almost every week

---

11. African Americans in Biloxi, Mississippi, were attacked and arrested in April 1960 while attempting to swim at an "all-white" beach maintained by public funds.

12. Quoted in Loudon Wainwright, "Martyr of the Sit-Ins: Dr. Martin Luther King Gets New Woe, Prestige," Life, 7 November 1960, p. 132.

13. See King, "Equality Now," 4 February 1961, p. 140 in this volume.

14. Although the Federal Housing Administration (FHA) pledged to extend benefits to people regardless of race, color, creed, or national origin in 1950, the U.S. Commission of Civil Rights estimated that less than two percent of FHA funds were allocated to African Americans in 1959. In Levittown, New Jersey, the FHA insured the builder's development despite his public intention to enforce segregation.

throughout Southern communities with funds from the Hill-Burden Act.[15] Yet, these hospitals practice open discrimination. The same thing in businesses and industries receiving big money—receiving government contracts—and yet they refuse in many instances to employ Negroes and if they do, in many instances they are employed in discriminatory capacities.[16] So this is what I mean.

WALLACE: Whose fault is it that this situation exists?

KING: Well, it's the fault of the government itself on the one hand, and the fault of the people on the other hand for not pressing the government more to end the situation.

WALLACE: In your article you say, "It is leadership and determination that count, and these have been lacking in recent years."[17] Are you pointing the finger at President Eisenhower on that score, Dr. King?

KING: Well, honesty impels me to say that I don't think Mr. Eisenhower gave the leadership that the problem demanded. I would say that I don't think he's a man of ill will, but I don't think he ever understood the depths and dimensions of this problem. And I am convinced that if he had taken a strong forthright stand, many of the problems and the tensions that we face in the South today would be non-existent.[18]

WALLACE: You say in this article, "A truly decisive President would work passionately and unrelentingly to change these shameful conditions."[19] Do you think that President Kennedy will meet this challenge?

KING: I think he has a real opportunity. I think he understands the problem and I think he has a real concern and I'm very hopeful. I hope I'm not engaging in a superficial optimism, but I'm very hopeful about the possibilities. Now, I don't think he will do it without the aid and the support that will come from forces working to implement the Supreme Court's decision in the community itself. Unless the people act, the President himself may not act. The people can greatly strengthen the President as he moves on in this type of action.

WALLACE: When he was still a Senator, and running for President just before the election, Mr. Kennedy made a phone call to your wife expressing his sympathy on your arrest down in Georgia. And recently a New York Times reporter said, "There is considerable evidence that the telephone call enhanced the Democratic nominee's standing with the Negro voters."[20]

---

15. In 1946 Senators J. Lister Hill and Harold Burton sponsored the Hospital Survey and Construction Act, which sought to modernize hospitals.

16. In May 1961, the President's Committee on Equal Employment Opportunity, headed by Vice President Lyndon B. Johnson, threatened to seek contract cancellation with Lockheed Aircraft Corporation unless Lockheed desegregated its facilities and provide its African American employees more training and job advancement opportunities.

17. See King, "Equality Now," 4 February 1961, p. 144 in this volume.

18. King made a similar claim in a 6 November 1960 interview, adding that, given Dwight D. Eisenhower's popularity, "he could have at least used moral persuasion to get people to see that this is the law of the land, it is morally right, and this is something that we as a nation must do in order to maintain our position in the world" (King, Interview by Zenas Sears on "For Your Information," in *Papers* 5:549).

19. See King, "Equality Now," 4 February 1961, pp. 141, 144 in this volume.

20. In a 27 November 1960 *New York Times* article, Anthony Lewis cited Kennedy's call to Coretta Scott King as "the most important single campaign move" (Anthony Lewis, "Negro Vote Held Vital to Kennedy," *New York Times*, 27 November 1960). For more on Kennedy's call, see Introduction in *Papers* 5:36–40.

And then only two months later, an attempt by Senate liberals to change the filibuster rule was defeated, as you remember, and another reporter observed that one phone call from President Kennedy at that time might have swung the vote to the liberals.[21] Were you disappointed about the fact that Mr. Kennedy did not make that phone call, or try to swing that vote, to change the filibuster rule.

## What Can President Do?

KING: Well, of course, many people would argue that it's changed, we will not get the type of meaningful legislation in civil rights that we so desperately need. And I would certainly hope that the President will take a determined stand on this issue and seek to use the whole weight of his office to do it, and if he failed to do it this time, I think it's a mistake, and I think he should seek to do it next time.

WALLACE: What, specifically, can he do? You have said, "The President could give segregation its death blow through the stroke of a pen."[22] What can Kennedy do?

KING: Well, I think he can work in three main areas. I think he should use his influence with the legislative branch of the government—this can be done, and it has been done in the past, and I think he can do it in this situation, using his influence to cause the legislative branch to render meaningful legislation.

Secondly, the President can move in the realm of moral persuasion. His very personal power can be a great force in bringing about integration and solving the problems which we face in this area. If the President refuses to participate in any way in anything that is segregated, if he from time to time will counsel the nation on television about the moral implications involved, this would be great. And finally, probably, I think, the most decisive area is that of executive order.

The President has the power, with a stroke of the pen, as I said in that article, to end many of these conditions in housing that I mentioned earlier, in employment, and in hospital and health areas. These are some of the things that he could end almost overnight. And we must never forget that the Emancipation Proclamation was an executive order, as well as ending segregation in the Army.[23] And there are many, many areas where the President can end segregation in this way.

## Serious Suggestion

WALLACE: You've even talked about a Secretary of Integration.
KING: Yes.
WALLACE: Did you make that suggestion seriously?
KING: I certainly did. I think this is vital. I think this is necessary. And if we are going to solve this problem, I think ultimately we must mobilize all of the forces that

---

21. When the Senate convened in early January 1961, a motion to change the requirements needed to filibuster was tabled by fifty senators favoring the change. Senate Majority Leader Mike Mansfield recommended tabling the bill out of fears that it "could disrupt the party unity needed" to pass Kennedy's legislative program ("Mansfield Urges Filibuster Foes to Defer a Fight," *New York Times*, 12 December 1960).

22. See King, "Equality Now," 4 February 1961, p. 145 in this volume.

23. Abraham Lincoln signed the Emancipation Proclamation on 22 September 1862, and it went into effect on 1 January 1863. On 26 July 1948 Harry S. Truman issued Executive Order 9981 mandating the desegregation of the military.

we can possibly gain behind the process of integration, and I think one of the ways is through a Secretary of Integration.[24]

WALLACE: Do you have a man in mind for the job?

KING: No, I haven't gone that far. I think there are many, many capable persons who could work in this area.

WALLACE: Are you hopeful that President Kennedy will do some of these things you suggest?

KING: I certainly am, and I plan to submit these plans to him—some of the things that I suggested in the article.[25] And I certainly hope that he will follow through.

PD. *New York Post*, 14 February 1961.

15 Feb
1961

15 February 1961
New York, N.Y.

WALLACE: Dr. King, your name has been mentioned in the same breath with Christ, Thoreau, Gandhi. You've been called a saint by some. Does that sort of thing please you or does it ever worry you a bit?

KING: Well, I would say that it proves to be quite embarrassing sometimes, because when I compare myself with all these great persons that have entered human history, I can see such a great difference. I am sure that the commitment of all proved to be much greater than my commitment. Their ideas were greater, and I feel that I am dependent upon them, and I've been greatly inspired by them and influenced by them.

WALLACE: You understand the necessity, though, of people comparing you, of using you as a symbol?

KING: Well, I always appreciate people holding me in high esteem and I think we all have a desire to be appreciated and to be respected, but I don't want anybody to feel that I'm a Christ, or that I'm a Gandhi or that I'm a Thoreau.

## Ideas Personified

WALLACE: But when discussing your importance as a symbol recently, you said this: You said, "People cannot become devoted to Christianity until they find Christ, to democracy until they find [*Abraham*] Lincoln and [*Thomas*] Jefferson and [*Franklin D.*] Roosevelt, to communism until they find [*Karl*] Marx and [*Vladimir*] Lenin and [*Joseph*] Stalin."[26]

KING: Well, I think it's quite true that people are often led to causes and often become committed to great ideas through persons who personify those ideas. They have to find the embodiment of the idea in flesh and blood in order to commit themselves to it.

---

24. For a fuller discussion on King's idea of a Secretary of Integration, see King, "Equality Now," 4 February 1961, and King to Percival Leroy Prattis, 26 April 1961, pp. 149 and 208–209 in this volume, respectively.

25. Despite several requests since March 1961 to meet with Kennedy, King did not meet with the president until October 1961 (King to Kennedy, 16 March 1961, King, Press Conference after Meeting with John F. Kennedy, 16 October 1961, pp. 175 and 308–311 in this volume, respectively).

26. Quoted in Wainwright, "Martyr of the Sit-Ins," p. 123.

WALLACE: What happens to a man when he becomes owned by a cause? What happens to you as you become the symbol of the segregation struggle? As a man?

KING: It has its advantages and its disadvantages.

When you are aware that you are a symbol, it causes you to search your soul constantly, to go through this job of self-analysis, to see if you live up to all of the high and noble principles that people surround you with, and to try at all times to keep the gulf between the public self and private self at a minimum—to bridge this gulf so that it serves at least to inspire the individual to seek to rise from the is-ness of his present nature to the eternal ought-ness that forever confronts him. On the other hand, it has its disadvantages in that you do lose some of your individual life, your private life. You lose something of the time that you would give to your family and to many of the other things that are important.

## Growing Up

WALLACE: What about you when you were a much younger person, before your every thought and act were channeled toward a cause? How did you feel about whites when you were a boy?

KING: Well, I went through stages. As a young boy, I had the same experiences that most children have, Negro and white. That is, I had no feeling about it. I wasn't aware of it until I was about 5 or 6 years old and some of my playmates, who happened to have been white, suddenly couldn't play with me any more.

Their parents ran a store in front of our home and we played together for all these years and then the time came when we couldn't. And my mother went through the process of explaining the best way that she could to me at my young age the meaning of this system and the history of it, and at the same time saying to me that this should not give you any sense of inferiority, that you must feel that you are as good as anyone else.[27]

Then I went through the experience as I came to the point of adolescence, of developing a resentment. I experienced segregation in all its dimensions living in the South and I did develop this feeling of resentment. I don't think it ever went to the point of being an extreme bitterness, but it was certainly a resentment where I for a period just felt like all white people were bad. Now, this was a temporary experience. It was never something that took its toll in terms of damaging my whole personality and giving me an eternal bitterness and hate.

WALLACE: You can say, with all candor, that there is little bitterness—there is no hate in you now about white people?

KING: I don't think so. This is something that I always try to say to myself—that we must not become bitter and we must not hate the white man—and this is part of my basic philosophy of nonviolence. And I really feel that I have risen above all of the bitterness and hate that can engulf the human personality in a conflict situation.

WALLACE: When the Negro youngsters started to go to formerly white public schools in New Orleans recently, one segregationist in the state legislature down

---

27. This story is recounted in William Peters, "Our Weapon Is Love," *Redbook*, August 1956; Ted Poston, "Fighting Pastor: Martin Luther King," *New York Post*, 8 April 1957; and *Stride Toward Freedom: The Montgomery Story* (New York: Harper & Row, 1958), pp. 18–19.

there warned—his direct quote was: "The burr-headed Congolese raping our daughters."[28]

Now, when you hear something like this, are you really able to satisfy your feelings by turning the other cheek, or explaining it away with historical theories or psychological theories? Do you never allow yourself the momentary luxury of a little human anger, or hate?

KING: I'm sure that I'm human enough to go through those moments of righteous indignation. I think we all do. When I hear things like this—these very tragic statements—I have a sort of mixed response. On the one hand, I do have this temporary sense of resentment. On the other hand, I pity the person, and I find myself saying, "This person is really to be pitied more than condemned"—although we must condemn them also.

### It's the System

And I try to keep the struggle centered on the system, and I think when we do that we can rise above many of these experiences of anger. When we seek to defeat the evil system, the system which causes individuals to make statements like that, we somehow develop the attitude that "this person is misguided, he is caught up in an evil system and we must free him." And so the struggle is not merely a struggle to free the Negro, but a struggle to free many of our white brothers from their fears, from their prejudices and from their bigotry.

WALLACE: In the current Harper's magazine, James Baldwin says: "I think it is of the utmost importance to realize that King loves the South. Many Negroes do."[29] What's there to love, from your point of view?

KING: Well, it's like a parent who loves a prodigal child, a child who strays away. Here is a section of the country that has some beauty, that has been made ugly by segregation. There is an intimacy of life that can be beautiful if it is transformed in race relations from a sort of lord-servant relationship to a person-to-person relationship. And I think there are other things about the South that will make it one of the finest sections of our country once we solve this problem of segregation.

### North and South

WALLACE: If you had your choice and you were not the symbol that you are, would you rather live North or South?

KING: Well, I don't know about that. I would say that there are some things in the North that are much better than some things in the South.

At least in the North, the problem of desegregation is solved to a great extent. It's not thoroughly integrated, but the legal barriers are broken down, so you have desegregation, whereas in the South we still have segregation and I don't like it.

---

28. The previous November, Leander Henry Perez, a leading segregationist in the Louisiana state legislature, told a New Orleans crowd of 5,000: "Don't wait for your daughter to be raped by these Congolese. Don't wait until the burr-heads are forced into your schools. Do something about it now" ("Segregation Planner: Leander Henry Perez, Sr.," *New York Times*, 28 November 1960).

29. Baldwin, "The Dangerous Road Before Martin Luther King," *Harper's Magazine*, February 1961, p. 38.

WALLACE: Chances are you might move North, then?

KING: Well, I'm sure that there is a possibility that I would. On the other hand, before I entered the movement, before I became involved in the Montgomery struggle, I went back South mainly because I felt that there were great opportunities there to transform a section of the country into something rich. I mean rich in spirit and beautiful. And I had an opportunity to live in the North because I had one or two jobs offered. So I went back mainly because I saw the vast potentials there.[30]

WALLACE: You're used to being called names, of course, by Southern whites, Dr. King. But again, according to the New York Times article by Claude Sitton: "Some Negroes regard King as a pious interloper, bent on personal aggrandizement."[31] How do you feel when members of your own race say that about you?

## Friends and Enemies

KING: Well, I don't think one can ever be involved in a movement of this nature, or, to put it in more general terms, one cannot be a public figure without constant attacks and without being criticized. So that I take it two ways. On the one hand, I'm again human enough not to want to be attacked from an unwarranted point of view. On the other hand, sometimes your best friends can be the people who call themselves your enemies, because they cause you to examine yourself. And certainly I have no pretense to absolute goodness, or to omniscience. I don't know all of the answers. And it's good every now and then for somebody to remind you so that you keep your feet on the ground. And also, sometimes criticisms are constructive criticisms and you must look at them as that.

WALLACE: After the successful Montgomery bus boycott in 1957, you said, in regard to your nationwide publicity: "Frankly, I'm worried to death." You said, "A man who hits the peak at 27 has a tough job ahead. People will be expecting me to pull rabbits out of the hat for the rest of my life. If I don't, or if there are no more rabbits to be pulled, they'll say I'm no good."[32] Are you still worried to death about that?

KING: Well, I don't think about it now. I think at that point I did have these worries to a degree, but now I'm bent on doing what I think is right, and I think this is a great cause and I'm caught up in it and I get a great internal satisfaction as a result of this. I'm not worried about the future and my own career.

PD. *New York Post*, 15 February 1961.

---

30. In *Stride Toward Freedom*, King wrote that he had offers from churches in Massachusetts and New York (King, *Stride Toward Freedom*, p. 16). King was also recommended as a possible candidate for the open pastorate at Mount Zion Baptist Church in Dayton, Ohio (Melvin H. Watson to King, 27 April 1954). In a 1957 interview, King's wife, Coretta, said that she would have preferred staying in the North because of the greater opportunities to pursue her own career in music (Poston, "Fighting Pastor").

31. Sitton, "Dr. King, Symbol of the Segregation Struggle."

32. Quoted in Ted Poston, "Where Does He Go From Here?," *New York Post*, 14 April 1957.

# To Diane Nash and Charles Sherrod

17 February 1961
[*Atlanta, Ga.*]

*On 31 January 1961—the eve of the first anniversary of the Greensboro sit-in—*
*nine protesters in Rock Hill, South Carolina, were arrested after conducting a*
*sit-in at a local segregated lunch counter.*[1] *A week later the Student Nonviolent*
*Coordinating Committee (SNCC) sent four members, including Diane Nash and*
*Charles Sherrod, to Rock Hill to aid the demonstrations. In the following letter,*
*King expresses support for Nash and Sherrod following their decision to serve thirty*
*days in jail for requesting service at a segregated drug store.*[2] *King praises the*
*students for their decision to remain jailed, believing that every day they remain*
*in jail scars the "conscience of that immoral city. You are shaming them into*
*decency. "*

Miss Dianne Nash
Mr. Charles Sherrard
County Jail
Rock Hill, South Carolina

TO THE FREEDOM FIGHTERS:

I do want you to know that you have my prayers for your sustained Christian witness in this dark hour in Rock Hill. You have inspired all of us by such demonstrative
courage and faith. It is good to know that there still remains a creative minority who
would rather lose in a cause that will ultimately win than to win in a cause that will
ultimately lose.

Your actions are moral, democratic, Christian and non-violent. You transcend the

---

1. CORE field secretary Thomas Gaither and eight students from Friendship Junior College were
found guilty of trespassing and sentenced to thirty days in jail or pay a $100 fine. All opted to remain in
jail.

2. Charles Jones and Ruby Doris Smith, both of SNCC, were also arrested and chose to remain in
jail. While serving time in jail, the male protesters were made to work on a chain gang. Diane Judith
Nash (1938– ), born in Chicago, Illinois, attended Howard University for a year before transferring to
Fisk University in Nashville. In 1960 she became active in the student sit-in movement in Nashville, and
later became one of the founding members of SNCC. In the spring of 1961, Nash was instrumental in
continuing the Freedom Rides after CORE decided to cease the campaign following several acts of
violence against the riders. Her leadership of that campaign led to her appointment as head of SNCC's
direct action division. In 1961 she married fellow activist James Bevel and later joined him on the SCLC
staff in 1962 as a field staff organizer. The pair worked on the Birmingham, March on Washington, and
Selma campaigns, efforts that won them SCLC's Rosa Parks Award in 1965. Charles Sherrod (1937– ) was
born in Petersburg, Virginia. He received a B.A. (1958) and B.Div. (1961) from Virginia Union University,
and an M.Div. (1967) from Union Theological Seminary in New York. While in college, Sherrod organized sit-ins, and became SNCC's first field secretary in 1961. Later that year, Sherrod went to Albany,
Georgia, where he served until 1964 as project director of SNCC's southwest Georgia voter registration
project. Sherrod later returned to Albany and in 1996 ran an unsuccessful campaign for the Georgia
State Senate.

judgments of evil men who decry the powerful weapon you are using. Every day that you remain behind bard sears the conscience of that immoral city. You are shaming them into decency.

Great numbers of us will be with you on Sunday—giving thanks for your courageous spirit and asking God's special presence in your lives.

Faithfully yours,
Martin Luther King, Jr.

km
Dictated by Dr. King, but signed in his absence.

TLc. MLKP-MBU.

# From Lonnie C. King and Mary Ann Smith

25 February 1961
Atlanta, Ga.

*On 15 February an estimated 1,600 people filled Atlanta's Warren Memorial Methodist Church for a rally in support of seventy-seven students and eight ministers arrested for violating the state's antitrespassing laws.[1] In his address that evening, King maintained that the protesters were "expressing the highest respect for the law" by willingly violating an unjust law.[2] In the following letter, Lonnie C. King and Mary Ann Smith, officials of the Committee on Appeal for Human Rights, thank King for his address, affirming that "you have been an inspiration to all of us."[3]*

Rev. Martin Luther King, Jr.
407 Auburn Avenue
Atlanta 12, Georgia

---

1. Among the ministers arrested was Walter McCall, pastor of Providence Baptist Church and a former classmate of King's at Morehouse College and Crozer Theological Seminary (Keeler McCartney, "8 Ministers Seized in Sit-In, Vow to Remain in Fulton Jail," *Atlanta Constitution*, 16 February 1961; Charles Moore, "Negroes Here Plan Huge Rally at Jail," *Atlanta Constitution*, 16 February 1961). The previous October, Atlanta student protesters had convinced King to participate in a sit-in at Rich's department store, resulting in his arrest along with fifty-one other protesters (see Introduction in *Papers* 5:36–40).

2. In addition to King, William Holmes Borders (1905–1993), pastor of Wheat Street Baptist Church, also addressed the crowd (Moore, "Negroes Here Plan Huge Rally at Jail").

3. For more on the Atlanta sit-in agreement, see Introduction, pp. 4–5 in this volume. Mary Ann Smith Wilson (1940– ), born in Atlanta, earned a B.A. from Morris Brown College (1961), an M.A. from University of California, Berkeley (1965), and an M.D. from the School of Medicine at the University of California, San Francisco (1975). The older sister of SNCC activist Ruby Doris Smith Robinson, Wilson was a leader in the Atlanta sit-in movement. In 1961 she was arrested at the Atlanta train terminal after requesting service at the whites-only restaurant.

Dear Rev. King:

We want to express our appreciation for the eloquent address that you rendered at the Warren Memorial Methodist Church on February 15, 1961. We have received many, many favorable comments both from students and adults concerning the content of your message. You have been an inspiration to all of us.

Yours in the struggle,
[*signed*] Lonnie C King, Jr.
Lonnie C. King, Jr., Chairman

[*signed*]
Mary Ann Smith, Executive Secretary

LCK:eml

TLS. MLKP-MBU.

## To the Editor

[*March 1961*]
[*Atlanta, Ga.*]

*In a speech before the National Civil Liberties Clearing House on 23 March, special assistant to the president Harris Wofford defended the Kennedy administration's strategy of using executive action to end segregation. To the ire of some civil rights groups, Wofford also suggested that organizations should abandon their "well established methods" of protesting and litigation in favor of getting in "better gear with the Government."[1] Responding to an editorial critical of Wofford published in the Washington* Afro-American, *King defends Wofford's record, citing proof of his civil rights activism and maintaining that "his counsel is responsible for a good part of the executive action" taken by the administration.[2] The letter was not published in the* Afro-American.

To the editor:

Since you were good enough to suggest me as one of the persons President Kennedy might call on for advice on civil rights, I want to comment on your inaccurate and unfair description of Harris Wofford, one of President Kennedy's special assistants who is working both on the Peace Corps and on civil rights problems.[3]

---

1. Wofford, "New Frontiers in Civil Rights," 23 March 1961. Responding to Wofford's contention that civil rights organizations should work more closely with the government, NAACP executive secretary Roy Wilkins argued that the group has been a "pioneer in trying to be 'in better gear with the government'" (Wilkins to Wofford, 5 April 1961).

2. "Wofford vs. Civil Rights," Washington *Afro-American*, 15 April 1961.

3. An editorial in the Washington *Afro-American* suggested Kennedy turn to King or other black

Harris Wofford has been an apostle of the civil rights {—and never delay—} during all the years I have known him. ~~I am sure that his counsel is responsible for a
good part of the President's new program of executive action.~~

Mr. Wofford has been actively engaged in the struggle for civil rights ever since
his studies of Gandhi in India in 1949 and his book, <u>India Afire</u>.[4] Although from a
southern white family, he attended and graduated from Howard Law School—and
later taught there.[5] In 1955, before the Montgomery bus boycott began, he gave a
talk at Hampton Institute, calling for non-violent direct action against segregation.[6]
This talk and other talks and articles by him on civil disobedience were widely distributed in the South, helping to create better understanding of what we were doing
in Montgomery—and of what the sit-in students have been doing since.[7]

Mr. Wofford was one of the first persons to offer help to us during the bus boycott,
and his advice has been available and useful ever since.[8] His role in the Civil Rights
Commission, as counsel to Father Hesburgh, as director of the studies and hearings
on discrimination in housing, and then as an editor of the Commission's Report, was
an ~~important~~ {valuable} one.[9]

He was one of the authors—probably the main author, I understand—of the
strong Democratic civil rights platform of 1960.[10] All of us who know him know that
his efforts inside the new Administration will be to see that this platform is carried
out.

---

leaders including New York Congressman Adam Clayton Powell, NAACP lawyer Thurgood Marshall,
labor leader A. Philip Randolph, or Roy Wilkins to "find out something about civil rights and how the
colored man feels about it" ("Wofford vs. Civil Rights," 15 April 1961).

4. In *India Afire,* co-authored with his wife, Clare, Wofford detailed conditions in India, noting that
Gandhi had special relevance for "the challenge of America's social frontier which runs roughly through
the millions of Negroes, unorganized Southern workers, and landless farm laborers" (*India Afire* [New
York: John Day, 1951], p. 338).

5. Harris Wofford received his J.D. in 1954 from Howard and was a visiting lecturer there in 1956.

6. Wofford argued that Gandhian civil disobedience "permits peaceful, civil resistance" and "rein-
forces the process of persuasion, and the basis for law" (Wofford, "Gandhi the Civil Rights Lawyer,"
*Mankind* 1, no. 1 [August 1956]: 70–74).

7. For example, see Wofford, "Nonviolence and the Law," 7 November 1957; "The Law and Civil
Disobedience," 20 November 1959. In *Stride Toward Freedom* (New York: Harper & Row, 1958), King drew
on Wofford's "Nonviolence and the Law," a version of which Wofford delivered at the "Non-Violence and
Social Change" conference at Howard University in 1957; King also spoke at the conference. Wofford
also delivered the speech at an MIA gathering that King attended in December 1957 (see note 131,
Introduction in *Papers* 4:32).

8. For more on Wofford's role during the boycott, see Wofford to King, 25 April 1956, in *Papers*
3:225–226.

9. Wofford was acknowledged for his work in the 1959 report by the U.S. Commission on Civil Rights
(*Report of the United States Commission on Civil Rights 1959* [Washington, D.C.: U.S. Government Printing
Office, 1959], p. viii).

10. According to Wofford's memoir *Of Kennedys & Kings: Making Sense of the Sixties* (New York: Farrar,
Straus, Giroux, 1980), Chester Bowles, chairman of the Democratic Platform Committee, assigned
Wofford to draft a civil rights platform with aides Thomas Hughes and Abram Chayes (pp. 51–52).
Among other issues, the plank pledged to eliminate literacy tests and poll taxes, enforce the 1954 *Brown*
decision, and end discrimination in federally assisted housing (Paul A. Smith and Richard E. May, eds.,
*Official Report of the Proceedings of the Democratic National Convention and Committee* [Washington, D.C.:
National Document Publishers, 1964], pp. 71–73).

The speech on which your editorial "Wofford vs. Civil Rights" was based, is no counsel of delay but instead was a call for executive action—and for public efforts to secure executive action.[11] I am sure that his counsel is responsible for a good part of the executive action which the Administration has already undertaken, and that he will be a significant factor in the further steps which still must be taken.

THD. MCMLK–RWWL: 2.4.0.140.

---

11. Denouncing what was perceived as an approach designed to "not rock the boat too fast," the editorial argued Wofford's image as a "'spokesman' for the colored community's desired pace of progress," should be "deplored." The editorial concluded: "We don't need any Mr. Harris Wofford speaking for us in this area, thank you, and the less he advises, the happier we'll be" ("Wofford vs. Civil Rights," 15 April 1961).

# To John F. Kennedy

1 March 1961
Atlanta, Ga.

*Responding to the opposition of Benjamin E. Mays's appointment to the United States Commission on Civil Rights by Georgia senators Herman E. Talmadge and Richard B. Russell, King sends this telegram to President Kennedy expressing support for Mays.[1] King defends Mays's character and talent, warning Kennedy that black voters will be "gravely disappointed" if Mays is not appointed due to "untrue attacks" by the senators. Although Kennedy expressed his high regard for Mays in a 21 March 1961 reply to King, he acquiesced to the southern senators' demand, and Mays was not seated on the Commission.[2] The following telegram was partially reprinted in the* Atlanta Daily World.[3]

---

1. A vacancy had recently been created on the commission by the resignation of George M. Johnson, an African American. Mays was president of Morehouse College from 1940 until 1967. Long-time opponents of the civil rights movement, Russell and Talmadge objected to Mays's appointment to the commission because they believed his identification with the civil rights movement would render him partial. The senators also accused Mays of associating with Communist-front organizations (Harold Davis, "Senators Oppose Mays Appointment," *Atlanta Journal*, 1 March 1961; "Russell Talmadge Rap Plan to Select Dr. Mays," *Atlanta Journal*, 1 March 1961).
2. In his reply to King, Kennedy called Mays "an outstanding American who has ably served his country in the past." Fearing a fight in the Senate over Mays's confirmation, Kennedy relented to pressure from Russell and Talmadge and instead appointed Spottswood William Robinson, dean of Howard University Law School (Harold Davis, "Dr. Mays Not to Get Rights Panel Post," *Atlanta Journal*, 2 March 1961; "Fighter for Civil Rights," *New York Times*, 28 July 1961). Southern senators also opposed Robinson's nomination. Senator James O. Eastland of Mississippi called Robinson's nomination "equally as reprehensible a choice for such a position as would be Roy Wilkins or Thurgood Marshall." Robinson's nomination was confirmed 73–17 (U.S. Congress, Senate, *Congressional Record*, 87th Cong., 1st sess., 1961, Vol. 107, pt. 10, 13669, 13695).
3. "Two Atlantans Wire Kennedy for Dr. Mays," 2 March 1961.

AN ARTICLE WHICH APPEARED IN THE ATLANTA JOURNAL REVEALED THAT DR BENJAMIN E MAYS IS BEING CONSIDERED FOR A POSITION IN THE ADMINISTRATION BUT THAT THERE IS A POSSIBILITY THAT HE WILL NOT RECEIVE AN APPOINTMENT BECAUSE SENATORS RUSSELL AND TALMADGE HAVE RAISED CERTAIN QUESTIONS CONCERNING HIS ELIGIBILITY.[4] IT WOULD BE TRAGIC IF SUCH A DISTINGUISHED AMERICAN WERE DEPRIVED OF THE OPPORTUNITY TO SERVE HIS COUNTRY IN A UNIQUE POSITION MERELY BECAUSE OF UNWARRANTED AND FALSE ACCUSATIONS MADE BY THE TWO SENATORS OF GEORGIA. IT SEEMS OBVIOUS THAT THE REAL OBJECTION THAT THE SENATORS HAVE TO DR. MAYS IS THAT HE HAS NOT BEEN AN ACCOMMODATING ULTRA CONSERVATIVE LEADER. HE HAS BEEN A MAN OF GENUINE HUMANITARIAN CONCERN AND REAL INTEGRITY. IT WOULD BE A CREDIT TO THE NATION AND TO YOUR ADMINISTRATION TO HAVE A MAN OF DR MAYS CALIBER SERVING IN SOME POSITION BY ALL STANDARDS OF MEASUREMENT HE IS ONE OF THE TRULY GREAT MEN OF OUR GENERATION HE HAS ALWAYS EVINCED UNSWERVING DEVOTION TO THE PRINCIPLES OF AMERICAN DEMOCRACY AND HAS LABORED UNTIRINGLY ACROSS THE YEARS TO EXTEND THE FRONTIERS OF JUSTICE. ALL MEN OF GOOD WILL AND NEGRO VOTERS IN PARTICULAR WILL BE GRAVELY DISAPPOINTED IF THE UNETHICAL AND UNTRUE ATTACKS BY THE SENATORS FROM GEORGIA WILL PREVENT DR MAYS FROM BEING APPOINTED.

MARTIN LUTHER KING JR.

PWSr. JFKWHCSF-MBJFK.

---

4. Harold Davis, "Morehouse's Dr. Mays Studied for Rights Post," *Atlanta Journal*, 28 February 1961. In his 21 March 1961 reply to King, Kennedy denied that Russell or Talmadge had contacted him "with any criticism" of Mays. Talmadge was incensed that the White House leaked to the press that Mays was being considered for the post. Talmadge wrote to Reverend Dow Kirkpatrick of Atlanta's St. Mark Methodist Church, who had written to Talmadge in support of Mays: "Appearances would indicate that the story was leaked with the view of trying to leave the impression in certain quarters that the President would be glad to consider such an appointment and leave the responsibility on Senator Russell and me for killing it" (Kirkpatrick to Talmadge, 6 March 1961; Talmadge to Kirkpatrick, 14 March 1961).

# To Kivie Kaplan

6 March 1961
[Atlanta, Ga.]

*Since 1958 NAACP board member Kivie Kaplan had attempted to recruit King to join the organization's national board without success.[1] In early 1961 Kaplan*

---

1. See note 1, King to Kaplan, 3 May 1960, in *Papers* 5:451.

*wrote four letters urging King's participation.[2] Citing a busy schedule, King
again declines Kaplan's offer but responds to Kaplan's query about the Nation of
Islam, better known as the Black Muslims.[3] King calls the sect a black supremacist
organization, but acknowledges that some blacks might be attracted to the group:
"As long as doors are closed in the faces of millions of Negroes and they feel dejected
and dis-inherited, an organization like this will appeal to some." In his 13 March
1961 reply, Kaplan thanked King for the note.*

Mr. Kivie Kaplan
Colonial Tanning Company, Incorporated
195 South Street
Boston 11, Massachusetts

Dear Kivie:

I am just returning to the office after having been out more than two weeks getting some much-needed rest.[4] I would have answered your letters long before now
but this absence from the city as well as the accumulation of other responsibilities
stood in my way.

First, let me try to answer your question concerning the NAACP Board. After
giving this matter serious consideration I have come to the conclusion that it would
probably be too much added to my schedule to accept a position on the Board of
NAACP at this time. Recently I have had to adopt a policy of spending much more
time in the south because of the temper of events in this section of the country. This
means that I have had to cut down on my outside travel a great deal. A position on
the Board of NAACP, while being a cherished one and one that I would be honored
to accept, would certainly increase my responsibilities and I am afraid that I would
not be able to make as many of the meetings as a good Board member would be
expected to attend. For these reasons, I think it would be better not to bring my
name before the Board at this time.

Second, you raise the question concerning the Muslims.[5] I regret to say that I
know very little about the inner workings of this organization. My knowledge is limited to what I have read in the papers. I have never met Elijah Mohammed or any of

---

2. Kaplan to King, 16 January 1961; Kaplan to Dora E. McDonald, 17 January 1961; Kaplan to King, 20 January 1961; and Kaplan to McDonald, 20 February 1961. In a letter to Dora E. McDonald, King's secretary, Kaplan wrote that "it is very, very frustrating to be on one end of a non-answering correspondence" (Kaplan to McDonald, 20 February 1961).

3. In his 20 February letter to McDonald, Kaplan wrote: "If he would tell me about the Muslims— what he knows about them—I would appreciate knowing as fully as I could about them." In a 9 January 1962 letter to Larry P. Silvey, a senior at Oklahoma State University, King called the Black Nationalist movement a "much more serious threat" than communism to African Americans, but suggested that as long as the United States continues to move toward a desegregated society, the threat will diminish (Silvey to King, 29 October 1961; King to Silvey, 9 January 1962).

4. King vacationed in the Bahamas for several days beginning on 19 February.

5. King refers to the members of the Nation of Islam (NOI), a black nationalist religious organization advocating spiritual, social, and political separatism. The group, led by Elijah Muhammad from
1934 until his death in 1975, based their teachings on the Prophet Mohammad and the Islamic religion.

his followers. Therefore, I would not like to be accused of giving false information concerning the organization.

In general terms, the Muslims, under the guise of the great religion of Islam (Islam, which is one of the great religions of the world, would disclaim any connection with the so-called Muslim sect of the United States) preaches a doctrine of racial separation rather than racial integration. They have some kind of strange dream of a black nation within the larger nation. At times the public expressions of this group have bordered on a new kind of race hatred and an unconscious advocacy of violence. It has also preached a doctrine of black supremacy. I must, however, say that the challenge which an extremist organization like this offers is that of demanding of us to work with renewed vigor to get rid of racial discrimination and all other conditions which such an organization thrives on. As long as doors are closed in the faces of millions of Negroes and they feel dejected and dis-inherited, an organization like this will appeal to some. It derives its membership largely from uneducated and underpriviledged Negroes who have lost the sense of belonging and have often felt forgotten.

It is always good to hear from you.

Thanks again for all of the nice things that you sent us at the birth of our new son.[6] I am happy to report that Dexter Scott (the new baby) and Coretta are doing very well. It is the inspiration that come from the friends like you and your lovely wife that give us the courage and vigor to carry on.[7]

Sincerely yours,
Martin

Km

TLc. MLKP-MBU.

---

6. After the birth of the Kings' son Dexter Scott on 30 January 1961, Kaplan and his wife sent clothes for the new baby (Kivie and Emily Kaplan to Martin and Coretta Scott King, 1 February 1961).

7. King refers to Kaplan's wife, Emily.

To John F. Kennedy

16 Mar
1961

16 March 1961
Atlanta, Ga.

*King congratulates Kennedy on his victory in the 1960 presidential election and requests a meeting with the president within the next month to discuss civil rights in the United States.[1] King met with Kennedy on 16 October 1961, nine months after Kennedy's inauguration.[2]*

President John F. Kennedy
The White House
Washington 25, D.C.

Dear President Kennedy:

First, let me offer my belated congratulations to you for being elected President of our great nation. You conducted a marvelous campaign and stood up superbly against tremendous odds. May I assure you that you will have my support and prayers as you lead us through the difficult yet challenging days ahead.

If it is at all possible, I would like to have a conference with you within the next three or four weeks to discuss some important matters concerning the civil rights issue. I realize that this is asking a great deal in the light of your extremely busy schedule, but I am sure that a brief discussion on the present status of the civil rights struggle may prove to be mutually beneficial. If a date can be worked out I would appreciate hearing from you as soon as possible so that I can re-arrange my schedule accordingly.

With warm personal regards, I am,

Sincerely yours,
[*signed*] Martin L. King Jr.
Martin Luther King, Jr.

Km

TLS. JFKWHCSF-MBJFK: Box 358.

---

1. There was considerable discussion within the White House regarding a meeting with King. Kennedy's special assistant for civil rights, Harris Wofford, who had also served as an unofficial advisor to King, was among those aides advocating for a meeting (see Wofford to Kenneth P. O'Donnell, 20 March 1961; Frank D. Reeves to O'Donnell, 22 March 1961; and O'Donnell to King, 25 March 1961). Dora E. McDonald sent another request on 28 April 1961, suggesting several dates in May (McDonald to Reeves, 28 April 1961). Throughout the summer and early fall, Wofford and Reeves urged the White House to arrange a formal meeting between King and President Kennedy (Reeves to Kennedy, 5 May 1961; Wofford to O'Donnell, 4 October 1961).

2. For King's remarks following his meeting with Kennedy, see Press Conference after Meeting with John F. Kennedy, 16 October 1961, pp. 308–311 in this volume.

175

**Martin Luther King, Jr.**
Ebenezer Baptist Church
407 Auburn Avenue, N. E.
Atlanta, Georgia

▬▬▬▬▬

Jackson 2-4395

March 16, 1961

President John F. Kennedy
The White House
Washington 25, D. C.

Dear President Kennedy:

First, let me offer my belated congratulations to you for
being elected  President of our great nation.  You conducted
a marvelous campaign and stood up superbly against tremendous odds.  May I assure you that you will have my
support and prayers as you lead us through the difficult yet
challenging days ahead.

If it is at all possible, I would like to have a conference with
you within the next three or four weeks to discuss some important matters concerning the civil rights issue.  I realize
that this is asking a great deal in the light of your extremely
busy schedule, but I am sure that a brief discussion on the
present status of the civil rights struggle may prove to be
mutually beneficial.  If a date can be worked out I would
appreciate hearing from you as soon as possible so that I can
re-arrange my schedule accordingly.

With warm personal regards, I am,

Sincerely yours,

Martin Luther King, Jr.

Km

King congratulates John F. Kennedy on his election and requests a conference with him
to talk over civil rights issues. Courtesy of the John F. Kennedy Presidential Library.

[*22 March 1961*]
[*Atlanta, Ga.*]

*King agreed to a request for an interview with Lester Margolies, a graduate
student at Southern Illinois University in Carbondale, who was working on his
master's thesis.*[1] *In the interview, which was held in King's office at Ebenezer, he
discusses the importance of the black vote, his role in the controversy over ending
desegregation protests in Atlanta, and competition between foreign aid and
domestic programs. Calling for a "broader distribution of wealth," King asserted:
"I have strongly supported all of the social welfare legislation that came into being
through the Roosevelt era and coming on up, because I think that this is the only
way that we can grapple with many of the problems that we face in our nation,
particularly this gulf between sometimes superfluous, inordinate wealth and over
here abject, deadening poverty." The following transcript was taken from an audio
recording.*

[*Margolies*]:   First question: What do you feel will be the general repercussions
of this movement on contemporary North American politics and contemporary
American thought?

[*King*]:   Well, I'm sure that this movement will have a tremendous impact on both
the political structure of our nation as well as the thought. I think, first, to deal with
the political side: I'm sure that the whole movement of the Negro, or to put it another
way, the whole civil rights struggle will tend to liberalize both political parties to a
degree, because the more the Negro secures the ballot, the more the Democratic
Party, for instance, will have to break away from the Southern Dixiecrats and move
more in line with its basic principles. And I think, to a degree, the more this movement goes on, the more it will break down the coalition in Congress between right-
wing Northern Republicans and Southern Dixiecrats, which in the long run will
make for a greater liberal bent and more progressive legislation in several areas.

Now, as far as the movement's influence on contemporary thought: I think it will
have a great impact there. For instance, the movement represents certainly a new
and creative dimension in the struggle in the United States. In the past, it has been
mainly legalistic. And now we see the birth of this new approach, not new approach,
but new in America on a mass scale, namely, nonviolent resistance. And I'm sure
that with this new dimension coming in, more and more people will begin to study
the meaning of nonviolent resistance as a philosophy and as a technique of social

---

1. Margolies to King, 13 February 1961; Dora E. McDonald to Margolies, 9 March 1961. Lester
Margolies (1937– ), born in Brooklyn, New York, received a B.A. (1959) and an M.A. (1961) from Southern
Illinois University. While an undergraduate, Margolies participated in efforts to integrate local businesses. His master's thesis, "The Political Theory of Martin Luther King, Jr.," was completed in 1961.
Afterward, Margolies moved to Berkeley to pursue further graduate study. From 1966 until his retirement in 2002, Margolies taught various political science and constitutional law classes at the high school
and college level in Alameda County, California.

change. I think also many of the stereotypes concerning the Negro are gradually being removed from the thinking of people because of this movement. They've come to see a different type of Negro than the Negro that they had in their minds as a result of these stereotypes that have been set up. So that I'm sure the movement will have a tremendous impact on both the political structure and the thought of our nation.

[*Margolies*]: Martin, has there been any transition in your thinking since the whole movement began in Montgomery [*as you are able to?*]?

[*King*]: Well, not basically. I'm sure that I've tried to clarify my thinking on certain issues more as we have moved on with the struggle, but I am still convinced that nonviolence as a philosophy and a method is the most potent weapon available to oppressed people in their struggle for freedom and human dignity. I, in Montgomery, came to see the necessity of carrying out both sides of a truly nonviolent struggle. The one is the protest side, the side of noncooperation with evil. But also there's the side of the constructive program, which is as important as the side of noncooperation. And I guess, more and more, I have come to see the necessity of this other side, on the one hand, seeking to remove the system of segregation which makes for unjust conditions and discrimination and also for lagging standards within the Negro community. So that, remove the system on the one hand, and work to improve the standards on the other hand, which has in many instances been brought into being as a result of the system itself. But to answer the question in short, I think my thinking is just about the same as that stated in *Stride Toward Freedom*.[2]

[*Margolies*]: OK, Dr. King. You've answered this one partially, I think, in the first question. Maybe you can expand on it a bit more. Should the Negro get the ballot? How do you think this would affect policy on the Southern and on the national level?

[*King*]: Yes, well, as I said, I think it would do a great deal both in this section of the country and on a national level. If it's true that when Negroes are voting in a particular community, when they are voting to a degree where an impact is palpable, things are better, conditions are better, the climate is much more reasonable, the atmosphere is much more peaceful. Now, I'm convinced that as this continues in various communities across the South, the transition from the segregated to the desegregated society will take place more, much more smoothly because public officials come to see that they must represent all people to get elected, and they need the Negro vote to get elected.

Now, I think the same thing will be true on a national scale: the more Negroes we have voting, the more the Congressmen of the nation, as well as the President and the executive branch of government, will see the necessity of implementing just and right laws that will make for freedom and human dignity for all people. So that I'm sure that the ballot is one of the most significant needs at this hour, and as I said to open, I think one of the most significant steps that the Negro can take is that short walk to the voting booth. It will change many, many conditions.

---

2. King published the story of the Montgomery bus boycott in *Stride Toward Freedom: The Montgomery Story* (New York: Harper & Row, 1958).

[*Margolies*]:  I hadn't planned on asking this—perhaps I should, if you can answer it briefly. Do you think there's any chance of getting the unit system abolished here in Georgia?[3]

[*King*]:  I think so. I think the signs are very encouraging now. Actually, the last time it went to the Supreme Court, I think the vote was five-four. It was very close, I think it was five-four.[4] So that if it goes back to the Supreme Court, I believe we have a greater possibility of getting it changed now than ever before. Now, on the other hand, there are those within the state who are coming to see that it can be changed and that there is a great possibility that it will be changed by the Supreme Court, so that they are seeking to make some changes through the state legislature to save the change that will come from the Supreme Court, which will probably be much greater than they would want. It will certainly be much greater than they would want, so they are trying to get through some immediate change that would at least represent token fair representation and thereby weaken the possibility of getting a decision from the Supreme Court. In any case, I'm convinced that it's going to be changed in the next few months, either by the Supreme Court or by a legislative act here in the state.

[*Margolies*]:  That's very encouraging. What are your future plans in the way of a program of action for getting civil rights now?

[*King*]:  Well, I would say that we have, and as you know I'm president of the Southern Christian Leadership Conference

[*Margolies*]:  Yeah.

[*King*]:  which is an organization that came into being to serve as a channel through which local protest groups in the South could coordinate their protest activities. And our main interest is that of securing citizenship rights for Negro people through nonviolent means. Now, through the Conference, we have many things in mind, many plans ahead. We plan to intensify our efforts in the area of voter registration, for instance, to try to double the number of Negro registered voters. Out of five million eligible Negro voters in the South, we only have 1,300,000, which means we have a big job to do in that area. Also, we are starting a citizenship training school in the South.[5] And this school has as its main purpose training leaders who in turn will

---

3.  The county unit system in Georgia was established in 1917, when the Georgia legislature passed the Neill Primary Act. The act allocated the vote in state elections by county population, awarding six unit votes to the eight most populous counties, four unit votes to the next thirty most populous counties, and two unit votes to the remaining 121 smallest counties. The candidate receiving a plurality of the popular vote received the entire unit vote from that county, allowing less populated rural counties to equal the votes of larger urban counties. In *Gray v. Sanders,* 372 U.S. 368 (1963), the U.S. Supreme Court ruled the act unconstitutional because "the practical effect of this system is that the vote of each citizen counts for less and less as the population of his county increases."

4.  King refers to the 1950 U.S. Supreme Court case *South v. Peters,* 339 U.S. 276. The final vote was in favor of the unit system.

5.  In late 1960, SCLC was pursuing a partnership with the Highlander Folk School in Monteagle, Tennessee, to establish citizenship training schools across the South. Since 1956, Highlander had conducted educational programs that focused on literacy, teaching constitutional rights, and preparing for voter registration tests. After the State of Tennessee closed Highlander for allegedly violating its tax-exempt status, SCLC used Highlander's curriculum models to establish its own affiliate citizenship training schools in southern communities (see Memo, "Leadership Training Program and Citizenship Schools," December 1960–January 1961, pp. 136–138 in this volume).

train many people within the various communities for citizenship responsibilities. And in cases where there will be various tests given for voters or people attempting to register and vote, we plan to do a great deal in that area.

Now, this is all a part of the constructive program on the side of creative protest. We intend to have as many nonviolent, mass nonviolent direct action programs as we can possibly work out within the course of a year. Now, things have centered on sit-ins at lunch counters in the past few months by the students, but there are still many other areas, as you know, where segregation is a glaring reality. And we are deeply committed to the idea of using mass nonviolent direct action as a technique to remove the barriers of segregation from all of these particular areas where we find segregation—whether it's in restaurants, theaters, hotels, and so many other areas in the South. Now, along with this, we are intensifying our work in nonviolent institutes because we know that [*phone rings*], we cannot expect people to do a real [*phone rings*] job in this area unless they know exactly what they are doing. I'll have to stop this. [*phone rings*]

[*Margolies*]:   OK.

[*King*]:   Hello. Hi. [*gap in tape*]

[*Margolies*]:   Perhaps, along the same lines, you can answer this. What role do you think the boycott, or selective buying, and/or selective buying will have in the nonviolent protests in the future?

[*King*]:   I think it will have a very important role. The buying power of the Negro is a very, very important factor in the whole struggle, and I think now the national or rather the annual income of the Negro collectively is about twenty billion dollars. Now, in any urban area, this is true. South, North and South, it may even be truer in the South, where you have smaller cities, in any urban area, the Negro has enough buying power to make the difference between profit and loss in any, in a particular business. And this can be used very effectively. The refusal to cooperate with a store that lends its support to a system of segregation and discrimination is the logical follow-through of the nonviolent direct action approach. And I think that the economic withdrawal approach will, to a great degree, bring many merchants around—and not only merchants but other agencies around—that would not come around ordinarily.

Now, I've seen this—we certainly saw it in Montgomery, in the struggle there. The bus company was ready to give in the first week after the boycott. It was the city commission that refused and held out, but the bus company was ready because they just couldn't stand the loss that they were facing. And this has been true in most of the sit-in movements where the boycott followed—and I think in most of them, the selective buying program followed the sit-ins. And in most cases, they just haven't been able to maintain the system of segregation and at the same time sustain the losses that they faced. So that I do think this will be a very, very effective instrument.

[*Margolies*]:   Do you think we ought to be even more concerned with foreign aid than we are now, or should we concentrate more upon the destitute here at home and put less emphasis on the foreign?

[*King*]:   Well, I think it's a both-and, not an either-or. I think we must be greatly concerned about foreign aid. Now, on the one hand, there are those who would say we ought to be concerned about foreign aid because Communism is a potent force in the world, and in order to compete with the Communists, we need to do this. And there is no doubt about the fact that if we go all out in foreign aid, it will help us prestige-wise in the world. But I don't think this is the reason it should be done. I think it should be done because it is morally right to do it and because of the interdependent structure of mankind. We can't live alone, independently of our neighbors, whether they are in other countries close by or the countries a long ways off; we must live together. And actually, we are not secure unless all of the nations of the world are secure. We are tied in a sort of inescapable network of mutuality. And therefore I think we must do it because it is right and because we are interdependent, and whatever affects one directly affects all indirectly.

Now, some of the problems in other countries are much greater than the problems in our own country. My travels in Africa, Asia, and South America have revealed to me that poverty is so great in these countries, many of the countries in these particular continents that it cannot be dealt with other than through the aid and the support and the backing of some of the nations of the world that have the resources.[6] And I think we should go all out to increase our foreign aid, and I don't mean military aid alone here. I think sometimes we have spent far too much money establishing military bases around the world rather than bases of genuine concern and understanding.

So I would strongly favor that, while strongly favoring all of the social welfare and economic approaches that are being used and advocated in our country to lift the standards of those who are deprived of the basic necessities of life. I have strongly supported all of the social welfare legislation that came into being through the Roosevelt era and coming on up, because I think that this is the only way that we can grapple with many of the problems that we face in our nation, particularly this gulf between sometimes superfluous, inordinate wealth and over here abject, deadening poverty. And while I don't advocate a socialistic economy, I do think there are some things that we must do that will make for a broader distribution of wealth. And therefore I think that as far as dealing with this problem is concerned, we must be concerned about foreign aid and also dealing with our own problems here in the nation, so [*phone buzzes*] it's both-and rather than either-or. [*someone enters and speaks to King*]

[*King*]:   OK. Tell him. OK, I'll be ready in about ten more minutes.

[*Margolies*]:   Well, I think that at the rate we're going, ten minutes may just be enough time, Doctor. You just answered another question that I had for you on the next collection.

[*King*]:   Oh, is that so?

[*Margolies*]:   That's what I was getting at anyway. I wanted your basic approach. A Negro sociologist not too long ago pointed out that, in quotes, "Many Negro leaders, while affiliated with Republican party organizations, have been forced to take into consideration the fact that the interests of the Negro man [*phone rings*] have been with the liberal program of the Democratic Party."[7] Can you comment on that?

---

6. King refers to his travels to Ghana in 1957, India in 1959, South America in early 1960, and Nigeria in November 1960. For more details on King's travels, see Introductions in *Papers* 4:7–10 and *Papers* 5:2–12, 32, 40.

7. Margolies quotes from sociologist E. Franklin Frazier's 1957 book, *Black Bourgeoisie* (London: Collier-Macmillan, 1957): "Although many of the middle-class leaders of the Elks have been connected with Republican Party organizations, they have been forced to take into consideration the fact that the interests of the Negro masses have been with the liberal program of the Democratic Party" (pp. 82–83).

[*King*]:  Yes, I think that that is true. Is the implication here that the Negro masses have supported the Democratic Party or that the Democratic Party has had a, is better, so to speak, for the Negro in lifting his economic—

[*Margolies*]:  Yes, I think the second one is more. The policies they've advocated

[*King*]:  Yes.

[*Margolies*]:  I think, would tend more to be better

[*King*]:  Yes.

[*Margolies*]:   for the Negro masses

[*King*]:  Yes.

[*Margolies*]:  It's liberal.

[*King*]:  Yes. Well, I think that's quite true. There's no doubt in my mind about that. But, and this isn't, I'm not taking a partisan point of view here, because I have not, I'm not a registered Democrat at all. But I do think the policies of the Democratic Party have been—certainly on economic questions and on social welfare questions, the policies have been much better for the Negro. Now, I don't approve, naturally, of the schizophrenic character of the Democratic Party, where you get a true liberalism in one area and then you come to the South and get the very conservative element of the Democratic Party. And this I'm very much concerned about when we think of the fact that the major committees are in the hands of Southerners, and they often block very aggressive legislation in various areas. But on the whole, when we look at the Democratic Party as a whole and its basic philosophy, it has advocated policies that are more helpful to not only the Negro but to the common man in general. And I'm sure this is the reason that the vast majority of Negroes still vote the Democratic ticket because of its policies in this area. [*phone rings*]

[*Margolies*]:  Do you have to get that?

[*King*]:  No, she answers that.

[*Margolies*]:  In regards to this recent agreement, I found it difficult to believe as was reported that you said that this is something that we can live with.[8] Would you like to comment on that for me? This can be on or off the record; I don't care.

[*King*]:  Well, I never made a comment pro [*phone buzzes*] or con on the agreement.

[*Margolies*]:  Oh, I see. I thought that it was understood that some had reported that—[*Someone enters and speaks to King*]

[*King*]:  Well, I guess we'll have to make it at 3:30. All right.

[*Unknown person*]:  OK.

[*King to unknown person*]:  Darling, maybe we better even make it for later than that. Let me call him, and maybe I'll have to come by there.

---

8. Margolies refers to the Atlanta lunch counter desegregation agreement of 6 March 1961. Although King did not sign the agreement, news reports indicated that he called the plan "workable and urged its support" (Bruce Galphin, "Negroes Agree to End Sit-Ins," *Atlanta Constitution*, 8 March 1961). In March 1960, sit-ins and boycotts of segregated lunch counters in downtown Atlanta prompted many department and drug stores to close. Members of the Atlanta Chamber of Commerce and the Student-Adult Liaison Committee that had been supporting the protest agreed to call an end to demonstrations in exchange for the timely desegregation of downtown Atlanta; in the meantime, the lunch counters would be allowed to reopen on a segregated basis (Galphin, "Negroes Agree to End Sit-Ins," 8 March 1961).

[*King to Margolies*]:    Many misinterpretations have gotten out about the agreement as far as my position is concerned. I never made any statement pro or con. I had my private convictions about it, which I still have, even in the mass meeting, where there was a great deal of disagreement and misunderstanding.[9] I came to the rostrum, and my position on it was mainly not to say whether the agreement was right or wrong, but that we had to be united, that the agreement may have some mistakes in it, but there could be something that could do even greater harm and that would be to go out and be inflicted with, the phrase that I used was the "cancerous disease of disunity."[10] So that we must somehow be united, even though we can't follow a way of uniformity here, because there will be differences.

And I think it was very unfair for, as many people were saying that their leaders had sold out, this wasn't true. They were grappling with a difficult problem; nobody got any money as some of the people were trying to say.[11] It was that they were just in a difficult situation, and they did what they felt was the right thing to do. If I had been there, I would have argued that we shouldn't have done it till the end. But after they did it, I felt a moral responsibility to at least somehow justify the leaders—not their actions, but at least try to keep the people to a point that they would maintain respect for the leaders and disagree with the agreement, but not say the leaders sold out. Because we go right back to the thing that the Negro has suffered from so long and that is not having any leadership and tearing up, you see, among ourselves, and the whole method of divide and conquer was the thing used.

So, and I never said this is something we can live with. What happened: the press felt that, I think they wanted to settle this thing, and I guess they felt that a lot of people, some people would listen to me, and if they knew they had my weight behind it, it would probably get over better. And naturally they wanted to settle it because they get thousands of dollars a week from Rich's and Davison's in advertisements, you see.[12] And I know the press willfully put certain statements in my mouth three, on three different occasions. At first, it came out that I signed the agreement. Well, they backed up, and they had to change that. Then the second thing came out was a state-

---

9.  On 10 March 1961, the Student-Adult Liaison Committee held a mass meeting of an estimated 1,500 people at Warren Memorial Methodist Church in Atlanta to discuss the agreement. Student protesters criticized the lack of a specific date for lunch counter desegregation and the fact that segregated facilities would remain open until after Atlanta school desegregation was completed in the fall. Despite assurances from the Student-Adult Liaison Committee that desegregation of downtown facilities would take place, many students repudiated the adult leaders, including Martin Luther King, Sr. (Claude Sitton, "Negroes to Keep Atlanta Boycott," *New York Times*, 11 March 1961; Sitton, "Atlanta Accord Arouses Dispute," *New York Times*, 12 March 1961).

10.  Before the hostile crowd, King pleaded with student protesters: "Calm reasonableness is need [*sic*], along with mutual trust and mutual respect. No greater tragedy could befall the Negro in Atlanta now . . . than to be inflicted with the Cancerous disease of disunity. Misunderstanding there will be, but disunity there must never be" ("Adult-Youth Liaison Committee Meets Tuesday," *Atlanta Daily World*, 12 March 1961).

11.  The Associated Negro Press reported that students felt they had been "sold down the river" by the agreement (Press release, "Martin Luther King calms uprising over Atlanta agreement; Students claim they were 'sold down the river' in 'deal,'" 13 March 1961).

12.  Both Davison's and Rich's had been targets of boycotts and sit-in demonstrations. Despite previous refusals, both stores joined in the settlement ("Atlanta Stores to Drop Jim-Crow Policy," *Chicago Daily Defender*, 8 March 1961).

ment that my father made, and they quoted this as *my* statement: Dr. Martin Luther King, Jr. Now, this was a statement that my father made for the radio station WGFT.

[*Margolies*]:   Is this the one I listened to?

[*King*]:   That's the one.

[*Margolies*]:   That's the one?

[*King*]:   I think that's the—well, they've made two. That's one. The other one was the statement that I said, "I think the plan is workable," and I called for full support. Now, that was my father—see, I was out of town.[13]

[*Margolies*]:   You were in Detroit, isn't that right?

[*King*]:   That's right. I was in Detroit.[14] But they quoted me as making this statement, you see? And then the other one came out that I think it is something we can live with, which I have never said. So this was all a part of the tragedy of errors in this whole thing.

[*Margolies*]:   All right, let's get off this. I'm cleared up on it. I was even before I asked it, I think. In regard to civil disobedience, some Southerners now are claiming to be resisting the Supreme Court decision on a strictly ethical basis. How does this position differ with your own nonviolent one?

[*King*]:   First, I haven't seen any Southerners really resisting it on an ethical basis. But I will say this: if they do, I think they should have a right to do that. If one is committed purely to the legalistic way, through the courts, you must give the opposition the right to appeal, to use the same approach. I mean he uses the same method, he can go to court, he can go up to the Supreme Court. He may lose, or he may win, but you give him that same, he has that same right. I think the same way in a nonviolent campaign: that if you insist that it is right to break what conscience tells you is an unjust law, then you must also give this man over here the right to break an unjust law, a law that conscience tells him is unjust, you see.

[*King to unknown person*]:   Tell him I'll be out in just a minute.

[*King to Margolies*]:   And the [*door closes*] only thing that I would say is this: that in breaking that unjust law, the individual must first be nonviolent. He should be peaceful in breaking it, he should have a loving attitude, he shouldn't be cursing, and he shouldn't be throwing out all of these vitriolic expressions that we find in New Orleans.[15] I don't think that's civil disobedience; I think it's uncivil disobedience.

And third, he must be willing to voluntarily and cheerfully accept the penalty for breaking an unjust law. Now, this is different from evading the law. This is what I think the Southern reactionaries are doing. They are defying the law, which I think is wrong. They are seeking to evade the law, which I think is wrong. But the individual [*phone buzzes*] who breaks an unjust law, a law which conscience tells him is unjust,

13. Articles in the *Atlanta Constitution* and *Atlanta Journal* erroneously reported that King had endorsed the agreement; however, another news source indicated that his father Martin Luther King, Sr., one of the signers of the agreement, said the deal was "workable" (Galphin, "Negroes Agree to End Sit-Ins," 8 March 1961; Margaret Shannon, "Sit-in Cases Stand Despite Accord," *Atlanta Journal,* 8 March 1961; and "Clarification Mass Meeting at Warren Church Tonight," *Atlanta Daily World,* 10 March 1961).

14. In Detroit on 6–7 March, King preached at Central Methodist Church as part of the Detroit Council of Churches' Noon Lenten Series.

15. King most likely refers to widespread resistance to court-ordered school desegregation in New Orleans.

and willingly accepts the penalty for it is expressing the highest respect for law. And he's not an anarchist, you see. He respects law, but he sees that there are two types of laws: there are just laws and there are unjust laws. A just law, from a purely moral point of view, is one that squares with what is morally right and certain basic principles of respect for the dignity and worth of human personality, so that any law that degrades human personality is unjust.

But not only that. An unjust law is a law in which the majority imposes upon the minority a code that it does not impose upon itself, that is not binding on itself. It is also a law which the majority imposes on the minority, which that minority had no power in creating or enacting because they don't have the right to vote in many instances.

So that most of the legislative bodies in the South can make these anti-trespass laws or what have you, I would contend, are not legally elected; the people did not elect them. In Mississippi only twenty thousand Negroes vote over the whole state, and yet they're about 48 percent of the population. So that this is an unjust law not on the basis of morality but on the basis of just observable facts, you see.

[*Margolies*]:   Dr. King, suppose [*phone buzzes*] that the Supreme Court had made a decision [*door opens*] confirming—

[*King*]:   Tell him I'll have to call him back. [*words inaudible*]

[*Margolies*]:   Suppose the Supreme Court had made a decision confirming segregation.

[*King*]:   What, you mean, what would I advocate? (*Yes, in this case*) I would say if the Supreme Court rendered a decision advocating segregation, I would urge people to resist that decision nonviolently. People have resisted the Supreme Court decisions before. In 1857 the Supreme Court rendered the *Dred Scott* decision.[16] This decision was morally wrong. It said in substance that the Negro is not a citizen of the nation, he is merely property. He had no rights that the white man is bound to respect. Now, this was morally wrong. Even the *Plessy* doctrine of 1896 was morally wrong, I think, and people resisted that decision.[17] Most of the resistance was legal, but there has been nonviolent resistance to it. So, I would say, today if the Supreme Court rendered a decision declaring segregation constitutional, I would urge people to resist that decision nonviolently, peacefully, and if necessary to break some law that was set up on the basis of the decision, to accept the consequences and stay in jail in order to arouse the conscience of the community so that the law can be altered.

Now, there is nothing new about civil disobedience, as you well know. I mean, academic freedom, to a degree, is a reality today because Socrates practiced civil disobedience. The early Christians mastered civil disobedience to the point of being thrown before the lions and everything else, refusing to accept certain laws that had come down through the Roman Empire and that they had to worship certain gods that the Roman Empire set up.[18] They practiced open civil disobedience. Everything

---

16.  *Dred Scott v. Sandford*, 60 U.S. 393 (1857).

17.  *Plessy v. Ferguson*, 163 U.S. 537 (1896).

18.  The earliest official persecution of Christians by the Romans began in the first century A.D. Despite a prevailing culture of religious tolerance, Romans mistrusted Christianity as a dangerous cult. Christians were persecuted for a variety of offenses with punishments that included burning, crucifixion, and being fed to lions and other wild animals.

that [*Adolf*] Hitler did in Germany was "legal," in quotes.[19] Everything that the Hungarian freedom fighters did in Hungary was illegal.[20] Now, it was legal, I mean illegal to aid and comfort a Jew during the time of Hitler in Germany. If I had lived in Germany I would have openly, I believe, advocated disobeying this and would have urged people to practice civil disobedience. The Boston Tea Party in our own history was a clear cut case of civil disobedience; even, to a degree, the Underground Railroad and the revolt against the Fugitive Slave Law.[21]

So that it just so happens now, which is a wonderful thing in the United States, that what we find in conscience to be right, we find in fact to be constitutional and this is good. This isn't true in South Africa, so I would tell the people in South Africa to disobey those laws.[22] But what we find in the United States is that we are practicing civil disobedience as far as local laws [*down in the South?*] are concerned, but we are really practicing civil disobedience to the federal law. We are really just trying to affirm the Constitution. And the question about the Supreme Court is just a hypothetical one because so far the Supreme Court has been consistent in upholding the laws as they relate to the question of integration. So that's about my answer on the whole question of civil disobedience.

[*Margolies*]:  Well, that's been extremely illuminating. I don't know—do we have time for one more?

[*King*]:  Yes, I'll take—I've got to go. I'm late for this other meeting, but I'll get there.

[*Margolies*]:  Well, OK—make this a quickie. I have a few more questions; I don't even know which one to ask. How about the coercive tendencies involved in nonviolence? Perhaps you could comment on that. It has coercive aspects [*words inaudible*].

[*King*]:  Well, that's a question that would take a little time. Basically, nonviolence says that persuasion is

[*Margolies*]:  Yeah.

[*King*]:  much better than coercion. Now, mainly it's thinking—when it talks against coercion, it's certainly thinking mainly of physical coercion, where you use physical violence and physical methods to bring about social change. When we think of persuasion, we're thinking of peaceful methods, peaceful demonstrations, peaceful picketing, peaceful sit-ins, or what have you, peaceful boycotts to do the job.

---

19. German legislation such as the 1935 Nuremberg Laws divided people into racially based categories which determined their legal rights.

20. On 23 October 1956, Hungarian citizens revolted against the policies of their government, which was backed by the Soviet Union. The revolutionaries quickly established a new democratic government, led by Prime Minister Imre Nagy. On 4 November, a large Soviet force invaded and crushed the resistance, regaining control of the Hungarian state by 7 November.

21. On 16 December 1773, a group of protesters dumped 342 chests of British East India Company tea into Boston Harbor rather than allow it to be off-loaded and sold. The Americans were protesting a tax on tea (taxation without representation) and the alleged monopoly of the East India Company. The Underground Railroad was a network of people that smuggled escaping slaves out of the South and into free states in the North. The 1850 Fugitive Slave Act secured the right of slaveholders to reclaim escaped slaves as lost property and made it illegal for anyone to aid a fugitive slave.

22. King is referring to the system of apartheid in South Africa, which legalized racial segregation and denied full citizenship to nonwhite South Africans. Apartheid remained in effect from 1948 to 1994.

On the other hand, I know the argument is that even in these so-called peaceful methods, in the boycott approach, you are coercing in the sense that you are withdrawing your economic support in order to make this man do something. Now, I would say there that it's a matter ultimately of intent. What is your ultimate purpose? Is your purpose to put the man out of business? Or is your purpose to create a situation in which a new relationship, a new relationship of understanding goodwill exists between you, your group, and this particular businessman, and all of the businesses involved? The intention is never to put the man out of business but, as I've said so often, to put justice in business. And this becomes, if it's coercion, it becomes the highest level of moral coercion.

Now, I must frankly say that there is a fine line of distinction here, because I believe that an element of coercion is necessary in life. I mean, I believe that you've got to have laws; I'm not an anarchist. For instance, I believe in the intelligent use of police power, so that I think we've got to have policemen. I think we've got to have a state. I don't feel that we can ever get by coercion totally because of man's capacity for evil. I think [*phone rings*] his capacity for goodness makes persuasion a very powerful instrument, but his [*phone rings*] inclination for evil makes coercion a necessity. And I don't throw it out all together. I think [*phone rings*] the only difference is that I believe in moral, non-violent coercion and never violent [*phone rings*] or physical, immoral coercion.

Excuse me. Operator, could that call come back in about a half an hour . . . in about a half an hour . . . I'm involved in an interview right now. Yes, yes. It is now two o'clock. Yes. [*recording interrupted*]

At. MLKJP-GAMK: Tape 88.

# To Sammy Davis, Jr.

28 March 1961
[*Atlanta, Ga.*]

*King thanks Davis for organizing the successful Carnegie Hall "Tribute to Martin Luther King, Jr.," and praises the work of musical artists like Davis, Harry Belafonte, Sidney Poitier, and Mahalia Jackson, who use their "enormous prestige" to "move the struggle forward."[1] Davis's tribute, which took place on 27 January, netted $22,577.47 for SCLC.[2]*

Mr. Sammy Davis, Jr.
THE SANDS
Las Vegas, Nevada

Dear Sammy:

The endless problems generated by our great FREEDOM MOVEMENT can only be compared to a river that never stops flowing. Fortunately, its progress too is like a river. Slowly—but surely and relentlessly—the Movement keeps pressing insistently forward, step by step. One such step, in my opinion, was the historic affair at Carnegie Hall on February 27, which you personally initiated and organized, then crowned with your astonishing artistry.

Not very long ago, it was customary for Negro artists to hold themselves aloof from the struggle for equality, in the belief that the example of their personal success was in itself a contribution in that it helped to disprove the myth of Negro inferiority—which indeed it did.

Today, however, our great Negro artists feel that this is an essentially defensive position which does not meet the needs of our time when the Negro people as a whole are vigorously striding towards freedom. Today greats like Harry Belafonte, Sidney Poitier, Mahalia Jackson and yourself, of course, are not content to merely identify with the struggle. They actively participate in it, as artists and as citizens,

---

1. Davis began organizing the tribute in late 1960. The idea for the benefit originated while members of the Rat Pack, a group of Hollywood entertainers including Davis and Frank Sinatra, were relaxing during the filming of *Ocean's 11* in Las Vegas (King to Davis, 20 December 1960, in *Papers* 5:582–583; "Sammy Davis Tells How Benefit Show for Rev. King was Born," *Jet*, 19 January 1961). According to a *Jet* magazine article, performances by Davis, Poitier, and Jackson were well received before the packed audience. Belafonte, an actor and friend of King's, read a congratulatory telegram from President Kennedy and introduced the civil rights leader to the audience at Carnegie Hall. Entertainers Jan Murray, Buddy Hackett, Nipsy Russell, Tony Bennett, and Count Basie also participated in the tribute (Robert E. Johnson, "Starry Tribute to King By Sinatra Clan Raises $50,000," *Jet*, 9 February 1961).

2. Abernathy, "Southern Christian Leadership Conference, treasurer's report," 1 September 1960–31 August 1961. The tribute committee gathered sponsorship for the evening from former first lady Eleanor Roosevelt, theologian Harry Emerson Fosdick, labor leader George Meany, New York governor W. Averell Harriman, and other well-known figures (A. Philip Randolph and Harry Belafonte to Meany, 27 November 1960; Meany to Randolph and Belafonte, 19 December 1960).

adding the weight of their enormous prestige and thus helping to move the struggle forward.[3]

Who can measure the impact, the inspirational effect, upon the millions of Negroes who have learned through thousands of grapevies that one of their idols, Sammy Davis, Jr., was responsible for rallying some of the greatest stars of Hollywood to come forward and publicly support the great cause of Negro freedom? On campuses and in communities throughout the south they are still talking about it and will continue to, I assure you, for many a long month to come.

It is primarily in behalf of these people—the embattled students and the many other thousands of southern freedom fighters, including my colleagues, the four ministers now being legally persecuted by the State of Alabama, that I wish to thank you deeply and sincerely for the truly significant contribution you have made, and, I am certain, will continue to make in the future.[4]

I hope our schedules will dovetail sometime soon so that we can spend a little time together under more relaxed conditions.

With warm personal regards to you and your charming wife, I am[5]

Sincerely yours,
Martin Luther King, Jr.

Km

TLc. MLKP-MBU.

---

3. Prior to the event, Belafonte told a reporter that "we as artists are told that we should not be identified with causes or political parties," but that he believed artists "have a responsibility to help create a social consciousness and lend economic support to men like Reverend King" (Johnson, "Starry Tribute to King," 9 February 1961).

4. King refers to the lawsuits filed against Ralph Abernathy, S. S. Seay, Joseph Lowery, and Fred L. Shuttlesworth by Alabama officials alleging that the four ministers and the *New York Times* slandered them by publishing an ad in the *Times* (see Introduction and "Heed Their Rising Voices," 19 March 1960, in *Papers* 5:25–26 and 382, respectively). The lawsuit resulted in the landmark defamation case, *New York Times Co. v. Sullivan*, 376 U.S. 254 (1964).

5. King refers to May Britt, Davis's wife.

# To John H. Herriford

31 March 1961
[*Atlanta, Ga.*]

*Herriford, a student at the University of Minnesota, wrote King on 11 November*
*1960 to offer suggestions for an upcoming televised debate against segregationist*
*James J. Kilpatrick.*[1] *Following the debate, Herriford wrote again, expressing*
*disappointment at King's performance.*[2] *Although King indicates that he did*
*not read Herriford's letter prior to the debate, he thanks him for his helpful*
*suggestions.*

Mr. John H. Harriford
3918 Portland Avenue
Minneapolis 7, Minnesota

Dear Mr. Harriford:

I guess you have concluded by now that either I have not received your letters or
that I am the most negligent person in the world concerning my correspondence.
The fact is that I received both of your recent letters and I am just getting to the
point of answering them. The only answer that I can give concerning my seeming
negligence is that I have had so many accumulated responsibilities, problems, and
mail over the last few months that I have remained behind almost constantly since
November. All of this, [*coupled?*] with several weeks away from the office as a result of
my physician's demand that I get some rest, accounts for the delay in replying to your
letters.[3] I hope you will accept my sincere apology.

Words are inadequate for me to express my appreciation to you for your very helpful suggestions concerning the debate that I had with Mr. Kilpatrick of Virginia. I
only regret that I did not receive your first letter until a week after the debate. I am
sure that I would have made a better showing if I had had the sound and able arguments you presented concerning the breaking of a tyrannous law.[4] As you know, I

---

1. On 26 November 1960, King debated Kilpatrick on the topic "Are Sit-in Strikes Justifiable," on the
television show "The Nation's Future" (see *Papers* 5:556–564). John Harold Herriford (1917–1984) first
entered the University of Minnesota in 1941 but did not complete a B.S. in political science until 1962. In
1965, he earned a second B.S. from the University of Minnesota in English. Herriford had urged King
to argue that businesses licensed by the public cannot defend racial discrimination (Herriford to King,
11 November 1960; Herriford to King, 19 December 1960).

2. Herriford to King, 19 December 1960. SNCC students were similarly disappointed by King's
appearance on the show (see Introduction in *Papers* 5:40–41).

3. King vacationed in the Bahamas from 19–26 February and shortened his Detroit speaking
engagement in March, after heeding a "demand from my physician that I get some much needed rest"
(King to G. Merrill Lenox, 15 February 1961). After another physical examination in May, King was
ordered to take six weeks of rest during the summer or "face the possibility of ominous consequences"
(King to Ewald Bash, 15 May 1961).

4. In his 11 November 1960 letter to King, Herriford wrote that there is a legal basis for disobeying a
tyrannous law: "A 'tyrannous' law is a law which compels the minority to do things which the majority

had undergone a great deal of stress before the debate. I spent seven days in jail after participating in the Atlanta sit-ins and immediately after my release I had to take a hasty trip to Nigeria, West Africa to attend the inaugural ceremonies of Governor General Azikewe.[5] I got back just in time to make the debate. With such a heavy [*schedule?*] in the background, I simply did not have time to prepare for the debate as I had hoped. Also, the question of civil disobedience is new in the minds of many people and it is difficult to explain in a half hour discussion. If the debate had been one hour, I am sure that many more fruitful points could have been brought out from my point of view.

May I say that I have found the points that you presented to Miss Bluford in the letter which you enclosed to be most helpful to me in discussions since the debate.[6] I think you have done more to clarify my thinking on this issue than anyone with whom I have talked. I plan to do an article for some major magazine on this question in the very near future. I would appreciate any suggestions that you may have. Also, I would like to have your permission to use the arguments that you set forth in the letter with reference to the difference between tyrannous and non-tyrannous laws.[7]

In closing, let me express my sincere gratitude to you for your interest in and support of the struggle which we are facing in the south. Such moral support is of inestimable value for the continuance of my humble efforts. Please feel free to write me at any time, and I hope we will become more personally acquainted in the not too distant future.

Very sincerely yours,
Martin Luther King, Jr.

Km

TLc. MLKP-MBU.

---

is <u>not</u> compelled to do. Or, such a law grants privileges to the majority which are denied the minority. Thus, there is no tyranny in a law which compels the minority to adhere to the <u>same</u> standards that apply to the majority."

5.  King and a group of student activists were jailed on 19 October 1960, after requesting service at the Magnolia Room, a segregated restaurant in Rich's department store in Atlanta. King was released on bond on 27 October 1960. From 14–18 November, King was in Lagos, Nigeria, for the swearing-in of Governor-General and Commander-in-Chief Nnamdi Azikiwe, the first person of African descent to be head of state in Nigeria. For more on King's arrest and Azikiwe's swearing-in ceremony, see Introduction in *Papers* 5:35–41.

6.  On 17 December 1960, Herriford wrote a lengthy letter to Lucile H. Bluford, of the newspaper *The Call*, in response to an editorial titled, "Must Obey Laws or Pay the Penalty," which discussed the King and Kilpatrick debate. Herriford felt the editorial mistakenly supported Kilpatrick and segregationists, and he presented various issues for Bluford to consider including the difference between tyrannous and nontyrannous laws, the authority of a democracy where not all citizens have the right to vote, King's need to attack segregation on a legal and moral basis, and the difference between individual anarchy and group protest of tyrannous laws.

7.  Herriford replied to King's letter on 11 April 1961, giving him permission to use any or all of the information from his earlier two letters. King later discussed the difference between just and unjust laws from a legal rather than a moral perspective in his September 1961 article "The Time for Freedom Has Come" (pp. 275–276 in this volume).

# "What Is the World's Greatest Need?"

2 April 1961
New York, N.Y.

*In a 21 November 1960 telegram, J. G. Stewart of the* New York Times Magazine
*asked King to write a short statement on what he believes to be "the world's greatest
need today."[1] Drawing upon the ideas of Harry Emerson Fosdick and Henry
David Thoreau, King claims that the world needs "modern man to keep the moral
and ethical ends for which he lives abreast with the scientific and technological
means by which he lives."[2]*

Modern man has built a complex and awe-inspiring civilization. One after
another the forces of the universe have been harnessed for our service.[3]

Yet there is something missing. In spite of man's tremendous mastery over the
scientific means of life, there is an appalling lack of mastery over those primitive
forces of social stagnation which result in wars and conflicts between races, nations
and religious groups.[4]

The world grows smaller as science advances. The elements of life are being
welded by the synthesis of time. Yet, man stumbles along vainly trying to maintain
racial, social and political separateness, to perpetuate ideas and systems that degrade
human personality. How much of our modern life is summarized in that great
phrase of Thoreau—"improved means to an unimproved end."[5]

Unless we can re-establish the moral ends for living in personal character and
social justice, our civilization will destroy itself by the misuse of its own instruments.[6]
In a world of thermonuclear weapons, the alternative to understanding, goodwill
and brotherhood may well be a civilization plunged into the abyss of annihilation.

---

1. King was one of ten individuals asked to contribute to the feature story. The other contributors
were British scientist and novelist C.P. Snow, former army chief of staff Maxwell D. Taylor, historian
Arnold Toynbee, managing director of the United Nations Special Fund Paul G. Hoffman, industrialist
Clarence B. Randall, Episcopal bishop James A. Pike, lawyer Charles P. Taft, and U.S. senators Margaret
Chase Smith and Mike Mansfield.

2. King expressed a similar message in 1949, while he served as associate pastor of Ebenezer Baptist
Church (King, "Civilization's Great Need," 1949, in *The Papers of Martin Luther King, Jr.*, vol. 6: *Advocate of
the Social Gospel, September 1948–March 1963*, ed. Clayborne Carson, Susan Carson, Susan Englander, Troy
Jackson, Gerald L. Smith [Berkeley and Los Angeles: University of California Press, 2007]: pp. 86–88).
Harry Emerson Fosdick (1878–1969), who King once called "the greatest preacher of this century," was
the founding minister of Riverside Church in New York City (King, Inscription to Fosdick, November
1958; see also Fosdick to King, 17 November 1958, in *Papers* 4:536–537). Henry David Thoreau (1817–1862)
was an American poet, essayist, and philosopher well known for his theory of civil disobedience.

3. Cf. Fosdick, *The Hope of the World* (New York and London: Harper & Brothers, 1933), p. 39. King
had a copy of Fosdick's book in his personal library.

4. Cf. Fosdick, *The Hope of the World*, p. 39.

5. Cf. Thoreau, *Walden: or, Life in the Woods* (Boston: Ticknor and Fields, 1854), p. 57. Fosdick, *The
Hope of the World*, p. 40: "'Improved means to an unimproved end'—how much of our modern life is
summarized in that shrewd phrase of Thoreau!"

6. Cf. Fosdick, *The Hope of the World*, p. 41.

The greatest need in the world today is for modern man to keep the moral and ethi- cal ends for which he lives abreast with the scientific and technological means by which he lives.

PD. *New York Times Magazine,* 2 April 1961.

## To Carlton B. Goodlett

10 April 1961
*[Atlanta, Ga.]*

*On 28 March 1961, one day after King concluded a fundraising tour through the Bay Area, an article in the* San Francisco Chronicle *reported that King chided the local black leadership for their lack of unity around the appointment of James E. Stratten as the first African American member of the San Francisco Board of Education.[1] King's alleged remarks elicited letters from local black leaders, including one from Goodlett, a local activist and the editor of the* Sun-Reporter, *who cautioned King to be "careful" when making statements about situations he knows little about: "When men of your national reputation allow themselves to be involved in a local controversy without a clear background, our burden is made heavier."[2] In response, King denies making any statement on that issue. Although King professes to be far from perfect, he is certain that he had not "come to the point that I would go into a local community and pass judgment on an issue that I am not informed about."[3]*

1. The article quoted King as saying that "it's little wonder Negroes are so rarely named to these responsible positions" as "Negroes can't even get behind their own people" (Donovan McClure, "Dr. King Leaves—Upset," *San Francisco Chronicle,* 28 March 1961). King's four-day visit was sponsored by the Western Christian Leadership Conference (WCLC), the West Coast fundraising arm of SCLC, and included engagements at Monterey Peninsula College and the Oakland Auditorium. California governor Edmund G. Brown authorized police escorts and security for King (King to Brown, 4 April 1961).

2. In his letter, Goodlett explained that his opposition to Stratten's appointment was due to the fact that he was director of a community center "subsidized in the main by the big industrialist." He added, "We wanted to place upon the board a distinguished minister who is beholden to no one but the Negro people" (Goodlett to King, 30 March 1961). San Francisco attorney Terry A. François sent a similar letter to King in which he warned King to "steer clear of complicated local issues and beware of newspaper reporters who invite your comment on same" (François to King, 29 March 1961; King to François, 12 April 1961). Carleton Benjamin Goodlett (1914–1997), born in Chipley, Florida, earned a B.A. from Howard University in 1935 and a Ph.D. in psychology from the University of California, Berkeley, in 1938. Goodlett completed a medical degree from Meharry Medical College in Nashville (1944), and the following year he opened a private practice in San Francisco's predominately black Fillmore District. Throughout his long career, Goodlett led and was a member of several civic rights organizations, including the NAACP (1947–1949) and the California Black Leadership Council (1951). He helped found the Black Press Archives (1973) at Howard University's Moorland Spingarn Research Center and the Morehouse School of Medicine (1975). In the 1966 Democratic gubernatorial primary, he ran unsuccessfully against incumbent Edmund G. Brown. He retired from medicine in 1983.

3. While Goodlett offered some praise of King and the work of SCLC, he further scoffed that he would never visit Atlanta and comment publicly on local disagreements like the discord between the

Dr. Carlton B. Goodlett
1380 Turk Street
San Francisco 15, California

Dear Dr. Goodlett:

Enclosed is a copy of a letter which I just sent to the editor of the San Francisco CHRONICLE.[4] I am very sorry that the impression was given that I made some critical statement of those who were raising questions concerning the Stratton appointment. I made no statement pro or con, privately or publicly. In fact, I was never even questioned by the press concerning the Stratton appointment. And I was so busy during my visit that I never had a chance to delve into the details of the whole issue.

I am sure you realize that one of the perils of being a leader is that of being constantly misrepresented, misquoted and misconstrued. This happens to me so often that I have had to develop the art of living with it. Whenever I can I seek to correct misrepresentations. However, it happens so often that in many instances I go on without even answering.

Certainly, I have no pretense to infallibility or to excellence of judgment at every point, but I do not believe that I have come to the point that I would go into a local community and pass judgment on an issue that I am not informed about. I sincerely regret that this whole thing occurred. While I do not feel that there was any malicious attempt on the part of the CHRONICLE, I am sure that the sentiments expressed were those of someone else and I was chosen as a person to state them.

I must also make it clear that I have made no statement concerning the San Francisco ministers. Actually, it never occurred to me that they were not cooperating. I never heard anyone discuss the matter at any time.[5] As I said in the letter to the Editor, I left the Bay Area so tremendously inspired and moved that I did not have time to think of any local division. Far from leaving upset, I left with new courage and vigor to carry on.

Please know that you have my prayers and best wishes for the significant work that

---

Atlanta student leaders, who wanted the desegregation of downtown Atlanta businesses immediately, and the adult leaders, who had recently reached an agreement with the Chamber of Commerce to gradually desegregate (Goodlett to King, 30 March 1961). For more on King's involvement in the Atlanta sit-in agreement, see Introduction, pp. 4–5 in this volume.

4. King to Editor of *San Francisco Chronicle*, 12 April 1961. Excerpts of King's letter were published in the *Chronicle* on 21 April 1961: "Actually I made no comment concerning this appointment. I recall hearing of disagreement over the appointment, but I did not feel sufficiently informed to make a statement. I sincerely regret that the article gave this impression . . . along with the one that I left the Bay area upset. I left tremendously inspired. I do not know when I have had an experience that gave me a feeling of such massive, overwhelming support from friends of good will (King, "Calm and Inspired," *San Francisco Chronicle*, 21 April 1961).

5. King closed out his tour of the Bay Area with a 26 March address before a capacity crowd of over 8,000 at the Oakland Auditorium where approximately $10,000 was raised for SCLC. Citing an unnamed source, a news article claimed that no San Francisco ministers had joined WCLC and that King was disappointed by the lack of support (McClure, "Dr. King Leaves—Upset," 28 March 1961; McClure, "8,000 Hear Dr. King in Oakland," *San Francisco Chronicle*, 27 March 1961). In his letter to King, Goodlett said that the local ministers would join WCLC soon, but that the comments attributed to King in the newspaper "have done to our cause in San Francisco" a "grievous injury" (Goodlett to King, 30 March 1961).

you are doing in the Bay Area. I quite agree with you concerning the insidious and subtle forms of discrimination in sections outside of the south. I can appreciate some of the problems which you are confronting. If I can be of any assistance, please do not hesitate to call on me. I have kept up with the dedicated and significant work you are doing with a great deal of inner pride.

Very sincerely yours,
Martin Luther King, Jr.

Km
Dictated by Dr. King, but signed in his absence.

TLc. MLKP-MBU.

## Lecture Delivered to Christian Ethics Class at Southern Baptist Theological Seminary and Question and Answer Period

[*19 April 1961*]
[*Louisville, Ky.*]

*After delivering "The Church on the Frontier of Racial Tension" at the Southern Baptist Theological Seminary (SBTS) chapel, King answers questions regarding nonviolence, black nationalism, and civil disobedience from an audience of approximately 500 students.[1] Distinguishing between private property and privately owned but publicly used enterprises, King postulates that America will not "rise to its full maturity" until all businesses no longer discriminate on the basis of race or color. When a business owner has the "freedom to choose his customers on the basis of race or religion," King says, freedom is taken "too far." Although King's visit drew positive responses from the students and faculty, it prompted a backlash from within Southern Baptist circles, including the withdrawal of donations earmarked for the seminary by several churches.[2] In response to the criticism, the SBTS board of trustees and seminary president*

---

1. The seminary invited King to speak on "some such topic as 'Christianity Confronts Race Relationships'" as part of its Julius Brown Gay Lectureship series (Allen Willis Graves to King, 1 June 1960). Following the question and answer session, King addressed the faculty, then presented a petition signed by an estimated 251 seminary students supporting desegregated facilities to the mayor's committee on integration in downtown Louisville. He concluded his afternoon by speaking at Quinn Chapel AME Church in support of the local sit-in campaign to desegregate restaurants in the downtown area. A week after King's visit, demonstrations escalated, prompting mayor Bruce Hoblitzell to call for downtown restaurants to desegregate by 1 May ("Police Brutality, Racial Violence Now Very Evident," *Louisville Defender*, 27 April 1961; Ora Spaid, "Dr. King Says 'Segregation Is Dead,'" *Louisville Courier-Journal*, 20 April 1961).

2. Baptist Press, Press release, "King's seminary talk draws Alabama critic," 28 April 1961. SBTS Christian ethics professor Nolan Howington afterward wrote that "the standing ovation which [the students] gave you at the conclusion of your second message is indicative of the genuineness of their

*Duke McCall released a statement expressing "regret for any offense caused by the recent visit of The Rev. Martin Luther King Jr."[3] Due to the poor quality of the audio recording, the questions from the audience could not be heard; the following transcript reflects only King's answers.*

[*King*]:   Thank you very kindly, Dr. Barnette and to the other faculty members who are here and to all of the members of the student body who are here.[4] I'm very happy to have this privilege, and I want most of this period to be your period. You've heard me talk long enough; I happen to be a Baptist preacher and I find it very difficult to control my time and face these time limits. As I go around the country preaching, they often send me a letter saying, "You will have twenty minutes for the sermon." And of course I find it much more difficult to preach a twenty-minute sermon than I do to preach an hour sermon. I have to prepare a little more to preach a twenty-minute sermon than an hour, you know that. [*laughter*] But I'm sure you'll have questions that you would like to raise concerning the whole question of integration and desegregation and also questions concerning the method being used and the movement generally, and I will be very happy to try to answer them. I must say to you in advance that I have no pretense to omniscience. I don't know everything. And I can only say that I'll try to answer the questions that you raise as we go on in this common search for truth and this common search for a solution to this big problem.

I would like to say just briefly something about the method that I have tried to advocate along with many, many other leaders in this struggle. There are three characteristic ways that oppressed people can deal with their oppression. Take one way, is to acquiesce, to resign oneself to the fate of oppression. And this method has been used through history. You remember when Moses was leading the children of Israel out of Egypt toward the Promised Land and they got out into the wilderness, there were some who wanted to go back to Egypt.[5] They preferred the flesh pots of Egypt to the challenges ahead. I remember when I was coming up in Atlanta, there was a man who used to play a guitar, and he had favorite songs that he would sing, and

---

appreciation for your spirit and for your grasp of a very perplexing problem" (Howington to King, 21 April 1961). Among other critics, W. D. Malone, chairman of the board of trustees of the First Baptist Church of Dothan, Alabama, wrote that if the seminary persists "in entertaining or encouraging those attempting to upset the good relation of the races in the South, I shall feel it my duty—insofar as I can—to strongly oppose any financial support for the Seminary" (Malone to Duke McCall, 15 May 1961). In a later letter, Malone expressed his fear that if "certain religious leaders generally continue their open and covert efforts to induce the South to accept integration, then the Southern Baptist Convention will be crippled, many good men will lost their pastorates, many churches dwindle and our church-supported institutions will lose prestige and much financial support" (Malone to McCall, 5 July 1961). McCall later estimated that King's visit cost the seminary between $200,000 and $500,000 in contributions (McCall to Henlee H. Barnette, 1 June 1993).

3. Baptist Press, Press release, "Southern trustees make King statement," 9 August 1961. The press release also quotes a letter from SBTS board of trustees chairman Ernest L. Honts: "You may be assured of our primary desire to place the advancement of the cause of Christ through our beloved denomination above any force which might attempt to divide us."

4. Henlee H. Barnette (1911–2004) taught Christian ethics at SBTS from 1951 to 1977.

5. Exodus 10.

one day I discovered that he was singing a little song like this: "Been down so long that down don't bother me."[6] Now, there a lot of people that get to this point; they achieve the freedom of exhaustion. And [*laughter*] this is, but of course this isn't the way because noncooperation with evil is as much a moral obligation as is cooperation with good.[7]

The second method that has been used is that of corroding hatred and physical violence. And of course we know about this method. It has been something of the inseparable twin of Western materialism and the hallmark of its grandeur. And I would not say at all that violence has never worked in the sense that it has never brought about a temporary victory. I know that nations have often received independence through the use of violence, and it has worked temporarily. But I would go on to say that although it may bring about temporary victory, it never brings permanent peace. And violence ends up creating many more social problems than it solves.

But there is a third way: mainly nonviolent resistance. And this is a method which makes it possible for the individual to stand up against an unjust system, to resist that system, and yet not hate in the process and not use violence in the process. Now, there are many things that can be said for this method. First, it gives one the possibility of working for a moral end through moral means. And this is where nonviolent resistance would break with all of those systems that would argue that the end justifies the means. I remember some time ago, when the student movement first started, a former president of the United States, the only thing he said about it was that it was Communism inspired, and I'm sure that students all over were very insulted by that.[8] Number one, it's an insult on one's intelligence to say to him that if somebody's standing on his neck, he doesn't have the intelligence to rise up against it and protest unless Mr. [*Nikita*] Khrushchev of Russia comes over and tells him that somebody's standing on his neck. But the other reason is even more deeper than that, and that is that this is a spiritual movement. It has a spiritualistic worldview rejecting the materialistic worldview of Communism and also rejecting the ethical relativism of Communism. [*Vladimir*] Lenin said on one occasion that any method is justifiable in order to bring about the classless society. So he says lying, deceit, violence, anything, just as long as it brings about the classless society that he talks about.[9]

But in the method of nonviolent resistance, when one is committed to it as a way of life, he does not succumb to the temptation of believing that an immoral, that immoral means can bring about moral ends, because he realizes that the end is

---

6. Blues singer Ishman Bracey's 1931 recording of "Trouble Hearted Blues" included the following lyrics: "Down so long, down don't worry me." Billie Holiday's 1954 recording of "Stormy Blues" had similar lyrics: "I've been down so long that down don't worry me."

7. Cf. M.K. Gandhi, *Satyagraha* (Ahmadabad: Navajivan Publishing House, 1951), p. 165: "Non-co-operation with evil is as much a duty as co-operation with good." See also Gandhi, "The Poet's Anxiety," *Young India*, 1 June 1921.

8. Among other critics, former president Harry S. Truman claimed that the 1960 sit-ins were engineered by Communists (King to Harry S. Truman, 19 April 1960, in *Papers* 5:437–439).

9. Robert J. McCracken, "What Should Be the Christian Attitude to Communism?," in *Questions People Ask* (New York: Harper & Brothers, 1951), pp. 168–169: "'We must be ready,' wrote Lenin, 'to employ trickery, deceit, lawbreaking, withholding and concealing truth.'" King frequently used McCracken as a source for his sermon material. For more on King's reference to *Questions People Ask*, see King, Index of Sermon Topics, 20 February–4 May 1951, in *Papers* 6:119.

pre-existent in the means. And the method of nonviolence makes it possible for one to seek to secure moral ends through moral means. It also makes it possible for one to struggle with determination to break down the unjust system and yet not defeat the individuals who may be caught up in that unjust system. So one who is committed to this method seeks to defeat segregation and not the segregationists; he seeks to convert the segregationist. And this is the tragedy of violence, you see; it seeks to annihilate the opponent rather than convert the opponent. Another thing about it is that it says that you must not only avoid internal violence, I mean external physical violence but also internal violence of spirit. And this is something of the love ethic that I talked about this morning.[10]

And as you know, Mohandas K. Gandhi who made, who used this method in a magnificent way to free his people from the domination of the British Empire, was greatly influenced by the Sermon on the Mount. And he read the Sermon on the Mount, he said that this was one of the most moving experiences of his life, particularly the part that says turn the other cheek and the other: resist not evil, resist the evil not with evil but with good.[11] And these aspects and these teachings within the Sermon on the Mount greatly influenced Gandhi. And I do remember, I do know when we started our movement in Montgomery, Alabama, long before the people heard the name of Mohandas K. Gandhi and Mahatma Gandhi, they had heard of Christ, and we made it very clear that this was a movement of Christian love. This was a movement based on the Christian ethic of love. And this is why I say that our movement there received its spirit and its inspiration from Christ and its operational technique from Gandhi. So that it is very important, I think, to get over that when we, to get over the point that when we talk about nonviolence, we are not merely talking about something that was advocated and used by Gandhi of India but also by Jesus of Nazareth. And I think that this is a very important aspect of nonviolence.

Now, nonviolence also says—and this is the final point I want to bring out—that there is an element of good, that is, that there are amazing potentialities for goodness within human nature and that it is possible for human beings to be transformed. This is basic in nonviolence. Now, I don't think it is necessary to be superficial in one's optimism at this point, and I think at times those who have believed in nonviolence have been a little too superficial in their optimism concerning human nature. Man is not all good; there is some, some bad in him. Carlyle said on one occasion that there are heights in man which go up to the highest heaven and depths which go down to the lowest hell, "for are not both Heaven and Hell made out of him, everlasting Miracle and Mystery that he is?"[12] And I think there is this aspect of man's nature that we must at least think about when we think of the nonviolent way. It's not enough to just say that man, man has potentialities for goodness; we must say man

10. King, "The Church on the Frontier of Racial Tension," Lecture delivered at Southern Baptist Theological Seminary, 19 April 1961: "Now, many people ask me over and over again, 'What do you mean when you say love these people who are oppressing you, these people who will bomb your home and threaten your children, and seek to block your desires and aspirations for freedom, what do you mean when you say love them?' And I always have to stop and try to define the meaning of love in this context."

11. Cf. Matthew 5–7; Gandhi, *An Autobiography: The Story of My Experiments with Truth* (Boston: Beacon Press, 1957), p. 68.

12. Cf. Thomas Carlyle, *The French Revolution* (1837), vol. 3, book 1, chap. 4.

has potentialities for evil also and be realistic in our anthropology. So, I don't want to give anybody the impression that in order to believe in this philosophy of nonviolence, it is necessary to go to the extreme that even liberalism within Protestantism has often gone to of seeing man evolving up some ladder of goodness that will finally be worked out in the long run of things. The fact is that we have too much evidence to refute this. But man does have potentialities for goodness as well as potentialities for evil, and the nonviolent resister believes that these things can be brought out and that the image of God is not totally destroyed. Man is not totally depraved. Although the image is terribly scarred, there is a possibility to transform human nature. And so these are just some of the things about the basic philosophy of nonviolence that I wanted to mention. Now I'm sure that you would like to raise some questions about the more practical aspects of the technique itself and the rightness of this method and the practicality of it. So with these introductory remarks I will turn it over to you to start firing the questions.

[*Indecipherable Question*]

[*King*]: Yes on the first question. I don't know what will be done in Atlanta, whether this will be repeated in Atlanta. Up to now, it hasn't been discussed; I mean it hasn't been definitely planned for May seventeenth. There is a possibility that something will be done on May seventeenth in Atlanta.[13] However, on a larger scale, May seventeenth is a very significant day in the Negro community, as well as in the white community for those who are allies in this struggle. Many demonstrations across the country take place on this day as a reminder to the nation that we have not fulfilled the American dream, we have not implemented the Supreme Court's decision. So that I'm sure there will be demonstrations in various sections of the country to dramatize this issue and the need to move on toward implementing the Supreme Court's decision.[14]

The second, on the second point, we have sought conferences with many Southern governors who have turned us down. I know in Alabama we sought conferences with Governor [*John*] Patterson, who consistently turned us down. The same thing in Georgia; we've tried to see Governor [*S. Ernest*] Vandiver, and he has turned us down. I have not sought personally, and I can't speak for others, to discuss this matter with Senator [*Herman Eugene*] Talmadge or [*Richard*] Russell of Georgia. But we have contacted other senators, and there's always a convenient way to just turn Negro groups down when they seek conferences with the political leaders. Now, I would imagine that there would be a great difference here in, say, I know in border states but even in the middle states—and when I say "middle states," I'm thinking of Tennessee, North Carolina, Texas, Florida, and Virginia—there would probably be no difficulty here. I think the governors of these states on the whole would see

---

13. On 17 May 1960, the sixth anniversary of the *Brown* decision, approximately 1,500 students in Atlanta attempted to march to the state Capitol but were turned away by highway patrol and city police. The students then marched to Wheat Street Baptist Church, where they were addressed by King (Claude Sitton, "Atlantans Block Negro Marchers," *New York Times*, 18 May 1960).

14. On 17 May 1954, the Supreme Court ruled in *Brown v. Board of Education* that segregated schools were unconstitutional. Three years later, some 20,000 demonstrators congregated at the Prayer Pilgrimage for Freedom in Washington, D.C., to push for the federal government to enforce the decision. For King's address at the 1957 Prayer Pilgrimage, see King, "Give Us the Ballot," Address Delivered at the Prayer Pilgrimage for Freedom, 17 May 1957, in *Papers* 4:208, 210–215.

Negro leaders and talk with them about the problem and probably the senators in these states. But in the Deep South, we do have this problem of the political leaders not being too open to conversations with Negro leaders.

Now, on the third question concerning the efficacy or rather the morality of the boycott technique, I can only say that it is a matter of intent here. I have never seen the boycott as a violent method. Certainly those who use it are not participating in physical violence. It's not physical violence, so that automatically says it isn't violence in a physical sense, and we have always said that we shouldn't have any violence of spirit when we go into boycotts. We stress the need for loving and maintaining this understanding goodwill so that the intent is not to destroy, not to put anybody out of business. The intent is to put justice in business and really to make a better business because if these values are broken down, these merchants will make more money. And this is why I, it is a matter of intent. I have never seen it just as a negative something that you do because you hate the merchant or you're trying to put him out of business. But it is a massive withdrawal of support from a system of evil in order to bring about some ultimate change and transformation, and certainly, we hope we will convert some of the merchants in the process. It is noncooperation with an unjust system and certainly not any attempt to destroy the individuals who are caught up in this unjust system. Now, we know that some people as a result of boycotts suffer on both sides. In Atlanta, when we had the boycott, three hundred and some people lost their jobs.[15] They would come to see me almost every day to help them get jobs. I mean Negro people who worked at these lunch counters. And this is something of the risk and something of the temporary sacrifice that you must go through in order to bring about the social change and transformation that we are seeking. But just to come back to this point, I don't think the boycott is fighting fire with fire, because the intention is not to defeat the merchant, not to put him out of business, but to make for a better business and to bring justice and freedom and human dignity into business which will make for a better society for everybody.

[*Indecipherable Question*]

[*King*]:   Well, I would only, I could only say that there are two types of laws. There are just laws and there are unjust laws. I would be the first person to say to everybody, "Obey just laws." Now, that not just, that puts us into the position of asking what are just laws and what are unjust laws. I would say that a just law is a law that squares with the moral law of the universe. A just law is a man-made law that is in line with what the religionist would call the law of God. Well, somebody would say, "Well, that's too abstract; that doesn't have any relevance in concrete terms. Well, what in the world do you mean by the law of God and the moral law?"

So, you would have to move to something maybe more concrete terms for some people. And I would certainly think that any law that degrades human personality is unjust from a moral point of view. But I would say in just sheer practical terms, any law in which the majority imposes a code on the minority that it does not impose on

---

15. In exchange for ending the sit-ins and other boycotts of downtown businesses in Atlanta, black leaders and local business owners in March 1961 agreed to desegregate by the fall of 1961 ("Atlanta's Sit-ins Ended by Accord," *New York Times*, 8 March 1961). For more on the Atlanta sit-in agreement, see Introduction, pp. 4–5 in this volume.

itself is an unjust law. On the other hand, a just law is when the majority imposes a 19 Apr
code on the minority that it imposes on itself. You can go on to say an unjust law is
one in which the majority imposes a code on the minority that that minority had no
part in creating or enacting because that minority had no right to vote. So the legislatures of most of the states in the Deep South are not even democratically elected.
And on the other hand, the just law would be the law in which you do have these
things existing, where people have the right to vote, they're democratically elected,
where the majority imposes a code on the minority that it imposes on itself.

Now, after one clears this up, I think we see that you do have two types of laws
here; you have just and unjust laws. I urge everybody to obey just laws. I also say that
a Christian not only has a right but a responsibility to stand up against an unjust
law. But now in doing this, he must do it peacefully; he must do it nonviolently; he
must do it in a loving spirit; and he must be willing to accept the penalty. He must
not seek to evade the law; he must not seek to subvert the law; he must do it openly.
He must not seek to defy the law, because he becomes an anarchist then. But the
individual who decides to break a law that conscience tells him is unjust, and willingly, cheerfully, and voluntarily accepts the penalty is at that moment expressing
the highest respect for law. And he is not an anarchist, but he's expecting, expressing the very highest respect for law. Now, what we see in the Deep South today is
not civil disobedience but uncivil disobedience. It is defying the law; it is evading
the law and an unwillingness to accept the penalty. But he who is willing to do this
and go to jail if necessary and stay there in order to arouse the conscience of the
community so that that unjust law will be altered and finally brought to the point
that the law squares with the moral law, that person is expressing the very highest
respect for law.

Now, let me mention just a few instances of this. It's nothing new about it. There's
nothing new about this. To a degree, academic freedom is a reality today because
Socrates practiced civil disobedience. The early Christians, the master of the art of
civil disobedience, they did not obey the Roman law; they just refused. They were
thrown to the lions for this. They would not bow down and worship the gods that the
Roman Empire wanted them to worship. They were determined to worship Christ,
and they disobeyed a law, and they were often killed for it. They were disobeying the
law that conscience told them was unjust.

Let us move on up to the modern day. Everything that Hitler did in Germany was
legal—end quote. Everything that the Hungarian freedom fighters did in Hungary
was illegal—end quotes. It was a crime to aid and comfort the Jewish people during
the days of Hitler. I believe that if I had lived in Germany, if I had the attitude that
I have now, I would have disobeyed the law. I would have aided and comforted my
Jewish brothers. In South Africa today, apartheid is the law of the land, and I would
be the first person to say to the African people, if you can organize yourself to disobey the extreme laws of white supremacy in South Africa, you should do it.

In our own history, the Boston Tea Party was a noble example of civil disobedience. The Underground Railroad—most of the abolitionists practiced civil disobedience. If I lived in a Communist country today where certain Christian customs
cannot take place in Christian worship—I would urge people to disobey the law
where they couldn't have Christian baptism and they couldn't have Christian communion. I would just say, "Disobey this law." So that I think that the students today in
disobeying laws that they know are unjust are really in noble company. They are in

the company of people throughout history. And I, this is the way I justify it, and this is my basic philosophy on it.

[*Indecipherable Question*]

[*King*]:    No, I cannot conceive of a situation where it would be better to renounce the nonviolent method and turn to violence. Now, I have sense enough to know that there will be times that people, individuals will renounce the nonviolent method and turn to violence, but still I would have to say that I don't think it is the best method from a practical point of view or a moral point of view. I think it is both impractical and immoral. And even if it were expedient in a particular instance, I would still say that it would be morally wrong. So that I would be absolute in my position at this point in saying that violence is absolutely wrong in our struggle, morally wrong, and I think, as I said, I think it's impractical. And particularly in America where we're seeking integration.

Integration is much more complex and even difficult than independence, because in one instance you are seeking to drive a foreign invader out. In the instance of our struggle in America, it's not driving a foreign invader out, but it's seeking a new level of creative life and existence with the very people that you're going to have to live with the very minute the struggle ends. You're going to have to live with these same people tomorrow morning at nine o'clock if segregation ends at eight o'clock tonight. Where in a colonial struggle, you are driving another force out that has dominated politically and otherwise. And I think in our situation it is even more imperative to practice nonviolence because we have this job of living with the very people and being friends with the very people that we are struggling against at this time. You can be next with the—

[*Indecipherable Question*]

[*King*]:    Well I'm an extremist. [*laughter*] I believe in the extreme of love, not the extreme of hate, I believe in the extreme of goodwill and not the extreme of ill will. I'm never worried about being an extremist. I think the world is in great need of extremists, and I say that very seriously.[16] But the other thing that I would like to say and a context is that it is not right to equate the NAACP with the White Citizens' Council, and I think this has too often been done. The NAACP has done nothing but work through the most dignified channels of legal democracy to make justice a reality for Negro people. It has not been an organization that advocated violence; it hasn't been an organization that advocated hatred; it has gone through the very dignified channels of the courts to achieve citizenship rights for Negro people. The NAACP is seeking to live in line with the Constitution of the United States. It's seeking to bring about the birth of justice, where in the White Citizens' Council, or Councils, are standing against the Constitution of the United States. They are, through their vitriolic expressions, they are creating the atmosphere for violence. They would say they don't advocate violence, but their defiance of the law and their words inevitably create the atmosphere for violence. So that they are seeking to prevent the birth of freedom and justice in society, wherein the NAACP is seeking in

---

16. King, "The Church on the Frontier of Racial Tension": "I think that all men of goodwill must be maladjusted to all of these things, for it may well be that the salvation of our world lies in the hands of the maladjusted."

a very disciplined way to bring into being the fulfillment of the Constitution of the United States.

And therefore I don't think the two should be equated. I think one is in line with the highest traditions of our nation, wherein I think the other is out of line with all that is noble and all that is true in our democratic dream. And I would say that people of goodwill should join and should cooperate with the NAACP. I'm very proud to be a life member of the NAACP. I'm not an official of the organization, but I'm very proud of it because I think the NAACP has done more than any other organization to achieve citizenship rights for Negroes, and I think it has served as the one organization to keep Negroes from turning to some extreme group like the Muslims or to some extreme philosophy as Communism or some foreign ideology.[17] It's the one organization that reminded the Negro that he could achieve his rights and his justice through these channels. And it gave him a way out wherein if he did not have something like this, he would have turned to Communism and other systems and other forms of, or other methods rather, that would have defeated in the long run the real democratic process.

Gentleman in the back is next.

[*Indecipherable Question*]

[*King*]: Well, I would say that we must continue to condemn the philosophy of this movement. And all of the major Negro leaders do condemn the philosophy of the black nationalist movement generally; there are about five of them. We must condemn the philosophy and the fact that they too can create the atmosphere for violence and very bitter feelings. So on the one hand, we will continue, I'm sure, to condemn the basic philosophy.

On the other hand, this movement came into being as a result of something. It is symptomatic of the frustration, the discontent, the disappointment of Negro people. And while we condemn the philosophy, we must work with vigor and new determination to remove the conditions that brought such a movement into being. And that means the federal government must do this, white people of goodwill must do this, and Negroes must do this.

The other thing is this: it should also bring us to see now that the leaders that we've been calling extremists and the leaders that we've been, movements that we've been calling extremist movements are really moderating influences within the Negro community. I know it's a difficult adjustment for some people to see that sit-ins serve as moderating influences. But it's one of the creative developments that people who have not seen a way out now see a way out nonviolently. And they've come to see that they don't have to hate to get free, and they don't have to use violence. So that it should help people of goodwill to support more these organizations and leaders that are guiding the Negro community into a channel of creative love and nonviolence and all of that.

The other thing I'd like to say is that I don't believe that this movement will ever have any great growth or great gains in the Negro community. It, right now it isn't

---

17. Since 1958 Kivie Kaplan, board member of the NAACP, had unsuccessfully tried to recruit King to join the organization's national board (see King to Kaplan, 6 March 1961, pp. 172–174 in this volume; see note 1, King to Kaplan, 3 May 1960, in *Papers* 5:451).

as large as we would think because we hear a lot about it. It's the kind of movement that will get a great deal of publicity anyway, no matter how small it is. But I don't believe that it will ever reach or influence the vast majority of Negroes. I think the predominant sentiment in the Negro community is opposed to this. We don't want to substitute one tyranny for another; we don't want get away from one kind of segregation and get into another kind of segregation. They said there's the most recent book out on this movement and probably the most definitive estimates the numbers at a hundred thousand.[18] The FBI estimates that it's sixty thousand. Now this sounds maybe large, but this is very small when you think of the fact that you have more than nineteen million Negroes in the United States. I can think of ten Negro churches in the United States with a hundred thousand members. And so that this is not large when you think of the number; it shows that it has not had a *great* impact. And the thing that amazes me is not how many people they've appealed to or they've gained, but how many they haven't gained. So that I don't think it will ever have any impact in terms of large numbers of Negroes, but I do think it will continue to exist and will continue to appeal to certain people as long as the conditions of discrimination exist, as long as the Negro faces all of these economic injustices and the other problems that I mentioned this morning.[19]

[*Indecipherable Question*]

[*King*]:   On the first question, I would say that there is a distinction between private property that is purely private and private property that is privately owned but publicly used, publicly supported, publicly sustained. I think there is a great difference between the two. I think the anti-trespass law is all right, for instance, because I don't think anybody should have the right to just come in my house that I may privately own and not leave if I wanted them to leave. I think that that's a private right that we should certainly protect on the basis of the First Amendment to the Constitution. But now if I turn my house into a store, if I turn it into a department store, if I turn it into a lunch counter or anything like that, then I have certain obligations to the public beyond my particular whims and caprices. For instance, if I deny, this is what was said in the Sherman anti-trespass act, that if a business is in the public market it cannot deny access, if it's in the public market it cannot deny access to this public market.[20] And I think the same thing applies here. It's one thing to say that you own a, that an individual owns a private piece of property and another thing to say that this property is now a private enterprise, where it is actually dependent on the public for its very survival. And this is why we feel very strong about this: that a man should not have the right to say that on the basis of color or religion, one cannot use a lunch counter that is open to everybody else in another racial group but

---

18.  King likely refers to C. Eric Lincoln's *The Black Muslims in America* (Boston: Beacon Press, 1961), p. 4.

19.  In "The Church on the Frontier of Racial Tension," King discussed the gap between white and African American incomes, automation, and segregation in churches as "injustices" where "the church must go out and take a stand."

20.  Initially passed in 1890, the Sherman Antitrust Act prohibited trusts and illegal monopolies that could be shown to restrain competition. In 1961 the U.S. Justice Department began investigating whether restrictive housing covenants violated the Sherman Antitrust Act, which also makes illegal any contract that imposes unreasonable constraints on trade or commerce.

not to these particular people; he has an obligation to the public. Now, I certainly wouldn't mind if they had some stipulation that people drunk couldn't come there, that people disorderly in that sense, but on the basis of race and religion, I don't think America will ever rise to its full maturity until all over this country we say that anybody who is in a public business cannot deny anybody, on the basis of race or color, access to that business. He should not have the freedom to choose his customers on the basis of race or religion, and I think this has really taken freedom too far.

On the second point, I think it may be an economic risk, I don't know how great, for a church to integrate. It may be an economic risk for a church where you have most of the people are believing in segregation. On the other hand, I think we have another obligation. We are citizens of two worlds. And there is something that says to us at all times that we must always move on the basis of our commitment to the kingdom of God and not merely on the expedient, on the basis of the expedient, what happens to be expedient for the moment. And I think in the long run, even in these situations where there may be some economic losses, there is this great gain that comes from committing oneself to the basic precept of the kingdom and committing oneself to the teachings of Jesus Christ. I think this is more important than thinking in terms of the economic side of it.

[*Dr. Barnette*]:   We regret that the time is up. And Dr. King, we express again our deep appreciation for your coming and lecturing to the class today. [*applause*]

At. MLKEC.

# From Rosa Parks

19 April 1961
Detroit, Mich.

*Parks, who relocated to Detroit in 1957 with her husband, Raymond, thanks King for a gift of twenty dollars. She also updates him on the status of her family's health.*[1]

Dear Dr. and Mrs. King:

I am sorry that it has taken me such a long time to write my thanks for your generous gift of $20.00 when you were here.[2]

I mislaid the card while looking up your address, and I kept putting off writing.

---

1. Rosa Parks (1913–2005). King's gift may have been a contribution to a fundraising campaign to ease Parks's financial troubles. For more on King's efforts to assist Parks financially, see Parks to King, 14 March 1960, in *Papers* 5:389.

2. King was in Detroit multiple times, first on 21 August 1960 and again 6–7 March 1961. It is uncertain during which visit King and Parks saw each other.

We ~~arg~~ are keeping up very well inspite of poor health and other problems.[3]

My family joins me in wishing the best of health, happiness and success for you and yours.

Sincerely yours,
[*signed*] Rosa Parks

ALS. MLKP-MBU.

---

3. The Parks family suffered from medical problems: Raymond caught pneumonia in July 1958 and was unemployed from January to August 1959, while Rosa Parks was hospitalized for stomach ulcers and a throat tumor, which resulted in a $560 medical bill (Alex Poinsett, "The Troubles of Bus Boycott's Forgotten Woman," *Jet*, 14 July 1960, pp. 12–15).

# To Andrew Young

25 April 1961
[*Atlanta, Ga.*]

*On 24 March 1961 Young wrote King asking him for advice on accepting a position at Highlander Folk School.[1] Although Young was satisfied working for the National Council of the Churches of Christ he wanted to return to the South and take a more active role in the civil rights struggle. Below, King writes Young to congratulate him on being invited to join the Highlander staff, but cautions him that he may be unemployed if the school is closed by the State of Tennessee.[2] Young accepted the Highlander position in June 1961. Three months later he became a member of the SCLC staff.[3]*

---

1. Andrew J. Young (1932– ), born in New Orleans, Louisiana, received his B.S. from Howard University in 1951 and a B.D. from Hartford Theological Seminary in 1955. Following graduation, Young became pastor of United Church of Christ in Thomasville, Georgia, until his resignation in 1957 to become the associate director in the Department of Youth Work for the National Council of the Churches of Christ. In 1961 he accepted a position in the adult citizenship program at Highlander, which was later transferred to SCLC. By 1964 Young had become executive director of SCLC, a position he held until 1970. In 1972 Young became the first African American from Georgia to be elected to Congress since 1870. He remained a congressman until 1977, when President Jimmy Carter appointed him U.S. Ambassador to the United Nations. Young later served two terms as mayor of Atlanta.

2. The state of Tennessee brought charges against Highlander for running a bootleg alcohol operation. After a series of investigations and appeals, the school was closed and the property confiscated by the state in late 1961. Nevertheless, the school reopened as the Highlander Research and Education Center in Knoxville, Tennessee, the same year.

3. See Young to King and Wyatt Tee Walker, 11 September 1961, pp. 279–281 in this volume.

The Reverend Andrew J. Young                                      25 Apr
National Council of the Churches of Christ in the U.S.A.          1961
475 Riverside Drive
New York 27, New York

Dear Andrew:

Please accept my apology for being so tardy in replying to your letter of March 24. Absence from the city and the accumulation of a great deal of mail account for the delay.

I am very happy to know that you have been invited to join the staff of Highlander Folk School.[4] As you know, I am intensely interested in the program of Highlander and I have found it to be one of the most significant institutions in the south. It has served in the unique capacity of providing leadership training programs that are so desperately needed in this period of transition. Because it has pioneered in interracial activities, it has faced many problems and has received the complimentary term of being considered a controversial institution.

Now the question of whether you should come to Highlander is one that I must answer in the light of the present difficulties that they are now facing. As you probably know, the State Supreme Court of Tennessee has upheld a lower court decision to close the school.[5] Since the decision was rendered on the basis of certain false accusations that have no constitutional questions involved, there is a possibility that this issue cannot be taken to the United States Supreme court.[6] If this is the case, Highlander may have to close temporarily. Just what the legal process is at the present time, I do not know. I have not had a chance to talk with Myles Horton recently. Certainly I would not advise you to leave the position that you are now holding unless you can be sure that Highlander will remain open. This can only be answered by Myles Horton and the lawyers.

If it remains open and you accept the position, I am sure that you will be able to render a unique service in the south. The south is in dire need of dedicated leaders who are committed to the great ideal of freedom and human dignity, and who are committed to the principle of Christian non-violence as the method to grapple with the problem of racial injustice.

I know that the foregoing does not completely answer your question but this is

----

4. In March Horton wrote King asking him for his opinion of Young. In King's response, he wrote: "I cannot for the world of me place Andrew Young!" (Myles Horton to King, 24 March 1961; King to Horton, 25 April 1961). King then wrote a letter to Stanley D. Levison telling him of the March 1961 letter he received from Young. Although King did not remember meeting Young, he was interested in determining "whether he is the kind of man who could work with me at SCLC." He asked Levison and New York minister Thomas Kilgore to assess Young's "ability, background and technical competence" (King to Levison, 25 April 1961).

5. *Highlander Folk School et al. v. State ex rel. Sloan*, 345 S.W.2d 667 (1961).

6. In the State Supreme Court ruling, the justices found that the question of integration at Highlander was not the major issue in the case, but rather whether Horton operated the school for his own personal and private gain and if the sale of alcohol on the premises violated state law. In October 1961 the U.S. Supreme Court declined to review the State Supreme Court's decision upholding the revocation of Highlander's charter (*Highlander Folk School et al. v. Tennessee ex rel. Sloan, cert. denied*, 368 U.S. 840 [1961]).

about all that I can say in the light of the present circumstances. Please know that you have my prayers and best wishes as you seek to make this important decision.

Very sincerely yours,
Martin Luther King, Jr.

Km

TLc. MLKP-MBU.

## To Percival Leroy Prattis

26 April 1961
Atlanta, Ga.

*King thanks Prattis, executive editor of the* Pittsburgh Courier, *for his recent letter regarding an article King wrote for* The Nation, *and reiterates his support for the creation of a Secretary of Integration, an idea that came to him after a 1959 trip to India.[1] Prattis had expressed skepticism regarding the establishment of such a position.[2]*

Mr. P. L. Prattis, Editor
PITTSBURGH COURIER
2628 Centre Avenue
Pittsburgh 19, Pennsylvania

Dear Mr. Prattis:

I am deeply grateful to you for your very kind and full letter of February 17. Please accept my apologies for being so tardy in my reply. A brief trip out of the country, other absences from the city and the accumulation of a great deal of mail account for the delay.

I am deeply grateful to you for your comments concerning my article in NATION magazine. I can well understand your fear that a Secretary of Integration may bring into being a new bureaucracy which would have as much interest in keeping segregation alive as in promoting integration. Certainly this is one of the risks that would be taken in setting up such a secretaryship. However, I am convinced that we have never

---

1. Prattis to King, 17 February 1961; King, "Equality Now," 4 February 1961, pp. 139–150 in this volume.

2. Although Prattis mostly praised King's article, he was unenthusiastic about King's idea of a Secretary of Integration. Prattis maintained that the president should make his position for integration "unmistakably clear," and make it known to his administration "that he wants action" and "that he is not playing." Prattis was optimistic about the president's response to racial matters, since he had received personal confirmation from Kennedy, who told him: "P. L., I would get up off my fanny and do something" (Prattis to King, 17 February 1961).

fully mobilized the forces of our nation behind the integration process. We have, in the past, moved only in a piecemeal fashion, and politicians always have rationalizations to give for not moving faster. I see the position as Secretary of Integration as one way that the federal government can express its determination to bring an end to the long desolate night of segregation. This agency would coordinate all of the government's activity in this field and make sure that all of the other governmental departments will enforce non-discriminatory operations. Frankly, this idea came to me as a result of my visit to India a few years ago. In seeking to end caste untouchability, the national government of India set up a department with a special minister to deal with the problem of ending untouchability.[3] I was so impressed with the amazing advances that have been made in India in ending discrimination against untouchables that I felt that a similar move on the part of the federal government of the United States would be the most meaningful.[4]

At any rate, I have no pretense to omniscience and I am sure that I could be altogether wrong in my contention at this point. My only concern is that we use all of our resources to solve a problem that has existed far too long and one that will determine the destiny of our nation. I do not conceive that any of the ideas that I have projected are the ultimate solutions to the race problem. Like Gandhi, I think we are all engaged in an experiment with truth.[5] I think that by our constant working together and unswerving devotion to the idea of freedom and human dignity, we will come up with the right answer.

It is always good to hear from you. Please feel free to write at any time. May the days ahead bring us nearer to the "beloved" community and a society where the brotherhood of man is a reality.

Very sincerely yours,
[*signed*] Martin L. King Jr.
Martin Luther King, Jr.

K.m

TLS. PLPC-DHU-MS.

---

3. Article 338 of the Indian Constitution established a Commissioner of Scheduled Castes and Scheduled Tribes, placed under the Ministry of Home Affairs, to investigate matters concerning the protection and welfare of lower castes. Lakshmidas Mangaldas Shrikant served as the first Commissioner from 1950–1961.

4. Several months after his trip to India, King published an account of his tour in *Ebony* magazine that included a section on India's form of atonement for past injustices to untouchables (King, "My Trip to the Land of Gandhi," July 1959, in *Papers* 5:236).

5. King refers to Mahatma Gandhi's 1927 book *An Autobiography: The Story of My Experiments with Truth* (Ahmadabad: Navajivan Publishing House).

# "After Desegregation—What"

[*27 April 1961*]
[*Atlanta, Ga.*]

> *On 2 December 1960,* Coronet *magazine offered King $600 to write an article about the challenges facing the next generation of African Americans "after the civil rights battles have been won."*[1] *In the following draft sent to* Coronet, *King explores adjustments that students active in the movement will make in a society that is both "unsegregated and yet not really integrated."*[2] *He asks: "Will the same forthrightness be shown in admitting whites to Negro clubs, fraternities and other voluntary associations that is now being shown in pressing for admittance to restaurants and theatres?"*[3] *Concluding the article, King observes: "There will come from this cauldron a mature man, experienced in life's lessons, socially aware, unafraid of experimentation, and most of all imbued with the spirit of service and dedication to a great ideal." The magazine folded in October 1961, before the article was published.*[4]

To the Negro college student of today—especially in the south—desegregation is the vidid moment of life. To grapple with Jim Crow directly and personally is real excitement. Most likely it would involve facing police, court-trial and jail. It might also include winking at the disapproval of a cautious Dean or an ultra-conservative college president. For once, it could be possible to instruct one's own parents, instead of the other way around.

There are no evenings quite like those spent in the student council office hammering out strategy or putting together the slogans for tomorrow's picket line. Sacrifice and daring, action and the common cause—these make a heady mixture for idealistic youth.

The dynamism of the student movement can be understood only if we realize that it is part of a revolt of all youth—Negro and White—against the world they never made; a revolt not alone to achieve desegregation but a social order consistent with the high principles on which the nation was founded. Youth has moved out to take

---

1. King's literary agent, Marie F. Rodell, had forwarded the offer (Rodell to King, 2 December 1960). *Coronet* magazine had initially proposed that King collaborate on the article with writer Louis E. Lomax. Instead, King suggested writing the article himself to avoid angering the NAACP, which had objected to an article Lomax published, arguing that the NAACP was "no longer the prime mover of the Negro's social revolt" because of the organization's reluctance to initiate direct action protest (King to Rodell, 30 November 1960, in *Papers* 5:565–566; Lomax, "The Negro Revolt against 'The Negro Leaders,'" *Harper's Magazine*, p. 41).

2. King had three other drafts of this article, one of which was handwritten (King, Drafts, "After Desegregation—What," April 1961).

3. *Coronet* executive editor James A. Skardon called the article "well-written and thoughtful," but asked King to revise it and add "more facts and examples" illustrating his points (Skardon to King, 12 May 1961).

4. King was still revising the article in June 1961 when Rodell notified him that *Coronet* was ceasing publication in October: "If the rewrite on your article isn't done by now, we might just as well forget it" (Rodell to King, 21 June 1961).

over leadership from what it perceives to be faltering hands. Negro youth has surged
into a vanguard position because it has the most desperate need and has been
gripped by a sense of destiny.

The Negro student knows he is not alone but is fortified by support of tens of millions of white and Negro citizens of all ages, of all classes, of all political persuasions. He is deadly serious and fiercely determined. He is not engaged in a lark nor superficially thrilled by the excitement and "kicks" of a moment. He is a part of a world-wide thrust into the future to abolish colonialism and racism; to replace institutionalized handicaps with free opportunity.

These are the moods and thoughts of Negro students—and many white ones—as I meet and talk with them from Washington to Houston, and in many Northern cities, too.

Many students and their elders temporarily away from the pounding struggle, pause in reflective moments to ask what will be the shape of things after desegregation is accomplished. These youthful partisans of today, know that the battle of desegregation will not last forever. Actually, one of its greatest attractions is the bright promise of triumph.

For example, lunch counter victories have been astounding and though school desegregation has been slow, federal judges, such as the Honorable Skelly Wright of Louisiana, and Honorable W.A. Bootle of Georgia, are becoming less patient with recalcitrant school boards and politicians.[5] Negro voter registration is on [*strikeout illegible*] the upswing. At least in the urban South, public opinion, on the whole, is beginning to accept the inevitability of compliance with "the law of the land" as determined by the United States Supreme Court. Throughout the nation the trend toward equality is increasingly favorable. And almost everywhere in the world the tides roll forward against colonialism and racism.

Accordingly, students who now mass their sit-ins, kneel-ins (churches), stand-ins (theatres) and wade-ins (beaches and swimming pools) are confident that at least the main campaigns [*strikeout illegible*] in the desegregation ~~war~~ {struggle} will be won before the end of the current decade.

And so, many bright young men and women, in their quiet moments, are asking themselves about life after college—especially after the big exciting hand-to-hand struggle with Jim Crow is done.

Almost all of them realize that the new frontier will be "integration" rather than "desegregation" and {that} this makes quite a difference. The latter means the removal of legal and customary barriers that have separated individuals and groups. These are mostly tangible and external such as laws and "For White Only" signs. In a word, desegregation is the opening up of public facilities and services to everyone.

---

5. In May 1960, Wright ordered the New Orleans school board to begin desegregation efforts by September 1960 and, thereafter, continue to desegregate one additional grade each year. Wright's decision came four years after his initial ruling that the school board must abide by the Supreme Court's *Brown* decision and desegregate "with all deliberate speed" (Claude Sitton, "U.S. Court Orders New Orleans to Start Pupil Integration in Fall," *New York Times*, 17 May 1960; *Brown et al. v. Board of Education of Topeka et al.*, 349 U.S. 294 [1955]). The University of Georgia admitted its first black students on 10 January 1961, after Judge Bootle enjoined Georgia governor S. Ernest Vandiver from cutting funding and closing public schools (Sitton, "2 Negro Students Enter Georgia U.," *New York Times*, 11 January 1961).

On the other hand, integration is much more subtle and internal, for it involves attitudes: the mutual acceptance of individuals and groups. Desegregation usually preceeds integration, the former making the latter possible. But this is not automatic. Once the laws between them have been struck down, both Negroes and Whites will still need to win friends across the invisible, though nonetheless real, psychological color line. Such a challenge will be more difficult and less glorious.

Many Negro students are aware, at least in a preliminary fashion of the shifts that they themselves will have to make in a society that will be unsegregated and yet not really integrated. However, the question remains: Will Negroes generally find it as easy to give up their own prejudices as it now is to <u>demand</u> their rights of others? Will the same forthrightness be shown in admitting whites to Negro clubs, fraternities and other voluntary associations that is now being shown in pressing for admittance to restaurants and theatres.

Moreover, after the fight has succeeded in unlocking the doors to rights and opportunities, there will be the very real obligation to "deliver the goods," that is, to behave well and perform excellently.

As the color differential fades, so will the racial point of view. Less and less will it be possible to speak with accuracy of Negro newspapers, Negro churches or the Negro vote. More and more, economic, social, and professional status will be more decisive in determining a man's orientation than the color of his skin.

Some may well ask whether students are gaining from the present movement the necessary resources and insights to make the psychological shift from a desegregated to an integrated society. Are studies being neglected? Will half-trained graduates typify this generation? Are deeper lessons of race relations being absorbed or is a simple "race against race" conception dominating immature minds?

There is undeniably a risk that some students will stumble into error. No movement of essentially revolutionary quality can be neat and tidy. Yet I am confident that the Negro college student, who is today in the thick of the desegregation fight will successfully make the transition to the campaign for integration and its consequent responsibilities. I have special reasons for my faith.

The public may have noticed that the student movement is based on broad principles. It has never advocated justice for Negroes as such; rather justice for all men, Negroes included, of course. The students realize that the festering sore of segregation debilitates the white man as well as the Negro. Therefore, the removal of this unjust system will create a moral balance in society which will allow all men, Negro and white, to rise to higher levels of self-completion. In workshop after workshop they have been inbued with the principle that the problem is not a purely racial one, with Negroes set against white; rather, it is a tension between justice and injustice. Therefore, their resistance is not aimed against oppressors but against oppression. The students have opposed "Black Supremacy" as vigorously as they have stood against "White Supremacy." They are not in any sense seeking to rise from a position of disadvantage to one of advantage, thereby subverting justice; rather, they are seeking to achieve democracy for everybody. They have gone out of their way to enlist whites in their ranks so that the movement itself would symbolize the society that they hope to bring about.

Then there is a factor that may have escaped public notice. So much attention has been given to the movement's emphasis on non-cooperation with evil, that is, with Jim Crow laws and customs, that not much light has been shed on its cooperation with good, that is, its constructive program.[6] This constructive program is a basic part of any genuine non-violent movement, for non-violence is essentially a positive concept. Its corollary must always be growth. Without this broad range of positive goals, non-cooperation ends where it begins. The students have revealed an amazing degree of understanding concerning the need for such a constructive program. So, on the one hand, they apply non-violent resistance to all forms of racial injustice, including state and local laws and practices, even when this means going to jail. On the other hand, they see the need for imaginative, bold, constructive action to end the demoralization caused by the legacy of slavery and segregation, inferior schools, slums, and second class citizenship. Certainly the creative thrust of the student's non-violent struggle will in itself help end the demoralization; but they realize that a new frontal assault on the poverty, disease, and ignorance of a people too long ignored by America's conscience will make the victory more certain.

In admitting that there are lagging standards in the Negro community which must be improved through a constructive program, the students are not in the least giving aid to the reactionaries who argue that the Negro is not ready for integration. The only answer that one can give to those who would question the readiness of the Negro for integration is that the standards of the Negro lag behind at times not because of an inherent inferiority, but because of the fact that segregation and discrimination do exist. There is no more torturous logic than to use the tragic effects of segregation as an argument for its continuation. The fact that so many Negroes have made lasting and significant contributions to the ongoing life of America in spite of such crippling restrictions is sufficient to refute any argument of his unreadiness.

Yet, the students have not allowed the fact that they are the victims of injustice, economic deprivation and social isolation lull them into abrogating responsibility for their own lives. They seek to make the lagging standards the basis for creative reconstruction. Their contest with segregation is merely the preliminary task of clearing away the obstacles to self-fulfillment to the release of human energy and talent for the goal of all. They seek to tear down what is restrictive, corrupting and inhibiting in order to build a society in which men may work and live in harmony with nature and each other. They believe in man's creative potential and the whole movement is dedicated to the proposition that if the Negro could but free himself of the frustrations of an unjust social order, the achievements of the human mind and heart would be limitless.

But more than anything else, the type of education that the students are gaining as a result of this movement will assure a meaningful transition. The overwhelming truth penetrating through the whole fabric of this extraordinary youth movement is

---

6. King's handwritten draft included the following sentences: "The [*contact?*] with segregation in this sense is merely the preliminary task of clearing away the obstacles to self-fulfillment, to the release of human energy and talent for the good of all. So the students seek to tear down what is restrictive, corrupting and inhibiting in order to build a society in which men may work and live in harmony with nature and each other. They believe in man's creative potential and the whole movement is dedicated to the proposition that if the Negro could but free himself of the frustrations of an unjust social order, the achievements of the human mind and heart would be limitless" (King, Draft, "After Desegregation—What").

the fact that the Negro student is gaining a double education. Indeed, the answer to the quest for a more mature, more educated American to compete successfully with the young people of other lands may be present in this spontaneous, new movement.

The Negro youth is learning social responsibility; he [*is?*] learning to earn through his own direct sacrifice and effort the result he seeks. There is no one to coddle him—to make him soft, pliable and conformist. He cannot be an uncreative organization man nor a mechanical status seeker. His experience is as harsh and demanding as that of the pioneer on the untamed frontier.

For those who falter and weaken, the penalty is immediate failure in wide public view. On the other hand, serious, planned action produces equally immediate victory and acclaim. Because this struggle is complex, especially pursued in a spirit of resistance and non-violence, there is no place for the frivolous or the rowdy. Knowledge and discipline are as indispensable as courage and self-sacrifice.

Hence, the forging of priceless qualities of character is taking place daily and monthly as the struggle for a goal of a high moral end is pursued. What will this mean to the future? There will come from this cauldron a mature man, experienced in life's lessons, socially aware, unafraid of experimentation, and most of all imbued with the spirit of service and dedication to a great ideal. Does America need such men and women? Asking the question answers it.

Often in the past educators have pondered the paradox that the academically brilliant student with superior grades failed frequently to realize the bright promise of his student days. More scholarships, more degrees, more training turned to dross as life's demands found them wanting in ability to relate to associates, motivate and to lead. The answer is in the one dimensional quality of learning. To learn for one's own advancement alone is inevitably self-defeating. To learn in order to become an instrument of social advancement has always been a keystone of achievement. It is this quality at the heart of the student movement today which guarantees the additional dimension of wisdom accompanying knowledge.

A new generation of Negro graduates schooled in life's tensions and changes will emerge on tomorrow's stage. Not a hot-house product, not a privileged elite, but an outgoing, though serious, person who will confront a world he not only understands but has helped to shape.

This is the double education most students will acquire and, in turn, contribute to his fellow-man who has already been his comrade-in-arms—white and Negro, rich and poor.

To face the awesome challenges of automation, space conquest, economic security and world peace, nothing less than the doubly educated man is indispensably necessary. I am both proud and confident that the Negro student of today is on his way to becoming that person. He will give to the nation a leadership ability and dedicated performance which will make the old myth of the inferior individual an ugly memory which will be difficult to recall in the luminous presence of his effective and creative performance.

TADd. MLKP-MBU.

# To Barbara Lindsay

3 May 1961
*[Atlanta, Ga.]*

*In an attempt to overthrow Cuba's dictator Fidel Castro, the United States
sponsored an invasion by Cuban rebels at the Bay of Pigs in April 1961. After
the coup failed, Lindsay wrote a lengthy letter to King, expounding her fears
and opinions on the political situation in Cuba.[1] Below, King echoes Lindsay's
disapproval of the Cuban situation, warning that "unless we as a nation join
the revolution and go back to the revolutionary spirit that characterized the birth
of our nation, I am afraid that we will be relegated to a second-class power in the
world with no real moral voice to speak to the conscience of humanity."*

Miss Barbara Lindsay
498 N. 2nd Street
San Jose, California

Dear Miss Lindsay:

This is just a note to acknowledge receipt of your letter of recent date. Let me say
emphatically that I absolutely share your views on the Cuban situation.[2] I think our
country has done not only a dis-service to its own citizens but to the whole of humanity in dealing with the Cuban situation. For some reason, we just don't understand
the meaning of the revolution taking place in the world. There is a revolt all over
the world against colonialism, reactionary dictatorship, and systems of exploitation.
Unless we as a nation join the revolution and go back to the revolutionary spirit
that characterized the birth of our nation, I am afraid that we will be relegated to a
second-class power in the world with no real moral voice to speak to the conscience
of humanity.

---

1. Lindsay was concerned that U.S. relations with Cuban exiles would put both countries on the
brink of war. She also compared the Cuban situation with the Civil Rights Movement and hoped that
civil rights and other leaders would "speak out for peace and against intervention in the Cuban matter"
(Lindsay to King, April 1961). Barbara Sterne Lindsay (1920–1978), grew up in Wilton, Connecticut, and
received a B.A. in linguistics (1961) from San Jose State University. An active member of the Communist
Party of the United States of America, the Women's International League for Peace and Freedom, and
SNCC, Lindsay also helped organize farm workers in Marysville and Watsonville, California, after
attending the California Labor School in San Francisco. Additionally, Lindsay wrote a number of books
for children and juveniles. Clarence B. Jones, King's attorney, later urged King in November 1962 to
address the Cuban Missile Crisis with the president: "There are those who feel someone of 'Dr. King's
stature' should say something 'forcefully' on the Cuban crisis." Jones further admonished other black
leaders of "stature" who had remained "silent on this question." Jones's letter included a draft statement
(Jones to King, 1 November 1962).

2. Tensions between the U.S. and Cuba increased between January 1959, when Castro assumed
power in Cuba, and April 1961. Due to Cuba's communist policies and alignment with the Soviet Union,
the U.S. imposed an embargo on trade with Cuba, and eventually severed all diplomatic ties with the
country. The Bay of Pigs highlighted the growing animosity between the U.S. and Cuba, culminating in
the Cuban Missile Crisis of October 1962.

I have already signed one statement which is to appear in one of the major newspapers concerning disapproval of our participation in the Cuban invasion.[3] I did this because I am as concerned about international affairs as I am about the civil rights struggle in the United States.

Thank you for your letter, and for the book which you enclosed. I will look forward to reading Dr. Mills' book as soon as time will permit.[4]

Very sincerely yours,
Martin Luther King, Jr.

K.m

TLc. MLKP-MBU.

---

3. On 28 April 1961 socialist leader Norman Thomas asked King to sign an open letter to President Kennedy protesting the United States-backed attack on Cuba. The letter, which was published in *New America* on 19 May 1961 did not include King's signature ("An Open Letter to the President: No Intervention in Cuba!").

4. In a handwritten addendum to her letter, Lindsay suggested that King read C. Wright Mills's 1960 book *Listen, Yankee: The Revolution in Cuba*: "It's an interesting book. Probably you have read it" (Lindsay to King, April 1961).

# To Robert F. Kennedy

4 May 1961
Atlanta, Ga.

*King pleads for Kennedy to grant clemency to Morton Sobell, who was convicted with Julius and Ethel Rosenberg on charges of spying for the Soviet Union.[1] King writes that Sobell's guilt or innocence has no consequence because the Communist hysteria around Sobell's conviction prevented a "calm and dispassionate" ruling. Sobell was eventually released from prison in 1969.*

---

1. In a 26 January 1961 letter, Sobell's wife, Helen, requested that King write Kennedy on her husband's behalf. Helen Sobell was the chairman of the Committee to Secure Justice for Morton Sobell. King had earlier signed a national appeal to free Morton Sobell (Peter Braestrup, "Sobell's Release Is Sought by 1,800," *New York Times*, 20 November 1960). Morton Sobell (1917– ) was born in New York and graduated from the College of the City of New York (CCNY) with a degree in electrical engineering (1938). He later earned a master's degree from the University of Michigan (1942). While a student at CCNY, Sobell befriended Julius Rosenberg. The pair were arrested with several others in the spring of 1951, and tried for conspiring to pass atomic bomb secrets to the Soviet Union. The Rosenbergs were executed in 1953 for espionage, and Sobell was given a thirty-year sentence for conspiracy of which he served nearly nineteen years. In a 2008 interview with the *New York Times*, Sobell admitted that he had leaked military but not atomic secrets to the Soviet Union (Sam Roberts, "Figure in Rosenberg Case Admits to Soviet Spying," 12 September 2008).

The Honorable Robert F. Kennedy                                           8 May
Attorney General                                                          1961
Department of Justice
Washington, D.C.

Dear Mr. Kennedy:

Traditionally, American jurisprudence has held the application of justice in the assignment of punishment resulting from violations of law as a most high estate. The rising tide of consciousness of the world's people to the rights of individuals gives added importance to the application of justice in the affairs of men in relation to their society.

Morton Sobell, now serving the eleventh year of a thirty year sentence on a charge of conspiracy to commit espionage, was convicted at a time when a climate of hysteria pervaded the country. At such a moment it was difficult to gain a calm and dispassionate dispensing of justice. The conclusiveness of the evidence which convicted him has been debated many times by notables of the legal profession. Many devoted and patriotic Americans are firmly convinced of Sobell's innocence.

But whether Sobell was guilty or innocent, I am firmly of the opinion that his thirty year sentence constituted a cruel and unusual punishment. To extend clemency to Morton Sobell would be in keeping with the highest ideals of jurisprudence and justice in America. His continued imprisonment will do a great deal to undermine our constitutional freedoms and safeguards of due process. I would hope that President Kennedy will respond affirmatively to this simple humane plea for clemency.

Respectfully yours,
Martin Luther King, Jr.

TLc. MLKP-MBU.

# From Gordon R. Carey

8 May 1961
New York, N.Y.

*On 4 May 1961 the Congress of Racial Equality (CORE) launched the Freedom Rides, an interracial group traveling by bus together to challenge segregation on interstate buses and in transportation terminals.*[1] *Below Carey confirms King's*

---

1. The group planned to ride buses from Washington, D.C., to New Orleans, Louisiana, arriving on 17 May, the seventh anniversary of the 1954 *Brown v. Board of Education* decision (CORE, "Freedom Ride Itinerary," 24 April 1961). In 1947, CORE and the Fellowship of Reconciliation (FOR) organized the Journey of Reconciliation, an interracial bus ride throughout the upper South to test compliance with the U.S. Supreme Court's ruling in *Morgan v. Virginia*, 328 U.S. 373 (1946), which outlawed segregation on interstate buses. In 1960 the Supreme Court extended the ruling in *Morgan* to include public facilities

*attendance at a public meeting and dinner with the freedom riders when the group*
*passes through Atlanta on 13 May. The public meeting was canceled, but King met*
*the riders for dinner at Paschal's restaurant.*[2]

DR. MARTIN LUTHER KING JR,
EBENEZER BAPTIST CHURCH
407 AUBURN AVE NORTHEAST ATLA

THIS CONFIRMS YOUR PRESENCE AT FREEDOM RIDE PUBLIC MEETING AS DISCUSSED
BY TELEPHONE AND LETTER[3] MEETING IS 8PM MAY 13 WARREN MEMORIAL METHODIST
CHURCH WOULD ALSO APPRECIATE YOUR MEETING WITH FREEDOM RIDERS PRIVATELY
FOR DINNER ABOUT 6PM WE WILL CONTACT YOU AGAIN ABOUT DINNER MEETING.
YOUR KIND COOPERATION DEEPLY AND SINCERELY APPRECIATED

GORDON R CAREY

PHWSr. MLKP-MBU.

---

such as waiting rooms, restaurants, and restrooms in bus and train terminals (*Boynton v. Virginia,* 364 U.S. 454 [1960]). Several weeks before the start of the campaign, CORE field director Gordon Carey asked for SCLC's "wholehearted support" for the rides and asked King if he knew of any potential recruits "experienced in nonviolent direct action and willing to accept violence and a jail term if they occur" (Carey to King, 31 March 1961).

2. "'Freedom Riders' Arrive in City," *Atlanta Daily World,* 14 May 1961. In his autobiography, *Jet* reporter Simeon Booker, who was riding the buses for a series of articles about the campaign, wrote that King took him aside at the dinner and said, "I've gotten word you won't reach Birmingham. They're going to waylay you" (Simeon Booker and Carol McCabe Booker, *Shocking the Conscience: A Reporter's Account of the Civil Rights Movement* [Jackson: University Press of Mississippi, 2013], p. 189).

3. Carey to Dora E. McDonald, 18 April 1961.

# Statement at Lawyers Advisory Committee Meeting

8 May 1961
New York, N.Y.

*On 29 March 1960, a full-page ad titled "Heed Their Rising Voices" ran in the*
New York Times, *criticizing Alabama officials who opposed the protest movement.*
*In response, Montgomery city commissioner L. B. Sullivan, Montgomery mayor*
*Earl James, former commissioner Clyde Sellers, and Alabama governor John*
*Malcolm Patterson each filed libel suits against the* New York Times *and SCLC*
*executive board members Ralph Abernathy, Joseph Lowery, S. S. Seay, and Fred*
*L. Shuttlesworth.*[1] *In the following address, King urges the Lawyers Advisory*

---

1. The Alabama officials each sued the ministers and the *Times* for $500,000. The suits were eventually resolved in *New York Times Co. v. Sullivan,* 376 U.S. 254 (1964). For more on the libel case, see Introduction and facsimile of the ad in *Papers* 5:25–26, 382, respectively.

*Committee (LAC), headed by New York lawyer Theodore Kheel, to give financial and legal support to the four SCLC ministers.[2] Emphasizing the economic impact of the charges on the defendants, King argues that an "economic lynching has terrors not fundamentally less destructive than physical lynching." King later acknowledged that the LAC's formation "was a significant contribution" to the movement.[3]*

It is not always that a case can properly be described as historic, but we are on safe ground when we declare that the implication of these cases profoundly affects the political and social interests of our nation. If these judgments are not reversed, no newspaper can publish truthful accounts of injustice without risk of bankruptcy and without hazard to its reporters of criminal indictment. If these judgments are not reversed, victims of injustice dare not express opposition to their oppressors. If these judgments are not reversed, the supporters of those seeking social advancement dare not act, nor reveal their sympathy, lest they be sued in tribunals where due process is elusive but power is almost unlimited. These cases are a classic example of tyranny over the minds and tongues of men making a nullity of the First Amendment to the Constitution.

It may be asked why authorities in the State of Alabama have acted with such unrestrained recklessness. In general this conduct is a part of their determined refusal to permit those social changes which emancipation of the Negro requires. More particularly, it reflects the counter-offensive of Alabama political rulers to reverse some of the progress attained in integration. Following the successful integration of buses in Montgomery, a new spirit of dignity and independence was felt in the heart of every Negro.[4] This small beginning was too much for the recalcitrant segregationist to accept. When, therefore, the students sought to integrate lunch counters, there was unleashed against them and the Negro community as a whole a reign of terror backed by a military display of force which would have been appropriate to combat an armed invasion by a foreign enemy. We were not secure even in our churches. Armed police were posted outside, and in one case a platoon invaded a church to disrupt a meeting in progress there.[5] In this context it can be understood how furious rage would result when an advertisement describing these conditions, and in strong terms denouncing them, was published in THE NEW YORK TIMES. That Negroes and their supporters should dare to speak out boldly and clearly profoundly shocked

2. Theodore Woodrow Kheel (1914–2010), a former president of the National Urban League and an arbitrator in New York labor disputes, organized the eighteen-member LAC in May 1961 to fight this "flagrant abuse of legal and judicial process for purposes other than those for which a legitimate civil action in libel was designed" (Kheel to William Hammatt Davis, 27 April 1961). Other members of the committee included Judge Hubert T. Delany and lawyer Lloyd K. Garrison (LAC, Press release, "Lawyers committee formed to assist defense in Alabama libel actions," 8 May 1961).

3. King to Kheel, 11 December 1961.

4. The U.S. Supreme Court ruled in *Gayle v. Browder,* 352 U.S. 903 (1956) that Alabama's laws requiring segregated public transportation were unconstitutional.

5. In March 1960, King wrote a telegram to President Dwight D. Eisenhower protesting a Montgomery police assault on the Alabama State College campus that halted demonstrations and interfered with religious services (King to Eisenhower, 9 March 1960, in *Papers* 5:385–387).

the segregationists. They were long accustomed to our submissive silence in the face of oppression. The Declaration of Independence could not have outraged the imperial sensibilities of King George more than this.[6] Such privileges of free expression are reserved for free men, and the Negro of the south was forgetting that he was not free. But physical intimidation can be sustained only for a limited period. Other complementary methods are required for long term effect.

Brutality and intimidation can wear many disguises. They need not openly be flaunted, as in Mississippi, by setting police dogs trained in viciousness on human beings, nor need they be expressed only by the howling lynch mob.[7] These have the disadvantages that the sense of decency and justice of the American people can in revulsion turn upon the perpetrators. So a more subtle form of attack needed to be designed. In this sense the misuse of legal process is a new and potent weapon in the arsenal of the segregationists. It is a sword with two cutting edges. It not only deprives the victim of his economic security, but it undermines his confidence in law as he finds himself led through all the processes of a juridical system traditionally designed to insure justice, but which for him is perverted to accomplish oppression and injustice. That ours is a government of laws not men becomes a bitter mockery when it is not only men who can misrule but the law itself.

The effect of accumulating millions of dollars in judgments against leaders in an integration struggle goes far beyond those directly involved. Every Negro senses the threat to his own security and his own dignity, when he witnesses his leaders stripped of their means of transportation, small parcels of land, and the garnishment of their salaries.[8] When the line between poverty and subsistence is paper thin, an economic lynching has terrors not fundamentally less destructive than physical lynching.

When I speak of the thin line separating so many of us from poverty, I do not exclude most of the defendants in these cases. They are ordained ministers; all but one are college trained. Yet none has a salary of as much as $100 a week. Reverend Seay is paid $50 a week; Rev. Abernathy $75 a week; and Rev. Shuttlesworth $70 a week. These are the men against whom 2–1/2 millions of dollars in judgments are sought.[9] But even beyond this, contemplate this fact: the Negro parishioners in most of our churches who are expected to carry financial burden of lawsuits, suffrage campaigns and organizations to achieve school and public facility desegregation, earn

---

6. The Declaration of Independence blamed King George III for tensions between America and Great Britain. On 23 August 1775 the King had declared the colonies in rebellion and refused to accept the Second Continental Congress's "Olive Branch Petition" for peace, which would have granted the colonists' rights while promising loyalty to the King.

7. King refers to a 29 March 1961 demonstration outside the courthouse in Jackson, Mississippi, where students were chased by dogs and club-wielding police officers as they protested the trials of demonstrators arrested for a previous sit-in ("Dogs, Clubs Used on Negroes; Ask Whites to Leave," *Atlanta Daily World*, 30 March 1961).

8. Seay, one of four ministers being sued for libel, wrote an urgent plea for financial aid to Stanley D. Levison, noting that his property was set to be sold a few weeks later (Seay to Levison, 9 April 1961). The four ministers attempted to obtain a federal injunction to stop the state from repossessing their property, but district court judge Frank M. Johnson dismissed the complaint because the issue was pending in the state court ("Federal Court Rejects Petition in Libel Case," *Birmingham News*, 17 March 1961).

9. On 27 March 1961 Clyde Sellers filed his own $500,000 claim after Sullivan and James had already won favorable verdicts ("Another Libel Action Filed against Times," *Birmingham News*, 28 March 1961).

between $12 and $15 per week. When so little separates a family from literal hunger, a massive economic threat can have a paralyzing effect.

If we, in struggling for our most elementary rights, find ourselves also defending the integrity of the Constitution for all Americans, we are, I feel, justified in asking for support not only because it is a common fight but because we have so little in financial resources for so great a struggle.

May I point out with pride that at no point in the conflicts of recent years, despite the most brutal periods of terror and intimidation, were we lacking in people to take any action required. There were always Negroes of courage to squarely face the mobs seeking to keep our children out of schools. There were always Negro students to sit at lunch counters. There were always Negroes to march to the State Capitols for redress of grievances. And always the Negroes adhered with iron discipline to non-violence. We will not sully our struggle by answering violence with violence nor hatred with hatred. But we cannot be complacent and rely upon inexhaustible courage. History teaches us that a people can at least temporarily be beaten into passivity and retreat.

Because we know we are in times that try men's souls, because we are living hundreds of Valley Forges across the south, we need your help to move out of the midnight of man's inhumanity to man, into that society of Brotherhood which the Declaration of Independence and the Constitution designed but which is still on the road ahead, for us.[10]

TD. WHDP-WHi: US MS AW, Box 33.

---

10. King refers to the statement in "The American Crisis," Thomas Paine's 1776 Revolutionary War pamphlet: "These are the times that try men's souls."

# From Lawrence Dunbar Reddick

9 May 1961
Baltimore, Md.

*In a 4 May 1961 letter, King invited Reddick, who accompanied him on his trip to India and wrote the first biography on King in 1959, to attend a 10 May luncheon of SCLC's administrative committee, prior to an executive board meeting in Montgomery.[1] In the letter below, Reddick regrets his inability to attend the meeting but suggests a few items to discuss with the members, including commending*

---

1. The executive board of SCLC met 10–11 May 1961. For Reddick's account on King's first press conference upon his arrival in India, see Account by Lawrence Dunbar Reddick on Press Conference in New Delhi on 10 February 1959, in *Papers* 5:125–129.

*Attorney General Robert F. Kennedy for his statement that schools would be
integrated as mandated by the Supreme Court.*[2]

Dr. Martin Luther King, Jr.
Ebernezer Bapist Church
407 Auburn Ave N.E.
Atlanta, Georgia

Dear Martin:

Greetings! It's been a long time! However, I keep up with you somewhat through
the newspapers and magazines. I hope that all are well at home and that SCLC is
now sailing along smoothly.

I really wish that I could make it to the Board Meeting. My re-entry at Montgomery,
as well as yours, would be symbolic.[3] However, here at school, we are in the pre-
closing festival season: ever day or night there is some event, and since I am taking
the whole summer off, I thought that I ought to stick around just now. During the
summer, if you and Wyatt [*Tee Walker*] are available, we can consult daily, if necessary,
since I'll be in Atlanta.

There are several matters that I trust you and Wyatt will be sure to place before
the Board:

I. The students of Jackson Mississippi deserve special commendation.[4]

II. Bob Kennedy should be commended for his candor and political courage in
coming to Athens, Georgia and telling a white, Southern audience that Civil
Rights laws and U.S. Supreme Court decisions will be enforced. (In the course
of his remarks, he stated a theory of obeying any and every law. Even though we
do not agree with him in this, please let us not be drawn into debating that now.
Let's get the full effect of his warning to those who defy the law and courts on
Civil Rights.)

---

2. On 6 May, Kennedy delivered his first formal address as attorney general at the University of
Georgia Law School in Athens, Georgia. Kennedy told the audience: "You may ask: Will we enforce the
civil rights statutes? The answer is: Yes, we will." Regarding the rule of law, Kennedy remarked: "The decisions of the courts, however much we might disagree with them, in the final analysis must be followed
and respected. If we disagree with a court decision and, thereafter, irresponsibly assail the court and
defy its rulings, we challenge the foundations of our society" ("Text of Attorney General Kennedy's Civil
Rights Speech at University of Georgia," *New York Times*, 7 May 1961). At the 10 May meeting the executive
board expressed its "sincere appreciation for the Attorney General Robert Kennedy and his forthright
leadership he is giving the enforcement arm of the Federal Government" (SCLC, Press release, "King
and SCLC meet in Montgomery," 12 May 1961).

3. In June 1960 Reddick was fired from his post as chair of the history department at Alabama State
College in Montgomery because of his support for student activists at the college. Reddick then moved
to Baltimore, Maryland, and became a professor of history at Coppin State Teachers College. For more
on Reddick's firing, see King to Patrick Murphy Malin, Roy Wilkins, and Carl J. Megel, 16 June 1960, in
*Papers* 5:471–472.

4. At SCLC's executive board meeting, the members declared their support for the Mississippi
students and avowed their "complete opposition to the inexcusable brutality directed against peaceful
Negroes by Mississippi police and the use of dogs and weapons" (SCLC, Press release, "King and SCLC
meet in Montgomery").

III. John Kennedy should be commended for making a good start in restoring the faith of Negro Americans in the concern and fairness of the federal government. His fair employment order is as sound as words could make it—now let's urge full and immediate implementation.[5]

IV. Our Board should urge President Kennedy, specifically, to do two things:

    1) use more Negro Americans in the diplomatic and foreign service with African Nations. (This is most important or we will be left out of the redemption of Africa. The supporting evidence is included in the enclosed speech)[6]

    2) the President should make a positive statement on the meaning of the Civil War Centennial or the Confederates will turn the war into a festival for reaction. This will build a psychological (and political) wall of resistance to desegregation and social welfare legislation. I also make that point in the speech.

Perhaps this is enough suggestions and advice for now.

Give my best to all—especially [*Ralph*] Abernathy, [*Joseph*] Lowery and [*Fred*] Shuttleswurth,

Our cause speeds on.

Sincerely yours,
[*signed*] Lawrence
Lawrence D. Reddick

LDR/obg

P.S. I'm sending a copy of this to Wyatt and in care of Abernathy just in case your copy to Atlanta misses you.

TLS. MLKP-MBU.

---

5. On 6 March 1961 Kennedy signed Executive Order 10925, which prohibited employment discrimination based on race in businesses contracting with the federal government and established the President's Committee on Equal Employment Opportunity to investigate, regulate, and sanction employers not meeting the requirements of the order.

6. In the enclosed speech Reddick argued that "the strongest and most natural bond between Africa and America is that between the African people and their transplanted Negro American brothers." Reddick further argued that the greatest weakness of the Kennedy administration's policy toward Africa is its "abysmal failure to use Negro Americans" in diplomacy with African nations ("Africa, the Confederate Myth and the New Frontier," 22 April 1961).

# To Members of the United
# Packinghouse Workers of America

17 May 1961
Atlanta, Ga.

*King writes an open letter to members of the United Packinghouse Workers of
America (UPWA), who raised over $11,000 in the first "Fund for Democracy"
campaign to benefit SCLC in October 1957.[1] Touting the success of SCLC's
leadership training program and voter registration and direct action campaigns,
King claims that his organization's methods "make up the cutting edge of our
attempt to tackle America's most grievous problems." Concluding, King notes the
solidarity between the labor and civil rights movement, arguing that the struggle
"could not continue nor expand were it not for our friends, who understand so
well that the struggle of which we are a part is of great importance not only to
us, but to the destiny of our nation, and perhaps our world."[2] By the 15 June 1961
deadline, the UPWA's drive netted $14,565.27 of its $25,000 goal.[3]*

Members of United Packing House Workers of America
608 Dearborn Street
Chicago, Illinois

Attention: Mr. Ralph Helstein[4]

Dear Friends of Freedom:

It gives me great pleasure to know that the members of the United Packing House
Workers of America are again instituting a Fund for Democracy. The Southern
Christian Leadership Conference greatly benefited from your last fund, and your
generous gift was really the means by which our then infant organization was able to
begin its work across the south.

Since that time, SCLC has become more definitely structured and is working

---

1. King to Executive Board Members, 8 October 1957. Russell R. Lasley, vice president of the UPWA,
forwarded King's letter to district directors and local unions, asking them to urge members to donate to
the campaign (Lasley to Local Unions, 9 June 1961; Lasley to District Directors, 9 June 1961).

2. As a member of the AFL-CIO's Public Review Advisory Committee since 1959, King reviewed in
February 1961 an investigative report on alleged communist infiltration of the UPWA (King to Nathan
Paul Feinsinger, 6 February 1961, pp. 150–151 in this volume).

3. Lasley to District Directors, 20 September 1961; Lasley to Local Unions, 9 June 1961. Because
the union did not meet its intended goal, the drive was extended and the union raised $22,326 by 1962
(Harry L. Alston to G. R. Hathaway, 8 February 1968).

4. Ralph Helstein (1908–1985), born in Duluth, Minnesota, received a B.A. (1929) and law degree
(1934) from the University of Minnesota. In 1942 he was named general counsel for the Packinghouse
Workers Organizing Committee (later the UPWA), and served as international president of the UPWA
from 1946 until the union's merger with the Amalgamated Meat Cutters union in 1968. In June 1964
Helstein joined a small group of King's closest advisors known as the "research committee," and periodi-
cally offered King advice through conference calls and private meetings.

untiringly to achieve freedom and human dignity for Negro people in the south. We now have almost fifty affiliate organizations covering every southern state.

From the beginning, SCLC has taken a primary interest in voter registration. The campaign to gain the ballot for Negroes in the south has profound implications. It will liberalize the total political structure of the nation. Negroes exercising a free suffrage would march to the polls to support those candidates who would be partial to social legislation. Negroes in the south, whether they elected Negro or white Congressmen, would be placing in office a liberal candidate. Here we can see the kinship of interests of labor and the Negro people. By extending the ballot to the Negro in the south, it will be much easier for labor to organize and establish a Congress which would be more responsive to liberal legislation. We, the Negro people, and labor, by extending the frontiers of Democracy to the south, inevitably will sow the seeds of liberalism where reaction has flourished unchallenged for decades. For all of these reasons we in SCLC contend that one of the most important steps the Negro can take is that short walk to the voting booth. Just the other day in our annual Board meeting, we voted to intensify our efforts in voter registration so that the vote of the southern Negro would be profoundly effective in the 1962 Congressional election.[5]

Aside from intensified work in voter registration, we are continuing our efforts in non-violent direct action. It has been demonstrated again and again that SCLC played a great role in giving direction to the sit-in movement of 1960 that still continues. The Student Non-Violent Coordinating Committee (SNCC), the coordinating organization of the student movement, was born as a result of a conference called by SCLC at Raleigh, North Carolina, in the spring of 1960.[6] Some of the most significant victories of the sit-in movement of southern college students have come as a result of the leadership and guidance of SCLC affiliates, e.g. The Nashville Christian Leadership Conference (NBC White Paper #2), The Petersburg Improvement Association (Look, August 30, 1960; Life, September 12, 1960).[7]

Since August 1, our staff has been expanded and we have embarked on a bold new approach to solving our human relations problems in the south.[8] We call this

---

5. SCLC's executive board met in Montgomery, Alabama, 10–11 May 1961.

6. Ella Baker, interim director of SCLC from 1959–1960 and veteran civil rights organizer, invited college students who had participated in the early 1960 sit-ins to a conference at Shaw University in Raleigh, North Carolina, on Easter weekend, 15–17 April 1960. At Shaw, the students voted to establish a temporary coordinating body, which became the permanent Student Nonviolent Coordinating Committee (SNCC). For more on SCLC's involvement in the founding of SNCC, see Introduction in *Papers* 5:26–27.

7. "Sit-in," the second of NBC's *White Paper* documentary series, was broadcast 20 December 1960, and reported on the movement for desegregation of public accommodations in Nashville, Tennessee. The Petersburg Improvement Association was featured in "School for Sit-Ins," *Look*, 30 August 1960, pp. 78–81. The *Life* magazine article discussed the efforts of protesters to desegregate downtown Jacksonville, Florida ("Racial Fury over Sit-Ins," *Life*, 12 September 1960, p. 37). Although King offered to make a visit to Jacksonville, his proposal was rejected by the local NAACP. For more on King and the Jacksonville movement, see Introduction in *Papers* 5:34–35.

8. In August 1960 three members of the Petersburg Improvement Association joined the SCLC staff: Wyatt Tee Walker, executive director; James R. Wood, administrative assistant; and Dorothy Cotton, an administrative assistant who later became education director of SCLC's Citizenship Education program.

our Leadership Training Program.[9] It is directed at bringing together at some central place in the south the second-line leadership of our protest communities, and training them in the skills of adult education. They then return to their respective communities and set up citizenship schools to train the "grass roots" population in the basic skills required for achieving full citizenship. This program is already operative and has been declared by the Health, Education and Welfare Department of the United States as one of the best known in this phase of adult education.

Our activity in voter registration, the use of the non-violent philosophy as a means of creative protest in an action program, and our Leadership Training Program make up the cutting edge of our attempt to tackle America's most grievous problems. We are faced with the task of attacking the causes of segregation and at the same time giving our hands to healing the effects of segregation.

We see a striking parallel in the present struggle of the Negro Community and that of organized labor some years ago. You were faced then with providing every individual worker at the bench with the right to a fair living wage and relief from the misery and misfortune of economic exploitation; the Negro community is faced with the herculean task of securing the right of the ballot for every citizen by which he may relieve himself of the misery and humiliation of the evil system of segregation. Both struggles are permeated with a genuine concern for the individual and an exaltation of the human personality.

Our work could not continue nor expand were it not for our friends, who understand so well that the struggle of which we are a part is of great importance not only to us, but to the destiny of our nation, and perhaps our world.

Very sincerely yours,
Southern Christian Leadership Conference
[*signed*] Martin Luther King Jr.
Martin Luther King, Jr.
President

Km

TLS. UPWR-WHi: Box 395.

---

9. The May 1961 edition of the SCLC *Newsletter* described voter registration as a primary goal of the newly launched Leadership Training and Citizenship School programs, which initially brought together members of SCLC affiliate organizations to Highlander Folk School in Monteagle, Tennessee, to learn how to teach "Reading and Writing, Civics, Simplified Politics, the Philosophy of Nonviolence, Picketing, and other subjects necessary for understanding How our Nation Works" (*Newsletter* 1, no. 1, May 1961).

226

# Address at Freedom Riders Rally
# at First Baptist Church

21 May 1961
Montgomery, Ala.

*On 14 May two buses carrying thirteen freedom riders departed from Atlanta bus terminals for Alabama. One bus, carrying eight riders, was firebombed in Anniston, while the other five riders were attacked as they tried to enter the bus terminal in Birmingham.[1] Despite the violence, the freedom riders voted to soldier on and continue the next leg of the trip from Birmingham to Montgomery; however, they could not find a bus driver willing to take them. Realizing that it might be days before they could leave Birmingham, the riders decided to fly to New Orleans instead. A mob of angry whites greeted the riders at the airport, and the flight was eventually canceled after bomb threats. A day after first arriving in Birmingham, a majority of the riders reluctantly agreed to end the Freedom Ride.[2]*

*Diane Nash and students from the Nashville student movement vowed to resume the campaign and organized volunteers to participate. After some setbacks, the new group of freedom riders arrived in Montgomery on 20 May and was attacked by a mob of segregationists.[3] King canceled his scheduled engagement at Dartmouth College and went to Montgomery to address a mass meeting in support of the freedom riders at Ralph Abernathy's First Baptist Church.[4] By the time the formal program*

---

1. "Buses of 'Freedom Riders' Burned and Stoned in South," *New York Herald Tribune*, 15 May 1961; "Bus Is Burned, Young Negro Beaten in Separate Alabama Race Clashes," *Washington Post*, 15 May 1961; and Genevieve Hughes, "Freedom Ride Report," 15 May 1961.

2. "Bi-Racial Group Cancels Bus Trip," *New York Times*, 16 May 1961; James Peck, *Freedom Ride* (New York: Grove Press, 1962), pp. 100–101. Justice Department official John Seigenthaler arranged for a flight to take the riders to New Orleans in time for the 17 May rally to commemorate the seventh anniversary of the *Brown* decision (Seigenthaler, Interview with William Finger and Jim Tramel, 24, 26 December 1974; Simeon Booker, "Jet Team Braves Mob Action 4 Times within 2-Day Period," *Jet*, 1 June 1961).

3. The new group left Nashville on 17 May for Montgomery, and upon their arrival in Birmingham, they were arrested by commissioner of public safety Theophilus Eugene "Bull" Connor. Late the following evening, Connor and other policemen drove the riders to the Tennessee-Alabama border and ordered them out of the car. The next morning riders were picked up by sit-in leader Leo Lillard, who immediately drove them back to Birmingham by car (John Lewis and Michael D'Orso, *Walking with the Wind: A Memoir of the Movement* [New York: Harcourt Brace & Company, 1998], pp. 147–154; Howard Zinn, *SNCC: The New Abolitionists* [Boston: Beacon Press, 1964], pp. 44–45). After intense negotiations between the Kennedy administration and local and state officials in Montgomery, the riders left Birmingham on 20 May under heavy guard provided by local and state police. Although FBI officials had alerted Montgomery police of the group's planned arrival, local officials arrived at the bus station too late to protect the riders (Memo to Byron R. White, 20 May 1961). Montgomery police commissioner L.B. Sullivan explained the delay, saying "we have no intention of standing guard for a bunch of troublemakers coming into our city and making trouble" ("Freedom Riders Attacked by Whites in Montgomery," *New York Times*, 21 May 1961). Seigenthaler and freedom riders John Lewis, William Barbee, and Jim Zwerg were among at least twenty people injured by the mob ("Freedom Riders Attacked by Whites in Montgomery," 21 May 1961; Don Martin, "U.S. Official Is Knocked Unconscious," *Washington Post*, 21 May 1961).

4. "Dr. King Cancels Visits at College, Returns to South for Race Crisis; Tension Increases in Montgomery," *The Dartmouth*, 22 May 1961. The mass meeting was sponsored by the Montgomery Improvement Association (MIA) and included addresses by King, S.S. Seay, and James Farmer (MIA, Program, "Salutes the 'freedom riders,'" 21 May 1961).

*began at 8:00 PM, a mob of several hundred surrounded the church, trapping
freedom riders and their supporters inside and vandalizing automobiles and
buildings.[5] In the following draft of his speech, King declares the violence against
protesters "comparable to the tragic days of Hitler's Germany," stressing that the
"ultimate responsibility for the hideous action in Alabama" must "be placed at the
doorsteps" of Alabama governor John Patterson. King urges his audience to heed
the "magnificence" of the freedom riders' nonviolent example and to "continue to be
strong spiritual anvils that will wear out many a physical hammer." No complete
recording of King's remarks are extant, but news coverage of the rally indicates
King gave a version of this address.[6]*

The words that I will utter tonight were written this morning as I flew at an altitude of 38,000 feet on a jet plane from New York to Atlanta, Georgia. As that giganic
instrument stretched its wings through the air like an eagle and moved smoothly
toward its destination, many thoughts ran through my mind. On the one hand I
thought of how the technological developments of the United States had brought
the nation and the world to an awe-inspiring threshold of the future. I thought of
how our scientific genius had helped us to drawf the distance and place time in
chains. I thought of how we had carved highways through the stratosphere, and how
our jet planes had compressed in to minute distances that once took days. On the
other hand I thought of that brutal mob in Alabama and the reign of terror that had
engulfed Anniston, Birmingham and Montgomery. I thought of the tragic expressions of man's inhumanity to man that still exist in certain sections of our country. I
could not help being concerned about this glaring contrast, this tragic gulf. Through
our scientific and technological developments we have lifted our heads to the skys
and yet our feet are still firmly planted in the muck of barbarism and racial hatred.
Indeed this is America's chief moral dilemma. And unless the Nation grapples with
this dilemma forthrightly and firmly, she will be relegated to a second rate power
in the world. The price that America must pay for the continued oppression of the
Negro is the price of its own destruction. America's greatest defense against communism is to take the offense for justice, freedom, and human dignity.

The Freedom Ride grew out of a recognition of the American delimma and
a desire to bring the nation to a realization of its noble dream. We are all deeply
indebted to CORE for this creative idea. These courageous freedom riders have
faced ugly and howling mobs in order to arouse the dozing conscience of the nation.
Some of them are now hospitalized as a result of physical injury. They have accepted
blows without retaliation. One day all of America will be proud of their achievements.

Over the past few days Alabama has been the scene of a literal reign of terror.
It has sunk to a level of barbarity comparable to the tragic days of [*Adolph*] Hitler's
Germany.[7]

---

5. "Rampaging Mob Stirs Governor into Action," *Montgomery Advertiser,* 22 May 1961; Stuart H.
Loory, "Marshals' Tear Gas Stops Mob of 1,000 at a Negro Church," *New York Herald Tribune,* 22 May 1961.
6. "Rampaging Mob Stirs Governor into Action," 22 May 1961; "Stop Violence, Tensions, President
Kennedy Urges," *Atlanta Daily World,* 23 May 1961.
7. After the riders were attacked in Alabama, King sent telegrams to Governor Patterson and
Attorney General Kennedy, denouncing "the disgraceful and unprovoked violence . . . inflicted upon

Now who is responsible for this dark night of terror in Alabama? Certainly the mob itself must be condemned. When people sink to such a low level of hatred and evil that they will beat unmercifully non-violent men and women, they should be apprehended and prosecuted on the basis of the crime they have committed.[8] But the ultimate responsibility for the hideous action in Alabama last week must be placed at the doorsteps of the Governor of this State. His consistent preaching of defiance of the law, his vitriolic public prouncements, and his irresponsible actions created the atmosphere in which violence could thrive.[9] When the governor of a atate will urge people to defy the Law of the Land, and teach them to disrespect the Supreme Court, he is consciously and unconsciously aiding and abetting the forces of violence.

Among the many sobering lessons that we can learn from the events of the past week is that the deep South will not impose limits upon itself. The limits must be imposed from without. Unless the Federal Goernment acts forthrightly in the South to assure every citizen his constitutional rights, we will be plunged into a dark abyss of chaos. The federal government must not stand idly by while blood thirsty mobs beat non-violent students with impunity.

The familiar cry of state rights will certainly come up at this time. The South will argue that Federal intervention is an invasion of the Rights of States. We must answer this argument by making it clear that we too believe in State Rights. We are commit-

---

interstate passengers and the failure of law enforcement officials to give adequate protection reeks of Hitlerism" (SCLC, Press release, "Freedom riders attacked in Alabama," 15 May 1961).

8. Birmingham and Montgomery police arrested several men for their role in the bus bombing and mob violence. The Justice Department charged ten men for bombing the bus in Anniston: Frank Tolbert, 54; Frank B. Johnson, 42; Dalton L. Roberts, 42; Kenneth Adams, 41; William Chappell, 40; Jerome Byron Couch, 25; Jerry Willingham, 23; Jerry Ronald Eason, 23; Cecil L. Lewallyn, 22; and Roger Dale Couch, 19. Eight of the ten men went on trial in October 1961, but the trial ended in a hung jury. Before the men could be tried again, six plead guilty and received a year of probation. One of the men, Roger Dale Couch, was already in jail on a burglary conviction and was sentenced to a year and a day to be served concurrently with his burglary sentence. Of the remaining four men, Roberts was arrested but not indicted by a grand jury, Adams and Tolbert were freed for lack of evidence, and Lewallyn was indicated by a federal Grand Jury, but he was never tried because of severe injuries sustained in an automobile accident in August 1961 ("Bus Burning Trial Tomorrow," *Birmingham Post-Herald*, 30 October 1961; Tommy Hill, "Jury Weighs Bus Burning at Anniston," *Birmingham News*, 3 November 1961; "Six Guilty in Bus Burning," *Birmingham News*, 16 January 1962). Six men were arrested for the violence at the Trailways bus station in Birmingham: Jesse Thomas Faggard, 48; Jesse H. Thompson, 47; Melvin Dove, 40; Herschel W. Acker, 30; Howard Thurston Edwards, 32; and Jesse Oliver Faggard, 20. Jesse Thomas Faggard, Thompson, Dove, and Jesse Oliver Faggard were sentenced to thirty days in jail and fined twenty-five dollars, and Edwards and Acker were acquitted ("Three Get Jail Terms in City Race Riot Case," *Birmingham News*, 13 July 1961; "Defendant Acquitted Here in Racial Violence Case," *Birmingham News*, 29 November 1961; Lou Isaacson, "Jury Here Clears Suspect in Beating," *Birmingham News*, 14 September 1961). Claude Henley, 37, was charged with assault and battery for the attack on two reporters at the Greyhound bus station in Montgomery. Henley, convicted, was ordered to pay a hundred dollar fine ("Arrest in Montgomery," *New York Times*, 24 May 1961; "Henley Pays Fine following 'Freedom Rider' Clash Here," *Montgomery Advertiser*, 13 February 1962).

9. On 17 May, Patterson threatened future freedom riders with arrest and said, "we can't act as nursemaids to agitators. They'll stay at home when they learn nobody is there to protect them. The state of Alabama can't guarantee safety of fools, and that's what they are" (Bob Ingram, "Patterson Vows Arrest for Integration Testers," *Montgomery Advertiser*, 18 May 1961).

ted to Jeffersonian democracy and would not want to see a complete centralization of government. But although States must have Rights, no State must have the right to do wrong. We must not allow state wrongs to exist under the banner of State Rights. To deny individuals the right to vote through threats, intimidations and other insidious methods is not a State Right, But a State Wrong. To trample over a people with the iron feet of economic exploitation is not a State Right, but a State Wrong. To keep a group of people confined to nasty slums and dirty hovels is not a State Right, but a State Wrong. To confine certain citizens to segregated schools and deprive them of an equal education is a State Wrong moving under the guise of a State Right. To allow hooded perpetrators of violence and vicious mobs to beat, kick and even kill people who only want to be free is a State Wrong without one scintilla of right. We are for <u>State Rights</u> when they are <u>Right</u>.

The other familiar cry that we will hear is that freedom riders, the federal government and no other agency can force integration upon the South. Morals, they argue, cannot be legislated.

To this we must answer it may be true that morals cannot be legislated, <u>but</u> behavior can be <u>regulated</u>. It may be true that laws and federal action cannot change bad internal <u>attitudes</u>, but they can control the external effects of those internal <u>attitudes</u>. The law may not be able to make a man <u>love</u> me, but it can keep him <u>from lynching</u> me. The fact is that the habits, if not the hearts of men have been, and are being changed everyday by <u>federal action</u>.

The recent developments in Alabama should challenge us more than ever before to delve deeper into the struggle for freedom in this State. There must be a full scale non-violent assault on the system of segregation in Alabama. In a few days I will call a meeting of the executive board of the Southern Christian Leadership Conference to map plans for a massive campaign to end segregation in Alabama.[10] This will include an intensified voter registration drive, a determined effort to integrate the public schools, lunch counters, public parks, theaters etc. In short, we will seek to mobilize thousands of people, committed to the method of non-violence, who will physically identify themselves with the struggle to end segregation in Alabama. We will present our physical bodies as instruments to defeat the unjust system.

We cannot in all good conscience sit complacently while Alabama has no respect for law and order and while it continues to impose upon the Negro the most inhuman form of oppression. We must stand up now not for ourselves alone, but in order to carry our nation back to those great wells of democracy which were dug deep by the founding fathers in the formulation of the Constitution and the Declaration of Independence. If Alabama continues to follow its present course of defiance, lawless-

---

10. On 26 May 1961 King and eight others, including Gordon Carey, Kelly Miller Smith, Metz Robbins, Constance Curry, Edward King, Len Holt, A.D. King, and James Wood, gathered at Ebenezer to discuss ways to "intensify the Freedom Ride so that national public attention can be brought to examine the denial of legal rights of interstate travellers." At the meeting, the group organized the Freedom Ride Coordinating Committee, which consisted of four members: Gordon Carey of CORE; Wyatt Tee Walker of SCLC; Diane Nash of the Nashville Christian Leadership Council; and Edward King of SNCC. The committee assumed responsibility for recruiting freedom riders, scheduling and coordinating trips, and raising funds for transportation and legal costs (James R. Wood, SCLC, Report on meeting of the Freedom Ride Coordinating Committee, 26 May 1961).

ness, and Hitlerism, the image of the United States will be irreparable scarred and the results may be fatal in terms of our national survival.

As I close may I strongly urge you to continue to follow the path of non-violence. The freedom riders have given us a magnificence example of strong courageous action devoid violence. This I am convinced is our most creative way to break loose for the paralyzing shackles of segregation. As we intensify our efforts in Alabama, Mississippi, and the deep South generally, we will face difficult days. Angry passions of the opposition will be aroused. Honesty impells me to admit that we are in for a season of suffering. I pray that recognizing the necessity of suffering we will make of it a virtue. To suffer in a righteous cause is to grow to our humanity's full stature. If only to save ourselves, we need the vision to see the ordeals of this generation as the opportunity to transform ourselves and American society.

So in the days ahead let us not sink into the quicksands of violence; rather let us stand on the high ground of love and non-injury. Let us continue to be strong spiritual amvils that will wear out many a physical hammer.

TAD. MLKJP-GAMK: Box 8.

## Statement Delivered at Freedom Riders Rally at First Baptist Church

[*21 May 1961*]
Montgomery, Ala.

*As a menacing mob swells outside Abernathy's church, King encourages supporters inside to remain calm, observing that "maybe it takes something like this for the federal government to see that Alabama is not going to place any limit upon itself. It must be imposed from without." After supporters were trapped in the church for more than six hours, federal marshals used tear gas to disperse the mob.[1] The following transcript is taken from an audio recording.*

---

1. "Montgomery under Martial Law; Troops Called After New Riot; Marshals and Police Fight Mob," *New York Times*, 22 May 1961. Newspaper reports indicated that King remained in contact with Attorney General Kennedy throughout the siege ("Negroes Leave Church after Long Stay," *Montgomery Advertiser*, 23 May 1961). Kennedy sent federal marshals to Montgomery on 20 May after Alabama governor John Patterson refused to ensure the safety of the bus riders (Bob Ingram, "Patterson Vows Arrest for Integration Testers," *Montgomery Advertiser*, 18 May 1961). In a telegram to President Kennedy, Patterson stressed that the federal government was not wanted in Alabama: "We have not asked federal marshals to help us, and we do not need their help. We do not want their help and in fact we do not want them here in Alabama." The governor then demanded that the President rescind the order for federal marshals as "Alabama is perfectly able to enforce all state laws" (Patterson to Kennedy, 21 May 1961). Faced with the possibility that the U.S. Army would be sent to Montgomery, Patterson declared Montgomery under martial law and instructed the National Guard to restore order throughout the city ("Rampaging Mob Stirs Governor into Action," *Montgomery Advertiser*, 22 May 1961).

[*King*]:   Now, we've had an ugly mob outside. They have injured some of the federal marshals. They, they've burned some automobiles [*Audience:*] (*Will justice come?*), but we, we are not . . . we are not giving in for what we are standing for. And maybe it takes something like this (*That's right*) for the federal government to see (*Yeah*) that Alabama is not going to place any limit upon itself. It must be imposed from without. [*gap in tape*]

[*Unknown voice*]:   [*words inaudible*], come on up here. Will you come up here please. Thank you. [*gap in tape*]

[*King*]:   The first thing that we must do here tonight is to decide that we aren't going to become panicky (*That's right, First thing*), that we're going to be calm, and that we are going to continue to stand up for what we know is right (*Yes*), and that Alabama will have to face the fact that we are determined to be free. (*Amen, Yes sir, Yes*) The main thing I want to say to you is fear not. (*That's right*) We've gone too far to turn back. (*That's right, Yeah*) Let us be calm, we are together, we are not afraid (*Amen*), and we shall overcome. (*That's right*) So just remain calm. [*speaker interrupted by disturbance*] [*recording interrupted*]

At. MMFR.

# From Septima Poinsette Clark

23 May 1961
Monteagle, Tenn.

*"As one Freedom Fighter to another," Clark commends King for his support of the freedom riders who met violent opposition in Alabama. She writes: "I could not sit on this mountain top and not let you know how much taller you have grown in my estimation." King replied on 13 June 1961.*[1]

Dr. Martin Luther King
407 Auburn Avenue N.E.
Atlanta, Georgia

Dear Dr. King;

Once more you have endeared yourself to the Peoples of the World as a real leader of the American People.

To read about you flying into strife torn Montgomery to be with your beloved people is a great feat and I commend you for it.

I saw the Broadcast on Monday night and heard you speak in eloquent simple

---

1. In his reply, King wrote that Clark's "words came as a great spiritual lift," and "your courage strengthens my courage."

terms to the courageous who braved the violence of the mob to unite their prayers and cement their determination for justice.

You did not wire a statement but went into the thickest fight as a real symbol of courage to the grass roots people.

I am writing, not as a representative of Highlander but as one Freedom Fighter to another. I could not sit on this mountain top and not let you know how much taller you have grown in my estimation.

My heart thrilled when I read the article in the Afro-American which gave your statement about Braden and Wilkinson.[2] Yes the road ahead, as James Baldwin says, is dangerous but I see you are not attempting to bypass it.[3] May God continue to pour His blessings upon you and your family and keep you ever in His care.

We cannot turn back, the future lies bright before us. We have a great job to do. The White Southerner must be educated. We, the American Negro must educate him.

Sincerely yours,
[*signed*]
Septima P. Clark

TALS. MLKP-MBU.

---

2. In 1958 Carl Braden and Frank Wilkinson appeared before the House Un-American Activities Committee (HUAC) and refused to answer questions about their communist ties. They were convicted of contempt of Congress and sent to federal prison in 1961. An article appeared in the *Chattanooga News-Free Press* quoting King as saying the recent jailing of Braden and Wilkinson is evidence of "McCarthyism" and that they were "being punished—particularly Mr. Braden—for their integration activities" ("King Claims Braden, Wilkinson Jailing Evidence of 'McCarthyism,'" 2 May 1961).

3. Clark refers to Baldwin's article "The Dangerous Road Before Martin Luther King," *Harper's Magazine*, February 1961, pp. 33–42.

# Press Conference Announcing the Continuation of the Freedom Rides

[*23 May 1961*]
[*Montgomery, Ala.*]

*King, Ralph Abernathy, John Lewis, James Farmer, and Wyatt Tee Walker host a news conference at Abernathy's home to announce the continuation of the Freedom Rides after violence against the riders temporarily halted the campaign.[1] During the press conference, King addresses concerns that the rides are negatively*

---

1. The night before the news conference, representatives from SNCC and SCLC including King, Wyatt Tee Walker, Ralph Abernathy, James Farmer, Ed King, Diane Nash, Bernard Lee, Paul Brooks,

*affecting America's international image, declaring that "it is not only impractical but it is immoral to urge people to accept injustices, oppression, and second class citizenship" just to "satisfy the whims and caprices of a few people who would say that this is hurting us in international affairs."[2] The following transcript is taken from two sources of film footage of the press conference.*

[*Walker*]:  Lewis. L-E-W-I-S.

[*Reporter*]:  John Lewis?

[*Walker*]:  John Lewis from Troy, Alabama. [*gap in film*]

[*King*]:  Mr. James Farmer, the national director of CORE, will be here in a few minutes. He had difficulty getting a cab [*recording interrupted*]

[*words inaudible*] as a way of opening this conference that we met with the students some four hours last evening and discussed many matters concerning the whole Freedom Ride and the goals ahead. And it was a unanimous feeling of all of the students present that the Freedom Ride should and must continue. So that we would like to make it palpably clear that the students will continue the Freedom Ride.[3]

---

among others, met at the Montgomery YMCA to discuss the future of the rides. According to John Lewis, some students at the meeting pleaded with King to go on the next Freedom Ride. King, who was on probation following a 1960 traffic violation, declined (Lewis and Michael D'Orso, *Walking with the Wind: A Memoir of the Movement* [New York: Harcourt Brace, 1998], pp. 163–164; Samuel Hoskins, "'Freedom Riders' Vow to Continue," *Chicago Daily Defender*, 24 May 1961; see also "A Disappointing King," *The Crusader* 2, no. 31 [5 June 1961]). James Farmer (1920–1999), the grandson of a slave, was born in Marshall, Texas. He earned a B.S. (1938) from Wiley College and a B.D. (1941) from Howard University. Farmer, a conscientious objector, worked as race relations secretary for the Fellowship of Reconciliation (FOR) from 1941 to 1945. In 1942, at the behest of FOR, Farmer cofounded the Congress of Racial Equality (CORE), a nonviolent, direct action organization, for which he would later serve as national director from 1961–1966. After leaving FOR, Farmer became a union organizer. From 1959–1960 Farmer was program director of the NAACP, and left the organization to devote full-time to CORE. Under his direction, CORE organized the 1961 Freedom Rides, a campaign modeled after the Journey of Reconciliation, an interracial bus ride in 1947 to test compliance of the Supreme Court ruling declaring segregation in interstate travel unconstitutional. Throughout the late 1960s Farmer served as assistant secretary of the U.S. Department of Health, Education, and Welfare (1969–1970), executive director of the Coalition of American Public Employees (1977–1982), and a distinguished professor at several universities, including Mary Washington College (1985–1994). Farmer's autobiography *Lay Bare the Heart* was published in 1985.

2.  King also spoke of the possibility that protesters may be killed on the campaign: "We would not like to see anyone die. We do not consider ourselves martyrs. We all enjoy life and want to live, but the philosophy of the non-violence involves the spirit of willingness to die for a cause. We are willing to face anything—even if it is death" ("'Freedom Riders' Sight Miss. as Next Target," *Los Angeles Times*, 24 May 1961). The day after the press conference, Attorney General Kennedy pleaded with protesters for a cooling-off period: "It would be wise for those traveling through these two states to delay their trips until the present state of confusion and danger has passed and an atmosphere of reason and normalcy has been restored" ("Attorney General's Pleas," *New York Times*, 25 May 1961).

3.  On 24 May two groups of freedom riders traveled from Montgomery, Alabama, to Jackson, Mississippi, under military escort by the Alabama and Mississippi National Guards. Both groups were arrested at the Trailways station in Jackson after seeking service at the lunch counter and attempting to use the men's restroom reserved for whites. The following day, demonstrators, led by Yale chaplain William Sloane Coffin, and SCLC representatives Abernathy, Walker, Bernard Lee, and Fred Shuttlesworth were arrested on charges of conspiracy to breach the peace after seeking service at the

Now we will not specify the exact time that the ride will resume, but it will continue. The students decided today that they will have a workshop on nonviolence for the rest of the day in order to purify themselves and in order to delve deeper into the meaning of the philosophy and method of nonviolence. The Reverend James Lawson of Nashville, Tennessee, the project director of the Nashville Christian Leadership Conference and staff consultant of Southern Christian Leadership Conference will be flying in at noon in order to begin the workshop this afternoon and Mr. Farmer and I will assist him in this.

[*Reporter*]: Can you repeat his name, sir?

[*King*]: The person coming in?

[*Reporter*]: Yes [*recording interrupted*]

[*King*]: [*recording interrupted*] and I'll add onto that is how soon will things develop after that, whether it'll be a matter of days. I would simply say that the ride will take place in the not too distant future. It is not far off. Now a lot of this will be determined by our conference later on and as soon as Reverend Lawson comes in. But we all, we have all agreed, to the fact that it should continue and it shouldn't be too long.

[*Reporter*]: By continuing, do you mean it will go through Mississippi and basically end up in New Orleans?

[*King*]: Yes, the destination is New Orleans and—

[*Reporter*]: Through Jackson?

[*King*]: this will go the same route as has been announced in the past.[4]

[*Reporter*]: Dr. King, do you expect, sir, that you will have the escort of federal marshals or have you made any arrangements to obtain any such escorts?

[*King*]: The students have made it crystal clear that [*phone rings*] the ride will take place with or without federal protection. This will be requested but if it is not given, this will not at all block the Freedom Ride. [*doorbell rings*][5]

[*Reporter*]: What about reports that other students are coming in from other states to augment the Freedom Rides?

[*King*]: There are other students who are standing by in other states and students from all over the country who are willing to join this massive campaign to break down segregation in waiting rooms, at lunch counters within the waiting rooms, and on the buses.

[*Unidentified speaker*]: [*You?*] Ryan.

---

white lunch counter at the Trailways bus terminal in Montgomery (Claude Sitton, "27 Bi-Racial Bus Riders Jailed in Jackson, Miss., as They Widen Campaign," *New York Times*, 25 May 1961; "Yale, Wesleyan Professors Jailed in Tense Montgomery," *Boston Globe*, 26 May 1961; see also Stuart LeRoy Anderson, 5 June 1961, pp. 245–246 in this volume).

4. The Freedom Ride was originally scheduled to begin in Washington, D.C., on 4 May and make stops in Virginia, North Carolina, South Carolina, Georgia, Alabama, Mississippi, and Louisiana (CORE, "Freedom Ride Itinerary," 24 April 1961).

5. On 23 May, Ed King, administrative secretary of SNCC, sent President Kennedy a telegram requesting authorization for the attorney general to "'take all necessary steps to handle the situation'" and issue a statement affirming the constitutional rights of the freedom riders "as they seek to use the various modes of inter-state travel" (Edward B. King to Kennedy, 23 May 1961).

[*Reporter*]:    Have any of the students involved in the current ride been notified of any difficulties with their schools because of absence?

[*King*]:    I think John Lewis can answer that.

[*Lewis*]:    There's a possibility for the students at Tennessee State University—It is possible for them to be expelled—[6]

[*Reporter*]:    Can't hear. [*gap in film*]

[*Lewis*]:    About ten I believe for the most part.

[*Reporter*]:    Dr. King when you started off you [*recording interrupted*]

[*King*]:    Well there will be white students. I don't know how many at this point, but it will definitely be interracial when it resumes.

[*Reporter*]:    Do you mean new white students who have not participated, in other words, not ones who have left?

[*King*]:    Well whether those who have left will come back is something I, I don't know at this time but there will be new white students.

[*Reporter*]:    Dr. King, Governor Barnett of Mississippi has said he will give a full escort to the riders non-stop through Mississippi. Would that be in your mind a satisfactory conclusion to the Freedom Ride?[7]

[*Walker*]:    Can I interrupt just a moment [*recording interrupted*]

[*Abernathy*]:    Could you lean over, Jim? Speak louder.

[*Farmer*]:    Yes, certainly. Well my own feeling is it would not be a successful culmination of the trip in as much as one of the purposes of the Freedom Ride is to test the unsegregated use of all facilities at bus terminals and rest stops for interstate passengers and if it's a nonstop trip across Mississippi under escort it means that such testing will not be possible. This, I think, would be in a sense a frustration of the goals of the Freedom Ride.

[*Abernathy*]:    Then I might add this: the final destination will be Louisiana but it certainly will not be the first stop. And we feel that it would be a grave infringement upon the rights of individuals to take them where they do not wish to go at that particular time and there will be some stops in Mississippi. [*gap in film*]

Would you call this kidnapping, taking individuals beyond their destination against their will? And I said in my thinking, I'm not an attorney, rather I certainly think that it would be a form of kidnapping.

[*Farmer*]:    May I add, Reverend Abernathy, I think it would also be deportation, by taking people from one state line to the other state line without stop.

[*Unidentified speaker*]:    [*words inaudible*] [*gap in film*]

---

6. Tennessee governor Buford Ellington told a reporter on 22 May that the State Board of Education had authorized the expulsion of students enrolled in state colleges if they are found guilty of personal misconduct. In June 1961 thirteen riders were dismissed from Tennessee A&I University; however, a federal judge ruled in December 1961 that the students deserved a hearing before being expelled from the school ("Youths Face Penalty," *New York Times*, 23 May 1961; "Judge Backs 13 Ousted Tenn. Student 'Riders,'" *Chicago Daily Defender*, 18 December 1961). Some students returned to the school in January 1962 (Pauline Knight-Ofosu, Interview by King Papers Project staff, September 2012).

7. Barnett stated that Mississippi did not want or need federal intervention to protect the freedom riders and that he would instruct the State Highway Patrol to usher the riders through the state without allowing them to stop ("Mississippi Escort," *New York Times*, 23 May 1961; Claude Sitton, "Bi-Racial Riders Decide to Go On," *New York Times*, 24 May 1961).

[*Abernathy*]:  Countries like Ghana and Lib—[*recording interrupted*]. The question is what type of effect do you feel that the incidents [*recording interrupted*]

F. NyNyFMN.

[*King*]:  My only answer to that is the answer that I gave a few minutes ago: that it is not only impractical but it is immoral to urge people to accept injustices, oppression, and second class citizenship in an attempt to wait until the so-called opportune time. The time is always right to do right and we cannot wait, we cannot continue to accept these conditions of oppression in order to satisfy the whims and caprices of a few people who would say that this is hurting us in international affairs.[8] The thing that is hurting us most is the continued existence of segregation and discrimination, and we think we're rendering a great service to our nation. For this is not a struggle for ourselves alone; it is a struggle to save the soul of America.[9]

F. WSB-TV-GU.

---

8.  A few days following the launch of the Freedom Rides, Attorney General Kennedy warned in an address at the University of Georgia's Law Day celebration that racial conflicts in the South harm not only those involved, but "such incidents hurt our country in the eyes of the world" ("Text of Attorney General Kennedy's Civil Rights Speech at University of Georgia," *New York Times*, 7 May 1961). Several editorials on the Freedom Rides and the violent attacks hurled at them lamented the international ramifications to America's image, and reported on international coverage of the events in Asia and Africa (John Hughes, "Just a Stone's Throw Spatters Mud," *Christian Science Monitor*, 22 May 1961; "Moscow Sees 'Savagery,'" *New York Times*, 23 May 1961). One op-ed piece published in the *Washington Post* reported that the Russian newspaper *Izvestia* regarded the violence against freedom riders in Alabama "as another example of 'wild bestial mores in a country pretending to teach others how to live'" ("Soviet Paper Raps 'Bestial' U.S. Mores," *Washington Post*, 23 May 1961).

9.  During a question and answer period with students and faculty of Inter-American University in Puerto Rico, King said that segregation in the United States is negatively affecting the nation's image (King, Interview by Inter-American University Students and Faculty, 14 February 1962, p. 401 in this volume).

# From Ruby Dee and Ossie Davis

25 May 1961
Mt. Vernon, N.Y.

*Black entertainers Ruby Dee and Ossie Davis send a message of encouragement to the freedom riders via King.[1] They express support for the decision to continue the protests despite violent resistance from segregationists.*

---

1.  Ruby Dee (1924–2014), born Ruby Ann Wallace in Cleveland, Ohio, joined the American Negro Theater in Harlem while earning a B.A. (1945) from Hunter College. She made her Broadway debut in the play *Jeb* in 1946, where she met her future husband, Ossie Davis. Ossie Davis (1917–2005), born Raiford Chatman Davis in Cogdell, Georgia, attended Howard University before moving to Harlem

THE FREEDOM RIDERS, CARE THE REV MARTIN LUTHER KING
407 AUBURN AVE NORTHEAST ATLA

OUR HUMBLE THANKS FOR DECISION TO CONTINUE THIS TRULY NOBLE STRUGGLE FOR THE DIGNITY OF THE BLACK MAN AND FOR THE DIGNITY AND SALVATION OF OUR COUNTRY

RUBY DEE AND OSSIE DAVIS

PWSr. MLKP-MBU.

---

to begin a career on the stage. Davis and Dee married in 1948, and they wrote and appeared in many successful stage, film, and television projects. Alongside their acting careers, Davis and Dee maintained relationships with many civil rights activists, including Malcolm X and King. In 1998 the pair published an autobiography titled *With Ossie and Ruby: In this Life Together.*

# From Anne Braden

30 May 1961
Louisville, Ky.

*Braden, a field organizer for the Southern Conference Educational Fund (SCEF), updates King on the imprisonment of her husband, Carl Braden, for refusing to testify before the House Un-American Activities Committee.[1] King had agreed to sign a clemency petition for Braden on the condition that he was part of a group rather than the sole initiator.[2] The petition was delivered to the White House on 17 August 1961.[3]*

---

1. Carl Braden (1914–1975), born in Louisville, Kentucky, was a white journalist and union organizer. In 1948 he married Anne Gambrell McCarty (1924–2006). The couple left their jobs as reporters for Louisville's daily newspaper and became editors of a local industrial labor union newspaper there for a time. In 1954 the Bradens purchased a home in a white Louisville suburb on behalf of a black family. After the home was dynamited, Kentucky officials arrested the Bradens and five other white leftists who had supported the purchase, and charged them with sedition. Only Carl Braden was tried and convicted after a highly sensationalized trial in 1954; the conviction was overturned in 1956. Unable to secure jobs in Louisville after the controversy, the Bradens became regional organizers for SCEF, and edited its newspaper, *Southern Patriot.* Upon his release from prison in February 1962, Braden continued his work with SCEF, and served as its co-executive director with Anne from 1967 to 1972. For details about King's relationship with Anne Braden, see Braden to King, 14 October 1958, in *Papers* 4:510–511; Braden to King, 23 September 1959, and King to Braden, 7 October 1959, in *Papers* 5:290–293 and 306–307, respectively.
2. Anne Braden to James A. Dombrowski, 20 April 1961. In early May, King told reporters that his support for Carl Braden was not in defense of communism, but to protest HUAC's efforts to thwart the integration movement by imprisoning Braden ("Braden's Term Hit in Pleas to President," *Atlanta Daily World,* 3 May 1961).
3. Besides King, nearly 2,000 signed the petition, including Abernathy, Wyatt Tee Walker, James M. Lawson, writer Lillian Smith, and Bishop Edgar Love (Carl Braden Clemency Appeal Committee,

Dear Martin:

In a recent letter, Carl sent the following message to you:

30 May
1961

"Please tell Martin, when you write him, how much I appreciate what he is doing in our behalf and how sorry I am that he didn't get in to see me. I'm sure the jailor wouldn't have allowed him to visit me. What a benighted creature!"[4]

This latter refers to a letter I wrote Carl after I talked with you on the telephone that Saturday afternoon some time ago, while he was still in the Fulton County Jail; I wrote Carl that you were going to try to visit him and Frank on the following day.[5] I don't know whether you managed to get out there or not, but I learned later that it is very likely that you would have been unable to get in even if you did, as the authorities were not allowing them to have any visitors at all except lawyers.

As you may know Carl is now at a Federal Prison Camp in Greenville, S.C. The situation on visiting may be somewhat better there. Certainly conditions are better. He is not supposed to have visits from anyone but family, but I should think ministers might be an exception. So if you should ever happen to be in the neighborhood of Greenville and have the time, you might want to try to visit him as a minister. I'm sure that a visit from you would be much more of a contribution to his spiritual well-being than a visit from the minister of his own church, who of course can't get there anyway. The location of the Federal Prison Camp is at the Donaldson Air Force Base which is six miles southwest of Greenville, I understand.

The events in Alabama and Mississippi, while tragic in a way, are thrilling in the new opportunities they offer to those who are working for a new South, and all of you [down?] there are doing a magnificent job of lifting the whole struggle to a new level.[6] I myself have been pretty much wrapped up in these developments for the past week or so, doing what I can from a distance to help on getting people down there and getting protests directed to the right people.[7] In the process, I'm afraid

---

Press release, "Statement by Dr. Ralph D. Abernathy, spokesman for the committee," 17 August 1961). A delegation of southern leaders led by Abernathy presented the petition to White House aides Harris Wofford and Lee White (Carl Braden Clemency Appeal Committee, Press release, "Statement by Ralph D. Abernathy, spokesman for the committee").

4. Carl Braden to Anne Braden, 18 May 1961. On 6 May 1961 King and Anne Braden had discussed plans for King to visit Carl (Anne Braden to Carl Braden, 10 May 1961).

5. Frank Wilkinson (1914–2006), born in Charlevoix, Michigan, graduated with a B.A. (1936) from the University of California, Los Angeles. Wilkinson was denounced as a communist after trying to build public housing units in Los Angeles. In 1955 and 1958 Wilkinson refused to answer questions before the House Un-American Activities Committee's subcommittees, and was imprisoned with Carl Braden in 1961. Following his release from prison, Wilkinson remained active in the National Committee Against Repressive Legislation, and served as executive director of the First Amendment Foundation. In 1999 Wilkinson received a lifetime achievement award from the American Civil Liberties Union (ACLU).

6. Beginning 4 May 1961, interracial groups of freedom riders from CORE, SNCC, and other groups tested the 1960 Supreme Court decision in *Boynton v. Virginia*, 364 U.S. 454, which ruled segregation in interstate travel facilities unconstitutional. Riders encountered mob violence in Anniston, Birmingham, and Montgomery, Alabama, and were arrested upon arrival in Jackson, Mississippi.

7. After receiving a call from Fred L. Shuttlesworth, Braden attempted to find potential recruits to continue the Freedom Rides, and wrote to Carl that she entertained thoughts of joining the rides herself.

I like everybody else pretty much forgot about Carl and what needs to be done on that situation. However, I feel that I must now get back to it, as, if anything, the new developments make it even more necessary that we clear away the cobwebs of the witch-hunt. I noticed that the Alabama Legislature has revived the idea of setting up its own Un-American Committee since the Freedom Rides.[8] And actually, if you trace the present troubles back to their source, I personally think that the fact that people like Patterson and [*strikeout illegible*] Connor are in control in Alabama today can be attributed to the fear that the segregationists have been able to create by the red scare back through the years.[9] In other words, if it had not been for the debilitating effect of McCarthyism, and the segregationists' own special use of it, we might have an entirely different element of people running things in Alabama today. As it is, the ~~rebels~~ {liberals} have been rendered impotent for the moment.

So we'll move ahead with plans to present the petitions to Kennedy. I discussed this on the telephone with Jim Wood the other night and he also agrees we should not delay.[10] I will be in touch with Wyatt about it as soon as he is out of jail, and I will probably calling on you for advice from time to time.[11]

I am enclosing a form letter which I have written to friends I have not had time to write otherwise, which may interest you as it will bring you up-to-date on Carl's present situation etc.[12] I am sending this letter to your home, rather than your office,

---

She decided not to participate after Carl pointed out that "with three children, one of a family in jail at a time was enough" (Braden to Friend, 1 August 1961; Anne Braden to Carl Braden, 21 May 1961 and 28 May 1961; Carl Braden to Anne Braden, 24 May 1961). On 23 May, Anne Braden spoke at a Detroit gathering to raise funds for the Freedom Rides (Marvel Raskin to Edward B. King, 1 June 1961).

8. On 2 May, Alabama state congressman John Hawkins proposed a bill establishing an un-American activities committee (Bob Ingram, "'Controversial' Bill Delayed by Debates," *Montgomery Advertiser,* 4 May 1961). After much heated debate, the Alabama House passed a weakened version of the bill on 14 July; however, the Alabama Senate did not discuss the bill before the general session closed in September because other items on the agenda took precedence, particularly redistricting after Alabama lost a federal congressional seat after the 1960 census (Bob Ingram, "Red Probe Group Gets House Okay," *Montgomery Advertiser,* 15 July 1961; "Senators Talk Jefferson Carve-Up Bill to Death in Violent Session," *Montgomery Advertiser,* 2 September 1961).

9. John Malcolm Patterson was governor of Alabama from 1959 to 1963. Theophilus Eugene "Bull" Connor served as commissioner of public safety in Birmingham, Alabama, from 1937 to 1953, and from 1957 to 1963.

10. James R. Wood, King's administrative assistant and SCLC's director of public relations, helped Braden gather sponsorship for the petition (Anne Braden to Wood and Dombrowski, 27 March 1961).

11. Wyatt Tee Walker was arrested 25 May 1961 for attempting to desegregate a Montgomery, Alabama, lunch counter with freedom riders headed for Jackson, Mississippi. Walker was released on 29 May 1961 ("Yale's Chaplain among 11 Seized in Montgomery," *New York Times,* 26 May 1961; "Drive Pushed Inside Jail, Mixers Say," *Montgomery Advertiser,* 30 May 1961).

12. In a May 1961 letter, Braden updated friends on Carl's imprisonment, noting that his spirits remain high as they usually do "when a person goes to jail for what he feels is a matter of high principle." She also assured Carl's supporters that the "positive program" that SCEF has started will continue in Carl's absence and that the organization's newsletter the *Southern Patriot* will continue to "keep our readers well-informed on developments in the integration movement." On a personal note, Braden reported that she and the couple's three children are adjusting just "fine" while Carl is in jail (Braden to Friends, May 1961).

as I thought that Coretta might also be interested in reading the form letter. Please pass it along to her.

31 May
1961

Warm regards,
[*signed*] Anne
Anne Braden

AB/dj

TALS. MLKP-MBU.


# From Robert F. Williams

31 May 1961
Monroe, N.C.

*Though SNCC representatives pleaded with King to join them on the Freedom Rides, he declined, citing his probation for a May 1960 traffic violation.*[1] *In this telegram, Williams, who had clashed with King in 1959 over the role of self-defense in the movement, calls King a "phony" for refusing to participate and challenges him to "lead the way by example."*[2]


REV MARTIN LUTHER KING
208 AUBURN AVE NE ATLA

THE CAUSE OF HUMAN DECENCY AND BLACK LIBERATION DEMANDS THAT YOU PHYSICALLY RIDE THE BUSES WITH OUR GALLANT FREEDOM RIDERS. NO SINCERE LEADER ASKS HIS FOLLOWERS TO MAKE SACRIFICES THAT HE HIMSELF WILL NOT ENDURE. YOU ARE A PHONY. GANDHI WAS ALWAYS IN THE FOREFRONT SUFFERING

---

1. For more on King's probation, see note 187, Introduction in *Papers* 5:37. On 22 May representatives from SNCC and SCLC met at the Montgomery YMCA to discuss the future of the Freedom Rides. During the meeting the students asked King to ride the buses with them (see Lewis and D'Orso, *Walking with the Wind: A Memoir of the Movement* [New York: Harcourt Brace, 1998], pp. 163–164).

2. Following King's refusal to join the Freedom Rides, Williams wrote in his newsletter *The Crusader* that many freedom riders were angered by King's refusal to join the campaign because they, too, had suspended sentences: "It is pathetic that some of the students are under suspended sentences and some are three and four time losers for freedom, yet they are participating. Maybe, in King's estimation, they are just students and only stand to lose their lives or careers while he stands to lose a fortune in struggle and blood money" (*The Crusader* 2, no. 31 [5 June 1961]). Williams also criticized King for wanting to "ride the great wave of publicity but not the buses" and purported that if King is the "undisputed leader as the white folks claim he is," he needs to ride the buses or "quit the scene" (*The Crusader*, 5 June 1961). Robert Franklin Williams (1925–1996), the grandson of a former slave, was born in Monroe, North Carolina. After serving in the U.S. Army and Marine Corps, Williams returned to Monroe in the mid-1950s, where he became president of the local chapter of the NAACP. In 1959, Williams was suspended from the NAACP after he advocated self-defense in response to the acquittal of a white man charged with raping a black woman. His statement sparked a debate between himself and King on the efficacy of nonviolence (see Introduction in *Papers* 5:17–18). In 1961 Williams was indicted for kidnapping a white

241

WITH HIS PEOPLE[3] IF YOU ARE THE LEADER OF THIS NON VIOLENT MOVEMENT LEAD
THE WAY BY EXAMPLE. YOU ARE BETRAYING OUR CAUSE BY ATTEMPTING TO APPEASE
OUR ENEMIES RIDE THE BUSES AS THE STUDENTS HAVE ASK YOU TO. IF YOU LACK THE
COURAGE, REMOVE YOURSELF FROM THE VANGUARD. I PERSONALLY CHALLENGE YOU
TO RIDE FOR FREEDOM. NOW IS THE TIME FOR TRUE LEADERS TO TAKE TO THE FIELD
OF BATTLE

ROBERT F WILLIAMS
PRESIDENT UNION COUNTY BRANCH NAACP.

PWSr. MLKP-MBU.

---

couple in Monroe, but fled to Cuba with his family. While there, he wrote his memoir, *Negroes with Guns* (1962), continued to publish his newsletter *The Crusader*, and started "Radio Free Dixie," a revolutionary radio program. At the invitation of Mao Zedong, Williams moved to China in 1965, staying until he returned to the U.S. in 1969. In Detroit, Williams worked at the University of Michigan's Center for Chinese Studies for a year and played a significant role in the opening of diplomatic relations between the U.S. and China. The kidnapping charges were dropped in 1976.

3. Williams elaborated on this point in his 5 June 1961 newsletter: "Gandhi was a leader who lead by example and suffered with his people. Gandhi never asked his followers to make any sacrifice that he was not himself willing to make."

# From Amrit Kaur

[*May 1961*]
Simla, India

*Amrit Kaur, an Indian official King had met during his 1959 visit to India, writes a letter of support to King after escalating violence against freedom riders.[1] Endorsing King's methods of nonviolence, she says "I wish I were in the States because I would then, old as I am, join your non-violent movement." She also reassures him that as long as the "struggle remains non-violent the victory of integration over segregation is assured." King replied on 12 June 1961.*

Rev Martin Luther King
Dexter Avenue Baptist Church
454 Dexter Avenue
Montgomery 4, Alabama, USA

---

1. For a photograph of King with Kaur, see *Papers* 5:79. Amrit Kaur (1889–1964), born in Lucknow, India, was a disciple of Mahatma Gandhi and an active participant in the Indian independence movement. A champion of women's rights in India, she served as Minister of Health from 1947–1957. From 1957 until shortly before her death, Kaur was a member of the Rajya Sabha, the Indian Parliament.

{Dear Friend,}

You and all those who are suffering today in Alabama and the two adjoining States who have taken up the wrong stand of Alabama in favour of segregation have been in the thoughts and prayers of my brother and me ever since we read in the press of your recent troubles.[2] Last night's news over the radio was disturbing inasmuch as it seems that the Government is going to imprison even the non-violent resisters.[3]

I pray with all my heart that you with your belief in Non-violence will be able to keep all American negroes in control for I have no doubt whatsoever that if the struggle remains non-violent the victory of integration over segregation is assured.

Can we here help you in any way? Unfortunately there are very few of us who really believe in Non-violence. I wish I were in the States because I would then, old as I am, join your non-violent movement.

President Kennedy is on your side but I do not think that your people need military aid if they remain non-violent because God is on their side.[4]

With every kind thought and prayers on your behalf,

Believe me,
{Very sincerely yours}
[*signed*] Amrit Kaur

TALS. MLKP-MBU.

5 June
1961

----

2. Kaur refers to her brother Kanwar Sir Dalip Singh, a lawyer and judge.

3. Kaur may be referring to the 24 May arrest of twenty-seven freedom riders, who were convicted of breaching the peace, fined $200 each, and given a suspended sixty-day jail term in Jackson, Mississippi (Claude Sitton, "Mississippi Court Fines 27 for Test at Bus Terminal," *New York Times,* 27 May 1961).

4. Kaur may refer to the events of 21 May when a large mob gathered outside of First Baptist Church in Montgomery where King addressed a mass meeting of supporters of the Freedom Rides. Though federal marshals were on the scene, Alabama governor John Patterson eventually sent out the Alabama National Guard to disperse the mob (see King, Address at Freedom Riders Rally at First Baptist Church, 21 May 1961, pp. 231–232 in this volume; "More Marshals Sent Into Montgomery; Church Attacked," *Atlanta Daily World,* 23 May 1961). Following the siege at the church, King told reporters that he had sent telegrams to the President and the Attorney General urging them "not to withdraw federal marshals from Montgomery at this crucial moment" ("King Asks Feds Stay on Job Here," *Montgomery Advertiser,* 26 May 1961).

# Press Release, Statement Calling for Executive
## Order Declaring Segregation Illegal

5 June 1961
New York, N.Y.

*At the Sheraton-Atlantic Hotel in New York, King urges President Kennedy to sign*
*a second Emancipation Proclamation "declaring all forms of racial segregation*

*illegal."[1] The order is needed, King affirms, because "the nation has moved all too
slowly toward the goal of justice and equality for all of its citizens."*

There is a mighty stirring in this land. The courageous young men and women
who are participating in the sit-ins at lunch counters and freedom riders on buses
are making it palpably clear that segregation must end and that it must end soon.[2]
They are no longer willing to adjust to meaningless delays and a crippling gradualism. They know that the nation has moved all too slowly toward the goal of justice
and equality for all of its citizens. The moods and the actions of these determined
youth reveal that the South cannot maintain segregation devoid of chaos and social
stagnation.

The time has now come for the President of the United States to issue a firm
executive order declaring all forms of racial segregation illegal.[3] This would be a
second emancipation proclamation. While such an executive order would be rather
far-reaching it would not be too much to ask, since it would be falling almost one
hundred years after the first emancipation proclamation. Such a creative and forthright move on the part of the President would serve as a great beacon light of hope
to millions of disinherited people and would convince people all over the world that
we are dead serious in our commitment to the democratic ideal. Just as Abraham
Lincoln had the vision to see almost one hundred years ago that this nation could
not exist half slave and half free, the present administration must have the insight to
see that today the nation cannot exist half segregated and half integrated.[4]

**********

There is a strange and tortuous logic being eloquently expressed in editorials of
great newspapers and decisions of Federal judges.[5] It is a reasoning that condemns

---

1. "President Urged to End Race Laws," *New York Times*, 6 June 1961. In a speech in Chattanooga in
December 1960, King began advocating for a second Emancipation Proclamation (see note 18, King,
"The Negro and the American Dream," Emancipation Day Address Delivered at Municipal Auditorium,
2 January 1961, p. 118 in this volume). The first Emancipation Proclamation was issued by Abraham
Lincoln on 1 January 1863.

2. By the end of May, forty-four freedom riders, mostly students, had traveled to Jackson, Mississippi.
They were arrested for breach of peace, disobeying an officer, and breaking local segregation laws that
had already been declared unconstitutional by the Supreme Court 1960 ruling in *Boynton v. Virginia*, 364
U.S. 454 (Cliff Sessions, "27 Bus Riders Arrested on Entry in Mississippi," *Washington Post*, 25 May 1961;
"17 More Freedom Riders Are Jailed in Mississippi," *New York Times*, 29 May 1961).

3. In an article for *The Nation*, King commented that "the power inherent in Executive orders has
never been exploited; its use in recent years has been microscopic in scope and timid in conception"
(King, "Equality Now," 4 February 1961, p. 145 in this volume).

4. King refers to Lincoln's "A House Divided" speech, delivered on 16 June 1858 in Springfield,
Illinois (*The Collected Works of Abraham Lincoln*, vol. 2, ed. Roy P. Basler [New Brunswick: Rutgers
University Press, 1953], p. 461).

5. On 2 June, federal district judge Frank M. Johnson issued a temporary injunction preventing the
Ku Klux Klan from threatening interstate passengers, and a temporary restraining order prohibiting
civil rights organizations, such as SCLC and CORE, from sponsoring the Freedom Rides in Alabama.

the robbed as well as the robbers. It is a reasoning that equates the peaceful, non-violent, {WITH THE} hateful mobs seeking to defy the law of the land. This strange logic is further expressed in the tendency which is so prevalent to refer to the recent violence in Alabama as a race riot. This type of thinking fails to see that a riot is when two conflicting groups are engaged in mutual violence. The freedom riders and the Negroes have not engaged in one act of retaliatory violence. So what happened in Alabama was mob actions and not a race riot.

THD. MCMLK–RWWL: 2.5.0.70.

---

Although sponsorship of the protests "is agitation within the law of the United States," Johnson wrote, it "is agitation that constitutes an undue burden upon the free flow of interstate commerce" (*United States v. U.S. Klans, Knights of Ku Klux Klan, Inc.*, 194 F. Supp. 897 [M.D. Ala. 1961]).

# To Stuart LeRoy Anderson

5 June 1961
Atlanta, Ga.

*King apologizes to Anderson, president of the Pacific School of Religion in Berkeley, for canceling his scheduled commencement address at the last minute because four SCLC staff members were in jail and one had been shot in Montgomery.[1] Anderson replied on 9 June 1961 expressing his disappointment, but professing to "understand perfectly the pressures" that forced King to cancel.*

Dr. Stuart LeRoy Anderson, President
Pacific School of Religion
1798 Scenic Avenue
Berkeley 9, California

Dear Dr. Anderson:

It is always a painful experience for me to have to cancel a speaking engagement. I am sure you can realize the feeling of regret that came to me when I found it necessary to get word to you that it would not be possible for me to make your commence-

---

1. King was scheduled to arrive in San Francisco on the afternoon of 25 May; however, that same day, Fred L. Shuttlesworth, Wyatt Tee Walker, Ralph Abernathy, and Bernard Lee were arrested when they accompanied seven freedom riders led by Yale chaplain William Sloane Coffin into the Montgomery Trailways bus station. Just a day before, two groups of freedom riders had been served at the lunch counter at the station without incident. Two days after their arrest, Shuttlesworth posted $1,000 bond, while the other three were released on 29 May. Also on 25 May six white youths fired shots at Reverend S.S. Seay's house in Montgomery, hitting him in the wrist (Dora E. McDonald to Frank Clarke, 22 May 1961; "Six Charged in Shooting of Rev. Seay," *Montgomery Advertiser*, 28 May 1961; "Yale's Chaplain among 11

ment exercises at the Pacific School of Religion.[2] I had looked forward to this experience with such great anticipation. The honor of delivering the commencement address and receiving an honorary degree from such a great theological seminary is a privilege that comes only once in a lifetime.[3] I can assure you that I would not have missed this if I could have found any other alternative. But I need not tell you of the critical state of things here in the south at this time.

At the very hour that I was planning to leave for San Francisco, four of my staff members were in jail and one had been shot. Certain emergency contacts and situations faced me that could not have waited until I made a trip to California.[4] Nothing short of my concern for and commitment to the struggle for freedom and human dignity could have made me miss your commencement.

May I thank you again for inviting me and for offering the honorary degree. I do hope it will be possible to come at another time. Please do not hesitate to call on me.

Very sincerely yours,
[*signed*] Martin L. King Jr.
Martin Luther King, Jr.

Km
Dictated by Dr. King, but signed in his absence.

TLS. CBPaC.

---

Seized in Montgomery," *New York Times*, 26 May 1961; and "Drive Pushed Inside Jail, Mixers Say," *Montgomery Advertiser*, 30 May 1961). Stuart LeRoy Anderson (1912–1995), born in Elmore, Ohio, received a B.A. from Albion College in 1933 and a B.D. from Chicago Theological Seminary in 1936. Following graduation from the seminary, he was ordained as a Congregational minister and pastored churches in Los Angeles, Glendale, and Long Beach, California. In 1950, he became president and a professor of homiletics at the Pacific School of Religion, and held both posts until 1971. Anderson also wrote *A Faith to Live By* (1959), a book of sermons and religious addresses.

2. Pacific School of Religion professor Georgia Elma Harkness spoke in King's place.

3. King was to receive an honorary doctoral degree in divinity from the school, and the announced topic of his commencement address was "The Church in a New Age" (Pacific School of Religion, Program, "Ninety-fourth annual commencement," 26 May 1961).

4. Immediately upon hearing the news of the arrest and shooting of SCLC staff members, King sent the president and attorney general telegrams urging them not to remove federal troops from Montgomery: "There is still need for federal marshals to remain in Montgomery. Knowing of your determination to preserve law and order and to protect all citizens, I strongly urge you not to withdraw federal marshals from Montgomery at this crucial moment" ("King Asks Feds Stay on Job Here," *Montgomery Advertiser*, 26 May 1961).

## To J. Raymond Henderson

6 June 1961
[*Atlanta, Ga.*]

*King urges family friend J. Raymond Henderson, a Los Angeles minister, to give financial support to the Freedom Rides through SCLC, emphasizing the "central*

Dr. J. Raymond Henderson
Second Baptist Church
Griffith Street at 24th Street

Dear Dr. Henderson:

I wanted very much to respond to your suggestion immediately, but I am sure you are sympathetic with how many other duties are crowded into my schedule at such a time as this.[2]

May I take a minute to describe the role of the Southern Christian Leadership Conference in the 'continued' Freedom Ride that has attracted international attention so that you can best judge as to where the funds you mentioned should be forwarded.

The Nashville students who picked up the Freedom Ride where CORE left off are directly supported and counseled by the Nashville Christian Leadership Confreence, the Nashville unit of SCLC. In Birmingham supportive help was given them by the Alabama Christian Movement for Human Rights, which is another unit of the SCLC.[3] As they came on to Montgomery, which was the center of the whole Freedom Ride operation until Wyatt Walker, Ralph Abernathy and Fred Shuttlesworth were jailed, is still another unit of SCLC. At the end of last week Jim Lawson, staff consultant of SCLC, and C. T. Vivian were in jail in Jackson, Mississippi; Wyatt, Ralph, Fred and Bernard Lee (a student member of SCLC) were in jail in Montgomery.[4] The responsibility of the three lawyers involved and the larger job of all transportation expenses and board and lodging has been borne by SCLC and/or its units.[5] I have drawn this picture on a factual basis, and on this basis it would be my feeling that the

---

1. An article published in the *Atlanta Constitution* said that King and SCLC had virtually "taken over direction of the movement" started by CORE ("Sit-In Lull Won't Last, King Warns," 27 May 1961). King answered a similar letter for funds a month later where he acknowledged other organizations raising funds for the rides (see King to A. Lincoln James, 11 July 1961, pp. 253–254 in this volume).

2. Beginning 3 June, King began a fundraising tour throughout several cities, including appearances in New York City and Albany, New York.

3. The Alabama Christian Movement for Human Rights, a coalition of local churches working toward various civil rights goals, was founded in Birmingham in 1956, after an Alabama court outlawed the NAACP.

4. Lawson and Vivian were two of twenty-seven freedom riders arrested in Jackson, Mississippi, on 24 May after arriving from Montgomery under police escort. The next day, Walker, Abernathy, Shuttlesworth, and Lee accompanied a group of seven freedom riders led by William Sloane Coffin, chaplain of Yale University, to the Trailways terminal lunch counter, where the last group of riders ate before departing. They were arrested for disorderly conduct and breach of peace (Claude Sitton, "27 Bi-Racial Bus Riders Jailed in Jackson, Miss., as They Widen Campaign," *New York Times*, 25 May 1961; "Yale's Chaplain Among 11 Seized in Montgomery," *New York Times*, 26 May 1961).

5. The three lawyers involved were Fred D. Gray, Charles S. Conley, and S.S. Seay (Seay to Walker, 7 December 1961). In an August 1961 treasurer's report, SCLC reported expending nearly $30,000 on appeal bonds, legal defense, and travel and aid for the freedom riders (Abernathy, "Southern Christian Leadership Conference treasurer's report," 1 September 1960–31 August 1961).

funds you raise should be forwarded to SCLC.[6] We do honestly admit (and have done so several times in the press) that the Freedom Rides were originated by CORE.[7] This is not in any way to detract from the initiation of the project, but the central involvement since May 17th organizational wise has been SCLC oriented. However we will be constrained to abide by your decision.

Let me now turn to the very creative suggestion concerning the Freedom Ride bus of noted clergymen. I have discussed this with several people who are very close to me and conversant with the Southern scene, and everyone agrees that this is a tremendous idea and should be done.[8] At this moment as you know we are under a Federal restraining order not to encourage, finance, organize, etc. any Freedom Rides through Alabama.[9] Thus we would like to delay a final decision for a few days until this matter is cleared up as to how the mechanics of such a ride would be carried out.[10] Please keep us advised of your decision and if it is as I have suggested you would want to know that checks and money orders can be made payable to SCLC and forwarded to the address indicated above.

Sincerely yours,
Martin Luther King, Jr

---

6. The Freedom Ride Coordinating Committee (FRCC) had established on 26 May that it would be the central organization for fundraising for the Freedom Rides (James R. Wood, Report on meeting of the FRCC, 26 May 1961).

7. See Wood, Press release, Freedom Ride Coordinating Committee formed, 24 May 1961.

8. Eighteen clergymen undertook a Freedom Ride sponsored by CORE from Washington, D.C., to Tallahassee, Florida, from 13 to 16 June. Ten were arrested after being refused service at the Tallahassee airport ("2 Bus Trips Planned," *New York Times*, 13 June 1961; "Ten Freedom Pastors Land in Florida Jail," *Chicago Daily Tribune*, 17 June 1961). Later, an interracial group of approximately fifteen priests affiliated with the Episcopal Society for Cultural and Racial Unity were arrested on 13 September for trying to desegregate interstate facilities in Jackson (Claude Sitton, "Episcopal Group Held in Jackson," *New York Times*, 14 September 1961).

9. On 2 June, federal district judge Frank M. Johnson issued a temporary injunction preventing the Ku Klux Klan from threatening interstate passengers and SCLC, CORE, and other civil rights organizations from sponsoring, financing, or encouraging the rides in Alabama (*United States v. U.S. Klans, Knights of Ku Klux Klan, Inc.*, 194 F. Supp. 897 [M.D. Ala. 1961]). In response to the injunction, King and Wyatt Tee Walker released a statement vowing to fight the court order: "We are seeking immediate relief through our counsel to have the order removed for we believe it is an abridgement of our constitutional privilege to insist on transportation within the bounds of interstate travel unencumbered by the customs of the segregated South" (SCLC, Press release, "Integration organization answers restraining order," 3 June 1961). On 12 June, Johnson allowed the restraining order to lapse after postponing a hearing to determine if it would be replaced by a lengthier injunction and warned that he would reinstate the order "if it becomes necessary" ("Judge Ends Curbs on Freedom Rides," *New York Times*, 13 June 1961).

10. Following a 2 June strategy meeting in Atlanta with Wyatt Tee Walker and other black leaders, King hinted that freedom riders might disobey the injunction: "I think we have revealed through many experiences that we have no fear of going to jail and staying to serve time when it is necessary" ("Willing to Go to Jail: King Indicates Defiance of Judge's Injunction," *Montgomery Advertiser*, 3 June 1961). The freedom riders did not break the injunction; instead an interracial group of five resumed the Alabama-based campaign on 20 June after Judge Johnson's injunction expired. They traveled through Alabama, stopping in Montgomery, but did not try to enter the bus terminal ("Riders Re-Enter Alabama Capital," *New York Times*, 21 June 1961).

(Dictated by Dr. King)     16 June
MLK/cg     1961

TLc. MLKP-MBU.

# From George Meany

16 June 1961
Washington, D.C.

*At its annual board meeting in May 1961, SCLC passed a resolution condemning
the recent firing of African American labor leader Theodore Brown as assistant
director of the civil rights division of the American Federation of Labor-Congress of
Industrial Organizations (AFL-CIO).[1] In a likely effort to ameliorate controversy
surrounding Brown's dismissal, Meany, president of the AFL-CIO, writes King
a telegram of support, highlighting the close alliance between the civil rights
movement and labor. He underscores organized labor's opposition to racial
discrimination in education, employment, and voter registration, concluding:
"These are our goals. I am sure they are yours."[2] No reply to Meany's telegram
has been found.*

= REVEREND MARTIN LUTHER KING JR, PRESIDENT SOUTHERN CHRISTIAN LEADER-
SHIP CONFERENCE

---

1. The resolution said: "Mr. Brown has been an outspoken critic of discrimination in any form. This
is a sad recompense for the courageous fight he has waged. The AFL-CIO has severely damaged its image
in the eyes of the Negro community" ("SCLC to Carry Libel Suit to Supreme Court," *Atlanta Daily World*,
14 May 1961). Other African American leaders, such as Adam Clayton Powell, Roy Wilkins, and L. Joseph
Overton, also blasted the AFL-CIO and called for a protest demanding Brown's reinstatement ("Negroes
War on Top Labor Heads," *New York Amsterdam News*, 6 May 1961). A news report indicated that Brown
was dismissed without cause by William Schnitzer, secretary-treasurer of the AFL-CIO, and that sources
within the labor movement said that Brown's firing may be related to the public feud between Meany
and A. Philip Randolph, who had taken Meany to task for failure to end racial discrimination in unions
affiliated with the AFL-CIO ("Negro Labor Leader Fired," *New York Amsterdam News*, 29 April 1961; see
also King, Press Release, Statement in Defense of A. Philip Randolph, 13 October 1961, and King, Address
Delivered at the Fourth Constitutional Convention of the AFL-CIO, 11 December 1961, pp. 306–308 and
333–341, respectively). When writing a section of his book *Stride Toward Freedom*, King relied heavily on a
piece Brown wrote about black workers and trade unions (See Introduction in *Papers* 4:32).

2. King echoed Meany's sentiments about the relationship between labor and the civil right movement in an 11 December 1961 speech at the Fourth Constitutional Convention of the AFL-CIO: "The
duality of interests of labor and Negroes makes any crisis which lacerates you a crisis from which we
bleed. And as we stand on the threshold of the second half of the twentieth century, a crisis confronts
us both. Those who in the second half of the nineteenth century could not tolerate organized labor
have had a rebirth of power and seek to regain the despotism of that era, while retaining the wealth and
privileges of the twentieth century. . . . Their target is labor, liberals, and Negro people" (see p. 336 in
this volume).

16 June
1961

CARE REVEREND D L SYLVESTER ODOM[3]
= WESTERN CHRISTIAN LEADERSHIP CONFERENCE
1177 W 25TH ST LOSA =

= LET ME CONVEY TO YOU WARMEST GREETINGS AND ADMIRATION FOR YOUR CONTRIBUTIONS TO ADVANCE THE CAUSE OF EQUALITY FOR ALL OUR CITIZENS. IT IS A GOAL THE AFL-CIO FULLY SUPPORTS.

RACIAL DISCRIMINATION IS MORALLY WRONG AND WEAKENS AMERICA. IT MUST BE ABOLISHED. IT IS NOT MERE COINCIDENCE THAT WHERE CIVIL RIGHTS ARE MOST STRONGLY SUPPRESSED, UNIONS ARE MOST VIGOROUSLY OPPOSED. NOR IS IT COINCIDENCE THAT WHERE NEGROES EXIST UNDER MISERABLE SOCIAL AND ECONOMIC CONDITIONS, WAGES ARE LOWEST FOR ALL WORKERS, SOCIAL LEGISLATION LEAST ADVANCED AND ANTI-LABOR LEGISLATION MOST SEVERE.

THE CONGRESSIONAL ROLL CALLS TELL THE STORY. THE SAME CONGRESSMEN WHO VOTE CONSISTENTLY AGAINST CIVIL RIGHTS LEGISLATION LINE UP JUST AS SOLIDLY IN OPPOSITION TO LABOR.

LABOR WANTS A BETTER DAY FOR ALL AMERICANS. WE WANT TO INVIGORATE OUR NATIONAL ECONOMY AT THE SAME TIME THAT WE ERADICATE DISCRIMINATION SO THAT ALL OUR CITIZENS CAN ENJOY FULL EMPLOYMENT AT DECENT WAGES.

WE WANT OUR EDUCATIONAL SYSTEM TREMENDOUSLY IMPROVED AND AT THE SAME TIME WE WANT TO INSURE THAT EVERY AMERICAN CHILD HAS EQUAL ACCESS TO EDUCATION. WE WANT A FULLER DEMOCRACY AND THAT IS POSSIBLE ONLY WHEN ALL CITIZENS HAVE A FULL OPPORTUNITY TO VOTE#

THESE ARE OUR GOALS. I AM SURE THEY ARE YOURS =

GEORGE MEANY
PRESIDENT AFL-CIO..

PWSr. MLKP-MBU.

---

3. Odom was the president of the Western Christian Leadership Conference and pastor of Ward AME Church in Los Angeles, California. King spoke at a rally in Los Angeles on 18 June to raise money for the Freedom Rides (Western Christian Leadership Conference, Program, "Freedom Rally," 18 June 1961; Odom to Friend, June 1961).

# From Gardner C. Taylor

7 July 1961
Brooklyn, N.Y.

*In the following letter, Taylor, pastor of Concord Baptist Church in Brooklyn, requests that King join him and seventeen others on a Freedom Ride to Jackson, Mississippi.[1] King's secretary Dora McDonald responded that King was out of town.[2] The proposed ride did not occur.*

Dr. Martin L. King, Jr.
407 Auburn Avenue, N.E.
Atlanta, Georgia

My dear Dr. King:

I believe that all men of honor and of belief in a democratic America look with gratitude upon the courage and moral strength of the hundreds of young student Freedom-Riders, white and Negro, who are confronting the nation with the option of fulfilling its democratic pledges.

I believe that the hour has struck when we who love this nation must spare nothing to cleanse it of the stain of segregation. Therefore, I am writing to you and 17 other outstanding Americans, asking that we join in a Freedom Ride to the Jackson, Mississippi Airport or Bus Station. I believe that the enormous prestige of your name, along with the others whose names I attach, will give to this effort the dramatic impact which may well set the nation firmly on a program of integration of public facilities. We can proceed with details as soon as we have agreed on the wisdom of the suggestion. I trust that I may have favorable and early reply.

Yours Sincerely,
[*signed*]
Gardner Taylor

GT: wll
Encl.

TLS. MLKP-MBU.

---

1. In a 6 June 1961 letter to J. Raymond Henderson, King stated that he had discussed the idea of a minister-led Freedom Ride with several people and "everyone agrees that this is a tremendous idea and should be done" (p. 248 in this volume). Among those invited were: John F. Kennedy, Adam Clayton Powell, A. Philip Randolph, John H. Johnson, Roy Wilkins, Ralph Abernathy, Hubert Humphrey, Jacob Javits, Francis Cardinal Spellman, George Meany, Walter Reuther, Bishop James Pike, C. Stanton Gallup, Henry Luce, James Farmer, and Benjamin Mays.
2. McDonald to Taylor, 10 July 1961.

# From Jim Zwerg

9 July 1961
Appleton, Wis.

*Zwerg, a Nashville Movement freedom rider severely beaten by a mob in
Montgomery on 20 May, thanks King for forwarding a donation sent on behalf of
St. Mark's Lutheran Church in San Francisco.[1] King was impressed by Zwerg's
"deep commitment to the cause of freedom" after he donated most of the money to
the Nashville Christian Leadership Council (NCLC).[2]*

Dr. Martin Luther King, Jr.
208 Auburn Ave., N.E.
Atlanta 3, Georgia

Dear Dr. King:

Thank you for forwarding the letter and check from St. Mark's congregation in
San Francisco.

I was very grateful for their Christian concern, but since my suit is still serviceable
after drycleaning and repairs, it seemed only right to me to pass their generosity
along to those still involved in this great effort. I hope both you and they will be
pleased to know that I have kept only $10.00 of their gift for personal use and have
forwarded the remaining $50.00 to the N.C.L.C.

Sincerely,
[*signed*] James W. Zwerg

TLS. MLKP-MBU.

---

1. Don Martin, "U.S. Official Is Knocked Unconscious," *Washington Post*, 21 May 1961. The church
sent Zwerg $60 to buy a new suit after his was damaged when segregationists attacked him on 20 May
1961 in Montgomery, Alabama (King and Walker to Zwerg, 28 June 1961). James William Zwerg (1939– )
was born in Appleton, Wisconsin, and graduated from nearby Beloit College in 1962. In his junior year,
Zwerg studied at Fisk University in Nashville as an exchange student and became involved in local demonstrations. In September 1961 Zwerg earned a "Freedom Award" from SCLC for his heroism during the
Freedom Rides (SCLC, Certificate of Merit for Jim Zwerg, 27 September 1961). At King's urging, Zwerg
followed his calling to be a minister and enrolled at Garrett Theological Seminary in Evanston, Illinois.
He was ordained in the United Church of Christ. After serving ten years in the ministry, Zwerg worked
at IBM as a manager until he retired in 1999.

2. King to Zwerg, 24 July 1961.

# To A. Lincoln James

11 July 1961
*[Atlanta, Ga.]*

*King thanks the chairman of Chicago's Freedom Action Committee for offering to
raise funds for the Freedom Rides and asserts that SCLC has provided significant
financial support for the protests.*[1]

Rev. A. Lincoln James
Greater Bethesda Baptist Church
Michigan Avenue At 53rd Street
Chicago 15, Illinois

Dear Dr. James:

Thank you for your letter of July 2, 1961. We are happy to know that the Freedom
Action Committee of Chicago is concerned and eager to help with the Freedom
Ride project.

The official position of SCLC as it relates to the Freedom Ride is one of absolute
endorsement. From the moment the Nashville Christian Leadership Conference
decided to continue the Freedom Ride originated by CORE, we have been intimately
involved. The supporting groups in both Birmingham and Montgomery are two of
our strongest affiliates as is NCLC.[2] The international focus drawn to Montgomery
in the very critical days was due largely to the events surrounding the Freedom
Riders and our being trapped in Dr. Abernathy's church.[3]

We have supplied staff, transportation costs to and from Jackson, legal counsel
($10,000.00 in Alabama alone) and cash bail bond fees for released riders.[4] We have

---

1. In an earlier letter written to J. Raymond Henderson, King had requested that the funds raised
for the Freedom Rides be forwarded to SCLC (King to Henderson, 6 June 1961, pp. 247–248 in this
volume). Abraham Lincoln James (1920–2010), born in Houston, Texas, received a B.A. (1945) from
Virginia Union University and an M.Div. (1947) from Virginia Union Theological Seminary. After serving
as pastor of First Baptist Church in Suffolk, Virginia, he become pastor of Chicago's Greater Bethesda
Baptist Church in 1954, a position he held for more than forty-five years. James became chairman of the
Freedom Action Committee of Chicago, a group founded to provide financial support for the Freedom
Rides. He also served on the Illinois Civil Rights Commission and was vice-president of the local NAACP
branch. Active in the National Baptist Convention, James became a member of the organization's board
of directors in 1982 and served as president of the National Baptist Congress of Christian Education.

2. King refers to the Alabama Christian Movement for Human Rights and the Montgomery
Improvement Association, respectively.

3. "Marshals Averted Major Bloodshed," *Times* (London), 23 May 1961; "Martial Law Proclaimed
after New Racial Riot," *Times* (London), 23 May 1961; and "How the World Press Viewed the Days
of Tension," *Newsweek*, 5 June 1961, p. 22. For more on the siege at Abernathy's First Baptist Church,
see King, Address at Freedom Riders Rally at First Baptist Church, 21 May 1961, and King, Statement
Delivered at Freedom Riders Rally at First Baptist Church, 21 May 1961, pp. 227–231 and 231–232 in this
volume, respectively.

4. During the fiscal year, SCLC reported that the organization had spent over $29,000 on the
Freedom Rides (Abernathy, "SCLC, treasurer's report," 1 September 1960–31 August 1961).

recently added Mr. Marion Barry to our staff to work in Jackson, Mississippi with the Freedom Ride operation there.[5]

We are in full cooperation with the Freedom Ride Coordinating Committee that has offices not only in Atlanta and Nashville, but also in Montgomery, Jackson, and New Orleans. There offices are manned and subsidized by the participating organizations. Our Representative on the committee is Mr. Wyatt Tee Walker, our executive director who is custodian of the funds and Public Information Office.[6]

The seed money for the Committee has been advanced by CORE ($1,000.00) and SCLC ($2,000.00). SNCC and NCLC have supplied much of the volunteer personnel.

It would be difficult for us to say to whom Funds should be directed. The Freedom Ride Fund is almost defunct again and needs replenishing, yet it will have to be replenished from the organizations involved. We are sure we would be persuaded by your judgement as to whom the monies should be sent.

Very truly yours,
Martin Luther King, Jr. President

Wyatt Tee Walker, Director

WTW/es

cc: NCLC
    SNCC
    CORE
    FRCC

TLc. MLKP-MBU.

---

5. On a three-week trial basis, the Freedom Ride Coordinating Committee sent Barry to Jackson, Mississippi, to recruit freedom riders. Barry drew a salary of $35 a week from SCLC and his room and board was paid by CORE (SNCC, Minutes of July meeting, 14 July–16 July 1961).

6. The Freedom Ride Coordinating Committee (FRCC) was formed on 26 May to "organize, coordinate, schedule and otherwise implement the travel of Freedom Riders" (James R. Wood, Report on meeting of FRCC, 26 May 1961). Walker, Gordon R. Carey from CORE, Diane Nash from the Nashville Christian Leadership Council, and Ed King from SNCC made up the four permanent members of FRCC.

# To George M. Houser

19 July 1961
Atlanta, Ga.

*King, an avid supporter of the American Committee on Africa (ACOA) since 1957, expresses horror at the violence occurring in Angola to Houser, the executive director of the ACOA: "The whole world should rise up and protest these unbelievable atrocities perpetuated by the Portuguese government."[1] While King agrees that a group of Americans should go to Angola to investigate conditions in the country, he declines Houser's request to join such a committee.[2]*

Mr. George M. Houser
American Committee on Africa
801 Second Avenue
New York 17, New York

Dear George:

First, let me apologize for being so tardy in my reply to your letter of June 21. Absence from the city and a rather extended lecture and fund-raising tour account for the delay.[3]

I know of no situation in the world that concerns me more than the brutality and barbarity taking place in Angola today.[4] The whole world should rise up and protest these unbelieveable atrocities perpetrated by the Portuguese government against the people of Angola. I think the idea of sending a group of Americans to Angola as an unofficial commission is very much needed. Certainly, I would like to be a part of such a commission. Unfortunately, some roadblocks stand in the way of my joining you. As you know, the southern struggle is gaining momentum every day. We have some definite projects in mind for the fall in the area of non-violent action which will demand my presence. I feel a moral obligation to be on hand as much as possible as things happen in the south. I am sure you can understand my feeling at this point. I am sure that two or three weeks away from the struggle will be difficult, if not impos-

1. In 1957 King joined the National Committee of the ACOA, and at Houser's request, he later agreed to add his name to an appeal letter to raise funds for the ACOA's Africa Defense and Aid Fund (King to Chester Bowles, 8 November 1957, in *Papers* 4:311–314; King to Friend, 12 November 1959, in *Papers* 5:320–321). On 15 March 1961, rebels based in northern Angola initiated an insurrection targeted at the Portuguese government and settlers in the region. In response, Portugal used armed force to break the rebellion, including bombings against native Angolans, and blamed the insurrection on outside agitators influenced by Communism and Protestantism. Estimates of the causalities vary. A United Nations report indicated that by early June 1961, Portuguese accounts estimated that 1,000 Europeans and 8,000 Africans had been killed. During Security Council debates on Angola, the number of African causalities was estimated at 30,000. In addition to those killed, a spike in refugees in African republics grew from 20,000 in April 1961 to 100,000 in June (U.N. General Assembly, Sixteenth Session, Official Records, Supplement 16, *Report of the Sub-Committee on the Situation in Angola*, prepared in pursuance of U.N. General Assembly Resolution 1603 [XV], A/4978, 1962, p. 14).

2. Houser to King, 21 June 1961. In January 1962, Houser and John A. Marcum, a specialist in African affairs at Lincoln University, went to Angola on a fact-finding mission to determine if American weapons given through the North Atlantic Treaty Organization (NATO) were being used against the Angolan rebels (Houser, "A report on a journey through rebel Angola," January 1962).

3. King was on a speaking tour throughout much of June; he attended the 52nd annual NAACP convention in Philadelphia on 10 July 1961.

4. King became personally aware of the struggles in Angola in 1959 when Deolinda Rodrigues Francisco de Almeida, a twenty-year-old Angolan student who was later jailed for her participation in the Angolan independence movement, wrote him requesting advice and support (see King to Rodrigues, 21 July 1959, and King to Rodrigues, 21 December 1959, in *Papers* 5:250–251; 345–346, respectively).

sible, in the light of the aforementioned conditions. When I talked with Mr. Weiss I felt that I could possibly work it out but since that time some things have happened which makes it difficult for me to leave.[5]

Thank you very much for writing me. Please know that I am always interested in what is taking place in Africa and the great work that you and your associates are doing in the the American Committee on Africa. Whenever I can be of assistance, I will always respond. Please do not hesitate to call on me.

Sincerely yours,
[*signed*] Martin
Martin Luther King, Jr.

Km

TLS. ACOA-ARC.

---

5. King refers to his discussion with ACOA vice-chairman Peter Weiss about joining the commission (Houser to King, 21 June 1961).

# From Ranganath Ramachandra Diwakar

22 July 1961
Bangalore, India

*The chairman of the Gandhi National Memorial Fund thanks King for granting him permission to publish an excerpt of* Stride Toward Freedom *in his journal.[1] Diwakar sends his best wishes to King and notes that in India he occasionally discusses how "Gandhiji's teaching is a living gospel for our struggling brethren in U.S.A."[2]*

---

1. King to Diwakar, 30 June 1961. During King's 1959 trip to India, Diwakar gave King a tour of the Mani Bhavan, Gandhi's residence in Bombay. Ranganath Ramachandra Diwakar (1894–1990), born in Dharwar in southwest India, attended Fergusson College in Pune, India, where he obtained an M.A. in English (1918) and an LL.B. (1919). Diwakar participated in the Indian independence movement and was imprisoned for a number of years as a result. Following independence, he became governor of Bihar State, a position he held from 1952–1957. He also served as the trustee and editor of several Indian publications, including *Kasturi*, a Kannada language monthly publication dedicated to literature. Diwakar published several books on Gandhian nonviolence, most notably *Satyagraha: Its History and Technique* (1946).

2. In his consent letter King echoes Diwakar's sentiment about the use of Gandhi's nonviolent technique in the South: "Mahatma Gandhi, in the most amazing manner, continues to live not only in India but even in the southern part of the United States" (King to Diwakar, 30 June 1961).

Dr. Martin Luther King                                   22 July
407 Auburn Avenue N.E.                                1961
Atlanta 12, Georgia
USA

My dear Friend Rev. Dr. King:

Re: Stride Towards Freedom and a Kannada condensation

I am extremely thankful to you for your very sympathetic and warm letter and for giving me permission to give a condensation in my Kannada Digest Kasturi of your book.

I presume that the number of words is 'five thousand' asked for and not 'fifty' as indicated in the second line of your letter.[3]

The humble royalty offered should be accepted when sent by us on our receiving a formal letter from you mentioning the fact of the royalty. That letter is necessary for purposes of the Reserve Bank of India rules here.

I often recall my brief stay at Atlanta, and the heartening talk I had there and elsewhere in U.S.A.[4] On occasions, I mention here that Gandhiji's teaching is a living gospel for our struggling brethren in U.S.A.

You may be pleased to know that the Gandhi National Memorial Fund has sanctioned Rs. 12,000/ = for Dr. Stuart Nelson's visit to India for three months. He pleaded that he could not get together any money for his passage; hence this sanction. I have yet to know as to when he is proposing to come over here.[5]

Let me convey my best wishes for the heroic struggle you and your colleagues are carrying on.

Please remember me to friends and to your sweet wife and children.

With best regards,

Yours sincerely,
[*signed*] R. R. Diwakar

TLS. MLKP-MBU.

---

3. Diwakar's initial request of 27 May 1961 indicated five thousand words. King's reply on 30 June indicated fifty.

4. Diwakar toured the United States from 8 September to 1 November 1960, and had stopped in Atlanta in October, attending Ebenezer to hear King preach and sharing a meal at King's home (James R. Wood to William H. Hadley, 19 September 1960).

5. Nelson, who had visited India in 1946–1947, 1950, and 1958–1959, did not travel to India in the early 1960s.

# To Benjamin Elijah Mays

1 August 1961
[*Atlanta, Ga.*]

*King accepts Mays's request to teach a social philosophy seminar at Morehouse
College during the 1961–1962 school year.*[1]

Dr. Benjamin E. Mays, President
Morehouse College
Atlanta, Georgia

Dear Dr. Mays:

After giving your offer serious and prayerful consideration, I have decided to do
thesseminar on Social Philosophy at Morehouse College beginning in September,
1961, and extending through May, 1962.[2] The salary of $1500.00 is quite agreeable
with me.

I am assuming that the seminar will be held on Tuesdays. As I said to you, there
are about four long standing commitments that I have on Tuesday which I will find
difficult to cancel.[3] With the exception of that, and the possibility of some unfore-
seen development which we discussed, I will be available every Tuesday.

Sincerely yours,
Martin Luther King, Jr.

Km

TLc. MLKP-MBU.

---

1. Mays's request, which was marked "Strictly Confidential," asked King not to discuss the salary
with anyone other than his wife (Mays to King, 20 July 1961). The seminar, which King co-taught with
Morehouse professor Samuel W. Williams, covered a variety of classical philosophers such as John Locke,
Friedrich Nietzsche, and Karl Marx, but also included a section examining nonviolence through the
works of Henry David Thoreau, Leo Tolstoy, and Mahatma Gandhi (King, "Outline of Lecture in Social
Philosophy," 3 October 1961, and King, Notes, Seminar in Social Philosophy, 3 October 1961–23 January
1962, pp. 288–291 and 291–304 in this volume, respectively; King, "What Is Justice," Lecture outline, 3
October 1961–23 January 1962; and King, Notes for seminar in Social Philosophy, October 1961–May
1962).

2. King fulfilled his agreement but decided not to teach another year (see King to Mays, 6
September 1962).

3. King's calendar indicated engagements in Philadelphia on 24 October 1961; Hot Springs,
Arkansas, on 23 January 1962; New York on 20 March 1962; Virginia on 27 March 1962; Denver on 17 April
1962; and Chattanooga on 15 May 1962 (King, "National Diary, 1961–1962," 1 January 1961–27 December
1962).

# To Robert F. Kennedy

5 Aug
1961

5 August 1961
*[Atlanta, Ga.]*

*After weeks of escalating racial tensions between segregationists and black
demonstrators in Monroe, North Carolina, SCLC sent Paul Brooks to investigate
the situation and consult with local black activists led by Robert F. Williams,
who had in 1959 challenged King's belief in the usefulness of nonviolence in the
movement.[1] In this telegram, Wyatt Tee Walker and King petition the attorney
general to begin an immediate investigation into the reports of violence against
activists in Monroe.[2] Although SCLC did not hear directly from Kennedy, Justice
Department official John Doar contacted Brooks to inquire about the severity of
the situation but did not indicate whether or not the government would open an
investigation.[3]*

ATTORNEY GENERAL ROBERT KENNEDY
DEPT OF JUSTICE

DEAR SIRS

SCLC RESPECTFULLY REQUEST THE IMMEDIATE ATTENTION OF INVESTIGATION
BY THE CIVIL RIGHTS DIVISION OR THE JUSTICE DEPARTMENT AND TO THE HIGHLY
EXPLOSIVE SITUATION AT MONROE NORTH CAROLINA THE REV PAUL BROOKS FIELD
REPRESENTATIVE OF SCLC ON SPECIAL ASSIGNMENT REPORTS LAW AND ORDER HAVE
BROKEN DOWN OUR CHIEF CONCERN IS THE SAFETY OF HUMAN RIGHTS AND PROPERTY
AND THE AVOIDANCE OF POSSIBLE VIOLENCE

VERY TRULY YOURS
WYATT T WALKER
EXECUTIVE DIRECTOR

---

1. On 22 June, Williams threatened a "wade-in" to protest the city's segregated swimming pool. In response to Williams's proposed demonstration, city officials closed the pool. With tacit cooperation from law enforcement, Monroe whites launched a campaign of intimidation, including four attempts on Williams's life and nightly gunfire in black neighborhoods. Monroe's black population responded with armed self-defense (Don Gray, "Closed Pool Is Picketed by Negroes," *Charlotte Observer,* 24 June 1961; *The Crusader* 3, no. 5 [7 August 1961]; "Monroe, N.C., Editor Defies Bigots Who Threaten Life," *Pittsburgh Courier,* 5 August 1961). On 4 August 1961, King and Walker wrote Brooks a letter of introduction stating that Brooks would be "used as Mr. Williams deems best." For more on King's relationship with Williams, see Introduction in *Papers* 5:17–18.

2. King and Walker also sent telegrams to Justice Department officials Burke Marshall and John Seigenthaler (King and Walker to Marshall and Seigenthaler, 5 August 1961).

3. In a conversation with Brooks, Doar said he had received several telegrams and phones calls about the situation in Monroe and gave Brooks his direct contact information (Walker, Memo to King, Burke Marshall, and James M. Lawson, 9 August 1961). For more on the situation in Monroe, see Monroe Non-Violent Action Committee to King, 21 August 1961, pp. 262–263 in this volume.

PWc. MLKP-MBU.

# To Nelson A. Rockefeller

9 August 1961
*[Atlanta, Ga.]*

*Following a series of speaking engagements in Albany, New York, King thanks
Rockefeller for his "genuine humanitarian concern" and "unswerving devotion" to
justice.[1] Rockefeller replied on 22 August 1961, writing that "the importance of your
work to make the American dream come true for all our citizens demands that all
who truly share in that dream shall do everything possible to assist you."*

The Honorable Nelson A. Rockefeller
State Capitol
Albany, New York

Dear Governor Rockefeller:

So many things have happened since I spent the very pleasant evening with you
some weeks ago that this note is long overdue. I simply want to say how deeply grateful I am to you for taking time out of your extremely busy schedule to discuss with
me one of the vital issues of our day, and to demonstrate anew your support for the

---

1. Rockefeller met King for dinner on 16 June and then accompanied him as he spoke at a fundraising rally at Wilborn Temple First Church of God in Christ ("Governor Attends Rally with Dr. King," *New
York Times*, 17 June 1961; King, "The American Dream," Address at Wilborn Temple First Church of God
in Christ, 16 June 1961). Nelson Aldrich Rockefeller (1908–1979), grandson of Standard Oil founder John
D. Rockefeller, received his B.A. from Dartmouth in 1930. After appointments in the Roosevelt, Truman,
and Eisenhower administrations, Rockefeller became governor of New York in 1958. As governor,
Rockefeller expanded New York's social welfare programs and endorsed the civil rights movement. In
1960, Rockefeller mounted the first of two unsuccessful campaigns for the Republican Party presidential
nomination. Rockefeller spoke in support of King after his October 1960 arrest in the Atlanta sit-ins,
noting that "when the great spiritual leader, the Rev. Dr. Martin Luther King, finds himself in jail today
because he had the courage to love, we have a long way to go in America" (Douglas Dales, "Governor
Turns to Lay Preaching," *New York Times*, 24 October 1960). After being reelected governor of New
York in 1970, Rockefeller moved politically toward the right, and recanted his support for social welfare
programs. When inmates at Attica Correctional Facility rioted and took hostages in 1971, Rockefeller
refused to negotiate with the prisoners and instead sent New York State troopers to quell the rebellion.
Over forty people were killed and critics condemned his handling of the situation. In 1973, he resigned
as governor to devote more time to his charitable work; however, this was short lived, as he accepted the
vice presidency of the United States when vice president Gerald Ford became president after Nixon's
resignation in 1974. He served for two years and declined to be renominated for the position.

on-going struggle to make the American dream a reality. Certainly all men tof good will are indebted to you for your genuine humanitariam concern and your unswerving devotion to the ideals of justice and human dignity.

I must mention the many personal courtesies extended to me, chief among them, the convenient arrangement that facilitated so much my travel schedule.[2]

Your statement in the public meeting gave not only new inspiration and hope to us who work on the front line, but also to the many people of color who are burdened by racial discrimination.[3]

I hope that the video tape of my speech turned out well, and I mention here in passing that here again you have provided another opportunity for my message to be more broadly distributed. I appreciate so much Mr. Hugh Morrow's skillful handling of the arrangements for making the tape at the Syracuse meeting.[4]

My best wishes to you, and I trust that your stay in Venezuela was most restful and rewarding.[5] I hope our paths will cross again in the not too distant future.

Very truly yours,
Martin Luther King, Jr.

Km

TLc. MLKP-MBU.

---

2. Rockefeller and King flew together on the governor's private plane from New York City to Albany to address the rally ("Governor Attends Rally with Dr. King," 17 June 1961).

3. In his introductory remarks before the rally at Wilborn Temple First Church of God in Christ, Rockefeller praised King as a great spiritual leader who is as "similarly motivated and similarly dedicated" as Gandhi (Rockefeller, Remarks at Wilborn Temple First Church of God in Christ, 16 June 1961).

4. King delivered "The American Dream" at Syracuse University on 13 July. Hugh Morrow (1915–1991) was Rockefeller's speechwriter and special assistant.

5. Rockefeller vacationed at his Venezuelan ranch from 16 July to 26 July.

# From the Monroe Non-Violent Action Committee

21 August 1961
Monroe, N.C.

*Following the arrest of SCLC representative Paul Brooks and the beating of a
photographer, the Monroe Non-Violent Action Committee (MNAC) petitions
King to aid their anti-discrimination campaign.[1] SCLC sent Wyatt Tee Walker to
Monroe on 29 August.[2]*

REV MARTIN LUTHER KING JR
AUBURN ST ATLA

WE THE MONROE NON VIOLENT ACTION COMMITTEE PLEAD FOR YOU TO COME
TO MONROE TO STUDY THE SITUATION STOP WE ARE A NEWLY COMPOSED GROUP OF
FREEDOM RIDERS AND MONROE CITIZENS STOP YOUR REPRESENTATIVE PAUL BROOKS
HAS BEEN ARRESTED AND ONE OF OUR FELLOWS HAS BEEN BEATEN FOR TAKING PIC-
TURES OF THE 30 MINUTE PICKET OF THE JAIL IN WHICH PAUL WAS IMPRISONED STOP
THIS SHOWS ONCE MORE THE DANGEROUS SITUATION EXCEEDING HEREWHICH MR
BROOKS HAS PREVIOUSLY EXPRESSED TO YOU IN HIS REPORT STOP BAYARD RUSTIN
HAS ADVISED US TO CONTACT YOU AND MR WILLIAMS, THE PERSON WE RECOGNIZE
AS THE COMMUNITY LEADER, HAS AUTHORIZED THIS CORRESPONDENCE STOP MR
WILLIAMS IS COMMITTED TO NON VIOLENCE ON PICKET LINES BUT HAS ARMS FOR

---

1. On 19 August freedom riders and local activists from Monroe organized the MNAC with Richard
J. Crowder as chairman (MNAC, "Minutes," Founding meeting of the Monroe Non-Violent Action
Committee, 19 August 1961; MNAC, "List of motions passed to date," 22 August 1961). That same day,
Brooks was arrested for running a stop sign, and after spending the night in jail, he was released on
twenty dollars bond. Photographer and New York native Richard Griswold was choked and thrown to
the ground by three white men as he took pictures of the demonstration outside the jail where Brooks
was being held ("Traffic Violator Didn't Want Bond," *Monroe Journal*, 22 August 1961).

2. Two days before Walker arrived in Monroe, a white mob gathered near picketers and began rioting when an interracial group entered a taxi together. The violence made national headlines as shots
were fired on both sides. Fearing a full-fledged assault by armed segregationists, residents in black neighborhoods prepared to defend their homes. G. Bruce and Mabel Stegall, a white couple from Marshville,
North Carolina, drove into the neighborhood of local NAACP leader Robert F. Williams where local
blacks ordered them from their vehicle. Williams came out of his home and assured the couple they
would not be harmed, and that they were free to leave at any time. Williams, however, declined to
provide the couple with an escort out of the neighborhood. The Stegalls left but before returning to
Marshville, they filed a report with the Monroe police. The following day, Williams was charged with
two counts of kidnapping ("Raid, Kidnap Charge Follow Race Rioting," *Washington Post*, 29 August
1961; Williams, *Negroes with Guns* [New York: Marzani and Munsell, 1962], pp. 84–88). At SCLC's annual
meeting in September, Walker said that albeit difficult, SCLC assuaged the tensions between whites and
blacks in Monroe. He also opined that the "dreadful experience" was a result of "unfortunate leadership" (Walker, "Report of the director," 28 September 1961; see also Walker, "The Deep South in Social
Revolution," 10 November 1961).

DEFENSE OF HIS HOME AND HIS FRIENDS[3] THIS CRISIS REQUIRES THE ATTENTIONS
OF PERSONS EXPERIENCED IN THE PRACTICE AND THEORY OF NON VIOLENCE IF THE
CORRECT PATHS TO THE JUST END WE SEEK ARE TO BE TAKEN STOP THANK YOU FOR
YOUR ATTENTION STOP

THE MONROE NON VIOLENT ACTION COMMITTEE.

PWSr. MLKP-MBU.

---

3. Brooks claimed that Williams, despite publicly advocating self defense, was "misunderstood" by
those unfamiliar with the situation in Monroe. Brooks recalled an incident where Williams, who was
threatened by whites shouting offensive language, urged his guards not to shoot unless absolutely necessary (Walker to King, Burke Marshall, and James M. Lawson, 9 August 1961).

# From James R. Wood

[*September 1961*]

*Wood, public relations director for SCLC, denies accusations that he was involved
in a "vulgar plan to discredit SCLC" and that he made disparaging comments
about the organization's leadership, namely King and Wyatt Tee Walker. "If this
results in my leaving the conference," Wood wrote, "I will feel the loss deeply."
Wood resigned from SCLC in February 1962 at the behest of Walker.*[1]

Daar Martin,

I have been thinking constantly about our conversation of this afternoon. There
seems to be no way I can make sense of it. As I sat there I thought of all the things
that have been said to me about SCLC and the men who lead it. Things I have not
chosen to repeat nor even accept as truth. At one point I felt the need to talk of these
but, decided it would would only degrade the whole thing further. Nothing is to be
gained by adding charges and countercharges.

The question in my mind is why all this is happening. With God as my witness
I did not say these things. As I listened to the things I was charged with saying I
recognized them as things I've heard many times in many places here in Atlanta,

---

1. By November 1961 SCLC had begun searching for a new administrative assistant (Stanley D.
Levison to King, 1 November 1961, pp. 318–319 in this volume). SCLC hired New York journalist Gould
Maynard for the job in January 1962. In an 18 January 1962 letter to Walker, Wood requested an "indefi-
nite leave" from SCLC to spend more time on a new organization he had started. Two months later,
Wood wrote King saying that his resignation from SCLC was involuntary and that the date was set by
Walker (Wood to King, 18 March 1962). James Richard Wood (1918–1976), born in Washington, D.C.,
attended the Hampton Institute and New York University before receiving training in the U.S. Marine
Corps School of Organization. He established military training centers during World War II and worked
with the United Mine Workers and the United Automobile Workers. While working as a data processing
instructor at Virginia State College, Wood met Wyatt Tee Walker and together they founded the Petersburg

Petersburg and others.[2] Much of this I've attributed to the usual gossip. All of it I've chosen not to repeat.

My work with SCLC has been a strange experience for me. First I was felt unable or incapable of doing the work assigned to me. When the meeting with the committee took place I felt that was the time to present a detailed explanation of my position. Two things caused me not to do this. First, I had no knowledge of the matters to be discussed and was completely surprised to learn what they were after the discussion started. Not having had time to prepare a defense I chose simply to answer questions. I made no attempt to contact committee members later and explain my position because of the new questions it would raise. I preferred to rest on their collective judgement. Then too, I felt that if the organization was to conduct its business in that fashion then it may be better for me to resign.

Secondly, my principle desire was and still is, to work at the job of changing social patterns. If I had gotten into a fight about the rightness and wrongness of judgements and opinions it would result in nothing but greater bitterness between Wyatt and me. This, I felt would only serve to make matters worse.

Recently, things have been exceptionally good in our office relationships, or at least I thought so. When the shift to voting came for me I felt this would open a new phase of good relationships. I would be serving where my best abilities and experience would be in use and the conference needs a successful program in this area. I knew I could make a substantial contribution that would meet the needs of the conference and satisfy my desire to work in the field I've chosen.

Now it appears that I have been involved in some vulgar plan to discredit SCLC and the men in it. Furthermore, I find myself unable to defend myself against it. One thing that bothers me is that had I chosen to tell some person the things in question I certainly would not have chosen Edwina to tell them to.[3] She has always shown loyalty to Wyatt as a person. Even when conversation in the office was negative in this regard she would defend Wyatt. I have listened to it many times.

Edwina has had much difficulty resulting from her position in the office. At one time there were very bitter relationships with the other personnel. The only possible reason I can construct for these alleged statements attributed to me is that she may have been seeking to solidify her position in relation to Wyatt and you. This is purely a guess on my part since ther is nothing I can point to as fact. People do strange things and I have been witness to many of them in the forty-six years of my life.

If this results in my leaving the conference I will feel the loss deeply. I have sincerely wanted to work with your image because it is the only tangible thing present today with which motivation of the Negro can be made possible. Then too, SCLC needs people with experience if it will do the job that needs to be done. I regret this

---

Improvement Association. Wood became Walker's administrative assistant and moved with him to Atlanta to join SCLC in 1960. From August 1960 until his resignation in February 1962, Wood served as King's administrative assistant and SCLC's director of public relations. Wood later worked for WAOK Radio in Atlanta, for Lockheed Corporation as assistant to the director of public relations, and for IBM as a communications specialist.

2. After Walker accepted the position of executive director of SCLC he brought Wood and Dorothy Cotton from the Petersburg Improvement Association with him.

3. Wood refers to Edwina Smith, Walker's secretary.

whole thing and wish there were something I could do about it. At present, I can see nothing I can do to refute these charges that would not create more harm than good.

I had thought of resigning. But, this would in fact be an implication of guilt. I could not have this hanging over me in the years to come since I will continue in this work. If I am discharged I have no choice but to accept this. If I stay I could disprove this by action. No matter what happens I will continue to have complete loyalty to the ideas and principles on which SCLC is founded because I believe in them. None of us are perfect. If we are to do the job we must all put principle above personality. I have tried to do this.

[*signed*] Jim

TLS. MLKJP-GAMK: Box 27.

Invocation Delivered at the Funeral of John Wesley
Dobbs at Big Bethel AME Church

[*2 September 1961*]
*[Atlanta, Ga.]*

*King delivers the invocation at the funeral service for family friend and Atlanta community leader John Wesley Dobbs, who died at age seventy-nine. He praises Dobbs's personal life and social activism: "We thank Thee for his matchless love and affection for his wife and children and for the example that he has left for all of us to follow."[1] On 21 September 1961, Dobbs's wife, Irene, thanked King for his "words of inspiration and consolation," which "helped to sustain our spiritual strength." The following transcript is taken from an audio recording.*

May we pray. Eternal God, before whose face the generations rise and fall. In moments made dark by the mystery of death, we are usually so absolved in our natural sadness that we find it difficult to raise our voices in joyous thanksgiving to Thee. But today, we pause to pay our last tribute of respect to one of Thy servants whose life has been so packed with purpose and so saturated with meaningful achievements that our usual "Lord, have mercies" are transformed into a joyous "Lord, we thank Thee." And so, like a mighty chorus we cry out to Thee, thank Thee for the life of John Wesley Dobbs. [*Audience:*] (*Amen, Yeah*)

We thank Thee for his Christian commitment and for his dedicated public service. We thank Thee for his love for people (*Yes*) and his unswerving devotion to the cause of freedom and human dignity. Especially do we thank Thee for the beauty of his

---

1. William Holmes Borders, pastor of Wheat Street Baptist Church in Atlanta, delivered the eulogy (Big Bethel AME Church, Program, Funeral service for John Wesley Dobbs, 2 September 1961).

265

*1*

Eternal God, Out of Whose Mind this
great cosmic universe has been created.
Before whose face the generations rise
and Fall. ~~It is out of~~ ~~that in~~
~~the midst of the sadness~~ of death, we
~~can lift our voices to thee in~~
~~joyous thanksgiving.~~

In moments made dark by the mystery of
death we usually ~~find it difficult~~ usually
so absorbed in (our) natural sadness that we
find it difficult to lift our voices to thee
in joyous thanksgiving. But ~~the~~ life of
our deceased friend has ~~been so~~ packed
~~with meaning~~ and so saturated with creative fulfillment
~~that we temporarily hold back our Lord have~~
~~mercies do give thee thanks.~~
Today we pause to pay our last tribute of
respect to one of thy servants who by life
has been so packed with meaning and creative

Two pages from handwritten draft of the invocation delivered at the funeral of family friend
and Atlanta community leader John Wesley Dobbs. King departed from his draft when
delivering this invocation. Courtesy of the Atlanta University Center, Robert W. Woodruff
Library Archives and Special Collections.

2

fulfillment, that our Lord have mercine"
"Lord we thank thee".
More than an stumbling can express, we
thank thee for the life of John Wesley
Dobbs. We thank thee for his Christian
character, his dedicated public service, his
sensitivity to the needs and problems of
the common man, and his genuine humanitarian
concern. Born at a time when the vast majority
of the Negro people could neither own counts,
he rose up with inner determination and communed
with the insights of poets and philosophers,
political scientist and historians and with his
retentive memory became the chief of
a legacy of knowledge. For this disciplined search for
thankful to thee. Born just a few years
after the Negro child emerged from the long and
desolate night of the Egypt of slavery, he
developed a restless determination to enter
the promised land of freedom and become an

family life, for his greatness as a husband and his magnanimity as a father. We thank Thee for his matchless love and affection for his wife and children (*Yes*) and for the example that he has left for all of us to follow.[2] (*Go ahead*) In these days when all too many people look upon marriage as little more than a convenient arrangement to be entered at will and dissolved at whim, grant, O God, that the nobility of the family life of John Wesley Dobbs will remind us anew (*Yes*) that marriage is holy ground (*Yeah sir*), and that through its sacred portals men and women enter the realm of their immortality. (*Yes*) We pray, O God, for this bereaved family, for this devoted wife, who for lo these many years has surrounded him with a strong canopy of love and loyalty. And for these lovely daughters (*Yes*), whose accomplishments individually and collectively have plunged against cloud-filled nights of oppression new and blazing stars of inspiration. (*Yeah*) Grant, O God, that they will gain a little consolation from the universality of this experience, realizing that death is the irreducible common denominator of all men (*Yeah*), that it is not an aristocracy for some of the people, but a democracy for all of the people. (*Yeah*) Grant, O God, that they will be strengthened by their awareness of Thy divine presence. (*Yes*) Help them to realize that like the ever-flowing waters of the river (*Yeah*), life has its moments of drought and its moments of flood. Like the ever-recurring cycle of the seasons, life has the piercing chill of its winters (*Yeah*) and the glittering sunlight of its summers. Help us to know and help them to know that in all of the changes and the vicissitudes of life (*Yes*) Thou art forever with Thy children. And that Thou art able in our most difficult moments to lift us from the fatigue of despair to the buoyancy of hope and transform dark and desolate valleys of disappointment into sunlit paths of inner peace.

And, O God, grant that all of us will gain consolation from our Christian faith, which reminds us that man is immortal. (*Yeah*) May we go out with this invincible surmise (*Yes*), convinced that death is not a period which ends this great sentence of life (*No*), but a comma (*Yeah*) that punctuates it to more loftier significance.[3] Death is not a blind alley that leads the human race into a state of nothingness, but an open door that leads men into life eternal.[4] (*Yeah*) And now, O God, as we come to the afternoon of the earthly departure of this princely servant of humanity, we do not come here to question Thee (*No*), but to praise Thee (*Yeah, Yes*) for giving to Atlanta, for giving to Georgia (*Yeah*), for giving to the Masons, for giving to America (*Yes*), such a noble life that has for seventy-nine years stood as a refreshing oasis in the midst of a desert world sweltering with the heat of oppression and cynicism.[5] And allow us, O God, to say to him as Horatio said at the death of Hamlet (*Yes*), "Good night, sweet prince (*Yes*), and may the flight of angels take Thee to Thy eternal rest."[6] In the name and spirit of Jesus we pray. Amen. (*Holy Jesus*)

At. JWD-ARC.

---

2. Dobbs had six daughters. The King and Dobbs families became well acquainted when the Kings moved to Boulevard Street, near the Dobbs's house, in 1941. Their children played together.

3. Amos John Traver, *The Christ Who Is All* (Philadelphia: The United Lutheran Publication House, 1929), p. 95.

4. King paraphrases from Victor Hugo's poem "Shall We Live Again" (Grenville Kleiser, comp., *Models for Study: Practical English Series* [New York: Funk & Wagnalls, 1911], pp. 51–52: "The tomb is not a blind alley; it is a thoroughfare. It closes on the twilight, it opens on the dawn."

5. Dobbs was grand master of the Prince Hall Masons of Georgia from 1932 to 1961.

6. Cf. *Hamlet*, act 5, scene 2, lines 312–313.

# To Ruby Doris Smith

6 September 1961
[*Atlanta, Ga.*]

*King and Walker notify Smith that she is the recipient of a $200 scholarship from SCLC for her participation in the Freedom Rides.*[1]

Miss Ruby Doris Smith
702 Wall Street
McComb, Mississippi

Dear Miss Smith:

This is to certify that you have been awarded a $200.00 scholarship for the school year 1961–62 as a part of SCLC's Scholarship aid to Freedom Riders Program.

Please indicate by return mail at which College or University you intend to register. As soon as we receive information you will be forwarded a certified check for the amount indicated above.

Dependent upon more finances being made available it is possible that additional scholarship aid may be available in the future.

Sincerely,
Martin Luther King, Jr.,
President

Wyatt Tee Walker,
Director

MLK: WTW/vmb

TLc. MLKP-MBU.

---

1. Nearly twenty students, including John Lewis, Jim Zwerg, and Paul Brooks, received scholarships. Eligible recipients were movement activists who demonstrated a financial need and were in good academic standing at the college or university at which they were enrolled (SCLC, "Briefs," September 1961; "Ten 'Riders' Given Grants by M.L. King," *Montgomery Advertiser*, 29 September 1961; Walker, "Report of the director," 28 September 1961). In September 1961, the American Baptist Convention (ABC), a predominately white and Northern religious organization, announced a partnership with SCLC to provide scholarships to college students active in the movement. With the help of the Field Foundation, ABC provided SCLC with $16,000 in scholarship aid, which would be administered by both organizations ("Baptist Unit to Aid Rights Campaigners," *New York Times*, 24 September 1961; Walker, "Report of the director," 28 September 1961). Ruby Doris Smith Robinson (1942–1967), born in Atlanta, Georgia, was a sophomore at Spelman College when she joined the nascent Atlanta student movement in early 1960. She attended SNCC's founding meeting at Shaw University, and was one of four SNCC demonstrators who spent a month in prison in early 1961 in Rock Hill, South Carolina. A member of SNCC's executive committee, she succeeded James Forman as SNCC's executive secretary in 1966. Smith graduated from Spelman in 1965 and died in 1967 after a ten-month battle with cancer.

# "The Time for Freedom Has Come"

10 September 1961
New York, N.Y.

*In the following* New York Times Magazine *article, King describes the impact that young black students have had on the African American freedom struggle. He asserts that students are not revolting against "conservative leadership" but are rather "carrying forward a revolutionary destiny of a whole people consciously and deliberately." Insisting that students are "seeking to save the soul of America," he adds that "in sitting down at the lunch counters, they are in reality standing up for the best in the American dream."*

On a chill morning in the autumn of 1956, an elderly, toil-worn Negro woman in Montgomery, Ala., began her slow, painful four-mile walk to her job. It was the tenth month of the Montgomery bus boycott, which had begun with a life expectancy of one week. The old woman's difficult progress led a passer-by to inquire sympathetically if her feet were tired. Her simple answer became the boycotters' watchword. "Yes, friend, my feet is real tired, but my soul is rested."[1]

Five years passed and once more Montgomery arrested the world's attention. Now the symbolic segregationist is not a stubborn, rude bus driver. He emerges in 1961 as a hoodlum stomping the bleeding face of a Freedom Rider. But neither is the Negro today an elderly woman whose grammar is uncertain; rather, he is college bred, Ivy League-clad, youthful, articulate and resolute. He has the imagination and drive of the young, tamed by discipline and commitment. The nation and the world have reacted with astonishment at these students cast from a new mold, unaware that a chain reaction was accumulating explosive force behind a strangely different facade.

Generating these changes is a phenomenon Victor Hugo described in these words: "There is no greater power on earth than an idea whose time has come."[2] In the decade of the Sixties the time for freedom for the Negro has come. This simple truth illuminates the motivations, the tactics and the objectives of the students' daring and imaginative movement.

The young Negro is not in revolt, as some have suggested, against a single pattern of timid, fumbling, conservative leadership. Nor is his conduct to be explained in terms of youth's excesses.[3] He is carrying forward a revolutionary destiny of a whole people consciously and deliberately. Hence the extraordinary willingness to fill the

---

1. A 10 January 1956 *Montgomery Advertiser* profile on minster Robert S. Graetz included a quote from an elderly boycotter: "Well, my body may be a bit tired, but for many years now my soul has been tired. Now my soul is resting" (Tom Johnson, "The Mechanics of the Bus Boycott"). King later attributed the quote to Mother Pollard (*Strength to Love* [New York: Harper & Row, 1963], p. 116).

2. Victor Hugo, *The History of a Crime: Deposition of a Witness* (New York: P.F. Collier & Son, 1877), p. 429.

3. King wrote this article likely with the help of Stanley Levison (Dora E. McDonald to Levison, 17 May 1961; McDonald to King, 2 August 1961). The first draft of King's article that is deposited at Morehouse College [MCMLK-RWWL] included the following sentence: "He is different in quality and degree from other college youth" (King, Draft, The Time for Freedom has Come, July 1961).

jails as if they were honors classes and the boldness to absorb brutality, even to the point of death, and remain nonviolent. His inner strength derives from his goal of freedom and the leadership role he has grasped even at a time when some of his white counterparts still grope in philosophical confusion searching for a personal goal with human values, searching for security from economic instability, and seeking relief from the haunting fear of nuclear destruction.

The campuses of Negro colleges are infused with a dynamism of both action and philosophical discussion. The needs of a surging period of change have had an impact on all Negro groups, sweeping away conventional trivialities and escapism.

Even in the Thirties, when the college campus was alive with social thought, only a minority was involved in action. Now, during the sit-in phase, when a few students were suspended or expelled, more than one college saw the total student body involved in a walkout protest.[4] This is a change in student activity of profound significance. Seldom, if ever, in American history has a student movement engulfed the whole student body of a college.

In another dimension an equally striking change is altering the Negro campuses. Not long ago the Negro collegian imitated the white collegian. In attire, in athletics, in social life, imitation was the rule. For the future, he looked to a professional life cast in the image of the middle-class white professional. He imitated with such energy that Gunnar Myrdal described the ambitious Negro as "an exaggerated American."[5]

Today the imitation has ceased. The Negro collegian now initiates. Groping for unique forms of protest, he created the sit-ins and Freedom Rides. Overnight his white fellow students began to imitate him. As the movement took hold, a revival of social awareness spread across campuses from Cambridge to California. It spilled over the boundaries of the single issue of desegregation and encompassed questions of peace, civil liberties, capital punishment and others.[6] It penetrated the ivy-covered walls of the traditional institutions as well as the glass-and-stainless-steel structures of the newly established colleges.

A consciousness of leadership, a sense of destiny have given maturity and dedication to this generation of Negro students which have few precedents. As a minister, I am often given promises of dedication. Instinctively I examine the degree of sincerity. The striking quality in Negro students I have met is the intensity and depth

---

4. Following the first Montgomery sit-in on 25 February 1960, Alabama governor John Malcolm Patterson pressured Alabama State College president H. Councill Trenholm to expel the thirty-five student protesters. In response, on 1 March, about one thousand students from Alabama State marched to the State Capitol (Lawrence Dunbar Reddick, "The Montgomery Situation," April 1960). For more on the Alabama State College demonstrations, see Introduction and King to Dwight D. Eisenhower, 9 March 1960, in *Papers* 5:24–25 and 385–387, respectively.

5. Gunnar Myrdal, *An American Dilemma: The Negro Problem and Modern Democracy* (New York: Harper & Brothers, 1944), p. 811.

6. In March 1960, the National Student Association (NSA), with chapters in over four hundred universities nationwide, expressed support for the sit-in movement and coordinated sympathy protests targeting department stores such as Woolworth's in northern cities. Fourteen months later, the NSA endorsed nationwide demonstrations in support of the Freedom Rides at Greyhound and Trailways bus terminals. The NSA also endorsed the Peace Corps and called for the abolition of the House Un-American Activities Committee.

of their commitment. I am no longer surprised to meet attractive, stylishly dressed young girls whose charm and personality would grace a Junior Prom and to hear them declare in unmistakably sincere terms, "Dr. King, I am ready to die if I must."

Many of the students when pressed to express their inner feelings, identify themselves with students in Africa, Asia and South America.[7] The liberation struggle in Africa has been the greatest single international influence on American Negro students. Frequently I hear them say that if their African brothers can break the bonds of colonialism, surely the American Negro can break Jim Crow.

African leaders such as President Kwame Nkrumah of Ghana, Governor General Nnamdi Azikiwe of Nigeria, Dr. Tom Mboya of Kenya and Dr. Hastings Banda of Nyasaland are popular heroes on most Negro college campuses.[8] Many groups demonstrated or otherwise protested when the Congo leader, Patrice Lumumba, was assassinated. The newspapers were mistaken when they interpreted these outbursts of indignation as "Communist-inspired."[9]

Part of the impatience of Negro youth stems from their observation that change is taking place rapidly in Africa and other parts of the world, but comparatively slowly in the South. When the United States Supreme Court handed down its historic desegregation decision in 1954, many of us, perhaps naively, thought that great and sweeping school integration would ensue. Yet, today, seven years later, only 7 per cent of the Negro children of the South have been placed in desegregated schools.[10] At the current rate it will take ninety-three more years to desegregate the public schools of the South. The collegians say, "We can't wait that long" or simply, "We won't wait!"[11]

---

7. King's draft [MCMLK-RWWL] included these additional sentences: "They are keenly aware that in the liberation struggles of these countries students have been social levers which have overturned governments, altered the compositions of legislatures and frequently entered high office to implement new policies and programs. Our students want deeply to influence their world particularly because they find themselves heading a struggle to win democratic rights for themselves which became the property of other Americans one hundred and seventy-five years ago. In this respect, they find similarities in their circumstances with the students in historically deprived and under-developed lands."

8. At the invitation of Nkrumah, King attended Ghana's independence celebrations in 1957 and was present for Azikiwe's 1960 inauguration as governor-general of Nigeria. Mboya, a prominent politician and labor activist in Kenya, visited King in 1959, while on a five-week tour of the United States. For more on King's relationships with Nkrumah, Mboya, and Azikiwe, see Introductions in *Papers* 4:7–10 and *Papers* 5:16, 40. Banda was the leader of an independence movement that created the state of Malawi in 1966; he served as president of Malawi until 1994.

9. Lumumba was the leader of the movement that resulted in the Congo's independence from Belgium in June 1960; but he was overthrown soon after in a military coup and killed on 17 January 1961. Various pro-Lumumba demonstrations worldwide occurred after Congo officials announced his death on 13 February. In New York, African American demonstrators stormed the United Nations in protest and were dispersed by police. According to the *New York Times*, several United States officials "asserted that Communist agitators had stirred up the pro-Lumumba demonstrations" ("Riot in Gallery Halts U.N. Debate," 16 February 1961).

10. The Southern Education Reporting Service, a nonpartisan agency, reported that 6.9 percent of Negroes were enrolled in previously all-white schools at the end of the 1960–1961 school year ("7.3 Per Cent Negro Students in Dixie Schools," *Chicago Daily Defender*, 11 December 1961).

11. In a second draft of this article, from the King Center [MLKJP-GAMK], King included the following paragraph: "This manifest impatience is even deeper than that. Its roots are in the very nature of the revolt of Negro youth. The obvious fight is against racial segregation, the mass of laws and customs,

Negro students are coming to understand that education and learning have become tools for shaping the future and not devices of privilege for an exclusive few. Behind this spiritual explosion is the shattering of a material atom.

The future of the Negro college student has long been locked within the narrow walls of limited opportunity. Only a few professions could be practiced by Negroes and, but for a few exceptions, behind barriers of segregation in the North as well as the South. Few frustrations can compare with the experience of struggling with complex academic subjects, straining to absorb concepts which may never be used, or only half-utilized under conditions insulting to the trained mind.

A Negro interne blurted out to me shortly after his patient died, "I wish I were not so well trained because then I would never know how many of these people need not die for lack of proper equipment, adequate post-operative care and timely admission.[12] I'm not practicing good medicine. I'm presiding over tragedies which the absence of good medicine creates."

The Negro lawyer knows his practice will bulk large with criminal cases. The law of wills, of corporations, of taxation will only infrequently reach his office because the clientele he serves has had little opportunity to accumulate property. In his courtroom experience in the South, his clients and witnesses will probably be segregated and he, as well as they, will seldom be referred to as "Mister." Even worse, all too often he knows that the verdict was sealed the moment the arrest was made.[13]

These are but a few examples of the real experience of the Negro professional, seen clearly by the student who has been asked to study with serious purpose. Obviously his incentive has been smothered and weakened. But today, more than ever, the Negro realizes that, while studying, he can also act to change the conditions which cripple his future. In the struggle to desegregate society he is altering it directly for himself as well as for future generations.

There is another respect in which the Negro student is benefiting, and simultaneously contributing to, society as a whole. He is learning social responsibility; he is learning to earn, through his own direct sacrifice, the result he seeks. There are those who would make him soft, pliable and conformist—a mechanical organization man or an uncreative status seeker. But the experience of Negro youth is as harsh and demanding as that of the pioneer on the untamed frontier. Because his struggle is complex, there is no place in it for the frivolous or rowdy. Knowledge and discipline

the humiliation of black by white. The more subtle [*strikeout illegible*] struggle is against authority, in all of its forms—black, white, individual and institutional. Not only are white policemen and mayors and governors often looked upon as 'natural enemies' but these same young people have strong feelings against Negro college presidents and deans, who are overly conservative yet domineering and parents who are 'always telling us what to do!' So strong is this rebellion against adult authority that leaders of the NAACP, ~~Core~~ CORE and my own organization, SCLC (Southern Christian Leadership Conference), occasionally find our advice rejected mainly, it appears to us, because the young people want to make their own decisions. As one of them put it: 'let us make some of the mistakes.'"

12. King's draft [MCMLK-RWWL] included a slightly different version of this sentence: "A Negro intern in an all too typical Negro hospital blurted out to me his bitter fury shortly after his patient died in these words."

13. King's draft [MCMLK-RWWL] included an additional sentence: "Justice is violated hourly and daily in the south so openly and notoriously that the attorney for the defendant is degraded by his participation in the farcical proceedings."

are as indispensable as courage and self-sacrifice. Hence the forging of priceless qualities of character is taking place daily as a high moral goal is pursued.

Inevitably there will emerge from this caldron a mature man, experienced in life's lessons, socially aware, unafraid of experimentation and, most of all, imbued with the spirit of service and dedication to a great ideal. The movement therefore gives to its participants a double education—academic learning from books and classes, and life's lessons from responsible participation in social action. Indeed, the answer to the quest for a more mature, educated American to compete successfully with the young people of other lands, may be present in this new movement.[14]

Of course, not every student in our struggle has gained from it. This would be more than any humanly designed plan could realize. For some, the opportunity for personal advantage presented itself and their character was not equal to the challenge. A small percentage of students have found it convenient to escape from their own inadequacies by identifying with the sit-ins and other activities.[15] They are, however, relatively few because this is the form of escape in which the flight from responsibility imposes even greater responsibilities and risks.[16]

It is not a solemn life, for all of its seriousness. During a vigorous debate among a group of students discussing the moral and practical soundness of nonviolence, a majority rejected the employment of force. As the minority dwindled to a single student, he finally declared, "All I know is that, if rabbits could throw rocks, there would be fewer hunters in the forest."

This is more than a witty remark to relieve the tensions of serious and even grim discussion. It expresses some of the pent-up impatience, some of the discontent and some of the despair produced by minute corrections in the face of enormous evil. Students necessarily have conflicting reactions.[17] It is understandable that violence presents itself as a quick, effective answer for a few.

---

14.  King's draft [MCMLK-RWWL] included the following additional paragraph: "A persistent question is put by many wondering if the distraction of social action does not militate against serious fruitful study. This legitimate question was answered by one student I know in an interesting way. This bright young man had always affected a cynical attitude toward grades. If he did poorly or failed a subject he was quick to find the joke or remark that deflected attention from it. As a defense mechanism he prided himself on the scope and sophistication of his dating and drinking. One evening he came to me startled and with a curious mixture of flippancy and concern stated, 'I'm becoming a scholar in spite of myself. I can't give them any excuse for expelling me now that I'm in the movement, so I've put some fast system in my study and it works. The books used to keep secrets from me but now I know what's in them and I it's pretty embarrassing when I hear myself sound like a grind. But I'll do anything for this fight—even study.'"

15.  In King's draft [MCMLK-RWWL] the above two sentences were reversed and followed by this additional sentence: "Others have abandoned their studies and pretended they were sacrificing themselves."

16.  The following sentence appeared in both drafts [MCMLK-RWWL and MLKJP-GAMK] of King's article: "The demands of the student movement are heavy. Discipline, alertness, sacrifice and danger are all involved and the student who enters weak in any quality faces the iron necessity to remake himself or risks disgracing himself."

17.  King's draft [MCMLK-RWWL]: "Their learning has enabled them to understand that merely ~~six~~ {seven} percent of the Negro children have been placed in desegregated schools after nearly one hundred years of legal emancipation and after seven years of a Supreme Court decision. They know, if white students do not, that 43% of Negro families earn less than $2,000.00 per year. These facts and others sum up for them the failure of the nation and the emptiness of the 'American Dream.' Hence while they hope and work, they must struggle with the weight of frustration and disappointment."

For the large majority, however, nonviolent, direct action has emerged as the bet- ter and more successful way out. It does not require that they abandon their discontent. This discontent is a sound, healthy social response to the injustice and brutality
they see around them. Nonviolence offers a method by which they can fight the evil
with which they cannot live. It offers a unique weapon which, without firing a single
bullet, disarms the adversary.[18] It exposes his moral defenses, weakens his morale,
and at the same time works on his conscience.[19]

Another weapon which Negro students have employed creatively in their nonviolent struggle is satire. It has enabled them to avoid corrosive anger while pressing the
cutting edge of ridicule against the opponent. When they have been admonished to
"go slow," patiently to wait for gradual change, with a straight face they will assure you
that they are diligently searching for the happy medium between the two extremes
of moderation and gradualism.

It is perhaps the special quality of nonviolent direct action, which sublimates
anger, that explains why so few students are attracted to extreme nationalist sects
advocating black supremacy.[20] The students have anger under controlling bonds
of discipline. Hence they can answer appeals for cooling-off periods by advocating
cooling-off for those who are hot with anger and violence.[21]

Much has been made of the willingness of these devotees of nonviolent social
action to break the law.[22] Paradoxically, although they have embraced Thoreau's and
Gandhi's civil disobedience on a scale dwarfing any past experience in American
history, they do respect law.[23] They feel a moral responsibility to obey just laws. But
they recognize that there are also unjust laws.

10 Sept
1961

---

18. King's drafts [MCMLK-RWWL and MLKJP-GAMK]: "It has demonstrated that when sacrifice
and courage enable the unarmed and non-violent to take up a position, the guns of the city and state
police are seldom used lest the wrath of the whole nation disarm and defeat them. Indeed the experience of the Freedom Riders has shown that the sense of fair play of the American people demands that
law enforcement agencies protect, rather than assault, non-violent demonstraters."

19. In his draft [MLKJP-GAMK], King handwrote this sentence.

20. King's draft [MCMLK-RWWL] indicated that students were "attracted to Muslim or other
extreme nationalist sects advocating black supremacy."

21. On 24 May Attorney General Robert F. Kennedy called for a suspension of the Freedom Rides,
but failed to persuade the riders ("Attorney General's Pleas," *New York Times*, 25 May 1961). King's draft
[MCMLK-RWWL] included an additional sentence: "They consider themselves, in the words of their
current vernacular, 'cool cats for change.'"

22. This sentence does not appear in King's first draft [MCMLK-RWWL], but is included in the
second draft [MLKJP-GAMK].

23. King's draft [MCMLK-RWWL] includes the following sentence: "The immature outbursts of conflict with town police or raids on girl's dormitories which now herald spring on the campus in many college communities are unknown on the Negro campus as they calmly and carefully plan a lunch counter
sit-in or a bus ride." His second draft [MLKJP-GAMK] contains the following addition, but it is also partially crossed out: "I quite agree with their willingness to break Jim Crow laws—or any law that degrades
man. This is not at all irresponsible lawlessness; rather, it shows a high respect for law that benefits man.
When they violate laws, unlike the {'uncivil disobedience' of the} segregationist, they are willing to suffer
the consequences of their acts. They do not run and hide. They are quite willing to endure the penalities,
whatever they are, for in this way the public comes to re-examine the law in question and will thus decide
whether it uplifts or downgrades man. Their appeal is to conscience. The pointless outbursts of conflict
with town police or raids on girl's dormitories which now herald spring on the campus in many college
communities are unknown on the Negro campus as they calmly and carefully plan a lunch counter sit-in
or a bus ride."

From a purely moral point of view, an unjust law is one that is out of harmony with the moral law of the universe. More concretely, an unjust law is one in which the minority is compelled to observe a code that is not binding on the majority. An unjust law is one in which people are required to obey a code that they had no part in making because they were denied the right to vote.

In disobeying such unjust laws, the students do so peacefully, openly and nonviolently. Most important, they willingly accept the penalty, whatever it is, for in this way the public comes to re-examine the law in question and will thus decide whether it uplifts or degrades man.

This distinguishes their position on civil disobedience from the "uncivil disobedience" of the segregationist. In the face of laws they consider unjust, the racists seek to defy, evade and circumvent the law, and they are unwilling to accept the penalty. The end result of their defiance is anarchy and disrespect for the law. The students, on the other hand, believe that he who openly disobeys a law, a law conscience tells him is unjust, and then willingly accepts the penalty, gives evidence thereby that he so respects that law that he belongs in jail until it is changed. Their appeal is to the conscience.

Beyond this, the students appear to have perceived what an older generation overlooked in the role of law. The law tends to declare rights—it does not deliver them. A catalyst is needed to breathe life experience into a judicial decision by the persistent exercise of the rights until they become usual and ordinary in human conduct. They have offered their energies, their bodies to effect this result. They see themselves the obstetricians at the birth of a new order. It is in this manner that the students have related themselves to and materialized "the idea whose time has come."

In a sense, the victories of the past two years have been spectacular and considerable. Because of the student sitters, more than 150 cities in the South have integrated their lunch counters. Actually, the current break-throughs have come about partly as a result of the patient legal, civil and social ground clearing of the previous decades.[24] Then, too, but slowly, the national Government is realizing that our so-called domestic race relations are a major force in our foreign relations. Our image abroad reflects our behavior at home.[25]

Many liberals, of the North as well as the South, when they list the unprecedented progress of the past few years, yearn for a "cooling off" period; not too fast, they say,

---

24. King's draft [MLKJP-GAMK]: "Moreover, the South, as 'backward' as it may appear when the riots break out, is much more enlightened today than it was say, twenty-five years ago. Also, it is more prosperous, urbanized and industrialized."

25. Robert F. Kennedy's 24 May statement urging a suspension of the Freedom Rides also included the plea to "keep in mind that the President is about to embark on a mission of great importance. Whatever we do in the United States at this time which brings or causes discredit on our country can be harmful to his mission" ("Attorney General's Pleas," 25 May 1961).

we may lose all that we have gained if we push faster than the violent ones can be persuaded to yield.

This view, though understandable, is a misreading of the goals of the young Negroes. They are not after "mere tokens" of integration ("tokenism," they call it); rather theirs is a revolt against the whole system of Jim Crow and they are prepared to sit-in, kneel-in, wade-in and stand-in until every waiting room, rest room, theatre and other facility throughout the nation that is supposedly open to the public is in fact open to Negroes, Mexicans, Indians, Jews or what-have-you. Theirs is total commitment to this goal of equality and dignity. And for this achievement they are prepared to pay the costs—whatever they are—in suffering and hardship as long as may be necessary.

Indeed, these students are not struggling for themselves alone. They are seeking to save the soul of America. They are taking our whole nation back to those great wells of democracy which were dug deep by the Founding Fathers in the formulation of the Constitution and the Declaration of Independence. In sitting down at the lunch counters, they are in reality standing up for the best in the American dream. They courageously go to the jails of the South in order to get America out of the dilemma in which she finds herself as a result of the continued existence of segregation. One day historians will record this student movement as one of the most significant epics of our heritage.

But should we, as a nation, sit by as spectators when the social unrest seethes? Most of us recognize that the Jim Crow system is doomed. If so, would it not be the wise and human thing to abolish the system surely and swiftly? This would not be difficult, if our national Government would exercise its full powers to enforce Federal laws and court decisions and do so on a scale commensurate with the problems and with an unmistakable decisiveness.[26] Moreover, we would need our religious, civic and economic leaders to mobilize their forces behind a real, honest-to-goodness "End Jim Crow Now" campaign.

This is the challenge of these young people to us and our ideals. It is also an expression of their new-found faith in themselves as well as in their fellow man.[27]

In an effort to understand the students and to help them understand themselves, I asked one student I know to find a quotation expressing his feeling of our struggle. He was an inarticulate young man, athletically expert and far more poetic with a basketball than with words, but few would have found the quotation he typed on a card and left on my desk early one morning:

---

26. King discussed a number of ways executive power could be used to end segregation in an earlier essay for *The Nation* ("Equality Now," 4 February 1961, pp. 139–150 in this volume).

27. The preceding four paragraphs were not in King's first draft [MCMLK-RWWL].

*I sought my soul, but my soul*
*I could not see,*
*I sought my God, but he eluded*
*me,*
*I sought my brother, and I*
*found all three.*[28]

PD. *New York Times Magazine*, 10 September 1961, pp. 25, 118–119.

---

28.   "The Search," by Ernest Howard Crosby (1899): "No one could tell me where my Soul might be./I searched for God, but God eluded me. /I sought my Brother out, and found all three" (Crosby, "The Search," in *Plain Talk in Psalm & Parable* [Boston: Small, Maynard and Co., 1899], p. 137). King admitted later that "I do not know the author of the poem that I quoted at the end of the article. I have always liked it, and I have used it many times in speeches. For some reason, I have never come across the author" (King to B.S. Weiss, 5 October 1961).

# To J. H. Jackson

10 September 1961
*[Atlanta, Ga.]*

*On 6 September during the 81st annual National Baptist Convention (NBC) in Kansas City, Missouri, a fight broke out between supporters of incumbent president Jackson and Gardner C. Taylor, a challenger backed by King. During the mêlée, sixty-four-year-old Arthur Wright, a Jackson supporter, fell four feet from the podium and suffered a fatal head injury. Three days later, Jackson reportedly said that King "masterminded the invasion of the convention floor . . . which resulted in the death of a delegate."[1] Below, King demands that Jackson retract the "libelous" allegation, fearing it would cause "irreparable harm to the freedom movement." Jackson replied on 12 September 1961.[2]*

DR J H JACKSON

AM DEEPLY DISTRESSED ABOUT STATEMENT WHICH APPEARED IN HEADLINE COV-
ERAGE IN SEVERAL LEADING NEWSPAPERS ACROSS THE COUNTRY IN WHICH YOU ARE
QUOTED AS SAYING THAT I MASTERMINDED AN INVASION OF THE NATIONAL BAPTIST

---

1.   "Church Conclave Violence Blamed on Martin King," *Birmingham News*, 10 September 1961. Both Jackson and Taylor claimed the presidency of the NBC at the 1960 convention held in Philadelphia. In 1961, both ministers asserted the right to preside over the Kansas City convention where members of Taylor's group descended on the dais and were blocked by Jackson supporters. Two days after the incident, Taylor conceded the presidency after gaining only 1,519 votes to Jackson's 2,732 votes. Jackson served as president of the NBC from 1953 until 1982. For more on the 1960 convention, see Introduction in *Papers* 5:34.

2.   See pp. 281–282 in this volume.

CONVENTION WHICH RESULTED IN THE DEATH OF REVERAND WRIGHT[3] IN SUBSTANCE
THE STATEMENT ACCUSES ME OF GIVING IMPETUS TO A CONSPIRACY WHICH HAD AS
ITS GOAL A HOMICIDE. SUCH AN UNWARRENTED UNTRUE AND UNETHICAL STATEMENT
IS LIBELOUS TO THE CORE AND CAN DO IRREPARABLE HARM TO THE FREEDOM MOVE-
MENT IN WHICH I AM INVOLVED. THE FACT IS THAT I WAS NOT IN THE AUDITORIUM
WHEN THE VIOLENCE OCCURRED AND I PARTICIPATED IN NO STRATEGY SESSION PRIOR
TO THE CONVENTION BECAUSE I DID NOT ARRIVE IN KANSAS CITY UNTIL AFTER MID-
NIGHT TUESDAY. WHILE I FEEL THAT DR TAYLOR AND HIS SUPPORTERS WERE ALWAYS
HONORABLE AND NON VIOLENT IN THEIR ACTION, I HAD NOTHING TO DO WITH MAP-
PING THE STRATEGY. IN FACT MY OVERCROWDED SCHEDULE MADE IT IMPOSSIBLE FOR
ME TO ATTEND A SINGLE STRATEGY SESSION OF THE TAYLOR TEAM. AS YOU KNOW MY
WHOLE PHILOSOPHY OF LIFE AND SOCIAL ACTION IS ONE OF LOVE AND NON VIOLENCE
AND FOR ONE TO GIVE THE NATION THE IMPRESSION THAT I AM LITTLE MORE THAN
A HOODLUM WITH A RECKLESS DISREGARD OF THE LIVES AND SAFETY OF PERSONS IS
BOTH LIBELOUS AND INJURIOUS TO MY PUBLIC IMMAGE. I THEREFORE ASK YOU IN A
CHRISTIAN SPIRIT TO RETRACT THIS STATEMENT IMMEDIATELY AND URGE THE PRESS
TO GIVE AS MUCH ATTENTION TO THE RETRACTION AS IT GAVE TO THE ORIGINAL
ACCUSATION.[4] PLEASE SEND A COPY OF RETRACTION TO ME.

MARTIN LUTHUR KING JR

PWc. MLKP-MBU.

---

3. The day after Jackson made the accusation, the *New York Times*, *Washington Post*, and *Chicago Tribune* each ran stories about Jackson's claim ("Dr. King Is Accused in Baptist Dispute," *New York Times*, 10 September 1961; Wallace H. Terry, "Baptist Leader Charges Dr. King Sparked 'Invasion' of Rival Forces," *Washington Post*, 10 September 1961; "Calls Dr. King 'Master Mind' of Fatal Riot," *Chicago Tribune*, 10 September 1961).

4. The Associated Negro Press published excerpts from King's telegram to Jackson on 11 September (Press release, "Dr. King denies link in violence at Baptist meet in K.C.; Asks President Jackson to retract statement," 11 September 1961).

# From Andrew Young

11 September 1961
New York, N.Y.

*Concerned and anxious about his new position as administrator of SCLC's*
*Citizenship Education Program (CEP), Young asks for "guidance and patience"*
*as he becomes familiar with the organization. Young, who was initially hired by*
*Highlander, admits to King that he feels "like an intruder in the SCLC," because*
*"you really never asked for me."*[1]

---

1. Due to Highlander's legal troubles the citizenship program was placed under SCLC administration and Young was appointed to direct the program. For more on Young and his relationship to

Dr. Martin L. King
Southern Christian Leadership Conf.
208 Auburn Ave. N.E.
Atlanta 3, Ga.

Rev. Wyatt Tee Walker
Southern Christian Leadership Conf.
208 Auburn Ave. N.E.
Atlanta 3, Ga.

Gentlemen:

The hour cometh, and I meet it with extremely mixed reactions. I will arrive in Atlanta on Thursday morning and will come to SCLC office. Today marked the end of my stay with the National Council and closed a very meaningful period of my life.[2] I've been so secure here that moving to Atlanta seems a fearful prospect. But then the one or two Negroes are always secure in this kind of set up, so the very token-ism that makes life so good for me is also the reason I am glad to leave if it offers an opportunity to share in the struggle for a better life for all.

The thing that worries me most is the fact that I feel like an intruder in the SCLC set up. You really never asked for me. I am sure that this whole project could go on without me. But I also feel that there are things that I might contribute with the help of your guidance and patience during this awkward period of getting acquainted. I know that time is a great luxury with you folk, and I want to consume as little of your time as possible, but I do think it will be necessary for me to have the benifit of your counsel and orientation for a while so that I may learn to fit into your pattern of thinking and operating. Once I feel that I understand SCLC a bit, I will feel free to make decisions concerning the Citizenship Education Project which are in keeping with SCLC policy.

I am sorry that I could not write more, sooner, but summer is always our busi-est time in the Youth Dept., and I was trying to get our house sold, consult with Hotchkiss and the Field Foundation on this in addition to the normal work load.[3] Now I am anxious to get to work. The longer I sit up here, the more troubles I can anticipate.

---

Highlander, see King to Young, 25 April 1961, pp. 206–208 in this volume. In his 1996 memoir, Young wrote that he lacked the experience to join "such a high-profile operation" and that SCLC "was dominated by emotional Baptist preachers and I was a self-contained Congregationalist" (*An Easy Burden: The Civil Rights Movement and the Transformation of America* [Waco: Baylor University Press, 2008], p. 131).

    2. Young served as associate director of the Department of Youth Work for the National Council of Churches from 1957 to 1961.

    3. Wesley Akin Hotchkiss was the general secretary of the Division of Higher Education and the American Missionary Association of The Board of Home Missions of the Congregational and Christian Churches, which helped sponsor the Citizenship Education Project. The Field Foundation provided SCLC with an initial $26,500 grant. Due to the fact that SCLC did not have tax-exempt status, the American Missionary Association administered the funds (Maxwell Hahn to Hotchkiss, 13 July 1961).

Hoping to see you Thursday, or whenever you get back in town, I am,

Sincerely yours,
[*signed*] Andy
Andrew Young

TLS. MLKP-MBU.

# From J. H. Jackson

12 September 1961
Chicago, Ill.

*Jackson replies to King's 10 September demand that he retract a statement blaming
King for the death of a delegate at the National Baptist Convention (NBC).
Jackson insists that he was misquoted and has been "victimized" by the press. King
later commented that, while Jackson's statement was not a real retraction, he would
not sue him for libel.[1]*

Dr. Martin Luther King, Jr.
2873 Dale Creek Rd. N.W.
Atlanta, Georgia

Dear Dr. King:

Please find enclosed a statement that was given to Mr. Joe Dell of the Associated
Press last night.[2] I repeated to him the statement that I made to you on the 'phone
Sunday morning to the effect that I did not say that you had master-minded the
invasion of the convention hall that resulted in a delegates' death.[3] The rest of the
enclosed statement is the same as I attempted to give you on the telephone last
Sunday morning.

I have been victimized so much in the public press that I have no desire to occasion any other person the pain and suffering of misrepresentation.

---

1. In an interview with the Associated Negro Press, King said: "Dr. Jackson has not apologized. I
don't consider his statement a real retraction. I think it should be made clear about who made the statement. All the reporters there said he did, but he says he didn't" (Eddie L. Madison, Press release, "Dr.
Martin Luther King, Jr., says he will not sue Dr. Jackson for alleged statement that he masterminded
convention violence 'at this time,'" 20 September 1961).

2. "Statement by Dr. J. H. Jackson, President National Baptist Convention of the United States of
America," 10 September 1961.

3. In his statement, Jackson claimed that King was "the master-mind behind the protest techniques"
of the sit-ins and Freedom Rides, not Taylor's challenge to the presidency of the NBC. He explained that
the statement was "not designed or intended to accuse Dr. King of any disorder," but was crediting King
"for his share in the philosophy of protest" ("Statement by Jackson").

I do not believe the reporters are malicious in this, but they can mistand, and therefore misrepresent. Allow me to quote several misrepresentations regarding me:

U.P.I. makes this statement September 8, 1961: "The Rev. Mr. Jackson who for all intent and purpose has been president for the last twelve months delivered the president's annual report. He collapsed after his one hour speech but was revived quickly."[4] There is not one iota of truth in the last sentence. I have never collapsed since I have been in public life.

An A.P. story in the New York Times, Sunday September 10th: "Mr. Jackson, an activist who favors freedom rides has held the presidential post several years. He and Dr. Gardner Taylor differ on how to achieve civil rights goals. Mr. Taylor favors reliance on court suits."[5] This quotation reveals another case of an error in the public press.

I hope the enclosed statement as given to the public press will receive as wide publicity as the former statement we seek to correct.

Best wishes to the family and friends.

Yours truly,
J. H. Jackson

JHJ:NM
Enclosures

TLc. MLKP-MBU.

---

4. "Preacher Hurt in Convention Rioting Dies," *Chicago Tribune*, 8 September 1961.

5. The quoted article was published in the *Times* on 9 September ("Chicagoan Elected at Baptist Parley"). Far from favoring reliance on court action over direct action, Taylor was a supporter of the Freedom Rides and even encouraged King's participation in a ministerial Freedom Ride (Taylor to King, 7 July 1961, p. 251 in this volume).

# From J. Pius Barbour

14 September 1961
Chester, Pa.

*Following Gardner C. Taylor's failed bid for the presidency of the National Baptist Convention (NBC), Barbour, King's mentor while in seminary, urges King to "stand up and fight" his removal as vice president of the National Sunday School and Baptist Training Union Congress (BTU) by the organization's president J. H. Jackson.[1] Despite Barbour's advice, King did not challenge his dismissal from the BTU.[2]*

---

1. King was elected vice president of the BTU at the June 1958 convention (see Introduction and King to O. Clay Maxwell, 18 July 1958, in *Papers* 4:18 and 455–456, respectively).

2. King was replaced by the Reverend Ernest C. Estell of Dallas.

CONVENTIONS HAS MORAL BUT NO LEGAL RIGHTS OVER THE CONGRESS[3] STAND UP
AND FIGHT AND TAKE ISSUE TO THE PEOPLE AT THE CONGRESS. DONY BE A RABBIT
LIKE GARDNER

J PIUS BARBOUR

PWSr. MLKP-MBU.

---

3.  The BTU is a nominally independent subsidiary body of the NBC.

# From Lawrence Dunbar Reddick

15 September 1961
Baltimore, Md.

*In preparation for the 27–29 September 1961 SCLC convention in Nashville,
Reddick advises the SCLC board and executive committee to establish concrete
plans as "many thoughtful persons are wondering why it is taking us so long to
build a mass movement in the South."*

Dr. Martin Luther King, Jr.
The Reverend Wyatt Tee Walker
Southern Christian Leadership Conference
208 Auburn Avenue, N.E.
Atlanta 3, Georgia

Dear Martin and Wyatt,

I had hoped to have a final huddle with you gentlemen before I left Atlanta but
the packing up kept me busy and you two were very much on the move.[1]

Let me say in passing, that Ruth and I are well settled here in circumstances about
as comfortable as Atlanta.[2] We like it fine.

I will be down for our three-day convention in Nashville and wish to raise two
questions in that connection. First, I am quite glad that we have such a good line-
up for our public program—Belafonte, Jim Lawson and Jim Farmer, etc.[3] I hope,

---

1.  A resident of Baltimore, Reddick stayed in Atlanta for the summer (Reddick to King, 9 May 1961,
p. 222 in this volume).

2.  Reddick refers to his wife, Ella Ruth Thomas Reddick.

3.  Entertainer and movement supporter Harry Belafonte was scheduled to open the convention
with a benefit concert honoring the freedom riders the evening of 27 September, but he canceled his

though, that we will not have those <u>long-drawn-out "country" meetings,</u> in which every "dignitary" present has to have his say and nobody will enforce a time limit on the speakers. We should be more modern and sophisticated than that.

Secondly, please let us plan to have time for the Board and our Executive Committee to do some thinking and looking ahead. Frankly, many thoughtful persons are wondering why it is taking us so long to build a mass movement in the South. We have done well with the crisis situations but we need to <u>plan</u> really for establishing affiliates on a wide basis and to service these affiliates.[4] I hope that we will not schedule so many concurrent operations during our Nashville Conference that the Board members can not be together for decision-making.[5]

The other point is about the SCLC Newsletter. Until we get a public relations man, I will be willing to do the newsletter.[6] Since I do not believe in getting paid for any services that I may render The Movement, I would only need coverage of any expenses involved. Accordingly, we could save me a trip to Atlanta, if I could get from you, when I see you in Nashville, information on the following topics:

I. Progress reports on projects—leadership training, etc.
II. New projects—joint voter registration campaign, etc.
III. Organizational and personnel changes and activities
IV. SCLC in the news
V. Vignette of Month (I hope that Fred Shuttlesworth comes, for I'd like to interview him for the coming issue)

Martin ask your secretary to send me a list of your speaking engagements (since the last one she prepared for me) and include programs and leaflets.

If I can get the above information from you in Nashville, I can prepare the copy, sending both of you copies for correction and approval and then pass it on to the printer. He could air-mail proofs, etc.

Let me close by coming back to the point that we need to make a number of important decisions—some policy, some political—at Nashville and we will not be able to do this if many of us are running here and yon during the deliberations.

---

appearance due to illness. The concert went on as scheduled with performances by folk singers Miriam Makeba and the Chad Mitchell Trio (SCLC, "Minutes of annual board meeting," 27 September 1961; "Belafonte III, Won't Be Here," *Nashville Tennessean*, 27 September 1961). Lawson gave the keynote address on the morning of 28 September and Farmer spoke that afternoon (SCLC, Program, "Annual meeting of SCLC," 27 September–29 September 1961).

4. The meeting's minutes indicated King's desire to expand direct action campaigns into South Carolina, Mississippi, and Alabama. In his annual report, Walker also expressed discontent with the organization's progress, noting that "our growth has not been as great as it might have been" (SCLC, "Minutes of annual board meeting," 27 September 1961; Walker, "Report of the director," 28 September 1961).

5. After the conference, Reddick wrote that "all things considered, we had a great time in Nashville" (Reddick to King and Walker, 6 October 1961).

6. After allegedly making disparaging comments about King and Walker, public relations director James R. Wood was ousted by the organization; he resigned on 28 February 1962 (Wood to Walker, 18 January 1962). For more about Wood and his troubles with SCLC, see Wood to King, September 1961, pp. 263–265 in this volume. SCLC hired journalist Gould Maynard in January 1962 to handle public relations. SCLC did not release a newsletter during the interim period between Wood's resignation and Maynard's hiring.

My home address: 3704 Winterbourne Road, Baltimore 16, Maryland. My tele- 19 Sept
phone number is 947–9326. 1961
Regards to all.

Sincerely yours,
[*signed*] Lawrence
L. D. Reddick

LDR/obg

TLS. MLKP-MBU.

# To Erma Jewell Hughes

19 September 1961
Atlanta, Ga.

*In a 16 September 1961 letter to J. H. Jackson, Hughes, a Houston educator,
castigated him for accusing King of playing a role in the death of Reverend
Wright at the National Baptist Convention (NBC) conference.[1] Calling King a
"brilliant young man," Hughes defended him as "a capable leader who is a builder
of humanity rather than a destroyer."[2] King thanks Hughes for her support,
acknowledging that this "unjust attack is just another cross that I must bear."
Hughes replied on 7 October 1961.*

Mrs. Erma J. Hughes
4214 Dowling Street
Houston 4, Texas

---

1. Hughes to Jackson, 16 September 1961; see also King to Jackson, 10 September 1961, and Jackson
to King, 12 September 1961, pp. 278–279 and 281–282 in this volume, respectively. Jackson also received
criticism from a group of thirty-one religious leaders including Benjamin Mays, Fred L. Shuttlesworth,
and Gardner C. Taylor, for his "vicious and un-Christian attack" on King. The group demanded that
Jackson "right this grievous wrong" by publicly repudiating his statement (Mays, Shuttlesworth, et al., to
Jackson, 12 September 1961; see also SCLC, Press release, "Religious leaders protest alleged attack on Dr.
Martin Luther King, Jr.," 12 September 1961). Erma Jewell Hughes (1913–1965) was raised in Houston and
attended high school in nearby Beaumont. She received a B.S. from Tennessee State College, an M.A.
from Columbia University, and an LVN from the Lincoln Institute of Nursing. She founded the Erma
Hughes Business College in September 1932 in Houston. Hughes corresponded regularly with King,
inviting him multiple times to speak at her college's commencement ceremony. He spoke at Hughes's
college on 18 May 1958 (Erma Hughes Business College, Program, Twenty-fifth annual baccalaureate
and commencement exercises, 18 May 1958).

2. Hughes to Jackson, 16 September 1961. Jackson responded: "Your whole letter was based on an
untrue statement" (Jackson to Hughes, September 1961).

Dear Mrs. Hughes:

This is just a note to thank you for your forthright and courageous letter to Dr. Jackson in my defense. I certainly wish it had been an open letter which could have been circulated to many, many papers. It goes without saying that such a vicious and unwarranted attack on my motives and integrity has served to confuse the minds of many people. Numberous friends have urged me to sue Dr. Jackson but I have decided that my commitment to the non-violent philosophy will not allow me to do this.[3] Therefore, this unjust attack is just another cross that I must bear.

It is always consoling to have the support of friends of good will. Your letter strengthened me immensely, and I know that you expressed the sentiments of thousands and millions of people of good will who are strongly backing us in this struggle for freedom and human diginity.

Enclosed is a copy of the telegram that I sent Dr. Jackson a few hours after the accusation was made.

Always grateful for your support and concern, I am

Sincerely yours,
Martin L. King, Jr
Martin Luther King, Jr

Km

TLc. CABP-ICHi: Box 386.

---

3. King stated publicly that he would not sue Jackson because his "non-violent philosophy causes me to temporarily hold back at this point" (Eddie L. Madison, Press release, "Dr. Martin Luther King, Jr., says he will not sue Dr. Jackson for alleged statement that he masterminded convention violence 'at this time,'" 20 September 1961).

# To James Baldwin

26 September 1961
*[Atlanta, Ga.]*

*King congratulates Baldwin on the publication of his book* Nobody Knows My Name, *and thanks him for "the many kind things you said about me and my work" in a 1961 article published in* Harper's Magazine.[1] *Baldwin replied on 15 November, writing that the appreciation "means more to me than I can say."*

---

1. The anthology, a reflection on race, was written while Baldwin was in Paris. Although pleased with the content of the *Harper's* article, "The Dangerous Road Before Martin Luther King," King considered asking Baldwin about his claim that he had fired Bayard Rustin under pressures from Congressman Adam Clayton Powell. King, however, decided that Rustin should address the matter himself (Rustin to

Mr. James Baldwin                                                26 Sept
c/o Dial Press, Inc.                                             1961
461 Park Avenue, South
New York 16, New York

Dear James:

Please excuse me for taking the perogative of addressing you by your first name, but I feel just that close to you. I have just finished reading <u>Nobody Knows My Name</u>, and I simply want to thank you for it. This collection of essays and lectures will certainly go down as a classic on the meaning of the social revolution that is taking place in the United States in the area of race relations. It is written with a lucidity of style and a profoundity of thought that inspires any serious reader. Your analysis of the problem is always creative and penetrating. Your honesty and courage in telling the truth to white Americans, even if it hurts, is most impressive.[2] I have been tremendously helped by reading the book, and I know that it will serve to broaden my understanding on the whole meaning of our struggle.

I would also like to express a rather belated thanks to you for the article which appeared in HARPER'S magazine. It, too, had a profound impact, and I am sure that as a result of it many people came to an appreciation of the dilemma that I confront as a leader in the civil rights struggle. I can assure you that the many kind things you said about me and my work in the article have been of inestimable value for the continuance of my humble efforts.

I hope you many more successful days as a writer. You are not only a great Negro writer; you are a great writer. In a most creative way you rose up from all of the crippling restrictions that a Negro born in Harlem faces, or anywhere in the United States for that matter, and plunged against a cloud-filled night of oppression new and blazing stars of inspiration. You make all of us proud to be Negroes.

With warm personal regards, I am,

Sincerely yours,
Martin Luther King, Jr.

Km


TLc. MLKP-MBU.

<hr />

King, 6 February 1961, p. 152 in this volume; and King to Rustin, 6 March 1961). In preparation for the article, Baldwin followed King around Atlanta in order to get a "dim approximation of what it is like to be in your position" (Baldwin to King, 26 May 1960, in *Papers* 5:460–461).

2. King later recommended Baldwin's book to a critic to help explain the impact of racism on the oppressed (King to Harold Courlander, 30 October 1961, pp. 315–316 in this volume).

# "Outline of Lecture in Social Philosophy"

[*3 October 1961*]
[*Atlanta, Ga.*]

*Outlining his introductory lecture for the Social Philosophy seminar he teaches at Morehouse College, King provides a broad overview of philosophy.[1] King's lecture was directly informed by Will Durant's* The Story of Philosophy, *which was listed as a source for subsequent lectures.[2]*

"Phi is that thinking which seeks to discover connected truth about all available experience.[3]

The meaning of Philosophy (phileia to love sophis—wisdom) It is the love of wisdom. Plato once called philosophy "that dear delight."[4] It is the wooing of wisdom. It is the delightful search for meaning. "Life has meaning," said Browning, to find its meaning is my meat and drink."[5] Thoreau once said "To be a philosopher is not merely to have subtle thoughts, or even to find a school, but so to love wisdom as to live according to its dictates, a life of simplicity, independence, magnanimity and trust"[6]

The Philosophy bitterly subpoenea every creed + institution to appear before the judgment seat of reason[7]

Science is analytical description, Philosophy is synthetic interpretation.[8]

Science observes processes and constructs <u>Means</u>. Phi criticizes and coordinate <u>En</u>

2. Philosophy includes <u>five</u> fields of study
   a. metaphysics or ontology
   b. epistimology
   c. logic
   d. esthetics

---

1. King taught the course with Morehouse professor Samuel W. Williams. He accepted the offer to teach on 1 August 1961 (see King to Benjamin Elijah Mays, 1 August 1961, p. 258 in this volume). Eight students enrolled in the course (Morehouse College, Class roll, Seminar in Social Philosophy, 27 January 1962).

2. See King, Notes for seminar in Social Philosophy, October 1961–May 1962.

3. Cf. Edgar Sheffield Brightman, *An Introduction to Philosophy* (New York: Henry Holt, 1925), p. 4. During his first year as a graduate student at Boston University, King took two courses—Philosophy of Religion and Seminar in Philosophy—with Brightman, earning an A- and B+, respectively (see Introduction and Courses at Boston University, in *Papers* 2:5, 18, respectively). King had a copy of Brightman's book in his personal library.

4. Will Durant, *The Story of Philosophy: The Lives and Opinions of the Greater Philosophers* (New York: Simon & Schuster, 1933), p. 1. King had a copy of Durant's book in his personal library.

5. Cf. Durant, *Story*, p. 1.

6. Cf. Henry David Thoreau, *Walden, or, Life in the Woods* (Boston: Ticknor and Fields, 1854), p. 18. Durant used the same Thoreau quote in his introduction (p. 1).

7. Cf. Durant, *Story*, p. 7.

8. Durant, *Story*, p. 2.

Outline of lecture in Social Philosophy
Oct. 3

"Phi. is actful thinking which seeks to discover connected truth about all available experience.

1. The meaning of Philosophy (philein to love sophia = wisdom)
It is the love of wisdom. Plato once called Philosophy "that dear delight." It is the wooing of wisdom. It is the delightful search for meaning. "Life has meaning," said Browning, "to find its meaning is my meat and drink." Thoreau once said "To be a philosopher is not merely to have subtle thoughts, or even to find a school, but so to love wisdom as to live according to its dictates, a life of simplicity, independence, magnanimity and trust."

The Philosophy literally subsumes every creed & whatnot it appears by the judical Scire is Analytical description, Philosophy is synthetic interpretation.

Science observes processes and constructs theories. Phi criticizes and coordinates Ends.

2. Philosophy includes five fields of study
a. metaphysics or ontology
b. Epistemology
c. logic
d. esthetics
e. ethics

Social Phi is the study of ideal social organization: monarchy; aristocracy; democracy; socialism; anarchism; feminism.

King's handwritten lecture outline for his course on social philosophy at Morehouse College. Courtesy of the Atlanta University Center, Robert W. Woodruff Library Archives and Special Collections.

3 Oct
1961

  e. ethics[9]

Social Phi is the study of <u>ideal social organization</u>: monarchy, aristocracy, democracy, socialism, anarchism, feminism.

3. Distinguish between ethics an csocial philosophy
 a. on deals with individuals an the other with society
 b. Aristotle's Golden mean and Kant's Categorial Imperative[10]
 c. But the ethics of the ind and society should be one.

4 Now before discussing the Republic, let us say a few words about Plato the man. It is impossible to discuss Plato without saying something about <u>Socrates</u>

 (a) He was a great phi. He had an unassuming simplicity that made him a teacher beloved of the finest youth in Athens[11]

 (b) They loved his modesty of wisdom. He did not claim to have wisdom, but only to seek it lovingly. He was wisdom's amateur, not its professional {Know thyself}[12]

 (c) There were philosophers before him. Thales + Heraclitus; Parmenides + Zeno; Pythagoras and Empedocles. But they were physical philosophers. They dealt with the nature of the external or measurable world. Socrates said what is man[13]

 (D) So he went about uncovering assumptions and questioning certainties. Socratic method is a way of teaching in which the master professes to impart no information, but draws forth more and more definite answers by means of pointed question. <u>It is a demand for accurate definition</u>.[14]

 e. It was this unswerving devotion to the search for truth that lead to his death and immortality. The rest of the story all the world knows, for Plato wrote it down in prose more beautiful than poetry.[15]

<u>The need for intelligence</u>

5. This was Plato teacher. He revered Socrates. "I thank God that I was born Greek and barbarian.."[16]

He returns to Athens in 387.

<u>He created for himself</u> a medium of <u>expression in which</u> both beauty and truth migh find room and play—the dialogue. At times Plato is difficult to understand

---

9. Durant, *Story*, p. 3: "Specifically, philosophy means and includes five fields of study and discourse: logic, esthetics, ethics, politics, and metaphysics."

10. In his notes for the class, King defined Aristotle's road to virtue as "the middle way, the Golden Mean. Excess and deficiency are Vices/ the Mean is Virtue" (King, Notes for seminar in Social Philosophy, October 1961–May 1962). In another set of notes, King quoted from Immanuel Kant's formulation of the Categorical Imperative: "'Treat every human being, including yourself, as an end in himself and not as a means to the advantage of anyone else.' In other words respect yourself and others" (King, Notes, Seminar in Social Philosophy, 3 October 1961–23 January 1962, p. 304 in this volume).

11. Cf. Durant, *Story*, pp. 7–8.

12. King wrote "Know thyself" in the margin. Cf. Durant, *Story*, p. 8.

13. Cf. Durant, *Story*, p. 9.

14. Cf. Durant, *Story*, p. 9.

15. Cf. Durant, *Story*, pp. 9, 11.

16. Cf. Durant, *Story*, p. 13.

because of this intoxicating mixture of phi and poetry[17] The Dialogues remain one of the priceless treasures of the world[18]

6. The most comprehensive of his dialogues is the Republic. He we find his metaphysics . . . It is a great document "It is a feast for the elite, served by an unstinting host.[19]

AD. MCMLK-RWWL: 5.1.0.220.

---

17. Cf. Durant, *Story,* p. 14.
18. Durant, *Story,* p. 15.
19. Durant, *Story,* p. 16.

## Notes, Seminar in Social Philosophy

*[3 October 1961–23 January 1962]*
*[Atlanta, Ga.]*

*In these handwritten notes, composed on lined paper in a notebook, King introduces his Morehouse students to the fundamental ideas of several well-known theologians and philosophers, including Plato, Aristotle, and Jean-Jacques Rousseau. King relied heavily upon the works of William Kelley Wright and Arthur Cushman McGiffert to inform his lectures.*

We are experiencing cold and whistling ~~words~~ winds of despair in a world packed with turbulence

While Russia is poisoning the ~~natural~~ physical atmosphere with megaton bombs, ~~we in Ame~~ Amirica is still poisoning the moral atmosphere with racial discrimination

We must invest our energies not in an hysterical anticommunism, but in a positive democratic dynamism which will lift the economic, social and political standard of the world.

Augustine and Aquinas

As the one great institution of antiquity that had survived the Dark [*remainder missing*].[1]

What are the four cardinal virtues wisdom, courage, temperance & justice These can be appreciated apart from divine grace. These are "natural virtues"

---

1. William Kelley Wright, *A History of Modern Philosophy* (New York: Macmillan, 1947), p. 15: "As the one great institution of antiquity that had survived the Dark Ages, the Christian Church became the chief civilizing agency in shaping the life and thought of the later Middle Ages." King had a copy of Wright's book, with marginal comments, in his personal library.

The Christian virtue—faith hope and charity—are imparted to man by divine grace.[2]

Volume 23
Machianvelli
    The Prince
    "The Art of War"
    "The Way Princes Keep Faith"[3]
Hobbes
    The Leviathan
        Part I    Natural Condition of Mankind
                 First and Second Natural Laws
                 Other Laws of Nature
        Part II   Causes, Generation and Definition of A Commonwealth
                 Rights of Sovereigns[4]
Aristotle (cont.)

Inferiority of Women. Woman is to man as the slave is to the master, the manual to the mental worker, the barbarian to the Greek.

The male is by nature superior; the one rules and the other is ruled. Woman is weak of will, and therefore incapable of independence of character or position[5]

Criticism of Aristotle
1. He was so enamored of the intellectual life that he failed to see the dignity of labor.[6]
2. This lead him to tolerate slavery. No man is good enough to own another man.
3. There is no evidence for his idea of the inferiority of women. Plato was nearer the truth at this point.
4. At point Aristotle is moderate in excess. His immoderate moderation has often been misused
5. His revolt against Plato's communism caused him to fail to see the truth in collectivism. He does not see that individual control of the mean of production was stimulating only when these means were so simple as to be purchasable by

---

2. Wright, History, p. 16: "St. Thomas recognizes the four cardinal virtues of wisdom, courage, temperance, and justice as 'natural virtues' which man can appreciate apart from divine grace. To these he adds the three 'Christian virtues' of St. Paul—faith, hope, and charity—which are imparted to man by divine beneficence."

3. Niccolò Machiavelli, *The Art of War* [*Dell'Arte della guerra*] (1521). "Concerning the Way in which Princes Should Keep Faith" is chapter XVIII in *The Prince* (Chicago: Encyclopædia Britannica, 1952). King had a copy of *The Prince* in his library.

4. Thomas Hobbes, *Leviathan, Or, Matter, Form, and Power of a Commonwealth Ecclesiastical and Civil* (Chicago: Encyclopædia Britannica, 1952). King had a copy of Hobbes's book in his personal library.

5. Cf. Will Durant, *The Story of Philosophy: The Lives and Opinions of the Greater Philosophers* (New York: Simon & Schuster, 1933), p. 66. King had a copy of Durant's book in his personal library.

6. Ernest Barker, *The Political Thought of Plato and Aristotle* (New York: Dover, 1959), p. 371.

any man; and that their increasing complexity and cost lead to a dangerous centralization of ownership, and finally disruptive inequality[7]

But after all, these are quite inessential criticisms of what remains one of the most marvelous and influential systems of thought ever put together by a single mind. It may be doubted if any other thinker contributed so much to the enlightenment of the world. Every later age has drawn upon Aristotle and stands upon his shoulders to see the truth[8]

## Augustine & Aquinas

The long period generally designated "medieval" extended from the beginning of the Christian era to the Renaissance. The two most outstanding thinkers of this period were Saint Augustine & S. Thomas Aquinas.[9]

## Augustine

Born in 354 at Tagaste, a small town in Morthern Africa. His father, a pagan, was an official of the town. His mother, Monnica, was a Christian of outstanding character.

His exceptional abilities were noted in his studies at Carthage.[10]

In his search for truth he became a Manichaean for nine years (373–384)[11] This system was a strange medley of idealism and materialism, asceticism and license, theosophy and rationalism.[12]

About 384 he began to turn away from the fanatical cosmological systems of the Manichaeans. It was at that time that he came under the influence of Neo-Platonism.[13]

The immediate results was his conversion to the Catholic Church. He was baptized by Bishop Ambrose in (387).[14]

He came to believe that Platonism and Catholic Christianity were at bottom one.[15]

---

7. Durant, *Story*, p. 72: "[*Aristotle*] forgets that Plato's communism was meant only for the élite, the unselfish and ungreedy few; and he comes deviously to a Platonic result when he says that though property should be private, its use should be as far as possible common. He does not see (and perhaps he could not be expected in his early day to see) that individual control of the means of production was stimulating and salutary only when these means were so simple as to be purchasable by any man; and that their increasing complexity and cost lead to a dangerous centralization of ownership and power, and to an artificial and finally disruptive inequality."

8. Cf. Durant, *Story*, pp. 72–73.

9. Cf. Gordon Haddon Clark, *Readings in Ethics* (New York: F.S. Crofts, 1935), p. 134.

10. Cf. Clark, *Readings*, p. 134.

11. Cf. J.L. Neve, "Augustine in Some Special Phases of His Development," *Bibliotheca Sacra* 89 (1932), p. 234.

12. Cf. Clark, *Readings*, p. 134.

13. Cf. Neve, "Augustine," p. 234.

14. Arthur Cushman McGiffert, *A History of Christian Thought*, vol. 2, *The West From Tertullian to Erasmus* (New York: Scribner's Sons, 1933), pp. 77, 79. McGiffert claimed that Augustine was baptized in 381 by Bishop Ambrose, while Clark put the correct date at Easter Sunday 387, but failed to specify by whom (see also Clark, *Readings*, p. 135).

15. Cf. McGiffert, *History*, p. 77.

In the Fundamental Principles of the Metaphysics of Morals and the Critique of Practical Reason, Kant endeavors to discover an a priori principle which ought the will, and put ethics upon an absolutely [certain foundation] What is that principle? The a priori principle which should regulate all conduct is a command or imperative, and since it admits of no exceptions it is categorical. Kant's name for it is the categorical imperative.

[margin: What is the difference between a hypothetical & categorical imperative?]

Kant is an uncompromising rationalist in moral philosophy, and will make no concession to Empiricism.

Kant believes that if an rational being is honest, he will admit as a self evident proposition that the only absolutely good thing conceivable in the world is "a good will," or as we should say, "good character." Even such virtues as courage & perseverance can be used for evil purposes, so they cannot be regarded as intrinsically good. But a good will is good in itself, in that it acts solely on the basis of duty regardless of consequences.

Such a good will obey the
<u>categorical imperative</u>. Kant gives
various formulations of this imperative

(1) "Act solely on that principle
which you would be willing might
become a universal law of nature
on which every other person would
also always act." (a) suicide (b) lying
about debts (3) the person who is tempted
to lead a life of idleness and not develop
his capacity. (4) the man who refuses to
give assistance to others when it is in
his power to do so.

Second
formulation (2) "Treat every human being, including
yourself, as an end in himself,
and not as a means to the advantage
of anyone else." In other words
respect yourself and others.

1. At the center of Augustine's thought was his doctrine of God.[16] His doctrine of God was at bottom Neo Platonic[17] God is <u>absolute being</u>. He is himself reality and the only reality. All else is temporary and changing.[18]

Being real and unchangeable, God is eternal, the only true and eternal substance. For the difference between eternity and time is not a matter of duration; eternity is not mere enless time. Where there is time there is change. Where there is eternnal there is no change.[19]

As God is the only real being, his is the only real good.[20]

Augustine adds the emphasis of God as personality, or more particularly he thinks of God in terms of will[21]

God is also creator. The world is not an emination from God; it is due to God's voluntary acts, an act of will.[22]

God sustains the world. Without this unbroken exercise of divine power, the world would lapse into nothingness[23]

Evil is non-being. The tendency of things to lapse again into the nothingness from which they came. Evil is nothing positive It is the absence of Good.[24]

The sin of man grows out of his constant tendency to lapse again into nothingness; to choose the less [*word illegible*] of the greater, the choice of self instead of God.[25]

He believes in original sin.

Adams sin was not due to the possession of a fleshly nature. His flesh was created good. His fall was due to pride[26]

Upon Augustine's idea of God as absolute will rested his famous doctrine of double predestination, the foreordaining of some to salvation and others to damnation.[27]

To those whom God predestines to eternal life he gives the gift of perseverance that they may endure to the end.[28]

---

2. Augustine's idea of the Church
(a) He distinguishes between the Church visible and the invisible Church, the eternal
      institution and the inner communion of saints[29]

---

16. Cf. McGiffert, *History*, p. 83.
17. Cf. McGiffert, *History*, p. 84.
18. Cf. McGiffert, *History*, p. 85.
19. Cf. McGiffert, *History*, pp. 85–86.
20. Cf. McGiffert, *History*, p. 86.
21. Cf. McGiffert, *History*, p. 87.
22. Cf. McGiffert, *History*, p. 88.
23. Cf. McGiffert, *History*, p. 88.
24. Cf. McGiffert, *History*, p. 89.
25. Cf. McGiffert, *History*, pp. 89–90.
26. Cf. McGiffert, *History*, p. 90.
27. Cf. McGiffert, *History*, p. 95.
28. Cf. McGiffert, *History*, p. 96.
29. Cf. McGiffert, *History*, p. 110.

There is no salvation outside of the Catholic Church, which is the body of Christ.[30]
The visible Church is identicle with the kingdom of God.[31]

The visible church provides the sacreements and is the channel of grace[32]

3. The City of God

The book is erected upon the conception of two states differing fundamentally
in their principles but continually touching each other—the people of God and the
people of this world.[33]

The city of God is made up of good angels and righteous men, the latter of the
fallen angels and wicked men. They had their origin in the strife that broke out
among the angels, and hence they antedate the creation of the world, but they are
perpetuated on earth, the one in the fellowship of true Christians, the other in
the rest of mankind, and they have visible embodiment, the former in the Cathilic
Church, and the latter in the Roman Empire[34]

"Why was the City of God written?"

Thomas Aquinas

Born in 1225 in central Italy. He died before he was fifty on his way to attend the
Council of Lyons in 1274

He sought to reinterpret the Christian faith in the light of Aristotelian philosophy.[35]

Western theology from the time of Plato was Augustine was dominated by Plato
or more especially Neoplatonism. Among the many differences between Plato and
Aristotle the most significant for our present purposes was epistemalolical. Plato
assumed that a knowledge of unseen things realities is possible quite apart from individual things, man has a faculty by which he can see the spirit world, while Aristotle
insisted that all knowledge come through the senses. How on the basis of Aristotle
thought could a Christian know God?[36]

Thomas grappled with this problem be drawing two sharp distinctions: the one
between natural and revealed theology and the other between the conditions of
knowledge in this life and in the next.[37]

Natural theology or philosophy begins with the creature and ascends to God; rev-
eled theology [or?] theology begins with God and decends to man or the creatures.[38]

Natural theology comprises all these truths concerning God and his relation to
man and the world that may be deduced from sense-experience.[39]

---

30. Cf. McGiffert, *History*, p. 112.
31. Cf. McGiffert, *History*, p. 110.
32. Cf. McGiffert, *History*, p. 112.
33. Cf. Neve, "Augustine," p. 243.
34. Cf. McGiffert, *History*, pp. 116–117.
35. Cf. McGiffert, *History*, pp. 259–260.
36. Cf. McGiffert, *History*, p. 260.
37. Cf. McGiffert, *History*, p. 260.
38. Cf. McGiffert, *History*, p. 261.
39. Cf. McGiffert, *History*, p. 261.

We see the shape that natural theology took in his greatest, and certainly most original work <u>Summa Contra Gentiles</u>[40]

In Book one he sets out to prove the existence of God He confined himself to a posteriori arguments from effect to cause.

He rejected Anselms ontological proof for a the idea of the most perfect being. He rejected the notion that the idea of God is inborn and therefore needs no proof[41]

Among the effects is motion, which can be accounted for only by trancing it back to an unmoved mover. Object are not selfmove but remain at rest until moved from without.[42]

He also argues for existence of things to a first cause.[43]

From Order to an Orderer

After asking how the existence of God can be proved on Aristotelian principles, Thomas turns to the nature of God:[44]

God is eternal[45]

He is necessary not contingent[46]

He has no admixture of potentiality but is Pure Actuality

He is Simple, not compound and divisible into parts

He is incorporeal[47]

God is perfect, for imperfection implies potentiality.

Being perfect God is God.[48]

God is infinite in goodness, power, and essence.[49]

God is intelligent. God is will.[50]

God is the cause of the being to all that is.[51]

All thing were created out of nothing.[52]

Creation was necessary to him, but was an act of free will motivated by goodness and controlled by wisdom.[53]

He believed in immortality[54]

The end of life is vision of God[55]

Aquinas Ethics

Man's last end is happiness which consist in vision of God.

---

40. Cf. McGiffert, *History*, p. 261.
41. Cf. McGiffert, *History*, p. 262.
42. Cf. McGiffert, *History*, p. 262.
43. Cf. McGiffert, *History*, p. 262.
44. Cf. McGiffert, *History*, p. 263.
45. Cf. McGiffert, *History*, p. 263.
46. Cf. McGiffert, *History*, pp. 263–264.
47. Cf. McGiffert, *History*, p. 264.
48. Cf. McGiffert, *History*, p. 264.
49. Cf. McGiffert, *History*, p. 264.
50. Cf. McGiffert, *History*, pp. 264–265.
51. Cf. McGiffert, *History*, p. 266.
52. McGiffert, *History*, p. 266.
53. Cf. McGiffert, *History*, p. 266.
54. McGiffert, *History*, pp. 267–268.
55. McGiffert, *History*, p. 268.

Eternal Law—the absolute principle of Wisdom by which God governs the universe

Natural Law—it is eternal law as exist in man. Since reason is the controling faculty of man, the natural law is the law of reason.

Human Law—the enactment of earthly governments. They are derived from and grounded in the natural law

Divine Law—it is revealed directly from God in its two historic forms—Judaism & Christianity.[56]


Niccolo Machiavelli (1469–1527)

In his political writings he attempted to avoid everything fantastic and visionary.[57]

He wanted Italy to ~~succeed~~ become united and great. He thought that a prince would be morally justified in seeking to accomplish this by any means whatsoever.

Discuss Means and ends[58]

He was the first political philosopher to try to understand politics as it actually goes on. Hence he is often call the father of modern political science.[59]

In Machiavelli there is a dualism between
Sacred & Secular
ind ethics & Group ethics


Hobbes How He sees man in his natural State

In a condition of nature, prior to the formation of a political state, everyone, according to Hobbes, would seek his own preservation, and the gratification of his own desires for selfish pleasure, such as gain and glory.[60] There would be no such thing as [*strikeout illegible*] law and injustice. The inevitable result would be a war of all against all. Man would alway be in war or in constant fear of attack.[61]

How does he justify his views? It is implied in the conduct of civilized men. When we go to bed we lock our doors[62]

---

56. Cf. McGiffert, *History*, p. 281.

57. Cf. Wright, *History*, p. 26.

58. Cf. Wright, *History*, p. 26; Machiavelli, *The Prince*, p. 25: "In the actions of all men, and especially of princes, which it is not prudent to challenge, one judges by the result. For that reason, let a prince have the credit of conquering and holding his state, the means will always be considered honest."

59. Cf. Wright, *History*, p. 26.

60. Hobbes, *Leviathan*, p. 85: "So that in the nature of man, we find three principal causes of quarrel. First, competition; secondly, diffidence; thirdly, glory. The first maketh men invade for gain; the second, for safety; and the third, for reputation. The first use violence, to make themselves masters of other men's persons, wives, children, and cattle; the second, to defend them; the third, for trifles, as a word, a smile, a different opinion, and any other sign of undervalue."

61. Cf. Wright, *History*, p. 63.

62. Hobbes, *Leviathan*, p. 85: "Let him therefore consider with himself: when taking a journey, he arms himself and seeks to go well accompanied; when going to sleep, he locks his doors; when even in his house he locks his chests; and this when he knows there be laws and public officers, armed, to revenge all injuries shall be done him . . . Does he not there as much accuse mankind by his actions as I do by my words?" Wright quotes this passage in *History*, p. 64.

In international relations we see that force and fraud are the cardinal virtue in time of war especially[63]

What do men do about this condition? Men naturally want peace and security, and to escape from the misery and horror of their natural condition. They ~~they~~ have effected this by the institution of a commonwealth, based on mutual consent, by which each ind. agrees to obey the commands of a common soverign which may be an individual (monarchy) or a group of men (aristocracy or democracy[64]

What is Hobbes' distinction between natural Right & Natural law?

Hobbes ethical & Political philosophy is based wholly on egotism and hedonism

Men do and should act only in accordance with their own interest. In the condition of nature a man has a <u>natural right</u> to do anything that he pleases, and to possess anything that he can take and hold against all comer.[65]

A Natural law is a general rule which man discovers by reason that it is his interest to obey, and so is his obligation to do so (In his naturalistic ethic interest and moral obligation are identical.)[66]

What are the natural law[67]
1. First & fundamental is that man should seek peace and follow it.
2. "that a man be willing, when others are so too This is his naturalistic interpreta of the Golden rule. The mutual and voluntary runication of natural rights is effected through a covenant or contract.
3. "that men perform their covenants made"
4. The obligation to good will
5. mutual accommodation
6. pardoning the offenses of the repentant.
7. infliction of punishments only for the correction of offenders, and not for vengeance
8. avoidance of contempt or hatred of others
9. Acknowledgment of all men as ~~equals~~ one's equal
10. a just or proportionate distribution of goods held in common; self conduct and settlement of dispute by judicial process.

<u>Rousseau</u> (1712–1778), a native of Geneva. Led an adventurous but unrestrained and unhappy life spent mostly in France.

During his last years he suffered from persication complexes and must have been at times partially insane. He was a man ~~of~~ with abnormally intense feelings and emotions. He lacked self control. His actual ~~life~~ conduct fell far short of the lofty ideals

---

63. Cf. Hobbes, *Leviathan*, p. 86; cf. Wright, *History*, p. 64.
64. Cf. Wright, *History*, p. 64.
65. Cf. Wright, *History*, p. 65.
66. Cf. Wright, *History*, p. 65.
67. Wright's *History of Modern Philosophy* covers Hobbes's natural laws on pp. 65–66.

which he proclaimed to the world. One redeeming feature is the honesty with which he acknowledges his weakneses and shortcomings in his Confessions.[68]

He was a ~~at~~ musician and had a great love for the Arts. He is considered the forerunner of the Romantic movement.[69]

He understood the common man, since he was povety stricken himself[70]

Almost all philosophers since Bacon had prided themselves upon the triumph of reason over emotion, and had looked to the unhampered progress of the arts and sciences for the liberation and advancement of man. Rousseau, on the contrary, regarded the evils of the times as the fruits of an artificial civilization, and in his early essays he praised the life of primitive man[71]

At this point he was confident that man was by nature good.

Even [*strikeout illegible*] in these early works Rousseau does not deny that civilization has brought some benefits[72]

In the Social Contract Rousseau is more constructive. It is possible for a critical reader today to eliminate from this book the vagaries and impracticalities, and to extract a valuable philosophy for a democratic state.

It exercised considerable influence in the development of republican ideals in France and the United States. It contributed to the Declaration of Independence[73]

Rousseau is still regard as the author who above all others inspired the French Revolution. His political philosophy represented the passing from the traditional theories rooted in the Middle Ages to the modern conception of the state. His influence may be seen in the moral philosophy of Kant and Goethe.

In the opening paragraph of Social Contract Roussau states: "Man is born free, and everywhere he is in chains" and poses the question, why? Society as opposed to a "state of nature" is only justified on the grounds that men, by nature free, may from the purposes of protection and self-improvement consent to a goverment, or form a social contract.[74]

He believes in direct government by the citizens, who should in public meetings and elections make the laws.

He recognized the civil and political rights of every citizen. In this he represented an advance over those who thought only of the Middle Class & the Aristocracy. In this work he realizes that true freedom is found in a state in which the natural rights of all men to life, liberty and property will be conserved by laws which the people impose upon themselves. Such laws should be the expression of the general will in which each citizens wills the common good.[75]

{Jan 16
Miss Adam        ab
" Worthy         ab.

---

68. Cf. Wright, *History*, p. 234.
69. Cf. Wright, *History*, pp. 234–235.
70. Cf. Wright, *History*, p. 235.
71. Cf. Wright, *History*, p. 235.
72. Cf. Wright, *History*, p. 236.
73. Cf. Wright, *History*, p. 236.
74. Jean-Jacques Rousseau, *The Social Contract and Discourses* (1762).
75. Cf. Wright, *History*, pp. 236–237.

Mr. Bond          ab

Mr. Black          ab

Mr. Brown          ab

Mr. Wright—ab.}[76]

### John Locke (1632–1704)

He was born the same year as Spinoza. Like Spinoza, he had delicate health and came of a consumptive family. He would probably have died young if he had not been prudent enough to study medicin and learn to conserve his health.

He lead a fairly active life, toward the close of which he was able to publish a series of books that determined the general course of philosophical thought for nearly a century.[77]

### Locke's Second Treatise On Civil Government.

Like Hobbes, Locke thinks of the establishment of the civil state as a result of a social contract, and that the state of nature that preceded it was one of perfect freedom and equality. Unlike Hobbes, however, he does not believe that the state of nature was a condition of license. In it man knew that no person should be harmed[78]

~~Compare the social Contract theories of Hobbes, Rosseau, Locke?~~

but to the community, so that thenceforth the decision of the community becomes law.[79]

What, for Locke, are the principle natural right that society should preserve? Life, Liberty and property.[80]

For the security of the people governmental powers should be divided between the legislative and the executive and if disputes arise between the two, the people, whose agents both are, have the right to make the final decision.

{What justifies Revolution}

If a government refuses to accede to the wishes of the people, the latter, after they have protested in vain in every peaceful manner, have a right to resort to arms, and make "an appeal to Heaven" to recognize the justice of the cause.[81]

The Declaration of Ind. of 1776 was conceived in accordance with the philosophy of Locke. In it the revolting colonist recount repeated violations of their natural rights.

The American Constitution of 1787 also shows the influence of Locke.

(1)  The division of government into executive & legislative

(2)  It is a compact of the people.[82]

### Locke on Property

The origin of property Locke found in first occupancy mixed with labor.

In primitive conditions, when there was land in abundance, the man who enclosed

---

76. In his seminar notes, King handwrote this list of students absent from his course on 16 January.

77. Cf. Wright, *History*, p. 141.

78. Cf. Wright, *History*, p. 166.

79. Wright, *History*, p. 167

80. Cf. Wright, *History*, p. 167.

81. Cf. Wright, *History*, p. 168.

82. Wright, *History*, p. 168.

a piece of land and cultivated it acquired the moral right to the ground as well as to its produce.[83]

~~Locke's~~ With the invention of money, Locke observes that men became able to accumulate wealth which need not be immediately consumed

Locke's view that capital is the product of labor was in the 19th century to give rise to socialistic theories of which Locke would have thoroughly disapproved.[84]

The Idealistic Period

Kant (1724–1804)

He spent his whole life in and near the province of Konigsberg in East Prussia.

He was brough up in humble circumstances. His mother died when he was 12 and his father when he was 21. His parent were strict adherents of the sect of the Pietists.

Kant was a brilliant student at the university, and after graduation for some years supported himself as a private tutor.[85]

In the <u>Fundamental Principles of the Metaphysics of Morals</u> and the <u>Critique</u> of Practical Reason, Kant endeavors to discover an a priori principle which ought the will, and put ethics upon an absolutely certain foundation What is that principle? The a priori principle which should regulate all conduct is a command or imperative, and since it admits of no exceptions it is categorical. Kant's name for it is the categorical imperative.

{What is the difference between a hypothetical & categorical Imperative?}

Kant is an uncompromising rationalists in moral philosophy, and will make no concession to empiricism.[86]

Kant believes that if a rational being is honest, he will admit as a self evident proposition that the only absolutely good thing conceivable in the world is "a good will," or as we should say, "good character". Even such virtues as courage & perseverance can be used for evil purposes, so they cannot be regarded as intrinsically good. But a good will is good in itself, in that it acts solely on the basis of duty regardless of consequences.[87]

Such a good will obey the <u>categorical imperative</u>. Kant gives various formulations of this imperative

(1) "Act solely on that principle which you would be willing might become a universal law of nature on which every other person would also always act." (a) suicide (b) lying about debts (3) the person who is tempted to lead a life of idleness and not develope his capacity. (4) The man who refuses to give assistance to others when it is in his power to do so.[88]

---

83. Cf. Wright, *History*, p. 168.
84. Cf. Wright, *History*, pp. 168–169.
85. Cf. Wright, *History*, pp. 255–256.
86. Cf. Wright, *History*, pp. 281–282.
87. Cf. Wright, *History*, p. 282.
88. Cf. Wright, *History*, pp. 282–283.

{Second formulation} (2) "Treat every human being, including yourself, as an end in himself and not as a means to the advantage of anyone else." In other words respect yourself and others.[89]

(3) "One must always act as if one were a member of an ideal Kingdom of ends, in which everyone would be at the same time sovereign and subject."[90]

In such a kingdom of ends every person would act in accordance with the categorical imperative which means that he would act rationally. Consequently the laws of such a kingdom would be willed by everybody and obeyed by everyone; everyone would be sovereign and make the laws which as subjects they obey.[91]

AD. MLKP-MBU.

---

89. Cf. Wright, *History*, pp. 283–284.
90. Cf. Wright, *History*, p. 285.
91. Cf. Wright, *History*, p. 285.

# To Robert F. Kennedy

6 October 1961
[*Atlanta, Ga.*]

*Following the murder of local farmer and SNCC supporter Herbert Lee in Amite County, Mississippi, King wires the attorney general requesting federal intervention.*[1]

ATTORNEY GENERAL ROBERT KENNEDY

JUSTICE DEPT

DEAR MR KENNEDY

IT APPEARS AN APPARENT RAIN OF TERROR HAS BEGUN IN MISSISSIPPI A LITTLE MORE THAN A WEEK AGO A MR. HERBERT LEE OF MCCOMB WAS SHOT AND KILLED

---

1. As a SNCC volunteer, Robert Moses led voter registration efforts in Mississippi. Lee had escorted Moses around Amite County canvassing for potential voters (SNCC, Minutes, July meeting, 14 July–16 July 1961; Claude Sitton, "Negro Vote Drive in Mississippi Is Set Back as Violence Erupts," *New York Times*, 24 October 1961). On 25 September, Mississippi state representative E. H. Hurst fatally shot Lee. Before a coroner's jury, Hurst testified that his pistol accidently discharged when he hit Lee on the head with it, after Lee threatened him with a tire iron. The all-white coroner's jury acquitted Hurst, ruling the case a justifiable homicide ("Amite Jury Clears Hurst," *Enterprise Journal*, 26 September 1961). Elizabeth Allen, the wife of witness Lewis Allen, testified before the Congressional House Subcommittee in 1964 that her husband had received death threats before he lied under oath to confirm Hurst's account (U.S. Congress, House, *Congressional Record*, 88th Cong., 2nd sess., 1964, Vol. 110, pt. 10, 14002–14003).

UNDER VERY QUESTIONABLE CIRCUMSTANCES BY REPRESENTATIVES HEARST OF THE 6 Oct
MISSISSIPPI LEGISLATURE YOU WOULD WANT TO KNOW THAT MR. LEE HAD BEEN VERY 1961
ACTIVE IN THE VOTE OF REGISTRATION PROJECT OF THE STUDENTS NON VIOLENT
COORDINATING COMMITTEE IN PIKE AND AMIT COUNTIES IT APPEARS THAT HIS
ASSOCIATION AND WORK WITH ROBERT MOSES CONTRIBUTED TO HIS DEATH AS OF
TODAY 113 STUDENTS HAVE BEEN ARRESTED FOR NON VIOLENTLY DEMONSTRATING
THE EXPULSION OF TWO FELLOW STUDENTS FROM HIGH SCHOOL ALL BUT 31 HAVE
BEEN RELEASED IN THE CUSTODY OF THEIR PARENTS[2] OF THOSE REMAINING 3 HAVE
BEEN VICTIMS OF POLICE BRUTALITY AND BEATINGS THESE INCLUDE ROBERT MOSES
CHARLES SHERROD AND CHARLES MCDEW[3] INTIMIDATION AND GENERAL HARASS-
MENT HAVE BECOME THE ORDER OF THE DAY COUPLED WITH AN OBVIOUS BLACK
OUT ON THE NEWS AS PRESIDENT OF SCLC AND AS A CONCERNED AMERICAN CITIZEN
I URGENTLY REQUEST AN IMMEDIATE INVESTIGATION BY FEDERAL AUTHORITIES IN
MCCOMB MISSISSIPPI

VERY TRULY YOURS
MARTIN LUTHER KING JR.
PRESIDENT SCLC


PHWc. MLKP-MBU.

---

2. After spending a month in jail for participating in a sit-in on 30 August, McComb residents and Burgland High School students Brenda Travis and Isaac Lewis were denied reenrollment in school. In protest, over one hundred Burgland High students walked out of school on 4 October and were joined by Moses and other SNCC workers in a march to City Hall where they were arrested. Although the underage demonstrators were released, the SNCC staff members and other adults were charged with breach of the peace and contributing to the delinquency of minors ("Trials Set for 119 in Race Protest," *Washington Post*, 6 October 1961; Charles B. Gordon, "15 Demonstrators Are Fined, Draw Sentences," *Enterprise Journal*, 31 October 1961). More than half the student protesters were later expelled from school for refusing to sign a statement condemning the demonstration and any future demonstrations (Sitton, "Hard-Core Segregationists City in Mississippi Is Nearing Crisis, *New York Times*, 21 October 1961).

3. On 29 August, after leading two McComb residents to the courthouse to register to vote, Moses was attacked by local resident Billy Jack Caston and suffered a head injury requiring stitches ("Negro Describes Beating," *Enterprise Journal*, 30 August 1961). At the 4 October march from Burgland High to City Hall, Bob Zellner, a white SNCC staff member, was beaten by a local white man, and when Moses and McDew came to his aid, they were struck by police and arrested (Tom Hayden, "Revolution in Mississippi: Special Report," January 1962). On the same day, SNCC field secretary Sherrod was charged with resisting arrest (Memo to Burke Marshall and J. Harold Flannery, 4 October 1961; "King Protests Dixie Vote Terror," Baltimore *Afro-American*, 14 October 1961).

# To Thurgood Marshall

11 October 1961
[*Atlanta, Ga.*]

*SCLC congratulates Marshall following his 23 September 1961 nomination by
President Kennedy to the United States Court of Appeals for the Second Circuit.
Southern senators delayed Marshall's confirmation until September 1962.*[1]

THURGOOD MARSHALL DIRECTOR
LEGAL DEFENSE AND EDUCATIONAL FUND
100 COLUMBUS CIRCLE

THE OFFICERS BOARD AND CONSTITUTENCY OF THE SOUTHERN CHRISTIAN LEAD-
ERSHIP CONFERENCE SALUTE YOU IN YOUR APPOINTMENT TO THE FEDERAL BRANCH
OF OUR NATION THE ADMINISTRATION KNOWS FULL WELL THAT THEY HAVE CHOSEN
THE BEST EQUIPPED MAN FOR THIS TASK IT MAKES US VERY PROUD TO SAY THAT WE
KNOW YOU. [*strikeout illegible*] MAY GOD'S RICHEST BLESSINGS FOR YOU IN THIS NEW
RESPONSIBILITY

SINCERELY YOURS
MARTIN LUTHER KING JR
PRESIDENT

WYATT T WALKER
DIRECTOR
SOUTHERN CHRISTIAN LEADERSHIP CONFERENCE

PWc. MLKP-MBU.

---

1. Mississippi Senator James O. Eastland, chairman of the Judiciary Committee, delayed action on
Marshall's nomination for eight months, and then held four months of hearings. The Senate confirmed
Marshall 54–16 (Warren Weaver, "Thurgood Marshall Confirmed by Senate, 54–16, for Judgeship," *New
York Times*, 12 September 1962).

# Press Release, Statement in Defense
# of A. Philip Randolph

13 October 1961
[*Atlanta, Ga.*]

*At the AFL-CIO's quarterly meeting in October 1961, A. Philip Randolph, vice
president of the federation of unions, was censured after recommending that
the organization require all affiliated national and international unions to*

*desegregate and integrate.*[1] *In the press release below, King defends the beleaguered*
*union leader, who he says epitomizes "faultless dedication, integrity and honor"*
*and who is "second to none, not only in our nation but in the world."*[2] *King*
*implores the AFL-CIO to lift the rebuke and refocus its efforts so the "struggle for*
*justice" can continue "with all honorable forces united."*

For more than a quarter of a century, A. Philip Randolph has been a labor leader
of faultless dedication, integrity and honor.

The leadership of the AFL-CIO has repeatedly held him forth as a sterling
example of a labor statesman, second to none, not only in our nation but in the
world. It is therefore, shocking and deplorable that a report replete with inaccura-
cies and groundless insults should have been adopted by the Executive Council of
the AFL-CIO.

As a friend of organized labor, I hope that sober second thoughts will cause it to
re-examine its actions and formally withdraw the report, replacing it with constructive proposals to deal with a grave evil which disfigures the image of our nation
everywhere in the turbulent world of today.

A. Philip Randolph has been attacked because he is speaking bluntly and power-
fully on behalf of millions of Negro workers. The truth that discrimination is not
being with either vigor or determination can no longer be concealed or obscured.[3]
The electrifying progress being made by peoples of Africa and Asia serve to high-

---

1. In May 1960 Randolph and other African American leaders formed the Negro American Labor
Council (NALC) to address discrimination and segregation in unions. King addressed the council at its
founding conference (NALC, Announcement, "Founding convention call," 27 May–29 May 1960). The
following February, the NALC, under Randolph's leadership, issued fifteen recommendations to top
officials of the AFL-CIO. Besides the request to end segregation in unions, the NALC also demanded
the election of black trade unionists to policy-making posts and the hiring of qualified black staff in all
departments at the AFL-CIO's headquarters in Washington, D.C. (NALC, Press release, Institute and
workshop mark launch of drive against job discrimination, 17 February–18 February 1961). The censure
was part of a twenty-page report that disputed Randolph's claims and accused the civil rights leader of
racial discrimination, claiming that the Brotherhood of Sleeping Car Porters only employed nonwhites
(Jacob S. Potofsky, George M. Harrison, and Richard F. Walsh, "Report to the Executive Council of the
AFL-CIO," 12 October 1961). All members of the AFL-CIO's executive council, with the exception of
Randolph, voted to impose the censure (AFL-CIO, Press release, "Council rejects Randolph's charges,
backs AFL-CIO rights record," 13 October 1961). Announcing the AFL-CIO's actions against Randolph at
its October meeting, Meany said: "We can only get moving on civil rights if he comes over to our side and
stops throwing bricks at us." He continued: "I think we could do a lot with his cooperation. But it seems
in the last two or three years he's gotten close to these militant groups and he's given up cooperation for
propaganda" (Stanley Levey, "A.F.L.-C.I.O. Chiefs Score Randolph," *New York Times*, 13 October 1961).

2. Later in the year, King defended Randolph again at the AFL-CIO's Constitutional Convention
(see King, Address Delivered at the Fourth Constitutional Convention of the AFL-CIO, 11 December
1961, p. 338 in this volume).

3. Randolph and Meany had also clashed about racial bias in unions in September 1959, at the AFL-
CIO's third biennial convention. There Randolph announced that he would press for the expulsion of
two unions that failed to integrate and for the elimination of segregated locals in all AFL-CIO-affiliated
unions. Angered by Randolph's criticisms of the AFL-CIO's anti-discrimination measures, Meany asked
Randolph: "Who the hell appointed you as the guardian of all the Negroes in America?" (A.H. Raskin,
"Meany, in a Fiery Debate, Denounces Negro Unionist," *New York Times*, 24 September 1959).

light the sluggish pace of change in our own nation. Tokenism and words of good will cannot answer the needs nor raise the dignity of people abused and deprived for generations.

A. Philip Randolph is the conscience of the labor movement. It would be as tragic for some leaders of labor to attempt to surpress this conscience as it is when an individual seeks to silence the inner spiritual warning that his deeds fall short of his obligations. The Negro people have always looked upon organized labor as one of the leaders in the struggle for Civil Rights.

I urge them to keep that faith because I deeply feel this unsound policy will be reversed and the struggle for justice will be resumed with all honorable forces united.

That's 40

TD. RPP-NN-Sc: Box 3.


# Press Conference after Meeting
# with John F. Kennedy

*[16 October 1961]*
*[Washington, D.C.]*

*Following a one-hour discussion at the White House with President Kennedy regarding violence against Mississippi civil rights workers, King calls for a second Emancipation Proclamation, and suggests an executive order ending housing discrimination.*[1] *This transcript was taken from film footage of the press conference.*

[*Reporter #1*]:   Dr. King, would you tell us about your visit with the president?

[*King*]:   Yes, I had a very fruitful visit with the president. I discussed with him some of the problems that we are facing in the South and tried to report some of the conditions firsthand that we face in the South at this time. He listened very sympathetically, and we had a most fruitful and rewarding discussion together.

[*Reporter #2*]:   Could you be any more specific about the particular problems that you were discussing?

[*King*]:   Well, I discussed some of the problems in Mississippi that we are facing at this time—the problems in McComb, Mississippi, and also many of the problems that students are facing in seeking to get Negro citizens in the South registered and voting. Also, I proposed to the president an idea that I have been discussing for several weeks now, and that is a need for a sort of second Emancipation Proclamation declaring all segregated facilities unconstitutional and illegal on the basis of

---

1. King had first requested a meeting with Kennedy on 16 March 1961 (King to John F. Kennedy, pp. 175–176 in this volume).

the Fourteenth Amendment of the Constitution.[2] Just as the first Emancipation Proclamation was an executive order, I don't think it is too much to ask for a second Emancipation Proclamation bringing an end to segregation almost a hundred years after the first Emancipation Proclamation was issued.[3]

[*Reporter #3*]: What was the president's reaction to your suggestion? Can we expect this to be forthcoming?

[*King*]: There again, the president listened very sympathetically and said that he would certainly take all of these things under consideration, but you would have to speak to him concerning the possibilities of this actually becoming a reality.[4]

[*Reporter #4*]: Did you make any specific proposals, Dr. King, for action that he might take in McComb, or in Mississippi, or that his administration might take?

[*King*]: Well, I know that the Justice Department is in the situation right now, seeking to determine if any violations have taken place in the area of voting; that is, the Justice Department can move in this area, and they are moving in Mississippi. There is very little that can be done otherwise—that is from the point of view of the Justice Department—but the situation can be investigated by the Civil Rights Commission, and I suggested to the president that some things like this could be done and certainly called by the president himself.[5]

[*Reporter #1*]: On this second Emancipation Proclamation, did you specify particular kinds of segregated facilities, or is this any area in which there's segregation?

[*King*]: Any area in which there is segregation. Segregation is still a glaring reality in the South, and we still face it in its hidden and subtle forms all over the nation. And I suggested to the president that the time had come for an executive order outlawing all forms of segregation, whether it is in housing, whether it is in public facilities, other areas where it still exists.

---

2. After Kennedy's election in November 1960, King began publicly calling for the president to issue a second Emancipation Proclamation that would ban segregation (see note 18, "The Negro and the American Dream," Emancipation Day Address Delivered at Municipal Auditorium, 2 January 1961, p. 118 in this volume).

3. Abraham Lincoln signed the Emancipation Proclamation on 22 September 1862. It became effective 1 January 1863.

4. Referring to the Kennedy administration's handling of civil rights issues in an essay for *The Nation*, King wrote that "the year 1961 was characterized by inadequacy and incompleteness in the civil-rights field." King also pointed to the administration's failure to employ executive power to rein in Southern senators as an example of its timidity (King, "Fumbling on the New Frontier," 3 March 1962, pp. 414, 416–417 in this volume).

5. Regarding voter registration conditions in Marshall County, Mississippi, Burke Marshall wrote that "we have evidence that registration officials in the county have engaged in racially discriminatory acts and practices depriving Negro citizens of the county of their right to register to vote without distinction because of race or color" and that he had informed the state attorney general of his responsibility to correct that problem (Marshall to L. G. Fant, 8 September 1961). The Civil Rights Commission had received several reports of police brutality against African American voters from the Mississippi State Advisory Committee. In October 1962 the Civil Rights Commission scheduled hearings in Mississippi, but postponed them at the request of the U.S. Justice Department (Hedrick Smith, "U.S. Again Defers Mississippi Study," *New York Times*, 7 January 1963).

[*Reporter #5*]:   Dr. King, can you tell us how this meeting came about, and why on apparently such short notice?

[*King*]:   Well, I requested the conference with the president. I wanted to talk with him concerning some of these problems—I think they are pressing problems—and of course I have been discussing the idea of an executive order in the area of outlawing all segregation for some time, and I felt that I should present it to the president instead of talking about it elsewhere, so I wanted to come to him and present it direct. Also I suggested the need for an executive order in housing as a specific executive order, because so much of housing, most of the housing financing, falls under the federal government either through FHA, PHA, urban renewal, or veterans loans.[6] And this is one area where we need an executive order. And as long as there is housing segregation, as I said to the president, we will have segregation in public schools; we will have segregation in recreational facilities and all areas. So that this is a pressing need, and I think it would solve a great problem if we could get such an order.

[*Unidentified Reporter*]:   About how long—

[*Reporter #1*]:   Do you consider housing the keystone now?

[*King*]:   Well, I would certainly say it is one of the most important areas. I know that we must work in all of these areas and must work simultaneously in all of them, but I do think that this is very important, because as long as we have housing segregation, we will face segregation in these other areas.

[*Reporter #4*]:   What was his reaction to that suggestion to the housing executive order?

[*King*]:   Well, this is not new for the president. He has been studying this, and other suggestions have been made, so that he made it very clear that he had this under advisement.[7]

[*Reporter #6*]:   How long were you with the president?

[*King*]:   About an hour. Just about an hour.

[*Reporter #6*]:   Just the two of you?

[*King*]:   No. Mr. Louis Martin and Mr. Harris Wofford were in on the conference.[8]

[*Reporter #7*]:   Dr. King, did the subject of interstate travel come up? [*words inaudible*] Freedom Riders?

---

6. In his 1961 essay in *The Nation*, King specified that the collective failure of the Federal Housing Administration (FHA), the Public Housing Administration (PHA), the Urban Renewal Administration, and the Veterans Administration Loan Program to enforce anti-discrimination clauses demonstrated that "the federal government has participated directly and indirectly in the perpetuation of housing discrimination" (King, "Equality Now," 4 February 1961, p. 146 in this volume).

7. Despite urges from the National Committee Against Discrimination in Housing, of which King was a member, and the Civil Rights Commission, Kennedy did not issue an executive order on housing discrimination until November 1962 (Peter Braestrup, "Ban on Color Line in Housing Is Due," *New York Times*, 28 September 1961; "Text of the Kennedy Order Barring Discrimination in Housing," *New York Times*, 21 November 1962).

8. Louis E. Martin was a Kennedy advisor and deputy chairman of the Democratic National Committee.

[*King*]:   No, it didn't. I had an opportunity to discuss that with the Jus—[*recording interrupted*]⁹

30 Oct
1961

---

9. King met separately with Attorney General Robert F. Kennedy earlier that day to discuss segregation in interstate travel ("King Asks Kennedy to Declare Bias Illegal," *Atlanta Daily World*, 17 October 1961). Following the meeting, the attorney general announced that the Illinois Central, Southern, and Louisville and Nashville Railroads would desegregate (Tom Wicker, "Three Railroads in South to Desegregate Stations," *New York Times*, 17 October 1961).

# To Tom Roland

30 October 1961
[*Atlanta, Ga.*]

*Following reports that he had accepted a minor role as a Southern senator in the upcoming movie* Advise and Consent, *King responds to a critical letter from a white CORE activist who expressed shock that King would trivialize the "Negro's problems" by agreeing to appear in the film and accused the SCLC president of publicity seeking.¹ King denies that he ever agreed to play the role and calls Roland's criticisms and "misconceptions" so "groundless that I need not take the time to answer them."²*

---

1. Roland dismissed Preminger's idea that there could be an African American senator in Congress, claiming that no African American in Georgia could gain such political support "unless a revolution occurred there yesterday." He also charged that King was out of touch with the movement, arguing that King was "moving in one direction, and the struggle for democracy is moving in the opposite direction" (Roland to King, 20 October 1961). The screenplay was based on Allen Drury's 1959 Pulitzer Prize winning novel *Advise and Consent*. The film's producer Otto Preminger hoped that King's role would illustrate the possibility for a "Negro to be elected to the United States Senate at any time, now or in the future" (A.H. Weiler, "Dr. King to Play Georgia Senator in Movie of 'Advise and Consent,'" *New York Times*, 20 October 1961). Florida Senator Spessard L. Holland called the decision "bad taste," while an editorial in the *Atlanta Constitution* claimed that the role would add "nothing to the American Negro's worthwhile fight for a greater freedom" (Bruce Galphin, "King Rejects Film Role As Critics Rap Overture," *Atlanta Constitution*, 21 October 1961; "Dr. King Rightly Refuses to Be Used," *Atlanta Constitution*, 21 October 1961). Thomas Van Roland (1937–2013) obtained his B.S. from the University of Michigan, Ann Arbor, in 1960 and was active in the local CORE chapter. He also participated in the 1960 sit-in movement in Miami and in the Freedom Rides the following year. After attending the University of California at Berkeley, Roland taught mathematics until he obtained his J.D. in 1971 from the University of San Francisco Law School. Roland then started a family law practice in Alameda County, California.

2. In his letter, Roland called King's attempt to avoid fallout in the National Baptist Convention (NBC) fracas "disturbing," while deprecating King's support for the Freedom Rides: "One could have asked for much more support from the SCLC in the Freedom Rides this summer, but your reluctance to become more involved could be partially explained by the possible infeasibility of the project in financial terms" (Roland to King, 20 October 1961). For more on King and the NBC, see King to J.H. Jackson, 10 September 1961, and J.H. Jackson to King, 12 September 1961, pp. 278–279 and 281–282 in this volume, respectively.

I will not be playing a role in the motion picture Advise And Consent. While many associates of mine felt that a positive contribution might be made by my appearance in a film as a Negro Senator and the producers of the film were aware of these deliberations, However, I had not given any final consent nor signed any agreement. In considering it, in addition to other factors, I feel that the brief role could not be of any significant in advancing civil rights, and

King drafts a press release denying having accepted an acting role in the film *Advise and Consent*. Courtesy of the Howard Gotlieb Archival Research Center, Boston University.

accordingly I have not accepted
the proposal.

# PAUL'S LETTER
# TO
# AMERICAN CHRISTIANS

Ki 3-3589

A SERMON PREACHED

in the

DEXTER AVENUE BAPTIST CHURCH

By The Minister

DR. MARTIN LUTHER KING, JR.

November 4th 1956

MONTGOMERY, ALABAMA

Mr. Tom Roland
2248 Blake Street
Berkeley 4, California

Dear Mr. Roland:

   I am in receipt of your letter of recent date expressing shock over the announcement of my appearing in "Advise and Consent." I can only say that the news releases that you saw on this matter were far from accurate.[3] I never gave my consent to act in the film.[4] My brief words to the press after the announcement came out will clarify my position on the whole matter. They were as follows:

> "I will not be playing a role in the motion picture 'Advise and Consent.' Well-meaning associates of mine felt that a positive contribution might be made by my appearance in a film as a Negro Senator, and the producers of the film were aware of these deliberations. However, I had not given my final consent nor signed any agreement. In considering it, in addition to the other factors, I feel that the brief role could not be of any significant value in advancing civil rights, and therefore, have not accepted the proposal."[5]

   In reading your letter I find that you have many misconceptions concerning my work and my commitment. I hope you will not consider my overlooking your criticisms if I will not take the time to answer them. But I must frankly say that most of them are so groundless that I need not take time to answer them. I hope some day I might have a chance to meet you and know you. As the days unfold let us continue to move on in the solution of a problem which plagues our nation and is destroying the peace of the world.

Sincerely yours,
Martin Luther King, Jr.

Km
Dictated by Dr. King, but signed in his absence.

TLc. MLKP-MBU.

---

   3. In his letter, Roland referenced a 20 October article in the *New York Times* (Roland to King, 20 October 1961; Weiler, "Dr. King to Play Georgia Senator in Movie," 20 October 1961).
   4. In a 19 October SCLC administrative committee meeting, it was unanimously agreed upon that King would accept the role. Wyatt Tee Walker sent Nathan Rudich, Preminger's executive assistant, conditions to be included in the contract for King's performance. The conditions included King's filming schedule, a nonrefundable $5,000 contribution to SCLC, and the right to withdraw from the movie should King's appearance "damage his unusual and unique symbolism" (SCLC, Minutes, Administrative committee meeting, 19 October 1961; Walker to Rudich, 19 October 1961).
   5. King made this statement on 20 October after arriving in New York en route to a speaking engagement in Connecticut ("Dr. King Rejects Movie Role of Georgia Senator," *New York Times*, 21 October 1961).

# To Harold Courlander

30 October 1961
[*Atlanta, Ga.*]

*In August 1961 Courlander, a writer sympathetic to the movement, sent King
a letter criticizing the Freedom Rides as too dependent on publicity and outside
support to succeed in the South.[1] In response, King defends the strategy of the
rides, noting that "in the absence of justice in the established courts of the region,
non-violent protesters are asking for a hearing in the court of world opinion."
Courlander replied on 5 November 1961.*

Mr. Harold Courlander
5523 Brite Drive
Bethesda 14, Maryland

Dear Mr. Courlander:

Thank you for your thoughtful letter of August 30. Certainly, one reason that you
have not received an answer is that your letter deserved more time than my schedule of the past months would allow for an answer. Fortunately, I think that time has
answered some of your questions, or has at least enabled us to be a bit more sure of
our position.[2] Might I say that we are never without some reservations in this struggle,
but usually it is impossible to anticipage all the objections and misunderstandings of
a movement such as this.

Public relations is a very necessary part of any protest of civil disobedience. The
main objective is to bring moral pressure to bear upon an unjust system or a particularly unjust law. The public at large must be aware of the inequities involved in such
a system. In effect, in the absence of justice in the established courts of the region,
non-violent protesters are asking for a hearing in the court of world opinion. Without
the presence of the press, there might have been untold massacre in the South. The
world selfom believes the horror stories of history until they are documented via
mass media. Certainly, there would not have been sufficient pressure to warrant a
ruling by the ICC had not this situation been so well-publicized.

---

1.   Courlander wrote: "When demonstrations carry with them the flavor of Yankee interference, outside organization, Madison Avenue publicity, and an intent to 'stir things up,' the chances for strategic
loss are as great as the chance of tactical gain" (Courlander to King, 30 August 1961). Despite the criticism, Courlander enclosed a donation to support the Freedom Rides. Harold Courlander (1908–1996)
earned a B.A. in English at the University of Michigan in 1931. He farmed for several years before
traveling to the Caribbean, Africa, the Pacific, and also the Deep South to document folk traditions.
Courlander's travels were the basis for many of his novels, including *The African* (1967), which he claimed
had been plagiarized by Alex Haley in *Roots*.

2.   In the time between Courlander's August letter and King's reply, the Interstate Commerce
Commission (ICC) relented to pressure by Attorney General Robert Kennedy and passed regulations
enforcing a ban on segregated interstate travel (James E. Clayton, "Attorney General Asks ICC to Back
Pledge to Abolish Bus Segregation," *Washington Post*, 16 August 1961; ICC, Resolution MC-C-3358,
"Discrimination in operations of interstate motor carriers of passengers," 22 September 1961).

Your other question in regard to outside interference must be answered with the question whether any United States citizen is an outsider in any part of this nation.[3] Especially is this true of Northern Negroes, most of whom are from the South with relatives still living there. You cannot imagine the pain that it causes when you are afraid to bring your children to the homes of their grandparents for fear of the abuse they might suffer due to their lack of acquaintance with 'respected, time-honored Southern tradition'.

Local persons could never run the risk of rebelling against the laws of their states alone. It is difficult for many to express an interest in voting in elections, a situation well documented by the reports of the Civil Rights Commission.[4] There are thousands of known cases of reprisal which never come to the attention of the world, and in some parts of the South there are persons who might even question your assumption that South African apartheid is catagorically different from the situation of the un-lettered Negro in the rural counties of the South of these United States.[5]

May I refer you to a new book by James Baldwin: NOBODY KNOWS MY NAME. It may provide some additional insights into the racial situation from the viewpoint of the oppressed. While I could not endorse all of Mr. Baldwin's opinions, they do make very stimulating reading.[6] I also enclose a lecture on Civil Disobedience by Harris Wofford.[7]

I trust that your book is going well. We look forward to its publication. Every viewpoint on this situation is certainly to be encouraged.[8]

Sincerely yours,
Martin Luther King, Jr.

---

3. In his 30 August letter, Courlander recommended limiting the campaign to local involvement as in the sit-ins, writing that "it is a sad but hard fact that the Southern communities have for a long time had an extreme neurotic sensitivity to 'interference' from the outside. As unreasonable—stupid, if you will—as this attitude is, it is there and must be reckoned with."

4. The Civil Rights Commission stated in its first report that "our investigations have revealed further that many Negro American citizens find it difficult, and often impossible, to vote" (U.S. Commission on Civil Rights, *Report of the United States Commission on Civil Rights 1959* [Washington, D.C.: U.S. Government Printing Office, 1959], p. 134).

5. In Courlander's 30 August letter he questioned the term "freedom rider," contending that "the term signifies that the struggle here is identical with that in South Africa, that the United States is a mean and contemptible colonialist nation." He added: "There are Africans and Asians today who equate the Freedom Riders with the guerrillas fighting the Portuguese authorities in Angola. Although both are fighting a good cause, as they see it, there is more than a subtle difference in those causes."

6. *Nobody Knows My Name* (New York: Dial Press), published in 1961, is a collection of essays on race written during Baldwin's stay in Europe. Courlander criticized Baldwin's book in his reply, writing: "There is in his approach and manner an element of thinly disguised extremism which can only be deplored" (Courlander to King, 5 November 1961).

7. In his speech "The Law and Civil Disobedience," Wofford uses his legal background to provide a defense of civil disobedience as a necessary corrective for unjust laws (Wofford, "The Law and Civil Disobedience," 20 November 1959).

8. King refers to Courlander's book *The Big Old World of Richard Creeks* (Philadelphia: Chilton, 1962), a fictional work set in Alabama that explores the impact of white racism on African Americans. Courlander enclosed a copy of the manuscript in his 5 November response to King.

Km

enc

1 Nov
1961

TLc. MLKP-MBU.

## To Thomas Kilgore

1 November 1961
*[Atlanta, Ga.]*

*King congratulates Kilgore, director of SCLC's New York office and family friend,
on his twenty-fifth anniversary in the ministry and praises his "unswerving
devotion to the principles of Freedom and Justice."[1] On 22 November 1961 Kilgore
thanked King for making his anniversary one "that will never be forgotten."*

The Reverend Thomas Kilgore, Jr.
Friendship Baptist Church
144 West 131st Street
New York 27, New York

Dear Tom:

May I take this way to congratulate you on the occasion of your Twenty-fifth
Anniversary as a pastor. In these years you have revealed that you are a dedicated
servant of God, a stalwart Christian statesman, and a prophetic preacher. You have
represented in every way what a Christian minister ought to be. You have proved to
be a great administrator, a loving pastor, and a powerful preacher. I am sure that in
your twenty-five years as a pastor, you have led hundreds of people to a new understanding of the Christian faith and to a new commitment to Jesus Christ.

You have not limited your gospel to the realm of personal salvation, but you
have extended it to the heights of social salvation, realizing that the gospel always
deals with the whole man. Your never-ceasing support of the civil rights movement
and your unswerving devotion to the principles of Freedom and Justice will always
remain one of the glowing epics of your ministry.[2] I can only say that you have my
prayers and best wishes as you continue your noble work.

---

1. Kilgore served at several churches for eleven years before being called to New York's Friendship
Baptist Church in 1947. Kilgore later gave the King children a dog named Topsy (Dora E. McDonald to
Kilgore, 21 November 1961).
2. From 1943–1944 Kilgore helped organize citizenship schools and participated in the unionization
of tobacco workers in Winston-Salem, North Carolina. In 1957 Kilgore directed the Prayer Pilgrimage for
Freedom in Washington, D.C., and from 1959 to 1963 he supervised SCLC's New York office.

I cannot close without expressing just a word of thanks to you for the support that you have given to me personally in the movement which I am seeking to lead. I can never express in words what this has meant to me. Certainly your constant moral and financial support have been of inestimable value for the continuance of my humble efforts.

I hope for you many more years of Christian service.[3] I will continue to pray that the years ahead will be packed with meaningful fulfillment.

Sincerely yours,
Martin Luther King, Jr.

Km

TLc. MLKP-MBU.

---

3. In 1985 Kilgore retired as senior pastor of Second Baptist Church in Los Angeles.

# From Stanley D. Levison

1 November 1961
New York, N.Y.

*Levison, a Jewish lawyer from New York and a King advisor since late 1956, expresses concern after reading reports that King was heckled while speaking at a London rally.[1] He also notes several administrative tasks that need King's immediate attention.*

Dear Martin,

I'm sorry I missed your call yesterday, but I was happy to know you returned safely. The New York Times in a small item reported you were heckled by a small group, and knowing that many of the British bigots are derived from facist elements, I was concerned about a possible use of violence against you. It was bizarre enough to have you attacked in the North by a Negro; it would be worse to have you injured in England by a hoodlum with a British accent.[2]

---

1. Shouts of "keep Britain white" and "go back to your own country" were heard during King's hour-long address at a rally sponsored by Christian Action, a British group opposed to South African apartheid ("Britons Taunt Dr. King," *New York Times*, 31 October 1961). While in London, King was interviewed by the British Broadcasting Corporation (Interview by John Freeman on "Face to Face," 29 October 1961).

2. Levison refers to King's 20 September 1958 stabbing while in Harlem (see Introduction in *Papers* 4:34–35).

There are two items which need your immediate attention. Enclosed is a draft of the appeal letter I have written. If you have any corrections call me on the phone because to save time, we are having the printer start on it at once in order to get mail out as fast as humanly possible.[3]

Also enclosed is a letter drafted by Clarence to go on your stationery to the lawyers who have promised varied assistance which could be substantial if they feel you are aware of their contribution.[4] This, too, should go out promptly. Have Dora send me a copy so we will know when to follow up.[5]

Jack [*O'Dell*] and I are contacted candidates for the Administrative Assistant job and/or Voting, Registration Director.[6] Randy White is calling us today to set the time for an appointment.[7] We are checking to get Twiddy's address but have not yet obtained it.[8] If you have it handy send it on, in any case. We are also trying to reach a young man who has been highly recommended from Chicago. He has a background in N.A.A.C.P. youth leadership work, was a founder of the N.S.A., U.N. employment, a masters from Spellman and is now completing his doctorate in Sociology.

I'll be talking to you on the phone, so I won't extend this letter any further. Take care of yourself—warmest and best regards.

Sincerely,

[*signed*]

Stan

SDL/ah
enclosures

SPECIAL DELIVERY—AIR MAIL

TLS. MLKP-MBU.

---

3. Levison, Draft, Letter to Friend, 1 November 1961. A fundraising appeal to support SCLC voter registration work, "Appeal for Human Dignity Now," alternatively known as "Dollars for Dignity," was sent on 11 November 1961 under King's signature. The appeal had the support of labor unions that asked their members to make a minimum donation of one dollar to SCLC (United Electrical, Radio and Machine Workers of America, "Contributions received on 'Dollars for Dignity' campaign of SCLC," 15 March–16 March 1962).

4. Levison refers to King's lawyer and advisor Clarence B. Jones (Jones, Draft, King to Harry H. Wachtel, 1 November 1961). In a 2 November 1961 letter, King thanked lawyers Eugene Cotton and Richard Watt for their work on a countersuit in the Alabama libel cases against Ralph Abernathy, Fred L. Shuttlesworth, S.S. Seay, and Joseph Lowery. The countersuit, which sought an injunction against legal harassment by the Montgomery city government, was unsuccessful. King also sent a 7 November letter to lawyer Harry H. Wachtel soliciting his support (pp. 325–327 in this volume).

5. McDonald to Levison, 2 November 1961.

6. New York journalist Gould Maynard was hired as both the administrative assistant and public relations director in January 1962, while O'Dell became SCLC's acting director of voter registration.

7. Randy White had expressed interest in SCLC's public relations position (Shirley Cummings to King, 18 September 1961).

8. John C. Twitty was an editor for *Ebony* and the *New York Amsterdam News*, among other publications.

# To William Berry Hartsfield

1 November 1961
*[Atlanta, Ga.]*

*On 1 November, the day the Interstate Commerce Commission's (ICC) ban on segregated interstate travel facilities took effect, SNCC members James Forman, Charles Jones, James Bevel, and Bernard Lafayette were arrested for trespassing at Jake's Fine Foods, a privately owned restaurant located in Atlanta's Trailways terminal.[1] In the following telegram, King urges outgoing Mayor Hartsfield to intervene.[2] In his reply, Hartsfield expressed his "regret that this sort of case had to come out of Atlanta."[3]*

MAYOR WILLIAM B HARTSFIELD
CITY HALL

DISTRESSED THAT OUR CITY AFTER HAVING MOVED FORWARD SO CREATIVELY IN RACE RELATIONS HAS TODAY TAKEN A STEP BACKWARDS. WE KNOW THIS IS NOT THE DESIRE OF YOUR HEART. REQUEST THAT YOU USE THE GREAT INFLUENCE OF YOUR OFFICE TO RESOLVE THE FOUR ARRESTS MADE IN VIOLATION OF THE NEW ICC RULING AND TAKE WHATEVER STEPS NECESSARY TO THWART ANY FUTURE VIOLATIONS.

VERY TRULY YOURS
SOUTHERN CHRISTIAN LEADERSHIP CONFERENCE

MARTIN LUTHER KING
PRESIDENT

WYATT TEE WALKER
DIRECTOR

PWc. MLKP-MBU.

---

1. "Four Arrested in ICC Ruling Test," *Atlanta Daily World,* 2 November 1961. In the wake of the attacks on the freedom riders, Attorney General Robert F. Kennedy petitioned the ICC to order desegregation of all terminal facilities, including waiting rooms, restrooms, restaurants, and ticketing areas. The ICC did so in September 1961, but the order did not take effect until 1 November (ICC, Resolution MC-C-3358, "Discrimination in operations of interstate motor carriers of passengers," 22 September 1961). A similar test case occurred in Jackson, Mississippi, where activists were arrested for entering the station's "whites-only" waiting room (Claude Sitton, "I.C.C. Travel Rule Is Defied in South," *New York Times,* 2 November 1961).

2. King also sent a similar telegram to Everett Hutchinson, chairman of the ICC (King and Walker to Hutchinson, 1 November 1961). In June 1961, Hartsfield had announced his intention to retire after serving six terms as mayor.

3. In a letter to Walker marked "personal," Hartsfield contended that "had I or Chief Jenkins, or some discreet higher officer been in touch, probably the situation would not have occurred" (Hartsfield to Walker, 2 November 1961).

# To I. Logan Kearse

2 November 1961
*[Atlanta, Ga.]*

*Citing his policy against endorsing political candidates, King declines to publicly
support Kearse's bid for Maryland's Fourth Congressional District seat.[1] Kearse
was ultimately defeated by incumbent George H. Fallen.[2]*

The Rev. Logan Kearse
Cornerstone Baptist Church of Christ
1627 Bolton Street
Baltimore 17, Maryland

Dear Logan:

It is always difficult to say 'no' to a friend. The only consolation that I gain when
necessity demands my saying no is that I am sure a friend will understand. I have
checked my calendar very scrutinizingly to determine if it would be at all possible for
me to be with you in Baltimore sometime before the election in order to stress the
importance of voter registration. Two problems confront me at this time. One is the
matter of an extremely crowded schedule.

Because of the temper of events in the south, I have had to adopt a policy of
spending much more time in this section of the country. My calendar reveals to me
that I have accepted the maximum number of engagements that is possible and
remain true to my work in the south.

The second problem is at points more potent. For many reasons I have had to follow a course of not endorsing candidates running for political offices. Whenever I

---

1. Kearse to King, 25 September 1961. Until the 1964 presidential election, King did not publicly
endorse political candidates (SCLC, Press release, Statement on nomination of Barry M. Goldwater, 16
July 1964). In a letter to E. F. Rodriguez, King explains: "I might say that my position all along has been
that the Negro should be more of an independent voter than a Republican or a Democrat. This would
give him more of a bargaining power, and by following such an approach he would vote for the party that
gives the greatest security to the nation" (King to Rodriguez, 19 September 1956). Kearse continued to
press for King's support after hearing that in February 1962 King supported Theodore Trammell's bid
for a Mississippi congressional seat (Kearse to King, 6 April 1962). King later explained to Kearse that he
was not planning to endorse Trammell, but instead "happened to have made an appearance at a meeting which, at the time, was not designed to be a political rally" (King to Kearse, 11 April 1962). Ingraham
Logan Kearse (1921–1991) was born in South Boston, Virginia. He received his undergraduate degree
from Stillman College (1939). In 1954 Kearse became pastor of Ebenezer Baptist Church in Baltimore,
and four years later he founded Cornerstone Baptist Church of Christ, also in Baltimore. Active in the
local movement, Kearse helped lead a sit-in campaign to desegregate Baltimore restaurants in 1961 and
participated in a ministerial protest at City Hall Plaza in support of the Albany Movement in August
1962. Kearse rendered support to the civil rights movement in Albany. In 1964 Kearse was a part of the
entourage who went to Oslo, Norway, to see King receive the Nobel Peace Prize, and in 1980 he became
president of the Metropolitan Spiritual Churches of Christ.

2. Nathan Miller, "Wilkinson Takes Lead Over Sickles," *Baltimore Sun*, 16 May 1962.

have done this, I have confronted many unnecessary problems.[3] While the meeting that you are inviting me to speak for will be in the interes of voter registration, I am sure that it is impossible to keep the press, and many people, from interpreting it as an endorsement for your candidacy. I am sure you understand these problems and the reasons why I find it necessary to decline your gracious invitation.

May I say, however, that if there is anything that I can do in the background to aid your election, I will be happy to know what it is. You have my private support, and I will be hoping and praying that you win the election.

God's blessings to you in all of your significant work. I hope to see you in the not too distant future.

Very sincerely yours,
Mike

MLKjr.m

TLc. MLKP-MBU.

-------------------

3. During the 1960 presidential election, King articulated a similar policy and did not publicly endorse Kennedy or Richard Nixon (Statement on presidential endorsement, 1 November 1960, in *Papers* 5:537–540).

# From Charles C. Diggs

6 November 1961
Washington, D.C.

*Acknowledging that King does not endorse political candidates "except to urge people to exercise their privilege of voting," Diggs, an early supporter of the Montgomery bus boycott and an SCLC advisory board member, thanks King for showing "abiding interest" in the unsuccessful campaign of African American candidate Russell Brown for Michigan's First Congressional District seat.[1] King had denied endorsing Brown in late October, after Michigan governor John*

-------------------

1. King visited Detroit on 8 October to speak at New Calvary Baptist Church. While in Detroit King stated that more African American congressmen were needed: "If I were a resident of Detroit and lived in the First District, I would be waiting for the polls to open to vote for Russell S. Brown" ("Diggs Endorses Brown," *Michigan Chronicle*, 14 October 1961). Brown, a former state parole agent and bail bondsman who had run for the First District seat in 1958 and 1960, was one of nine Democrats running for Congressman Thaddeus M. Machrowicz's vacant seat. Diggs, who served in Congress from 1954–1980, had sent a form letter to local leaders endorsing Brown because he was "not only the best qualified of ALL the candidates but is the ONLY NEGRO CANDIDATE WHO HAS A CHANCE TO WIN" (Diggs to Reverend, 9 October 1961). For more on King's relationship with Diggs, see Diggs to King, 20 April 1956, in *Papers* 3:218; King to Diggs, 6 January 1958.

Swainson called for the Fair Campaign Practices Commission to investigate whether King had made a racially based endorsement.[2] No reply from King has been found.

6 Nov
1961

The Reverend Martin Luther King
Ebenezer Baptist Church
Atlanta, Georgia

Dear Martin:

I presume you know by now that the Brown for Congress Campaign missed its objective by less than a thousand votes. The final results dramatized our contention that we had all the ingredients of an historical achievement. We had predicted that if we failed it would be due to apathy and division among our sources of strength.[3] We had just enough of both, but much less of each factor to encourage us to believe our efforts were not in vain. Although the other two Negro candidates had no substantial support, they drained off enough votes from Russell Brown to prevent certain victory.[4] This experience served as a classical object lesson that will be permanently remembered by many people.

Some elements in the community, principally the daily press have attempted to distort the motivation behind my personal participation in the campaign and the implications of a letter sent to registered voters over my signature accompanied by a circular we published containing the picture we took with you along with certain supporting statements. The fact that Brown's race was referred to was interpreted by them as a "racist" appeal. In my opinion, which is shared by almost everyone in the so-called Negro community, such an interpretation was so completely distorted that it obviously was designed to serve the nefarious purposes of its perpetrators. They were undoubtedly attempting to galvanize and alert the anti-Negro elements

---

2. In its report, the commission stated, "Mr. King has advised us that he never endorses a local candidate," although Diggs asserted publicly that King was aware that his quote would be printed on literature distributed by the Brown campaign. According to the commission, King's alleged endorsements were "direct appeals to racial emotions" and "an affront ... to our concepts of the dignity and goals of American democracy" ("Prosecution Hinted in Quiz on Bias in Congress Race," *Detroit News*, 28 October 1961; Glenn Engle, "State Charges Bias in 1st District Vote," *Detroit News*, 27 October 1961). In a letter to Detroit resident Georgia Harris, King rejected the claim that he had made an endorsement: "I had a picture taken with Congressman Diggs and Mr. Brown, as I do with many people, and I had no idea what the picture would be used for. Being a public figure, however, I have accepted the fact that I will constantly be misused, misrepresented, and misunderstood" (King to Harris, 2 November 1961; "Diggs, King Push Brown for Congress," *Michigan Chronicle*, 14 October 1961).

3. Diggs to Fellow Voter, October 1961: "IF OUR CANDIDATE LOSES, IT WILL BE BECAUSE YOU OR OTHERS STAYED AT HOME. Our opposition is depending upon our APATHY and DIVISION to defeat us."

4. Brown placed second in the primary, receiving 9,015 votes to Lucien N. Nedzi's 10,063 votes. The other three African American candidates, W. Venoid Banks, James Bradley, and J. Alexander Burchett, received 3,140, 2,446, and 146 votes, respectively, out of over forty thousand cast.

in that district to overcome the manifest growing unity behind Russell Brown's candidacy.[5]

I am proud of the campaign we conducted. There was only one issue—who was the best qualified candidate in terms of background, experience and temperament to represent such a diversified district in the Congress of the United States.[6]

We contended it was Russell Brown, a member of one of America's most accomplished Negro families.[7] What was wrong with identifying his race? The newspapers themselves did it in every story they printed about the campaign. This is the way they also identify me, you and others I could name. We constantly ask Negroes to vote for "other" candidates; what was wrong with asking them to vote for Brown if we thought he was capable of doing the job?

Additionally, you and I both know how under-represented we are at every level of government. Until we reach some level of fair representation from our group we have to focus particular attention on qualified "Negro" candidates whenever certain opportunities present themselves. We cannot always rely upon others to discover the capacity of our talented people to serve their government. Within this context it is certainly legitimate to appeal to the pride of our people to help stimulate their interest in group achievement. To call this "racism" or "discrimination" in reverse is ridiculous. On the contrary if Brown had won, his victory would have been heralded in the daily press and through the Voice of America as a great expression of democracy at work.

I know you do not as a general rule become involved in politics except to urge people to exercise their privilege of voting. I certainly respect and understand this policy in light of the particular leadership role you play. We were very delighted, however, that your policy was flexible enough to have expressed such obviously abiding interest in our candidate's success when we took that picture during your last visit to Detroit. I think we handled the publicity about your interest with the kind of taste befitting a person of your stature. It was certainly inspirational to those of us who worked so hard for our common cause. Its effectiveness can be gauged by the reaction of the daily press who was opposed to us anyway and sought to seize upon any turn of events to thwart our efforts. However, their attacks upon the King-Diggs

---

5. Brown claimed that King's support was not "solely because I was a Negro," but because "he felt I was more suited for the office. My being a Negro was coincidental to this fact" ("Await Decision in Probe of Racism in 1st District," *Michigan Chronicle*, 4 November 1961).

6. African Americans comprised forty percent, voters of Polish descent comprised about thirty percent, and other white ethnic groups comprised the rest of the voting population of the First Congressional District, which contained the east side of Detroit and nearby Hamtramck, an industrial city enclosed within Detroit's borders.

7. Brown was the son of Russell Brown, Sr., who served as general secretary and financial officer of the AME Church, and grandson of Charles S. Smith, who founded the first black business school at Wilberforce University. Brown's brother Charles worked as an attorney, and his brother-in-law Howard Jenkins, Jr., was a Labor Department official and in 1963 was the first African American elected to the National Labor Relations Board.

"intervention" merely angered the Negro community and <u>raised our stock in its</u> <u>eyesight for fighting for a valid principle.</u>

I am not surprised that you were discerning enough not to have been drawn into commenting upon references to you with respect to this matter. Whatever you might say would be distorted by our detractors in the same degree as their original interpretation. The situation is over; let our common enemies worry about where we might "strike" next.

With best wishes and warmest regards to you and family, I remain

Faithfully yours
[*signed*]
Charley

TLS. MLKP-MBU.

# To Harry H. Wachtel

7 November 1961
[*Atlanta, Ga.*]

*King enumerates ways Wachtel's legal background could assist SCLC.[1] Wachtel replied on 5 December 1961, informing King that he was interested in contributing in the "not too distant future."[2]*

Harry Wachtel, Esq.
Attorney at Law
Wachtel and Michaelson
711 Fifth Avenue
New York, New York

---

1. Clarence B. Jones wrote a draft of this letter, which Levison sent to King (see Levison to King, 1 November 1961, pp. 318–319 in this volume; Jones, Draft, King to Wachtel, 1 November 1961). Harry H. Wachtel (1917–1997) was born in New York and received his B.S. from New York City College (1938) and his LL.B. from Columbia (1940). Following his admission to the New York Bar that same year, Wachtel served as legal counsel for several chain store corporations and established his own practice. In 1962 Wachtel was introduced to King, and later advised King on legal matters and provided him with access to business and other legal contacts. With King's endorsement, he co-founded the Gandhi Society for Human Rights, a tax-exempt charitable organization that raised funds for the civil rights movement. In 1964, Wachtel and his wife accompanied King to Norway to receive the Nobel Peace Prize. Wachtel later served as Coretta Scott King's lawyer and offered legal counsel to the King Center from 1969–1982.

2. King and Wachtel continued this discussion in an early February 1962 meeting in New York (see King to Wachtel, 12 February 1962, pp. 397–398 in this volume).

Dear Mr. Wachtel:

Clarence B. Jones has informed me of his conference with you and John Powell, Esq. of your office.[3] I was particularly delighted to learn of your interest and offer to assist the Southern Christian Leadership Conference in the conduct of its legal work.

Undoubtedly the material left with you by Clarence and his remarks gave you a partial picture of our program and problems. However, I would like to take this occasion to outline to you in broad terms how lawyers like you can be most helpful.

Broadly speaking, the problems confronted by the Southern Christian Leadership Conference in its efforts to achieve full equality for Negro citizens in the South in particular and in our nation as a whole have been of two types:

1.  The acquisition of a continuing reservoir of legal services, and
2.  Financial.

The need for maximum legal assistance has been imposed upon our Conference as a result of the institution in May of 1960 of a series of libel suits by various state officials of the State of Alabama against four members of our Executive Board and The New York Times.[4] I will not go into the details and legal background of that litigation. I believe the enclosed material prepared by our Northern office sufficiently accomplishes this.[5]

Instead, I would like to call your attention to the Conference of Lawyers held at the Lotus Club last Spring and the Lawyers Advisory Committee which arose therefrom.[6] The actions and public statements of that Committee, under the leadership of Theodore W. Kheel, Esq. was the first major significant public support given to our Conference in the libel actions since these suits were filed against four of our Executive Board members and The New York Times.[7] It is our objective, with the assistance of Mr. Jones, to again enlist the support of outstanding counsel from the City of New York. We would like to involve you not only as part of that assistance rendered to us around the libel cases but we also would like your help in the preparation of a memorandum of law in support of the historic Executive Order which was the subject of my recent conference with the President of the United States.[8] The objective of such an order is the elimination of all segregation laws from the statute books of respective states of the Union.

The preparation of a memorandum, to be submitted oto the Attorney General and President of the United States, is one of the most important components of our

---

3. John H. Powell, Jr. (1931–1994), a lawyer in Wachtel's law firm, provided legal assistance to protesters in Edenton, North Carolina.

4. King refers to the Alabama libel cases against SCLC pastors Ralph Abernathy, Joseph E. Lowery, S.S. Seay, and Fred L. Shuttlesworth.

5. See "Background, The Alabama Libel Suits," 8 May 1961.

6. A handwritten comment on Jones's draft of the letter noted that material regarding the conference and committee were left with Wachtel and Powell. The Lawyers Advisory Committee was a group of eighteen lawyers formed to support those accused in the Alabama libel suits (see King, Statement at the Lawyers Advisory Committee, 8 May 1961, pp. 218–221 in this volume).

7. Kheel served as president of the National Urban League from 1956–1960 and was a New York lawyer who specialized in mediating labor disputes.

8. King met with President Kennedy on 16 October to discuss, among other things, an executive order declaring all segregated facilities unconstitutional (King, Press Conference after Meeting with John F. Kennedy, 16 October 1961, pp. 308–311 in this volume).

program for the coming year. Obviously, the issuance of such an Executive Order on or about the Centennial of the Emancipation Proclamation would be a tremendous step forward in the area of race relations as well as give great moral prestige and standing to our country at home and abroad. A brief outline of this memorandum and the method of its preparation will be the subject of a conference planned by our Northern office. Mr. Jones has informed me that all relevant material around this Proposed Executive Order is being forwarded to you.

Another and equally important part of our civil rights program for the coming year which will inevitably require legal assistance is our campaign to double the registration of Negroes in the South. You may have already been informed of this drive by articles in <u>The New York Times</u>.[9] The areas of concentration will be Alabama, Louisiana, Georgia and Mississippi. We anticipate that as our registration program unfolds we will be required to take certain steps legally to protect and advance the participants in this program.

Thus, from the standpoint of legal problems, the Southern Christian Leadership Conference requires assistance on three levels:

1. The continued defense and preparation of the Alabama libel actions.
2. The research and writing of a thoroughly documented memorandum supporting our request for an Executive Order declaring null and void all segregation laws on the statute books of the respective States of the Union.
3. The maintenance of a reservoir of legal services to aid our registration campaign.

The activities of our Conference on all three levels will involve the necessity of using facilities and personnel from as many lawyers as we can call upon. It will also involve, in certain instances, the enlistment of financial support to sustain the activities of our Conference on the three levels outlined.

Financial support can obviously take two forms—that which is indirect and that which is direct. The donation of the use of personnel and/or facilities of your firm from time to time would be a most welcomed form of financial assistance. Naturally, we, of course, are also receptive to any other form of financial assistance which enables us to carry on our legal program. I would deeply appreciate it if you would extend to Mr. Jones on a regular basis from time to time whatever assistance, both in personnel and facilities, he would need to carry on the coordination and research preparation of our legal work.

I am looking forward to the opportunity, on one of my trips to New York, to meet and talk with you and Mr. Powell.

Very truly yours,
Martin Luther King, Jr.

Km
encls

TLc. MLKP-MBU.

---

9. The *Times* ran two articles in late September on SCLC's voter registration drive (Wilma Dykeman and James Stokely, "'The Big Cure for Segregation,'" 24 September 1961; "Southern Negroes Map a Voter Drive," 30 September 1961).

# From Anne Braden

24 November 1961
Louisville, Ky.

*After learning that film advisor Bertram Edises was a former member in the
Communist Party, Anne Braden reassures King regarding his participation in
a documentary about the House Un-American Activities Committee (HUAC).
Braden insists that King's "philosophy is so unmistakably clear and you believe in
it with such strong conviction and state it so lucidly that no misinterpretation is
possible."[1] Despite Braden's reassurances, King opted out of the project.[2]*

Dear Martin:

I had a letter today from Bert Edises, one of the people working on that film on
the House Un-American Activities Committee and civil liberties, about which I wrote
you previously.[3]

I had written him, after receiving your letter, that you had said you would be glad
to appear in the film.[4]

He is trying to work out the mechanics of getting you on film, and I talked to him
by phone yesterday too. At that time, he told me that after writing the letter which I
received today he had spoken with Wyatt on the phone and that Wyatt will work with
him on the mechanics—time and arrangements, etc. What he is thinking of now is
a four-way conversation in the film, between you and Fred [*Shuttlesworth*] and Ralph
[*Abernathy*] and Wyatt if they are all agreeable (Fred has told me he is, but I have not
heard directly from Ralph).[5]

I think this would be very dynamic and effective if it is possible for all of you to

---

1. King was initially chosen for an interview to discuss HUAC's negative impact on desegregation
efforts. Edises was a civil rights lawyer from Oakland, California, who successfully challenged a HUAC
charge of contempt in *Fagerhaugh v. United States*, 232 F.2d 803 (1956).

2. In a letter to Robert Cohen, the film's producer, Wyatt Tee Walker explained that although King
agreed to participate in the film, the announcement that Edises had been a member of the Communist
Party "necessitated a revaluation of the prior decision," noting Edises's political associations would "create more problems than we have time to deal with as it relates to the major work of Dr. King" (Walker
to Robert Carl Cohen, 30 January 1962). In 1959 King had spoken out against HUAC following the committee's accusations of communist involvement in the United Packinghouse Workers of America. King
vouched for the integrity of the union, arguing that "it is tragic indeed that some of our reactionary
brothers in America will go to the limit of giving Communism credit for all good things that happen in
our nation. It is a dark day indeed when men cannot work to implement the ideal of brotherhood without
being labeled communist (King, Statement on House Committee on Un-American Activities Hearings
on the United Packinghouse Workers of America, 11 June 1959, in *Papers* 5:226–227).

3. Edises to Braden, 21 November 1961.

4. King to Braden, 7 November 1961.

5. Only Walker appeared in the film.

get together. However, since Wyatt will be working on this, I need not go into details on mechanics here.

However, I am writing to you now because there is a paragraph in Bert's letter pertaining to something else, which I should pass on to you and the others right away. He writes:

"In all fairness, Dr. King and the others should be told that while Robert Cohen, and not Bertram Edises, is the producer, still I am in a sense the inspirer of this film, and that while I am not a Communist I <u>was</u> one ten years ago, and that in the eyes of HUAC (House Un-American Activities Committee) I am still one—and will always be until I consent to join HUAC's stable of informers—which will be never. If this means that the ministers will feel unable to participate, it is the film's loss, and I think the nation's loss too. Nevertheless there must be absolute honesty as far as myself and my role in the making of the film are concerned. The ministers, like all others who volunteer to participate, will have the right to delete their contribution if the final version of the film does not meet with their approval."[6]

Since I did not have this information when I wrote you about this project originally, I of course feel obligated to send the information along now. I must say though that it seems a little bit of too bad to me that a person in Bert Edises position should feel obliged to go into what his politics were <u>ten years ago</u> in approaching people about what is obviously a good project <u>now</u>. But I suppose this is a part of the crazy times we live in, and in light of this, I feel that it is very fair and considerate of him to bring this up now.

I will be interested in knowing what your feeling about this is. My own feeling is that the key question here is not what the <u>past</u> politics of someone connected with the film are; rather the key thing is what the film itself, intrinsically, is going to say and do. If it were going to be a film promoting communism, that would be a very different matter. But in reading the outline and discussing the concept with those making it it, I find no indication that there will be even an inkling of such an idea in the film. Rather, it appears that its only purpose will be to promote democracy and civil liberties. If it doesn't turn out that way in the finished product, of course, all participants, as Bert notes, will have the right to withdraw.

I assume of course that the film will be attacked by HUAC and its followers, but this would not be because of Edises but because of what the film will say and could be expected in any event, if it were made by anyone. However, as I have told you before, I think you are far above any such attack and absolutely invulnerable, in the deepest sense, to it—because your own philosophy is so unmistakably clear and you believe in it with such strong conviction and state it so lucidly that no misinterpretation is possible. I assume that you would state it in the film and that this in itself would make it impossible for anyone to misunderstand.

Edises sent a copy of his letter to me to Wyatt, but I also want to get the information covered in this letter to Fred and Ralph. I am leaving town shortly to go spend tomorrow (Saturday) with Carl, and in the interest of saving time, I am just

---

6. Edises to Braden, 21 November 1961.

going to send Fred and Ralph copies of this letter.[7] A copy also goes to Wyatt for his information.

Warm regards,
[*signed*] Anne
Anne Braden

TLS. MLKP-MBU.

---

7. Braden's husband Carl was serving a one-year prison sentence for refusing to testify before HUAC (see Braden to King, 30 May 1961, pp. 238–241 in this volume).

# To Carter Zeleznik

28 November 1961
[*Atlanta, Ga.*]

*In an 11 September 1961 letter to King, Zeleznik, a clinical psychologist, noted similarities between King's philosophy of nonviolence and his own "logic of relations" theory.[1] He invited King to collaborate; however, King declines, explaining that one day he hopes "to correlate into a philosophy many of the things which experience is now teaching us," but "my role at present is that of an actionist."*

Dr. Carter Zeleznik
The Jefferson Medical College of Philadelphia
1025 Walnut Street
Philadelphia, Pennsylvania

Dear Dr. Zeleznik:

First, I would like to apologize for being rather tardy in replying to your letter of recent date. Absence from the city, the accumulation of a large volume of mail, and the many problems incident to moving our offices account for the delay.[2]

Let me take this opportunity to thank you for shaing with me your article entitled "The Concept of Power in Political Science," and your thoughts concerning my

---

1. Zeleznik (1925–2010), born in Detroit, Michigan, received a B.A. (1948) and an M.A. (1950) from the University of Michigan. After graduating, Zeleznik taught in Ethiopia for several years before joining Jefferson Medical College's Psychiatry department in 1958. In 1969, he became associate director of Jefferson's Office of Medical Education. He earned his Ph.D. from University of Pennsylvania in 1978.

2. SCLC had recently relocated their offices to 41 Exchange Place in Atlanta.

article.[3] I certainly appreciate your views as to the predictability of the forces at work in our midst. I find your views quite stimulating. It will be interesting to test them in my observances of group behavior in our struggle.

At the present time, I don't see how I could work with you in the 'logic of relationships' experiment. It so happens that any bent that I have toward philosophy has been absorbed by the pressures of everyday decisions. Too often we are forced to make existential decisions and then seek a rationale for them in this work. Experiment and reality have become one for us.

I would like to encourage you in these studies. A great deal of thought must go into the work which is involved in persons of different backgrounds living together. It remains for you, in the disciplines of Philosophy and Psychology to point directions for our struggle. This is extremely important, as I am sure you realize. However, my role at present is that of an actionist. There are times when I would prefer it otherwise, and perhaps some day I will be able to correlate into a philosophy many of the things which experience is now teaching us.

I will appreciate being kept abreast of your future work, and look forward to meeting you personally sometime in the not too distant future.

Sincerely yours,
Martin Luther King, Jr.

Km

TLc. MLKP-MBU.

---

3. "The Concept of Power in Political Science," *Il Politico* 25 (1960): 875–879. Zeleznik praised King's 10 September 1961 article "The Time For Freedom Has Come" (pp. 270–278 in this volume; Zeleznik to King, 11 September 1961).

## To Herman Jackson

28 November 1961
*[Atlanta, Ga.]*

*Less than two months away from his scheduled execution, Jackson, a Florida convict, pleaded for King's help in appealing his conviction for raping a thirteen-year-old white girl in February 1960.[1] King explains that SCLC does not have a legal fund to cover such cases, suggesting Jackson contact the NAACP Legal Defense and Educational Fund. In closing, King offers Jackson solace as he faces*

---

1. Jackson to King, 7 November 1961. Herman Jackson, Jr. (1939–2001) worked as a laborer in West Palm Beach, Florida, before his rape conviction. After discovering that potentially exculpatory evidence had not been disclosed to the defense, Jackson appealed his conviction to the Supreme Court of Florida,

*death: "We know that we have a Father and Creator who cares for us, who forgives*
*our sins and who promises us life with Him in His Kingdom." Jackson was later*
*retried and spent fifteen years in prison before being paroled in 1984.*

Mr. Herman Jackson, Jr.
c/o Attorney I. C. Smith[2]
412 Rosemary Avenue
West Palm Beach, Florida

Dear Mr. Jackson:

This is to acknowledge receipt of your letter of recent date. While I am in no position to make any judgments as to your alledged crime, I am very much concerned about your well-being.

I regret so much that the Southern Christian Leadership Conference, the organization of which I am president, is not in a position to give you any legal aid. We do not have a legal department to handle cases such as yours. I would suggest that you contact the NAACP Legal Defense Fund, Inc., 10 Columbus Circle, New York, New York with the hope that they may be of assistance to you. If your crime is clearly a result of lack of justice due to racial implications of the case, the U.S. Government, Department of Justice may offer some hope.

Yours is certainly not an unusual case, however. There are so many problems concerning the Negro's ability to receive justice in our courts.[3] These are not neces-

---

which ruled the evidence "indefinite" and affirmed the death sentence on 6 September 1961 (*Jackson v. State of Florida*, 132 So. 2d 596). In *Jackson v. L. L. Wainwright* (390 F.2d 288 [1968]), the Fifth Circuit Court of Appeals reversed the Florida Supreme Court's decision, claiming that the prosecution had a duty to disclose the exculpatory evidence to the defense, and ordered that the state retry Jackson. Jackson was again found guilty in a 1969 trial, and resentenced to life imprisonment. He was paroled on 28 February 1984.

2. Isiah C. Smith (1922–2012) was a pioneering black attorney who played an instrumental role in the desegregation movement in Palm Beach County, Florida. After working as a lawyer for more than thirty years, he became a judge in 1986.

3. A week after King wrote Jackson, SCLC released a statement decrying a U.S. District Court judge's denial of a motion for a stay of execution for Willie Seals, a black man convicted of raping a white woman in Alabama in 1958. The press release quoted King as saying: "We are distressed that Southern justice continues to penalize the Negro community. The Seals' case, as so many others, underscores the violation of the 'due process' clause of the Fourteenth Amendment. Negroes are systematically excluded from grand and petit juries. Mr. Seals was tried in a segregated courtroom and within the framework of a state-enforced segregated judicial system." King went on to argue that "there has always been the practice of Southern juries and judges to sentence Negroes more heavily than whites for the same offense, as demonstrated here by the state of Alabama. SCLC sincerely feels that Mr. Seals has been denied a fair trial and the issues involved strike at the very heart of the constitutional guarantees of all Negroes" (SCLC, "SCLC charges injustice in Seals case," 5 December 1961). Seals was granted an emergency stay of execution, and in 1962 the Alabama Fifth Circuit Court of Appeals ruled that the exclusion of blacks from the jury rolls in Alabama was a violation of the Constitution. Seals was found guilty of the rape again in 1964 and sentenced to life in prison. He was released in 1971. Prior to the Seals case, King had protested the 1958 electrocution of Jeremiah Reeves, a seventeen-year-old black boy who was sent to death row after being convicted of raping a white woman in Montgomery. Shortly after Reeve's electrocution, King told a crowd gathered at the Alabama capital: "The issue before us now is not the innocence or guilt of Jeremiah Reeves. Even if he

sarily deliberate attempts to deprive us always, sometimes faulty identification or the
anxiety to catch the criminal lead to the victimizing of one who happens to be in the
vicinity. This is one reason that we are working so hard to do away with the patterns
of life which make it unsafe for any Negro to walk the streets of our nation. This
offers very little hope for those who are made to suffer in the meantime.

As a minister of the Christian church, however, I can offer you the hope which our
Lord offered to us all, starting with the thief who was crucified with Him on Calvary.[4]
This is man's only real hope. We know that we have a Father and Creator who cares
for us, who forgives our sins and who promises us life with Him in His Kingdom.
You are not alone as you face death. Many have innocently faced death before you,
and many more choose to face death in this freedom struggle daily in order that we
may make it possible that Liberty and Justice is attained for everyone in these United
States. Our prayers are with you.

Sincerely yours,
Martin Luther King, Jr.

Km


TLc. MLKP-MBU.

---

were guilty, it is the severity and inequality of the penalty that constitutes the injustice" (King, Statement Delivered at the Prayer Pilgrimage Protesting the Electrocution of Jeremiah Reeves, 6 April
1958, in *Papers* 4:397).

    4. Cf. Luke 23:39–43.


# Address Delivered at the Fourth Constitutional Convention of the AFL-CIO

*[11 December 1961]*
Miami, Fla.

*On 26 October 1961, George Meany, president of the AFL-CIO, asked King
to address the federation's annual convention.[1] In his address King extols the
common struggle between the civil rights and labor movements: "Labor has no
firmer friend than the twenty million Negroes whose lives will be deeply affected
by the new patterns of production."[2] Detailing the ways that automation and
reactionary politicians threaten both groups, King recommends that labor tap
into the "vast reservoir of Negro political power," first by addressing the lack of*

---

    1. Meany to King, 26 October 1961.

    2. According to an FBI memorandum, Stanley Levison had reportedly written King's AFL-CIO
speech (J. Edgar Hoover to Robert F. Kennedy, 8 January 1962, Bureau file 100–392452–131; King, Draft,
Address at the fourth constitutional convention of the AFL-CIO, 11 December 1961).

*integration within its own ranks and secondly through financial support for the movement." King also chastises the federation for its treatment of labor leader A. Philip Randolph, who since July 1959 had criticized some unions for practicing discrimination. "When a Negro leader who has a reputation of purity and honesty, which has benefited the whole labor movement, criticizes it, his motives should not be reviled nor his earnestness rebuked."[3] "Labor must honestly admit these shameful conditions," King maintains, and should "design the battle plan which will defeat and eliminate them." A news report indicated that the labor audience initially gave King a "cool reception but warmed up during his attack on anti-union employers."[4] The following transcript was taken from an audio recording of the event.[5]*

President [*George*] Meany, distinguished platform associates, delegates to the Fourth Constitutional Convention of AFL-CIO, ladies and gentlemen. I need not pause to say how very delighted I am to be with you today. It is a privilege indeed to have the opportunity of addressing such a significant gathering, and I have looked forward to being with you with great anticipation. One while I thought that the forces of nature wouldn't cooperate with me enough in order to be here, for I left Los Angeles early this morning, and when I got to the airport, I discovered that the flight that I was to take out of Los Angeles had been canceled because of weather in Dallas and in Atlanta, so I was lucky enough to get a flight through Chicago, and certainly that was a joyous moment when I heard that I could go another way and get here.[6] Course the flight was rather bumpy all the way from Chicago to Miami, and I was very happy when we landed. Now I don't want to give you the impression that I don't have faith in God in the air; it's simply that I've had more experience with him on the ground. [*laughter*] But it is a delightful privilege to be here, and I want to express my great appreciation to President Meany and the committee for extending the invitation.

Less than a century ago, the laborer had no rights, little or no respect, and led a life which was socially submerged and barren. He was hired and fired by economic despots whose power over him decreed his life or death. The children of workers had no childhood and no future; they too worked for pennies an hour, and by the

---

3. The AFL-CIO censured Randolph on 12 October 1961 (Jacob S. Potofsky, George M. Harrison, and Richard F. Walsh, "Report to the Executive Council of the AFL-CIO," 12 October 1961; see also King, Press Release, Statement in Defense of A. Philip Randolph, 13 October 1961, pp. 306–308 in this volume). Afterward Randolph charged the federation with "moral paralysis, pessimism, defeatism and cynicism" regarding segregation in its organization (Stanley Levey, "Negro Union Head Scores A.F.L.-C.I.O.," *New York Times*, 12 November 1961). Meany met with Randolph at the beginning of the convention in Miami, and on 13 December both sides agreed to strike their criticisms from the official record (Levey, "Labor Approves Formula to Settle Internal Fights," *New York Times*, 14 December 1961).

4. "AFL-CIO Told It Must Do More to End Bias," *Atlanta Daily World*, 13 December 1961. In a 22 December 1961 letter Meany thanked King for his "interesting and most significant address."

5. Transcripts of King's address were published in the *Proceedings of the Fourth Constitutional Convention of the AFL-CIO* (Washington, D.C.: AFL-CIO, 1962), vol. 1, pp. 282–289; and *Hotel*, 12 February 1962, pp. 4, 6.

6. King was in Los Angeles from 7–10 December on a speaking tour.

time they reached their teens, they were worn-out old men, devoid of spirit, devoid 11 Dec 1961
of hope, and devoid of self-respect. Jack London described the child worker in these
words: "He did not walk like a man. He did not look like a man. He was a travesty of
the human. It was a twisted and stunted and nameless piece of life that shambled like
a sickly ape, arms loose-hanging, stoop-shouldered, narrow-chested, grotesque and
terrible."[7] American industry organized misery into sweatshops and proclaimed the
right of capital to act without restraints and without conscience. Victor Hugo, literary
genius of that day, commented bitterly that there was always more misery in the lower
classes than there was humanity in the upper classes.[8]

The inspiring answer to this intolerable and dehumanizing existence was economic organization through trade unions. The worker became determined not to
wait for charitable impulses to grow in his employer. He constructed the means by
which a fairer sharing of the fruits of his toil had to be given to him, or the wheels
of industry, which he alone turned, would halt and wealth for no one would be
available. This revolution within industry was fought bitterly by those who blindly
believed their right to uncontrolled profits was a law of the universe, and that without the maintenance of the old order, catastrophe faced the nation. But history is a
great teacher. Now everyone knows that the labor movement did not diminish the
strength of the nation but enlarged it by raising the living standards of millions.
Labor miraculously created a market for industry and lifted the whole nation to
undreamed-of levels of production. Those who today attack labor forget these simple
truths, but history remembers them.

Labor's next monumental struggle emerged in the thirties, when it wrote into
federal law the right freely to organize and bargain collectively. It was now apparently
emancipated. The days when workers were jailed for organizing and when in the
English parliament, Lord Macaulay had to debate against a bill decreeing the death
penalty for anyone engaging in a strike were grim but almost-forgotten memories.[9]
Yet the Wagner Act, like any other legislation, tended merely to declare rights but
did not deliver them.[10] Labor had to bring the law to life, by exercising in practice its
rights over stubborn, tenacious opposition. It was warned to go slow, to be moderate,
not to stir up trouble.[11] But labor knew it was always the right time to do right, and it
spread its organization over the nation and achieved equality, organizationally, with
capital, and the day of economic democracy was born.

Negroes in the United States read this history of labor and find that it mirrors

7. Jack London, "The Apostate: A Child Labor Parable," *Woman's Home Companion* 33, no. 9 (Sept. 1906): 5–7, 49.

8. Victor Hugo, *Les Misérables* (New York: A.L. Burt, 1862), p. 11.

9. Lord Thomas Babington Macaulay served in Parliament from 1830–1847 and 1852–1856.

10. The National Labor Relations Act (1935), also called the Wagner Act after Senator Robert F. Wagner, guaranteed unions the right to organize and established the National Labor Relations Board to arbitrate disputes between workers and employers.

11. The following sentence was in King's draft of the speech: "Tom Girdler summed it up in his auto-biography when he said, 'We had had industrial peace until reckless and selfish union organizers made unprovoked war on our workers'" (King, Draft, Address at the fourth constitutional convention of the AFL-CIO).

their own experience. We are confronted by powerful forces, telling us to rely on the goodwill and understanding of those who profit by exploiting us. They deplore our discontent, they resent our will to organize so that we may guarantee that humanity will prevail and equality will be exacted. They are shocked that action organizations, sit-ins, civil disobedience, and protests are becoming our everyday tools, just as strikes, demonstrations, and union organization became yours to ensure that bargaining power genuinely existed on both sides of the table. We want to rely upon the goodwill of those who would oppose us. Indeed, we have brought forward the method of nonviolence to give an example of unilateral goodwill in an effort to evoke it in those who have not yet felt it in their hearts. But we know that if we are not simultaneously organizing our strength, we will have no means to move forward. If we do not advance, and the crushing burden of centuries of neglect and economic deprivation will destroy our will, our spirits, and our hopes. In this way, labor's historic tradition of moving forward to create vital people as consumers and citizens has become our own tradition and for the same reasons.

This unity of purpose is not an historical coincident. Negroes are almost entirely a working people. There are pitifully few Negro millionaires and few Negro employers. Our needs are identical with labor's needs: decent wages, fair working conditions, livable housing, old-age security, health and welfare measures, conditions in which families can grow, have education for their children, and respect in the community. That is why Negroes support labor's demands and fight laws which curb labor. That is why the labor-hater and labor-baiter is virtually always a twin-headed creature, spewing anti-Negro epithets from one mouth and anti-labor propaganda from the other mouth. [*applause*]

The duality of interests of labor and Negroes makes any crisis which lacerates you a crisis from which we bleed. And as we stand on the threshold of the second half of the twentieth century, a crisis confronts us both. Those who in the second half of the nineteenth century could not tolerate organized labor have had a rebirth of power and seek to regain the despotism of that era, while retaining the wealth and privileges of the twentieth century. Whether it be the ultra-white right wing in the form of Birch Societies the alliance which former President [*Dwight D.*] Eisenhower denounced, the alliance between big military and big business, or the coalition of southern Dixiecrats and northern reactionaries—whatever the form, these menaces now threaten everything decent and fair in American life. Their target is labor, liberals, and Negro people, not scattered Reds or even Justice [*Earl*] Warren, former Presidents Eisenhower and [*Harry S.*] Truman, and President [*John F.*] Kennedy, who are in truth beyond the reach of their crude and vicious falsehoods.

Labor today faces a grave crisis, perhaps the most calamitous since it began its march from the shadows of want and insecurity. In the next ten to twenty years, automation will grind jobs into dust as it grinds out unbelievable volumes of production. This period is made to order for those who would seek to drive labor into impotency by viciously attacking it at every point of weakness. Hard-core unemployment is now an ugly and unavoidable fact of life, and like malignant cancer, it has grown year by year and continues its spread. But automation can be used to generate an abundance of wealth for a people or an abundance of poverty for millions as its human-like machines turn out human scrap, along with machine scrap, as a by-product of production. And I am convinced that our society, with its ability to perform miracles with machinery, has the capacity to make some miracles for men, if it values men as highly as it values machines.[12] [*applause*]

To find a great design to solve a great problem, labor will have to intervene in the political life of the nation, to chart a course which distributes the abundance to all instead of concentrating it among a few. The strength to carry through such a program requires that labor know its friends and collaborate as a friend. If all that I have said is sound, labor has no firmer friend than the twenty million Negroes whose lives will be deeply affected by the new patterns of production.

Now to say that we are friends would be an empty platitude if we fail to behave as friends and honestly look to weaknesses in our relationship. And unfortunately, there are weaknesses. Labor has not adequately used its great power, its vision and resources to advance Negro rights. Undeniably, it has done more than other forces in American society to this end. Aid from real friends in labor has often come when the flames of struggle heighten, but Negroes are a solid component within the labor movement and a reliable bulwark for labor's whole program and should expect more from it, exactly as a member of a family expects more from his relatives than he expects from his neighbors. Labor, which made impatience for long-delayed justice for itself a vital motive force, cannot lack understanding of the Negro's impatience. It cannot speak with the reactionary's calm indifference of progress around some obscure corner, yet not yet possible even to see. That is a maximum in the law: justice too long delayed is justice denied.[13]

When a Negro leader who has a reputation of purity and honesty, which has benefited the whole labor movement, criticizes it, his motives should not be reviled nor his earnestness rebuked. Instead the possibility that he is revealing a weakness in the labor movement, which it can ill afford, should receive thoughtful examination. A man who has dedicated his long and faultless life to the labor movement cannot be raising questions harmful to it any more than a lifelong devoted parent can become the enemy of his child. And the report of a committee may smother with legal constructions, a list of complaints and dispose of it for a day, but if it buries a far larger truth, it has disposed of nothing and made justice more elusive.[14]

Discrimination does exist in the labor movement.[15] It is true that organized labor

---

12. King made similar comments in an earlier speech to the Transport Workers Union of America: "We are neither technologically advanced nor socially enlightened, if we witness this disaster for tens of thousands, without finding a solution. And by 'solution' I mean a real and genuine alternative, providing the same living standards and opportunities which were swept away by a force called 'progress' but which for some is destruction" (America's Greatest Crisis, Address at the Eleventh Constitutional Convention of the Transport Workers Union of America, 5 October 1961). For more on King's views on automation, see "People in Action: Nothing Changing Unless," 28 April 1962, pp. 449–451 in this volume.

13. The quote is most often attributed to William Gladstone, leader of the House of Commons and Chancellor of the Exchequer, who made a similar remark during a 16 March 1868 address to the House of Commons: "But, above all, if we be just men we shall go forward in the name of truth and right, bearing this in mind—that, when the case is proved and the hour is come, justice delayed is justice denied." It has also been linked to William Penn, *Fruits of Solitude in Reflections and Maxims Relating to the Conduct of Human Life* (1682): "Our law says well, 'To delay justice, is injustice.'"

14. King refers to labor leader A. Philip Randolph.

15. Jacob S. Potofsky, George M. Harrison, and Richard F. Walsh, "Report to the Executive Council of the AFL-CIO," 12 October 1961. For more on the report, see King, Press Release, Statement in Defense

has taken significant steps to remove the yoke of discrimination from its own body. But in spite of this, some unions govern by the racist ethos, have contributed to the degraded economic status of the Negro. Negroes have been barred from membership in certain unions and denied apprenticeship training and vocational education. In every section of the country, one can find labor unions existing as a serious and vicious obstacle when the Negro seeks jobs or upgrading in employment.[16] Labor must honestly admit these shameful conditions and design the battle plan which will defeat and eliminate them. In this way, labor would be unearthing the big truth and utilizing its strength against the bleakness of injustice in the spirit of its finest traditions.

How can [applause], how can labor rise to the heights of its potential statesmanship and cement its bonds with Negroes to their mutual advantage? First, labor should accept the logic of its special position with respect to Negroes and the struggle for equality. Although organized labor has taken actions to eliminate discrimination in its ranks, the standard expected of you is higher than the standard for the general community. Your conduct should and can set an example for others, as you have done in other crusades for social justice. You should root out vigorously every manifestation of discrimination so that some internationals, central labor bodies, or locals may not besmirch the positive accomplishments of labor. I am aware that this is not easy, nor popular, but the eight-hour day was not popular, nor easy to achieve, nor was a closed shop, nor was the right to strike, nor was outlawing anti-labor injunctions.[17] But you accomplished all of these with a massive will and determination. And out of such struggle for democratic rights you won both economic gains and the respect of the country, and you will win both again if you will make Negro rights a great crusade.

Second, the political strength you are going to need to prevent automation from becoming a Moloch, consuming jobs and contract gains, can be multiplied if you tap the vast reservoir of Negro political power.[18] Negroes, given the vote, will vote liberal and labor, because they need the same liberal legislation labor needs. To give just an example of the importance of the Negro vote to labor, I might cite the arresting fact that the only state in the South which repealed the right-to-work law is

---

of A. Philip Randolph, 13 October 1961, pp. 306–308 in this volume. The following sentence was in King's draft of the speech: "A useful committee report would be that one which squarely faced the fact and designed the battle plan which will defeat and eliminate it. In this way, labor would be unearthing the big truth and utilizing its strength against evil and for justice in the spirit of its finest traditions."

16. The United States Commission on Civil Rights, in its 1961 report on employment, noted that the labor movement celebrates civil rights goals "at the higher levels, but fundamental internal barriers tend to preserve discrimination at the workingman's level" (*1961 U.S. Commission on Civil Rights Report Book 3: Employment* [Washington, D.C.: U.S. Government Printing Office, 1961], p. 151).

17. In the 1870s the eight-hour workday became a central demand of the United States labor movement. It was not until the Fair Labor Standards Act of 1938 was passed that a maximum forty-four-hour, seven-day workweek was established. The 1947 Taft-Hartley Act banned the closed shop. The Norris-La Guardia Act of 1932 barred federal courts from issuing injunctions in labor disputes.

18. Cf. Leviticus 20:2–5.

Louisiana.[19] And this was achieved because the Negro vote in that state grew large enough to become a balance of power, and it went along with labor to wipe out anti-labor legislation.

Thus [*applause*], thus support to assist us in securing the vote can make the difference between success and defeat for us both. You have organizing experience we need. And you have an apparatus unparalleled in the nation. You recognized five years ago a moral opportunity and responsibility when several of your leaders—including Mr. Meany, Mr. Reuther, Mr. Dubinsky and Mr. McDonald and others—projected a $2 million campaign to assist the struggling Negroes fighting bitterly in handicapped circumstances in the South.[20] A $10,000 contribution was voted by the ILGWU to begin the drive, but for reasons unknown to me, the drive was never begun. The cost to us in lack of resources during these turbulent, violent years is hard to describe. We are mindful that many unions, thought of as immorally rich, in truth have problems in meeting the budget to properly service their members, so we do not ask that you tax your treasuries. Indeed, we ask that you appeal to your members for $1 apiece to make democracy real for millions of deprived American citizens. For this, you have the experience, the organization, and, most of all, the understanding.[21] And if you would do these two things now, in this convention resolve to deal effectively with discrimination and provide financial aid for our struggle in the South this convention will have a glorious moral deed to add to an illustrious history.

The two most dynamic and cohesive liberal forces in the country are the labor movement and the Negro freedom movement. Together we can be architects of democracy. In a South now rapidly industrializing, together we can retool the political structure of the South, sending to Congress steadfast liberals who, joining with those from Northern industrial states, will extend the frontiers of democracy for the whole nation. Together, we can bring about the day when there will be no separate identification of Negroes and labor. There is no intrinsic difference, as I have tried to demonstrate. Differences have been contrived by outsiders who seek to impose disunity by dividing brothers because the color of their skin has a different shade.

I look forward confidently to the day when all who work for a living will be one, with no thought of their separateness as Negroes, Jews, Italians, or any other distinctions. This will be the day when we shall bring into full realization the dream of American democracy, a dream yet unfulfilled. A dream of equality of opportunity, a privilege and property widely distributed. A dream of a land where men will not take necessities from the many to give luxuries to the few. A dream of a land where

---

19. Louisiana's "right-to-work" law banned labor unions from requiring employees to join.

20. Walter Reuther (1907–1970) was the president of the United Automobile Workers from 1946–1970. David Dubinsky (1892–1982) was the president of the International Ladies' Garment Workers' Union (ILGWU) from 1932–1966. David McDonald (1902–1979) headed the United Steelworkers of America from 1952–1965.

21. SCLC sent out its "Appeal for Human Dignity Now," also known as "Dollars for Dignity," in November 1961 requesting a minimum $1 individual contribution collected by labor unions. In his appeal letter, King wrote, "we have the courage in our ranks, we have the skill and capacity. We lack most desperately funds to organize and educate" (King to Friend, 11 November 1961; United Electrical, Radio and Machine Workers of America, "Contributions received on 'Dollars for Dignity' campaign of SCLC," 15 March–16 March 1962).

men will not argue that the color of a man's skin determines the content of his character. A dream of a nation where all our gifts and resources are held not for ourselves alone, but as instruments of service, for the rest of humanity. The dream of a country where every man will respect the dignity and worth of human personality—that is the dream. And as we struggle to make racial and economic justice a reality, let us maintain faith in the future. At times we confront difficult and frustrating moments in the struggle to make justice a reality, but we must believe somehow that these problems can be solved.[22]

There is a little song that we sing in the movement taking place in the South; it goes something like this: "We shall overcome / We shall overcome / Deep in my heart / I do believe / We shall overcome." And somehow all over America, we must believe that we shall overcome and that these problems can be solved and they will be solved.

Before the victory's won, some of us will have to get scarred up, but we shall overcome. Before the victory of justice is a reality, some may even face physical death, but if physical death is the price that some must pay to free their children and their brothers from a permanent life of psychological death, then nothing could be more moral. Before the victory's won, some more will have to go to jail. We must be willing to go to jail and transform the jails from dungeons of shame to havens of freedom and human dignity. Yes [*applause*], before the victory's won [*applause*], before the victory's won, some will be misunderstood; some will be dismissed as dangerous rabble rousers and agitators; some will be called Reds and Communists merely because they believe in economic justice and the brotherhood of man.

But we shall overcome, and I am convinced that we shall overcome because the arc of the moral universe is long but it bends toward justice. We shall overcome because Carlyle is right: "No lie can live forever."[23] We shall overcome because William Cullen Bryant is right: "Truth crushed to earth, will rise again."[24] We shall overcome because James Russell Lowell is right: "Truth forever on the scaffold / Wrong forever on the throne / Yet that scaffold sways the future. . . . "[25]

And so if we will go out with this faith, and with this determination to solve these problems, we will bring into being that new day, and that new America. When that day comes, the fears of insecurity and the doubts clouding our future will be transformed into radiant confidence, into glowing excitement to reach creative goals, and into an abiding moral balance where the brotherhood of man will be undergirded by a secure, and expanded prosperity for all. Yes, this will be the day when all of God's children—black men and white men, Jews and Gentiles, Protestants and Catholics—will be able to join hands all over this nation and sing in the words of

22. The text of this paragraph resembles the conclusion of King's address at the 11 May 1959 Religious Leaders Conference (see *Papers* 5:202).

23. Cf. Thomas Carlyle, *The French Revolution* (1837), vol. 1, book 6, chap. 3.

24. Cf. William Cullen Bryant, "The Battlefield" (1839), stanza 9.

25. James Russell Lowell, "The Present Crisis" (1844), stanza 8: "Truth forever on the scaffold, Wrong forever on the throne,—/ Yet that scaffold sways the future, and, behind the dim unknown / Standeth God within the shadow, keeping watch above his own."

the old Negro spiritual, "Free at last, free at last / Thank God almighty, we are free at last." [*applause*] Thank you.

At. GRVVL-MiEM.

## To James M. Ault

14 December 1961
[*Atlanta, Ga.*]

*At the request of Ault, dean of Union Theological Seminary (UTS), King writes
a glowing recommendation of Gurdon Brewster, who spent the previous summer
interning at Ebenezer for the Student Interracial Ministry (SIM) Project.[1] King
notes that church members wanted Brewster to return and believes seminarians
like him give hope for "a better atmosphere in race relations and a new social
consciousness on the part of the churches."*

Mr. James M. Ault, Dean of Students
Union Theological Seminary
Broadway at 120th Street
New York 27, New York

Dear Mr. Ault:

I am very happy to respond to your inquiry regarding the work of Gurdon
Brewster in our church last summer.

I think I can say without fear of successful contradiction that Gurdon rendered a
great and lasting service in our church last summer. He proved to be a real influence
for good. His radiant personality, genuine sincerity, and helpful manner made him

---

1. Ault to King, 28 November 1961. SIM, organized by students from Gammon Seminary in Atlanta
and UTS, sought to build cross-racial ties by placing white seminarian interns at black churches for a
summer, and vice versa. During his time at Ebenezer, Brewster worked with the youth program, assisted
in Sunday services, visited parishioners, and facilitated dialogue between local black and white churches.
James Mase Ault (1918–2008), was born in Sayre, Pennsylvania, and served in the U.S. Army during
World War II. He graduated from Colgate University in 1949 and received his B.D. from UTS in 1952.
Ault pastored three churches in Massachusetts and New Jersey before returning to UTS as dean of students in 1961. He was dean of Drew Theological School in New Jersey from 1968 to 1972. In 1972, Ault was
elected bishop, a position he held until retiring in 1988. As a United Methodist Bishop, Ault lobbied the
World Council of Churches to support economic sanctions against South Africa due to its apartheid policies. Gurdon Brewster (1937– ), born in New York City, earned a B.A. (1959) from Haverford College and
a B.D. (1962) from UTS. After teaching in India for two years, he became chaplain at Cornell University,
where he remained until his retirement in 1999. In 1966 King, Sr., asked Brewster to join him and his son
as assistant minister at Ebenezer. Brewster turned down the offer but spent the summer ministering at
the church. Brewster wrote an account of his experience at Ebenezer titled *No Turning Back: My Summer
with Daddy King* (2007).

most acceptable to the youth. He was able to develop our youth program in a way that it had never developed, and he gave many areas of religious education in our church a new shot in the arm. He was also extremely helpful in developing creative interracial activities. As you know, it is not easy to bring people together of different racial groups in the south, consequently we end up living in monologue rather than dialogue. But Gurdon was able to bring several white students and adults in contact with our members, thereby developing the climate for creative dialogue.[2]

I have always strongly advocated the need for an interracial church in order to make our witness known as to our oneness in Jesus Christ. I am happy to say that we were able to move a great deal in that direction as a result of Gurdon's work with us. Let me close by saying that Gurdon Brewster's work was so significant and he got into the heart of the people so much that many of them wanted him to come back on a permanent basis.[3] I am sure that if persons of his competence and dedication will continue to work with churches across the south, many meaningful steps will be made toward a better atmosphere in race relations and a new social consciousness on the part of the churches.

Very sincerely yours,
Martin Luther King, Jr.

Km

TLc. MLKJP-GAMK: Box 6.

---

2. Brewster convinced over forty white participants to attend a one-day conference with twenty-five members of the Ebenezer Youth Organization (Brewster, *No Turning Back* [Maryknoll, N.Y.: Orbis Books, 2007], pp. 175–179).

3. Martin Luther King, Sr. and Alberta Williams King offered Brewster a job as associate minister at Ebenezer in 1966, which Brewster declined (Brewster, *No Turning Back*, pp. 224–225).

## Address Delivered at Albany Movement Mass Meeting at Mt. Zion Baptist Church

[*15 December 1961*]
[*Albany, Ga.*]

*On 10 December, Albany police arrested eleven freedom riders outside the train station for obstructing traffic and failure to obey an officer.*[1] *When local residents*

---

1. The arrests came after SNCC workers and some local residents conducted tests during November and December of Albany's compliance with the ICC's September ruling banning segregation in interstate transportation facilities ("Albany, Ga., Jails 267 Negro Youths," *New York Times*, 13 December 1961).

*protested, police arrested more than 700 demonstrators.*[2] *Worried about the lack
of bail funds and the difficulties of coordinating a large campaign, Albany
Movement president William G. Anderson asked King and SCLC for help.*[3] *King
arrived in Albany on 15 December and addressed a crowd of nearly 1,000 at Mt.
Zion Baptist Church.*[4] *The following transcript was taken from a film recording of
that mass meeting.*

Dr. Anderson [*recording interrupted*] something that it so desperately needs to
hear [*Audience:*] (*Well, That's right*) and that is that you do not like segregation. (*Yes,
That's right, Amen*) You are saying that segregation is still the Negroes' burden and
America's shame. (*Amen, That's right*) [*Applause*] You are saying as you assemble here
tonight and as you continue to move on in your movement that you are willing to
struggle, to suffer, to sacrifice, and even die if necessary (*Yes, Yes*) in order to be free
in this day and in this age. (*That's right, Yes sir*) This is what you are saying in this
most significant way. And I can only bid you God speed (*Yes sir*) as you continue. As
it has been said so eloquently tonight, what we are doing in the South and what we
are seeking to do all over the nation (*Well*) is something bigger than Negro rights.
(*Amen*) For we are not struggling for ourselves alone. (*No*)

As you assemble here tonight, you can think of the fact that there are approximately [*break in tape*] two others who are telling us to slow up, who are telling us that
we are pushing things too fast. We must say to them that the hour is late (*That's right,
That's right*) That the clock of destiny is ticking out. (*Yes*) And we must act now before
it is too late. For the shape of the world today does not afford us the luxury of an
anemic democracy and the price that America must pay for the continued oppression of the Negro is a price of its own destruction. (*Yes sir, That's right*) This is [*break*

---

2. "Alert Guard in Georgia Race Strife," *Chicago Daily Defender,* 16 December 1961. To accommodate
the mass arrests, Albany police chief Laurie Pritchett arranged for jails in neighboring counties to house
demonstrators (SNCC, Press release, "Latest from Albany," 13 December 1961).

3. Prior to King's arrival, Anderson and the Albany Movement had attempted to negotiate with
Albany city officials. In return for ceasing any further demonstrations, the Albany Movement demanded
that charges be dropped against those arrested days earlier and called for the enforcement of the ICC's
desegregation ruling. Mayor Asa Kelley refused: "At this point, it is the feeling of the city commission
that there is no area of possible agreement" (Claude Sitton, "202 More Negroes Seized in Georgia," *New
York Times,* 14 December 1961). William Gilchrist Anderson (1927– ), born in Americus, Georgia, pursued
premedical studies at Fort Valley State College in Georgia before serving as a medic during World War II.
After the war, he attended Atlanta College of Mortuary Science and moved to Montgomery, Alabama, to
practice. Continuing his studies, Anderson attended Alabama State College, receiving his B.S. in 1949.
He obtained his D.O. in 1956 from Des Moines Still College of Osteopathy and Surgery in Des Moines,
Iowa, and completed an internship in Flint, Michigan. After his residency, Anderson moved to Albany,
Georgia, and set up a private practice. The newly created Albany Movement elected Anderson its first
president in November 1961. In 1963 Anderson and other Albany leaders were charged with conspiracy
to boycott a juror's business, but this prosecution ended in a mistrial. After moving to Detroit in late 1962,
Anderson finished his training in general surgery and joined a group medical practice. He later became
associate dean of Kirksville College of Osteopathic Medicine in Michigan.

4. Ralph Abernathy, Wyatt Tee Walker, and Ruby Hurley of the NAACP also spoke at the rally.
King also addressed a capacity crowd at Shiloh Baptist Church, located across the street from Mt. Zion
("Albany Balks at Truce Price; Rev. King Rallies Negroes," *Atlanta Constitution,* 16 December 1961).

*in tape*] I can say nothing to you this evening, but continue in your determination to be free. All over the South we must continue to engage in creative protest to break down the system of segregation. Now we've got to get rid of two myths in order to do this. [*recording interrupted*]

F. WSB-TV-GU.

# From Herschelle Sullivan

16 December 1961

*Sullivan, a former Spelman student arrested with King in October 1960, sends
a jocular note updating King on her studies at Johns Hopkins University.[1] She
offers encouragement to King, who was arrested in Albany on 16 December while
leading a prayer demonstration: "My thoughts and prayers are dominated by
concern for you and the other Americans who are being punished for exercising
their constitutional rights."*

Dear Rev. King,

Recent radio and television reports lead me to believe that you are still "an Arrogant Negra". Needless to say I am overjoyed.

I feel so left out of things here. During the Thanksgiving vacation I had hoped to chat with you if only for a moment.

Johns Hopkins is without questionnone of the most stimulating schools I've attended.[2] They work the. . . . with all due respects to the ecclesiastical order. . . . devil out of you, but somehow you don't mind. The students by and large come from Ivy league schools and many have expressed an interest at least from a sociological point of view in the advent of the "New Negro".[3] This is especially true of the other students majoring in the African area who are searching in the American Negro some correlation with the so called "African Personality", and some identification

---

1. King, Sullivan, and several others were arrested on 19 October 1960 for participating in a sit-in at Rich's department store in Atlanta. For more on their arrest, see King to Female Inmates, in *Papers* 5:527–528. Herschelle Sullivan Challenor (1938– ), born in Atlanta, attended nearby Spelman College, where she was elected student body president. In 1960, Sullivan became involved in the Atlanta student movement. Following her graduation from Spelman in 1961, Sullivan pursued graduate studies in international relations, receiving an M.A. from Johns Hopkins (1963) and a Ph.D. from Columbia University (1970). Later Sullivan held several academic positions, including the directorship of the Washington Liaison Office of the United Nations Educational, Scientific and Cultural Organization. In 1994, she was nominated by President Bill Clinton to the National Security Education Board.

2. In a 9 March 1962 letter, King encouraged Sullivan's graduate studies, writing that her "experience at Johns Hopkins will broaden your insights and extend your intellectual horizon."

3. Sullivan may refer to Alain Locke's groundbreaking essay "The New Negro" (*The New Negro: An Interpretation*, ed. Alain Locke [New York: Albert and Charles Boni, 1925]).

with Senghor's ideas of Negritude.[4] Being the one of the two Negroes here (out of an enrollment of about 100, only 10 of which are girls) who had participated in the sit-ins, they come to me occasionally with questions.

My roommate, a white student from California, is one such student. Many hours have been spent in examing the entire problem. It has been a good experience for me to defend my point of view to really sharp students arguing from an academic rather than an emotional point of view. One night we stayed up until 4:00a.m. planning an armed invasion of Mississippi. (smiles) I remember the night she and I went out with some graduate students from Howard. It was her first date with a Negro and she was rather apprehensive fearing that he would not like her, and would be disappointed that she was white (it was a blind date), so I hastily reminded her that all Negro men wanted to marry white women, putting her at ease.

Although the conditions there cannot possibly equal the luxury of the "Fulton Bars", I hope you are resonably comfortable and that your diet is not limited to corn bread and buttermilk.[5] It is after 2:30a.m. so I must close. I want you to know that my thoughts and prayers are dominated by concern for you and the other Americans who are being punished for exercising their constitutional rights. It is, however, a relief to know your are there to give the spiritual guidance and moral strength that those who perhaps have been arrested for the first time may need.

Sincerely,
Herschelle

P.S. Sorry you had to put up with my poor typing, but I could not find my pen

TLc. MLKJP-GAMK: Box 19.

---

4. Léopold Sédar Senghor was the first president of Senegal (1960–1980). A critic of colonization and western assimilation, he promoted Negritude, a literary movement that emphasized the inherent value of African culture.

5. Sullivan refers to the Fulton County Jail.

# From Ralph Abernathy

17 December 1961
Atlanta, Ga.

*On 16 December, King, Abernathy, and Albany Movement president William
G. Anderson were arrested for parading without a permit, congregating on a
sidewalk, and obstructing traffic, after leading a crowd of over 260 people to pray
at Albany City Hall.[1] The three were taken to the Albany city hall but were later
booked into the Sumter County Jail in Americus, Georgia.[2] While King vowed
to remain in jail until Christmas, Abernathy posted bond that night and called
for a nationwide pilgrimage to Albany.[3] Abernathy writes King a telegram of
encouragement, lamenting that "I should be with you," and "I anxiously await
the time when I can rejoin you."*

= DR MARTIN LUTHER KING JR =

COUNTY JAIL ALBANY GA =

= NOW THAT THE CHURCH DAY IS OVER, THE PREACHING FOR THE WEEK COM-
PLETED, AND I AM BACK IN THE COMFORT OF MY HOME, I MUST CONFESS TO YOU AND
DOCTOR ANDERSON THAT THERE IS AN EMPTINESS IN MY SOUL THAT NONE OF THE
EXPERIENCES THIS DAY HAVE BEEN ABLE TO FILL I PREACHED THE GOSPEL TODAY TO
THE BEST OF MY ABILITY AT WEST HUNTER, AND I CARRIED YOUR PERSONAL MES-
SAGE TO THE PEOPLE OF EBENEEZER, BUT AS I LISTEN TO THE SWEET CHRISTMAS
MUSIC NOW I KNOW THAT I WOULD NOT BE HERE BUT THAT I SHOULD NOT BE HERE
BUT I SHOULD BE WITH YOU AND WITH THE HUNDREDS OF SONS AND DAUGHTERS OF
SLAVES WHO HAVE THE COURAGE TO SAY TO THE SONS AND DAUGHTERS OF FORMER
SLAVE HOLDERS THAT THIS IS A NEW DAY AND WE WANT OUR FREEDOM NOW.[4] I AM
CONCERNED ABOUT YOUR COMFORT AND WELFARE. I HAVE TRIED TO DO ALL THE
THINGS WHICH YOU ASKED ME TO DO, BUT I ANXIOUSLY AWAIT THE TIME WHEN I CAN
REJOIN YOU. THE SERMON WHICH YOU PREACHED TO MEN AND WOMEN ALL ACROSS
THE NATION THROUGH YOUR BEING THERE WAS MUCH MORE PROFOUND THAN ANY

---

1. King reportedly planned to stay in Albany only for "a day or so and return home after giving
counsel" (David Miller, "Non-Violence: Police Chief and Minister," *New York Herald Tribune*, 18 December
1961; Bruce Galphin, "Albany Shaping Racial Settlement," *Atlanta Constitution*, 15 December 1961).

2. Facsimile of Sumter County Jail ledger, 16 December 1961, p. 347 in this volume. The FBI claimed
that King was moved from the Albany City Hall to the Sumter County Jail for his safety (Special Agent
in Charge, Atlanta, Ga., to J. Edgar Hoover, 17 December 1961, Bureau File 157–6–2–2). Although he did
not find the jail conditions harsh, King complained that jailers called him "boy" and that Sheriff Fred
Chappell was the "meanest man in the world" (Bill Shipp, "U.S. Pilgrimage Is Urged As Albany Negroes
Call Halt," *Atlanta Constitution*, 18 December 1961; "Rev. King Meets 'Meanest Man in World' in Jail," *Jet*,
4 January 1962).

3. SCLC, Press release, "Abernathy issues call for nation-wide protest at Albany, Ga.," 17 December
1961; "King Vows to Spend Yule in Ga. Jail," *Chicago Daily Defender*, 19 December 1961.

4. According to the *Atlanta Daily World*, King was scheduled to preach on "God's Love" at Ebenezer,
while Abernathy was slated to preach on "Light of Hope in the Midst of Darkness" at West Hunter on 17
December ("'God's Love' To Be Topic At Ebenezer on Sunday," *Atlanta Daily World*, 16 December 1961;
"'Light of Hope in Midst of Darkness,' Abernathy," *Atlanta Daily World*, 16 December 1961).

Following their 16 December 1961 arrest in Albany, Georgia, King, Ralph Abernathy, and William G. Anderson are transferred to Sumter County Jail in Americus. On this jail ledger, King is listed as number forty-five and is referred to as a "[*Niger?*] male." Reprinted with the permission of the Sumter County Clerk of the Court's Office, Americus, Ga.

WORDS I COULD HAVE EVER UTTERED. JUANITA AND THE CHILDREN JOIN ME AND SENDING BEST WISHES AS WELL AS VINCENT AND ROSE MARY HARDING WHO ARE WITH US AT THIS TIME =[5]

RALPH D ABERNATHY.

PWSr. MCMLK-RWWL: 1.1.0.70.

---

5. Abernathy refers to his daughters, Juandalynn and Donzaleigh, and his son, Ralph David III. Vincent Harding and his wife, Rosemarie, moved to Atlanta in 1961 as representatives of the Mennonite Central Committee and established Mennonite House, an interracial community center.

Abernathy, Ralph

AA97

A AND19 (A LLA779) LONG PD=ATLANTA GA 17 VIA AMERICUS GA 18

=DR MARTIN LUTHER KING JR= 1961 DEC 18 AM 11 26

COUNTY JAIL ALBANY GA=

=NOW THAT THE CHURCH DAY IS OVER, THE PREACHING FOR
THE WEEK COMPLETED, AND I AM BACK IN THE COMFORT OF MY
HOME, I MUST CONFESS TO YOU AND DOCTOR ANDERSON THAT
THERE IS AN EMPTINESS IN MY SOUL THAT NONE OF THE
EXPERIENCES THIS DAY HAVE BEEN ABLE TO FILL I PREACHED
THE GOSPEL TODAY TO THE BEST OF MY ABILITY AT WEST
HUNTER, AND I CARRIED YOUR PERSONAL MESSAGE TO THE
PEOPLE OF EBENEEZER, BUT AS I LISTEN TO THE SWEET
CHRISTMAS MUSIC NOW I KNOW THAT I WOULD NOT BE HERE BUT
THAT I SHOULD NOT BE HERE BUT I SHOULD BE WITH YOU AND
WITH THE HUNDREDS OF SONS AND DAUGHTERS OF SLAVES WHO
HAVE THE COURAGE TO SAY TO THE SONS AND DAUGHTERS OF
FORMER SLAVE HOLDERS THAT THIS IS A NEW DAY AND WE WANT
OUR FREEDOM NOW. I AM CONCERNED ABOUT YOUR COMFORT AND
WELFARE. I HAVE TRIED TO DO ALL THE THINGS WHICH YOU
ASKED ME TO DO, BUT I ANXIOUSLY AWAIT THE TIME WHEN I
CAN REJOIN YOU. THE SERMON WHICH YOU PREACHED TO MEN
AND WOMEN ALL ACROSS THE NATION THROUGH YOUR BEING THERE
WAS MUCH MORE PROFOUND THAN ANY WORDS I COULD HAVE EVER
UTTERED. JUANITA AND THE CHILDREN JOIN ME AND SENDING
BEST WISHES AS WELL AS VINCENT AND ROSE MARY HARDING WHO
ARE WITH US AT THIS TIME= E SUGGEST        RALPH D ABERNATHY. E

After posting bail following his 16 December 1961 arrest, Ralph Abernathy sends the following telegram to King, who is in jail in Americus, Georgia. Courtesy of the Atlanta University Center, Robert W. Woodruff Library Archives and Special Collections.

# To John F. Kennedy

17 December 1961
Atlanta, Ga.

*King, Abernathy, and Anderson urge President Kennedy to issue a second*
*Emancipation Proclamation and to use his influence to free those arrested in*
*Albany.[1] No reply from the White House has been located. On 18 December,*
*negotiations between Albany officials and the Albany Movement resulted in the*
*release of King and all jailed protesters, and King left Albany later that day.[2]*

THE PRESIDENT
THE WHITE HOUSE

WE URGE YOU ISSUE AT ONCE BY EXECUTIVE ORDER A SECOND EMANCIPATION
PROCLAMATION TO FREE ALL NEGROES FROM SECOND CLASS CITIZENSHIP. FOR UNTIL
THE GOVERNMENT OF THIS NATION STANDS AS FORTHRIGHTLY IN DEFENSE OF DEMO-
CRATIC PRINCIPLES AND PRACTICES HERE AT HOME AND PRESSES AS ENCEASINGLY
FOR EQUAL RIGHTS OF ALL AMERICANS AS IT DOES IN AIDING FOREIGN NATIONS WITH
ARMS.[3]AMMUNITION AND THE MATERIALS OF WAR FOR ESTABLISHMENT DEFENSE OF
HUMAN RIGHTS BEYOND OUR SHORES, THEN AN ONLY THEN, CAN WE JUSTIFY THE
CLAIM TO WORLD LEADERSHIP IN THE FIGHT AGAINST COMMUNISM AND TYRANNY.
WE URGE YOU FURTHER TO USE EVERY MEANS AVAILABLE TO RELEASE AT ONCE THE
HUNDREDS OF PERSONS NOW IN JAIL IN ALBANY GEORGIA FOR SIMPLY SEEKING TO
EXERCISE CONSTITUTIONAL RIGHTS AND TO STAND UP FOR FREEDOM

DR MARTIN LUTHER KING JR

---

1. This telegram was likely sent from Atlanta by Abernathy, who had bailed out of the Sumter
County Jail on 16 December. King had previously called for Kennedy to sign a second Emancipation
Proclamation (see note 18, King, "The Negro and the American Dream," Emancipation Day Address
Delivered at Municipal Auditorium, 2 January 1961, p. 118 in this volume).

2. Following seven hours of closed-door negotiations, the Albany Movement agreed on 18 December
to cease all protests in return for the immediate release of protesters on bond, an opportunity to present their demands to the Albany City Commission, and police compliance with the ICC's ruling against
segregated bus and rail terminals. King's bond was signed by William G. Anderson (Bill Shipp, "Albany,
Negroes Seal Peace; Prisoners to Go Free on Bail," *Atlanta Constitution*, 19 December 1961; "Dr. King Is
Freed," *New York Times*, 19 December 1961). Attorney General Kennedy called Albany mayor Asa Kelley
to congratulate him on reaching a settlement "under difficult conditions" (Shipp, "Albany, Negroes
Seal Peace," 19 December 1961). Before leaving Albany, King told a crowd gathered at Shiloh Baptist
Church that "it wasn't necessary" for him to remain in jail since one of his goals, the desegregation of
bus terminals and train stations, had been achieved. In addition, King did not want "to stand in the way
of meaningful negotiations," by remaining in jail. King also denied rumors of a rift between SCLC and
the Albany Movement leadership (Shipp, "Albany, Negroes Seal Peace," 19 December 1961; "Dr. King Is
Freed," 19 December 1961).

3. Congress passed, with strong backing from the Kennedy administration, an expansive foreign
aid program of nearly $4 billion, with $1.6 billion earmarked for military aid—several hundred million below what the administration called its "rock bottom" acceptable figure (Felix Belair, "Defense
Leaders Demand Arms Aid," *New York Times*, 9 June 1961; Belair, "Congress Votes Aid Compromise of
$3,900,000,000," *New York Times*, 27 September 1961).

PRES SCLC

DR W G ANDERSON
PRES ALBANY NON-VIOLENT MOVEMENT

RALPH D ABERNATHY
SEC OF TREAS SCLC.

PWSr. JFKWHCSF-MBJFK.

# Letter to the Editor, "Rev. M. L. King
## Clarifies Stand"

19 December 1961
Nashville, Tenn.

*In this letter published in the* Nashville Tennessean, *King writes Edward Ball,
the newspaper's editor, to refute a recent editorial claiming that King suggested
that black Americans should turn to communism or black nationalism if more
progress is not made in civil rights.*[1] *King disputes the statement, insisting he said:
"There can be no doubt that if the problem of racial discrimination is not solved in
the not too distant future, some Negroes, out of frustration, discontent, and despair
will turn to some other ideology." King continues: "How anyone can take this
analysis of an actual situation on my part and interpret it as advocacy of turning
to a new ideology is a mystery to me." He concludes that "I only advocate adhering
to an ideology as old as the insights of Jesus of Nazareth and as meaningful as the
techniques of Mohandas K. Gandhi."*

To the Editor:

It is very seldom that I attempt to answer the numerous criticisms and misinterpretations of my work and ideas. However, a misinterpretation which appeared in your paper a few days ago is so glaring that I feel compelled to answer it.

In an editorial entitled "Dr. King Does His Cause a Dis-Service" you gave the impression that I had advocated that the Negro turn to a new ideology in his struggle for freedom and human dignity—the ideology being either communism or the Muslim movement.

Such an idea is so far out of harmony with my general thinking that I am sure

---

1. On 29 November the *Nashville Tennessean* published the editorial "Mr. King Does His Cause a Disservice." Per King's request, Ball published King's entire letter in the newspaper (King to Ball, 14 December 1961). King wrote a similar letter to Joseph B. Cumming, *Newsweek's* Atlanta bureau chief, after an article with the same claims was published in the magazine ("The Inside Story," *Newsweek*, 11 December 1961; King to Cumming, 22 December 1961). *Newsweek* did not publish King's letter.

many people will wonder why I even take the time to answer it. Maybe I should give you just a little background of the situation that led to the false impressions given by several news channels.

I was appearing on a television program called "Open Circuit" in Cleveland, Ohio in which I was called upon to answer questions which came from the general public.[2] One of the questions that came in was: "If the Negro does not receive freedom within a certain period of time, will he turn to communism or some other movement such as the Muslim movement?"

My answer was simply this:

"There can be no doubt that if the problem of racial discrimination is not solved in the not too distant future, some Negroes, out of frustration, discontent, and despair will turn to some other ideology. However, it is amazing and commendable that so few have turned to the Communist movement in spite of extreme proselytizing on the part of the Communists. I think this can be attributed to the fact that the vast majority of Negroes have found a ray of hope in the framework of American democracy."[3]

How anyone can take this analysis of an actual situation on my part and interpret it as advocacy of turning to a new ideology is a mystery to me. Certainly I would not be true to the facts if I gave the impression that some Negroes would not turn to new ideologies such as the Muslim movement and even communism if the problem of racial discrimination is not solved.

The week before I appeared on the television program in Cleveland it was reported in the press that one of the most brilliant Negro scholars in America had joined the Communist party, and many authorities estimate that the Muslim movement has a following of more than 75,000.[4] In a real sense, the growth of this movement is symptomatic of the deeper unrest, discontent and frustration of many Negroes because of the continued existence of racial discrimination.

To acknowledge this basic fact is not to advocate turning to the movement or justify its validity. Suffice it to say that I can see no greater tragedy befalling the Negro than a turn to either communism or Black Nationalism as a way of out of the present dilemma. It is my firm conviction that communism is based on an ethical relativism, a metaphysical materialism, a crippling totalitarianism, and a denial of freedom which I could never accept.

Moreover, the Black Nationalism is based on an unrealistic and sectional perspective that I have condemned both publicly and privately. It ends up substituting the tyranny of black supremacy for the tyranny of white supremacy.

I have always contended that we as a race must not seek to rise from a position of disadvantage to one of advantage, thus subverting justice. Our aim must always

---

2. The show aired on 26 November 1961.

3. An article in the *Cleveland Call and Post* reported that King said that if segregation is not eradicated, the Black Muslims may "pull the rug from under responsible Negro leadership" (Charles Price, "Dr. King Attacks Muslims," 2 December 1961).

4. The Communist Party announced on 22 November that black activist and scholar W. E. B. DuBois had become a member of the group (Peter Kihss, "Dr. W. E. B. DuBois Joins Communist Party at 93," *New York Times*, 23 November 1961).

be to create a moral balance in society where democracy and brotherhood will be a reality for all men.

May I say in conclusion that the Negro is American in culture, language, and loyalty and I am convinced that the vast majority of us will continue to struggle with the weapons of love and non-violence to establish a better social order. Fortunately, we are making significant strides, and with such progress being made I am confident that the number of Negroes turning to other ideologies will continue to remain relatively small.

I hope this clears up my thinking, and I am sorry that the public has been given the impression that I have advocated that the Negro turn to a new ideology. I only advocate adhering to an ideology as old as the insights of Jesus of Nazareth and as meaningful as the techniques of Mohandas K. Gandhi.

MARTIN LUTHER KING, JR.,
41 Exchange Place, S.E.
Atlanta, Ga.

PD. *Nashville Tennessean*, 19 December 1961.

# To O. Clay Maxwell

20 December 1961
[*Atlanta, Ga.*]

*After being stripped of the vice presidency of the National Sunday School and Baptist Training Union Congress (BTU) due to his support of Gardner Taylor's failed bid for the presidency of the NBC, King declines the BTU president's offer to attend the upcoming executive committee meeting. He states that continuing to protest against his removal "would make me look little rather than big, and my involvement in the struggle for the rights of my people must always keep me above the level of littleness."[1]*

The Rev. O. Clay Maxwell
114 West 120th Street
New York 27, New York

---

1. Maxwell's offer was made "on the basis of the fact that the Congress elected you for the period to expire in June, 1962" (Maxwell to King, 14 December 1961). In his memoir, NBC president J. H. Jackson claimed that while he was not personally opposed to King keeping his position, the Board of Directors voted on 9 September 1961 to strip King of his rank "because of the type of militant campaign carried on against his own denomination and his own race" (Jackson, *A Story of Christian Activism: The History of the National Baptist Convention, U.S.A., Inc.* [Nashville: Townsend Press, 1980], pp. 483–484, 486; see also King to J. H. Jackson, 10 September 1961, and Jackson to King, 12 September 1961, pp. 278–279 and 281–282 in this volume, respectively).

My Dear Friend Dr. Maxwell:

Thank you for your very kind letter of December 14. As you probably know, I was just getting out of jail that day and I can think of no-one that I would like to hear from more than you after a brief sojourn in a very mean Georgia prison.[2] The Movement is still moving and we are still trying to carry on even when it means suffering and sacrifice in order to solve this big problem which faces America.

I am very happy that you raised the question with me concerning the Congress. I had intended writing you a long, long time ago to share with you some of my ideas. First, I should say that it came as a real disappointment to me to discover that I had been removed from my position as Vice President in such an undemocratic manner.[3] I had come to the point of really loving the Congress and cherishing the relationship I had with you. This was why I stretched a point to be at almost every meeting of the Executive Committee and the Executive Board, and to stay through all of the sessions of the Congress itself, even though this meant a great sacrifice in terms of my man-killing schedule.[4] It was a sacrifice that I enjoyed making and I will always remember the creative moments we spent together in the Congress.

Now that Dr. Jackson has seen fit to move me, I do not feel that I am of the temperament to put up a struggle at this point.[5] I think it may give the impression that I am fighting to maintain an office. Wherever I can serve my denomination, I will gladly do it, but I do not think I should do it by seeking to force myself in. So I have decided to accept the decision of Dr. Jackson and the Board as final. Many people feel that there should be some type of protest in Hot Springs and in Denver since I was elected by the people in St. Louis.[6] I am not altogether opposed to this, for I think that Dr. Jackson will continue his un-Christian, unethical and dictatorial tactics as long as no-one openly oposes him. But I could not in all good conscience lead such a protest. It would make me look little rather than big, and my involvement in the struggle for the rights of my people must always keep me above the level of littleness. I do plan to be in Denver and I have no intention of severing my relationship with the Congress. I will simply attend as an ordinary delegate.

It goes without saying that our friendship is larger than the Congress and my being removed from the position of Vice President will, in no way, lessen our personal relationship. I consider you and Mrs. Maxwell among the most dedicated and royal people I have ever met.[7] If I can ever be of assistance to you in the Congress, or

2. King was released from jail in Americus on 18 December 1961.

3. Washington, D.C., area pastors and members of the NBC wrote to Maxwell protesting the "undemocratic removal" of King from the BTU (Baptist Pastors and Lay Leaders of the NBC to Maxwell, 9 October 1961).

4. Maxwell earlier thanked King for the contributions that King had "been making across the years" to attend the BTU meetings and help plan its conferences (Maxwell to King, 26 July 1961).

5. J. Pius Barbour had previously pushed King to challenge his removal from the leadership of the BTU, noting that the NBC had no "legal rights" to remove him (Barbour to King, 14 September 1961, p. 283 in this volume).

6. The NBC Board of Directors met annually in Hot Springs, Arkansas. The 1961 convention was held in St. Louis, and the 1962 convention was scheduled for 18–24 June 1962 in Denver.

7. King refers to Maxwell's wife, Lillie.

any other area, please feel free to call on me. You have been a real personal inspiration to me and I should say a real spiritual father.

Please give my best regards to Mrs. Maxwell. I hope for you a most Joyous Christmas and a New Year packed with meaningful fulfillment. I look forward to seeing you when I am in New York. Incidently, you mention my not getting in touch with you when I am in your city.[8] I must say that I walways come to New York intending to talk with you but my schedule is usually so crowded that I end up running to the airport at break-neck speed. My visits to New York are usually very brief, sometimes only twelve or fifteen hours long. I am very seldom there more than a day. But I do plan to get in touch with you soon.

May God continue to bless you in all of the great work that you are doing.

Sincerely yours,
Martin Luther King, Jr.

Km

TLc. MLKJP-GAMK: Box 15.

---

8. Maxwell wrote in his 14 December 1961 letter, "I told your Father that I was just a bit surprised that you could be in New York so often and I not hear from you."

# From Nicholas W. Raballa

20 December 1961
Westport, Conn.

*A Kenyan exchange student financially supported by King and SCLC asks King for money and comments on his experience living in the North.[1] Raballa later thanked King for sending fifty dollars.[2]*

Dear Rev. King Jr.

I hope this letter finds at home. I was wondering if it would be possible for you to

---

1. At the request of Kenyan nationalist leader Tom Mboya, King arranged in 1959 for Dexter Avenue Baptist Church and SCLC to support Raballa, who was one of a group of eighty-one Kenyan students flown to the United States to attend American colleges and universities (see King to Tom Mboya, 8 July 1959, in *Papers* 5:242–243). By 1961 King was no longer paying for Raballa's tuition, but promised to send funds "from time to time" (Dora E. McDonald to Raballa, 14 November 1961). Nicholas Wandia Raballa (1931–1996), born in Samia, Kenya, attended local Catholic mission schools. Raballa enrolled at Tuskegee Institute in 1959, and in the fall of 1961, he transferred to the University of Bridgeport. Raballa graduated from Hope College in 1965 with a B.A. in political science and became a lawyer in Kenya in 1977.

2. Raballa to King, 30 January 1962, pp. 376–377 in this volume.

send me some more money as I have exhausted the $50 you sent last including my savings from earnings in summer. I do get some assistance in the neighbourhood like rides apart from the board and lodging and this is why things have not been so extreme with me.

It provides deep experience living in this apparently exclusively sophisticated community but nonetheless our differences are imminent although we do hold them to a simmering ebb and dare not drive them to an obvious division.

I am following the trend of events there with much interest and deep concern. That certain legislations should be operative locally and not statewide or nationwide is [*word illegible*] of the hipocrisy inherent in this democratic nation.

Wishing you and every one nice Christmas and happy new year

Yours sincerely
[*signed*] N.W. Raballa

AHLS. MLKJP-GAMK: Box 20.

# To Herbert H. Eaton

21 December 1961
[*Atlanta, Ga.*]

*Following his release from jail, King thanks his successor at Dexter Avenue Baptist Church for a letter of concern.[1] He tells Eaton that although the agreement reached in Albany was less than he hoped for it was "a real victory for the Negro community."*

The Rev. Herbert H. Eaton
Dexter Avenue Baptist Church
454 Dexter Avenue
Montgomery 4, Alabama

Dear Herb:

This is just a note to thank you for your very kind letter of recent date. I am now a free man again after a brief sojourn in a rather depressing Georgia jail. While we did not achieve all that we had anticipated in the Albany situation, I think it was a real victory for the Negro community. Your encouraging words were most inspiring. Such moral support is of inestimable value for the continuance of my humble efforts.

---

1. In his letter, Eaton wrote: "We sang the song of faith 'Fight the good fight with all thy might! Christ is thy strength, and Christ thy right;' in dedication to you and all of the freedom fighters who now are facing the battle lines throughout the country" (Eaton to King, 20 December 1961). King was arrested in Albany on 16 December and released two days later.

sorN

Please extend my warm best wishes to all of the members of Dexter. I hope for you a most joyous Christmas and a New Year packed with meaningful fulfillment.

Wish every good wish, I am,

Sincerely yours,
Martin Luther King, Jr.

Km

TLc. MLKJP-GAMK: Box 8.

# From Hazel R. Gregory

21 December 1961
Montgomery, Ala.

*MIA secretary Gregory thanks the Kings for their $25 donation to the organization.*[1]

Dr. and Mrs. M. L. King, Jr.
563 Johnson Avenue, N.E.
Atlanta, Georgia

Dear Friends:

Thank you very kindly for your recent contribution in the amount of twenty-five dollars ($25.00).

We, here at the MIA, will always miss your presence. There is still much to be done in the freedom struggle and we must not give us now. We are very proud of the stand taken in Albany. Maybe in the not too distant future, we will have the courage here in Montgomery to sit-in, stand-in or stay-out.

We wish for you and the family a most joyous holiday season.

Very sincerely,
[*signed*]
Hazel R. Gregory

Enclosure: Receipt #11790

TLS. MLKJP-GAMK: Box 16.

---

1. Hazel Robinson Gregory (1920–2011), a native of Montgomery, worked as a clerk at St. Jude Catholic Hospital before being hired as secretary of the MIA in 1956. After nearly ten years with the MIA, Gregory retired in 1966. She also worked for the Alabama Department of Corrections and for the Montgomery Board of Education.

# To Evelyn R. Spraitzar

# To Evelyn R. Spraitzar

29 December 1961
[*Atlanta, Ga.*]

*King responds to a student's request for a "Southern Minister's comment" on the Freedom Rides.[1] He praises the rides for remaining "nonviolent to the core" and adds: "I think it has done a great deal to add to the vitality of American Democracy."*

Mrs. Evelyn R. Spraitzar
1 Joanna Way
Chatham, New Jersey

Dear Mrs. Spraitzar:

I have just come across your letter asking me to comment on the Freedom Rides. As you probably realize, I consider the Freedom Ride Movement one of the most significant events in our struggle for freedom and human dignity. It had tremendous social value because it served to point up to the nation the fact of injustices and indignities the Negro still confront in inter-state travel. In a most dramatic manner, it brought out the fact that segregation is still the Negro's burden and America's shame. Beyond this, the movement brought about real practical achievements. As a result of the Freedom Rides, a firm ICC ruling came into being declaring all segregated facilities illegal in inter-state travel. I am happy to say that almost all of the cities in the south have complied with this decision. There are just a few scattered communities holding out, and it is only a matter of time before they will have to comply.

The most magnificent thing about the Freedom Ride Movement is that it has been nonviolent to the core. The Freedom Riders have been willing to accept physical violence without retaliating. And they have willingly gone to jail and suffered inconveniences in order to make their witness know. It is only natural that many white southerners would be against this movement. Their criticisms run from the absurd statement that the movement is Communist inspired to the rather subtle argument that the end sought is fine but the methods used are bad. All of these arguments are groundless and serve as highly colored excuses for those who really want to maintain the status quo. In the meantime, the movement continues, and I think it has done a great deal to add to the vitality of American Democracy.

---

1. Spraitzar was writing a report on the rides for a social psychology class (Spraitzar to King, 1 December 1961). Evelyn Ruth Spraitzar (1920– ), born in Somerville, Alabama, graduated from St. Vincent's Nursing School in Birmingham in 1940, and served as a nurse in the U.S. Army during World War II. After the war, Spraitzar worked in a number of hospitals and nursing homes. In 1973 she moved to Boston, where she worked at the Jamaica Plains Veterans Hospital and attended Boston College, receiving a B.A. in psychology in 1982.

Sincerely yours,
Martin Luther King, Jr.

Km

TLc. MLKJP-GAMK: Box 10.

# To Audrey V. Mizer

29 December 1961
[*Atlanta, Ga.*]

*During a Q&A session following a speech at the Freedom Forum in Schenectady,
New York on 9 October, King called for the United Nations (U.N.) to admit the
People's Republic of China (PRC).*[1] *In a 3 December 1961 letter to King, Mizer,
a realtor from Coshocton, Ohio, disagreed with King, claiming that China was
starving its people in order to produce enough heroin "to drug the world."*[2]
*Defending his comment, King insists he does not endorse China's human rights
abuses but points out the "realistic recognition" that universal disarmament is
unlikely if China remains outside the U.N. King adds: "It is an old saying that
one can better watch his enemy at close range."*

Mrs. Audrey V. Mizer
170 Park Avenue
Coshocton, Ohio

Dear Mrs. Mizer:

I have just come across your letter raising some questions concerning my position
on admitting Red China to the United Nations. Let me assure you that my advocacy
of admitting Red China to the U.N. is not to be construed as endorsement of the
many brutal and vicious things done by the government of China. It simply grows
out of my realistic recognition of the fact that disarmament will be meaningless as

---

1. "U.S. Negro Urges UN Seat for Peking," *Christian Science Monitor*, 11 October 1961. The Freedom
Forum bought notable lecturers to spur interest in contemporary civic and educational topics. King
had earlier expressed similar sentiments about China in a letter to supporter Ingeborg Teek-Frank
(23 December 1959 in *Papers* 5:346–347). In 1971, the United States recognized the PRC as China's sole
representative.

2. Mizer referenced a *Christian Economics* article inserted in the *Congressional Record* by Ohio con-
gresswoman Frances Bolton (Lawrence Sullivan, "Dope—Red China's Secret Weapon," 13 December
1960, in U.S. Congress, House, *Congressional Record*, 87th Cong., 1st sess., 1961, Vol. 107, pt. 2, 2272–2273).
Audrey Virginia Mizer (1890–1968) was born in Bakersville, Ohio. She became the first woman realtor
in the town, serving as vice president of the local district's realtors association and also on the state's Real
Estate Board of Examiners. Mizer was also a charter member with the local Young Women's Christian
Association and the Business and Professional Women's Club.

long as the largest nation in the world is not somehow brought under the scrutiny of Jan
the agency of disarmament. It is an old saying that one can better watch his enemy at 1962
close range. Therefore, it is my contention that we will only be able to deal with the
inhuman and brutal methods of the government of Communist China by bringing
it to the point where it has to sit down and negotiate with the nations of the world.

I know this is a very touchy subject and one packed with emotional content. But
I do think sonner or later we must think through this problem in a very sober and
realistic manner.

Very sincerely yours,
Martin Luther King, Jr.

Km

TLc. MLKJP-GAMK: Box 61.

## "Gandhi and the World Crisis: A Symposium"

January 1962
New Delhi, India

*Seeking to launch a new symposium for* Gandhi Marg, *the journal's editor G.
Ramachandran requested a statement from King on how Gandhian nonviolent
direct action can "compel Governments to commit themselves unreservedly to
total disarmament without delay and hesitation."[1] King's contribution to the
symposium appeared in the magazine's January 1962 edition.*

*Non-violent direct action must not be seen as merely a method to be used in conflicts within
nations, but as a method which can be creatively used to resolve conflicts among the power blocs
in the world today. . . .*

. . .

The civilized world stands on the brink of nuclear annihilation. No longer can
any sensible person talk glibly about preparation for war. The present crisis calls
for sober thinking, reasonable negotiation and moral commitment. More than
ever before the Gandhian method of non-violent direct action must be applied in
international affairs. This method must not be seen as merely a method to be used

---

1. Ramachandran to King, 6 December 1961. Ramachandran was also secretary of the Gandhi
Smarak Nidhi, a sponsor of King's 1959 trip to India. For more on their relationship, see Ramachandran
to King, 27 December 1958, in *Papers* 4:552–553; King to Ramachandran, 19 May 1959, in *Papers* 5:211–212.
At the request of Norman Cousins and Clarence Pickett, co-founders of the National Committee for a
Sane Nuclear Policy, King supported a ban on nuclear testing in 1958 when he allowed the organization
to use his name in an advertisement published in the *New York Herald Tribune* (Cousins and Pickett to 359
King, 9 March 1958, in *Papers* 4:379–380).

in conflicts within nations. It must be seen as a method which can be creatively used to resolve conflicts among the power blocs in the world today. Moreover, it must be used to arouse the conscience of these nations on the whole question of disarmament. Through such non-violent demonstrations as sit-ins, stand-ins and picketing, the leaders of the Western Powers and the Soviet Union must be reminded of the dark night of destruction which hovers over all of us. Without this kind of non-violent direct action, mankind may well come to an untimely grave on this planet. The choice is no longer between violence and non-violence, it is either non-violence or non-existence.

PD. *Gandhi Marg* 6 (January 1962): 23–24.

# To Roy Wilkins

3 January 1962
Atlanta, Ga.

*Following the 1 January tribute in honor of Wilkins's thirty years of service to the NAACP, King offers him his congratulations.[1] Wilkins replied on 11 January 1962.[2]*

ROY WILKINS, NAACP
20 WEST 40 ST NY

AS A RESULT OF BEING OUT OF THE OFFICE TWO WEEKS I TOTALLY FORGOT THE TRIBUTE IN HONOR OF YOUR 50 YEARS OF DEDICATED SERVICE IN THE FIGHT FOR FREEDOM. PLEASE ACCEPT MY BELATED CONGRATULATIONS YOU HAVE PROVED TO BE ONE OF THE GREAT LEADERS OF OUR TIME THROUGH YOUR EFFICIENCY AS AN ADMINISTRATOR YOUR GENUINE HUMANITARIAN CONCERN AND YOUR UNSWERVING DEVOTION TO THE PRINCIPLES OF FREEDOM AND HUMAN DIGNITY YOU HAVE CARVED FOR YOURSELF AND IMPERISHABLE NICHE IN THE ANNALS OF CONTEMPORARY HISTORY MAY GOD CONTINUE TO BLESS YOU IN YOUR SIGNIFICANT WORK AND MAY THE NEW YEAR BRING OUR WHOLE NATIONAL CLOSER TO GOAL OF DEMOCRACY AND BROTHERHOOD THAT YOU HAVE WORKED SO UNTIRINGLY TO ACHIEVE

MARTIN LUTHER KING JR

PWSr. NAACPP-DLC.

---

1. Wilkins began his career with the NAACP as chief assistant to executive secretary Walter White. When White died in 1955, Wilkins succeeded him.

2. Wilkins wrote: "There can be no doubt that victory in our cause will be achieved when we note the emergence of inspirational leaders like yourself who have fired the conscience of the nation and the world in this issue."

4 January 1962
*[Atlanta, Ga.]*

*In response to Pamp's request, King agrees that Vinoba Bhave, a disciple of*
*Gandhi, whom King met in 1959, is worthy of a Nobel Peace Prize.[1] King calls*
*Bhave a humanitarian who "embodies the true spirit of Mahatma Gandhi*
*probably more than anyone alive today."*

Mr. Oke G. Pamp
603 S. Batavia Avenue
Batavia, Illinois

Dear Mr. Pamp:

I am very happy to join you and many others in recommending Vinoba Bhave for
the Nobel Peace Prize. I can think of very few, if any, persons alive today who have
given as much of their energy and labors to achieve peace than Vinoba Bhave. He
is a humanitariam of the first magnitude. His genuine humanitarian concern, his
complete unselfishness, and his unswerving devotion to the principles of justice and
freedom conjoin to make him superbly qualified to receive the Nobel Peace Prize.
He embodies the true spirit of Mahatma Gandhi probably more than anyone alive
today. For all of these reasons, I would like to give him an unqualified recommendation for the Nobel Peace Prize.

Sincerely yours,
Martin Luther King, Jr.

Km

TLc. MLKJP-GAMK: Box 18.

---

1. Pamp told King he sent similar requests to other notable leaders such as Martin Niemöller,
Eleanor Roosevelt, Karl Menninger, and Norman Cousins (Pamp to King, 17 December 1961). Scientist
Linus Pauling received the 1962 Nobel Peace Prize for his efforts to ban worldwide nuclear testing.
During his March 1959 trip to India, King met with Vinoba twice, calling the Indian leader "one of
the most moving personalities that I have met" (King to Robert M. Bartlett, 3 April 1959; see also
Introduction in *Papers* 5:9–10 and "Dr. Martin Luther King with Vinoba," *Bhoodan* 3 [18 March 1959]:
369–370). Pamp lived in Batavia, Illinois, and frequently wrote letters to the editors of several Chicago
newspapers.

# To David Johnson

9 January 1962
[*Atlanta, Ga.*]

*King gives Johnson, a senior at Ball State Teachers College in Muncie,*
*Indiana, suggestions for leading an integration campaign on his campus.*[1]
*King recommends contacting the local press and encourages Johnson's efforts:*
*"Committed persons, like yourself, are making a definite contribution to the*
*moral strength of our nation when you concern yourself with such matters."*[2]

Mr. David Johnson
307 N. Tillotson
Muncie, Indiana

Dear Mr. Johnson:

I am very pleased that you feel concerned about the complete integration of your campus to the extent that you want to take some positive steps toward accomplishing this end. Negro students suffer severe psychological damage in such a partially integrated set-up. These campuses are the source of much of the racial bitterness which is growing in the young intellectual class. Committed persons, like yourself, are making a definite contribution to the moral strength of our nation when you concern yourself with such matters.

Your course of action seems to be quite sound. It was right and proper that you consult the campus officials first.[3] I think a second course of action might be to docu-

---

1. Johnson wrote to King seeking advice on how to challenge local segregation practices (Johnson to King, 22 November 1961). While Ball State was officially desegregated, black students who lived off-campus could only live in the black section of Muncie six to twelve miles away from campus. In spring 1961, Johnson met with veterans of the Greensboro, North Carolina, sit-ins, and organized an interracial student group, which put pressure on local restaurants to change their unofficial policy of barring black students unaccompanied by white friends (David Johnson, Interview by King Papers Project staff, 20 February 2009). David Wolcott Johnson (1940– ), grew up near Muncie, Indiana, and attended Ball State Teachers College from 1958–1962. Johnson had met King while working as a student staff member at the American Baptist Assembly in the summer of 1959. Johnson was one of two recipients of the 1962 Russell Bull Scholarship, awarded by the United Packinghouse Workers of America to college students for their civil rights work. After graduating with a B.S. in English, Johnson earned an M.A. (1964) and Ed.D. (1966) in social psychology from Columbia University and was involved with SNCC, teaching black history at a freedom school in Harlem and assisting with preparations for the 1964 Mississippi Freedom Summer project.

2. By the time King responded, the administration and local restaurants had already complied with the student group's demands (Johnson, Interview by KPP staff).

3. Johnson described the Ball State administration as willing to work on integration, but were "extremely anxious not to have the slightest conflict with the community." The administration maintained separate housing lists based on race because it insisted that students did not desire to live in integrated conditions. The student group refuted the administration's claim by finding white families willing to house black students and students willing to have a black roommate (Johnson, Interview by KPP staff).

ment the situation as to exactly how many Negro students are there, how many have tried to secure residence at certain places, etc. You might then contact the press of Muncie. A particularly crusading journalist might accomplish more than demonstrations, for he is able to bring this particular injustice before the public eye in such a way that the conscience of the community might be quickened to action.[4]

The Negro students themselves must be ready to take some action also. Southern Negro and white students have been quite effective in dramatically protesting the inequities of this partial democracy.

You might also write to The Rev. William Coffin, Chaplain, Yale University, New Haven, Connecticut. They have done a splendid job at Yale in this respect.[5] He will certainly be able to give you some advice concerning desegregation of college communities.

Very truly yours,
Martin Luther King, Jr.

Km

TLc. SCLCR-GAMK: Box 63.

---

4. As past editor of the *Ball State News*, the school newspaper, Johnson had ready access to the campus press. The student group threatened both negative press coverage and demonstrations to compel campus administration to integrate (Johnson, Interview by KPP staff).

5. William Sloane Coffin was the chaplain of Yale University from 1958 to 1975. Yale was among the first Ivy League schools to alter their admission standards in respect to race. During the 1961–1962 school year, the university began recruiting academically qualified black students from specific high schools.

# Stanley D. Levison to the Editor of *Time* Magazine

11 January 1962
New York, N.Y.

*Levison questions* Time *magazine's slant in its 12 January 1962 article that claimed student activists had accused King of "status seeking."*[1] *He argues that the article is biased and that King's "unique self sacrifice" and "courage of conviction and deed" are unparalleled.*

---

1. "Confused Crusade," *Time*, 12 January 1962, p. 15. NAACP executive secretary Roy Wilkins also sent a letter to the editor of *Time* in which he dispelled rumors of discord between the major civil rights organizations, namely SCLC, NAACP, SNCC, and CORE (Wilkins to Editor of *Time* magazine, 10 January 1962).

Editor of Time Magazine
Time & Life Building
Rockefeller Center
New York 20, New York

Dear Sir:

In your story on "Races" in the January 12th issue, some anonymous students are quoted as critizing Dr. Martin Luther King for status seeking in taking offices in a white building in Atlanta; for failing to go to jail in Mississippi; and for not remaining in jail long enough in Albany, Ga.[2]

Ordinary fairness to Dr. King would require that a reasonable balance of facts be presented. Certainly, if Dr. King is status seeking by moving his organizations offices to an all white building, it is curious for his critic to question how long he remains in jail. Status seekers do not generally go to jail, even for limited periods. Ignored by the comment is the fact that in moving to downtown Atlanta a new front of segregation was breached.

Beyond this, and of more importance, the unidentified critic seeks to discredit Dr. King for insufficient jail internment. Dr. King is the only major civil rights leader in the country who has been in jail every year in the past five years and during the past year, more than once.[3]

If this were not enough to establish his unique self sacrifice, it should be remembered that at the height of the tension of the Freedom Rides, after bloodthirsty gangs had brutally beaten the first group of Riders, Dr. King went to Montgomery, Alabama and was beseiged by a mob of more than a thousand, who attempted to burn down the church in which he was speaking.[4] His coolness under fire was an inspiring example of leadership courage which should evoke admiration and respect from any fair minded person, uninfluenced by envy.

It is also noteworthy that as recently as last month in Indianapolis, threats were made to bomb the hall in which he was speaking (to raise money for the movement),

---

2. According to the article, there was an apparent split among the "leading Negro civil rights groups," namely between King's SCLC and SNCC members who began to "turn against" King after he declined to participate in the Freedom Rides. The students expressed frustration that "King is far more interested in making speeches across the U.S. than in head-on action." Tensions were further exacerbated after SCLC relocated to new offices at 41 Exchange Place in Atlanta. Although the realtor had told King that facilities in the building were desegregated, King and his staff were denied service in the restaurant on the ground floor. Other occupants of the building joined King in trying to desegregate the restaurant, but the owner refused. Additionally, the students were disappointed when in December 1961, King was arrested in Albany along with over 250 other protesters and, rather than spend Christmas in jail as he had promised, he was bailed out. For more on King's efforts to desegregate SCLC's new office building and the bailout following his December 1961 arrest in Albany, see King to Benjamin J. Massell, 9 June 1962, and King, Anderson, and Abernathy to John F. Kennedy, 17 December 1961, pp. 470–473 and 349–350 in this volume, respectively.

3. In his 10 January 1962 letter to the editor of *Time*, Wilkins also defended King's jail record: "TIME's paragraph hand-off on Dr. Martin Luther King is typical of its weakness for the pat phrase and the neat niche at any cost. If jailings are the hallmark of leadership, Dr. King's record has been clear."

4. See King, Address at Freedom Riders Rally at First Baptist Church, 21 May 1961, and King, Statement Delivered at Freedom Riders Rally at First Baptist Church, 21 May 1961, pp. 227–231 and 231–232 in this volume, respectively.

and again he defied the terrorists and completed his speech.[5] Finally, it is still fresh in memory that his home was twice bombed, once when his children and wife were asleep there.[6]

Ironically, there are those who have argued that Dr. King is so extraordinarily self sacrificing he must be seeking martyrdom, while now a new voice charges that he avoids sacrifice. He is indeed damned if he does and damned if he does not.

Fortunately, facts are more eloquent than words, and our nation can well be proud of a man whose courage of conviction and deed is unequalled in our day.

Very truly yours,
Stanley D. Levison

TLc. SCLCR-GAMK: Box 36.

---

5. King was accompanied by a police guard during his 24 November 1961 visit to Indianapolis because threats to bomb the hall where he was speaking were sent to a local newspaper.
6. King's home in Montgomery, Alabama, was first attacked on 30 January 1956. On 27 January 1957, a bundle of dynamite was thrown onto King's porch, but it did not explode (see Introduction in *Papers* 3:10–11, and Introduction in *Papers* 4:6–7).

# "I Predict: Twenty-five Farseeing People Tell What They Hope, Fear and Imagine for 1987"

16 January 1962
New York, N.Y.

*Responding to a request from Daniel D. Mich, King offers a statement for the January 1962 issue of* Look.[1]

"I hope that world peace will have become secure, not because a balance of terror will have paralyzed mankind, but because most of the world's people will have realized that nonviolence in the nuclear age was life's last chance.[2] I hope that militarism and mass ignorance will have become ugly relics of a vain quasi-civilization.[3] I would

---

1. Mich to King, 6 July 1961. Other contributors included President John F. Kennedy, Eleanor Roosevelt, former U.S. ambassador to Italy Clare Boothe Luce, and socialist leader Norman Thomas.
2. King's draft was slightly different from the published version: "I would hope that world peace would have become secure not because a balance of frightful terror paralyzed mankind, but because a majority of the world's people, regardless of their political systems, realized that non-violence in the nuclear age was life's last chance, and no ruler anywhere was strong enough to defy this monumental truth" (King, Draft, I Predict, 4 August 1961).
3. King's draft: "I would expect a world in which poverty, race prejudice, militarism, and mass ignorance would have become ugly relics of vain quasi-civilization. I would expect the Christian era to begin" (Draft, I Predict, 4 August 1961).

expect the world to blush with shame to recall that, three decades earlier, a human being was graded by the color of his skin and degraded if that color was not white. I would expect the Christian era to begin."

PD. *Look*, 16 January 1962, p. 19.

# From Allan Knight Chalmers

18 January 1962
New York, N.Y.

*Chalmers informs King of an upcoming meeting of the Joint Consultative Council (JCC), which will focus on resolving tensions between civil rights organizations.[1] Recognizing that open communication has been established among the groups, Chalmers maintains additional steps are needed to quell issues "which could hurt the common cause." In a handwritten addendum, he stresses that King's "presence is indispensable," given the potentially negative consequences of intramovement discord. King attended the meeting in Greenwich, Connecticut, on 20–21 March.[2]*

Reverend Martin Luther King
407 Auburn Avenue N.E.
Atlanta, Georgia

Dear Martin:

I'm glad you have March 20th and 21st on your schedule for the next, and most important, meeting of the Joint Consultative Council. Informal discussions we have had with each other, at many affairs, have made it clear that the next meeting of the JCC should be a long enough one for us to get down to brass tacks in solving some of our problems of inter-organizational cooperation.[3]

---

1. Initially organized by Chalmers, the JCC was an informal gathering of prominent leaders from various national, religious, civic, and labor organizations created to address the immediate needs and overall direction of the civil rights movement in the south. King attended the first JCC meeting on 10 December 1960 at the Belmont Plaza Hotel in New York City. The group continued to meet regularly over the course of the next few years.

2. At the meeting, King pleaded for unity among the civil rights organizations and suggested a united fundraising campaign, which was not well received by NAACP representatives (SNCC, "Minutes of SNCC regional meeting," 24 March 1962).

3. By early 1962, tensions had arisen between various civil rights groups, particularly the NAACP, SCLC, SNCC, and CORE, regarding differences in philosophy, goals, and tactics. Reporting back to SNCC members about the meeting, SNCC's executive secretary James Forman commented that SNCC was "a thorn in the flesh to many of the groups." Forman also noted that NAACP leaders were concerned that their organization was being supplanted due to the creation of locally-based SCLC and CORE chapters (SNCC, "Minutes of SNCC regional meeting"). In January 1962 King responded to an SCLC donor's letter expressing hopefulness that the reports of conflicts between groups were "exaggerated." King conceded that each organization has a different approach to techniques and methods and was

We have communication well established but need to work out some solutions on dangers in the situation which could hurt the common cause.

Therefore, we have proposed for the next meeting, originally scheduled just for the 21st, that a conference beginning at suppertime (March 20th at 6:00 PM) is to be held at Seabury House in Greenwich (this is a retreat and consultation center run by the Episcopal Church). We shall be together overnight and continue until after lunch on March 21st.

In addition to yourself, I have seen the following informally at other conferences—Roy Wilkins, Oscar Lee, Bill [*William*] Oliver, Whit [*Whitney*] Young, Jim [*James*] Farmer, plus Jack Greenberg and myself—and all of us plan, definitely, to be there.[4]

Anyone may bring one other person along, but we want to make it a small concentrated group of friends who share this responsibility for the moment. Since we have to make definite reservations by name, I shall appreciate your letting me know officially that you will be there and who, if anyone, will accompany you.[5]

The cost will be $10.00 for the overnight stay, including three meals. If out of town members will notify me of their travel plans, we'll see that you get there from New York.

The agreed presence of so many, already, insures a good conference. I am very anxious that we face, with complete honesty and uninhibited frankness, some very real difficulties. Come prepared to do a job in depth.
Sincerely,
[*signed*] Allan
Dr. Allan Knight Chalmers
Executive President

AKC: jcb

{Please keep firmly in mind that this is potentially a crucial meeting and your presence is indispensible. If you are not in jail, I count on your supporting me in this.}

TALS. MCMLK-RWWL: 1.1.0.7470.

---

troubled about the media's propensity to emphasize these differences, while the "larger and more positive significance can be found in the great amount of inter-organizational cooperation that goes on many times un-noticed" (Joseph S. Clark to King, 30 December 1961; King to Clark, 16 January 1962).

4. Chalmers refers to representatives of the NAACP, National Council of Churches, United Auto Workers, National Urban League, and Congress of Racial Equality, respectively. Greenberg, like Chalmers, worked for the NAACP Legal Defense and Educational Fund.

5. King was accompanied by SCLC executive director Wyatt Tee Walker (Chalmers to King, 28 March 1962).

# To Leslie Dunbar

19 January 1962
*[Atlanta, Ga.]*

*In the wake of violence against freedom riders in the spring of 1961, the Kennedy
administration urged civil rights organizations to move away from potentially
explosive protests and toward voter registration efforts.[1] In late 1961, the Southern
Regional Council (SRC) submitted a grant request to the Taconic Foundation
seeking funding for the Voter Education Project (VEP), a tax-exempt, nonpartisan
voter registration effort to be conducted by civil rights organizations.[2] Despite
an earlier decision that no joint announcement would take place, King writes to
Executive Director Leslie Dunbar recommending that the participating civil rights
organizations hold a press conference introducing the VEP.[3] According to King,
the press conference would be a demonstration of unity that "would do much to
dispel any doubt in the minds of our supporters and counter-act the indictments
of our detractors." NAACP head Roy Wilkins opposed the idea and no press
conference was held.[4]*

Mr. Leslie Dunbar
Southern Regional Council
5 Forsyth Street, S.W.
Atlanta 3, Georgia

Dear Leslie:

This is my attempt to put into writing my suggestion made to you a few days ago
in conversation.

---

1. In a 1964 interview, Attorney General Robert Kennedy argued that voter registration would be a more effective approach to civil rights reform: "A great deal could be accomplished internally within a state if the Negroes participated in elections and voted." Kennedy also recalled trying to convince civil rights groups to focus on voter registration, suggesting that philanthropic organizations would donate money tax free (Robert F. Kennedy and Burke Marshall, Interview by Anthony Lewis, 4 December 1964).

2. Five organizations took part in the two-year program: CORE, NAACP, National Urban League, SCLC, and SNCC. The five organizations would work collaboratively to divide up geographic areas of responsibility (Dunbar to King, James Farmer, Roy Wilkins, Whitney M. Young, Wyatt Tee Walker, Charles McDew, and Timothy L. Jenkins, 13 September 1961; Dunbar to Stephen R. Currier, 10 November 1961; SCLC, "Southwide Voter Registration Prospectus," 1961). According to VEP records, its efforts helped register 551,328 people in Southern states from April 1962 through March 1964 (SRC, Press release, Results of Voter Education Project programs, 3 August 1964).

3. Leslie Wallace Dunbar (1921– ) was born in Lewisburg, West Virginia, and graduated from Cornell University with an M.A. (1946) and a Ph.D. (1948). Following graduation, he taught political science at Emory University from 1948–1951 and at Mt. Holyoke College from 1955–1958. He then moved to SRC as director of research until 1961, when he became executive director. Dunbar served four years as executive director of SRC before becoming executive director of the Field Foundation, a position he held until 1980. He has published several books addressing social policy toward the poor and serves on the board of directors of several nonprofits.

4. Wilkins objected to the press conference because the possibility of misinterpretations about the project exceeded the potential benefit of a press conference (Wilkins to Dunbar, 24 January 1962). The SRC eventually announced the start of the VEP in a 29 March 1962 press release.

It is my sincere feeling that my earlier comment that a press conference, held in conjunction with the public announcement of the Southwide Drive, might be beneficial in some way. I am more persuaded now due to the reports in the various news media that there is 'division' and 'disunity' among the agencies.[5] This coordinated effort could get off to a tremendous start. At the same moment, the visual impact of the titular heads of the major civil rights organizations assembeled for such an announcement would do much to dispel any doubt in the minds of our supporters and counter-act the indictments of our detractors.

My final suggestion would be in the vein of suggesting that if a press conference is held, Roy Wilkins should be the spokesman for the agencies since he is the head of the senior organization involved.

I trust that this matter will be given the studied concern of all those involved.

Very truly yours,
Martin Luther King, Jr.

Km

cc: Messrs. Roy Wilkins, Wiley Branton, James Farmer, James Forman, Whitney Young.[6]

Dictated by Dr. King, but signed in his absence.

TLc. MLKJP-GAMK: Box 22.

---

5. A 12 January article in *Time* magazine asserted that there was a split and tension between the various civil rights organizations and that King had "began to lose status" among student activists for his timidity during the Freedom Rides and the Albany campaign ("Confused Crusade," p. 15). For more on the article, see Levison to the Editor of *Time* Magazine, 11 January 1962, pp. 363–365 in this volume.

6. Branton (1923–1988), a lawyer from Pine Bluff, Arkansas, who represented the students in the Little Rock school desegregation cases in 1957, served as VEP Project Director. Forman (1928–2005) was executive secretary of SNCC from 1961 until 1966. Young (1921–1971) was executive director of the National Urban League from 1961 until 1971.

# To Glenn E. Smiley

22 January 1962
[*Atlanta, Ga.*]

*King endorses Smiley's proposal for a national FOR conference of ministers to convene in March 1962. Although FOR had to postpone the conference and King was unable to speak at a later proposed October date, King addressed an interracial group of ministers a year later at the National Conference on Religion and Race.*[1]

---

1. For more on King's participation on the National Conference on Religion and Race, see King to J. Oscar Lee, 2 July 1962, pp. 493–494 in this volume.

Mr. Glenn E. Smiley
The Fellowship of Reconciliation
Box 271
Nyack, New York

Dear Glenn:

I notice that I have three letters on my desk from you.[2] My answer to each of them is long overdue. Please accept my apology for being so tardy in replying. Absence from the city, a brief sojourn in jail, and the accumulation of a flood of mail account for the delay.[3]

Let me respond first to your letter concerning the proposed meeting in Montgomery on March 13 and 14. I will give my reaction to each of your points.

1. I think it will be good to begin the meeting Tuesday night and go through Thursday.

2. I think it will be a good idea to have a processional from Dexter Avenue Baptist Church to the First Baptist Church on the opening afternoon. This would draw attention to the fact that we are there and it may also have a real spiritual impact. I would go along with having Borders of Atlanta serve as speaker for the banquet.[4]

3. I would be very glad to give the keynote address on Tuesday evening, and I think the idea of a thirty-minute concert by John Raitt would be excellent.[5] I am not sure whether Mahalia Jackson would be willing to furnish music for the reception after the evening meeting. I think she performs better in a concert before larger groups.[6]

4. I would heartily agree with the Wednesday session beginning with prayers, and the workshop having such men as Howard Thurman and Douglas Steere.[7] I would also add the name of Jim Lawson.

5. I think the idea of dividing into smaller groups and going to the local churches is an excellent one. While I am not optimistic about most of the white churches opening their doors for such a gathering, it would be well to confront their conscience with it.

---

2. Smiley sent letters on 2 November 1961, 29 November 1961, and 5 January 1962. The letter concerning the FOR conference has not been found.

3. King refers to his involvement in the Albany campaign and the three days he spent in the Sumter County Jail in Americus, Georgia, from 16–18 December.

4. William Holmes Borders was minister of Wheat Street Baptist Church in Atlanta and on SCLC's executive board.

5. Raitt, a famous Broadway singer in the 1940s and 1950s most known for his roles in "Carousel" and "The Pajama Game," had endorsed FOR's Food for China program in 1961.

6. Jackson, also known as the "Queen of Gospel," regularly performed at large-scale civil rights events such as the 1957 Prayer Pilgrimage for Freedom.

7. Thurman was a theologian and dean of Boston University's Marsh Chapel. Steere was an author and professor of philosophy and theology noted for his relief work with the American Friends Service Committee (AFSC) in Europe after World War II.

6. I am completely in accord with this suggestion. I believe we could get Dorothy Maynor, and since Dr. Sockman has retired, his schedule may allow him to appear.[8]

7. This is an excellent suggestion and would certainly be one of the most significant moves of the whole conference. I think everyone should be willing to face any physical danger that may emerge as a result of such a door-to-door confrontation.

8. I can add nothing to this suggestion. It is fine.

9. I think a concluding communion service would certainly be fitting and proper.

Let me say just a word concerning some of the other questions you raised. I think the program is quite feasible. It seems to me that we must aim high if we are going to cause this meeting to have the kind of national impact that it can well have. I think it may well prove to be one of the most creative steps in our struggle. Such a step on the part of religious leaders, both Negro and white, in the cradle of the Confederacy cannot be ignored. Of course, there may be some intimidation by the Klan and other reactionary groups in Alabama. We must also face the fact that there may be attempts at physical violence. But this is the risk that we must be willing to take in order to redeem the southern community. I can see nothing but good coming out of this proposed conference. The presence of 500 Negro and white ministers from all over the United States would probably restrain the violent element, but even if it does not, the conscience of so many millions of people all over this country would be aroused that it would be a blessing in disguise.

I am not sure whether Grover Hall would go along with a full page ad.[9] As you know, he is rather unpredictable. But if he is properly approached, I rather feel that he would go along with it.

There is one other thing that I must say, The Southern Christian Leadership Conference will certainly be delighted to serve as co-sponsor. I must admit, however, that the demands on our time are so great during this period that it will not be possible for us to do much of the planning and real leg work. We are seeking to get an intensified voter registration drive started in the south, and we are also making plans for nonviolent direct action which would tax almost all of our time.[10] But we will certainly do all that we possibly can to make it a tremendous success.

I will be happy to serve as one of the sponsors of your Shelter Program. I will also be willing to do a television interview on this issue.[11] Unfortunately, however, I am so

---

8. Maynor, a soprano soloist, founded the Harlem School of the Arts to provide affordable lessons in the arts to poor children. Ralph W. Sockman retired on 31 December 1961 after serving forty-four years as pastor at Christ Church Methodist in New York City.

9. Hall was editor of the *Montgomery Advertiser*, the city's primary newspaper.

10. On 5 April 1962, King launched the drive with the goal of doubling the number of registered black voters within two years (King, Press Release, Statement on Intensified Voter Registration Drive, 5 April 1962, pp. 433–435 in this volume).

11. Smiley had asked King if he would help sponsor FOR's Shelter for the Shelterless program and also appear in a promotional interview on television (Smiley to King, 5 January 1962). Criticizing the construction of fallout shelters to protect against nuclear attacks as not only ineffectual but also selfish in light of worldwide homeless rates, FOR sent out appeals to contributors to donate money to build housing for the poor.

involved now that I cannot give a specific time. I am trying to do some writing, get the voter registration drive started, and take a tour of our affiliates across the south. These, and other pressing responsibilities, are taking all of the time that I have at this period. As soon as I have a little let-up, I will let you know.

Very sincerely yours,
Martin Luther King, Jr.

Km

TLc. MLKJP-GAMK: Box 10.

## To Robert F. Kennedy

25 January 1962
[*Atlanta, Ga.*]

*In this telegram to the attorney general, King requests that the Justice Department monitor the safety of Fred L. Shuttlesworth, who had been jailed in Birmingham for an earlier conviction.*[1] *Although the Justice Department refused to intervene, Shuttlesworth was released on $300 bond on 1 March.*[2]

ATTORNEY GENERAL KENNEDY
DEPT OF JUSTICE

DEAR MR KENNEDY THIS AFTERNOON THE REV FRED SHUTTLESWORTH—SECRE-TARY OF THE SOUTHERN CHRISTIAN LEADERSHIP CONFERENCE SURRENDERED HIM-SELF TO THE AUTHORITIES OF BIRMINGHAM ALABAMA TO BEGIN SERVING A 90 DAY SENTENCE GROWING OUT OF THE VIOLATION OF A BUS SEATING LAW THAT HAS SINCE BEEN DECLARED UNCONSTITUTIONAL.[3] WHEREAS MR SHUTTLESWORTH DOES NOT

---

1. On 21 October 1958, Shuttlesworth surrendered to Birmingham police after leading James S. Phifer and twelve others in a protest against segregated seating practices by the Birmingham Transit Company the day before. Shuttlesworth and Phifer were fined $100 each and received ninety and sixty day sentences, respectively, for breach of the peace. During their appeal process, United States district judge Harlan Hobart Grooms ruled on 23 November 1959 that violating bus segregation laws did not constitute a breach of the peace; however, the United States Supreme Court refused to overturn the conviction on 8 January 1962 because Shuttlesworth's lawyer did not file the appeal in time.

2. In a 1 February 1962 letter to King, assistant attorney general Burke Marshall explained that "there is no basis at this time to assume that the people of Birmingham will be lawless or that the local officials will not take the necessary steps to provide for Reverend Shuttlesworth's safety." For more details on Shuttlesworth's release from jail, see King, "People in Action: Most Abused Man in Nation," 31 March 1962, pp. 429–432 in this volume.

3. On 8 November 1961, District Judge Grooms ruled in *Shuttlesworth et al. v. Gaylord et al.* (202 F. Supp. 59) that the city's public recreational facilities be desegregated. Following the verdict, Birmingham city officials drastically cut funding for recreational facilities, effectively shutting them down. Only the

SHRINK FROM JAIL-GOING, I HAVE GRAVE FEARS FOR HIS SAFETY IN THE LIGHT OF THE RECENT RASH OF BOMBINGS AND GENERAL BITTERNESS DIRECTED TOWARD THIS COURAGEOUS NON-VIOLENT LEADER[4] IT IS CLEAR THAT HUNDREDS OF SEGREGATIONISTS IN AND OUT OF JAIL WOULD LIKE NOTHING BETTER THAN TO DO BODILY HARM TO REV SHUTTLESWORTH. WE RESPECTFULLY REQUEST IMMEDIATE SURVEILANCE BY YOUR OFFICE OF THIS SITUATION AS A PRECAUTIONARY MEASURE TO INSURE HIS SAFETY

VERY TRULY YOURS

MARTIN LUTHER KING JR

PRESIDENT

SOUTHERN CHRISTIAN LEADERSHIP CONFERENCE

PHWSr. MLKJP-GAMK: Box 14.

---

Birmingham Zoo, Art Museum, Municipal Airport, Legion Field, Vulcan Park, and Woodrow Wilson Park were left operating; however, the city charged an entrance fee to cover the operating costs of the zoo, and considered leasing some of the park properties to private groups.

4. King refers to three local churches that were bombed on 16 January.

# To Gardner C. Taylor

25 January 1962
[Atlanta, Ga.]

*King congratulates Taylor on his appointment to the Brooklyn Democratic Party's executive committee and invites him to speak at an event celebrating the 75th anniversary of Ebenezer. Taylor agreed to speak, if the event was postponed to 27 May.[1]*

The Rev. Gardner Taylor
Concord Baptist Church
833 Marcy Avenue
Brooklyn 16, New York

Dear Gardner:

Pursuant to our conversation concerning the Anniversary Observance of our church, the committee has decided on the date May 20, 1962. As I said in our telephone conversation, this will be the occasion of the 75th Anniversary of the Ebenezer

---

1. Taylor to King, 29 January 1962. Ebenezer's week-long celebration from 21–27 May also featured local Atlanta pastors William Holmes Borders of Wheat Street Baptist Church and Ralph Abernathy of West Hunter Baptist Church (Ebenezer Baptist Church, Program, Seventy-fifth anniversary diamond jubilee, 21 May–27 May 1962).

Baptist Church. We are seeking to make this the greatest event that has ever taken place in these seventy-five years. Your presence and your message could do so much to climax this event. Both our members and the Atlanta community look forward to your coming. Please let me know as soon as possible whether this date is satisfactory to you, and we will make this a firm commitment.

I should say that we would want you to preach for the eleven o'clock service. This would be your only responsibility. We can offer a modest honorarium of $150.00 plus travel expenses and all other expenses incident to your visit.

I saw the article in the New York TIMES concerning your elevation to the leadership of the Democratic Party in Brooklyn. There was also a long article and a picture in the ATLANTA DAILY WORLD this morning.[2] Let me congratulate you for such a significant achievement. A good man cannot be defeated even by the conniving methods of J. H. Jackson and the shortsightedness of the National Baptist Convention.[3] May God continue to bless you in your great work.

Let me hear from you as soon as possible concerning the Anniversary.

Very sincerely yours,
(Mike)
Martin Luther King Jr.

Km
Dictated by Dr. King, but signed in his absence.

TLc. MLKJP-GAMK: Box 9.

---

2. Leo Egan, "3 of Mayor's Men Succeed Sharkey," *New York Times*, 19 January 1962; "Dr. Taylor Named to Brooklyn Demo Party," *Atlanta Daily World*, 24 January 1962. New York councilman and Brooklyn Democratic leader Joseph T. Sharkey resigned after opposing Mayor Robert Wagner's nomination for a third term in office. Taylor, along with industrialist Aaron Jacoby and banker John Lynch were appointed as a three-man council to serve in Sharkey's place until the next primary in the fall.

3. King refers to Taylor's 1961 failed bid for the presidency of the National Baptist Convention.

# To William H. Rhoades

26 January 1962
[*Atlanta, Ga.*]

*King writes the executive secretary of the American Baptist Home Mission Societies (ABHMS) regarding Ebenezer's and Ralph Abernathy's West Hunter Baptist Church's votes to join the predominantly white American Baptist Convention (ABC).[1] In his response to King, Rhoades indicated that he was "greatly pleased"*

---

1. King had previously expressed interest in joining the convention before his 1959 trip to India (King to Reuben E. Nelson, 23 March 1959, in *Papers* 5:157–158). Despite joining the ABC, King maintained

*by Ebenezer's vote to join the convention and that he hoped the new association*
*"will prove to be a source of fellowship and strength to the church."*[2] *The churches*
*were voted in during the ABC's annual convention in May.*[3]

26 Jan
1962

Dr. William H. Rhodes
164 Fifth Avenue
New York 10, New York

Dear Dr. Rhodes:

In our annual church meeting a few weeks ago, the members unanimously voted to have our church affiliate with the American Baptist Convention. This decision was made because of our awareness of the great work that your Convention is doing for Kingdom building, and our strong conviction concerning an integrated church. Although our congregation is predominantly Negro, (we have only two white members), we have never been a segregating church. I am sure that our association with the American Baptist Convention could strengthen immeasurably our position on this issue.[4] I should also mention that the West Hunter Baptist Church of this city, pastored by The Rev. Ralph D. Abernathy, formerly of Montgomery, Alabama, also voted to join the American Baptist Convention.

We would appreciate your apprising us of the necessary procedures to become affiliated with the American Baptist Convention. If it is possible to have Mr. Hansen

---

that Ebenezer would also remain affiliated with the National Baptist Convention (NBC). In 1845 the issue of slavery divided the American Baptist Home Mission Society into separate northern and southern conventions. The northern Baptists, later renamed the American Baptist Convention in 1950, had a progressive approach to dealing with civil rights and interracial relations. From 1950 to 1966, the American Baptist Convention adopted a yearly resolution regarding race relations, and in 1963, the organization passed a resolution pledging the Convention's support for King and Abernathy's efforts to maintain a nonviolent movement (Baptist Press, "Detroit Convention Condemns Race Bias," 24 May 1963). William Hosler Rhoades (1900–1970) graduated from Denison University with a bachelor's degree and the University of Toledo with a master's degree before passing the Ohio bar in 1927. During World War II, he was decorated by the Chinese Nationalist Party for his service in the United States Army Air Force. He became treasurer of the ABHMS in 1947 and served as executive secretary from 1957–1968.

2. Rhoades to King, 31 January 1962.

3. The acceptance of the two congregations was announced shortly before King addressed the convention in Philadelphia ("Many Arming in South King Warns Baptists," Philadelphia *Afro-American*, 2 June 1962; King, "The Mission to the Social Frontiers," 24 May 1962).

4. The ABC passed a resolution during its 1957 convention agreeing that "membership in each Baptist church shall be open to all people of its community regardless of their race or national origin" (Year Book of the American Baptist Convention, 1957, p. 95). The following year, the ABC issued an "Affirmation of Welcome" reiterating the convention's commitment to accepting Baptist organizations regardless of race or cultural background (ABC, "Affirmation of Welcome," 14 March 1958). In 1960 they also passed a resolution supporting the sit-ins, calling for others "to bear witness to their concern in creative techniques" (Year Book of the American Baptist Convention, 1960, p. 68). In September 1961 the ABC and SCLC partnered to give scholarships to college students involved in the civil rights movement. For more on the scholarship, see note 1, King to Ruby Doris Smith Robinson, 6 September 1961, p. 269 in this volume.

to come down and talk with our official boards, I am sure that this would be most helpful.[5]

Thank you very kindly for your cooperation.

Very sincerely yours,
Martin Luther King, Jr.

Km

TLc. MLKJP-GAMK: Box 9.

---

5. King refers to Clifford G. Hansen, the General Missionary for the South of the ABHMS. Hansen planned to meet with King in February. King, however, canceled the appointment because he was due to appear in court in Albany, Georgia (Hansen to King, 1 February 1962; King to J. Timothy Boddie, 26 February 1962).

# From Nicholas W. Raballa

30 January 1962
Westport, Conn.

*Appreciative of King's continued financial support of his education at the University of Bridgeport in Connecticut, Kenyan student Raballa regrets missing King's appearance at a local high school.[1] He also updates King on the political situation in Kenya, expressing hope that the tension between leaders Jomo Kenyatta and Tom Mboya "will subside to a peaceful and promising settlement."[2]*

Rev. M. L. King.
The Ebenezer Baptist Church
Atlanta Georgia

---

1. A month earlier, Raballa wrote King asking for money, stating that "I have exhausted the $50 you sent last including my savings from earnings in summer" (Raballa to King, 20 December 1961, p. 355 in this volume). King spoke at Central High School in Bridgeport on 15 January 1962. The event was jointly sponsored by the local Interdenominational Ministerial Alliance and the NAACP of Bridgeport and the Vicinity.

2. Kenyan president Kenyatta and African trade unionist and nationalist Mboya were active in the Kenyan independence movement. Early in their careers they worked closely together in the Kenya African National Union (KANU), the colony's first black-majority party, but Mboya became an outspoken critic of corruption in Kenyatta's government; and Kenyatta was rumored to have been involved in an assassination plot against Mboya. In May 1959 King and SCLC honored Mboya at an "African Freedom Dinner" (King, Remarks Delivered at Africa Freedom Dinner at Atlanta University, 13 May 1959, in *Papers* 5:203–204).

Dear Rev. King.

This is to acknowledge with much thanks the receipt of $50 check sent to me from your office. It is unfortunate, I was not able to meet you the last time you spoke in Bridgeport. The time you spoke I was doing a test and I made several telephone calls to contanct you in the hall but all in vain.

Some friends of mine undergoing special training at Princenton University Graduate School are anxious to meet you. I gave your address to one of them, Mr. Abraham Wabuti, who is assistant secretary to the Treasury in Kenya, to write to you directly on their behalf and explore with you their interests.

Back home things are not getting on well. There is slim hope that neither Kenyatta nor Mboya—both of whom are now tied up in an intense struggle to oust each other, will be the man to be. Whatever the case, I do hope that all will subside to a peaceeful and promising settlement.

Hoping to write again

Yours sincerely
[*signed*] N W Raballa

ALS. MLKJP-GAMK: Box 6.

## "People in Action: Turning Point of Civil Rights"

3 February 1962
New York, N.Y.

*In King's first biweekly column in the* New York Amsterdam News *he identifies two turning points in the civil rights struggle.[1] He describes the Supreme Court's 1954 decision in* Brown v. Board of Education *as the "inevitable culmination of the years of spirit-breaking legal battles." Following the legal victory came a "psychological turning point" with the wave of direct action protest, most notably the Montgomery bus boycott, the student sit-in movement of the 1960s, the Freedom Rides, and the Albany Movement. Acknowledging that the legal battles will continue, King remains optimistic that the "fight for full freedom will surely be won."*

Within the last decade, we have reached two significant turning points in the civil rights movement. The first was the legal turning point which took place on May 17,

---

1. On 15 January 1962, Clilan B. Powell, president and editor of the *New York Amsterdam News*, expressed his delight that King agreed to write the column. Powell noted that other civil rights leaders, including Lester Granger, Roy Wilkins, and Jackie Robinson, would contribute columns as well. From 1962 to 1966 King wrote articles for the newspaper highlighting his views on contemporary issues, including the efficacy of nonviolence, the state of the civil rights movement, and the role of the church in the freedom struggle.

1954, when the United States Supreme Court rendered its precedent-making school desegregation decision.

This decision was the inevitable culmination of the years of spirit-breaking legal battles fought throughout the length and breadth of these United States. This history-making decision paved the way for all future action. In effect, the Supreme Court dealt the coup de grace to the Plessy doctrine which held Negroes to be less deserving of any legal rights than any of the beasts of the field.[2]

Court decisions (rendered from no matter how a source), cannot deliver rights; they can only chart the paths along which they can be truly achieved.

## Turning Point

What was obviously indicated immediately after the May 17, 1954 decision, was a psychological turning point that would spell out, make indisputedly clear, and irrevocably permanent, the fact that Negroes were the equal of all other men.

The Negro peoples of Montgomery provided the prime impetus for this psychological change. Stung into action by the decisively defiant stand of Mrs. Rosa Park when the Montgomery city and transit authority pushed her one point past the limit of human dignity, they gathered together in a protesting boycott that fired the imagination of the entire world.[3]

Bear in mind that these were the so called "little people." These were the traditionally disenfranchised, the down trodden, the historically fearful, and historically humble.

But from somewhere within their vitals, they mustered the strength and God gave them the spirit to stand fast and stand together to defeat the forces of injustice and discrimination.

## Non Violent

Bear in mind that these were non violent, serene human instruments of decisive action who demonstrated once and for all time, the Negro's ability to animate himself and create a climate in which justice would be rendered without benefit of skin coloration.

The young people, who first participated in the sit-ins demonstrations, were still another instant of the Negro's initiative imagination in non violently challenging structures which could not be breached by routine court cases.[4]

No honest historian of the future can possibly continue the history of those who made America great and ignore the names of those young people.

---

2. The *Plessy v. Ferguson* decision of 1896 declared that public facilities could be segregated along racial lines as long as the quality of facilities was equal.

3. After Rosa Parks was arrested on 1 December 1955 for refusing to give up her seat for a white man on a city bus, the Women's Political Council organized a day-long protest of the Montgomery bus system. Motivated by the success of this boycott, the Montgomery Improvement Association (MIA) was formed to coordinate a more long-term movement. Black residents of Montgomery refused to ride the city's buses for 381 days before the U.S. District Court stated that bus segregation was unconstitutional.

4. The sit-in movement began on 1 February 1960 when four black students sat at the Woolworth's lunch counter reserved for white customers in Greensboro, North Carolina. Similar protests quickly followed along with workshops on nonviolent action, which ultimately resulted in the creation of SNCC (see Introduction in *Papers* 5:23).

The freedom rides which were also begun by the young, grew to such proportion that they eventually encompassed people of all ages, and the halt, lame and blind.

Not even the mad dogs of southern sheriffs were able to deter these brave peoples from their chosen destinations, and the bombs of the would-be murderers stopped not one Freedom Rider until it was completed, or its participants were in jail.[5]

It must be clear to even the most biased observer, that the dramatic Albany Movement protest was the climax to this phychological forward thrust.

This most recent drive by Negroes to highlight the injustices wrecked by those who, even in this enlightened day, strive to be their master, cut clear across sex, age and class lines.

It brought together in one mighty army domestics, doctors of medicine, law and philosophy to stand 700-odd strong and say, "We are willing to go to jail for our rights—because we know, deep in our hearts, we shall overcome!"[6]

The legal battles are by no means over. They will continue in every southern state, but coupled now with this indomitable spirit, the fight for full freedom will surely be won.

PD. *New York Amsterdam News*, 3 February 1962.

---

5. In May 1961, student activists began traveling on buses throughout the South, confronting segregation both on interstate buses and terminals. The riders were met with violent opposition, prompting international press coverage. The Kennedy administration eventually pressured the Interstate Commerce Commission (ICC) to ban segregation from all of their facilities. For more on the Kennedy administration's influence on the ICC ruling, see Introduction, p. 15 in this volume.

6. In late 1961, the Albany Movement, a coalition of civil rights organizations, was founded to deal with racial issues in Albany, Georgia. The movement's mission was broad in scope and its activities utilized a wide range of methods to target discrimination and segregation in a number of public arenas. For more on the founding of the Albany Movement and its goals, see Introduction, pp. 23–24 in this volume.

# Form Letter to Doctor

6 February 1962
[*Atlanta, Ga.*]

*In this form letter, King urgently requests fellow pastors to collect an offering for the financially strapped SCLC. Due largely to fundraising appeals, SCLC went from a $6,500.78 deficit at the end of November 1961 to a $4,662.78 surplus by the end of February 1962.*[1]

---

1. Ralph Abernathy, "Treasurer's Report," 1 September 1961–30 April 1962. King's appeal went out to many black churches, including Dexter Avenue Baptist Church, and the New York churches of allies Thomas Kilgore, Gardner Taylor, and O. Clay Maxwell, who boasted that his congregation of Mount Olivet Baptist Church could do much better than the requested $100 and enclosed $500 (Maxwell to King, 12 February 1962; Herbert H. Eaton to King, 12 February 1962; Kilgore to King, 19 February 1962; and Taylor to King, 20 February 1962).

Dear Doctor:

It has become necessary that I turn to you to make a very special and personal request. An emergency has arisen that we are unable to cope with at the moment and I need your immediate help. You have been sensitive to the struggle here in the Deep South and have supported the work we are doing so loyally, that it is with reluctance that I turn to you again. However, were it not for this crisis, I'm sure this letter would not be in your hands.

As you probably know, this struggle is such that there is rarely ever a chance to prepare for each eventuality. We have been thrown into serious financial arrears by several unexpected circumstances that have conjoined to place us in this dilemma.

Fred Shuttlesworth is now in the Birmingham city jail serving a 90 day sentence growing out of the violation of the bus-segregation law. None of us ever dreamed he would actually have to serve time. We had to secure additional counsel to perfect the legal steps we are taking to free him. William Kunstler, Esq., of New York City is now in our employ on this matter.[2] Mrs. Shuttlesworth is not well; to relieve both her and Fred of unnecessary anxiety, we have committed ourselves to fill his pulpit in Cincinnati in his absence.[3] SCLC is responsible for all these expenses. Trial, costs for the Freedom Ride along with attorney's fees still remain to be met. The three million dollar libel suits continue against Ralph Abernathy, Fred Shuttlesworth, Joseph Lowery and S. S. Seay, Sr.[4] The day-to-day operation must continue, but with this sudden drain on us, we cannot keep pace with program needs and field service necessary to keep the movement here in the Deep South accelerated. I would not like to see our work here bogged down because of lack of adequate funds.[5]

The only way I can see through this dilemma is to turn to a few of the men I know personally and who are dedicated to this movement and seek their help. I would not do this if the need were not so immediate.

Would you possible arrange to take an after-offering this coming Sunday in order that your people might have an opportunity to respond to this crisis that effects the entire Negro community. It would give us a tremendous boost if we could receive early next week at least $100.00 from the inner circle of men to whom I am writing. We do not want to lose the momentum that we have built up in the last several months.

My prayers and good wishes are ever with you.

---

2. Kunstler, a lawyer with the American Civil Liberties Union, worked on several cases, including defending freedom riders in Jackson, Mississippi, and Monroe, North Carolina.

3. While Shuttlesworth was in jail, his wife, Ruby, stated publicly that her husband's imprisonment "could tax my physical stamina to the very limit" (Woody L. Taylor, "Wife of Martyred Rev. Shuttlesworth Undergoing Ordeal," *Pittsburgh Courier*, 17 February 1962). During Shuttlesworth's jailing, King, Wyatt Tee Walker, SCLC executive board members C. K. Steele and Joseph Lowery, and SCLC regional representative Otis Moss, an Ohio resident, volunteered to fill Shuttlesworth's pulpit at Revelation Baptist Church in Cincinnati. Shuttlesworth had moved to Cincinnati from Birmingham on 20 August 1961.

4. See Introduction in *Papers* 5:25–26.

5. According to SCLC's treasurer report, from 1 December 1961 to 28 February 1962, legal defense for freedom riders, the Shuttlesworth case, and the libel suits cost $4,309.74 (Abernathy, "Treasurer's Report," 1 September 1961–30 April 1962).

Faithfully,                                                                                          9 Feb
Martin Luther King, Jr.                                                                              1962

MLK/dm

TLc. MLKJP-GAMK: Box 1.

## Notes on Recruitment of Volunteers

[*7 February–9 February 1962*]
[*Atlanta, Ga.*]

*In February, King began a series of trips through the South to recruit volunteers*
*for SCLC's voter registration and direct action campaigns.[1] Through these People*
*to People tours, he hoped to connect personally with African Americans in regions*
*of the South that he might not otherwise reach. These notes reflect King's thoughts*
*about his first tour through the Mississippi Delta.[2]*

The immediate aim of this tour is ~~personally~~ to recruit hundreds of volunteers
to work in our [*strikeout illegible*] intensified southwide voter registration drive and
[*strikeout illegible*] ~~enlist a small number of persons for a non-violent army that will~~
~~speahead direct actions~~ [*strikeout illegible*] enlist a small number of volunteers to serve
in [*strikeout illegible*] a nonviolent army.[3] [*strikeout illegible*] This NVA will be composed
of persons who can be on call to engage in direct action programs and who will be
[*strikeout illegible*] will be prepared for prolonged jailing when necessary.
    Along with the ecomic [*word illegible*] that the whole state of Mississippi inflicts

---

1. The direct action volunteers, also called the "nonviolent army," would be a group of on-call volunteers who would be available for mass demonstrations or open-ended jail stays (SCLC, Press release,
Martin Luther King Jr. to begin People to People program, 1 February 1962). The plan for the voter
registration campaign was discussed at SCLC's annual convention held in Nashville in September 1961.
The goal was to double the number of black voters in the South (SCLC, "Minutes of annual board meeting," 27 September 1961; "Southern Negroes Map Voter Drive," *New York Times*, 30 September 1961; King,
"Nonviolence on Tour," 17 March 1962). In December 1959, SCLC in conjunction with the NAACP had
launched a similar voter registration campaign aimed at registering over one million new black voters
by the November 1960 presidential election (Charles Moore, "Drive Launch Here Seeks Million More
Negro Voters," *Atlanta Constitution*, 29 December 1959).
2. On 7 February King began his tour in Clarksdale, Mississippi, joined by Wyatt Tee Walker and
Dorothy Cotton. Over the next three days, he delivered more than a dozen speeches at churches and
schools in six different towns throughout Mississippi's Third Congressional District. More than 150
people from the Mississippi Delta volunteered for the Voter Registration Crusade (SCLC, Press release,
"King's 'People to People' tour sweeps Delta," 21 February 1962; Jack O'Dell to Harry Blake, 22 February
1962).
3. King conducted similar tours of other southern states over the next few months, including
Alabama, Georgia, South Carolina, and Virginia.

Memo... FROM THE DESK OF MARTIN LUTHER KING, JR. DATE_____

*The immediate aim of this tour is ~~personally~~ to recruit hundreds of volunteers to work in our ~~——~~ intensified southside voter registration drive and ~~enlist a small number of persons for a non violent army that will spearhead direct actions.~~ enlist a small number of volunteers to serve in ~~——~~ a non violent army. this NVA will be composed of persons who can be on call to engage in direct action programs and ~~——~~ prepared for prolonged jailing when necessary.*

Handwritten notes on recruitment of Freedom Corps volunteers during SCLC's People to People tours. Courtesy of the Atlanta University Center, Robert W. Woodruff Library Archives and Special Collections.

Along with the economic exploitation that the whole state of Mississippi inflicts upon the Negro, there is the ever present problem of physical violence. As we rode along the roads of the Delta our riding companion cited unbelievable cases of police brutality and incidents of brutal lynchings that are totally unknown to the outside world.

In spite of this there is hope

upon the Negro, there is the ever present problem of physical violence. As we rode along the roads of the Delta our riding companion cited ~~about~~ unbelievable cases of police brutality and ~~brutal~~ incidents of brutal lynchings that are totally unknown to the outside world.[4]

In spite of this there is hope

The immediate aim of this tour is is Recruitment of a "Freedom Corps." This "freedom Corps" will be composed of two units. On the one hand, it will consist of volunteers to work in the intensified southwide voter registration drive. On the other hand, [*remainder missing*]

ADf. MCMLK-RWWL: 2.6.0.390.

---

4. Much of the language of these notes resurfaced in King's longer editorial "People in Action: Pathos and Hope," published in the *New York Amsterdam News* on 3 March 1962 (pp. 419–421 in this volume).

## To Carl Braden

9 February 1962
Atlanta, Ga.

*King welcomes Braden home following his 1 February release from prison after serving a nine-month sentence for refusing to testify before HUAC in 1958. SCLC executive director Wyatt Tee Walker read King's letter at a Southern Conference Educational Fund (SCEF) reception in Braden's honor on 9 February.[1] Braden's wife, Anne, replied, expressing her appreciation "for the beautiful message that you sent to Carl."[2]*

Mr. Carl Braden
C/O Hotel Biltmore
New York, New York

Dear Carl:

I am forwarding this message by our mutual friend, Wyatt Tee Walker. You cannot imagine how good it is to say to you, "Welcome Home".

The days you have spent away from your family and friends have not been spent in vain. They have become a part of the catalogue of sacrifices by which freedom is earned.

All of us are indebted to you. It is a debt that can never be repaid. Our dedication

---

1. King had just begun his People to People tour in Mississippi and was unable to attend the event.
2. Braden to King, 19 February 1962. King's letter was reprinted in the March 1962 SCEF newsletter *The Southern Patriot.*

and determination has been fired by the example of your selflessness. Democracy has a better chance of being realized here in America because of you.

11 Feb
1962

My continued good wishes,
[*signed*] Martin
Martin Luther King Jr., President
Southern Christian Leadership Conference

TLS. CAABP-WHi: Box 11.

# A Knock at Midnight, Sermon Delivered
## at the Installation Service of Ralph Abernathy
### at West Hunter Baptist Church

[*11 February 1962*]
[*Atlanta, Ga.*]

*After orchestrating a letter-writing campaign urging the congregation of Atlanta's West Hunter Baptist Church to extend a call to Abernathy, King delivers "A Knock at Midnight," a sermon based largely on D. T. Niles's homily "Evangelism," at his friend and colleague's installation service.[1] King insists that although this nation was founded on the principle that "all men are created equal," Americans are "still arguing over whether the color of a man's skin determines the content of his character." He instructs the members of West Hunter to help those in need and to confront the moral failure of churches that have "left men disappointed at the darkest hour of life." West Hunter, King maintains, is embarking on a "great experience" with a "great minister to the gospel" who has a "peculiar awareness" of "the problems that individuals face in life." The following transcript is taken from an audio recording of the sermon.*

[*gap in tape*] It is midnight in this parable, but I would like to remind you this afternoon, my friends, that it is also midnight in our world today. At points we are

---

1. Daniel Thambyrajah Niles (1908–1970) was a Sri Lankan evangelist and ecumenical leader. See Niles, "Evangelism," Address at the second assembly of the World Council of Churches, 16 August 1954. Niles later published this sermon as "Summons at Midnight" (Niles, *Christian Century* 71 [1 September 1954]: 1037–1039). On his copy of Niles's homily that he kept in his sermon file, King wrote "A Knock at Midnight." Following the death of A. Franklin Fisher in November 1960, Samuel L. Spear, a parishioner at West Hunter, asked King if he might be interested in filling the vacancy. King declined but recommended Abernathy for the job (King to Spear, 16 December 1960, in *Papers* 5:581–582). Two months later, King wrote a letter to the chairman of West Hunter's board of deacons highlighting Abernathy's qualifications to assume the pastorate of the church (King to J.R. Butts, 8 February 1961, pp. 153–154 in this volume). On Abernathy's behalf, King also solicited letters of recommendations from fellow pastors O. Clay Maxwell and Gardner C. Taylor (King to Maxwell, 9 February 1961; King to Taylor, 9 February 1961). Abernathy accepted the call to West Hunter in August 1961.

385

experiencing a darkness so deep that we hardly know which way to turn.[2] Certainly, it is midnight in the social order. When we look out on the international horizon, we see the nations of the world engaged in a bitter and colossal contest for supremacy. There is a danger now that this contest will lead to the annihilation of the human family on this globe. Atomic warfare has just begun, and bacteriological warfare is yet unused. These things can destroy us. It is dark; it is midnight. This midnight in the social order expresses itself even in our own nation in race relations. While Russia is poisoning the physical atmosphere with fifty-megaton bombs [*Congregation:*] (*Make it plain*), the United States is still poisoning the moral atmosphere with the continuation of racial prejudice. And it is one of the ironies of history that in a nation founded on the principle that all men are created equal, we're still arguing over whether the color of a man's skin determines the content of his character. It's midnight (*Yes*) in the social order. (*Amen*)

But not only is it midnight out there; it is midnight in here. We preachers know that. Whenever I'm in town, I can hardly find enough hours in the day to counsel with people who are confronting problems. Psychopathic wards of our hospitals today are filled. People are haunted by day and plagued by night with crippling anxieties and paralyzing fears. It's midnight in the psychological order. What are the popular books in psychology today? *Man against Himself, The Neurotic Personality of Our Time, Modern Man in Search of a Soul.* What are the popular books in religion today? *Peace of Mind* (*Make it plain*), *Peace of Soul.*[3] And who are the popular preachers today? Preachers who can preach nice little sermons on how to relax and how to be happy. And so we have retranslated the gospel to read, "Go ye into all the world, and keep your blood pressure down, and, lo, I will make you a well-adjusted personality."[4] [*laughter*] All of this is indicative of the fact that it is midnight (*Yes*) in the psychological order.

But not only that, it is midnight in the moral order. Midnight is a time when all colors lose their distinctiveness and become merely a dirty shade of gray.[5] Midnight is a time when all moral values lose their distinctiveness. Morality becomes a thing that is measured in terms of what the people are doing. At midnight, absolute standards pass away. A dangerous ethical relativism comes into being, so at midnight, men begin to say that there is nothing absolutely right and absolutely wrong; it's just a matter of what the majority of people are doing. So at midnight, men live by some

---

2. See Niles, "Evangelism": "It is midnight in the parable. It is also midnight in the world today. The night is so deep that everything has become just an object to be avoided, and obstacle in the dark against which men must take care not to bump."

3. King cites Karl A. Menninger, *Man against Himself* (New York: Harcourt, Brace, 1938); Karen Horney, *The Neurotic Personality of Our Time* (New York: Norton, 1937); C. G. Jung, *Modern Man in Search of a Soul* (New York: Harcourt, Brace, 1933); Joshua Loth Liebman, *Peace of Mind* (New York: Simon and Schuster, 1946); and Fulton J. Sheen, *Peace of Soul* (New York: Whittlesey House, 1949).

4. King parodies Mark 16:15–16: "And he said unto them, Go ye into all the world, and preach the gospel to every creature. He that believeth and is baptized shall be saved; but he that believeth not shall be damned." See also Halford E. Luccock, "Life's Saving Tension," in *Marching Off the Map* (New York: Harper & Brothers, 1952), p. 75: "They are almost on the verge of rewriting the Scriptures to read, 'If any man will come after me, let him relax,' or 'Go into all the world and keep down your blood pressure.'"

5. Niles, "Evangelism": "Besides, at midnight, every colour loses its distinctiveness and becomes merely a dirty shade of grey."

such philosophy as this: everybody is doing it, so it must be all right. [*laughter*] And so we have come to feel that we discover what is right by taking a sort of Gallup poll of the majority opinion: everybody's doing it, it is all right. Midnight is a time when everybody seeks to get by. (*Well*) Midnight is a time when men live by the philosophy that right is getting by and wrong is getting caught. (*Yes*) [*laughter*] So we see that today we live by philosophy that is somewhat different from the Darwinian survival of the fittest. It is now the survival of the slickest: do anything but just don't get caught. And so nobody today is much concerned about the Ten Commandments; they are not important at midnight.[6] Everybody is busy obeying the eleventh commandment: thou shall not get caught. [*laughter*] It's all right to lie, [*laughter*] but just lie with a bit of finesse. It's all right to exploit, but be a dignified exploiter. (*Yeah, Lord*) [*laughter*] It's all right even to hate, but dress your hate up in the garments of love and make it appear that you are loving when you are actually hating—just get by. (*Yeah*) [*laughter*] (*Yes, Yes, Yes, Yes*) This is the philosophy at midnight.

This is what we face in our world today: a threefold midnight experience. It is midnight in the social order, midnight in the psychological order, midnight in the moral order. But in the midst of this midnight experience, the deep darkness is interrupted by a knock in the parable. And in our world today, it is a knock of the world on the door of the church.[7] This is it, West Hunter; this is it, Ebenezer; this is it, Friendship; this is it, Wheat Street; this is it for every other church here this afternoon. It is dark and it is midnight, but there is a knock. (*Yes sir*) And it is the knock of the world (*Yes*) on the door of the church. And no one is more conscious of this than the minister of the gospel of Jesus Christ. He knows that it is dark (*Yes, Yes*), but he has the strange capacity to hear the knock at midnight. Men all over this world are knocking. I just read two days ago in the *New York Times* an article by Harrison Salisburg who's doing a series of articles on Russia. He's saying that something strange is happening in Russia, starting out with its communistic dialectical materialism and its atheism—it felt that there was no God in the universe, but it said that the Russian scientists are now coming around to feeling that there's something spiritual in the cosmos. And he said this is disturbing the Communist Party. They're especially disturbed because so many young people are piling into the churches in Russia.[8] He says they are disturbed because for forty years of propaganda against religion, for forty years of oppression, for forty years of trying to get rid of God and the church, the churches are now more packed than ever before. (*Amen, Amen*) Even in Soviet Russia, you can't get rid of God because men know that they need God in the church at midnight. (*Amen, Yes, Yes, Yes*) Even if you try to push Him out of the front door, religion has a way of sneaking back in the back door. (*Yes sir*) [*laughter*] (*Preach, Yes, Yes, Yes*)

Men are turning, knocking on the door of the church at midnight. This parable said they wanted three loaves—this man wanted three loaves of bread, physical

---

6. Exodus 20.

7. Niles, "Evangelism": "But, as in the parable, so in our day, the tense silence of the midnight is disturbed by the sound of a knock. It is the door of the Church on which somebody is knocking."

8. King may be referring to the fifth in a series of eight articles by Harrison Salisbury: "Khrushchev's Russia—5: Anti-Semitism and Religious Upsurge Are Said to Baffle the Soviet Regime," *New York Times*, 12 September 1959.

bread. Men and women today are seeking three loaves, not physical bread but spiritual bread.[9] (*Yes, Yes, Yes*) Men are seeking the bread of faith. (*Yes*) Points so many people have lost faith in themselves, faith in their neighbors, faith in God. And in the midst of this, they are reaching out for the bread of faith. They want the bread of hope. Young people want this; old people want this. Living under the threat of nuclear and atomic annihilation, people are crying out today for a ray of hope. So many today feel like crying with the philosopher Schopenhauer that life is an endless pain with a painful end.[10] Others feel like crying with Shakespeare's Macbeth life is "a tale/Told by an idiot, full of sound and fury, /Signifying nothing."[11] (*Go ahead*) Others feel like crying out with [*laughter*] Paul Laurence Dunbar [*laughter*]:

> A crust of bread and a corner to sleep in, (*Go on*)
> A minute to smile and an hour to weep in,
> A pint of joy to a peck of trouble, [*laughter*] (*Go on*)
> And never a laugh that the moans come double;
> And that is life![12] (*Yes sir, Yes*)

In the midst of this darkness and hopeless situation men are crying out today for the bread of hope. (*Amen, Yes sir, Preach*) Then they want the bread of love. (*Yes*) Three loaves they want (*Yes*): faith, hope, and love. [*laughter*] (*Yes*) And everybody wants a little love. (*Amen*) Oh, [*laughter*] we are hovered up today in big cities in mass populations, and so often we live in systems that are oppressive and discriminatory. They take from us our sense of personhood and our sense of selfhood, and so many people feel that they don't count, that they don't belong. (*My God*)

With the depersonalization of modern life, all too often we feel that we are little more than numbers. (*Well*) When the mother goes to the hospital to have a child, she becomes maternity patient number 10–82. When the child is born, after he's fingerprinted and foot-printed, he becomes number 12–65. Then when the child grows up and decides to go out and work in a big factory, he's simply number 12–06. Or even if he becomes a little criminal in his tendencies, he goes into jail and he becomes 5–8–7–5 in Cell B. And even when he comes to the point [*laughter*] of his last days of death, he goes into Parlor B in the funeral home (*Yes, Yes, Yes*) and he is carried out by preacher 14, who preaches the sermon, and singer 19, and the flowers and the decorations become class B. [*laughter*] And this is how modern man finds

---

9. Luke 11:5–6: "And he said unto them, Which of you shall have a friend, and shall go unto him at midnight, and say unto him, Friend, lend me three loaves; For a friend of mine in his journey is come to me, and I have nothing to set before him?"

10. Cf. Arthur Schopenhauer, *The World as Will and Idea*, trans. R. B. Haldane and J. Kemp (London: Kegan Paul, Trench, Trubner, and Co., 1891), vol. 3, p. 462: "In the whole of human existence suffering expresses itself clearly enough as its true destiny. Life is deeply sunk in suffering, and cannot escape from it; our entrance into it takes place amid tears, its course is at bottom always tragic, and its end still more so."

11. Shakespeare, *Macbeth*, act 5, scene 5: "Life's but a walking shadow, a poor player/That struts and frets his hour upon the stage/And then is heard no more: it is a tale/Told by an idiot, full of sound and fury, /Signifying nothing."

12. King quotes the first verse of Dunbar's poem "Life" (1895).

himself (*Yes*) caught up in the depersonalization of modern life.[13] This is where he
is. (*Yes, Yes sir*) So he reaches out in the midst of this for the bread of love (*Oh Yes*): I
want to be somebody; I want to count; I'm *more* than just a *number* (*Yes*); I'm *more* than
an *index* card. (*Yes*) I'm a child of God (*Yes*), and I want the bread of love. (*Yes*) This is
what he's looking for today. [*laughter*] This is what modern man is seeking. (*Yes*) He's
running to the church of God trying to find a little bread. (*Amen*)

But I want you to follow me a little more here. (*Amen, Go ahead*) This is an installation sermon, and I'm (*Yes*) trying to challenge the church and the Christian family and all of us this afternoon. (*Yes Lord, Yes, Yes, Yes*) I want you to follow me here.
(*Walk on, Preach, Walk on*) Said when that man knocked on the door trying to get
some bread, he knocked and he knocked, the man inside wouldn't open the door.
He said in substance, "I'm tired, I'm sleepy, the children are in bed, don't bother me,
don't worry me now." So this man outside was left disappointed at midnight. Oh, my
friends, I hate to say this afternoon, so often the church left men disappointed at the
darkest hour of life. (*Well, Yes Lord*)

Men have cried out in Asia and Africa for the bread of justice. Look at South
Africa, if you will. (*Yes*) There you will find about 10 million black men dominated
politically, exploited economically, segregated on 2 percent of their own land. (*Yes*)
You know who stands out probably more than anybody else for the policy of apart-
heid, the policy of segregation in South Africa? Nothing less than the Dutch Reform
Protestant Church.[14] (*Go on, Amen*) Chief Lutuli and his followers have gone up over
and over again to the church trying to get the bread of justice, and the church has
said, "Leave me alone. I'm *busy* with my creeds; I'm *busy* with my worship of God.
Leave me alone." And these people have left—been left disappointed at midnight.[15]
(*Amen*)

We can come right on here to America. (*Go on, Preach*) When we stand on Sunday
morning to sing "In Christ There Is No East or West," (*Go on*) we stand in the most
segregated hour of Christian America.[16] (*Yes Lord*) The most segregated school of
the week is the Sunday school.[17] How often has the white church had a high blood

---

13. Cf. Ralph Borsodi, *This Ugly Civilization* (New York: Simon and Schuster, 1929), p. 199: "The
modern mother is merely maternity case number 8,434; her infant after being finger and foot printed,
becomes infant number 8,003. By virtue of the same mania for system, a modern corpse becomes number 2,432; while a modern funeral becomes one of a series scheduled for parlor 4B for a certain day at
a certain hour, with preacher number fourteen, singer number 87, rendering music number 174, and
flowers and decorations class B." Borsodi (1886–1977), an agrarian theorist and modern critic, tested the
idea of moving back to the land and embraced the concept of simple living.

14. Daniel François Malan (1874–1959), a former clergyman in the Dutch Reformed Church, instituted the country's apartheid policies during his tenure as South Africa's prime minister from 1948 until
1954.

15. Nobel laureate Albert John Mvumbi Lutuli (1898?–1967), chief of the Umvoti Reserve commu-
nity near Groutville, South Africa, was a long-time leader of the African National Congress (ANC). At
Lutuli's request, King sent him a copy of *Stride Toward Freedom* (King to Lutuli, 8 December 1959, in
*Papers* 5:344–345).

16. King evokes John Oxenham's hymn "In Christ There Is No East or West" (1908).

17. National Council of Churches official Helen Kenyon labeled eleven o'clock on Sunday morning
the "most segregated time" in the United States ("Worship Hour Found Time of Segregation," *New
York Times*, 4 November 1952; see also Robert J. McCracken, "Discrimination—The Shame of Sunday
Morning," *The Pulpit* 26, no. 2 [February 1955]: 4–5).

pressure of creeds and an anemia of deeds? (*Yes sir*) This is the tragedy. (*Yes*) This is it. (*This is it*) Bread of social justice has not been provided by the Christian church in so many instances. (*Yes*) Yes, some of them will give thousands of dollars to Africa for the missionary effort—you know about it. (*Yes*) Southern Baptist Convention probably give more money for missions than any church that you can find anywhere. (*Yes sir*) I tell you, if this morning a young man came over to the United States from Kenya or from Ghana or from Nigeria, any point in Africa, and tried to worship in the First Baptist or the Second Ponce de Leon or the Druid Hill Baptist Church even in Atlanta, Georgia, they would put him out (*Oh yeah*) in spite of the fact that they send thousands of dollars to Africa.[18] (*Yes sir, Amen*) Seem that I can hear the almighty God saying, "Get out of my face. Move away from me because your hands are full of blood. (*Yes, Yes, Yes*) I'm not interested merely in your dollars unless those dollars have human love within them. (*Yes Lord, Yes*) I'm not interested in your checks unless those checks are signed with the ink of compassion. (*Yes, Preach*) I'm not interested, my (*Yes sir, Yes Lord*) friend in all of your beautiful hymns and all of your long prayers. (*No*) You must discover that you must "let justice roll down like waters (*Yes, Yes*) and righteousness like a mighty stream."[19] (*Yes Lord, Yes*) That is what you must do." (*Make it plain*) This is what God is saying even to the church today when we leave men disappointed. (*Yes*)

Now, I don't want to stop with the white church. (*No, Come on over*) [*laughter*] Unfortunately [*laughter*], unfortunately, we have these differences—we have a white church and a Negro church. That day must pass. (*Yes, Yes*) I want to say that often the Negro church has left men and women disappointed at the midnight hour. (*Yes, That's right*) Let nobody fool you. Now, you know there are two types of Negro churches that have left people disappointed. One of them freezes up and the other one burns up. (*Yes, That's right, Come on*) [*laughter*] One of them is a church that boasts of the fact that it's a dignified church. (*Lord*) It's a church that says, you know, we, we don't sing spirituals—no we don't do that (*No*)—and we have so many doctors and so many lawyers and so many schoolteachers in our church (*Only way to go*) [*laughter*], and of course [*laughter*], we are dignified. [*laughter*] (*Yes, Yes*) This church [*laughter*] has often substituted a sort of a, a sort of social acceptance for the genuine power of the gospel. (*Yes Lord, Yes Lord*) This dignified church becomes a little more than a secular social club with a thin veneer of religiosity. (*Look out*) And it has so often left the warmth of religion, and the power of the gospel, wanting. (*Yes*) It has somehow lost the power of the whosoever-will-let-him-come doctrine.[20] (*Yes*) [*laugh-*

---

18. In 1961, the Southern Baptist Convention (SBC) had 377 missionaries stationed in eight African countries and devoted almost $3.5 million of the $17 million Foreign Mission Board budget to these locations (Southern Baptist Convention, *Annual of the Southern Baptist Convention 1962*, comp. James W. Merritt [1962], pp. 125–137, 271–275). Despite their focus on cultivating Christianity abroad, Southern Baptists were divided over the issue of integration, as many congregations remained segregated. Druid Hills Baptist pastor and former SBC president Louie D. Newton indicated his personal support for a 1958 call by more than three hundred Atlanta area religious leaders in favor of public school integration but two years later black college students were prevented from worshiping at his church (Claude Sitton, "Atlanta Clerics Bid South Yield," *New York Times*, 23 November 1958; "Students Try 'Kneel-in' at 10 Churches," *Washington Post*, 15 August 1960).

19. Cf. Amos 5:24.

20. Cf. Mark 8:34.

*ter*] Oh, the church must never stand up talking about "certain kinds of people are in it" (*That's right, Preach*); God's church is for everybody. (*Amen, Yes*) It's for the Ph.D.s and the no-Ds (*That's right*); it's for the ups and ins and the downs and outs (*Preach*); it's for the rich and it's for the poor; it's for the young and for the old (*Yes*) [*laughter*]. But this church which freezes up is nothing but a social club. (*Yeah*) It leaves so many people disappointed. (*Yes, Go on, Preach*)

*ter*] Oh, the church must never stand up talking about "certain kinds of people are in it" (*That's right, Preach*); God's church is for everybody. (*Amen, Yes*) It's for the Ph.D.s and the no-Ds (*That's right*); it's for the ups and ins and the downs and outs (*Preach*); it's for the rich and it's for the poor; it's for the young and for the old (*Yes*) [*laughter*]. But this church which freezes up is nothing but a social club. (*Yeah*) It leaves so many people disappointed. (*Yes, Go on, Preach*)

Then there's another church that becomes little more than an entertaining center. The other one freezes up and this one burns up. It majors in gymnastics. (*Yeah*) [*laughter*] It confuses "muscle-ality" with spirituality. [*laughter*] So often, the members of that church [*laughter*] have more religion in their hands and their feet than they have in their hearts and in their souls. [*laughter*] (*Yeah*) They play with the gospel. (*Yeah, That's right, Lord*) They think only about the volume of their voices rather than the quality of their service to humanity and to God. (*Yes sir*) I can hear the almighty God saying, "Both of these churches [*laughter*] leave men disappointed." (*Preach, Come on now*) I can hear Him saying, "I'm not concerned about all of that, but what I am concerned about is that you will love mercy, and that you will do justice (*Amen*) and that you will walk humbly with your God."[21] (*Yes, Yes*) That's what I'm concerned about. (*Yes, Yes, Yes*) So my friends, let us be sure here in this church and in this community all over, we will not leave men disappointed. (*Amen*)

There's another point—I'm moving on toward my conclusion now. (*Go on*) But you know [*laughter*] it's a strange thing—that man kept knocking; he didn't leave. [*laughter*] That's strange, isn't it? (*Yes, Yeah, Go on, Preach*) The man wouldn't open the door. [*laughter*] (*That's right, Amen*) He was disappointed, but he kept knocking. (*Yes*) There's a big word there: *importunity*. It says because of his importunity—that merely means because of his persistence (*Yeah*)—because of because of his stick-to-it-ness (*Yes, All right*), because of his willingness to keep on keeping on (*All right*), finally that man opened the door. But I tell you—we may use our imagination here—why on, why he didn't, I mean, why that man kept knocking, and we can say on the one hand that he was desperate and he needed some bread. That's true. But I'll tell you why he stayed there and kept knocking: he stayed there because he knew there was some bread in there. (*Yeah*) And no matter how much that man in there had disappointed him, he knew that there was some bread in there. He wouldn't have stayed if he didn't think there was any bread in there. But he stayed because, in spite of the disappointment that he faced, he knew that there was some bread in that house. (*Yes, Yes*)

Oh, if I can leave anything with you this afternoon as you embark on this great experience with a great minister to the gospel and a great man of God, let me say to you, West Hunter, that you have the bread of life here. (*Yeah, Well, Amen*) I can only urge you to keep the bread fresh. (*Yeah*) Don't let it get stale on you (*Yeah*) because somebody will want it. Some young boy or some young lady will make a mistake one day; they will run around the nightclubs and pick up all of the bottles that they can find, trying to drown out a sense of guilt. (*All right*) One day they will discover that they can't find it in the nightclub (*Yes, Amen*), and they will come back by here (*Yes, Yes, Yes, Yes*) to find the bread of forgiveness. (*Yes, Yes, Yes, Amen*) One day (*Yes, Yes*) someone will move toward the evening of life. (*All right*) They will be afraid of

---

21. Cf. Micah 6:8.

bad health and afraid of old age and afraid of death. They will try in many ways to grapple with it. One day they will come by here. (*Amen, Yes*) They will want you to give them the bread that will carry them across the chilly Jordan. They will want a little bread (*Yes, Yes*) that will tell them that death is not a period which ends this great sentence of life, but a comma that punctuates it to more loftier significance.[22] (*All right*) They will want a little bread (*Yes, Yes*) to tide them over. (*Yes*) God grant that the church of God will *always* keep the bread fresh. (*Yes Lord*) If the church will do this, it would be a great church; it would be a powerful church.

God has blessed West Hunter. (*Yes*) He has given to you a man who's had a peculiar awareness of the need for the bread of social justice. (*Yes, Lord, Well*) He's given to you a man who has a peculiar awareness the problems that individuals face in life. (*Yes*) It is a marvelous thing to be able to move out right here (*All right*) and provide that bread on this corner. (*Yes, Lord*)

I'm closing now. There's something implied here that I want to leave. He said he wanted some bread, but it is implied that he just wants enough bread to tide him over until the dawn (*Amen, All right*), just enough bread to tide him over until the dawn. He knew it was midnight; he knew it was dark. But, but something reminded him that daybreak was coming (*Yeah, Yes, Lord*), and he just wanted enough to hold him until, until daybreak emerged (*Yeah*), enough to tide him over until the dawn.[23] This is our message to the world; this is what Ralph Abernathy has been preaching; this is what West Hunter has to say to Atlanta and to the members of this church: it may be dark; it may be difficult; it may be a dangerous world in which we live, but midnight is only a temporary phenomenon in the universe. (*Yes, Yes*) You know our slave foreparents used to deal with this problem. (*All right*) Sometimes they'd cry out, "Nobody knows the trouble I see (*Yeah*),/Nobody knows but Jesus."[24] (*Yeah*) It was midnight then. (*Yes, Yes*) Then they recognized something and they could sing, "I'm so glad (*Yeah*) the trouble don't last always."[25] (*Yeah, That's it*) Then they could cry out, "I got shoes, you got shoes (*Go ahead*), / All of God's children got shoes. (*Yes, Lord*)/When I get to heaven going to put on my shoes/And I'm just going to walk all over God's heaven" (*Yeah, Go ahead*) because daybreak is coming.[26] (*Yes, Lord, Yes, Well, Preach*) Let it get dark in your individual life; let it get dark in race relations, but never forget that there is a God in this universe (*Yes sir, Yes*) who can transform dark and desolate valleys (*Yes, Lord*) into sunlit paths of joy (*Yes*), who can lift us from the fatigue of despair to the buoyancy of hope. (*Yes there is*) This is our hope. This is the power of our gospel.

My friends from Montgomery will remember this closing experience that I would like to mention to you. We went through some dark days there in our struggle. (*Yes,*

----

22. Amos John Traver, *The Christ Who Is All* (Philadelphia: United Lutheran Publication House, 1929), p. 95: "Life is one, death is but a comma in the unending sentence . . . To change the thought demands a period, and that is just what we are too often making of death, a period."

23. Niles, "Evangelism": "Midnight is a difficult hour in which to be faithful or successful: but we shall find grace as we seek to minister to the real need of him who comes to us in the midnight. For the traveller by midnight who is asking for bread is really asking for the dawn."

24. King quotes from part of the spiritual "Nobody Knows the Trouble I've Seen."

25. King refers to the spiritual "I'm So Glad Trouble Don't Last Always."

26. King references a verse from the spiritual "Going to Shout All Over God's Heaven."

*Yes, Well*) We faced midnight so often. (*Yes, Go on, Go on*) And I can remember after we had struggled together for several months, walked the streets, we had developed a carpool—had, friends from over the nation had helped us to develop. Many of you from Atlanta and all over sent money down there so that we could buy station wagons and we could provide a carpool to help get people to and from work. Oh, Dr. Seay will remember; Reverend Abernathy and Brother Nesbitt and all people from Montgomery will remember. One day the mayor of the city came out in the paper and said: "We are tired of this mess, and we are going to file a suit in the court of Montgomery, Alabama, to bring an end to the carpool."[27] It was announced that the city commission would seek an injunction against a carpool.[28] Now, we knew that they would get it; we knew the courts in Alabama. And I never will forget that morning when I read it in the paper. I started calling Ralph and others and asking, "What are we going to do now?" It was moving toward Monday night when we had our regular weekly mass meeting, and I stayed back in my den in despair and in a disillusioning moment, and I was, I was at the point that I was faltering and I, I didn't have the strength to face the people and go to the mass meeting. I would speak every Monday night and try to give encouragement and hope and courage to the people along with the other leaders. This night I, I didn't want to face them, for I knew that carpool would be enjoined, and all I could say was what's going to happen now. We are, we are set back, and the people are going to lose faith in us, and all of this that we have done will be in vain. You can never know the lonely moments and the agonizing moments that a leader in a struggle like this goes through. (*Well*) And I remember it was getting toward eight o'clock and I finally mustered up enough courage to go on to the meeting. As I walked in that night, I could see that the people themselves were worried a little about this, and I looked into their eyes and I could see, figuratively speaking, clouds of sorrow floating in their little mental skies. I could see cold waves of pessimism flowing around that congregation in the Bethel Baptist Church. I got up and I tried to talk and I said, in substance, "We've come to many dark moments before. Often we didn't see our way clear. We didn't know the way out, but in our darkest moments, God always came to make a way out of no way." (*Yes, Yes Lord, Yes, Yes Lord*) I said, "I know tomorrow morning that, that our carpool will be enjoined and I can't exactly tell you now what we're going to do, but, but God will make a way for us." (*Yes, Yes Lord, Well*) Even after I said that, I could still feel that faltering element within myself and within the people, oh it was dark that night (*Yes, Yes, Yes*), blacker than a thousand midnights. (*It's true*) It was midnight in Montgomery. (*Yes*)

Got up that morning, Ralph came by and picked me up, and we moved on down to the court with our wives and other friends. Since I was the chief defendant, they had me sitting at the table with the lawyers, and they started the case, and attorney [*Arthur*] Shores and attorney [*Fred*] Gray and the other lawyers argued brilliantly before Judge [*Eugene*] Carter, and yet I could see that Judge Carter was going to rule against us. The city argued that we were operating a business without a franchise,

---

27. W.A. Gayle (1895–1965) was mayor of Montgomery from 1951–1959.

28. S.S. Seay (1899–1988), pastor of Mt. Zion AME Zion Church from 1947–1962, and Robert D. Nesbitt (1908–2002), longtime clerk of Dexter Avenue Baptist Church, were both members of the Montgomery Improvement Association's executive board.

and they argued, and our lawyers argued that, that wasn't true—that this was a nonprofit corporation, that this was a nonprofit situation. In all of the arguments, I could see which way Judge Carter was going to rule. Then it came to the point that it was about twelve o'clock. I was sitting there, and I had gone down at that moment in the deepest despair. (*All right*) I could see nothing but darkness even though it was physical daylight—darkness, midnight, was surrounding us. (*All right*) Then I started noticing that people were walking around in the courtroom. I looked over to the mayor, and I saw him walking back to a little room. Then I saw Commissioner [*Clyde*] Sellers, and he started moving back to a little room. (*Preach on*) [*laughter*] Then Judge Carter said, "The court is recessed for ten minutes." [*laughter*] (*All right*) Then as I was sitting there at that table [*laughter*], Rex Thomas, the AP reporter, came to me and said, "Dr. King (*Yes, Yes sir*), I have a little statement that I want you to read. It has just come out, and we want a comment from you. We need your comment." [*laughter*] And I took that little piece of paper; [*laughter*] it read something like this: "This morning [*laughter*] the United States Supreme Court unanimously declared bus segregation unconstitutional [*laughter*] in Montgomery, Alabama."[29] [*applause*] I say to you today (*Come on*), for it was midnight a few hours ago [*laughter*] (*Yes Lord, Yes*), somebody cried out, "God has spoken from Washington." (*Yeah*) [*laughter*] Many times God has spoken. (*Yes*) So we left that court that day knowing that it didn't matter what decision was rendered. (*Yes, Amen*) We didn't *need* a carpool [*laughter*] anymore because we were going *back* to integrated buses. (*Amen, All right*)

Don't you worry, my friends. (*Amen*) It may be dark, but daybreak is coming. (*That's right*) Darker yet may be the night, right may often yield to might, but if you are right, God will fight your battles.[30] (*Yes*) [*laughter*] (*Yeah*) Don't worry tonight; (*That's right*) don't worry this afternoon. (*That's right*) Midnight is not here to stay. (*Yes sir*) "Truth forever on the scaffold, Wrong forever on the throne,—/Yet that scaffold sways the future, and, behind the dim unknown, / Standeth God within (*Yes*) the shadow, keeping watch above his own."[31] (*Oh yes*) So this afternoon, I can walk around the city of Atlanta; (*Yes, Yes, Yes*) I can fly around America; (*Yes*) I can face temporary setbacks in the civil (*Yes, Yes, Yes*) rights struggle, but I can say to you, "Walk together, children. (*Yes sir*) [*laughter*] Don't you get weary, for there is a great camp meeting in the Promised Land."[32] (*Amen*) [*applause*] (*Amen, Amen, Amen, Amen*)

At. BAA-CSt-KPP.

---

29. On 13 November 1956, the United States Supreme Court declared the segregation of Montgomery buses unconstitutional in the case of *Gayle v. Browder*, 352 U.S. 903 (1956). King retells this story in *Stride Toward Freedom: The Montgomery Story* (New York: Harper & Row, 1958), pp. 158–160.

30. King paraphrases the lyrics of Charles Albert Tindley's "Some Day": "Harder yet may be the fight, / right may often yield to might. / Wickedness awhile may reign, / Satan's cause may seem to gain./There is a God that rules above, /With hand of power and heart of love./If I am right, He'll fight my battle, /I shall have peace some day."

31. James Russell Lowell, "The Present Crisis" (1844), stanza 8.

32. King paraphrases from the spiritual "There's a Great Camp Meeting."

# To Luther White

12 February 1962
[*Atlanta, Ga.*]

*Citing his leadership role in the civil rights movement, King declines White's
request to make a public show of support for embattled Teamster Union president
Jimmy Hoffa.[1] Acknowledging that the Teamsters are "doing some significant work
to increase the benefits of the Negro worker," King explains that because his "every
word is dissected" and his "motives can be so easily misinterpreted," he cannot
publicly defend the controversial union leader.[2]*

Mr. Luther White
1222 Prospect Avenue
Cleveland 15, Ohio

Dear Luther:

First, let me apologize for being rather tardy in getting this letter off to you after
our telephone conversation a few days ago.[3]

I have given our many discussions serious and prayerful attention. I have read a
great deal of the literature that has been forwarded to me. There is no doubt in my
mind that the Teamsters have, in many areas, done a great deal to break down racial

---

1. Luther Randolph White (1902–1978) was born in Marianna, Florida. After attending college at
Florida A&M College and Boston University, White settled in Cleveland and founded Triangle Realty in
1924. He founded the *Cleveland Eagle*, a black community newspaper, in 1936 before establishing White
and White, a public relations firm, and becoming director of the Cleveland chapter of the American
Negro Emancipation Centennial Authority. James Riddle Hoffa (1913–1975?) was born in Brazil, Indiana.
After the death of his father, Hoffa dropped out of high school to help support his family. In Detroit,
Michigan, Hoffa went to work for a grocery store where he organized his first labor strike. In the 1930s,
he joined the International Brotherhood of Teamsters, and eventually became the president of the
union's Detroit chapter. In 1952 he was elected vice president of the Teamsters. Five years later, Hoffa
was elected president of the union and was investigated for both attempting to bribe a public official and
for racketeering by the Senate Select Committee on Improper Activities in the Labor Management Field
headed by Senator John L. McClellan and with Robert F. Kennedy as chief counsel. Although he was
acquitted in both trials, the Senate committee continued to investigate him and union corruption until
his imprisonment in 1967. Hoffa was also suspected of elevating known Mafia members to positions of
leadership within the union. After serving four years in prison, Hoffa was pardoned by President Richard
Nixon in 1971 with the stipulation that he would not hold any leadership positions in the Teamsters until
1980. In 1975 Hoffa disappeared. His body has never been found.

2. In December 1957, the AFL-CIO charged that the Teamsters Union was dominated by corrupt
elements and voted to expel it from the federation. Realizing the value of black support during the
ongoing investigations, Hoffa and the Teamsters Union became outspoken proponents of integration
in organized labor. As early as 1958 the Teamsters implemented a policy of no race discrimination in
their chapters ("Hoffa Calls for 'No Discrimination,'" *The International Teamster*, May 1958). Following
the 1961 censure of A. Philip Randolph by the AFL-CIO, the Teamsters issued an executive resolution in
support of Randolph and accused the AFL-CIO of maintaining Jim Crowism ("Randolph Defended by
Teamster Board," *The International Teamster*, January 1962).

3. Phone message slips indicate that White called King's office on 5, 8, and 9 February.

barriers, raise wages, and upgrade Negroes.[4] I have also weighed and find much merit in the claims that Mr. Hoffa is "target for tonight" for some of his opponents.[5] I cannot disagree with the contention that on the whole, the Teamsters are doing some significant work to increase the benefits of the Negro worker.

However, I have come to the conclusion that I should not take a public stand on this issue. This is in no way a re-treat, nor is it an expression of faith. It simply grows out of my position that I now hold in the civil rights movement. The weight of the civil rights struggle on my shoulders is such that I lack the time and the energy to take on a task which will abruptly place me in a defensive position. Being in this struggle is equivalent to being in a glass house. My every word is dissected. My every move examined. My motives can be so easily misinterpreted. There are always those cynics and opponents who would argue that I was "paid off" to take a stand for Hoffa and the Teamsters Union.[6] I have not come to this decision without serious thinking and talking with some of my close associates. All of them concur that I should not make this move. I also talked with some outstanding Negroes in the ranks of labor, and while they are genuinely sympathetic with Mr. Hoffa, they feel that it would be a mistake for me to intervene in this situation.[7]

I am sure you can understand how much I regret coming to this conclusion. It is even more regrettable in the light of our personal friendship and my warm regard for you. I trust that you will be sympathetic to my position and commitment to the larger cause to which you also are committed. Believe me, because you are my friend and you ask this of me, it pains me not to be able to comply with the request.

May God bless you in all of the noble work you are doing, and I hope you success at every point. I am off to Puerto Rico now where I will be speaking on tour for about a week.[8] I hope I will be able to get some much needed rest in the process.

---

4. According to *Pittsburgh Courier* reporter Trezzvant Anderson, around five hundred thousand African Americans were part of the Teamsters Union, the second largest membership behind only the National Baptist Convention ("Reporter Can't See Hoffa Win as Rigged," 2 December 1961). In 1959, White coordinated with Associated Negro Press founder Claude Barnett the publishing of several articles on Hoffa.

5. Anderson quoted King as saying that Hoffa was "the 'whipping-boy' of those who were anti-labor" ("King Meets Negro Labor Before Confab," *Pittsburgh Courier*, 9 December 1961). Following Hoffa's successful reelection as president in July 1961, several locals in San Diego, Cincinnati, and Philadelphia voted to leave the Teamsters Union, charging that Hoffa had centralized too much power.

6. In mid-1957, questions about the motives of boxer Joe Louis's public support of Hoffa were mounting. Walter Sheridan, a federal investigator, asked Louis to sign an affidavit confirming that Hoffa did not pay Louis for his support. Louis crossed out most of the affidavit, but signed the last paragraph insisting that he did not receive any money from Hoffa ("McClellan Says Teamsters Paid Joe Louis' Hotel Bill during Hoffa Trial: Dio Linked to Garment Workers," *Wall Street Journal*, 2 August 1957; Walter Sheridan, *The Fall and Rise of Jimmy Hoffa* [New York: Saturday Review Press, 1972], pp. 35–36).

7. A. Philip Randolph in December 1961 publicly supported the Teamsters' unsuccessful bid to be reinstated into the AFL-CIO because "I don't think the labor unions are qualified to sit in moral judgment" of the Teamsters, who were "less guilty of racial discrimination than most of the other unions" (Lee Blackwell, "A. Philip Randolph Speaks His Mind," *Chicago Daily Defender*, 16 December 1961).

8. King spoke at Inter-American University, the Evangelical Seminary, and the University of Puerto Rico on a speaking tour from 13–16 February, and then took an eight-day vacation before returning on 24 February. For more on King's trip to Puerto Rico, see Interview by Inter-American University Students and Faculty, 14 February 1962, pp. 399–410 in this volume.

Very truly yours,

Martin Luther King, Jr.

Km

Dictated by Dr. King, but signed in his absence.

TLc. MLKJP-GAMK: Box 6.


# To Harry H. Wachtel

12 February 1962
*[Atlanta, Ga.]*

*At a 1 February meeting with King, Wachtel proposed the establishment of a tax-exempt organization that would eventually become the Gandhi Society for Human Rights.[1] In the letter below, King thanks Wachtel for his "moral" and "practical" support for the civil rights struggle and suggests that the foundation's focus should be on citizenship education and legal aid.[2] In his 16 February 1962 reply, Wachtel confessed his "deep respect" for King's "historic and selfless fight against encrusted injustice and humanity," saying that the hours he spent with the civil rights leader "stirred me and afforded me new perspectives."*


Mr. Harry Wachtel
Wachtel & Michelson
711 Fifth Avenue
New York 22, New York

Dear Mr. Wachtel:

I hope that though we both were rushing to catch trains, I managed to convey to you the warm appreciation I feel for your interest in the integration work we are trying to accomplish. It is not exaggerating to say that without the depth of concern certain people like you feel, we would be unable to make real progress. Several centuries of neglect coupled with tenacious resistance to change from the established elements, are immense burdens to carry. When, with these handicaps, the job must be done by a people who are largely impoverished, our road is rough and long. Therefore, the help we receive has special significance because it is moral support and practical aid, both of which one needs in this kind of struggle.

I want to re-state my confidence in you and Ted Kheel and to urge you to pursue

---

1. Labor arbitrator Theodore Kheel also attended the meeting. The organization Wachtel suggested was to address King's earlier observation that the lack of legal and financial support were roadblocks to SCLC's integration efforts (King to Wachtel, 7 November 1961, pp. 325–327 in this volume).

2. King sent a similar letter to Kheel (King to Kheel, 12 February 1962).

the project with assurance that I will be available at any time. I will be in touch with you regarding a special trip to New York where our discussion can continue.[3]

Responding to your suggestion that I indicate some of the objectives of a Foundation, there are two principal areas which are keys for progress in the South. The first is education in the exercise of constitutional rights. Under this heading the most important is registering and voting. Educational activity here would encompass publications, workshops, schools to teach reading and writing, conferences, etc. A staff would be required to develop materials and to work in the field where large numbers of American citizens are without the franchise, some because of artificial obstacles interposed to prevent Negro suffrage, others because apathy and tradition and lack of understanding of rights inhibit the use of the ballot even though no otherfforms of opposition exist.

There are other constitutional rights which are frequently unused because knowledge of them does not exist or techniques are not known. These include the right to travel on public conveyances, the right to employment on an equal basis in industry or in Federal Government jobs and others.[4]

The second major area is legal defense, especially in situations arising from activity in seeking to exercise constitutional rights. Many people who are poor find themselves in legal actions, and the heavy cost of defense is a crippling difficulty, thus hindering the progress of citizens who may be informed of their rights but lack the means to carry on. Also, there are areas where positive legal steps should be taken in the form of injunctive suits or other actions to remove illegal obstacles, and again where the financial means do not exist to see a project to completion.

I think this is a general statement of needs which are significant, and which reach a substantial part of the work that must be done to bring the South culturally, politically and socially up to the level of the rest of the nation.

Warmest personal regards.

Very cordially yours,
Martin Luther King, Jr.

Km

TLc. MLKJP-GAMK: Box 25.

---

3. King was in Connecticut 20–21 March at a meeting of the Joint Consultative Council and may have met with Wachtel on the evening of 21 March (Charles B. Markham to King, 28 March 1962). Wachtel had also made plans to meet with King in Atlanta on 23 April (Clarence B. Jones to King, 18 April 1962).

4. In 1960 the Supreme Court outlawed segregation in public transportation facilities in *Boynton v. Virginia* (364 U.S. 454). The Kennedy administration affirmed equal access to federal employment in Executive Order 10925, which established a committee led by Vice President Lyndon B. Johnson. For more on the committee, see Johnson to King, 13 April 1962, pp. 435–437 in this volume.

[*14 February 1962*]
San Germán, Puerto Rico

*In a 22 October 1959 letter, Robert Brank Fulton, a professor of religion and
philosophy at Inter-American University (IAU) in Puerto Rico, invited King to
the island to give a series of lectures.*[1] *After initially agreeing to speak in Puerto
Rico in l961, King had to reschedule for early 1962 due to SCLC commitments and
the birth of his third child.*[2] *Sponsored by the IAU and the Puerto Rico chapter of
the Fellowship of Reconciliation (FOR), the four-day speaking tour included an
appearance on a local television program and an engagement at the University
of Puerto Rico in Rio Piedras. In the following question and answer session
after delivering "Non-Violence and Racial Justice" at the IAU in Puerto Rico,
King discusses the struggle to end nuclear proliferation, racial prejudice, and
segregation in all aspects of American life.*[3] *For King, the basis of success in any of
these movements lies in the philosophy of nonviolence because of its "persistence."
Although it may not produce an instantaneous victory, the nonviolent approach
"leaves an aftermath of brotherhood," says King, whereas violence "always leaves
an aftermath of bitterness."*[4] *Due to the poor quality of the audio recording,
the questions from the audience could not be heard; only King's answers are
transcribed below.*

[*King*]:    I frankly didn't know that this situation existed with reference to soldiers.
This is new to me. I would certainly feel that if this existed any soldier would have the
kind of redress, or would have the possibility of appealing to higher authorities in the
nation so that that particular situation could be changed. I don't think, for instance,
the federal government could stand to have these conditions existing, and I'm pretty
sure that the federal government would go out, all out to protect soldiers more than

---

1. Fulton first invited King to Puerto Rico in October 1958, but the civil rights leader declined
because he was still recuperating from surgery following a near fatal stabbing in New York a month
earlier (Fulton to King, 18 October 1958; Maude L. Ballou to Fulton, 29 November 1958). For more on
King's September 1958 stabbing, see Introduction in *Papers* 4:34–35.
2. King to Fulton, 5 October 1960.
3. In addition to the addresses at Inter-American University, King also spoke at the Evangelical
Seminary of Puerto Rico in Río Piedras, at the University of Puerto Rico's Mayagüez campus, and at
a public meeting in Río Piedras (Inter-American University, Program, "Toward a World of Understanding," 12 February–15 February 1962; King, Nonviolence and Racial Justice, Address delivered at
Inter-American University, 14 February 1962; King, "The Future of Integration," Address delivered
at Inter-American University, 14 February 1962; King, Stride Toward Freedom, Address delivered at
Inter-American University, 15 February 1962).
4. Local FOR chairman Lillian Pope assessed the impact of King's Puerto Rico trip: "Apparently you
deepened the thinking of many people here, and made many give serious consideration for the first time
to the merits of non-violent direct action as a technique and as a philosophy" (Pope to King, 4 March
1962). Fulton concurred, noting that the topics of many of his students' term papers echoed the themes
of King's addresses (Fulton to King, 15 May 1962).

that.[5] I mean, with conditions existing like this, it would be not only injurious to the soldiers involved but also to the image of the nation. So, I am sure that if they once existed, these conditions do not exist as much at this time. As you know, there's also a pretty—I would say, generally speaking, the armed forces of the United States have been integrated. And I mean, this includes all branches of the service, so that along with the integration that has taken place, I'm sure that other conditions have been changed and other conditions have been rectified where unjust conditions existed.[6]

[*King*]:  Well, I would say that many things must be done to meet the Russian threat. Many things must be done to meet the whole threat of atomic and nuclear annihilation. Now, I must say that I'm not optimistic about getting any whole nation in the world—certainly not the United States, or any other nation—to disarm unilaterally. I think that we have to be realistic enough to know that this will not be, even though there may be a good case for advocating this. But when we come down to the practical realism of the situation, this probably won't happen. Consequently, we must work through channels such as the United Nations to bring about disarmament, to bring about suspension of nuclear tests, and this means that there must be a greater willingness to negotiate on the part of the nations of the world.[7]

Now, the other thing that I would say here is that somehow the conscience of the world must be aroused on this issue—the conscience of the United States as well as the conscience of Russia. And I think that there is a great deal that can be done through individuals through peace movements to arouse the conscience of the world. This has already been done in some parts of the world. It has been done a great deal in England through Lord Russell and others.[8] It's been done in the United States and in other places of the world.[9] This attempt to say through civil disobedi-

---

5.  In a June 1961 memo, the Defense Department restated their assurance of "equal treatment for all members of the Armed Forces without regard to race, creed or color" (Roswell Gilpatric, "Memo to the Secretary of the Army, the Secretary of the Navy, and the Secretary of the Air Force," 19 June 1961).

6.  Although President Truman desegregated all branches of the armed forces in 1948, the Leadership Conference on Civil Rights accused the Defense Department in 1961 of not providing servicemen with legal assistance for civil cases confronting racial discrimination. The study also found that segregation and discrimination still existed throughout the military, including in the National Guard, the reserve units, the officer training programs, and military academies ("Report on discrimination by the federal government," 29 August 1961).

7.  Charged in its founding charter with addressing arms regulation, the United Nations General Assembly brought representatives of the United States, Canada, Britain, France, and the Soviet Union together to discuss nuclear disarmament in February 1955. After being unable to bring about a ban on the use of nuclear weapons, however, the General Assembly voted unanimously four years later to empower a previously established ten-nation committee to resolve the issue, including the United States, Britain, and the Soviet Union. The three countries would sign a partial test ban treaty on 5 August 1963.

8.  On 17–18 September 1961, over 1,300 Britons were arrested in London at a demonstration against nuclear weapons organized by the Committee of 100. In an attempt to prevent the demonstration, five days earlier thirty-two members of the Committee, including founder and president Bertrand Russell, were imprisoned for terms from seven days to two months after refusing to pledge to keep the peace (Drew Middleton, "Bertrand Russell Jailed over Atom Protests," *New York Times*, 13 September 1961).

9.  For example, in October 1961, thirteen Americans, sponsored by the Committee for Nonviolent Action, completed a ten-month walk for disarmament from San Francisco to Moscow. Although they had hoped to hold a rally at Red Square, the group met with students at Moscow University and shared tea

ence if necessary that survival must be a foremost concern, and that if we consider, rather, if we feel that we have a right to survive, then we must find some alternative to war. So that I think nonviolence can work in bringing about disarmament. And in this kind of disarmament, we would certainly think of disarming the whole world, and I think we must continue to pursue this path of peaceful negotiation so that the whole world can be disarmed. And a sort of international police power would be set up through the United Nations, but as far as the continuation of the arms race and as far as continuation of nuclear tests which can only serve to poison the atmosphere with radioactive fallout, all of this should come to an end.

[*King*]: [*recording interrupted*] definitely think the continued existence of racial segregation or racial discrimination in the United States is doing a great deal to tarnish the image of the United States in the eyes of the world. I have seen this in many instances as I have traveled around the world, whether it's in Europe or in South America or in Africa or Asia. There's always a great concern about the problem of racial injustice in the United States, and there's always the statement that if the United States doesn't solve this problem, and if it doesn't solve it in a hurry, it will certainly be relegated not only to a second rate political power but relegated in terms of its moral force and its moral power and that it will fail to be a moral voice in the world. So that there can be no gainsaying of the fact that it is hurting the reputation of the United States.[10] However, I think the hopeful thing is, I think the hopeful sign is the fact that although the problem is there, and no one can deny it, there are numerous people working passionately to get rid of it and to change the situation. And I think that this will probably continue to grow so that there's an awareness of the problem and a new determination to solve it.

[*King*]: Well, I would say first that I don't quite agree that laws represent a sort of organized violence. Now, it is quite true that there have been persons who believed in nonviolence very firmly who were anarchists. Thoreau, Henry David Thoreau was an anarchist at points.[11] Tolstoy was an anarchist at points.[12] I don't happen to be an

---

with the wife of Soviet premier Nikita Khrushchev (Seymour Topping, "'West Sobers Up'—According to Moscow," *New York Times*, 8 October 1961).

10. Discussing the mobs that attacked the Freedom Riders, Ralph Bunche called them a "discredit to a civilized society" who "give much aid and comfort to our communist detractors" ("Dr. Bunche Supports Freedom Riders," Baltimore *Afro-American*, 17 June 1961). *Jet* magazine reported that news of the violence was "like a shot around the globe," hurting American prestige, a point later reiterated by Edward R. Murrow, director of the United States Information Agency, in testimony to the House Committee on Education and Labor ("Label U.S. Racial Violence 'Shot Heard 'Round World,'" *Jet*, 22 June 1961; "Murrow Cites Reaction," *New York Times*, 25 June 1961; Report, "A United States Information Agency report summary world-wide reactions to racial incidents in Alabama," June 1961).

11. In *Civil Disobedience*, Thoreau argued that a majority will maintain power not because they do what is right, but because they are the strongest. "It is not desirable to cultivate a respect for the law," he contended, "so much as for the right. The only obligation which I have a right to assume is to do at any time what I think right" (Thoreau, *Civil Disobedience* [Harrington Park, N.J.: 5 x 8 Press, 1942], p. 3).

12. Although he did not agree violence was needed to bring about change, Russian author Leo Tolstoy agreed with anarchists "in the negation of the existing order and in the assertion that, without Authority there could not be worse violence than that of Authority under existing conditions" ("On Anarchy," 1900).

anarchist. I believe that the state serves a vital purpose. I believe that we must have laws to regulate behavior, and this is why I think that some persons who believe in nonviolent resistance have been over-optimistic concerning human nature, and they could see the goodness in man but not the evil. And I live with the idea that man is neither innately good or innately bad, but he has potentialities for both. And because he has potentialities for evil, it is necessary to have the kind of restraining agencies that you have through the state and through laws that, as I said, serve to maintain order in society and to regulate behavior. So that I don't think this is organized violence at any point. I think laws only serve the purpose to maintain a degree of order within society.

Now, the second point is that I can't see that nonviolent resistance, when one is committed to it, represents a sort of psychological violence. You do not seek to demoralize the opponent. You do not seek to injure the opponent. Your ultimate aim is, as I said earlier, to win his friendship and understanding and to convert him. And even if he is hurt in the process, this is not your intention. If you are engaged in a boycott, for instance, it may mean that the man will get put out of business, but this is certainly not your intention. Your intention is to put justice in business and not to put this man out of business, and you're seeking to create a moral balance in society, which will help that man as well as it will help those who are in the struggle to break it down.

I happen to believe that segregation hurts the white man as well as it hurts the Negro, and that when we fight to get rid of segregation, we are fighting not merely for the Negro, but we are fighting to free the soul of the white man. So, I don't think of nonviolent resistance as psychological violence, first, because it avoids physical violence, and, second, because the intent is always to create the beloved community. The intent is to make a better situation for all of the people involved, not just a better situation for yourself but a better situation for that opponent who is also misguided and who often has this system set up, and he follows it because he's been taught that way. So, I think it must always be interpreted in terms of intent, and this is the only way that we can really deal with this, deal with the problem of which you termed "psychological violence." I believe that nonviolent resistance represents nonviolence in spirit as well as nonviolence in physical terms.

[*King*]:    I would say, first, that there is no doubt about the fact that nonviolence is based on the theory that you are able to carry on a movement when you have a potential ally in the conscience of your opponent. There is no doubt about that. Second, I must admit that I think this method does work better in a situation where you have democratic processes, where you have freedom of press, where you have freedom of assembly. Even, I don't think there's anywhere—I just left Mississippi last week, and that's, and I was in the Mississippi Delta trying to recruit people to engage in a extended voter registration campaign. And even there, which is the most difficult state in the United States in race relations, we had public meetings. I addressed three or four public meetings, and nothing stopped that.[13] So that even in the most

---

13. King spent three days making appearances at local churches, schools, and mass meetings in an effort to register voters and recruit demonstrators for a "nonviolent army" (SCLC, Press release, "King's 'People to People' tour sweeps delta," 21 February 1962). For more on the trip, see King, "People in Action: Pathos and Hope," 3 March 1962, pp. 419–421 in this volume.

difficult places, we can at least have meetings, and we can at least organize. Wherein
in South Africa, Chief Lutuli couldn't call a meeting, a mass meeting, next week and
have it.[14] And I can assure you that it would be much more difficult to organize a
nonviolent movement in such a situation than in a country where you do have some
commitment to democracy. I think also that it is true that when you have a condition
that is not a totalitarian one, you are able to do more in nonviolence.

But after saying this, I think we must go to the other side and say that we have
no empirical evidence that nonviolence cannot work in these situations that are
extremely difficult. I would only say that there was never any organized mass nonviolent movement against Hitler. We must make a distinction between nonresistance
and nonviolent resistance, and it may well be that if there had ever been a mass nonviolent organized campaign against Hitler, the casualty list would have been less. This
is speculation, naturally. I cannot say, because it's impossible to know, but I think this
is a real possibility that if there had been an organized nonviolent movement and a
nonviolent movement resisting the inhuman and brutal and vicious methods being
used by Hitler, the casualty list may have been less. In South Africa, the only movement that has worked—when I say "that has worked," I mean the only movement that
has brought the government to its knees—has been a nonviolent direct action mass
movement. A few years ago, they had a bus boycott in South Africa, and this was so
effective that the government had to give in. So, that it has worked already in South
Africa.[15] And I think as difficult as it is, it wouldn't be as easy as it would in some parts
of the United States, but as difficult as it is [*recording interrupted*]

Here again, we have an extremely difficult situation, with a statement being made
at points, at least Lenin said on one occasion that any method, violence, deceit, lying,
or any other method is justifiable in order to bring about the end of the classless
society.[16] Now, whenever you get this idea and this kind of ethical relativism, certainly it is more difficult to grapple with the problem there with nonviolence than
in a situation where that idea doesn't emerge. But I submit to you that the people
in Russia have consciences, I believe. I think that there are some people who live in
Russia, who I think they love their children, and I think they respond to some of the
same human things that other human beings respond to. And I think sometimes
we overplay the goodness and the conscience of the British and the Southerners
in the United States. I think some of them are mighty bad and mighty misguided.
And the difference is that in Russia, I believe firmly that they are under the power
of a system that I totally disagree with in terms of its philosophical structure and in

---

14. Zulu chief Albert Lutuli fought against apartheid as president of the African National Congress
in South Africa. Due to his ANC activities, Lutuli was banned by Justice Minister Charles R. Swart from
attending any meetings or gatherings in South Africa for five years.

15. For three months in 1957, fifty thousand South Africans chose to walk the twenty-mile round-trip
from their segregated homes in the township of Alexandra to their jobs in Johannesburg after the transit
company raised the fare twenty-five percent. On 1 April 1957 the city's chamber of commerce ended the
boycott when they agreed to subsidize the price increase by selling vouchers at the previous price of four
pence to Alexandra residents ("Bus Strike Ends in South Africa," *New York Times*, 2 April 1957).

16. Robert J. McCracken, "What Should Be the Christian Attitude to Communism?," in *Questions
People Ask* (New York: Harper & Brothers, 1951), pp. 168–169: "'We must be ready,' wrote Lenin, 'to
employ trickery, deceit, lawbreaking, withholding and concealing truth.'"

terms of its moral projection. But the people themselves, they have consciences that can be aroused, and I think we must always see this—that maybe we've gone too far in thinking that other people have had good consciences and that all of the people in Russia are bad people. And I think that there are people of conscience in Russia, and that conscience can be aroused even though at points they are under an evil and a vicious system. I think someone. Yes.

[*King*]:  I think the problem, as I've said so often, is a national problem and is not just a sectional problem. It is a problem facing the whole nation. It may be more conspicuous, more glaring in the South than in the North, but it certainly exists in its subtle forms all over the country. Therefore, every citizen of the United States should be concerned about getting rid of segregation and discrimination, because injustice anywhere is a threat to justice everywhere. And no person who lives inside the United States can be considered an outsider. Therefore, I have welcomed Northerners in the movement, and I think it helps to make it clear to those who live in the South and those who live in the North that the problem is a national problem, and it must be a concern of every citizen.[17]

Now, certainly I don't think the Northern help in the struggle should be a substitute for the determination of Southerners themselves, for I am convinced that the more people in the South that you get to rise up, the more you are able to refute the idea that Negroes like segregation. This is what many of the Southern politicians say: that Negroes really like segregation and that it's only the agitators that stir them up, but basically they are content.[18] Now, the only way this can be refuted is through the people in the situation to engage in a determined, forthright way in the movement that is taking place. So that I would say that it is necessary to have Southerners themselves, as you had in the lunch counter sit-ins, to make it crystal clear that they do not like segregation. But on the other hand, I think it is good to have people from all sections of the country rising up and supporting the movement so that it is clear all over the nation that this is a problem, which must be the concern of every citizen of the nation.

---

17. In 1961 District Court judge Irving Kaufman ordered that black students be allowed to transfer out of Lincoln Elementary School after he ruled the New Rochelle, New York, board of education had "deliberately created and maintained the Lincoln School as a racially segregated school" (*Taylor et al., v. Board of Education of City School District of City of New Rochelle et al.*, 195 F. Supp. 231). Later that year the Federal Commission on Civil Rights blamed the Chicago board of education for allowing overcrowding of classrooms and hiring inferior teaching staffs at the city's predominantly black schools. A group of parents had already filed suit against the board for establishing districts along racial lines (Donald Janson, "School Quarrel Grows in Chicago," *New York Times*, 1 October 1961).

18. After a white mob attacked a group of freedom riders arriving in Birmingham, Alabama, Governor John Patterson described the integrationists as "agitators" who journeyed to the state to "deliberately break the law" and who were "looking for trouble" (Bob Ingram, "Patterson Vows Arrest for Integration Testers," *Montgomery Advertiser*, 18 May 1961). In the midst of SNCC-led sit-ins and voter registration campaigns in McComb, Mississippi, in October 1961, the mayor, C.H. Douglas, blamed "outside interference" for bringing an end to the city's eighty-eight years of racial harmony (Claude Sitton, "Hard-Core Segregationist City in Mississippi Is Nearing Crisis," *New York Times*, 21 October 1961).

[*King*]: Why, I quite agree that you do have that third man, and at points maybe
this third man is to be criticized even more than those who are brutal and those who
are vocal in their opposition. I think I said somewhere today that it may well be that
we will have to repent in this generation not merely for the loud words of the bad
people but for the appalling silence of the so-called good people. I have been disappointed in many instances with the Christian church. I've been disappointed with
many ministers in particular and the church in general. It may be that the church
has been a little slow on this point, because it didn't read or didn't translate or didn't
quite understand some biblical passages. There is a passage in the New Testament
which talks about the light of the world, and many have felt that this could at least
apply to the church—that the church should be the light of the world.[19] But I think
many of the preachers and Christians feel that this meant the taillight instead of the
headlight. [*laughter*] So, I guess they've kind of misinterpreted the Bible. But it is true
that the church has often been the taillight.

I remember last year in Atlanta when the schools were getting ready to be integrated. The church announced, the bishop, the Catholic bishop announced that the
Catholic schools, the parochial schools would be integrated after the public schools
are successfully integrated.[20] So that was the taillight again. The same thing happened in New Orleans. Archbishop Rummel announced back in '55 that they would
integrate the parochial schools there. And there was a great deal of pressure and
opposition, which lead to a retreat. And finally, last year it was said that they would
wait a while to see how the public school integration worked out and then the church
schools would be integrated.[21] And of course, I don't even need to talk about many
of my fellow Protestants because they haven't even had the idea in mind of starting
at all. [*laughter*]

But this is disappointing, and I think that the failure of the church in this period
to be a great moral voice is certainly one of the tragedies of this whole period. And
I think it would be one of the tragedies of history if a future [*given?*], a future historian is able to look back and cry out in the history books that the Christian church
proved to be the bulwark, the last bulwark of segregated power in the United States.
This would be a great tragedy. I think though that there is a new awareness, at least
a new nagging of consciousness on the part of many ministers and many Christians.
They are coming to realize that the church has failed to stand out in its witness at
this point, and many are trying to do something about it. So, there is a ray of hope
even amid the fact that, amid the darkness and the fact that they have not stood out
in the past.

---

19. John 8:12: "Then spake Jesus again unto them, saying, I am the light of the world: he that fol-
loweth me shall not walk in darkness, but shall have the light of life."

20. Atlanta's public schools were integrated at the beginning of the 1961 school year, when nine students integrated local high schools. Although the Archdiocese of Atlanta integrated its schools the next
fall, those run by the Presbyterian and Episcopal Churches integrated only reluctantly between 1963 and
1966.

21. Calling it "morally wrong and sinful," Archbishop Joseph Rummel of New Orleans announced
his intention to integrate the archdiocese's school system in February 1956. Faced with protests over the
decision, including an appeal to Pope Pius XII to prevent integration, the schools were not integrated
until the fall of 1962, four years after the public schools ("Catholics End Segregation at Schools in New
Orleans," *New York Times*, 28 March 1962).

[*King*]:   Well, one would have to go into the whole idea, and I guess this can lead to a long philosophical debate—the whole idea of who is religious and who isn't religious. And there have been people who believe firmly in nonviolence who consider themselves atheist. There are still people who are strong believers in nonviolence who don't believe in God in the same sense that other people believe in. Even Gandhi did not believe in a personal God in the sense that a theist would believe in a personal God. The whole Hindu tradition has believed more in an impersonal absolute, an impersonal Brahman.[22] And I think it goes into this whole idea of who is religious. But there have been people and there are people today—I read a book the other day, *The Conquest of Violence*, written by a woman who contends that this philosophy of nonviolence has relevance to the world beyond the religious side of it, because it is the first answer to the problem that I have discussed earlier: means and ends. And she says in the beginning, in the preface of the book, that she is a humanist and that there was so much that she couldn't accept that Gandhi taught, but the one thing she could accept was nonviolence as a practical technique to grapple with a social situation and to solve the problem which nobody else has solved on such a great level as Gandhi, namely, the problem of means and ends.[23]

I do think, though, that while it is possible for a nonreligious person to believe in nonviolence as a technique and as a passing strategy, in order for a person to really believe in nonviolence as a way of life, he must have some religious orientation. I believe that if it is to become more than just a passing technique to be used in a particular social situation for the moment, if it is to become a way of life, a creed, so that it touches the individual in his everyday life and in his every attitude, then I do believe that it is necessary to have some religious orientation.

[*King*]:   I quite agree with you that prejudice is at the center of this thing, and that when we move into the realm of prejudice, we are moving into the realm of emotional problems. I think at points in this whole struggle, we are grappling with a sort of mass psychosis, a mass neurosis or whatever we want to call it. People are caught up in a system that they really can't explain. They don't know how they got there. It's irrational and all of that. Now, I think it is necessary to understand this in analyzing the problem, and I think it is true that in understanding this, it can help bring about a broader understanding, and I think this is what nonviolence does in its deeper dimensions. It is that understanding goodwill.

On the other hand, I don't think it should lead one to the point of retreating and not trying to change certain conditions. In other words, it would not be fair to say to

---

22. In the Hindu tradition, Brahman represented ultimate reality, and multiple beings were worshipped, including the gods Shiva and Vishnu. In his autobiography, Gandhi admitted that he did not have a deep faith in any god, but rather the "conviction that morality is the basis of things, and that truth is the substance of all morality" (Mahatma Gandhi, *An Autobiography: The Story of My Experiments with Truth* [Boston: Beacon Press, 1957], p. 34).

23. A self-described "rationalist and humanist" suspicious of religion and "obscurantist approaches," Joan V. Bondurant argued it was unnecessary, however, to "subscribe either to the asceticism so characteristic of Gandhi nor to his religious notions in order to understand and to value the central contribution of his technique of non-violent action" (*Conquest of Violence: The Gandhian Philosophy of Conflict* [Princeton: Princeton University Press, 1958], vi–vii).

oppressed people that you should wait and just patiently accept injustice until all of the oppressors have their prejudices removed. I think it's necessary to work to help to 1962 move these prejudices, and one of the ways to do it is to get rid of the system itself. I believe firmly that the only way we're going to get rid of some of the fears in the white South concerning desegregation is to present them with desegregation.

Feb
1962

I was reading the other day of a psychiatrist who had this little boy to come to him. The mother brought a little boy who had had a series of bad dreams about a bear who just tried to attack him every night. And every night he had a nightmare about this bear. And so the psychiatrist got the little boy and said, "Now, that bear really likes you, and he wants to play with you." He said, "Now, tonight when he comes back, and he's coming back tonight, when he comes back," he says, "put your arms around him, and he's going to like you and you'll like him." And he went on, and his bad dream that night, and the bear came, and he embraced the bear, and the bear embraced him, and he didn't dream about the bear anymore. And if I could use the analogy here, there are many people who have fears in our nation concerning integration, and the only way they're going to get rid of these fears is to be presented with the fact that they will have to accept it. And sometimes I think just a shock is necessary, the shock method is necessary, the shock treatment is necessary to get people back to reality when there are emotional problems. There has to be occasionally a sort of creative shock in society in order to get people back to reality.[24]

So that I think we must work on these two levels. I think there must be that understanding goodwill.

On the other hand, I think we must continue to work to remove the conditions so that it will be easier for the people to get rid of the prejudices. It is true that, as I've said this morning, laws cannot change attitudes maybe, but they can certainly control the external effects of bad internal attitudes. It is true, I know, in many situations that laws have made it easier for people to rise out of their prejudices. In Montgomery, Alabama, the buses are now integrated, and I'm sure that the people who struggled against integration as we struggled to bring about bus integration felt that they couldn't live with it. But now the buses are integrated and they go on and ride them, and they discovered that the sun still got up that next morning after the buses were integrated and things are moving on fine. And the fact itself helped to do something, and I think the more we can present the facts to people, even though it's painful in the beginning, the more they will change. Just as certain laws had to come into being in the United States to rectify certain unjust business practices, I'm sure that the people today have changed their attitudes concerning these very things that were once done, because the law helped to create the situation where attitudes could be changed much easier than they could with the continued existence of the system itself.[25]

------

24. "A little rebellion now and then is a good thing," Thomas Jefferson wrote, believing it provided "a medicine necessary for the sound health of government" (Jefferson to James Madison, 30 January 1787, in *The Papers of Thomas Jefferson*, vol. 11, ed. Julian P. Boyd, Mina R. Bryan, Fredrick Aandahl [Princeton: Princeton University Press, 1955], pp. 92–97).

25. The Sherman Antitrust Act (1890), the Clayton Antitrust Act (1914), and the Federal Trade Commission Act (1914) were all passed with the intent of protecting consumers by eliminating monopolies, price-fixing, and other business agreements designed to lessen competition.

407

[*King*]:    I don't know if you're speaking of, you're thinking of any specific religion at this point. I think it is true that some religions contend that they have the answer. I think in a sense all religions would have certain contentions to make at this point. I would say this: that I'm a Christian, and as a Christian I believe in the saving power of Jesus Christ for instance, but my Christianity has not lead me to the point of believing that God has limited his revelation to Christianity. I think that God has revealed himself in some way in all religions, and even though I believe that Jesus Christ represents the most unique revelation of God, I believe firmly that God has revealed himself in other religions, and he has not left himself without a witness.[26] And there are other sheep that are not of this fold, even the Christian fold.[27] So that I'm not so narrow as to say that only within Christianity do you have ultimate truth. I would say that there are truths revealed in the other great religions of the world. Now, I'm sure that there are some people who would disagree with me at this point. There are many people who would, but I would hold the theory and the idea that there is an aspect of God's revelation in all religions.

[*King*]:    Let me start off by saying that I think you've raised a very serious question and one of the real questions that one who is committed to nonviolence has to face whether there is that moral feeling or conscience that can be appealed to.

The initial response of the oppressor when oppressed people rise up is bitterness whether you use violence or nonviolence. The initial response is bitterness. I don't think the people in Montgomery, Alabama, or in Jackson, Mississippi, or in Albany, Georgia, just to mention some examples—I don't think they were inspired at all by the fact that the Negroes were using nonviolence when the movement first started.[28] I think their initial reaction was bitterness.

Prime Minister Nehru said he never saw the British officials more angry than when they first turned the other cheek. That's when they would beat them a little more, because sometimes this can arouse the guilt feeling more than anything else, and there are two ways that we respond to guilt feelings.[29] One is to try to repent and to change our ways and allow this guilt to so arouse the conscience that we really try to get better and make a right about [*face?*]. On the other hand, the guilt feeling can cause the individual to try to drown that sense of guilt by engaging even more in the guilt-evoking act. And I have seen this in so many instances. I believe that many

---

26. Christianity, Judaism, and Islam all draw on the faith of ancient Israel for their foundation and each looks to prophets as responsible for revealing God's message. Jesus and Muhammad are the main figures in Christianity and Islam, respectively, whereas Judaism recognizes a number of prophets, including Moses and Isaiah.

27. Cf. John 10:16.

28. During the bus boycott in Montgomery, the homes of King and E. D. Nixon were bombed, and city officials charged over eighty leaders of violating an anti-boycotting law. Twenty-seven freedom riders were jailed and charged with breach of the peace when they attempted to integrate the bus terminal in Jackson, Mississippi, on 24 May 1961. In December 1961, over 700 protesters were arrested when the Albany Movement sought to end segregation throughout Albany, Georgia.

29. Nehru believed that the use of nonviolent techniques in the independence movement provided the British "no handle, no grip, no opportunity for forcible suppression" and ultimately led them to open fire on a crowd in Amritsar on 13 April 1919, killing over 300 people (*Toward Freedom: The Autobiography of Jawaharlal Nehru* [New York: John Day, 1941], p. 70).

of the people in any struggle—whether it's in the white South of the United States or in other places, many of the people who use violence are really fighting offensive guilt, and they are trying to drown that sense of guilt by engaging more in the very act which brought it into being.

Now, after saying this though, I do feel that if there is a persistence in nonviolence, it does eventually get over. It does eventually arouse the conscience. It does eventually appeal to that moral sense. It doesn't do it overnight. It doesn't do it the next week. But if one continues, if the group continues, I do feel that it eventually gets over. And I think the virtue of it is that it leaves an aftermath of brotherhood, of reconciliation, wherein violence always leaves an aftermath of bitterness.

If I can give an example on a large scale, I think that one of the beautiful things is the kind of friendship that exists today between the British and the Indian people. I never will forget when I was in India a few years ago. We were having dinner with Prime Minister Nehru, and two of the visitors that night, two of the persons who had dinner with us were, one was Lady Mountbatten and the other was the daughter. Now, Lord Mountbatten was the viceroy, I believe, of India when India received its independence.[30] But now there is a level of friendship and understanding. They are having dinner with Prime Minister Nehru, and there is this level of friendship and understanding that would not have been there if that had been won through violence. So that they didn't have the problem of spending the next hundred years getting rid of the bitterness that came into being as a result of the situation. So, this is the first thing that I would say.

The second point is that while it may be true that groups and people that have used nonviolence have not been in the position of controlling the agencies of violence, I don't necessarily feel that they have been the weak people. Gandhi use to say that if one has to choose between cowardice and violence, it is better to fight, because cowardice is on a lower moral level than violence.[31] And I quite agree with Gandhi. If one is nonviolent merely because he doesn't have the weapons of violence or because he's afraid, he isn't truly nonviolent. And this was something that was taught over and over again by Gandhi, and we could say well he was rationalizing, because they really didn't have the weapon and they really didn't have the know-how, the techniques of violence. But I think there was a deep commitment to nonviolence and all of its dimensions. And I believe the same thing in our struggle today: that we should not use it merely because we don't have the instruments of violence, but we must follow this method because it is the method of the strong.

I can give an example in my own life. When we started our struggle in Montgomery, Alabama, a few years ago, I had the gun in the house, just as many other people. And I went to my wife one day, and we talked about this thing. I said, "Now, as a leader in the nonviolent movement, I just cannot in all good conscience have a gun in the

---

30. On 10 February 1959, King dined with Edwina Mountbatten and her daughter Pamela at Nehru's home in New Delhi. Louis Mountbatten was the viceroy of India when it received its independence on 15 August 1947.

31. "I would rather have India resort to arms in order to defend her honor," Gandhi wrote, "than that she should in a cowardly manner become or remain a helpless witness to her own dishonor" ("The Doctrine of The Sword," *Young India*, 11 August 1920).

house. I don't think I need it, and I don't want it," and we discussed it. And I said, "Now, I know that the vast majority of people, Negro people in Montgomery would not follow this, but it is also necessary for a leader to take an absolute position in order to get the followers to take a relative position." So, I felt it absolutely necessary, and finally, we finally agreed to get rid of the gun. And I haven't had a gun in my house since then, and I have been less afraid without a gun than I was when I had the gun in the house.[32] [*laughter*] But I do think there is a power that can come within, which causes the individual to engage in a nonviolent movement not because he can't go in his house and get a gun and come out and shoot somebody. I think there are cases in the United States where Negroes could do pretty well with violence, at least for a few minutes anyway. [*laughter*] But I think it would defeat the end.

And I think another thing is this: that it is much more difficult in the situation where you're struggling to bring about integration. You are not—there is difference between integration and independence—you are not driving out a foreign invader, but you've got to live the next morning with the very people that you are struggling with at this hour. And there's a much greater difficulty in grappling with it there. The other thing is that in most places and most situations where you have a struggle for independence, it is a numerical majority struggling in a situation where a numerical minority is there in the political controlling situation, wherein in our struggle in the United States it's a numerical minority seeking to develop a new relationship and a brotherly relationship with a numerical majority. So that I think in both situations, whether it is a struggle for independence or integration, nonviolence is necessary and workable. But I think it's even more necessary in a situation where you're working for integration.

[*Moderator*]:   Dr. King has been most generous with his time, certainly most inspiring, and we're extremely grateful. He will speak again tomorrow morning at 9:30 in this auditorium, and all are invited.[33] I should also like to say that there will be an informal gathering at Casa Maria after this meeting, and you are invited to come up and meet Dr. King. This message is for university students and for learners of all ages. Thank you very much. [*applause*]

At. RBFP.

---

32.   King recounts this decision in *Stride Toward Freedom: The Montgomery Story* (New York: Harper & Row, 1958), pp. 140–141. According to Bayard Rustin, however, when he and writer Bill Worthy visited King's house in late February 1956, Worthy nearly sat on a gun lying on a chair, and armed guards almost shot a telegram delivery boy (Rustin, Interview by T. H. Baker, 17 June 1969).

33.   "Stride Toward Freedom" would be King's topic on 15 February.

# Statement to *Newsweek* Magazine on the Proposed
## Department of Urban Affairs

26 February 1962
[*Atlanta, Ga.*]

*Five days after the United States House of Representatives voted against President
Kennedy's proposed Department of Urban Affairs, King sends the following
statement to* Newsweek.[1] *Given the controversy surrounding the appointment
of Robert C. Weaver, an African American, to head the department, King warns
that the black community could wield their political power to defeat politicians who
"allowed the race question to sabotage" Weaver's appointment.[2] Excerpts from this
statement were published a week later in an article on black perspectives on the role
of race in the proposal's failure.[3]*

Many factors have conjoined to produce the smashing defeat of a Department
of Urban Affairs that obstensibly would have placed a Negro in the government at
Cabinet level. There is no gainsaying however, that the issue of race was one of the
primal factors. Negroes cannot help but interpret this as a vote by Congress against
the full acceptance of the Negro in American life. Negroes may use their political
power at the polls this Fall to defeat Congressmen who allowed the race question to
sabotage one of the most cherished dreams of the Negro community—a Negro in
the Federal government at the cabinet level.

MLK Jr

TD. MLKJP-GAMK.

---

1. Kennedy proposed the creation of the new Cabinet department in December 1960 to aid cities
with transportation, housing, and urban renewal projects.

2. Weaver was the head of the Housing and Home Finance Agency and would have been the first
African American to hold a cabinet position. A newspaper article also quoted King as saying he was
"filled with disgust over the hypocrisy of the Republican Party," and that the vote against the new
department was a "vote against civil rights" ("Racism Tag Put on GOP Urban Affairs Vote," Baltimore
*Afro-American*, 3 February 1962). For more on Weaver, see King to Weaver, 13 February 1961, pp. 155–156
in this volume.

3. *Newsweek* quoted King's last two sentences in "The Weaver Case: Negro Views," *Newsweek*, 5 March
1962.

# To C. Kenzie Steele

26 February 1962
[*Atlanta, Ga.*]

*After returning from a speaking tour in Puerto Rico, King belatedly congratulates*
*Steele, a cofounder of SCLC, on his tenth anniversary as pastor of Bethel Baptist*
*Church in Tallahassee, Florida.*

REV C K STEELE
BETHEL BAPTIST CHURCH POBN1003

JUST RETURNED TO THE COUNTRY AND DISCOVERED THAT YOUR TENTH ANNIVER-
SARY WAS CELEBRATED YESTERDAY REGRET THAT I DID NOT KNOW IN TIME TO GET
YOU A MESSAGE YOUR HUMANITARIAN CONCERN WILL BE AN INSPIRATION TO GENERA-
TIONS YET UNBORN SMALL CONTRIBUTION WILL FOLLOW[1]

MARTIN LUTHER KING JR
SOUTHERN CHRISTIAN LEADERSHIP CONFERENCE

PHWSr. MLKJP-GAMK: Box 23.

---

1. On the same day this telegram was sent, King's secretary mailed Steele a check for $25 as a "per-
sonal contribution" (Dora E. McDonald to Steele, 26 February 1962).

# "Fumbling on the New Frontier"

3 March 1962
New York, N.Y.

*A year after* The Nation *published King's article "Equality Now," the journal's*
*editor Carey McWilliams asked King to write another piece reflecting on the*
*Kennedy administration's handling of civil rights issues over the past year.[1] In*
*this largely critical piece, King assails the administration for being too "cautious*
*and defensive," claiming that Kennedy's failure to end discrimination in housing*
*"did more to undermine confidence in his intentions" than can be counterbalanced*
*by his achievements. King acknowledges Kennedy's political quandary but points*
*to the courage of Abraham Lincoln to pass the Emancipation Proclamation*
*despite fear of alienating slave owners. He advises the president not to allow the*

---

1. McWilliams to King, 15 December 1961; King, "Equality Now," 4 February 1961, pp. 139–150 in this
volume.

*segregationist South to hold "hostage his legislative program." King warns that
Kennedy "may become a tragically helpless figure" if the president did not break
from his metaphorical "prison" and take control of his legislative agenda or use
his executive powers.*[2]

The Kennedy Administration in 1961 waged an essentially cautious and defensive struggle for civil rights against an unyielding adversary. As the year unfolded, Executive initiative became increasingly feeble, and the chilling prospect emerged of a general Administration retreat. In backing away from an Executive Order to end discrimination in housing, the President did more to undermine confidence in his intentions than could be offset by a series of smaller accomplishments during the year.[3] He has begun 1962 with a show of renewed aggressiveness; one can only hope that it will be sustained.[4]

In any case, it is clear that the vigorous young men of this Administration have displayed a certain *élan* in the attention they give to civil-rights issues. Undaunted by Southern backwardness and customs, they conceived and launched some imaginative and bold forays. It is also clear that this Administration has reached out more creatively than its predecessors to blaze some new trails, notably in the sensitive areas of voting and registration.[5] Moreover, President Kennedy has appointed more Negroes to key government posts than has any previous administration.[6] One Executive Order has been issued which, if vigorously enforced, will go a long, long way toward eliminating employment discrimination in federal agencies and in industries where

---

2. On 25 February 1962, SCLC issued a press release about the article's publication entitled "King disappointed with Kennedy administration." Later that same day, SCLC released a revised press release, containing paragraphs "inadvertently omitted" from the earlier press release. The statement conceded that the Kennedy administration had made "some significant gains," namely the appointment of African Americans to government positions (SCLC, Press release, Omitted paragraphs from earlier press release, 25 February 1962).

3. In the 7 October presidential debate with Republican candidate Richard Nixon, Kennedy observed that "equality of opportunity in the field of housing" could be achieved "on all federal supported housing by a stroke of the president's pen." King endorsed this idea in "Equality Now," observing that "it is no exaggeration to say that the President could give segregation its death blow through a stroke of the pen" (King, "Equality Now," 4 February 1961, p. 145 in this volume). Although a draft of the executive order was ready for Kennedy's signature in late November 1961, the *New York Times* reported that Kennedy held off signing for fear of alienating Southern votes for his tariff program and other proposals (Peter Braestrup, "Order to Ban Bias in Housing Ready," *New York Times*, 27 November 1961). On 20 November 1962, Kennedy issued Executive Order 11063 barring racial discrimination in federal housing.

4. King may be referring to Kennedy's support of legislation in early 1962 to end literacy tests and poll taxes in federal elections and primaries.

5. During Robert F. Kennedy's first year as Attorney General, the Justice Department filed fourteen new cases and investigated complaints regarding violations in voter registration in sixty-one counties (Kennedy, Report to the President on the Department of Justice's activities in the field of Civil Rights, 29 December 1961).

6. Among the more than fifty African Americans appointed were Housing and Home Finance Agency administrator Robert C. Weaver, appeals judge Thurgood Marshall, and Norway ambassador Clifton R. Wharton.

413

government contracts are involved.[7] So it is obvious that the Kennedy Administration has to its credit some constructive and praiseworthy achievements.

With regard to civil rights, then, it would be profoundly wrong to take an extreme position either way when viewing the Administration. While the President has not yet earned unqualified confidence and support, neither has he earned rejection and withdrawal of support. Perhaps his earnestness of attitude, fed with the vitamins of mass action, may yet grow into passionate purpose. The civil-rights movement must remain critical and flexible, watchful and active.

It is fortunate that the initiatives that President Kennedy has directed toward the reduction of international tensions present no contradictions with respect to civil rights. The Administration need have no fear that the white South will punish it for its desegregation attitudes by withholding support for a new foreign policy. While white and Negro Southerners have not yet mastered the art of living together in a relaxed society of brotherhood, they are united in the desire to remain alive. Indeed, Negroes *need* an international *détente*, because in a period of tensions and crisis their needs are easily forgotten, and a political rigidity grips the nation that sharply inhibits social change.

The year 1961 was characterized by inadequacy and incompleteness in the civil-rights field. It is not only that the Administration too often retreated in haste from a battlefield which it has proclaimed a field of honor, but—more significantly—its basic strategic goals have been narrowed. Its efforts have been directed toward limited accomplishments in a number of areas, affecting few individuals and altering old patterns only superficially. Changes in depth and breadth are not yet in sight, nor has there been a commitment of resources adequate to enforce extensive change. It is a melancholy fact that the Administration is aggressively driving only toward the limited goal of token integration.

It is important to understand the perspective from which this criticism develops. The paradox of laudable limited progress on the one hand, and frustrating insufficiency of progress on the other, is understandable if it is realized that the civil-rights struggle can be viewed from two quite dissimilar perspectives. Many people of good will accept the achievement of steady advances, even when fractional. They feel simple addition must eventually accumulate a totality of social gains which will answer the problem. Others, however, viewing the task from the long perspective of history, are less sanguine. They are aware that the struggle being waged is against an opposition capable of the most tenacious resistance, either actively or through inertia. Such forces are not overcome by simple pressures, but only through massive exertion. This is a law not alone of physics, but of society as well.

To illustrate, it is not practical to integrate buses, and then over an extended period of time expect to add another gain, and then another and another. Unfortunately,

---

7. On 6 March 1961, Kennedy issued Executive Order 10925, establishing the President's Committee on Equal Employment Opportunity. The committee focused on eliminating discrimination within the federal government and possessed the power to cancel government contracts for failure to comply. Led by Vice President Lyndon B. Johnson, the committee accepted "Plans for Progress" from various industries pledging to employ African Americans but drew criticism from the NAACP for its failure to urge mandatory compliance. As head of the new committee, Johnson wrote King on 13 April 1962 updating him on the progress on black federal employment in Atlanta (pp. 435–437 in this volume).

resistance stiffens after each limited victory; inertia sets in, and the forward movement not only slows down, but is often reversed entirely. What is required to maintain
gains is an initial sweep of positive action so far-reaching that it immobilizes and
weakens the adversary, thus depriving him of his power to retaliate. Simultaneously,
in order that public officials are not left free to circumvent the law by local devices, an
extensive campaign to put the franchise in the hands of Negroes must be conducted.
These programs, in turn, require for their success that a corps of responsible leaders
be trained and developed—that ample legal defense skills and financial resources
be available. In short, what is required is massive social mobilization uniting the
strength of individuals, organizations, government, press and schools.

It is clear that to date no Administration has grasped the problem in this total
sense and committed the varieties of weaponry required for constructive action on
so broad a scale.

Beyond this, the American Negro is impelled by psychological motives not fully
understood even by his white allies. Every Negro, regardless of his educational or
cultural level, carries the burden of centuries of deprivation and inferior status. The
burden is with him every waking moment of his life—and often, through his dreams,
dominates his sleeping moments as well. It diminishes his confidence and belittles
his achievements. He is tormented by the overwhelming task of catching up. This
problem sharpens to a razor edge when he confronts a new struggle and is aware of
the pitiful inadequacy of his resources.

When the nation feels threatened by war, a military budget of some $50 billion
is freely spent each year to achieve security.[8] Not even $1 billion a year is spent by
government on behalf of 20,000,000 Negroes seeking to defend themselves from
the persistent attack on their rights. When Negroes look from their overworked,
undermanned civil-rights organizations to their government, they see in Washington
only a tiny bureau, equally undermanned and overworked, hopelessly incapable of
doing what is necessary. They cannot feel certain that progress is over tomorrow's
horizon, or even that the government has any real understanding of the dimensions
of their problems.

Their sense of inadequacy is further heightened when they look at Africa and
Asia and see with envy the bursting of age-old bonds in societies still partially at a
tribal level, but ablaze with modern vitality and creativity. An Alliance for Progress
for South America, to cost $20 billion, is forward-looking and necessary.[9] An Alliance
for Progress for the turbulent South is equally necessary.

From this perspective, the New Frontier is unfortunately not new enough; and the
Frontier is set too close to the rear.

In the year that has just passed, certain significant developments occurred in the
South that are worthy of comment. Despite tormenting handicaps, Negroes moved
from sporadic, limited actions to broad-scale activities different in kind and degree

---

8. Both houses of Congress unanimously approved a then-record $46 billion dollar defense budget
on 10 August 1961.

9. On 13 March 1961, Kennedy announced the Alliance for Progress, offering Latin American
nations $20 billion over ten years in low-interest loans to help develop their economies and "to satisfy the
basic needs of the American people for homes, work and land, health and schools" (*Public Papers of the
Presidents of the United States: John F. Kennedy, 1961* [Washington, D.C.: U.S. Government Printing Office,
1962], p. 172).

from anything done in the past. City after city was swept by boycotts, sit-ins, freedom rides and registration campaigns. A new spirit was manifest in the Negro's willingness to demonstrate in the streets of communities in which, by tradition, he was supposed to step aside when a white man strode toward him.

The change in spirit was even more dramatically exemplified by the Negroes' willingness, in communities such as Albany, Georgia, to endure mass jailing. Words cannot express the exultation felt by the individual as he finds himself, with hundreds of his fellows, behind prison bars for a cause he knows is just. This exultation has been felt by businessmen, workers, teachers, ministers, housewives, housemaids—in ages ranging from the early teens to the seventies. Significantly, these people were not gathered from across the nation; all were local residents, except for a few "outsiders" and "aliens"—including this writer, who is from far-off Atlanta, Georgia.[10]

To the depth of these movements was added breadth when areas such as Mississippi and rural Georgia, hitherto quiescent, were churned into turbulence by registration campaigns and freedom rides.

Thus 1961 saw the Negro moving relentlessly forward against an opposition that was occasionally reasonable, but unfortunately more often vicious. It was a year of the victory of the nonviolent method: though blood flowed, not one drop was drawn by a Negro from his adversary. Yet the victories were scored by the victims, not by the violent mobs.

These highlights are cited to illustrate that Negroes, despite shortcomings and a flood of unresolved problems, were spiritedly meeting their obligation to act.

It is against this backdrop that the inquiry into the experience of 1961 turns us again to the Administration and its responsibilities. At the beginning of the year, the cautious approach of the Administration turned a possible spectacular victory into a tragic defeat. A move was made in the Senate to end the two-thirds cloture rule—the legislative incinerator that burns into ashes all civil-rights bills. At the climactic moment, the Administration remained mute instead of carrying out its pledge of active leadership. Even so, the measure was defeated by a narrow 50–46 vote.[11] No one doubts that had the Administration spoken, a historic victory would have resulted.

The Administration then brought forth a plan to substitute Executive orders for legislative programs. The most challenging order, to end discrimination in federal housing, while no adequate substitute for the many legislative acts promised in campaign platforms and speeches, nevertheless was alluring, and pressure abated for Congressional action. The year passed and the President fumbled. By the close of the year, a new concept was adopted: the President now wished to "move ahead in a way which will maintain a consensus."[12] According to Washington observers,

---

10. Over seven hundred Albany demonstrators, ranging from high school protesters to Albany Movement president William G. Anderson, were jailed during December 1961 (Howard Zinn, "Albany: Special report of the Southern Regional Council," 8 January 1962).

11. On 11 January 1961, the Senate voted 50–46 for a motion to send to the Rules Committee a proposed plan to modify Rule XXII, which stipulated that any motion to cut off a potential filibuster, or cloture, has to be approved by two-thirds of senators present and voting.

12. In a 15 January 1962 press conference, Kennedy added: "I think a proper judgment can be made on this and all other matters relating to equality of rights at the end of this year, and at the end of our

this concept derived from the President's concern that his legislative programs in other areas, notably his trade program, might suffer at the hands of key Southern Congressmen—if he upset them by moving "too fast" on civil rights.[13]

For years, Abraham Lincoln resisted signing the Emancipation Proclamation because he feared to alienate the slaveholders in the border states. But the imperatives of the Civil War required that slavery be ended, and he finally signed the document and won the war, preserved the nation, and gave America its greatest hour of moral glory.[14] President Kennedy may be tormented by a similar dilemma, and may well be compelled to make an equally fateful decision—one which, if correct, could be found a century later to have made the nation greater and the man more memorable.

Though one can respect the urgency of trade legislation to facilitate competition with the European Common Market, the 20 million Americans who have waited 300 years to be able to compete as human beings in the market place at home have the right to question whether, this year, trade agreements are more important than their long-postponed freedom. Should Americans favor the winning of the welfare and trade programs in Congress at the cost of the Negro citizen's elementary rights?

Are we seeking our national purpose in the spirit of Thomas Jefferson, who said: "All men are created equal . . . endowed with certain inalienable rights. . . . Among these are life, liberty and the pursuit of happiness"? Or are we pursuing the national purpose proclaimed by Calvin Coolidge, who said: "The business of America is business"?[15]

It may be an electrifying act to shelve trade bills for human-rights legislation because it has never been done before. Perhaps that alone is reason enough to do it.

Even apart from morality, practical considerations require a different course. The defensive posture of the President against adversaries seasoned in the art of combat, and older than the nation itself, will increase his impotence, not release his strength. They have already paralyzed his Executive power by holding hostage his legislative program. If he cannot break out of this prison, he will be unable either to influence

---

term" (*Public Papers of the Presidents of the United States: John F. Kennedy, 1962* [Washington, D.C.: U.S. Government Printing Office, 1963], p. 21). Robert F. Kennedy defended his brother's actions in a televised interview, claiming that "it would have been the easiest thing in the world for him, and the most politically expedient matter for him to sign that Executive Order some months ago. But there are other considerations which he as President must take into mind and before he takes certain actions" (Robert F. Kennedy, Interview by Martin Agronsky on *Today*, 30 January 1962).

13. The Senate eventually voted 78–8 to approve the Trade Expansion Act of 1962, which sought to accelerate the economy by giving the President authority to reduce tariffs between the United States and the European Common Market; Kennedy signed the bill into law on 11 October 1962.

14. During King's February 1962 trip to Puerto Rico he told an audience that on a visit to the White House, likely in October 1961, President Kennedy showed him the table where Abraham Lincoln signed the Emancipation Proclamation in 1862. King told the President: "I would like you to sign a Second Emancipation Proclamation on this very table" (Antonio Quiñones Calderón, "King in the UI Believes Second Emancipation Declaration Is Needed," [in Spanish.] trans. Anena Otii, *El Mundo*, 16 February 1962).

15. Coolidge, Address to the American Society of Newspaper Editors, "The Press under a Free Government," 17 January 1925: "After all, the chief business of the American people is business" (Calvin Coolidge, *Foundations of the Republic: Speeches and Addresses* [New York: Charles Scribner's Sons, 1926], p. 187).

legislation or use his Executive powers, and in this confinement he may become a tragically helpless figure.

Impotence at a moment of kaleidoscopic world change is even worse than error. The President is seeking compromises acceptable to his jailers, but they would rather paralyze him than accept compromises. It is deeply significant that the activities of the ultra-right-wing organizations are aimed principally at the President, and that the one issue uniting all the disparate rightist groups is their virulent opposition to civil rights. He has already challenged them, boldly, but holding to the offensive on civil rights is part of the challenge.[16]

The President and the Administration are impressively popular. The President will have to take his fight to the people, who trust him. He must now trust *them*. He can be confident that correct policy, sound issues and an aroused people are a fortress mightier than a hundred reactionary committee chairmen. An illustrious predecessor, Franklin Roosevelt, relied more on the weight of the people than on maneuvering in Congressional cloakrooms.[17]

If the President acts, his leadership will communicate strength to waiting millions. Firm, decisive direction from him will galvanize the forces that can turn a program into an actuality. "Nothing in the world is stronger," Victor Hugo said, "than an idea whose time has come."[18] The nation is ready and eager for bold leadership in civil rights. This is evident in the scope and quality of the actions conducted last year even in the absence of sustained, strong, national leadership.

The opportunity is not yet lost, nor has the sincerity of the Administration been irrevocably discredited. But the clock of history is nearing the midnight hour and an upsurge in governmental activity is an inescapable necessity. The Negro in 1962—almost one hundred years after slavery's demise—justifiably looks to government for comprehensive, vital programs which will change the totality of his life.

Civil rights will continue for many decades to remain a political football unless the national government abandons the traditional piecemeal approach and constructs a long-term plan. India and other underdeveloped nations, confronting the monumental challenge to liquidate centuries of backwardness, have relied upon detailed plans of two years, four years, six years.[19] The plans define the specific steps to be taken by stages which will lift the nation into a new era. We are not strangers to such conceptions. The President has proposed a ten-year plan to put a man on

---

16. At a Democratic Party dinner in Los Angeles on 18 November, Kennedy lashed out at right-wing extremist organizations, like the John Birch Society, for their attempts to equate the Democratic Party with socialism and further provoking disunity: "There have always been those fringes of our society who have sought to escape their own responsibility by finding a simple solution, an appealing slogan or a convenient scapegoat" (Tom Wicker, "Kennedy Asserts Far-Right Groups Provoke Disunity," *New York Times*, 19 November 1961).

17. Throughout his presidency, Roosevelt used radio broadcast and fireside chats in an ongoing dialogue with the public, keeping them apprised of his political goals in an effort to gain their support.

18. Victor Hugo, *The History of a Crime: Deposition of a Witness* (New York: P.F. Collier & Son, 1877), p. 429.

19. In a July 1959 article published in *Ebony* magazine, King praised efforts by Indian leaders to atone for centuries of injustices against untouchables (King, "My Trip to the Land of Gandhi," July 1959, in *Papers* 5:236).

the moon.[20] We do not yet have a plan to put a Negro in the State Legislature of Alabama.

The development of a plan for the nation-wide and complete realization of civil rights would accomplish several purposes. It would affirm that the nation is committed to solve the problem within a stated period of time; it would establish that the full resources of government would be available to that end, whatever the cost. (In this connection, it is well to remember that our country built its foundations on a cotton economy based on two centuries of virtually unpaid labor by millions of Negroes.) Finally, a plan would enable the nation to assess progress from time to time, and would declare to those who dream that segregation and discrimination can still be preserved that they must begin to live with the realities of the twentieth century.

PD. *The Nation* 194, no. 9 (3 March 1962): 190–193.

---

20. On 25 May 1961, Kennedy urged more spending to put a man on the moon before the Soviet Union, leading to a projected $40 billion budget.

## "People in Action: Pathos and Hope"

3 March 1962
New York, N.Y.

*In early February, King launched SCLC's People to People campaign with a three-day tour of the Mississippi Delta, the "symbol of hard-core resistance" in the South. Aimed at registering new voters and nurturing local leadership to serve in a "nonviolent army," the campaign included stops in Georgia, Alabama, Virginia, South Carolina, and Louisiana. Talking "with thousands of people," King recalls in this* New York Amsterdam News *article that he "listened to their problems, learned of their fears, felt the yearnings of their hope." Concluding, King maintains that "we must encourage our people in Mississippi to rise up by the hundreds and thousands and demand their freedom—now!"[1]*

I have just returned from the heart of the Mississippi Delta. It is a strange experience to see hope and pathos at the same time. Yet, this is the story of the Third Congressional District of dark Mississippi.

As part of SCLC's "people-to-people" program, several members of our staff and

---

1. Following the tour, Clarksdale resident and Mississippi NAACP activist Aaron Henry thanked SCLC on behalf of the city (Henry to Wyatt Tee Walker, 10 February 1962).

I travelled the fertile and sometime depressing Delta country.[2] This was the initial visit of a tour that will take me into every State in the South.

The immediate aim of this tour is to recruit hundreds of volunteers to work in our intensified Southwide voter registration drive and to enlist a smaller number of volunteers to serve in a nonviolent army.

This nonviolent army will consist of persons who can be on call to engage in direct action programs across the South and who will be prepared for prolonged jailings when necessary.

This trip provided me with an opportunity to talk with thousands of people on a personal basis. I talked with them on the farms and in the village stores, on the city streets and in the city churches. I listened to their problems, learned of their fears, felt the yearnings of their hope.

### Bits Of Hope

There are some flesh and blood scenes that I can never dispel from my memory. One of our earliest stops was a Catholic school that included the elementary and high school grades.

The sister in charge in each classroom, asked the question, "Where are you going tonight?" The answer was chorused, "To the Baptist Church!" They were referring to the Baptist Church where I was to speak for the mass meeting.[3] The sister had strongly urged them to attend.

How marvelous that the struggle for freedom and human dignity rises above the communions of Catholic and Protestant. This was a bit of the hope I glimpsed in the Mississippi Delta.

Then, of course, there was the pathos. How sobering it is to meet people who work only six months in the year and whose annual income averages $500.00 to $600.00.

We were informed that one plantation of 40,000 acres owned by a British syndicate and worked by a thousand Negro families, has a 95% illiteracy rate among the adults.[4]

### Violence Is Fear

Along with the economic exploitation that the whole State of Mississippi inflicts upon the Negro, there is the ever-present problem of physical violence.

As we rode along the dusty roads of the Delta country, our riding companions cited unbelievable cases of police brutality and incidents of Negroes being brutally murdered by white mobs, which never became known to the outside world. In spite of this, there is a ray of hope.

---

2. Wyatt Tee Walker, who went with King to Mississippi, later commented that one "cannot imagine how much humanity can be compressed into two and a half days of hour by hour scheduling" ("Report of the director," April 1962).

3. King spoke at the Centennial Baptist Church in Coahoma County, Mississippi (SCLC, Press release, "King's 'People to People' tour sweeps Delta," 21 February 1962).

4. The Fine Cotton Spinners and Doublers Association, later known as the Delta and Pine Land Company, was owned by several private textile mill companies, and in 1911, they purchased thirty-eight thousand acres in the area surrounding Scott, Mississippi. Over three thousand sharecroppers, who represented one thousand tenant families, were employed by the company.

This ray of hope is seen in the new determination of the Negroes themselves to be free.

As we talked with the "saints of the soil" at one country store, we recruited some twenty-odd volunteers, some unable to write their own names![5]

Functionally illiterate, but desiring freedom nevertheless. Pathos and hope.

### Editor Was Wrong

And speaking of hope, despite a blistering editorial in the Clarksdale daily decrying the advent of "professional agitators," the two public meetings held in Clarksdale were packed and jammed Wednesday and Thursday nights.[6]

The editor had predicted that most of the Negroes in Clarksdale and its environs would ignore our presence. However, the Centennial Baptist and the First Baptist Churches whose sanctuaries seat more than a thousand, were filled hours before the meeting time. This was evidence that Negroes in Mississippi are not satisfied with segregation. Hope and pathos.

You have already read in the national press that The Reverend Theodore Trammell, minister of the Haven Methodist Church in Clarksdale has filed as a candidate for the Congress of the United States from the Third District.[7] He is reportedly the first candidate for high office since Reconstruction.

He has been joined by another clergyman from the Fourth District in Jackson. Think of it! Two Negro candidates for Congress from Mississippi.

It is not improbable that if pending legislation in Washington outlawing literacy requirements above the sixth grade is enacted, and a concerted drive is made on the part of the Negro community itself in voter registration, Mississippi could have four or five Negro Congressmen in the next few years.[8]

### A Beginning

During the week of our visit, the Reverend James Lawson of Nashville, Tennessee, our Special Projects Director, conducted nonviolent workshops in Laurel, Cleveland, and Jackson, Mississippi. We joined each other on Friday at Tougaloo College and shared a morning of fruitful workshops and discussion with some of the young people who are prodding forces in the social revolution of the South.

When I reflect on our visit to the state that has become the symbol of hard-core resistance, the enormity of the task is inescapable. We could put the field staffs of SCLC, NAACP, CORE, SNCC and a few other agencies to work in the Delta alone. However, no matter how big and difficult a task it is, we have begun. We must encourage our people in Mississippi to rise up by the hundreds and thousands and demand their freedom—now!

PD. *New York Amsterdam News*, 3 March 1962.

---

5. King stopped at a country store in Sherard, Mississippi, on 8 February (SCLC, Press release, "King's 'People to People' tour sweeps Delta").

6. "Time for Questions," *Clarksdale Press Register*, 6 February 1962.

7. Despite his policy of not endorsing political candidates, King spoke at a "Trammell for Congress" rally on 8 February (see King to I. Logan Kearse, 2 November 1961, pp. 321–322 in this volume).

8. In 1986, Mississippi elected Alphonso Michael Espy, its first black congressman in over a hundred years.

# From Virginia Foster Durr

6 March 1962

*Montgomery activist Durr urges King to lead the fight against discrimination on military bases in the South.[1] She declares that when a black soldier "is asked and commanded to die for his country, he is certainly entitled to be treated as a first class citizen while he is wearing its uniform." On 31 March 1962, King responded that segregation in the military was a "matter in which all of us are intensely interested," and assured her that he would discuss her letter with his colleagues.[2]*

Dear Martin:

I hope to see you tomorrow when I come to Atlanta, but if I do not, I will hand this to Coretta for you.

As you can see from the enclosed, the CRC [*Civil Rights Commission*] is interested in the amount of discrimination that goes on at the Military Bases in the South.[3] As we both know, there is a great deal still actually on the bases, such as schools, etc. but where the greatest injustice is done is when men are sent here, by no wish of their own, and because they are doing their duty by their country, they have to put with segregation and discrimination which many of them have never had to suffer before, or at least not to as great an extent.

---

1. Virginia Foster Durr (1903–1999), grew up in Birmingham, Alabama, and attended Wellesley College. In the 1930s and 1940s, she worked with Eleanor Roosevelt to end the poll tax in the South. Durr was a leader of the interracial Southern Conference for Human Welfare, and, in 1948, campaigned unsuccessfully for the Senate as a member of the Progressive Party. In 1955, she and her husband, attorney Clifford J. Durr, posted bail for Rosa Parks after she was arrested for refusing to move to the back of a Montgomery bus. Durr remained active in state and local politics until her early nineties.

2. On 20 March 1962, King received a letter from De Witt Paul Garth, a member of the United States Air Force, stationed at the Ellsworth base in South Dakota. Garth complained about the racial situation in the city, asking King how he is expected to "protect and defend the rights of our free United States," when "I am not able to exercise the liberty granted to me by the law of this country?" King responded on 2 April 1962 that he had been in contact with the Kennedy administration regarding numerous claims from black servicemen around the world, and officials within the administration are "beginning to make some effort to insure equal treatment." In June 1962, Kennedy created the President's Advisory Committee on Equal Opportunity in the Armed Forces under the chairmanship of Washington lawyer Gerhard A. Gesell. When asked if the President was acting in response to particular complaints about racial discrimination in the armed forces, White House press secretary Pierre Salinger said: "No. This is a study the President felt should be undertaken at this time" ("Kennedy Attacks Prejudice in Service," *New York Times*, 24 June 1962).

3. Durr enclosed a copy of a 1961 Defense Department memorandum reiterating that "the policy of equal treatment for all members of the Armed Forces without regard to race, creed or color," is well established in the department (Roswell Gilpatric, Memo to the Secretary of the Army, the Secretary of the Navy, and the Secretary of the Air Force, 19 June 1961). She also included a letter from Berl Bernhard, of the U.S. Commission on Civil Rights, suggesting that Durr should express her concerns to Senator Kenneth Keating of New York, who himself served in both world wars (Bernhard to Durr, 28 February 1962). Keating, a staunch supporter of civil rights, was a member of the Senate Judiciary Committee. In 1957, he helped draft the 1957 Civil Rights Act, and in 1961 he vocally urged President Kennedy not to dismantle the U.S. Commission on Civil Rights.

From my conversations with various people from Washington, I am convinced that if the Negro people, or you as their spokesman, will press continuously on this point, that something will be done by Executive Order. The right of a man or woman in the uniform of Uncle Sam to travel and to eat and to sleep is so obvious that only the most bigoted people will dare to defend any such practice as segregation of the Military Personnel. Of course we want all segregation barriers to go down, but here is one opening that I feel sure will go if the pressure is put there.

As the letter says, Senator Keating of New York is also interested in this, and if no action is forthcoming from the Administration, then I think he should be appealed to.

I hope you will press hard on this point as it is something that is even embarrassing to the deepest dyed white supremacist. After all when a man is asked and commanded to die for his country, he is certainly entitled to be treated as a first class citizen while he is wearing its uniform, and this is so obvious that the most rampant racist will have to invent something to avoid its obvious injustice.

Sincerely yours,
[*signed*]
Virginia Durr

TLS. MLKJP-GAMK: Box 7.

## To T.Y. Rogers

8 March 1962
[*Atlanta, Ga.*]

*Writing to his former assistant at Dexter, King shares his views regarding the formation of the Progressive National Baptist Convention (PNBC) as a rival to the National Baptist Convention (NBC).[1] King expresses his reservations regarding the PNBC's formation but notes its potential for "possibilities far exceeding any of our expectations."*

The Rev. T.Y. Rogers, Jr.
Galilee Baptist Church
457 Roxborough Avenue
Philadelphia 28, Pennsylvania

---

1. Rogers, who solicited King's views on the split, helped organize in 1960 the Baptist Foreign Mission Bureau, a NBC program that conducted missionary work in Nigeria, Bahamas, and Haiti. In 1961 the NBC and the PNBC split, and after several years of support from both organizations, the PNBC accepted full sponsorship of the Bureau. Although he was partial to the Bureau, Rogers admitted that his lack of experience led him to consult with King on the matter (Rogers to King, 16 February 1962).

Dear T.Y.:

Let me apologize for being somewhat tardy in my reply to your letter of February 16. A trip out of the country and the accumulation of a huge volumn of mail account for the delay.[2]

I, too, am sorry that you could not make yourself available for the First Baptist Church in Montgomery. I had looked forward to having you as a new associate in the Southern Christian Leadership Conference and the struggle for freedom in the South. Let us hope that something else will open in the near future.[3]

It is difficult for me to properly advise you on the Progressive Baptist Convention, since I have not had an opportunity to attend any of its sessions. I must confess that I had hoped that a split would not take place.[4] Also, I was taken aback a bit when I noticed the procedures used to call the meeting which led to the formation of the Progressive Baptist Convention. I felt that a small group of about twenty or twenty-five men should have gotten together and discussed all the pros and cons of organizing a new Convention and then if the concensus was for organizing, the meeting should have been jointly called by this particular group. But, as you know, it ended up that only one man called the meeting, namely, Rev. [*L. Venchael*] Booth.[5] This greatly weakened the potential effectiveness of the new Convention.[6] Whether it has now gotten over this initial blunder, I do not know.

———————

2. King went to Puerto Rico on a speaking tour and vacation from 13–24 February.

3. After Ralph Abernathy moved to West Hunter Baptist Church in Atlanta in August 1961, King encouraged Rogers to consider applying to First Baptist Church, Abernathy's old pastorate (King to Rogers, 13 September 1961). In his 16 February 1962 letter to King, Rogers expressed "a strange feeling of guilt" for not considering the position. Instead, Rogers accepted the call at Galilee Baptist Church in Philadelphia. In 1964 Rogers moved to First African Baptist Church in Tuscaloosa, Alabama, and joined the SCLC executive board that same year.

4. In the aftermath of the September 1961 NBC convention, King joined presidential challenger Gardner C. Taylor in publically advising against forming a separate organization, explaining "what ever is wrong with the convention cannot be corrected by a split" ("New Split Threatens Baptists; Jackson Denies Rapping Dr. King," *Jet*, 28 September 1961). For more on Taylor and the NBC, see King to J. H. Jackson, 10 September 1961, and Jackson to King, 12 September 1961, pp. 278–279 and 281–282 in this volume, respectively.

5. On 11 September 1961, Booth, pastor of Zion Baptist Church in Cincinnati, announced a meeting to form a new convention not connected to Taylor's earlier bid for the presidency of the NBC. According to Booth, the meeting was open to all "freedom loving, independent and peace loving Baptists," except those that did not want to organize a new convention. The new convention's proposed constitution included amendments supporting the civil rights movement and tenure limits for elected officers ("National News Release," 11 September 1961, and Program, "A Volunteer Committee for the Formation of a New National Baptist Convention," 14–15 November 1961, in William D. Booth, *A Call to Greatness* [Lawrenceville: Brunswick Publishing, 2001], pp. 178 and 114–119, respectively). The participants who attended the 14–15 November meeting elected T. M. Chambers, pastor of Zion Hill Baptist Church in Los Angeles, president of the new convention.

6. In a letter to Booth, Morehouse College president Benjamin Mays wrote that he also would have preferred "to have had a meeting of 12, 15, or 20 people before announcing the separate convention." In a handwritten postscript on his letter, Mays wrote, "You & I differ on procedure only" (Mays to Booth, 21 September 1961).

On the other side of the ledger, I must say that I well understand the frustrations and the discontent that those who started the new Convention face. I am sure that most of the men in this Convention are motivated by a desire to see our denomination do something positive and meaningful for Kingdom building. So it may very well be that the Progressive Baptist Convention has possibilities far exceeding any of our expectations. Therefore, I would say that we should observe the developments of the new Convention and see which direction it will be taking. I plan to attend its next session as an observer, and also attend the other Convention for a day or so in order to keep contact with the brethren.[7] This is not an attempt to be a sort of 'Mister In Between' or playing both sides but it is an attempt to grapple with the dilemma which we will all face from now on it.

Please give my best regards to the family.[8] I hope I will see you soon.

Very truly yours,
Martin Luther King, Jr.

Km

TLc. MLKJP-GAMK: Box 20.

---

7. The PNBC and the NBC met 4–9 September 1962 in Philadelphia and Chicago, respectively. King did not attend either convention.

8. King refers to Rogers' wife, La Pelzia, and daughter, Gina.

# To Eugene Exman

9 March 1962
[*Atlanta, Ga.*]

*King promises the vice president of Harper & Brothers' religious book department
that he will finish his book of sermons in time to meet a spring 1963 publication
date.*[1] *Although King spent much of the summer focused on the Albany campaign,*
Strength to Love *was published in June 1963.*[2]

Dr. Eugene Exman
Harper & Brothers
49 East 33d Street
New York 16, New York

Dear Gene:

I am happy to know that my book was selected by the American Booksellers
Association as one of the 500 books presented to President Kennedy.[3] I was not aware
of this and I am grateful to you for calling it to my attention.

Again I am confronting problems with the manuscript of sermons. So many
things have come up in the Civil Rights struggle recently that I have had to give
virtually all of my time to the movement. Frankly, I cannot see a let-up for the next
few months so I have decided to take a month off this Summer and finish the manuscript. I deeply regret the delay because I had so much wanted to finish the book by
last December. As it stands now, we would have to think in terms of a publication date
around the Spring of 1963. As things develop, I will let you hear from me.

Very truly yours,
Martin Luther King, Jr.

Km

TLc. MCMLK-RWWL: 2.1.1.10.

---

1. King had already devoted August 1961 to work on the manuscript, hoping to meet a November
deadline, but missed it "for the usual reasons" (King to Exman, 4 December 1961). Eugene Exman
(1900–1975), born in Blanchester, Ohio, received a B.Phil. from Denison University in 1922 and an M.A.
from the University of Chicago in 1925. After working at the University of Chicago Press as a salesman
from 1925–1928, Exman joined Harper & Brothers as editor-manager of its religious books department.
Exman became director of the department in 1944 and vice president in 1955. After retiring in 1965,
Exman wrote two books on Harper's history, *The Brothers Harper, 1817–1853* (1965) and *The House of Harper*
(1967).

2. For more on *Strength to Love's* publication, see Introduction in *Papers* 6:35–44.

3. Following Herbert Hoover's inauguration in 1929, the American Booksellers Association (ABA)
donated five hundred books to the White House to start a private library. Every four years since, the ABA
donates two hundred books, including various genres reflecting contemporary trends, to the library's
collection. King's book *Stride Toward Freedom* was one of the two hundred books donated by the ABA
to President Kennedy on 18 January 1961 (American Booksellers Association, Press release, "The 1961
Presentation to the Home Library of the White House," 18 January 1962; "Zoo Books Given to White
House," *New York Times*, 19 January 1962).

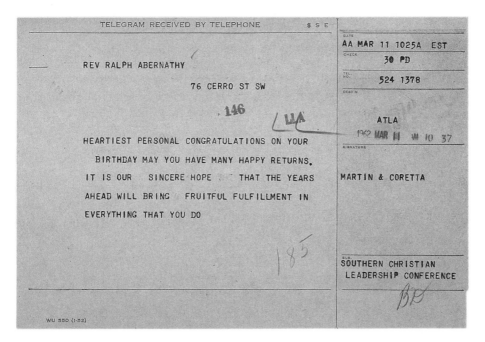

King and his wife, Coretta, wish Ralph Abernathy a happy thirty-sixth birthday. Courtesy of the Atlanta University Center, Robert W. Woodruff Library Archives and Special Collections.

# To Aaron Henry

17 March 1962
[*Atlanta, Ga.*]

*King, Abernathy, and Walker send the following telegram in a show of support for Mississippi activist and NAACP member Henry, who was convicted on 14 March of making sexual advances toward a white male hitchhiker.*[1]

DR AARON HENRY
220 FOURTH ST
CLARKSDALE MISS

---

1.  Henry was sentenced to six months in prison and fined $500. The eighteen-year-old hitchhiker Sterling Eilert testified that the sexual overture took place on 3 March near Alligator, Mississippi, while he was a passenger in Henry's car. Henry maintained his innocence, claiming that his conviction was a "diabolical plot" by attorney Thomas H. Pearson and Clarksdale police chief Ben C. Collins to discredit the movement ("Mississippi NAACP Leader Convicted on Youth's Charge," *Montgomery Advertiser*, 15 March 1962). Pearson and Collins sued Henry for libel and won; however, the Supreme Court cleared Henry in 1965 of the libel charges in *Henry v. Collins* (380 U.S. 356). On appeal, the Supreme Court also vacated Henry's March 1962 conviction on 18 January 1965 (*Henry v. Mississippi* [379 U.S. 443]).

DEAR AARON

WE HAVE JUST READ ACCOUNT OF TRAIL IN MONTGOMERY ADVERTISER WANT YOU TO KNOW THAT WE RECOGNIZE THIS AS GROWING TECHNIQUE OF WHITE RACIST OPPOSITION TO DEFAME MILITANT NEGRO LEADER SHIP THEY HAVE DISCOVERED THE SOUTHERN NEGRO CAN NO LONGER BE CONTAINED IN HIS BID FOR FULL EQUALITY AND THE CHARGES AGAINST YOU ARE BUT A PLOT TO DISCREDIT YOUR LEADERSHIP WE ARE WITH YOU 100 PERCENT

SINCERELY YOURS
MARTIN LUTHER KING JR
RALPH D ABERNATHY
AND WYATT TEE WALKER
SOUTHERN CHRISTIAN LEADERSHIP CONFERENCE

PWSr. MCMLK-RWWL: 6.2.0.2180_002.

# To John F. Kennedy

30 March 1962
Atlanta, Ga.

*Following a vacancy in the United States Supreme Court, King urges President Kennedy to consider Judge William H. Hastie or Judge Thurgood Marshall for the position, claiming that appointing a black man to the Court could be a good way to show "commitment to the ideal of equality of opportunity."*[1] *Lawrence O'Brien, special assistant to the president, thanked King for the recommendation, but added*

---

1. On 29 March, Kennedy announced associate justice Charles Whittaker's retirement due to medical concerns. Judge Hastie of the U.S. Court of Appeals for the 3rd Circuit was strongly considered to fill the position. Kennedy sought to avoid a Senate dispute over confirmation of his first appointment, and was advised by Theodore Sorensen, that "You cannot appoint both Hastie and Weaver to HEW without appearing to be guilty of reverse racism," and to "save Hastie for the next vacancy before 1964" (Sorensen to John F. Kennedy, 29 March 1962; "President's Choice," Baltimore *Afro-American*, 14 April 1962). Although not a leading candidate in the discussions surrounding Whittaker's potential successor, Marshall went on to become the first black U.S. Supreme Court justice in 1967. Starting in 1962, the FBI had begun a wiretap on Stanley Levison's office phone. A memo to J. Edgar Hoover indicated that Wyatt Tee Walker had called Levison on behalf of King to ask whether King should publicly pressure Kennedy to nominate Hastie. Levison allegedly said: "My tendency is for MARTIN (LUTHER KING) to issue a statement on it and speak of it as a superb opportunity coming at a critical juncture in history" (SAC, New York, to Hoover, 30 March 1962, Bureau File 100–106670–33). William Henry Hastie (1904–1976), born in Knoxville, Tennessee, earned his B.A. (1925) at Amherst College and later his law degree (1930) and doctorate of juridical science from Harvard University (1933). In 1943, he was awarded the Spingarn Medal by the NAACP after he resigned from his position as civilian aide to the Secretary of War because of discriminatory practices in the military. In 1946 Hastie was appointed governor of the Virgin Islands, a position he held until 1949. That same year, he became the first African American to be appointed to the U.S. Circuit Court of Appeals and served as a judge for the 3rd Circuit for twenty-one years, spending three of them as chief judge.

THE PRESIDENT
THE WHITE HOUSE

URGENTLY REQUEST YOUR SERIOUS CONSIDERATION OF JUDGE WILLIAM H HASTIE AND JUDGE THURGOOD MARSHALL FOR APPOINTMENT TO THE SUPREME COURT BENCH. BOTH MEN ARE EMMINENTLY QUALIFIED TO FILL VACANCY. THIS IS SUPERB OPPORTUNITY FOR THE ADMINISTRATION TO REVEAL TO WORLD ITS SERIOUS DETER-MINATION TO MAKE THE NEGRO A FULL PARTICIPANT IN EVERY PHASE OF AMERICAN LIFE, IN THIS CRUCIAL PERIOD OF HISTORY SUCH AN APPOINTMENT WOULD BE ONE OF THE FINEST WAYS TO DEMONSTRATE THE NATIONS COMMITMENT TO THE IDEAL OF EQUALITY OF OPPORTUNITY

YOURS VERY TRULY.
MARTIN LUTHER KING JR
PRESIDENT SOUTHERN CHRISTIAN LEADERSHIP CONFERENCE

PWSr. JFKWHCNF-MBJFK: Box 1478.

---

2. O'Brien to King, 5 April 1962. White (1917–2002) was confirmed by the Senate on 11 April 1962 and served on the Supreme Court until his retirement in 1993.

# "People in Action: Most Abused Man in Nation"

31 March 1962
New York, N.Y.

*On 8 March 1962, SCLC organized a testimonial dinner and mass meeting honoring Birmingham civil rights leaders Fred Shuttlesworth and J. S. Phifer, who were released from jail on 1 March.*[1] *Below, King dedicates his biweekly column for the* New York Amsterdam News *to Shuttlesworth, calling him "one of Dixie's most fearless freedom fighters." King's tribute concludes: "When that day dawns on which Negro men and women and children can walk with their heads high and finally breathe the free air as do all other men, the name of Fred Shuttlesworth will shine like a guiding star among the names of those who gave of themselves in full measure, for freedom for us all."*

---

1. In October 1958 Shuttlesworth and Phifer were convicted of violating bus segregation laws in Birmingham. Fined $100 each and sentenced to ninety and sixty days in jail, respectively, the pair surrendered to Birmingham authorities on 25 January 1962.

Last Thursday night the good citizens of Birmingham gathered together to pay well deserved tribute to Reverends Fred Shuttlesworth and J. S. Phifer who, on the previous Thursday, had been released from "Bull" Connor's city jail after serving 36 days.

Present also at the testimonial dinner, was a representative of civil rights leaders from across the country who had felt it their duty to journey to Birmingham to pay tribute to these latest of the Christian victims of brutal and seditious segregation. The NAACP's Roy Wilkins delivered the principal address.[2]

The two ministers were jailed on January 25th, after the U.S. Supreme Court refused to review an appeal from a conviction on charges growing out of a protest of segregated seating on local buses.

The refusal by the high court was based on a legal technicality (the failure of the legal defense to meet a deadline set for the filing of the initial appeal).

When the case was reentered in state courts, the two ministers were denied bail and were then required to start serving the 60 and 90 day terms to which they were originally sentenced.

During the time they were in prison, they mopped the prison floors and scrubbed the greasy dishes used for the mass meals.

Far from being daunted or discouraged by this treatment, however, their spirits and courage flared like banners of defiance in the faces of their tormentors. Even while they were imprisoned, the two ministers were among the signers of a petition to Birmingham's Mayor Arthur J. Hanes, asking for improved race relations.[3]

### "Jailbirds"

When Mayor Hanes replied that he had thrown their petition in the wastebasket, the two ministers retorted, "Colored citizens do not consider asking for their rights the same as waving a red flag in front of a furious animal."

They stated that. "Your calling us extraordinary people, or jailbirds, can only be interpreted as official knowledge of our determination to win freedom, even if we must suffer the indignities of working 12 hours, 7 days a week in jail, washing thousands of dishes and lifting heavy garbage cans and cartons of food."

In conclusion, they told the Mayor that if "serving this or other terms will hasten that day when there is freedom and justice for all, then we are at your service."[4]

Throughout their travail, the ministers received the full support of their congregations, their organizations and their colleagues.

### Furnished Ministers

The Southern Christian Leadership Conference, of which I am president, sup-

---

2. Nashville Christian Leadership Council president Kelly Miller Smith, Wyatt Tee Walker, Ralph Abernathy, and A.D. King also attended the events (Citizens of Birmingham, Alabama and SCLC, Program, "A testimonial honoring Rev. F.L. Shuttlesworth and Rev. J.S. Phifer," 8 March 1962).

3. Hanes (1916–1997) served as mayor of Birmingham from 1961 to 1963. A copy of the petition was published in the *Birmingham World* ("Officials Asked to Wipe Out Racial Bias in City," 10 February 1962).

4. King quotes from a letter to Hanes written by Shuttlesworth and Phifer in response to the mayor's dismissal of their petition. The letter was published in the *Birmingham World* ("Shuttlesworth, Phifer Renew Request to City to End Bias; Both Serving Hard Labor Terms," 17 February 1962).

plied ministers to fill his pulpit while Reverend Shuttlesworth was away.[5] The
expenses for supplying these ministers were paid by S.C.L.C., as its contribution to
the struggle, so that there would be no extra burden on his congregation.

S.C.L.C. also retained William Kunstler, American Civil Liberties Union lawyer, of
New York City, to aid the defense attorneys, Arthur D. Shores and Orzell Billingsley.[6]

This ordeal was just one in a long series suffered by this gallant servant of humanity. Back in Christmas, 1956, Shuttlesworth's home was bombed and completely
demolished.[7] In winter of 1957, his church, Bethel Baptist was dynamited by racists,
and late in 1957, Shuttlesworth and his wife were mobbed, beaten, and stabbed.[8]
They were also jailed eight times, four times during the Freedom Rides.[9]

He was sued for three million dollars by state officials of Alabama, his automobile
and personal property sold at public auction, and his driver's license revoked for a
whole year.[10] The three Shuttlesworth children were illegally arrested and beaten at
Gadsden, Alabama.[11]

## 27 Actions

One of Dixie's most fearless freedom fighters, he is currently involved in twenty-
seven criminal and civil actions. He has received sentences totaling three and a half
years in time and $5000 in fines.[12] Fred Shuttlesworth is without a doubt one of the
most abused and arrested ministers in the nation.

---

5. During Shuttlesworth's jailing, members of the SCLC executive board volunteered at
Shuttlesworth's Revelation Baptist Church in Cincinnati, Ohio (SCLC, Press release, "Civil rights leaders volunteer to fill Reverend Shuttlesworth's pulpit," 31 January 1962).

6. Although some of his fees were paid for by the ACLU, Kunstler charged SCLC a $250 retainer fee
to represent Shuttlesworth (Kunstler & Kunstler, Bill for attorney services, 30 March 1962).

7. The bomb's blast caved in the roof and shattered every window of the parsonage, though
Shuttlesworth's family only suffered minor injuries.

8. On 29 June 1958, Shuttlesworth's body guard removed a bomb near Bethel Baptist Church, but
not before it caused minor damage to the church and shattered windows up to six blocks away. In 1980,
Klan member Jesse Benjamin Stoner was convicted of involvement in the crime. Also, on 9 September
1957, Shuttlesworth's family was surrounded by a mob while leading schoolchildren to integrate all-white
Phillips High School. Shuttlesworth suffered a damaged kidney, his wife, Ruby Keeler Shuttlesworth,
was stabbed in the leg and slugged with a blunt object, and his daughter Ruby Fredricka Shuttlesworth
suffered a fractured ankle when someone closed a car door on her leg.

9. Shuttlesworth was also jailed for violating bus segregation laws in October 1958; violating a city
ordinance during the sit-ins in March 1960; and for refusing to obey an officer, for breach of the peace,
and twice for conspiracy during the Freedom Rides.

10. Effective 31 August 1960, Shuttlesworth's driver's license was suspended for one year for two
speeding violations. In addition to Shuttlesworth, Ralph Abernathy, Solomon Snowden Seay, and Joseph
E. Lowery were sued for three million dollars for libel by Alabama officials. King was sued for one million
dollars by Alabama governor John Patterson. For more on the libel suits against the five ministers, see
Introduction in *Papers* 5:25–26.

11. On 16 August 1960, Shuttlesworth's children Patricia, Ruby, and Fred Jr., were arrested in
Gadsden, Alabama, for refusing to move to the back of a Greyhound bus. King sent a telegram to
Attorney General William P. Rogers to investigate the confirmed "police brutality" the children experi-
enced (King to William P. Rogers, 18 August 1960, in *Papers* 5:496–497).

12. By July 1961, Shuttlesworth had been convicted of six criminal charges with punishments totaling
over two years in jail and $1,400 in fines for his involvement in Birmingham demonstrations, all of which
he appealed. Additionally he was fined $10 and spent one day in jail on 2 June 1961 after he "refused

Birmingham has been described as the worst city this side of Johannesburg, South Africa.[13]

## Impact

Despite the likes of Eugene (Bull) Connor and deeply entrenched habits of segregation in both the Negro and white community, Fred Shuttlesworth and the ACMHR have had an impact that Birmingham will long remember.

The desegregation of the city buses, delayed through seemingly endless litigation and police harassment, is now a reality.

Visitors of Birmingham today are shown street lights, paved streets, Negro policemen—all credited to Shuttlesworth and ACMHR. In the North Birmingham section, residents will point out "Shuttlesworth School," "Shuttlesworth Park," and "Shuttlesworth Pool," each hurriedly built to stave off the persistent demands of Shuttlesworth and Company for adequate tax supported facilities.

## In Demand

Nationally famous in the civil rights struggle, Mr. Shuttlesworth is in demand all over the nation. His personal magnetism attracts great crowds wherever he speaks. He has travelled and lectured in Europe. He is founder and Secretary of S.C.L.C.

When that day dawns on which Negro men and women and children can walk with their heads high and finally breathe the free air as do all other men, the name of Fred Shuttlesworth will shine like a guiding star among the names of those who gave of themselves in full measure, for freedom for us all.

PD. *New York Amsterdam News,* 31 March 1962.

---

to promise not to break any segregation laws for the next year" ("Revolving Doors Jailing, Suite Haunt Alabama Leader," *Chicago Daily Defender,* 1 July 1961).

13. An article in the *New York Times* on Birmingham quoted an anonymous African American as saying: "The difference between Johannesburg and Birmingham is that here they have not yet opened fire with the tanks and big guns" (Harrison E. Salisbury, "Fear and Hatred Grip Birmingham," 12 April 1960).

# From Alfred Daniel King

2 April 1962
Birmingham, Ala.

*Following his installation service at First Baptist Church of Ensley on 18 March, A. D. King thanks his older brother for speaking.*[1]

---

1. A.D. King's installation lasted two days. His father spoke at the morning service, and King, Jr. delivered the afternoon sermon (Program, "Installation services of Rev. A. D. Williams King," 18 March–19

Rev. M. L. King Jr.                                                          5 Apr
407 Auburn Avenue                                                            1962
Atlanta 12, Georgia

Dear M. L.,

It was certainly a great deal of pleasure and inspiration to have you share in our Installation Services. Thank you so much for the message in the afternoon. Our people have shown a new spirit for work, and I believe that this new spirit is a result of your thorough explanation of the importance of a preacher.

Please express my deepest thanks to the very fine people of Ebenezer for their more than generous contribution.[2]

Give our love to the family.

A. D.

TLI. MLKJP-GAMK: Vault Box 1.

---

March 1962). Ralph Abernathy also participated in A. D. King's installation service and wrote a letter of recommendation for A. D. King to the chairman of the board of deacons at First Baptist. The letter was similar to the recommendation King, Jr., wrote to West Hunter Baptist Church on Abernathy's behalf (Abernathy to Meredith McCaroll, 22 November 1961; King to J. R. Butts, 8 February 1961, pp. 153–154 in this volume). A. D. King began serving at First Baptist Church on 7 January 1962. The King family also participated in his 1959 installation as pastor of Mount Vernon First Baptist Church in Newnan, Georgia (Program, Installation of Alfred Daniel King, 12 April 1959).

2. The Ebenezer Baptist Church choir performed at the service.

# Press Release, Statement on Intensified Voter Registration Drive

5 April 1962
[*Atlanta, Ga.*]

*On the heels of the official announcement of the start of the Voter Education Project (VEP), King sends this press release describing SCLC's quest to double the number of registered African American voters within two years.*[1]

---

1. The Southern Regional Council (SRC) announced on 29 March that the new tax-exempt organization would coordinate and fund voter registration efforts of the major civil rights organizations (SRC, Press release, Voter Education Project to study voter registration in the South, 29 March 1962). From 15 February to 1 September, SCLC received $11,500 from the VEP and spent $34,000 of the organization's own funds on voter registration (Jack H. O'Dell, "Report on voter registration work, February 15–September 1 1962," 28 September 1962).

I am happy to announce that the Southern Christian Leadership Conference has begun its intensified voter registration drive. We are actively participating in this effort with the Voter Education Project of the Southern Regional Council. We now visualize the doubling of the number of Negro registered voters within the next two years.

For practical reasons we have carved out a territory for ourselves in which our work will not duplicate the work of the other participating civil rights organizations.

That segment of the South comprises South Carolina {(Charleston)}, Georgia, Alabama, the Fourth Congressional District or the Southside of Virginia, Eastern North Carolina, Northern Louisiana, the Delta area of Mississippi from Vicksburg to Clarksdale; East Tennessee and West Texas {(Marshall)}.

We have been working in this territory on our own from the beginning of this year with our limited staff. Now that our program has moved into high gear, we have been forced to expand our field staff to cope with it.

These six new staff persons are: John H. Calhoun, Herbert V. Coulton, James L. Bevel, Fred C. Bennette, Jr., Bernard S. Lee, and Harry Blake.

John H. Calhoun will serve as Georgia State Organizer for 1962–63 in the voter registration drive. Herbert V. Coulton of Petersburg, Virginia, will serve as Field Secretary in the drive in Virginia, Tennessee and North Carolina. Mr. Coulton will concentrate his efforts in the 4th Congressional District in the South end of Virginia. James L. Bevel is Field Secretary in the area of Mississippi. Field Secretary for Georgia is Fred C. Bennette, Jr. Bernard S. Lee will serve as Student Liaison in the five key states (South Carolina, Alabama, Georgia, Mississippi and Louisiana). Harry Blake will serve as Field Secretary in North Louisiana from Shreveport to the Mississippi Delta. In addition, three or four specialists will be added in the future.[2]

During my "people-to-people" trips, I have recruited more than 1000 volunteers in Georgia, Mississippi and Virginia alone.[3] I am happy that I have been able to be a part of this drive personally, I am more than gratified with the response which my pleas for volunteers for voter registration and the "non-violent" army received in the rural areas of the South. I will continue to participate personally.[4]

Our procedure is to go into a town to recruit volunteers. We then send these volunteers to our McIntosh training center, one of our other schools for specialized training. These trainees then return to their home communities and recruit and train other volunteers to continue the voter registration drive and the spread of citizenship education.

To date we have trained over 930 persons in the Citizenship Education Program in

---

2. Among the others added to SCLC staff were Golden Frinks and Fred H. LaGarde in North Carolina, Benjamin Mack in South Carolina, Hosea Williams in Georgia, and Annell Ponder in Mississippi (Young to Wiley A. Branton, September 1962).

3. During the People to People tours, King spoke with local leaders to help build grassroots leadership. For more on King's tours of the Mississippi Delta and Virginia, see King, "People in Action: Pathos and Hope," 3 March 1962, and King, "People in Action: Virginia's Black Belt," 14 April 1962, pp. 419–421 and 437–440 in this volume, respectively.

4. As part of the People to People tours, King also traveled to South Carolina in April and to Louisiana in June (see Introduction, and King, "People in Action: New Harassment," 23 June 1962, pp. 29 and 486–488 in this volume, respectively).

the 95 schools which we are operating in Louisiana, Alabama, Georgia, Mississippi,
Virginia, and South Carolina.[5]

We are totally committed to this work and fully intend to carry it through to its fruitful objective—full citizenship for Negroes everywhere in the United States.

THD. DABCC.

-----

5. Headed by Andrew Young, SCLC's Citizenship Education Project invited potential leaders to attend a five-day training session with expenses paid at Dorchester Center in Midway, Georgia. After training on community organizing and voter registration methods, the attendees were expected to establish local Citizenship Schools in their communities.

# From Lyndon B. Johnson

13 April 1962
Washington, D.C.

*As head of the newly established President's Committee on Equal Employment Opportunity, the vice president informs King of an upcoming meeting regarding federal employment in Atlanta.[1] Johnson, who had received criticism for the committee's lack of enforcement, promises King that "some very searching questions are going to be asked" if progress had not been made.[2]*

Doctor Martin Luther King
413 Auburn Avenue
Atlanta, Georgia

-----

1. On 6 March 1961 President Kennedy signed executive order 10925, which established the President's Committee on Equal Employment Opportunity to ensure equality, regardless of race, creed, color, or national origin, for qualified employees seeking to work in the federal government and under government contracts. In addition, the committee had the authority to cancel any government contract if a business working for the government was found discriminating against its employees. For nearly two hours on 9 April, King had met with Johnson to discuss equal employment opportunities for African Americans (SCLC, Press release, "Vice-President promises Dr. King compliance with job opportunity mandate," 11 April 1962).

2. In Spring 1961, after two African American workers complained of discrimination at the Lockheed Aircraft Corporation plant in Marietta, Georgia, the committee threatened to cancel the company's billion-dollar contract with the federal government unless it pledged to desegregate facilities and provide African American employees with more opportunities for advancement (Peter Braestrup, "Kennedy to Fight Curbs on Negroes in Federal Work," *New York Times*, 8 April 1961). On 5 April 1962, NAACP labor secretary Herbert Hill criticized the administration's program, noting that it had "resulted in more publicity than progress" and was "simply a euphemism for what a previous Administration called voluntary compliance" (Peter Braestrup, "N.A.A.C.P. Accuses Kennedy on Jobs," *New York Times*, 6 April 1962). Lockheed president Courtlandt Gross and Vice President Johnson signed an anti-discrimination plan on 25 May 1961 (Peter Braestrup, "Lockheed Signs Equal-Jobs Pact," *New York Times*, 26 May 1961).

Dear Doctor King:

I have carefully looked into the situation involving Federal employment in Atlanta.[3] Last July 20th, members of the Committee staff and a Civil Service Commission representative met in Atlanta with the top people of twelve agencies involving about 20,000 people in that area.

In that meeting, the determination of the President and the Committee to improve the employment situation was stressed heavily. The Committee staff and the Civil Service Commission also offered their full cooperation in carrying out the President's order.

Another meeting is planned in Atlanta for May 14, 15, and 16. At this meeting, members of the staff and the Civil Service Commission will meet separately with each of the agencies that were contacted last July. In advance of this meeting, the agencies have been asked to submit statistics on employment distribution so that we will have a picture of the situation before we actually enter Atlanta.[4] We will know how far each agency has gone and what should be done. We will discuss the problems and make whatever suggestions are deemed advisable. The meetings as such will not be opened to the public because it is desired that the discussions be as frank as possible. But I will certainly keep you advised with the progress that is being made, step by step, and if progress has not been made since the July 20th meeting, some very searching questions are going to be asked.

I enjoyed meeting with you and I hope you will keep in touch with me.[5] I value your advice and your counsel and this office is always open to you.[6]

---

3. On behalf of twenty-five workers, the NAACP filed a complaint against the Atlantic Steel Company in Atlanta charging it with hiring African American workers specifically for menial jobs, barring them from enrollment in training programs, and collusion with the local branch of the United Steel Workers of America in negotiating separate racial seniority lines ("NAACP Files Bias Charges against Industry, Unions," *Atlanta Daily World*, 7 December 1961). The National Labor Relations Board's regional director in Atlanta dismissed the complaint and his ruling was upheld by the Board's general counsel ("Board Rules Atlanta Firm Was Not Biased," *Atlanta Daily World*, 10 April 1963).

4. By 15 January 1962, fifty-two companies participating in "Plans for Progress" submitted base plans calling for specific commitments to improve their employment practices ("The First Nine Months: Report of the President's Committee on Equal Employment Opportunity," 15 January 1962). Of these fifty-two companies, twenty-four had facilities in the Atlanta area. The "Plans for Progress" subcommittee became a source of contention between committee members who preferred compulsory compliance versus voluntary compliance. As such only seven of the twenty-four Atlanta-based companies participating in "Plans for Progress" produced any evidence of compliance with their pledges. Only three firms, Lockheed Aircraft, Goodyear Tire & Rubber Company, and Western Electric, demonstrated "a vigorous desire to create job opportunities" (SRC, Special report, "Plans for Progress: Atlanta Survey," January 1963).

5. King declined Johnson's invitation to attend a 19 May conference sponsored by the President's Committee on Equal Employment Opportunity (Johnson to King, 27 April 1962; Johnson to King, 15 June 1962).

6. In June 1963 King sent Johnson a telegram informing him that he had filed a discrimination complaint with the committee against the Atlantic Steel Plant (King to Johnson, Hobart Taylor, and Frank W. McCulloch, 4 June 1963). Committee vice chairman Hobart Taylor replied on behalf of the vice president promising an immediate investigation (Taylor to King, 4 June 1963).

Sincerely yours,
[*signed*]
Lyndon B. Johnson

TLS. MCMLK-RWWL: 1.1.0.24130.

## "People in Action: Virginia's Black Belt"

14 April 1962
New York, N.Y.

*Continuing his People to People tour, King made multiple stops in Virginia in
late March 1962. In the following* New York Amsterdam News *article, King
praises the local movement's perseverance despite efforts by the state to maintain
segregation. Although King asserts that these obstacles can be eradicated by the
executive and legislative branches of government, the "major responsibility of
securing our full freedom depends upon the Negro himself." King cautions that if
African Americans do not "rise up by the hundreds and the thousands, community
by community, and demand their rights through nonviolence and creative protest"
the freedoms guaranteed by the Constitution will remain out of reach.*

I did not realize until our "People to People" tour swung through the Black Belt of
Virginia last week that the South gave to our nation nine of its first twelve Presidents.
Seven of them were Virginians.[1] How strange it is, that this southern Commonwealth
has failed so miserably in giving moral leadership to the South. The idea of "massive resistance" was spawned not in Georgia or Alabama—but in the heart of the
Southside Virginia, commonly known as the Black Belt.[2]

This section of Virginia is the bulwark of Harry Byrd's political dynasty that
holds Virginia's liberal bent in a strangle-hold. The anti-NAACP laws, the infamous
trespass ordinances aimed at thwarting the Sit-Ins, the Pupil Placement laws—all
children of "massive resistance," had their origin and loudest support from this
same Negro majority section of Virginia that makes up most of the Fourth U.S.
Congressional District.[3]

---

1. George Washington, Thomas Jefferson, James Madison, James Monroe, William Harrison, John
Tyler, and Zachary Taylor were all born in Virginia, while Andrew Jackson and James Polk were born in
South and North Carolina, respectively.

2. Senator Harry Flood Byrd (D-Va.) coined the term "massive resistance" when he suggested in a
25 February 1956 statement that Southern refusal to accept the 1954 *Brown* decision would lead the "rest
of the country" to "realize that racial integration is not going to be accepted in the South."

3. In September 1956 Virginia governor Thomas Stanley signed several laws aimed at thwarting
the *Brown* decision and preserving legal segregation within the state. Some of the laws were specifically
aimed at the NAACP, the predominant civil rights organization in Virginia, by requiring the group to
register with the state and report membership and finances. Stanley's plan also prohibited the use of
state funds for integrated schools and made available tuition grants for students affected by public

What a pity that this state of such early historical distinction has missed an opportunity for real greatness in one of her nation's most critical hours!

## Led Backwards

It may well have been that the severe social change that is taking place in the South today might have been considerably accelerated had not Virginia, "the mother of Presidents" led the South backward into "massive resistance."

It is refreshing, however, to observe even from this brief vantage point of the struggle's history, that social crises at times produce their greatest need. The nonviolent thrust of the Negro community in the South and Virginia has met "massive resistance" with "massive insistence."

This is a part of the aim of the Southern Christian Leadership Conference "People to People" program. I am convinced, as I have said many times, that the salvation of the Negro is not in Washington, D.C.

The Supreme Court, The Justice Department, the President of the United States, and the Congress can aid immeasurably in the emancipation process of the Negro, but the major responsibility of securing our full freedom depends upon the Negro himself.[4]

Our constitutional guarantees will not be realized until Negroes rise up by the hundreds and the thousands, community by community, and demand their rights through nonviolence and creative protest.

As our SCLC task force traveled over the Black Belt of Virginia last week, I could see the potential of this.[5] In just two days, we touched the lives of nearly 10,000 people. We could see the deep hope and yearning for freedom in the eyes of thousands of Negroes and the sincere commitment to human equality in many whites.

## 100,000 Potential

The Black Belt of Virginia has a potential of 100,000 voters in the Negro community but there are barely 17,000 registered at the present. The Fourth District is similar to many parts of Mississippi with many Negroes who are tied to the land as sharecroppers. Economic suppression is the rule rather than the exception and the poll tax requirement adds to the burden of general apathy in Negro voter registra-

---

school closures to enroll in private schools. Taking advantage of the Supreme Court's failure to set a specific timetable for school integration, the Virginia legislature passed the pupil placement law, allowing a three-member board to assign students to public schools and authorize any student transfers between schools. Additionally, the law gave the governor power to close any schools ordered to integrate. By mid-1960, when Virginia's Fourth Circuit Court of Appeals ordered the admission of four African American students into white schools in Norfolk, no African Americans had been transferred to white schools under the pupil placement law. In response to the 1960 sit-in movement, Virginia governor James Almond signed into law three anti-trespassing laws.

4. In articles published in *The Nation*, King discusses how executive power could assist the movement (King, "Equality Now," 4 February 1961, and King "Fumbling on the New Frontier," 3 March 1962, pp. 139–150 and 412–419 in this volume, respectively).

5. The SCLC task force included King, Ralph Abernathy, former Virginia pastor Wyatt Tee Walker, field secretaries Bernard Scott Lee and Herbert Coulton, and SCLC's educational consultant and former Virginia resident Dorothy Cotton.

tion. It is towards this enormous task in Virginia's Black Belt that our "People to
People" tour was directed.

As I indicated in an earlier column, the "People to People" program is aimed at
the recruitment of our Freedom Corps and Nonviolent Army in the Negro majority
areas of every southern state.[6]

Mississippi was our initial tour and then Virginia.

We joined Fourth District leaders in Petersburg on the first day of our visit and
spent the afternoon literally knocking on doors in the First Ward in a voter registration canvass.

We could discern from the response of the occupants of the more than eighty
homes visited, that many of our people just need the information as to what they
must know and exactly where they must go and what they must do.[7]

In Lynchburg the same evening, up in the western half of the state, along with
Ralph Abernathy and Wyatt Tee Walker, we recruited 118 volunteers to work in voter
registration. I was overwhelmed by a nine-year-old white lad, Chuck Moran, who
came forward and said he wanted to help in this struggle. The example of this tender
spirit triggered the response of many of the others who joined the Freedom Corps
that night.[8]

Nine a.m. the next day, we saw first-hand the tragedy of Prince Edward County.
This is the Virginia county that closed down its public schools rather than comply
with the Supreme Court Decision of 1954.[9] This is the third year that there has been
no public schools for any child white or black.

We could see the obvious lines of strain and weariness in the face of Prince
Edward's peerless leader, the Rev. L. Francis Griffin.

He has refused the compromise of a half loaf of freedom and the parents and
children have backed him unanimously in this position.[10] Think of it! Closed schools
in Virginia, the mother of Presidents.

---

6. See King, "People in Action: Pathos and Hope," 3 March 1962, p. 420 in this volume.

7. One homeowner greeted King saying, "'Come on in, but don't start talking 'till I get the neighbors here!'" (SCLC, Press release, "Martin Luther King, Jr. moves into Virginia," 30 March 1962).

8. An estimated 2,400 people attended the mass meeting at E.C. Glass High School to hear King
speak. Of the 118 voter registration volunteers, more than twenty were white. The mass meeting raised
$1,626 (SCLC, Press release, "Martin Luther King, Jr. moves into Virginia"). For a photograph of King
and Moran, see p. 100 in this volume.

9. In response to a 1959 federal court order to integrate its public schools, Prince Edward County
officials voted to withdraw all funding from public education, effectively closing down its schools. Aided
by state grants, most of the white students attended segregated private schools organized by the Prince
Edward School Foundation. Under the leadership of Reverend L. Francis Griffin, the Prince Edward
County Christian Association established "activity centers" to keep more than 600 African Americans
off the streets. Three hundred black students transferred to schools outside the county, while approximately 800 students received no formal education (Claude Sitton, "Prince Edward County Adamant on
Refusing School Integration," *New York Times*, 17 April 1961).

10. Leslie Francis Griffin (1917–1980) was the pastor of First Baptist Church in Farmville, Virginia.
In 1959 and 1961, he turned down several proposals from Prince Edward County school board officials
to reopen a few closed schools on a segregated basis. After a federal district judge postponed orders to
desegregate Prince Edward County public schools on 3 October, King sent Griffin a telegram of support,
saying: "America will never be able to calculate what your leadership will mean in the future to public
education" (King to Griffin, 5 October 1962). A week later, a federal judge said Prince Edward County

Virginia State College afforded us another thrill. This was a homecoming for Mrs. Dorothy Cotton, Director of the Citizenship Schools, who accompanied us.[11] The students jam-packed Virginia Hall auditorium (capacity 2500) in a voluntary assembly that a college official said was the first such occasion in history.

It evidences a new breed and a new generation in our Negro community with this kind of enthusiasm and interest.

We rounded out our Virginia tour by attending the trials of 62 Sit-Inners in Hopewell, Virginia and visiting two rural communities in Dinwiddie County, just south of Petersburg.[12]

More than 400 people talked with us informally and expressed their interest in the freedom struggle.

The last public meeting held at Petersburg's First Baptist Church was a standing room only affair where 158 joined our Freedom Corps to work in voter registration.

As we winged our way back to Atlanta, it came to me that the tremendous response we had found in Virginia held promise of changing the political climate in Virginia, and perhaps—perhaps, Virginia might once again produce a president.

PD. *New York Amsterdam News*, 14 April 1962.

---

could not keep the schools closed but did not issue any further orders to allow time for an appeal. On 25 May 1964, in *Griffin v. Prince Edward School Board* (377 U.S. 218 [1964]), the Supreme Court ordered the public schools to reopen on an integrated basis.

11. A graduate of Virginia State College in 1954, Cotton was also the secretary of the Petersburg Improvement Association. She moved to Atlanta and joined the staff of SCLC in September 1960.

12. The demonstrators, arrested between August 1960 and January 1961 on charges of trespassing, were convicted; the adults were sentenced to thirty days in jail and the juveniles to probation. King attended the trial of Hopewell resident Curtis Harris, who was charged with contempt for refusing to answer questions regarding his integration activities before the Virginia Legislative Committee on Offenses against the Administration of Justice. Harris was found guilty of contempt but was not fined or sentenced. Harris's attorney, Len Holt, wrote that King's presence, as well as that of other black ministers, "was a substantial factor" in the victory (Holt to King, 3 April 1962).

# "The Meaning of Easter," Sermon Delivered at Ebenezer Baptist Church

[*22 April 1962*]
Atlanta, Ga.

*Drawing upon II Corinthians for his Easter sermon, King describes the African American experience of Good Friday: "We've known our Good Fridays in something called separate but equal, where there was always a strict enforcement of the separate without the slightest intention to abide by the equal." Despite the bleak outlook of Good Friday, King maintains, "Easter is always around the corner" and Jesus's resurrection serves as a contemporary "affirmation of the ultimate triumph of good." Confronting those in his congregation who fear death, King concludes that they "don't believe in God" and are not true Christians. "The Meaning of Easter," King claims, is that "evil will not triumph in the universe," and death is "an open door that leads men into life eternal." In conclusion, King calls upon those in the church who have not yet claimed a spiritual home: "This is the moment of supreme opportunity. And what is a better day to unite with the church of God than on the day when we celebrate the resurrection of our Lord and Savior Jesus Christ?" The following transcript is taken from an audio recording of the service.*

[*choir sings*] Now, will we now hum that very softly. [*congregation hums*] In the fourth chapter and the eighteenth verse of Paul's second letter to the Corinthians, "while we look not at the things which are things, but at the things which are not things: for the things which are things are temporary; but the things which are not things are eternal." Well, we come again to Easter Sunday, and it is notorious indeed that this day brings people to church who will not be seen again in twelve months. For some, the Easter festival is little more than a fashion show; for others, it is little more than a national holiday with no semblance of a religious holy day. But perhaps for most of you assembled here this morning, Easter represents something more enduring and something deeper. It is a day above every day. It is a day that even surpasses the mystery and marvel of Christmas with all of the glory of the incarnation, for Easter asserts that man's extremity is God's opportunity. Easter affirms that what stops us does not stop God. (*Yes*) And that miracle is as much a part of the end as of the beginning. Above all, Easter provides the answers to the deepest queries of the human spirit, for Easter is more than a day of ostentatious show. It is the day that commemorates an event which provides answers to the questions which have puzzled the probing minds of philosophers and theologians and ordinary people of every generation. And so this morning I would like to use our text and the second letter of the Corinthians as a basis for our thinking together on the meaning of Easter.

Now let me say very quickly that Easter is an affirmation of the meaningfulness of the universe. There are those who try to tell us that the universe doesn't have any meaning beyond the years that we spend on Earth and beyond the material objects that we are able to see or touch or feel. Professor Sorokin of Harvard University talks of the sensate civilization and so many people living this type of sensate civilization and this type of sensate life feeling that only those things which we can see and touch and feel and apply our five senses to have existence.[1] Those people believe that the whole of life is little more than a fortuitous interplay of atoms and electrons and that at bottom the universe is going nowhere.

But then Easter comes to remind us that this universe has meaning, that it is not an accidental collision of atoms and electrons; that it is not an accidental interplay of other forces, but that at bottom there is a God in this universe who has injected meaning in it. And if we fail to see that, we fail to see the meaning of Easter, for that message still rings across the ages. The things that are seen are temporal, but the things that are unseen are eternal.

---

1. Pitirim Alexandrovitch Sorokin (1889–1968) was a Russian-born sociologist who characterized twentieth-century Western industrial society as "sensate," possessing a reality that is perceived largely through the senses.

And so Easter tells us something about ourselves; it tells us something about man; it tells us that we are more than bodies. It tells us that we are more than the stuff out of which we are made from a material point of view. Easter tells us that there is something deeper than all of this. I've mentioned to you before that a certain group of chemists who had a flair for statistics got together some years ago and thought to work out the value of man's body in terms of the market value of that day. And after they had worked with this research for several weeks, they came out with this conclusion that the average man has enough fat in him to make about seven bars of soap, enough iron to make a medium-sized nail, enough sugar to fill a shaker, enough lime to whitewash a chicken coop, enough phosphorous to make about twenty-two hundred match sticks, enough magnesia, for about a dose of—enough magnesium, rather—for about a dose of magnesia, and a little sulfur. And when all of that was added up in terms of the market values of that day, it came to ninety-eight cents.[2] Now that's pretty cheap, isn't it? I guess in these days when the standards of living are a little higher, you could get about a dollar and ninety-eight cents for the average man—and when I say man, I'm speaking in the generic sense; that includes women too. [*Congregation:*] (*Yes*) I guess you could get a dollar ninety-eight cents.[3]

But think of this, that this is about all you can get for the bodily makeup of man; this is all you can get for the, the material stuff of your being. But can you explain the poetic genius of a Shakespeare in terms of ninety-eight cents? Can you explain the artistic genius of a Michelangelo in terms of ninety-eight cents? (*Make it plain, Make it plain*) Can you explain the spiritual genius of a Jesus of Nazareth in terms of ninety-eight cents? Can you explain the mystery of the human heart, the magic of the human soul in terms of ninety-eight cents? Oh no! There is something in there that cannot be explained in dollars and cents. There is something in man that cannot be reduced to materialistic and biological terms. Man is a child of the Almighty God, made in His image, and he's more than a tiny vagary of whirling electrons or whiffs of smoke from a limitless smolder. And oh no! Man is more than that, and Easter comes to tell us that over and over again—that you can't explain man in terms of ninety-eight cents. There is something deep down within him that the Bible calls the image of God. There is something deep down within him that causes the psalmist to be right when he said that God "made him a little lower than the angels" and "crowned him with glory and honor."[4] (*Yes sir, Yes Lord*) There is something within man that tells us that he is a child of God and he is a being of spirit. The things that are seen are temporal; the things that are unseen are eternal, and there's something in us that cannot be seen, but this is the eternality within man. And so Easter comes to refute materialism and to tell us once more that life is more than a physiological process with a physiological meaning. Life is the realm where God reigns (*Yes*) and injects His being into the veins of the universe. Easter comes to tell us that.

---

2. Harry Emerson Fosdick, pastor of Riverside Church, also used this illustration in his sermon "There Is No Death" (*Successful Christian Living* [New York: Harper & Brothers, 1937], pp. 265–266). King annotated a copy of Fosdick's book and kept it in his personal library.

3. Cf. Marshall Dawson, *Nineteenth Century Evolution and After: A Study of Personal Forces Affecting the Social Process, in the Light of the Life-Sciences and Religion* (New York: Macmillan, 1923), p. 19.

4. Cf. Psalm 8:5.

Now Easter means something else. It is an affirmation of the ultimate triumph of good. So often we are in despair because evil takes over. There is hardly anyone here this morning who has not seen evil on the throne. (*Yes sir*) You've seen it in your own individual life. (*Yes*) You try to be good and you try to do right, and you suffer. And then you see somebody out here who has never had any commitment to anything right or good and yet they seem to be prospering. (*Preach*) The eternal question comes to you that came in the book of Job years ago. This question always comes anew in every generation. Well, it does look at times that evil is winning out and let nobody fool you, evil is a reality. Now there are those who try to say that that evil doesn't have any existence; they say it's an illusion. And there are others who would say that it is an error of the mortal mind. They would try to deny the objectivity of evil. But Christianity has never affirmed this. It contends that evil does exist. Sometimes it sees it in a serpent who comes to inject the discord in the beautiful symphony of life in a garden.[5] Sometimes it sees it in vicious men hanging the world's most precious character on a cross between two thieves.[6] (*Yes*) Sometimes it sees it in nagging injustice (*Make it plain*) and agonizing oppression. The Bible and Christianity are always clear on the fact that evil is a reality, but it goes on to contend that evil does not have the final word. It goes on to say that evil carries the seed of its own destruction.

There is a checkpoint in the universe. Evil cannot permanently organize itself. History is the long and tragic story of evil forces rising high only to be crushed by the battering rams of the forces of justice. There is a law in the moral universe, a silent, invisible imperative akin to the laws in the physical universe, which reminds us that life will only work a certain way. The Hitlers and the Mussolinis may have their day, and for a period they may wield great power, spreading themselves like a green bay tree. But soon they are cut down like the grass and wither as the green herb. This is the story of life, and my friends, this morning Easter comes to tell us that Good Friday may occupy the throne for a day, but ultimately it must give way to the triumphant beat of the drums of Easter. Somehow, my friends, Easter comes to remind us that evil may so shape events that Caesar will occupy the palace and Christ the cross, but one day that same Christ will rise up and split history into A.D. and B.C. (*Right*) so that even the life of Caesar must be dated by his name. There is something in Easter to remind us that evil cannot last forever (*Yes*) and that the forces of goodwill eventually triumph.

Now we've seen this in the modern world, I've pointed it out to you before. An evil got loose in this world called colonialism. And you know what happened as a result of this evil. The major Western powers got together, and what did they do? Many of them went over in Africa and Asia, where most of the peoples of the world live, and they got those people and dominated them politically and exploited them economically, segregated them and humiliated them. You look in those countries, and you see how they have had to live under the dark and oppressive night of colonialism. It looked like they would never get out. Something started happening (*Yes*); the wind of change started blowing; forces of the modern universe started working. And all of

---

5. Genesis 3:1–7.
6. Cf. Luke 23:33.

these things came to the point of bringing an end to colonialism, and do you know that out of the one billion seven hundred million people in Asia and Africa who were formerly colonial subjects, more than one billion five hundred million of them have their independence today. Back just twenty-five years ago there were only three independent countries in the whole of Africa. (*That's right*) I remember when Mrs. King and I went to Ghana in West Africa to attend the independence celebration in 1957, there were only eight independent countries in the whole of Africa.[7] And did you know that this morning there are twenty-nine independent countries in the continent of Africa. (*Yes sir*)

All of these things reveal to us that evil may occupy the throne for a day (*Make it plain*), it cannot last forever. No, we in America have known our Good Fridays. (*Yes sir*) They've come to us in various forms. (*Well*) We've known our Good Fridays in the long nights of economic injustice. We've known our Good Fridays in something called separate but equal (*Yes sir*), where there was always a strict enforcement of the separate without the slightest intention to abide by the equal.[8] We've known our Good Fridays. (*Yes sir*) In the past, thousands and millions of Negroes have been stripped of their personhood. We've known our Good Fridays in the fact that we've seen with our own eyes police brutality. We've known our Good Fridays in the fact that we've known tens and twenties and thirties and forties and fifties of Negroes being lynched in one year. We've known our Good Fridays in the fact that we've often gone downtown to get a little coffee and a hamburger only to be told that we couldn't stop. We've known our Good Fridays (*Yes*) in the fact that we've so often had to go to the back. We've known our Good Fridays in the fact that so often we have had to live with the Ku Klux Klan marching on [*the?*] outside of our doors. (*Yes, Yes*) But I tell you Easter is always around the corner: never forget. (*Yes sir, Yes*)

In these same places where we've known Good Friday, we've known Easter. And this morning, in those same stores (*Make it plain*) that would not feed us last year, we can eat there this morning: Easter has come. This morning, in those same places where we had to go to the back, we can now go to the front: (*Yes*) Easter has come. (*Yes*) In those same places where lynchings occurred, the Tuskegee Institute had the report last year that there was not a single lynching (*Make it plain*): Easter has come.[9] And all I am saying this morning is that Good Friday may occupy the throne for a day, but one day (*One day*) Easter is coming. (*Make it plain, Yes*)

There is a third day (*Third day*), and I'm here to tell you this morning (*We're on our way*), segregation is on its death bed. (*Yes sir*) Why is it on its death bed? (*It's done*) Not merely because the Supreme Court of this nation examined the legal body of segregation and pronounced it constitutionally dead. (*Yes sir*) Not merely because millions of white people gained a nagging conscience about segregation. (*Yes*) Not merely because the Negro himself is finally against it. But segregation is dead today because there is always an Easter in this universe to come to block out the darkness

---

7. For more on the Kings' trip to Ghana, see Introduction in *Papers* 4:7–10.

8. In 1896 the Supreme Court in *Plessy v. Ferguson* established the doctrine of "separate but equal."

9. The Tuskegee lynching study noted that, including the killings of Emmett Till (1955) and Mack Charles Parker (1959), three African Americans were lynched in 1955, one in 1959, and one in 1961. No African Americans were lynched in 1960.

of Good Friday. (*Yes*) And this is the story of the Easter message: it says to us that right will ultimately triumph. (*Yes*)

And so this morning—I don't know about you, but I'm not worried. (*Not worried brother*) I'm not worried because there is a [*final?*] law in this universe which justifies a man like Carlyle in saying, "No lie can live forever."[10] I'm not worried this morning because Victor Hugo was right in *Les Misérables* when he talked about when he talked about Napoleon and the fact that Waterloo "is not merely a crease on the map, but it is a symbol of the eternal doom of every Napoleon."[11] I'm not worried this morning (*Not worried*) because there is something in this universe which justifies William Cullen Bryant in saying, "Truth, crushed to earth, will rise again."[12] (*Yes*) I'm not worried this morning because there is something in this universe that justifies the Bible in saying, "You shall reap what you sow."[13] I'm not worried this morning (*Not worried*) because there is something in this universe that justifies James Russell Lowell in saying, "Truth forever on the scaffold, Wrong forever on the throne (*Yes*),—/ Yet that scaffold sways the future, and, behind the dim unknown, / Standeth God within the shadows (*Yes*), keeping watch above his own."[14] I'm not worried this morning (*Worried*) because Easter is coming (*Yes, It is*), and the Easter message is always the message of hope. The Easter message says that ultimately evil must give way (*Yes*) to the triumphant march of the drums of goodness.

And there is a final thought I want to bring out: it is Easter is an affirmation of the fact that death is not the end. (*Yes sir, Talk to me*) Somebody here this morning is worrying about death. Well, if you are, you're not a Christian. (*That's right, Make it plain*) If you are, you don't believe in God. (*Go ahead*) Somebody here this morning is afraid to get up in an airplane because it might drop. If you are, you don't have any faith in God. (*Make it plain*) If it drops, so what? (*So what, Yeah*) The Christian affirmation is that a man or a woman developed the capacity that he does not fear death (*That's right*) because he knows that death is not the end. (*Amen, All right, Amen*) Death is merely a sort of turn in the road of the universe; it's not the end. (*No sir*) And this earthly life is merely the embryonic prelude to a new awakening. This is the Easter affirmation (*Yes sir*), and that tomb is empty. That tomb where they laid Jesus—is empty (*Yes*) and it's empty forever. He, in His own life and in His own death and in His own resurrection, came to reveal to us that death is not the end. What are you [*worried?*] about? (*Not worried*) You come now to the evening of life (*Yes sir*), then to the morning of childhood, move through the noon of adulthood, and now you are moving toward the evening of life—are you worried (*No*) that death is around the corner? What are you worrying about? (*Nothing*) Jesus has fixed that up eternally

---

10. Cf. Thomas Carlyle, *The French Revolution* (1837), vol. 1, book 6, chap. 3.

11. Cf. Victor Hugo, *Les Misérables* (New York: A. L. Burt, 1862), pp. 337–338.

12. Cf. William Cullen Bryant, "The Battlefield" (1839), stanza 9.

13. Cf. Galatians 6:7.

14. Cf. James Russell Lowell, "The Present Crisis" (1844), stanza 8. King's phrasing closely resembles a sermon by Harry Emerson Fosdick: "There is something in this universe beside matter and motion. There is something here that justifies Carlyle in saying, 'No lie can live for ever'. . . . and Lowell in saying, 'Truth forever on the scaffold, Wrong forever on the throne,—/ Yet that scaffold sways the future'" (Fosdick, "Why We Believe in God," *On Being Fit to Live With: Sermons on Post-War Christianity* [New York: Harper & Brothers, 1946], p. 94). King annotated his copy of Fosdick's book.

(*Yes*), that death is not the end.[15] This morning somebody will see that. Something will happen in your life to cause you to go through life not worrying about death (*Yes*) because you know that this has been eternally fixed. (*Yes*)

And there is something that we call the immortality of the soul. And it must be true in order for the universe to be rational. If everything ends with the grave, this universe doesn't have a bit of rationality. (*Not a bit, Not a bit*) In order for this universe to have meaning, there must be something beyond death. (*Right*) There must be a wedding of virtue and happiness, and we don't get it in this world as I said a few minutes ago. The Bible is right when it stresses the point, back from Deuteronomy on up, that there must be a wedding of virtue and happiness. And it is no sign that if you are virtuous in this world, you will always be happy. So there must be life after this world in order to make for the final (*Yes*) wedding of virtue and happiness, for what do we see in this life?[16] We see many situations where there is a triumph of that which is unjust for the moment. We see that for the moment where there is a triumph of that which is evil, as I just said a few minutes ago. But in order for the universe to be just and rational, there must be a wedding of happiness and virtue.

The other thing is this: that God has given all of us an infinite duty and yet we only have finite time to finish it. What is every life but Schubert's *Unfinished Symphony*?[17] No man or woman ever finishes what he starts out to do. God always gives us an infinite duty and we need infinite time to complete it. And so there must be immortality in order to allow us to finish the unfinished work that we can never finish in this life. (*That's right*)

And then another thing that tells us that there is something beyond this is the fact that that everything that we see is a shadow cast by that which we do not see. (*Yes*) You see, they're temporal (*Yes*)—most things that we see are temporal (*Yes*), but the unseen is eternal. The things about you that are eternal are things you can never see. (*Yes, Amen*) Look in the mirror, and you can see your body, but one day that's gone. (*Yes*) Look in the mirror—you can see your beautiful face, but one day that's going. (*Yes*) Look in the mirror—you can see your beautiful hair with all of its black strands, but one day the long winters of night will creep up upon you. (*Yes*) The long days of the years will creep up upon you. That's going; there is nothing permanent about that. (*Amen*)

There is something that you can never see through a mirror, because it is eternal. That is your soul (*Yes sir*); that is your personality (*Yes, Yes*); and that is that something that lives on. (*Yes, Yes*) Go out at night and look up at the stars. You can see them; they are temporal. (*Yes, Yes*) But there is something that holds them there called the law of gravitation—you can never see that. (*That's right*) Look at Ebenezer Church today;

---

15. Amos John Traver, *The Christ Who Is All* (Philadelphia: The United Lutheran Publication House, 1929), p. 95: "Death is but a comma in the unending sentence."

16. In his notes on Jeremiah 12:1, King wrote: "If God is justice there must somehow and ~~sometime~~ {somewhere} be a wedding of virtue and happiness. This doesn't always take place in life as Jeremiah so candidly points out. What then is the solution? It seems to me that the only solution to this problem is found in the doctrine of personal immortality" (King, Notecards on Books of the Old Testament, 22 September 1952–28 January 1953, in *Papers* 2:166).

17. Franz Schubert (1797–1828), an Austrian composer, completed only two movements of his eighth symphony.

this old building one day is going down. (*Yes sir*) You can see that; you can see this building that we are trying to pay out of debt right now; you can see it. One day it's going down, but there is something behind it that you can never see. You can never see the love and the faith and the hope of these people who are struggling to raise seventy-five dollars to pay it out of debt.[18] (*Yes*) You can never see the mind of the architect who drew the blueprint. And this goes right through life and the universe: everything that we see is something cast by that (*Yes*) which we do not see.

And so this morning, even though you can't see the soul, it has reality. And I'm convinced more than ever before in the immortality of the soul. I'm sorry this morning that I can't describe heaven to you. Reinhold Niebuhr has reminded us that it is dangerous to try to give the temperature of hell or the quality of heaven.[19] I'm sorry I can't give it to you this morning. I don't know all of the, I don't know all of the makeup of heaven (*Not right here*), but the beautiful thing is that that I know who's there. (*Who's there, Yes*) Somebody here tonight may have a son up in New York City and you've never been there—maybe you've lived in the rural area all of your life, you've gotten to Atlanta, but way off is a son or daughter up in New York. And there with all of its skyscraping buildings (*Yes*), there with its dashing subways (*Make it plain*), and there with all of the fascinating things that have been created by man—and one day he sends you a little money to come to visit him in New York. And you get on the train—trains are not the thing that inspires you about New York as you ride up the road on the Silver Comet.[20] It's not its skyscraping buildings—you aren't concerned about that. (*Yes*) You wouldn't know how to picture them because you've never seen a skyscraper maybe. (*Preach*) You wouldn't know how to picture the Empire State Building because you've never seen it maybe. You will never know how to picture the subway because you've never seen it. But as you move across the continent, something inspires you as you go on up there, and that is the fact that you know who's in New York. (*Amen*) And it is the pull of that son (*Yes*) and the power of that son (*Yes*) that makes the trip meaningful. (*Yes*) Not the skyscraping buildings, not the externals of New York (*No*), but the internal longing to see your son.

And I close this morning by saying I do not know what heaven is like. (*Yes, Make it plain*) I do not know the furniture of heaven or what the streets are made like. (*Yes*) I don't even know if heaven is a place in the sense that we know place, but I know who's there. (*Yes*) And I know that Jesus is there. (*Oh yes*) I know that some loved one is there. (*Yes*) I know that someone who's struggled along the way of life is there. (*Yes*) This is the thing that gives meaning to heaven, and therefore I say that this corruptible shall take on incorruption (*Yes sir*), and this mortal shall take on immortality.

Once more we must say over and over again that the things seen are temporal and the things unseen are eternal. This is what the Easter message tells us. Go out

---

18. Ebenezer Baptist Church had launched a fundraising drive to pay off its $50,000 debt in honor of its 75th anniversary, asking each of its members to contribute a minimum of seventy-five dollars (King, Notes on Ebenezer's 75th anniversary fundraising drive, December 1961–May 1962).

19. Niebuhr, *The Nature and Destiny of Man: A Christian Interpretation*, vol. 2, *Human Destiny* (New York: Scribner's, 1953), p. 294: "It is unwise for Christians to claim any knowledge of either the furniture of heaven or the temperature of hell."

20. The Silver Comet, a passenger train operated by Seaboard Air Lines, ran between New York and Birmingham, Alabama.

this morning—go out into your homes, into your communities knowing that Easter has brought out the new ray of hope (*Yes sir*) that tells us that there is meaning in the universe. It tells us that evil will not triumph in the universe, and it tells us that death is not the end. It is an open door (*Yes*) that leads men into life eternal.

We open the doors of the church now, and there may be someone here this morning (*That's right*) who has never been a member of the church. I'm sure there is someone here this morning who has not united with the church although you live in this community. If you are here this morning as we sing together "He Lives," hymn number 279, as we think of a living Christ (*Yes*), we think of the living Savior, who this morning will make the decision. Wherever you are, come this morning at this time, at this [*organ plays*] moment, will you make that decision? Wherever you are, I know there is someone here this morning who needs to come into the church (*Yes, Lord, Yes, Lord*), who needs to accept Christ. Are you here this morning? [*congregation sings*] Is there one who make that decision this morning? All, let us stand on the next stanza. We still bid you come, wherever you are. Who this morning will make that decision? [*congregation sings*]

Now, just before we sing that last stanza, I know this morning that there is someone here, I know that this morning there's someone here who is not a member of a church in Atlanta. There's someone here this morning waiting for a more appropriate time. There's someone here saying that that "I can make up my mind a little later." But I want to say to you this morning that this is your opportunity now. Don't let it be said too late. (*That's right*) This is the moment of supreme opportunity. (*Yes sir*) And what is a better day to unite with the church of God (*Yes, Yes*) than on the day when we celebrate the resurrection of our Lord and Savior Jesus Christ? Who will this morning allow Him to live in your life by making a decision? I don't know your name; I don't know where you are sitting; but you are here, and we sing this last stanza for you. Wherever you are, come now. [*congregation continues singing*]

Thank you. May we remain standing. We are asking that all of you will be back for the evening worship service this evening at 7:30. Will we all be back on time at 7:30 this evening. May we all turn now to the closing hymn. It's not a hymn this morning; it is the Hallelujah Chorus, one of the greatest anthems in all Christendom. (*Hymn number 3, now*) After that, all members will remain seated. We'll take those seats after the benediction. We want to see all members of the church, and we're strongly urging you to stay, every member, please stay for just a few minutes. Hallelujah Chorus. [*congregation sings*]

The Lord bless Thee and keep Thee; the Lord make His face to shine upon Thee and be gracious unto Thee; the Lord lift up the light as his count [*recording interrupted*][21]

At. MLKEC.

---

21. Cf. Numbers 6:24–26.

## "People in Action: Nothing Changing Unless"

28 April 1962
New York, N.Y.

*In the following article, drafted prior to Kennedy's 15 March 1962 signing of the Manpower Development and Training bill, King implores the administration to strengthen the multi-million dollar plan, calling it a "drop-in-the-bucket" for its failure to address the more than 4.5 million unemployed workers.[1] For African American workers, King said, the bill is a "clear case of too little, too late," as automation threatens to render the worker obsolete. King insists that the bill must give African Americans the "rightful opportunity to participate in the nation's job market without restriction and discrimination." In conclusion, King admonishes the government, saying: "To deny any group honest work and fair play is not only immoral, it is almost murderous. It is deliberate strangulation of physical and cultural development." The article was published in the* New York Amsterdam News.

Negroes, traditionally the "last to be hired, and the first to be fired," may find themselves in an even more precarious position in the years to come, unless they pressure the administration to put sharp teeth in the new $435 million job training bill.

This manpower training bill is judged to be enough to train a "drop-in-the-bucket" million persons. In addition to unemployed workers, other eligibles for training include members of farm families with a total income of less than $1,200 a year and youths between 16 and 22.

Training allowances will be paid to trainees, equal to the unemployment compensation in the trainee's state, for a maximum of 52 weeks. Youths between 16 and 19 will get no training allowance and those between 19 and 22 will get $20 a week.

However successful this program becomes, it is a clear case of too little, too late.

The mass of Negroes in the United States are already suffering from the results of long exclusion from trades and job categories in which they could have acquired training and experience.

Now, even while this belated attempt is being made to salvage a segment of the unemployed and potentially employable, "computers and automation threaten to create vast unemployment and social unrest."

### Job Study

A recent job study predicted that the advent of mass automation "would eliminate entire job categories ranging from factory workers to bank tellers and middle-management executives."[2]

---

1. The "Manpower Development and Training Act of 1962" authorized a new three-year program to retrain unemployed workers displaced by automation. To qualify, trainees must be either unemployed youths, the head of a family or household that has been unemployed at least three years, or from a farm family with net income of less than $1,200 a year.

2. See quote in "Automation Report Sees Vast Job Loss," *New York Times*, 29 January 1962. King refers to Donald N. Michael's study *Cybernation: The Silent Conquest*, which focused on the difficulties brought

The Study foresaw a severe displacement of blue collar workers, especially in dock, factory and mine operations, "where Negroes have hitherto found their steadiest employment."[3] An unhealthy effect of automation, it added, may be the lack of jobs for "untrained adolescents," 26,000,000 of whom will be seeking work in this decade.[4]

Recently, Secretary of Labor Arthur Goldberg, pointed out that as United States population increases and introduction of automatic machinery displace workers on land and in offices and factories, between one million and 1.5 million new jobs have to be found every year . . . and this at a time when there are already 4.5 million unemployed.[5]

The nation's manpower shortage in certain areas and excessive unemployment can be compensated immeasurably, if the administration sees to it that Negroes get their fair share of benefits under the first main provision of the new manpower bill.

That first provision authorizes the Secretary of Labor to make a survey of the nation's manpower, the skills needed, and then to set up the training programs in those skills found to be in short supply.

## U.S. Would Benefit

Affording just one million of the nation's Negro unemployed and untrained their just opportunity to acquire this much needed job training, would benefit not only the Negro population, but the economy of the entire nation.

Secretary Goldberg made a case for the administration by saying that there is no practical way of providing jobs or security for the United States unles it finds new markets at home and abroad.[6] Mr. Goldberg and the administration can take part, they need only to put down their buckets where they are.

---

about by automation (Michael, *Cybernation: The Silent Conquest* [Santa Barbara: Center for the Study of Democratic Institutions, 1962], p. 10). Automation, according to Michael, makes blue-collar workers and middle management obsolete, while skilled workers are overworked, and too many adolescents are untrained to take on the skilled jobs. Michael proposed shorter hours for the same pay and an expanded public works program as alternate solutions to these problems, noting that "retraining has not always been successful, nor have new jobs based on that retraining been available" (p. 24).

3. In Michael's study, he argues that one and a half million manufacturing jobs had been cut in the last six years, which impacted the already "increasingly lopsided Negro-to-white unemployment ratio as the dock, factory, and mine operations where Negroes have hitherto found their steadiest employment are cybernated" (pp. 14–15).

4. Michael listed four choices for unskilled adolescents to join the automated workforce: "They can stay in school, for which they are unsuited either by motivation or by intelligence; they can seek training that will raise them out of the untrained work force; they can compete in the growing manpower pool of those seeking relatively unskilled jobs, or they can loaf. If they loaf, almost inevitably they are going to become delinquent. Thus, without adequate occupational outlets for these youths, cybernation may contribute substantially to further social disruption" (pp. 22–23).

5. See James Reston, "Washington: The Cold War Switches to the House," *New York Times*, 14 March 1962.

6. Arthur J. Goldberg noted that while ninety thousand jobs would be lost due to imports allowed by lowering tariffs, one hundred fifty thousand jobs would be created with every additional billion dollars of exports. He made this observation while defending Kennedy's trade bill, which sought to lower tariffs with the European Common Market (John D. Morris, "Goldberg Says Tariff Cuts Will Spur Net Gains in Jobs," *New York Times*, 14 March 1962).

They need only to provide the Negroes of the United States with their rightful opportunity to participate in the nation's job market without restriction and discrimination, and allow the United States to benefit from the increased spending power which will then be afforded these Negroes.

### Moral Confusion

The nation's failure to grapple forthrightly with this problem of economic injustice can lead only to a darker night of moral confusion. We need not look very far to see the injurious effect that discrimination has upon the psychological and moral life of its victims. To deny any group honest work and fair play is not only immoral, it is almost murderous. It is deliberate strangulation of physical and cultural development.[7]

Few practices are more detrimental to our national welfare than the discrimination with which the economic order is rife. Few practices are more thoroughly sinful.

PD. *New York Amsterdam News*, 28 April 1962.

----

7. King made similar comments in a speech to the Eleventh Constitutional Convention of the Transport Workers Union of America, AFL-CIO, on 5 October 1961, calling automation's impact on labor a catastrophe: "We are neither technologically advanced nor socially enlightened, if we witness this disaster for tens of thousands, without finding a solution. And by 'solution,' I mean a real and genuine alternative, providing the same living standards and opportunities which were swept away by a force called 'progress,' but which for some, means destruction."

# To Mrs. E. D. Johnston

30 April 1962
[*Atlanta, Ga.*]

*Johnston, a white British woman married to a black man, wrote King asking for his advice for her twenty-year-old biracial son, who viewed his heritage as a "burden and source of inferiority."*[1] *Below, King acknowledges the "frustration" Johnston's son must feel, noting that "it is tragic that so many of us make the mistake in life of being overly concerned with the externals of life, e.g. color, skin, hair, wealth, position." He prays that her son will "lose himself in working for a great humanitarian cause" for "it is only when he loses himself that he will find himself."*[2]

----

1. In her letter, Johnston said her son feels like a "fraud" when he does not disclose his mixed-race background (Johnston to King, 17 April 1962).

2. King paraphrases from Harry Emerson Fosdick's *On Being a Real Person* (New York: Harper & Brothers, 1943), p. 92: "No man can be himself until he gets out of himself into work with which he identifies himself." King had a copy of Fosdick's book in his personal library. King also paraphrases Matthew 10:39: "He that findeth his life shall lose it; and he that loseth his life for my sake shall find it." Using the same passage for the text of his 11 August 1957 sermon "Conquering Self-Centeredness" at Dexter

30 Apr   Mrs. E. D. Johnston
1962      R.R. 1 Box 102
          Lakeshore Drive
          St. Joseph, Illinois

Dear Mrs. Johnston:

This is to acknowledge receipt of your letter of recent date. I am very happy to know that you liked my message and that you found it helpful.[3]

I am very much in sympathy with your son and can understand the frustration he often feels. I am sure that he could make a fine, worthwhile contribution to the cause of freedom and human dignity if he could take his mind away from himself. He must recognize that the most meaningful life is a life whose center is a fixed point outside of his own being. Someone has said that the smallest package they had seen was a man all wrapped in himself.[4] To a large measure, this is very true. Every person can have the confidence that God did not make a mistake when he was created in his own individuality. The acme of the human spirit is for each of us to exploit our five talents, our three talents, or our one talent to his fullest potential.[5] It is tragic that so many of us make the mistake in life of being overly concerned with the externals of life, e.g. color, skin, hair, wealth, position, when really the essentials of life are the internals: self-respect, integrity, human dignity, selflessness, etc. I pray that your son will soon lose himself in working for a great humanitarian cause. It is only when he loses himself that he will find himself.

Let me also take this opportunity to thank you for your very encouraging words concerning my work. Your words are of inestimable value in the continuance of our humble efforts. Our struggle is often difficult and the moments are often frustrating, but we gain new courage to carry on when we realize that persons of good will, such as you, are supporting us.

---

Avenue Baptist Church, King said: "I think one of the best ways to face this problem of self-centeredness is to discover some cause and some purpose, some loyalty outside of yourself and give yourself to that something" (in *Papers* 4:253).

3. After seeing King on television, Johnston said she felt that he had the "right approach to the race question" (Johnston to King, 17 April 1962). Johnston may have seen King's 15 April address before the Chicago Sunday Evening Club, which was televised on local station WTTW (King, "Remaining Awake Through a Great Revolution," Address delivered at the Chicago Sunday Evening Club, 15 April 1962; "Television Programs for Sunday," *Chicago Tribune*, 15 April 1962).

4. Fosdick, *On Being*, pp. 83–84: "At the very best, a person completely wrapped up in himself makes a small package." On the top of page 93 of King's copy of Fosdick's book, he wrote: "There is nothing more tragic than a self-focused, unextended life."

5. Matthew 25:14–18: "For the kingdom of heaven is as a man travelling into a far country, who called his own servants, and delivered unto them his goods. And unto one he gave five talents, to another two, and to another one; to every man according to his several ability; and straightway took his journey. Then he that had received the five talents went and traded with the same, and made them other five talents. And likewise he that had received two, he also gained other two. But he that had received one went and digged in the earth, and hid his lord's money." King had used the Parable of the Talents as a text of a sermon he delivered at Dexter Avenue Baptist Church in 1955 (King, "Opportunity, Fidelity, and Reward," Sermon at Dexter Avenue Baptist Church, January 1955, in *Papers* 6:207–209).

Very truly yours,
Martin Luther King, Jr.

Km

TLc. SCLCR-GAMK: Box 63.

## "A Prayer"

4 May 1962
*[Atlanta, Ga.]*

*King contributes an intercessory prayer for a book of devotions being assembled by*
*Reverend Frank Madison Reid, pastor of St. James AME Church in St. Louis.*
*The book was intended to be a guide for Reid's congregation during a hundred-*
*hour prayer vigil.*[1]

Eternal God, our Father, out of whose mind this great cosmic universe has been created; before whose face the generations rise and fall; toward whom men of all ages turn for consolation, we thank Thee for the many blessings of life. We are grateful to Thee for the challenging opportunities that lie before us. We are not unmindful of our sins and shortcomings. All too often, we have chosen injustice rather than justice, hate rather than love, the low road rather than the high road. Forgive us for yielding to our low impulses. Help us to realize that we are made for the stars and created for eternity. In these days of emotional tension, when the problems of the world are gigantic in extent and chotic in detail, give us broad understanding, penetrating vision, and power of endurance. Save us from the paralysis of crippling fears. May we commit ourselves to the task of working with renewed vigor for a warless world, for a better distribution of wealth, and for a brotherhood that transcends race or color. In the name and spirit of Jesus, we pray.
 Amen.

TD. MLKJP-GAMK: Box 64.

---

 1. In a 1 May 1962 letter, Reid asked King to write a prayer for "<u>all</u> those who must suffer in the social upheaval for which we strive." For a similar prayer, see King, "Prayers," 5 July–6 September 1953, in *Papers* 6:138.

# "People in Action: Unknown Heroes"

12 May 1962
New York, N.Y.

*In April 1962 SCLC's People to People tour stopped in South Carolina where*
*King met with local heroes Esau Jenkins and Billie Fleming. As part of King's*
*biweekly column in the* New York Amsterdam News, *he writes of discovering*
*"literally thousands of unknown heroes across our Southland," like Jenkins and*
*Fleming, who keep the "threadbare hopes of the Negro community intact against*
*insurmountable odds."*[1]

I never realized how many unknown heroes there were in the Freedom struggle of the Negro in the South until I began our "people to people" tours. Out of the Montgomery Bus protest experience, Ralph Abernathy and I had learned, that through a quirk of fortune and circumstances, public exposure, national and international, came to us. We honestly faced through all the days that followed the truth that there were literally hundreds of others in Montgomery who were more deserving than ourselves. It was but a whim of history that made us the titular leaders.[2]

Thus the awareness of unknown heroes in our struggle has always been present, but never to the degree that it now exists. However, after spending the better part

---

1. Following his visit to South Carolina, King thanked Jenkins for his hospitality and commended the civil rights leader for his "deep dedication and genuine commitment to the cause of freedom and human dignity" (King to Jenkins, 24 April 1962). Esau Jenkins (1910–1972), born on Johns Island, South Carolina, left school after the fourth grade to help his father work in the cotton and rice fields. By the 1930s Jenkins owned his own farm and a trucking company to transport his vegetables to the market in Charleston, South Carolina. As his trucking company prospered, Jenkins invested in several other businesses, including a fruit stand, a motel, and a restaurant. As a prominent member of the Johns Island community, Jenkins began lobbying for a black high school on the island and purchased a bus to transport students living on the island to the city to attend school. Three years later, Jenkins bought additional buses to transport islanders who commuted into Charleston to work. It was during one of these trips that Jenkins began teaching riders to read parts of the Constitution to prepare them for the voter registration test. In 1954 Jenkins at the urging of Septima Clark attended a workshop at the Highlander Folk School in Monteagle, Tennessee. In 1956, Jenkins, Clark, and Bernice Robinson with the help of Highlander set up one of the citizenship schools on Johns Island. Throughout the 1960s Jenkins continued to play a pivotal role in the civil rights movement. He served on the boards of the Charleston chapter of the NAACP and SCLC, and was president of the Citizens Committee of Charleston. In 1966 Jenkins founded the CO Federal Credit Union. Just before his death, Jenkins was appointed to the state advisory committee for the U.S. Commission on Civil Rights. Billie Sunday Fleming (1923–1992) was born in Manning, South Carolina. After receiving a B.A. from South Carolina State College, Fleming served as a lieutenant in the U.S. Navy during World War II. Fleming worked to improve race relations in Clarendon County, as president of the Manning branch of the NAACP for thirty-two years and co-founder and president of the Clarendon County Improvement Association. Before the Senate Subcommittee on Constitutional Rights in 1959, Fleming testified to economic and violent retaliation for his participation in the civil rights movement. Following his death, Fleming was recognized by the South Carolina General Assembly for his long-time civil rights work.

2. King expressed similar sentiments in a sermon "Conquering Self-Centeredness" on 11 August 1957 (*Papers* 4:255).

of three days in the Negro-majority counties of the First and Second Congressional Districts of South Carolina on our third "people to people" tour, I see now, that in nearly every hamlet, every town, every county seat, every rural community, there is some staunch lover of Freedom—unknown and unpublicized—who kept the threadbare hopes of the Negro community intact against insurmountable odds. Esau Jenkins and Billy Fleming are two of these.

Esau Jenkins is a rather portly, dark-skinned Negro who has lived on John's Island all his life. John's Island is one of a number of the Sea Islands of South Carolina where there is the unique admixture of French, Negro and white family strain, very similar to the Creoles of New Orleans.

Esau Jenkins is an industrious business man who has parlayed one small business into a network of restaurants and bus-service lines to the islands in the Charleston area.

### Involved

For as long as he can remember, he has been "involved" in the drive for Negro rights, many times spending his own money and giving uncalculated time. Yet by his own testimony he told us that though in many quarters of the community both Negro and white, he is persona non grata, his businesses have flourished and all of his seven children educated.[3]

The most remarkable thing about Esau Jenkins is that the Citizenship School Program of SCLC which now represents nearly a $100,000.00 a year operation, was born on one of his buses.[4]

Several years ago, while waiting to make a run into Charleston from the islands, Esau Jenkins conceived the idea to use the time between trips to teach his riders "their letters."

Thus he began teaching reading and writing to his adult riders in order that they could qualify to vote.

### Idea Spreads

It was not too long before the classes outgrew the bus and were transferred to a back room of his store. Soon the idea began to spread all over the Sea Islands.

Then, with the help of the Field Foundation, schools were established and staffed throughout the islands. This program has now been developed on a South-wide basis through SCLC.

In less than six months, we have trained 200 teachers and there are presently 105 Citizenship Schools operative in nine states across the South, six in Mississippi.[5] And all of this began with Esau Jenkins on his bus at John's Island, South Carolina.

He is one of the unknown heroes of the Freedom struggle in the South.

---

3. Jenkins's seven children were Abraham, Marie, Ethel, James, Lorretta, Francena, and Elaine.

4. From July 1961–June 1962, the proposed budget for the citizenship schools was $40,500 of which $31,500 came from a Field Foundation grant (Citizenship Education Program, Financial statement, "Citizenship Education Program in the South, Field Foundation," 11 December 1961).

5. From January to June 1962, 334 people attended SCLC's training seminars held in Dorchester Center in Midway, Georgia, and 125 schools were established in Alabama, Georgia, Louisiana, Mississippi, South Carolina, Virginia, and Texas (SCLC, Citizenship School attendance records, 1962).

Billy Fleming is another.

On our people to people tour the second day, we headed northeast early in the morning.

## Clarendon County

Our next stop was a little hamlet called Manning. Manning is in Clarendon County! This is the county where the suit that resulted in the Supreme Court Decision of 1954 originated.[6]

In some magisterial districts, Negroes outnumber whites, five to one. An old friend, Billy Fleming, is the leader there. Tall and robust, easily six feet three or four, Billy Fleming's gentleness was disarming when contrasted with his physical size.

You could not miss a definite grimness in his copper-colored countenance. I later learned there was good reason.

Billy Fleming related to me a story of bombings, economic reprisals, mayhem threatenings and intimidations that would make Alabama and Georgia seem tame.[7]

## Reprisals

He explained that during the last three years, the farm people of Clarendon County (there is no other industry of any kind) have had grain standing in the field that couldn't be harvested; the White Citizens Councils pressured the withdrawal of commercial combines.

On other occasions, men with money in their hands couldn't buy seed and fertilizer and fuel for their machinery.

This latter condition existed with some farmers at the very moment he talked with us. Billy Fleming happens to be an undertaker. Negroes who indicate they desire his services, are pressured and investigated by the WCC. Yet Billy Fleming hangs on, holding together the integrity and dignity of the Negro community despite the tremendous pressures he faces from every quarter.

---

6. In March 1948, local citizen Levi Pearson brought a suit requesting that the state provide public transportation for students attending Scott's Branch High School in Clarendon County. Although the suit was dismissed on legal technicalities, local citizens gave their support to a lawsuit filed by the NAACP to declare school segregation unconstitutional. On 23 June 1951 the U.S. District Court in Charleston ruled in *Briggs v. Elliott* (98 F. Supp. 529 [E.D.S.C. 1951]) that Clarendon County must improve its black public schools, but that segregated schools by themselves were legal. After the NAACP appealed the decision on the basis that segregated facilities by nature violated the Fourteenth Amendment, *Briggs* was combined with *Davis v. County School Board of Prince Edward County* (103 F. Supp. 337 [1952]), *Brown v. Board of Education* (98 F. Supp. 797 [D. Kan. 1951]), *Bolling v. Sharpe* (347 U.S. 497 [1954]), and *Belton v. Gebhart* (87 A. 2d [Del. Ch. 1952] *aff'd* 91 A. 2d 137 [Del. 1952]).

7. As retaliation for his efforts to desegregate schools in Manning, shots were fired into Fleming's home in 1955. Fleming's funeral home suffered economic hardship when his name appeared on a list maintained by the White Citizens Council (WCC) warning blacks not to do business with him. In 1959 Fleming testified before a Senate subcommittee that he founded the Clarendon County Improvement Association to provide economic aid to NAACP members and *Briggs* plaintiffs blacklisted by the local WCC. According to Fleming's testimony, WCC pressure led to white farmers refusing to rent out harvesting equipment to NAACP members and wholesalers refusing to sell goods to merchants affiliated with the NAACP (*Civil Rights–1959*, Part One [Washington, D.C.: U.S. Government Printing Office, 1959], pp. 526–544).

## How?

Just before we left Manning, I had the opportunity to shake hands with several of the original plaintiffs in the Clarendon County school desegregation suit. Very seldom have I been as inspired as when I met the simple people of the land who possessed such great courage and persistent devotion to freedom.

If you ever visit Clarendon County, you will wonder as I did, "How on earth did a school desegregation suit begin here in the early fifties?" It was begun because of an unknown hero named Billy Fleming and his faithful followers of Clarendon County, South Carolina.

### Unknown Heroes

There must be literally thousands of unknown heroes across our Southland. There's one at John's Island, South Carolina and another at Manning in Clarendon County. Remember their names. Esau Jenkins and Billy Fleming.

Unknown Heroes.

PD. *New York Amsterdam News,* 12 May 1962.


# Address at the Formation of the Gandhi Society
# for Human Rights

17 May 1962
Washington, D.C.

*Discussions in late 1961 between King and New York attorneys Harry Wachtel
and Theodore Kheel led to the formation of the Gandhi Society for Human Rights,
a tax-exempt organization aimed at educating the public about nonviolence
and providing legal and financial support to the civil rights movement.[1] In the
following address, delivered on the eighth anniversary of the* Brown *decision,
King describes the purpose of the new organization and announces that SCLC had
asked President John F. Kennedy to issue a second Emancipation Proclamation,
thereby ending all forms of segregation in the United States.[2] A hundred years
after Abraham Lincoln abolished slavery "with a stroke of the pen," King argues
that like Lincoln, Kennedy, too, has the power to change the lives of millions of*

---

1. For more on King's discussions with Wachtel and Kheel, see King to Wachtel, 7 November 1961 and 12 February 1962, pp. 325–327 and 397–398 in this volume, respectively. Kheel was the Society's first president, while Clarence B. Jones served as acting executive director. King, who did not have a formal role in the organization, was honorary chairman. Twenty-five people agreed to serve on the executive board ("Gandhi Society for Rights Formed; King Presents Documents to JFK," *Atlanta Daily World,* 20 May 1962).

2. Washington SCLC representative Walter Fauntroy gave the proposal to Brooks Hays, special assistant to the president, who reportedly said that Kennedy would take a "great deal of interest in the document" and would "be sympathetic to the sentiments expressed within" (King, "An Appeal to the Honorable John F. Kennedy, President of the United States for National Rededication to the Principles of the Emancipation Proclamation and for an Executive Order," 17 May 1962; Wallace Terry, "Race Group

*southern blacks.*[3] *According to King, even though the nation survived the Civil War, it continues to be plagued by issues of race as millions of qualified black voters are barred from participating in full citizenship just as their enslaved ancestors had been. As part of a growing revolution taking place all over the world, King proclaims that in America "we have the power, the resources and the moral support of the majority of the nation to institute long-delayed reforms." In conclusion, King claims that blacks and sympathetic whites have forged an "invincible will of justice and democracy."*

This occasion might well signalize not one anniversary but several apparently disparate events. Actually they are components of one tapestry of human experience—a tapestry which depicts justice's stubborn struggle to be dominant in the affairs of men. The historic supreme court decision on school desegregation; the threshold of the centennial anniversary of the Emancipation Proclamation; the founding of the Gandhi Society for Human Rights and the 100th anniversary of the death of Henry David Thoreau are all celebrated this year.[4]

Thoreau has said "there are a thousand hacking at the branches of evil to one who is striking at the roots."[5] I believe that we who are here today are those striking at the root of evil, not at its branches.

It is altogether fitting that on these overlapping anniversaries of liberal triumphs a distinguished group of public citizens should form a new society dedicated to progress through non-violence. Thoreau's anniversary reminds us that the concepts of civil disobedience and non-violence are part of the American tradition. But it is only now that its use in widespread practice has engaged the American people and established itself irrevocably as a primary social lever. Non-violence is not woven into the fabric of American life in hundreds of boycotts across the South; it is marked on the jail walls of thousands of cells of freedom riders; it sits in majestic, democratic dignity upon thousands of lunch counter stools. Non-violent protest is no longer a bizarre or alien concept. It wins battles for justice with as much lethal effectiveness as the blazing six-shooters of the old frontier or the more contemporary "punch in the jaw." It may well mark a new stage for mankind in which his conduct acquired a

to Stress Gandhi Non-Violence," *Washington Post*, 18 May 1962). At a press conference following his address, King clarified that the Gandhi Society was not a "direct action" organization, nor would it be concerned with the use of nonviolence on an international scale, but rather an organization aimed at solving race issues in the United States (King, Excerpts, Press conference on the formation of the Gandhi Society for Human Rights and the appeal for a second Emancipation Proclamation, 17 May 1962). A month after the luncheon, Jones sent a memorandum to the society's board members highlighting the "adaptation of Gandhi's Satyagraha or 'truth force'" as the foundation of the new organization (Jones, Memo, "The formation of the Gandhi Society for Human Rights, Inc.," 20 June 1962). For more on King's request for Kennedy to sign a second Emancipation Proclamation, see note 18, King, "The Negro and the American Dream," Emancipation Day Address Delivered at Municipal Auditorium, 2 January 1961, p. 118 in this volume.

3. Lincoln issued the Emancipation Proclamation on 1 January 1863.
4. Henry David Thoreau (1817–1862) was an American author, philosopher, and abolitionist.
5. Cf. Thoreau, *Walden: or, Life in the Woods* (Boston: Ticknor and Fields, 1854), p. 82.

more civilized quality even as he continues a bitter struggle for broader democratic freedoms.[6]

Because this day is so filled with historic significance, my organization, the Southern Christian Leadership Conference, chose it to deliver to President Kennedy a document we consider to be a landmark contribution in the struggle for civil rights. We have asked the President, on the centennial anniversary of the Emancipation Proclamation, to issue an executive order which would rededicate the nation to the principles of that noble proclamation. The rededication we seek would not be limited to hollow words, however. We ask that he proclaim all segregation statutes of all southern states to be contrary to the constitution and that the full powers of his office be employed to avoid their enforcement. Just as Abraham Lincoln made the tragic sacrifices of the civil war worth enduring when he ended human chattel slavery with a stroke of the pen, President Kennedy can change the totality of life of the Negro in the South by the issuance of this executive order we have proposed.

1.  That the full powers of your office will be used to eliminate all forms of statutory-imposed segregation and discrimination from and throughout the respective states of this nation.

2.  Effective January 1, 1963, that as of the school year, September 1963, all school districts presently segregated must desegregate. Such a proclamation should be accompanied by a Directive authorizing the Department of Health, Education and Welfare to immediately prepare, in consultation with local school officials, a program of integration in compliance with the mandate of Brown v. Board of Education.[7]

3.  That racial segregation in Federally assisted housing is henceforth prohibited and unlawful.[8]

---

6. In King's draft of this address, he handwrote at the end of this paragraph: "This society will assist in a very significant way in educating the public on the [many?]" (King, Draft, Address at the formation of the Gandhi Society for Human Rights, 17 May 1962).

7. In a press conference after his speech, King further explained that the executive order would "declare in firm, crystal clear terms that segregation is against the national policy of the United States and against the best interests morally and politically of our country" (King, Excerpts, Press conference, 17 May 1962). At the president's weekly press briefing also on 17 May 1962, Kennedy responded to a reporter who asked if progress in school desegregation was occurring fast enough: "Well, I think we can always hope that more progress can be made in the area of civil rights, or equal opportunity, whether it's in employment or education or housing or anything else. There is a good deal left undone, and while progress has been made I think we can always improve equality of opportunity in the United States" (*Public Papers of the Presidents of the United States: John F. Kennedy, 1962* [Washington, D.C.: Government Printing Office, 1963], p. 404). Although no formal decree or order was issued, President Kennedy announced on 9 September 1963 that 144 school districts in eleven Southern states peacefully desegregated their public schools since 1954. In spite of other states' progress, Alabama under Governor George C. Wallace refused to comply with federal integration laws (*Public Papers of the Presidents of the United States: John F. Kennedy, 1963* [Washington, D.C.: U.S. Government Printing Office, 1964], pp. 661–662; William O. Bryant, "Kennedy Warns Wallace, U.S. Will do Whatever Necessary to Desegregate Schools in Alabama," *Atlanta Daily World*, 10 September 1963).

8. Although the executive order ending discrimination in federally funded housing was ready for Kennedy's signature in November 1961, he held off signing it for fear of losing support among Southern members of Congress for his tariff program. In a March 1962 article published in *The Nation*, King criticized Kennedy for refusing to sign the initial draft of the order: "In backing away from an Executive

4. That any and all laws within the United States requiring segregation and discrimination because of race or color are contrary to the national policy of the
   Government of the United States and are detrimental and inimical to the best
   interest of the United States at home and abroad.

One hundred years ago today it was far from certain that our republic would
survive. It has survived through all the turbulent upheavals of a century and the
President securely occupies his office under the mandates of the constitution.
But who would have thought that the President, one hundred years after the
Emancipation Proclamation, would be confronted with a grotesque array of race
problems? Who would have thought that despite the spectacular growth of the
nation, backward and brutal institutions of segregation and discrimination would
cling like ugly parasites to the ship of state? Who would have thought that the particular President in the White House in 1962 would himself have been a victim of
prejudice and discrimination because he is of a minority religion?[9] Who would have
thought that 100 years after the Emancipation Proclamation and the enactment
of the 14th amendment, millions of qualified Negroes still would have no vote and
would be as totally excluded from the democratic electoral process as their slave
forebears had been? Our republic did survive but it lived and grew with visible scars
which a century still has failed to heal.

One hundred years is a long time. Even one year is too long if you are deprived of
your rights. Even one day is too long. We believe with the Supreme Court that "justice too long delayed is justice denied."[10]

That is why we are here today. That is why Thoreau's observation about striking
at branches or roots is so pertinent. For so long, so many have grimly torn away

---

Order to end discrimination in housing, the President did more to undermine confidence in his
intentions than could be offset by a series of smaller accomplishments during the year" (King, "Fumbling on the New Frontier," 3 March 1962, p. 413 in this volume). Kennedy eventually issued Executive Order 11063 on 20 November 1962.

9. During Kennedy's 1960 presidential bid, some critics, particularly in the South, expressed con-
cern that Kennedy, a Catholic, might be unduly influenced by the Roman Catholic Church (Edward T.
Folliard, "Kennedy's Religion Held Rising Factor," *Washington Post*, 24 August 1960; Cabell Phillips, "The
Catholic Issue: Use of Religion against Kennedy in South May Help Him in the North," *New York Times*, 4
September 1960). Before the Ministerial Association of Houston, Senator Kennedy addressed concerns
about his religious affiliation, claiming that there are far more important issues for which the country
should be concerned. Although he questioned why his religion would be important to anyone other than
himself, Kennedy emphatically stated: "I believe in an America where the separation of church and state
is absolute—where no Catholic prelate would tell the President (should he be Catholic) how to act, and
no Protestant minister would tell his parishoners for whom to vote." He also warned that while today he
is the "victim," tomorrow "it may be you" ("Text of Kennedy's Address Before Ministerial Association in
Houston," *Washington Post*, 13 September 1960). Responding to the attacks on Kennedy, King told reporters that he doubted that African American voters would object to any candidate on the basis of religion
and drew the conclusion that "individuals who are anti-Catholic are usually anti-Negro" ("Negro Vote
Seen Mostly on Rights," *New York Times*, 15 September 1960).

10. The quote is most often attributed to William Gladstone, leader of the House of Commons and
Chancellor of the Exchequer, who made a similar remark during a 16 March 1868 address to the House
of Commons: "But, above all, if we be just men, we shall go forward in the name of truth and right, bearing this in mind—that, when the case is proved and the hour is come, justice delayed is justice denied."
It has also been linked to William Penn, *Fruits of Solitude in Reflections and Maxims Relating to the Conduct
of Human Life* (1682): "Our law says well, 'To delay justice, is injustice.'"

branches of evil only to find they were to grow again. The day has come to dig to the roots and put an end to these evils for all time.

All over this seething world stubborn roots of injustice are being ripped from deep soil frequently with fire and sword. Over a billion people are proclaiming a permanent end to an intolerable existence. We are busily engaged seeking new policies, experimenting with varied forms of aid, sitting at countless counsel tables, designing and planning far-reaching changes. Yet here at home we have the power, the resources and the moral support of the majority of the nation to institute long-delayed reforms which would transform the restricted lives of tens of millions of our own citizens. We need only the will and the leadership of our government to act and we will initiate a new century of growth. It is interesting that today our nation is deeply concerned with foreign trade, the preservation and expansion of our foreign markets.[11] It would be well not to forget that we enjoyed our greatest industrial growth during the 19th century in the development of our internal market, particularly to the west. We still have great reserves of an internal market among the 20 million Negro citizens whose present living standards are less than half of the national average.[12]

While on the subject of economic growth, it might be pertinent to ask if today the prosperous leaders of the south, who are boastful of its new growth, would like to return to the old order. Would they like to go back to the anti-bellum south—would they restore slavery if they could and with it the limitations it imposed upon the development of the whole region? Of course their answer would be no. Looking forward from today it can still be said that the potential of the south remains restricted by an outworn as well as unjust "peculiar institution."[13] Indeed, let us say it frankly and candidly. When the south is freed from institutionalized injustice it will first realize its full potential socially, politically and economically. Many southern leaders are pathetically trapped by their own devices. They have pandered to the lowest passion to develop political support, proclaiming themselves faithful and devoted to segregation and discrimination. Yet many of them know that the perpetuation of this archaic, dying order is hindering the rapid growth of the south. Yet they cannot speak this truth—they are imprisoned by their own lies. It is history's wry paradox that when Negroes win their struggle to be free those who have held them down will themselves be freed for the first time.[14]

We know where we were 100 years ago—we know where we are today. Where will our nation be 100 years from now? We can bend its moral arc towards justice if

---

11. At his 1962 State of the Union Address, Kennedy lobbied for passage of a foreign trade bill, which would give his administration latitude in negotiating the reduction and removal of tariffs with the European Economic Community (*Public Papers of the Presidents: John F. Kennedy, 1962*, pp. 14–15). Kennedy signed the Trade Expansion Act on 11 October 1962.

12. The 1960 U.S. Census reported that the annual median income of the average white man, between the ages of 25 and 64, was $5,278, while nonwhite men of the same age range earned $3,037 (U.S. Bureau of the Census, *U.S. Census of Population: 1960; Subject Reports: Occupation by Earnings and Education* [Washington, D.C.: U.S. Government Printing Office, 1963], pp. 2–3).

13. The "peculiar institution" was a euphemism for slavery popularized by Civil War historian Kenneth M. Stampp's 1956 book, *The Peculiar Institution: Slavery in the Ante-bellum South* (New York: Knopf).

14. In his draft, King handwrote: "The problem of racial injustice will not be solved until enough."

we unroot the twisted tangle of evil statutes which unlawfully deprived Negroes of elementary rights. To that noble task nearly 20 million Negroes are dedicated—millions of sincere white Americans stand with us—the invincible will of justice and democracy undergird our struggle. All of the armies of the earth—all of the parliaments—all of the presidents, prime ministers and kings—are not stronger than one single moral idea which tenaciously demands fulfillment.[15] That fulfillment will come because from the first day an American farmer shouldered a musket for liberty, to this day, a national character was being formed, which could grow only if it lived in a climate of decency and fair play.[16] That fulfillment will come because America must do it to remain American in the next 100 years.

TD. MLKP-MBU.

---

15. In King's draft the following sentence begins with an introductory clause: "I have faith to believe."
16. King's draft included the following additional sentence: "Before it comes some will get scarred up a bit."

# From Adelaide Tambo

17 May 1962
Cholmeley Park, England

*Adelaide Tambo, wife of exiled African National Congress (ANC) leader Oliver Tambo, requests King's assistance in drawing attention to the abuses suffered by women leaders of the anti-apartheid movement in South Africa.[1] No response from King has been located.*

Dear Dr. King,

You may not remember from whom this letter comes from, but I will remind you a little my name is Adelaide Tambo (Mrs) we met at the home of Canon Collins (Christian Action) the last time when you were in London I was also one of the

---

1. Adelaide Tambo (1929–2007), born in Vereeniging, South Africa, tried at fifteen to join the ANC after witnessing her grandfather being beaten by police. She eventually joined the ANC at eighteen and was soon elected chair of the local branch. In 1956 she married ANC leader Oliver Tambo. Following the Sharpesville Massacre and the banning of the ANC in 1960, the Tambos fled South Africa; Adelaide Tambo went to London while her husband went to Zambia. She was a founding member of the Afro-Asian Solidarity Movement in 1957 and the founder of the Pan-African Women's Organisation in 1962. The Tambos returned to South Africa after the unbanning of the ANC in 1990. Four years later, she became one of the first democratically elected members of the South African Parliament.

Sponsors of the function we held for you at the Africa Unity House.[2] I had thought I would be in a position to write to you earlier but as a housewife who is a student and also doing political work there is always very little time to keep in touch with friends.

Once again the South African Government is hitting viciously at the Women's leaders who are opposed to racial discrimination and the principle of "Apartheid" After the deportation of Mrs Mafekeng the mother of 11 Children, now Mrs Lillian Ngoyi our president has been banned from attending meetings for 5 years and also barred from leaving the township in which she leaves.[3] So that he Cannot get near any industrial area to look for work to keep her family going Others who have been or rather who are Victims of this Cruel banning are Mrs Matomela a prominont Womans leader also Mrs Florence Mkhize and Florence Baard who were both with Mrs Ngoyi in the Mamoth South African Treason Trial which ended in March 1961.[4] Because of all this bannings and other Arrests of Women's leaders the A.N.C. Women's League is Appealing to you to give Material help to the Organization and to use your influence so that other Sympathetic people Can also give Material help to enable the organizetion to help the deported and banned mothers and also to look after the Children of those arrested and to pay school fees and clothes those children {P.T.O.} whose parents had to go underground and those whose parents had to flee the country for political reasons.

I am enclosing some press cuttings and shall also be sending you some of our pablications and News letters.

Fondest Regards to you and your family

Yours in the South African Struggle.
[*signed*] Adelaide Tambo.

ALS. MLKJP-GAMK: Box 23.

---

2. King was in London from 28–31 October 1961 for a series of appearances. He spoke at the African Unity House, a center dedicated to promoting unity among African students, on 30 October. John Collins (1905–1982), a priest and political activist, was canon of St. Paul's Cathedral for thirty-three years. In 1946, he founded Christian Action, an organization dedicated to connecting Christianity to economic, political, and social life. He also served as President of the International Defence and Aid Fund for Southern Africa.

3. Elizabeth Mafikeng (1918–2009), a long-time union leader, was vice-president of the ANC Women's League. She was deported in 1959 after leading a large demonstration protesting laws requiring African women to carry passes. Lilian Ngoyi (1911–1980), politician and activist against apartheid, served as the President of the ANC Women's League from 1953–1960.

4. Florence Matomela (1910–1969) served as an organizer for the ANC Women's League and vice-president of the Federation of South African Women. Florence Mkhize (1932–1999) was one of the founding members of the United Democratic Front and an organizer of the South African Congress of Trade Unions. Frances Baard (1901–1997), an anti-apartheid activist, worked for the ANC Women's League and later became secretary and treasurer of the League's Port Elizabeth branch in South Africa. On 1 August 1958, ninety-one South Africans went on trial in Pretoria on charges they violated the state's anti-communist laws. In 1961, the court in South Africa ruled that the state had failed to prove the ANC was communist. All of the accused were acquitted of treason.

# From Chauncey Eskridge

22 May 1962
Chicago, Ill.

*Responding to what Eskridge calls King's "screams of anguish" over recent*
*negative press about SCLC in the* Pittsburgh Courier, *he assures King that the*
*situation has been addressed.*[1] *No reply from King has been found.*

Reverend Martin Luther King, Jr.
41 Exchange Place, SE
Atlanta 3, Georgia

Dear Martin:

As a result of your screams of anguish with respect to the article written in the
Courier by McCray of South Carolina, and Trezz Anderson, of Atlanta, Mr. McCoy
read the riot act to the people involved.[2] So forthright was he that it is now contem-
plated that in June, after you have moved, they will send Frank Bolden from the
Pittsburgh office to do a long series of articles on you and SCLC.[3] This should be our
opportunity to set the record straight concerning your own financial condition, your
income and your estate. It is also an opportunity to set the record straight about the
financial affairs of SCLC. I would suggest the granting of permission for the writer,

---

1. *Courier* columnist John H. McCray had asserted that SCLC was attempting to usurp the NAACP's
position in the South and that it "ram-rodded or joined in on a great many sit-ins, sent hundreds of
youths into activities costing money in bail and fines, and then ducked out and left NAACP to foot the
bills" ("Need for Changing," *Pittsburgh Courier,* 5 May 1962). Wyatt Tee Walker disputed McCray's claims
in a *Courier* interview, asserting that "there's no death struggle between Southern Christian Leadership
Conference and National Association for the Advancement of Colored People," and accused McCray
of being "uninformed of the facts" (Ted Watson, "Struggle between NAACP-SCLC Denied," *Pittsburgh
Courier,* 26 May 1962). Chauncey Eskridge (1917–1988) graduated from Tuskegee Institute in 1939 with a
B.S. in Business Administration. He served as a field artillery officer and spotter pilot during World War
II before receiving his LL.B. from John Marshall Law School in 1949. Eskridge joined Moore, Ming, and
Leighton (later McCoy, Ming, and Leighton) in 1954 as a tax specialist. Eskridge was one of six lawyers
on King's legal team during his 1960 Alabama perjury trial for tax evasion and became King's personal
financial attorney. He also served as legal counsel for SCLC and as Muhammad Ali's lawyer when Ali
was indicted for draft evasion in 1967. In 1981 he was elected a Cook County district judge and held the
position until retiring in 1986.
2. Fleetwood McCoy was senior partner of the law firm McCoy, Ming, and Leighton and simultaneously represented King and the *Pittsburgh Courier*. In a 15 June 1962 letter to McCray, *Courier* editor
William Nunn wrote that King's relationship with McCoy is the only reason the newspaper has "not been
embarrassed" by the "pot-shots you are taking at" King. Nunn (1900–1969) was managing editor of the
*Pittsburgh Courier* from 1940 until his retirement in 1963.
3. SCLC was in the process of moving its offices due to a dispute with the owners regarding the
desegregation of a restaurant in the same building. For more, see King to Benjamin J. Massell, 9 June
1962, pp. 470–473 in this volume. Frank Bolden (1913–2003), a longtime *Courier* reporter, was an accred-
ited World War II correspondent and interviewed international figures including Mahatma Gandhi and
Jawaharlal Nehru.

Bolden, to see the last audit reports made by Bonser and, if you wish, copies of your 1959, 1960 and 1961 returns.[4]

Moreover, since the information that we gave to the Treasury Department, along with our application for exempt status for SCLC, is now a public record, we might even exhibit those financial statements to the writer.[5] This would also permit exposure nationally of the work we are doing in voter registration and what our connections are with the Southern Regional Council with respect to financing the voter registration drive.[6]

Bill Nunn assures me, most vociferously that the Courier has no policy which is inimicable to your interest. However, he is curious about the rumors that he has heard, he says, about your "Take" from SCLC.[7]

If you approve of this idea, I suggest that you write a letter to Bill Nunn and invite Frank Bolden to come and do this series of articles and suggest a time when you would be available to Frank. Frank Bolden is a man I have known nearly all of my life, as is true with Bill Nunn.

Because of my relationship with them, I would chance the observation that they would seek to please me. If you think that my presence there along with Bolden is necessary, please advise. If there is anything else that you think I may do in the premises, please advise.

Note the enclosed clipping from the Wall Street Journal how your name is curiously connected with the subject person of the article.[8]

Fraternally yours,
[*signed*] Chauncey
Chauncey Eskridge

msk

TLS. MLKJP-GAMK: Box 9.

---

4. Allan Bonser worked for the IRS as a revenue agent in Atlanta.

5. SCLC applied for federal tax exemption on 10 August 1961 and was granted a 501(c)(4) exemption in May 1962.

6. For more on SCLC's financial relationship with the VEP, see King to Leslie Dunbar, 19 January 1962, pp. 368–369 in this volume.

7. In a May 1962 SCLC board meeting, King tabled a motion from several board members to pay him a salary "commensurate with [*his*] office and in keeping with the budget," noting that his salary as a co-pastor of Ebenezer Baptist Church, supplemented with six thousand dollars from speaking fees, was "enough to live on." King officially received a salary of one dollar from SCLC in order to be eligible for the organization's health insurance benefits (Minutes, SCLC board meeting, 15 May 1962).

8. The *Wall Street Journal* ran an article covering President Kennedy's civil rights plan, noting that several civil rights leaders, including King, were "far from satisfied" with the administration's progress toward issuing an executive order on housing and its failure to promote broad civil rights legislation (William M. Beecher, "Kennedy Plans a Series of Actions to Soothe Critics, Sway Voters," *Wall Street Journal*, 10 May 1962).

# "People in Action: Literacy Bill Dies"

26 May 1962
New York, N.Y.

*Incensed by Congress's failure to pass a bill banning literacy test requirements for voter registration, King criticizes President Kennedy for not ensuring its success, noting that "it may well be that we will have to repent in this generation not merely for the bitter words and actions of the bad people but for the appalling silence of the good people." Mentioning probable global news coverage of the debate, King insists that "any democratic nation that cannot guarantee all of its citizens the elemental right to vote is suffering from a moral sickness that must be cured if it is to survive."[1] The following article was published in the* New York Amsterdam News.

A few days ago newspapers across the country carried the headlines, "Literacy Bill Dies in Senate." This disappointing headline referred to the second attempt in less than a week to shut off debate on a civil rights bill. By a vote of 54–42 the Senate refused to impose cloture (limit debate) and the bill in question, the administration's literacy test measure, was thereby a dead issue.[2]

This measure was designed to end discriminatory use of literacy tests by southern voting registrars.

It would have declared anyone with a sixth grade education literate for voting purposes. No honest person can deny the critical need for such a measure. The so called literacy tests have been used in the most vicious and undemocratic manner to prevent Negroes across the South from becoming registered.

Negroes with college degrees, have been denied the right to vote because they were not "literate" enough.[3] Even more ludicrous is the fact that there have been Negroes with Ph.D. degrees who could not qualify as registered voters because they were not literate according to southern registrars.[4]

---

1. Roy Wilkins, executive secretary of the NAACP, also criticized the Senate's failure to pass the literacy test bill in his *New York Amsterdam News* column: "How good is our political system if it not only cannot deliver on basic human rights, but actually and actively perpetuates that meanest of exploitation—discrimination based upon skin color?" ("How Long? How Long?," *New York Amsterdam News*, 19 May 1962).

2. On 9 May, the Senate voted 53–43 against imposing cloture, which required a two-thirds majority vote, to end the filibuster (Anthony Lewis, "Senate Rejects Bid for Closure; Right Bill Dead," *New York Times*, 10 May 1962). The following week, a second attempt to impose cloture also failed by a vote of 52–42 ("Senate Rejects New Move to End Debate on Rights," *New York Times*, 15 May 1962).

3. In September 1958, the Justice Department filed an injunction against registrars in Terrell County, Georgia, for discrimination against African Americans, naming five black college graduates who failed the literacy test. According to chairman of the board of registrars J. G. Raines, the applicants were disqualified for writing illegibly or mispronouncing and slurring words (Claude Sitton, "Georgia Vote Aide Says He Knew Rejected Negroes Held Degrees," *New York Times*, 6 September 1958).

4. Professors Daniel Wynn, J. N. Blankenship, and S. T. Nero testified before the Volunteer Civil Rights Commission that they had attempted to register to vote, but their applications had been denied. Blankenship, who was from Saline, Louisiana, also noted that other teachers in his area with M.A. or Ph.D. degrees had their applications denied ("Transcript of proceedings before the Volunteer Civil Rights Commission," 31 January 1960).

Yet, in spite of these obvious and notorious expressions of discrimination against Negroes, the highest legislative body of the nation refused to pass a bill that would have been just a step in guaranteeing the right to vote.

## Lessons

There are several lessons that we should learn from the defeat of this all-important measure. First it reminds us anew that the Senate rules must be changed if any meaningful civil rights legislation is ever to be enacted. The two-thirds cloture rule is the legislative incinerator that burns to ashes all strong civil rights bills.

It provides a legal channel through which a recalcitrant minority can block and even bury the wishes of a right thinking majority. For years the southern senators have relied on this rule to stall any legislation that would destroy the backward and brutal institutions of segregation and discrimination. Unless Senate rule 22 is changed we will continue to see civil rights bills fade into a tragic death.[5]

The defeat of the literacy bill also reveals that the forces of goodwill must become more vigorous. We must face the tragic fact that this bill failed to pass because those who were for it were far less vigorous, forthright and determined than those who were against it.

## Kennedy Inactive

It was a clear and pathetic example of the children of darkness being more zealous and unrelenting than the children of light.

This lack of forthrightness was especially present in the White House. I have no doubt that President Kennedy wanted the bill, but he did very little, if anything, in its behalf.

He never spoke out for its passage nor did he seek to arouse national public opinion on the issues involved.[6] Even the Senate Majority Leader, Mr. Mansfield, who talked so eloquently for the need of the measure, made the hours for the debate so brief each day that the southern senators had little possibilities of tiring out.[7]

---

5. Adopted in 1917 at the urging of President Woodrow Wilson, Senate Rule 22 allowed for the ending of debate with a two-thirds majority vote. Even with the cloture rule, the filibuster remained an effective means to block legislation because a two-thirds majority was difficult to attain. When the Senate convened in early January 1961, a motion to change the requirements for cloture from two-thirds present and voting to sixty percent was tabled by a 50–46 vote. When the bill was brought up nine months later, the Senate voted 43–37 against imposing cloture, effectively dooming the bill. In an article for *The Nation*, King argued that if Kennedy had actively campaigned for the bill in January, "a historic victory would have resulted" ("Fumbling on the New Frontier," 3 March 1962, p. 416 in this volume).

6. Journalist Anthony Lewis, who covered the debate on the bill for the *New York Times*, argued that Kennedy "said little in its behalf and did not make it a major concern or attempt to rouse the public in its behalf" ("Civil Rights Defeat," *New York Times*, 11 May 1962). Attorney General Robert F. Kennedy did testify on behalf of the bill on 10 April, arguing that "there was ample proof" of racial discrimination in voter registration (Anthony Lewis, "Robert Kennedy Debates Ervin on Literacy Tests," *New York Times*, 11 April 1962).

7. Michael Mansfield (1903–2001) served as the Senate majority leader from 1961–1977. Between 25 April and 15 May, the Senate met for an average of six hours per day to discuss the bill, and avoided weekend debates. Vice President Lyndon B. Johnson criticized the Senate's limited debate hours, saying that when he was Senate majority leader, "we stayed right at it and we passed a bill" ("Johnson Jabs Leadership on Rights Defeat," *Chicago Daily Tribune*, 20 May 1962).

Somewhere along the way men of goodwill must come to see that we are struggling against a stubborn and unyielding adversary. Its massive resistance must be met with massive insistance. The lovers of democracy are still all too silent and timid.

It may well be that we will have to repent in this generation not merely for the bitter words and actions of the bad people but for the appalling silence of the good people.

### No Fulfillment

A third thing revealed in the defeat of the literacy bill is the agonizing fact that the American Dream is still far from fullfilment. Any democratic nation that cannot guarantee all of its citizens the elemental right to vote is suffering from a moral sickness that must be cured if it is to survive. I suspect that the death of the literacy bill was reported in newspapers over the world, yes in Asia and Africa.

Think of the response of inhabitants of the newly independent nations in Africa when they read that an American Negro is not supported in his efforts to vote by this nation's highest legislative body.

### The Omission

Think of the response of the teeming millions in India when they read that an American Negro with a Ph.D. degree is denied the right to vote, knowing that the most illiterate peasant in India can vote with no restrictions.

No longer can America preach democracy abroad—and practice the democracy at home—and practice the very opposite of that democracy at abroad. Yes, the headlines were correct—the literacy bill died in the Senate.

But those headlines omitted something that we must never forget: when the literacy bill died a bit of the American Dream died and it will never be resurrected until that day emerges when every Negro is guaranteed the right to vote.

PD. *New York Amsterdam News*, 26 May 1962.

## From Carl L. Manfred

8 June 1962
Minneapolis, Minn.

*Manfred, newly elected executive secretary of the Luther League of the Lutheran Church in America (LCA), regretfully withdraws his invitation for King to speak at the organization's Constituting Convention in San Francisco.[1] "It has been brought to my attention that in some areas of our Church," Manfred wrote, "you are considered to be a somewhat 'controversial' person." On 14 June 1962 King's*

---

1. Manfred to King, 29 May 1962. Carl Lawrence Peterson Manfred (1918–2011), born in St. Peter, Minnesota, earned a B.A. (1939) from Gustavus Adolphus College, a B.D. (1943) from Augustana Seminary, and a D.D. (1963) from Luther Seminary. He pastored at St. Mark's (1943–1946) in Cedar Rapids, Iowa, and Gloria Dei (1946–1952) in Duluth, Minnesota. Manfred served as youth director of the LCA from 1963–1964, when he become assistant to the president of the LCA, Minnesota Synod

*secretary replied that King could not attend the convention anyway and that he was not offended by the matter as he has become "accustomed to being considered 'controversial' by many who do not share his position."*



Dr. Martin Luther King
Pastor, Ebenezer Baptist Church
Atlanta, Georgia

Dear Dr. King:

A week ago I spoke to you on the phone (and later confirmed the message in a letter) inviting you to address the Constituting Convention of the Luther League—Lutheran Church in America—on Saturday afternoon or evening, August 25, at San Francisco.

Now, with a heavy heart, I find that I must withdraw this invitation.

I will explain the situation as candidly as I can. It has been brought to my attention that in some areas of our Church you are considered to be a somewhat "controversial" person. Of this, of course, I was fully aware at the time the invitation was extended. However, my advisors have raised this question: Is it wise for us to introduce the note of controversy at the initial convention of the official youth auxiliary of a newly merged Church, when the emphasis at this strategic time should be given to issues which will unite rather than divide the delegation?[2]

In all candor, let me say that those who have counseled with me on this matter were not opposed to you, personally, nor to your message. They felt, to the contrary, that it is important that the youth of our new Church be exposed to the stimulation of new and dynamic insights into all areas of thought and life. The only question which was raised, as I indicated above, was the matter of timing.

I want to assure you that we are very interested in having you address a national convention of our Luther League at a future date. I am persuaded, however, that we will best serve the youth of our Church if we make arrangements for such an address after we have perfected the organization of our church-wide auxiliary, and that this will provide for you a more favorable climate of acceptance.

Perhaps you will feel that by our withdrawal of this invitation we have also forfeited our chances to hear you at a later date, but I earnestly hope that this is not the case.

We have not given any publicity of any kind to our invitation to you, and thus are hopeful that its withdrawal will not be a source of any embarrassment to you.

I have not yet heard from you with respect to the invitation. I realize that I could

---

from 1965–1976. Manfred published several books, including *Facing Forward: The Minnesota Synod of the Lutheran Church in America, 1963–1987* (1987). He retired in 1982.

2. King had addressed the youth department of the American Lutheran Church in Miami on 16 August 1961. Prior to the convention in Miami, Reverend David Brown, the executive director of the youth department, reported he had received an official censure from the Council of Bishops for inviting King to speak (Brown to King, 23 August 1961). On 28 June 1962, the United Lutheran Church in America, the Augustana Lutheran Church, the Finnish Evangelical Lutheran Church, and the American Evangelical Lutheran Church merged to form the Lutheran Church in America, representing 3.2 million people.

hold up this letter until I receive your response, reasoning to myself that if it is negative, no more need be said. However, this strategy to my way of thinking would be something less than being entirely honest with you—an honor which you deserve.

Again, my deep regrets for the situation which compels the withdrawal of my invitation of last week.

Sincerely yours,
[*signed*]
Carl L. Manfred

CLM:kt

TLS. MLKJP-GAMK: Box 47.

# To Benjamin J. Massell

9 June 1962
[*Atlanta, Ga.*]

*Following sit-in protests at the Tasty Coffee Shop on the ground floor of the building that houses SCLC headquarters, King, in this unusually long letter, informs the building's owner that he is breaking the lease because the restaurant refuses to serve black patrons.[1] Embarrassed by the situation, King explains that he is being questioned "all over the nation" about "the inconsistency of taking a stand against segregation on the one hand and having my office in a building with a segregated restaurant on the other." King pledges to dedicate his life to ending segregation: "I am willing to give every ounce of my energy to get rid of it, and, if necessary, I am willing to die, to give a redemptive witness to the ideal of the brotherhood of man." By the end of June, SCLC relocated their offices to the Prince Hall Masonic Temple on Auburn Ave.*

Mr. Ben J. Massell
40 S. Pryor Street, S.W.
Atlanta 3, Georgia

Dear Mr. Massell:

The Executive Board of the Southern Christian Leadership Conference has unanimously voted to embark on a course of action which I, as president, feel morally

---

1. "Brief 'Sit-in' Staged Here at Coffee Shop," *Atlanta Daily World*, 22 March 1962. Benjamin Joseph Massell (1886–1962), born in Lithuania, immigrated to Atlanta where he embarked on a successful career in real estate and construction. Massell built more than 1,000 commercial buildings in Atlanta and was consequently hailed as the "Father of Atlanta's Skyline" for his contributions to its development into a major metropolis. He was also an active philanthropist who made significant contributions to various Jewish causes, educational institutions, and health-related organizations.

bound to call to your attention. After serious and prayerful consideration, we have decided to move our office from your building at 41 Exchange Place. This decision resulted from a situation existing in the building which we can no longer endure.

When we signed the lease for the office space at 41 Exchange Place, we were told by your Realtor that all the facilities of the building, including the ground floor restaurant, were desegregated. With this understanding and assurance, we signed the lease and moved in about eight months ago. Before the moving van had completely unloaded our furniture and equipment, we discovered that we had been grossly misinformed. On that same day, Mr. James Forman, a young Negro student leader, who had come to visit one of the offices in the building, was denied service in the restaurant.[2] My first impulse was to move from 41 Exchange Place immediately, even though we had signed the lease. But after thinking the matter through, I decided to go on and try to work out the problem within.

I immediately authorized my staff head, the Rev. Wyatt Tee Walker, to look into the matter. Following the true spirit of the non-violent movement, we began, not with direct action, (i.e. sitting-in), but with sincere negotiation. Mr. Walker talked first with your agent who had told us that the restaurant was not segregated, and he responded by asserting that he was not aware of its segregation policies. He went on to say that the restaurant was not operated by the owner of the building, but was leased to another person. On discovering this, Mr. Walker, under my authorization, went directly to Mr. Carswell, the operator of the restaurant. For well-nigh three months we talked patiently and calmly with him about this matter. We made it clear that we were issuing neither threats nor ultimatums, but that we were seeking, through peaceful negotiation, to work out a problem that was a constant drain i on our sense of dignity and self-respect. The occupants of almost every other office in the building joined us in requesting that Mr. Carswell operate his restaurant on a racially integrated basis. We even made studies to prove to him that on the basis of other places that had integrated eating facilities, he would not face an economic loss. In spite of all of these good faith efforts on our part, Mr. Carswell remained adamant, and insisted that he would not integrate his restaurant.

When we saw the futility of our negotiating efforts, we felt that we had no alternative but to present our very bodies as a witness to the truth as we saw it, and as a means to arouse the oconscience of the perpetrators of this unjust condition. Under my authorization, members of our staff and other concerned citizens began sitting in the restaurant. Not only were they refused service, but at times were the objects of abusive language from waitresses and Mr. Carswell consistently called the police and threatened them with arrest. To add insult to injury, I received a rather unkind letter from Mr. Sam A. Goldberg stating that you had authorized him to demand that we cease and desist in our effort to desegregate the restaurant.[3] When I received

---

2. Forman (1928–2005) was executive secretary of SNCC.

3. As president of the Allan-Grayson Realty Company, Goldberg managed Massell's real estate holdings. In his letter to King, Goldberg demands an end to SCLC demonstrations against V.J. Carswell's restaurant because of their harmful effects on the business, claiming that if Carswell were to integrate the restaurant, he would go out of business. He suggests that an integrated restaurant would not be able to pay as much rent as a segregated restaurant. He concludes by asking King to "use your influence to

this letter I called my staff in and said: "The cup of endurance has run over. We can take it no longer. We must move." A few days later the matter was called to the attention of our Executive Committee and they unanimously concurred with my recommendation.

Mr. Massell, I cannot begin to express in words the agonizing and frustrating hours I have spent as a result of this situation. It has caused me undue embarrassment. All over the nation people have questioned me about the inconsistency of taking a stand against segregation on the one hand and having my office in a building with a segregated restaurant on the other. My only explanation has been that we were given the impression that the restaurant was integrated when we moved in only to find that we had been inadvertently misled.

Before closing, I think I should give just a brief statement of my personale conviction on this matter. I am convinced that segregation is evil. It is against all of the noble precepts of our Judeo-Christian heritage. Therefore, I cannot cooperate with this evil system in any form. I am willing to give every ounce of my energy to get rid of it, and, if necessary, I am willing to die, to give a redemptive witness to the ideal of the brotherhood of man. And may I say, Mr. Massell, that I take this position not merely on behalf of my people, whose lives have for centuries been fettered by the chains of oppression and the manacles of exploitation; I take this position because of my devotion to democracy, justice, and truth. The festering sore of segregation dibilitates the white man as well as the Negro. America faces its midnight hour. The clock of destiny is ticking out. If we fail to get rid of this cancerous disease of segregation in the next few years, America will be relegated to second rate power in the world with no moral or political voice. So I believe firmly that we were helping America when we sat in at the restaurant in your building.

While sitting down, paradoxical as it may sound, we were standing up for the best in the American dream. I also believe that we were helping Mr. Carswell when we sat in his restaurant. We were helping him face truth and to know himself. For some strange reason, Mr. Carswell will never know himself until he knows that every Negro, however dark his skin may be, is his brother.

I must mention a final reason whi I personally must leave your building. A few days ago my little six year old daughter went to my office with me.[4] As we entered the building, she looked over and noticed the restaurant. She immediately said: "Daddy, will you take me in for some ice cream?" As I stood there trying to work out my answer, she ran in the restaurant and took a seat. I went in behind her and said: "Come on darling, you can't have ice cream now." Then came the inevitable "why" from the inquisitive spirit of a child. Behind that why is America's greatest tragedy. Behind that why is a system that has caused millions of Negroes to think they are nobody and sent them through life with a terrible sense of inferiority. It is difficult for others to see what segregation has done to the Negro. But just imagine your little six year old child asking you why he or she can't go in a certain place, and your having to answer you can't go because you are colored. Yes, I must move because my children and the children of the members of my staff are too precious to walk to

---

dissuade these people against any continuance of their harrassing tactics which can only result in loss of a tenant on the ground floor of the building" (Goldberg to King, 3 April 1962).

4. King refers to his daughter Yolanda Denise.

their father's offices in a building where they can't sit down in the restaurant and eat a little ice cream. 14 June 1962

This letter is far too long, longer than any I have written in the last few years. But I felt morally bound to explain our position. In moving we are not unmindful of the fact that we are breaking a lease. I must honestly admit that, as a cause organization, our funds are far too limited to face a suit. But if this comes, we will have to face it with the same faith that has sustained our humble effort over the last few years.[5] If taken to court, I will honestly present the facts to the leaders in the Negro community and our friends in the white community, and I am certain that they will support our decision. In short, we cannot in all good conscience continue to have an office in a building where we are constantly embarrassed, daily stripped of our personhood, and where our fundamental rights as human beings are blatantly violated.

I hope you will not take this as an attack on you. Although I have not had the privilege of meeting you, I understand that you are a man of good will, deeply concerned about the progress of Atlanta, and I believe that if you will look objectively and sympathetically at our situation, you will understand why we reached this decision.

With every good wish, I am

Very truly yours,
Martin Luther King, Jr.

Km

CC:  Mr. Sam Goldberg
Mr. H. J. Carswell
Mr. Sam Massell.

TLc. SMP-GAHi: Box 84.

---

5. Massell died three months later and no law suit was filed against SCLC.

# To Lillian Eugenia Smith

14 June 1962
Atlanta, Ga.

*In April 1962, King invited National Book Award–winning author Smith to speak at Ebenezer's Annual Women's Day but, due to the worsened state of her cancer, Smith was unable to attend.[1] In the following letter, King offers Smith assistance in whatever way he can and indicates his wish that he and Coretta can visit Smith at her home in Clayton, Georgia, soon.[2]*

---

1. King to Smith, 3 April 1962; Smith to King, 7 May 1962.
2. In a message left with King's secretary, Smith requested that King visit on 16 July (Dora E. McDonald to King, 10 July 1962).

17 June
1962

Miss Lillian Smith
Box 208
Clayton, Georgia

Dear Lillian:

Thank you for your very kind letter informing me that it would not be possible for you to speak to our congregation in July. Naturally, I understand why you cannot come. I regret so much to hear of your present health situation. Please know that you are constantly in my prayers, and if ever there is anything that I can do to ease the load in any way, do not hesitate to call on me. I am always deeply inspired by your great spirit. In spite of your suffering, you always maintain such a wholesome and creative attitude.

Coretta and I would like to come to Clayton to spend a few hours with you in the not too distant future. I will have to be out of the city for the next two weeks, but I will be in Atlanta most of July.[3] If you are home during July, we could plan to come down. At any rate, we will be calling you in a few days concerning this.

Thank you for your constant support. It gives me renewed courage and vigor to carry on.

Sincerely yours,
[*signed*] Martin
Martin Luther King, Jr.

Km

THLS. LSP-GU-HR.

---

3. King spent the following weeks at various meetings and speaking engagements across the country. He returned to Atlanta briefly at the beginning of July before returning to Albany to commence demonstrations. On 19 July 1962, King's secretary Dora McDonald sent Smith a letter saying that King would be writing and visiting her soon.

# "The Dilemma and the Challenge Facing the Negro Today," Address Delivered at Zion Hill Baptist Church

[*17 June 1962*]
Los Angeles, Calif.

*At the end of a whirlwind speaking tour through Southern California, King addressed a packed audience on the challenges African Americans face in*

*obtaining racial equality.*[1] *Using a personal anecdote to demonstrate the effects
of segregation, King admits struggling for words when his six-year-old daughter,
Yolanda, asked to go to Funtown, a segregated amusement park in Atlanta.*[2] *"I'd
been speaking across the country, talking about segregation and discrimination"
for years, King said, but "I didn't know how to explain it." With his wife at his
side, King explains: "Yoki, even though you can't go to Funtown, I want you to
know that you are as good as anybody who goes into Funtown."*

*Shifting his focus from the South to Los Angeles, King urges the audience to
reject "token" integration, insisting that "we want all of our rights; we want them
here; and we want all of them not next year, not next week, but we want them
now, at this hour." The ballot box, King says, is "one of the most significant steps"
African Americans can take to rid the community of housing and employment
discrimination and police brutality, an issue highlighted by the April murder of Los
Angeles Nation of Islam (NOI) leader Ronald Stokes.*[3] *In closing, King warns those
who have become "psychologically" defeated not to turn to racial separatism: "Black
supremacy is as dangerous as white supremacy."*[4] *He adds: "God is interested in the
freedom of the whole human race and the creation of a society where all men will live
together as brothers." The following transcript is taken from an audio recording of
the event.*

I think this is the last public appearance that I will make on this brief visit to the
state of California and the city of Los Angeles. And I want to say on this last public

1. The tour was cosponsored by the American Friends Service Committee (AFSC) and the Western
Christian Leadership Conference. King arrived in Los Angeles on 15 June and departed the morning of
19 June. California governor Edmund G. Brown, Los Angeles mayor Sam Yorty, and Los Angeles County
Board of Supervisors member Kenneth Hahn declared Sunday, 17 June 1962, "Freedom Sunday." King's
address at Zion Hill climaxed a busy schedule, which included four addresses, one of which was before
a large crowd gathered at Bovard Auditorium on the University of Southern California campus ("King
Gives Progress Formula: Reveals 3 Simple 'Wants,'" *Los Angeles Sentinel*, 21 June 1962).

2. Funtown opened in 1961. Rather than admit an interracial group of teens, the amusement
park temporarily closed in June 1963 (Dick Hebert, "Funtown Is Closed by Integration Bid," *Atlanta
Constitution*, 17 June 1963). During the last half of 1963, Funtown desegregated, and King took his daughter Yolanda to the park: "Pleasantly, word came to me later that Funtown had quietly desegregated, so
I took Yolanda. A number of white persons there asked, 'Aren't you Dr. King, and isn't this your daughter?' I said we were, and she heard them say how glad they were to see us there" (Quoted in Alex Haley,
"Playboy Interview: Martin Luther King," *Playboy* 12 [January 1965]: 65–68, 70–74, 76–78).

3. On 28 April, Los Angeles police clashed with members of the NOI, resulting in the shooting
death of NOI secretary Ronald Stokes and injuries to six other NOI members and three police officers.
As a result of the violence, nine NOI members were arraigned on assault charges. The local NAACP
and other black leaders claimed that the murder was an act of police brutality and joined the NOI
in calling for the removal of chief of police William Parker, who had previously been accused of bias
against minorities. Malcolm X, minister of Mosque No. 7 in New York, said in a press conference at the
Statler Hilton in Los Angeles on 4 May that the Muslims were unarmed and that the police were guilty
of murder. The following day, Stokes was buried (Bill Becker, "Cultists on Coast Denounce Police," *New
York Times*, 6 May 1962; "Muslim Leader Accuses Police of Murder," *Los Angeles Times*, 5 May 1962; "Black
Muslims Conduct Rites for Riot Victim," *Los Angeles Times*, 6 May 1962).

4. Just two days before King spoke at Zion Hill, a reporter asked him his thoughts on the "Black
Muslim religion." King said: "First I must make it palpably clear that the Black Muslim movement must

appearance something that I have been saying on platforms over the last two days—and this happens to be I think the tenth speech that I have made since I landed in Los Angeles last Friday afternoon. But I have said, as I have gone from platform to platform and the various areas of this community, that I always come to California with a great sense of belonging and a great sense of appreciation because I am sure that the state of California has given more financial and moral support to the Southern struggle in general and the Southern Christian Leadership Conference in particular than any other state in the United States. [*applause*] We will remain eternally grateful to you for this, for this type of consistent rapport, support is of inestimable value for the continuance of our humble efforts. I want to thank these ministers of the gospel for the leadership that they are giving in this community at this significant hour, and I want to thank them for the support that they have given us in our work in the South. I want to thank Dr. Chambers, my good friend, for opening the doors of his church and making it possible for us to meet here this afternoon.[5]

There are many things I'm sure that one could say coming up from the Deep South, coming up from the front line of the struggle for freedom and justice in the South, but I would like to try to develop what I have to say this afternoon by using as a subject "The Dilemma and the Challenge Facing the Negro Today." The dilemma and the challenge facing the Negro today. You will remember that it was in the year of 1619 when the first Negro slaves landed on the shores of this nation. They were brought here from the soils of Africa, and the Negro lived amid this system of slavery for 244 years. For all of these years, he was a thing to be used, not a person to be respected. And even after slavery ended, the Negro discovered that he was confronting a new type of slavery because racial segregation is nothing but slavery covered up with certain niceties of complexity. [*Audience:*] (*Yeah, Yeah, Yes, Yeah*) And so the Negro lived with physical slavery 244 years [*whistle*], and he has been a victim of racial segregation for almost one hundred years.

Now the Negro's dilemma is this and it's a serious dilemma. In spite of the fact that we have been victims of slavery for 244 years, in spite of the fact that we have lived with segregated conditions for one hundred years, the demands of history require that we be as productive, as resourceful, and as responsible as the people who never had these disadvantages. (*Right, Yeah, Yeah, Right*) Here we are, as a people, having experienced political domination, economic exploitation, segregation, and

---

be distinguished from the religion of Islam, one of the great religions of the world. The Muslim movement, headed by Mr. Muhammed, is not a religion <u>per se</u>. To be sure, it has some religious reference taken from the religion of Islam, but it is primarily a socio-economic movement in a religious frame of reference. Now as far as my attitude towards the Black Muslim movement; I have said many times before, we ought not be so concerned with what they represent, but we must consider the forces and conditions that brought the Muslim movement into existence." King's reply disturbed Muslim entertainers Talib Dawud and Dakota Stanton, who felt King's statement condemned Islam. In an effort to ward off additional misunderstandings, SCLC sent out a press release with King's entire statement about Black Muslims (SCLC, Press release, Wyatt Tee Walker clarifies statement of Martin Luther King, Jr. regarding Black Muslims, 22 June 1962).

5. Reverend T. M. Chambers (1895–1977) was pastor of Zion Hill Baptist Church and president of the Progressive National Baptist Convention.

humiliation for well now 344 years, and yet the demands of history make it necessary for us to be as productive and as responsible as the people who never had these experiences. This is our dilemma. (*Go on*) He who gets behind in a race must forever remain behind or run faster than the man in front. (*Go on*) This is our dilemma. (*Yeah, Yeah, Yeah*)

But this dilemma is at one and the same time a great challenge. We are challenged to mobilize our resources and to mobilize all of the constructive forces that we can muster to make a creative contribution in the life of our nation. And I would like to suggest this afternoon some of the things that we must do to grapple with this dilemma and meet the challenge of the hour.

I would like to say first that we must develop and maintain a sense of dignity and self-respect. (*Yeah, Yeah, Yeah, Yeah*) [*applause*] We must [*applause*], we must not allow anybody or any force to make us feel that we do not count. We must believe in our souls that we are somebody (*Amen, Right*), that we are significant (*Yeah*), that we are worthful. (*Yeah*) And we must walk the streets of life every day with this sense of dignity and this sense of somebody-ness. (*Yeah, Yeah, Yeah*) [*applause*]

Now, I know that this has often been difficult because we have lived with so many conditions that told us that we were nobody. (*Yeah, Right*) Segregation does this, and one of the things that the Supreme Court said in its decision of 1954 was that segregation generates a feeling of inferiority within the segregated.[6] (*That's right*) And this is what this system does. But every parent must remind his or her child, every minister of the gospel must remind his congregation (*All right*), every Negro must remind his neighbor, his brother, and his sister (*Yeah*) that we are God's children (*That's right, That's right, Amen*), and that every man from a bass black to a treble white is significant on God's keyboard (*Yeah, Amen, Amen*) that nobody is to make us feel that we are nobody.

This is what the old slave preacher used to do. He didn't always have his grammar right. He had never heard of Plato and Aristotle. He would never have understood [*Albert*] Einstein's theory of relativity. But he knew God, and he knew that the God that he worshiped (*Yeah, Yeah, Amen*) was not a God that would subject some of his children and exalt the others. (*All right*) And so he looked at his black brothers and sisters and said, "You ain't no niggers. (*No*) You ain't no slaves. But you're God's children." (*Yeah, That's right, That's right*) And this gave them a new sense of dignity and a new sense of somebody-ness. And in the midst of the darkness of slavery, they had a bit of hope, as expressed, as is expressed in many of the beautiful spirituals that have come down to us. And we must continue to do this, to get over this idea that we do count. We must have this sense of dignity and this sense of self-respect.

I came to see something of what this system does to us more than ever before just a few weeks ago. God has blessed our home with three little children. We have a daughter six years old, a son, four, and another son, eighteen months.[7] My little daughter

---

6. In *Brown v. Board of Education* (1954), the Supreme Court unanimously concluded that "to separate [children] from others of similar age and qualifications solely because of their race generates a feeling of inferiority as to their status in the community that may affect their hearts and minds in a way unlikely ever to be undone."

7. King refers to his daughter, Yolanda Denise, and his sons, Martin Luther III and Dexter Scott.

loves to ride to the airport with me. She says to me so often, "Daddy, you just go over and over and over again." [*laughter*] And so one of the ways she consoles herself in the fact that her daddy has to be away so much is to ride to the airport whenever I'm going in or coming back into town or going out of town, and she can do it if she isn't in school. And as we pass on the expressway going to the airport in Atlanta, we pass by what is known as Funtown. Now this is an amusement center where little children go to play and where they go for recreation, something like Disneyland and something like the very fine amusement centers across the country for young people. And as we pass Funtown so often in the car, she would look over to me and say, "Daddy, I want to go to Funtown."

Well, I could always evade the question when we were going by in the automobile because we were passing by and I could jump to another subject. And I didn't want to have to tell my little daughter that she couldn't go to Funtown because of the color of her skin. (*That's right*) But then the other day, we were at home, and like most children, she likes to look at television, and she was looking at television, and they were advertising Funtown, and she ran downstairs and said, "Daddy, you know I've been telling you I want to go to Funtown, and they were just talking about Funtown on the television, and I want you to take me to Funtown." And, oh, I stood there speechless. How could I explain to a little six-years-old girl that she couldn't go to Funtown because she was colored? (*Go ahead*) I'd been speaking across the country, talking about segregation and discrimination, and I thought I could answer most of the questions that came up, but I was speechless for the moment. I didn't know how to explain it.

Then I said to myself, I've got to face this problem once and for all. And I took her and called over—my wife was sitting on the other side of the table—and I took my little daughter and told her to have a seat on my knees. And she jumped up in my lap, and I looked at her, and I said, "Yolanda, we have a problem." Said, "You know, some people don't do the right things, and they are misguided. And so they have developed a system where white people go certain places and colored people go certain places." And I said, "They have Funtown like that, so that they don't allow colored children to go to Funtown."

And then I looked at her at that point because I didn't want her to develop a sense of bitterness. I didn't want her to grow up with a sense of hatred and bitterness in her heart, and so I had to rush on and say, "But now, all white people aren't like this. There are some white people right here in Atlanta who would like for you to go to Funtown, and there are some all over the country who are right on this issue. (*Yeah, That's right*) And still, there are those who have been misguided." (*Yeah*) And then I looked down into her eyes, and I said to her at that point, and I saw tears flowing from her eyes at that point, I said, "Yoki, even though you can't go to Funtown, I want you to know that you are as good as anybody who goes into Funtown. (*Yes*) [*applause*] And I want you to know, Yoki, that some of us are working hard every day to get Funtown open and to get many other places open. And I say to you that in the not too distant future, Funtown and every other town will be open to all of God's children [*applause*] because we're going to work for it." (*Yes*) [*applause*]

I only give this illustration to say that it is often difficult for us to have this sense of dignity and this self-respect because we live every day with a system glaring us in the face, saying you are less than, you are not equal to. But in the midst of that we must know that we do count, that we are somebody. (*Yes, Yes*) And we must be able to cry out, even if it's unconsciously, with the eloquent poet:

> Fleecy locks and black complexion
> Cannot forfeit nature's claim;
> Skin may differ, but affection
> Dwells in black and white the same. (*Yeah, Yeah*)
>
> Were I so tall as to reach the pole
> Or to grasp the ocean at a span,
> I must be measured by my soul,
> The mind is the standard of the man.[8] (*Right*)

We must believe this (*Yeah*) [*applause*], and we must live by this. [*applause*]

Now, another thing that we must do is something that I've mentioned to you before. I know I've mentioned it in California before. If we are going to grapple with this dilemma and at the same time meet the challenge, we must work hard and with determination to achieve excellence (*That's right*) in our various fields of endeavor. (*That's right*) Doors are opening now that were not opened in the past. We were just speaking about, Dr. Chambers was just mentioning the fact that even here in your city hall, new opportunities have opened within the last few months.[9] And this will be even greater all over the United States: doors will be opening that have not been opened in the past to Negroes. And the great challenge that we face is to be ready to enter these doors when they open. (*Yeah, That's right, Amen*) [*applause*] Ralph Waldo Emerson [*applause*], Ralph Waldo Emerson said in a lecture back in 1871 that if a man can write a better book or preach a better sermon or make a better mousetrap than his neighbor, even if he builds his house in the woods, the world will make a beaten path to his door.[10] (*Yeah, Amen*) This will become increasingly true. That means that we're going to have to work hard. We're going to have to burn the midnight oil sometimes. We're going to have to take advantage of new opportunities.

But we must set out to do our life's work so well that *nobody* could do it better. (*That's right, That's right*) We must set out to do a good job. (*Yes*) And we must not seek merely to do a good Negro job. If you are setting out to be merely a good Negro doctor or a good Negro lawyer, a good Negro teacher, a good Negro preacher or a good Negro skilled laborer, a good Negro barber, a good Negro beautician, you have

---

8. For the first four lines, cf. "The Negro's Complaint" (1788) by William Cowper, and for the remaining lines, cf. "False Greatness," *Horae Lyricae* (1706) by Isaac Watts.

9. Thanks largely to strong support in predominantly black districts, Samuel W. Yorty defeated incumbent C. Norris Poulson in the 1961 Los Angeles mayoral election (Carlton Williams, "Switch in Vote Trends Noted in City Election," *Los Angeles Times*, 9 June 1961). In the year following his election, Yorty named six African Americans to the city commission and made public statements decrying racial discrimination in the city's fire department, the hiring of city employees, and housing ("Poll Reveals Why Negoes Backed Yorty," *Los Angeles Sentinel*, 24 August 1961; "Fire Dept. Bias Out—Yorty," *Los Angeles Sentinel*, 21 December 1961; "Mayor Pushes Probe of City Job Bias, Upgrading," *Los Angeles Sentinel*, 22 March 1962; "Mayor Backs Fair Housing," *Los Angeles Sentinel*, 19 April 1962).

10. The source of this quotation, generally attributed to Emerson, is uncertain (see note 6, "Mother's Day in Montgomery," 18 May 1956, in *Papers* 3:266).

already flunked your matriculation exam for entrance into the university of integration. (*That's right*) [*applause*] We must get ready. [*applause*]

We must set out to do a good job (*Amen*) and to do that job so well that the living, the dead, or the unborn couldn't do it better. (*That's right, Yeah*) As I've said so often, if it falls your lot to be a street sweeper (*Yes*), go on out and sweep streets like Michelangelo carved marble (*Yes*), sweep streets like Raphael painted pictures (*That's it*), sweep streets like Beethoven composed music, and like Shakespeare wrote poetry. (*That's right*) Sweep streets so well that all the hosts of heaven and earth will have to pause and say, "Here lived a great street sweeper who swept his job well."[11] [*applause*] This is it. [*applause*] If you can't be a pine on the top of the hill, be a scrub in the valley, but be the best little scrub on the side of the rill. (*Yeah*) Be a bush if you can't be a tree. (*Yes*) If you can't be a highway, just be a trail. (*Yes*) If you can't be the sun, be a star (*Preach*), for it isn't by size that you win or you fail—be the best of whatever you are.[12] [*applause*] (*Yes, That's it*) And if we will do this, we will grapple with our dilemma (*Yes sir*), and we will meet the challenge of this hour. (*I hope*)

I would like to suggest another thing. We must develop and maintain a keen sensitivity to the social evils of the world today. (*Yeah*) There are three major social evils alive in our world today. One is the evil of war, the other is the evil of economic injustice, and the third is the evil of racial injustice. My friends, this afternoon let me say to you that we must never adjust to war. Somehow, deep down in our hearts, something should tell us that there's something wrong with war. (*Yes sir, Amen*) War is wrong because it ends up stacking up national debts higher than mountains of gold. (*Yes sir, Yes sir*) War is wrong because it fills our nations with widows and orphans. (*Yes sir*) War is wrong because it sends men home maimed and mutilated. (*Yes sir, Yes sir*) War is wrong because it sends men home psychologically deranged and mentally handicapped. (*Yes, Yes sir, That's true*) And God has reminded us over and over again through Jesus Christ that man is too precious to die on the battlefields of the world. And I don't know about you, but I will never cease reminding this nation and the world that war is wrong. (*Yes sir, Yes, Yes sir, Amen*) And in a day when Sputniks and Explorers are dashing through outer space, and guided ballistic missiles are carving highways of death through the stratosphere (*Yes*), no nation can win a war. (*Amen*) It is no longer a choice between violence and nonviolence it is either nonviolence or nonexistence. (*That's right*) And the alternative to disarmament, the alternative to suspension of nuclear tests, the alternative to strengthening the United Nations and thereby disarming the whole world may well be a civilization plunged into the abyss of annihilation. And I never intend to adjust myself to war. [*applause*] War is evil. [*applause*]

Then there is the problem of economic injustice. All over this world, this problem is still alive. It grows out of exploitation. It grows out of taking necessities from the masses to give luxuries to the classes. (*That's true, Right*) And I never intend to adjust

---

11. King once attributed this quotation to Morehouse College president Benjamin Mays (see King, "Facing the Challenge of a New Age," Address Delivered at NAACP Emancipation Day Rally, 1 January 1957, in *Papers* 4:79).

12. King paraphrases Douglas Malloch's poem "Be the Best of Whatever You Are" (1926).

myself to this. Just last Sunday, I was at the table, the breakfast table with my children and my wife, and after the prayer, I had my usual devotional message with the children and the family, and I said some things that I don't think they quite understood because they are too young. They did not understand the conditions existing in the world. And I looked across that table and I said, "Yolanda and Marty and Dexter, you are having breakfast this morning, you're getting ready to eat a nice breakfast. But I want to remind you, and I want you to know that millions of people all over this world went to bed hungry last night. (*Yes, That's true, All right*) People in this very nation that you live in will not have a breakfast this morning. But I want you to know that those people are your brothers and your sisters. (*Yeah, Absolutely*) And I'm going to work, do what I can, to see that you have the proper meals, and I'm going to work to see that you get your education. But I want you to realize that, as you get your education, that there are millions of people who did not have the privilege and the opportunity to get an education, and they are your brothers and your sisters. (*Yes*) And never get so high that you forget them. [*applause*] I want you to know that." [*applause*]

And I will never adjust myself to economic injustice. (*Yes sir, Yes sir*) I will never adjust myself to the fact that some people can live in inordinate superfluous wealth while others live in abject, deadening poverty. (*That's right*) And I don't believe God intended it that way. (*No*) One tenth of 1 percent of the population of this nation controls more than 50 percent of the wealth, and I will say this afternoon or this evening without any hesitation, that there is something *wrong* with a system where some people can wallow in wealth and others do not have the basic necessities of life. (*That's it*) [*applause*] I'll say that. (*Preach*) [*applause*] And Communism is not the answer to this problem (*No it isn't*), for Communism is based on an ethical relativism, a metaphysical materialism, a totalitarianism, and a denial of human freedom which I could never accept. But we *can* work within the framework of our democracy to make for a better distribution [*applause*] of wealth. [*applause*]

Wyatt talked about our trip down in Mississippi.[13] And I walked around, in the cotton fields and around the villages in that state, down in what is known as the Delta of Mississippi, and I met hundreds and thousands of people who earn less than seven hundred dollars a year. And I said to myself, "God doesn't like this. (*No indeed*) And God didn't mean for it to be like this." When I was in India some few years ago, I saw with my own eyes millions of people sleeping on the sidewalks at night.[14] They had no beds to sleep in, no houses to go in, and I said to myself, "God doesn't like this." (*No, No*) And I started thinking of the fact that right here in America, we spend more than a million dollars a day to store surplus food. (*Yes*) And I said to myself, I know where we can store that food free of charge (*Yes sir*): in the wrinkled stomachs of the millions of people in Asia and Africa, in South America, and in our own nation who go to bed hungry at night. (*Yes sir*) [*applause*] And maybe we've spent far too

---

13. Wyatt Tee Walker accompanied King on his trip to California. On 7–9 February 1962, King visited the Mississippi Delta region on a People to People tour. For more on the trip, see King, "People in Action: Pathos and Hope," 3 March 1962, pp. 419–421 in this volume.

14. King toured India from 9 February–17 March 1959. For more on his trip to India, see Introduction in *Papers* 5:2–12.

much [*applause*], maybe we've spent far too much of our national budget establishing military bases around the world (*Yes*) rather than bases of genuine concern and understanding.[15] (*All right*)

All I am saying, my friends, is this: that all life is interrelated. (*Yeah*) We are caught in an inescapable network of mutuality, tied in a single garment of destiny. And whatever affects one directly affects all indirectly. (*Yeah*) And no individual in this world can feel that he is divorced or separated from any other individual. We are all tied together. And we must be concerned about economic injustice wherever we see it. (*Yeah*)

And the third evil in our world is the evil of racial injustice. (*All right*) We know about this evil, for we have lived with it for all too many years. We knew about it during the days of slavery, when even the Supreme Court back in 1857 said in the *Dred Scott* decision that the Negro wasn't a citizen of the United States; he was merely property, subject to the dictates of his owner. It went on to say that the Negro had no rights that the white man was bound to respect.[16] We have known about racial injustice. We have known about it through the brutality and viciousness of lynching mobs. We've known about it through the voice of a little Emmett C. Till, crying from the mad waters of Mississippi. We've known about it (*Yeah, All right*) through the screaming voice of a little Mack C. Parker being pulled through the streets of Mississippi and taken and lynched.[17] We've known about it (*Yeah, That's true*) because we've heard the voice of an old Negro woman, after shopping all day in a downtown store in a Southern city, going up to get a little coffee to drink and a hamburger to eat, only to be told that we don't serve niggers here. We've heard about it (*Yes, Yeah, Yes*) even in Los Angeles, California. We've heard about it in housing discrimination and in employment discrimination. [*applause*] We've heard about it. [*applause*] (*Good Lord, Go on*) And I can only say to you this evening, let us never rest (*Yeah, No*) and be content until *all* of the walls of segregation and discrimination are torn down. (*Yeah, Yes*) [*applause*] And we must make it clear [*applause*], we must make it clear that we are determined to be free. (*Yeah*)

We don't need to utter but three words to tell this nation what we are talking about. They aren't big words; you don't need to have a great vocabulary to utter them. You don't need to have a philosophical bent to grasp them. (*No*) They are three little words, but we want to let the world know that these words describe what we mean and what we are determined to do about racial injustice. One is the word "all." We don't want some of our rights. (*That's right, Come on now*) We don't want a few token handouts here and there. We want (*Yeah, Amen*) all of our rights. (*Amen*) [*applause*] The other word is "here." There are some people who say that we need to go back to Africa (*Yes sir, Yes sir, Yes sir*), and then there are some others who tell Negroes in the South to leave the South: you can't be free, so get out. But down in Alabama and

---

15. King made a similar statement in "The Three Dimensions of a Complete Life" at the Unitarian Church of Germantown on 11 December 1960 (in *Papers* 5:577).

16. *Dred Scott v. Sandford*, 60 U.S. 393 (1857).

17. Till, at age fourteen, was murdered in August 1955 for allegedly whistling at a white woman, while Mack Charles Parker was abducted from jail and murdered in April 1959. For more on Parker's murder, see King to James P. Coleman, 25 April 1959, in *Papers* 5:190–191.

Mississippi and Georgia and South Carolina, we are saying something else now. (*Yes* sir, Yes sir*) We want all of our rights, and we want all of our rights *here* in Alabama and Mississippi [*applause*] and South Carolina. (*Yeah*) [*applause*] And then there's a third word; it is the word "now." [*laughter, applause*] We are not willing to wait a hundred years for our rights. We are not willing to wait fifty years for what is ours (*That's right, Yes sir*) on the basis of the Constitution of this United States and the authority of God himself. (*Yes sir, That's it, All right*) No, we are not willing to wait another twenty-five years for our rights. (*Yes sir, Yes sir*) We can hear voices telling us to slow up. We can hear voices telling us to cool off. (*Yes sir*) Our only answer in calm, patient term must be that we have cooled off too long, and if we keep cooling off we'll end up in a deep freeze.[18] [*laughter, applause*] We must go on and say [*applause*], "Know what we are saying to this nation is that we want all of our rights; we want them here; and we want all of them not next year (*Yes*), not next week (*Yes*), but we want them now [*applause*], at this hour." [*applause*] This is what we are saying. [*applause*]

We must work through the courts, through legislation, through the ballot. This is what we've been talking about over these last few meetings: the necessity of registering and the necessity of voting. And this is one of the most significant steps that the Negro can take at this hour (*That's right, That's right*): going to the ballot box. (*That's right*) And many of the conditions that exist right here in Los Angeles will be changed. (*That's right, Amen*) They tell me that you have a problem of pollut—of police brutality here in Los Angeles. [*applause*] One of the ways of this problem will be rectified and dealt with is to go out with a determined effort to get the ballot so that you can say to the political leaders of this city, "We are determined that this particular chief of police or this particular person will have to *go* because (*Right*) they have not committed [*applause*] themselves to democracy." (*Yeah*) [*applause*]

These are the things we face, and we must develop a determination. But I would like to give you a warning signal. I've tried to talk in militant terms for the last few minutes, but in the midst of this militancy, let us always realize that we don't have to hate as we try to straighten this situation (*No*) out. (*That's right, Go ahead*) Let us always [*applause*] realize that we don't have to become bitter as we try to straighten this situation out. (*No, Go ahead, Right*) And oh, my friends if there is any one thing that I would like for you to remember this evening, it is the fact that somebody must have some sense in this world. (*Yeah*) Somebody must have sense enough to meet hate with love. (*Yes*) Somebody must have sense enough to meet physical force with soul force. (*Yes sir, Yes sir, Yes sir, Yes sir*) If we will but try this way, we will be able to change these conditions and yet at the same time win the hearts and souls of those who have kept these conditions alive. (*Yes, Yes*) [*applause*]

And I know the temptation. [*applause*] I know the temptation which comes to all of us. We've been trampled over so long. (*Lord, Jesus*) I know the temptation that comes to all of us. We've seen the viciousness of lynching mob with our own eyes. We've seen police brutality in our own lives. We are still the last hired and the first fired. (*Yeah, That's right*) So many doors are closed in our faces and that is a tempta-

17 June
1962

---

18. In response to Attorney General Robert F. Kennedy's request for a cooling off period, CORE executive director James Farmer said: "We've had 100 years to cool off and we're in a deep freeze now" ("Acid Tossed in Face of Freedom Fighter," Baltimore *Afro-American*, 12 August 1961).

tion for us to end up bitterness, with bitterness. And I understand these people who have ended up in despair.

I understand why there are some who have been a little misguided, and they've ended up feeling that the problem can't be solved within, and so they talk about racial separation rather than racial integration. I understand their response. I have analyzed it psychologically, and I understand it. But in spite of the fact that I understand it I must say to them in patient terms that that isn't the way. (*No it isn't*) I must say to them in patient terms that black supremacy is as dangerous as white supremacy. (*Yeah*) [*applause*] And God is not interested merely [*applause*], and God is not interested merely in the freedom of black men and brown men and yellow men (*Yes sir, Yes sir*), but God is interested in the freedom of the whole human race (*Yeah*) and the creation [*applause*] of a society where all men will live together as (*Yes*) brothers. (*That's it*)

No, we need not hate. (*Yes sir*) We need not use violence. (*Yes sir*) There is another way (*Yes sir, Yes sir*), a way as old as the insights of Jesus of Nazareth (*Go on, Go on, Go on*) and as modern as the techniques of Mohandas K. Gandhi. (*Go on*) There is another way (*Yes sir, Well*), a way as old as Jesus saying, "Love your enemies (*Yeah, Watch out*), bless them that curse you (*Yes, Yeah*), pray for them that despitefully use you."[19] (*Yeah, Yeah, Yes sir*) And as modern as Gandhi saying through Thoreau, "Non-cooperation with evil is as much a moral obligation as is cooperation with good."[20] (*That's right*)

There is another way (*Yes sir*), a way as old as Jesus saying, "Turn the other cheek." (*Yes, Yes*) And when he said that, he realized that turning the other cheek might bring suffering sometimes.[21] (*Yes he did, Yeah*) He realized that it may get some home bombed sometimes. (*All right*) He realized that it may get you stabbed sometimes.[22] (*Right*) He realized that it may get you scarred up sometimes. (*Yeah*) But he was saying in substance that it is better to go through life with a scarred-up body (*Yes*) than a scarred-up soul. (*Yeah*) [*applause*]

There is another way. [*applause*] This is what we've got to see. [*applause*] (*Preach*) And oh, there is a power in this way. (*That's right, Yeah*) And if we will follow this way, we will be the participants in a great building process (*That's right*) that will make America a new nation. (*That's right, Yes*) And we will be able to transform the jangling discords of our nation into a beautiful symphony of brotherhood. This is our chal-

---

19. Cf. Matthew 5:44.

20. Cf. M.K. Gandhi, *Satyagraha* (Ahmadabad: Navajivan Publishing House, 1951), p. 165: "Non-co-operation with evil is as much a duty as co-operation with good"; see also Gandhi, "The Poet's Anxiety," *Young India*, 1 June 1921. In a 12 October 1929 letter to English writer and reformer Henry S. Salt, Gandhi wrote: "My first introduction to Thoreau's writings was I think in 1907 or later when I was in the thick of passive resistance struggle. A friend sent me Thoreau's essay on civil disobedience. It left a deep impression upon me" (Gandhi, *The Collected Works of Mahatma Gandhi*, vol. 41 [Ahmadabad, Navajivan Press, 1970]).

21. Cf. Matthew 5:39.

22. King's home in Montgomery, Alabama, was bombed on 30 January 1956 (see Introduction in *Papers* 3:10–11). The following year, segregationists attempted a second bombing of his home, but it failed (see Introduction in *Papers* 4:6–7). On 20 September 1958 King was stabbed by a mentally deranged woman while signing copies of *Stride Toward Freedom* in a Harlem department store (see Introduction in *Papers* 4:34–35).

lenge. (*That's right*) This is the way we must grapple with this dilemma (*Yes sir*), and we will be a great people. (*Yes*)

And let us have faith in the future. I know it's dark sometimes. And I know all of us begin to ask, "How long will we have to live (*Go on*) with this system?" (*Yes sir now*) I know all of us are asking, "How long will prejudice blind the visions of men (*Yes*) and darken their understanding and drive bright-eyed wisdom from her sacred throne? When will wounded justice lying prostrate on the streets of our cities be lifted from this dust of shame to reign supreme among the children of men? Yes, when will the radiant star of hope be plunged against the nocturnal bosom of this lonely night (*Well*) and pluck from weary souls the manacles of death and the chains of fear? (*How long*) How long will justice be crucified (*Yeah, All right, Preach, Well*) and truth buried, how long?" (*How long*) I can only answer this evening, "Not long." (*Oh, That's right, Not long*)

There's a little song that we sing in our movement down in the South; I don't know if you've heard it, but it has become the theme song. "We shall overcome (*Yeah, That's right*), we shall overcome. Deep in my heart, I do believe (*Yeah*) we shall overcome." (*Yeah, Yes sir, That's it*) Though I joined hands so often with students and others behind jail bars singing it—"We shall overcome." (*Yes sir, Yeah*) Sometimes, we've had tears in our eyes when we joined together to sing it (*Well*), but we still decided to sing it, we shall overcome. (*Yes, That's it, Yes*) And oh, before this victory is won some will have to get thrown in jail some more, but we shall overcome. (*Yes*) Don't worry about us. Before the victory's won, some of us will lose jobs, but we shall overcome. (*Oh, That's right, Yes*) Before the victory's won, even some will have to face physical death. (*Yes*) But if physical death is the price that some must pay (*Yes*) to free their children from a permanent psychological death (*Yes*), then nothing shall be more redemptive—we shall overcome. (*That's right, Yes*) Before the victory's won, some will be misunderstood and called bad names and dismissed as rabble-rousers and agitators, but we shall overcome (*Yes sir, That's right*), and I'll tell you why.

We shall overcome because the arc of the moral universe is long (*Yes*), but it bends toward justice. (*All right*) We shall overcome because Carlyle is right: "No lie can live forever."[23] (*Yes sir, Yeah*) We shall overcome because William Cullen Bryant is right (*Yes sir, Come on*): "Truth crushed to earth, will rise again."[24] (*Come on, Yes sir, That's right*) We shall overcome because James Russell Lowell is right: "Truth forever on the scaffold/Wrong forever on the throne/Yet that scaffold sways the future, and, behind the dim unknown/Standeth God within the shadow (*Come on*), keeping watch above his own."[25] (*That's right*) We shall overcome because (*Preach*) the Bible is right (*Preach*): "You shall reap what you sow."[26] (*Yes, Come on*) We *shall* overcome. (*That's right*) Deep in my heart, I do believe (*Yes*) we shall overcome. (*Yes*) And with this faith (*Well*) we will go out and adjourn the councils of despair (*Yeah, Yes sir*) and

23. Cf. Thomas Carlyle, *The French Revolution* (1837), vol. 1, book 6, chap. 3.
24. Cf. William Cullen Bryant, "The Battlefield" (1839), stanza 9.
25. James Russell Lowell, "The Present Crisis" (1844), stanza 8. King's phrasing closely resembles a sermon by Harry Emerson Fosdick (see note 14, "The Meaning of Easter," Sermon Delivered at Ebenezer Baptist Church, 22 April 1962, p. 445 in this volume).
26. Cf. Galatians 6:7.

bring new light into the dark chambers of pessimism. (*Yes*) And we will be able to rise from the fatigue of despair to the buoyancy of hope, and this will be a great America. We will be the participants in making it so. And so as I leave you this evening, I say, "Walk together children. Don't you get weary. [*applause*] There's a great camp meeting in the Promised Land."27 (*Yeah*) [*applause*]

At. MLKEC.

---

27. King quotes from the spiritual "There's a Great Camp Meeting."

## "People in Action: New Harassment"

23 June 1962
New York, N.Y.

*As King prepared to address a rally at Little Union Baptist Church in Shreveport on 8 June, local police arrested SCLC officials Wyatt Tee Walker and Harry Blake and subjected them to a mental competency examination.*[1] *In this article published in the* New York Amsterdam News, *King decries the "lunacy test" as an example of the "absurdity of the lengths to which the racist opposition will go to thwart the Freedom Movement in the South." Concluding the article, King asks if segregationists will learn that their efforts to stop integration are "as vain as trying to hold back the tides of the sea." Walker and Blake were found mentally competent and permitted to post bond on 9 June.*

The racist opposition in the Deep South has worked far into the night dreaming up the many not-so-subtle devices to thwart the accelerated civil rights thrust of the Negro community. The most familiar since the outlawing of the old devices—the grandfather clause and the white primary—have been the literacy tests, polltaxes etc.[2] However, with the advent of the Sit-In movement in 1960, architects of evil

---

1. The stop in Shreveport was part of SCLC's People to People tours. Walker and Blake were arrested for loitering as they checked security around the church after King had received death threats (Claude Sitton, "2 Negro Leaders Seized in South," *New York Times*, 10 June 1962). Harry Blake (1934– ), born in Portland, Arkansas, graduated from Bishop College in Dallas, Texas, in 1959. In 1960, Blake, who was serving as interim pastor of Elizabeth Baptist Church in Belcher, Louisiana, was hired as a field secretary for SCLC, a position he held until 1963. From 1961 until 1966 he was pastor of Lake Bethlehem Baptist Church in Shreveport. Blake had served as pastor of Shreveport's Mount Canaan Baptist Church since 1966. A lifetime member of the NAACP, Blake also served as general secretary of the National Baptist Convention (2000–2009) and president of the Louisiana Baptist State Convention (1995–2010).

2. Oklahoma's "grandfather clause," which exempted from literacy tests those who were descended from pre-1866 voters, was ruled unconstitutional in *Guinn and Beal v. United States* (238 U.S. 347 [1915]). The Democratic Party of Texas's resolution that only white citizens could become members and, therefore, vote during the primary election was deemed unconstitutional in *Smith v. Allwright* (321 U.S. 649 [1944]).

went to work anew. They have now developed such legal devices (aimed primarily at
the nonviolent approach) as "anti-trespass" ordinances that carry heavy penalties,
breach of the peace and inciting to riot statutes, and more recently in the sovereign
state of Louisiana, criminal anarchy charges that require cash bail in cash in excess
of $10,000.00 on each charge.[3]

Now another device of harassment is born again in the sovereign state of
Louisiana. The criminal anarchy statute was invoked in Baton Rouge. The new
harassment is the coroner's commitment or lunacy test. The lunacy test statute was
applied in Shreveport, bastion of the White Citizens Council.

Just last Friday, the Reverend Wyatt Tee Walker, executive director of SCLC,
Bernard Lee, Field Secretary and myself were scheduled to go into Shreveport to aid
in kicking off an intensified voter registration drive. Two and one-half hours before
plane time, Harry Blake, our SCLC Field Secretary in north Louisiana telephoned
the home office in Atlanta to advise us that the racists threatened to kill us if we came
to Shreveport. Naturally, we decided to go anyway, despite the fact that the climate
of law and order in this north Louisiana city is very bad.[4]

Director Walker and Harry Blake made some precautionary arrangement (as
much as can be taken in this kind of circumstance) particularly in the immediate
area of the Little Union Baptist Church, site of the rally.

While they were checking on the men who were guarding the church, the
Commissioner of Public Safety and the Chief of Police, J. Earl Downs and Harvey
D. Teasley, accosted Walker and Blake and insisted that they go inside the church.
Previously, the Commissioner had refused police protection for "that nigger King
and his crowd" when asked by the local leaders. Our staff director questioned Downs
as to whether his change of heart about police protection would include the area of
the church. When Mr. Walker insisted on an answer to his query, he and Blake were
arrested on a "loitering" charge and taken to the Shreveport city jail where they were
booked and finger printed.[5]

In an affidavit, filed with the Department of Justice, Mr. Walker describes their

---

3. On 12 February Ronnie Moore, chairman of the Baton Rouge chapter of CORE, was charged
with criminal anarchy for his membership in "an organization seeking to 'subvert' the government of
the state," with bond set at $12,500 (CORE, Newsletter, "*CORE-lator*, no. 95," April 1962).

4. Prior to King's visit, local SCLC affiliates were subjected to bouts of violence. On 18 February
1962, the home of C. O. Simpkins, head of SCLC's Shreveport affiliate known as the United Christian
Movement, was bombed. Three months later, Simpkins's summer home was also bombed and burned
to the ground (King, "People in Action: Can We Ever Repay Them?," *New York Amsterdam News*, 9
June 1962). Additionally, Blake had suffered minor wounds from a drive-by shooting in October 1960
("Attempt Made on Life of Local Civil Rights Leader," *Shreveport Sun*, 22 October 1960). King's draft of
the article appended the following sentence: "We are confronted with many hard decision like this but
it is part of the code of our work: If we knew for sure that we would not be coming back, we would still
go!" (Draft, "New Harassment: The Lunacy Test," 23 June 1962).

5. Teasley offered a different account, stating that several whites from a local segregationist group
were picketing the church and had drawn the attention of local blacks, including Walker and Blake.
Fearing violence, the police ordered everyone to disperse, but Walker and Blake refused to obey and
were arrested (Sitton, "2 Negro Leaders Seized in South," 10 June 1962). According to his affidavit,
Walker agreed to go inside the church, but first wanted to insure that police protection extended around
the back of the church. While he awaited confirmation, Walker was arrested and charged with loitering
(Walker, Affidavit, 11 June 1962).

amazement when they were mysteriously transferred to the Caddo Parish (county) jail under coroner commitments signed by Chief Teasley. They were to be held without bond until the county coroner could examine them and determine whether they were "mentally competent."[6]

The Chief of Police was reported in the New York Times as saying this was regular procedure. The Times indicated that they checked with other law enforcement officials around the state and no one could explain the practice and had never heard of it.

Interestingly enough, Wyatt Tee Walker graduated at the top of his class in undergraduate school with a B.S. in chemistry and physics and from graduate school with a B.D. in theology. He compiled a brilliant record during the eight years he served the 1000-member Gillfield Baptist Church in Petersburgh, Virginia. In the two-year period of his administration as director of SCLC, our organization has developed from a five-member staff, $63,000 a year program to a thirty-member staff, $475,000 program. This is the man whose mental competence the Louisiana officials doubted.

The lesson of this account is but to demonstrate once again the absurdity of the lengths to which the racist opposition will go to thwart the Freedom Movement in the South. Will they ever learn that it is as vain as trying to hold back the tides of the sea.[7]

PD. *New York Amsterdam News*, 23 June 1962.

---

6. According to Walker, the examination consisted of forty minutes of questions such as "if you had the choice to defend the state of Georgia or the United States, which would you choose?"; "do you feel people are against you?"; and "you really do believe what you say, don't you?" (Walker, Affidavit). After the men's competence was established by county coroner Stuart DeLee, the United Christian Movement bonded Walker and Blake out on 9 June. In a 27 June 1962 letter to Walker, Burke Marshall, assistant attorney general, said the Justice Department had made contact with local officials in Shreveport to ensure that Walker and Dr. King would be protected. "I understand that adequate police action was taken," Marshall wrote. Marshall also said that his department had investigated Walker's arrest and found "no basis for any federal action with respect to it."

7. King references the legend of "King Canute on the Seashore."

# To Harold Edward Fey

27 June 1962
Atlanta, Ga.

*Following the Gandhi Society's founding on 17 May, the* Christian Century *and the Episcopal Society for Cultural and Racial Unity (ESCRU), liberal Christian supporters of the movement, publicly expressed their fears that the Gandhi Society represented a dangerous turn toward a humanistic secularism with*

*Gandhi replacing Christ as a central figure.*[1] *King responds to these criticisms* 27 June
*in a private letter to* Century *editor Fey, explaining that the Gandhi Society is* 1962
*to be an educational organization supporting the movement.*[2] *He also clarifies*
*his theological views regarding interfaith efforts, asserting that his Christian*
*convictions did not conflict with his belief "that in some marvelous way, God*
*worked through Gandhi, and the spirit of Jesus Christ saturated his life." King*
*says he was "shocked" that Fey and Morris of the Episcopal Society had not*
*checked with him "to clarify the facts," adding it is a "Christian courtesy that*
*I would expect from a dedicated Priest who is an ally in the struggle, and from*
*a responsible periodical that does not hesitate to use my name as an Editor-at-*
*Large." Fey later apologized, expressing his "regret that you feel we contributed to*
*a misunderstanding of the Gandhi Organization."*[3] *King granted permission for*
*the* Century *to quote sections of the letter for an explanatory editorial clarifying*
*the Gandhi Society's auxiliary role.*[4]

Dr. Harold E. Fey, Editor
THE CHRISTIAN CENTURY
407 South Dearborn Street
Chicago 5, Illinois

Dear Dr. Fey:

It is very seldom that I pause to answer criticisms that are directed toward me and my work. If I stopped to answer all of the criticisms that come across my desk, I would find little time to do anything else and my office staff would be almost completely involved in this task. However, the editorial which appeared in The Christian

---

1. The *Christian Century* published an editorial expressing its fear that the Society's leaders, focused on "penultimate human rights instead of ultimate human unity," would substitute "Gandhi's laudable humanistic creed for the power of reconciliation which they possess in the Lord of all history" ("A Gandhi Society?," *Christian Century* 79 [13 June 1962]: 735–736). John B. Morris, executive director of ESCRU, an independent organization seeking to promote integration efforts both within and outside of the Episcopal Church, asserted that the Society's founding indicated a shift where "Gandhi displaces Christ as the source of power and motivation for those who call themselves Christian" and that "new prophets must come foreward now if Christ is not to be shunted aside in favor of humanistic loyalties which man elevates higher than faith" (ESCRU, Press release, John Burnett Morris statement on disappointment in religious divergence, 29 May 1962). King called both of these statements a "'misunderstanding' of the nature and purpose" of the Society ("Gandhi Unit Criticized by Journal," *Washington Post*, 16 June 1962).
2. Harold Edward Fey (1898–1990), received his B.A. from Cotner College in 1922 and a B.D. from Yale Divinity School in 1927. Ordained a minister of the Disciples of Christ in 1923, Fey served as pastor of First Christian Church in Hastings, Nebraska, after graduating from Yale and from 1929–1931 taught sociology abroad at Union Theological Seminary in Manila. In 1932, Fey became editor of *World Call,* a monthly magazine tied to the Disciples of Christ. He was executive secretary of the Fellowship of Reconciliation and editor of *Fellowship* from 1935–1940. Fey joined the *Century* staff in 1940 and served as editor from 1956–1964. He published several books, including his autobiography *How I Read the Riddle* (1982).
3. Fey to King, 6 July 1962. *Century* managing editor Kyle Haselden also wrote King reassuring him "that we are deeply devoted to the causes which you serve, and that we want to do you good and not harm" (Haselden to King, 16 July 1962).
4. See Dora E. McDonald to Fey, 16 July 1962; "Gandhi Society Explained," *Christian Century* 79 (1 August 1962): 929–930.

489

Century and the statement released by The Rev. John Morris, of the Episcopal Society for Cultural and Racial Unity, reveal such a blatant misunderstanding of the new Gandhi Society for Human Rights that I feel compelled to answer it.

First, I should give you some idea of the circumstances that led to the formation of the Gandhi Society. Several months ago I met with a group of distinguished lawyers in New York and solicited their support in the libel cases that several Alabama officials had brought against four ministers of the Southern Christian Leadership Conference. These lawyers were so outraged at this tragic misuse of the judicial process that they immediately formed a lawyer's committee to give legal and financial assistance to these victims of injustice.[5] When one realizes that the SCLC has already spent over $40,000.00 on the libel cases, it is not too difficult to see what a tremendous lift it was to me to get the support of these lawyers.[6]

As these men came closer and closer to the struggle, they came to a realization of the overwhelming financial burden that we were facing in the non-violent movement. They saw how our all-too-limited financial resources were constantly drained by the legal maneuvers and vicious attacks of those who opposed our efforts. As a result of this, many felt that a tax extmpt fund should be set up through which large scale financial support could be channelized for the non-violent movement. Along with this, the idea emerged that this fund could also serve as a medium through which educational material on non-violence could be disseminated on a broad scale and support for voter education on a non-partisan basis could be developed.[7] Out of this interplay of ideas and concern the Gandhi Society had its birth. It is not a new civil rights organization such as NAACP, Urban League, SCLC or CORE. It is rather an educational fund or foundation which was established to serve as a crucible for new ideas in non-violent direct action, and to provide support for the movement to increase the number of Negro registered voters, and to provide legal aid to those leaders and individuals who are legally attacked because of their involvement in the non-violent movement.

It is clear from the foregoing that the founders of the Gandhi Society had not the slightest desire to set up an organization that would displace the church or repudiate the Christian gospel. This question never came up, and I am sure that no one in the group considered this new thrust as a substitute for the social action program of the Christian church.

At this point, I think I should state my personal convictions on the issue. Both

---

5. King refers to the Lawyers Advisory Committee, a group of eighteen lawyers assembled by Theodore Kheel. For more on the committee, see King, Statement at Lawyers Advisory Committee meeting, 8 May 1961, pp. 218–221 in this volume.

6. According to SCLC's financial reports, around $20,000 had been spent on costs related to the libel cases from September 1960 to April 1962 (Abernathy, "SCLC, treasurer's report," 1 September 1960–31 August 1961; Abernathy, "Treasurer's report," 1 September 1961–30 April 1962).

7. King once noted that SCLC, "with respect to active legal support, is like an Army engaged in battle without a medical corps" (King to Theodore Woodrow Kheel, 11 December 1961). In his 12 February 1962 correspondence with New York lawyer Harry Wachtel, one of the architects of the Gandhi Society, King raised the need for educational material about voting rights and funding for legal assistance for local voter registration campaigns (pp. 397–398 in this volume).

you and Mr. Morris imply in your statements that I am now forsaking the Christian church in order to turn to a new kind of American sectarianism. You seem to have the idea that the Gandhi Society will replace the Southern Christian Leadership Conference. This is implied in your statement that "they are likely to be disappointed with the results of this organizational re-shuffling and re-naming."[8] Suffice it to say that the SCLC, of which I am president, is more alive than ever before. We have some seventy-five affiliate organizations covering every Southern State. We work mainly through the churches to achieve citizenship rights for Negroes and to instill the philosophy of Christian non-violence. There is not the slightest idea of giving up this approach. My connection with SCLC is that of Executive President and most of my time and energy are given to the implementation of its program. The Gandhi Society has no organic or structural connection with SCLC. My only connection with the Society is that of Honorary Chairman. How anyone could interpret my relation with the Gandhi Society as a turn away from the church is a real mystery to me.

As far as my Christology goes, I believe as firmly now as ever that God revealed Himself uniquely and completely in Jesus Christ. Like Thomas of old, I, too, can affirm in the presence of Christ, "My Lord, and my God."[9] I believe with every Christian in the Lordship of Jesus Christ and I am more convinced than ever before that we will only find the solution to the problems of the world through Christ and His way.

One's commitment to Jesus Christ as Lord and Savior, however, should not mean that one cannot be inspired by another great personality that enters the stage of history. I must confess that I saw in your statement and that of Mr. Morris a narrow sectarianism and a degree of religious intolerance that caused me real concern. While I firmly believe that God revealed Himself more completely and uniquely in Christianity than any other religion, I cannot make myself believe that God did not reveal Himself in other religions. I believe that in some marvelous way, God worked through Gandhi, and the spirit of Jesus Christ saturated his life. It is ironic, yet inescapably true that the greatest Christian of the modern world was a man who never embraced Christianity.[10] This is not an indictment on Christ but a tribute to Him—a tribute to his universality and His Lordship. When I think of Gandhi, I think of the Master's words in the fourth gospel: "I have other sheep that are not of this fold."[11] This is not to make of Gandhi a new Jesus Christ—this he can never be. It is fallacious to think of the Gandhi Society as an attempt to deify Gandhi or establish a cult around his name. It seems only natural for this new foundation to take the name of Gandhi since he, more than anyone in the modern world, lifted the method of non-violence to a powerful level of socio-political action. To say that a Society formed with the name of Gandhi to give aid to those engaged in the non-violent struggle for justice is the establishment of a new cult, is as illogical as saying that a foundation

---

8. "A Gandhi Society?," p. 736.

9. Cf. John 20:28.

10. King expressed a similar sentiment in his 1959 Palm Sunday sermon on Gandhi's life (Palm Sunday Sermon on Mohandas K. Gandhi, Delivered at Dexter Avenue Baptist Church, 22 March 1959, in *Papers* 5:147–148).

11. Cf. John 10:16.

established in the name of Albert Schweitzer or Tom Dooley to aid in medical care for Asian and African people is the development of a new cult.[12]

To sum up all that I have said: you have been misinformed on at least two points.

(1) You have the impression that the Gandhi Society is a new civil rights organization. This, it is not. It is an educational fund.
(2) You have the impression that the Gandhi Society is made up of Christian leaders who have deserted Christ and the church. Nothing could be further from the truth. The Christian leaders on the Board of the Gandhi Society are more involved in making the gospel relevant in this period of social change than ever before.

I must say in conclusion that I was somewhat shocked to discover that you and Mr. Morris would so vehemently attack the Gandhi Society without first getting a statement from me concerning its nature and purpose.[13] Certainly I do not wish to imply that my views and my work should not be criticized when necessary. But for one to criticise without knowing all of the facts is both unjust and unfair. Just a telephone call or a letter could have cleared up most of your misconceptions. Naturally I would not expect most journalists to speak to me to clarify the facts before releasing a statement, but it is a Christian courtesy that I would expect from a dedicated Priest who is an ally in the struggle, and from a responsible periodical that does not hesitate to use my name as an Editor-at-Large. I have come to see over the past few years that most misunderstanding in the world develops because of a lack of communication—the tragic tendency to live in monologue rather than dialogue. I am extremely sorry that your editorial and the statement of Mr. Morris will spread so many unfortunate misconceptions about the Gandhi Society and will cause many Christian leaders to look upon it with strange suspicion and doubt my own commitment to Christ and the church. It may even cause some to withhold financial support—and this can be a tragedy when one considers the burden and the strain that all of us face in seeking to raise funds for the civil rights struggle.

I am sure, however, that, as in the past when our humble efforts have been misinterpreted, and temporary setbacks have been our fate, we will be sustained by Him whose grace and power will keep us from falling.[14]

Very sincerely yours,
[*signed*] Martin L. King Jr
Martin Luther King, Jr.

Km

---

12. Schweitzer was a medical missionary who founded the Schweitzer Hospital in present-day Gabon; Dooley was a physician who established several clinics for locals in Laos.

13. In his response to King, Fey explained, "we should have checked with you before issuing our statement but, frankly, we have tried so many times to get in touch with you and have failed. We have written so many letters and have not received responses that we had unconsciously accepted the erroneous assumption that nothing we could do would attract your attention" (Fey to King, 6 July 1962).

14. Cf. Jude 1:24.

P.S. I am not writing this letter for publication. MLK

TLSr. CCFA-ICarbS.

2 July
1962

# To J. Oscar Lee

2 July 1962
[*Atlanta, Ga.*]

*King accepts Lee's offer to serve on the steering committee of the upcoming
interfaith National Conference on Religion and Race.[1] He addressed the
convention in Chicago on 17 January 1963.[2]*

Dr. J. Oscar Lee, Executive Director
National Council of the Churches of Christ
475 Riverside Drive
New York 27, New York

Dear Oscar:

I am in receipt of your letter of June 22. Please accept my apologies for being somewhat tardy in replying. Absence from the city accounts for the delay.

I will be more than happy to serve on the Steering Committee for the National
Conference on Religion and Race. Apparently Mr. Miller did not receive my letter
stating my willingness to serve. I dictated it to my secretary fully four weeks ago.[3] I
also made it clear that the Southern Christian Leadership Conference would be
very happy to serve as a participating member of the Conference. While it will not be
possible for me to attend all of the meetings of the Steering Committee, I am sure

---

1. Lee to King, 22 June 1962. James Oscar Lee (1910–1995), born in Washington, D.C., graduated
from Lincoln University (1931) before receiving a B.D. from Yale Divinity School (1935) and an M.A.
from Union Theological Seminary in New York (1940). In 1946, Lee became the first African American
to receive a Ph.D. in theology from the Union Theological Seminary in Richmond, Virginia. He served
as assistant director of the Connecticut Council of Churches from 1943 to 1946. Lee joined the Federal
Council of Churches in 1946 and later became director of the Department of Racial and Cultural
Relations after the organization merged into the National Council of Churches. He was the only African
American on the professional staff. In 1965, he became vice president of the National Conference of
Christians and Jews, a position he held until retiring in 1978.

2. The convention began on the 14th of January and lasted through the 17th. On the last day, King
delivered "A Challenge to the Churches and Synagogues" (Program, National Conference on Religion
and Race, 14 January–17 January 1963).

3. NCC president J. Irwin Miller sent King a formal invitation on 15 May 1962 and asked whether
SCLC would join in the planning. In his reply to Miller, King said he wanted to be kept abreast of the
plans for the conference and that he had designated Wyatt Tee Walker as liaison between the NCC and
SCLC (King to Miller, 5 October 1962).

that I will be able to attend some of them. When that is not possible, I will follow your suggestion and have a person from the New York area represent me.[4]

As I said to Mr. Mathew Ahmann in a letter the other day, I feel that this can be the most significant conferences ever held on Religion and Race.[5] It is unprecedented, and certainly the possible good effects of such a conference are inexhaustible. Please keep me informed on the meetings and all developments.

Very truly yours
Martin Luther King, Jr.

Km

TLc. MLKJP-GAMK: Box 17.

---

4. In a handwritten note to Wyatt Tee Walker, King suggested that either George W. Lawrence or Thomas Kilgore serve as King's representative (Ahmann to King, 3 May 1962).

5. King to Ahmann, 14 June 1962. Ahmann (1932–2002), executive director of the National Catholic Conference for Interracial Justice, also served as secretariat for the conference.

# Press Interview on Atlanta Hotel and Restaurant Desegregation

[5 July 1962]
Atlanta, Ga.

*More than a thousand delegates arrived in Atlanta for the NAACP's fifty-third annual convention to find that some local hotels refused accommodations to African American patrons.[1] On the second day of the convention, more than one hundred attendees began demonstrations at sixteen hotels, motels, and restaurants that refused to serve African Americans.[2] King predicts in the following interview that through negotiation, legal methods, and nonviolent direct action, the desegregation of Atlanta hotels and restaurants "will come in the very near future." In January 1964, fourteen major hotels and motels publicly pledged to*

---

1. The NAACP's convention lasted from 2 July through 8 July 1962. On the eve of the convention, Roy Wilkins, executive secretary of the NAACP, announced that the Atlanta Cabana Motor Hotel refused accommodations to Dr. Eugene Reed, president of the New York branch of the NAACP, and William Booth, vice president of the New York branch. Additionally, Ralph J. Bunche, United Nations undersecretary for Special Political Affairs, was refused hotel accommodations at the Dinkler Plaza Hotel ("NAACP Says Atlanta Motel Barred Two," *Chicago Daily Defender*, 3 July 1962; Stanley S. Scott, "Seek All Rights in a World Where Hopes for Permanent Peace Live, Bunche Urges," *Atlanta Daily World*, 7 July 1962). Reed filed a $10,500 suit against the Atlanta Cabana Motor Hotel, which was dismissed in September 1962 on grounds that the hotel did not violate his Fourteenth Amendment rights ("Delegate Files Suit Against Hotel Here," *Atlanta Daily World*, 5 July 1962; *Reed v. Sarno et al.*, Civil Action no. 7982 [N.D. Ga. 1962]).

2. See Al Kuettner, "Hotels Picketed by NAACP Groups," *Atlanta Daily World*, 4 July 1962.

[*Interviewer*]:  How long will your speech tonight last?

[*King*]:  About thirty, thirty-five minutes, I think.

[*Interviewer*]:  Okay, thanks. Dr. King, you've been active in trying to register Negro delegates to the convention . . .

[*Voice off-camera*]:  Take it from the top. [*gap in film*]

[*Interviewer*]:  Dr. King, you've been active in trying to register Negro delegates to the convention at hotels here in Atlanta. What— . . . do you think the complete desegregation of Atlanta hotels and restaurants is a possibility?

[*King*]:  Yes, I definitely feel that this is something that will come in the not-too-distant future. There are still a few recalcitrant hotel owners who don't want to give in at all, but I think the vast majority of them know that this is inevitable and they are working to get it done. So that I would say it will come in the very near future.

[*Interviewer*]:  Well, what methods will be used to try to achieve this desegregation?

[*King*]:  Well, we will continue to negotiate, and of course there may be some legal methods used—that is a real possibility. And I would not throw out direct action, nonviolent direct action as a possibility—having sit-ins and wait-in in hotel lobbies. We have discussed this, and we will use the best method possible if the negotiation breaks down.

[*Interviewer*]:  Dr. King, what progress is being made for the Negro here in Atlanta and throughout the South?

[*King*]:  Well, I think we're making some significant strides in Atlanta and all over the South. At least massive resistance has about broken down, with the exception of Mississippi, Alabama, and South Carolina. Most states have come to see the need of complying with the Supreme Court's decision. Now our big problem now is a problem of dealing with tokenism. Although there are some states realizing that they must comply with the Supreme Court's desegregation decision, they're still only complying in a token manner. And we feel that token integration is little more than token democracy and that we must revolt against this as much as we did massive resistance.

[*Interviewer*]:  Do the different Negro organizations such as your Southern Christian Leadership Conference and the NAACP agree on the, on the methods to be used to achieve this desegregation?

[*King*]:  Well, there are differences of emphasis, but certainly we all are united on the goal we seek. I would say that we're working and moving up the same road. It may be a three-lane road with some working mainly in nonviolent direct action, others mainly through litigation and by mobilizing political forces for meaningful legislation, and others working through education and research, but all are moving up the same road toward the same goal, which is freedom and first-class citizenship.

F. NyNyFMN.

---

3.  Stanley S. Scott, "14 Leading Hotels, Motels to Desegregate Voluntarily," *Atlanta Daily World*, 11 January 1964.

# Address Delivered at the "Freedom Fund Dinner" at the Fifty-third Annual Convention of the NAACP

[*5 July 1962*]
Atlanta, Ga.

*In an effort to dispel rumors of disunity between the NAACP and SCLC, John Morsell, assistant to Roy Wilkins, invited King to address the NAACP annual convention.*[1] *Speaking to an audience of over 1,500 gathered at the Morehouse College gymnasium for the NAACP's Freedom Fund Dinner, King debunks six myths about the civil rights movement: time will solve the race problem, only education and not legislation will resolve racial conflict, the South had peaceful race relations prior to the movement, the African American vote has no impact, disunity amongst the civil rights organizations and leadership undermines the movement, and nonviolent direct action is ineffective. To the proponents of gradualism, King argues that change comes through persistence and that time is neutral: "It can be used either constructively or destructively and it may well be that we will have to repent in this generation not merely for the bitter words and actions of the bad people, but for the appalling silence of the good people." He dismisses rumors of disunity among SCLC, SNCC, CORE, and the NAACP, asserting that "we are all moving down the same road toward the same beautiful city of freedom and first-class citizenship." In conclusion, King urges his audience to refrain from complacency and challenges everyone to actively push forward in the nonviolent struggle for civil rights. The following transcript is taken from an audio recording of the event.*

My good friend Judge Delany, my good friend Mr. [Roy] Wilkins, other distinguished dais guests, delegates to this the fifty-third convention of the National Association for the Advancement of Colored People, ladies and gentlemen.[2] I sincerely welcome the opportunity to be with you on this auspicious occasion. We reaffirm our appreciation to you for all of the significant work that you have done across the years. As a result of the work of the NAACP, America is a better nation, and we as Negroes are the heirs of a legacy of dignity and courage. One day all America will be proud of your achievements.

As a citizen of Atlanta, I would like to say how much I regret that short-sightedness, moral laxity, and downright prejudice on the part of some made it impossible for the hotels to be open for this convention. I know that this has been an insult to your dignity and an affront to your person. You ought to be commended for protesting this

---

1. In his invitation to King, Morsell wrote that "our joint presence should speak with unmistakable clarity to the whole nation" (Morsell to King, 18 May 1962). Also appearing at the dinner was Coretta Scott King, who sang a solo, and comedian Dick Gregory, who was presented with a citation by Roy Wilkins (Program, "N.A.A.C.P. Fight for Freedom Fund and Awards Dinner," 5 July 1962).

2. Hubert Thomas Delany (1901–1990) was a justice in the New York City Domestic Relations Court from 1942 to 1955 and a longtime member of the NAACP and its Legal Defense and Educational Fund.

grave injustice. Your picket lines have eloquently laid the issue before the conscience of the community. This whole episode reveals that Atlanta is far from where it ought to be in human relations.

Now, it is very hot tonight, and since it is very hot, it makes it difficult for the speaker to speak, and it makes it difficult for the listeners to listen. But for the moments left, I would like to attempt to assess the progress that has been made in the civil rights struggle and determine from that the challenges and responsibilities which lie ahead.

On the one hand, we can affirm with almost inexpressible joy that we have made some significant strides in our long trek up freedom's road. In the words of Prime Minister Macmillan, "The wind of change is blowing and with almost hurricane force, it is sweeping away an old and unjust order."[3] Probably the most overt expression of this change is a gradual breakdown of the system of segregation. We all know the legal history of this system. It had its beginning in 1896 when the Supreme Court of the nation rendered the *Plessy versus Ferguson* decision, establishing the doctrine of separate but equal as the law of the land. Of course, we know what happened as a result of the *Plessy* doctrine. There was always a strict enforcement of the separate without the slightest intention to abide by the equal. [*applause*] And so the Negro ended up being plunged into the abyss of exploitation, where he experienced the bleakness of nagging injustice.

The minute the *Plessy* decision was rendered, there were those who saw its injustice. About twelve years later, the NAACP came into being, and then followed its brilliant, diligent, and courageous work on behalf of justice and Negro rights. It was mainly the work of this great organization which led to the decision of May seventeenth 1954. In this decision, the Supreme Court of the nation examined the legal body of segregation and pronounced it constitutionally dead. It said in substance that the old *Plessy* doctrine must go, that separate facilities are inherently unequal, that to segregate a child on the basis of his race is to deny that child equal protection of the law. This decision came as a refreshing oasis in a desert sweltering with the heat of injustice.

When this *Brown* decision was rendered, seventeen states and the District of Columbia practiced absolute segregation in the public schools. Today, all but three of these states have made some move, most of them token, toward integrating their schools. So there are only three states now seeking to hold out with determined resistance: the state of South Carolina, the state of Alabama, and the great sovereign state of Mississippi. [*laughter*] Segregation has broken down in other areas. When the Montgomery bus boycott started in 1955, most communities in the South had segregated bus systems. Today segregation is almost totally eliminated on city buses in the major urban areas of the South. Since the sit-in movement started in 1960, more than 150 cities of the South have integrated their lunch counters. Since the freedom

---

3. Maurice Harold Macmillan (1894–1986) was prime minister of the United Kingdom from 1957 to 1963. King paraphrases Macmillan's "Wind of Change" speech in which he criticized apartheid before the South African Parliament on 3 February 1960: "The wind of change is blowing through this continent, and whether we like it or not, this growth of national consciousness is a political fact. We must all accept it as a fact, and our national policies must take account of it."

Presiding Officer, Mr. Wilkins, delegates to the 53rd Convention of the National Association For the Advancement of Colored People, Ladies and Gentlemen.

I sincerely welcome the opportunity to be with you on this auspicious occasion. ~~always considered it a great honor to~~ ~~different officers and are unable to attend these~~ ~~NAACP convention~~ I bring warm greetings to you from the Southern Christian Leadership Conference. We reaffirm our appreciation to you for all of the significant work that you have done across the years. As a result of the work of the NAACP, America is a better nation, and we as Negroes are ~~heirs~~ heirs of a legacy of courage and dignity. One day all of America will be ~~proud~~ of your achievements.

As a citizen of Atlanta I would like to say how much I regret that shortsightedness, moral laxity and downright prejudice on the part of some made it impossible for the hotels to be opened for this convention. I know that ~~it the could~~ this has been an insult to your dignity and ~~you~~ an affront to you person. You are to be commended for

10-16

responsibilities which lie ahead.

On the one hand we can affirm with almost inexpressible joy that we have made some significant strides in our long trek up freedom's road. In the words of Prime Minister McMillan, the wind of change is blowing, and with almost hurricane force it is sweeping away an old and unjust order. Probably the most overt expression of this change is the gradual breakdown of the system of segregation. We all know the legal history of this system. It had its beginning in 1896 when the Supreme Court rendered the Plessy v Ferguson decision establishing the doctrine of separate but equal as the law of the land. Of course we know what happened as a result of the Plessy decision; there was always a strict enforcement of the separate, without the slightest intention to abide the equal, and so the Negro ended up being plunged into the abyss of

10-18

rides began in 1961, segregation in interstate travel has all but been eliminated.[4] So in a real sense, the system of segregation is on its death bed today, and the only thing uncertain about it is how costly the South will make the funeral. [*applause*]

Now, this would be a wonderful place for me to bring an end to my speech. On such a hot night it would mean making a short speech, and of course this would be a magnificent accomplishment for a Baptist preacher. [*laughter*] But it would also mean that the problem is about solved [*and?*] now and that we can sit comfortably by the wayside and wait on the coming of the inevitable. But if I stop at this point, I will merely be stating a fact and not telling the truth. You see, a fact is merely the absence of contradiction, but truth is the presence of coherence; truth is the relatedness of facts. Now, it's a fact that we have made meaningful strides in civil rights over the last few years, but it isn't the whole truth. We've got to go on and add the other side, and that is that we still have a long, long way to go.

And so if I stop at this point, I am afraid that I will leave you the victims of a dangerous optimism. If I stop now, I will leave you the victims of an illusion wrapped in superficiality. So in order to tell the truth, it is necessary to move on and say we are far from the Promised Land in civil rights. We need not look very far to see this. There are still legislative halls in the South ringing loud with such words as interposition and nullification. The Negro still confronts numerous problems in seeking to register and vote in many sections of the South. Economic injustice is still an ugly reality where the Negro is involved. All over the nation, the Negro is still the last hired and the first fired.

Above all, we must not overlook the fact that segregation is still with us. It still exists in the South in its overt and glaring forms. It still exists in the North in its hidden and subtle forms. It is true as I just said, figuratively speaking, that Old Man Segregation is on his death bed, but history has proven that social systems have a great last minute breathing power, and the guardians of the status quo are always on hand with their oxygen tents to keep the old order alive. [*applause*] But we know as we assemble here for this convention that segregation is a cancer in the body politic which must be removed before our democratic health can be realized. [*applause*] In fact if [*applause*], in fact if democracy is to live, segregation must die. [*applause*]

America does not have long to solve this problem. I know that there are those— some well-intentioned—who are telling us to slow up and cool off for a while. They urge us to adopt a policy of moderation. Well, if moderation means moving on toward the goal of justice with wise restraint and calm reasonableness, then moderation is a great virtue which all men of goodwill must seek to achieve in this tense period of transition. But if moderation means slowing up in the move for freedom and capitulating to the undemocratic practices of the guardians of the evil system of segregation, then moderation is a tragic vice which all men of goodwill must condemn. We can't afford to slow up. We have our self respect to maintain. But even

---

4. In the spring of 1961, members of the Congress of Racial Equality (CORE) launched the Freedom Rides to challenge segregation on interstate buses and bus terminals. Traveling on buses from Washington, D.C., to New Orleans, Louisiana, the riders met violent opposition in the Deep South, garnering extensive media attention and eventually forcing federal intervention from the Kennedy administration.

more, we can't afford to slow up because of our love for America and the democratic way of life. The jet-like pace of modern world events does not afford America the luxury of oxcart movement in civil rights.

There are approximately two billion eight hundred million people in the world. The vast majority of these people live in Asia and Africa. For years, they have been dominated politically, exploited economically, segregated, and humiliated by some foreign power. But the wind of change began to blow, and what a jostling wind it is. Just fifteen years ago, the British Empire had under its political domination in Asia and Africa more than six hundred fifty million people. Today that number has been reduced to less than fifty million. Twenty-five years ago, there were only three independent countries in the whole of Africa.[5] With the birth of three new nations in the last two weeks, including Algeria, there are now thirty-two independent nations in Africa.[6] [*applause*] As these former colonial subjects gain their independence, they are saying in no uncertain terms that racism and colonialism must go. And they are making it clear that they will not respect any nation that will subject a segment of its citizenry on the basis of race or color. So the hour is late. The hands of the clock of destiny are fastly moving toward midnight. To put it another way, the motor is now cranked up and we are moving up the highway of freedom toward the city of equality, and we can't afford to stop now because our nation has a rendezvous with destiny. [*applause*] We must keep moving. [*applause*]

Now, if we are to bring a final end to the system of segregation and discrimination we must continue to explode and refute several time-worn myths. The first myth is the idea that time will solve all problems. It lingers around in many quarters; it is expressed in many familiar phrases: "It takes time, you know." "This thing can't be done overnight." "Just be patient and the problem will work itself out in a few generations." Proponents of this myth fail to see that time is neutral. It can be used either constructively or destructively, and it may well be that we will have to repent in this generation not merely for the bitter words and actions of the bad people but for the appalling silence of the good people. Human [*applause*], human progress never rolls in on the wheels of inevitability. It comes through the tireless efforts and the persistent work of dedicated individuals. Without this hard work, time itself becomes the ally of the insurgent and primitive forces of irrational emotionalism and social stagnation. We must always be up and doing and realize that the time is always right to do right. [*applause*]

The second myth affirms that only education can solve problems of racial conflict. The devotees of this cherished myth contend that legislation, court orders, and executive decrees are ineffective because they cannot change the heart. They also go on to argue that you can't legislate morals. Well, it may be true that morality cannot

---

5. King refers to Ethiopia, Liberia, and Egypt.

6. Burundi and Rwanda gained their independence on 1 July, and Algeria became independent on 5 July. As of July 1962, the following countries in Africa were also independent: Benin (1960), Burkina Faso (1960), Cameroon (1960), Central African Republic (1960), Chad (1960), Congo (1960), Democratic Republic of Congo (1960), Cote d'Ivoire (1960), Egypt (1922), Gabon (1960), Ghana (1957), Guinea (1958), Liberia (1847), Libya (1951), Madagascar (1960), Mali (1960), Mauritania (1960), Morocco (1956), Niger (1960), Nigeria (1960), Senegal (1960), Sierra Leone (1961), Somalia (1960), South Africa (1931), Sudan (1956), Togo (1960), and Tunisia (1956).

be legislated, but behavior can be regulated. In short, the law may not make a man love me, but it can keep him from lynching me, and I think that's pretty important also. [*applause*] The law may not change the heart, but it can restrain the heartless. It will take education and religion to change bad internal attitudes, but legislation and court orders can control the external effects of bad internal attitudes. And so we are challenged to work diligently for meaningful legislation. There is need for civil rights legislation now. [*applause*] It is appalling [*applause*], it is appalling and tragic that in this enlightened year of 1962, the United States has a do-nothing Congress in civil rights.[7] [*Audience:*] (*Go ahead*)

The third myth that must be exploded is the idea that the South had peaceful race relations until NAACPers, sit-inners, freedom riders, and the Supreme Court began their vigorous action. Now, the proponents of this myth argue that we are going backwards instead of forward in race relations. They constantly talk about tension being created and hostilities being aroused. They have the strange illusion that there can be a tensionless social transition. But they must be reminded that there is a kind of creative tension which is necessary for growth. They must be reminded that we do not now and we have never had true peace in race relations in the South. [*applause*]

I remember when I still lived in Montgomery, Alabama, one of the friends from the white community came by my office one day and he was very disturbed. He said, "Brother King, the thing that worries me is that over so many years we've had such wonderful and such harmonious and peaceful race relations. And now you people have started this boycott and destroyed all of the peace that once existed. And we used to love the Negroes; I used to give contributions to your church, and I just don't feel like giving it now. I don't have the same attitude that I once had." [*laughter*] And I looked at him—I knew he was sincere—and I said, "My friend, we've never had peaceful race relations in Montgomery. We may have had a sort of negative peace in which the Negro patiently adjusted to and accepted second-class citizenship. And you must know that true peace is not merely the absence of some negative force; it is the presence of some positive force. True peace is not merely the absence of tension, but it is the presence of justice."[8]

---

7. King may be referring to the watered-down Manpower and Development Training Act (MDTA) passed in March 1962. The act did little for African Americans, who had long been excluded from jobs that required training and experience. He may have also been referring to Congress's failure in May 1962 to pass the ill-supported literacy bill, which would have ended literacy tests as a requirement for voting. For more on King's thoughts about the MDTA and the literacy bill, see King, "People in Action: Nothing Changing Unless," 28 April 1962, and "People in Action: Literacy Bill Dies" 26 May 1962, pp. 449–451 and 466–468 in this volume, respectively. Besides King, others, like the Anti-Defamation League of B'nai B'rith, criticized Congress's failure to enact civil rights reforms. In January 1962, the Anti-Defamation League published a civil rights review, summarizing that "While more than seven years have passed since the Supreme Court had outlawed school segregation, only token desegregation has thus far been achieved in the South. Negro employment still follows the grim pattern of last to be hired and first to be fired, and the Negro jobless rate is still more than three times the white" (Warren Kornberg, "'61 Civil Rights Record Disappointing to ADL," *Washington Post*, 2 January 1962).

8. King gives a similar account of this story in his 1956 sermon "When Peace Becomes Obnoxious," in *Papers* 3:208.

And I think this is what Jesus meant when he looked at his disciples one day and said, "I come not to bring peace but a sword."[9] Now, certainly he didn't mean he came to bring a physical sword. Certainly he didn't mean that he did not come to bring true peace. But Jesus was saying this, in substance: that I come not to bring an old negative peace, which makes for deadening passivity and stagnant complacency. And whenever I come, a conflict is precipitated between the old and the new. Whenever I come, tension sets in between justice and injustice. Whenever I come, a division takes place between the forces of light and the forces of darkness. I come not to bring an old-negative peace which is merely the absence of tension, but I come to bring a positive peace which is the presence of justice, which is the presence of love, which is the presences of brotherhood. And we must get rid of the myth once and for all that we have peaceful race relations in the South. The tension which we see in the South today is a necessary tension that comes when the oppressed rise up and start to move forward toward a permanent, positive peace. And this we must see.

Another myth that must be refuted is the idea that the Negro vote can do very little to alter conditions in the nation in general and the South in particular. Strangely enough, the supporters of this myth are not the whites but the Negroes. The white ruling class in the South has always recognized the power of the Negro vote. This is why they have fought so long and hard to deprive the Negro of this right. There are still all too many Negroes devoid of motivation, caught in the clutches of apathy and expressing the attitude that "My vote does not count." We have the job of going out into the hedges and the highways to arouse the motivation of our people and lift them from their apathetic slumber. I am still convinced that one of the most significant steps that the Negro can take at this hour is that short walk to the voting booth. [applause] And I commend you [applause], and I commend you for making this issue the theme of your convention.[10]

I would like to urge everyone here to take this matter seriously. Let us go back into our communities and develop intensive voter registration campaigns. This job cannot be done through eloquent speeches and emotion-packed mass meetings, although both may be useful means of arousing interest and enthusiasm. But after the interest is aroused, it must be followed through with block-to-block, door-to-door organization. We must go to the grassroots level and mobilize every segment of the community for this massive drive.

Fortunately, some exciting things are already happening in this area. It is significant, indeed, that the major civil rights organizations—the NAACP, CORE, SCLC, SNCC, and the Urban League—have come together to develop the most thorough and effectively coordinated campaigns ever seen in voter registration. Already we are getting results. In Georgia alone, we were able to register more than thirty thousand Negroes in less than ninety days. Take a community like Macon, Georgia. The leaders of that community came together a few months ago and organized a massive

---

9. Cf. Matthew 10:34.

10. An NAACP press release announced that voter registration, employment discrimination, school desegregation, urban renewal, and the role of direct action in the movement would be topics for the upcoming convention (NAACP, Press release, "Voting, schools and jobs, NAACP convention topics," 22 June 1962).

voter registration campaign. Little did we know in SCLC when we invested staff and money in that campaign that in sixty days six thousand new persons would be registered, thereby doubling the number of Negro registration in that community. Just a few days ago, the NAACP and SCLC began a joint drive in Chattanooga, Tennessee. Mr. Patton of the NAACP, Mr. John Calhoun, and the Reverend Fred Bennette of SCLC began working with the community.[11] In slightly less than thirty days, some 2,800 persons have been registered.

This, I believe, is the answer. If we can do this all over the South, things will change. With the ballot, we will be able to liberalize the total political climate of the South. With the ballot, we will be able to elect Negro congressmen right here in the South. With the ballot, we will be able to transform the salient misdeed of bloodthirsty mobs into the blessed good deeds of orderly citizens. With the ballot, we will be able to end police brutality and bring a halt to the dastardly acts of hooded perpetrators of violence. With the ballot, we will be able to house our courts with judges who will do justly, love mercy, and walk humbly with God. We will be able to send to the sacred halls of Congress men who will not sign the Southern Manifesto, because of their commitment to the manifesto of justice and love.[12] [*applause*] This is our challenge. [*applause*]

I would like to discuss briefly the next myth and I know [*you would?*] like for me to be honest and candid as I discuss it, for I think the time has come to discuss it publicly. The fifth mist, myth expresses the idea that the civil rights movement is a confused admixture of organizations seething with disunity. Disunity in the civil rights movement is becoming a favorite topic for a certain number of newspapers and magazines. Recently *Time* magazine offered opinions of observers whom it styled as spokesmen but whose identities are not revealed, evidently to encourage them to make sensational charges about other civil rights leaders.[13]

Frankly, I believe we are being victimized. We are enticed into self-serving statements and borderline slander about others to furnish gossip and colorful copy. And certainly we all know that none of us is immune to error. We frequently have different views on some questions. And thankfully, we are creative and intellectually bold enough to reach in new directions. We can and should criticize each other in fair and free exchange, but we must be watchful of a growing tendency to encourage and stimulate rancor within us by forces outside.

---

11. W.C. Patton (1913–1997) was a civic leader who worked for voter registration and headed the Birmingham branch of the NAACP. John H. Calhoun (1899–1988) was a civil rights activist in Atlanta, Georgia, and cofounded the Negro Voters League. Fred C. Bennette, Jr. (1928–1994) was director of security for SCLC. The five-week long NAACP voter registration campaign in Chattanooga, Knoxville, Memphis, and Clarksville resulted in 8,000 newly registered voters. The campaign in Chattanooga, conducted in cooperation with the SCLC, resulted in the registration of 1,400 new voters, bringing the total number of black registered voters to 15,000 ("Along the N.A.A.C.P. Battlefront," *The Crisis* [August–September 1962]: 412).

12. In March 1956, seventy-seven Southern congressman and nineteen Southern senators signed the Declaration of Constitutional Principles, also known as the Southern Manifesto, which opposed racial integration in public places (U.S. Congress, Senate, *Congressional Record*, 84th Cong., 2nd sess., 1956, Vol. 102, pt. 4, 4459–4460).

13. "Confused Crusade," *Time*, 12 January 1962; see also Stanley D. Levison to the Editor of *Time* Magazine, 11 January 1962, pp. 363–365 in this volume.

The civil rights movement necessarily has weaknesses and the people who lead it have faults. But in the past few years, this movement has meant more to America than even its civil rights objectives.

It is singularly a mass movement, vibrant with idealism, with goodwill, with honest zeal which has inspired tens of millions. Its wholesome qualities have refreshed the spirit of mature adults, young people, and children. Amidst seas of corruption, reported in detail in the press, this movement has been an island of purity of purpose. This generation has had little to hold on to against the storms of cynicism other than the spiritual grandeur of our struggle.

Our differences are relatively minor. Our criticisms of each other are not deep or intense. Yet when they are sensationally presented, they have the illusion of importance, and if repeated often enough, a new image of our movement will emerge: that of leaders and followers smiling at each other over trivialities and proving by this conduct how unworthy they are of freedom's responsibility. When I say "trivialities," let me be very clear. It is not the disclosure that there are criticisms which disturb me. In any movement, absence of criticism means limited depth of bureaucratic dictation. But when our differences of opinion are exploited to disfigure our appearance, we must send petty gossipmongers on their way empty-handed but educated in the strength of our dignity.

I would like to directly deal with the alleged issue of disunity. The dictionary defines disunity as alienation, as the severing of parts. By this definition, we do not have disunity at all. We have instead differences of opinion, of interests, but not disunity. Indeed, I think few movements of broad scope have had some of the features of unity which characterizes ours. In looking over my schedule the other day, I found that I, president of the Southern Christian Leadership Conference, had addressed NAACP chapters in more than twenty states and appeared at its national convention three years out of the past five.[14] The chairmen of several SCLC affiliates are presidents of the NAACP chapters in their communities, and right here in Atlanta, the Reverend Sam Williams, the host, is a president of the NAACP and also a vice president of the Southern Christian Leadership Conference.[15] The NAACP has given significant legal assistance to CORE and SNCC. SCLC has contributed cash and personnel to SNCC. Beyond this intimacy organizationally, I believe a flexible unity and diversity of views characterizes our work.

And so let us stay together, remembering that we are all moving down the same road. It may be a three-lane road, with some emphasizing the way of litigation and mobilizing forces for meaningful legislation and others emphasizing the way of nonviolent direct action and others moving through research and education and building up forces to prepare the Negro for the challenge of a highly urbanized society.

---

14. King delivered addresses at the 1956, 1957, and 1959 NAACP conventions ("The Montgomery Story," Address Delivered at the Forty-seventh Annual NAACP Convention, 27 June 1956, in *Papers* 3:299–310; "Remarks in Acceptance of the Forty-second Springarn Medal at the Forty-eighth Annual NAACP Convention," 28 June 1957, in *Papers* 4:228–233; Address at the Fiftieth Annual NAACP Convention, 17 July 1959, in *Papers* 5:245–249).

15. Samuel Woodrow Williams (1912–1970) also cotaught a philosophy course with King at Morehouse College in 1961–1962 (see King to Mays, 1 August 1961, p. 258 in this volume).

But we are all moving down the same road toward the same beautiful city of freedom and first-class citizenship. [*applause*] (*And we'll achieve it?*) [*applause*]

Another myth that is alive today—this is the last one that I would like to discuss—is the idea that nonviolent direct action is weak, is a weak and ineffective method that lulls people to sleep. How this idea ever emerged is strange indeed. Can one honestly refer to the fifty thousand Negroes of Montgomery, Alabama, the thousands of sit-inners and the hundreds of freedom riders as weak and asleep? Of course not, and so this method is for the strong and well-disciplined. It does not overlook the need for court action; only the misinformed and short-sighted would seek to minimize the importance of litigation. Many of the current breakthroughs have come because of the groundwork laid by the diligent work through the courts across the years, and so nonviolent direct action should not minimize work through the courts. But it recognizes that legislation and court orders can only declare rights; they can never thoroughly deliver them. Only when the people themselves begin to act are rights on paper given life blood. A catalyst is needed to breathe life experience into a judicial decision by the persistent exercise of the rights until they become usual and ordinary in human conduct.

The method of nonviolent direct action is also effective in that it has a way of disarming the opponent. It exposes his moral defenses; it weakens his morale; and at the same time, it works on his conscience, and he just doesn't know what to do. If he seeks to beat you, you develop the capacity to accept it without retaliation. If he doesn't beat you, fine. If he doesn't put you in jail, wonderful; nobody likes to go to jail who has any sense. If he puts you in jail, you go in that jail and transform it from a dungeon of shame to a haven of freedom and human dignity. [*applause*] Even if he tries to kill you [*applause*], even if he tries to kill you, you develop the quiet courage of dying if necessary without killing. And he just doesn't know how to handle it.[16]

And then this method also makes it possible for the individual to struggle to secure moral ends through moral means.[17] There has been a long debate through, in history on the whole question of ends and means. There have been those, from Machiavelli on down, who argued that the end justifies the means.[18] Sometimes, systems of government will argue this, and I think this is the great weakness of Communism. Communism says somewhere that the end justifies the means. Read Lenin and you will hear him saying that "Lying, deceit, and even violence are justifiable means for the achievement of the end of the classless society."[19] This is where we would break with Communism and any movement that would argue that the end justifies the means, because the end is pre-existent in the means. The means represent the ideal in the making and the end in process. In the long run of history, destructive means cannot bring about constructive ends. Immoral methods cannot achieve moral goals, and we must work to secure moral ends through moral means.

---

16. King used this explanation of the method of nonviolent direct action in "The Future of Race Relations in the United States," a speech delivered at Dartmouth College on 23 May 1962.

17. Immanuel Kant, *The Metaphysics of Morals* (1797).

18. Niccolò Machiavelli (1469–1527) was a political theorist and philosopher from Florence, Italy.

19. Robert J. McCracken's *Questions People Ask* (New York: Harper & Brothers, 1951), pp. 168–169: "'We must be ready,' wrote Lenin, 'to employ trickery, deceit, lawbreaking, withholding and concealing truth.'"

Nonviolent resistance also provides a creative force through which men can channelize their discontent. It does not require that they abandon their discontent. This discontent is sound and healthy. Nonviolence saves this discontent from degenerating into morbid bitterness and hatred. Hate is always tragic. It is as harmful to the hater as it is to the hated. It distorts the personality and scars the soul. Psychiatrists are telling us now that many inner conflicts, many of those strange things that happen deep down in the subconscious, are rooted in hate. And so they are now saying, "Love or perish." This is the beauty of nonviolence. It says you can struggle without hating, you can fight war without violence, and this is where we find the ethic of love standing at the center of this movement. And at the center of nonviolent resistance stands the idea that noncooperation with evil is as much a moral obligation as is cooperation with good.[20] Now, this is the whole idea of civil disobedience. This is probably the most misunderstood aspect of the nonviolent movement. [*gap in tape*]

Well, first I would say that a just law is a law that squares with the moral law of the universe. A just law is a law that is in line with the law of God. An unjust law is a law that is out of harmony with the law of the universe, the moral laws of the universe. Well, somebody said, "Now you're talking in religious terms, and I don't have much religion, and I don't believe in those abstract things called moral laws. Make it a little more concrete." Well, I would say that an unjust law is a code which a majority inflicts on the minority, which is not binding on itself so this becomes difference made legal. By the same token a just law is a code which the majority compels the minority to follow because it is willing to follow it itself. This is sameness made legal. And then an unjust law is a code which a majority inflicts on a minority which that minority had no part in enacting or creating because it was denied the right to vote. We could say that the legislative body of Mississippi or Georgia or Alabama which brought into being many of these laws was democratically elected. The fact is that Negroes cannot vote in many of these situations, and so they have no power in enacting or creating these laws. And therefore an unjust law is a code that is inflicted on a group that that group had no part in enacting or creating, because it was denied the right to vote.

Now, when the individuals do this and engage in civil disobedience, they do it peacefully and openly if they are in line with the nonviolent movement. Most important, they willingly accept the penalty, whatever it is, for in this way the public comes to re-examine the law in question and will thus decide whether it uplifts or degrades man. And so they do not seek to subvert, they do not seek to evade or defy the law. This would be anarchy; this is what many of the segregationists would do. But I submit to you that any individual who decides to break a law that conscience tells him is unjust and willingly accepts the penalty for it is at that moment expressing the very highest respect for law. [*applause*]

There is nothing new about this. [*applause*] There is nothing new about this. Go back with me, if you will, to the Old Testament. See Shadrach, Meshach, and

---

20. Cf. M.K. Gandhi, *Satyagraha* (Ahmadabad: Navajivan Publishing House, 1951), p. 165: "Non-co-operation with evil is as much a duty as co-operation with good"; see also Gandhi, "The Poet's Anxiety," *Young India*, 1 June 1921.

Abednego as they stand before King Nebuchadnezzar. They made it clear: we cannot bow. [21] Come if you will to Plato's *Dialogues*, open to *Crito* or the *Apology*, and see
Socrates practicing civil disobedience.[22] And academic freedom is a reality today
because Socrates practiced civil disobedience. Come to the early Christians; see them
practicing civil disobedience to the point that they are willing to be thrown to the
lions to stand up for what they believe. Listen to Peter as he says, "We must obey God,
rather than man."[23] Come up to the modern world. Never forget that everything that
Hitler did in Germany was legal. It was illegal to aid and comfort a Jew in the day of
Hitler's Germany, but I believe if I had lived there, with my present attitude, I would
have disobeyed that law, and I would have encouraged people to aid and comfort our
Jewish brothers. [*applause*] If I lived [*applause*], if I lived in South Africa today, I would
join Chief [*Albert*] Lutuli as he says to his people, "Break this law. Don't take this unjust
pass system, where you must have passes. Take them and tear them up and throw them
away."[24] We come up through history and see it, even in our own nation, for what is the
Boston Tea Party [*applause*] but a massive act of civil disobedience? [*applause*]

So, I say that those who practice civil disobedience are in noble company, and
I'm still willing in Atlanta, Georgia, to break a law that conscience tells me is unjust.
[*applause*] So today, my friends, I say we are challenged more than ever before. Let
us explode these myths. May we not let up in our determination.

We must make it palpably clear that three simple words describe the meaning of
our struggle. They are the words *all, here,* and *now.*

We do not want some of our rights. (*No*) We shall not be content with a few token
handouts here and there. We must be ever mindful of a dangerous trend that is
developing in the South. It is a trend toward planned and institutionalized tokenism.
Token integration as a good-faith start may have some merit, but it is too often a bad,
faithless, evasive scheme. It is the old resistance dressed in sophisticated garments.
It is nothing but a new form of discrimination covered up with certain niceties of
complexity. But we will not settle for token integration. (*No*) We want all of our rights
[*applause*], and we must make it clear. [*applause*]

We do not plan to run to some distant land to get our rights. We will join neither
a Back to Africa movement, nor a White Citizens' Council freedom-ride-north movement.[25] [*applause*] We want our freedom here in America, here in the black belt
of Mississippi, here behind the cotton curtain of Alabama, here on the red clay of
Georgia. [*applause*] We want all of our rights, and we want them here.

And we are not willing to wait a hundred years for our rights. (*No*) We have lived
with gradualism and we know that it is nothing but do-nothingism and escapism,

21. Cf. Daniel 3:16–18.

22. Cf. Plato, *The Dialogues of Plato*, trans. B. Jowett (New York: Scribner's, 1911).

23. Cf. Acts 5:29.

24. Following the March 1960 Sharpeville massacre, in which more than sixty protesters were killed
for demonstrating against South Africa's pass system, ANC president Albert Lutuli publicly burned his
pass and urged others to follow suit. For his actions, Lutuli was sentenced to six months in prison, but
he was released due to poor health and exiled to Groutville. At Lutuli's request, King sent him a copy of
*Stride Toward Freedom* in 1959 (King to Lutuli, 8 December 1959, in *Papers* 5:344–345).

25. King likely refers to Marcus Garvey's Universal Negro Improvement Association.

which ends up in stand-stillism. No, we are not willing to wait any longer. We want freedom now. [*sustained applause*]

Honesty impels me to admit—as I leave you in my conclusion—as we continue our struggle in the days ahead, the journey will not always be easy. Before we reach the Promised Land, we will confront gigantic mountains of resistance and prodigious hilltops of opposition. Some will have to get scarred up a bit. Some more will have to go to jail. And I do not know, maybe some will have to face physical death. If physical death is the price that some must pay to free their children from a permanent psychological death, then nothing can be more redemptive. Before the victory is won, some will be misunderstood and called bad names. Some will be dismissed as dangerous rabble-rousers and agitators. Some will lose their jobs. Some will have restless nights and will be forced to stand amidst the chilly winds of adversity.

You have been here for these days, and in a few days, you will be going back to your communities. Some will be going into the hard-core states and the hard-core communities. It will be difficult, but I would say to you as you go back, that you go back with cosmic companionship. Go back knowing that as you struggle, you do not struggle alone. We must continue with the faith that unearned suffering is redemptive and that "Truth, crushed to earth, will rise again."[26] Go back with the faith that "no lie can live forever."[27] Go back to the faith that "Truth forever on the scaffold, Wrong forever on the throne—/Yet that scaffold sways the future, and, behind the dim unknown,/Standeth God within the shadow, keeping watch above his own."[28] Go back with the faith that the Bible is right: "Ye shall reap what you sow."[29] Go back with the faith that there is something to remind us that one day "Every valley will be exalted, and every mountain and hill will be made low. The rough places will be made plain, and the crooked places will be made straight. And the glory of the Lord will be revealed, and all flesh shall see it together."[30] (*All right*) [*applause*] And with this faith [*applause*], with this faith we will be able right here in America to adjourn the councils of despair and bring new light into the dark chambers of pessimism. We will be able to transform the jangling discords of our nation into a beautiful symphony of brotherhood.

This is our challenge. Let us use this moment creatively; let us continue to work. Wait not until next week, wait not until tomorrow morning, wait not an hour from now. For somewhere there's a little poem which says, "A tiny little minute, just sixty seconds in it. I didn't choose it. I can't refuse it. It's up to me to use it. A tiny little minute, just sixty seconds in it. But eternity is in it, and God grant you to use it."[31] [*sustained applause*]

At. PHBC.

---

26. Cf. William Cullen Bryant, "The Battlefield" (1839), stanza 9.

27. Thomas Carlyle, *The French Revolution* (1837), vol.1, book 6, chap. 3.

28. James Russell Lowell, "The Present Crisis" (1844), stanza 8.

29. Cf. Galatians 6:7.

30. Cf. Isaiah 40:4–5.

31. King paraphrases an anonymous poem, often attributed to Benjamin Mays, titled "God's Minute": "I have only a moment/Only sixty seconds in it/Forced upon me, /Can't refuse it, /Didn't seek it, /Didn't choose it/But it's up to me to use it. /I must suffer if I lose it/Give account if I abuse it/Just a tiny little minute/But eternity is in it."

# Press Release, King and Abernathy Choose Jail
## Time over Fine

10 July 1962
Atlanta, Ga.

*In this statement released from the SCLC office in Atlanta, King and Ralph
Abernathy announce their decision to spend forty-five days in jail rather than pay
a fine following their conviction the previous February for demonstrating without
a permit in Albany.[1] "Peaceful protest is a part of our American tradition," King
said, and "if we succumb to this unjust sentence and pay the fines levied, we would
be partners in the crime of whittling away our freedom." After spending two days
in jail, the two were released on 12 July when an anonymous person paid the fine.[2]*

"We have elected to serve out our 45 day sentences handed down today by Judge
A. N. Durden of the Recorders Court.[3] We sincerely feel that neither of us is guilty.
Peaceful protest is a part of our American tradition. If we succumb to this unjust
sentence and pay the fines levied, we would be partners in the crime of whittling
away our freedom. Therefore, we chose to serve our sentences to give moral witness
that it is better to go to jail with dignity and self respect than to pay an unjust fine
and cooperate with evil and immorality. We willingly deferred bond because we are
concerned about the fate of the more than 700 others similarly situated. We do earnestly pray that the deeper meaning of our action may be redempted {redeem} and
reclaimed a sense of justice and morality in Mr. Durden and the officials of Albany.
Our conviction today was a mortal wound in the body of justice. Jail-staying can possibly bring justice to life again in this community."

Both King and Abernathy were sentenced by Recorder Court Judge, A. N. Durden,
to fines of $178.00 or 45 days "on the streets" in Albany, Georgia in a conviction stem-
ing from a series of demonstrations against segregation in this south-side Georgia
city.

Wyatt Tee Walker, executive assistant to Dr. King, indicated following a visit with

---

1. On 16 December 1961, King, Abernathy, and William G. Anderson led a group of over 260 to
Albany City Hall to protest the failure of local officials to respond to the Albany Movement's desegregation plan. On 27 February 1962, King and Abernathy appeared in an Albany courtroom to answer
charges of unlawful assembly. At the end of the trial, the judge said he would not make his ruling for at
least sixty days. According to the *Washington Post*, Coretta Scott King hugged her husband following the
conviction and said through tears: "I know you are doing the right thing" ("King Refuses to Pay Fine,
Goes to Jail," 11 July 1962).

2. Rumors circulated about the anonymous donor who posted their bonds. The *New York Times*
reported that local whites wanting King to leave Albany posted the bail; however, Albany police chief
Laurie Pritchett said he did not know who paid the fines. Following their release, King and Abernathy
held a news conference where King was quoted as saying: "This is one time I'm out of jail that I'm not
happy to be out" (Claude Sitton, "Dr. King Is Freed against His Will," 13 July 1962).

3. Adie Norman Durden (1898–1979) was a Georgia native and recorders' court judge in Albany
from 1962 to 1966.

King and Abernathy, that both were in "high spirits" and had begun fasting. Both SCLC officials told Walker and their wives that they would neither eat nor drink for the first 24 hours in order to purify their own sprits for the jail term ahead.

Dr. W.G. Anderson, leader of the Albany movement, pledged the total support of all the Albany community to this sacrificial gesture on the [*part?*] of Dr. King and Rev. Abernathy. Members of the Negro community in Albany were seen shortly after a mid-day mass meeting wearing black arm bands, which Walker says was a symbol of "mourning for dead justice" in Albany. The people in Albany have pledged to wear these black arm bands until Abernathy and King are free. It is their badge of belonging to the [*Freedom?*] Army of Dr. King. This could spread all over the nation.[4]

THD. SCLCR-GAMK: Box 120.

---

4. Walker contacted King supporters asking them to send telegrams demanding King and Abernathy's immediate release to President John F. Kennedy, Attorney General Robert F. Kennedy, Georgia governor S. Ernest Vandiver, and police chief Laurie Pritchett (Walker to Friends, 10 July 1962). Numerous people answered Walker's call, including Harry Golden, a prominent Jewish journalist who sent a telegram to Vandiver: "Interesting that on the day Telestar revolutionized world communication that down at Albany, Georgia, they imprisoned Martin Luther King and Ralph D. Abernathy to remind us that perhaps the time is not yet to rejoice at our scientific advances" (Golden to Vandiver, 11 July 1962).

## Albany Jail Diary from 10 July–11 July 1962

10 July–11 July 1962
[*Albany, Ga.*]

*In this handwritten journal, composed on a yellow legal pad, King recounts the events preceding his 10 July trial, resulting from his arrest the previous December. Following his conviction for parading without a permit, King reports being escorted to the jail, which he says is "by far the worst I've ever been in." Describing the jail as a "dingy, dirty hole with nothing suggestive of civilized society," King reflects on the emotional impact of his confinement: "Jail is depressing because it shuts off the world. It leaves one caught in the dull monotony of sameness. It is almost like being dead while one still lives." Despite the emotional toll, King looks forward to visits from family and friends, especially his wife, Coretta, whom he credits with providing him with "love, understanding, and courage." With forty-three more days left of his sentence, King reminds himself "that this self-imposed suffering is for a great cause and purpose."*

### Tuesday, July 10

We left Atlanta in a party of seven [*strikeout illegible*] via Southern airline to attend court trial in Albany Georgia. The party included Juanita and Ralph Abernathy,

Handwritten diary composed while jailed in Albany, Georgia, from 10 July–11 July 1962. Courtesy of the Atlanta University Center, Robert W. Woodruff Library Archives and Special Collections.

month. But if the sentence were three
months or less we would serve the time.
With this decision we left for court.

At 10:00 A.M. Judge Durham called
the court to order. He immediately began by
reading a prepared statement. He said in
short that he had found all four defendants
guilty. The four defendants were Ralph Abernathy,
Eddie Jackson, Solomon Walker and myself. Ralph
and I were given a fine of $178.00 or
45 days on the streets. Jackson and Walker were
given lesser fines and days since, according to
the judge, they were not the leaders.

Ralph and I immediately notified the
court that we could not in all good conscience
pay the fine, and therefore chose to serve the
time. Eddie Jackson joined us in this decision.
Mr. Walker decided to appeal.

After a brief press conference in the
vestibule of the court we were brought
immediately to the Albany City Jail which is
in the basement of the same building
which houses the court and the city hall.

Wyatt Walker, Ted Brown, Vincent Harding, Coretta and myself.[1] We left Atlanta around 7:45 A.M. and arrived in Albany promptly at 8:50. We were met at the airport by Andy Young, who had preceded us the night before, Dr. William Anderson and the two detectives who had been assigned to us by the city. We proceeded directly to Dr. Anderson's residence. There we had breakfast and discussed our possible actions in the event we were convicted. Dr. Anderson brought us up to date on the temper of the Negro community. He assured us that the people were generally enthusiastic and determined to stick with us to the end. He mentioned that several people had made it palpable clear that they would go to jail again and stay indefinitely. From all of these words we gradually concluded that we had no alternative but to serve the time if we were sentenced. Considering Church and organizational responsibilities we concluded that we could not stay in more than three months. But if the sentence were three months or less we would serve the time. With this decision we left for court

At 10:00 A.M. Judge Durden called the Court to order. He immediately began by reading a prepared statement. It said in short that he had found all four defendants guilty.[2] The four defendants were Ralph Abernathy, Eddie Jackson, Solomon Walker and myself.[3] Ralph and I were given a fine of $178.00 or 45 days on the streets. Jackson and Walker were given lesser fines and days, since, according to the Judge, they were not the leaders.

Ralph and I immediately notified the court that we could not in all good conscience pay the fine, and thereby chose to serve the time. Eddie Jackson joined us in this decision. Mr. Walker decided to appeal.[4]

After a brief press conference in the vestibule of the court we were brought immediately to the Albany City jail which is in the basement of the same building which houses the Court and the city hall.[5] This jail is by far the worst Ive ever been in. It is a dingy, dirty hole with nothing suggestive of civilized society. The cells are saturated with filth and what mattresses there are [*for?*] the bunks are as hard as [*strikeout illegible*] solid rocks and as nasty as anything that one has ever seen. The companionship of roaches and ants is not at all unusual. In several of the cells there are no mattresses at all. The occupants are compelled to sleep on the bare hard steel.

When we entered our cell—Ralph and I were placed together in a single cell—we found it as filthy as all the rest. However, conscience of the fact that he had some

---

1. Vincent Gordon Harding (1931–2014) founded along with his wife, Rosemarie, Mennonite House in Atlanta to support the southern civil rights struggle. Theodore E. Brown (1915–1983) was assistant director of the civil rights department of the AFL-CIO.

2. Judge Durden upheld the validity of the city ordinance under which the defendants were charged and stated that King and Abernathy were given stiffer penalties because they were "leaders" (Vic Smith, "King, Abernathy Go to Jail Here," *Albany Herald*, 10 July 1962).

3. Eddie Jackson, an Albany native, was twenty years old at the time of his arrest. Solomon W. Walker (1936–2013), of Atlanta, Georgia, received a B.A. in business from Morehouse College (1958), and was in charge of publicity for the Albany Movement.

4. Walker decided to appeal the court's decision, stating his insurance business would suffer if he was jailed (Bill Shipp, "Albany Jails Rev. King; Negroes Vow to March," *Atlanta Constitution*, 11 July 1962).

5. At the press conference, King said he chose jail "not in any spirit of martyrdom or for publicity purposes but to demonstrate to the world how strongly I feel about this whole situation" (Smith, "King, Abernathy Go to Jail Here," 10 July 1962).

political prisoners on hand who could make these conditions known around the nation, the chief immediately ordered the entire cell block to be cleaned. So with water, soap and lysol the boys got to [*strikeout illegible*] work and gave the a cleaning it so desperately needed.

The rest of the day was spent getting adjusted to our home for the next 45 days. There is something inherently depressing about jail, especially when one is confined to his cell. We soon discovered that we would not be ordered to work on the streets because, according to the chief, "it would not be safe." This, to me, was bad news. I wanted to work on the streets at least to give some alternative to the daily round. Jail is depressing because it shuts off the world. It leaves one caught in the dull monotony of sameness. It is almost like being dead while one still lives. To adjust to such a meaningless existence is not easy. It is The only way that I adjust to it is to constantly remind myself that this self-imposed suffering is for a great cause and purpose. This realization takes a little of the agony and a little of the depression away. But, in spite of this, the painfulness of the experience remains. It is something like the mother giving birth to a child. While she is temporarily consoled by the fact that her pain is not just bare meaningless pain, she nevertheless experiences the pain. In spite of the fact that she realizes that beneath her pain is the emergence of life in a radiant infant, she experiences the agony right on. So is the jail experiece. It is life without the singing of a bird, without the sight sight of the sun moon and stars, without the felt presence of the fresh air. In short, it is life without the beauties of life; it is bare existence—cold cruel and degenerating.

One of the things that takes the monotony out of jail is the visit of a relative or a friend. About 1:32—three hours after we were arrested—our wives came by to see us.[6] As usual Coretta was calm and sweet, encouraging me at every poit. God blessed my faith a great and wonderful wife. Without her love understanding and courage, I would have faltered long ago. We talked about the movement. I asked about the children. She told me that Yolanda cried when she discovered that her daddy was in jail. Somehow I have never quite adjusted to bringing my children up under such inexplicable conditions. How do you explain to a little child why you have to go to jail? Coretta has developed an answer. She tells them that daddy has gone to jail to help the people.

The rest of the day was spent sleeping, adjusting to the unbearable heat, and talking with the friends—Wyatt, Dr Anderson, Andy Young., Ted Brown Vincent Hardin and Att. [C. B.] King—who floated in.[7] Around 11:00 P.M. I fell asleep. Never before have I slept under more miserable conditions. My bed was so hard; my mattress was so back was so sore, and the jail was so ugly

### Wednesday July 11

I awake bright and early. It was around 6:00 to be exact. My back was still sore. Around 8:00 breakfast came. We had fasted all day Tuesday in order to prepare our-

---

6. King refers to his wife Coretta and Abernathy's wife Juanita.

7. Chevene Bowers "C.B." King (1923–1988), the first African American lawyer in Albany, provided legal services for the Albany Movement, the freedom riders, and other incarcerated civil rights protesters.

selves spiritually for the ordeals ahead. We broke the fast by eating breakfast. The food is generally good in this jail. This may be due to the fact that the food is cooked, not in the jail itself, but in a cafe adjacent to the jail. For breakfast we had link sausage, eggs and grits. I was pleasantly surprised when I discovered that the coffee had cream and sugar. In all other jails that I have inhabited we were not permitted to have sugar or cream in the coffee.

At 10:00 we had a visit from C.K. Steele, Andy Young and Henry Elkins, my summer assistant pastor. He had brought me some articles that my wife sent from Atlanta. They told us about the mass meeting. It was lively and extremely well attended.[8] They wispered to us that a group was planning to march to the city hall around noon.

Around noon the group did march. They were led by C.K. Steele. All were arrested—about fifty. They were first brought to the city jails. We heard them as they approached singing freedom songs. Naturally this was a big lift to us.[9]

As the group neared the jail, two of the jailers came over and ordered Ralph and I to move over to what is known as the bull pen. This is a dark and desolate call that holds nine persons. It is unbelievable that such a cell could exist in a supposedly civilized society.

AD. MCMLK-RWWL: 2.6.0.90.

---

8. A news report estimated that approximately 200 people gathered the morning of 11 July at Shiloh Baptist Church in "a 'now or never' effort to obtain [King's] release and break down racial barriers" (Claude Sitton, "Protest in Georgia," *New York Times*, 12 July 1962). Henry G. Elkins (1937– ) received a B.A. from Yale College (1959), his B.D. from Southeastern Baptist Theological Seminary (1962), and his Ph.D. from University of Chicago (1970). Elkins served as campus pastor at North Carolina College at Durham from 1962–1966. During the summer of 1962, Elkins was assistant pastor to King and Daddy King at Ebenezer. His primary responsibilities as assistant pastor were working with the Ebenezer youth group.

9. After the mass meeting at Shiloh, the Reverends C.K. Steele of Tallahassee and Robert Alfred, a minister from Albany, led a group of thirty-two in a march on Albany City Hall. All were jailed for demonstrating without a permit (Sitton, "Protest in Georgia," 12 July 1962; Howard Zinn, "Albany: A Study in National Responsibility," 1962). In a show of support for King and Abernathy, members of the African American community in Albany were seen wearing black arm bands, which Wyatt Tee Walker said symbolized "dead justice" (SCLC, Press release, "Joint statement of Drs. Martin Luther King, Jr., and Ralph D. Abernathy, president and treasurer of SCLC respectively," 10 July 1962).

# To Otto Kerner

[*10 July–12 July 1962*]
Albany, Ga.

*From the Albany jail, King wires Kerner, governor of Illinois, asking him to spare the life of Paul Crump, an African American on death row for murder since 1953.*[1] *Crump, who was scheduled to be electrocuted on 3 August, garnered mass public support from individuals, including King, who believed he had been rehabilitated.*[2] *Crump's execution, King says, "would be one of the great tragedies of this generation," and it will discourage other prisoners from hoping "they could ever return to usefulness in society." Thirty-six hours before Crump was scheduled to die, Kerner granted him clemency, arguing that the goal of prison is rehabilitation and that the justice system should "be able to hold forth to others the hope that they can look forward to a useful life."*[3] *In 1993 Crump was released from prison.*

12 July
1962

HIS EXCELLENCY OTTO KERNER
GOVERNOR
STATE OF ILLINOIS
STATE CAPITOL
SPRINGFIELD, ILLINOIS

DEAR GOVERNOR

WHILE CONFINED HERE IN THE ALBANY CITY JAIL MY MIND TURNS TOWARD PAUL CRUMP. HIS IS ONE OF THE MOST BEAUTIFUL RESCUE STORIES OF MODERN HISTORY. HIS MAGNIFICENT REHABILITATION IS ONE OF THE SIGNIFICANT EPICS OF OUR DAY. FOR HIM TO BE ELECTROCUTED WOULD BE ONE OF THE GREAT TRAGEDIES OF THIS GENERATION. IT WILL CAUSE MANY PRISONERS TO GIVE UP HOPE THAT THEY COULD EVER RETURN TO USEFULNESS IN SOCIETY. I IMPLORE YOU, IN THE NAME OF GOD, HUMAN DECENCY AND HUMANITY, TO GRANT EXECUTIVE CLEMENCY TO PAUL CRUMP AND SAVE HIS LIFE SO BEAUTIFULLY REHABILITATED FROM SO TRAGIC A [*strikeout*

---

1. In 1959 Paul Orville Crump (1930–2002) sent King a letter professing his innocence and asking the civil rights leader for financial assistance to fund his appeal. In his response to Crump, King suggested other ministers in the Chicago area that might know more about the case, such as J.H. Jackson, J.C. Austin, or Morris Tynes. King apologized for being unable to do anything further, but assured Crump that he had his "prayers and best wishes for a speedy reversal of your conviction" (Crump to King, 9 February 1959; King to Crump, 15 April 1959). Otto Kerner, Jr. (1908–1976), born in Chicago, earned a B.A. (1930) at Brown University and a J.D. (1934) at Northwestern University Law School. In 1935 Kerner became a partner in his father's firm, Kerner, Jaros, and Tittle. After serving in World War II with distinction, Kerner was appointed U.S. attorney for the Northern District of Illinois, spent six years as a Cook County judge, and was elected governor of Illinois in 1960. In 1967 President Lyndon B. Johnson appointed Kerner to head the President's National Advisory Commission on Civil Disorders (known as the "Kerner Commission"). In 1968 he resigned as governor of Illinois to serve on the United States Court of Appeals for the Seventh Circuit, but he was later convicted and served a three-year prison term for income tax evasion, mail fraud, and other charges.
2. While in prison, Crump penned a novel, *Burn, Killer, Burn* (1962), and his case became a cause célèbre with supporters like Billy Graham and Mahalia Jackson.
3. "Kerner Tells Why He Saved Crump's Life," *Chicago Tribune*, 2 August 1962.

517

*illegible*] {DEATH}. IF YOU {do this you} WILL ALLOW THE EXAMPLE OF PAUL CRUMP TO STAND AS AN INSPIRATION AND BEACON LIGHT OF HOPE TO MANY A WAYWARD BOY WHOSE ILL-JUDGED ACTION PLACED HIM BEHIND PRISON WALLS.

FAITHFULLY YOURS
MARTIN LUTHER KING, JR.

THWc. MLKJP-GAMK: Box 61.

# Address Delivered at Mass Meeting
## at Shiloh Baptist Church

[*12 July 1962*]
Albany, Ga.

*To a crowd of 1,500 gathered at Shiloh Baptist Church, King explains the circumstances surrounding his and Ralph Abernathy's release from jail earlier that day, despite their resolve to serve their forty-five day sentence.[1] A dismayed King tells the audience that he does not "appreciate the subtle and conniving methods being used to get us out of jail" and vows to remain in Albany until justice is "properly worked out in this community."[2] Within hours of his release from jail, King and members of the Albany Movement had met with police chief Laurie Pritchett for further negotiations. A news report indicated that after the two sides emerged from the two-hour meeting, King expressed optimism that "definite progress" was being made toward resolving the city's racial problems.[3] The following transcript is taken from an audio recording of the mass meeting.*

President Anderson, and my dear friend and close associate Ralph Abernathy and all of my friends and fellow strugglers for freedom and first-class citizenship of the city of Albany, ladies and gentlemen: I, like Ralph Abernathy, find myself in a difficult position tonight. Now, I don't want to give anybody the impression that I have a great joy in going to jail—and a great desire to appreciate the subtle and conniving methods being used to get us out of jail. Now, several people have asked today since we've been out, "Why do you think they did that?" Well, I don't

---

1. King was introduced by Abernathy, who hailed him as "the Moses of the twentieth century."

2. Desperate to avoid the political and media fallout of jailing King again, white Albany officials secretly arranged for B.C. Gardner, a colleague of Mayor Asa Kelley, to pay the fines owed by King and Abernathy (Norma L. Anderson and William G. Anderson, *Autobiographies of a Black Couple of the Greatest Generation* [n.p.: privately printed, 2004], p. 220). Chief Pritchett told the public that an "unidentified 'tall, well-dressed Negro'" paid the fines (Bill Shipp, "Freed by Mystery Fine Donor, Rev. King Meets Police Chief," *Atlanta Constitution*, 13 July 1962).

3. Shipp, "Freed by Mystery Fine Donor," 13 July 1962.

know; I don't have the answer. There are probably several reasons that could be given for this action on the part of those who decided to follow this course. I do remember the chief saying to me, "God knows, Reverend, I don't want you in my jail."[4] [*laughter*]

Now [*laughter*], we had decided that we would be in the chief's jail for forty-five days, and I say to you in all seriousness that we had come to this decision on the basis of what we thought was the right position to take. Last December we joined with many of you in going down in a nonviolent pilgrimage to have prayer at the city hall. We knew we were not doing anything wrong. This is a right that every American citizen should have. We were not in a parade, as they said later. We were not violent as we moved forth, but we were nonviolent to the core. And finally, we were arrested and we were convicted on the basis of a statute which said that it is not legal to parade without a permit.[5]

We felt, and we still feel, that this law was unjustly applied to all of the people who engaged in this nonviolent demonstration. [*Audience:*] (*Yes*) And consequently, we felt that since we had been convicted on the basis of a law that was unjustly applied, we could not in all good conscience pay the fine because we would have been cooperating with an unjust law.

And so we decided as we stood in the courtroom and as we listened to the decision of Judge Durden the other day that we would not and we could not pay the fine of $178. And we said, "Instead, we will accept the forty-five days to work on the streets of Albany, Georgia," in order to make our moral witness clear and in order to make it clear to this city and to this nation that never again would we adjust to an unjust law. (*No*) This was why we decided to do it, and we were prepared to stay every minute of that time. We had no idea that anything would be done—whether it would be done in legitimate ways or whether it would be done in underhand ways—to get us out, because we'd made it clear to our families, we'd made it clear to the Albany Movement, and we'd made it clear to friends that we felt that we should serve this time.

Now, another reason we decided to serve the time was the fact that 750-some-odd persons still have hanging over them these cases and these possible trials. And we wanted it to be known all over Albany and all over this nation that we were not concerned about ourselves alone, but we were concerned about our more-than-700 brothers and sisters (*That's right*) who still have these cases hanging over them. And we will not be content, and we will not cease our determined activities (*Amen*), until these 750-odd-people here in the city of Albany (*Amen*) are dealt with in a proper

---

4. In a statement following his release from jail, King said he told Albany police chief Pritchett that he wanted to serve his entire sentence, but the police chief responded: "God knows, Reverend, I don't want you in my jail" (King, Press conference following release from Albany Jail, 12 July 1962).

5. During his trial in February, King testified that the demonstration was strictly a nonviolent march to city hall "to pray and seek to have talks with the Commissioners." Albany officials, however, maintained that the march constituted an official "parade" ("Dr. King Is Jailed for Georgia Protest," *New York Times*, 11 July 1962).

manner (*Yes, Yes*), and that these cases will not continue to hang over their heads.[6]
[*applause*]

Now, after we made it clear to the chief of police, Chief Pritchett, that we had been dealt with unjustly and that we had been deprived of our constitutional rights, having fines paid against our wills, and after he had made it clear that we had to leave, that they could not hold us, that they had to release us on the basis of the fine being paid, we did not go over to some place or some corner and make a decision to leave Albany. We made it clear that we were still concerned and we were still determined to see justice properly worked out in this community.

And so we decided that we needed to open channels of communication and channels of negotiation. And we got together and decided to go back to Chief Pritchett and talk with him concerning the conditions in Albany. I joined the Reverend Abernathy, attorney C.B. King, and your own president, Dr. Anderson, in talking with Chief Pritchett.

Now, you will remember that your leaders set forth five simple yet important proposals, and these things have been offered to the city commission, to the police chief, and to the city manager in an attempt to work out the problems in this community. They have been offered in good faith.

These are the five things that you have asked for: Number one: That the ICC ruling, which was handed down on November 1 or, rather took effect on November 1, 1961 (*Yes*), would be vigorously enforced here in Albany. Now, this ruling says in substance that there can be no segregation (*No*) in interstate travel, no segregated facilities in the bus terminals, and no segregation on the buses themselves. Now, there has been some harassment at this point in Albany. And this ICC ruling has never thoroughly been enforced. And so one of the things that you insisted on was that this ruling would be vigorously enforced. Number two: You asked and demanded that if the city buses are returned, that there would be no segregation on these buses and that the police force would not seek to enforce segregation on the buses. Number three: You asked and made it clear that you wanted to see developed in this community a biracial committee that would serve as a channel through which you could discuss and grapple with the other problems that you still confront in this community. Number three, number four: You asked that *all* of the money that had been paid for cash bonds would be returned to the individuals who put up this money. (*That's right*) Number five: You asked that all of the charges against the more than seven hundred citizens of this community who engaged in the nonviolent demonstrations would be dropped. These are the five things that you asked for.

We talked about two hours with Chief Pritchett about these things. We made it clear that the community was still determined. We made it clear that [*recording interrupted*]

At. Nashville, Tenn.: Creed Records, Nashboro Record Company, 1984.

---

6. A *New York Times* article indicated that from 10 December through 16 December 1961, 749 people had been arrested in Albany (Claude Sitton, "Dr. King Among 265 Negroes Seized in March on Albany, Ga., City Hall," *New York Times*, 17 December 1961). Of the more than 700 protesters arrested in December, only King, Abernathy, and two others had been brought to trial by July 1962 ("Rev. King Set Free; Not Happy about It," *Chicago Daily Tribune*, 13 July 1962).

# "Albany Manifesto"

15 July 1962
Albany, Ga.

*Negotiations between the Albany Movement and city officials collapsed again when movement leaders learned that decisions made in a meeting on 12 July with Albany police chief Laurie Pritchett were not binding.[1] On 15 July, King, Anderson, Abernathy, and Slater King sent Albany mayor Asa D. Kelley and the City Commission the following manifesto along with a telegram requesting a "special meeting" no later than 17 July to discuss their grievances.[2]*

The Albany Movement totally rejects the response of the city of Albany toward its requests as transmitted through Chief of Police, Laurie Pritchett. We have discovered over the last six months that it is the intention of the city fathers to maintain the system of segregation throughout the community regardless of the constitutional rights and just demands of the Negro citizenry.

We have learned through bitter experience that Chief Laurie Pritchett has not the power to make or keep the decisions for which he is purportedly responsible. We submit a long history of double-talk, unkept promises, subtle intimidation and lack of integrity as it relates to the just resolution of our grievances against the system of segregation as it exists in our city; and

WHEREAS we insist it is our right under the Constitution and the Bill of Rights to peacefully protest our grievances; and whereas it is a true saying that no Negro can exercise that right without provoking arrest and conviction; be it therefore resolved that we shall never bargain away our First Amendment privelege to so peacefully protest; and

WHEREAS there remain more than 700 cases pending presently on the docket of the Recorder's Court since December of last year, which have yet to be adjudi-

---

1. After King and Abernathy were unexpectedly released from jail on 12 July, they and other Albany leaders met informally with Pritchett. King later claimed that Pritchett had approved the creation of a biracial committee to settle disputes and agreed to return bond money paid by previously arrested demonstrators, two points of contention during stalled negotiations the previous December. Pritchett, however, denied any deals were made (Claude Sitton, "Dr. King's Release Reduces Tensions," *New York Times*, 14 July 1962). At a press conference from Ralph Abernathy's West Hunter Baptist Church in Atlanta, King said of Pritchett: "The police chief is a fine man with the best of intentions but because of difficult conditions in the city he can't engage in good faith negotiations." He continued: "He says one thing behind closed doors and another when he meets the press." King also said that the "situation" in Albany "is much more serious," warning that "if the City Commission doesn't meet with us there is no alternative but to engage in a nonviolent direct action movement to open channels of negotiation" (William Hannah, "Albany Negroes Urge Mayor to Renew Talks," *Atlanta Constitution*, 16 July 1962; "Albany Officials Refuse to Parley," *Birmingham News*, 16 July 1962).

2. The manifesto was likely drafted by King aide Wyatt Tee Walker (Walker, Interview by King Papers Project staff, 11 August 2012). In the telegram, the movement leaders expressed dissatisfaction with the negotiations over the past year: "Terms relayed to us by Chief (Laurie) Pritchett are unsatisfactory. Long records of broken promises and bad faith agreements reveal conferences with Chief Pritchett are of no avail" (Hannah, "Albany Negroes Urge Mayor to Renew Talks," 16 July 1962).

cated, we demand under the Sixth Amendment, as interpreted in the Fourteenth Amendment, that they be granted a fair and speedy trial at once or be summarily discharged from prosecution; and

WHEREAS there continues only intermittent compliance, at the city bus terminals, with the ICC ruling which became effective as of September, 1960, we do further resolve that we petition the Attorney General of the United States to initiate immediately a suit pursuant to a Federal Court injunctive order to restrain public officials or private interests from interference with the use of all such facilities; and[3]

WHEREAS desegregation is the order of the day with support of the Constitution, Supreme Court of the United States, the climate of world opinion, the moral order and the laws of God, we resolve to address all of our energies to the removal of every vestige of segregation from our midst; and

WHEREAS Christian nonviolence has demonstrated its power in application, technique and discipline, we resolve that the instruments with which we work shall be those alone that are consistent with nonviolent principles; and

WHEREAS the inspiration and support afforded to the Albany Movement by Dr. Martin Luther King, Jr., Dr. Ralph D. Abernathy, The Southern Christian Leadership Conference, Student Nonviolent Coordinating Committee, National Association for the Advancement of Colored People and other individuals and organizations similarly dedicated, we do resolve to make a career, publicly and privately, that they are here by invitation and we heartily welcome their presence; and

WHEREAS in some quarters of the community, state and nation there are spurious reports of a truce, we do resolve that all may know there is no truce and we band ourselves together to do whatever must be done to deliver the death-knell once and for all to the system of segregation in the city of Albany, Georgia with earnest hope that the example we set here shall spread across the South.

THD. SCLCR-GAMK: Box 34.

3. In May 1961, Attorney General Robert F. Kennedy petitioned the Interstate Commerce Commission (ICC) to desegregate all terminal facilities, including waiting rooms, restrooms, restaurants, and ticketing areas. The ICC complied in September 1961, but the order did not take effect until 1 November.

# Address Delivered at Albany Movement Mass Meeting at Shiloh Baptist Church

[16 July 1962]
Albany, Ga.

*Reacting to the Albany City Commission's public refusal to meet with the Albany Movement and the commission's reluctance to uphold terms of earlier negotiations,*

*King reiterates his promise to remain in Albany until a settlement is reached.[1] He* 16 July
*calls on his audience to prepare themselves for renewed demonstrations, saying: "If* 1962
*they will not listen to our words, they will have to face our bodies." Declaring this a*
*"decisive moment" in the Albany Movement, King implores his audience to remain*
*committed to the end: "I want you to be committed now. I don't want you to wait*
*until next week. I don't want you to wait until eighty-four hours from now. I don't*
*want you to wait until two days from now to get committed. I don't want you to*
*wait until an hour from now to get committed. I want you to become committed this*
*minute." The following transcript is taken from an audio recording of the meeting.*

Again, I address you as fellow citizens of Albany, and I address you that way
because I no longer feel like a person living outside of Albany, but I feel like a person
living in Albany.[2] [*applause*] I regret that we are a little late tonight—at least that we
were late getting to the meeting. But I'm sure that you will all agree that the situation that made us late was a situation that merited our attention and our concern.
We journeyed over to Camilla, Georgia, where we had the privilege of visiting the
Reverend Doctor C. K. Steele and the other courageous, freedom-loving citizens of
this community who are still in jail.[3] And they said they are willing to stay there until
the walls of segregation come tumbling down. [*Audience:*] (*Yes*) [*applause*] We are
all proud of these people and deeply grateful to them for their dedication, for their
commitment to freedom and their unswerving devotion to the ideals and principles
of the Albany Movement.

Now, there can be no denying of the fact that the Negro citizens of Albany have
been dominated politically, exploited economically, and humiliated over and over
again. And these conditions exist because of a system known as racial segregation.
These conditions exist in Albany today because there are still individuals in the
power structure of this community who are determined to maintain segregation at
any cost.

But you have made it clear in the past and you are making it clear now that you are
absolutely opposed to segregation. You know that segregation is unconstitutional; it
is against the law of the land. But deeper than that, segregation is against the noble
precepts of our democratic and Christian heritage. And we want it known all over
Albany tonight, all over Georgia, all over the South, and all over the United States
that we are no longer willing to accept segregation. [*applause*]

But the thing that makes me so happy, and I think the thing that makes men and
women all over this nation of goodwill so happy is that you have been willing to stand
up against segregation courageously and nonviolently. I remember when I came here

---

1. For more on the December 1961 negotiations, see King, Anderson, and Abernathy to John F.
Kennedy, 17 December 1961, pp. 349–350 in this volume.

2. In his introduction of King, William G. Anderson said, "It gives me a good deal of pleasure at this
time to again present to Albany, one who is now one of us, pledged to stay with us throughout the civil
rights struggle, none other than the twentieth-century Moses, Dr. Martin Luther King."

3. In a show of solidarity with King after his 10 July sentencing in Albany, C. K. Steele and thirty-two
other demonstrators were arrested as they marched from Shiloh Baptist Church on 11 July. All declined
bail and were later transferred to jail in Camilla, Georgia ("King Batters 'Walls of Albany,'" Baltimore
*Afro-American*, 21 July 1962).

last December along with Dr. Ralph Abernathy to join you in this struggle, I was so deeply inspired and deeply moved by your determined efforts, by your willingness to suffer and sacrifice and stand up nonviolently against segregation.[4] Now, we've demonstrated good faith at every point. They called Dr. Abernathy and I, along with Mr. [*Eddie*] Jackson and Mr. [*Solomon*] Walker, to trial the other day. We came back. And after we were convicted and given the alternative to pay $178 or serve forty-five days in jail, you remember that we decided to serve the forty-five days and work on the streets of Albany. But they tricked us out of jail, thinking [*laughter*] that this would stop the movement. [*applause*] And when they tricked us out, I guess they thought that this would mean that we would get the first plane back to Atlanta and that the mass meetings would come to an immediate halt and that the Negro citizens of Albany would go back to their homes willing to accept their conditions as they existed. (*Yeah*) But your presence here tonight demonstrates that we are more determined now than ever before. [*applause*]

Now, we have tried to talk and negotiate. We are not a rabble-rousing group; we are not a violent group; we are not a group of individuals saturated with hate in our hearts. And so we have said all along that we want to sit down at the conference table and air our grievances and talk about these problems. We've made that clear. We've talked with Chief Pritchett, and I sincerely believe that Chief Pritchett is a nice man, a basically decent man, but he's so caught up in the system that he ends up saying one thing to us behind closed doors and then we open the newspapers and he's said something else to the press.[5] (*Yeah*) [*applause*]

And so we know now that the problem is far from solved and that we need to go not to the chief of police to talk, but we want to talk with the city commission itself (*Yes*), the chief legislative and executive power in the government of this city. (*Yes*) We sent a telegram requesting a meeting with the city commission.[6] We did this in good faith, for we feel that you have a right through your leaders to talk with the people who are supposed to be representing all of the people. (*Yeah*) The city commission of Albany, the mayor of Albany, and all of the people in the city government are not to be representing some of the people; they are to be representing all of the people. And we sought to talk with them.

They made it clear this afternoon that they will not talk with us. And they said they will not talk with lawbreakers.[7] This is what they call us: lawbreakers. Now, first we don't feel that we have done anything wrong. We know that deep down in the democratic creed is the whole idea that individuals can protest for that which they

---

4. Responding to Anderson's invitation, King traveled to Albany on 15 December 1961. The next day, he and a group of over two hundred protesters were arrested as they marched to City Hall (see King, Address Delivered at Albany Movement Mass Meeting at Mt. Zion Baptist Church, 15 December 1961, pp. 342–344 in this volume).

5. See Claude Sitton, "Dr. King's Release Reduces Tensions," *New York Times*, 14 July 1962.

6. Citing a history of unfulfilled promises made in meetings with Pritchett, the telegram requested a direct meeting with the commissioners no later than 17 July (Vic Smith, "'No Deal', City Informs Negro Violators of Law," *Albany Herald*, 16 July 1962).

7. The city commission acknowledged the request, but declared they would not "deal with Law Violators" (Albany City Commission, Statement regarding special meeting with Albany Movement, 16 July 1962).

consider right. It is embedded in the First Amendment of the Constitution and when we engage in nonviolent, orderly, peaceful pilgrimages to pray and to seek an audience with the city commission, we are just doing that in line with our great American heritage. (*Yes*) And so we do not consider ourselves dangerous lawbreakers, but we consider ourselves children of almighty God made in his image (*Yeah*), created equal as all men (*Yeah, Yeah*), and that we have a right to stand up and protest in a peaceful way. (*Yeah*) [*applause*] Now, since they refused to talk with us, since they refuse to meet us across the conference table, we must make it palpably clear that they will have to meet us in some way. (*Yeah*) [*sustained applause*]

We've tried to talk, and we've tried to negotiate, but if they will not listen to our words, they will have to face our bodies and our bare lives so that we can witness to the truth as we see it. (*Yes, Yes*) And we must begin now to purify ourselves and prepare ourselves because we must move all the way to the end in order to make it clear all over this city and all over this nation that we are determined to be free, and we must be willing to fill up jails all over the state of Georgia. [*sustained applause*]

Let us stay together, let us mobilize our forces, let us work together, let us pray together. More details will be given to you as the hours unfold, but let me conclude by saying this is the decisive moment. (*Yeah*) Let us realize that we have a great challenge and a great opportunity. And God grant that everybody assembled here tonight is committed. I want you to be committed now to go with us all the way. (*Yeah*) I want you to be committed now. I don't want you to wait until next week. I don't want you to wait until eighty-four hours from now. I don't want you to wait until two days from now to get committed. I don't want you to wait until an hour from now to get committed. I want you to become committed this minute, for somewhere I read a little poem which goes like this: "A tiny little minute,/just sixty seconds in it./I didn't choose it./I can't refuse it./It's up to me to use it./A tiny little minute,/just [*applause*] sixty seconds in it."[8] [*sustained applause*]

At. GDL-G-Ar.

---

8. Often attributed to Benjamin Mays, King paraphrases the anonymous poem "God's Minute": "I have only a moment/Only sixty seconds in it/Forced upon me, /Can't refuse it, /Didn't seek it, /Didn't choose it/But it's up to me to use it. /I must suffer if I lose it/Give account if I abuse it/Just a tiny little minute/But eternity is in it."

## To Albany City Commission and Asa D. Kelley

17 July 1962
Albany, Ga.

*A day after receiving a request from the Albany Movement for a meeting no later than 17 July to discuss the impasse in negotiations, Albany mayor Asa D. Kelley released a statement to the press on 16 July indicating that the City Commission*

*would "not deal with Law Violators."[1] In the following telegram, the Albany*
*Movement urges the mayor and City Commission to reconsider: "In the interest*
*of democracy and the brotherhood of man, we earnestly implore you to join us in*
*seeking reconciliation in our community."*


THE CITY COMMISSION =

CARE MAYOR ASA D KELLEY ALBANY GA =

HONORABLE SIRS:

REGRET PUBLIC PRESS INDICATES YOU REFUSE TO MEET AND TALK WITH US. STRONGLY URGE THAT YOU RECONSIDER AND CONSENT TO CONFERENCE. IN THE INTEREST OF DEMOCRACY AND THE BROTHERHOOD OF MAN, WE EARNESTLY IMPLORE YOU TO JOIN US IN SEEKING RECONCILIATION IN OUR COMMUNITY. UNDER SEPARATE COVER WE ARE FORWARDING TO YOU THE SPECIFIC AREAS OF DISCUSSION THAT ARE OUR DEEP CONCERN.[2]

VERY TRULY YOURS =

DR W G ANDERSON, SLATER KING, MARTIN LUTHER KING JR., RALPH D ABERNATHY FOR THE ALBANY MOVEMENT.


PWSr. DJG-GEU-S.

---

1. See "Albany Manifesto," 15 July 1962, pp. 521–522 in this volume; Albany City Commission, Statement regarding special meeting with Albany Movement, 16 July 1962. On 17 July, Kelley told reporters that he would not participate in any negotiations that included King and Ralph Abernathy; however, "any local person, white or Negro, will always receive consideration from the City Commission" ("Albany Stalemate Develops between Dr. King, Officials," *Atlanta Daily World*, 19 July 1962). In addition to Kelley, the Albany City Commission consisted of six members: James Buford Collins (1960–1971); T.H. McCollum (1962–1963); L.W. Mott (1959–1962); C.B. Pritchett (1959–1962); W.C. Holman (1962–1967); and Allen Fleming Davis (1961–1964). Asa Dempsey Kelley, Jr. (1922–1997), born in Albany, Georgia, earned a LL.B. from Emory University in 1943. For three years, Kelley worked as a judicial secretary and later taught at Atlanta Law School (1947–1948). After becoming a partner in two law firms, Kelley served in the Georgia State Senate (1957–1959) when he was elected mayor (1960–1964) and deputy assistant attorney general of Georgia (1959–1967). In 1967 Kelley was appointed director of the State Department of Corrections. After serving one year as director, he became a Superior Court judge in Dougherty County, a position he held for nearly three decades.

2. In addition to the telegram, Albany Movement officials may have sent a "Position Paper" on 17 July 1962, requesting the reopening of face-to-face negotiations with the City Commission, clarification of the city's position on the 1 November ICC ruling, the desegregation of buses, the return of cash bonds to those arrested, and the establishment of a biracial commission to discuss a timetable for further desegregation in the city.

[*19 July 1962*]
Washington, D.C.

*Despite efforts by southern members of the National Press Club to derail his invitation to address the organization, King became the first African American to speak before the organization.[1] Before a capacity crowd of 400, King calls for "full realization" of the "American dream," which is a "land where men no longer argue that the color of man's skin determines the content of his character." He dreams, he says, of a "land where every man will respect the dignity and the worth of human personality," and that one day the "jangling discords of our nation will be transformed into a beautiful symphony of brotherhood" where "men everywhere will know that America is truly the land of the free and the home of the brave."[2]*

*In the question and answer session immediately following his speech, King responds to a wide range of topics, including the federal government's role in the Albany Movement, the Supreme Court's recent ruling against prayer in public schools, and rumors of discord among the top civil rights organizations.[3] Responding to an Indian reporter, King acknowledges his indebtedness to Mahatma Gandhi, but draws a distinction between integration and independence, claiming that in India a "foreign invader is being driven out," but African Americans "are seeking to gain freedom within a situation where we will have to live with the same people the minute we get that freedom." The following transcript is taken from an audio recording of the event.*

Mr. Chairman, distinguished dais guests, members of the National Press Club, ladies and gentlemen. I warmly welcome the opportunity to address such a distinguished group of journalists. As has been said, I almost didn't make it. Just last week I was convicted in the city court of Albany, Georgia, for participating in a peaceful

---

1. The National Press Club was founded by Graham Nichol, a reporter at the *Washington Times*, who in March 1908 brought together thirty-two reporters to start a club as a meeting place for editors and reporters. In 1932 the club introduced a luncheon format featuring newsworthy individuals from around the world invited to address the club's members. Edward W. Scripps, chairman of the club's speakers committee, tentatively scheduled King to appear on 25 June, but southern members objected, claiming that King was an "extremist," resulting in an indefinite postponement of King's appearance. King was not aware of the dissention within the NPC and was instead told that a scheduling conflict made his appearance "unfavorable" (Edward W. Scripps to King, 1 June 1962; Dan Day, "Capital Spotlight," Baltimore *Afro-American*, 23 June 1962; and Scripps to King, 20 June 1962). Club president George Cullen (1901–1980) extended a formal invitation to King on 3 July 1962. At King's request, Harry Wachtel of the Gandhi Society, Theodore Kheel of the Lawyers Advisory Committee, and James Nabrit, president of Howard University, accompanied him to the event.

2. Senator Philip Hart (D-MI) inserted King's speech in the *Congressional Record* (U.S. Congress, Senate, *Congressional Record*, 87th Cong., 2nd sess., 1962, Vol. 108, pt. 2, 14247–14249).

3. An article in *Jet* expressed concerned about how King would perform on the "grueling questions" from a "crack press corps." Would he be "alert, quick minded on his feet?" After King's appearance, *Jet* quoted a veteran reporter as saying: "He's not to be denied. He ranks among the best who've come here" ("Rev. King at National Press Club Breaks Racial Precedent," *Jet*, 2 August 1962, pp. 6–7).

march protesting segregated conditions in that community. I decided on the basis of conscience not to pay the fine of $178 but to serve the jail sentence of forty-five days. Just as I was about to get adjusted to my new home for forty-five days, Reverend Abernathy and I were notified that some unknown donor had paid our fines and that we had to leave the jail.[4] As the *Atlanta Constitution* suggested the other day, we have now reached a new landmark in race relations.[5] We have witnessed persons being ejected from lunch counters during the sit-ins [*laughter*] and thrown into jails during the Freedom Rides. But for the first time, we witness persons being kicked out of jail.[6] [*laughter*]

Victor Hugo once said that there is nothing more powerful in all the world than an idea whose time has come.[7] Anyone sensitive to the present moods in our nation must know that the time for racial justice has come. The issue is not whether segregation and discrimination will be eliminated, but how they will pass from the American scene. During the past decade, some intelligent leadership in the South recognized inevitability, but others vainly tried to stop the wind from blowing and the tides from flowing. The recalcitrant forces offered such concepts as nullification and interposition along with uglier evils such as bombings, mob violence, and economic reprisals. But the idea whose time had come moved on, and over the rubble left by the violence of the mobsters, many communities resumed their normal activities and moved out on a new basis of partial integration. To be sure, the changes have been unevenly distributed, and in some communities even a small beginning is barely perceptible. Yet enough has been accomplished to make the pattern of the future sharply clear. The illusions of the die-hards have been shattered, and in most instances they have made a hurried retreat from the reckless notions of ending public education and closing public facilities.

But in the tradition of the old guard which dies but does not surrender, a new, hastily constructed roadblock has appeared in the form of planned and institutionalized tokenism.[8] Thus, we have advanced in some areas from all-out, unrestrained resistance to a sophisticated form of delay embodied in tokenism. In a sense, this is one of the most difficult problems that our movement confronts. But I'm confident that this tactic will prove to be as vain a hope as the earlier quest to utilize massive resistance to inhibit even a scintilla of change.

Now, what of the future? Will it be marked by the same types of action as the past periods? This question is not easy to answer with precision. Certainly there will continue to be resistance, but in spite of this, I am convinced that the opponents of

---

4. For more on King's arrest and release from jail, see Press release, King and Abernathy Choose Jail Time over Fine, 10 July 1962, pp. 510–511 in this volume.

5. "Another Landmark In Race Relations?," *Atlanta Constitution*, 16 July 1962.

6. After being released from jail, King joked that "this is one time that I'm out of jail and I'm not happy to be out" (King, Press conference following release from Albany Jail, 12 July 1962).

7. Victor Hugo, *The History of a Crime: Deposition of a Witness* (New York: P.F. Collier & Son, 1877), p. 429.

8. A draft of this address, which King deposited at Boston University [MLKP-MBU], included the following sentence: "Many areas of the South are retreating to a position which will permit a handful of Negroes to attend all-white schools or the employment in lily-white factories of one Negro to a thousand white employees."

desegregation are fighting a losing battle. The old South has gone, never to return again. Many of the problems that we are confronting in the South today grow out of a futile attempt of the white South to maintain a system of human values that came into being under a feudalistic plantation system and which cannot survive in a day of democratic equalitarianism.

First, if the South is to grow economically, it must continue to industrialize. We see signs of this vigorous industrialization with a concomitant urbanization throughout every southern state.[9] With the growth of industry, the folkways of white supremacy will gradually pass away. This growth of industry will also increase the purchasing power of the Negro, and this augmented purchasing power will result in improved medical care, greater educational opportunities, and more adequate housing. Each of these developments will result in a further weakening of segregation.

In spite of screams of "Over my dead body will any change come," one must not overlook the changes that have come to the South as a result of federal action. There are always those who argue that legislation, court orders, and executive decrees from the federal government are ineffective because they cannot change the heart. They contend that you cannot legislate morals. Well, it may be true that morality cannot be legislated, but behavior can be regulated. The law may not change the heart, but it can restrain the heartless.[10] Federal court decrees have altered transportation patterns and changed the educational mores.[11] The habits, if not the hearts, of people have been and are being altered every day by federal action. These major social changes have accumulated force, conditioning other segments of life.

More and more, the voice of the church is being heard. It is still true that the church is the most segregated major institution in America. As a minister of the gospel, I am ashamed to have to affirm that eleven o'clock on Sunday morning, when we stand to sing "In Christ There Is No East Nor West," is the most segregated hour of America.[12] But in spite of this appalling fact, we're beginning to shake the lethargy from our souls. And here and there churches are courageously making attacks on segregation.[13] As the church continues to take a forthright stand on this issue, the transition from a segregated to an integrated society will be infinitely smoother.

---

9. King's draft [MLKP-MBU] included an additional sentence: "Day after day the South is receiving new multi-million dollar industries."

10. King's draft [MLKP-MBU] included two additional sentences: "It will take education and religion to change bad internal attitudes, but legislation and court orders can control the external effects of bad internal attitudes. An executive order completely transformed the armed services."

11. In *Gayle v. Browder* (352 U.S. 903 [1956]), the Supreme Court affirmed an earlier ruling outlawing segregation in the Montgomery, Alabama, bus system. *Morgan v. Virginia* (328 U.S. 373 [1946]) and *Boynton v. Virginia* (364 U.S. 454 [1960]) made segregation in interstate travel illegal by integrating not only buses, but bus terminals, restaurants, and restrooms as well. *Brown v. Board of Education* (1954) desegregated schools.

12. John Oxenham, "In Christ There Is No East or West" (1908). In an address to the Women's Society of Riverside Church, Helen Kenyon, former moderator of the General Council of the Congregational Christian Churches, called eleven o'clock on Sunday mornings the "most segregated time" in the country ("Worship Hour Found Time of Segregation," *New York Times*, 4 November 1952; see also Robert J. McCracken, "Discrimination—The Shame of Sunday Morning," *The Pulpit* 26, no. 2 [February 1955]: 4–5). King's draft [MLKP-MBU] included this additional phrase: "And the Sunday School is the most segregated school of the week."

13. King's draft [MLKP-MBU] included this additional phrase: "And actually integrating their congregation."

Probably the most powerful force that is breaking down the barriers of segregation is a new determination of the Negro himself. For many years, the Negro tacitly
accepted segregation. He often, he was often the victim of stagnant passivity and
deadening complacency. And while there were always solo voices in the Negro community crying out against segregation, conditions of fear and apathy made it difficult
to develop a mass chorus. But through the forces of history, something happened to
the Negro. The social upheavals of two world wars, the Great Depression, and the
spread of the automobile have made it possible and necessary for the Negro to move
away from his former isolation on the rural plantation. The decline of agriculture
and parallel growth of industry have drawn large numbers of Negroes to urban
centers and brought about a gradual improvement in their economic status. New
contacts have led to a broader, a broadened outlook and new possibilities for educational advance.

Once plagued with a tragic sense of inferiority resulting from the crippling effects
of slavery and segregation, the Negro has now been driven to re-evaluate himself. He
has come to feel that he is somebody, and with this new sense of somebody-ness and
self-respect, a new Negro has emerged with a new determination to achieve freedom
and human dignity whatever the cost may be.[14]

This is the true meaning of the struggle that is taking place in the South today.
One cannot understand the Montgomery bus boycott and the sit-ins without understanding that there is a new Negro on the scene with a new sense of dignity and destiny. And thousands of Negroes have come to see that it is ultimately more honorable
to suffer indignity than accept segregation and humiliation.

A special feature of our struggle is its universal quality. Every social strata is
involved, every age—children, teenagers, adults, and senior citizens. The whole
nation was startled by the Montgomery bus boycott in 1956 chiefly because every
Negro allied himself in the cause with firm discipline. The same universal involvement is now appearing in Albany, Georgia. Last December, more than seven hundred Negroes from this community willingly went to jail to create an effective protest. I shall never forget this experience in which elderly women over seventy, young
teenagers, and middle-aged adults crowded the jail cells—some with professional
degrees in medicine, law, and education; some simple housekeepers and laborers;
others from business—all differences of age and social status but all united around
one objective. This is a powerful, growing force which no society may wisely ignore.

Fortunately, the Negro has been willing to grapple with a creative and powerful
force in his struggle for racial justice: namely, nonviolent resistance. This does not
mean that a new method has come into being to serve as a substitute for litigation
and legislation. Certainly, we must continue to work through the courts and legislative channels. But those who adhere to the method of nonviolent direct action rec-

14. In his essay "The New Negro," Alain LeRoy Locke noted a psychological shift in the black community "from social disillusionment to race pride, from the sense of social debt to the responsibilities
of social contribution, and offsetting the necessary working and commonsense acceptance of restricted
conditions, the belief in ultimate esteem and recognition." The end result, Locke argued, is that "the
Negro to-day wishes to be known for what he is," not the "sick man of American Democracy" (Locke,
"The New Negro," in *The New Negro: An Interpretation*, ed. Alain Locke [New York: Albert and Charles
Boni, 1925], p. 11).

ognize that legislation and court orders tend only to declare rights; they can never thoroughly deliver them. And only when the people themselves begin to act are rights on paper given life blood. A catalyst is needed to breathe life experience into a judicial decision by the persistent exercise of the rights until they become usual and ordinary in human conduct.

The method of nonviolent resistance is effective in that it has a way of disarming the opponent. It exposes his moral defenses, it weakens his morale, and at the same time it works on his conscience. It also makes it possible for the individual to struggle to secure moral ends through moral means. One of the most persistent philosophical debates of the centuries has been over the question of ends and means. There have been those from Machiavelli on down who have argued that the end justifies the means.[15] This I feel is one of the greatest tragedies of Communism. Read Lenin as he says, "Lying, deceit, and violence are justifiable means to bring about the end of a classless society."[16] This is where nonviolence breaks with Communism and any other method which contends that the end justifies the means. In a real sense, the means represent the ideal in the making and the end in process. And so in the long run, destructive means cannot bring about constructive ends, because the end is pre-existent in the means.

Nonviolent resistance also provides a creative force through which men can channelize their discontent. It does not require that they abandon their discontent. This discontent is sound and healthy, but nonviolence saves it from degenerating into morbid bitterness and hatred. Hate is always tragic. It is as injurious to the hater as it is to the hated.[17] Psychiatrists are telling us now that many of the inner conflicts and strange things that happen in the subconscious are rooted in hate. And so they are now saying, "Love or perish." This is the beauty of nonviolence. It says you can struggle without hating; you can fight war without violence. And it is my great hope that as the Negro plunges deeper into the quest for freedom, he will plunge even deeper into the philosophy of nonviolence.

As a race, we must work passionately and unrelentingly for first-class citizenship, but we must never use second-class methods to gain it. As I've said so often, we must never succumb to the temptation of using violence in our struggle, for if this happens, unborn generations will be the recipients of a long and desolate night of bitterness, and our chief legacy to the future will be an endless reign of meaningless chaos.[18] The nonviolent resisters can summarize their message in the following simple terms: We will take direct action against injustice without waiting for other

---

15. Niccolò Machiavelli (1469–1527) was an Italian philosopher best known for his contribution to political theory.

16. Robert J. McCracken, *Questions People Ask* (New York: Harper & Brothers, 1951), pp. 168–169: "'We must be ready,' wrote Lenin, 'to employ trickery, deceit, lawbreaking, withholding and concealing truth.'"

17. In King's draft [MLKP-MBU], this sentence was followed by: "It distorts the personality and scars the soul."

18. King's draft [MLKP-MBU] included the following sentences: "I feel that this way of nonviolence is vital because it is the only way to re-establish the broken community. It is the method which seeks to implement the just law by appealing to the conscience of the great decent majority who through blindness, fear, pride, or irrationality have allowed their consciences to sleep."

agencies to act. We will not obey unjust laws or submit to unjust practices. We will do this peacefully and openly because our aim is to persuade. We adopt the means of nonviolence because our end is a community at peace with itself. We will try to persuade with our words but if our words fail, we will try to persuade with our acts. We will always be willing to talk and seek fair compromise, but we are ready to suffer when necessary and even risk our lives to become witnesses to the truth as we see it.[19]

This approach to the problem is not without successful precedent. We have the magnificent example of Mohandas K. Gandhi, who challenged the might of the British Empire and won independence for his people by using only the weapons of truth, noninjury, courage, and soul force. Today we have the noble example of thousands of Negro students who have nonviolently challenged the principalities of segregation. Their courageous and disciplined activities have come as a refreshing oasis in a desert sweltering with the heat of injustice. They have taken the whole nation back to those great wells of democracy which were dug deep by the founding fathers in the formulation of the Constitution and the Declaration of Independence. And I believe that one day, all of America will be proud of their achievements.[20]

Along with our continued efforts in nonviolent direct action, we are determined to extend our exercise of constitutional privileges to areas heretofore neglected, particularly in the exercise of the ballot. We are embarked upon a campaign to involve millions of Negroes in the use of the franchise. Some of our workers have already suffered violence and arrests for their efforts, but we will continue. We believe that with our intensified actions, a correspondingly expanded federal government program of vigorous law enforcement is indispensable. A number of administrative initiatives have been useful, and the present Justice Department has certainly moved with forthrightness and concern in the sensitive area of voter registration.[21] But the coming period will undoubtedly require that the Justice Department utilize the Civil Rights Act of 1960 extensively and seek court-appointed referees in thousands of communities in which the right to vote is brutally denied to Negroes.[22]

Now, I have spent most of my time talking about the problem as it exists in the

---

19. King included a similar discussion of the fundamentals of nonviolent resistance in his 1958 book *Stride Toward Freedom: The Montgomery Story* (New York: Harper & Row, 1958), p. 216.

20. This paragraph in King's draft [MLKP-MBU] was slightly different: "This approach to the problem is not without precedent. We have the magnificent example of Gandhi who challenged the might of the British empire and won independence. for his people by using only the weapons of truth, noninjury, courage and soul force. Today we have the noble example of thousands of Negro students who have courageously challenged the principalities of segregation. For all of these months they have moved in a uniquely meaningful orbit imparting light and heat to distant satellites. Through their nonviolent, disciplined and courageous efforts they have been able to bring about integration at lunch counters in more than 150 cities of the south. One day all of America will be proud of their achievements."

21. After meeting with King and other SCLC members in April 1962, Attorney General Robert Kennedy promised action to address evidence of widespread discrimination in the voter registration process (SCLC, Press release, "Attorney General promises S.C.L.C. immediate attention to voting irregularities," 11 April 1962).

22. Signed by President Dwight D. Eisenhower on 6 May 1960, the law empowered Federal judges to appoint referees to register voters after the Department of Justice proved qualified citizens were denied the right to vote in some communities in the South.

South. But I hope this is not interpreted as my feeling that the problem is merely Southern. Indeed no section of our country can boast of clean hands in the area of brotherhood. Segregation may exist in the South in overt and glaring forms, but it exists in the North in hidden and subtle forms. Housing and employment discrimination are often as prominent in the North as they are in the South. In short, the racial issue that we confront in America is not a sectional but a national problem.

I must also clear up another impression which may have been conveyed. I have talked about the emerging new order of integration and the forces that are at work to assure its realization. From this, one may conclude that I am laboring under the impression that the problem is about solved now and that men can sit complacently by the wayside and wait on the coming of the inevitable. Nothing could be further from the truth. Human progress is neither automatic nor inevitable. The Darwinian theory of evolution is valid in the biological realm, but when a Herbert Spencer seeks to apply it to the whole of society, there is very little evidence for it.[23] Even a superficial look at history reveals that no social advance rolls in on the wheels of inevitability. It comes through the tireless efforts and persistent work of dedicated individuals. Without this hard work, time itself becomes an ally of the primitive forces of irrational emotionalism and social stagnation.

To outline the problem is to chart the course of the Negro freedom movement. We have come to the day when a piece of freedom is not enough for us as human beings nor for the nation of which we are part. We have been given pieces, but unlike bread, a slice of which does diminish hunger, a piece of liberty no longer suffices. Freedom is like life: You cannot be given life in installments. You cannot be given breath but no body, nor a heart but no blood vessels. Freedom is one thing. You have it all, or you are not free, and our goal is freedom. I believe we will win it because the goal of the nation is freedom.[24] Our destiny is bound up with the destiny of America. We built it for two centuries without wages. We made cotton king. We built our homes and homes for our masters and suffered injustice and humiliation but out of a bottomless vitality continued to live and grow. If the inexpressible cruelties of slavery could not extinguish our existence, the opposition we now face will surely fail.

We feel that we are the conscience of America. We are its troubled soul. We will continue to insist that right be done because both God's will and the heritage of our nation speak through echoing demands.

We are simply seeking to bring into full realization the American dream, a dream yet unfulfilled—a dream of equality of opportunity, of privilege and property widely distributed. A dream of a land where men no longer argue that the color of a man's skin determines the content of his character. A dream of a land where every man will respect the dignity and the worth of human personality. This is a dream, and when it is realized, the jangling discords of our nation will be transformed into a beautiful

---

23. An English philosopher and sociologist, Spencer (1820–1903) applied evolutionary theory to society, arguing that the most successful and happy societies were those that celebrated equal freedom and valued morality and justice.

24. King's draft [MLKP-MBU] included an additional sentence: "Yet we are not passively waiting for a deliverance to come from others moved by their pity for us."

symphony of brotherhood, and men everywhere will know that America is truly the land of the free and the home of the brave.[25] [*applause*]

[*George Cullen*]: Doctor, we'll get you right off to a good hot question here. The press reports that you used your influence to obtain a preferment for a bank charter with the Federal Home Loan Bank. Will you please explain fully your intersession and why?

[*King*]: I did make a telephone call to Mr. [*Joseph P.*] McMurray, the head of the Home Loan Bank Board some months ago on behalf of the Franklin Savings and Loan Association of Miami, Florida. A group came to me from this association expressing their interest in getting the charter, stating that there was no fiscal institution in the Negro community of Miami and stating that the board was interracial. After I talked with them, I felt that this was a worthwhile venture, I felt that there was a real need for a fiscal institution in that community, something that I have stressed over and over again that we must develop thrift, we must save and lift ourselves by our own economic bootstraps at points. So that because of my interest in seeing this and because of the fact that I do not know of any strong interracial savings and loan association in the South, I felt that it was something worthwhile. I simply called Mr. McMurray to make a character recommendation since I knew some of the men on the board and knew that they were men of great and genuine integrity. I also felt that this would be a new level in race relations with an interracial group in the South forming a savings and loan association. At that time, I did not know that another group was seeking a charter. It was only a month later, when I was in Miami addressing the AFL-CIO convention that I discovered that another group was competing or seeking a charter. So when I made the call to Mr. McMurray, I had no knowledge of another group.[26]

---

25. On a draft deposited at Atlanta University Center [MCMLK-RWWL], King handwrote an alternative ending: "With this faith and determination we will continue to work for a great America. With this faith we will go on to make not only a stride toward freedom, but a stride into freedom. With this faith we will be able to carve a tunnel of hope through the mountain of despair. With this faith we will be able to transform the jankling discord of our nation into a beautiful symphony of brotherhood, every man will be men all over the land will and men all over this vast land will 'do justly, love mercy, and walk humbly with their God;' and every man will respect the dignity and worthy of human personality. When this is realized men everywhere will know that America is the truely the land of the free and the home of the brave."

26. Edward Graham, pastor of Mount Zion Baptist Church in Miami, Florida, and Donald Van Koughnet, lawyer for the Franklin Savings and Loan Association, solicited King's assistance in securing a charter from the Federal Home Loan Bank Board (Graham to King, 20 July 1961; Van Koughnet to King, 9 August 1961). After allegations of misconduct were levied against King by the Roosevelt Savings and Loan Association, a group also competing for a charter, King defended his intervention: "The call I made to Mr. McMurray was nothing more than a character recommendation, something I am called on to do every week. There never was anything secret or furtive about the call. My motivating interest has been, and still is, broadening the economic strength of the Negro through the pooling of our financial resources. I stand on the record" (SCLC, Press release, "Dr. King invites investigation," 28 June 1962). During a 5 July press conference, President Kennedy acknowledged that the White House was looking into the case, but did not have any conclusive information regarding illegal conduct (*Public Papers of the Presidents of the United States: John F. Kennedy, 1962* [Washington, D.C.: U.S. Government Printing Office, 1963], pp. 542–543). A Washington, D.C., district court judge halted the issuance of a charter to the Franklin Savings and Loan Association pending further investigation into King's role; however, by the

[*Cullen*]:  We have a question here about your speech to the AFL convention, Doctor. Would you care to tell us whether the report is true that your friend Attorney Stanley Levison wrote the speech you made before the AFL convention?[27] [*laughter*]

[*King*]:  No, my friend Stanley Levison did not write the speech that I made before the AFL-CIO convention. I don't have the good fortune of having speech writers so that I write all of the speeches I make, including the one that I made at the AFL-CIO convention. [*applause*]

[*Cullen*]:  Has the federal government been giving the Albany movement sufficient help? If not, what suggestions do you have?

[*King*]:  Certainly the federal government has been concerned. The Justice Department has been in Albany, the FBI I think is on the job in Albany right now. I do think there is more that can be done because I think basic constitutional rights are being denied. The persons who are protesting in Albany, Georgia, are merely seeking to exercise constitutional rights through peaceful protest, nonviolent protest, and I think that the people in Albany are being denied their rights on the basis of the First Amendment of the Constitution. And I think it would be a very good thing for the federal government to take a definite stand on this issue even if it means joining with Negro attorneys who are working now in the situation and not only Negro attorneys but many attorneys are working in the situation, making it clear that these constitutional rights are being denied.

[*Cullen*]:  Would you comment on the recent Supreme Court decision on prayers in public school system?[28]

[*King*]:  I know that this decision has received a great deal of criticism.[29] I would say simply that this decision was a sound and a good decision reaffirming something that is basic in our constitution, namely separation of church and state. It was a reaffirmation of a basic constitutional principle and I think the principle,

---

time of King's address at the Press Club he had been cleared of any wrongdoing ("Court Bars Permit to S&L Firm Using Dr. King's Support," *Washington Post*, 20 July 1962; "Dr. King Faces Ga. Sentence," Baltimore *Afro-American*, 14 July 1962). In October 1962, following the conclusion of the federal investigation, Roosevelt Savings and Loan dropped its suit against the Federal Savings and Loan Board ("Firm Drops Suit Linking Dr. King," Baltimore *Afro-American*, 6 October 1962).

27. An April 1962 FBI memo indicated that Levison had written King's speech for the United Packinghouse Workers of America convention to be held in Minneapolis in May (Special Agent in Charge, New York, N.Y., Memo to J. Edgar Hoover, 12 April 1962, Bureau File 100–106670–43; see also King, Address at the thirteenth constitutional convention of the United Packinghouse Workers of America, 21 May 1962). FBI surveillance of Stanley Levison also indicated that Levison wrote King's speech for the National Press Club. A copy of King's National Press Club address was found in Levison's personal collection (Report, Physical surveillance of Stanley D. Levison, 11 June 1962, Bureau File 100–111180–57/58).

28. On 25 June, the Supreme Court ruled in *Engel v. Vitale* (370 U.S. 421 [1962]) that prayer in public schools violated the First Amendment of the Constitution, which prevents Congress from establishing a national religion.

29. For example, James Francis McIntyre, Archbishop of Los Angeles, criticized the Court's decision and Maryland congressman Thomas F. Johnson drafted a constitutional amendment to overturn the ruling out of fear it would cause "a marked deterioration of spiritual emphasis" in the country (Alexander Burnham, "Edict Is Called a Setback by Christian Clerics—Rabbis Praise It," *New York Times*, 26 June 1962; James E. Clayton, "Wave of Protests Follows Ruling on Prayers in School," *Washington Post*, 27 June 1962).

I mean the criticisms have been centered on issues that were nowhere in the decision. For those who believe in God, he is still on his throne and the Supreme Court decision did nothing to dethrone God and it did nothing to say that prayer is wrong. It simply reaffirmed this great principle of the separation of church and state. [*applause*]

[*Cullen*]: Since the Department of Justice and the courts are pressing for the enforcement of Negro rights, why do you condone extralegal activities such as sit-ins and demonstrations?

[*King*]: This question will take a little longer than others because it goes into a whole matter of civil disobedience and it is true at points that in the sit-ins and some of our other developments in the South, we have broken laws. And this is a very difficult thing to understand when on the one hand we say obey the law when it deals with the 1954 decision of the Supreme Court and on the other hand we say break the laws.

First I would like to say that while we are practicing civil disobedience in the South, we're practicing civil obedience to the Constitution and the federal government. The other thing is that I believe firmly that we must obey law, laws, we must respect law, I believe this firmly but there are two types of laws. There are just and unjust laws and I don't think any moral person can adjust to and patiently respect and follow unjust laws.

Now the question comes, what is an unjust law and what is a just law and who determines this? First I would say that an unjust law is a law that is out of harmony with the moral laws of the universe. Any law that degrades the human personality is out of harmony with the moral laws of the universe and therefore is an unjust law. By the same token, a just law is a law that is in line with the moral principles of the universe.

Well, somebody would say that's a little too abstract, I don't believe in those abstract things called moral laws, so make it a little more concrete. I would say that an unjust law is a code which a majority inflicts on the minority which is not binding on itself. This is difference made legal wherein a just law is a code that a majority compels the minority to follow which it is willing to follow itself. This is sameness made legal. I would also say that an unjust law is a code which a majority inflicts on a minority which that minority had no part in enacting or creating because it was denied the right to vote. Who can say that the legislative bodies of the South had brought in all of these legislative, I mean, all of these segregation laws were democratically elected—these persons who form the legislative bodies?

Now in order to protect ourselves from anarchy, we do not say defy the law, we do not say evade the law, we say that these laws are to be disagreed with or even broken openly and they are to be done publicly, they are to be done, they are to be broken nonviolently. And I submit that any individual who comes to the point that he has to break a law that conscience tells him is unjust and willingly accepts the penalty for it is at that moment expressing the very highest respect for law. And we are not practicing anarchy, we are merely saying that there are some laws unjust and the only way to call this to the attention of the community is to break them and suffer the penalty by staying in jail if necessary.

Now of course this is nothing new. It goes back into history for many years. In the Old Testament the three Hebrew boys in the fiery furnace so to speak and the early Christians practiced civil disobedience superbly to the point that they were thrown to the lions.[30] Socrates, to an extent academic freedom is a reality today because Socrates practiced civil disobedience. We must never forget that everything that Hitler did in Germany was legal in quotes. It was illegal to aid and comfort a Jew in Hitler's Germany and I believe firmly if I had lived there with my present attitude I would have broken that law. Everything that Chief Lutuli's doing in South Africa is against the law and certainly what is more in line with civil disobedience than the Boston Tea Party, so that even this nation came into being to an extent through civil disobedience.[31] [applause]

[Cullen]:   What is your frank appraisal of President Kennedy's civil rights efforts? Specifically, is he moving ahead fast enough?

[King]:   It is very difficult to give a yes or no answer to this question. I would say first that President Kennedy is friendly to civil rights. The new administration I feel has done much more than the predecessor administration in civil rights. I would say that the new administration has created a climate of concern for civil rights and as I said in my talk I think the Justice Department has moved in a very forthright manner in the sensitive area of voter registration.

On the other hand, there are some things to be desired. The fact that the president has not signed an executive order eliminating discrimination in federally assisted housing, the fact that the president has not taken a vigorous stand for civil rights legislation means that there is still a great deal to be done and I must honestly say that I do not think the president has yet given the kind of leadership in this area that the enormity of the problem demands.[32]

[Cullen]:   Do you feel that the news media have generally been fair in their treatment of your activities?

[King]:   Yes, I do. I think generally the press has been very fair. Now this would not apply to the press as a, I mean all of the press because we have the Southern press and some of the Southern papers are fair and objective in their reporting and in their editorials. On the other hand, we know that some are very unfair and some stand in the way of progress. But when we look at the picture as a whole, I would say that the press has done a good job in objective, clear, meaningful reporting.

[Cullen]:   How do you explain the growing competition between race relations organizations? Is it because many groups want to take credit for imminent victories or does it represent a philosophical split that will retard progress?

[King]:   I do not think we have a great deal of competition and disunity as we often feel, as is said so often. I think we do have many approaches coming into being, some new and I feel creative approaches. There is no one lane road that leads to the city of freedom. I think there are several avenues but they are all moving the same way. Some may move down the lane of litigation and stressing legislation, some may

---

30. Daniel 3:16–28.

31. As president of the African National Congress from 1952–1967, Albert Lutuli organized demonstrations against the apartheid laws of South Africa including sit-ins at segregated libraries and in rail cars. In response to the 1960 Sharpeville massacre, Lutuli publically burned his pass book which dictated where he could and could not go within the country. King wrote Lutuli a letter of support in 1959 (King to Lutuli, 8 December 1959, in *Papers* 5:344–345).

32. For more on King's assessment of the Kennedy administration, see "Fumbling on the New Frontier," 3 March 1962, pp. 412–419 in this volume.

move down the lane of nonviolent direct action, some may move down the lane of emphasizing education and research and preparing the Negro to face the challenges of a highly urbanized society. But it is all moving, they are all moving in the same direction, all toward this city, so to speak, of integration and first-class citizenship. I think what we have at this point is the fact that these new methods are coming into being and we are at the point where we are trying to bring them together as supplements rather than substituting for something else. And the differences are minor, I feel. They are human differences but there is no basic disunity in the Negro struggle and in the organizations guiding and leading this struggle. I think at bottom we are all moving the same way and we are all moving toward the same goal.[33]

[*Cullen*]:   How much do you owe to Mr. Gandhi in your philosophy and technique? How well does nonviolence work here? I might say that's an Indian correspondent, asked that question.

[*King*]:   Well I would say I owe a great deal to Mahatma Gandhi for my own commitment to nonviolence. I would say that we gained the operational technique for this movement from the great movement that took place in India. Now of course there are differences and we recognize these differences. We are in a different cultural situation, the Indian people constituted a numerical majority seeking to gain freedom in a situation where a numerical minority ruled wherein in the United States we are a numerical minority. Also there's a distinction between integration and independence. On the one hand, a foreign invader is being driven out, in America we are seeking to gain freedom within a situation where we will have to live with the same people the minute we get that freedom. And so there are differences but I think the basic philosophy itself, the basic method is the same and that is that it is possible to stand up against an unjust system, resist it with determination, and yet not stoop to violence and hatred in the process.

[*Cullen*]:   Do you feel that passive resistance could be effective against a Communist state or is it only possible against nations such as the U.S. and Britain?

[*King*]:   There can be no gainsaying of the fact that passive resistance works better in a situation where you have a potential ally in the conscience of your opponent. It works better in a democratic situation where you have the freedom of the press and freedom of speech and assembly. Or it's much more difficult to organize a passive resistance movement in a totalitarian situation.

On the other hand, we have no empirical evidence that this method cannot work in a situation where you have a totalitarian regime reigning. It has not been tried on a massive scale in situations like that and I still feel that it is a possibility even though it is more difficult. Certainly it is more difficult to have a passive resistance movement in South Africa than it is in the United States but one of the only successful movements in South Africa on the part of the Africans was a passive resistance

---

33. At his speech at the NAACP's Freedom Fund Dinner in July 1962, King addressed disunity among civil rights organizations: "We frequently have different views on some questions. And thankfully, we are creative and intellectually bold enough to reach in new directions. We can and should criticize each other in fair and free exchange, but we must be watchful of a growing tendency to encourage and stimulate rancor within us by forces outside. The civil rights movement necessarily has weaknesses and the people who lead it have faults. But in the past few years, this movement has meant more to America than even its civil rights objectives" (pp. 504–505 in this volume).

movement when they had the bus boycott back in 1956 or 7. And it actually brought the government to its knees so that even in a situation as difficult as South Africa, passive resistance has worked.[34] And I believe that although it is more difficult, it may work in a situation where you have a totalitarian regime.

[*Cullen*]:   To what extent have you been helped by progress in Africa?

[*King*]:   I think we've been helped a great deal by the progress in Africa. Certainly no one can ignore what has taken place in Africa and we are sensitive not only, when I say we I mean we as a nation, are sensitive to world opinion, we are concerned about this and the rolling tide of world opinion has helped I believe in our struggle. And I think the new determination of the African people, the new sense of dignity in a real sense has given to the Negro a new sense of dignity and a new sense of, a new determination. So in short I think we have been helped a great deal by what is taking place in Africa today.

[*Cullen*]:   Well, along that line Doctor, how do you feel [*cough*] about the totalitarian regimes in Ghana and Guinea?

[*King*]:   I think it is all too easy to oversimplify this point, oversimplify the problem and to make certain accusations that may not be valid if one takes a look at the whole situation. I will take Ghana first. I'm sure President Nkrumah has made some mistakes. On the other hand I think we will have to see the problems that he has confronted. It is not an easy thing to lift a nation from a tribal tradition into a democratic thrust without having problems and it may well be that if there had not been a strong leader in Ghana like Mr. Nkrumah we would have many of the same problems there that we had in the Congo for he confronted something of the same problem. Where you had Katanga province in the Congo, you had the Ashanti tribe in Ghana and the same problem could have developed if there had not been strong leadership.[35] I am not justifying any mistakes that have been made, I am simply saying that there are two sides and I think we have to see the problems that these men confront as they attempt to lead their nations on in the modern world.

[*Cullen*]:   [*cough*] What do you think of the Black Muslim Movement?

[*King*]:   Well it's only natural that I would disagree with the basic philosophy of this movement. I have said on many occasions that I firmly believe that black supremacy is as dangerous as white supremacy. I also feel that there are certain points in the movement that are unrealistic such as the attempt to separate rather than integrate and the whole talk about moving out to certain new areas and getting a certain area set aside for the Negro to live in separation. This I would disagree with because I believe in integration. On the other hand, I must affirm this movement

34.  Angered over a fare hike for the ride between Johannesburg and the segregated township of Alexandra, an estimated forty to sixty thousand black South Africans conducted a three-month boycott, ending in April 1957 when the Johannesburg Chamber of Commerce agreed to subsidize the price increase.

35.  After Ghana gained its independence in 1957, the state of Katanga, located in the southern portion of the Democratic Republic of the Congo, announced its secession from the country on 11 July 1960, sparking a bloody civil war. Kwame Nkrumah, president of Ghana, responded to opposition led by the Ashanti tribe, who clung to their tribal cultures, by exiling members of the opposing party, passing laws eliminating free press, and authorizing the detention of dissenters. In 1957 Nkrumah invited King to attend the independence ceremonies for Ghana (see Introduction in *Papers* 4:7–10).

did not come into being out of thin air. It is symptomatic of the deeper unrest, the frustrations, and the discontent of Negro people. In other words, some conditions brought the movement here and while on the one hand it is necessary to condemn the philosophy and disagree with it, I think it is just as important for people of good-will to work to remove the conditions that brought this movement into being. And so I'm not as worried about the Muslim movement as I am about these conditions that brought it here for as long as we have the conditions of social isolation and economic deprivation, discrimination in so many areas, movements like this will spring up. So it is at once a challenge to all people of goodwill to seek to remove the conditions that brought it into being.

[*Cullen*]: [*cough*] Before I ask the final question Doctor, I'd like to present to you with our certificate of appreciation and a copy of *Shrdlu,* fifty-years history of the Press Club.[36] [*cough*] Now for the final question. Your Albany, Georgia, appearance on T.V. was very exuberant and your audience rose to great excitement. Today your appearance is subdued and restrained. Do you have a split personality? [*laughter*]

[*King*]: Well I guess I'm trying to be a strong man. One great French philosopher said, "no man can be strong unless he bines, combines in his character antitheses strongly marked."[37] I guess the strong man must be militant and moderate. But in all seriousness I don't think I have a split personality. In Albany, Georgia, I am in a different situation and we are in the midst of a great struggle and a great movement there and the conditions are altogether different. Here, I am in the National Press Club in the capital of the nation and I'm sure that my analysis of the problem and my attempt to get over certain ideas would be totally different from Albany. For in Albany, I'm seeking to develop certain decisions and I think there is a difference here between getting a lecture over and getting something else over. The dominant point in a lecture is the subject to be explained but the dominant point in a speech in the civil rights movement where you're trying to arouse people is the object to be attained and pleading with people to make a decision for a great cause and a great movement. But basically my approach is always the same in philosophy and that is that we must adhere to nonviolence to the core and I believe that through this approach we will be able to transform not only . . .

[*Cullen*]: [*cough*]

[*King*]: . . . Albany, Georgia, but the whole of our nation and move on toward that great goal of brotherhood under the fatherhood of God. [*applause*]

At. MLKEC.

---

36. National Press Club, *Shrdlu: An Affectionate Chronicle* (Washington, D.C.: Colortone Press, 1958).

37. E. Stanley Jones, *Mahatma Gandhi: An Interpretation* (New York: Abingdon-Cokesbury Press, 1948), p. 17: "A French philosopher once said that 'no man is strong unless he bears within his character antitheses strongly marked.'" King annotated a copy of Jones's book and kept it in his personal library.

# Address Delivered at Albany Movement Mass
# Meeting at Third Kiokee Baptist Church

[*20 July 1962*]
Albany, Ga.

*After the Albany City Commission refused to negotiate with the Albany Movement,
King addresses a throng of more than 1,200 to garner support for a protest at
Albany City Hall the following day. King encourages his audience to get their
"marching shoes ready" for "we are going on in the name and spirit of our Lord
and Savior Jesus Christ, believing and knowing that our efforts and that the cause
that we stand for is a righteous cause. "[1] Although King admits that at times the
outlook may seem bleak, "we will see the sunlight of freedom shining with all of its
radiant beauty."*

    *Just hours before the march, King and other local leaders were served with a
federal injunction barring any further demonstrations in Albany.[2] Pritchett, who
had summoned more than 150 police officers and state troopers, threatened to arrest
anyone who marched. Although King and the other local leaders named in the
injunction did not march, 160 marchers led by Albany minister Samuel B. Wells
violated the federal order and were arrested.[3] The following transcript is taken from
an audio recording of the mass meeting.*

[*recording interrupted*] the incomes were meager because out of a population of
400 million people, more than 370 million made an income of less than $58 a year.
[*Audience:*] (*Yes*) And yet they had to pay these heavy taxes. Gandhi looked at them
and said, "We can't take this any longer." And he started what was known as a march
to the sea—it was known as the Salt March to the Sea.[4] Mrs. King and I were in India

---

    1.  Due to an "important turn of events in Albany," King canceled his appearance at a testimonial
dinner at the Waldorf-Astoria in New York honoring Jackie Robinson's induction to the National
Baseball Hall of Fame. Wyatt Tee Walker read the speech King had prepared for the event ("It was Jackie
Robinson's Week: Honored, Inducted," *New York Amsterdam News*, 28 July 1962; King, Address for Hall of
Fame Dinner in Honor of Jackie Robinson, 20 July 1962; also see King to Jackie Robinson Testimonial
Dinner, 20 July 1962, pp. 544–545 in this volume).

    2.  At the behest of Albany mayor Asa Kelley, city manager Stephen A. Roos, and police chief Laurie
Pritchett, U.S. District Court Judge J. Robert Elliott issued an injunction enjoining a planned demonstra-
tion by the Albany Movement. Those named in the injunction included: King, William G. Anderson,
Marion S. Page, Slater King, Charles Jones, Ralph Abernathy, Wyatt Tee Walker, Ruby Hurley, and mem-
bers of CORE, SCLC, SNCC, and NAACP ("U.S. Judge Halts Albany Negro Marchers," *Albany Herald*, 21
July 1962).

    3.  Don McKee, "Sweeping Order Halts Albany Demonstrations," *Americus Times Recorder*, 21 July
1962; Claude Sitton, "Negroes Defy Ban, March in Georgia," *New York Times*, 22 July 1962. Two days
before the planned protest, Anderson wrote Albany city manager Stephen Roos requesting a permit to
march to Albany City Hall. Requesting a police escort to help approximately 300–500 marchers cross the
street, Anderson described in detail the route the marches planned to take. The purpose of the march,
Anderson wrote, is to "manifest in the presence of God, the Albany community, and the world our great
concern over the inability of Negro citizens of Albany to effectively communicate to the city fathers their
community problems" (William G. Anderson to Roos, 19 July 1962).

    4.  On 12 March 1930, Mahatma Gandhi and seventy-eight volunteers began a 200-mile march from
Ahmadabad, India, to Dandi on the Gulf of Khambhat in protest of the British salt tax. Thousands had

just a few years ago, and we visited the ashram where Gandhi was living at the time and started his great march.[5] And he started with just a few people. (*Yes he did*) And he said to them, "Now, we just going to march. If you're hit, don't hit back. They may curse you; don't curse back. (*That's right, Yeah*) They may beat you and push you around, but just keep going. (*Yes*) They may even try to kill you, but just develop the quiet courage of dying if necessary, without killing and just keep on marching." (*Yeah, That's right, Amen*) Just a few men started out, but when they got down to that sea, more than a million people had joined in that march, and Gandhi and those people reached down in the sea and got a little salt in their hands (*Preach*) and broke that law. And the minute that happened (*All right*), seemed that I could hear the boys back at Number 10 Downing Street in London, England, saying, "It's all over now, boys."[6] (*All right, Go ahead, Preach*) [*applause*]

There is nothing in this world more powerful than the power of the human soul. (*Yeah*) And if we will mobilize this soul force (*All right*) right here in Albany, Georgia, we will be able to transform this community. (*Yeah*) And we will see something new (*Yes*) and powerful, and we will be eating where we couldn't eat before. (*Yeah*) We will be marching where we couldn't march before. (*Yeah*) We will be doing things that we couldn't do before. (*Yeah, go ahead*) And so let's get our marching shoes ready. (*Yeah*) For we are going [*sustained applause*]—we are going to Albany's "march to the sea" and we expect great things to happen. (*Go ahead*)

I need not remind you again that whatever we do, we are going to be peaceful (*Yeah*), we are going to be nonviolent (*That's right*), and we are going on in the name and spirit of our Lord and Savior Jesus Christ, believing and knowing that our efforts and that the cause that we stand for is a righteous cause. (*Yeah, All right*) When we stand up for our rights here in America, we are not standing up for something that we do not deserve.

Somebody wrote me a letter—I got it just a few days ago—and they raised the question, "What do you all want in Albany?" Well, it didn't have an address on it because I would've enjoyed answering that letter. [*laughter*] I could list many grievances. Somewhere along the way, I have come to see that there is a basic hurt that has come to the Negro in the South that no list of grievances can it quitely explain. I can only say that freedom is our goal (*Yeah*), and I know that we will win because freedom is the goal of America. (*Yeah*) We are bound up with the destiny of America. (*Yes*) For two centuries we worked here without wages; we made cotton king; we built our homes and homes for our masters and facing injustice and humiliation at every point. And yet out of a bottomless vitality, we continue to live and grow. And if the inexpressible cruelties of slavery could not stop us, certainly the opposition that we now face cannot stop us. [*applause*]

And so we go on with this faith, knowing that we are right (*Amen*), that we will win.

---

joined the protest by the time Gandhi reached the shore several weeks later and began to manufacture salt in violation of British law. This act of civil disobedience touched off similar protests across India and gained worldwide attention.

5. The Kings visited India during February and March 1959. For more on King's trip to India, see Introduction in *Papers* 5:2–12. King visited the Sabarmati ashram, the starting point of Gandhi's Salt March, on 1 March 1959.

6. Ten Downing Street is the official residence and office of the British Prime Minister.

(*Yeah*) Now I know that it gets dark sometimes, and we begin to wonder how long will we have to face this. How long will we have to protest for our rights? When will they begin to listen to us? When will we be able to sit down with men of wisdom and goodwill and solve our problems without the inconveniences and without the suffering that we have to face? I know you raise these questions, but I submit to you this evening that if we will only keep faith in the future (*Yeah*), we will be able to go on, and we will gain an inner consolation and an inner stability that will keep us powerful and strength—give us strength as we carry the struggle on. (*Yeah*)

I was in South America some months ago, and I never will forget the morning that I was getting ready to leave—coming back to the United States. It was one of those dark and desolate mornings. The clouds were hovering mighty low. I was down in Argentina—I'd gone there from Rio de Janeiro, Brazil—been attending a church meeting, and for the first time in some twenty-one years, it snowed in Argentina.[7] And so the clouds were hovering mighty low, and we waited there in the waiting room of the airport an hour and a half, feeling that that plane would not get off that morning. Then finally they had us board the plane. We went on the plane; everybody finally boarded. And that big jet plane started up, with all of the power of these great jets; then it moved on down what is known as the taxi lane; then it pulled over, and as it pulled over, we heard a voice coming over the system, saying "Welcome aboard Pan American's flight 409 to New York City. Our first stop will be in Caracas, Venezuela. The flying time is two hours and twenty-five minutes. We will fly at an altitude of 38,000 feet. Fasten your seatbelts and observe the No Smoking signs until we are aloft." Then that big jet plane moved on out into what is known as the takeoff lane, and it started moving down the takeoff lane with all of its power. It moved and moved and finally it started picking up off the ground. Finally that plane moved on up, and it moved on up and finally hit those very clouds that we had been noticing as we waited in the waiting room. It started moving on through the clouds, and it got a little choppy and turbulent, and in spite of this it was still going on up. (*Yeah*) It moved on, and still a little choppy and turbulent, but it still moved on, and finally it got way up. And I was reading a book and I heard a voice saying, "We have now reached our cruising altitude. We're getting ready to serve breakfast." (*Yeah*) And I looked out, and I looked beneath, and I could see nothing but the shining, silvery sheets of the clouds. I looked up, and I could see nothing but the dark, deep shadows of blue. Then I looked out, and I saw something else. I saw the radiant sun shining with all of its scintillating beauty. (*Yeah*) And I said to myself, "This is an analogy to life. Just a few minutes ago it was dark. (*Amen*) We couldn't see anything. (*Amen, Yes*) We didn't know whether we would get off. (*Yes*) But then we moved on out of the taxi lane into the takeoff lane and took off, and now the sun is shining." (*Yeah*)

And I say to you tonight, my friends (*That's good*), as I try to talk with you on the eve of a great action movement, don't despair. (*Yeah*) It may look dark now. (*Yeah*) Maybe we don't know what tomorrow and the next day will bring. (*Yeah*) But if you will move on out of the taxi lane of your own despair (*Yeah*), move out of the taxi lane of your worries and your fears (*Yeah*), and get out in the takeoff lane and move out on the wings of faith (*Yeah*), we will be able to move up through the clouds of disap-

---

7.   King attended the Baptist World Alliance conference in Rio de Janeiro from 28 June to 3 July 1960.

pointment. (*Yeah*) We will be able to face the dangers that lie ahead. (*Yeah*) We will be able to move through the clouds that may be gathered by state patrolmen. (*Yeah*) Then we will get up to a point and we will see the sunlight of freedom shining with all of its radiant beauty. (*Yeah*) This is what Longfellow meant, I believe, when he said:

> Be still, sad heart! and cease repining; (*Yeah*)
> For behind the dark cloud the sun is still shining; (*Yeah*)
> Thy fate is the common fate of all, (*Preach*)
> Into each life some rain must fall, (*Yeah*)
> Some days must be dark and dreary.[8] (*Yeah*)

Get on your walking shoes. (*Yeah*) Live together children. Don't you get weary! (*Yeah*) [*enthusiastic applause*] There's a great camp meeting.[9] [*sustained applause*] [*audience sings "We Shall Overcome."*]

At. Nashville, Tenn.: Creed Records, Nashboro Record Company, 1984.

---

8. Cf. Henry Wadsworth Longfellow's "The Rainy Day" (1842).

9. King paraphrases the lyrics of the spiritual "There's a Great Camp Meeting": "Walk together children/Don't you get weary/There's a great camp meeting in the Promised Land."

# To Jackie Robinson Testimonial Dinner

20 July 1962
Albany, Ga.

*Sending his regrets, King writes that he will be unable to speak at the Jackie Robinson Testimonial Dinner that evening.*[1]

THE JACIE ROBINSON TESTIMONIAL DINNER =
CARE REV WYATT T WALKER WALDORF-ASTORIA HOTEL
SUITE 14-R NYK =

WARMEST HEARTFELT GREETINGS TO ALL OF YOU ASSEMBLED ON THIS AUSPICIOUS OCASION. AN IMPORTANT TURN OF EVENTS IN ALBANY, = GEORGIA MADE IT IMPERATIVE FOR ME TO RETURN HERE IMMEDIATELY.[2]

HAD LOOKED FORWARD WITH GREAT ANTICIPATION TO BEING WITH YOU TONIGHT. CAN THINK OF NOTHING I REGRET MORE THAN HAVING TO MISS THIS OPPORTUNITY

---

1. The dinner was in honor of Robinson's election into the National Baseball Hall of Fame. All the estimated $20,000 proceeds from the dinner benefited SCLC's voter registration efforts.

2. When King sent this telegram, he and other Albany leaders were planning a mass demonstration for 21 July.

TO PERSONALLY JOIN WITH YOU IN THIS TESTIMONIAL TO ONE OF THE TRULY GREAT 22 July
MEN OF OUR NATION=[3] 1962

MARTIN LUTHER KING, JR. =

PWSr. JaRP-DLC.

---

3. Though King's name remained on the event program, in his absence Wyatt Tee Walker, who already was scheduled to attend, read King's prepared remarks (Program, "Jackie Robinson Hall of Fame Dinner," 20 July 1962; King, Address for Hall of Fame Dinner in Honor of Jackie Robinson, 20 July 1962; "It Was Jackie Robinson's Week," *New York Amsterdam News*, 28 July 1962). King's biweekly column in the *New York Amsterdam News* on 4 August 1962 was a tribute to Robinson (King, "People in Action: Hall of Famer").

# Press Conference Regarding Albany Injunction

[*22 July 1962*]
Albany, Ga.

*At a press conference held in W. G. Anderson's backyard, King and Anderson respond to the 20 July injunction banning leaders of the Albany Movement from participating in public protests, demonstrations, and marches in Albany. While vowing to obey the court order "out of our respect for the leadership of the federal judiciary," they insist they will continue to "work vigorously in higher courts to have said order dissolved."[1] They also clarify that the order is applicable to leaders only and that nothing will be done to "discourage the community at large from seeking their self-respect and human dignity."[2] The Albany Movement issued a press release of this statement. The following transcript is taken from NBC film footage of the press conference.*

[*gap in film*] However, in spite of the reactionary tendencies of some few federal judges, the judicial branch of our government has been the one branch of our republic that has given consistent, dynamic, and forthright leadership in this tense period of transition. Out of our respect for the leadership of the federal judiciary,

---

1. In response to a petition filed by lawyers of the Albany Movement, chief judge Elbert P. Tuttle of the Fifth Circuit overturned Judge Elliott's injunction, claiming that the "trial court had no jurisdiction to enter this order at all" (Claude Sitton, "Albany, Ga., Police Break Up Protest by 2,000 Negroes," *New York Times*, 25 July 1962). In a memorandum to the attorney general, Burke Marshall casted doubt on the legality of the injunction as well (Marshall, "Memorandum for the Attorney General—Monday Report," 24 July 1962).

2. On the evening of 21 July, 161 demonstrators defied the order and were arrested for marching to Albany City Hall (Claude Sitton, "Dr. King Denounces U.S. Judge for Ban on Georgia Protest," *New York Times*, 23 July 1962).

the enjoined parties and organizations have agreed to obey the order issued by Judge Elliot and to work vigorously in higher courts to have said order dissolved.[3]

We assume that the order applies to the defendants and those who are working in direct concert with them and is not applicable to the entire Negro community. Moreover, we sense an irrepressible desire among the Negroes in the Albany community to continue their movement for freedom. We respect this community aspiration certainly at least as much as we respect the temporary order. Therefore, we cannot rightfully consider the restraining order to be applicable to the city at large. We, as defendants, do not feel any responsibility to conduct any campaigns to discourage the community at large from seeking their self-respect and human dignity.

We still feel it is tragic that the city officials of Albany, Georgia, are laboring under the illusion that the legitimate aspirations of the Negro community for freedom and human dignity can be snuffed out by a series of evasions and legal maneuvers. History has proven that a movement for freedom cannot be enjoined. Reasonable and responsible public officials would have sought a just resolution to these grievances long ago.

In such a moment as this, we believe that men of goodwill and firm moral conviction must take, make their voices heard. Surely there are many such white persons in Albany, and we call upon them to join with us in this search for a community of justice, mutual respect, and brotherhood, urging them to use every means of influence at their command.

---

3. According to a news report, King told reporters: "We regret to say that recent events have revealed to us that there are some federal judges in the South who are engaged in a conspiracy with state and local political leaders to maintain the evil system of segregation." When pressed further to comment on whether Judge Elliott was part of the conspiracy, King said: "I would not go so far as to say that he is engaged in a conspiracy to the extent that some others are" (Bill Hannah, "Albany Ban Is Unjust, King Says," *Atlanta Constitution*, 23 July 1962).

## To Robert F. Kennedy

[*23 July 1962*]
[*Albany, Ga.*]

*King, Anderson, and James Forman of SNCC inform Attorney General Kennedy of the "inhumane treatment and unhealthy conditions" at Mitchell County Jail where twenty-one demonstrators were being held.[1] Assistant Attorney General Burke*

---

1. In protest of King's jailing on 10 July, thirty-two demonstrators were arrested at Albany City Hall. The eleven youths involved were sent to the Juvenile Detention Center in Camilla, and the remaining twenty-one adults were sent to the Mitchell County Jail (Claude Sitton, "Protest in Georgia," *New York Times*, 12 July 1962).

*Marshall responded by stating that "the internal administration of a state penal institution is not a matter over which this Department would have any jurisdiction in the absence of an indication of a violation of federal law," but he agreed to investigate whether there was such a violation.*[2]

Hon. Robert F. Kennedy
U.S. Department of Justice
Washington, D.C.

Dear Mr. Kennedy:

Strongly urge immediate investigation of inhumane treatment and unhealthy conditions at Mitchell County Jail at Camilla, Georgia. Peaceful demonstrators are political prisoners and committed to accept jail as a matter of conscience. We insist that jail conditions for any prisoner should conform to minimal standards of sanitation and decency. Will forward under separate cover specific conditions existing.[3]

Very truly yours
Martin Luther King, Jr.
SCLC (Southern Christian Leadership Conference)

W. G. Anderson
Albany Movement

James Foreman
SNCC (Student Nonviolent Coordinating Committee)

cc:  Albany Movement
 SCLC
 SNCC

TWc. MLKJP-GAMK: Box 13.

---

2. Burke Marshall to King, 26 July 1962.

3. The leaders of the Albany Movement sent a follow-up memo to Kennedy outlining six complaints, including: "1. Clergymen refused visitation, 2. Inadequate and unstable diet, 3. No bedding and/or mattresses, 4. Refusal to accept supplementary food, 5. General overcrowding that borders on inhumanity, 6. Non-acceptance of clothes for prisoners" (Albany Movement, Memo to Robert F. Kennedy, 23 July 1962). Reverend Benjamin Gay, chairman of the Albany Movement Church Division, sent a similar list of unsatisfactory conditions at the Mitchell County Jail to Police Chief Laurie Pritchett. Gay called the jailed demonstrators "political prisoners" who will "remain in jail as long as conscience dictates" (Gay to Pritchett, 23 July 1962).

# To Albany City Commission and Asa D. Kelley

24 July 1962
Atlanta, Ga.

*King sat in the front row of an Atlanta courtroom while attorneys for the Albany*
*Movement presented their appeal to vacate the injunction issued by Judge J.*
*Robert Elliott.[1] Deciding in favor of the Albany Movement, Fifth Circuit Court*
*judge Elbert Tuttle dissolved the order, allowing the civil rights leaders to*
*resume demonstrations.[2] Describing Tuttle's ruling as "sober and sound," King,*
*Anderson, and Slater King plead with the city commission and the mayor to sit*
*down immediately as "brothers" to "discuss ways and means to grant citizenship*
*rights that can no longer be postponed."[3] Outside of the courtroom, King told*
*a reporter that city officials would be given twenty-four hours to respond to the*
*telegram, and if the movement's overtures were ignored, peaceful demonstrations*
*would resume.[4]*

CITY COMMISSION OF ALBANY, CARE MAYOR ASA KELLEY =
CITY HALL ALBANY GA =

WE DO NOT CONSIDER THE LIFTING OF THE INJUNCTION A VICTORY. WE FEEL THAT
IT IS A SOBER AND SOUND DECISION ON THE PART OF JUDGE TUTTLE TO PRESERVE
BASIC CONSTITUTIONAL RIGHTS. THE REAL VICTORY WILL COME WHEN WE AS BROTH-
ERS SIT DOWN AND DISCUSS WAYS AND MEANS TO GRANT CITIZENSHIP RIGHTS THAT
CAN NO LONGER BE POSTPONED. WE IMPLORE YOU TO REALIZE THAT OUR LIGITIMATE

---

1. Albany Movement lawyers initially appealed to U.S. District Court Judge W.A. Bootle in Macon,
Georgia, but he refused, stating that he did not have jurisdiction in the case (Vic Smith, "Judge Tuttle
Rules with Negro Leaders," *Albany Herald*, 24 July 1962). In addition to the appeal, lawyers for the Albany
Movement filed two class action lawsuits against Albany city officials. The first sought to enjoin city leaders from enforcing segregation in public facilities (*W. G. Anderson et al., v. Asa D. Kelly et al.*, 32 F.R.D. 355
[M.D. Ga. 1963]). In the second case, the Albany Movement sought to restrain the City of Albany and its
officials from infringing upon Albany's black residents' First Amendment right to peacefully assemble,
protest, and picket. In addition to W. G. Anderson, Elijah Harris, Slater King, and Emanuel Jackson, King
was named a plaintiff in this case (*W. G. Anderson et al., v. City of Albany et al.*, 321 F.2d 649 [5th Cir. 1963]).
The City of Albany filed a cross-complaint in the second case, requesting a permanent injunction against
further demonstrations by the Albany Movement.
2. In his ruling Tuttle claimed that the "trial court had no jurisdiction to enter this order at all"
(Claude Sitton, "Albany, Ga., Police Break Up Protest by 2,000 Negroes," *New York Times*, 25 July 1962).
Tuttle also made clear that his order did not interfere with Elliott's planned injunction proceedings on
30 July.
3. Slater Hunter King (1927–1969) was born in Albany, Georgia, into one of the town's most
prominent African American families. A graduate of Fisk University, King earned a B.A. in economics
in 1946 and later opened his own real estate office. In November 1961 King was elected vice president of
the Albany Movement before becoming president in 1963. That same year, he became the first African
American to run, albeit unsuccessfully, for mayor of Albany. For several years King used his real estate
experience to purchase property in all-white areas of Albany and sell them to African Americans. Before
he was killed in an automobile accident in 1969, he was soliciting funds to build housing for the elderly.
4. John H. Britton, "Injunction in Albany Is Voided by Judge Tuttle; Negotiations Meet Urged,"
*Atlanta Daily World*, 25 July 1962.

ASPIRATIONS FOR FREEDOM CANNOT BE SNUFFED OUT BY A SERIES OF EVASIONS AND LEGAL MANEUVERS. WE THEREFORE BEG OF YOU ONCE MORE, IN THE NAME OF DEMOCRACY, HUMAN DECENCY AND THE WELFARE OF ALBANY TO GIVE US AN OPPORTUNITY TO PRESENT OUR GRIEVANCES TO THE CITY COMMISSION IMMEDIATELY =

W G ANDERSON MD SLATER KING
AND MARTIN LUTHER KING JR.

PWSr. AMR-GAMK: Box 1.

## Address Delivered at Albany Movement Mass Meeting

[*24 July 1962*]
Albany, Ga.

*Immediately after the injunction was lifted, a vindicated King returned to Albany, where he spoke to audiences at Shiloh and Mt. Zion Baptist Churches. In the following address, King calls for a continuation of demonstrations, insisting that there is no shame in going to jail because like Indian prime minister Jawaharlal Nehru and Ghanaian president Kwame Nkrumah, you can "rise from prison to power."[1] Surveying the crowd, King asks: "Who will go? Who will be a part of greater ongoing movement who made God's kingdom a reality?" In closing, King insists that if Albany officials continue to deny demonstrators the right to protest, "we will have to present our very bodies and our lives and lay this issue squarely before the conscience of this community." At the end of the mass meeting, a group of three hundred protesters, led by Marvin Rich of CORE, spontaneously marched on Albany City Hall, and when police moved in to disperse the crowd, bystanders began throwing rocks and bottles, injuring two law enforcement officers.[2] The following transcript is taken from an audio recording of the mass meeting.*

Some three or four years ago, Mrs. King and I had the great privilege of spending about six weeks in that great country in Asia known as India.[3] You may be aware of the fact that India is the second most populous nation in the world. It has a popula-

---

1. Nkrumah spent a year in prison after being convicted of sedition in 1950. As the leader of the Indian National Congress, Nehru spent more than thirteen years in prison for his protest activities.

2. According to newspaper reports, a crowd of about two thousand African American bystanders had gathered at city hall. King and other movement leaders did not participate in the unplanned march. Forty people were arrested during the demonstration. The following day, King vehemently denied any Albany Movement involvement in the violence (Vic Smith, "Uneasy Calm Prevails Here As M.L. King Cries 'Penance,'" *Albany Herald*, 25 July 1962; Claude Sitton, "Dr. King Sets a Day of Penance After Violence in Albany, Ga.," *New York Times*, 26 July 1962).

3. King, his wife, Coretta, and SCLC historian Lawrence D. Reddick toured India from February to March 1959. For details about King's trip to India, see Introduction in *Papers* 5:2–12.

tion of more than four hundred million people. That's larger than the United States and the whole continent of Africa put together. You may also know that for many, many years, the Indian people were dominated politically, exploited economically, segregated and humiliated by some foreign power. So in a sense, the problems that the Indian people faced were not too different from the problems we face in Albany, Georgia, today for we too are dominated politically, we too are exploited economically, we too are segregated and humiliated on a day-to-day basis.

When I landed in India, in Bombay, we journeyed the next day to New Delhi, which is the capital of that great nation. We had dinner that evening with the prime minister, a man by the name of Jawaharlal Nehru—a great man, one of the great statesmen of the world.[4] But I want you to know this tonight: that Mr. Nehru was placed in jail exactly fourteen times in his life as he struggled for the independence of his people. The next day, we had dinner with President Prasad.[5] A great man, a great legal mind; he was a lawyer. I want you to know that as we talked with President Prasad, he reminded us that he had spent three years of his life in jail. The next day, we had dinner with a man who is a great philosopher. He taught at Oxford. He is the vice president—at that time he was the vice president of India, a man by the name of Radhakrishnan.[6] Doctor Radhakrishnan told us of hours he'd spent in the independence struggle and the times he'd spent in jail. Not long after that, we met with Mrs. Indira Gandhi, the daughter of Prime Minister Nehru—beautiful, charming young lady.[7] And she told us in beautiful terms, in joyous terms, that she had been arrested seven times in her life during the independence struggle.

Not long after that, we began our journey over that vast country. We moved into Madras, we moved into Trivandrum, we moved to Calcutta.[8] We were entertained and we were the guests of the various governors in every province of India. I didn't meet a single governor who had not spent time in jail. And out of the thousands and thousands of people that we met all over India, I doubt seriously if we met one hundred people who had not been to jail as they struggled to free themselves from the conditions that they faced in India.

Well, a few years before that, Mrs. King and I journeyed to Africa.[9] It was the first time that we had been to Africa. We went over to join thousands and millions of people in celebrating the independence of the new nation of Ghana. This was the country known as the Gold Coast in West Africa. And I never will forget that night when Prime Minister [Kwame] Nkrumah came out on that stage and stood before some three hundred thousand people. When Prime Minister Nkrumah stood there, he cried out, "We are now a free and an independent people," and I looked at that point and I saw a flag coming down and another flag going up. The flag coming down

4. King and his companions arrived in Bombay [Mumbai] on 9 February 1959. The following day King had dinner with Nehru at the prime minister's home in New Delhi.

5. King had tea with Rajendra Prasad on 12 February.

6. King met India's vice president Sarvepalli Radhakrishnan on 10 February.

7. King met Indira Gandhi on 10 February 1961, while a guest at Nehru's home in Delhi.

8. King arrived in Calcutta on 15 February, in Madras on 18 February, and in Trivandrum on 22 February.

9. King attended the independence ceremonies in the Gold Coast from 4 March to 12 March 1957. For more on King's trip to Ghana, see Introduction in *Papers* 4:7–10.

was the Union Jack flag of the British Empire; the flag going up was the flag of the new nation of Ghana. And I looked around and we heard young men and women, old men and women crying as they had never been able to cry it before: "Freedom [*Audience:*] (*Yes*), freedom, freedom." Then we looked up at, around Prime Minister Nkrumah and the members of his cabinet were assembled with him and they had on some funny little caps, and I inquired of the person who was taking us around, the guide, what did the caps mean? And the guide looked over and said, "Those are prison caps. You see all of those men went to prison to get our independence."[10] (*Yes, That's right*) Whether you realize it or not, Prime Minister Nkrumah was elected the prime minister of the Gold Coast while he was in jail.

I say all of this in a round-about way to try to tell you tonight that there's nothing wrong with going to jail because you can rise from prison to power (*Yes*), and we have something. [*applause*]

I want to leave that with you tonight. I want you to think about it tonight. We have problems in Albany. (*Amen*) God is speaking through the long vistas of eternity saying, "Who will go?" (*Well*) It is echoing through the centuries: Who will go? Who will be a part of greater ongoing movement who made God's kingdom a reality?

Now, today many of our hopes and many of our longings were vindicated. When I stood before you Sunday afternoon, I said to you that it was a little dark. I couldn't quite see my way clear. There are times that you do cry out, "Why?" (*Yes*), and I don't mind crying, "Why?" occasionally (*Well*) 'cause even our Lord and master found himself crying out one day, "My God, my God, why?" (*Why, Yes Lord*) Sunday I was crying "Why?" After we had become aroused and after we had gotten ourselves ready, [*recording interrupted*] participated in a magnificent drama (*Yes*) [*unfolding?*] onto the stages of history (*Yes*), the injunction came. (*Yes*) And I told you Sunday afternoon that we just needed to keep ourselves together and have faith and realize that sometimes the darkest hour (*Yes*) is just that hour before the dawn of a new day.[11] (*Yes, Yes, Yes*) This morning something came (*Yes*), transformed dark and desolate valleys into sunlit paths of [*peace?*]. (*Yeah*) This morning something happened. (*Yes*) It came to me to transform the fatigue of despair into the buoyancy of hope. This morning something happened (*Yeah*) that caused me to leave that court-room (*Yeah*) saying, not "Lord, why is all of this trouble coming?" Not, on the one hand, "Nobody knows the trouble we see," but I could leave crying, "I am so glad that trouble don't last always."[12] [*applause*]

And so we're all happy about the decision rendered by Judge [*Elbert*] Tuttle. It

---

10. King expressed similar recollections about his trip to Ghana in his April 1957 sermon "Birth of a New Nation" (see *Papers* 4:155–167).

11. On the afternoon of Sunday, 22 July, King and Anderson held a press conference in the backyard of Anderson's home. For the press conference, see pp. 545–546 in this volume. An Albany police surveillance report indicated that later that day King attended a mass meeting at Mt. Zion (Laurie Pritchett, J. Ed. Friend, Bill Manley, Statement of police officers concerning the demonstrations, 22 July 1962). The *Americus Times Recorder* reported that King told the crowd: "I will not go out on a door-knocking campaign trying to tell people not to take part in what their conscience tells them they ought to do" ("Judge Denies Hearing on Albany Injunction," *Americus Times Recorder*, 23 July 1962).

12. King quotes from the spirituals "Nobody Knows the Trouble I've Seen" and "I'm So Glad Trouble Don't Last Always."

gave us renewed faith in the judicial branch of our government. We know that there are some bad apples in the basket of the federal judiciary (*Yeah*), but we are happy and thankful to God that by and large (*Yes*) the men in this branch of our government are men who have decided to stand up for what is right on the basis of our Constitution. (*Yeah*) And we are appreciative of these men and their leadership in this tense period of transition.

As Charles Jones said, we do not need to go around with a victory complex (*Yes*), for when you begin to love God and when you begin to love humanity (*Yes*), you never see these temporary changes as victories for one particular group.[13] And God knows I am not interested in seeing a victory merely for twenty million Negroes in the United States. (*Yes*) My concern is that we will have a victory for justice (*Yes*), a victory for democracy (*Yes*), so that every child born in this world would be able to know that he can walk the earth with dignity and self-respect (*That's right*), knowing that he's somebody. (*Yeah*)

Tonight I would remind you that the tension in Albany is not tension merely between black people and white people—this isn't the tension. The tension in Albany is at bottom a tension between justice and injustice. (*Yes, That's right, That's right*) It is a tension between the forces of light and the forces of darkness. And this is why we say we welcome anybody in this movement (*Yes*) on the basis of conscience. This isn't a colored folks movement (*Well*); this is a movement for justice, and any white person who wants to join this movement, come on and get in it and let's get free. [*applause*]

So, my friends, we have an opportunity now—I must stress something that I always say and I never tire of saying it—so by now you know what I believe about this. I don't have but one speech. I don't have but one message as I journey around this country, and it is the message which says that I am convinced that the most potent weapon available to oppressed people (*Yes sir*) as they struggle for freedom and justice is the weapon of nonviolence. (*Yes, Yes*) Let us keep this weapon. Let's keep it in the forefront. (*Yes*)

Judge Tuttle made it clear today that on the basis of the First and the Fourteenth Amendment, people have a right to protest. And I believe this is the greatness of our nation. This is why I could never be a Communist; this is why my allegiance could never turn to Russia, for I know that deep down within this nation is a commitment to something even if it fails to live up to it. (*Yes*) Deep down within this nation is a commitment to freedom, which says that every man has a right to protest for right. (*Yeah*) And ever and again something comes to remind us that America was based and built on a great principle: "We hold these truths to be self-evident, that all men are created equal." (*Amen*) Not "some men," but "all men." (*All right*) Not "all white men," but "all men," which includes black men. (*All right*) This is deep down (*That's right*) in the very structure of our nation. (*Yes*) We have a right to do what we are doing. (*Yes*)

And I go on with a faith that as we engage in these peaceful demonstrations and these peaceful protests (*Yes*) that we are doing what is right because we are trying to say to Albany (*Well*), "If you won't sit down and talk with us and grant us those things which are ours on the basis of the Constitution of the United States (*Yes*), sanctioned

---

13. Jones (1937– ), field secretary of SNCC from 1961 to 1963, introduced King to the audience.

by heaven itself and endorsed by the forces of justice, if you won't do that, we will
have to present our very bodies and our lives and lay this issue squarely before the conscience of this community." (*Yes*) This is what we've got to do all over Albany. (*Yes*) There may be somebody here moving toward the evening of life. (*Well*) You may be sixty, you may be seventy. You've gone through the morning of childhood, somehow you've moved [*recording interrupted*]

At. GDL-G-Ar: Record Group 9.

# Press Conference Denouncing Violence in Albany

[*25 July 1962*]
Albany, Ga.

*Following the outbreak of violence in downtown Albany the previous night, King denies involvement of people from the Albany Movement in the mêlée, but assumes partial responsibility since the violence stemmed from "the ranks of the Negro community." Calling for a day of penance, King halts all demonstrations for the next twenty-four hours to refocus "our commitment to nonviolence and our determination to keep our protests peaceful."[1] While King states that he abhors the violence and does not seek to justify it, he is not "unmindful of the fact that the Negroes in Albany have confronted so much oppression" that it may be impossible for "those of us who believe in nonviolence and who give our lives to this method and philosophy to control violent outbreaks." The following transcript is taken from a film recording of the press conference.*

[*King*]:   While we are certain that neither the peaceful demonstrators nor persons active in the Albany Movement were involved in the violence that erupted last night, we abhor violence so much that when it occurs in the ranks of the Negro community we assume part of the responsibility for it. In order to demonstrate our commitment to nonviolence and our determination to keep our protests peaceful, we declare a day of penance beginning at twelve o'clock noon today. [*recording interrupted*] on all members and supporters of the Albany Movement to pray for their brothers in the Negro community who have not yet found their way to the nonviolent discipline during this day of penance. [*gap in film*]

[*recording interrupted*] nonviolence to our people with every ounce of energy in our bodies we fear that these admonitions will fall on some deaf ears if Albany does not engage in good faith negotiations. We sense a great deal of satisfaction and joy on the part of some public officials when violence erupted in the ranks of the onlookers.[2]

---

1. King and William G. Anderson also issued a written statement about the violence (King and Anderson, Statement on violence in Albany, Ga. and declaration of day of penance, 25 July 1962).

2. Responding to the violence, Police Chief Laurie Pritchett asked a reporter: "Did you see them nonviolent rocks?" (Claude Sitton, "Dr. King Sets a Day of Penance after Violence in Albany, Ga.," *New York Times*, 26 July 1962).

553

This betrays the fact that a community has fallen to a new low in moral degeneracy when it uses such an unfortunate incident for their own political capital.[3] [*gap in film*]

[*Reporter 1*]: [*recording interrupted*] members of the, or any city officials communicated to you their concern about further violence?

[*King*]: No, they—

[*Reporter 1*]: [*Any incidents?*]

[*King*]: No, they have not. I have not talked with any city officials since last night.[4]

[*Reporter 2*]: Does your statement mean that there won't be any more demonstrations today, for the next twenty-four hours?

[*King*]: Yes there will be, during the day of penance, there will be no demonstrations. This afternoon, I will go along with a team of persons who are well-disciplined in nonviolence and who are well-grounded in the philosophy of nonviolence to the Harlem section of the community and talk with persons in the business establishments there, the pool rooms and the taverns, urging them to follow nonviolence and doing some teaching and we may even have some sidewalk meetings calling for absolute commitment to nonviolence. Now, we must make it very clear that while we will not use past incidents as excuses for what occurred last night, we can give them as explanations. For we are not unmindful of the fact that the Negroes in Albany have confronted so much oppression and have been the victims of so much violence. For instance, a Negro was killed a few weeks ago by a policeman, a Mr. Walter Harris.[5] Mrs. Slater King was brutally beaten and knocked down by policemen in Camilla just two days ago.[6] All of these things developed within the people a sense of discontent and at times a sense of bitterness. And, while we are not using these things as excuses, I don't think the community can overlook the fact that that if they continue it would be very difficult for those of us who believe in nonviolence and who give our lives to this method and philosophy to control violent outbreaks. [*gap in film*]

[*Reporter 3*]: [*recording interrupted*] demonstrations as such?

[*King*]: Well I think we will have to reconsider night demonstrations. We did have some reluctance about having night demonstrations all along, and I think now we will think in terms of having all of our demonstrations in the day.

---

3. Georgia governor S. Ernest Vandiver threatened to send 12,000 National Guardsmen to Albany, warning that "agitators from within and without Georgia, and this includes Martin Luther King, that I will use all forces available to me to maintain peace" (Vic Smith, "Uneasy Calm Prevails Here As M.L. King Cries 'Penance,'" *Albany Herald*, 25 July 1962).

4. King met with Chief Pritchett on the evening of 24 July 1962. Following the meeting, King and Abernathy visited jailed protesters (Laurie Pritchett, J. Ed. Friend, and Bill Manley, Statement from police officers concerning activities of the Albany Movement, 24 July 1962).

5. Walter Harris, a forty-nine-year-old restaurant owner, was killed on 15 April by an Albany police officer, who accused him of assault with a knife after being questioned about carrying illegal whiskey. The officer shot Harris three times in the chest but sustained no injuries himself ("Protest against Shooting Jails 25 Albany Negroes," *Chicago Daily Defender*, 26 April 1962; "Negro with Knife Slain by Policeman," *Albany Herald*, 16 April 1962).

6. On 23 July, Marion King, wife of Albany Movement leader Slater King, was beaten by two officers while delivering food and clothing to protesters jailed in Camilla, Georgia. When she did not move out of the jail yard fast enough, the officers knocked her to the ground and repeatedly kicked her while she held her three-year-old daughter. Mrs. King was five months pregnant at the time and later suffered a stillbirth (Marion King, Statement on beating at Mitchell County Jail, 23 July 1962; Slater King to John F. Kennedy, 26 December 1962).

[*Reporter 4*]:   Will the demonstrations will [*recording interrupted*]

[*King*]:   I sense a real desire to at least accept nonviolence as a tactic. I realize that the vast majority of Negroes in the United States aren't going to the point of accepting nonviolence as a creed and as a way of life. But even if we sense a willingness to follow it as a tactic, then we will certainly resume demonstrations. But I must confess that if I sense at all a large-scale desire for violence on the part of the Negro community, I cannot in all good conscience call for demonstrations at this time.[7] My impression is that this is a very small minority and that the people, the Negro people of Albany are willing to be nonviolent just as they've done in most difficult moments. Night before last, after we had gotten the word that Mrs. King had been beaten, this was a difficult situation and the community was certainly aroused about this. But no violence occurred and that demonstrated, I think, the commitment on the part of the vast majority of people to nonviolence.

[*Reporter 5*]:   Well [*recording interrupted*]

[*King*]:   [*recording interrupted*] implement a plan and a program for a four-prong attack on the system of segregation consisting first [*recording interrupted*].

F. WSB-TV-GU.

---

7.  After the day of penance ended peacefully, King called for demonstrations to resume. On 27 July, King and twenty-seven others, including Ralph Abernathy and William G. Anderson, were jailed for holding a series of prayer vigils in front of city hall (Claude Sitton, "Dr. King Is Jailed Again at Prayer Rally in Georgia," *New York Times*, 28 July 1962; "28 Negroes Pray, Then Land in Jail," *Chicago Daily Tribune*, 28 July 1962).

# Statement on Nonviolence at Pool Hall

[*26 July 1962*]
Albany, Ga.

*After King's announcement of a day of penance on demonstrations in Albany,
he and representatives from SCLC and SNCC spent the afternoon walking
the streets of Albany's predominately African American district of Harlem,
talking to locals about the previous night's violence and garnering support for a
nonviolent movement.[1] At Dick's Pool Room, King warns that violence is "what
our opposition would like to see" and insists that "all we need is the very power of*

---

1.  According to surveillance conducted by two Albany police officers, Ralph Abernathy and SNCC representatives Charles Jones and Charles Sherrod accompanied King on stops at a shoe shine parlor, a cleaners, a drug store, and a bar in addition to the pool hall. They also held two impromptu meetings on street corners (Laurie Pritchett, Bill Manley, and J. Ed. Friend, Statement of police officers concerning activities of Martin Luther King, Jr., 25 July 1962).

*our souls and our commitment and our determination to be free."2 The following
transcript is arranged for clarity from several individual clips taken from film
recordings of the event.*

[*King*]:   [*recording interrupted*] as you know we are in the mid—[*recording interrupted*] great movement here in Albany and we—why don't you come on over.

[*Unidentified people*]:   Come on up. Come on in. Come on up fellas. Come on in.
Come on here. Come on up in here please. You, too, come on in [*and?*] tell everyone
to come on in. Come on in the door. Good.

[*King*]:   And as I was saying, we are in the midst of a great movement here in
Albany, and we want and solicit the support of everybody in this community—all of
the Negro citizens and even white citizens of goodwill who join with us. And as you
know we have had our demonstrations and marches, making it very clear that we
will no longer accept segregation and discrimination. And the one thing about this
movement is that it's a nonviolent movement. [*Spectators:*] (*Go ahead, brother*) It's been
that way from the very beginning. [*gap in film*]

. . .

[*King*]:   Now as you know—maybe you've heard—last night some violence broke
out. There was some bottle throwing. In fact, a policeman was injured, an automobile was cut—that is the top of a convertible automobile and maybe some other
things. Now, we know that nothing can hurt our movement more than this kind of
performance. [*gap in film*]

. . .

[*King*]:   [*recording interrupted*] exactly what our opposition would like to see,
and they will use this to defeat all of our efforts. And in order for our movement to
continue to be a great movement and continue to be based on our great Christian
heritage, based on love and nonviolence, we will have to keep it peaceful. Now, we
come to you because we know that you meet people, and you have friends, and you
know people, and we want you to talk with your friends and, and everybody that you
come in contact with about this movement and urge them to be nonviolent and, and
not to throw bottles or not to do anything that would keep our demonstration from
being peaceful. And I know that if we do this, we are destined to win this struggle.
[*gap in film*]

. . .

[*King*]:   [*words inaudible*] for us to all of the people that you come in contact
with—all of your friends—and we will continue to stress it as we get around the city.

. . .

---

2. Jones reportedly accused Chief Pritchett of provoking the violence and paying individuals to
throw rocks and bottles (Pritchett, et al., Statement of police officers).

[*King*]: We want thousands of people to be involved in our movement and demonstrations. And it is marvelous to see the number of people who have already been willing to go to jail in this great movement. And we want others to go by the hundreds, but above all we want it to be nonviolent. We're not going to hate anybody; we don't need to do that. We don't need our guns; we don't need any ammunition. All we need is the very power of our souls and our commitment and our determination to be free. [*gap in film*]

. . .

[*King*]: [*recording interrupted*] two mass meetings, one at Shiloh and one at Mount Zion—right in front of Shiloh—and we invite you to come to the mass meetings and be with us in these sessions and these discussions and get this over also to your friends and to your relatives. Thank you so much for giving us these few minutes.[3] And thank you [*recording interrupted*]

. . .

[*King*]: [*recording interrupted*] first of all be in the movement, for we need every one of you, and we need the support, and we are all together in this—in a common struggle for freedom and human dignity. And God bless you as the days unfold. Thank you so much. Okay.

[*Charles Jones*]: We want to talk specifically [*words inaudible*]. Obviously, last night, the city and the state [*words inaudible*]—[4]

[*King*]: Alright. [*Laughter*]

[*Jones*]: —provoked some violence on our part because Pritchett never has come down this far with all those men. You know it, and I know it too. And this was an attempt to get some of you to do exactly what you did last night, so that if this happens again, or at any point we are engaged in action, do—don't throw anything. The most important thing is our nonviolent demonstration that's going downtown,

---

3. At a mass meeting that evening, marking the end of the self-imposed penance period, six hundred people heard William G. Anderson announce a resumption of demonstrations in order to teach the city's government a "lesson" ("Albany, Ga., Negroes Warned to Expect New Violence," *New York Times*, 27 July 1962). On 27 July, King and twenty-seven others, including Abernathy and Anderson, were arrested during multiple prayer demonstrations in front of Albany's city hall (Claude Sitton, "Dr. King Is Jailed Again at Prayer Rally in Georgia," *New York Times*, 28 July 1962). The Albany Movement held mass meetings on the evening of King's arrest and on 28 July (Sitton, "Dr. King Is Jailed Again," 28 July 1962; Sitton, "Negro Lawyer Is Beaten, 37 Arrested in Albany, Ga.," *New York Times*, 29 July 1962).

4. Joseph Charles Jones (1937– ), born in Chester, South Carolina, received a B.A. (1958) from Johnson C. Smith University and a J.D. (1966) from Howard University School of Law. While enrolled at Johnson C. Smith Theological Seminary, Jones led students in sit-in demonstrations in downtown Charlotte, North Carolina. As a founding member of the Student Nonviolent Coordinating Committee (SNCC) in 1960, Jones left theological seminary to become director of the organization's voter registration program. The following year, he participated in the 1961 Freedom Rides and the desegregation and voter registration campaigns in McComb, Mississippi, and Albany, Georgia. In 1965 Jones became project director for the Prince George County Anti-Poverty Project in Washington, D.C., followed by a two-year post as chairman and executive director of the Action Coordinating Committee to End Segregation in the Suburbs (ACCESS).

so don't give the city or the state the opportunity of saying to the country, "You see, here's what we mean. These Negroes are violent. They want to destroy, they want to have mob action," and if we don't control this, each of us, each of you, then we give them the opportunity to say it. You understand this matter truly—that there are some people last night just got a little out of hand. So let's keep this word going around and keep—if this happens again, make sure you tell the person next to you, or anybody who's gathered like that, just to constrain themselves and hold themselves and don't hit back—don't throw back regardless of what happens, alright?

. . .

[*King*]:  Here's just a word from Dr. Abernathy—Dr. Ralph Abernathy.

[*Abernathy*]:  [*recording interrupted*] challenging you this afternoon to select this strong, powerful weapon of love and of nonviolence, but continue to press for your rights. If new demonstrations are called for then we expect every Negro in house to join in these demonstrations. If they become necessary, we expect you to [*follow through?*] and come on and march with us in the demonstration. But as we march, we want to march in love with hate toward nobody and remember whenever anything happens, as it did last night, then you bring shame and disgrace upon the leaders. I don't mean you do it, but I mean whoever threw the bottles on last night or cut the top of this automobile was not helping the cause, whatsoever, because Mr. Pritchett has trained his men [*recording interrupted*]

. . .

[*Abernathy*]:  [*gap in film*] I want to say this because so often it is difficult for us to understand the meaning of nonviolence, and I don't want anybody here today to go away with the impression that we are making an appeal to you to slacken up in the struggle, or to stop resisting this evil system of segregation. In fact, we're making an appeal to you to fight more now and in the future than in—than you have in the past. Nonviolence is the way for the strong, and not for the weak. It takes a strong man to be a nonviolent man.

F. WSB-TV-GU.

# Albany Jail Diary from 27 July–31 July 1962

Albany, Ga.

*On 27 July, King and nine others marched to Albany City Hall to pray and request a meeting with the City Commission. After refusing an invitation by Chief*

*Pritchett to talk privately in his office, the protesters were arrested.*[1] *During his incarceration, King kept a handwritten diary. In the following excerpt, published on 23 August in* Jet *magazine, King writes of his commitment to remain in jail. From his cell, King formulates strategy for continued demonstrations in Albany with SCLC executive director Wyatt Tee Walker. He instructs Walker to scale back the large demonstrations in favor of smaller ones because "there is so much tension in the town." Before heading to J. Robert Elliott's courtroom to hear oral arguments about the injunction placed on demonstrations in Albany, King confers with his lawyers C. B. King and Donald Hollowell about the importance of waging a four-pronged "battle" to end segregation in Albany through the courts, demonstrations, economic boycotts, and a voter registration campaign.*

**Friday, July 27**—Ralph Abernathy and I were arrested again in Albany at 3:15 p.m. (for the second time in July and the third time since last December.) We were accompanied by Dr. W. G. Anderson, Slater King, the Rev. Ben Gay and seven ladies. This group held a prayer vigil in front of the City Hall, seeking to appeal to the City Commission to negotiate with leaders of the Albany Movement. When we arrived at the City Hall, the press was on hand in large numbers and Police Chief Laurie Pritchett came directly over to us and invited us into his office. When we declined, he immediately ordered us arrested.[2]

Around 9 p.m., one of the officers came to the cell and said Chief Pritchett wanted to see me in his office. I responded suspiciously, remembering that two weeks ago, we were summoned to Pritchett's office, only to discover that we were being tricked out of jail. (A mysterious donor paid the fine, $178 for each of us.)[3] Today, we were deter-

---

1. Among the nine arrested with King were Abernathy, Anderson, Albany Movement vice president Slater King, Albany Movement chaplain Benjamin Gay, and five women—Emma Lou Louketis, Betty William, Gloria Courtney, Evelyn Toney, and Alvonia Dorsey. All were charged with disorderly conduct, failure to obey an officer, and congregating on the sidewalk. After King's arrest, a second wave of demonstrators, led by Charles Jones, marched to city hall, where eighteen more protesters were arrested (Bill Shipp, "King, 27 Others Jailed for Prayer-Protests at Albany's City Hall," *Atlanta Constitution*, 28 July 1962; J. Edgar Hoover, Memo to Robert F. Kennedy regarding the racial situation in Albany, Georgia, 28 July 1962, Bureau File 157-6-2-513). According to a newspaper report, the day before the demonstrations, King called Albany mayor Asa Kelley requesting a meeting between city officials and African American leaders. Kelley told King he "would not consider such a request as long as he and other outsiders are still in the city." King replied that if his presence prevented negotiations he would consider leaving Albany ("Mayor of Albany Says U.S. Official Asked About Friday Arrests," *Atlanta Daily World*, 28 July 1962).

2. Just prior to their arrest, King asked Abernathy to lead the group in prayer: "We pray, O God, that Thou will touch the hearts of the leaders of this city and have them to know that there will be no peace in this community until those elected to higher office will rise to stature and through the understanding that they will be willing to sit down and to talk and to discuss their problems with the leaders of the Negro people of this community. We pray that our, those of us who keep this vigil, this prayer vigil here at city hall, may have our hearts fixed aright and let there be no hate or animosity in our hearts. And may we be willing to go with Thee all the way, to take up our cross and to follow after Thee. Bless Dr. Anderson, our spokesman. Bless Dr. King, our leader. Bless reverend Gay, and all of those who have now participated in this" (Abernathy and King, Prayer vigil and arrests at Albany, Ga., City Hall, 27 July 1962).

3. For more on King's release from jail, see Press Release, King and Abernathy Choose Jail Time over Fine, 10 July 1962, and King, Address Delivered at Mass Meeting at Shiloh Baptist Church, 12 July 1962, pp. 510–511 and 518–520 in this volume, respectively. According to William G. Anderson's auto

mined that this would not happen again. So, I told the officer that Pritchett would have to step back to our cell. The officer reacted very bitterly, but he apparently got the message to Pritchett because the Chief came immediately and said: "Come on, Doctor. I am not trying to get you to leave. There is a long-distance call for you from a man named Spivak."

The call turned out to be Lawrence Spivak from Meet The Press TV program. I was scheduled to be on the program, Sunday, July 29. He was very upset and literally begged me to come out on bond. I immediately called Atty. (C.B.) King and the Rev. Wyatt Walker, my assistant, to the jail and sought their advice. We all agreed that I should not leave and suggested that Dr. Anderson, president of the Albany Movement, get out on bond and substitute for me. Dr. Anderson agreed and I decided to remain in jail.[4]

**Saturday, July 28**—I was able to arrange with Chief Pritchett for members of my staff to consult with me at any time. We held our staff meetings right there in jail. My wife, Coretta, also came to see me twice today before returning to Atlanta.

When Wyatt came to the jail, I emphasized that more demonstrations must be held with smaller numbers in front of the City Hall instead of large marches because there is so much tension in the town.

A little while after I talked with Wyatt, 15 more demonstrators were arrested as they appeared before City Hall and they all came in the jail singing loudly.[5] This was a big lift for us. This group was immediately shipped out to another jail in the state.

Later, that day, Pritchett came and asked me to leave jail for good. He said that someone had actually sent the cash money for my bond and technically he could make me leave. I told him I certainly did not want to be put in the position of being dragged out of jail, but that I had no intention of leaving because I wanted to serve my sentence. (Rep. John Lamula, a New York Republican, sent bond money for Dr. King, but later turned the funds over to the Albany Movement.)[6]

Pritchett told us: "You don't know how tense things are, do you? Do you know what happened?" When we said no, he replied: "Somebody almost busted C.B. King's head wide open." It sounded horrible and we became excited. I asked him who and he said calmly: "the sheriff over in the County Jail."[7] I immediately sent for Wyatt and

---

biography, it was later revealed that B.C. Gardner, a law partner of Mayor Asa Kelley, paid the bond for King and Abernathy's release (Norma L. Anderson and William G. Anderson, *Autobiographies of a Black Couple of the Greatest Generation* [n.p.: privately printed, 2004], p. 220).

4. Anderson posted a $400 property bond and appeared on "Meet the Press" on 29 July 1962.

5. Thirty-seven demonstrators were arrested on 28 July for picketing and staging a kneel-in at city hall (Vic Smith, "Sheriff Campbell Whacks C.B. King; Protesters Jailed," *Albany Herald*, 29 July 1962).

6. Lamula, an assistant clerk for the New York Assembly, raised the initial bail money for King's 12 July arrest by asking Poughkeepsie, New York, residents to contribute one dollar each. After an anonymous donor paid the bail, Pritchett returned the money, and Lamula, who believed King's effort in Albany was "the most important social issue of our generation," forwarded it to SCLC with another two hundred dollar contribution (Lamula to King, 19 July 1962; King to Lamula, 22 August 1962).

7. Soon after King's arrest on 27 July, SNCC workers Charles Jones and William Hansen led fourteen teenagers on a prayer vigil and were themselves arrested and jailed. According to Hansen, he was attacked by police and suffered a fractured jaw. News of Hansen's injuries reached attorney C.B. King, who went to Dougherty county sheriff D.C. Campbell's office to obtain medical relief for Hansen.

asked him to send a telegram to the President and to call Atty. Gen. Robert Kennedy and the Burke Marshall of the Justice Dept.[8] I told them I was very much concerned about this kind of brutality by law enforcement agencies and that something had to be done.

**Sunday, July 29**—Everything was rather quiet this morning. We had our regular devotional services among all the prisoners. I read from the Book of Job. We hold services every morning and evening and sing whenever we feel like it. Since only Ralph and I are in a cell together, we can't see the other prisoners, but we can always hear them. Slater is two cells away. Marvin Rich, Ed Dickenson and Earl Gorden (some white demonstrators) are across the hall in another cell block but they join us in services.[9] After devotion, I started reading some of the books I had with me.

They brought us the usual breakfast at 8 o'clock. It was one link sausage, one egg and some grits, two pieces of bread on a tin plate with a tin cup of coffee.

We were astonished when the jailer returned at 10 minutes after 10 this morning with a plate of hash, peas and rice and corn bread. He said it was supper and the last meal we were going to get that day because the cook was getting off early. Soon, the Rev. Mr. Walker came over with Dr. Roy C. Bell from Atlanta and Larry Still, a writer from Jet. Roy inspected Ralph's teeth and said he would arrange with Chief Pritchett to get us some "food packages." I told him this was needed because we would starve on the jail house food. The Albany Jail is dirty, filthy and ill-equipped. I have been in many jails and it is really the worse I have ever seen.[10]

---

Campbell told King to leave his office, and, after King refused, Campbell then hit him over the head with a walking cane, causing a cut in his forehead that required eight stitches. Campbell claimed that King was "interfering with business in the office" (Claude Sitton, "Dr. King Is Jailed Again at Prayer Rally in Georgia," *New York Times*, 28 July 1962; Bill Shipp, "3 Albany Negroes Protest in Prayer," *Atlanta Constitution*, 30 July 1962; "Sheriff Says He Struck Negro Who Interfered," *Los Angeles Times*, 30 July 1962).

8. Walker sent a telegram to movement supporters asking them to contact Pritchett, President Kennedy, Attorney General Kennedy, Mayor Asa D. Kelley, and Governor S. Ernest Vandiver about the "in humane and insufferable" jail conditions and the violation of the protesters' First Amendment rights (Walker to Supporters, 28 July 1962). Several responded to Walker's request, including Roy Wilkins, James Farmer, and Congressional leader Robert N.C. Nix (Wilkins to John F. Kennedy, 30 July 1962; Farmer to John F. Kennedy, 29 July 1962; Nix to Vandiver, 31 July 1962). For a list of additional supporters who sent letters to government officials, see note 3, Seay to King, 1 August 1962, p. 566 in this volume. Walker also made a call to the leaders of the Western Christian Leadership Conference requesting help coordinating West Coast prayer vigils in support of King and the others arrested. Vigils were staged at city halls in San Francisco, Los Angeles, Fresno, and other locals (WCLC, Press release, Western Christian Leadership Conference calls for nation-wide public prayer demonstration, 30 July 1962; "Rev. King Trial Set for Friday," *Los Angeles Sentinel*, 9 August 1962; "Prayer Vigil," *Fresno Bee*, 31 July 1962).

9. Rich (1929– ), community relations director for CORE, arrived in Albany on 24 July after receiving William G. Anderson's request for a CORE representative. He was arrested leading a demonstration the night of his arrival (CORE, Minutes, "Steering committee of the National Action Council," 28 July 1962). Dickerson (1941– ), from Cambridge, Maryland, had participated in local demonstrations earlier that year.

10. Bell (1926–2011), a dentist, was also Special Projects Director of Atlanta's local chapter of SCLC in 1962 and participated in efforts to desegregate Atlanta's Grady Hospital and the American Dental Association. Still (1923–2001), an associate editor at *Jet* magazine, described King's jail conditions in a feature article ("Courts Take Time, We Want Freedom Now—Albany Leaders," *Jet*, 16 August 1962).

Friday, July 27, 1962

Ralph Abernathy and I were ~~arrested~~ arrested again with six others for July at 3:15 P.M. We were accompanied by Dr. Anderson, Slater King, Rev. Ben Gay and seven other ladies. This group held a prayer vigil in front of the City Hall seeking to appeal to the City Commission to negotiate. When we arrived at the city hall the press was on hand in large numbers, and Chief Pritchett came directly to us and invited us to his office. When we declined this in favor of seeing the City Commission he immediately ordered us arrested.

Ralph and I were ~~soon~~ given the same cell that we occupied two weeks before. We immediately began singing freedom songs. A brief worship service was held Friday evening, and all of the persons arrested in our group made a statement of personal witness.

Around 9:00 P.M. one of the officers came to the cell and said the Chief Pritchett wanted to see me in his office. I immediately responded with

Handwritten diary composed while jailed in Albany, Georgia, from 27 July–28 July 1962. Courtesy of the Howard Gotlieb Archival Research Center, Boston University.

suspicion; remember that two weeks before we were summoned to Pritchett office; only to discover that we were being tricked out of jail (a mysterious donor paid the fine of $178.00 for each of us — to this day it has not been revealed who paid — of course I am convinced that the whole thing was a arrangement made by the city); I was determined that this would not happen again. So I told the officer to phone Pritchett to step back...to the call. The officer reacted very bitterly, but he apparently got the message over to Pritchett, for when I came he immediately said "Come on Doctor I am not trying to get you to leave; there is a long distance call for you from a man named Spivak"

This turned out to be Spivak from "Meet the Press". I was scheduled to be on the program Sunday July 28. He was very upset about my being in jail and literally begged me to clear my...good. I told him that I would have to think about it. I immediately summoned atty King and W. L. Walker to the jail and sent their advice. We all agreed that I shouldn't leave. I suggested that Dr. Anderson substitute for me. This he agreed to do.

These handwritten notes, likely written after King's arrest on 27 July 1962 while leading a prayer vigil at Albany City Hall, indicate his reasons for remaining in jail: "1. After weighing the total situation, I think it will be a blow to the morale of the people if I leave at this point. 2. It will be misinterpreted and distorted by the press in view of the fine being mysteriously paid in the other instance of my arrest here." Courtesy of Manuscript, Archives, and Rare Book Library, Emory University.

**Monday, July 30**—I spent most of the day reading and writing on my book on Negro sermons before our hearing in Federal court started.[11] The heat was so unbearable, I could hardly get anything done. I think we had the hottest cell in the jail because it is back in a corner. There are four bunks in our cell, but for some reason, they never put anybody in with us. Ralph says everytime we go to the wash bowl we bump into each other. He is a wonderful friend and really keeps our spirits going. The food seemed to be worse than usual today. I could only drink the coffee.

I talked with Wyatt and he told me the demonstrations were still going as planned. We soon heard about them because they brought in about 15 more they had arrested.[12] We were then told to get ready to go to court to begin the hearing on the city's request for a Federal injunction against the demonstrations. I was informed that Atty. Connie [*Constance Baker*] Motley was here from the New York office of the NAACP and I was very happy. Lawyers [*C. B.*] King and Donald L. Hollowell of Atlanta came to see me before the hearing started. We discussed how the Albany battle must be waged on all four fronts. A legal battle in the courts; with demonstrations and kneel-ins and sit-ins; with an economic boycott and, finally, with an intense voter registration campaign. This is going to be a long summer.

**Tuesday, July 30**[13]—I was very glad to get to court today because I had a chance to see my wife and my friends and associates who are keeping the Albany Movement going. I also had chance to consult with Wyatt during the recesses. He told demonstrations were going on while we were in court and that some of the youth groups led by the Student Non-Violent Coordinating Committee were testing places like drug stores and drive-ins and motels.[14]

Later, my father came to me with the Rev. Allen Middleton, head of Atlanta's SCLC chapter, I was happy to hear that my mother has adjusted to my role in the Albany Movement.[15] She understood that I still had to remain in jail as long as neces-

---

11. In 1957 King discussed producing a book of sermons with Harper Brothers publishing house, but his commitments to the Montgomery Improvement Association and SCLC made it impossible for him to complete the manuscript before 1962. King's book, titled *Strength to Love*, was published in 1963. For more on *Strength to Love*, see Introduction in *Papers* 6:35–44. King refers to the hearing scheduled to determine if Judge J. Robert Elliott's injunction against the Albany Movement would be made permanent.

12. On the night of 30 July, sixteen protesters led by Albert L. Dunn, a student at the Interdenominational Theological Seminary in Atlanta, were arrested while singing and praying in front of city hall. Nearly 300 protesters were arrested during the month of July (Hedrick Smith, "Dr. King Set Back in U.S. Court Test," *New York Times*, 31 July 1962).

13. This entry was erroneously dated 30 July instead of 31 July.

14. While court was in session, thirty-nine demonstrators conducted prayer protests in front of Carnegie Public Library and city hall in Albany. All thirty-nine demonstrators were arrested (Bill Shipp, "39 More Negroes Jailed in 3 Protests at Albany City Hall and Library," *Atlanta Constitution*, 1 August 1962). Additionally, SNCC executive secretary James Forman was arrested along with four students after attempting to integrate three Albany stores and the local Holiday Inn, while field secretary Charles Jones organized demonstrations against lunch counters and the city's swimming pool ("Jail SNCC Leader in Albany, Ga.," *Chicago Daily Defender*, 7 August 1962; Claude Sitton, "Negroes Rally in Albany, Ga.; 80 Driven from a Public Pool," *New York Times*, 19 July 1962).

15. King refers to John Albert Middleton (1914–1975), pastor of Allen Temple AME Church of Atlanta from 1956 to 1965 and president of Morris Brown College from 1965 to 1973. From 1962 to 1967 Middleton served as president of the Atlanta chapter of SCLC.

sary. I told dad to invite some preachers in to help him carry on the church, but he told me: "As long as you carry on in jail, I'll carry on outside."

PD. *Jet*, 23 August 1962, pp. 14–21.

# From S. S. Seay

1 August 1962
Montgomery, Ala.

*While King remains in jail following his 27 July arrest for leading a prayer vigil outside Albany City Hall, MIA president Seay sends a letter of encouragement.*[1] *This might be "the greatest test of your experience as a leader," Seay writes, but "please keep in mind that I am as ever WITH MARTIN WITH ALL THAT I HAVE."*

Dr. Martin L. King, Jr.
c/o The City Jail
Albany, Georgia

Dear Martin:

You would have heard from me before now but I kept thinking it would be like it was before, just about time I got ready, along with others, to come over, the news came that you were out.[2] In talking with Wyatt I got the idea that you just might be in jail at least for the duration of the hearing and that the hearing might last for the week.

We have sent telegrams to the President, Robert Kennedy, Governor [*S. Ernest*] Vandiver, Mayor [*Asa*] Kelly, and Chief of Police Pritchett.[3] We are calling on the churches of Montgomery to take time out Sunday for prayer for you and Ralph and the Albany movement.[4]

---

1. King also received letters of support from other Montgomery colleagues such as MIA board member Irene West, who wrote that "We are so proud of your Courageous leadership. Good will soon triumph over wrong" (West to King and Abernathy, 1 August 1962).

2. King served two days in jail following his arrest in Albany on 16 December 1961, and two days of his forty-five-day sentence of 10 July 1962. For more on King's jailing in July, see King, Albany Jail Diary from 10 July–11 July 1962, pp. 511–516 in this volume.

3. In his telegram to Robert F. Kennedy, Seay urges the attorney general to use the "power of your office to persuade the authorities in Albany, Georgia, to return to reason and desist from the shameful conduct they have exemplified before the world" (Seay to Kennedy, 30 July 1962). Others who sent telegrams of support included Connecticut governor John Dempsey, Congressman Adam Clayton Powell, and labor leaders Walter Reuther and A. Philip Randolph (Dempsey to Vandiver, 30 July 1962; Powell to John F. Kennedy, 2 August 1962; Bluestone to Walker, 1 August 1962; and Randolph to John F. Kennedy, 30 July 1962).

4. In a 27 July 1962 form letter addressed to "Friends of Freedom," Walker asked churches to mobilize their membership in a show of support for those arrested by sending telegrams to government and

Perhaps, you are facing the greatest test of your experience as a leader. It might be possible for you to feel the slacking of some cords of loyalty that have helped you sustain all along the path you have chosen to take. When that time comes to me I have one prayer that I keep: "<u>If the Lord will go with me and keep me in the way that I go, bread to eat and raiment to put on, And bear my spirit above the crushing waves that threaten to overwhelm me, He is my God!</u>"[5]

I do not know all the things I can do. Neither do all the things I shall do. But please keep in mind that I am as ever WITH MARTIN WITH ALL THAT I HAVE.

Yours for freedom,
[*signed*] S. S. Seay
S. S. Seay, Sr.

SSS/hg

TLS. MLKJP-GAMK: Box 21.

---

local Albany officials, mobilizing prayer vigils in their communities, and wearing black arm bands "symbolic of murdered justice in Albany" (Walker to Friend of Freedom, 27 July 1962).
   5. Cf. Genesis 28:20.

# To John F. Kennedy

2 August 1962
Albany, Ga.

*From the jail in Albany, Georgia, King thanks President Kennedy for his recent statement chastising Albany city officials for refusing to negotiate with Albany Movement leaders.*[1]

THE PRESIDENT
THE WHITE HOUSE

DEAR MR PRESIDENT,

---

   1. In response to a reporter's question regarding the situation in Albany, Kennedy said: "Let me say that I find it wholly inexplicable why the City Council of Albany will not sit down with the citizens of Albany, who may be Negroes, and attempt to secure them, in a peaceful way, their rights. The United States Government is involved in sitting down at Geneva with the Soviet Union. I can't understand why the government of Albany, City Council of Albany, cannot do the same for American citizens. We are going to attempt, as we have in the past, to try to provide a satisfactory solution and protection of the constitutional rights of the people of Albany, and will continue to do so" (*Public Papers of the Presidents of the United States: John F. Kennedy, 1962* [Washington, D.C.: U.S. Government Printing Office, 1963], pp. 592–593).

GRATIFIED BY DIRECTNESS OF YOUR STATEMENT TO ALBANY CRISIS. REV ABERNA-
THY AND I EARNESTLY HOPE YOU WILL CONTINUE TO USE THE GREAT MORAL INFLU-
ENCE OF YOUR OFFICE TO HELP THIS CRUCIAL SITUTATION. THERE IS NO NEED FOR
ANOTHER LITTLE ROCK HERE[2]

MARTIN LUTHER KING JR.

PWSr. JFKWHCSF-MBJFK.

---

2. King refers to President Dwight D. Eisenhower's use of federal troops to integrate Arkansas's
Little Rock Central High School in September 1957. For more on the integration of Central High, see
note 1, King to Eisenhower, 25 September 1957, in *Papers* 4:278.

# Albany Jail Diary from 1 August–7 August 1962

Albany, Ga.

*In the second part of King's diary, published on 23 August in* Jet *magazine,
he writes about a visit from his family, particularly his three children, whom he
has not seen in several weeks. The visit, King says, "certainly gave me a lift."[1]
Throughout the week, he continues to attend court proceedings on the July
injunction against demonstrations in Albany. Listening to testimony by the state's
witnesses, King tells Abernathy that it is "depressing to see city officials make a
farce of the court."*

**Wednesday, August 1**—My father and Dr. [*John A.*] Middleton came to see me
again this morning and told me they spoke at the mass meeting last night at Mt. Zion
Baptist Church.[2] The crowd was so large they overflowed into Shiloh Baptist across
the street, where nightly mass meetings are usually held. Dad said he would remain
through today's hearing and listen to Chief Pritchett's testimony about how he had to
arrest Negroes to protect the white people from beating them.[3] Dad said he told the
people I didn't come to Albany on my own but I was invited there by the city officials
to visit their jail.

**Thursday, August 2**—I learned about President Kennedy saying that the commissioners of Albany ought to talk to the Negro leaders. I felt this was a very forthright

---

1. King was allowed out of his jail cell for the visit with his family. In an interview following their
visit, Coretta said her husband "feels much better after seeing the children" (Hedrick Smith, "Dr. King's
3 Children Visit Him; He Is Allowed Out of Jail Cell," *New York Times*, 6 August 1962).
2. According to an FBI memorandum, King, Sr. encouraged an audience at Mt. Zion to demand better housing and to begin a comprehensive economic boycott of white businesses in Albany (FBI, Memo,
"Racial situation, Albany, Ga.," 2 August 1962, Bureau File 157–6–2–597).
3. Pritchett testified from 30 July–1 August and again on 8 August (Transcript of Trial Testimony,
*Kelly v. Page*, 335 F.2d 114 [5th Cir. 1964]).

statement and immediately dictated a statement to the President commending him on his action.[4]

**Friday, August 3**—They recessed the court hearing until Tuesday. I still have the feeling it is too long and drawn out and that the people should keep demonstrating no matter what happens.

**Saturday, August 4**—More demonstrators were arrested all day today and later on Pritchett came back and asked them to sing for him.[5] "Sing that song about *Ain't Going to Let Chief Pritchett Turn Me Around*, he asked. I think he really enjoyed hearing it. The other jailers would just stare and listen.

**Sunday, August 5**—Today was a big day for me, because my children, Yolanda, Martin Luther IV and Dexter came to see me. I had not seen them for five weeks. We had about 25 minutes together. They certainly gave me a lift.

**Monday, August 6**—I saw Coretta again before she left to take the children back to Atlanta. I devoted most of the day to reading newspapers and letters from all over the world. Some of them were just addressed to "Nation's No. 1 Troublemaker, Albany" without any state. I got a few bad ones like this, but most of them were good letters of encouragement from Negroes and whites.[6] After dinner and devotional period I continued writing on my book. I had planned to finish it this summer, but I have only written 11 of the 18 sermons to be included. I have written three sermons in jail. They all deal with how to make the Christian gospel relevant to the social and economic life of man. This means how the Christian should deal with the race relations, war and peace and economic injustices. They are all based on sermons I have preached. The sermons I wrote in jail are called "A Tender Heart and A Tough Mind;" "Love In Action" and "Loving Your Enemies." I think I will name the book *Loving Your Enemies*.[7]

**Tuesday, August 7**—We went back to court today. As I listened to the testimony of the state's witnesses about how they were trying to prevent violence and protect the people, I told Ralph it was very depressing to see city officials make a farce of the court.

PD. *Jet*, 23 August 1962, pp. 14–21.

---

4. *Public Papers of the Presidents of the United States: John F. Kennedy, 1962* (Washington, D.C.: U.S. Government Printing Office, 1963), pp. 592–593; King to Kennedy, 2 August 1962, p. 567 in this volume.

5. Thirteen demonstrators, one an expectant mother, were arrested at Albany City Hall after refusing to obey Chief Pritchett's orders to disperse ("Refuse to End Race Protest; 15 Arrested," *Chicago Daily Tribune*, 5 August 1962).

6. Wyatt Tee Walker had urged SCLC staff on 31 July 1962 to send King and Abernathy letters of encouragement, noting that "your message will abundantly aid them morally and amply supply them spiritually." SCLC board members Kelly Miller Smith and Samuel W. Williams complied and sent words of encouragement (Smith to King, 2 August 1962; Williams to King, 3 August 1962).

7. King had initially planned to take a month off during the summer to finish his book of sermons (King to Eugene Exman, 9 March 1962, p. 426 in this volume). Although the turn of events in Albany monopolized any free time King planned to have in the summer, he explained in a letter to Harper & Brothers editor Melvin Arnold that "I did get a chance to write two or three sermons while in jail. I am sure I would have been able to send you more if the Albany jail had not been so hot" (King to Melvin Arnold, 5 September 1962). In the preface to *Strength to Love*, King says that "Love in Action," "Loving Your Enemies," and "Shattered Dreams" were written while in jail in Albany (King *Strength to Love* [New York: Harper & Row, 1963], p. ix).

# Testimony in *Asa D. Kelly et al., v. M. S. Page et al.*

8 August 1962
Albany, Ga.

*Still detained after his 27 July arrest, King was escorted from the Albany jail to Judge J. Robert Elliott's courtroom to testify about his involvement in the Albany Movement.*[1] *Since 30 July Elliott had been hearing testimony from approximately thirty witnesses on the plaintiffs' case to make permanent the injunction against Albany Movement demonstrations.*[2] *In his testimony, King recalls the night of 24 July when violence erupted at an unplanned Albany Movement march. When asked by defense attorney Donald Hollowell if the entire community of Albany should assume some responsibility for the violence, King agreed, stating that "all of these accumulated injustices and indignities and the many brutal and inhuman things that have been inflicted upon many Negroes, have naturally brought about deep-seated resentment, which can develop in violent responses at times."*[3] *Under cross examination by E. Freeman Leverett, counsel for the plaintiffs, a calm King explains civil disobedience: "The individual is to decide in his own conscience whether the law is right; and, if he violates it, he must accept the penalty. He must not try to run from it, he must not seek to evade it, he must not seek to violate it in some sense of subverting the law. He must do it openly and in a non-violent spirit; and this becomes civil disobedience and not uncivil disobedience which we too often see by those who seek to take the law in their hands."*[4] *After King's testimony, attorneys for the Albany Movement and for the City of Albany rested their cases.*[5] *Judge Elliott concluded the hearing without setting a date for adjudication, saying: "I am not sure whether it might be in a couple of days, a week or a month."*[6]

---

1. Asa D. Kelley's name was misspelled in the published case.

2. Transcript of Trial Testimony, *Kelly v. Page*, 335 F.2d 114 (5th Cir. 1964), 30 July–26 September 1962.

3. In addition to Hollowell, the legal team consisted of C. B. King, Constance Baker Motley, Frank D. Reeves, Howard Moore, Jr., Carl Rachlin, William M. Kunstler, Clarence B. Jones, Horace T. Ward, and Norman Amaker. Donald Lee Hollowell (1917–2004), born in Wichita, Kansas, earned his high school diploma over six years while serving in the 10th Cavalry Regiment of the United States Army. He received his B.A. from Lane College (1947) and J.D. from Loyola University in Chicago (1951). During the 1950s and 1960s, Hollowell earned a reputation as an influential civil rights attorney, counseling student activists in Atlanta and successfully litigating the 1961 case which integrated the University of Georgia. In 1966, President Johnson appointed him the southeast regional director of the Equal Employment Opportunity Commission, a position he held until 1985. Hollowell also served as chairman of the board for the Voter Education Project from 1971 until 1986.

4. Ernest Freeman Leverett (1929–1997), born in Fort Valley, Georgia, earned a B.S. from Indiana Technical College in 1949 and an LL.B. from Emory University School of Law in 1951. Leverett began practicing law in 1951. When Georgia governor S. Ernest Vandiver requested Leverett's help defending the city of Albany against the Albany Movement, Leverett was in his third year as deputy assistant attorney general of Georgia, a position he held until 1966. That same year, Leverett co-argued the constitutionality of the Voting Rights Act of 1965 before the U.S. Supreme Court. He was a member of several organizations, including the National and Georgia School Boards Associations and the Disciplinary Board of the State of Georgia.

5. Just prior to the conclusion of the case, the U.S. Justice Department filed a "friend of the court" brief opposing the Albany city officials' request to halt any further demonstrations ("Justice Dept. Enters Case in Court in Albany," *Atlanta Daily World*, 9 August 1962).

6. "Justice Dept. Enters Case in Court in Albany," 9 August 1962. Four days after Kelley filed an injunction against mass demonstrations and protests in Albany, the Albany Movement filed two class

a party Defendant, and called in behalf of Defendants, being first duly sworn,
testified

DIRECT EXAMINATION BY MR. HOLLOWELL:

Q    You haven't been on the stand before during this trial, have you?

A    No sir.

Q    Would you give your full name for the record?

A    Martin Luther King, Jr.

Q    Rev. King, I believe you are the President of the Southern Christian Leadership
     Conference, is that correct?

A    Yes sir, that's correct.

Q    In connection with your official capacity, did you have the occasion to be in
     Albany, Georgia, during the month of December, 1961?

A    Yes sir, I did.

Q    How did you happen to come?

A    Well, I came at the invitation of the Albany Movement. I received a telephone
     call as well as a telegram from leaders of the Albany Movement, inviting me to
     come in an advisory capacity on the whole question of non-violence and also to
     join the movement.[7] I think the telegram stated in specific language that they
     were desirous of having me to join the non-violent movement in Albany.

Q    When did you arrive, sir?

A    As I recall, I arrived on the 15th of December, the afternoon of the 15th.[8]

---

action lawsuits asking the court to end racial discrimination in public facilities in Albany and to prohibit Albany city officials from interfering with Albany residents' right to protest peacefully (*W. G.
Anderson et al., v. Asa D. Kelly et al.*, 32 F.R.D. 355 [M.D. Ga. 1963]; *W. G. Anderson et al., v. City of Albany
et al.*, 321 F.2d 649 [5th Cir. 1963]). In response, the City of Albany filed a counter-claim, asking the
court to institute a permanent injunction against demonstrations in Albany. Due to the similarity of
the four cases and the large number of witnesses, they were consolidated for the purpose of trial, and
the hearings were conducted in stages, beginning 30 July 1962 and ending 26 September 1962. In
1963, *Anderson v. Kelly* (M.D. Ga. 1963) was dismissed after Judge Elliott found that the suit was not a
proper class action claim. The three remaining cases, *Kelly v. Page, Anderson v. City of Albany*, and *City
of Albany v. Anderson*, were decided together in 1963. Finding that race relations had improved since
the cases were first filed in 1962, Elliott denied all parties' applications for permanent injunctions.
The Fifth Circuit Court of Appeals later affirmed Elliott's decision to deny a permanent injunction to
Albany city officials, but remanded the Albany Movement's case back to district court. In 1964, Elliott
enjoined the City of Albany and its officials from preventing anti-segregation protests or retaliating
against protesters and from enforcing segregation in publicly owned or operated facilities and privately owned recreational and travel services open to the public (*Kelly v. Page*, 335 F.2d 114 [5th Cir.
1964]).

     7. King received a call from Albany Movement president William G. Anderson. The telegram invit-
ing King to Albany has not been located.

     8. See King, Address Delivered at Albany Movement Mass Meeting at Mt. Zion Baptist Church, 15
December 1961, pp. 342–344 in this volume.

Q   Now, on the day of the 16th of December, '61, between the hours of noon and 6 o'clock in the evening, did you have the occasion to be at the Shiloh Baptist Church in this City?

A   Yes sir, I was there.

Q   What were you there for?

A   Well, in the morning we had a prayer meeting and then around noon we had a regular worship service, and Dr. Abernathy preached at that service; and we had a regular worship service and mass meeting.

Q   Did you hear Rev. Abernathy or did you yourself make any suggestion as to the use of violence on the part of yourself or anybody in the sound of your voice or anybody in the community?

A   No, all of our statements were centered in the whole philosophy of non-violence. Every time I spoke to the group I stressed the importance of adhering absolutely to the principles of non-violence.

Q   Did you at any time have the occasion to address the City Commission of the City of Albany; that is, individually or in conference with any other persons?

A   Yes sir, I did have an opportunity, I think at that period. It was through a letter or through a telegram urging them to negotiate.[9]

Q   But face to face; did you ever have any face to face contact?

A   No sir, I did not have any face to face contact.

Q   Do you know whether any was sought?

A   Whether I sought this?

Q   Or the Albany Movement itself or the leaders of the Movement?

A   Oh yes sir, over and over again, this request was mde.

Q   Now, you've heard the testimony concerning the group that left the church on that day and moved on toward the City Hall; you were a part of that group, were you not?[10]

A   Yes sir.

Q   You were at the head of the line of walking and walking with whom?

A   Dr. Anderson.

---

9. On 16 December 1961, Anderson and Albany Movement secretary Marion Page sent a telegram to Kelley and the City Commission requesting negotiations. In response, Kelley wrote: "Since you have elected not to use the medium of the negotiating committee to submit your grievances and demands and since you apparently have no intention of living up to the truce and encouraging your people to avoid the occasion of the violation of valid ordinances and statutes, we feel that you are not acting in good faith and until you can do so we can give no response to your demand" (Vic Smith, "City Officials Reject Negro Group's Demands," *Albany Herald*, 16 December 1961; Kelley to Anderson and Page, 16 December 1961).

10. Other witnesses called to testify about the protest on 16 December 1961 included Albany police chief Laurie Pritchett, Albany city manager Stephen A. Roos, William G. Anderson, Slater King, and Ralph Abernathy (Transcript of Trial Testimony, *Kelly v. Page*, 335 F.2d 114 [5th Cir. 1964], 30 July–26 September 1962).

Q    Now, I will ask you whether or not you at any time made any statement to
     anybody from the time that you left the church uhtil the time that you were
     arrested, to the effect "Strike me first"?

A    No sir, absolutely not. I have made no such statement in Albany or anywhere
     else concerning "strike me first".

Q    Did you hear such a statement made?

A    Yes sir, I did hear the statement made.

Q    Who made it?

A    Dr. Anderson.[11]

Q    How long were you in Albany on that occasion?

A    Well, I came in on Friday afternoon and I was arrested Saturday, and I was here
     until Monday; through Monday, the following Monday.[12]

Q    Of the succeeding week?

A    That's right.

Q    After you got out, did you have occasion to remain in the City?

A    Yes, I remained through the evening meeting. There was a mass meeting that
     Monday night, as I recall; and I believe I remained for that mass meeting.[13]

Q    Would you indicate whether or not during the process of your walking with this
     group from the church in the direction of the City Hall by way of Whitney and
     then Jackson Street, you noticed any violence in any way whatsoever on the part
     of anybody?

A    No sir, I didn't notice any violence at all.

Q    Would you indicate what your reactions were at the time that you arrived at the
     corner of [*strikeout illegible*] Highland and South Jackson, insofar as whether
     you moved directly across the street or whether you stopped?

A    As I recall, I guess it was Highland and Jackson, we stopped for the red light.
     There was a light there and we stopped and after that, we went right on.

---

11. Anderson corroborated King's statement in his own testimony, explaining, "I made the statement
in response to the action of one of the police officers. As he approached the line . . . he raised his night-
stick and grasped it in both hands and held it up before him; and I said, 'If you hit anybody, hit me first'"
(Transcript of Trial Testimony, *Kelly v. Page*, 335 F.2d 114 [5th Cir. 1964], 30 July–26 September 1962).

12. After addressing a group of protesters at Shiloh Baptist Church on 16 December 1961, King,
Anderson, Abernathy, and over 260 demonstrators marched toward Albany's City Hall to pray. All were
arrested for parading without a permit, obstructing traffic, and blocking sidewalks. King, Abernathy,
and Anderson were taken to the Albany Jail but later transferred to the jail in Americus, Georgia (see
Abernathy to King, 17 December 1961, pp. 346–347 in this volume).

13. After his release from jail on 18 December 1961, King addressed a mass meeting at Shiloh Baptist
Church before leaving for Atlanta. He told the crowd that he did not want "to stand in the way of mean-
ingful negotiations" between the Albany Movement and city officials by remaining in jail (Bill Shipp,
"Albany, Negroes Seal Peace; Prisoners to Go Free on Bail," *Atlanta Constitution*, 19 December 1961; "Dr.
King Is Freed," *New York Times*, 19 December 1961).

Q    Now, do you agree that the testimony which you have heard, indicating that the group proceed on up South Jackson to Oglethorpe and at that point you were stopped; now, would you indicate by whom and what the occasion was?

A    We were stopped at that corner of Oglethorpe, I think, and we were stopped by Chief Pritchett. He came up to the front of the group, along with several policemen and maybe some State Troopers, I don't recall; and his question to me was, "Do you have a permit to parade?"

Q    Was this the first time that you had the occasion to be addressed by any officer along the line of walking?

A    Yes sir, that was the first time.

Q    Was this the first time that you had made any statement other than in conversation perhaps with Dr. Anderson?

A    Yes sir, that's correct, the first time that I made any statement.

Q    Now, when you left, you say the following day after your arrest or the following Monday, you made a speech that night and then you left the City?

A    Yes, that's right.

Q    When, if ever, did you return?

A    I did not return to Albany until the date of the trial, I don't recall the exact date, but it was in July, on a Tuesday. It was about the 13th or 14th, I guess. No, excuse me—

Q    Was that the trial or was that the sentence?

A    No, I'm sorry. I did return for the trial in February, February I believe.[14]

Q    How long were you here on that occasion?

A    Just a few hours. I came in that morning and went right out in the afternoon.[15]

Q    And then, the next time you returned to the City?

A    Was for the sentencing in July.

Q    That was about the 10th of July or thereabout?

A    That's correct, about that time.

Q    And after you were sentenced what, if anything, happened to you?

A    Well, after I was sentenced, I decided on the basis of conscience to serve the time, which turned out to be 45 days instead of paying the fine of $178.[16]

Q    Now, did you serve the time?

A    Well, I served about two days of the time.

Q    And then, what happened?

---

14. King came back to Albany on 27 February 1962 to stand trial before Judge A.N. Durden on charges stemming from his December 1961 arrest (see Introduction, p. 30 in this volume).

15. King was found guilty following the trial on 27 February, but Judge Durden postponed the verdict for sixty days. King returned to Atlanta after the trial (see Introduction, pp. 30–31 in this volume).

16. See Press Release, King and Abernathy Choose Jail Time over Fine, 10 July 1962, pp. 510–511 in this volume.

A       Well, we were called in Chief Pritchett's office on Thursday of that same week;
        again, I don't remember the date.[17]

Q       Now, who is "we"?

A       Rev. Abernathy was with me.

Q       Two of you?

A       The two of us. And we felt, in fact, they told us about 7 o'clock in the morning
        to get dressed, that the Chief wanted to see us; and we just assumed that we
        were being transferred to another jail. But when we got to Chief Pritchett's
        office, he talked with us a while and finally said that our fines had been paid
        and that we were now to leave.

Q       Did you inquire as to who paid them?

A       Yes, we did. We asked over and over again and Chief Pritchett said that he
        didn't know who paid the fines.

Q       Do you know now who paid them?

A       No, I don't. We still have no knowledge of who paid the fines.

Q       Was it paid at your behest?

A       No sir, I made it very clear to my family and to the leaders of the Albany
        Movement and anybody else that I had any close connections with that I did
        not want the fine paid, and Dr. Abernathy did the same.[18]

Q       Allright, now after you got out, did you leave the City on that occasion?

A       No sir, I didn't leave until, oh 4 or 5 days later.[19]

Q       Now, during that period of time, you had the occasion to make some speeches,
        did you not?

A       Yes sir, that's correct, in mass meetings.

Q       Did you attend 'most all of the mass meetings during the time you were here?

A       Yes sir, I think I made all of the mass meetings during that period.

Q       Did you yourself or did you hear any one who had the occasion to speak on the
        rostrum address themselves to the matter of violence?

A       Yes, over and over again.

Q       Did you—I'm sorry?

A       Yes, I said over and over again speakers addressed themselves to the question of
        violence and always discouraged it in the most vigorous and forthright terms.

Q       Now, there has been statement—excuse me just one moment—you heard the
        Chief's testimony a moment ago, did you not?[20]

---

17.  King was summoned to Pritchett's office on 12 July 1962.

18.  Police Chief Laurie Pritchett stated that an "unidentified 'tall, well-dressed Negro'" paid the fine
(Bill Shipp, "Freed by Mystery Fine Donor, Rev. King Meets Police Chief," *Atlanta Constitution*, 13 July
1962).

19.  King was released from jail on 12 July 1962. He went back to Atlanta on 14 July and returned to
Albany on 16 July.

20.  In his testimony given on 8 August 1962, Chief Pritchett said: "I have heard [King and other lead-
ers] through my own contact with them state that they were responsible for part of the violence that

A  Yes sir, I did.

Q  Would you indicate what you did say in connection with any assumption of responsibility for some alleged violence that, I believe, Is supposed to have occurred either on the 21st or the 24th of July; the 24th, I guess it was?

A  Yes, I made the statement that I was sure that none of the persons involved in the pilgrimage or in the line participated in any act of violence on that evening, and that I was also sure that no one connected with the Albany Movement participated in any violence; but that in this non-violent movement, we abhor violence so much that we felt a spiritual need of accepting some responsibility for the violence that occurred. This was the substance of my statement.[21]

Q  What did you mean by "spiritual"? I believe you said "a spiritual need to accept"; wasn't that your language, sir?

A  That's right.

Q  What did you mean by that?

A  Well, I meant that as long as there is any violence, as I have said on many occasions, taking place in a non-violent movement, even though the persons involved are not in any way connected with the movement, in order to make it a pure and spiritually rooted movement, it is necessary for the leaders of that movement always to take some step in the direction of making it clear that they are absolutely opposed to violence in any form.

Q  Did you mean to exclude any other part of the Albany community?

A  I'm sorry, I don't think I quite understand.

Q  In your statement about assuming of some spiritual responsibility, I asked you did you mean to exclude any other portion of the community from having some responsibility in connection with it?

A  Oh no, not at all.

Q  I'll ask you whether or not you feel that there is some responsibility on the part of the full community for anything that happened?

A  Yes sir, I do. I think the presence of injustice in society is always the presence in a potential sense of violence; and I think the long night of injustices, indignities and brutality, and all of the things that have been inflicted—

MR. LEVERETT: May it please the Court, I object again to this going into a speech and harangue.

MR. HOLLOWELL: May it please the Court—

---

has occurred here, because they were encouraging the people and inciting the people and they would have to take the responsibility of it; and that was the reason that Dr. Martin Luther King and Dr. Abernathy called a day of penitence." He then asserted that King never explained exactly what he meant by "assuming a part of the responsibility" for the violence of 24 July 1962 (Transcript of Trial Testimony, *Kelly v. Page*, 335 F.2d 114 [5th Cir. 1964], 30 July–26 September 1962).

21. On the evening of 24 July 1962, violence erupted during an unplanned march led by members of the Albany Movement. The following day King denounced the violence and called for a day of penance (Press Conference Denouncing Violence in Albany, 25 July 1962, pp. 553–555 in this volume).

THE COURT: Let's let him complete his statement and ask him to abbreviate it as much as possible.

A     The Witness: Yes sir, I was about to say that all of these accumulated injustices and indignities and the many brutal and inhuman things that have been inflicted upon many Negroes, have naturally brought about deep-seated resentment, which can develop in violent responses at times.

Q     Mr. Hollowell: Do you think that this responsibility that you are mentioning is a responsibility to be shared only by the spiritual association that you made with those who were the actual perpetrators or do you feel that there are broader connotations as relate to other people?

A     Yes sir, I definitely feel that there are broad connotations. I think it would have been a marvelous act of spiritual discipline and commitment for the whole community to take some part of the responsibility; but I felt that I could not and the leaders of the Albany Movement could not afford to wait for others to do this, feeling that they wouldn't do it. And so, we were willing to take this spiritual plunge, so to speak, and assume the responsibility, even though we knew we had nothing to do with it.

Q     I think, Doctor, you will recall on earlier testimony that there has been some considerable time spent upon your approach to unjust laws; I believe you heard the Chief's statement: I would like for you to indicate for the Court what you mean by an unwillingness to adhere to unjust laws?

A     Well, this could be a very long philosophical discussion, but in terms of this context, I would say that we are dealing or referring mainly to laws upholding the system of segregation.

MR. HOLLOWELL: I think we have no further questions for this witness.

THE COURT: Any questions for this witness?

MR. LEVERETT: Yes sir.

CROSS EXAMINATION BY MR. LEVERETT:

Q     Dr. King, when did you say was the first occasion that you came into Albany since the formation of the Albany Movement? What was the date on that?

A     December 14, I believe.

Q     Now, prior to the time that you received a telegram, had you been in communication with Dr. Anderson or any other leads of the Albany Movement?

A     Yes sir, I think I had talked with Dr. Anderson several times. In fact, I have known Dr. Anderson for a number of years and almost every time he came to Atlanta, he stopped by the office or called.

Q     You aren't saying, are you Doctor King, that the first occasion in which you discussed with any member of the Albany Movement the possibility of your participation was just the incident that you referred to as having occurred a day or two before you came down?

A     Yes sir, that was the first time that an invitation was extended and the first time that I ever considered coming to Albany.

Q     Assuming that was the first time an invitation had ever been extended, had you on any prior occasion volunteered your services?

A     No sir, I had not on any prior occasion, as I recall, volunteered my services.

Q    I believe you said that you arrived here on the afternoon of December 15?

A    I think it was the 14th, I believe. It was on a Friday. It may have been the 15th.

Q    And that you stayed over through Monday? What was the following Monday, what was the date, do you recall?

A    It was the 18th, I believe.

Q    Now, did you speak at the Shiloh Church on the night of the 16th?

A    On the night of the 16th? No sir, I think that was the night I was in jail, the 16th.

Q    Excuse me, go ahead?

A    That was the night I was in jail.

Q    Dr. King, do you know how many times you have actually spoken either at Shiloh or Mt. Zion Baptist Church? Shiloh Methodist, I believe and Mt. Zion Baptist?

A    Baptist. No sir, I don't recall the exact number of times. I've spoken there many times since the Movement started, especially this last period that I've been back.

Q    In fact, in your speeches you have encouraged the people to march and to protest, haven't you?

A    Yes sir, I have encouraged the people to protest, as I have done over and over again all over the South and the Nation.

Q    Also, Dr. King, did you on one, at least one occasion, I don't know the exact date, address the crowd and tell them to come and bring their walking shoes?[22]

A    I may have. I don't recall this particular statement. It's altogether possible.

Q    Now, is it your testimony that you were here only on this occasion in December for a period of several days and that the next occasion that you returned to Albany was in February, when the trial was held; is that right?

A    Yes sir, I think it was February or early March. I don't recall the date.

Q    You were tried in February?

A    That's correct.

Q    And you commenced serving your sentence when?

A    In July.

Q    You did not commence serving it in February when the trial was held?

A    No sir, at that time the Judge ruled or stated that, since there were several legal questions involved and since several motions were made that he had not had a chance to study, he would have both sides to file briefs and then he would render his decision after that period; and I think he said that would be a 60-day period.

Q    Was there any appeal ever instituted by way of certiorari or any other legal proceedings that are available to review decisions of Recorder's Court?

---

22. Leverett may have been referring to King's speech on 20 July 1962 when he exhorted the crowd of over 1,200 to "get on your walking shoes. Live together children. Don't you get weary! There's a great camp meeting" (King, Address Delivered at Albany Movement Mass Meeting at Third Kiokee Baptist Church, 20 July 1962, p. 544 in this volume).

A    No sir, I don't recall. I don't know of any.

Q    Did you request that your attorney appeal it?

A    Appeal, you mean—?

Q    Of your conviction?

A    In July?

Q    Whenever you were convicted; I believe you stated that you had the trial in February and the determination of the Court was made in July, is that right?

A    That's right, that's right, yes.

Q    The question was, did you ever request that your attorneys appeal?

A    No sir, I didn't make a request for them to appeal. I knew that one case was being appealed, which would test the legality of the arrests themselves; and I didn't make a request for an appeal to be made on my behalf.

Q    Now, Dr. King, a few minutes ago you drew some distinction between the people who were the actual marchers and the other groups who followed along behind or who were engaged in some of this violent activity: Did you hear—were you hear when the witness, Slater King, testified that the Albany Movement represented all of the Negroes in Albany?[23]

A    I didn't hear, I don't recall this particular statement, but I'm sure that it does represent all of the Negroes of Albany, in the sense that it is seeking to achieve justice and first-class citizenship for all of the citizens of Albany.

Q    Also, Dr. King, do you know whether or not Dr. Anderson has stated on occasions that he estimated that the Albany Movement represented approximately 10,000 people in the Albany area: are you familiar with his statement to that effect?

A    No sir, I don't know about that particular statement. In fact, I don't know the actual membership of the Albany Movement. I don't think there is a membership list, in the sense that you would have in some incorporated bodies.

Q    Now Dr. King, you stated on direct that in referring to your right to violate unjust laws, you had reference mainly to segregation laws, is that right?

A    In this particular context, yes sir.

Q    By the use of the word "mainly", I presume you meant you were not necessarily limiting it to segregation laws, is that right?

A    Well, in this particular situation, yes.

Q    Would that include court decrees as well as laws, if you felt a court decree was unjust, do you think that you would have a right to violate it or to advocate violating it?

A    Well, it's difficult to give a yes or no answer to that. I think it is so general and it involves so many philosophical complexities that it would take me a few minutes to really explain this.

---

23. On 30 July 1962, Slater King testified: "We have no formal membership. We consider most of the Negro community members of the Albany Movement" (Transcript of Trial Testimony, *Kelly v. Page*, 335 F.2d 114 [5th Cir. 1964], 30 July–26 September 1962).

Q   Now, in making this statement about violating the laws, have you ever made that statement at any of these meetings that you had a Shiloh or Mt. Zion churches?

A   No sir, I don't think I have gone into a discussion of unjust laws or the whole question of civil disobedience at any of the mass meetings.

Q   Now Dr. King, when you made these statements, I believe before the Press Club on one occasion, is that correct, about the unjust law situation?

A   Yes sir. Well, that was in a question that came up when I was addressing the National Press Club.[24]

Q   Now, of course, when you made those statements, you didn't undertake to elaborate upon any of these philosophical or metaphysical insights or reservations that you now have just expressed, did you?

A   Yes sir, I took at least eight minutes to explain that.

Q   Now Dr. King, do you think that the masses of people that have been involved in the Albany Movement are capable of comprehending and appreciating all of this philosophical insight that you've referred to?

A   Many would. I think it can be broken down to the point that it can be understood by almost anybody. I have in the past tried to explain the meaning of civil disobedience and just and unjust laws to people who may not have had a great deal of formal training, but who had intelligence; and this can't be measured by the number of years that an individual has been to school; and I think it can be broken down to the point that people who are not well trained in the formal sense can understand it.

Q   In fact, Dr. King, isn't it true that such a statement as that could very easily be interpreted by some peoplle as an open invitation to go out and violate the law generally?

A   No sir, I have never said it when I did not explain exactly what I meant because I have always argued that anarchy is much worse in the final analysis than some other things; and what we seek is to create a society where men will live together as brothers and to correct and point out the deficiencies of the law and not to develop a situation where people will disobey the law generally when it is a just law.

Q   Now, Dr. King, let me ask you this question: A lot of people, conscientious people, disagree with certain Supreme Court decisions, do you think those people are justified, if their conscience tells them, do you think they are justified in going out and violating those decrees and advocating to others that they violate them?

A   I think—yes sir, I think that they have that right if they will do it openly, if they will willingly accept the penalty, if they will do it in loving, non-violent spirit and not curse and use terms that deal with Negroes as if they are dogs; if they are willing to accept the penalty, if they do it openly, fine; but if they seek to

---

24.  See King, Address Delivered to the National Press Club and Question and Answer Period, 19 July 1962, p. 536 in this volume.

subvert, if they seek to evade the law, I think that's wrong; and I think that this
is what they've done.

Q   In other words, you think that an open defiance of the law is all right but that if a person tries to, as you say, evade or circumvent, that that's wrong?

A   No sir, I don't think an open—I would not like to see them defy, evade or seek to circumvent the law. I would say that it becomes right when conscience tells them it is unjust and they openly, non-violently, lovingly break that law and willingly accept the penalty by staying in jail, if necessary, to point out the deficiencies of the law and arouse the conscience of the community so that it will see that it is wrong.

Q   In other words, you're saying that it's a state of mind and motivation of the individual that's the determining factor?

A   I'm sorry, I don't think I understand your question.

Q   As I understand what you're saying, you are saying that it's in effect a subjective question, that it's a state of mind, whether it is lovingly, as you say, violation; is that the determining factor, the mental attitude of the person doing it, is that what you're saying?

A   Well, no sir, I don't think it's the state of mind only, but only if that state of mind is coupled with a deep-seated moral conviction and that moral conviction takes one to the point of seeking to secure the moral end which is in the mind through moral means. Now, what often happens is that people seek to secure what they think are moral ends through immoral means, and I think this is wrong because the end is pre-existent in the means.

Q   Right there, who is going to determine whether it is a moral or immoral end, Dr. King? Are you going to make that determination or is somebody else going to make it and, if so, who would it be?

A   Well, I = would hope that the community and the Nation and the people of good will would make it as a result of the self-inflicted suffering that people who move out on a moral principle are willing to undertake. I'm not saying that they take the law in their hands, but they believe so much in the sacredness of the law when it is a right law that they are willing to suffer in order to see that those laws which are not right are somehow made or re-made to square with that which is morally right.

Q   I follow your explanation, I understand your explanation, but I am still not certain who you are saying is to make this determination as to whether it's right or wrong?

A   Well, the individuals involved are the ones, the individual conscience is the issue at that point.

Q   The individual is to decide in his own conscience whether or not he will violate the law, is that right?

A   The individual is to decide in his own conscience whether the law is right; and, if he violates it, he must accept the penalty. He must not try to run from it, he must not seek to evade it, he must not seek to violate it in some sense of subverting the law. He must do it openly and in a non-violent spirit; and this becomes civil disobedience and not uncivil disobedience which we too often see by those who seek to take the law in their hands.

Q    Now, Dr. King, you stated that your method was method of non-violence?

A    Yes sir.

Q    The fact of the matter is though that you anticipated violence, didn't you?

A    Well, I had rather put it another way. I hoped and I still hope that there will be no violence in our struggle for first-class citizenship. I came to Albany when I came and joined the Movement, hoping that there would be no violence; and when I say that I mean violence from either side.

       However, in a non-violent movement, the one thing that you say is that you as a person committed to non-violence will never inflict violence upon another, but you will willingly accept it upon yourself. And it may be that before freedom is achieved in some places in the South some blood will flow, but I've always insisted that it must be our blood and not the blood of our white brothers.

Q    Back in that connection, Doctor, you are familiar with these clinics that have been held, are you not, in Albany, at which the participants in the Albany Movement are given instruction in how to receive acts of violence against them?

A    In the clinics here in Albany?

Q    Right?

A    I haven't attended; no, I haven't had a chance to attend any of them.

Q    You have had instruction along those lines yourself, have you not?

A    Yes sir, I have been in clinics.

Q    In fact, you have attended clinics at the Highland Folk School in Tennessee, have you not?

A    No sir, I never attended a clinic there.

Q    Have you ever attended any meetings there?

A    Yes, I addressed the 25th—I gave one of the addresses at the 25th Anniversary of the Highlander Folk School.[25]

Q    Was Mr. Miles Horton there?

A    Yes sir, he was a director.

Q    Did you go there at his invitation?

A    As I recall, the invitation came from—I really don't remember. I don't know if Mr. Horton extended it or somebody else on the Board.[26]

Q    Did you address the group there on the subject of non-violent protests?

---

25. See King, "A Look to the Future," Address Delivered at Highlander Folk School's Twenty-fifth Anniversary Meeting, 2 September 1957, in *Papers* 4:269–276. In 1959 Highlander came under scrutiny when the Tennessee government recommended its charter be revoked on charges that the school was being run for profit, which was a violation of its nonprofit requirements. Highlander closed in 1961 and reopened later that year as the Highlander Research and Education Center.

26. MIA activist and Highlander executive council member James E. Pierce invited King to attend the seminar (Myles Horton to King, 19 April 1957). King spoke on the last day of the seminar, which lasted four days.

A    I'm sure in the course of my lecture, as I always do in all of my speeches, I dealt
     much time I spent on it.

MR. HOLLOWELL: May it please the Court, I cannot see where some speech
that has been made in some years previous at some place outside of Albany, which
has nothing to do and had nothing to do with any of the activities which are here,
could have in any way have any relevancy or materiality to this particular issue, unless
counsel is seeking to show that this particular witness, Defendant and party, has at
some time made a speech in which he recommended violence or something other
than this which he is submitting here now. I would submit it would have absolutely
no materiality.

MR. LEVERETT: May it please the Court, this witness has testified of his advocacy
of non-violent protests, and I am going into the question of what preparation which
he and other members of his group may have had for violence.

MR. HOLLOWELL: I would submit that it wouldn't matter what his preparation
was, as long as this has been the advocation that has been made here in this suit
pertaining to all matters which are related to the subject case, this and this only.
What preparation, I think unless he was going to the original preparation from the
standpoint of his background, study and so forth, I think would be of no moment
and would have no materiality.

THE COURT: I think that's what, as I understood counsel's statement, that's what
he intends to do, is to show what training he's had in connection with the very thing
we're talking about. That's what I understood counsel to say.

MR. LEVERETT: Yes sir.

MR. HOLLOWELL: Training, if this is what it relates to, that's one thing; if it
merely relates to a matter of some speech which has been made at some prior time
and did not relate to this, then I don't think it is relevant.

THE COURT: Then, that would only go to possible impeachment to contradict
some other testimony which he has given; but, as I understood counsel, he said he
was going into the matter of training. So, I will allow the question.

Q    Mr. Leverett: Dr. King, the matter of these protests and the procedures to be
     utilized and the anticipation of violence, all of these things were in fact dis-
     cussed or there was instruction given at this Highlander Folk School, isn't that
     true?

A    I really couldn't say. I was only at the Highland Folk School one time and that
     was the time that I went in for that address, and I was there only 3 or 4 hours;
     I had to go right out; so, I don't know too many of the details. I do know that
     Highland Folk School has worked in the area of race relations across the years,
     but how much emphasis they place on training non-violent leaders, I don't
     know.

Q    Is it your testimony that you went there to speak or to attend other addresses
     that were made?

A    My testimony is that I went there to speak. I didn't hear any of the other
     addresses. I went in and made my speech and left, oh an hour or two after
     that.

Q    Dr. King, I hand you a document—

MR. HOLLOWELL: May we see that?

MR. LEVERETT: I want to present him with the pictures [*strikeout illegible*] not with the writing in the paper, but the pictures.

(Document tendered to counsel for Defendants)

MR. HOLLOWELL: May it please the Court, I will object to this particular document, which is P-22, on the ground that there is nothing in it which would show the source from which it came, or the name of the editors or publishers of it. There is no certificate of any kind attached to it. There is nothing to indicate that these photographs which are even on it were actually taken of the particular scene which they purport to have been taken of; or that any of the identifications that are attributed here are in fact true; and on the further ground that there is nothing here which would suggest anything dealing with the Albany Movement or with any preparation which this witness has at any time made, which would go to the development of a theory of non-violence and a philosophy dealing with the matter of unjust laws.

MR. LEVERETT: May it please the Court, I wanted to show the witness the paper, there are some pictures on here, and I wanted to ask him about if this is his picture there and this is his picture here; and he appears to be sitting here, and he just testified that he didn't hear any speeches but that he went there and spoke only. And I wanted to question him about these pictures.

MR. HOLLOWELL: The wording under it, Your Honor, I mean the wording itself, I think that again is objectionable as no evidence has been offered about the authenticity of it.

THE COURT: Mr. Hollowell, he hasn't offered it in evidence, the document hasn't been offered in evidence; and I'm going to proceed the same way that I did on a previous occasion when counsel was questioning the witness about a newspaper article, whether that was correctly represented, and the same rule would apply here. I will <u>allow</u> counsel to ask him questions about the pictures on cross-examination. Now, if it comes to the question of introduction of the document, then I will rule when we get to that.

MR. HOLLOWELL: Allright.

Q   <u>Mr. Leverett:</u> Dr. King, I ask you whether this picture in the top left-hand corner, is that your picture there?

A   Yes sir, that's my picture.

Q   Is that a true representation of you as you appeared at the Highlander Folk School?[27]

A   Yes sir, that's correct.

Q   Now, I call your attention to the picture over here in the top right-hand corner and ask you if that is you sitting in̶ the second from the right in that picture?

---

27. Following his address, billboards featuring King at Highlander appeared throughout the South with the headline "King At Communist Training School" (King, "A Look to the Future," 2 September 1957, in *Papers* 4:269–276; for a photograph of the billboard, see photographs in *Papers* 4).

A    Yes sir.

Q    And you're sitting down there, are you not?

A    That's correct.

Q    Who was speaking at the time that you were sitting there?

A    I don't recall. As I recall, and this is vague in my memory, someone was leading a devotional period, and I think it was Dr. Thompson of the University of Chicago, because he was up when I came in; and I spoke immediately after him.[28]

Q    Is this picture on the right, the one where you're sitting down, is that a true representation of you as you sat there on the occasion in question?

A    On the—?

Q    Is this a true picture?

A    Yes, that's my picture.

Q    Who is this party right here sitting, looking at the picture, to the right?

A    I don't know him.

Q    What about this party?

A    That's Mr. Aubrey Williams.[29]

Q    And what about this gentleman here?

A    I don't believe I know him; no, I don't know him.

THE COURT: Is that Aubrey Williams from Alabama?

The Witness: From Montgomery, Alabama; that's right.

Q    Mr. Leverett: Dr. King, I ask you whether or not a Miss or Mrs. Grace Lorch was also at that meeting?[30]

A    I don't know her, so I couldn't say.

Q    Now, getting back to the question that I asked you a few minutes ago, it is true, is it not Dr. King, that in this movement that you have engaged in, that you did anticipate that violence might be committed?

A    In Albany or the over-all?

Q    In Albany specifically?

MR. HOLLOWELL: May it please the Court, I think this is now about the third time that he has asked that and the witness has already answered the question.

---

28. John B. Thompson, one of Highlander's first staff members and dean of the University of Chicago's Rockefeller Memorial Chapel, introduced King.

29. Williams, president of the Southern Conference Education Fund, preceded King's address at Highlander's meeting in September 1957.

30. Grace Lorch, a former schoolteacher from Arkansas, first gained public attention in September 1957 when she defended fifteen-year-old Elizabeth Eckford against an angry mob after the girl had been turned away from all-white Central High School in Little Rock. The next month Mrs. Lorch was called before the Senate Internal Security Subcommittee to answer questions about her alleged communist involvement. When Senators James O. Eastland (D-MS) and William Jenner (R-IN) questioned her, she answered with a prepared statement that began, "I am here under protest." She was charged with contempt ("Little Rock Woman Defies Senate Unit," *New York Times*, 30 October 1957).

THE COURT: I think so. I think we've been over that and I don't see any use in going over that again. Let's move on to something else.

Q    Mr. Leverett: Dr. King, are you a member of CORE?

A    I'm a member of the advisory board, the National Advisory Board.

Q    Are you affiliated with the Student Non-Violent Coordinating Committee?

A    Yes sir, I am.

Q    In what capacity?

A    Adviser.

Q    As an adviser or are you on some board or committee?

A    Yes sir, it is called, I think, advisory board.

Q    Advisory board?

A    Yes sir.

Q    Is that the governing body of that group?

A    No sir, the governing body is another body altogether.

MR. LEVERETTS: That's all at this time.

MR. HOLLOWELL: Now, if it please the Court, I would respectfully request the Court to rule on our motion now pertaining to all of his testimony relative to this Highlander School, insofar as it is not relevant and it is immaterial and there is no way that it has been in any wise associated with anything that is the subject-matter of this particular case; and, therefore, I again move that it be stricken. It was not tied in in any way whatsoever.

THE COURT: I think your motion is too broad. Certainly the fact that he attended and so and testified that these matters were discussed there, I think that would be pertinent. Now, the question of whether the testimony given about these particular pictures, I don't see how that adds anything to the case; and I sustain the motion insofar as it relates to these pictures in question.

MR. HOLLOWELL: Thank you, sir.

MR. LEVERETT: May it please the Court, before the Court rules, my point on the pictures was that the witness testified that he went there only to make a speech, that he was not present when any other speeches were made; and I believe this picture shows him sitting down listening to some sort of speech, certainly something was going on.

THE COURT: I'm going to sustain the motion and exclude the reference to the pictures. I admit all of the other testimony about the Highlander School.

Anything further from this witness?

REDIRECT EXAMINATION BY MR. HOLLOWELL:

Q    One question, did you or did you not know who was to be present at the meeting just referred to?

MR. LEVERETT: May it please the Court, now if I can't go into it, I think that counsel certainly has no right to go into it.

THE COURT: I think his question only relates to the general meeting.

MR. HOLLOWELL: That is correct.

THE COURT: Go ahead.

Q    Mr. Hollowell: Did you or did you not know who was to be present?

A   No sir, I did not know who was to be present, only some of the people. I would 9 Aug
say 4 or 5; but the vast majority I didn't know. 1962

Q   No further questions.

RECROSS EXAMINATION BY MR. LEVERETT:

Q   Dr. King, in fact, several people there were acknowledged Communists, isn't that true?

A   I did not know any. In fact, all of the people I came in contact with and the people that I know who were there are not Communists and never have been. Now, if there were communists there, I knew nothing about it.

Q   You are disclaiming though any knowing association with those people now?

A   Any knowing association with the people at the Conference?

Q   Right?

A   I don't quite understand. You mean all of the people there?

Q   You've just stated that you did not know who was going to be there, which I presume was by means of ameliorating or explaining the fact that some people were there who apparently you were little unconcerned about?

MR. HOLLOWELL: May it please the Court, that's a matter, I think, of testimony and conclusion made by counsel and I would submit that it would be improper and ought to be stricken as a conclusion on his part.

THE COURT: Yes, that's simply a statement made by counsel and not a question. I strike that.

THE COURT: Now, do you want to ask the question over?

MR. LEVERETT: No further questions.

MR. HOLLOWELL: Come down.

THE COURT: We'll take a recess at this time for 10 minutes.

TD. Transcript of Trial at 1138–1170, *Kelly v. Page*, 335 F.2d 114 (5th Cir. 1964); copy at GEpNASR: Record Group 21.


# From Alabama Christian Movement
# for Human Rights

9 August 1962
Birmingham, Ala.

*On 8 August Jerome Heilbron of the Civil Rights Division of the U.S. Justice Department issued a "friend-of-the-court" brief opposing the request of Albany city officials for a permanent injunction banning further civil rights protests.[1] Buoyed by this federal intervention, the leaders of the Alabama Christian Movement for Human Rights (ACMHR), Fred Shuttlesworth, J. S. Phifer,*

---

1. Hendrick Smith, "U.S. Intervenes on Negroes' Side in Georgia Case," *New York Times*, 9 August 1962.

*Edward Gardner, Abraham Woods, and W. E. Shortridge, send King the following
telegram expressing their optimism that "victory is ours and our prayers are being
answered."*[2]

DR MARTIN LUTHER KING =

CITY JAIL ALBANY GA =

WE ARE ALL ENCOURAGED TODAY AFTER READING THAT THE JUSTICE DEPART-
MENT HAS ENTERED THE PICTURE IN ALBANY. WITH GOD, UNCLE SAM AND YOU, WE
ARE CONFIDENT THAT VICTORY IS OURS AND OUR PRAYERS ARE BEING ANSWERED.
KEEP UP YOUR COURAGEOUS FIGHT WITH CONFIDENCE, WYATT IS KEEPING US POSTED
AND DOING A GOD JOB. WE ARE IN CONSTANT TOUCH WITH A.D. ON NEW DEVELOP-
MENTS AND TRYING TO DECIDE ON A DELEGATION TO ATTEND HEARING, HOWEVER,
TELEPHONE COMMUNICATIONS WITH YOUR DAD SUGGESTS THAT WE REFRAIN.[3] BEST
WISHES FOR SUCCESS =

ALABAMA CHRISTIAN MOVEMENT FOR HUMAN RIGHTS
REV F L SHUTTLESWORTH
PRESIDENT

---

2. Fred L. Shuttlesworth (1922–2011). James S. Phifer (1915–1969), born in Lowndes County, was
pastor of Birmingham's Zion Star Baptist Church before moving to White Plains, New York, to become
pastor of Calvary Baptist Church. Phifer was active in the Birmingham struggle for civil rights and served
as second-vice president of the ACMHR. He was arrested several times for his participation in nonviolent
demonstrations and was honored with Fred Shuttlesworth in March 1962 for serving thirty-two days in
Birmingham City Jail (Citizens of Birmingham and SCLC, Program, "A Testimonial Honoring Rev. F. L.
Shuttlesworth and Rev. J. S. Phifer," 8 March 1962; see also King to Robert Kennedy, 25 January 1962,
pp. 372–373 in this volume). Edward Gardner (1907–2006), was born in Birmingham, Alabama, and
graduated from Parker High School. He became pastor of Mt. Olive Baptist Church in Birmingham
in 1947, a position he held for nearly sixty years. Gardner cofounded the ACMHR and served as the
organization's first vice president. He succeeded Fred Shuttlesworth as president of the organization in
1968. In 1962 Gardner was one of many who defended King when he was attacked by a white segregationist while he spoke at SCLC's sixth annual convention. Abraham Lincoln Woods (1928–2008), born
in Birmingham, Alabama, earned a B.A. (1953) in theology from Birmingham Baptist College, a B.A.
(1962) in sociology from Miles College in Fairfield, Alabama, and an M.A. (1975) from the University
of Alabama at Tuscaloosa. When the state outlawed the NAACP in 1956, he joined Fred Shuttlesworth
to form the ACMHR and became the organization's second vice president. In 1961, Woods became a
faculty member at his alma mater Miles College and worked with King to desegregate Birmingham and
organize the March on Washington in August 1963. William Eugene Shortridge (1900–1964) was born in
Birmingham, Alabama. He graduated from Howard University with a B.S. in commerce and finance in
1923. Following his father's death in 1925, Shortridge took over the operation of the Shortridge Funeral
Home in Birmingham. In 1956 Shortridge became treasurer of ACMHR, a position he held until his
death in 1964. Shortridge was a member of the SCLC executive committee from 1958–1964 and an
active member of the local NAACP for thirty-two years, serving in several posts during that time, including branch treasurer, branch president, and executive committee member. King spoke at Shortridge's
funeral on 2 May 1964, calling him a "great freedom fighter" (Emory O. Jackson, "Bishop I. H. Bonner
Says 'Some Day We Will Overcome,'" *Birmingham World*, 6 May 1964).

3. As a minister of a church on the outskirts of Birmingham, King's brother A. D. worked with the
ACMHR. The group likely refers to King's trial scheduled for 10 August for charges stemming from his
arrest on 27 July.

REV J S PHIFER
VICE

REV EDWARD GARDNER
VICE

REV ABRAHAM WOODS
VICE

BY W E SHORTRIDGE
TREASURER.

PWSr. MCMLK-RWWL: 6.1.0.150.

10 Aug
1962

## Albany Jail Diary from 8 August–10 August 1962

Albany, Ga.

*In King's last few days of his jail stay in Albany, he testified in two trials. In the
first trial on 8 August, King defends his First Amendment right to peacefully
protest against segregation. Although Judge J. Robert Elliott delayed making
a decision in the case, King is relieved that the hearings are over as he is
"exhausted," requiring medical attention from Dr. W. G. Anderson.[1] Two days
later, King is back in court to answer charges of disorderly conduct, failure
to obey an officer, and illegally congregating on a sidewalk in Albany on 27
July. Testifying before Judge A. N. Durden, King said he went to City Hall to
participate in a prayer vigil as a "last resort" in hopes that the "consciences of the
commissioners would be aroused so that they would comply with this very simple
request" to negotiate with the Albany Movement. In pronouncing sentence,
Durden said that blacks should seek redress in the courts rather than conducting
mass demonstrations. He fined King and three others two hundred dollars and
gave them each a sixty-day suspended sentence.[2] Calling the sentence "unjust,"
King agrees to leave Albany to give the commission "a chance to 'save face'" and
enter in "good faith" negotiations with the Albany Movement.[3]*

---

1. For more on King's testimony, see Testimony in *Asa D. Kelly et al., v. M. S. Page et al.*, 8 August 1962,
pp. 570–587 in this volume.

2. See Bill Shipp, "Rev. King Is Released, Leaves Albany to Give Negotiations a Chance," *Atlanta
Constitution*, 11 August 1962. King, Abernathy, Anderson, and Slater King were put on probation subject
to re-arrest should they participate in demonstrations during the next sixty days (Milton L. Carr, "Dr.
King, 3 Others Get Suspended Terms," *Atlanta Daily World*, 11 August 1962).

3. Reacting to her husband's release, Coretta Scott King said that "justice has come to Albany"
(Carr, "Dr. King, 3 Others Get Suspended Terms," 11 August 1962). King returned to Atlanta on the evening of 10 August, and the following day, Albany officials closed its public parks and libraries rather than
integrate them. Considering these new developments, a newspaper article reported that King promised
to return to Albany on Monday, 13 August (Hedrick Smith, "Albany, Ga., Closes Parks and Libraries to
Balk Integration," *New York Times*, 12 August 1962).

**Wednesday, August 8**—Today was the last day of the hearing and Ralph and I testified. Although the Federal court hearing offered some relief from the hot jail, I was glad the hearings were over. It was always miserable going back to the hot cell from the air-conditioned courtroom. I was so exhausted and sick that Dr. Anderson had to come and treat me for the second time.

**Thursday, August 9**—Even though we decided to remain in jail, *We Woke Up This Morning With Our Mind On Freedom.* Everyone appeared to be in good spirits and we had an exceptionally good devotional program and sang all of our freedom songs.

Later, Wyatt and Dr. Anderson came and told me that two marches were being planned if Ralph and I were sentenced to jail tomorrow. All of the mothers of many prisoners agreed to join their families in jail (including my wife, Mrs. Anderson, Wyatt's wife, Young's wife, Ralph's wife and the wife of Atty. William Kunstler.[4]

**Friday, August 10**—The suspended sentence today did not come as a complete surprise to me. I still think the sentence was unjust and I want to appeal but our lawyers have not decided. Ralph and I agreed to call off the marches and return to our churches in Atlanta to give the (Albany City) Commission a chance to "save face" and demonstrate good faith with the Albany Movement.

PD. *Jet*, 23 August 1962, pp. 14–21.

---

4. On 10 August Coretta Scott King was scheduled to lead a "mother's march" with Juanita Abernathy, wife of Ralph Abernathy; Norma L. Anderson, wife of W.G. Anderson; Theresa Walker, wife of Wyatt Tee Walker; Jean Young, wife of Andrew Young; and Margaret Kunstler, wife of William Kunstler. The second planned march was a prayer pilgrimage composed of local citizens and a group of out-of-state ministers, who had come to Albany to show support for the movement (Hedrick Smith, "Albany Negroes to Protest Today," *New York Times*, 10 August 1962; FBI, Memo, "Racial situation, Albany, Ga.," 10 August 1962, Bureau File 157–6–2–644). Both marches were canceled after King was released from jail (Smith, "Dr. King Set Free after Conviction," *New York Times*, 11 August 1962).

# Statement Delivered at the Ruins of Shady Grove Baptist Church

*[15 August 1962]*
*[Leesburg, Ga.]*

*Before dawn the Shady Grove Baptist Church, a center for voter registration activity in southwest Georgia, was bombed.[1] King, who visited the ruins in the*

---

1. "Negroes' Church Burns in Georgia," *New York Times*, 16 August 1962. There were no injuries and no reported witnesses to the fire. Leesburg sheriff R.A. Forrester and Albany fire chief E.F. Moody, an arson expert, speculated that the fire was started by lightning or faulty electrical wiring. Moody elaborated: "There is no evidence of arson and definitely no indication of an explosion" ("Fire Destroys Negro Church at Leesburg," *Americus Times Recorder*, 15 August 1962). Between August and September 1962, eight black churches were burned in southwest Georgia ("Macon Church Is Destroyed by Fire," *Atlanta Daily World*, 26 September 1962).

*morning, returns that evening and leads a group in prayer.[2] In October the FBI
charged two white men from nearby Smithville with the crime.[3] The following
transcript is taken from a film recording.*

We know that what happened here came from somebody who had the strange
illusion that they could block the aspirations of the Negro people for freedom and
justice by destroying property.[4] And it is not just ordinary property. All property is significant [*Congregation:*] (*Yes, Yes*), but this is a church of God. (*Yes, Amen*) And when
men will do this (*Well*), when men will seek to destroy the church of God, they have
degenerated to a tragic level of inhumanity and sin and evil. And so we come here
this evening to pray for them. I know it's hard to pray for our enemies, and to bless
those persons who curse us, and yet this is what Jesus commands us to do.[5]

F. CBSNA-NNCBS.

2. King pledged $500 to help rebuild the church (SCLC, Press release, "SCLC pledges special fund
to rebuild dynamited church," 15 August 1962). In an article titled "We're Ready to Build," published in
the SCLC *Newsletter* in December 1962, Jackie Robinson announced: "I am happy to say to the supporters
of the Southern Christian Leadership Conference and our many friends around the nation that we have
to date received $35,000.00 for the rebuilding of the burned churches in South Georgia." He continued:
"In about ten days, I will be meeting with the pastors of the churches, Dr. King, the architects and a
few other people who represent funds that have been gathered in addition to reports that the Atlanta
Constitution's fund is nearly $10,000.00 and there is possibly another $10,000.00 available through the
National Council of Churches. We propose to coordinate our efforts early in December in order that
these churches will be ready for use as soon as possible."

3. On 4 October 1962, FBI agents investigating the bombing of Shady Grove Baptist Church arrested
Jack P. Smith, 28, and detained Douglas Harold Parker, 18, in connection with the bombing, but a federal
grand jury failed to indict the two men ("Two Charged with Burning Lee County Church Where Voter
Meetings Were Held," *Atlanta Daily World*, 5 October 1962; "Dispute between Hoover and King: The FBI's
Answer to Criticisms," *U.S. News & World Report*, 7 December 1964).

4. In King's article "The Terrible Cost of the Ballot" published in the September 1962 issue of the
SCLC *Newsletter*, he said that efforts to register voters in Lee County were "tantamount to inviting death."
He also wrote that the "charred remains of the Shady Grove Baptist Church," was the "terrible cost of
the ballot in the Deep South."

5. Cf. Matthew 5:44.

# Address Delivered at Albany Movement Mass Meeting at Shiloh Baptist Church

[*15 August 1962*]
Albany, Ga.

*Less than an hour after negotiations between the Albany Movement and the
Albany City Commission collapsed, King vows before a large audience at Shiloh*

*Baptist Church to renew demonstrations in Albany.*[1] *King says: "The City Commission of Albany has again revealed to you, to the state of Georgia, to the United States, and to the world that it holds the Negro citizens of this community in utter contempt." He criticizes the commission for living in "1962 industrially" but in "1862 in human relations," insisting that if Albany is to grow as a community, it "cannot keep a man down in the valley without staying down there with him." Reminding the audience of the virtues of their grievances, King declares that "what we are doing is vindicated by history" and calls on white men and women to break their silence, for "we will have to repent in this generation not merely from the loud and bitter words of the bad people but for the appalling silence of the good people." In conclusion, King beseeches the audience to remain nonviolent and committed to the goal of creating a "moral balance" between whites and African Americans: "Our aim is not merely to get rid of a system called segregation, but our aim is to do something to people who have lived in the midst of segregation. Our aim is to make new creatures: better white men and better Negro men, better white women and better Negro women." The following address was taken from an audio recording.*

I noticed when I came in that they had listed on the program that I would make an address, the main address for the evening. Now, I want to relieve you a bit, and I want to relieve myself a bit, by saying to you that I don't plan to make an address of any length. I think you will all agree that it is mighty hot [*Audience:*] (*Yes, Yes it is, Sure enough*), and although many people don't believe it, but I am a Baptist preacher. (*Yes, Amen, All right*) And of course, I can get fired up just like Baptist preachers generally get fired up. [*laughter*] But in all seriousness, I want to say just a few brief words to you tonight, and then we will move on.

The City Commission of Albany has again revealed to you, to the state of Georgia, to the United States, and to the world that it holds the Negro citizens of this community in utter contempt. (*That's right, That's right*) The City Commission has revealed that it does not intend to negotiate in good faith, and when you won't talk to people, you don't even negotiate in bad faith. [*laughter*] (*That's right, You know that's right*) This is tragic for this city. This is tragic for the state of Georgia, and one day in the not too distant future (*Yes sir, Amen*), the City Commissioners will have to realize that this is 1962 (*That's right*) and not (*Amen*) 1855 (*Yes, 1855, That's right, Sure enough*), and you cannot hold on to ox cart methods in a jet age. (*That's right*) [*applause*]

And Albany is in a terrible dilemma—not its Negro citizens, because the Negro

---

1. A five-member African American delegation attended the packed City Commission meeting and sat in the back of the room. In what a reporter called an "unusual action," a crowd of whites applauded as the mayor and the six commissioners entered the room. The meeting had been the first between the Albany Movement and the entire City Commission since February 1962. Marion Page, executive secretary of the Albany Movement, presented the commission with a five-point desegregation petition, which included desegregation of bus and train terminals, the return of cash bonds for property bonds for those arrested, desegregation of city buses, no police interference with the right to protest, and quick disposition of cases of arrested demonstrators. Albany's mayor, Asa Kelley, dismissed the Albany Movement's requests, stating that the matter was already under consideration by the federal district court ("Albany, Ga., Hears Negro Pleas but Refuses to Take Any Action," *New York Times*, 16 August 1962; Don Kimsey, "Await Court Action, Mayor Tells Negroes," *Albany Herald*, 16 August 1962).

citizens of this community are standing on and living with what is right. (*Amen,* 15 Aug
*Amen*) And there is no losing where we're concerned. What we're doing (*That's true*)  1962
is vindicated by history (*Amen, That's right*), is sanctioned by all of the eternities, and
it is a part of the edicts of God himself (*Yes, That's right*) so that all of the stars in their
courses are working with us. We aren't in the dilemma. (*Go ahead, Amen, Go ahead*)

But, but the city, under the leadership of the City Commission, is in a terrible
dilemma. I'll tell you why. They want to live in 1962 (*That's right*) industrially, but
they want to live in 1862 in human relations, and [*applause*] they just aren't going to
work together. [*applause*] They are going around begging for industry (*That's right*)
all over the South. Let nobody fool you, these industries are not coming into these
communities that will stand up and defy the very law of the land and hold Negro
citizens in utter contempt. For when you have in Russia astronauts and cosmonauts
dashing through outer space in eighty-eight minutes per orbit, and we are still down
here in Albany, Georgia, can't even go in the library to read a book [*applause*], how
in the world can we compete? [*sustained applause*] We've got to say to them that the
two aren't going to work together. If you plan to grow and develop as a community, if
you plan to grow economically and otherwise, you are going to have to do something
about this race problem, for it is a fact of life that you cannot keep a man down in the
valley without staying down there with him (*That's right*) in order [*applause*] to hold
him there. [*applause*]

Now, this is the first thing that I would like to get over to you this evening. The
second thing is this. The City Commission is composed, I believe, of seven people.[2]
The population of this city, I believe, is about fifty-eight thousand. Some 60 percent
of these people are white, and I want to raise a question tonight. Where are the other
white people of Albany? (*Yes sir*) What are they saying about the absolute refusal of
the City Commission to negotiate? (*Well*) Tonight I want to call on white people
of goodwill (*Yes*) to rise up, gird their courage, and move on out and make it clear
(*That's right*) that they will not sit idly by the wayside on their stools of silence while
this community sinks more and more into moral degeneracy. The political structure
of any community is only one side of the power structure. (*Yes sir*) There's always a
economic power structure, and let nobody fool you, the boys in the political power
structure will always listen to the boys in the economic power structure. (*That's right*)
These are the people who run the politics of a city and a state. (*That's right*) [*applause*]
I want to know, where are the leading businessmen in the white community of
Albany (*That's right*) in this situation? [*applause*] I want to hear from them. [*applause*]
We need to hear from them now.

And I want to ask about another group because I'm intimately associated with it.
(*Talk about it, Come on, Preach*) I want to know where the Christian people, who go to
church every Sunday morning, stand. (*Amen, Well, Amen*) I want to hear from them
(*Yes, Amen*), for you see, it may well be that we will have to repent in this generation
(*Yes sir*) not merely from the loud and bitter words of the bad people but for the
appalling silence of the good people. (*That's right, Yes sir*)

This disturbs me (*Yes*), and I believe it disturbs you. (*Yes*) It disturbs me to see min-

2. Albany's Board of City Commissioners consisted of five members: T.H. McCollum, L.W. Mott,
C.B. Pritchett, W.C. Holman, and Allen Fleming Davis.

isters of the gospel (*All right*), laymen, trying to go to worship in churches in Albany, and they can't worship. (*Amen, Yes sir*) A Methodist minister, Reverend Ralph Roy from New York City, went to his own denomination with a Negro. (*That's right*) And do you know they turned him back?[3] (*Yes, Yes, Yes they did, Yes*) Oh, how tragic this is. (*It's tragic, Yes, Well, Right*) Eleven o'clock on Sunday morning, when we stand to sing "In Christ There Is No East or West," is the most segregated hour in America, and the Sunday school is the most segregated school of the (*That's right*) week.[4] (*That's right, That's right*) How tragic this is.

To use Dr. Anderson terms, Dr. Anderson's terms that he would use as a doctor, too often in the church and particularly the white church, we have a high blood pressure of creeds and an anemia of deeds. (*Yeah*) It's time now (*Amen*) that we begin to shake the lethargy from our souls. (*All right, Yes sir, Amen*) We are going to be children of the almighty God. If our white brothers are going to be Christians (*That's right*), they must go on back to the Old Testament (*That's right*), hear Amos crying out, "Let justice roll down (*Yes*) like water (*That's right, Go ahead*) [*applause*], and righteousness like a mighty stream."[5] [*applause*] They must go on over and turn till they get to Micah (*Yes sir*), hear him as he cries out in words that echo across the centuries (*Yes, That's right, Go on ahead*): "What doth the Lord require of thee (*Yes, Yes*), but to do justly, to love mercy (*Yes*), and to walk humbly with thy God."[6] (*Yes, Well, Go ahead, Go ahead*) Go with me, if you will, on over to the New Testament. (*Yes*) Stand with Paul as he stands on Mars Hill and cries out, "Out of one blood God made *all* men [*applause*] to dwell upon the face of the earth."[7] (*Yes, Amen, Go ahead, That's right*) [*applause*] Then stand with me. Watch our Lord and master as he moves (*Yes*) around the Galilean hills. (*All right, Yes sir*) Hear him as he said, "Blessed are the pure in heart (*Go on, Yeah, That's right, Oh yeah*), for they shall see God. (*Yeah, That's right*) Blessed are the meek, for they (*Yes*) shall inherit the earth. (*Yes, Yes, Well*) Do unto others as you would have them (*That's right*) do unto you."[8] (*Okay, Yes, That's true*) Our white brothers in Albany need to hear these words. (*That's true, Yes, That's right*) That's the second point I want to bring out.

The third point I want to bring out is something that I've been wanting to say to you, because something can be said to you so long that you come to believe it. I reread a book a few weeks ago written by a man named Adolph Hitler—you've heard of him. (*Yes, Yes*) It's a book called *Mein Kampf*; he says in that book, among other things, that if you are going to tell a lie—and he implies that to be a good dictator

---

3. Ralph Lord Roy (1928– ), a white CORE activist and pastor at Grace Methodist Church in New York, participated in an unsuccessful attempt to integrate several all-white churches in Albany with a small group of ministers on 12 August 1962. For more on Roy's efforts, see King to Roy, 22 August 1962, pp. 602–604 in this volume.

4. National Council of Churches official Helen Kenyon labeled eleven o'clock on Sunday morning as "the most segregated time" in the United States ("Worship Hour Found Time of Segregation," *New York Times*, 4 November 1952; see also Robert J. McCracken, "Discrimination—The Shame of Sunday Morning," *The Pulpit* 26, no. 2 [February 1955]: 4–5). King cites the title of John Oxenham's hymn "In Christ There Is No East or West" (1908).

5. Cf. Amos 5:24.

6. Cf. Micah 6:8.

7. Cf. Acts 17:26.

8. Cf. Matthew 5:8, 5:5, 7:12.

you have to do it—he says tell a big lie.[9] (*Yes, All right*) And if you tell it long and loud
enough, everybody will soon believe it, even yourself. (*That's right*) [*laughter*] So now,
we've been hearing a lot of things, and I'm afraid that we're going to come to believe
these things if we don't straighten them out. (*That's right*)

Now, they say we are lawbreakers, and they aren't going to negotiate with lawbreakers. (*That's right*) You've read that, haven't you?[10] (*Yes*) Now, I want to say to
you tonight that the 1,100-odd persons who have been arrested in this struggle are
not lawbreakers. (*That's right*) We don't even have to go to the point of explaining a
doctrine that is very dear to me, and I believe sincerely that there are times when it
is necessary to break laws. This is nothing new in history to break laws (*No*), but we
don't even have to go that far.

There's nothing new about breaking laws. Academic freedom wouldn't be a reality today if Socrates hadn't broke a law—hadn't broken a law. (*That's right, Go ahead*)
Go back and read Plato and look at his dialogues, the *Apology* and the *Crito*, and all
through it you see (*Go ahead*) Socrates making it clear (*Yes*) that he's got to drink
the hemlock (*Yes*) because he's practiced civil (*Go ahead*) disobedience.[11] (*Go ahead*)
That's nothing new. (*Yes*) The early Christians mastered lawbreaking to the point that
they were thrown to the lions (*Yeah*) in the midst of the lion's den. (*Yeah*) If you don't
want to go that far, go back to the Old Testament. (*Go ahead, Yeah*) Look at Shadrach,
Meshach, and Abednego (*That's right*) standing before King Nebuchadnezzar saying,
"We cannot bow."[12] (*That's right*) This is nothing new about lawbreaking. (*No, Go
ahead*) Let us never forget that everything that Hitler did in Germany was legal. It
was illegal to aid and comfort a Jew in the days of Hitler's Germany. If I had lived in
Germany and had my attitude, the attitude that I have now, I would have aided and
comforted my Jewish brothers even though the law said it was wrong. And even this
nation came into being with a massive act of lawbreaking, for what implied more civil
disobedience than the Boston Tea Party? (*That's right*) [*applause*] There's nothing
new about lawbreaking. [*applause*]

But we don't even have to go that far. (*Go on back*) We don't even have to go that
far. In 1954 the Supreme Court of our nation said in a decision, called the *Brown*
decision, that segregation is unconstitutional. Now, let me put it in legal terms just
like they said. They said that separate facilities are inherently unequal and that to
segregate a child on the basis of his race is to deny that child equal protection of the
law. (*That's right, That's right*) This is what it said. (*That's right*) It said that the old *Plessy*
doctrine of 1896 must go.[13] This is what it said. Now, the Supreme Court is the final
law of the land. The Supreme Court is the final judicial body of this land, and it rendered the decision. We didn't render it; the Supreme Court rendered the decision.
(*That's right*) Not only that, we have a Constitution, and it has a First Amendment,
and it talks about freedom of the press, freedom of assembly, freedom of speech.

---

9. Cf. Adolf Hitler, *Mein Kampf* (Boston: Houghton Mifflin, 1943), p. 134.

10. "'No Deal,' City Informs Negro Violators of Law," *Albany Herald*, 16 July 1962.

11. Cf. Plato, *The Dialogues of Plato*, trans. B. Jowett (New York: Scribner's, 1911).

12. Cf. Daniel 3:16–18.

13. The *Plessy* doctrine of 1896 established the "separate but equal" law, which was inherently unjust
and reinforced the subjugation of African Americans.

And this is what makes America great, 'cause in its best moments, it realized that there are some things so basic that they should never be taken from anybody.

This is the great weakness of Communism, isn't it? (*Well, Yes sir*) It takes these basic freedoms from men. But when our forefathers founded this nation, they said, "All men are created equal and endowed by their Creator." (*That's right*) In other words, they said that there are some basic rights that we all have (*Yes*), and in order to discover where they came from, it is necessary to go back behind the dim mist of eternity; they are God given. (*Yes indeed*) This stands at the basis of our nation. And yet they tell us that when we engage in peaceful protest, something guaranteed by the First Amendment, that we are lawbreakers.

Now I want to put it the other way around. (*That's right*) The City Commissioners of Albany are the real lawbreakers. [*sustained applause*] Let me tell you (*That's right*) the difference between what we are doing and what they are doing. Even if we were lawbreakers, we break the law openly; we don't seek to evade the law. (*That's right, That's right, That's right*) We haven't organized anything to defy the law. We believe too much in the sacredness of the law to defy it. (*That's right, Yes, That's right*) We do not seek to circumvent; we do not engage in violence and hatred as we do what we do. (*That's right, That's right*) And then when we go on and do all of this, we willingly accept the penalty. (*That's right*) But what do they do? (*That's right*) They seek to evade the law. (*That's right, Yeah, That's right*) They seek to defy the law with sophisticated methods and big words such as "interposition" and "nullification." This is what they seek to do. (*That's right*) They do it with hate, they do it with violence. (*Yes, Yes, That's right*) This is what they do. (*That's true*) And I would like to say to them this evening (*That's right, Go ahead*), "My white brothers, if you believe segregation is right (*That's right*), if you believe that it is eternally decreed from God himself, why don't you be Christians and go on and break the law openly, which is the law of the land?" (*Yeah, Yes*) Then after you break the law of the land and they tell you that you have a one-year sentence, sit up in jail, and I will believe that you are sincere. (*Yes*) But when you defy and evade the law, you make for nothing but anarchy, and you will destroy the very foundation of this country. (*Yes*)

And so God hath brought us here for this hour (*Go ahead*) to tell us to save America, because our white brothers (*Yes*) is carrying it more and more (*Go ahead*) to destruction (*Yes*) and damnation. (*That's right, Yes*) [*applause*] We are called to do it, and so that means we can't stop. (*That's right*) I'm going to sound like a Baptist preacher in a few (*Go ahead, Go ahead*) minutes. (*Preach, Start it out*) [*applause*] That means we can't stop. This should make us more determined than ever before.

Now, they always tell us to cool off (*Yes*), and I know that when you get people cooling off too much, they will end up in a deep freeze. (*Yes*) They tell us to slow up (*Yes, Slow up*), and some of them even say that the Negroes in Albany ought to go home and be quiet because there's a political campaign going on (*Yes, Go on*), and you may help elect some particular candidate that shouldn't be in office. (*That's right*) Well, I don't know if you have an answer for them, and I don't know if I have an absolute answer, but I want to say to those who are telling us to stop merely because a political campaign is going on that this is a moral issue for us. (*Yes, Yes*) We are moving on toward freedom's land. (*That's right, Yes*) We cannot stop our legitimate aspirations for freedom merely because some immoral person will use this for his own political aggrandizement. (*That's right, True*)

Then, go back and tell them that, in the final analysis, it doesn't matter who's

elected governor of Georgia; our movement is going on.[14] (*That's right*) [*applause*]
You may also say this to them (*That's right*): We live with 244 years of slavery. (*Yes sir,
All right*) We've lived with almost a hundred years of segregation. (*Right here, Right
here*) Right here in the state of Georgia, we live with two Talmadges. (*So true, That's it*)
Over in Mississippi, we live with Bilbo. (*Yes, Yes*) In Alabama, we live with Patterson.[15]
(*So true, Preach*) We worked in this very nation two centuries without wages. We made
cotton king. (*Yes*) We built our homes and the homes of our masters in the midst of
injustice (*Amen*) and exploitation; yet out of a bottomless vitality, we continued to
grow and to live. (*Amen, Amen*) And if the inexpressible cruelties of slavery couldn't
stop us, the opposition that we now face cannot stop us—and even Marvin Griffin
can't stop [*applause*] us. We're going on. (*Go on*) [*sustained applause*]

This is all we are asking for. (*Go ahead*) We are just saying we want to be free.
(*That's right, That's all, That's all*) They call us dangerous rabble-rousers, but deep
down within, we know that we are not rabble-rousers. (*That's right*) We just want to be
free. (*Yes, That's right*) They tell us that we are agitators in the negative sense (*That's
right*), but deep down within, we know that if we are agitators, it is creative agitation.
(*We know it, That's right*) We just want to be free. (*For sure, That's right*)

We can say, "America, we haven't deserted you." (*That's true*) We've stood with you
in all of your major difficulties. (*That's right*) Communism has never invaded our
ranks, America. We haven't turned to some foreign ideology to solve our problems.
(*No sir*) We, too, disagree with the philosophy of Communism, for we believe it is
based on principles that we could never accept. But, America, we do want to be free.
(*Yes, That's right, Yes*) Whenever you have been threatened from without, and even
within, America, we've been with you. For your security, America, our sons sailed
the bloody seas of two world wars. (*That's right, Amen*) For your security (*Amen*), our
sons died on the trenches, in the trenches of France (*That's true*), in the foxholes
of Germany, on the beachheads of Italy, and on the islands of Japan. And now,
America, we are saying we want to be free. (*Yes, That's right*) We know that without
freedom, we can't be (*Amen*) our true selves. (*Amen*) We can't be truly men, for, to
paraphrase the words of Shakespeare's *Othello*, "Who steals my purse steals trash; 'tis
something, nothing; 'twas mine, 'tis his, has been the slave of thousands. But he who
filches from me my freedom robs me of that which not enriches him but makes me
poor indeed."[16] We want to be *free*, America (*Yes*). [*applause*] And we are determined
to be free. [*applause*]

---

14. Carl Sanders, who was running for governor of Georgia against arch-segregationist Marvin
Griffin, stated that if elected governor, he would not interfere with local law enforcement and would
continue to support the courts until the segregation laws were changed: "I believe in law and order, I
believe in dignity and respect." Sanders defeated Griffin in the gubernatorial Democratic primary on
18 September 1962 (Sanders, Press conference on the events in Albany, Ga., 30 July 1962).

15. King refers to Georgia governor Eugene Talmadge, who held office from 1933–1937, 1940–1943,
and was reelected in 1946 but passed away before assuming office, and his son, Herman Talmadge, who
was governor of Georgia from 1948–1955 and served as a Georgia senator from 1957–1981. King also
mentions Theodore Bilbo in Mississippi, who was elected lieutenant governor between 1912–1916, twice
served as governor from 1916–1920 and 1928–1932, and represented the state in the Senate from 1908–
1912 and 1935–1947; as well as John Patterson, who served as attorney general of Alabama from 1955–1959
and governor from 1959–1963.

16. Cf. William Shakespeare, *Othello*, act 3, scene 3.

I must say, finally, the thing I always have to close with: We don't have to hate to be free. (*That's right, No, No*) We don't have to throw bottles to be free. (*That's right, All right, That's true*) And if there is any one thing—you may forget everything that I said tonight, but I can think of nothing that would injure our cause more than to resort to violence at any point in our struggle. We must make our white brothers know, even though they will refuse to understand it, that we are not trying to defeat them or to humiliate them but to win their friendship and understanding. We've been on the bottom. We've been on the bottom right in this nation for almost 344 years (*That's right, Go ahead*), and it would be almost human to want to retaliate and rise up to the top. But I believe we've made it clear that our aim is not to rise from the bottom to the top. Our aim is to create a moral balance.

We are not attempting to rise from a position of disadvantage to one of advantage, thus subverting justice. We just want to be a brother. (*That's true*) We just want to have the basic necessities of life. We just want the opportunity to grow and develop as individuals like anybody else. (*That's true*) This is all that we want. (*That's right*) We must get it over to our white brothers over and over again that we are forced because of problems of semantics, we are forced because of words that we must use, to talk about segregation and integration. And our aim is not merely to get rid of a system called segregation but our aim is to do something to people who have lived in the midst of segregation. (*Yes*) Our aim is to make new creatures: better white men and better Negro men (*Yes*), better white women (*Yes*) and better Negro women. (*Yes*) This is our aim. (*Amen*) If we can get this over, we can just get on out and pick up the ammunition of love (*True, Yes sir*) and just surround ourselves with kindness and prayer and put on the whole armor of God (*Yes, Amen*) and just march. (*Yes, Go on*)

And if we will do this, we'll be able to do this job in Albany (*Yes*) and all over the United States of America. And we have already a noble example through our Lord and Savior, for he lived amidst the intricate and fascinating military machinery of the Roman Empire. And he could've very easily talked about violence as a way, but he didn't do that. (*No*) He decided that he would follow the way of love; He went on to a cross and died (*Yes, Yes, Yes*), but when you have love in your hearts, a cross can't stop you. (*Well*) Pretty soon this same Christ rose up and split history into A.D. and B.C. Men and women all over ran out and started shaking the hinges from the gates of the Roman Empire. Not long after that, it started growing. It started off with just a few men, and now it's gone to more than seven hundred thousand. We can hear the glad echo of heaven saying, "Jesus shall reign where 'er the sun doth his successive journeys run; his kingdom spread from shore to shore, till moons shall wan and wax no more."[17] (*Amen*) We can hear another chorus saying, "In Christ there is no East or West (*Amen*), in him no North or South, but one great fellowship of love throughout the whole wide world."[18] (*Amen, Yes*) And then another group cries out from afar, "Jesus (*Jesus, Jesus, Jesus*), Jesus, the king of the universe." (*Yes, That's right, Yes*) Another group cries out, "All hail the power of Jesus' name. (*Amen*) Let angels prostrate fall (*Yes*); bring forth the royal diadem, and crown him Lord of Lords."[19]

17. Cf. Isaac Watts, "Jesus Shall Reign" (1719).
18. King paraphrases John Oxenham's hymn "In Christ There Is No East or West" (1908).
19. King paraphrases Edward Perronet's hymn "All Hail the Power of Jesus' Name" (1779).

(*Go ahead*) And then another chorus cries out, "He's Lord of Lords, King of Kings (*Yeah*), he shall reign forever and ever. Hallelujah, hallelujah."[20] (*Amen*)

If he had hated, he couldn't have done this. (*That's right*) If he had used violence, he couldn't have done this. (*No, Amen, That's right*) And so I'm saying, here in Albany, let us love. (*Yeah*) Let us use nonviolence (*Yes, That's right, Preach*), and we can do this job (*Yes*), and nothing will stop us. And to use the quote that they've used all kind of, kinds of ways, "If we will use nonviolence (*That's right*), we will be able to turn the upside-down structure of Albany right side up." (*Right side up*) [*applause*] This is what we will be able [*to do?*]. [*applause*] All of our children will grow up in a better world. (*Yes, That's right*) This is what we seek, and this is what we will develop right here in Albany, Georgia.

God bless you; don't let nobody (*Turn you around, Turn you around*) turn you around. (*Turn you around*) We've gone too far now (*Yes, Yes sir*) to turn back. (*Amen, That's right*) Don't let the City Commission turn you around. (*No*) Don't let any official turn you around. (*No*) And for God's sake, as I said to a group this afternoon, don't be afraid (*That's right, That's right*), for if you are afraid you are a slave.[21] You may get in a march and wonder why at your age are you marching. (*Yes*) Just look up enough to say, "I'm marching for my children and my grandchildren (*Go ahead, Yeah*), and I'm willing to suffer for them." (*Go ahead, Go ahead*) [*applause*] We may make this [*applause*], and you may make this significant witness at this hour, and this is our great opportunity to give a nonviolent witness.

We will be saying more to you about the plans, but I just want you to know now that we have requested all that we can request of the City Commission. (*Yes*) We've asked them to talk about these things. We haven't been dangerous rabble-rousers and agitators (*No*), even though for political reasons they called us that, but deep down within, they know that we have loving spirits and nonviolent hearts. (*Amen, Amen, Amen*) We have asked and we have pleaded with them (*Yes*), and now we have no alternative (*That's right*) but to put on our marching shoes (*Yeah, Yeah, All right, All right, All right*) [*applause*] and move on toward the city hall. (*Yes*) Not the city hall of Chief Pritchett (*No*), not the city hall of Mayor Kelley, not the city hall of the City Commission (*Well*), but the city hall of the people. (*Yes, Go ahead, Yes, That's right*) And we move there to pray and ask God's guidance. And if we don't get there (*Yes, Yes*), we are ready to fill up the jails all over the state of Georgia. (*Yes*) [*applause*]

And I know we shall overcome. (*Oh Yeah, Yes, Yes, One of these days*) I know we shall overcome. (*Yes*) We shall overcome because we are right. (*Yes*) And so I say, "Have faith in the future (*Yes*), and keep moving." As I've said so often: "If you can't run, walk (*Yes*); if you can't walk (*Crawl*), crawl (*Crawl, Yes*); if you can't crawl, just keep inching along. But by all means, keep moving." [*applause*]

At. Nashville, Tenn.: Creed Records, Nashboro Record Company, 1984.

---

20. King paraphrases the "Hallelujah Chorus" in George Frideric Handel's oratorio *Messiah* (1741).

21. Earlier that day King visited the burnt remains of the Shady Grove Baptist Church in Leesburg, Georgia.

# To Bertrand Russell

21 August 1962
New York, N.Y.

*On behalf of the American Committee on Africa (ACOA), King and Albert
Lutuli invite Russell to be one of the signers of the "Appeal for Action Against
Apartheid."[1] Russell was one of more than a hundred international sponsors of
the appeal published on Human Rights Day in December 1962.[2]*

Lord Bertrand Russell
c/o Anenaeum
London S.W.1
England

Dear Lord Bertrand Russell:

We write to ask you to join us in sponsoring the Appeal for Action Against Apartheid,
first printing of which is enclosed.[3] Designed to call attention to the deepening crisis in
South Africa, the Appeal aims at stimulating concerted action by people around the
world. The campaign starting now focuses toward Human Rights Day, December 10,
1962, as the first climax in a continuing movement to quarantine apartheid.

International action now is imperative: the recently enacted "Sabotage" law ultimately makes opposition to the government's apartheid system a capital offense.[4]

---

1. George Houser, executive director of ACOA, wrote King on 6 February 1962 asking if he would
team up with Lutuli, president of the African National Congress, and Eleanor Roosevelt, former first
lady, to invite international figures to sign the declaration. The "Appeal for Action Against Apartheid"
was signed by world leaders to mobilize support for a boycott of South African goods and economic
sanctions against the country. Bertrand Arthur William Russell (1872–1970), born in Monmouthshire,
Wales, attended Trinity College and earned First Class degrees in both part I of the school's mathemati-
cal tripos (1893), part II of the moral science tripos (1894), and an M.A. in moral science (1897), before
lecturing at the college from 1895–1916. Russell wrote on analytic philosophy for which he eventually
earned a Nobel Prize in 1950. Best known for his opposition to war and nuclear weapons, Russell was
dismissed from Trinity in 1916 and jailed for six months in 1918 for his anti-war activities. In 1961 he was
sentenced to two months in jail for organizing a nonviolent demonstration that officials said incited others to breach the peace. Only a few months before his death, Russell appealed to the United Nations to
investigate war crimes by American soldiers in South Vietnam.

2. More than 200,000 copies of the Appeal were distributed to individuals, organizations, student
groups, churches, and labor unions on Human Rights Day. In addition to seeking public support, the
ACOA sent letters protesting apartheid to President Kennedy and South African Prime Minister, H.F.
Verwoerd (ACOA, "A brief review of action taken on and around Human Rights Day, December 10, in
connection with the Appeal for Action Against Apartheid campaign," December 1962; "ACOA Urges
Action in Anti-Apartheid Campaign," *Africa Report*, December 1962, p. 31).

3. American Committee on Africa, "Appeal for Action against Apartheid," 1962.

4. Following several bombings in December 1961, the South African legislature proposed the
General Law Amendment Bill, which broadly defined sabotage as not only threats to property or life but
any action seeking to bring about social and political reform. The minimum punishment for sabotage
was five years in prison, and the maximum sentence was death. The controversial law also included a new
provision, "civil death," in which a lifetime of forced isolation under house arrest would be imposed.

The <u>Appeal</u> can become the base on which to unite the people of the world against the tragic and suicidal racist practices in South Africa.

In 1957, a similar campaign was built around the <u>Declaration of Conscience</u>, signed by international figures from all continents.[5] We believe the present effort, because it calls for action, can be significantly more effective. We cannot overestimate the significance of international pressure in influencing the course the South African Government may follow. Even more important, such pressure has been called for by those courageous South Africans now risking life itself to oppose their government's barbarous policy.

We therefore ask you to join us as sponsors of the <u>Appeal for Action</u>. To do so, simply sign the enclosed card and rush it to us at the American Committee on Africa.

Thank you,
[*signed*] A. J. Lutuli
Albert J. Lutuli
South Africa

[*signed*] Martin L. King Jr.
Martin Luther King
United States

encs.

P.S. We should like to have your signature by September 10 so that the names of signers can be issued three months before 1962's Human Rights Day.

TLS. LBRP-WRDA-OHMa.

---

5. In mid-1957 King joined the National Committee of the ACOA, and later sponsored with Eleanor Roosevelt and Reverend James A. Pike "The Declaration of Conscience," an international call for demonstrations on 10 December 1957 to protest South African apartheid (see King to Chester Bowles, 8 November 1957, in *Papers* 4:311–314).

# From Eubie Blake

21 August 1962
Brooklyn, N.Y.

*Blake, a renowned composer and songwriter, offers King the use of his pre-World War II arrangement "We Are Americans, Too" for a second time and assures King of his spiritual and financial support.[1] No reply has been found.*

---

1. Blake, along with Andy Razaf and Charles L. Cooke, composed "We Are Americans Too" in 1941. In 1956, King had received one hundred copies of the song to raise funds for the Montgomery

To: Rev. Dr. Martin Luther King Jr.

Dear Rev.

I was reading in the New york times, that music is helping your struggle for free-dom, in the South[2] If you will accept a marching Song Title "We Are American Too". I will send this one Copy to you, And you'll accept this music I will send as many cop-ies as you [*will?*] wish free of Charge. I will also Send a Brass Band Arrangent if you wish. I hope you'll get to read this letter.

I you do Please me know at once, again I will send you as many Copies as you wish. Thank I am with you both speritually & ~~finanacilly~~ financially.

[*signed*] Eubie Blake

ALS. SCLCR-GAMK: Box 3.

---

Improvement Association (King to Lovie M. Rainbow, 10 July 1956, in *Papers* 3:317). In a 23 March 1961 letter to Razaf, King called the song "most inspiring" and said he "always listened to it with deep appreciation." James Hubert Blake (1883–1983) was born to two former slaves in Baltimore, Mary-land. At a young age, Blake learned to play the pump organ and piano. After working in nightclubs for several years, Blake was hired in 1907 to play at the Goldfield Hotel in Baltimore, a night spot whose clientele included wealthy and prominent businesspeople and entertainers. In 1911, he left the Goldfield as a successful and popular ragtime pianist. Blake also composed several musicals, includ-ing *Shuffle Along* (1921) and *Chocolate Dandies* (1924) with Noble Sissle. During World War II Blake served as a bandleader with the United Servicemen Organizations (USO), and afterward attended New York University and graduated with a degree in music in 1950. Because of renewed interest in ragtime music, Blake signed recording deals with 20th Century Records and Columbia Records. He lectured and performed around the world, and in 1981 he was awarded the Presidential Medal of Freedom for his pioneering contributions to music.

2. Blake refers to an article written by *Times* reporter Robert Shelton regarding the impact freedom songs made on the civil rights movement. In the article, King was quoted as saying: "The freedom songs are playing a strong and vital role in our struggle. They give the people new courage and a sense of unity. I think they keep alive a faith, a radiant hope, in the future, particularly in our most trying hours" (Shelton, "Songs a Weapon in Rights Battle," *New York Times*, 20 August 1962).

# To Ralph Lord Roy

22 August 1962
Atlanta, Ga.

*After numerous attempts to negotiate with the Albany City Commission, King, in the telegram below, calls on clergy from the greater New York area to "bear witness to the prophetic faith of our Judeo-Christian tradition," and "stand with the people of Albany as they strive for freedom."[1] Roy, New York pastor of Grace United*

---

1. On 6 August New York pastors George W. Lawrence and Thomas Kilgore protested King's arrest in Albany on 27 July by leading a biracial "Minister's March on the White House" that attracted over

*Methodist Church and coordinator of the pilgrimage, assembled ten rabbis, eight*
*Catholic laypersons, and fifty-six Protestant leaders, all of whom would be arrested*
*leading a prayer vigil on 27 August in Albany.*[2]

22 Aug
1962

THE CLERGY OF THE NEW YORK AREA=
CARE REP RALPH ROY METROPOLITAN BAPTIST CHURCH
7 AVE AND=128 ST NYK=

THE ALBANY MOVEMENT IS IN ITS SECOND MONTH OF STRUGGLE TO BRING =ABOUT JUST RECONCILIATION OF THE COMMUNITY'S RACIAL GROUPS. =THE CRISIS HERE IN ALBANY IS NOT A LOCAL SITUATION BUT IS A =CRISIS IN THE NATIONAL LIFE OF THIS DEMOCRACY WHEN CITIZENS =ARE DENIED THE RIGHT TO PRAY AND PICKET IN PUBLIC, WHEN CHURCHES =ARE BURNED FOR THEIR USE AS VOTER REGISTRATION CENTERS OUR =NATION SUFFERS GREATLY.[3]

IN BEHALF OF THE ALBANY MOVEMENT AND THE SOUTHERN LEADERSHIP =CONFERENCE I EXTEND A CALL TO ALL THOSE WHO WOULD BEAR= WITNESS =TO THE PROPHETIC FAITH OF OUR JUDEO CHRISTIAN TRADITION TO =STAND WITH THE PEOPLE

---

one hundred Jewish, Catholic, and Protestant religious leaders. Although the ministers did not speak to the President, they met with assistant attorney general Burke Marshall, staff director of the Civil Rights Commission Berl Bernhard, and White House staffer Lee C. White. The ministers also scheduled a 10 August march in Albany should King be sentenced to jail. The march was canceled after King received a suspended sentence and was released from jail ("Ministers Take Albany Plea to White House, See JFK Aides," *Washington Post,* 7 August 1962; Hedrick Smith, "Dr. King Set Free after Conviction," *New York Times,* 11 August 1962).

2. Most of the seventy-five predominately white clergy and laymen came from New York, New Jersey, Connecticut, and Illinois, though Atlanta SCLC president John A. Middleton, Albany pastor Joseph Smith, and Reverend Robert Gaines of Dallas also participated. From 12–14 August, Roy joined several integrated groups attempting to worship at Trinity Methodist Church and receive service at Phoebe Putney Hospital's snack bar. Albany police chief Laurie Pritchett accused the clergy of coming to "aid and abet the law violators of this city" and urged them to instead "clear your own city of sin and of lawlessness before you come here to try and convert us" (Pritchett, Statement on arrest of clergy in Albany, Ga., 28 August 1962). Police arrested the group and charged them with congregating on the sidewalk, disorderly conduct, and failure to obey an officer. Chicago minister J. H. Jackson called the ministers hypocrites for going to Albany, which prompted a strongly worded response from William G. Anderson who called Jackson a "disgrace, not only to the Negro people, but to the human race. He's a Mississippi boy who's been away so long that he has no idea what the Negro in the Deep South is up against" ("Negro Baptist Chief Assails Racial Battles," *Los Angeles Times,* 5 September 1962; Albany Movement, Press release, "Albany Movement leader blasts National Baptist prexy on movement," 13 September 1962). Ralph Lord Roy (1928– ), born in St. Albans, Vermont, received his B.A. from Swarthmore College in 1950 and joined CORE while a student. He received a joint M.A. from Union Theological Seminary and Columbia University in 1952 and was ordained in the Methodist Church that same year. In 1957 Roy became assistant minister of Metropolitan Community United Methodist Church, an African American church in Harlem, and began teaching at Mills College of Education in Manhattan. From 1960–1963 Roy served as senior pastor of the English-language congregation of Grace Methodist Church. As the Freedom Rides extended into the summer of 1961, Roy joined an interfaith group of riders and was arrested in Tallahassee, Florida. Roy was also the author of two books, *Apostles of Discord* (1953) and *Communism and the Churches* (1960). He went on to serve churches in Brooklyn and Connecticut before his retirement in 2006.

3. King refers to the 14 August bombing of Shady Grove Baptist Church in nearby Leesburg, Georgia, which had been a site for voter registration.

OF ALBANY AS THEY STRIVE FOR FREEDOM. ==========ON MONDAY AUGUST 27TH
WE ARE ASKING YOU TO COME TO ALBANY AND =MAKE WITNESS IN BEHALF OF YOUR
CONGREGATION AGAINST THE SEGREGATED =WAY OF LIFE. YOUR PRESENCE WOULD BE
A GREAT BOOST TO THE FREEDOM=LOVING PEOPLE OF THAT COMMUNITY =[4]

MARTIN LUTHER KING JR. ===

PHWSr. ACRMtZ.

---

4. In letters sent to several of the clergy who answered King's call, he thanked them for doing "much to raise the right moral and religious questions" in Albany. He also marveled at how each demonstrator gave of themselves "that we may walk together as sons and daughters of God one day soon in these United States" (King to Stanley Terry, 10 October 1962). Additional recipients of the form letter included Ralph Lord Roy, Marian Kuzela, and John Papandrew, among others.

# To Alfred Daniel King

30 August 1962
*[Atlanta, Ga.]*

*In this letter to his brother A. D., King proclaims that a "real mobilization of our civil rights forces" is needed in Alabama and that the state will be the focus of SCLC activity in the coming year.[1] "We want to help you to help Alabama," King writes. King also invites his brother to Birmingham in September for a meeting, which coincides with SCLC's annual convention.[2]*

Reverend A. D. King
721 12th Street
Birmingham, Alabama

---

1. King sent out dozens of similar letters to ministers throughout the South, including Birmingham residents Edward Gardner, W.E. Shortridge, Orzell Billingsley, and John Cross (King to Gardner, 31 August 1962; King to Shortridge, Billingsley, and Cross, all dated 4 September 1962).
2. The sixth annual SCLC convention was held at Sixteenth Street Baptist Church from 25–28 September. The conference theme was the "Diversified Attack on Segregation." According to an SCLC press release, King said Birmingham was chosen as the site for the conference because "it represents the hardcore South, and our affiliate group here has carried on a relentless and sometimes lonely battle for freedom from segregation" (Program, "Annual Meeting of SCLC," 25 September–28 September 1962; SCLC, Press release, "SCLC sets annual meet in Birmingham," 22 August 1962). On the second day of the conference, King announced that SCLC would focus on increasing voter registration and desegregating public facilities and universities in Birmingham in 1963 ("State Target of '63 Mixing, King Declares," *Birmingham News*, 26 September 1962). The following day, King was attacked by a member of the American Nazi party as he addressed the conference (Peter Kihss, "Dr. King Assaulted at Meeting by Self-Styled American Nazi," *New York Times*, 29 September 1962).

Dear Rev. King:

31 Aug
1962

This is the first opportunity that I have had to express my regret that I could not meet with you in July. Ralph Abernathy and Wyatt Tee Walker were as disappointed as I was that we missed such a heart-warming meeting.[3]

I am writing to you personally for a two-fold reason. As you know, during this past year, I have devoted a great deal of my time to field work, conducting people to people tours, and recruiting for voter registration and teachers in our Citizenship Education program.[4] Our next program this year calls for a real mobilization of our civil rights forces in the State of Alabama. We want to help you to help Alabama.

Through our reciprocal efforts, we can bring a new day in the Deep South and your state.

Secondly, I want to invite you to meet with us for a follow-up meeting on September 25th in Birmingham. We propose a 10:30 A.M. meeting at the Sixteenth Street Baptist Church. This will provide you with an opportunity to look in on our Annual Convention that begins Tuesday night with a gala Freedom banquet featuring Jackie Robinson.[5] We hope that you will bring a carload of representatives from your area.

In a few days we will forward to you some of the details of our Annual Convention in order that you might plan to spend several days with us and "kill two birds with one stone."

I shall look forward to clasping hands with you on the 25th.

Faithfully yours,
Martin Luther King, Jr.

MLK/wm

TLc. MLKJP-GAMK: Box 1.

---

3. King may be referring to a meeting he scheduled for 16 July in Montgomery to discuss integration efforts in Alabama. King's involvement in the Albany Movement prevented him from attending the meeting in Montgomery (King, Form letter, July 1962; Andrew Young to Friends, 6 July 1962).

4. For more of King's People to People tours and SCLC's Citizenship Education Program, see Introduction, pp. 22–23 and 28–29 in this volume.

5. Robinson, Freedom Dinner Address at the Sixth Annual Convention of the Southern Christian Leadership Conference, 25 September 1962.

# To John F. Kennedy

31 August 1962
Albany, Ga.

*Following the arrest of seventy-five clergy and lay leaders in Albany, Georgia, on 28 August, King asks President Kennedy to appeal to the nation to safeguard the civil rights of millions of blacks and mediate negotiations between Albany*

605

*city officials and leaders of the Albany Movement.*[1] *Responding on behalf of the president on 2 September 1962, Attorney General Robert F. Kennedy reiterated the administration's dedication to defend the "rights of all Americans" regardless of "race color or creed."*[2] *He also reminded King that the desegregation of Albany is currently under judicial review in the federal courts.*[3]

THE PRESIDENT

THE WHITE HOUSE

DEAR MR. PRESIDENT. FIFTEEN PROTESTANT AND JEWISH RELIGIOUS LEADERS FROM AMONG THE SEVENTY FIVE UNJUSTLY ARRESTED TUESDAY, AUGUST 28, REMAIN IN JAIL AND ARE CONTINUING THE FAST BEGUN AT THE TIME OF ARREST IN HOPES THAT THEY WILL AROUSE THE CONSCIENCE OF THIS NATION TO THE GROSS VIOLATIONS OF HUMAN DIGNITY AND CIVIL RIGHTS, WHICH ARE THE RULE IN ALBANY AND SUR-ROUNDING COUNTIES.[4] IT IS MY HOPE THAT YOU WILL AS PRESIDENT OF THESE UNITED STATES #1 APPEAL TO THE NATION TO UPHOLD THE MORAL IDEALS AND DEMOCRATIC PRINCIPLES WHICH ARE NOW BEING THREATENED BY THE CONTINUED DEPRIVAL OF RIGHTS TO EIGHTEEN MILLION CITIZENS IN OUR NATION THROUGH THE COVERT SEG-REGATION OF THE SOUTH AND THE COVERT PATTERNS OF DISCRIMINATION OF THE NORTH[5] #2 SERVE AS MEDIATOR IN THE PRESENT CONFLICT IN ALBANY GEORGIA BY

---

1. At King's behest, seventy-five protesters mainly from northern and midwestern states descended upon Albany, Georgia, to aid desegregation efforts (King to Ralph Lord Roy, 22 August 1962, pp. 602–604 in this volume). On 28 August, the group was arrested as they staged a prayer vigil in front of Albany City Hall (Claude Sitton, "Albany, Ga., Jails 75 in Prayer Vigil," *New York Times*, 29 August 1962). King had previously petitioned President Kennedy to intervene and moderate discussions between the city officials and movement leaders on 9 August (Frank Hunt, "Dr. King Urges JFK to Mediate Ga. Crisis," Baltimore *Afro-American*, 11 August 1962).

2. Joining King in his appeal to Kennedy, eight of the imprisoned clergy penned an open letter ask-ing the president to intervene in Albany, and to "speak out clearly reminding our Nation and the world that America is firmly opposed to racial discrimination and segregation." The clergy also argued that "we are all agreed, Catholic, Jew and Protestant, that God wills the end of all racial discrimination and segregation in His world" ("Clerics in Albany Jail Urge Kennedy to Help," *Washington Post*, 3 September 1962). On 8 August, the Justice Department filed an amicus curiae brief in the District Court of Albany, opposing the request by Albany city officials for a court order barring demonstrations ("Justice Department Enters Albany Dispute," *Washington Post*, 9 August 1962).

3. Kennedy was likely referring to the four civil cases on the constitutionality of segregation in Albany and the rights of citizens to protest. For more on the cases, see note 6 of King's testimony of 8 August (pp. 570–571 in this volume).

4. Prior to the demonstration, the participants had voted to stage a fast for the first twenty-four hours of their confinement should they be arrested (William Hannah, "Albany Jails 50 Ministers from North," *Atlanta Constitution*, 29 August 1962). Most of the seventy-five protesters jailed made bail within twenty-four to forty-eight hours after their arrest. Eighteen protesters, many of whom refused food for the duration of their detention, remained in jail for six days (Robert E. Jones, "Ministers in Jail: Prayer Pilgrimage Proved to Negroes 'They Are Not Alone,'" *Boston Globe*, 11 September 1962).

5. After the arrest of the protesters, King said that President Kennedy would need to act toward ending segregation if he wanted to maintain the black vote: "Mr. Kennedy will have to do a great deal to implement his campaign promises in order to hold the support he received from Negro voters in the last election." King also addressed the possibility that blacks may support Republican New York governor Nelson Rockefeller if he decided to run for president: "Rockefeller certainly has taken a stand and if

INVITING MEMBERS OF THE ALBANY CITY COMMISSION AND THE ALBANY MOVEMENT      31 Aug
TO WASHINGTON FOR DISCUSSIONS OF THIS SITUATION.      1962

SINCERELY YOURS
DR. MARTIN LUTHER KING JR.

PHWSr. JFKWHCNF-MBJFK.

---

he continues and if he implements this (desegregation) in our state, then we will be greatly impressed"
(Hannah, "Albany Jails 50 Ministers from North," 29 August 1962). In June 1961 Rockefeller intro-
duced King when the civil rights leader spoke at Wilborn Temple First Church of God in Christ in
Albany, New York (Rockefeller, Remarks at Wilborn Temple First Church of God in Christ, 16 June
1961; King, "The American Dream," Address at Wilborn Temple First Church of God in Christ, 16
June 1961). After King missed his train from New York City to Albany, Rockefeller gave him a lift on
his private plane and later drove King to the rally at Wilborn Temple First Church of God in Christ
("Governor Attends Rally with Dr. King," *New York Times,* 17 June 1961).

Each volume of *The Papers of Martin Luther King, Jr.* includes a Calendar of Documents that provides an extensive list of significant King-related material for the period. The calendar includes research material relevant to the study of King's life and work that was not selected for publication in the volume. It is generated from an online database maintained at the King Project's Stanford University office.

Space limitations prevent the listing of all seven thousand documents from the online database: only the most important (approximately 1,660) have been selected by the editors for inclusion in the calendar. This inventory includes not only notable documents in the King collections at Boston University, King Center, and Atlanta University Center, but those obtained from King's relatives and acquaintances and material gathered during an intense search of over 165 archives such as the John F. Kennedy Library.

Owing to space constraints, full bibliographic citations are not provided in editorial annotations: complete references for individual documents mentioned in headnotes, footnotes, and the Introduction are found only in the calendar. The calendar includes significant King-authored material such as speeches, sermons, and articles; selected correspondence and other ephemera regarding events in which King participated; and press releases and notes of meetings he attended. Relatively mundane documents such as routine office correspondence and most unsolicited letters of support are not listed in the calendar, though they remain available in the online database. The calendar also includes a sampling of the following types of documents: correspondence with friends, religious leaders, political leaders, and activists in civil rights organizations; historically significant SCLC documents such as financial materials and correspondence with committee members; contemporary interviews; published articles with extensive King quotations; internal White House and Federal Bureau of Investigation memos; and other material documenting King's activities. The calendar also includes citations to documents that became available after the publication of the volume of the King Papers covering that time period. The listings of photographs or illustrations that appear in the current volume are printed in boldface type.

Each calendar entry provides essential bibliographic information about the document. Italics and brackets indicate information determined by the editors based on evidence contained in the document. The entry adheres to the following format:

Date        Author (Affiliation). Document title. Date. Place of origin. (Physical description codes) Number of pages. (Notes.) Archival location. King Papers Project identification number.

1/19/1961    King, Martin Luther, Jr. Letter to Carey McWilliams. 1/19/1961. [*Atlanta, Ga.*] (TLc) 1 p. (Contains enclosure 610119–005.) MLKP-MBU. 610119–001.

**DATE**. The date in the left margin is intended to aid the reader in looking up specific documents. Complete date information is provided in the entry. In those cases where the original bears no date the editors have assigned one and enclosed it in brackets. Those documents bearing range dates appear after precisely dated documents and are arranged by end date in the range, unless logic dictates another order. The date of photographs is presented without brackets if the donor provided a date. The date of published or printed papers is the date of publication or public release rather than the date of composition.

**AUTHOR.** A standardized form of an individual's name (based on *Anglo-American Cataloging Rules*, 2d ed.) is provided in both the author and title fields. Forms of address are omitted unless necessary for identification, such as a woman who used only her husband's name. For photographs, the photographer is considered the author. Since King's script is distinctive, his unsigned handwritten documents are identified as of certain authorship. Institutional authorship is provided when appropriate.

**AFFILIATION.** Affiliation information is provided if the author wrote in his or her capacity as an official of an organization. No brackets or italics have been used in the affiliation field.

**TITLE.** Titles enclosed in quotation marks have been drawn directly from the document with minor emendations of punctuation, capitalization, and spelling for clarity. Phrases such as "Letter to," "Photo of," are used to create titles for otherwise untitled documents; in such titles, words are generally not capitalized and names are standardized. The use of the word "delivered" in the titles of speeches and sermons connotes an audio version. Published versions of earlier speeches contain the date of delivery in the title.

**PLACE OF ORIGIN.** This field identifies where the document was completed or, in the case of a published document, the place of publication. If the document does not contain the place of origin and the information can be obtained, it is provided in brackets; such information is offered only for documents written by King or those written on his behalf.

**PHYSICAL DESCRIPTION.** This field describes the format of presentation, type of document, version of document, and character of the signature (see List of Abbreviations, pp. 85–94). Documents that consist of several formats are listed with the predominant one first.

**LENGTH.** The number of pages or the duration of a recording is indicated.

**NOTES.** In this optional field, miscellaneous information pertaining to the document is provided. This information includes enclosures to a letter, routing information (e.g., "Copy to King") since King often received copies of correspondence addressed to others, and remarks concerning the legibility of the document or the authorship of marginalia. For tapes, information about the media used is also indicated in this field.

**ARCHIVAL LOCATION.** The location of the original document is identified using standard abbreviations based on the Library of Congress's codes for libraries and archives (see List of Abbreviations, pp. 85–94). When available, box numbers or other archival location identification are provided.

**IDENTIFICATION NUMBER.** The nine-digit identification number, based on the date, uniquely identifies the document. Documents of the same date are listed in order of their identification number.

| | |
|---|---|
| 1925 | Brightman, Edgar Sheffield. *An Introduction to Philosophy, Revised Edition.* New York: Henry Holt & Co., 1925. (PHD) (Marginal comments by King.) CSKCH. 250000–002. |
| 1933 | Durant, Will. *The Story of Philosophy: The Lives and Opinions of the Greater Philosophers.* New York: Simon & Schuster, 1933. (PHD) (Marginal comments by King.) CSKCH. 330000–001. |
| 1937 | Fosdick, Harry Emerson. *Successful Christian Living: Sermons on Christianity Today.* New York: Harper & Brothers, 1937. (PHD) (Marginal comments by King.) CSKC. 370000–011. |
| 1943 | Fosdick, Harry Emerson. *On Being a Real Person.* New York: Harper & Brothers, 1943. (PHD) (Marginal comments by King.) CSKCH. 430000–012. |
| 1946 | Fosdick, Harry Emerson. *On Being Fit to Live With: Sermons on Post-War Christianity.* New York: Harper & Brothers, 1946. (PHD) (Marginal comments by King.) CSKCH. 460000–004. |
| 1947 | Wright, William Kelley. *A History of Modern Philosophy.* New York: Macmillan, [1947]. (PHD) (Marginal comments by King.) CSKCH. 470000–018. |
| 1947 | U.S. President's Committee on Civil Rights. *To Secure These Rights: The Report of the President's Committee on Civil Rights.* Washington, D.C.: U.S. Government Printing Office, 1947. (PD) (Inscription by Robert Kenneth Carr.) CSKCH. 470000–028. |
| 1948 | Jones, E. Stanley. *Mahatma Gandhi: An Interpretation.* New York: Abingdon-Cokesbury Press, 1948. (PHD) (Marginal comments by King.) CSKCH. 480000–033. |
| 1950 | Gandhi, Mahatma. *Satyagraha in South Africa.* Ahmedabad, India: Navajivan Publishing House, 1950. (PHD) (Inscription by L.D. Reddick.) CSKCH. 500000–053. |
| 1952 | Machiavelli, Niccoló and Thomas Hobbes. *The Prince; and, Leviathan: Or, Matter, Form and Power of a Commonwealth Ecclesiastical and Civil.* Chicago: Encyclopedia Britannica, 1952. (PD) CSKCH. 520000–000. |
| 7/8/1952 | Carey, Archibald J. (Chicago City Council). Address delivered to the Republican National Convention. 7/8/1952. Chicago, Ill. (TD) 5 pp. AJC-ICHi: Box 12. 520708–000. |
| 9/22/1952– 1/28/1953 | King, Martin Luther, Jr. (Boston University). Notecards on topics from "Jeremiah." [9/22/1952–1/28/1953]. [Boston, Mass.] (AD) 55 pp. MCMLK-RWWL: 4.7.0.20. 530128–036. |
| 4/27/1954 | Watson, Melvin H. (Morehouse College). Letter to Martin Luther King, Jr. 4/27/1954. Atlanta, Ga. (TALS) 1 p. MLKP-MBU. 540427–000. |
| 8/16/1954 | Niles, Daniel Thambyrajah. "Evangelism," Address at the second assembly of the World Council of Churches. 8/16/1954. (THD) 8 pp. (Marginal comments by King on verso.) MCMLK-RWWL: 2.2.0.960. 540816–000. |
| 9/19/1956 | King, Martin Luther, Jr. (MIA). Letter to E.F. Rodriguez. 9/19/1956. [Montgomery, Ala.] (TLc) 1 p. MLKP-MBU. 560919–002. |
| 4/1957 | King, Martin Luther, Jr. (Ebenezer Baptist Church). Questions that Easter Answers. [4/1957]. [Atlanta, Ga.] (ADd) 4 pp. MCMLK-RWWL: 2.2.0.1650. 570400–000. |
| 4/19/1957 | Horton, Myles (Highlander Folk School). Letter to Martin Luther King, Jr. 4/19/1957. Monteagle, Tenn. (THLS) 1 p. (Contains enclosure 570902–003.) MLKP-MBU. 570419–003. |
| 8/30/1957– 9/2/1957 | Highlander Folk School. Program, "The South Thinking Ahead: The Human Aspects of the Integration Struggle." 8/30/1957–9/2/1957. Monteagle, Tenn. (TD) 3 pp. (Enclosed in 570419–003.) DABCC. 570902–003. |
| 10/8/1957 | King, Martin Luther, Jr. (SCLC). Form letter to Executive Board Members. 10/8/1957. [Montgomery, Ala.] (TLc) 1 p. MLKP-MBU. 571008–001. |
| 11/7/1957 | Wofford, Harris. "Nonviolence and the Law." 11/7/1957. (TAD) 16 pp. (Enclosed in 611030–010, pp. 315–316 in this volume.) MCMLK-RWWL: 3.2.0.680. 571107–002. |
| 1/6/1958 | King, Martin Luther, Jr. (Dexter Avenue Baptist Church). Letter to Charles C. Diggs. 1/6/1958. Montgomery, Ala. (TLS) 1 p. CCDP-DHU-MS: Box 25. 580106–004. |
| 3/14/1958 | American Baptist Convention. "Affirmation of Welcome." 3/14/1958. Kansas City, Kan. (TD) 1 p. MLKP-MBU. 580314–009. |
| 5/18/1958 | Erma Hughes Business College. Program, "Twenty-fifth annual baccalaureate and commencement exercises." 5/18/1958. Houston, Texas. (PD) 4 pp. MLKP-MBU. 580518–007. |
| 10/18/1958 | [Fulton, Robert Brank]. Letter to Martin Luther King, Jr. 10/18/1958. (TAL) 1 p. RBFP. 581018–002. |
| 11/29/1958 | Ballou, Maude L. (Dexter Avenue Baptist Church). Letter to Robert Brank Fulton. 11/29/1958. (TLS) 1 p. RBFP. 581129–009. |

| | |
|---|---|
| 12/10/1958 | Truman, Harry S. Letter to Martin Luther King, Jr. 12/10/1958. Independence, Mo. (TLS) 1 p. MLKP-MBU. 581210–003. |
| 2/9/1959 | Crump, Paul. Letter to Martin Luther King, Jr. 2/9/1959. Chicago, Ill. (ALS) 3 pp. MLKP-MBU. 590209–005. |
| 3/18/1959 | Bhave, Vinoba. "Dr. Martin Luther King with Vinoba." *Bhoodan* 3 (18 March 1959): 369–370. (PD) MLKP-MBU. 590318–000. |
| 4/3/1959 | King, Martin Luther, Jr. Letter to Robert M. Bartlett. 4/3/1959. [*Montgomery, Ala.*] (TLc) 1 p. MLKP-MBU. 590403–008. |
| 4/12/1959 | Mount Vernon First Baptist Church. Program, Installation of Alfred Daniel King. 4/12/1959. Newnan, Ga. (PHD) 4 pp. (Marginal comments by King.) MLKP-MBU. 590412–004. |
| 4/15/1959 | King, Martin Luther, Jr. Letter to Paul Crump. 4/15/1959. Montgomery, Ala. (TLc) 1 p. MLKP-MBU. 590415–003. |
| 7/8/1959 | Helstein, Ralph (United Packinghouse Workers of America, AFL-CIO). Letter to Martin Luther King, Jr. 7/8/1959. Chicago, Ill. (TLS) 2 pp. MLKP-MBU. 590708–000. |
| 10/22/1959 | Fulton, Robert Brank (Inter-American University). Letter to Martin Luther King, Jr. 10/22/1959. (TLS) 1 p. MLKP-MBU. 591022–015. |
| 11/20/1959 | Wofford, Harris (University of Notre Dame). "The Law and Civil Disobedience." 11/20/1959. (THD) 4 pp. (Marginal comments by King. Enclosed in 611030–010, pp. 315–316 in this volume.) MCMLK-RWWL: 2.3.0.1010. 591120–008. |
| 1/31/1960 | "Transcript of proceedings before the Volunteer Civil Rights Commission." 1/31/1960. Washington, D.C. (THD) 59 pp. SCLCR-GAMK: Box 37. 600131–009. |
| 4/1960 | [*Reddick, Lawrence Dunbar*]. "The Montgomery situation." 4/1960. (TD) 23 pp. LDRP-NN-Sc: Box 2. 600400–023. |
| 5/6/1960 | Helstein, Ralph (United Packinghouse Workers of America). Letter to Martin Luther King, Jr. 5/6/1960. Chicago, Ill. (TLS) 1 p. (Contains enclosures 600506–008 & 600506–009.) MLKP-MBU. 600506–007. |
| 5/6/1960 | Helstein, Ralph (United Packinghouse Workers of America. AFL-CIO). Letter to Nathan Paul Feinsinger. 5/6/1960. Chicago, Ill. (TLc) 1 p. (Enclosed in 600506–007.) MLKP-MBU. 600506–008. |
| 5/6/1960 | Lasley, Russell R., Frank Schultz, Glenn Chinander, George Thomas, and Dave Hart. "Report of the subcommittee of the international executive board." [*5/6/1960*]. (TD) 20 pp. (Enclosed in 600506–007.) MLKP-MBU. 600506–009. |
| 5/27/1960–<br>5/29/1960 | Negro American Labor Council. Announcement, "Founding convention call." 5/27/1960–5/29/1960. Detroit, Mich. (PD) 3 pp. RPP-NN-Sc: Box 3. 600529–009. |
| 6/1/1960 | Graves, Allen Willis (Southern Baptist Theological Seminary). Letter to Martin Luther King, Jr. 6/1/1960. Louisville, Ky. (THLS) 2 pp. (Marginal comments by King.) MLKP-MBU. 600601–001. |
| 7/15/1960 | Kennedy, John F. (John Fitzgerald). "The New Frontier," Address at the Democratic National Convention. 7/15/1960. (PD) 7 pp. JFKPOF-MBJFK: JKPOF–137–003. 600715–004. |
| 9/7/1960 | Robinson, James R. (CORE). Letter to Martin Luther King, Jr. 9/7/1960. New York, N.Y. (TLS) 1 p. MLKP-MBU. 600907–001. |
| 9/19/1960 | Wood, James R. Letter to William H. Hadley. 9/19/1960. [*Atlanta, Ga.*] (TLc) 1 p. MLKP-MBU. 600919–001. |
| 10/5/1960 | King, Martin Luther, Jr. Letter to Robert Brank Fulton. 10/5/1960. [*Atlanta, Ga.*] (TLS) 1 p. RBFP. 601005–001. |
| 10/11/1960 | Cotton, Dorothy (SCLC). "Minutes of annual board meeting." [*10/11/1960*]. Shreveport, La. (TD) 3 pp. MLKJP-GAMK: Box 29. 601011–008. |
| 10/12/1960 | Kennedy, John F. (John Fitzgerald) (U.S. Congress. Senate). Remarks at National Conference on Constitutional Rights and American Freedom. 10/12/1960. New York, N.Y. (TTa) 3 pp. JFKCAMP-MBJFK. 601012–008. |
| 10/31/1960 | Carey, Gordon (CORE). Letter to Martin Luther King, Jr. 10/31/1960. New York, N.Y. (TLS) 2 pp. MLKP-MBU. 601031–011. |
| 11/3/1960 | McWilliams, Carey (*The Nation*). Letter to Martin Luther King, Jr. 11/3/1960. New York, N.Y. (THLS) 1 p. MLKP-MBU. 601103–005. |
| 11/11/1960 | Herriford, John H. (University of Minnesota). Letter to Martin Luther King, Jr. 11/11/1960. Minneapolis, Minn. (TLS) 2 pp. MCMLK-RWWL: 1.1.0.20770. 601111–001. |
| 11/21/1960 | Stewart, J.G. (New York Times Company). Telegram to Martin Luther King, Jr. 11/21/1960. New York, N.Y. (PHWSr) 1 p. MLKP-MBU. 601121–009. |

11/27/1960    Pollitt, Daniel H. (University of North Carolina). "The president's powers in areas of race relations: An exploration." [*11/27/1960*]. Chapel Hill, N.C. (PD) 65 pp. ASRC-RWWL: Reel 128. 601127–009.

11/27/1960    Randolph, A. Philip (Asa Philip), and Harry Belafonte (Care Tribute to Martin Luther King, Jr.). Telegram to George Meany. 11/27/1960. New York, N.Y. (PWSr) 1 p. ACCP-MdU. 601127–010.

11/30/1960    Fey, Harold Edward (*Christian Century*). Letter to Martin Luther King, Jr. 11/30/1960. Chicago, Ill. (TLS) 1 p. MLKP-MBU. 601130–004.

12/2/1960    Rodell, Marie F. (Marie Freid) (Marie Rodell and Joan Daves, Inc.). Letter to Martin Luther King, Jr. 12/2/1960. (TLS) 1 p. MLKP-MBU. 601202–000.

12/7/1960    Neal, H. Grady. Letter to J. H. (Joseph Harrison) Jackson. 12/7/1960. (TLc) 3 pp. (Enclosed in 601207–011. Copy to King.) MLKP-MBU. 601207–010.

12/7/1960    Neal, H. Grady. Letter to Gardner C. Taylor. 12/7/1960. (TLc) 1 p. (Contains enclosure 601207–010. Copy to King.) MLKP-MBU. 601207–011.

12/7/1960    Wagner, John (National Lutheran Council). Letter to Martin Luther King, Jr. 12/7/1960. Chicago, Ill. (TLS) 1 p. MLKP-MBU. 601207–012.

12/15/1960    King, Martin Luther, Jr. Letter to John Wagner. 12/15/1960. [*Atlanta, Ga.*] (THLc) 1 p. MLKP-MBU. 601215–007.

12/15/1960    Neal, H. Grady. Letter to Gardner C. Taylor. 12/15/1960. (TLc) 2 pp. (Copy to King.) MLKP-MBU. 601215–017.

12/16/1960    Dunbar, Leslie (Southern Regional Council). Letter to Charles H. Slayman. 12/16/1960. (TLc) 1 p. ASRC-RWWL: Reel 122. 601216–007.

12/17/1960    Herriford, John H. Letter to Lucile Bluford. 12/17/1960. Minneapolis, Minn. (TALc) 5 pp. (Enclosed in 601219–006. 610000–053 on verso.) MLKP-MBU. 601217–002.

12/19/1960    Duke, Angier Biddle (Abyssinian Baptist Church and the Citizen's Committee of 1,000). Letter to Martin Luther King, Jr. 12/19/1960. New York, N.Y. (THLS) 1 p. MLKP-MBU. 601219–000.

12/19/1960    Meany, George (AFL-CIO). Letter to A. Philip (Asa Philip) Randolph and Harry Belafonte. 12/19/1960. Washington, D.C. (TWc) 1 p. ACCP-MdU. 601219–003.

12/19/1960    Herriford, John H. Letter to Martin Luther King, Jr. 12/19/1960. (TL) 1 p. (Contains enclosures 601217–002 & 610000–053.) MLKP-MBU. 601219–006.

12/21/1960    King, Martin Luther, Jr. Letter to Harold Edward Fey. 12/21/1960. [*Atlanta, Ga.*] (TLc) 1 p. MLKP-MBU. 601221–001.

12/23/1960    Wood, James R. Letter to Septima Poinsette Clark. 12/23/1960. [*Atlanta, Ga.*] (TLc) 1 p. MLKP-MBU. 601223–006.

12/27/1960    King, Martin Luther, Jr. Letter to John Young. 12/27/1960. [*Atlanta, Ga.*] (TLc) 1 p. MLKP-MBU. 601227–000.

12/27/1960    Sheller, Aurelia. Letter to Martin Luther King, Jr. 12/27/1960. Mineral Ridge, Ohio. (TLS) 1 p. MLKP-MBU. 601227–003.

12/30/1960    King, Martin Luther, Jr. "The Negro and the American Dream," Address delivered at Memorial Auditorium. [*12/30/1960*]. [*Chattanooga, Tenn.*] (At) 34 min. (1 sound cassette: analog.) BTC. 601230–008.

12/31/1960    Ebenezer Baptist Church. Press release, "'How Big Is Your God?,' King Jr.'s topic at Ebenezer Sunday morning." 12/31/1960. Atlanta, Ga. (TD) 1 p. EBCR. 601231–000.

1961    SCLC. "This is SCLC." [*1961*]. Atlanta, Ga. (PDd) 8 pp. MCMLK-RWWL: 6.5.0.1300. 610000–007.

1961    King, Martin Luther, Jr. "The Road to Freedom." [*1961*]. [*Atlanta, Ga.*] (ATD) 2 pp. MCMLK-RWWL: 2.2.0.1730. 610000–026.

1961    King, Martin Luther, Jr. *Sit-In Story*. Englewood Cliffs, N.J.: Folkways/Scholastic Records, 1961. (Ff) 5 min. (1 videocassette.) 610000–033.

1961    SCLC. Pamphlet, "Southern Christian Leadership Conference." [*1961*]. Atlanta, Ga. (PHD) 4 pp. MLKP-MBU. 610000–037.

1961    Highlander Folk School. "Training leaders for citizenship schools." [*1961*]. Monteagle, Tenn. (TD) 11 pp. (Enclosed in 610100–021, pp. 136–138 in this volume). MLKJP-GAMK: Box 14. 610000–049.

1961    King, Martin Luther, Jr. Notes on sit-ins and nonviolence. [*1961*]. [*Atlanta, Ga.*] (AD) 3 pp. (Verso of 601217–002.) MLKP-MBU. 610000–053.

1960–1961    King, Martin Luther, Jr. (SCLC). Proposed staff salaries. [*1960–1961*]. [*Atlanta, Ga.*] (AD) 2 pp. MLKP-MBU. 610000–077.

1960–1961    King, Martin Luther, Jr. (SCLC). "Proposed budget." [*1960–1961*]. [*Atlanta, Ga.*] (AD) 1 p. MLKP-MBU. 610000–078.

| | |
|---|---|
| 1961 | SCLC. "Voter registration prospectus." 1961. Atlanta, Ga. (TD) 21 pp. (Enclosed in 610430–001.) MLKJP-GAMK: Box 35. 610000–081. |
| 1961 | SCLC. "Citizenship workbook." [*1961*]. [*Atlanta, Ga.*] (PD) 34 pp. CCC-NN-Sc: Box 3. 610000–092. |
| 1961 | SCLC. "Voter registration program outline." 1961. (TD) 2 pp. MLKP-MBU. 610000–095. |
| 1960–1961 | SCLC. "Budget analysis." 1960–1961. Atlanta, Ga. (TD) 1 p. SCLCR-GAMK: Box 57. 610000–100. |
| 1961 | Walker, Wyatt Tee (SCLC). Memo to Participating Agencies. [*1961*]. (TLS) 2 pp. JFKWHCSF-MBJFK: Box 8. 610000–109. |
| 1961 | SCLC. "Southwide Voter Registration Prospectus." [*1961*]. Atlanta, Ga. (TD) 14 pp. MLKP-MBU. 610000–111. |
| 1961 | SCLC. Program, "Crusade for citizenship." [*1961*]. Atlanta, Ga. (PD) 6 pp. MCMLK-RWWL: 6.5.0.810. 610000–121. |
| 1960–1961 | SCLC. "General program." 1960–1961. Atlanta, Ga. (TD) 15 pp. SCLCR-GAMK: Box 37. 610000–140. |
| 1961 | SCLC. Pamphlet, "Citizenship education program." [*1961*]. Atlanta, Ga. (PDS) 6 pp. MLKJP-GAMK: Box 90. 610000–180. |
| 1/1961 | King, Martin Luther, Jr. Letter to Major J. Jones. [*1/1961*]. [*Atlanta, Ga.*] (TLc) 1 p. MLKP-MBU. 610100–004. |
| 1/1961 | King, Martin Luther, Jr. Letter to John Thomas Porter. [*1/1961*]. [*Atlanta, Ga.*] (TLc) 1 p. MLKP-MBU. 610100–010. |
| 1/1961 | Southern Regional Council. "The federal executive and civil rights." 1/1961. Atlanta, Ga. (PD) 54 pp. ASRC-RWWL: Reel 219. 610100–019. |
| 12/1960–1/1961 | SCLC. "Citizenship school training program." [*12/1960–1/1961*]. Atlanta, Ga. (TD) 11 pp. (Enclosed in 610100–021, pp. 136–138 in this volume.) SCLCR-GAMK: Box 136. 610100–020. |
| 1/2/1961 | Brown, Johnnie. Letter to Martin Luther King, Jr. [*1/2/1961*]. Dawson, Ga. (ALS) 3 pp. MLKP-MBU. 610102–000. |
| 1/2/1961 | Emancipation Association. Program, "Emancipation Celebration." 1/2/1961. Savannah, Ga. (PHD) 4 pp. MCMLK-RWWL: 12.3.0.310. 610102–001. |
| 1/3/1961 | Alinsky, Saul David (Industrial Areas Foundation). Letter to John H. Wagner. 1/3/1961. Chicago, Ill. (TLS) 2 pp. (Enclosed in 610103–001, pp. 123–126 in this volume.) MLKP-MBU. 610103–000. |
| 1/3/1961 | Morris, John Burnett (Episcopal Society for Cultural and Racial Unity). Letter to Martin Luther King, Jr. 1/3/1961. Atlanta, Ga. (TALS) 1 p. MLKJP-GAMK: Box 9. 610103–006. |
| 1/5/1961 | Currier, Stephen R. (Taconic Foundation). Letter to Martin Luther King, Jr. 1/5/1961. New York, N.Y. (THLS) 2 pp. MLKP-MBU. 610105–001. |
| 1/5/1961 | King, Martin Luther. Letter to William A. Johnson. 1/5/1961. [*Atlanta, Ga.*] (TLc) 1 p. MLKP-MBU. 610105–002. |
| 1/9/1961 | King, Martin Luther, Jr. Letter to George C. Simkins. 1/9/1961. [*Atlanta, Ga.*] (TLc) 1 p. MLKP-MBU. 610109–007. |
| 1/9/1961 | Maxwell, O. Clay (Mount Olivet Baptist Church). Letter to Martin Luther King, Jr. 1/9/1961. New York, N.Y. (TLS) 1 p. MLKP-MBU. 610109–010. |
| 1/10/1961 | King, Martin Luther, Jr. Letter to Franklin H. Littell. 1/10/1961. [*Atlanta, Ga.*] (TLc) 1 p. MLKP-MBU. 610110–000. |
| 1/10/1961 | Reid, Milton A. (Virginia Christian Leadership Conference). Letter to Martin Luther King, Jr. 1/10/1961. Petersburg, Va. (THLS) 2 pp. MLKP-MBU. 610110–003. |
| 1/10/1961 | King, Martin Luther, Jr. Letter to Charles McDew. 1/10/1961. [*Atlanta, Ga.*] (THLc) 1 p. MLKP-MBU. 610110–007. |
| 1/10/1961 | Carman, Bernard R. (Union College). Telegram to Martin Luther King, Jr. 1/10/1961. Schenectady, N.Y. (PWSr) 1 p. MLKP-MBU. 610110–010. |
| 1/10/1961 | King, Martin Luther, Jr. (Ebenezer Baptist Church). Letter to Charles McDew. 1/10/1961. Atlanta, Ga. (TLS) 1 p. SNCCP-GAMK. 610110–011. |
| 1/11/1961 | Wood, James R. (SCLC). Press release, James Lawson to become staff consultant. 1/11/1961. Atlanta, Ga. (TD) 1 p. SAVFC-WHi. 610111–001. |
| 1/11/1961 | Exman, Eugene (Harper & Brothers). Letter to Martin Luther King, Jr. 1/11/1961. New York, N.Y. (THLS) 1 p. MLKP-MBU. 610111–002. |
| 1/11/1961 | McDonald, Dora E. Letter to Charles Moore. 1/11/1961. [*Atlanta, Ga.*] (THLc) 1 p. MLKP-MBU. 610111–011. |
| 1/11/1961 | King, Martin Luther, Jr. Letter to H. Grady Neal. 1/11/1961. [*Atlanta, Ga.*] (THLc) 1 p. MLKP-MBU. 610111–013. |

| 1/12/1961 | Gray, Fred D. Letter to Martin Luther King, Jr. 1/12/1961. Montgomery, Ala. (TLS) | Calendar |

1/12/1961    Gray, Fred D. Letter to Martin Luther King, Jr. 1/12/1961. Montgomery, Ala. (TLS) 1 p. MLKP-MBU. 610112–003.

1/12/1961    Anderson, Trezzvant W. (Pittsburgh Courier Publishing Co.). Letter to Martin Luther King, Jr. 1/12/1961. Pittsburgh, Pa. (THLS) 1 p. MLKP-MBU. 610112–005.

1/15/1961    King, Martin Luther, Jr. "The Future of Integration," Address at Canoga Park High School. 1/15/1961. Canoga Park, Calif. (TD) 10 pp. WHCCR. 610115–001.

1/15/1961    King, Martin Luther, Jr. Three Dimensions of a Complete Life, Sermon at Woodland Hills Community Church. [1/15/1961]. [Woodland Hills, Calif.] (TTa) 8 pp. FODC. 610115–002.

1/16/1961    Kaplan, Kivie (Colonial Tanning Company, Inc.). Letter to Martin Luther King, Jr. 1/16/1961. Boston, Mass. (THLS) 1 p. MLKP-MBU. 610116–008.

1/16/1961    Sheffield, Horace L. (International Union, United Automobile, Aircraft & Agricultural Implement Workers of America (CIO)). Letter to Martin Luther King, Jr. 1/16/1961. Detroit, Mich. (TLS) 1 p. MLKP-MBU. 610116–009.

1/16/1961    King, Martin Luther, Jr. Letter to Jimmie Flamer. 1/16/1961. [Atlanta, Ga.] (THLc) 1 p. MLKP-MBU. 610116–010.

1/17/1961    Lasley, Russell R. (United Packinghouse Workers of America, AFL-CIO). Telegram to Martin Luther King, Jr. 1/17/1961. Chicago, Ill. (PHWSr) 1 p. MLKP-MBU. 610117–001.

1/17/1961    Kaplan, Kivie (Colonial Tanning Company, Inc.). Letter to Dora E. McDonald. 1/17/1961. Boston, Mass. (THLS) 1 p. MLKP-MBU. 610117–004.

1/17/1961    Wood, James R. Letter to Elizabeth Knight. 1/17/1961. (THLc) 1 p. MLKP-MBU. 610117–006.

1/18/1961    Wood, James R. Letter to Ian H. Brown. 1/18/1961. [Atlanta, Ga.] (THLc) 1 p. MLKP-MBU. 610118–000.

1/18/1961    Louchheim, Katie (Inaugural Committee). Invitation for reception at the National Gallery of Art to Coretta Scott King. 1/18/1961. Washington, D.C. (PD) 3 pp. MLKJP-GAMK: Vault Box 2. 610118–005.

1/18/1961    Bentz, Betty (Hotel and Club Employees Union Local 6). Letter to Martin Luther King, Jr. 1/18/1961. New York, N.Y. (THLS) 1 p. (Contains enclosure 610118–014.) MLKP-MBU. 610118–011.

1/18/1961    Hotel and Club Employees Union, Local 6. "Candidates for Local Six 1960 better race relations award." [1/18/1961]. (TD) 2 pp. (Enclosed in 610118–011.) MLKP-MBU. 610118–014.

1/19/1961    King, Martin Luther, Jr. Letter to Carey McWilliams. 1/19/1961. [Atlanta, Ga.] (TLc) 1 p. (Contains enclosure 610119–005.) MLKP-MBU. 610119–001.

**1/19/1961    King, Martin Luther, Jr. Draft, Equality Now: The President Has the Power. [1/19/1961]. [Atlanta, Ga.] (ADd) 26 pp. MLKP-MBU. 610119–002.**

1/19/1961    Foley, Edward H. (Inaugural Committee). Invitation to the inaugural concert of John F. (John Fitzgerald) Kennedy. 1/19/1961. Washington, D.C. (PD) 2 pp. MLKJP-GAMK: Vault Box 2. 610119–003.

1/19/1961    King, Martin Luther, Jr. Equality Now: The President Has the Power. [1/19/1961]. [Atlanta, Ga.] (TAD) 16 pp. (Enclosed in 610119–001.) MLKP-MBU. 610119–005.

**1/20/1961    Foley, Edward H. (Inaugural Committee). Invitation to the inauguration of John F. (John Fitzgerald) Kennedy and Lyndon B. (Lyndon Baines) Johnson. 1/20/1961. Washington, D.C. (PD) 1 p. MLKJP-GAMK: Vault Box 2. 610120–005.**

1/20/1961    Woodward, Stanley, and Lindy Boggs (Inaugural Ball Committee). Invitation to the inaugural ball of John F. (John Fitzgerald) Kennedy and Lyndon B. (Lyndon Baines) Johnson. 1/20/1961. Washington, D.C. (PD) 2 pp. MLKJP-GAMK: Vault Box 2. 610120–006.

1/20/1961    Kaplan, Kivie (Colonial Tanning Company, Inc.). Letter to Martin Luther King, Jr. 1/20/1961. Boston, Mass. (THLS) 1 p. MLKP-MBU. 610120–007.

1/20/1961    McDonald, Dora E. Letter to Betty Bentz. 1/20/1961. [Atlanta, Ga.] (TLc) 1 p. MLKP-MBU. 610120–012.

1/20/1961    Wood, James R. Report to Martin Luther King, Jr. 1/20/1961. (TAD) 4 pp. CSKC. 610120–014.

1/20/1961    Duke, Angier Biddle (Africa League). Letter to Martin Luther King, Jr. 1/20/1961. New York, N.Y. (THLS) 1 p. MLKP-MBU. 610120–015.

1/21/1961    Feinsinger, Nathan Paul (United Packinghouse Workers of America, AFL-CIO). Press release, Public Review Advisory Commission held hearings on charges of violation of ethics codes. 1/21/1961. Chicago, Ill. (THD) 1 p. MLKP-MBU. 610121–000.

1/21/1961    Robinson, Cleophus (Bethlehem Missionary Baptist Church). Letter to Martin Luther King, Jr. 1/21/1961. St. Louis, Mo. (THLS) 1 p. MLKP-MBU. 610121–002.

| | |
|---|---|
| 1/19/1961–<br>1/21/1961 | SCLC. Program, "Training leaders for citizenship schools refresher workshop." 1/19/1961–1/21/1961. Monteagle, Tenn. (THD) 9 pp. MLKP-MBU. 610121–003. |
| 1/23/1961 | King, Martin Luther, Jr. Letter to A.S. Myklebust. 1/23/1961. [*Atlanta, Ga.*] (TLc) 1 p. MLKP-MBU. 610123–001. |
| 1/23/1961 | King, Martin Luther, Jr. Letter to Curtis Jackson. 1/23/1961. [*Atlanta, Ga.*] (TLc) 1 p. MLKP-MBU. 610123–004. |
| 1/23/1961 | King, Martin Luther, Jr. (Ebenezer Baptist Church). Letter to Fred O. Doty. 1/23/1961. Atlanta, Ga. (TLS) 1 p. FODC. 610123–019. |
| 1/23/1961 | King, Martin Luther, Jr. Letter to Willoughby Abner. 1/23/1961. [*Atlanta, Ga.*] (THLc) 1 p. MLKP-MBU. 610123–024. |
| 1/23/1961 | Doggett, John N. (Hamilton Methodist Church). Letter to Martin Luther King, Jr. 1/23/1961. Los Angeles, Calif. (THLS) 1 p. MLKJP-GAMK: Box 36. 610123–026. |
| 1/24/1961 | Wood, James R. Letter to Saul David Alinsky. 1/24/1961. [*Atlanta, Ga.*] (THLc) 1 p. MLKP-MBU. 610124–000. |
| 1/24/1961 | McWilliams, Carey (*The Nation*). Letter to Martin Luther King, Jr. 1/24/1961. New York, N.Y. (THLS) 1 p. MLKP-MBU. 610124–002. |
| 1/24/1961 | Sitton, Claude (New York Times Company). Letter to Martin Luther King, Jr. 1/24/1961. Atlanta, Ga. (THLS) 1 p. MLKP-MBU. 610124–007. |
| 1/24/1961 | Wood, James R. (SCLC). Press release, "SCLC denies endorsing Co-op Wholesale Mart." 1/24/1961. Atlanta, Ga. (THD) 2 pp. MLKP-MBU. 610124–010. |
| 1/25/1961 | Reid, Milton A. (Virginia Christian Leadership Conference). Letter to Martin Luther King, Jr. 1/25/1961. Petersburg, Va. (TLS) 2 pp. MLKP-MBU. 610125–004. |
| 1/25/1961 | Reid, Milton A. (Virginia Christian Leadership Conference). Letter to Wyatt Tee Walker. 1/25/1961. (TLS) 2 pp. MLKP-MBU. 610125–005. |
| 1/26/1961 | Sobell, Helen L. (Committee to Secure Justice for Morton Sobell). Letter to Martin Luther King, Jr. 1/26/1961. New York, N.Y. (THLS) 1 p. MLKP-MBU. 610126–002. |
| 1/27/1961 | Spiegel, Arthur (Associated Students of Stanford University and the Institute of International Relations). Letter to Martin Luther King, Jr. 1/27/1961. Stanford, Calif. (TLS) 2 pp. MLKP-MBU. 610127–002. |
| 1/27/1961 | King, Martin Luther, Jr. Letter to Lacy Harris. 1/27/1961. [*Atlanta, Ga.*] (TLc) 1 p. MLKP-MBU. 610127–011. |
| 1/27/1961 | Pamphlet, "Tribute to Martin Luther King, Jr." 1/27/1961. New York, N.Y. (PD) 4 pp. JWPC-DcWaMMB. 610127–021. |
| 1/28/1961 | Gray, Fred D. Letter to Martin Luther King, Jr. 1/28/1961. Montgomery, Ala. (TLS) 1 p. MLKP-MBU. 610128–001. |
| 1/29/1961 | Ebenezer Baptist Church. Program, Sunday services. 1/29/1961. Atlanta, Ga. (TD) 4 pp. EBCR. 610129–008. |
| 1/29/1961 | Chicago Sunday Evening Club. Program, "Chicago Sunday Evening Club." 1/29/1961. Chicago, Ill. (PD) 4 pp. MCMLK-RWWL: 12.3.0.200. 610129–010. |
| 1/30/1961 | Americans for Democratic Action. Program, "Thirteenth annual Roosevelt Day dinner." 1/30/1961. (PD) 28 pp. ADAR-WHi. 610130–009. |
| 1/31/1961 | Shull, Leon (Americans for Democratic Action). Letter to Martin Luther King, Jr. 1/31/1961. Philadelphia, Pa. (TLS) 1 p. MLKP-MBU. 610131–004. |
| 11/1/1960–<br>1/31/1961 | Abernathy, Ralph (SCLC). "Quarterly budget summary." 11/1/1960–1/31/1961. Atlanta, Ga. (TDS) 1 p. SCLCR-GAMK: Box 57. 610131–016. |
| 1/31/1961 | King, Martin Luther, Jr. "The Future of Integration" Address delivered at the University of Utah. [*1/31/1961*]. [*Salt Lake City, Utah*]. (At) 37.3 min. (1 sound cassette: analog.) CSS. 610131–019. |
| 12/1960–2/1961 | "The citizenship school." [*12/1960–2/1961*]. (TD) 11 p. CKFC. 610200–000. |
| 2/1961 | Department of Racial and Cultural Relations. "Membership of general committee." 2/1961. (THDf) 2 pp. NCCP-PPPrHi: Box 45. 610200–002. |
| 2/1961 | Canfield, Cass (Harper & Brothers). Letter to Martin Luther King, Jr. [*2/1961*]. New York, N.Y. (THLS) 1 p. MLKP-MBU. 610200–004. |
| 2/1961 | Baldwin, James. "The Dangerous Road Before Martin Luther King." *Harper's Magazine* (February 1961), 33–42. (PHD) 11 pp. 610200–005. |
| 2/1961 | Americans for Democratic Action. "Report on Roosevelt Day Dinner." *News of ADA* 8, no. 2 (February 1961), 1–2. (PD) 2 pp. ADAR-WHi. 610200–010. |
| 2/1/1961 | Kaplan, Kivie. Letter to Martin Luther King, Jr. and Coretta Scott King. 2/1/1961. Chestnut Hill, Mass. (TALS) 2 pp. (Contains enclosure 610201–001.) MLKP-MBU. 610201–000. |
| 2/1/1961 | Kaplan, Kivie, and Emily Kaplan. Telegram to Martin Luther King, Jr. and Coretta Scott King. 2/1/1961. (PWSr) 1 p. (Enclosed in 610201–000.) MLKP-MBU. 610201–001. |

| | |
|---|---|
| 2/1/1961 | Guthrie, Shirley C. (Columbia Theological Society). Letter to Martin Luther King, Jr. 2/1/1961. Decatur, Ga. (THLS) 1 p. MLKP-MBU. 610201–004. |
| 2/1/1961 | Porter, John Thomas. Letter to Martin Luther King, Jr. 2/1/1961. Detroit, Mich. (TLS) 1 p. MLKP-MBU. 610201–006. |
| 2/2/1961 | Americans for Democratic Action. "Citation to Martin Luther King, Jr." 2/2/1961. New York, N.Y. (PDS) 1 p. MLKP-MBU. 610202–001. |
| 2/3/1961 | Wood, James R. Letter to Edward Stovall. 2/3/1961. [*Atlanta, Ga.*] (THLc) 2 pp. MLKP-GAMK: Box 36. 610203–003. |
| 2/3/1961 | King, Martin Luther, Jr. Letter to Claude Sitton. 2/3/1961. [*Atlanta, Ga.*] (TLc) 1 p. MLKP-MBU. 610203–006. |
| 2/6/1961 | Roosevelt, Eleanor (United Feature Syndicate, Inc.). Press release, My day. 2/6/1961. Waltham, Mass. (PD) 2 pp. ERC-NHyF. 610206–000. |
| 2/6/1961 | Rustin, Bayard. Letter to the Editor of *Harper's Magazine*. 2/6/1961. New York, N.Y. (TLc) 2 pp. (Enclosed in 610206–003, p. 152 in this volume.) MLKP-MBU. 610206–002. |
| 2/7/1961 | Jones, M.A. (U.S. FBI). Memo to Cartha D. DeLoach. 2/7/1961. (THLI) 2 pp. FBIDG-NN-Sc: Bureau File 100–106670. 610207–012. |
| 2/7/1961 | King, Martin Luther, Jr. Interview by Mike Wallace, part one. 2/7/1961. (TTv) 7 pp. MWallP-NSyU. Box 6. 610207–013. |
| 2/8/1961 | King, Martin Luther, Jr. Letter to J.C. Austin. 2/8/1961. [*Atlanta, Ga.*] (TLc) 1 p. MLKP-MBU. 610208–002. |
| 2/8/1961 | Randolph, A. Philip (Asa Philip) (Negro American Labor Council). Letter to Martin Luther King, Jr. 2/8/1961. New York, N.Y. (TLS) 1 p. (Contains enclosure 610208–006. 610208–007 on verso.) MLKP-MBU. 610208–004. |
| 2/8/1961 | Negro American Labor Council. "A resolution." [*2/8/1961*]. (TD) 1 p. (Enclosed in 610208–004. 610208–006 on verso.) MLKP-MBU. 610208–006. |
| 2/8/1961 | Ballard, Ronald. Letter to Martin Luther King, Jr. [*2/8/1961*]. (AHLS) 1 p. (Enclosed in 610208–004. 610208–006 on verso. Marginal comments by King.) MLKP-MBU. 610208–007. |
| 2/8/1961 | King, Martin Luther, Jr. Letter to Goldie B. Schwarz. 2/8/1961. [*Atlanta, Ga.*] (TLc) 1 p. MLKP-MBU. 610208–010. |
| 2/8/1961 | King, Martin Luther, Jr. (SCLC). Form fundraising letter. 2/8/1961. Atlanta, Ga. (TLd) 1 p. MLKP-MBU. 610208–015. |
| 2/8/1961 | King, Martin Luther, Jr. Interview by Mike Wallace, part two. 2/8/1961. (THTv) 5 pp. MWallP-NSyU. Box 6. 610208–022. |
| 2/9/1961 | King, Martin Luther, Jr. Letter to James A. Peterson. 2/9/1961. [*Atlanta, Ga.*] (TLc) 2 pp. MLKP-MBU. 610209–007. |
| 2/9/1961 | King, Martin Luther, Jr. Letter to O. Clay Maxwell. 2/9/1961. [*Atlanta, Ga.*] (TLc) 1 p. MLKP-MBU. 610209–010. |
| 2/9/1961 | King, Martin Luther, Jr. Letter to Gardner C. Taylor. 2/9/1961. [*Atlanta, Ga.*] (TLc) 1 p. MLKP-MBU. 610209–012. |
| 2/10/1961 | Feinsinger, Nathan Paul (University of Wisconsin Law School). Letter to Martin Luther King, Jr. 2/10/1961. Madison, Wis. (TALS) 1 p. MLKP-MBU. 610210–001. |
| 2/10/1961 | King, Martin Luther, Jr. Letter to A. (Allen) A. Banks. 2/10/1961. [*Atlanta, Ga.*] (TLc) 1 p. MLKP-MBU. 610210–005. |
| 2/10/1961 | King, Martin Luther, Jr. Address on unjust laws, the necessity of jail and future hope of equality. [*2/10/1961*]. (F) 1.1 min. (1 video cassette) NBCNA-NNNBC. 610210–011. |
| 2/12/1961 | Ebenezer Baptist Church. Program, "The Ebenezer Youth Organization Presents?" 2/12/1961. Atlanta, Ga. (PD) 4 pp. EBCR. 610212–000. |
| 2/13/1961 | King, Martin Luther, Jr. (Ebenezer Baptist Church). Letter to Whitney M. Young. 2/13/1961. Atlanta, Ga. (TLS) 1 p. (Contains enclosure 610204–000, pp. 139–150 in this volume.) WYC-NNC. 610213–001. |
| 2/13/1961 | King, Martin Luther, Jr. (Ebenezer Baptist Church). Letter to Roy Wilkins. 2/13/1961. Atlanta, Ga. (TLS) 1 p. NAACPP-DLC. 610213–003. |
| 2/13/1961 | King, Martin Luther, Jr. Letter to Harris Wofford. 2/13/1961. [*Atlanta, Ga.*] (TLc) 1 p. MLKP-MBU. 610213–005. |
| 2/13/1961 | Margolies, Lester (Southern Illinois University). Letter to Martin Luther King, Jr. 2/13/1961. Carbondale, Ill. (THLS) 1 p. MLKP-MBU. 610213–020. |
| 2/14/1961 | Wood, James R. (SCLC). Press release, "SCLC starts leadership training program." 2/14/1961. Atlanta, Ga. (TD) 1 p. SAVFC-WHi. 610214–000. |
| 2/14/1961 | McDonald, Dora E. Letter to E.W. Williamson. 2/14/1961. [*Atlanta, Ga.*] (TLc) 1 p. MLKP-MBU. 610214–003. |
| 2/15/1961 | King, Martin Luther, Jr. (Ebenezer Baptist Church). Letter to Eleanor Roosevelt. 2/15/1961. Atlanta, Ga. (THLS) 1 p. ERC-NHyF. 610215–000. |

| | |
|---|---|
| 2/15/1961 | King, Martin Luther, Jr. Letter to Eugene Exman. 2/15/1961. [*Atlanta, Ga.*] (THLc) 1 p. MLKP-MBU. 610215–004. |
| 2/15/1961 | Powell, Adam Clayton (U.S. Congress. House of Representatives). Letter to Martin Luther King, Jr. 2/15/1961. Washington, D.C. (THLS) 1 p. MLKP-MBU. 610215–006. |
| 2/15/1961 | King, Martin Luther, Jr. Letter to G. Merrill Lenox. 2/15/1961. [*Atlanta, Ga.*] (TLc) 1 p. MLKP-MBU. 610215–009. |
| 2/15/1961 | King, Martin Luther, Jr. Letter to J. Raymond Henderson. 2/15/1961. [*Atlanta, Ga.*] (TLc) 1 p. MLKP-MBU. 610215–015. |
| 2/15/1961 | King, Martin Luther, Jr. (Ebenezer Baptist Church). Letter to Daniel H. Pollitt. 2/15/1961. Atlanta, Ga. (TLS) 1 p. DPC. 610215–021. |
| 2/15/1961 | United Packing House Workers of America, CIO. "Report of Public Review Advisory Commission of United Packinghouse, Food, and Allied Workers of America, AFL-CIO." 2/15/1961. (TDc) 53 pp. (Contains enclosure 610215–026.) MLKP-MBU. 610215–025. |
| 2/15/1961 | King, Martin Luther, Jr. "Concurring statement of Rev. Martin Luther King, Jr." [*2/15/1961*]. Atlanta, Ga. (TDc) 2 pp. (Enclosed in 610215–025.) UPWR-WHi: Box 162. 610215–026. |
| 2/16/1961 | King, Martin Luther, Jr. Letter to James Whitehurst. 2/16/1961. [*Atlanta, Ga.*] (TLc) 1 p. MLKP-MBU. 610216–000. |
| 2/16/1961 | King, Martin Luther, Jr. Letter to Philip Price. 2/16/1961. [*Atlanta, Ga.*] (TLc) 1 p. MLKP-MBU. 610216–004. |
| 2/16/1961 | McDonald, Dora E. Letter to A. Louise Jones. 2/16/1961. [*Atlanta, Ga.*] (TLc) 1 p. MLKP-MBU. 610216–006. |
| 2/16/1961 | King, Martin Luther, Jr. Letter to Gardner C. Taylor. 2/16/1961. [*Atlanta, Ga.*] (TLc) 1 p. MLKP-MBU. 610216–007. |
| 2/16/1961 | King, Martin Luther, Jr. Letter to Donald R. Raichle. 2/16/1961. [*Atlanta, Ga.*] (TLc) 1 p. MLKP-MBU. 610216–009. |
| 2/17/1961 | Prattis, Percival Leroy (Pittsburgh Courier Publishing Co.). Letter to Martin Luther King, Jr. 2/17/1961. Pittsburgh, Pa. (TLS) 3 pp. MLKP-MBU. 610217–000. |
| 2/17/1961 | King, Martin Luther, Jr. Letter to Robert F. Kennedy. 2/17/1961. [*Atlanta, Ga.*] (TLc) 1 p. MLKP-MBU. 610217–005. |
| 2/17/1961 | King, Martin Luther, Jr. Letter to Leon Green and the seventy-nine freedom fighters. 2/17/1961. [*Atlanta, Ga.*] (TLc) 1 p. MLKP-MBU. 610217–007. |
| 2/17/1961–2/18/1961 | Negro American Labor Council. Press release, Institute and workshop mark launch of drive against job discrimination. 2/17/1961–2/18/1961. Washington, D.C. (THD) 4 pp. RPP-NN-Sc: Box 3. 610218–002. |
| 2/17/1961–2/18/1961 | Negro American Labor Council. Program, "Race bias in trade unions, industry and government." 2/17/1961–2/18/1961. Washington, D.C. (PD) 4 pp. RPP-NN-Sc: Box 2. 610218–003. |
| 2/18/1961 | Ebenezer Baptist Church. Press release, "'I Am the Way,' Dr. King's sermon subject at Ebenezer." 2/18/1961. (TD) 1 p. EBCR. 610218–007. |
| 2/20/1961 | Kaplan, Kivie (Colonial Tanning Company, Inc.). Letter to Dora E. McDonald. 2/20/1961. Boston, Mass. (THLS) 1 p. MLKP-MBU. 610220–005. |
| 2/20/1961 | King, Martin Luther, Jr. (Ebenezer Baptist Church). Letter to Secretary of the Delegacy for Extra Mural Studies. 2/20/1961. [*Atlanta, Ga.*] (TLc) 1 p. MLKP-MBU. 610220–009. |
| 2/21/1961 | Roosevelt, Eleanor. Letter to Martin Luther King, Jr. 2/21/1961. New York, N.Y. (THLS) 1 p. MLKP-MBU. 610221–004. |
| 2/21/1961 | Weaver, Robert Clifton (U.S. Housing and Home Finance Agency). Letter to Martin Luther King, Jr. 2/21/1961. Washington, D.C. (THLS) 1 p. MLKP-MBU. 610221–005. |
| 2/21/1961 | Wood, James R. (SCLC). Press release, Ministers file complaint for relief in *Patterson v. New York Times* case. 2/21/1961. Atlanta, Ga. (TD) 1 p. BWOF-AB: File 1102. 610221–011. |
| 2/23/1961 | Rodell, Marie F. (Marie Freid) (Marie Rodell and Joan Daves, Inc.). Letter to Martin Luther King, Jr. 2/23/1961. New York, N.Y. (TLS) 2 pp. MLKP-MBU. 610223–001. |
| 2/23/1961 | Wood, James R. Letter to L. F. Palmer. 2/23/1961. [*Atlanta, Ga.*] (TLc) 2 pp. MLKP-MBU. 610223–003. |
| 2/26/1961 | Chicago Conference for Brotherhood, Inc. Program, "Annual brotherhood dinner." 2/26/1961. Chicago, Ill. (PD) 4 pp. MLKP-MBU. 610226–000. |
| 2/27/1961 | Thompson, R. A. (Atlanta Urban League). Letter to Martin Luther King, Jr. 2/27/1961. Atlanta, Ga. (TLS) 1 p. MLKP-MBU. 610227–006. |

| | |
|---|---|
| 2/28/1961 | Ling, Warren (Belafonte Enterprises, Inc.). Letter to Martin Luther King, Jr. 2/28/1961. New York, N.Y. (TLS) 1 p. MLKP-MBU. 610228–002. |
| 3/1961 | "Biographical sketch of Martin Luther King, Jr." [*3/1961*]. (TD) 5 pp. ICHi. 610300–007. |
| 3/1961 | SCLC. Memo to Supporters. 3/1961. Atlanta, Ga. (TL) 4 pp. MLKP-MBU. 610300–011. |
| 3/1961 | King, Martin Luther, Jr., and Wyatt Tee Walker (SCLC). Letter to the Student Interracial Ministry. [*3/1961*]. Atlanta, Ga. (TL) 2 pp. MLKJP-GAMK: Box 132. 610300–013. |
| 3/1/1961 | Kennedy, Robert F. (U.S. Dept. of Justice). Letter to Martin Luther King, Jr. 3/1/1961. Washington, D.C. (THLS) 1 p. MLKP-MBU. 610301–000. |
| 3/1/1961 | King, Martin Luther, Jr. Letter to Maya Angelou. 3/1/1961. [*Atlanta, Ga.*] (TLc) 1 p. MLKP-MBU. 610301–013. |
| 3/1/1961 | Megill, June. (Mission Orientation Program). Letter to Martin Luther King, Jr. 3/1/1961. Stony Point, N.Y. (THLS) 1 p. MLKP-MBU. 610301–014. |
| 3/2/1961 | Brown, Margaret. Letter to Martin Luther King, Jr. 3/2/1961. Los Angeles, Calif. (THLS) 1 p. MLKP-MBU. 610302–005. |
| 3/3/1961 | Merchants' Credit Guide Co. Letter to Martin Luther King, Jr. 3/3/1961. Chicago, Ill. (TL) 1 p. MLKP-MBU. 610303–004. |
| 3/3/1961 | Walker, Wyatt Tee (SCLC). Letter to Martin Luther King, Jr. 3/3/1961. Atlanta, Ga. (TLS) 1 p. MLKP-MBU. 610303–005. |
| 3/4/1961 | King, Martin Luther, Jr. "TV Interview with the Rev. Martin Luther King, Jr., Part One." Baltimore *Afro-American*, 4 March 1961, pp. 1, 4 (PD) 2 pp. 610304–001. |
| 3/5/1961 | Braden, Anne (Southern Conference Educational Fund). Letter to Martin Luther King, Jr. 3/5/1961. Louisville, Ky. (TALS) 2 pp. MLKP-MBU. 610305–000. |
| 3/6/1961 | O'Brien, Lawrence F. (U.S. White House). Letter to Martin Luther King, Jr. 3/6/1961. Washington, D.C. (THLS) 1 p. MLKP-MBU. 610306–004. |
| 3/6/1961 | King, Martin Luther, Jr. Letter to Bayard Rustin. 3/6/1961. [*Atlanta, Ga.*] (TLc) 1 p. MLKP-MBU. 610306–006. |
| 3/6/1961 | King, Martin Luther, Jr. The Man Who Was a Fool, Sermon delivered at the Detroit Council of Churches' noon Lenten services. 3/6/1961. Detroit, Mich. (At) 33.8 min. (1 sound cassette: analog.) MAWC. 610306–028. |
| 3/6/1961 | Kirkpatrick, Dow (St. Mark United Methodist Church). Letter to Herman E. (Herman Eugene) Talmadge. 3/6/1961. Atlanta, Ga. (THLS) 1 p. HETC-GU: Box 4. 610306–033. |
| 3/7/1961 | McDonald, Dora E. Letter to Annie Loggins. 3/7/1961. (TLc) 1 p. MLKP-MBU. 610307–000. |
| 3/7/1961 | King, Martin Luther, Jr. Letter to Thomas Long. 3/7/1961. [*Atlanta, Ga.*] (TLc) 1 p. MLKP-MBU. 610307–001. |
| 3/7/1961 | King, Martin Luther, Jr. Letter to Lester S. Levy. 3/7/1961. [*Atlanta, Ga.*] (TLc) 1 p. MLKP-MBU. 610307–002. |
| 3/7/1961 | Alexander, James T. (Dexter Avenue Baptist Church). Letter to Martin Luther King, Jr. 3/7/1961. Montgomery, Ala. (THLS) 1 p. MLKP-MBU. 610307–010. |
| 3/7/1961 | King, Martin Luther, Jr. Loving Your Enemies, Sermon delivered at the Detroit Council of Churches' noon Lenten services. 3/7/1961. Detroit, Mich. (At) 38.6 min. (1 sound cassette: analog.) MAWC. 610307–012. |
| 3/8/1961 | King, Martin Luther, Jr. Letter to Edward E. Hart. 3/8/1961. [*Atlanta, Ga.*] (TLc) 1 p. MLKP-MBU. 610308–006. |
| 3/8/1961 | Gentile, Dolores (Marie Rodell and Joan Daves, Inc.). Letter to Martin Luther King, Jr. 3/8/1961. New York, N.Y. (THLS) 1 p. MLKP-MBU. 610308–007. |
| 3/8/1961 | King, Martin Luther, Jr. Letter to G. Merrill Lenox. 3/8/1961. [*Atlanta, Ga.*] (TLc) 1 p. MLKP-MBU. 610308–011. |
| 3/8/1961 | King, Martin Luther, Jr. Letter to Jane Stembridge. 3/8/1961. [*Atlanta, Ga.*] (TLc) 1 p. (Contains enclosure 610308–016.) MLKP-MBU. 610308–015. |
| 3/8/1961 | King, Martin Luther, Jr. Letter of introduction for Jane Stembridge and Donna McGinty. 3/8/1961. [*Atlanta, Ga.*] (TLc) 1 p. (Enclosed in 610308–015.) MLKP-MBU. 610308–016. |
| 3/8/1961 | King, Martin Luther, Jr. Letter to Delores E. Thomas. 3/8/1961. [*Atlanta, Ga.*] (TLc) 2 pp. MLKP-MBU. 610308–017. |
| 3/9/1961 | Doar, John (U.S. Dept. of Justice). Letter to Martin Luther King, Jr. 3/9/1961. Washington, D.C. (THLS) 1 p. MLKP-MBU. 610309–000. |
| 3/9/1961 | King, Martin Luther, Jr. Telegram to Benjamin Blom. 3/9/1961. [*Atlanta, Ga.*] (PHWc) 1 p. MLKP-MBU. 610309–006. |

| | |
|---|---|
| 3/8/1961–<br>3/9/1961 | SCLC. Minutes, "First quarterly meeting of Administrative Committee." 3/8/1961–<br>3/9/1961. Atlanta, Ga. (TD) 3 pp. SCLCR-GAMK: Box 36. 610309–011. |
| 3/9/1961 | McDonald, Dora E. Letter to Lester Margolies. 3/9/1961. [Atlanta, Ga.] (TLc) 1 p.<br>MLKP-MBU. 610309–012. |
| 3/9/1961 | Shuttlesworth, Fred L. (SCLC). Memo to Administrative Committee [3/9/1961].<br>[Atlanta, Ga.] (THL) 2 pp. SCLCR-GAMK: Box 36. 610309–015. |
| 3/10/1961 | Burkhart, James A. (Stephens College). Telegram to Martin Luther King, Jr.<br>3/10/1961. Columbia, Mo. (PHWSr) 1 p. MLKP-MBU. 610310–011. |
| 3/11/1961 | McDonald, Dora E. Telegram to Elinor B. Bratton. 3/11/1961. [Atlanta, Ga.]<br>(PHWc) 2 pp. MLKP-MBU. 610311–006. |
| 3/11/1961 | King, Martin Luther, Jr. "TV Interview with the Rev. Martin Luther King, Jr., Part<br>Two." Baltimore Afro-American, 11 March 1961, pp. 3–4 (PD) 2 pp. 610311–007. |
| 3/10/1961–<br>3/11/1961 | SCLC. Program, "Institute on nonviolence." 3/10/1961–3/11/1961. Lynchburg, Va.<br>(PD) 8 pp. SCLCR-GAMK: Box 35. 610311–009. |
| 3/11/1961 | Ebenezer Baptist Church. Press release, "'I am the bread of life,' Dr. King Sr.'s topic<br>at Ebenezer Sunday." 3/11/1961. Atlanta, Ga. (TD) 1 p. EBCR. 610311–010. |
| 3/11/1961 | "First Amendment Of No Avail," Norfolk Journal and Guide, 11 March 1961. (PD) 1 p.<br>(Enclosed in 610323–012 & 610314–008.) MLKP-MBU. 610311–011. |
| 3/12/1961 | King, Martin Luther, Jr. The Question of Progress in the Area of Race Relations,<br>Address delivered at Temple Emanuel. [3/12/1961]. Worcester, Mass. (At) 68.5<br>min. (2 sound cassettes: analog.) TEC-MWTE. 610312–001. |
| 3/12/1961 | King, Martin Luther, Jr. Question and Answer Period at Temple Emanuel.<br>[3/12/1961]. Worcester, Mass. (At) 31.2 min. (1 sound cassette: analog.) TEC-<br>MWTE. 610312–003. |
| 3/13/1961 | Kaplan, Kivie (Colonial Tanning Company, Inc.). Letter to Martin Luther King, Jr.<br>3/13/1961. Boston, Mass. (THLS) 1 p. MLKP-MBU. 610313–003. |
| 3/13/1961 | Halsey, James H. (University of Bridgeport). Letter to Martin Luther King, Jr.<br>3/13/1961. Bridgeport, Conn. (TLS) 1 p. MLKP-MBU. 610313–009. |
| 3/13/1961 | University of Bridgeport. Program, "Tenth annual Frank Jacoby lecture."<br>3/13/1961. (TD) 7 pp. MWL-CtBU. 610313–011. |
| 3/13/1961 | Associated Negro Press. Press release, "Martin Luther King calms uprising over<br>Atlanta agreement; Students claim they were 'sold down the river' in 'deal.'"<br>3/13/1961. Chicago, Ill. (PD) 2 pp. 610313–012. |
| 3/14/1961 | Braden, Anne (Southern Conference Educational Fund). Letter to Martin Luther<br>King, Jr. 3/14/1961. Louisville, Ky. (TALS) 3 pp. (Contains enclosure 610311–011.)<br>MLKP-MBU. 610314–008. |
| 3/14/1961 | Talmadge, Herman E. (Herman Eugene) (U.S. Congress. Senate). Letter to<br>Dow Kirkpatrick. 3/14/1961. Washington, D.C. (TLc) 2 pp. HETC-GU: Box 4.<br>610314–010. |
| 3/15/1961 | Clarke, Frank (Ajaye Clarke Associates). Letter to Martin Luther King, Jr.<br>3/15/1961. Berkeley, Calif. (TLS) 1 p. (Contains enclosure 610326–004.) MLKP-<br>MBU. 610315–001. |
| **3/16/1961** | **King, Martin Luther, Jr. (Ebenezer Baptist Church). Letter to John F. (John<br>Fitzgerald) Kennedy. 3/16/1961. Atlanta, Ga. (TLS) 1 p. JFKWHCSF-MBJFK:<br>Box 358. 610316–000.** |
| 3/16/1961 | King, Martin Luther, Jr. Letter to Anastacia Hetelekis. 3/16/1961. [Atlanta, Ga.]<br>(TLc) 2 pp. MLKP-MBU. 610316–004. |
| 3/16/1961 | Kilgore, Thomas (Friendship Baptist Church). Letter to Martin Luther King, Jr. and<br>Coretta Scott King. 3/16/1961. New York, N.Y. (TLS) 1 p. MLKP-MBU. 610316–006. |
| 3/16/1961 | Wood, James R. Letter to Dan P. Frazier. 3/16/1961. [Atlanta, Ga.] (TLc) 2 pp.<br>MLKP-MBU. 610316–007. |
| 3/16/1961 | Kennedy, John F. (John Fitzgerald). Letter to Martin Luther King, Jr. 3/16/1961.<br>[Washington, D.C.] (THLc) 1 p. JFKWHCSF-MBJFK: Reel 8. 610316–012. |
| 3/17/1961 | King, Martin Luther, Jr. Letter to Jack Z. Krigel. 3/17/1961. [Atlanta, Ga.] (TLc) 1<br>p. MLKP-MBU. 610317–006. |
| 3/18/1961 | King, Martin Luther, Jr. "Martin Luther King: He Hates No One." Baltimore Afro-<br>American, 18 March 1961, pp. 4, 8. (PD) 2 pp. 610318–000. |
| 3/18/1961 | [King, Martin Luther, Jr.] Letter to Sammy Davis, Jr. 3/18/1961. [Atlanta, Ga.] (HLd)<br>4 pp. MLKP-MBU. 610318–001. |
| 3/19/1961 | Ebenezer Baptist Church. Program, "Anniversary observance: Church and pas-<br>tors." 3/19/1961. Atlanta, Ga. (PD) 10 pp. EBCR. 610319–000. |
| 3/20/1961 | McDonald, Dora E. Letter to Julian Huxley. 3/20/1961. [Atlanta, Ga.] (TLc) 1 p.<br>MLKP-MBU. 610320–006. |

| | | |
|---|---|---|
| 3/20/1961 | King, Martin Luther, Jr. Letter to Ed Sullivan. 3/20/1961. [*Atlanta, Ga.*] (TLc) 1 p. MLKP-MBU. 610320–009. | Calendar |

3/20/1961     Wofford, Harris (U.S. White House). Memo to Kenneth P. O'Donnell. 3/20/1961. Washington, D.C. (THLS) 1 p. JFKWHCSF-MBJFK: Reel 1. 610320–013.

3/21/1961     Kennedy, John F. (John Fitzgerald) (U.S. White House). Telegram to Martin Luther King, Jr. 3/21/1961. Washington, D.C. (PWSr) 1 p. MLKP-MBU. 610321–002.

3/21/1961     King, Martin Luther, Jr. Letter to Adolph Held. 3/21/1961. [*Atlanta, Ga.*] (TLc) 2 pp. MLKP-MBU. 610321–003.

3/22/1961     King, Martin Luther, Jr. (Ebenezer Baptist Church). Letter to Jawaharlal Nehru. 3/22/1961. Atlanta, Ga. (THLc) 1 p. (Enclosed in 610322–008.) MLKP-MBU. 610322–000.

3/22/1961     Reeves, Frank D. Memo to Kenneth P. O'Donnell. 3/22/1961. Washington, D.C. (TLS) 1 p. JFKWHCSF-MBJFK: Reel 1. 610322–002.

3/22/1961     McDonald, Dora E. Letter to Benjamin D. Brown. 3/22/1961. [*Atlanta, Ga.*] (TLc) 1 p. (Contains enclosure 610322–000.) MLKP-MBU. 610322–008.

3/23/1961     King, Martin Luther, Jr. Telegram to organizations interested in desegregating Macys. 3/23/1961. [*Atlanta, Ga.*] (TWc) 1 p. MLKP-MBU. 610323–003.

3/23/1961     King, Martin Luther, Jr. Letter to Andy Razaf. 3/23/1961. [*Atlanta, Ga.*] (TLc) 2 pp. MLKP-MBU. 610323–007.

3/23/1961     Wofford, Harris. "New Frontiers in Civil Rights," Address at the annual conference of the National Civil Liberties Clearing House. 3/23/1961. [*Washington, D.C.*] (TD) 3 pp. JFKWHCSF-MBJFK: Box 14. 610323–014.

3/24/1961     King, Martin Luther, Jr. Letter to Eleanor Roosevelt. 3/24/1961. Atlanta, Ga. (THLs) 2 pp. ERC-NHyF. 610324–001.

3/24/1961     Young, Andrew (National Council of the Churches of Christ in the United States of America). Letter to Martin Luther King, Jr. 3/24/1961. New York, N.Y. (TLS) 2 pp. MLKP-MBU. 610324–004.

3/24/1961     Horton, Myles (Highlander Folk School). Letter to Martin Luther King, Jr. 3/24/1961. Monteagle, Tenn. (TLS) 1 p. MLKP-MBU. 610324–006.

3/24/1961     King, Martin Luther, Jr. Letter to Harry Belafonte. 3/24/1961. (TLc) 1 p. SCLCR-GAMK: Box 3. 610324–009.

3/25/1961     O'Donnell, Kenneth P. (U.S. White House). Letter to Martin Luther King, Jr. 3/25/1961. Washington, D.C. (THLS) 1 p. MLKP-MBU. 610325–003.

3/23/1962– <br> 3/26/1961     Itinerary for Martin Luther King, Jr. 3/23/1961–3/26/1961. (TD) 1 p. (Enclosed in 610315–001.) MLKP-MBU. 610326–004.

3/27/1961     King, Martin Luther, Jr. Letter to Arthur J. Goldberg. 3/27/1961. [*Atlanta, Ga.*] (THLc) 1 p. (Contains enclosure 610327–024.) MLKP-MBU. 610327–008.

3/27/1961     King, Martin Luther, Jr. Letter to Adam Clayton Powell. 3/27/1961. [*Atlanta, Ga.*] (TLc) 1 p. MLKP-MBU. 610327–009.

3/27/1961     King, Martin Luther, Jr. Letter to James T. Alexander. 3/27/1961. [*Atlanta, Ga.*] (TLc) 1 p. MLKP-MBU. 610327–012.

3/27/1961     Wood, James R. Letter to June Megill. 3/27/1961. [*Atlanta, Ga.*] (TLc) 1 p. MLKP-MBU. 610327–015.

3/27/1961     [*King, Martin Luther, Jr.*] Letter to Patricia Jenkins. 3/27/1961. [*Atlanta, Ga.*] (TLf) 1 p. MLKP-MBU. 610327–016.

3/27/1961     Braden, Anne (Southern Conference Educational Fund). Letter to Martin Luther King, Jr. 3/27/1961. Louisville, Ky. (TALS) 1 p. MLKP-MBU. 610327–018.

3/27/1961     Braden, Anne. Memo to James R. Wood and James A. (James Anderson) Dombrowski. 3/27/1961. (THLc) 3 pp. (Enclosed in 610327–022.) SCLCR-GAMK: Box 116. 610327–020.

3/27/1961     Braden, Anne (Southern Conference Educational Fund). Letter to James R. Wood. 3/27/1961. Louisville, Ky. (TALS) 2 pp. (Contains enclosures 610327–020 & 610327–023.) SCLCR-GAMK: Box 116. 610327–022.

3/27/1961     Braden, Anne (Southern Conference Educational Fund). Memo to Initiators of Carl Braden clemency petition. [*3/27/1961*]. (TALc) 1 p. (Enclosed in 610327–022.) SCLCR-GAMK: Box 116. 610327–023.

3/27/1961     [*Mangham, Marvin C.*] "Marvin C. Mangham, personal data sheet." [*3/27/1961*]. (TD) 2 pp. (Enclosed in 610327–008.) MLKP-MBU. 610327–024.

3/28/1961     Roosevelt, Eleanor. Letter to Martin Luther King, Jr. 3/28/1961. New York, N.Y. (THLS) 1 p. (Enclosed in 610331–007. Marginal comments by King.) MLKP-MBU. 610328–001.

3/29/1961     McDonald, Dora E. Letter to Ian Ballantine. 3/29/1961. [*Atlanta, Ga.*] (TLc) 2 pp. MLKP-MBU. 610329–002.

| | |
|---|---|
| 3/29/1961 | King, Martin Luther, Jr. Letter to Donald A. Metts. 3/29/1961. [*Atlanta, Ga.*] (TLc) 1 p. MLKP-MBU. 610329–003. |
| 3/29/1961 | François, Terry A. Letter to Martin Luther King, Jr. 3/29/1961. San Francisco, Calif. (TLS) 2 pp. MLKP-MBU. 610329–004. |
| 3/29/1961 | King, Martin Luther, Jr. Letter to Frank Hampton. 3/29/1961. [*Atlanta, Ga.*] (TLc) 1 p. MLKP-MBU. 610329–006. |
| 3/29/1961 | McDonald, Dora E. Letter to David Evanier. 3/29/1961. [*Atlanta, Ga.*] (TLc) 1 p. MLKP-MBU. 610329–007. |
| 3/30/1961 | Goodlett, Carlton B. (Carlton Benjamin) (Sun-Reporter Publishing Company). Letter to Martin Luther King, Jr. 3/30/1961. San Francisco, Calif. (TLS) 2 pp. MLKP-MBU. 610330–005. |
| 3/30/1961 | "Power of attorney." 3/30/1961. Atlanta, Ga. (TFmS) 1 p. CSKC. 610330–012. |
| 3/31/1961 | King, Martin Luther, Jr. Letter to Edward Stovall. 3/31/1961. [*Atlanta, Ga.*] (TLc) 1 p. MLKP-MBU. 610331–000. |
| 3/31/1961 | Carey, Gordon (CORE). Letter to Martin Luther King, Jr. 3/31/1961. New York, N.Y. (THLS) 1 p. MLKP-MBU. 610331–003. |
| 3/31/1961 | McDonald, Dora E. Letter to Stanley D. Levison. 3/31/1961. [*Atlanta, Ga.*] (TLc) 1 p. (Contains enclosure 610328–001.) MLKP-MBU. 610331–007. |
| 12/1960–3/31/1961 | Levison, Stanley D. Report, "Tribute to Martin Luther King, Jr." 12/1960–3/31/1961. (TD) 3 pp. MLKJP-GAMK: Box 28. 610331–011. |
| 4/1961 | Lindsay, Barbara. Letter to Martin Luther King, Jr. [*4/1961*]. San Jose, Calif. (TALc) 4 pp. MLKP-MBU. 610400–000. |
| 4/1961 | Fortier, Lillian. Press release, Martin Luther King, Jr. speaks in Oakland, Calif. [*4/1961*]. Berkeley, Calif. (THD) 4 pp. MLKP-MBU. 610400–003. |
| 4/1961 | King, Martin Luther, Jr., and Martin Luther King (Ebenezer Baptist Church). Letter to Pastor. [*4/1961*]. Atlanta, Ga. (TLS) 1 p. MLKP-MBU. 610400–004. |
| 4/1961 | Gaither, Thomas Walter (CORE). *Jailed-In.* New York: League of Industrial Democracy, April 1961. (PD) 16 pp. MLKJP-GAMK. 610400–007. |
| 4/1961 | King, Martin Luther, Jr. Draft, "After Desegregation—What." [*4/1961*]. [*Atlanta, Ga.*] (ADd) 11 pp. MCMLK-RWWL: 2.4.0.20. 610400–009. |
| 4/1961 | King, Martin Luther, Jr. Draft, "After Desegregation—What?" [*4/1961*]. [*Atlanta, Ga.*] (TAHDd) 6 pp. MLKP-MBU. 610400–010. |
| 4/1961 | King, Martin Luther, Jr. Draft, After Desegregation—What? [*4/1961*]. [*Atlanta, Ga.*] (THDd) 4 pp. MLKP-MBU. 610400–011. |
| 4/1961 | Powell, Mary L. Letter to Martin Luther King, Jr. [*4/1961*]. (ALSr) 3 pp. MLKP-MBU. 610400–012. |
| 4/1/1961 | Ebenezer Baptist Church. Press release, Theme for Easter Sunday services. 4/1/1961. Atlanta, Ga. (THD) 1 p. EBCR. 610401–000. |
| 4/4/1961 | King, Martin Luther, Jr. Letter to Frank Clarke. 4/4/1961. [*Atlanta, Ga.*] (TLc) 1 p. MLKP-MBU. 610404–003. |
| 4/4/1961 | Eerdmans, William B. (Wm. B. Eerdmans Publishing Co.). Letter to Martin Luther King, Jr. 4/4/1961. Grand Rapids, Mich. (THLS) 1 p. MLKP-MBU. 610404–005. |
| 4/4/1961 | King, Martin Luther, Jr. Letter to Edmund G. (Edmund Gerald) Brown. 4/4/1961. [*Atlanta, Ga.*] (TLc) 1 p. MLKP-MBU. 610404–013. |
| 4/4/1961 | Craig, Leon Sampson (Birmingham Baptist Mission Center). Letter to Martin Luther King, Jr. 4/4/1961. Birmingham, Ala. (TLS) 1 p. MLKP-MBU. 610404–017. |
| 4/4/1961 | King, Martin Luther, Jr. Letter to Dorothy Norman. 4/4/1961. [*Atlanta, Ga.*] (TLc) 1 p. MLKP-MBU. 610404–019. |
| 4/4/1961 | King, Martin Luther, Jr. Letter to Barbara Jacobson. 4/4/1961. [*Atlanta, Ga.*] (THLc) 1 p. MLKP-MBU. 610404–020. |
| 4/4/1961 | King, Martin Luther, Jr. Letter to Nat Ratner. 4/4/1961. [*Atlanta, Ga.*] (TLc) 1 p. MLKP-MBU. 610404–021. |
| 4/5/1961 | Thelma X (Tribe of Shabazz). Letter to Martin Luther King, Jr. 4/5/1961. Chicago, Ill. (THLc) 3 pp. MLKP-MBU. 610405–003. |
| 4/5/1961 | Wilkins, Roy (NAACP). Letter to Harris Wofford. 4/5/1961. New York, N.Y. (TLS) 3 pp. JFKWHSFHW-MBJFK: Box 11. 610405–008. |
| 4/4/1961–4/5/1961 | [*Kennedy, Robert F.*] (U.S. Dept. of Justice). Desk diary. 4/4/1961–4/5/1961. (AD) 2 pp. RFKAG–MBJFK: Desk Diary Series, Box 146. 610405–009. |
| 4/8/1961 | Ebenezer Baptist Church. Press release, "'The Meaning of Freedom,' Dr. King Jr.'s subject Sunday at Ebenezer." 4/8/1961. Atlanta, Ga. (TD) 1 p. EBCR. 610408–001. |
| 4/9/1961 | Seay, S. S. (Solomon Snowden). Letter to Stanley D. Levison. 4/9/1961. Montgomery, Ala. (THLS) 1 p. (Copy to King.) MLKP-MBU. 610409–000. |
| 4/11/1961 | King, Martin Luther, Jr. Letter to Fred L. Shuttlesworth. 4/11/1961. [*Atlanta, Ga.*] (TLc) 1 p. MLKP-MBU. 610411–002. |

4/11/1961    McDonald, Dora E. Letter to Homer Alexander Jack. 4/11/1961. [*Atlanta, Ga.*]
             (TLc) 1 p. MLKP-MBU. 610411–007.

4/11/1961    King, Martin Luther, Jr. Letter to Faculty, Students and Friends of Columbia
             University. 4/11/1961. [*Atlanta, Ga.*] (TLc) 1 p. (Enclosed in 610411–012.) MLKP-
             MBU. 610411–011.

4/11/1961    King, Martin Luther, Jr. Letter to Gordon R. Hitchens. 4/11/1961. [*Atlanta, Ga.*]
             (TLc) 1 p. (Contains enclosure 610411–011.) MLKP-MBU. 610411–012.

4/11/1961    Dickinson College Chapel. Program, Chapel service. 4/11/1961. Carlisle, Pa. (TD)
             2 pp. SCWSL-PCarlD. 610411–017.

4/11/1961    Herriford, John H. Letter to Martin Luther King, Jr. 4/11/1961. Minneapolis, Minn.
             (TLS) 1 p. MLKP-MBU. 610411–019.

4/12/1961    King, Martin Luther, Jr. Letter to Harry Van Arsdale. 4/12/1961. [*Atlanta, Ga.*]
             (TLc) 2 pp. MLKP-MBU. 610412–000.

4/12/1961    King, Martin Luther, Jr. Letter to S. S. (Solomon Snowden) Seay. 4/12/1961. [*Atlanta,
             Ga.*] (TLc) 1 p. MLKP-MBU. 610412–003.

4/12/1961    King, Martin Luther, Jr. Letter to Harry Emerson Fosdick. 4/12/1961. [*Atlanta, Ga.*]
             (TLc) 2 pp. MLKP-MBU. 610412–006.

4/12/1961    King, Martin Luther, Jr. Letter to Terry A. François. 4/12/1961. [*Atlanta, Ga.*] (TLc)
             2 pp. MLKP-MBU. 610412–007.

4/12/1961    King, Martin Luther, Jr. Letter to Editor of *San Francisco Chronicle.* 4/12/1961.
             [*Atlanta, Ga.*] (TLc) 1 p. MLKP-MBU. 610412–017.

4/13/1961    King, Martin Luther, Jr. Letter to Alton Wintz. 4/13/1961. [*Atlanta, Ga.*] (TLc) 1 p.
             MLKJP-GAMK: Box 6. 610413–015.

4/16/1961    Thompson Memorial Chapel (Williams College). Program, Sunday services.
             4/16/1961. Williamstown, Mass. (PHD) 2 pp. MCMLK-RWWL: 12.3.0.1080.
             610416–001.

4/16/1961    Helen Hills Hills Chapel (Smith College). Program, "Morning worship." 4/16/1961.
             (THD) 2 pp. MCMLK-RWWL: 12.3.0.895. 610416–002.

4/17/1961    Douglas, William O. (William Orville). Telegram to Martin Luther King, Jr.
             4/17/1961. Washington, D.C. (PWSr) 1 p. (610418–005 in margin.) MLKP-MBU.
             610417–010.

4/17/1961    Associated Negro Press. Press release, "King featured in *Look* and *Holiday
             Magazine.*" 4/17/1961. (TD) 1 p. 610417–012.

4/17/1961    King, Martin Luther, Jr. (SCLC). Form letter for SCLC annual board meeting.
             4/17/1961. Atlanta, Ga. (TLc) 1 p. (Contains enclosure 610417–015.) SCLCR-
             GAMK: Box 129. 610417–013.

4/17/1961    SCLC. Agenda, "Annual board meeting of the SCLC." [*4/17/1961*]. [*Atlanta, Ga.*]
             (TD) 1 p. (Enclosed in 610417–013.) SCLCR-GAMK: Box 129. 610417–015.

4/18/1961    Carey, Gordon R. (CORE). Letter to Dora E. McDonald. 4/18/1961. New York, N.Y.
             (THLS) 1 p. MLKP-MBU. 610418–001.

4/18/1961    King, Martin Luther, Jr. Telegram to William O. (William Orville) Douglas.
             4/18/1961. [*Atlanta, Ga.*] (THW) 1 p. (In margin of 610417–010.) MLKP-MBU.
             610418–005.

4/18/1961    Wood, James R. (SCLC). Press release, "Cornell University hosts Dr. King."
             4/18/1961. Atlanta, Ga. (TD) 1 p. MLKP-MBU. 610418–007.

4/19/1961    King, Martin Luther, Jr. Letter to David S. King. 4/19/1961. [*Atlanta, Ga.*] (TLc) 1
             p. MLKP-MBU. 610419–002.

4/19/1961    King, Martin Luther, Jr. "The Church on the Frontier of Racial Tension," Lecture
             delivered at Southern Baptist Theological Seminary. 4/19/1961. Louisville, Ky.
             (At) 47.2 min. (1 sound cassette: analog.) KyLoS. 610419–015.

4/19/1961    King, Martin Luther, Jr. Letter to William McPeak. 4/19/1961. [*Atlanta, Ga.*] (TLc)
             2 pp. MLKP-MBU. 610419–026.

4/19/1961    Tatum, Arlo (War Resisters' International). Letter to James R. Wood. 4/19/1961.
             Enfield, England. (TLS) 1 p. MLKP-MBU. 610419–029.

4/20/1961    [*Braden, Anne*]. Letter to James A. (James Anderson) Dombrowski. 4/20/1961.
             (TAL) 1 p. SCLCR-GAMK: Box 116. 610420–008.

4/21/1961    King, Martin Luther, Jr. Letter to Benjamin Blom. 4/21/1961. [*Atlanta, Ga.*] (TLc)
             2 pp. MLKP-MBU. 610421–005.

4/21/1961    King, Martin Luther, Jr. Letter to Martin Grossack. 4/21/1961. [*Atlanta, Ga.*] (TLc)
             2 pp. MLKP-MBU. 610421–008.

4/21/1961    Howington, Nolan (Southern Baptist Theological Seminary). Letter to Martin
             Luther King, Jr. 4/21/1961. Louisville, Ky. (TLS) 2 pp. MLKP-MBU. 610421–012.

4/21/1961    SCLC. Press release, "3,500 hear M.L. King, Jr." 4/21/1961. Atlanta, Ga. (TD) 1 p.
             SCLCR-GAMK. 610421–019.

| | | |
|---|---|---|
| 4/22/1961 | Petition for clemency for Carl Braden. 4/22/1961. [*Atlanta, Ga.*] (TDdS) 3 pp. ERP-NHyF. 610422–000. |
| 4/22/1961 | King, Martin Luther, Jr. Letter to Robert F. Kennedy. 4/22/1961. [*Atlanta, Ga.*] (TLc) 1 p. MLKP-MBU. 610422–001. |
| 4/22/1961 | King, Martin Luther, Jr. Letter to Paul H. (Paul Howard) Douglas. 4/22/1961. [*Atlanta, Ga.*] (TLc) 2 pp. MLKP-MBU. 610422–002. |
| 4/22/1961 | Reddick, Lawrence Dunbar (Coppin State Teachers College). "Africa, the Confederate Myth and the New Frontier." [*4/22/1961*]. (TDf) 11 pp. MLKP-MBU. 610422–004. |
| 4/24/1961 | King, Martin Luther, Jr. Letter to Morton Stavis. 4/24/1961. [*Atlanta, Ga.*] (TLc) 3 pp. MLKP-MBU. 610424–004. |
| 4/24/1961 | CORE. "Freedom Ride Itinerary." 4/24/1961. New York, N.Y. (TD) 1 p. (Enclosed in 610426–022.) JFKWHCSF-MBJFK: Reel 7. 610424–015. |
| 4/25/1961 | King, Martin Luther, Jr. (Ebenezer Baptist Church). Letter to Myles Horton. 4/25/1961. Atlanta, Ga. (THLS) 1 p. HRECR-WHi: Box 13. 610425–000. |
| 4/25/1961 | King, Martin Luther, Jr. Letter to Stanley D. Levison. 4/25/1961. [*Atlanta, Ga.*] (TLc) 2 pp. MLKP-MBU. 610425–001. |
| 4/25/1961 | McDonald, Dora E. (Ebenezer Baptist Church). Letter to Carlton B. (Carlton Benjamin) Goodlett. 4/25/1961. Atlanta, Ga. (TLS) 1 p. (Contains enclosure 610412–017.) CBGP-WHi. 610425–013. |
| 4/26/1961 | King, Martin Luther, Jr. Letter to Ross W. Anderson. 4/26/1961. [*Atlanta, Ga.*] (TLc) 2 pp. MLKP-MBU. 610426–000. |
| 4/26/1961 | King, Martin Luther, Jr. Letter to Chester Bowles. 4/26/1961. [*Atlanta, Ga.*] (TLc) 1 p. MLKP-MBU. 610426–003. |
| 4/26/1961 | King, Martin Luther, Jr. Letter to Lonnie King. 4/26/1961. [*Atlanta, Ga.*] (TLc) 1 p. MLKP-MBU. 610426–004. |
| 4/26/1961 | King, Martin Luther, Jr. Letter to Nathan Paul Feinsinger. 4/26/1961. [*Atlanta, Ga.*] (TLc) 1 p. MLKP-MBU. 610426–005. |
| 4/26/1961 | McDonald, Dora E. Letter to Gordon Carey. 4/26/1961. [*Atlanta, Ga.*] (TLc) 1 p. MLKP-MBU. 610426–006. |
| 4/26/1961 | Farmer, James (CORE). Letter to John F. (John Fitzgerald) Kennedy. 4/26/1961. New York, N.Y. (THLS) 1 p. (Contains enclosure 610424–015 & 610426–023.) JFKWHCSF-MBJFK: Reel 7. 610426–022. |
| 4/26/1961 | CORE. "Freedom Ride, 1961 Participants." 4/26/1961. New York, N.Y. (TD) 1 p. (Enclosed in 610426–022.) JFKWHCSF-MBJFK: Reel 7. 610426–023. |
| 4/27/1961 | King, Martin Luther, Jr. Address at the twenty-fifth anniversary dinner of the International Union, United Automobile, Aerospace and Agricultural Implement Workers of America. 4/27/1961. Detroit, Mich. (TTa) 9 pp. MLKP-MBU. 610427–001. |
| 4/27/1961 | McDonald, Dora E. Letter to James Skardon. 4/27/1961. [*Atlanta, Ga.*] (TLc) 1 p. (Contains enclosure 610427–022, pp. 210–214 in this volume.) MLKP-MBU. 610427–014. |
| 4/27/1961 | King, Martin Luther, Jr. Telegram to Horatius H. Coleman. [*4/27/1961*]. [*Atlanta, Ga.*] (TWc) 1 p. MLKP-MBU. 610427–015. |
| 4/27/1961 | Kheel, Theodore Woodrow. Letter to William Hammatt Davis. 4/27/1961. New York, N.Y. (TLS) 2 pp. WHDP-WHi: Box 33. 610427–021. |
| 4/28/1961 | King, Martin Luther, Jr. and Wyatt Tee Walker (SCLC). Telegram to Robert F. Kennedy. 4/28/1961. [*Atlanta, Ga.*] (PHWc) 1 p. MLKP-MBU. 610428–000. |
| 4/28/1961 | McDonald, Dora E. Letter to Frank D. Reeves. 4/28/1961. Atlanta, Ga. (TLS) 2 pp. JFKWHCSF-MBJFK: Box 90. 610428–001. |
| 4/28/1961 | King, Martin Luther, Jr. (SCLC). Statement in support of union organization of voluntary hospital workers under joint sponsorship of Local 1199 and District 65. 4/28/1961. [*Atlanta, Ga.*] (TD) 1 p. (Enclosed in 610428–007.) KLMDA-NNCorI. 610428–003. |
| 4/28/1961 | King, Martin Luther, Jr. Letter to Leon J. Davis. 4/28/1961. Atlanta, Ga. (TLS) 1 p. (Contains enclosure 610428–003.) KLMDA-NNCorI: 5206-s, Box 30. 610428–007. |
| 4/28/1961 | Baptist Press. Press release, "King's seminary talk draws Alabama critic." 4/28/1961. Nashville, Tenn. (TD) 2 pp. MLKP-MBU. 610428–011. |
| 4/28/1961 | Hahn, Maxwell (Marshall Field Foundation). Letter to Martin Luther King, Jr. 4/28/1961. New York, N.Y. (TLS) 1 p. (Contains enclosure 610428–014.) MLKP-MBU. 610428–013. |
| 4/28/1961 | Hahn, Maxwell (Marshall Field Foundation). Letter to Charles Miles Jones. 4/28/1961. New York, N.Y. (TLS) 1 p. (Enclosed in 610428–013 & 610428–020. Copy to King.) MLKP-MBU. 610428–014. |

| | | |
|---|---|---|
| 4/28/1961 | Thomas, Norman. Letter to Martin Luther King, Jr. 4/28/1961. New York, N.Y. (THLS) 1 p. (Contains enclosure 610428–018.) MLKP-MBU. 610428–017. | Calendar |

4/28/1961     Thomas, Norman. "Statement to President Kennedy." [*4/28/1961*]. (TD) 4 pp. (Enclosed in 610428–017.) MLKP-MBU. 610428–018.

4/28/1961     Hahn, Maxwell (Marshall Field Foundation). Letter to James R. Wood. 4/28/1961. New York, N.Y. (TLS) 1 p. (Contains enclosure 610428–014.) SCLCR-GAMK: Box 136. 610428–020.

4/29/1961     SCLC. Telegram to SNCC. 4/29/1961. Atlanta, Ga. (PHWc) 1 p. MLKJP-GAMK: Box 23. 610429–004.

4/29/1961     Ebenezer Baptist Church. Press release, "'Who did sin,' Dr. King Sr.'s sermon topic at Ebenezer Sunday." 4/29/1961. (THD) 1 p. EBCR. 610429–005.

11/1/1960–     Walker, Wyatt Tee (SCLC). "Report of the director: Semi-annual report."
4/30/1961     [*11/1/1960–4/30/1961*]. Atlanta, Ga. (TD) 8 pp. (Contains enclosure 610000–081.) MLKJP-GAMK: Box 36. 610430–001.

11/1/1960–     [*Abernathy, Ralph*] (SCLC). Report of the treasurer. 11/1/1960–4/30/1961. Atlanta,
4/30/1961     Ga. (TD) 1 p. MLKJP-GAMK: Box 28. 610430–002.

**4/30/1961**     **Photo of Martin Luther King, Jr., James A. (James Anderson) Dombrowski, Carl Braden, Anne Braden, Frank Wilkinson, and Coretta Scott King. [*4/30/1961*]. Atlanta, Ga. (Ph) 1 p. CAABP-WHi. 610430–003.**

4/1/1961–     SCLC. "Monthly budget control sheet." 4/1/1961–4/30/1961. Atlanta, Ga. (TD) 1
4/30/1961     p. MLKP-MBU. 610430–004.

5/1961     SCLC. *Newsletter* 1, no. 1. 5/1961. Atlanta, Ga. (PD) 4 pp. SCLCR-GAMK: Box 122. 610500–008.

5/1961     Braden, Anne. Form letter to Friend. 5/1961. Louisville, Ky. (TLc) 2 pp. MLKP-MBU. 610500–010.

5/1961     Reid, Milton, A. (Virginia Christian Leadership Conference). "President's report." [*5/1961*]. (TD) 3 pp. MLKJP-GAMK: Box 35. 610500–013.

4/1961–5/1961     SNCC. *The Student Voice* 2, nos. 4 and 5. 4/1961–5/1961. Atlanta, Ga. (PD) 4 pp. SNCCP-GAMK: Reel 73. 610500–047.

5/1961     Telephone message to Martin Luther King, Jr. [*5/1961*]. [*Atlanta, Ga.*] (TL) 1 p. MLKP-MBU. 610500–048.

5/1/1961     King, Martin Luther, Jr., and Wyatt Tee Walker (SCLC). Form letter to T. H. Alexander. 5/1/1961. [*Atlanta, Ga.*] (TLc) 1 p. SCLCR-GAMK: Box 52. 610501–016.

5/2/1961     King, Martin Luther, Jr. Letter to Spottswood Robinson. 5/2/1961. [*Atlanta, Ga.*] (TLc) 1 p. MLKP-MBU. 610502–009.

5/2/1961     King, Martin Luther, Jr. Letter of recommendation for Janet Bond. 5/2/1961. [*Atlanta, Ga.*] (TLc) 1 p. MLKP-MBU. 610502–016.

5/2/1961     McDonald, Dora E. Letter to Helen L. Sobell. 5/2/1961. [*Atlanta, Ga.*] (TLc) 1 p. (Contains enclosure 610504–003, pp. 216–217 in this volume.) MLKP-MBU. 610502–011.

5/3/1961     Douglas, Paul H. (Paul Howard) (U.S. Congress. Senate). Letter to Martin Luther King, Jr. 5/3/1961. Washington, D.C. (TALS) 1 p. MLKP-MBU. 610503–000.

5/3/1961     King, Martin Luther, Jr., and Wyatt Tee Walker (SCLC). Letter to Stephen R. Currier. 5/3/1961. [*Atlanta, Ga.*] (TLc) 1 p. MLKP-MBU. 610503–007.

5/3/1961     King, Martin Luther, Jr. Letter to Spottswood Robinson. 5/3/1961. [*Atlanta, Ga.*] (TLc) 1 p. MLKP-MBU. 610503–012.

5/4/1961     King, Martin Luther, Jr. Letter to Lawrence Dunbar Reddick. 5/4/1961. [*Atlanta, Ga.*] (TLc) 1 p. (Enclosed in 610509–000, pp. 221–223 in this volume.) MLKP-MBU. 610504–005.

5/5/1961     Program, "All citizens voter registration drive luncheon meeting." 5/5/1961. (TD) 3 pp. MLKJP-GAMK: Box 35. 610505–009.

5/5/1961     Reeves, Frank D. (U.S. White House). Memo to John F. (John Fitzgerald) Kennedy. 5/5/1961. Washington, D.C. (THLS) 2 pp. JFKWHCSF-MBJFK: Box 358. 610505–010.

5/6/1961     Thompson, Elsa K. (KPFA (FM)). Letter to Martin Luther King, Jr. 5/6/1961. Berkeley, Calif. (THLS) 1 p. MLKP-MBU. 610506–000.

5/6/1961     Ebenezer Baptist Church. Press release, "'The other prodigal son,' Dr. King Jr.'s topic Sunday." 5/6/1961. Atlanta, Ga. (TD) 1 p. EBCR. 610506–001.

5/8/1961     Roosevelt, Eleanor, and William O. (William Orville) Douglas (Committee for Walter Reuther 25th Anniversary of Democratic Trade Unionism). Letter to Martin Luther King, Jr. 5/8/1961. (TLS) 2 pp. MLKP-MBU. 610508–009.

5/8/1961     Burkhart, James A. (Stephens College). Letter to Martin Luther King, Jr. 5/8/1961. Columbia, Mo. (TLS) 1 p. MLKP-MBU. 610508–013.

| | | |
|---|---|---|
| 5/8/1961 | | Lawyers Advisory Committee. Press release, "Lawyers committee formed to assist defense in Alabama libel actions." 5/8/1961. New York, N.Y. (PD) 3 pp. WHDP-WHi: Box 33. 610508–016. |
| 5/8/1961 | | "Background, The Alabama Libel Suits." 5/8/1961. (TD) 5 pp. WHDP-WHi: Box 33. 610508–017. |
| 5/9/1961 | | King, Martin Luther, Jr. Letter to Avraham Soltes. 5/9/1961. [*Atlanta, Ga.*] (TLc) 1 p. MLKP-MBU. 610509–005. |
| 5/9/1961 | | King, Martin Luther, Jr. Letter to Jerry M. Chance. 5/9/1961. [*Atlanta, Ga.*] (TLc) 2 pp. MLKP-MBU. 610509–007. |
| 5/9/1961 | | King, Martin Luther, Jr. Letter to Jerome Mettetal. 5/9/1961. [*Atlanta, Ga.*] (TLc) 1 p. MLKP-MBU. 610509–008. |
| 5/10/1961 | | High, Robert King (Miami. Office of the Mayor). Letter to Martin Luther King, Jr. 5/10/1961. Miami, Fla. (TLS) 1 p. MLKP-MBU. 610510–009. |
| 5/10/1961 | | Blanton, Sankey L. (Crozer Theological Seminary). Letter to Martin Luther King, Jr. and Coretta Scott King. 5/10/1961. Chester, Pa. (TLS) 2 pp. MLKP-MBU. 610510–010. |
| 5/10/1961 | | Braden, Anne. Letter to Carl Braden. 5/10/1961. (TALS) 2 pp. CAABP-WHi: Box 11. 610510–012. |
| 5/12/1961 | | SCLC. Press release, "King and SCLC meet in Montgomery." [*5/12/1961*]. Montgomery, Ala. (TD) 2 pp. MLKJP-GAMK: Box 1. 610512–000. |
| 5/12/1961 | | Skardon, James A. (*Coronet*). Letter to Martin Luther King, Jr. 5/12/1961. New York, N.Y. (TLS) 2 pp. MLKP-MBU. 610512–003. |
| 5/13/1961 | | Ebenezer Baptist Church. Press release, "'Crisis in the Modern Family,' Dr. King Jr.'s topic at Ebenezer." 5/13/1961. Atlanta, Ga. (TD) 1 p. EBCR. 610513–002. |
| 5/13/1961 | | Wells, I.J.K. (Alabama State Teachers College). Letter to Martin Luther King, Jr. 5/13/1961. Montgomery, Ala. (TLS) 1 p. MLKP-MBU. 610513–003. |
| 5/15/1961 | | King, Martin Luther, Jr. Letter to Ewald Bash. 5/15/1961. [*Atlanta, Ga.*] (TLc) 2 pp. MLKP-MBU. 610515–008. |
| 5/15/1961 | | King, Martin Luther, Jr. Letter to Richard M. Millard. 5/15/1961. [*Atlanta, Ga.*] (TLc) 1 p. (Enclosed in 610515–012.) MLKP-MBU. 610515–011. |
| 5/15/1961 | | McDonald, Dora E. Letter to Herschelle Sullivan. 5/15/1961. [*Atlanta, Ga.*] (TLc) 1 p. (Contains enclosure 610515–011.) MLKP-MBU. 610515–012. |
| 5/15/1961 | | SCLC. Press release, "Freedom riders attacked in Alabama." 5/15/1961. Atlanta, Ga. (TD) 1 p. SCLCR-GAMK: Box 129. 610515–019. |
| 5/15/1961 | | Transcript, Phone conversation between Robert F. Kennedy and George E. Cruit. 5/15/1961. (THD) 2 pp. RFKAG-MBJFK: Box 10. 610515–023. |
| 5/15/1961 | | Malone, W.D. Letter to Duke McCall. 5/15/1961. (TLS) 1 pp. MLKP-MBU. 610515–025. |
| 5/15/1961 | | Hughes, Genevieve (CORE). Press release, "Freedom Ride Report." 5/15/1961. Anniston, Ala. (TD) 2 pp. COREP-A-GAMK: Reel 25. 610515–026. |
| 5/16/1961 | | King, Martin Luther, Jr. Letter to Abraham Ribicoff. 5/16/1961. [*Atlanta, Ga.*] (THLc) 2 pp. MLKP-MBU. 610516–007. |
| 5/16/1961 | | CORE. "Statement by CORE National Director, James Farmer." 5/16/1961. New York, N.Y. (TD) 1 p. MLKJP-GAMK. 610516–011. |
| 5/17/1961 | | King, Martin Luther, Jr. Letter to Walter Reuther. 5/17/1961. [*Atlanta, Ga.*] (TLc) 1 p. (Enclosed in 610517–016.) MLKP-MBU. 610517–011. |
| 5/17/1961 | | McDonald, Dora E. Letter to Stanley D. Levison. 5/17/1961. [*Atlanta, Ga.*] (TLc) 1 p. MLKP-MBU. 610517–015. |
| 5/17/1961 | | McDonald, Dora E. Letter to William O. (William Orville) Douglas. 5/17/1961. [*Atlanta, Ga.*] (TLc) 1 p. (Contains enclosure 610517–011.) MLKP-MBU. 610517–016. |
| 5/17/1961 | | King, Martin Luther, Jr. Letter to Shirley Cummings. 5/17/1961. [*Atlanta, Ga.*] (TLc) 1 p. MLKP-MBU. 610517–022. |
| 5/17/1961 | | King, Martin Luther, Jr. Letter to Addine D. Drew. 5/17/1961. [*Atlanta, Ga.*] (TLc) 2 pp. MLKP-MBU. 610517–024. |
| 5/17/1961 | | King, Martin Luther, Jr., and Wyatt Tee Walker (SCLC). Letter to Eleanor Roosevelt. 5/17/1961. [*Atlanta, Ga.*] (TLc) 1 p. SCLCR-GAMK: Box 5. 610517–025. |
| 5/18/1961 | | Kennedy, Robert F. (U.S. Dept. of Justice). Letter to Martin Luther King, Jr. 5/18/1961. Washington, D.C. (TALS) 1 p. MLKP-MBU. 610518–000. |
| 5/18/1961 | | Wood, James R. (SCLC). Press release, "Dr. King calls for a stepped up assault on foes of integration." 5/18/1961. Atlanta, Ga. (TD) 1 p. SCLCR-GAMK. 610518–019. |
| 5/18/1961 | | Braden, Carl. Letter to Anne Braden. 5/18/1961. Greenville, S.C. (ALS) 2 pp. CAABP-WHi: Box 11. 610518–020. |

5/19/1961     King, Martin Luther, Jr. Agreement and contract with Southeastern Recording Company of America, Inc. 5/19/1961. Atlanta, Ga. (TFmS) 5 pp. MCMLK-RWWL: 11.0.0.30. 610519–005.

5/19/1961     King, Martin Luther, Jr. Letter to Edward E. Hart. 5/19/1961. [*Atlanta, Ga.*] (TLc) 1 p. MLKP-MBU. 610519–006.

5/19/1961     King, Martin Luther, Jr. (SCLC). Letter to John Collins. 5/19/1961. [*Atlanta, Ga.*] (THLc) 1 p. MLKP-MBU. 610519–014.

5/20/1961     Ebenezer Baptist Church. Press release, "'A misplaced emphasis,' Dr. King Sr.'s subject Sunday." 5/20/1961. Atlanta, Ga. (TD) 1 p. EBCR. 610520–002.

5/20/1961     [*Kennedy, Robert F.*] Summary of telephone conversation with John Malcolm Patterson. 5/20/1961. (TD) 2 pp. RFKAG-MBJFK: Box 10. 610520–006.

5/20/1961     Memo to Byron R. White. [*5/20/1961*]. (TL) 4 pp. RFKAG-MBJFK: Box 10. 610520–007.

5/21/1961     King, Martin Luther, Jr. Announcement of martial law in Montgomery. 5/21/1961. Montgomery, Ala. (TTa) 1 p. MLKJP-GAMK. 610521–002.

5/21/1961     MIA. Program, "Salutes the 'freedom riders.'" [*5/21/1961*]. Montgomery, Ala. (TD) 1 p. MCMLK-RWWL: 7.0.0.370. 610521–009.

5/21/1961     Patterson, John Malcolm (Alabama. Office of the Governor). Telegram to John F. (John Fitzgerald) Kennedy. 5/21/1961. (PHWSr) 4 pp. (Enclosed in 610522–024.) JFKWHCSF-MBJFK: Box 365. 610521–013.

5/21/1961     Braden, Anne. Letter to Carl Braden. 5/21/1961. Louisville, Ky. (TD) 2 pp. CAABP-WHi: Box 11. 610521–023.

5/22/1961     McDonald, Dora E. Letter to Frank Clarke. 5/22/1961. [*Atlanta, Ga.*] (TLc) 1 p. MLKP-MBU. 610522–011.

5/22/1961     King, Martin Luther, Jr. Statement on violence in Alabama. [*5/22/1961*]. (At) .8 min. (1 sound cassette: analog.) GRVVL-MiEM. 610522–022.

5/22/1961     Dutton, Fred. Memo to Robert F. Kennedy. 5/22/1961. (THLc) 1 p. (Contains enclosure 610521–013.) JFKWHCSF-MBJFK: Box 365. 610522–024.

5/22/1961     King, Martin Luther, Jr. Statement on future of freedom rides. [*5/22/1961*]. [*Montgomery, Ala.*] (At) .5 min. (1 sound cassette: analog.) GRRVL-MiEM: TN 651578. 610522–038.

5/22/1961     King, Martin Luther, Jr. Statement on need for federal intervention in Alabama. [*5/22/1961*]. [*Montgomery, Ala.*] (At) .9 min. (1 sound cassette: analog.) GRRVL-MiEM: TN 651232. 610522–039.

**5/21/1961– 5/22/1961**     **Schutzer, Paul George. Photo of Martin Luther King, Jr. and Ralph Abernathy waiting out a violent mob outside of First Baptist Church. [*5/21/1961–5/22/1961*]. Montgomery, Ala. (Ph) 1 p. GI-NNTI. 610522–041.**

5/23/1961     Randolph, A. Philip (Asa Philip) (Negro American Labor Council). Telegram to Martin Luther King, Jr. 5/23/1961. (TWc) 1 p. RPP-NN-Sc: Box 2. 610523–005.

5/23/1961     King, Martin Luther, Jr. Press conference during Freedom Rides. [*5/23/1961*]. [*Montgomery, Ala.*] (F) 1.8 min. (1 videocassette.) CLU-FT: Telenews volume 14. 610523–019.

5/23/1961     King, Edward B. (SNCC). Telegram to John F. (John Fitzgerald) Kennedy. 5/23/1961. Atlanta, Ga. (PWc) 6 pp. SNCCP-GAMK: Reel 4. 610523–023.

5/23/1961     Transcript, Phone conversation between Robert F. Kennedy and Ross R. Barnett. 5/23/1961. (TD) 2 pp. RFKAG-MBJFK: Box 10. 610523–027.

**5/23/1961**     **Davidson, Bruce (Magnum Photos). Photo of Martin Luther King, Jr., James Farmer, Wyatt Tee Walker, John Lewis, and Ralph Abernathy. 5/23/1961. Montgomery, Ala. (Ph) 1 p. NNMAGPC. 610523–028.**

**5/23/1961**     **Lockwood, Lee. Photo of Martin Luther King, Jr., Len Holt, David Dennis, Edward B. King, B. Elton Cox, Bernard LaFayette, Matthew Walker, Dion Diamond, Ernest Patton, and Henry Thomas. [*5/23/1961*]. Montgomery, Ala. (Ph) 1 p. GI-NNTI. 610523–031.**

5/24/1961     U.S. District Court (Georgia. Northern District. Atlanta Division). "Subpoena Ticket-Duces Tecum." [*5/24/1961*]. (TFmS) 2 pp. MLKP-MBU. 610524–001.

5/24/1961     King, Martin Luther, Jr. Statement on segregation. 5/24/1961. [*Montgomery, Ala.*] (TTa) 1 p. MLKJP-GAMK. 610524–002.

5/24/1961     Wood, James R. (SCLC). Press release, Freedom Ride Coordinating Committee formed. 5/24/1961. Atlanta, Ga. (TD) 2 pp. NAACPP-DLC: Group IIIA-289, A175. 610524–005.

5/24/1961     U.S. Dept. of Justice. Statement, Robert F. Kennedy on protection for freedom riders. 5/24/1961. Washington, D.C. (TD) 1 p. RFKAG-MBJFK: Box 10. 610524–026.

5/24/1961     King, Martin Luther, Jr. "Martin Luther King Liked Articles on His Work." *Los Angeles Mirror*, 24 May 1961. (PD) 1 p. 610524–033.

627

5/24/1961 Braden, Carl. Letter to Anne Braden. 5/24/1961. [*Greenville, S.C.*] (ALS) 2 pp. CAABP-WHi: Box 11. 610524–034.

5/25/1961 Poitier, Sidney, and Juanita Poitier. Telegram to Martin Luther King, Jr. and Freedom Riders. 5/25/1961. Mt. Vernon, N.Y. (PHWSr) 1 p. MLKP-MBU. 610525–005.

5/25/1961 McKinney, Harold C. (Detroit Council of Churches). Letter to Martin Luther King, Jr. 5/25/1961. Detroit, Mich. (THLS) 1 p. (Contains enclosures 610525–008, 610525–009, & 610525–010.) MLKP-MBU. 610525–007.

5/25/1961 McKinney, Harold C. (Michigan Council of Churches). Letter to John F. (John Fitzgerald) Kennedy. 5/25/1961. Lansing, Mich. (TLc) 1 p. (Enclosed in 610525–007.) MLKP-MBU. 610525–008.

5/25/1961 McKinney, Harold C. (Michigan Council of Churches). Letter to Robert F. Kennedy. 5/25/1961. Lansing, Mich. (TLc) 1 p. (Enclosed in 610525–007.) MLKP-MBU. 610525–009.

5/25/1961 McKinney, Harold C. (Michigan Council of Churches). Letter to John Malcolm Patterson. 5/25/1961. Lansing, Mich. (TLc) 1 p. (Enclosed in 610525–007.) MLKP-MBU. 610525–010.

5/25/1961 Kennedy, Robert F. (U.S. Dept. of Justice). Press release, "Statement by Attorney General Robert F. Kennedy." 5/25/1961. Washington, D.C. (TD) 1 p. RFKAG-MBJFK: Box 10. 610525–017.

5/15/1961– U.S. Dept. of Justice. Phone Log for Robert F. Kennedy. 5/15/1961–5/25/1961. (TD)
5/25/1961 4 pp. RFKAG-MBJFK: Box 10. 610525–019.

5/26/1961 Pacific School of Religion. Program, "Ninety-fourth annual commencement." 5/26/1961. Berkeley, Calif. (PHD) 4 pp. CBPaC. 610526–003.

5/26/1961 Wood, James R. (SCLC). Report on meeting of the Freedom Ride Coordinating Committee. 5/26/1961. Atlanta, Ga. (TDS) 4 pp. MLKP-MBU. 610526–009.

5/27/1961 Diwakar, Ranganath Ramachandra (Loka Shikshana Trust). Letter to Martin Luther King, Jr. 5/27/1961. Hubli, India. (TLS) 1 p. (Contains enclosure 610527–003.) MLKP-MBU. 610527–002.

5/27/1961 Diwakar, Ranganath Ramachandra (*Kasturi*). Letter to Harper & Brothers. 5/27/1961. Hubli, India. (THLc) 1 p. (Enclosed in 610527–002.) MLKP-MBU. 610527–003.

5/28/1961 Braden, Anne. Letter to Carl Braden. 5/28/1961. Louisville, Ky. (TALS) 2 pp. CAABP-WHi: Box 11. 610528–004.

5/29/1961 King, Martin Luther, Jr. Letter to John R. Yungblut. 5/29/1961. [*Atlanta, Ga.*] (TLc) 1 p. MLKP-MBU. 610529–002.

5/29/1961 King, Martin Luther, Jr. Letter to S.I. (Samuel Ichiye) Hayakawa. 5/29/1961. [*Atlanta, Ga.*] (TLc) 1 p. MLKP-MBU. 610529–016.

5/29/1961 King, Martin Luther, Jr. Letter to Kyle Haselden. 5/29/1961. [*Atlanta, Ga.*] (TLc) 1 p. MLKP-MBU. 610529–017.

5/29/1961 Kennedy, Robert F. (U.S. Dept. of Justice). "Petition for rule making." 5/29/1961. Washington, D.C. (TD) 7 pp. (Enclosed in 610606–020.) MLKJP-GAMK: Box 27. 610529–019.

5/30/1961 Blangsted, Eleanor. Letter to Martin Luther King, Jr. 5/30/1961. Tujunga, Calif. (ALS) 3 pp. MLKP-MBU. 610530–000.

5/30/1961 King, Martin Luther, Jr. Form letter to Friend. 5/30/1961. Montgomery, Ala. (THLS) 2 pp. NAACPP-DLC: Group III-A213. 610530–001.

5/30/1961 King, Martin Luther, Jr. Statement on Montgomery lawsuits. 5/30/1961. Montgomery, Ala. (THTa) 1 p. MLKJP-GAMK. 610530–004.

5/31/1961 Dhadda, Siddharaj (Akhil Bharat Sarva Seva Sangh). Letter to Martin Luther King, Jr. 5/31/1961. Rajghat, Kashi, India. (TLS) 1 p. MLKP-MBU. 610531–001.

5/31/1961 King, Martin Luther, Jr., Statement on Freedom Rides. 5/31/1961. Atlanta, Ga. (TTa) 1 p. MLKJP-GAMK. 610531–002.

5/31/1961 King, Martin Luther, Jr., and Ralph Abernathy. Press conference on Freedom Rides. [*5/31/1961*]. Montgomery, Ala. (F) 1.8 min. (1 videocassette.) CLU-FT: telenewsreel, Volume 14. 610531–021.

6/1961 King, Martin Luther, Jr. (Ebenezer Baptist Church). "The Man Who Was a Fool," *Pulpit* 32 (June 1961): 4–6. (PD) 3 pp. MCMLK-RWWL: 2.2.0.1130. 610600–000.

6/1961 Odom, Lawrence S. (Lawrence Sylvester) (Western Christian Leadership Conference). Form letter to Friend. [*6/1961*]. Los Angeles, Calif. (THLS) 2 pp. (Marginal comments by King.) MLKJP-GAMK: Box 123A. 610600–008.

6/1961 Report, "A United States Information Agency report summary world-wide reactions to racial incidents in Alabama." [*6/1961*]. (TD) 9 pp. (Enclosed in 610621–014.) USIA-MBJFK: Reel 6. 610600–019.

| | |
|---|---|
| 6/1/1961 | Brown, Ernestine (Lockheed Aircraft Corporation). Letter to Martin Luther King, Jr. 6/1/1961. Marietta, Ga. (TLS) 2 pp. MLKP-MBU. 610601–003. Calendar |
| 6/1/1961 | Raskin, Marvel (Michigan Friends of the South). Letter to Edward B. King. 6/1/1961. Huntington Woods, Mich. (TLS) 1 p. SNCCP-GAMK: Reel 14. 610601–010. |
| 6/2/1961 | Ku Klux Klan, et al., Defendants. "Summons," *United States v. Ku Klux Klan.* 6/2/1961. (TD) 1 p. MLKP-MBU. 610602–001. |
| 6/2/1961 | Ku Klux Klan, et al., Defendants. "Temporary restraining order," *United States v. Ku Klux Klan.* 6/2/1961. (TD) 2 pp. MLKP-MBU. 610602–002. |
| 6/2/1961 | Ku Klux Klan, et al., Defendants. "Order," *United States v. Ku Klux Klan.* 6/2/1961. (TD) 15 pp. MLKP-MBU. 610602–003. |
| 6/2/1961 | Lawrence, George (SCLC). Press release, "Dr. Martin Luther King, Jr., other southern leaders set to speak at series of New York protest meetings." 6/2/1961. Brooklyn, N.Y. (THD) 4 pp. MCMLK-RWWL: 6.5.0.1360. 610602–008. |
| 6/3/1961 | SCLC. Press release, "Integration organization answers restraining order." 6/3/1961. Atlanta, Ga. (TD) 1 p. SCLCR-GAMK: Box 120. 610603–004. |
| 6/4/1961 | University of Bridgeport. Program, Fortieth commencement. 6/4/1961. Bridgeport, Conn. (PHD) 6 pp. MLKP-MBU. 610604–000. |
| 6/4/1961 | King, Martin Luther, Jr. Letter to Harold Edward Fey. 6/4/1961. [*Atlanta, Ga.*] (TWd) 1 p. MLKP-MBU. 610604–013. |
| 6/5/1961 | King, Martin Luther, Jr. Letter to Grenville Clark. 6/5/1961. Atlanta, Ga. (TLS) 1 p. GCC-NhD. 610605–004. |
| 6/5/1961 | *The Crusader* 2, no. 31 (5 June 1961). Monroe, N.C. (THD) 8 pp. SCLCR-GAMK: Box 155. 610605–019. |
| 6/5/1961 | King, Martin Luther, Jr. Press conference at the Sheraton-Atlantic Hotel. [*6/5/1961*]. (F) 1.1 min. CBSNA-NNCBS. 610605–021. |
| 6/6/1961 | King, Martin Luther, Jr. Letter to Marie F. (Marie Freid) Rodell. 6/6/1961. [*Atlanta, Ga.*] (THLc) 1 p. (Contains enclosures 610527–002 & 610527–003.) MLKP-MBU. 610606–014. |
| 6/6/1961 | Wofford, Harris (U.S. White House). Letter to Martin Luther King, Jr. 6/6/1961. Washington, D.C. (TLS) 1 p. (Contains enclosure 610529–019.) MLKJP-GAMK: Box 27. 610606–020. |
| 6/6/1961 | King, Martin Luther, Jr. "The American Dream," Address delivered at Lincoln University Commencement. [*6/6/1961*]. Lincoln University, Pa. (At) 41.8 min. (1 sound cassette: analog.) PLuL. 610606–025. |
| 6/7/1961 | King, Martin Luther, Jr. (SCLC). Form letter to Pastor. 6/7/1961. Atlanta, Ga. (TLc) 2 pp. SCLCR-GAMK: Box 51. 610607–010. |
| 6/8/1961 | SCLC. Press release, "Stanford University student body supports Freedom Ride." 6/8/1961. Atlanta, Ga. (TD) 1 p. SCLCR-GAMK: Box 120. 610608–008. |
| 6/8/1961 | Minutes, Citizenship School Committee meeting. 6/8/1961. Monteagle, Tenn. (TD) 4 pp. SCLCR-GAMK: Box 136. 610608–009. |
| 6/9/1961 | Anderson, Stuart LeRoy (Pacific School of Religion). Letter to Martin Luther King, Jr. 6/9/1961. Berkeley, Calif. (THLS) 1 p. MLKP-MBU. 610609–005. |
| 6/9/1961 | Lasley, Russell R. (United Packinghouse Workers of America, AFL-CIO). Form letter to Local Unions. 6/9/1961. Chicago, Ill. (TLS) 1 p. (Contains enclosure 610517–003, pp. 224–226 in this volume.) UPWR-WHi: Box 395. 610609–015. |
| 6/9/1961 | Lasley, Russell R. (United Packinghouse Workers of America, AFL-CIO). Form letter to District Directors. 6/9/1961. Chicago, Ill. (TLS) 1 p. (Contains enclosure 610517–003, pp. 224–226 in this volume, & 610613–016.) UPWR-WHi: Box 395. 610609–016. |
| 6/10/1961 | Ebenezer Baptist Church. Press release, "'Mastering our fears,' Dr. King Jr.'s topic at Ebenezer Sunday." 6/10/1961. Atlanta, Ga. (THD) 1 p. EBCR. 610610–001. |
| 6/12/1961 | King, Martin Luther, Jr. (SCLC). Letter to Robert Cobb. 6/12/1961. [*Atlanta, Ga.*] (TLc) 2 pp. MLKP-MBU. 610612–004. |
| 6/12/1961 | King, Martin Luther, Jr. Letter to Amrit Kaur. 6/12/1961. [*Atlanta, Ga.*] (TLc) 1 p. MLKP-MBU. 610612–005. |
| 6/12/1961 | King, Martin Luther, Jr. Letter to Sargent Shriver. 6/12/1961. [*Atlanta, Ga.*] (TLc) 1 p. MLKP-MBU. 610612–008. |
| 6/12/1961 | King, Martin Luther, Jr. Letter to Ernestine Brown. 6/12/1961. [*Atlanta, Ga.*] (TLc) 1 p. MLKP-MBU. 610612–010. |
| 6/13/1961 | King, Martin Luther, Jr. Letter to Septima Poinsette Clark. 6/13/1961. [*Atlanta, Ga.*] (THLc) 1 p. MLKP-MBU. 610613–011. |
| 6/13/1961 | King, Martin Luther, Jr. Letter to William Sloane Coffin. 6/13/1961. [*Atlanta, Ga.*] (TLc) 1 p. MLKP-MBU. 610613–012. |

6/13/1961    [*United Packinghouse Workers of America, AFL-CIO*]. Report, "Fund for Democracy." [*6/13/1961*]. (TD) 7 pp. (Enclosed in 610609–016.) UPWR-WHi: Box 395. 610613–016.

6/14/1961    King, Martin Luther, Jr. (Ebenezer Baptist Church). Letter to Ralph Helstein. 6/14/1961. Atlanta, Ga. (TLSr) 1 p. UPWR-WHi: Box 164. 610614–002.

6/15/1961    [*McDonald, Dora E.*] Letter to Martin Luther King, Jr. [*6/15/1961*]. (TLc) 2 pp. MLKP-MBU. 610615–006.

6/16/1961    King, Martin Luther, Jr. "The American Dream," Address at Wilborn Temple First Church of God in Christ. 6/16/1961. Albany, N.Y. (TD) 10 pp. NARGR-NNttR. 610616–014.

6/16/1961    Rockefeller, Nelson A. (Nelson Aldrich) (New York. Office of the Governor). Remarks at Wilborn Temple First Church of God in Christ. 6/16/1961. Albany, N.Y. (TTa) 3 pp. NARGR-NNttR: Box 8. 610616–018.

6/18/1961    King, Martin Luther, Jr. "The American Dream," Address delivered at Los Angeles Freedom Rally. [*6/18/1961*]. From: Los Angeles, Calif.: Dootone Record Corporation, 1968. (At 30.7 min.) 610618–008.

6/18/1961    Western Christian Leadership Conference. Program, "Freedom Rally." 6/18/1961. Los Angeles, Calif. (PD) 16 pp. SCLCR-GAMK: Box 51. 610618–010.

6/19/1961    Drew, Addine D. (Alabama State Coordinating Association for Registration and Voting). Letter to Martin Luther King, Jr. 6/19/1961. Birmingham, Ala. (TLS) 1 p. MLKP-MBU. 610619–012.

6/19/1961    Gilpatric, Roswell (U.S. Dept. of Defense). Memo to the Secretary of the Army, the Secretary of the Navy, and the Secretary of the Air Force. 6/19/1961. Washington, D.C. (TLc) 1 p. (Enclosed in 620306–005, pp. 422–423 in this volume.) MLKJP-GAMK: Box 7. 610619–014.

6/21/1961    Houser, George M. Letter to Martin Luther King, Jr. 6/21/1961. New York, N.Y. (TLS) 2 pp. MLKP-MBU. 610621–001.

6/21/1961    Rodell, Marie F. (Marie Freid) (Marie Rodell and Joan Daves, Inc.) Letter to Martin Luther King, Jr. 6/21/1961. New York, N.Y. (TLSr) 1 p. MLKP-MBU. 610621–002.

6/21/1961    Cohen, Robert (Robert Cohen Productions). "The Un-Americans." 6/21/1961. Los Angeles, Calif. (TD) 7 pp. (Enclosed in 611031–011 & 611031–012.) MLKP-MBU. 610621–013.

6/21/1961    Murrow, Edward R. (Columbia Broadcasting System, inc.) Letter to Adam Clayton Powell. 6/21/1961. (TLc) 2 pp. (Includes enclosure 610600–019.) USIA-MBJFK: Reel 6. 610621–014.

6/25/1961    Central Baptist Church. Program, Sunday services. 6/25/1961. (PD) 1 p. EBCR. 610625–000.

6/28/1961    King, Martin Luther, Jr., and Wyatt Tee Walker (SCLC). Letter to Jim Zwerg. 6/28/1961. Atlanta, Ga. (TLS) 1 p. AFF-WBB. 610628–009.

6/29/1961    King, Martin Luther, Jr. Letter to Lonnie Parker and Lucille Parker. 6/29/1961. [*Atlanta, Ga.*] (TLc) 1 p. MLKP-MBU. 610629–002.

6/29/1961    King, Martin Luther, Jr. Letter to Cordie King Stuart and Marion H. Stuart. 6/29/1961. [*Atlanta, Ga.*] (TLc) 1 p. MLKP-MBU. 610629–010.

6/29/1961    King, Martin Luther, Jr. Letter to Addine D. Drew. 6/29/1961. Atlanta, Ga. (TLc) 1 p. MLKP-MBU. 610629–015.

6/29/1961    Wood, James R. (SCLC). Press release, Fundraising report. 6/29/1961. Atlanta, Ga. (TD) 1 p. SCLCR-GAMK. 610629–018.

6/30/1961    Virginia Christian Leadership Conference. Announcement, Martin Luther King, Jr. in mass inspirational service. 6/30/1961. Norfolk, Va. (PD) 1 p. MLKP-MBU. 610630–000.

6/30/1961    King, Martin Luther, Jr. Letter to Ranganath Ramachandra Diwakar. 6/30/1961. [*Atlanta, Ga.*] (TLc) 1 p. MLKP-MBU. 610630–002.

6/30/1961    Thomas, Norman, Reinhold Niebuhr, Grenville Clark, Junius Scales, and Robert F. Goheen. Letter to Martin Luther King, Jr. 6/30/1961. New York, N.Y. (THLS) 1 p. (Contains enclosure 610630–006.) MLKP-MBU. 610630–005.

6/30/1961    Memo in support of petition for reduction and suspension of sentence for Junius Scales. [*6/30/1961*]. (TL) 3 pp. (Enclosed in 610630–005.) MLKP-MBU. 610630–006.

6/30/1961    SCLC. Press release, Prayer pilgrimage from New Orleans to Detroit planned. 6/30/1961. Atlanta, Ga. (TD) 1 p. SCLCR-GAMK: Box 120. 610630–008.

7/1961    King, Martin Luther, Jr. Draft, The Time for Freedom Has Come. [*7/1961*]. [*Atlanta, Ga.*] (TADd) 6 pp. MCMLK-RWWL: 2.4.0.510. 610700–005.

| | | |
|---|---|---|
| 7/1961 | King, Martin Luther, Jr. Draft, The Time for Freedom Has Come. [8/2/1961]. [Atlanta, Ga.] (TAHDf) 12 pp. (Draft of 9/10/61 New York Times Magazine.) MLKJP-GAMK: Box 109. 610700–018. | Calendar |
| 7/1/1961 | Steele, C. Kenzie (Inter Civic Council of Tallahassee). Letter to Martin Luther King, Jr. 7/1/1961. Tallahassee, Fla. (TLS) 1 p. MLKP-MBU. 610701–004. | |
| 7/3/1961 | Dawkins, Maurice A. (People's Independent Church of Christ). Letter to Martin Luther King, Jr. 7/3/1961. Los Angeles, Calif. (THLSr) 1 p. MLKP-MBU. 610703–003. | |
| 7/3/1961 | Thomas, Francis. Letter to Martin Luther King, Jr. and Coretta Scott King. 7/3/1961. Albany, Calif. (TLS) 1 p. (Contains enclosures 610703–007 & 610703–008.) MLKP-MBU. 610703–005. | |
| 7/3/1961 | King, Martin Luther, Jr., John C. (John Coleman) Bennett, Sidney Akselrad, Edward Stovall, Richard Byfield, Charles Jones, James T. Carey, Russell Jorgenson, Cecil Thomas, and Charles S. McCoy. Invitation, "Mission to Mississippi." [7/3/1961]. Berkeley, Calif. (TL) 2 pp. (Enclosed in 610703–005.) ASRC-RWWL: Reel 4. 610703–007. | |
| 7/3/1961 | Thomas, Cecil. "Operation Jackson." [7/3/1961]. (THD) 2 pp. (Enclosed in 610703–005.) MLKP-MBU. 610703–008. | |
| 7/5/1961 | Malone, W.D. (First National Bank of Dothan). Letter to Duke McCall. 7/5/1961. Dothan, Ala. (TLS) 5 pp. JDGP-SBHLA: Box 3. 610705–007. | |
| 7/6/1961 | Mich, Daniel Danforth (Look). Letter to Martin Luther King, Jr. 7/6/1961. New York, N.Y. (THLS) 1 p. MLKP-MBU. 610706–003. | |
| 7/7/1961 | King, Martin Luther, Jr. Letter to Sammy Davis, Jr. and May Britt Davis. 7/7/1961. Atlanta, Ga. (THWc) 1 p. MLKP-MBU. 610707–002. | |
| 7/7/1961 | King, Martin Luther, Jr. Letter to Norman Thomas. 7/7/1961. [Atlanta, Ga.] (TLc) 1 p. MLKP-MBU. 610707–007. | |
| 7/8/1961 | Ebenezer Baptist Church. Press release, Invitation to worship at Ebenezer Baptist Church. 7/8/1961. (THD) 1 p. EBCR. 610708–004. | |
| 7/10/1961 | McDonald, Dora E. Letter to Gardner C. Taylor. 7/10/1961. Atlanta, Ga. (TLc) 1 p. MLKP-MBU. 610710–011. | |
| 7/12/1961 | King, Martin Luther, Jr. (SCLC), and G.L. Bedford (Western Christian Leadership Conference). Form letter to Pastor. 7/12/1961. Atlanta, Ga. (TLS) 1 p. MLKP-MBU. 610712–002. | |
| 7/12/1961 | [Horton, Aimee]. Minutes, Citizenship School Committee meeting. 7/12/1961. Atlanta, Ga. (TD) 2 pp. HRECR-WHi: Reel 7. 610712–004. | |
| 7/13/1961 | King, Martin Luther, Jr. "The American Dream," Address delivered at Syracuse University. 7/13/1961. Syracuse, N.Y. (At) 46 min. (1 sound cassette: analog.) MLKJP-GAMK. 610713–001. | |
| 7/13/1961 | Isenberg, Harry (Guardians of the Jewish Home for the Aged). Letter to Martin Luther King, Jr. 7/13/1961. Los Angeles, Calif. (THLS) 2 pp. (Marginal comments by King.) MLKP-MBU. 610713–005. | |
| 7/13/1961 | Hahn, Maxwell (Marshall Field Foundation). Letter to Wesley Hotchkiss. 7/13/1961. New York, N.Y. (TLS) 1 p. (Copy to King.) MLKP-MBU. 610713–013. | |
| 7/16/1961 | Ebenezer Baptist Church. Program, Women's Day services. 7/16/1961. Atlanta, Ga. (TD) 11 pp. EBCR. 610716–000. | |
| 7/16/1961 | Announcement, "Third annual Gospel-Spiritual-Folk Music Festival." 7/16/1961. New York, N.Y. (PD) 1 p. MLKP-MBU. 610716–001. | |
| 7/14/1961– 7/16/1961 | SNCC. Minutes, July meeting. 7/14/1961–7/16/1961. Baltimore, Md. (TD) 7 pp. MLKJP-GAMK: Box 23. 610716–002. | |
| 7/18/1961 | King, Martin Luther, Jr. Letter to Benjamin D. Brown. 7/18/1961. [Atlanta, Ga.] (TLc) 1 p. MLKP-MBU. 610718–000. | |
| 7/18/1961 | King, Martin Luther, Jr. Letter to Richard A. Battles. 7/18/1961. [Atlanta, Ga.] (THLc) 1 p. MLKP-MBU. 610718–004. | |
| 7/18/1961 | King, Martin Luther, Jr. Letter to J. William Rioux. 7/18/1961. [Atlanta, Ga.] (TLc) 1 p. MLKP-MBU. 610718–007. | |
| 7/19/1961 | King, Martin Luther, Jr. Letter to Harry Isenberg. 7/19/1961. [Atlanta, Ga.] (TLc) 1 p. MLKP-MBU. 610719–003. | |
| 7/20/1961 | King, Martin Luther, Jr. Letter to Paul Krassner. 7/20/1961. [Atlanta, Ga.] (TLc) 1 p. MLKP-MBU. 610720–000. | |
| 7/20/1961 | Battles, Richard A. (Mount Olive Baptist Church). Letter to Martin Luther King, Jr. 7/20/1961. Hartford, Conn. (TLS) 2 pp. MLKP-MBU. 610720–003. | |
| 7/20/1961 | Mays, Benjamin Elijah (Morehouse College). Letter to Martin Luther King, Jr. 7/20/1961. Atlanta, Ga. (TLS) 1 p. MLKP-MBU. 610720–007. | |

| | | |
|---|---|---|
| 7/20/1961 | Graham, Edward T. (Mount Zion Baptist Church). Letter to Martin Luther King, Jr. 7/20/1961. Miami, Fla. (THLS) 1 p. MLKP-MBU. 610720–008. |
| 7/23/1961 | Dinke, Berhanu (Ethiopia. Office of the Embassy). Invitation to Martin Luther King, Jr. 7/23/1961. Washington, D.C. (PD) 1 p. MLKP-MBU. 610723–001. |
| 7/23/1961 | Western Christian Leadership Conference. Announcement, "Come see and hear Rev. Martin Luther King, Jr. at the Freedom Rally." 7/23/1961. San Francisco, Calif. (PD) 1 p. MLKP-MBU. 610723–002. |
| 7/24/1961 | Friedrich, C.J. (Harvard University). Letter to Martin Luther King, Jr. 7/24/1961. Cambridge, Mass. (TLS) 2 pp. MLKP-MBU. 610724–008. |
| 7/24/1961 | King, Martin Luther, Jr. Letter to Jim Zwerg. 7/24/1961. [*Atlanta, Ga.*] (TLc) 1 p. MLKP-MBU. 610724–009. |
| 7/25/1961 | Rioux, J. William. Letter to Martin Luther King, Jr. 7/25/1961. Lakewood, Colo. (TLS) 1 p. MLKP-MBU. 610725–009. |
| 7/26/1961 | Maxwell, O. Clay (National Sunday School and Baptist Training Union Congress). Letter to Martin Luther King, Jr. 7/26/1961. New York, N.Y. (TLS) 1 p. MLKP-MBU. 610726–006. |
| 7/27/1961 | Lewis, John. Letter to Martin Luther King, Jr. 7/27/1961. (TLS) 1 p. MLKP-MBU. 610727–005. |
| 7/28/1961 | King, Martin Luther, Jr. Letter to Richard J. Brown. 7/28/1961. [*Atlanta, Ga.*] (TLc) 1 p. MLKP-MBU. 610728–007. |
| 7/28/1961 | King, Martin Luther, Jr. Letter to G. L. Bedford. 7/28/1961. [*Atlanta, Ga.*] (TLc) 1 p. MLKP-MBU. 610728–009. |
| 7/28/1961 | Committee for Better Human Relations. Program, Salute to the SCLC for its assistance to the freedom riders. 7/28/1961. New York, N.Y. (PD) 4 pp. MLKP-MBU. 610728–011. |
| 7/28/1961 | King, Martin Luther, Jr., and Wyatt Tee Walker (SCLC). Telegram to U.S. Interstate Commerce Commission. 7/28/1961. [*Atlanta, Ga.*] (PWc) 1 p. MLKP-MBU. 610728–012. |
| 7/28/1961 | Agenda and outline for meeting discussing voter registration. 7/28/1961. (TD) 6 pp. ASRC-RWWL: Reel 73. 610728–015. |
| 7/31/1961 | Dunbar, Leslie (Southern Regional Council). Memo to members of the Executive Committee. 7/31/1961. Atlanta, Ga. (TL) 2 pp. ASRC-RWWL: Reel 73. 610731–008. |
| 8/1961 | SCLC. *Newsletter* 1, no. 2. 8/1961. Atlanta, Ga. (PD) 4 pp. MLKP-MBU. 610800–001. |
| 8/1961 | "SCLC affiliates." 8/1961. (THD) 6 pp. SCLCR-GAMK: Box 50. 610800–009. |
| **6/1961–8/1961** | **Photo of Martin Luther King, Jr., and Gurdon Brewster in the office of Ebenezer Baptist Church. [*6/1961–8/1961*]. Atlanta, Ga. (Ph) 1 p. GBC. 610800–020.** |
| 8/1/1961 | Mays, Benjamin Elijah (Morehouse College). Letter to Martin Luther King, Jr. 8/1/1961. Atlanta, Ga. (TLS) 1 p. (Contains enclosure 610801–005.) MLKP-MBU. 610801–004. |
| 8/1/1961 | Warren, Edward J. Letter to Benjamin Elijah Mays. [*8/1/1961*]. Buffalo, N.Y. (TLS) 1 p. (Enclosed in 610801–004.) MLKP-MBU. 610801–005. |
| 8/1/1961 | Braden, Anne. Form letter to Friend. 8/1/1961. Louisville, Ky. (TD) 3 pp. CAABP-WHi: Box 20. 610801–011. |
| 8/2/1961 | McDonald, Dora E. Letter to Martin Luther King, Jr. 8/2/1961. Atlanta, Ga. (TLI) 1 p. (Contains enclosure 610802–003.) MCMLK-RWWL: 6.2.0.3030. 610802–002. |
| 8/2/1961 | King, Martin Luther, Jr. Draft, The Time for Freedom Has Come. [*8/2/1961*]. (TADf) 9 pp. (Enclosed in 610802–002.) MCMLK-RWWL: 2.4.0.520. 610802–003. |
| 8/2/1961 | Thompson, Elsa Knight (KPFA (FM)). Letter to Martin Luther King, Jr. 8/2/1961. Berkeley, Calif. (TLS) 1 p. MLKP-MBU. 610802–007. |
| 8/3/1961 | Brackeen, S. Amos (Jones Memorial Baptist Church). Letter to Martin Luther King, Jr. 8/3/1961. Philadelphia, Pa. (TLS) 1 p. MLKP-MBU. 610803–000. |
| 8/3/1961 | Mays, Benjamin Elijah (Morehouse College). Letter to Martin Luther King, Jr. 8/3/1961. Atlanta, Ga. (TLS) 1 p. MLKP-MBU. 610803–007. |
| 8/3/1961 | SCLC. Press release, "Freedom Ride Coordinating Committee." 8/3/1961. Atlanta, Ga. (TD) 1 p. SCLCR-GAMK: Box 34. 610803–014. |
| 8/4/1961 | Walker, Wyatt Tee, and Martin Luther King, Jr. Letter on behalf of Paul Brooks. 8/4/1961. (TLc) 1 p. MLKP-MBU. 610804–003. |
| 8/4/1961 | Connectional Laymen's Organization of the African Methodist Episcopal Church. "Citation of appreciation." 8/4/1961. Atlanta, Ga. (PDS) 1 p. MLKP-MBU. 610804–004. |
| 8/4/1961 | King, Martin Luther, Jr. Letter to Sherman Lawrence Greene. 8/4/1961. [*Atlanta, Ga.*] (TLc) 1 p. MLKP-MBU. 610804–007. |

| 8/4/1961 | King, Martin Luther, Jr. Draft, I Predict. 8/4/1961. [*Atlanta, Ga.*] (TDdI) 1 p. MLKP-MBU. 610804–016. | Calendar |

8/5/1961      Ebenezer Baptist Church. Press release, "Dr. Martin Luther King, Jr. at Ebenezer Sunday." 8/5/1961. Atlanta, Ga. (TD) 1 p. EBCR. 610805–003.

8/5/1961      King, Martin Luther, Jr., and Wyatt Tee Walker (SCLC). Telegram to Burke Marshall and John Seigenthaler. 8/5/1961. [*Atlanta, Ga.*] (PHWc) 1 p. MLKP-MBU. 610805–006.

8/6/1961      King, Martin Luther, Jr. "Paul's Letter to American Christians." [*8/6/1961*]. [*Atlanta, Ga.*] (TD) 10 pp. MLKP-MBU. 610806–000.

8/7/1961      *The Crusader* 3, no. 5. 8/7/1961. Monroe, N.C. (PD) 6 pp. SCLCR-GAMK: Box 155. 610807–014.

8/9/1961      Van Koughnet, Donald E. (Law Offices of Weaver & Van Koughnet). Letter to Martin Luther King, Jr. 8/9/1961. Washington, D.C. (TLS) 2 pp. MLKP-MBU. 610809–003.

8/9/1961      McDonald, Dora E. Letter to Charles A. McLean. 8/9/1961. [*Atlanta, Ga.*] (TLc) 1 p. MLKP-MBU. 610809–004.

8/9/1961      King, Martin Luther, Jr. Letter to Theodore Woodrow Kheel and Ann S. (Ann Sunstein) Kheel. 8/9/1961. [*Atlanta, Ga.*] (TLS) 1 p. TWKC. 610809–006.

8/9/1961      Baptist Press. Press release, "Southern trustees make King statement." 8/9/1961. Montgomery, Ala. (TD) 2 pp. MLKP-MBU. 610809–009.

8/9/1961      Walker, Wyatt Tee (SCLC). Memo to Martin Luther King, Jr., Burke Marshall, and James M. Lawson. 8/9/1961. (TLf) 7 pp. MCMLK-RWWL: 6.2.0.4820. 610809–010.

8/10/1961      King, Martin Luther, Jr. Letter to Sidney Poitier. 8/10/1961. [*Atlanta, Ga.*] (TLc) 2 pp. MLKP-MBU. 610810–017.

8/10/1961      Maguire, John David (Wesleyan University). Letter to Martin Luther King, Jr. 8/10/1961. Middletown, Conn. (TLS) 1 p. MLKP-MBU. 610810–023.

8/11/1961      Ku Klux Klan, et al., Defendants. "Order, Judgment and Decree," *United States v. Ku Klux Klan.* 8/11/1961. (TD) 2 pp. (Enclosed in 610814–005.) SCLCR-GAMK: Box 34. 610811–008.

8/11/1961      Dunbar, Leslie. Memo, "Notes on the morning session at the Taconic conference July 28, 1961." 8/11/1961. (TL) 3 pp. ASRC-RWWL: Reel 73. 610811–009.

8/12/1961      Fischer, Eleanor. Letter to Martin Luther King, Jr. 8/12/1961. New York, N.Y. (TLS) 1 p. MLKP-MBU. 610812–000.

8/12/1961      Ebenezer Baptist Church. Press release, "'The use and misuse of the Mizpah,' Anderson's topic at Ebenezer." 8/12/1961. [*Atlanta, Ga.*] (TD) 1 p. EBCR. 610812–001.

8/13/1961      Riverside Church. Program, Sunday services. 8/13/1961. New York, N.Y. (PD) 4 pp. CHAC. 610813–000.

8/13/1961      Ebenezer Baptist Church. Program, Sunday services. 8/13/1961. Atlanta, Ga. (PHD) 4 pp. EBCR. 610813–002.

8/14/1961      Conley, Charles S. Letter to Dorothy Cotton. 8/14/1961. (TLS) 1 p. (Contains enclosure 610811–008.) SCLCR-GAMK: Box 34. 610814–005.

8/15/1961      Walker, Wyatt Tee (SCLC). Statement before the U.S. Interstate Commerce Commission. 8/15/1961. Washington, D.C. (TD) 5 pp. MLKP-MBU. 610815–000.

8/15/1961      Smith, Dwight C. (John Milton Society). Letter to Martin Luther King, Jr. 8/15/1961. New York, N.Y. (THLS) 2 pp. MLKP-MBU. 610815–002.

8/16/1961      Poitier, Sidney. Letter to Martin Luther King, Jr. [*8/16/1961*]. (ALS) 1 p. (Enclosed in 610818–002.) MLKP-MBU. 610816–003.

8/16/1961      SCLC. Press release, SCLC annual meeting. 8/16/1961. Atlanta, Ga. (TD) 1 p. MLKP-MBU. 610816–004.

8/16/1961      King, Martin Luther, Jr. Christ Lives in the World, Address delivered at the American Lutheran Church Luther League convention. [*8/16/1961*]. Miami, Fla. (At) 74.6 min. (1 sound cassette: analog.) ICEL. 610816–010.

8/16/1961      King, Martin Luther, Jr. Press conference at the American Lutheran Church Luther League convention. [*8/16/1961*]. [*Miami, Fla.*] (F) .6 min. FMIA-FlMiMLW. 610816–011.

8/16/1961      King, Martin Luther, Jr. Press conference at the American Lutheran Church Luther League convention. [*8/16/1961*]. [*Miami, Fla.*] (F) .9 min. FMIA-FlMiMLW. 610816–012.

8/16/1961      King, Martin Luther, Jr. Question and answer session at the American Lutheran Church Luther League convention. [*8/16/1961*]. [*Miami, Fla.*] (F) 2.3 min. ICEL. 610816–013.

| | |
|---|---|
| 8/17/1961 | Currier, Stephen R. (Taconic Foundation). Telegram to Martin Luther King, Jr. 8/17/1961. New York, N.Y. (PWSr) 1 p. MLKP-MBU. 610817–001. |
| 8/17/1961 | Lyons, Jesse (Riverside Church). Letter to Martin Luther King, Jr. 8/17/1961. New York, N.Y. (ALS) 2 pp. MLKP-MBU. 610817–002. |
| 8/17/1961 | Carl Braden Clemency Appeal Committee. Press release, "Statement by Dr. Ralph D. Abernathy, spokesman for the committee." 8/17/1961. Washington, D.C. (TD) 2 pp. SCLCR-GAMK: Box 34. 610817–010. |
| 8/17/1961 | Carl Braden Clemency Appeal Committee. Press release, Committee presents clemency appeal petition to John F. (John Fitzgerald) Kennedy. 8/17/1961. (THD) 14 pp. (Contains enclosure 610817–013.) SCLCR-GAMK: Box 34. 610817–011. |
| 8/17/1961 | [*Carl Braden Clemency Appeal Committee*]. Partial list of signers of Carl Braden clemency petition. [*8/17/1961*]. (TD) 4 pp. (Enclosed in 610817–011.) SCLCR-GAMK: Box 34. 610817–013. |
| 8/18/1961 | Resnikoff, M. Bernard. Letter to Martin Luther King, Jr. 8/18/1961. Fairlawn, N.J. (TLS) 1 p. MLKP-MBU. 610818–000. |
| 8/18/1961 | McDonald, Dora E. Letter to Frances Freeborn Pauley. 8/18/1961. [*Atlanta, Ga.*] (TLc) 1 p. (Contains enclosure 610816–003.) MLKP-MBU. 610818–002. |
| 8/19/1961 | Monroe Non-Violent Action Committee. Minutes, Founding meeting of the Monroe Non-Violent Action Committee. 8/19/1961. Monroe, N.C. (TD) 1 p. MLKJP-GAMK: Box 33. 610819–000. |
| 8/21/1961 | Allen, Ivan. Letter to Martin Luther King, Jr. 8/21/1961. Atlanta, Ga. (THLS) 1 p. MLKP-MBU. 610821–000. |
| 8/22/1961 | Rich, Marvin (CORE). Letter to Martin Luther King, Jr. 8/22/1961. New York, N.Y. (THLS) 1 p. MLKP-MBU. 610822–000. |
| 8/22/1961 | Rockefeller, Nelson A. (Nelson Aldrich) (New York. Office of the Governor). Letter to Martin Luther King, Jr. 8/22/1961. Albany, N.Y. (THLS) 2 pp. MLKP-MBU. 610822–001. |
| 8/22/1961 | [*King, Martin Luther, Jr.*] Telegram to Richard Rettig. 8/22/1961. [*Atlanta, Ga.*] (PHWc) 1 p. MLKP-MBU. 610822–007. |
| 8/22/1961 | [*Monroe Non-Violent Action Committee*]. "List of motions passed to date." 8/22/1961. (TD) 2 pp. MLKJP-GAMK: Box 33. 610822–010. |
| 8/23/1961 | Brown, L. David (American Lutheran Church). Letter to Martin Luther King, Jr. 8/23/1961. Miami Beach, Fla. (TLS) 1 p. MLKP-MBU. 610823–001. |
| 8/23/1961 | King, Martin Luther, Jr. (SCLC). Letter to Stanley D. Levison. 8/23/1961. [*Atlanta, Ga.*] (TLc) 1 p. SCLCR-GAMK: Box 61. 610823–006. |
| 8/23/1961 | Southern Regional Council. Memo for discussion regarding Voter Education Project. [*8/23/1961*]. (THL) 7 pp. ASRC-RWWL: Reel 73. 610823–007. |
| 8/24/1961 | King, Martin Luther, Jr. (SCLC). Letter to Theodore Woodrow Kheel. 8/24/1961. [*Atlanta, Ga.*] (TLc) 1 p. MLKJP-GAMK: Box 14. 610824–000. |
| 8/25/1961 | Alexander, Cecil A. Letter to Martin Luther King, Jr. 8/25/1961. Atlanta, Ga. (TLS) 1 p. MLKP-MBU. 610825–000. |
| 8/26/1961 | Ebenezer Baptist Church. Press release, "'What time is it?' Rev. Brewster at Ebenezer." 8/26/1961. (TD) 1 p. EBCR. 610826–000. |
| 8/29/1961 | Freedom Riders. Telegram to Martin Luther King, Jr. 8/29/1961. Monroe, N.C. (PWSr) 2 pp. MLKP-MBU. 610829–000. |
| 8/29/1961 | Leadership Conference on Civil Rights. Report on discrimination by the federal government. 8/29/1961. New York, N.Y. (TD) 78 pp. JFKWHCSF-MBJFK. 610829–002. |
| 8/30/1961 | Rivera, Emilio (Adelphi College). Letter to Martin Luther King, Jr. 8/30/1961. Garden City, N.Y. (TLS) 1 p. MLKP-MBU. 610830–000. |
| 8/30/1961 | Courlander, Harold. Letter to Martin Luther King, Jr. 8/30/1961. Bethesda, Md. (THLS) 3 pp. MLKP-MBU. 610830–002. |
| 9/1/1960–<br>8/31/1961 | SCLC. "Bank balances." 9/1/1960–8/31/1961. (THD) 1 p. (Marginal comments by King.) MCMLK-RWWL: 6.3.0.660. 610831–001. |
| 9/1/1960–<br>8/31/1961 | Abernathy, Ralph. "Southern Christian Leadership Conference, treasurer's report." 9/1/1960–8/31/1961. (TD) 2 pp. MCMLK-RWWL: 6.3.0.660. 610831–004. |
| 8/31/1961 | Macomson, W. O. "Statement of receipts and expenditure for the fiscal year ended August 31, 1961." 8/31/1961. (TD) 2 pp. SCLCR-GAMK: Box 57. 610831–006. |
| 8/31/1961 | SCLC. Press release, "Lawson to keynote SCLC annual meeting in Nashville." 8/31/1961. Atlanta, Ga. (TD) 1 p. SCLCR-GAMK: Box 120. 610831–009. |
| 9/1961 | SCLC. "Briefs...," *Newsletter* 1, no. 3. (TDd) 1 p. MLKP-MBU. 610900–003. |
| 9/1961 | Jackson, J.H. (Joseph Harrison) (National Baptist Convention of the United States of America). Letter to Erma Jewell Hughes. [*9/1961*]. [*Chicago, Ill.*] (TLc) 1 p. MLKP-MBU. 610900–004. |

| | | |
|---|---|---|
| 9/1961 | [*Abernathy, Ralph*] (SCLC). Draft, "Treasurer's report." [*9/1961*]. Atlanta, Ga. (THD) 3 pp. (Marginal comments by King.) MCMLK-RWWL: 6.3.0.660. 610900–010. | Calendar |
| 9/1961 | SCLC. *Newsletter* 1, no. 3. 9/1961. Atlanta, Ga. (PD) 4 pp. MCMLK-RWWL: 6.5.0.1050. 610900–012. | |
| 9/1961 | "Wagner, King address packed meeting; Mayor backs $1.50 minimum in hospitals." *1199 Organization News* 28 (September 1961). (PDf) 1 p. KLMDA-NNCorI. 610900–013. | |
| **9/2/1961** | **King, Martin Luther, Jr. Draft, Invocation at funeral of John Wesley Dobbs. [*9/2/1961*]. [*Atlanta, Ga.*] (ADd) 8 pp. MCMLK-RWWL: 2.2.0.870. 610902–001.** | |
| 9/2/1961 | Big Bethel AME Church. Program, Funeral service for John Wesley Dobbs. 9/2/1961. Atlanta, Ga. (PD) 4 pp. MCMLK-RWWL: 12.3.0.110. 610902–005. | |
| 9/2/1961 | Ebenezer Baptist Church. Press release, "Dr. King, Jr. at Ebenezer Sunday." 9/2/1961. Atlanta, Ga. (TD) 1 p. EBCR. 610902–006. | |
| 9/5/1961 | Fischer, Eleanore (Canadian Broadcasting Corporation). Telegram to Martin Luther King, Jr. 9/5/1961. New York, N.Y. (PHWSr) 1 p. MLKP-MBU. 610905–003. | |
| 9/7/1961 | SCLC. Press release, "SCLC to meet to discuss deep south in social revolution." 9/7/1961. Atlanta, Ga. (TD) 1 p. SCLCR-GAMK: Box 120. 610907–012. | |
| 9/8/1961 | Marshall, Burke (U.S. Dept. of Justice). Letter to L. G. Fant. 9/8/1961. Washington, D.C. (TLc) 3 pp. BMPP-MBJFK: Reel 3. 610908–008. | |
| 9/9/1961 | Ebenezer Baptist Church. Press release, "Martin Luther King, Jr. at Ebenezer Sunday." 9/9/1961. Atlanta, Ga. (THD) 1 p. EBCR. 610909–000. | |
| 9/10/1961 | Jackson, J. H. (Joseph Harrison) (National Baptist Convention of the United States of America). "Statement by Dr. J. H. Jackson, President National Baptist Convention of the United States of America." 9/10/1961. (TD) 2 pp. (Enclosed in 610912–007, pp. 281–282 in this volume.) SCLCE-GEU-S: Box 543. 610910–007. | |
| 9/11/1961 | Zeleznik, Carter (Jefferson Medical College of Philadelphia). Letter to Martin Luther King, Jr. 9/11/1961. Philadelphia, Pa. (TLS) 2 pp. MLKP-MBU. 610911–002. | |
| 9/11/1961 | Toles, William, and Ernestine Toles. Letter to Martin Luther King, Jr. 9/11/1961. Philadelphia, Pa. (ALS) 2 pp. MLKP-MBU. 610911–004. | |
| 9/11/1961 | Walker, Wyatt Tee (SCLC). Form letter to Friend of Freedom. 9/11/1961. Atlanta, Ga. (TLc) 1 p. (Enclosed in 610912–014.) MCMLK-RWWL: 6.2.0.880. 610911–008. | |
| 9/11/1961 | Associated Negro Press. Press release, "Dr. King denies link in violence at Baptist meet in K.C.; Asks President Jackson to retract statement." 9/11/1961. (PD) 1 p. 610911–013. | |
| 9/12/1961 | SCLC. Press release, "Religious leaders protest alleged attack on Martin Luther King, Jr." 9/12/1961. Atlanta, Ga. (TD) 2 pp. MLKP-MBU. 610912–008. | |
| 9/12/1961 | Mays, Benjamin Elijah, Fred L. Shuttlesworth, Kelly Miller Smith, C. Kenzie Steele, Sandy F. Ray, William Holmes Borders, Gardner C. Taylor, D.E. (Dearine Edwin) King, M.C. (Millard Curtis) Williams, Samuel W. Williams, S. Howard Woodson, D.A. Holmes, L. Venchael Booth, E.W. Perry, Roland A. Smith, and Ralph Abernathy. Telegram to J.H. (Joseph Harrison) Jackson. 9/12/1961. (PWc) 5 pp. MLKP-MBU. 610912–009. | |
| 9/12/1961 | Cotton, Dorothy (SCLC). Letter to Martin Luther King, Jr. 9/12/1961. Atlanta, Ga. (TLS) 1 p. (Contains enclosures 610911–008 & 610912–015.) MCMLK-RWWL: 6.2.0.880. 610912–014. | |
| 9/12/1961 | SCLC. "Minimum operations budget for Citizenship School Program." [*9/12/1961*]. (TD) 1 p. (Enclosed in 610912–014.) MCMLK-RWWL: 6.2.0.880. 610912–015. | |
| 9/12/1961 | Clark, Septima Poinsette. Letter to J.H. (Joseph Harrison) Jackson. 9/12/1961. Atlanta, Ga. (TLc) 2 pp. SCLCE-GEU-S: Box 543. 610912–016. | |
| 9/13/1961 | King, Martin Luther, Jr. Letter to Robert F. Shannon. 9/13/1961. [*Atlanta, Ga.*] (TLc) 2 pp. MLKP-MBU. 610913–003. | |
| 9/13/1961 | King, Martin Luther, Jr. Letter to T.Y. Rogers. 9/13/1961. [*Atlanta, Ga.*] (TLc) 1 p. MLKP-MBU. 610913–008. | |
| 9/13/1961 | Dunbar, Leslie (Southern Regional Council). Letter to James Farmer, Roy Wilkins, Whitney M. Young, Wyatt Tee Walker, Charles McDew, and Timothy L. Jenkins. 9/13/1961. Atlanta, Ga. (TLS) 6 pp. (Copy to King.) SCLCR-GAMK: Box 36. 610913–010. | |
| 9/13/1961 | SCLC. Press release, "Belafonte and co. to open SCLC convention, in Nashville." 9/13/1961. Atlanta, Ga. (TD) 1 p. SCLCR-GAMK: Box 120. 610913–014. | |
| 9/14/1961 | Weaver, Edward K. (Atlanta University). Letter to Martin Luther King, Jr. 9/14/1961. Atlanta, Ga. (TLSr) 1 p. MLKP-MBU. 610914–002. | |
| 9/14/1961 | King, Martin Luther, Jr. Letter to William Toles and Ernestine Toles. 9/14/1961. [*Atlanta, Ga.*] (TLc) 1 p. MLKP-MBU. 610914–005. | |

635

| | | |
|---|---|---|
| 9/14/1961 | Braden, Anne. Letter to Carl Braden. 9/14/1961. Louisville, Ky. (TAHLS) 2 pp. CAABP-WHi: Box 11. 610914–009. |
| 9/15/1961 | Butler, Charles William (Metropolitan Baptist Church). Letter to Martin Luther King, Jr. 9/15/1961. Detroit, Mich. (TLSr) 1 p. MLKP-MBU. 610915–000. |
| 9/15/1961 | King, Martin Luther, Jr. Letter to Charlayne A. Hunter. 9/15/1961. [Atlanta, Ga.] (TLc) 1 p. MLKP-MBU. 610915–004. |
| 9/15/1961 | King, Martin Luther, Jr. Letter to Arthur Smith. 9/15/1961. [Atlanta, Ga.] (TLc) 1 p. MLKP-MBU. 610915–008. |
| 9/15/1961 | Dombrowski, James A. (James Anderson) (Southern Conference Educational Fund). Letter to Martin Luther King, Jr. 9/15/1961. New Orleans, La. (THLS) 1 p. MLKP-MBU. 610915–013. |
| 9/16/1961 | Raballa, Nicholas W. Letter to Martin Luther King, Jr. 9/16/1961. Westport, Conn. (ALS) 1 p. MLKP-MBU. 610916–000. |
| 9/16/1961 | Hughes, Erma Jewell (Erma Hughes Business College). Letter to J.H. (Joseph Harrison) Jackson. 9/16/1961. Houston, Texas. (TLS) 2 pp. MLKP-MBU. 610916–001. |
| 9/16/1961 | Ebenezer Baptist Church. Press release, "'Where God is found,' King Jr. at Ebenezer Sunday." [9/16/1961]. Atlanta, Ga. (TD) 1 p. EBCR. 610916–002. |
| 9/17/1961 | King, Martin Luther, Jr. Letter to Thane Read. 9/17/1961. [Atlanta, Ga.] (TLc) 1 p. MLKP-MBU. 610917–001. |
| 9/18/1961 | King, Martin Luther, Jr. Letter to William Peters. 9/18/1961. [Atlanta, Ga.] (TLc) 1 p. MLKP-MBU. 610918–003. |
| 9/18/1961 | King, Martin Luther, Jr. Letter to Loudon Wainwright. 9/18/1961. [Atlanta, Ga.] (TLc) 1 p. MLKP-MBU. 610918–004. |
| 9/18/1961 | Cummings, Shirley. Letter to Martin Luther King, Jr. 9/18/1961. New York, N.Y. (TLS) 1 p. MLKP-MBU. 610918–009. |
| 9/18/1961 | King, Joseph (New Calvary Baptist Church). Letter to Martin Luther King, Jr. 9/18/1961. Detroit, Mich. (TLSr) 1 p. MLKP-MBU. 610918–012. |
| 9/20/1961 | King, Martin Luther, Jr. Telegram to Vernon Parker Bodein. 9/20/1961. [Atlanta, Ga.] (TWc) 1 p. MLKP-MBU. 610920–006. |
| 9/20/1961 | King, Martin Luther, Jr. Letter to George Burr Leonard. 9/20/1961. [Atlanta, Ga.] (TLc) 1 p. MLKP-MBU. 610920–013. |
| 9/20/1961 | Lasley, Russell R. (AFL-CIO). Letter to District Directors. 9/20/1961. Chicago, Ill. (TLS) 2 pp. UPWP-WHi: Box 395. 610920–019. |
| 9/20/1961 | Madison, Eddie L. (Associated Negro Press). Press release, "Dr. Martin Luther King, Jr., says he will not sue Dr. Jackson for alleged statement that he masterminded convention violence 'at this time.'" 9/20/1961. Chicago, Ill. (PD) 4 pp. 610920–020. |
| 9/21/1961 | Dobbs, Irene T. Letter to Martin Luther King, Jr. 9/21/1961. Atlanta, Ga. (ALS) 1 p. MLKP-MBU. 610921–003. |
| 9/21/1961 | SCLC. Press release, "SCLC convention in Nashville, September 27–29." 9/21/1961. (TD) 1 p. SCLCR-GAMK: Box 129. 610921–005. |
| 9/21/1961 | Mays, Benjamin Elijah (Morehouse College). Letter to L. Venchael Booth. 9/21/1961. Atlanta, Ga. (TALS) 1 p. LVBP-DHU-S. 610921–007. |
| 9/22/1961 | King, Martin Luther, Jr. Letter to Carl T. Rowan. 9/22/1961. [Atlanta, Ga.] (TLc) 2 pp. MLKP-MBU. 610922–001. |
| 9/22/1961 | Sellers, Lilla A. Letter to Martin Luther King, Jr. 9/22/1961. [Atlanta, Ga.] (TLS) 1 p. MLKP-MBU. 610922–003. |
| 9/22/1961 | King, Martin Luther, Jr. Letter to Wilhelmie Bowden. 9/22/1961. [Atlanta, Ga.] (TLc) 1 p. (Contains enclosure 610922–016.) MLKP-MBU. 610922–008. |
| 9/22/1961 | King, Martin Luther, Jr. Testimonial statement for Edward Stovall. 9/22/1961. [Atlanta, Ga.] (TD) 1 p. (Enclosed in 610922–008.) MLKP-MBU. 610922–016. |
| 9/23/1961 | Sheffield, Horace L. (Trade Union Leadership Council). Letter to Martin Luther King, Jr. 9/23/1961. Detroit, Mich. (TLS) 1 p. (Contains enclosures 610923–001 & 610923–002.) MCMLK-RWWL: 1.1.0.42390. 610923–000. |
| 9/23/1961 | Dillard, Ernest C. (Trade Union Leadership Council). Press release, Telegram to J.H. (Joseph Harrison) Jackson. 9/23/1961. Detroit, Mich. (TD) 1 p. (Enclosed in 610923–000.) MCMLK-RWWL: 1.1.0.42390. 610923–001. |
| 9/23/1961 | "Rev. Jackson Rips Rev. King During Eulogy." *Michigan Chronicle*, 23 September 1961. (PD) 2 pp. (Enclosed in 610923–000.) 610923–002. |
| 9/24/1961 | Ebenezer Baptist Church. Program, Sunday services. 9/24/1961. Atlanta, Ga. (TD) 4 pp. EBCR. 610924–000. |

| | |
|---|---|
| 9/25/1961 | Kearse, I. Logan (Cornerstone Baptist Church of Christ). Letter to Martin Luther King, Jr. 9/25/1961. Baltimore, Md. (TLS) 2 pp. MLKP-MBU. 610925–000. |
| 9/25/1961 | Macomson, W.O. "Full audit for the SCLC for the fiscal year ended 8/31/61." 9/25/1961. (TD) 8 pp. MLKJP-GAMK: Box 28. 610925–009. |
| 9/25/1961 | King, Martin Luther, Jr. (SCLC). Form telegram to C.O. Simpkins. 9/25/1961. [*Atlanta, Ga.*] (PHWc) 1 p. MLKP-MBU. 610925–018. |
| 9/26/1961 | Daniel, Bradford (*Sepia*). Letter to Martin Luther King, Jr. 9/26/1961. Fort Worth, Texas. (TLS) 1 p. MLKP-MBU. 610926–005. |
| 9/26/1961 | SCLC. "Budget of additional needs for Citizen Education Project." 9/26/1961. (TD) 1 p. MLKP-MBU. 610926–008. |
| 9/26/1961 | Hardmond, Robert E.L. (Bethesda Baptist Church). Letter to J.H. (Joseph Harrison) Jackson. 9/26/1961. Port Chester, N.Y. (TLc) 1 p. MLKP-MBU. 610926–012. |
| 9/27/1961 | SCLC. "Minutes of annual board meeting, SCLC." 9/27/1961. Nashville, Tenn. (THD) 4 pp. MLKJP-GAMK: Box 29. 610927–001. |
| 9/27/1961 | SCLC. Certificate of Merit for Jim Zwerg. 9/27/1961. (PDS) 1 p. AFF-WBB. 610927–009. |
| 9/28/1961 | King, Martin Luther, Jr. Draft, Address at SCLC annual meeting. [*9/28/1961*]. Nashville, Tenn. (ADd) 1 p. MCMLK-RWWL: 6.1.0.250. 610928–001. |
| 9/28/1961 | Walker, Wyatt Tee (SCLC). "Report of the director." 9/28/1961. Nashville, Tenn. (TD) 13 pp. SCLCR-GAMK. 610928–004. |
| 9/28/1961 | King, Martin Luther, Jr. Press conference at SCLC annual meeting. [*9/28/1961*]. (F) 1.2 min NBCNA-NNNBC. 610928–005. |
| 9/27/1961–9/29/1961 | SCLC. Program, "Annual meeting of SCLC." 9/27/1961–9/29/1961. Nashville, Tenn. (PD) 12 pp. MCMLK-RWWL: 6.5.0.720. 610929–001. |
| 9/27/1961–9/29/1961 | SCLC. Flyer, "Everybody's coming to Nashville! Are you?" 9/27/1961–9/29/1961. (PD) 1 p. MCMLK-RWWL: 6.5.0.850. 610929–007. |
| 9/30/1961 | Ebenezer Baptist Church. Press release, "'Making life worth living,' Martin Luther King's topic at Ebenezer Sunday." [*9/30/1961*]. Atlanta, Ga. (TD) 1 p. EBCR. 610930–000. |
| 10/1961 | King, Martin Luther, Jr. "Crisis and the Church." *Council Quarterly* (October 1961). (PD) 3 pp. MLKP-MBU. 611000–000. |
| 10/1961 | "Integrationist Dr. King Praises Priests' Bus Ride." [*10/1961*]. [*Detroit, Mich.*] (PD) 1 p. MCMLK-RWWL. 611000–002. |
| 10/1961 | "Gandhi and the Deepening World Crisis." *Gandhi Marg* (October 1961): 277–280. (PD) 4 pp. (Enclosed in 611206–001.) MLKJP-GAMK: Box 11. 611000–003. |
| 10/1961 | Department of Political Science (Atlanta University). Program, "Town meeting." [*10/1961*]. [*Atlanta, Ga.*] (TD) 1 p. MLKP-MBU. 611000–007. |
| 10/1961 | SNCC. "Students face Mississippi violence for you." 10/1961. Atlanta, Ga. (TD) 1 p. SNCCP-GAMK: Reel 1. 611000–009. |
| 10/1961 | Urban League of Portland. "News Roundup." 10/1961. Portland, Ore. (PDf) 3 pp. PMC-OrHi. 611000–012. |
| 10/1961 | Diggs, Charles C. (U.S. Congress. House of Representatives). Form letter to Fellow Voter. 10/1961. (TLc) 1 p. CCDP-DHU-S: Box 50. 611000–015. |
| 10/3/1961 | King, Martin Luther, Jr. Letter to Gene E. Bartlett. 10/3/1961. [*Atlanta, Ga.*] (TLc) 2 pp. MLKP-MBU. 611003–004. |
| **10/3/1961** | **King, Martin Luther, Jr. (Morehouse College). "Outline of Lecture in Social Philosophy." [*10/3/1961*]. [*Atlanta, Ga.*] (AD) 3 pp. MCMLK-RWWL: 5.1.0.220. 611003–006.** |
| 10/3/1961 | King, Martin Luther, Jr. Letter to William Stuart Nelson. 10/3/1961. [*Atlanta, Ga.*] (TLc) 1 p. MLKP-MBU. 611003–012. |
| 10/4/1961 | King, Martin Luther, Jr. Letter to Nicholas W. Raballa. 10/4/1961. [*Atlanta, Ga.*] (TLc) 1 p. MLKP-MBU. 611004–001. |
| 10/4/1961 | King, Martin Luther, Jr. Letter to Walter S. Pinn. 10/4/1961. [*Atlanta, Ga.*] (TLc) 2 pp. MLKP-MBU. 611004–004. |
| 10/4/1961 | King, Martin Luther, Jr. Letter to Helen L. Sobell. 10/4/1961. Atlanta, Ga. (TLS) 2 pp. CJMSC-WHi: Box 31. 611004–007. |
| 10/4/1961 | King, Martin Luther, Jr. Letter to Harold I. Bearden. 10/4/1961. [*Atlanta, Ga.*] (THLc) 1 p. MLKP-MBU. 611004–010. |
| 10/4/1961 | Wofford, Harris (U.S. White House). Memo to Kenneth P. O'Donnell. 10/4/1961. Washington, D.C. (THLS) 1 p. JFKWHCSF-MBJFK: Box 358. 611004–017. |
| 10/4/1961 | Memo to Burke Marshall and J. Harold Flannery. 10/4/1961. (TLc) 2 pp. BMPP-MBJFK: Reel 3. 611004–018. |

| | |
|---|---|
| 10/5/1961 | King, Martin Luther, Jr. Letter to B.S. Weiss. 10/5/1961. [*Atlanta, Ga.*] (TLc) 1 p. MLKP-MBU. 611005–011. |
| 10/5/1961 | McDonald, Dora E. Letter to Welford P. Carter. 10/5/1961. [*Atlanta, Ga.*] (TLc) 2 pp. MLKP-MBU. 611005–014. |
| 10/5/1961 | King, Martin Luther, Jr. (SCLC). America's Greatest Crisis, Address at the Eleventh Constitutional Convention of the Transport Workers Union of America. 10/5/1961. New York, N.Y. (PD) 8 pp. TWUP. 611005–019. |
| 10/6/1961 | Reddick, Lawrence Dunbar (Coppin State Teachers College). Letter to Martin Luther King, Jr., and Wyatt Tee Walker. 10/6/1961. Baltimore, Md. (TLS) 1 p. MLKP-MBU. 611006–003. |
| 10/6/1961 | King, Martin Luther, Jr. Letter to Milton A. Reid. 10/6/1961. [*Atlanta, Ga.*] (TLc) 1 p. MLKP-MBU. 611006–005. |
| 10/6/1961 | Ebenezer Baptist Church. Press release, "'The earth is the Lord's,' Pastor King Sr.'s topic at Ebenezer Sunday." 10/6/1961. [*Atlanta, Ga.*] (TD) 1 p. EBCR. 611006–013. |
| 10/7/1961 | Williams, Howard (Bloomsbury Central Baptist Church). Letter to Martin Luther King, Jr. 10/7/1961. London, England. (AHLS) 1 p. (Marginal comments by King.) MLKP-MBU. 611007–000. |
| 10/7/1961 | Hughes, Erma Jewell (Erma Hughes Business College). Letter to Martin Luther King, Jr. 10/7/1961. Houston, Texas. (AHLS) 1 p. MLKP-MBU. 611007–001. |
| 10/9/1961 | Muste, A.J. (Abraham Johannes) (FOR). Letter to Martin Luther King, Jr. 10/9/1961. New York, N.Y. (TLS) 1 p. MLKP-MBU. 611009–006. |
| 10/9/1961 | Baptist Pastors and Lay Leaders of the National Baptist Convention of the United States of America. Letter to O. Clay Maxwell. [*10/9/1961*]. Washington, D.C. (THL) 1 p. MLKP-MBU. 611009–007. |
| 10/9/1961 | Freedom Forum. Program, "Freedom forum." 10/9/1961. Schenectady, N.Y. (PHDS) 5 pp. (Marginal comments by King.) RBC. 611009–011. |
| 10/9/1961 | Braden, Anne. Memo to advisors in Carl Braden clemency case. 10/9/1961. (TL) 1 p. SCLCR-GAMK: Box 34. 611009–012. |
| 10/9/1961 | Diggs, Charles C. (U.S. Congress. House of Representatives). Form letter to Reverend. 10/9/1961. Washington, D.C. (TLc) 1 p. CCDP-DHU-MS: Box 50. 611009–013. |
| 10/10/1961 | Johnson, Lyndon B. (Lyndon Baines) (Peace Corps). Letter to Martin Luther King, Jr., and Coretta Scott King. 10/10/1961. Washington, D.C. (TLS) 1 p. MLKP-MBU. 611010–000. |
| 10/10/1961 | Ferman, James (Associated Television Limited). Letter to Martin Luther King, Jr. 10/10/1961. (TLc) 1 p. MLKP-MBU. 611010–003. |
| 10/10/1961 | Edwards, Clarence C. Letter to Martin Luther King, Jr. 10/10/1961. Maywood, Ill. (TLS) 1 p. MLKP-MBU. 611010–006. |
| 10/11/1961 | King, Martin Luther, Jr. Letter to Emilio Rivera. 10/11/1961. [*Atlanta, Ga.*] (TLc) 1 p. MLKP-MBU. 611011–002. |
| 10/11/1961 | Meyer, Leonard S. (*Christian Century*). Letter to Martin Luther King, Jr. 10/11/1961. Chicago, Ill. (TLS) 1 p. MLKP-MBU. 611011–008. |
| 10/11/1961 | King, Martin Luther, Jr., and Wyatt Tee Walker (SCLC). Telegram to Jack Greenberg. 10/11/1961. [*Atlanta, Ga.*] (PHWc) 1 p. MLKP-MBU. 611011–010. |
| 10/12/1961 | Carter, Welford P. (Calvary Baptist Church). Letter to Martin Luther King, Jr. 10/12/1961. Santa Monica, Calif. (THLS) 1 p. MLKP-MBU. 611012–002. |
| 10/12/1961 | King, Martin Luther, Jr. Letter to the Shifflett family. 10/12/1961. [*Atlanta, Ga.*] (TLc) 1 p. MLKP-MBU. 611012–004. |
| 10/12/1961 | SCLC. "Preliminary report of the annual convention." 10/12/1961. Atlanta, Ga. (TD) 1 p. MLKP-MBU. 611012–008. |
| 10/12/1961 | Horton, Myles (Highlander Folk School). Letter to Andrew Young. 10/12/1961. Monteagle, Tenn. (TLS) 1 p. SCLCR-GAMK: Box 136. 611012–013. |
| 10/12/1961 | Potofsky, Jacob S. (Jacob Samuel), George M. Harrison, and Richard F. Walsh (AFL-CIO). "Report to the Executive Council of the AFL-CIO." 10/12/1961. New York, N.Y. (TD) 29 pp. APRP-DLC: Box 23. 611012–015. |
| 10/13/1961 | Henderson, J. Raymond. Letter to L. Venchael Booth. 10/13/1961. (TLc) 2 pp. MLKP-MBU. 611013–002. |
| 10/13/1961 | AFL-CIO. Press release, "Council rejects Randolph charges, backs AFL-CIO rights record." 10/13/1961. New York, N.Y. (TD) 2 pp. RPP-NN-Sc. 611013–008. |
| 10/13/1961 | Cook, Samuel DuBois (Atlanta University). Letter to Martin Luther King, Jr. 10/13/1961. Atlanta, Ga. (TALS) 1 p. MLKP-MBU. 611013–010. |
| 10/14/1961 | Ebenezer Baptist Church. Press release, "Martin Luther King, Jr. at Ebenezer Sunday." 10/14/1961. Atlanta, Ga. (TD) 1 p. EBCR. 611014–000. |

| | |
|---|---|
| 10/15/1961 | NAACP. Program, Martin Luther King, Jr. at Goler Metropolitan Church. 10/15/1961. Winston-Salem, N.C. (PDS) 12 pp. MCMLK-RWWL: 12.3.0.670. 611015–001. |
| 10/16/1961 | King, Martin Luther, Jr. Statement after meeting with John F. (John Fitzgerald) Kennedy. 10/16/1961. Washington, D.C. (TTa) 1 p. MLKJP-GAMK. 611016–002. |
| **10/16/1961** | **Associated Press. Photo of Martin Luther King, Jr. addressing the press outside of the White House. 10/16/1961. Washington, D.C. (Ph) 1 p. NNAPWW. 611016–023.** |
| 10/17/1961 | Wilkins, Roy (NAACP). Letter to Leslie Dunbar. 10/17/1961. New York, N.Y. (TLS) 3 pp. ASRC-RWWL: Reel 73. 611017–014. |
| 10/18/1961 | SCLC. Press release, "King urges JFK to issue second Emancipation Proclamation." 10/18/1961. Atlanta, Ga. (TD) 1 p. MLKP-MBU. 611018–001. |
| 10/18/1961 | United Kingdom. Ministry of Labour. Foreign Labour Division. Alien work permit order for Martin Luther King, Jr. 10/18/1961. London, England. (TFmS) 2 pp. MCMLK-RWWL: 11.0.0.20. 611018–002. |
| 10/18/1961 | SCLC. Press release, "British TV audiences to hear SCLC president." 10/18/1961. Atlanta, Ga. (TD) 1 p. MLKP-MBU. 611018–004. |
| 10/18/1961 | Tatum, Arlo (Conference to Establish a World Peace Brigade). Form letter to Martin Luther King, Jr. 10/18/1961. Brummana, Lebanon. (TLS) 1 p. MLKP-MBU. 611018–006. |
| 10/19/1961 | Walker, Wyatt Tee (SCLC). Letter to Nathan M. Rudich. 10/19/1961. (TLc) 2 pp. MLKP-MBU. 611019–002. |
| 10/19/1961 | Cochrane, W.R. (Warren Robert) (YMCA). Letter to Martin Luther King, Jr. 10/19/1961. Atlanta, Ga. (TLS) 1 p. MLKP-MBU. 611019–005. |
| 10/19/1961 | SCLC. Minutes, Administrative committee meeting. 10/19/1961. Atlanta, Ga. (AD) 5 pp. MLKP-MBU. 611019–009. |
| 10/20/1961 | Roland, Tom. Letter to Martin Luther King, Jr. 10/20/1961. Berkeley, Calif. (TLS) 2 pp. MLKP-MBU. 611020–001. |
| 10/20/1961 | Harris, Georgia. Letter to Martin Luther King, Jr. 10/20/1961. Detroit, Mich. (ALS) 1 p. MLKP-MBU. 611020–011. |
| 10/21/1961 | Ebenezer Baptist Church. Press release, "'The impotent man,' King Sr.'s topic for Sunday." 10/21/1961. Atlanta, Ga. (TD) 1 p. EBCR. 611021–003. |
| **10/21/1961** | **King, Martin Luther, Jr. Draft, Press release on King's appearance in "Advise and Consent." [*10/21/1961*]. [*Atlanta, Ga.*] (ADd) 3 pp. MLKP-MBU. 611021–007.** |
| 10/22/1961 | King, Martin Luther, Jr. Paul's Letter to American Christians, Sermon delivered at White Rock Baptist Church. [*10/22/1961*]. Philadelphia, Pa. (At) 41.9 min. (1 sound cassette: analog.) WRBC. 611022–002. |
| 10/23/1961 | King, Martin Luther, Jr. Letter to Ernest R. Rather. 10/23/1961. [*Atlanta, Ga.*] (TLc) 1 p. MLKP-MBU. 611023–001. |
| 10/23/1961 | King, Martin Luther, Jr. Letter to George Holmes. 10/23/1961. [*Atlanta, Ga.*] (TLc) 1 p. MLKP-MBU. 611023–008. |
| 10/24/1961 | King, Martin Luther, Jr. Letter to Robert Rankin. 10/24/1961. [*Atlanta, Ga.*] (TLc) 1 p. MLKP-MBU. 611024–003. |
| 10/24/1961 | King, Martin Luther, Jr. Form letter to G. Ramachandran. 10/24/1961. [*Atlanta, Ga.*] (TLc) 1 p. MLKP-MBU. 611024–005. |
| 10/24/1961 | Goldburg, Robert Eugene (Congregation Mishkan Israel). Letter to Martin Luther King, Jr. 10/24/1961. Hamden, Conn. (THLS) 1 p. MLKP-MBU. 611024–007. |
| 10/24/1961 | King, Martin Luther, Jr. Letter to Glenn E. Smiley. 10/24/1961. [*Atlanta, Ga.*] (TLc) 2 pp. MLKP-MBU. 611024–010. |
| 10/25/1961 | King, Martin Luther, Jr. (SCLC). Letter to Russell Buckner. 10/25/1961. [*Atlanta, Ga.*] (TLc) 2 pp. MLKP-MBU. 611025–000. |
| 10/25/1961 | [*Crane, Sylvia E.*] Telegram to Robert F. Kennedy. 10/25/1961. (THWc) 1 p. (Enclosed in 611025–010.) MLKP-MBU. 611025–003. |
| 10/25/1961 | Crane, Sylvia E. Letter to Martin Luther King, Jr. 10/25/1961. New York, N.Y. (THLS) 1 p. (Contains enclosure 611025–003.) MLKP-MBU. 611025–010. |
| 10/26/1961 | Meany, George (AFL-CIO). Letter to Martin Luther King, Jr. 10/26/1961. Washington, D.C. (THLS) 2 pp. MLKP-MBU. 611026–004. |
| 10/27/1961 | SCLC. Program, "A Conference on Freedom and the First Amendment." 10/27/1961. Chapel Hill, N.C. (PD) 4 pp. MLKP-MBU. 611027–002. |
| 10/27/1961 | *Columbia Owl.* Invitation to reception honoring Martin Luther King, Jr. 10/27/1961. New York, N.Y. (TL) 1 p. MLKP-MBU. 611027–008. |
| 10/27/1961 | Nuyl, P. te (Omroepvereniging Vara). Letter to Martin Luther King, Jr. 10/27/1961. Hilversum, Holland. (TLS) 1 p. MLKP-MBU. 611027–010. |

| | | |
|---|---|---|
| 10/27/1961 | SCLC. Press release, "Dr. King departs for London." [*10/27/1961*]. Atlanta, Ga. (TD) 1 p. MLKP-MBU. 611027–013. |
| 10/27/1961 | *Columbia Owl.* Program, Columbia University affair. 10/27/1961. New York, N.Y. (THD) 1 p. MLKP-MBU. 611027–015. |
| 10/27/1961 | Cox, John W. (Bell Neighborhood Center). Letter to Martin Luther King, Jr. 10/27/1961. Cleveland, Ohio. (THLS) 1 p. MLKP-MBU. 611027–016. |
| 10/29/1961 | King, Martin Luther, Jr. Interview by John Freeman on "Face to Face." [*10/29/1961*]. [*London, England.*] (At) 30 min. (1 sound cassette: analog.) MLKJP-GAMK. 611029–001. |
| 10/29/1961 | Silvey, Larry P. Letter to Martin Luther King, Jr. 10/29/1961. Stillwater, Okla. (TLS) 2 pp. MLKJP-GAMK: Box 65. 611029–002. |
| 10/30/1961 | Penney, Marjorie (Fellowship House and Farm). Letter to Martin Luther King, Jr. 10/30/1961. Philadelphia, Pa. (TALS) 2 pp. MLKP-MBU. 611030–009. |
| 10/30/1961 | King, Martin Luther, Jr. Progress in the Area of Race Relations, Address at Central Hall Westminster. 10/30/1961. London, England. (THTad) 13 pp. LJCC-UK-LoLPL: MS3297. 611030–014. |
| 10/31/1961 | King, Martin Luther, Jr. Letter to David A. Vermilyea. 10/31/1961. [*Atlanta, Ga.*] (TLc) 1 p. MLKP-MBU. 611031–001. |
| 10/31/1961 | Braden, Anne (Southern Conference Educational Fund). Letter to Martin Luther King, Jr. 10/31/1961. Louisville, Ky. (TLS) 2 pp. (Contains enclosures 611031–012 & 610621–013.) MLKP-MBU. 611031–011. |
| 10/31/1961 | Cohen, Robert. Form letter outlining qualifications. [*10/31/1961*]. (TLS) 1 p. (Enclosed in 611031–011. Contains enclosure 610621–013.) MLKP-MBU. 611031–012. |
| 10/31/1961 | Baldrige, Letitia (U.S. White House). Telegram to Martin Luther King, Jr. 10/31/1961. Washington, D.C. (PHWSr) 1 p. MLKP-MBU. 611031–013. |
| 1/1961–11/1961 | "Meetings and special events for 1961." 1/1961–11/1961. (TD) 1 p. MLKP-MBU. 611100–001. |
| 11/1961 | King, Martin Luther, Jr. (SCLC). Form letter to Brother-in-Christ. 11/1961. Atlanta, Ga. (TLS) 1 p. MLKJP-GAMK: Vault Box 4. 611100–002. |
| 11/1961 | H.M. Inspector of Taxes (United Kingdom). Letter to Martin Luther King, Jr. 11/1961. London, England. (TL) 2 pp. MLKP-MBU. 611100–006. |
| 11/1/1961 | [*Levison, Stanley D.*] Draft, Letter to Friend. [*11/1/1961*]. (TLd) 1 p. (Enclosed in 611101–005, pp. 318–319 in this volume.) MLKP-MBU. 611101–000. |
| 11/1/1961 | Tilly, Dorothy Rogers (Southern Regional Council). Letter to Martin Luther King, Jr. 11/1/1961. Atlanta, Ga. (THLS) 1 p. MLKP-MBU. 611101–002. |
| 11/1/1961 | Suudi, Ann E.G. (Granada TV Network Limited). Letter to Martin Luther King, Jr. 11/1/1961. London, England. (TLS) 1 p. MLKP-MBU. 611101–010. |
| 11/1/1961 | King, Martin Luther, Jr., and Wyatt Tee Walker (SCLC). Telegram to Everett Hutchinson. 11/1/1961. [*Atlanta, Ga.*] (TWc) 1 p. MLKP-MBU. 611101–021. |
| 11/1/1961 | Jones, Clarence B. Draft, Letter to Harry H. Wachtel. [*11/1/1961*]. New York, N.Y. (THLd) 4 pp. (Enclosed in 611101–005, pp. 318–319 in this volume.) MLKP-MBU. 611101–022. |
| 11/2/1961 | McDonald, Dora E. Letter to Stanley D. Levison. 11/2/1961. [*Atlanta, Ga.*] (TLc) 1 p. (Contains enclosure 611102–005). MLKP-MBU. 611102–004. |
| 11/2/1961 | King, Martin Luther, Jr. Letter to Eugene Cotton and Richard Watt. 11/2/1961. [*Atlanta, Ga.*] (TLc) 2 pp. (Enclosed in 611102–004). MLKP-MBU. 611102–005. |
| 11/2/1961 | Smiley, Glenn E. (FOR). Letter to Martin Luther King, Jr. 11/2/1961. Nyack, N.Y. (TLS) 1 p. MLKP-MBU. 611102–009. |
| 11/2/1961 | Standish, Thomas A. (Yale University). Letter to Martin Luther King, Jr. 11/2/1961. New Haven, Conn. (TLS) 1 p. MLKP-MBU. 611102–010. |
| 11/2/1961 | King, Martin Luther, Jr. Letter to Marjorie Penney. 11/2/1961. [*Atlanta, Ga.*] (TLc) 1 p. MLKP-MBU. 611102–011. |
| 11/2/1961 | King, Martin Luther, Jr. Letter to Georgia Harris. 11/2/1961. [*Atlanta, Ga.*] (TLc) 1 p. MLKP-MBU. 611102–012. |
| 11/2/1961 | Hartsfield, William Berry (Atlanta. Office of the Mayor). Letter to Wyatt Tee Walker. 11/2/1961. Atlanta, Ga. (TLS) 2 pp. SCLCR-GAMK: Box 33. 611102–013. |
| 11/2/1961 | "Basic questions for interview with Martin Luther King, Jr." 11/2/1961. (THD) 6 pp. MLKP-MBU. 611102–014. |
| 11/2/1961 | King, Martin Luther, Jr., and Wyatt Tee Walker (SCLC). Letter to Robert F. Kennedy. [*11/2/1961*]. [*Atlanta, Ga.*] (TLc) 1 p. MLKP-MBU. 611102–015. |
| 11/3/1961 | Wood, James R. (SCLC). Press release, "SCLC wins desegregation suit." 11/3/1961. Atlanta, Ga. (TD) 1 p. MLKP-MBU. 611103–001. |

| | |
|---|---|
| 11/3/1961 | King, Martin Luther, Jr. Letter to George Meany. 11/3/1961. [*Atlanta, Ga.*] (TLc) 2 pp. MLKP-MBU. 611103–003. |
| 11/3/1961 | King, Martin Luther, Jr. Letter to Herbert C. Nelson. 11/3/1961. [*Atlanta, Ga.*] (TLc) 2 pp. MLKP-MBU. 611103–005. |
| 11/3/1961 | King, Martin Luther, Jr. Letter to Robert F. Kennedy. 11/3/1961. [*Atlanta, Ga.*] (TLc) 1 p. MLKP-MBU. 611103–006. |
| 11/3/1961 | Congregation Temple de Hirsch. *Temple Tidings* 53, no. 10 (3 November 1961). Seattle, Wash. (TD) 2 pp. THSR-WaU-AR. 611103–009. |
| 11/5/1961 | Courlander, Harold. Letter to Martin Luther King, Jr. 11/5/1961. Bethesda, Md. (TLS) 2 pp. MLKP-MBU. 611105–000. |
| 11/6/1961 | MIA. Program, "A testimonial of love and appreciation." 11/6/1961. [*Montgomery, Ala.*] (TD) 2 pp. HG-GAMK. 611106–000. |
| 11/6/1961 | Wilkins, Tommy. Letter to Martin Luther King, Jr. 11/6/1961. Atlanta, Ga. (TLS) 1 p. MLKP-MBU. 611106–009. |
| 11/6/1961 | King, Martin Luther, Jr. "Philosophy behind the Student Movement," Address at the annual meeting of the Fellowship of the Concerned of the Southern Regional Council. [*11/6/1961*]. [*Atlanta, Ga.*] (TAD) 14 pp. MCMLK-RWWL: 2.3.0.20. 611106–011. |
| 11/7/1961 | Jackson, Herman. Letter to Martin Luther King, Jr. 11/7/1961. Raiford, Fla. (ALS) 2 pp. MLKP-MBU. 611107–001. |
| 11/7/1961 | King, Martin Luther, Jr. Letter to Robert Brank Fulton. 11/7/1961. Atlanta, Ga. (THLS) 2 pp. RBFP. 611107–002. |
| 11/7/1961 | King, Martin Luther, Jr. Letter to L. John (Lewis John) Collins. 11/7/1961. [*Atlanta, Ga.*] (TLc) 1 p. MLKP-MBU. 611107–008. |
| 11/7/1961 | King, Martin Luther, Jr. Letter to John L. Moore. 11/7/1961. [*Atlanta, Ga.*] (TLc) 1 p. MLKP-MBU. 611107–009. |
| 11/7/1961 | King, Martin Luther, Jr. Letter to Elton Trueblood. 11/7/1961. [*Atlanta, Ga.*] (TLc) 1 p. MLKP-MBU. 611107–010. |
| 11/7/1961 | King, Martin Luther, Jr. Letter to Hugh Carney. 11/7/1961. [*Atlanta, Ga.*] (TLc) 1 p. MLKP-MBU. 611107–011. |
| 11/7/1961 | King, Martin Luther, Jr. Letter to Anne Braden. 11/7/1961. [*Atlanta, Ga.*] (TLc) 1 p. MLKP-MBU. 611107–012. |
| 10/31/1961–11/7/1961 | King, Martin Luther, Jr. (SCLC). Form letter to Brother-in-Christ. 10/31/1961–11/7/1961. Atlanta, Ga. (TLS) 1 p. SCLCR-GAMK: Box 116. 611107–013. |
| 11/8/1961 | Smothers, James R. (United Negro College Fund). Letter to Martin Luther King, Jr. 11/8/1961. New York, N.Y. (TLS) 1 p. MLKP-MBU. 611108–009. |
| 11/8/1961 | Gaylord, Dan, et al., Defendants. "Declaratory judgment and a permanent injunction," *Shuttlesworth v. Gaylord*. 11/8/1961. (TD) 7 pp. JTWP-AB: Box 7. 611108–012. |
| 11/9/1961 | King, Martin Luther, Jr. Press release, Secretary of Defense consents to address segregated meeting. 11/9/1961. (TD) 1 p. MLKJP-GAMK: Box 108. 611109–000. |
| 11/9/1961–1/10/1961 | Mount Zion Baptist Church. "Itinerary—Martin Luther King, Jr." 11/9/1961–11/10/1961. Seattle, Wash. (TD) 1 p. MLKP-MBU. 611110–003. |
| 11/10/1961 | Mount Zion Baptist Church. Program, "Third annual lecture." 11/10/1961. Seattle, Wash. (PD) 4 pp. MLKP-MBU. 611110–005. |
| 11/10/1961 | Walker, Wyatt Tee (SCLC). "The Deep South in Social Revolution," Address at the fifteenth annual conference of the National Association of Intergroup Relations Officials. 11/10/1961. San Francisco, Calif. (TD) 16 pp. SCLCR-GAMK: Box 37. 611110–012. |
| 11/10/1961 | Dunbar, Leslie (Southern Regional Council). Letter to Stephen R. Currier. 11/10/1961. (TLc) 3 pp. ASRC-RWWL: Reel 73. 611110–015. |
| 11/11/1961 | King, Martin Luther, Jr. (SCLC). Form letter to Friend. 11/11/1961. Atlanta, Ga. (TLS) 1 p. (Contains enclosure 611111–002). JBMP-NcD: Box 498. 611111–000. |
| 11/11/1961 | Taylor, Gardner C., Fred L. Shuttlesworth, Harry Belafonte, Harry Emerson Fosdick, Edward E. Klein, and Harry Van Arsdale. Donation card, "Appeal for human dignity now." 11/11/1961. Atlanta, Ga. (TDS) 2 pp. (Enclosed in 611111–000.) UERR-PPiU-IS. 611111–002. |
| 11/12/1961 | Wesley Foundation at Mankato State College. Program, "Third annual lectureship." 11/12/1961. Mankato, Minn. (PD) 4 pp. MLKP-MBU. 611112–001. |
| 11/12/1961 | Chalmers, Allan Knight (NAACP Legal Defense and Educational Fund). Letter to Martin Luther King, Jr. 11/12/1961. New York, N.Y. (TALS) 1 p. MLKP-MBU. 611112–003. |
| 11/14/1961 | McDonald, Dora E. Letter to Nicholas W. Raballa. 11/14/1961. [*Atlanta, Ga.*] (TLc) 1 p. MLKP-MBU. 611114–008. |

| | |
|---|---|
| 11/29/1961 | Eskridge, Chauncey (McCoy, Ming & Leighton). Letter to Martin Luther King, Jr. 11/29/1961. Chicago, Ill. (ALS) 1 p. (Contains enclosure 611129–008.) MCMLK-RWWL: 11.0.0.30. 611129–007. |
| 11/29/1961 | "Power of attorney." 11/29/1961. (THD) 1 p. (Enclosed in 611129–007.) MCMLK-RWWL: 11.0.0.30. 611129–008. |
| 12/1/1960–11/30/1961 | Ebenezer Baptist Church. "Annual report." 12/1/1960–11/30/1961. Atlanta, Ga. (TD) 37 pp. (Marginal comments by King.) EBCR. 611130–003. |
| 11/30/1961 | Nelson, Boris Erich (University of Toledo). Letter to Martin Luther King, Jr. 11/30/1961. Toledo, Ohio. (THLS) 1 p. MLKJP-GAMK: Box 42. 611130–007. |
| 12/1961 | King, Martin Luther, Jr. "Martin Luther King says: 'I'd Do It All Again,' An Interview by Bradford Daniel." *Sepia* (December 1961). (PD) 5 pp. 611200–005. |
| 12/1961 | Young, Andrew. Memo to SCLC, Citizenship School Committee, American Missionary Association, Marshall Field Foundation. [*12/1961*]. (TD) 3 pp. SCLCR-GAMK: Box 136. 611200–019. |
| 12/1/1961 | King, Martin Luther, Jr. Telegram to Nelson A. (Nelson Aldrich) Rockefeller. 12/1/1961. [*Atlanta, Ga.*] (TWc) 1 p. MLKP-MBU. 611201–000. |
| 12/1/1961 | Ebenezer Baptist Church. Press release, "'The Secret of Adjustment,' King Jr.'s topic at Ebenezer." 12/1/1961. Atlanta, Ga. (TD) 1 p. EBCR. 611201–005. |
| 12/1/1961 | Spraitzar, Evelyn R. Letter to Martin Luther King, Jr. 12/1/1961. Chatham, N.J. (TALS) 1 p. MLKJP-GAMK: Box 10. 611201–008. |
| 12/3/1961 | Mizer, Audrey V. Letter to Martin Luther King, Jr. 12/3/1961. Coshocton, Ohio. (TLS) 2 pp. MLKJP-GAMK: Box 61. 611203–001. |
| 12/4/1961 | King, Martin Luther, Jr. Letter to Eugene Exman. 12/4/1961. [*Atlanta, Ga.*] (TLc) 1 p. MCMLK-RWWL: 2.1.1.10. 611204–008. |
| 12/4/1961 | Ebenezer Baptist Church. Program, "Installation service." 12/4/1961. Atlanta, Ga. (TD) 4 pp. MLKJP-GAMK: Vault. 611204–010. |
| 12/5/1961 | Wachtel, Harry H. (Wachtel & Michaelson). Letter to Martin Luther King, Jr. 12/5/1961. Washington, D.C. (TLS) 1 p. MLKJP-GAMK: Box 25. 611205–007. |
| 12/5/1961 | SCLC. Press release, "SCLC charges injustice in Seals case." 12/5/1961. Atlanta, Ga. (TD) 1 p. SCLCR-GAMK. 611205–011. |
| 12/6/1961 | Ramachandran, G. (*Gandhi Marg*). Letter to Martin Luther King, Jr. 12/6/1961. New Delhi, India. (TALS) 1 p. (Contains enclosure 611000–003.) MLKJP-GAMK: Box 11. 611206–001. |
| 12/6/1961 | King, Martin Luther, Jr., and Wyatt Tee Walker (SCLC). Form letter to Friends. 12/6/1961. [*Atlanta, Ga.*] (TLc) 1 p. SCLCR-GAMK: Box 153. 611206–003. |
| 12/7/1961 | King, Martin Luther, Jr. (SCLC). "The Future of Integration," Address delivered at Los Angeles Valley College. 12/7/1961. Van Nuys, Calif. (At) 55 min. (1 sound cassette: analog.) CVnL. 611207–002. |
| 12/7/1961 | Seay, S. S. (Solomon Snowden). Letter to Wyatt Tee Walker. 12/7/1961. Montgomery, Ala. (TLS) 1 p. SCLCR-GAMK: Box 35. 611207–004. |
| 12/8/1961 | Maguire, John David (Wesleyan University). Letter to Martin Luther King, Jr. 12/8/1961. Middletown, Conn. (TALS) 2 pp. MLKP-MBU. 611208–000. |
| 12/9/1961 | Lewis, William (International Brotherhood of Teamsters Local 237). Letter to Martin Luther King, Jr. 12/9/1961. New York, N.Y. (THLS) 1 p. MLKJP-GAMK: Box 50. 611209–005. |
| 12/10/1961 | King, Martin Luther, Jr. Racial Justice and Nonviolent Resistance, Address delivered at Chapman College. 12/10/1961. Orange, Calif. (At) 47.5 min. (1 sound cassette: analog.) FMPL-SCA-COrC. 611210–001. |
| 12/11/1961 | King, Martin Luther, Jr. Draft, Address at the fourth constitutional convention of the AFL-CIO. [*12/11/1961*]. (TADd) 5 pp. MCMLK-RWWL: 2.3.0.140. 611211–002. |
| 12/11/1961 | King, Martin Luther, Jr. Letter to Theodore Woodrow Kheel. 12/11/1961. [*Atlanta, Ga.*] (TLc) 2 pp. MLKP-MBU. 611211–005. |
| 12/11/1961 | King, Martin Luther, Jr. Letter to Virgil A. Wood. 12/11/1961. [*Atlanta, Ga.*] (TLc) 1 p. MLKJP-GAMK: Box 27. 611211–017. |
| 12/11/1961 | Citizenship Education Program. Financial statement, "Citizenship Education Program in the South, Field Foundation." 12/11/1961. (TD) 1 p. SCLCR-GAMK: Box 136. 611211–026. |
| 12/12/1961 | SCLC. Press release, "Two-hundred fifty arrested in pray-in." 12/12/1961. Atlanta, Ga. (TD) 1 p. MLKJP-GAMK: Box 28. 611212–006. |
| 12/13/1961 | SNCC. Press release, "Latest from Albany." 12/13/1961. Atlanta, Ga. (TD) 4 pp. ACLUR-NjP-SC. 611213–000. |
| 12/13/1961 | King, Martin Luther, Jr. Letter to Edward D. Ball. 12/13/1961. [*Atlanta, Ga.*] (TLc) 2 pp. (Enclosed in 611214–010.) SCLCR-GAMK: Box 3. 611213–003. |

643

| | | |
|---|---|---|
| 12/13/1961 | SCLC. "Revised list of executive board." 12/13/1961. Atlanta, Ga. (TD) 4 pp. SCLCR-GAMK: Box 36. 611213–004. |
| 12/13/1961 | King, Martin Luther, Jr. Letter to Mamie Massey. 12/13/1961. [*Atlanta, Ga.*] (TLc) 1 p. MLKJP-GAMK: Box 61. 611213–006. |
| 12/13/1961 | King, Martin Luther, Jr. Letter to John M. Pierson. 12/13/1961. [*Atlanta, Ga.*] (TLc) 2 pp. MLKJP-GAMK: Box 61. 611213–008. |
| 12/14/1961 | SCLC. Press release, "King answers southern editor's blast." 12/14/1961. Atlanta, Ga. (TD) 2 pp. SAVFC-WHi. 611214–002. |
| 12/14/1961 | Maxwell, O. Clay (National Sunday School and Baptist Training Union Congress). Letter to Martin Luther King, Jr. 12/14/1961. New York, N.Y. (TLS) 1 p. MLKJP-GAMK: Box 15. 611214–004. |
| 1/1/1961–<br>12/14/1961 | "1961 speaking engagements, Dr. Martin Luther King, Jr." 1/1/1961–12/14/1961. (TD) 2 pp. MLKJP-GAMK: Box 12. 611214–008. |
| 12/14/1961 | King, Martin Luther, Jr. Letter to Edward D. Ball. 12/14/1961. [*Atlanta, Ga.*] (TLc) 1 p. (Contains enclosure 611213–003.) MLKJP-GAMK: Box 16. 611214–010. |
| 12/14/1961 | King, Martin Luther, Jr. Letter to Robert T. Handy. 12/14/1961. [*Atlanta, Ga.*] (TLc) 1 p. MLKJP-GAMK: Box 6. 611214–012. |
| 12/14/1961 | SCLC. Press release, "Southern integration leader to speak here." 12/14/1961. Atlanta, Ga. (TD) 1 p. MLKJP-GAMK: Box 33. 611214–017. |
| 12/15/1961 | Pierce, Harold E. (West Park Clinic). Letter to Martin Luther King, Jr. 12/15/1961. Philadelphia, Pa. (TLS) 4 pp. MLKJP-GAMK: Box 7. 611215–001. |
| 12/15/1961 | McWilliams, Carey (*The Nation*). Letter to Martin Luther King, Jr. 12/15/1961. New York, N.Y. (TLS) 1 p. MLKJP-GAMK: Box 17. 611215–003. |
| 12/15/1961 | Page, Marion S., et al. "Complaint," *Page v. Kelley*. 12/15/1961. Albany, Ga. (THDc) 4 pp. AMR-GAMK: Box 1. 611215–008. |
| **12/16/1961** | **United Press International. Photo of Laurie Pritchett reading Martin Luther King, Jr., and William G. Anderson their rights. 12/16/1961. Albany, Ga. (Ph) 1 p. UPIR-NNBETT. 611216–001.** |
| 12/16/1961 | King, Martin Luther, Jr. (SCLC). Form letter to Pastor. 12/16/1961. Atlanta, Ga. (TL) 1 p. MLKJP-GAMK: Box 33. 611216–003. |
| 12/16/1961 | Kelley, Asa D. (Albany. Office of the Mayor). Letter to William G. Anderson and Marion S. Page. 12/16/1961. (TLc) 1 p. AMR-GAMK: Box 1. 611216–010. |
| **12/16/1961** | **Sumter County Jail ledger. 12/16/1961. Americus, Ga. (AD) 2 pp. SCCO. 611216–012.** |
| 12/17/1961 | Ebenezer Baptist Church. Press release, "'God's love,' Dr. King Jr. at Ebenezer." 12/17/1961. Atlanta, Ga. (THD) 1 p. EBCR. 611217–004. |
| 12/17/1961 | McGowan, C.L. (U.S. FBI). Memo to Alex Rosen. 12/17/1961. (THLI) 3 pp. FBIDG-NN-Sc: Bureau File 157-6-2-229. 611217–005. |
| 12/17/1961 | Pamp, Oke G. Letter to Martin Luther King, Jr. 12/17/1961. Batavia, Ill. (ALS) 1 p. MLKJP-GAMK: Box 18. 611217–006. |
| 12/17/1961 | SCLC. Press release, "Abernathy issues call for nation-wide protest at Albany, Ga." 12/17/1961. Atlanta, Ga. (TD) 3 pp. MLKJP-GAMK: Box 28. 611217–007. |
| **12/17/1961** | **Abernathy, Ralph. Telegram to Martin Luther King, Jr. 12/17/1961. Atlanta, Ga. (PWSr) 1 p. MCMLK-RWWL: 1.1.0.70. 611217–008.** |
| 12/17/1961 | Special Agent in Charge, Atlanta, Ga. (U.S. FBI). Telegram to J. Edgar Hoover. 12/17/1961. Atlanta, Ga. (THW) 2 pp. FBIDG-NN-Sc: Bureau File 157-6-2-2. 611217–009. |
| 12/18/1961 | Auer, Bernhard M. (*Time*). Letter to Martin Luther King, Jr. 12/18/1961. New York, N.Y. (TLS) 1 p. MLKJP-GAMK: Box 23. 611218–008. |
| 12/18/1961 | Overton, L. Joseph (Negro Labor Committee). Telegram to Robert F. Kennedy. 12/18/1961. New York, N.Y. (PWSr) 1 p. CRDPad-DJ: Department File 144–101–19M–9. 611218–021. |
| 12/18/1961 | Levison, Stanley D. (American Jewish Congress). Telegram to Robert F. Kennedy. 12/18/1961. New York, N.Y. (PWSr) 1 p. CRDPad-DJ: Department File 144–101–19M–9. 611218–025. |
| 12/19/1961 | King, Martin Luther, Jr. (SCLC). Form letter to Friend. 12/19/1961. Atlanta, Ga. (TLS) 1 p. JWWP-DHU-S: Box 13. 611219–000. |
| 12/19/1961 | Liggett, Thomas J. (Evangelical Seminary of Puerto Rico). Letter to Martin Luther King, Jr. 12/19/1961. Río Piedras, Puerto Rico. (TLS) 1 p. MLKP-MBU. 611219–003. |
| 12/20/1961 | McDonald, Dora E. Letter to G. Ramachandran. 12/20/1961. [*Atlanta, Ga.*] (TLc) 1 p. MLKJP-GAMK: Box 11. 611220–001. |
| 12/20/1961 | Barnett, Claude (Associated Negro Press). Letter to Martin Luther King, Jr. 12/20/1961. Chicago, Ill. (THLS) 1 p. MLKJP-GAMK: Box 62. 611220–003. |

| | | |
|---|---|---|
| 12/20/1961 | King, Martin Luther, Jr. Letter to Welford P. Carter. 12/20/1961. [*Atlanta, Ga.*] (TLc) 1 p. MLKP-MBU. 611220–004. | Calendar |
| 12/20/1961 | Eaton, Herbert H. (Dexter Avenue Baptist Church). Letter to Martin Luther King, Jr. 12/20/1961. Montgomery, Ala. (TLS) 1 p. MLKJP-GAMK: Box 8. 611220–006. | |
| 12/20/1961 | King, Martin Luther, Jr. Letter to Donald E. Secord. 12/20/1961. Atlanta, Ga. (TLS) 2 pp. DSEC. 611220–009. | |
| 12/20/1961 | Potter, John (KYW-TV). Letter to Martin Luther King, Jr. 12/20/1961. Cleveland, Ohio. (THLS) 1 p. MLKP-MBU. 611220–012. | |
| 12/21/1961 | King, Martin Luther, Jr. Letter to George M. Houser. 12/21/1961. [*Atlanta, Ga.*] (TLc) 1 p. LewBP. 611221–001. | |
| 12/22/1961 | King, Martin Luther, Jr. Letter to Joseph B. Cumming. 12/22/1961. [*Atlanta, Ga.*] (TLc) 2 pp. MLKJP-GAMK: Box 18. 611222–000. | |
| 12/22/1961 | Meany, George (AFL-CIO). Letter to Martin Luther King, Jr. 12/22/1961. Washington, D.C. (THLS) 1 p. MLKP-MBU. 611222–002. | |
| 12/23/1961 | Ebenezer Baptist Church. Press release, "Martin Luther King, Jr. will fill pulpit at Ebenezer Sunday." 12/23/1961. Atlanta, Ga. (TD) 1 p. MLKP-MBU. 611223–000. | |
| 12/26/1961 | Handy, W.T. (William Talbout) (St. Mark Methodist Church). Letter to Martin Luther King, Jr. 12/26/1961. Baton Rouge, La. (TLS) 2 pp. MLKJP-GAMK: Box 4. 611226–001. | |
| 12/27/1961 | Jordan, Elizabeth S. Letter to Martin Luther King, Jr. [*12/27/1961*]. (TLI) 1 p. MLKP-MBU. 611227–000. | |
| 12/29/1961 | Kennedy, Robert F. (U.S. Dept. of Justice). Report to the President on the Department of Justice's activities in the field of Civil Rights. 12/29/1961. [*Washington, D.C.*] (THD) 4 pp. JFKWHSFHW-MBJFK: Box 14. 611229–002. | |
| 12/30/1961 | Ebenezer Baptist Church. Press release, "These all died in the faith." 12/30/1961. Atlanta, Ga. (TD) 1 p. EBCR. 611230–000. | |
| 12/30/1961 | Carey, Altina (Educational Communications Corporation). Letter to Martin Luther King, Jr. 12/30/1961. Beverly Hills, Calif. (THLS) 1 p. MLKJP-GAMK: Box 61. 611230–001. | |
| 12/30/1961 | Clark, Joseph S. Letter to Martin Luther King, Jr. 12/30/1961. Brooklyn, N.Y. (TALS) 1 p. MLKJP-GAMK: Box 62. 611230–004. | |
| 12/31/1961 | King, Martin Luther, Jr. "Remaining Awake Through a Great Revolution." [*12/31/1961*]. (At) 32.9 min. (1 sound cassette: analog.) MLKJP-GAMK: Box 62. 611231–001. | |
| 1962 | Gandhi Society for Human Rights, Inc. Pamphlet, "...striking at the root." [*1962*]. New York, N.Y. (TDc) 6 pp. MCMLK-RWWL: 1.1.0.48640. 620000–029. | |
| 1962 | King, Martin Luther, Jr. Outline, "The Meaning of the Present Struggle." [*1962*]. [*Atlanta, Ga.*] (ADf) 4 pp. MCMLK-RWWL: 2.3.0.1020. 620000–035. | |
| 1962 | King, Martin Luther, Jr. "Nonviolence and Racial Justice." From: Harold Fey and Margaret Frakes, eds. *The Christian Century Reader*, New York: Association Press, 1962. (PD) 6 pp. (Reprint of 2/6/57 *Christian Century*). 620000–038. | |
| 1961–1962 | King, Coretta Scott. SCLC contribution card. 1961–1962. Atlanta, Ga. (TD) 2 pp. CSKC. 620000–074. | |
| 1962 | SCLC. "The SCLC voter registration prospectus for 1962." 1962. (TD) 22 pp. (Enclosed in 620322–004.) CSKC. 620000–075. | |
| 1962 | SCLC. Citizenship School attendance records. [*1962*]. (TD) 4 pp. SCLCR-GAMK: Box 137. 620000–144. | |
| 1962 | King, Martin Luther, Jr. (SCLC). Form letter to Friend of Freedom. [*1962*]. Atlanta, Ga. (TLS) 1 p. SCLCR-GAMK: Box 63. 620000–196. | |
| 1962 | Zinn, Howard (Spelman College). *Albany: A Study in National Responsibility*. Atlanta: Southern Regional Council, 1962. (PD) 41 pp. FFPP-GEU-S: Box 27. 620000–239. | |
| 1962 | American Committee on Africa. "Appeal for Action Against Apartheid." [*1962*]. New York, N.Y. (TD) 3 pp. SCLCR-GAMK: Box 34. 620000–240. | |
| 1962 | Student Interracial Ministry. "Statement of purpose." [*1962*.] (TD) 10 pp. MLKJP-GAMK: Box 132. 620000–246. | |
| 1/1962 | King, Martin Luther, Jr. Telegram to Gardner C. Taylor. [*1/1962*]. Atlanta, Ga. (TLc) 1 p. MLKJP-GAMK: Box 7. 620100–002 | |
| 1/1962 | Draft, Press release, United drive to increase voter registration announced. 1/1962. Atlanta, Ga. (TDd) 2 pp. MLKJP-GAMK: Box 22. 620100–004. | |
| 1/1962 | Houser, George M. (American Committee on Africa). "A report on a journey through rebel Angola." [*1/1962*]. New York, N.Y. (TD) 11 pp. ACA-OYesA: Box 79. 620100–015. | |
| 1/1962 | Hayden, Tom (Students for a Democratic Society). *Revolution in Mississippi: Special Report*. 1/1962. (PD) 32 pp. MJMCRC-MsHaU: Box 2. 620100–018. | 645 |

| | | |
|---|---|---|
| 1/3/1962 | SCLC. Press release, "King lauds NAACP head as great American leader." 1/3/1962. Atlanta, Ga. (TD) 1 p. MLKJP-GAMK. 620103–000. |
| 1/3/1962 | Updyke, Elaine L. (United Liberal Church). Letter to Martin Luther King, Jr. 1/3/1962. Atlanta, Ga. (TLS) 1 p. MLKP-MBU. 620103–003. |
| 1/4/1962 | Special Agent in Charge, New York, N.Y. (U.S. FBI). Memo to J. Edgar Hoover. 1/4/1962. New York, N.Y. (THL) 1 p. RFBI-DNA: Bureau File 100–392452–132. 620104–005. |
| 1/5/1962 | Smiley, Glenn E. (FOR). Letter to Martin Luther King, Jr. 1/5/1962. Nyack, N.Y. (TLS) 1 p. MLKJP-GAMK: Box 10. 620105–004. |
| 1/5/1962 | Peters, James D., and Richard A. Battles (SCLC). Telegram to Martin Luther King, Jr. 1/5/1962. Bridgeport, Conn. (PHWSr) 1 p. MLKJP-GAMK: Box 4. 620105–008. |
| 1/4/1962–1/5/1962 | SCLC. Minutes, "SCLC board-staff consultation." 1/4/1962–1/5/1962. Atlanta, Ga. (TD) 5 pp. MLKJP-GAMK: Box 29. 620105–009. |
| 1/6/1962 | Ebenezer Baptist Church. Press release, "'The ultimate triumph of goodness,' Martin Luther King's topic at Ebenezer." 1/6/1962. Atlanta, Ga. (TD) 1 p. EBCR. 620106–001. |
| 1/6/1962 | Ebenezer Baptist Church. Press release, "Martin Luther King Jr. to give New Year sermon at Ebenezer Sunday." 1/6/1962. Atlanta, Ga. (THD) 1 p. (Marginal comments by King.) EBCR. 620106–002. |
| 1/8/1962 | Zinn, Howard (Spelman College). "Albany: Special report of Southern Regional Council." 1/8/1962. Atlanta, Ga. (TD) 37 pp. ACLUR-NjP-SC. 620108–000. |
| 1/8/1962 | Hoover, J. Edgar (U.S. FBI). Memo to Robert F. Kennedy. 1/8/1962. (THL) 1 p. RFBI-DNA: Bureau File 100–392452–131. 620108–004. |
| 1/9/1962 | Wilson, John M. (Ohio Council of Churches). Letter to Martin Luther King, Jr. 1/9/1962. Columbus, Ohio (TALS) 1 p. (Contains enclosure 620131–001.) MLKP-MBU. 620109–000. |
| 1/9/1962 | King, Martin Luther, Jr. Letter to Larry P. Silvey. 1/9/1962. [*Atlanta, Ga.*] (TLc) 2 pp. MLKJP-GAMK: Box 65. 620109–004. |
| 1/10/1962 | Langlie, Arthur B. (National Safety Council). Letter to Martin Luther King, Jr. 1/10/1962. Chicago, Ill. (THLS) 1 p. (Contains enclosure 620110–005.) MLKJP-GAMK: Box 17. 620110–002. |
| 1/10/1962 | Wilkins, Roy (NAACP). Letter to Editor of *Time* magazine. 1/10/1962. (THLc) 2 pp. NAACPP-DLC: Group III-A263. 620110–003. |
| 1/10/1962 | National Safety Council. "Purposes, operating principles and policies." 1/10/1962. [*Chicago, Ill.*] (TD) 7 pp. (Enclosed in 620110–002.) MLKJP-GAMK: Box 17. 620110–005. |
| 1/11/1962 | Wilkins, Roy (NAACP). Letter to Martin Luther King, Jr. 1/11/1962. New York, N.Y. (TLS) 1 p. MLKJP-GAMK: Box 17. 620111–004. |
| 1/11/1962 | King, Martin Luther, Jr., and Wyatt Tee Walker (SCLC). Form letter to Fellow Americans. 1/11/1962. [*Atlanta, Ga.*] (TLS) 1 p. MLKJP-GAMK: Box 35. 620111–006. |
| 1/12/1962 | King, Martin Luther, Jr. Statement to *Time* on new civil rights legislation. 1/12/1962. [*Atlanta, Ga.*] (TD) 1 p. MLKJP-GAMK: Box 23. 620112–000. |
| 1/13/1962 | Ebenezer Baptist Church. Press release, "Such as I have," Martin Luther King's sermon topic at Ebenezer Baptist Church. 1/13/1962. Atlanta, Ga. (THD) 1 p. EBCR. 620113–000. |
| 1/15/1962 | SCLC. Telegram to Martin Luther King, Jr. [*1/15/1962*]. Atlanta, Ga. (PWSr) 1 p. MLKJP-GAMK: Box 6. 620115–001. |
| 1/15/1962 | Powell, Clilan B. (*New York Amsterdam News*). Letter to Martin Luther King, Jr. 1/15/1962. New York, N.Y. (THLS) 2 pp. MLKJP-GAMK: Box 3. 620115–002. |
| 1/16/1962 | King, Martin Luther, Jr. Letter to Joseph S. Clark. 1/16/1962. (TLS) 1 p. MLKJP-GAMK: Box 62. 620116–008. |
| 1/18/1962 | Wood, James R. Letter to Wyatt Tee Walker. 1/18/1962. (TL) 1 p. MLKJP-GAMK: Box 27. 620118–004. |
| 1/18/1962 | King, Martin Luther, Jr., and Coretta Scott King. Telegram to A.W. Wilson. 1/18/1962. [*Atlanta, Ga.*] (TWc) 1 p. MLKJP-GAMK: Box 6. 620118–007. |
| 1/18/1962 | American Booksellers Association. Press release, "The 1961 Presentation to the Home Library of the White House." [*1/18/1962*]. New York, N.Y. (PD) 7 pp. MLKPP. 620118–019. |
| 1/20/1962 | Ebenezer Baptist Church. Press release, "The choice is urgent," Martin Luther King's topic at Ebenezer Baptist Church. 1/20/1962. Atlanta, Ga. (TD) 1 p. EBCR. 620120–002. |
| 1/22/1962 | King, Martin Luther, Jr. Letter to Nat King Cole. 1/22/1962. (TLc) 2 pp. MLKJP-GAMK: Box 6. 620122–005. |

1/22/1962    King, Martin Luther, Jr. (SCLC). Form letter to S.S. (Solomon Snowden) Seay. 1/22/1962. Atlanta, Ga. (TLc) 1 p. MLKJP-GAMK: Box 21. 620122–007.

1/22/1962    Marshall, Burke (U.S. Dept. of Justice). Letter to Martin Luther King, Jr. 1/22/1962. Washington, D.C. (TLS) 1 p. MLKJP-GAMK: Box 24. 620122–008.

1/22/1962    King, Martin Luther, Jr. Letter to Allan Knight Chalmers. 1/22/1962. [*Atlanta, Ga.*] (THLc) 1 p. MLKJP-GAMK. 620122–010.

1/22/1962    King, Martin Luther, Jr. Letter to Franklin H. Littell. 1/22/1962. [*Atlanta, Ga.*] (TLc) 1 p. MLKJP-GAMK: Box 64. 620122–012.

1/22/1962    Press release, "Martin Luther King to visit Puerto Rico." 1/22/1962. San Germán, Puerto Rico. (TD) 2 pp. RBFP. 620122–019.

10/3/1961–    King, Martin Luther, Jr. Outline, "What is justice." [*10/3/1961–1/23/1962*]. [*Atlanta,*
1/23/1962    *Ga.*] (AD) 4 pp. MCMLK-RWWL: 5.1.0.275. 620123–004.

10/3/1961–    King, Martin Luther, Jr. "Outline of seminar in Social Philosophy, first semes-
1/23/1962    ter." [*10/3/1961–1/23/1962*]. [*Atlanta, Ga.*] (TD) 1 p. MCMLK-RWWL: 5.1.0.270. 620123–005.

1/23/1962    Moody, Curt (American Friends Service Committee). Letter to Martin Luther King, Jr. 1/23/1962. Pasadena, Calif. (TLS) 1 p. (Contains enclosure 620123–010.) MLKJP-GAMK: Box 2. 620123–009.

1/23/1962    Moody, Curt (American Friends Service Committee). Form letter to Friend. 1/23/1962. Pasadena, Calif. (TLS) 1 p. (Enclosed in 620123–009.) MLKJP-GAMK: Box 2. 620123–010.

**10/3/1961–    King, Martin Luther, Jr. Notes, Seminar in Social Philosophy. [*10/3/1961–***
**1/23/1962    *1/23/1962*]. Atlanta, Ga. (AD) 34 pp. MLKP-MBU. 620123–017.**

1/24/1962    King, Martin Luther, Jr. (SCLC). Letter to Claude Barnett. 1/24/1962. Atlanta, Ga. (TLS) 1 p. CABP-ICHi: Reel 4. 620124–000.

1/24/1962    King, Martin Luther, Jr. Letter to Arthur B. Langlie. 1/24/1962. [*Atlanta, Ga.*] (TLc) 1 p. MLKJP-GAMK: Box 17. 620124–004.

1/24/1962    King, Martin Luther, Jr. (SCLC). Telegram to Jackie Robinson. 1/24/1962. [*Atlanta, Ga.*] (TWc) 1 p. MLKJP-GAMK: Box 20. 620124–005.

1/24/1962    King, Martin Luther, Jr. Letter to Leslie Dunbar. 1/24/1962. Atlanta, Ga. (TLc) 1 p. MLKJP-GAMK: Box 22. 620124–009.

1/24/1962    Wilkins, Roy (NAACP). Letter to Leslie Dunbar. 1/24/1962. New York, N.Y. (THLc) 1 p. COREP-WHi: Reel 4. 620124–010.

1/25/1962    King, Martin Luther, Jr. "Semester examination, seminar in Social Philosophy." 1/25/1962. [*Atlanta, Ga.*] (TD) 1 p. MCMLK-RWWL: 5.1.0.280. 620125–001.

1/25/1962    King, Martin Luther, Jr. Letter to William Sloane Coffin. 1/25/1962. Atlanta, Ga. (TLS) 1 p. WSCC-CtY: Box 4. 620125–002.

1/25/1962    King, Martin Luther, Jr. Letter to John David Maguire. 1/25/1962. [*Atlanta, Ga.*] (TLc) 1 p. MLKP-MBU. 620125–003.

1/25/1962    King, Martin Luther, Jr. Letter to Edward B. Gulick. 1/25/1962. [*Atlanta, Ga.*] (TLc) 1 p. MLKP-MBU. 620125–008.

1/26/1962    King, Martin Luther, Jr. Letter to Benjamin L. Hooks. 1/26/1962. (TALc) 1 p. MLKJP-GAMK: Box 12. 620126–003.

1/26/1962    Henry, Aaron. Letter to Wyatt Tee Walker. 1/26/1962. (TLS) 1 p. (Contains enclosure 620208–011.) SCLCR-GAMK: Box 35. 620126–007.

1/26/1962    SCLC. Press release, "To all city editors." 1/26/1962. Atlanta, Ga. (TD) 1 p. CAABP-WHi: Box 57. 620126–009.

1/27/1962    Morehouse College. Class Roll, Seminar in Social Philosophy. 1/27/1962. (TFm) 1 p. MLKP-MBU. 620127–001.

1/28/1962    Mt. Olivet Baptist Church. Program, "The Mt. Olivet annual youth day." 1/28/1962. Columbus, Ohio. (TD) 10 pp. MCMLK-RWWL: 12.3.0.600. 620128–000.

1/28/1962    Pope, Lillian and Robert Pope. Letter to Martin Luther King, Jr. 1/28/1962. Santurce, Puerto Rico (TLS) 2 pp. MLKP-MBU. 620128–001.

1/29/1962    Taylor, Gardner C. (Concord Baptist Church of Christ). Letter to Martin Luther King, Jr. 1/29/1962. Brooklyn, N.Y. (TLS) 1 p. MLKJP-GAMK: Box 9. 620129–002.

1/30/1962    Walker, Wyatt Tee (SCLC). Letter to Robert Carl Cohen. 1/30/1962. Atlanta, Ga. (TLc) 1 p. MLKJP-GAMK: Box 12. 620130–000.

1/30/1962    King, Martin Luther, Jr. Letter to Samuel W. Williams. 1/30/1962. (TLc) 2 pp. (Contains enclosure 620130–005.) MLKJP-GAMK: Box 15. 620130–004.

1/30/1962    King, Martin Luther, Jr. (Morehouse College). Grades, Seminar in Social Philosophy, first semester 1961–1962. 1/30/1962. (TD) 1 p. (Enclosed in 620130–004.) MLKJP-GAMK: Box 15. 620130–005.

1/30/1962    Kennedy, Robert F. (U.S. Dept. of Justice). Interview by Martin Agronsky on *Today*. 1/30/1962. (TTv) 8 pp. RFKAG-MBJFK: Box 1. 620130–011.

| | |
|---|---|
| 1/31/1962 | SCLC. Press release, "Civil rights leaders volunteer to fill Reverend Shuttlesworth's pulpit." 1/31/1962. Atlanta, Ga. (TD) 1 p. NCCR-PPPrHi: Box 47. 620131–000. |
| 1/28/1962–1/31/1962 | Program, "Forty-third annual Ohio pastor's convention." 1/28/1962–1/31/1962. Columbus, Ohio. (TD) 1 p. (Enclosed in 620109–000.) MLKP-MBU. 620131–001. |
| 1/31/1962 | Rhoades, William H. (American Baptist Home Mission Societies). Letter to Martin Luther King, Jr. 1/31/1962. New York, N.Y. (TLS) 1 p. MLKJP-GAMK: Box 9. 620131–002. |
| 1/31/1962 | King, Martin Luther, Jr. Letter to Thor Andersen. 1/31/1962. [Atlanta, Ga.] (TLc) 4 pp. SCLCR-GAMK: Box 1. 620131–004. |
| 1/31/1962 | King, Martin Luther, Jr. Letter to Agnes Bridges. 1/31/1962. [Atlanta, Ga.] (TLc) 1 p. MLKJP-GAMK: Box 62. 620131–010. |
| 2/1962 | SCLC. Newsletter 1, no. 4. 2/1962. Atlanta, Ga. (PD) 4 pp. ASRC-RWWL: Reel 173. 620200–007. |
| 2/1962 | SCLC. "Church affiliates." 2/1962. (TD) 4 pp. (Enclosed in 620718–005.) ASRC-RWWL: Reel 173. 620200–008. |
| 2/1/1962 | SCLC. Press release, Martin Luther King, Jr. to begin People to People program. 2/1/1962. Atlanta, Ga. (TD) 1 p. NCCR-PPPrHi: Box 47. 620201–000. |
| 2/1/1962 | Hansen, Clifford G. (American Baptist Home Mission Society). Letter to Martin Luther King, Jr. 2/1/1962. New York, N.Y. (TLS) 1 p. MLKJP-GAMK: Box 9. 620201–002. |
| 2/1/1962 | Marshall, Burke (U.S. Dept. of Justice). Letter to Martin Luther King, Jr. 2/1/1962. Washington, D.C. (TLS) 1 p. MLKJP-GAMK: Box 24. 620201–003. |
| 2/2/1962 | SCLC. Agenda, "Southwide meeting of SCLC state and local leaders." 2/2/1962. Atlanta, Ga. (THD) 1 p. (Comments by King on verso.) MLKJP-GAMK: Vault Box 9. 620202–001. |
| 2/2/1962 | SCLC. "Roster of participants in President's meeting." 2/2/1962. Atlanta, Ga. (TD) 2 pp. MLKJP-GAMK: Box 29. 620202–004. |
| 2/3/1962 | Ebenezer Baptist Church. Press release, "'The worth of man,' King, Jr.'s topic at Ebenezer Sunday." 2/3/1962. Atlanta, Ga. (TD) 1 p. EBCR. 620203–003. |
| 2/3/1962 | King, Martin Luther, Jr. (SCLC). Letter to Alfred Daniel King. 2/3/1962. Atlanta, Ga. (TLc) 1 p. (Contains enclosure 620203–006.) MLKJP-GAMK: Box 28. 620203–004. |
| 2/3/1962 | SCLC. Memo to Affiliate heads. 2/3/1962. (TLc) 2 pp. (Enclosed in 620203–004.) MLKJP-GAMK: Box 29. 620203–006. |
| 2/5/1962 | King, Martin Luther, Jr. Letter to H. Beecher Hicks. 2/5/1962. [Atlanta, Ga.] (TLc) 1 p. MLKP-MBU. 620205–000. |
| 2/5/1962 | McDonald, Dora E. Letter to Martin E. Marty. 2/5/1962. [Atlanta, Ga.] (TLc) 1 p. (Contains enclosure 620205–004.) MLKJP-GAMK: Box 6. 620205–003. |
| 2/5/1962 | King, Martin Luther, Jr. Memo to Christian Century. 2/5/1962. [Atlanta, Ga.] (TLc) 1 p. (Enclosed in 620205–003.) MLKJP-GAMK: Box 6. 620205–004. |
| 2/5/1962 | Kline, Reamer (Bard College). Letter to Martin Luther King, Jr. 2/5/1962. Annandale-on-Hudson, N.Y. (THLS) 1 p. MLKP-MBU. 620205–009. |
| 2/5/1962 | Holmes, Harold J. (National Safety Council). Letter to Martin Luther King, Jr. [2/5/1962]. Chicago, Ill. (TLS) 1 p. MLKJP-GAMK: Box 17. 620205–012. |
| 2/6/1962 | Houser, George M. (American Committee on Africa). Letter to Martin Luther King, Jr. 2/6/1962. New York, N.Y. (THLS) 1 p. MLKP-MBU. 620206–000. |
| 2/6/1962 | Rockefeller, Nelson A. (Nelson Aldrich) (New York. Office of Governor). Letter to Martin Luther King, Jr. 2/6/1962. Albany, N.Y. (TALS) 1 p. MCMLK-RWWL: 1.1.0.39800. 620206–001. |
| 2/6/1962 | SCLC. Press release, "Police brutality in Edenton, North Carolina." 2/6/1962. Atlanta, Ga. (TD) 1 p. SNCCP-GAMK. 620206–010. |
| 2/6/1962 | King, Martin Luther, Jr. Letter to Maxwell Hahn. 2/6/1962. [Atlanta, Ga.] (TLc) 3 pp. MLKJP-GAMK: Box 57. 620206–013. |
| 2/6/1962 | SCLC. Press release, "Dr. King and staff head for delta country of Mississippi." 2/6/1962. Atlanta, Ga. (TD) 1 p. ASRC-RWWL: Reel 173. 620206–015. |
| 2/7/1962 | King, Martin Luther, Jr. Letter to Arlo Tatum. 2/7/1962. [Atlanta, Ga.] (THLc) 1 p. MLKJP-GAMK: Box 27. 620207–007. |
| 2/8/1962 | Shortridge, W. E. (Alabama Christian Movement for Human Rights). Letter to Martin Luther King, Jr. 2/8/1962. Birmingham, Ala. (THLS) 1 p. MLKP-MBU. 620208–002. |
| 2/8/1962 | SCLC. Press release, "King says Mississippi can elect five Negro congressmen." 2/8/1962. Atlanta, Ga. (TD) 1 p. SNCCP-GAMK. 620208–003. |

| | |
|---|---|
| 2/8/1962 | Liggett, Thomas J. (Evangelical Seminary of Puerto Rico). Letter to Martin Luther King, Jr. 2/8/1962. Río Piedras, Puerto Rico. (TLS) 1 p. MLKP-MBU. 620208–009. |
| 2/7/1962– 2/8/1962 | "General program outline for visit of Rev. Martin L. King, Jr." [2/7/1962–2/8/1962]. (THDc) 1 p. (Enclosed in 620126–007.) SCLCR-GAMK: Box 35. 620208–013. |
| 2/9/1962 | Davis, Jerome. Letter to Martin Luther King, Jr. 2/9/1962. Zephyrhill, Fla. (THLS) 1 p. MLKJP-GAMK: Box 62. 620209–005. |
| 2/9/1962 | King, Martin Luther, Jr. Letter to H. H. Benware. 2/9/1962. [Atlanta, Ga.] (TLc) 1 p. MLKJP-GAMK: Box 62. 620209–008. |
| **2/7/1962– 2/9/1962** | **King, Martin Luther, Jr. Notes on recruitment of volunteers. [2/7/1962–2/9/1962]. [Atlanta, Ga.] (ADf) 4 pp. MCMLK-RWWL: 2.6.0.390. 620209–009.** |
| 2/10/1962 | Henry, Aaron. Letter to Wyatt Tee Walker. 2/10/1962. Clarksdale, Miss. (TLS) 1 p. SCLCR-GAMK: Box 35. 620210–001. |
| 2/12/1962 | King, Martin Luther, Jr. (SCLC). "If the Negro Wins, Labor Wins." *Hotel* (12 February 1962), 4, 6. (PD) 2 pp. 620212–000. |
| 2/12/1962 | King, Martin Luther, Jr. Letter to Nelson A. (Nelson Aldrich) Rockefeller. 2/12/1962. [Atlanta, Ga.] (TLc) 1 p. MCMLK-RWWL: 1.1.0.39800. 620212–001. |
| 2/12/1962 | Maxwell, O. Clay (Mount Olivet Baptist Church). Letter to Martin Luther King, Jr. 2/12/1962. New York, N.Y. (TLS) 1 p. MLKJP-GAMK: Box 22. 620212–004. |
| 2/12/1962 | McDonald, Dora E. Letter to George Riemer. 2/12/1962. [Atlanta, Ga.] (TLc) 3 pp. (Contains enclosure 620212–009.) MLKJP-GAMK: Box 12. 620212–008. |
| 2/12/1962 | King, Martin Luther, Jr. Statement for *Good Housekeeping*. 2/12/1962. (THD) 2 pp. (Enclosed in 620212–008.) MLKJP-GAMK: Box 12. 620212–009. |
| 2/12/1962 | King, Martin Luther, Jr. Letter to Theodore Woodrow Kheel. 2/12/1962. [Atlanta, Ga.] (TLc) 2 pp. MLKJP-GAMK: Box 14. 620212–010. |
| 2/12/1962 | Eaton, Herbert H. (Dexter Avenue Baptist Church). Letter to Martin Luther King, Jr. 2/12/1962. Montgomery, Ala. (TLS) 1 p. MLKJP-GAMK: Box 22. 620212–011. |
| 2/14/1962 | King, Martin Luther, Jr., and Wyatt Tee Walker (SCLC). Letter to George W. Lawrence. 2/14/1962. (TLc) 1 p. SCLCR-GAMK: Box 52. 620214–002. |
| 2/14/1962 | King, Martin Luther, Jr. Letter to Arthur Reed. 2/14/1962. [Atlanta, Ga.] (THLc) 1 p. MLKJP-GAMK: Box 20. 620214–004. |
| 2/14/1962 | McWilliams, Carey (*The Nation*). Letter to Martin Luther King, Jr. 2/14/1962. New York, N.Y. (TLS) 1 p. MLKJP-GAMK: Box 17. 620214–010. |
| **2/14/1962** | **Hoover, J. Edgar (U.S. FBI). Memo to Robert F. Kennedy. 2/14/1962. From: Garrow, David J. ed., *Centers of the Southern Struggle* [*microfilm*], (University Publications of America, 1988). (THL) 1 p. FBIDG-NN-Sc: Bureau File 100– 106670. 620214–014.** |
| 2/14/1962 | [*Hoover, J. Edgar*] (U.S. FBI). Letter to Kenneth P. O'Donnell. 2/14/1962 (THLc) 1 p. FBIDG-NN-Sc: Bureau File 100–106670–24. 620214–015. |
| 2/14/1962 | King, Martin Luther, Jr., and Wyatt Tee Walker. Letter to Fred H. LeGarde. 2/14/1962. [Atlanta, Ga.] (TLc) 2 pp. SCLCR-GAMK: Box 52. 620214–016. |
| 2/14/1962 | King, Martin Luther, Jr. "The Future of Integration," Address delivered at Inter-American University. [2/14/1962]. San Germán, Puerto Rico. (At) 46.4 min. (1 compact disc.) RBFP. 620214–017. |
| 2/14/1962 | King, Martin Luther, Jr. Nonviolence and Racial Justice, Address delivered at Inter-American University. [2/14/1962]. San Germán, Puerto Rico. (At) 28.9 min. (1 compact disc.) RBFP. 620214–018. |
| 2/14/1962 | Program, "Servicio de Adoración." 2/14/1962. (TD) 1 p. RBFP. 620214–020. |
| 2/15/1962 | King, Martin Luther, Jr., and Wyatt Tee Walker. Letter to Richard Battle. 2/15/1962. [Atlanta, Ga.] (TLc) 1 p. SCLCR-GAMK: Box 51. 620215–002. |
| 2/15/1962 | [*McDonald, Dora E.*] Letter to Martin Luther King, Jr. 2/15/1962. [Atlanta, Ga.] (TLc) 2 pp. MLKJP-GAMK: Box 15. 620215–006. |
| 2/15/1962 | King, Martin Luther, Jr. "Stride Toward Freedom," Address delivered at Inter-American University. [2/15/1962]. San Germán, Puerto Rico. (At) 34.6 min. (1 compact disc: digital.) RBFP. 620215–010. |
| 2/12/1962– 2/15/1962 | Inter-American University. Program, "Toward a world of understanding." 2/12/1962–2/15/1962. San Germán, Puerto Rico. (PD) 3 pp. RBFP. 620215–011. |
| 2/16/1962 | Hollis, Harvey W. (Denver Area Council of the Churches of Christ). Letter to Martin Luther King, Jr. 2/16/1962. Denver, Colo. (TLS) 1 p. MLKP-MBU. 620216–001. |
| 2/16/1962 | Rogers, T.Y. (Galilee Baptist Church). Letter to Martin Luther King, Jr. 2/16/1962. Philadelphia, Pa. (THLI) 1 p. MLKJP-GAMK: Box 20. 620216–002. |

| | | |
|---|---|---|
| 2/16/1962 | Wachtel, Harry. Letter to Martin Luther King, Jr. 2/16/1962. New York, N.Y. (THLS) 1 p. MLKJP-GAMK: Box 25. 620216–003. |
| 2/16/1962 | Announcement, Martin Luther King, Jr. to speak at the University of Puerto Rico. 2/16/1962. [*San Juan, Puerto Rico.*] (PD) 2 pp. RBFP. 620216–008. |
| 2/17/1962 | Ebenezer Baptist Church. Press release, "All for good," Martin Luther King's sermon topic. [*2/17/1962*]. Atlanta, Ga. (TD) 1 p. EBCR. 620217–000. |
| 2/17/1962 | King, Martin Luther, Jr. "People in Action: The President's Record." *New York Amsterdam News*, 17 February 1962. (PD) 1 p. 620217–001. |
| 2/19/1962 | SCLC. Press release, "King predicts 'stand-ins' at polls next civil rights move." 2/19/1962. Atlanta, Ga. (TD) 1 p. MLKJP-GAMK: Box 34. 620219–002. |
| 2/19/1962 | Braden, Anne (Southern Conference Educational Fund). Letter to Martin Luther King, Jr. 2/19/1962. Louisville, Ky. (TALS) 2 pp. MLKJP-GAMK: Box 4. 620219–006. |
| 2/19/1962 | Southern Conference Educational Fund. Press release, Arrest of Charles McDew and Robert Zellner. 2/19/1962. New Orleans, La. (TD) 2 pp. MLKJP-GAMK: Box 23. 620219–007. |
| 2/19/1962 | King, Martin Luther, Jr., and Wyatt Tee Walker (SCLC). Telegram to Burke Marshall. 2/19/1962. [*Atlanta, Ga.*] (TWc) 2 pp. MLKJP-GAMK: Box 24. 620219–013. |
| 2/19/1962 | Kilgore, Thomas (Friendship Baptist Church). Letter to Martin Luther King, Jr. 2/19/1962. New York, N.Y. (TALS) 1 p. MLKJP-GAMK: Box 22. 620219–017. |
| 2/20/1962 | Taylor, Gardner C. (Concord Baptist Church of Christ). Letter to Martin Luther King, Jr. 2/20/1962. Brooklyn, N.Y. (TLS) 1 p. MLKJP-GAMK: Box 22. 620220–007. |
| 2/21/1962 | SCLC. Press release, John H. Calhoun and Herbert V. Coulton added to staff. 2/21/1962. Atlanta, Ga. (TD) 1 p. MLKJP-GAMK: Box 34. 620221–000. |
| 2/21/1962 | SCLC. Press release, "King's 'People to People' tour sweeps delta." 2/21/1962. Atlanta, Ga. (TD) 2 pp. MLKJP-GAMK: Box 34. 620221–001. |
| 2/22/1962 | New York Friends of the SCLC. Program, "Tribute to Mrs. Martin Luther King, Jr. at Mother A.M.E. Zion Church." 2/22/1962. New York, N.Y. (PD) 1 p. MCMLK-RWWL: 6.5.0.540. 620222–000. |
| 2/22/1962 | King, Martin Luther, Jr., and Wyatt Tee Walker (SCLC). Letter to Stewart L. Udall. 2/22/1962. [*Atlanta, Ga.*] (TLc) 1 p. MLKJP-GAMK: Box 24. 620222–004. |
| 2/22/1962 | O'Dell, Jack H. Letter to Harry Blake. 2/22/1962. (TLc) 1 p. SCLCR-GAMK: Box 135. 620222–007. |
| 2/25/1962 | SCLC. Press release, "King disappointed with Kennedy administration." 2/25/1962. Atlanta, Ga. (TD) 2 pp. MLKJP-GAMK: Box 34. 620225–000. |
| 2/25/1962 | SCLC. Press release, Omitted paragraphs from earlier press release. 2/25/1962. Atlanta, Ga. (TD) 1 p. SCLCR-GAMK: Box 120. 620225–001. |
| 2/26/1962 | King, Martin Luther, Jr. Letter to J. (James) Timothy Boddie. 2/26/1962. Atlanta, Ga. (TLc) 2 pp. MLKJP-GAMK: Box 22. 620226–004. |
| 2/26/1962 | King, Martin Luther, Jr. Letter to Vivian Carter Mason. 2/26/1962. [*Atlanta, Ga.*] (TLc) 2 pp. MLKJP-GAMK: Box 19. 620226–005. |
| 2/26/1962 | Tonnaire-Taylor, Lillian (LYNX). Letter to Martin Luther King, Jr. 2/26/1962. Paris, France (THLS) 1 p. (Contains enclosure 620226–007.) MLKJP-GAMK: Box 14. 620226–006. |
| 2/26/1962 | Tonnaire-Taylor, Lillian (LYNX). Interview questions for Martin Luther King, Jr. 2/26/1962. Paris, France. (THLS) 1 p. (Enclosed in 620226–006.) MLKJP-GAMK: Box 14. 620226–007. |
| 2/26/1962 | McDonald, Dora E. Letter to C. Kenzie Steele. 2/26/1962. [*Atlanta, Ga.*] (TLc) 1 p. MLKJP-GAMK: Box 23. 620226–008. |
| 2/26/1962 | SCLC. Letter to J.F. Worley. 2/26/1962. Atlanta, Ga. (TLc) 3 pp. SCLCR-GAMK: Box 35. 620226–012. |
| 2/27/1962 | King, Martin Luther, Jr. Statement at Albany, Ga. courthouse. [*2/27/1962*]. [*Albany, Ga.*] (F) 1 min. CBSNA-NNCBS. 620227–008. |
| 2/28/1962 | King, Martin Luther, Jr. Letter to Paul M. Stevens. 2/28/1962. [*Atlanta, Ga.*] (TLc) 1 p. MLKJP-GAMK: Box 65. 620228–011. |
| 2/28/1962 | SCLC. Press release, "Hoods bomb S.C.L.C. leader's home." 2/28/1962. Atlanta, Ga. (TD) 1 p. SCLCR-GAMK: Box 120. 620228–014. |
| 2/28/1962 | Bernhard, Berl I. (U.S. Commission on Civil Rights). Letter to Virginia Foster Durr. [*2/28/1962*]. Washington, D.C. (TLS) 1 p. (Enclosed in 620306–005, pp. 422–423 in this volume.) MLKJP-GAMK: Box 9. 620228–015. |
| 3/1962 | SCLC. *Newsletter* 1, no. 5. 3/1962. Atlanta, Ga. (PD) 4 pp. SCLCR-GAMK: Box 122. 620300–005. |

| | |
|---|---|
| 3/1962 | King, Martin Luther, Jr. "Not Spent in Vain," *Southern Patriot* 20 (March 1962) (PD) Calendar 1 p. 620300–017. |
| 3/1962 | [*SCLC*]. Staff roster. [*3/1962*]. (THD) 4 pp. SCLCR-GAMK: Box 36. 620300–019. |
| 3/1/1962 | King, Martin Luther, Jr. Letter to J.L. LeFlore. 3/1/1962. [*Atlanta, Ga.*] (TLc) 1 p. MLKJP-GAMK: Box 21. 620301–001. |
| 3/1/1962 | King, Martin Luther, Jr. Letter to Samuel Newman. 3/1/1962. [*Atlanta, Ga.*] (TLc) 1 p. MLKJP-GAMK: Box 6. 620301–002. |
| 3/1/1962 | King, Martin Luther, Jr. (SCLC). Form letter to Friend. 3/1/1962. Atlanta, Ga. (TLS) 1 p. URWR-WHi: Box 399. 620301–003. |
| 3/1/1962 | King, Martin Luther, Jr. Letter to John Burnett Morris. 3/1/1962. [*Atlanta, Ga.*] (TLc) 2 pp. MLKJP-GAMK: Box 41. 620301–004. |
| 3/1/1962 | SCLC. Press release, SCLC to partner with other organizations to desegregate Atlanta hospital. 3/1/1962. Atlanta, Ga. (TD) 1 p. SCLCR-GAMK: Box 51. 620301–011. |
| 3/2/1962 | SCLC. Press release, "Flash news from S.C.L.C." 3/2/1962. Atlanta, Ga. (THD) 2 pp. SCLCR-GAMK: Box 125. 620302–003. |
| 3/4/1962 | Pope, Lillian (FOR). Letter to Martin Luther King, Jr. 3/4/1962. Santurce, Puerto Rico. (TLS) 1 p. MLKP-MBU. 620304–001. |
| 3/6/1962 | King, Martin Luther, Jr. Letter to Lillian Tonnaire-Taylor. 3/6/1962. Atlanta, Ga. (TLc) 4 pp. MLKJP-GAMK: Box 14. 620306–006. |
| 3/6/1962 | Hughes, Langston. Telegram to Martin Luther King, Jr. 3/6/1962. New York, N.Y. (PWSr) 1 p. MLKJP-GAMK: Box 6. 620306–023. |
| 3/7/1962 | King, Martin Luther, Jr. Letter to Elizabeth Rose. 3/7/1962. Atlanta, Ga. (TLc) 2 pp. MLKJP-GAMK: Box 64. 620307–006. |
| 3/7/1962 | King, Martin Luther, Jr. Letter to Jane Hamman. 3/7/1962. (TLc) 2 pp. SCLCR-GAMK: Box 63. 620307–007. |
| 3/8/1962 | King, Martin Luther, Jr. Letter to Lawrence Dunbar Reddick. 3/8/1962. [*Atlanta, Ga.*] (TLc) 2 pp. MLKJP-GAMK: Box 20. 620308–003. |
| 3/8/1962 | King, Martin Luther, Jr. (SCLC). Letter to J.F. Worley. 3/8/1962. [*Atlanta, Ga.*] (TLc) 6 pp. MLKJP-GAMK: Box 32. 620308–006. |
| 3/8/1962 | Citizens of Birmingham, Ala. and SCLC. Program, "A Testimonial Honoring Rev. F.L. Shuttlesworth and Rev. J.S. Phifer." 3/8/1962. Birmingham, Ala. (PD) 3 pp. SAVFC-WHi: Box 44. 620308–008. |
| 3/9/1962 | King, Martin Luther, Jr. Letter to Herschelle Sullivan. 3/9/1962. [*Atlanta, Ga.*] (TLc) 1 p. MLKJP-GAMK: Box 6. 620309–007. |
| 3/9/1962 | King, Martin Luther, Jr. Letter to John David Maguire. 3/9/1962. [*Atlanta, Ga.*] (TLc) 2 pp. MLKJP-GAMK: Box 39. 620309–008. |
| **3/11/1962** | **King, Martin Luther, Jr., and Coretta Scott King (SCLC). Telegram to Ralph Abernathy. 3/11/1962. Atlanta, Ga. (PWc) 1 p. MCMLK-RWWL: 1.1.0.70. 620311–000.** |
| 3/11/1962 | Catalina Methodist Church. Program, Sunday services. 3/11/1962. Tucson, Ariz. (TD) 3 pp. AzTCM. 620311–002. |
| 3/13/1962 | Bowman, Gloria (Atlanta University). Letter to Martin Luther King, Jr. 3/13/1962. Atlanta, Ga. (THLS) 1 p. MLKP-MBU. 620313–005. |
| 3/13/1962 | SCLC. Press release, "SCLC's 'People to People' tour heads for Virginia's black belt." 3/13/1962. Atlanta, Ga. (TD) 1 p. SCLCR-GAMK: Box 120. 620313–008. |
| 3/13/1962 | Southern Regional Council. "Executive support of civil rights." 3/13/1962. Atlanta, Ga. (PD) 52 pp. ASRC-RWWL: Reel 219. 620313–010. |
| 3/14/1962 | McDonald, Dora E. Letter to Thomas H. Wilkins. 3/14/1962. [*Atlanta, Ga.*] (TLc) 1 p. MLKP-MBU. 620314–002. |
| 3/14/1962 | Udall, Stewart L. (U.S. Dept. of the Interior). Letter to Martin Luther King, Jr. 3/14/1962. Washington, D.C. (TLS) 1 p. MLKJP-GAMK: Box 24. 620314–003. |
| 3/15/1962 | SCLC. Press release, "The white south must speak for integration." 3/15/1962. Atlanta, Ga. (TD) 1 p. MLKJP-GAMK: Box 109. 620315–000. |
| 3/15/1962 | SCLC. Press release, Martin Luther King, Jr. sends telegram to Clarence T. Lundquist. 3/15/1962. Atlanta, Ga. (THD) 1 p. SCLCR-GAMK: Box 120. 620315–001. |
| 3/15/1962 | King, Martin Luther, Jr. (SCLC). Telegram to Clarence T. Lundquist. 3/15/1962. [*Atlanta, Ga.*] (PWc) 2 pp. MLKJP-GAMK: Box 24. 620315–008. |
| 3/16/1962 | SCLC. Press release, Announcement of new SCLC staff. 3/16/1962. Atlanta, Ga. (TD) 2 pp. DABCC. 620316–000. |
| 3/15/1962– 3/16/1962 | United Electrical, Radio and Machine Workers of America. "Contributions received on 'Dollars for Dignity' campaign of SCLC." 3/15/1962–3/16/1962. (THD) 4 pp. UERR-PPiU-IS. 620316–008. |

| | | |
|---|---|---|
| 3/17/1962 | King, Martin Luther, Jr. "Nonviolence on tour." 3/17/1962. [*Atlanta, Ga.*] (TD) 4 pp. MLKJP-GAMK: Box 109. 620317–000. |
| 3/18/1962 | Wood, James R. Letter to Martin Luther King, Jr. 3/18/1962. Atlanta, Ga. (TLS) 1 p. MLKJP-GAMK: Box 27. 620318–001. |
| 3/19/1962 | King, Martin Luther, Jr. Letter to Bernard L. Isaacs. 3/19/1962. [*Atlanta, Ga.*] (TLc) 1 p. MLKP-MBU. 620319–004. |
| 3/19/1962 | King, Martin Luther, Jr. Letter to Shirley Bird. 3/19/1962. [*Atlanta, Ga.*] (TLc) 1 p. MLKP-MBU. 620319–005. |
| 3/19/1962 | King, Martin Luther, Jr. Letter to T. W. Brown. 3/19/1962. [*Atlanta, Ga.*] (TLc) 1 p. MLKP-MBU. 620319–006. |
| 3/19/1962 | Community Service Committee. Program, "Community Service Committee presents Dr. King." [*3/19/1962*]. Huntsville, Ala. (THD) 4 pp. OUA-AHO. 620319–010. |
| 3/19/1962 | Announcement, "Ebony survey: Martin Luther King, Jr. second most influential Negro." [*3/19/1962*]. (APD) 1 p. MLKJP-GAMK: Box 123A. 620319–011. |
| 3/19/1962 | King, Martin Luther, Jr., and Coretta Scott King (SCLC). Telegram to the McCall family. 3/19/1962. [*Atlanta, Ga.*] (PWc) 1 p. CSKC. 620319–012. |
| 3/19/1962 | King, Martin Luther, Jr. Ways Toward Nonviolent School Integration, Address delivered at Oakwood College. [*3/19/1962*]. Huntsville, Ala. (At) 40.8 min. (1 sound cassette: analog.) AlHvCFS. 620319–015. |
| 3/18/1962–<br>3/19/1962 | First Baptist Church. Program, "Installation services of Rev. A. D. Williams King." 3/18/1962–3/19/1962. Ensley, Ala. (PD) 6 pp. MCMLK-RWWL: 12.3.0.330. 620319–017. |
| 3/20/1962 | King, Martin Luther, Jr. Letter to John C. (John Coleman) Bennett. 3/20/1962. [*Atlanta, Ga.*] (TLc) 2 pp. MLKJP-GAMK: Box 6. 620320–000. |
| 3/20/1962 | Midorikawa, Toru (Iwanami Shoten, Publishers). Letter to Martin Luther King, Jr. 3/20/1962. Tokyo, Japan. (TLS) 1 p. MLKJP-GAMK: Box 6. 620320–001. |
| 3/20/1962 | King, Martin Luther, Jr., and Wyatt Tee Walker (SCLC). Telegram to Ella Trammell. 3/20/1962. [*Atlanta, Ga.*] (PHWc) 1 p. CSKC. 620320–003. |
| 3/20/1962 | Garth, DeWitt Paul. Letter to Martin Luther King, Jr. 3/20/1962. Ellsworth Air Force Base, S.D. (THLS) 1 p. MLKJP-GAMK: Box 63. 620320–007. |
| 3/20/1962 | Special Agent in Charge, New York, N.Y. (U.S. FBI). Memo to J. Edgar Hoover. 3/20/1962. New York, N.Y. (TL) 1 p. SLFBI-DJ: Bureau File 100–392452–147. 620320–008. |
| 3/21/1962 | Chapman, Earl (Improved, Benevolent, Protective Order of Elks of the World). Letter to Martin Luther King, Jr. 3/21/1962. New York, N.Y. (THLS) 1 p. MLKJP-GAMK: Box 62. 620321–003. |
| 3/22/1962 | King, Martin Luther, Jr. Letter to James M. (James Madison) Nabrit. 3/22/1962. [*Atlanta, Ga.*] (TLc) 2 pp. MLKJP-GAMK: Box 6. 620322–002. |
| 3/22/1962 | O'Dell, Jack H. (SCLC). Letter to Martin Luther King, Jr. 3/22/1962. (TLS) 1 p. (Contains enclosure 620000–075.) CSKC. 620322–004. |
| 3/22/1962 | King, Martin Luther, Jr., and Coretta Scott King (SCLC). Telegram to Ralph McGill. [*3/22/1962*]. [*Atlanta, Ga.*] (PHWc) 1 p. MCMLK-RWWL: 1.1.0.29960. 620322–008. |
| 3/23/1962 | King, Martin Luther, Jr. Letter to Stewart L. Udall. 3/23/1962. [*Atlanta, Ga.*] (TLc) 1 p. MLKJP-GAMK: Box 24. 620323–002. |
| 3/23/1962 | Program, "Testimonial banquet in honor of Rev. F. L. Shuttlesworth." 3/23/1962. (PD) 8 pp. BWOF-AB: File 1102.2.7.18. 620323–006. |
| 3/24/1962 | SNCC. "Minutes of SNCC regional meeting." 3/24/1962. Atlanta, Ga. (THD) 7 pp. SNCCP-GAMK: Reel 3. 620324–003. |
| 1/7/1962–<br>3/25/1962 | Sunday Evening Forum. Program, The Sunday Evening Forum. 1/7/1962–3/25/1962. Tucson, Ariz. (TD) 3 pp. MLKP-MBU. 620325–000. |
| 3/26/1962 | King, Martin Luther, Jr. (SCLC). Telegram to Robert F. Kennedy. 3/26/1962. [*Atlanta, Ga.*] (PWSr) 1 p. DJG-GEU-S: Box 1.1. 620326–007. |
| 3/26/1962 | SCLC. Press release, Church members urged to attend contempt trial. 3/26/1962. Atlanta, Ga. (TD) 2 pp. SCLCR-GAMK: Box 120. 620326–010. |
| 3/27/1962 | King, Martin Luther, Jr. "The American Dream," Address delivered at E. C. Glass High School. [*3/27/1962*]. Lynchburg, Va. From: Suitland, Md.: Business & Social (B & S) Recordings, 1986. (At) 54 min. (1 sound cassette: analog.) 620327–001. |
| 3/27/1962 | King, Martin Luther, Jr. Letter to Carey McWilliams. 3/27/1962. [*Atlanta, Ga.*] (TLc) 1 p. MLKJP-GAMK: Box 17. 620327–008. |
| 3/27/1962 | King, Martin Luther, Jr. Letter to Daniel C. (Daniel Calbert) Thompson. 3/27/1962. [*Atlanta, Ga.*] (TLc) 2 pp. MLKJP-GAMK: Box 28. 620327–009. |
| 3/27/1962 | Dunbar, Leslie (Southern Regional Council). Letter to Martin Luther King, Jr. 3/27/1962. Atlanta, Ga. (THLS) 1 p. (Contains enclosure 620327–021 & 620329–007.) MLKJP-GAMK: Box 22. 620327–010. |

| | |
|---|---|
| 3/27/1962 | King, Martin Luther, Jr. Letter to Kivie Kaplan. 3/27/1962. [*Atlanta, Ga.*] (TLc) 1 p. MLKJP-GAMK: Box 13. 620327–013. |
| 3/27/1962 | Walker, Wyatt Tee (SCLC). Letter to Harry Walker. 3/27/1962. (TLc) 1 p. MLKP-MBU. 620327–014. |
| 3/27/1962 | Dunbar, Leslie (Southern Regional Council). Letter to James Farmer. 3/27/1962. Atlanta, Ga. (TLS) 1 p. (Contains enclosures 620327–021 & 620329–007.) COREP-WHi: Reel 5. 620327–020. |
| 3/27/1962 | Southern Regional Council. "Guides for answering of inquiries from the press or others." [3/27/1962]. (TD) 1 p. (Enclosed in 620327–010.) CORER-WHi: Reel 5. 620327–021. |
| **3/27/1962** | **A. L. Adams Photo Studio. Photo of Martin Luther King, Jr. shaking hands with Chuck Moran at E. C. Glass High School. [3/27/1962]. [*Lynchburg, Va.*] (Ph) 1 p. WTWP. 620327–023.** |
| 3/28/1962 | Fauntroy, Walter E. (SCLC). Form letter to Friends. 3/28/1962. Atlanta, Ga. (TLS) 1 p. MLKJP-GAMK: Vault Box 1. 620328–000. |
| 3/28/1962 | Chalmers, Allan Knight (NAACP Legal Defense and Educational Fund). Letter to Martin Luther King, Jr., and Wyatt Tee Walker. 3/28/1962. New York, N.Y. (THLS) 1 p. MLKJP-GAMK. 620328–002. |
| 3/28/1962 | SCLC. Press release, "Mrs. Martin Luther King Jr. flies to Geneva disarmament conference." 3/28/1962. Atlanta, Ga. (TD) 1 p. SAVCR-WHi. 620328–003. |
| 3/28/1962 | Markham, Charles B. (Battle, Fowler, Strokes & Kheel). Letter to Martin Luther King, Jr. 3/28/1962. New York, N.Y. (TLS) 1 p. (Contains enclosure 620328–005.) MCMLK-RWWL: 1.1.0.30900. 620328–004. |
| 3/28/1962 | [*Markham, Charles B.*] Article, Untitled. [3/28/1962.] (TD) 23 pp. (Enclosed in 620328–004.) CSKC. 620328–005. |
| 3/27/1962–3/28/1962 | SCLC. Program, "Dr. Martin Luther King, Jr. in a People to People tour." 3/27/1962–3/28/1962. (PD) 1 p. CAABP-WHi: Box 37. 620328–009. |
| 3/29/1962 | McPherson, Thomas (Morris Brown College). Letter to Martin Luther King, Jr. 3/29/1962. Atlanta, Ga. (TLS) 1 p. MLKP-MBU. 620329–002. |
| 3/29/1962 | Bentz, Betty (Hotel and Club Employees Union Local 6). Letter to Martin Luther King, Jr. 3/29/1962. New York, N.Y. (TLS) 1 p. SCLCR-GAMK: Box 5. 620329–003. |
| 3/29/1962 | Burton, T. N. (SCLC). Letter to Wyatt Tee Walker. 3/29/1962. Lynchburg, Va. (TLc) 1 p. SCLCR-GAMK: Box 52. 620329–004. |
| 3/29/1962 | Southern Regional Council. Press release, Voter Education Project to study voter registration in the South. 3/29/1962. Atlanta, Ga. (TD) 2 pp. (Enclosed in 620327–010.) MLKJP-GAMK: Box 22. 620329–007. |
| 3/29/1962 | Sorensen, Theodore C. Memo to John F. (John Fitzgerald) Kennedy. 3/29/1962. (THL) 1 p. JFKPOF-MBJFK. 620329–013. |
| 3/27/1962–3/29/1962 | Walker, Wyatt Tee (SCLC). "Fifty-three Hours with Martin Luther King Jr." [3/27/1962–3/29/1962]. (THD) 7 pp. SCLCR-GAMK: Box 37. 620329–025. |
| 3/30/1962 | SCLC. Press release, "Martin Luther King, Jr., moves into Virginia." 3/30/1962. Atlanta, Ga. (TD) 3 pp. SCLCR-GAMK: Box 120. 620330–000. |
| 3/30/1962 | Special Agent in Charge, New York, N.Y. (U.S. FBI). Memo to J. Edgar Hoover. 3/30/1962. New York, N.Y. (TL) 2 pp. FBIDG-NN-Sc: Bureau File 100–106670–33. 620330–004. |
| 3/30/1962 | Kunstler & Kunstler. Bill for attorney services. 3/30/1962. New York, N.Y. (TFm) 1 p. NNU-LA. 620330–010. |
| 3/31/1962 | Roosevelt, Eleanor. Letter to Martin Luther King, Jr. 3/31/1962. New York, N.Y. (THLS) 1 p. MCMLK-RWWL: 1.1.0.40140. 620331–002. |
| 3/31/1962 | King, Martin Luther, Jr. Letter to Toru Midorikawa. 3/31/1962. [*Atlanta, Ga.*] (TLc) 1 p. MLKJP-GAMK: Box 6. 620331–006. |
| 3/31/1962 | King, Martin Luther, Jr. Letter to Virginia Foster Durr. 3/31/1962. [*Atlanta, Ga.*] (TLc) 1 p. MLKJP-GAMK: Box 7. 620331–007. |
| 3/31/1962 | King, Martin Luther, Jr. Letter to R. A. Rollins. 3/31/1962. [*Atlanta, Ga.*] (TLc) 1 p. MLKJP-GAMK: Box 64. 620331–009. |
| 10/1961–4/1962 | Walker, Wyatt Tee (SCLC). "Report of the director." 10/1961–4/1962. Atlanta, Ga. (TD) 10 pp. MLKJP-GAMK: Box 36. 620400–003. |
| 4/1962 | SCLC. *Newsletter* 1, no. 6. 4/1962. Atlanta, Ga. (PD) 4 pp. HRECR-WHi: Box 26. 620400–005. |
| 4/1962 | American Clergymen. "Mr. President: Assert your moral leadership!" [4/1962]. (PD) 1 p. MLKJP-GAMK: Box 20. 620400–006. |
| 4/1962 | CORE. Newsletter, *CORE-lator*, no. 95. 4/1962. (PHD) 4 pp. SCLCR-GAMK: Box 125. 620400–007. |
| 4/1/1962 | King, Martin Luther, Jr. Form letter to Friend. 4/1/1962. Atlanta, Ga. (TLS) 1 p. SAVFC-WHi: Box 44. 620401–000. |

4/2/1962    Brown, Paul D. (Allied Real Estate Board, Inc.). Letter to Martin Luther King, Jr. 4/2/1962. Lawrence, N.Y. (TALS) 2 pp. MLKP-MBU. 620402–000.

4/2/1962    King, Martin Luther, Jr. (SCLC). Form letter to Pastor. 4/2/1962. Atlanta, Ga. (TLS) 1 p. MLKJP-GAMK: Vault Box 4. 620402–002.

4/2/1962    King, Martin Luther, Jr. Letter to Thomas McPherson. 4/2/1962. [Atlanta, Ga.] (TLc) 1 p. MLKP-MBU. 620402–005.

4/2/1962    King, Martin Luther, Jr. Letter to DeWitt Paul Garth. 4/2/1962. [Atlanta, Ga.] (TLc) 1 p. MLKJP-GAMK: Box 63. 620402–009.

4/2/1962    King, Martin Luther, Jr. Address at Tabernacle Baptist Church. [4/2/1962]. Augusta, Ga. (F) 7.6 min. (1 videocassette.) WSB-TV-GU. 620402–010.

4/2/1962    King, Martin Luther, Jr. Address at Tabernacle Baptist Church. [4/2/1962]. Augusta, Ga. (F) 7.9 min. (1 videocassette.) WSB-TV-GU. 620402–011.

4/3/1962    King, Martin Luther, Jr. (Ebenezer Baptist Church). Letter to Lillian Eugenia Smith. 4/3/1962. Atlanta, Ga. (TLS) 2 pp. (Enclosed in 620504–003.) LSP-GU-HR. 620403–000.

4/3/1962    King, Martin Luther, Jr. Letter to Earl Kjer. 4/3/1962. [Atlanta, Ga.] (TLc) 1 p. MLKP-MBU. 620403–003.

4/3/1962    King, Martin Luther, Jr. Letter to Wallace Douma. 4/3/1962. [Atlanta, Ga.] (TLc) 1 p. MLKP-MBU. 620403–004.

4/3/1962    King, Martin Luther, Jr. (Ebenezer Baptist Church). Letter to Lillian Eugenia Smith. 4/3/1962. Atlanta, Ga. (TLS) 2 pp. (Enclosed in 620504–003.) MLKJP-GAMK: Box 9. 620403–007.

4/3/1962    Goldberg, Sam A. (Allan-Grayson Realty Company). Letter to Martin Luther King, Jr. 4/3/1962. Atlanta, Ga. (THLS) 2 pp. MLKJP-GAMK: Box 15. 620403–008.

4/3/1962    Marshall, Burke (U.S. Dept. of Justice). Letter to Martin Luther King, Jr. 4/3/1962. Washington, D.C. (TLS) 1 p. MLKJP-GAMK: Box 24. 620403–012.

4/3/1962    Holt, Len (Jordan, Hawley, & Holt). Letter to Martin Luther King, Jr. 4/3/1962. Norfolk, Va. (TLS) 2 pp. MLKJP-GAMK: Box 12. 620403–013.

4/3/1962    SCLC. Press release, King to hold a press conference on the voter registration program. 4/3/1962. Atlanta, Ga. (TD) 1 p. EJBC-NN-Sc. 620403–014.

4/3/1962    King, Martin Luther, Jr. (SCLC). Letter to Maxwell Hahn. 4/3/1962. [Atlanta, Ga.] (TLc) 1 p. MLKJP-GAMK: Box 57. 620403–019.

4/4/1962    [King, Martin Luther, Jr.] Letter to Anne Farnsworth. 4/4/1962. [Atlanta, Ga.] (TLf) 3 pp. MLKJP-GAMK: Box 29. 620404–001.

4/4/1962    Jenkins, Esau (Citizens Committee of Charleston County). Letter to Martin Luther King, Jr. 4/4/1962. Charleston, S.C. (TLS) 1 p. MLKJP-GAMK: Box 22. 620404–003.

4/4/1962    SCLC. Press release, "Dr. King 'masters' Augusta." 4/4/1962. Atlanta, Ga. (TD) 2 pp. SCLCR-GAMK: Box 120. 620404–004.

4/5/1962    O'Brien, Lawrence F. (U.S. White House). Letter to Martin Luther King, Jr. 4/5/1962. Washington, D.C. (TLS) 1 p. MLKJP-GAMK: Box 14. 620405–003.

4/5/1962    SCLC. Press release, "SCLC's People to People tour touches 10,000 in Virginia's black belt." 4/5/1962. Atlanta, Ga. (TD) 3 pp. SAVFC-WHi. 620405–007.

4/5/1962    King, Martin Luther, Jr. Letter to William L. Muttart. 4/5/1962. Atlanta, Ga. (TLc) 2 pp. MLKJP-GAMK: Box 64. 620405–008.

4/5/1962    King, Coretta Scott, Dagmar Wilson, and Anne Eaton. Telegram to John F. (John Fitzgerald) Kennedy. 4/5/1962. Geneva, Switzerland. (PWSr) 1 p. JFKWHCNF-MBJFK: Box 1478. 620405–014.

4/6/1962    King, Martin Luther, Jr., and Wyatt Tee Walker (SCLC). Letter to Wiley A. Branton. 4/6/1962. Atlanta, Ga. (TLS) 1 p. ASRC-RWWL: Reel 173. 620406–000.

4/6/1962    Kearse, I. Logan (Cornerstone Baptist Church of Christ). Letter to Martin Luther King, Jr. 4/6/1962. Baltimore, Md. (TLS) 1 p. MLKJP-GAMK: Box 13. 620406–002.

4/9/1962    King, Martin Luther, Jr. Letter to Ralph Schoenman. 4/9/1962. [Atlanta, Ga.] (TLc) 1 p. MLKJP-GAMK: Box 20. 620409–003.

4/9/1962    King, Martin Luther, Jr., and Wyatt Tee Walker (SCLC). Letter to Southern Conference Educational Fund. 4/9/1962. [Atlanta, Ga.] (TLc) 1 p. MLKJP-GAMK: Box 8. 620409–004.

4/9/1962    King, Martin Luther, Jr. Letter to Basil A. Paterson. 4/9/1962. [Atlanta, Ga.] (TLc) 2 pp. MLKJP-GAMK: Box 28. 620409–006.

4/9/1962    King, Martin Luther, Jr. Letter to Eleanor Roosevelt. 4/9/1962. [Atlanta, Ga.] (TLc) 1 p. MLKJP-GAMK: Box 11. 620409–008.

4/10/1962   McDonald, Dora E. Letter to Samuel T. Daniels. 4/10/1962. [Atlanta, Ga.] (TLc) 1 p. MLKP-MBU. 620410–005.

| | | |
|---|---|---|
| 4/11/1962 | Pettigrew, Thomas F. (Harvard University). Letter to Martin Luther King, Jr. 4/11/1962. Cambridge, Mass. (THLS) 2 pp. MLKJP-GAMK: Box 7. 620411–001. | Calendar |

4/11/1962   King, Martin Luther, Jr. Letter to I. Logan Kearse. 4/11/1962. [*Atlanta, Ga.*] (TLc) 1 p. MLKJP-GAMK: Box 13. 620411–005.

4/11/1962   SCLC. Press release, "Attorney General promises S.C.L.C. immediate attention to voting irregularities." 4/11/1962. Atlanta, Ga. (TD) 2 pp. SAVFC-WHi. 620411–007.

4/11/1962   SCLC. Press release, "Vice-President promises Dr. King compliance with job opportunity mandate." 4/11/1962. Atlanta, Ga. (TD) 1 p. SCLCR-GAMK: Box 120. 620411–019.

4/12/1962   King, Martin Luther, Jr. Letter to Louis Lyons. 4/12/1962. [*Atlanta, Ga.*] (TLf) 2 pp. (Enclosed in 620412–003.) MLKJP-GAMK: Box 11. 620412–002.

4/12/1962   McDonald, Dora E. Letter to Bruce Galphin. 4/12/1962. [*Atlanta, Ga.*] (TLc) 1 p. (Contains enclosure 620412–002.) MLKJP-GAMK: Box 11. 620412–003.

4/12/1962   Special Agent in Charge, New York, N.Y. (U.S. FBI). Memo to J. Edgar Hoover. 4/12/1962. New York, N.Y. (TL) 1 p. FBIDG-NN-Sc: Bureau File 100–106670–43. 620412–007.

4/12/1962   SCLC. Press release, "Atlanta SCLC calls meet to aid Birmingham victims." 4/12/1962. Atlanta, Ga. (TD) 1 p. SCLCR-GAMK: Box 120. 620412–012.

4/13/1962   Walker, Wyatt Tee (SCLC). Letter to Norman B. Houston. 4/13/1962. (TLc) 2 pp. SCLCR-GAMK: Box 36. 620413–002.

4/12/1962–   SCLC. "South Carolina 'People to People' tour." 4/12/1962–4/13/1962. Atlanta,
4/13/1962   Ga. (TD) 2 pp. MLKJP-GAMK: Box 34. 620413–003.

4/13/1962   Osborne, H. Paul (Unitarian Church). Letter to Martin Luther King, Jr. 4/13/1962. Charleston, S.C. (THLS) 1 p. MLKJP-GAMK: Box 35. 620413–006.

4/14/1962   Daniels, Samuel T. (Most Worshipful Prince Hall Grand Lodge). Letter to Martin Luther King, Jr. 4/14/1962. Baltimore, Md. (TLS) 1 p. MLKP-MBU. 620414–001.

4/15/1962   King, Martin Luther, Jr. "Remaining Awake Through a Great Revolution," Address delivered at the Chicago Sunday Evening Club. [*4/15/1962*]. [*Chicago, Ill.*] (At) 28.8 min. (1 sound cassette: analog.) MLKJP-GAMK. 620415–000.

4/15/1962   King, Martin Luther, Jr. Palm Sunday prayer delivered at Ebenezer Baptist Church. 4/15/1962. Atlanta, Ga. (At) 6.5 min. (1 sound cassette: analog.) MLKEC: S-5. 620415–001.

4/17/1962   Crawford, Evans E. (Howard University). Letter to Martin Luther King, Jr. 4/17/1962. Washington, D.C. (TLS) 1 p. MLKJP-GAMK: Box 12. 620417–002.

4/17/1962   Johnston, Mrs. E.D. Letter to Martin Luther King, Jr. 4/17/1962. (AHLS) 2 pp. MLKJP-GAMK: Box 63. 620417–007.

4/18/1962   Denver Area Council of Churches. Program, "Holy week service." 4/18/1962. Denver, Colo. (TD) 4 pp. CSKC: Sermon file. 620418–000.

4/18/1962   Jones, Clarence B. Letter to Martin Luther King, Jr. 4/18/1962. New York, N.Y. (TLS) 1 p. MLKJP-GAMK: Box 11. 620418–012.

4/19/1962   King, Martin Luther, Jr. (SCLC). Form letter to Brother-in-Christ. 4/19/1962. Atlanta, Ga. (TLS) 1 p. SCLCR-GAMK: Box 52. 620419–002.

4/19/1962   SCLC. Press release, "Martin Luther King signs up 332 volunteers in South Carolina." 4/19/1962. Atlanta, Ga. (TD) 4 pp. SCLCR-GAMK: Box 120. 620419–009.

4/20/1962   King, Martin Luther, Jr. Letter to Milton C. Froyd. 4/20/1962. [*Atlanta, Ga.*] (TLc) 1 p. MLKJP-GAMK: Box 7. 620420–001.

4/23/1962   King, Martin Luther, Jr. Letter to Evans E. Crawford. 4/23/1962. [*Atlanta, Ga.*] (TLc) 1 p. MLKJP-GAMK: Box 12. 620423–004.

4/24/1962   King, Martin Luther, Jr. Letter to Ruth H. Bunche. 4/24/1962. Atlanta, Ga. (TLS) 3 pp. (Contains enclosure 620424–010.) RJBP-NN-Sc. 620424–002.

4/24/1962   King, Martin Luther, Jr. Letter to Harvey W. Hollis. 4/24/1962. [*Atlanta, Ga.*] (TLc) 1 p. MLKP-MBU. 620424–003.

4/24/1962   King, Martin Luther, Jr. List of guests invited to luncheon for Gandhi Society for Human Rights, Inc. 4/24/1962. [*Atlanta, Ga.*] (TD) 1 p. (Enclosed in 620424–002.) UPWP-WHi: Box 399. 620424–010.

4/24/1962   King, Martin Luther, Jr. Letter to Esau Jenkins. 4/24/1962. [*Atlanta, Ga.*] (TLc) 1 p. MLKJP-GAMK: Box 22. 620424–015.

4/24/1962   Chapman, Earl (Improved, Benevolent, Protective Order of Elks of the World. Grand Lodge Elks). Letter to Martin Luther King, Jr. 4/24/1962. New York, N.Y. (TLS) 1 p. MLKJP-GAMK: Box 62. 620424–017.

4/24/1962   Goldberg, Max. Letter to Martin Luther King, Jr. 4/24/1962. Denver, Colo. (THLS) 1 p. MLKJP-GAMK: Box 63. 620424–018.

4/24/1962    King, Martin Luther, Jr. Letter to M.C. (Millard Curtis) Williams. 4/24/1962. (TLc) 1 p. SCLCR-GAMK: Box 65. 620424–022.

4/24/1962    King, Martin Luther, Jr. Form letter to Lloyd K. Garrison. 4/24/1962. Atlanta, Ga. (THLS) 3 pp. LKGP-MH-L: Box 2. 620424–023.

4/25/1962    SCLC. Press release, "Attorney General promises immediate aid in voting complaints." 4/25/1962. Atlanta, Ga. (TD) 1 p. SCLCR-GAMK: Box 120. 620425–010.

4/25/1962    SCLC. Press release, "SCLC sets annual board meeting for Chattanooga." 4/25/1962. Atlanta, Ga. (TD) 2 pp. SCLCR-GAMK: Box 120. 620425–011.

4/27/1962    Johnson, Lyndon B. (Lyndon Baines) (U.S. Office of the Vice President). Letter to Martin Luther King, Jr. 4/27/1962. Washington, D.C. (TLS) 1 p. MCMLK-RWWL: 1.1.0.24130. 620427–001.

4/27/1962    Alfred Duckett Associates, Inc. Press release, Martin Luther King, Jr. to speak at Newark's Mosque Theatre. 4/27/1962. New York, N.Y. (TD) 2 pp. SCLCR-GAMK: Box 34. 620427–004.

4/26/1962–    Princeton University. Program, "Biennial religious conference." [4/26/1962–
4/29/1962    4/29/1962]. Princeton, N.J. (PD) 4 pp. CSKCH. 620429–002.

4/29/1962    Princeton University Chapel. Program, "Order of worship." 4/29/1962. (PD) 4 pp. SGMM-NjP. 620429–004.

4/30/1962    Javits, Jacob K. (Jacob Koppel) (U.S. Congress. Senate). Letter to Martin Luther King, Jr. 4/30/1962. Washington, D.C. (THLS) 1 p. MLKJP-GAMK: Box 11. 620430–007.

9/1/1961–    Abernathy, Ralph (SCLC). "Treasurer's report." 9/1/1961–4/30/1962. (THDc) 7
4/30/1962    pp. MLKJP-GAMK: Box 32. 620430–008.

4/30/1962    King, Martin Luther, Jr. Letter to L. K. Jackson. 4/30/1962. [Atlanta, Ga.] (TLc) 2 pp. SCLCR-GAMK: Box 63. 620430–015.

4/30/1962    Baptist Minister's Conference of Philadelphia and Vicinity. Announcement, "President's first award night." 4/30/1962. Philadelphia, Pa. (PD) 2 pp. CORER-WHi: Reel 3. 620430–017.

4/1962–5/1962    SCLC. "Crusade for the ballot." [4/1962–5/1962]. Atlanta, Ga. (PD) 6 pp. MCMLK-RWWL: 6.5.0.820. 620500–006.

10/1961–5/1962    King, Martin Luther, Jr. Notes for seminar in Social Philosophy. [10/1961–5/1962]. [Atlanta, Ga.] (AD) 16 pp. MCMLK-RWWL: 5.1.0.240. 620500–009.

5/1962    [King, Martin Luther, Jr.] Form letter to Supporters. 5/1962. [Atlanta, Ga.] (TLd) 2 pp. SCLCR-GAMK: Box 4. 620500–011.

5/1962    King, Martin Luther, Jr. Draft, Form letter to Member. 5/1962. [Atlanta, Ga.] (AD) 1 p. MCMLK-RWWL: 9.0.0.140. 620500–012.

5/1962    King, Martin Luther, Jr. (Ebenezer Baptist Church). Form letter to Members. 5/1962. Atlanta, Ga. (TLS) 1 p. EBCR. 620500–013.

5/1962    World Constitution Coordinating Committee. "Call to all nations of the world." [5/1962]. Phoenix, Ariz. (PD) 2 pp. MLKJP-GAMK: Box 27. 620500–014.

5/1/1962    Mays, Benjamin Elijah (Morehouse College). Letter to Martin Luther King, Jr. 5/1/1962. Atlanta, Ga. (TLS) 1 p. MLKJP-GAMK: Box 11. 620501–002.

5/1/1962    Lewis, Claude A. (Newsweek). Letter to Martin Luther King, Jr. 5/1/1962. New York, N.Y. (THLS) 1 p. MLKJP-GAMK. 620501–003.

5/1/1962    Reid, Frank Madison (St. James AME Church). Letter to Martin Luther King, Jr. 5/1/1962. St. Louis, Mo. (TLS) 2 pp. MLKJP-GAMK: Box 64. 620501–005.

5/2/1962    King, Martin Luther, Jr., and Wyatt Tee Walker (SCLC). Form letter to Ralph J. (Ralph Johnson) Bunche. 5/2/1962. Atlanta, Ga. (TLS) 1 p. (Contains enclosure 620502–012.) RJBPC-CLU-AR: Box 26. 620502–004.

5/2/1962    Helstein, Ralph (United Packinghouse Workers of America, AFL-CIO). Letter to Martin Luther King, Jr. 5/2/1962. Chicago, Ill. (TLS) 1 p. MLKJP-GAMK: Box 11. 620502–005.

5/2/1962    Abernathy, Ralph, Ralph J. (Ralph Johnson) Bunche, Harry Belafonte, Martin Luther King, Jr., John La Farge, George Meany, Herbert H. (Herbert Henry) Lehman, James A. (James Albert) Pike, A. Philip (Asa Philip) Randolph, Jackie Robinson, Eleanor Roosevelt, Walter Reuther, Clarence Pickett, Fred L. Shuttlesworth, Lillian Eugenia Smith, Wyatt Tee Walker, and Roy Wilkins. Petition, "For an executive order outlawing segregation in American life." 5/2/1962. Atlanta, Ga. (TD) 3 pp. (Enclosed in 620502–004.) RJBPC-CLU-AR: Box 26. 620502–012.

5/3/1962    SCLC. Press release, "SCLC leader bombed out second time." 5/3/1962. Atlanta, Ga. (TD) 1 p. SAVFC-WHi. 620503–007.

| | |
|---|---|
| 5/3/1962 | Ahmann, Mathew H. (National Catholic Conference for Interracial Justice). Letter to Martin Luther King, Jr. 5/3/1962. Chicago, Ill. (THLS) 1 p. (Marginal comments by King.) MLKJP-GAMK: Box 17. 620503–008. |
| 5/3/1962 | SCLC. Press release, "SCLC protests jailing of expectant mother in Jackson Mississippi." 5/3/1962. Atlanta, Ga. (TD) 1 p. SCLCR-GAMK: Box 120. 620503–011. |
| 5/4/1962 | McDonald, Dora E. Letter to Lillian Eugenia Smith. 5/4/1962. (TLc) 1 p. (Contains enclosure 620403–007.) MLKJP-GAMK: Box 9. 620504–003. |
| 5/4/1962 | King, Martin Luther, Jr. Letter to Irving Horowitz. 5/4/1962. [*Atlanta, Ga.*] (THLc) 2 pp. MLKJP-GAMK: Box 29. 620504–007. |
| 5/4/1962 | McDonald, Dora E. Letter to Frank Madison Reid. 5/4/1962. [*Atlanta, Ga.*] (TLc) 1 p. (Contains enclosure 620504–011, p. 453, in this volume.) MLKJP-GAMK: Box 64. 620504–010. |
| 10/22/1961– 5/6/1962 | Chapman College. Announcement, "Artist lecture series." 10/22/1961–5/6/1962. Orange, Calif. (PD) 1 p. FMPL-SCA-COrC. 620506–000. |
| 5/7/1962 | Smith, Lillian Eugenia. Letter to Martin Luther King, Jr. 5/7/1962. Clayton, Ga. (TALS) 1 p. MLKJP-GAMK: Box 9. 620507–001. |
| 5/7/1962 | Jones, Clarence B. Letter to Martin Luther King, Jr. 5/7/1962. New York, N.Y. (TLS) 2 pp. MLKJP-GAMK: Box 11. 620507–004. |
| 5/7/1962 | King, Martin Luther, Jr. Letter to Max Greenberg. 5/7/1962. [*Atlanta, Ga.*] (THLc) 2 pp. MLKJP-GAMK: Box 14. 620507–010. |
| 5/8/1962 | Randolph, A. Philip (Asa Philip) (Brotherhood of Sleeping Car Porters and Maids). Letter to Martin Luther King, Jr. 5/8/1962. New York, N.Y. (TLS) 1 p. MLKJP-GAMK: Box 11. 620508–003. |
| 5/10/1962 | Salem Methodist Church. Program, "Fourth annual F.A. Cullen achievement award banquet honoring Martin Luther King, Jr." 5/10/1962. New York, N.Y. (PD) 4 pp. WAWP. 620510–003. |
| 5/10/1962 | SCLC. Press release, "King to present emancipation document to JFK." 5/10/1962. Atlanta, Ga. (TD) 2 pp. SCLCR-GAMK: Box 120. 620510–010. |
| 5/10/1962 | King, Martin Luther, Jr. (Gandhi Society for Human Rights, Inc.). Form telegram to Lee C. White. 5/10/1962. (PWSr) 2 pp. JFKWHCNF-MBJFK: Box 1478. 620510–013. |
| 5/11/1962 | King, Martin Luther, Jr. (SCLC). Form letter to Friend of Freedom. 5/11/1962. Atlanta, Ga. (TLc) 1 p. SCLCR-GAMK: Box 116. 620511–012. |
| 5/14/1962 | King, Martin Luther, Jr. (SCLC). Letter to Jackie Robinson. 5/14/1962. [*Atlanta, Ga.*] (TLc) 1 p. MLKJP-GAMK: Box 20. 620514–004. |
| 5/15/1962 | Minutes, SCLC board meeting. 5/15/1962. Chattanooga, Tenn. (TD) 11 pp. MLKJP-GAMK: Box 29. 620515–000. |
| 5/15/1962 | National Conference on Religion and Race, Chicago, 1963. Memo, "Conference on Religion and Race: Challenge to Justice and Love." [5/15/1962]. (TL) 2 pp. (Enclosed in 620515–005.) MLKP-MBU. 620515–004. |
| 5/15/1962 | Miller, J. Irwin, William E. Cousins, and Julius Mark (National Council of the Churches of Christ in the United States of America, National Catholic Welfare Conference and Synagogue Council of America). Letter to Martin Luther King, Jr. 5/15/1962. Chicago, Ill. (THLS) 2 pp. (Contains enclosure 620515–004.) MLKP-MBU. 620515–005. |
| 5/15/1962 | Fulton, Robert Brank (Inter-American University). Letter to Martin Luther King, Jr. 5/15/1962. San Germán, Puerto Rico. (TLc) 1 p. RBFP. 620515–014. |
| 5/16/1962 | Minutes, SCLC board meeting. 5/16/1962. Chattanooga, Tenn. (TD) 7 pp. SCLCE-GEU-S: Box 1. 620516–000. |
| 5/15/1962– 5/16/1962 | SCLC. Program, "Board meeting of the SCLC." 5/15/1962–5/16/1962. Chattanooga, Tenn. (PD) 2 pp. MLKJP-GAMK: Box 29. 620516–005. |
| 5/16/1962 | Marshall, Burke (U.S. Dept. of Justice). Letter to Martin Luther King, Jr. 5/16/1962. Washington, D.C. (TLS) 1 p. MLKJP-GAMK: Box 24. 620516–007. |
| 5/16/1962 | Maynard, Gould (SCLC). Press release, "Belafonte head deep-south for first time." 5/16/1962. Atlanta, Ga. (TD) 2 pp. SCLCR-GAMK: Box 120. 620516–009. |
| 5/17/1962 | King, Martin Luther, Jr. (SCLC). "An Appeal to the Honorable John F. Kennedy, President of the United States for National Rededication to the Principles of the Emancipation Proclamation and for an Executive Order." 5/17/1962. Atlanta, Ga. (TD) 60 pp. BRP-DLC: Reel 3. 620517–002. |
| 5/17/1962 | King, Martin Luther, Jr. Excerpts, Press conference on the formation of the Gandhi Society for Human Rights and the appeal for a second Emancipation Proclamation. [5/17/1962]. [*Washington, D.C.*] (At) 16.2 min. (1 sound cassette: analog.) MMFR. 620517–006. |

| | | |
|---|---|---|
| 5/17/1962 | Gandhi Society for Human Rights, Inc. Press release, Founding of Gandhi Society for Human Rights in Washington, D.C. 5/17/1962. Washington, D.C. (TD) 3 pp. MLKJP-GAMK: Box 11. 620517–010. |
| 5/17/1962 | McDonald, Dora E. Letter to Walter Reuther. 5/17/1962. (TLc) 1 p. (Contains enclosure 620517–013.) MLKJP-GAMK: Box 20. 620517–012. |
| 5/17/1962 | King, Martin Luther, Jr. Letter to Edward L. Cushman. 5/17/1962. [*Atlanta, Ga.*] (TLc) 1 p. (Enclosed in 620517–012.) MLKJP-GAMK: Box 20. 620517–013. |
| 5/17/1962 | King, Martin Luther, Jr. Interview on progress toward integration. [*5/17/1962*]. [*Washington, D.C.*] (F) 1.8 min (1 videocassette.) CBSNA-NNCBS. 620517–017. |
| 5/17/1962 | SCLC. Press release, "Mrs. Martin Luther King, Jr. named mother of the year." 5/17/1962. Atlanta, Ga. (TD) 1 p. SCLCR-GAMK: Box 120. 620517–019. |
| 5/17/1962 | SCLC. Press release, "SCLC kicks off national petition campaign." 5/17/1962. Atlanta, Ga. (TD) 1 p. SCLCR-GAMK: Box 120. 620517–020. |
| 5/17/1962 | King, Martin Luther, Jr. Draft, Address at the formation of the Gandhi Society for Human Rights. 5/17/1962. [*Washington, D.C.*] (TAHDd) 8 pp. MLKJP-GAMK: Box 4. 620517–021. |
| 5/18/1962 | Morsell, John A. (NAACP). Letter to Martin Luther King, Jr. 5/18/1962. New York, N.Y. (THLS) 1 p. MLKP-MBU. 620518–003. |
| 5/20/1962 | King, Martin Luther, Jr. Interview by Paul Niven on "Washington Conversation." 5/20/1962. Washington, D.C. (TTv) 17 pp. MCMLK-RWWL: 3.3.0.720. 620520–000. |
| 5/20/1962 | Galphin, Bruce (*Atlanta Constitution*). Letter to Martin Luther King, Jr. 5/20/1962. (TLS) 1 p. MLKJP-GAMK: Box 11. 620520–002. |
| 5/21/1962 | King, Martin Luther, Jr. Address at the thirteenth constitutional convention of the United Packinghouse Workers of America. 5/21/1962. Minneapolis, Minn. (TD) 23 pp. UPWR-WHi: Box 21. 620521–003. |
| 12/1961–5/21/1962 | King, Martin Luther, Jr. (Ebenezer Baptist Church). Notes on Ebenezer's 75th anniversary fund raising drive. [*12/1961–5/21/1962*]. [*Atlanta, Ga.*] (AD) 14 pp. MCMLK-RWWL: 3.3.0.720. 620521–009. |
| 5/21/1962 | SCLC. Press release, "Belafonte heads deep-south for first time." 5/21/1962. Atlanta, Ga. (TD) 1 p. SCLCR-GAMK: Box 120. 620521–010. |
| 5/22/1962 | Ebenezer Baptist Church. Program, Seventy-fifth anniversary diamond jubilee service. 5/22/1962. Atlanta, Ga. (TD) 1 p. CKFC. 620522–000. |
| 5/23/1962 | King, Martin Luther, Jr. (SCLC). Form letter to Walter Reuther. 5/23/1962. Atlanta, Ga. (TLS) 2 pp. WPRC-MiDW-AL: Box 523. 620523–000. |
| 5/23/1962 | Brown, Paul D. (Allied Real Estate Board, Inc.). Letter to Martin Luther King, Jr. 5/23/1962. Lawrence, N.Y. (THLS) 2 pp. MLKP-MBU. 620523–002. |
| 5/23/1962 | King, Martin Luther, Jr. "The Future of Race Relations in the United States," Address delivered at Dartmouth College. 5/23/1962. Hanover, N.H. (At) 61 min. (1 sound cassette: analog.) GIDC-NhD. 620523–003. |
| 5/23/1962 | King, Martin Luther, Jr. (Ebenezer Baptist Church). Letter to Thomas Kilgore. 5/23/1962. [*Atlanta, Ga.*] (TLc) 1 p. MLKJP-GAMK: Box 14. 620523–012. |
| 5/23/1962 | SCLC. Press release, "King at Philadelphia's convention hall." 5/23/1962. Atlanta, Ga. (TD) 1 p. SCLCR-GAMK: Box 120. 620523–020. |
| 5/24/1962 | Kassel, Virginia. Letter to Dora E. McDonald. 5/24/1962. (TLS) 2 pp. (Contains enclosure 620524–002.) MLKJP-GAMK. 620524–001. |
| 5/24/1962 | King, Martin Luther, Jr. Statement on desegregation. [*5/24/1962*]. [*Atlanta, Ga.*] (TD) 3 pp. (Enclosed in 620524–001.) MLKJP-GAMK. 620524–002. |
| 5/24/1962 | King, Martin Luther, Jr. "The Mission to the Social Frontiers," Address at the American Baptist Convention. 5/24/1962. Philadelphia, Pa. (TD) 17 pp. ABHSR-GaAaBHS. 620524–003. |
| 5/25/1962 | King, Martin Luther, Jr. (Belafonte Concert Committee). Form letter to Friend. 5/25/1962. Atlanta, Ga. (TLc) 1 p. MCMLK-RWWL: 6.1.0.3830. 620525–002. |
| 5/25/1962 | Williams, Nelson and Edith Dixon (Salem Methodist Church). Letter to Martin Luther King, Jr. 5/25/1962. New York, N.Y. (TLS) 1 p. MLKP-MBU. 620525–004. |
| 5/25/1962 | Bodein, Vernon Parker (Hampton Institute). Letter to Martin Luther King, Jr. 5/25/1962. Hampton, Va. (TLS) 1 p. (Contains enclosure 620629–000.) MLKP-MBU. 620525–005. |
| 5/25/1962 | King, Martin Luther, Jr. (SCLC). Form letter to Friend. 5/25/1962. Atlanta, Ga. (TLS) 1 p. MLKP-MBU. 620525–006. |
| 5/26/1962 | Press release, "M.L. King will address NAACP's Atlanta meeting." 5/26/1962. Atlanta, Ga. (TD) 1 p. NAACPP-DLC: Group 3–A177. 620526–003. |

| | | |
|---|---|---|
| 5/26/1962 | Thomas, Joseph A. (Grace Baptist Church). Letter to Martin Luther King, Jr. 5/26/1962. Westmont, N.J. (THLS) 1 p. MLKJP-GAMK: Box 6. 620526–004. | Calendar |

5/21/1962–
5/27/1962
Ebenezer Baptist Church. Program, Seventy-fifth anniversary diamond jubilee. 5/21/1962–5/27/1962. Atlanta, Ga. (PD) 49 pp. EBCR. 620527–002.

5/28/1962
King, Martin Luther, Jr. Letter to Paul D. Brown. 5/28/1962. [*Atlanta, Ga.*] (TLc) 1 p. MLKP-MBU. 620528–001.

5/28/1962
King, Martin Luther, Jr., and Wyatt Tee Walker (SCLC). Form letter to Roy Wilkins. 5/28/1962. (TLc) 1 p. SCLCR-GAMK: Box 5. 620528–013.

5/29/1962
[*Williams, Samuel W.*] "Social Philosophy, final examination." 5/29/1962. [*Atlanta, Ga.*] (AD) 1 p. MCMLK-RWWL: 5.1.0.290. 620529–000.

5/29/1962
King, Martin Luther, Jr. Letter to the Committee on Character and Fitness, Appellate Division of the Supreme Court of the State of New York. 5/29/1962. Atlanta, Ga. (TLc) 1 p. MLKJP-GAMK: Box 13. 620529–002.

5/29/1962
Manfred, Carl L. (Luther League). Letter to Martin Luther King, Jr. 5/29/1962. Minneapolis, Minn. (TLS) 1 p. MLKJP-GAMK: Box 47. 620529–005.

5/29/1962
[*King, Martin Luther, Jr.*] "Examination for Martin Luther King, Jr.'s class." [*5/29/1962*]. [*Atlanta, Ga.*] (THD) 1 p. (Marginal comments by King.) MCMLK-RWWL: 5.1.0.290. 620529–008.

5/29/1962
Episcopal Society for Cultural and Racial Unity. Press release, John Burnett Morris statement on disappointment in religious divergence. 5/29/1962. Atlanta, Ga. (PD) 1 p. MLKJP-GAMK: Box 11. 620529–009.

5/31/1962
McDonald, Dora E. Letter to Social Secretary. 5/31/1962. [*Atlanta, Ga.*] (TLc) 1 p. MLKJP-GAMK: Box 26. 620531–001.

5/31/1962
SCLC. Press release, "Belafonte helps Atlanta push forward in race relations." 5/31/1962. Atlanta, Ga. (TD) 1 p. EJBC-NN-Sc. 620531–006.

5/1962–6/1962
King, Martin Luther, Jr. Interview on progress toward integration. [*5/1962–6/1962*]. [*Atlanta, Ga.*] (F) 2.4 min. (1 videocassette.) CBSNA-NNCBS. 620600–018.

6/1/1962
Scripps, Edward W. (National Press Club). Letter to Martin Luther King, Jr. 6/1/1962. Washington, D.C. (THLS) 1 p. MLKP-MBU. 620601–008.

6/3/1962
Gray, William Herbert (Bright Hope Baptist Church). Letter to Martin Luther King, Jr. 6/3/1962. Philadelphia, Pa. (TLS) 1 p. (Contains enclosure 620603–001.) MLKJP-GAMK: Box 20. 620603–000.

6/3/1962
Bowser, Charles W. Statement prepared for Martin Luther King, Jr. on voter registration and voting. 6/3/1962. Philadelphia, Pa. (TD) 1 p. (Enclosed in 620603–000.) MLKJP-GAMK: Box 20. 620603–001.

6/4/1962
King, Martin Luther, Jr. (SCLC). Telegram to Robert F. Kennedy. 6/4/1962. Atlanta, Ga. (TWc) 1 p. MCMLK-RWWL: 1.1.0.25650. 620604–000.

6/4/1962
King, Martin Luther, Jr. Letter to Gene Martin Lyons. 6/4/1962. [*Atlanta, Ga.*] (TLc) 1 p. MLKP-MBU. 620604–001.

6/4/1962
King, Martin Luther, Jr. Letter to George E. Johnson. 6/4/1962. [*Atlanta, Ga.*] (TLc) 1 p. MLKP-MBU. 620604–009.

6/5/1962
Kennedy, John F. (John Fitzgerald) (U.S. White House). Invitation to Martin Luther King, Jr. 6/5/1962. Washington, D.C. (PD) 2 pp. MCMLK-RWWL: 1.1.0.25610. 620605–000.

6/5/1962
Yungblut, John R. (Quaker House). Letter to Martin Luther King, Jr. 6/5/1962. Atlanta, Ga. (TLS) 1 p. MLKJP-GAMK: Box 2. 620605–001.

6/5/1962
NAACP. Announcement, "All roads lead to Atlanta." 6/5/1962. New York, N.Y. (TD) 1 p. MLKJP-GAMK: Box 17. 620605–005.

6/6/1962
[*SCLC*]. Press release, Refusal of restaurant to seat Belafonte. 6/6/1962. (TD) 1 p. MLKJP-GAMK: Box 4. 620606–007.

6/6/1962
SCLC. Program, "Belafonte." [*6/6/1962*]. Atlanta, Ga. (PHDd) 25 pp. SCLCR-GAMK: Box 51. 620606–008.

6/8/1962
King, Martin Luther, Jr. (SCLC). Telegram to J.H. Lewis. 6/8/1962. (PWc) 2 pp. MLKJP-GAMK: Box 7. 620608–002.

6/9/1962
King, Martin Luther, Jr. "People in Action: Can We Ever Repay Them?" *New York Amsterdam News*, 9 June 1962, p. 11. (PD) 1 p. 620609–000.

6/11/1962
Eskridge, Chauncey (McCoy, Ming, & Leighton). Letter to Martin Luther King, Jr. 6/11/1962. Chicago, Ill. (THLS) 1 p. (Contains enclosure 620615–007.) MLKJP-GAMK: Box 9. 620611–006.

6/11/1962
Walker, Wyatt Tee (SCLC). Affidavit. 6/11/1962. Fulton, Ga. (TD) 7 pp. SCLCR-GAMK: Box 36. 620611–007.

6/11/1962
U.S. FBI. Report, Physical surveillance of Stanley D. Levison. 6/11/1962. New York, N.Y. (TADf) 6 pp. RFBI-DNA: Bureau File 100–111180–57/58. 620611–008.

| | |
|---|---|
| 6/12/1962 | Pawlicki, Audrey. "1,500 Hear Rev. King at Gary Freedom Rally." *Gary Post-Tribune*, 12 June 1962 (PD) 3 pp. 620612–001. |
| 6/12/1962 | U.S. FBI. Report, "Martin Luther King Security Matter." 6/12/1962. New York, N.Y. (THD) 2 pp. FBIDG-NN-Sc: Bureau File 100–106670–73. 620612–005. |
| 6/12/1962–6/13/1962 | National Sunday School and Baptist Training Union Congress. Program, "Fifty-eighth annual session." 6/12/1962–6/13/1962. Atlanta, Ga. (TD) 4 pp. EBCR. 620613–002. |
| 6/13/1962 | SCLC. Press release, "Belafonte dazzles Atlanta in first deep south appearance." 6/13/1962. Atlanta, Ga. (TD) 2 pp. SCLCR-GAMK: Box 120. 620613–007. |
| 6/14/1962 | King, Martin Luther, Jr. Letter to Mathew H. Ahmann. 6/14/1962. Atlanta, Ga. (TLc) 1 p. MLKJP-GAMK: Box 17. 620614–010. |
| 6/14/1962 | McDonald, Dora E. Letter to Carl L. Manfred. 6/14/1962. [*Atlanta, Ga.*] (TLS) 1 p. MLKJP-GAMK: Box 47. 620614–013. |
| 6/15/1962 | Johnson, Lyndon B. (Lyndon Baines) (U.S. Office of the Vice President). Letter to Martin Luther King, Jr. 6/15/1962. Washington, D.C. (TLS) 1 p. MCMLK-RWWL: 1.1.0.24130. 620615–000. |
| 6/15/1962 | Rockefeller, Nelson A. (Nelson Aldrich) (New York. Office of the Governor). Letter to Martin Luther King, Jr. 6/15/1962. Albany, N.Y. (TALS) 1 p. MCMLK-RWWL: 1.1.0.39800. 620615–001. |
| 6/15/1962 | Klein, Jerome E. (Lane Bryant Annual Awards). Letter to Martin Luther King, Jr. 6/15/1962. New York, N.Y. (TLS) 2 pp. (Contains enclosure 620615–005.) MLKJP-GAMK: Box 14. 620615–004. |
| 6/15/1962 | Lane Bryant Annual Awards. "Citation as Semi-Finalist." 6/15/1962. (TD) 2 pp. (Enclosed in 620615–004.) MLKJP-GAMK: Box 14. 620615–005. |
| 6/15/1962 | SCLC. Press release, "SCLC officials pass 'lunacy test,'" 6/15/1962. Atlanta, Ga. (TD) 2 pp. SCLCR-GAMK: Box 120. 620615–006. |
| 6/15/1962 | Nunn, William G. (*Pittsburgh Courier*). Letter to John H. McCray. 6/15/1962. (THLc) 1 p. (Enclosed in 620611–006.) MLKJP-GAMK: Box 9. 620615–007. |
| 6/16/1962 | Nixon, Richard M. (Richard Milhous). Telegram to Martin Luther King, Jr. 6/16/1962. (TWc) 1 p. PPRN-CYIRMN. 620616–000. |
| 6/16/1962 | American Friends Service Committee. Announcement, "Martin Luther King, Jr. speaks on 'Powers Greater than Violence.'" [*6/16/1962*]. Pasadena, Calif. (TD) 1 p. (Enclosed in 620622–006.) SCLCR-GAMK: Box 51. 620616–002. |
| 6/20/1962 | Jones, Clarence B. (Gandhi Society for Human Rights, Inc.). Memo, "The formation of the Gandhi Society for Human Rights, Inc." 6/20/1962. New York, N.Y. (TL) 3 pp. WGAC-GAMK. 620620–001. |
| 6/20/1962 | Scripps, Edward W. (National Press Club). Letter to Martin Luther King, Jr. 6/20/1962. Washington, D.C. (PWc) 1 p. MLKP-MBU. 620620–009. |
| 6/21/1962 | U.S. FBI. Report on Martin Luther King, Jr. 6/21/1962. New York, N.Y. (THD) 2 pp. FBIDG-NN-Sc: Bureau File 100–106670–80. 620621–004. |
| 6/22/1962 | King, Hardin W. (University of Georgia). Letter to Martin Luther King, Jr. 6/22/1962. Athens, Ga. (THLS) 1 p. MLKP-MBU. 620622–000. |
| 6/22/1962 | Lee, J. Oscar (National Council of the Churches of Christ in the United States of America. Dept. of Racial and Cultural Relations). Letter to Martin Luther King, Jr. 6/22/1962. New York, N.Y. (THLS) 1 p. MLKJP-GAMK: Box 17. 620622–001. |
| 6/22/1962 | King, Martin Luther, Jr. Draft, Invitation to a nonviolence seminar at the Dorchester Center, Midway, Ga. 6/22/1962. (TLd) 1 p. SCLC-GAMK: Box 35. 620622–002. |
| 6/22/1962 | Moody, Curt (American Friends Service Committee). Letter to Wyatt Tee Walker. 6/22/1962. Pasadena, Calif. (TLS) 1 p. (Contains enclosure 620616–002.) MLKJP-GAMK: Box 51. 620622–006. |
| 6/22/1962 | SCLC. Press release, Wyatt Tee Walker clarifies statement of Martin Luther King, Jr. regarding Black Muslims. 6/22/1962. Atlanta, Ga. (TD) 2 pp. SCLCR-GAMK: Box 120. 620622–008. |
| 6/22/1962 | NAACP. Press release, "Voting, schools and jobs, NAACP convention topics." 6/22/1962. New York, N.Y. (TD) 6 pp. TeM-TNJ. 620622–009. |
| 6/23/1962 | King, Martin Luther, Jr. Draft, "New Harassment: The Lunacy Test." [*6/23/1962*]. [*Atlanta, Ga.*] (THDd) 6 pp. (Draft of 6/23/1962 *New York Amsterdam News*.) MLKJP-GAMK. 620623–000. |
| 6/23/1962 | McDonald, Dora E. Letter to Kyle Haselden. 6/23/1962. Atlanta, Ga. (TLc) 1 p. (Contains enclosure 620623–004.) MLKJP-GAMK: Box 6. 620623–003. |
| 6/23/1962 | King, Martin Luther, Jr. Letter to Harold Edward Fey. 6/23/1962. Atlanta, Ga. (TLc) 5 pp. (Enclosed in 620625–001 & 620623–003.) MLKJP-GAMK: Box 6. 620623–004. |

| | |
|---|---|
| 6/23/1962 | Bard College. Program, "The One hundred and second Annual Commencement." 6/23/1962. Annandale-on-Hudson, N.Y. (PD) 7 pp. NAnB. 620623–007. |
| 6/25/1962 | McDonald, Dora E. Letter to Mordecai W. (Mordecai Wyatt) Johnson. 6/25/1962. Atlanta, Ga. (TLc) 1 p. (Contains enclosure 620623–004.) MLKJP-GAMK: Box 6. 620625–001. |
| 6/25/1962 | Daniels, Samuel T. (Most Worshipful Prince Hall Grand Lodge). Letter to Martin Luther King, Jr. 6/25/1962. Baltimore, Md. (TLS) 1 p. MLKP-MBU. 620625–007. |
| 6/27/1962 | Marshall, Burke (U.S. Dept. of Justice). Letter to Wyatt Tee Walker. 6/27/1962. Washington, D.C. (TLS) 1 p. MLKJP-GAMK: Box 36. 620627–002. |
| 6/28/1962 | SCLC. Press release, "Dr. King invites investigation." 6/28/1962. Atlanta, Ga. (TD) 2 pp. SCLCR-GAMK: Box 120. 620628–009. |
| 6/25/1962–6/29/1962 | Hampton Institute. Program, "Forty-eighth annual Hampton Institute ministers conference." [6/25/1962–6/29/1962]. Hampton, Va. (PHD) 16 pp. (Enclosed in 620525–005.) MLKP-MBU. 620629–000. |
| 7/1962 | Kunstler, William M. (William Moses) (Kunstler & Kunstler). Letter to William G. Anderson. 7/1962. New York, N.Y. (ALS) 1 p. (Contains enclosure 620700–007.) WGAC-GAMK. 620700–006. |
| 7/1962 | State of Georgia, Respondent. "Petition for removal," *Martin Luther King, Jr. v. State of Georgia.* 7/1962. (TDd) 3 pp. (Enclosed in 620700–006.) WGAC-GAMK. 620700–007. |
| 7/1962 | King, Martin Luther, Jr. "Civil Disobedience." 7/1962. Albany, Ga. (D) 3 pp. AJYP-GA: Box 11. 620700–008. |
| 6/1962–7/1962 | King, Martin Luther, Jr. Book review, *The Desegregated Heart* by Sarah-Patton Boyle. [6/1962–7/1962]. Atlanta, Ga. (TD) 1 p. MLKJP-GAMK: Box 4. 620700–014. |
| 7/1962 | King, Martin Luther, Jr. (Gandhi Society for Human Rights, Inc.). "Draft of proposed covering letter to first issue of newsletter." [7/1962]. [Atlanta, Ga.] (TLd) 1 p. MLKJP-GAMK: Box 11. 620700–022. |
| 7/1962 | King, Martin Luther, Jr. (Gandhi Society for Human Rights, Inc.). Draft, "The Rev. Martin Luther King, Jr.—Human rights reporter." [7/1962]. [Atlanta, Ga.] (TDd) 3 pp. UPWP-WHi: Box 179. 620700–024. |
| 7/1962 | King, Martin Luther, Jr. (SCLC). Form letter. [7/1962]. Atlanta, Ga. (TLS) 2 pp. SCLCR-GAMK: Box 50. 620700–031. |
| 7/1962 | SCLC. Press release, Martin Luther King, Jr. speaks out against the dangers of tokenism. [7/1962]. [Atlanta, Ga.] (TDf) 1 p. SNCCP-GAMK: Reel 9. 620700–039. |
| 7/2/1962 | King, Martin Luther, Jr. Letter to Peggy Brooks. 7/2/1962. [Atlanta, Ga.] (TLc) 2 pp. (Contains enclosure 620702–013.) SPCC-ScCC. 620702–000. |
| 7/2/1962 | King, Martin Luther, Jr. Letter to Benjamin Elijah Mays. 7/2/1962. Atlanta, Ga. (TLc) 1 p. MLKJP-GAMK: Box 15. 620702–006. |
| 7/2/1962 | King, Martin Luther, Jr., and Wyatt Tee Walker (SCLC). Telegram to Burke Marshall. 7/2/1962. Atlanta, Ga. (TWc) 1 p. MLKJP-GAMK: Box 24. 620702–007. |
| 7/2/1962 | Gandhi Society for Human Rights, Inc. Mission statement. 7/2/1962. (TD) 7 pp. MLKJP-GAMK: Box 11. 620702–010. |
| 7/2/1962 | King, Martin Luther, Jr. Book review, *Echo in My Soul* by Septima Poinsette Clark. 7/1962. [Atlanta, Ga.] (TD) 1 p. (Enclosed in 620702–000.) SPCC-ScCC: Box 3. 620702–013. |
| 7/3/1962 | King, Martin Luther, Jr., and Wyatt Tee Walker (SCLC). Telegram to Roy Wilkins. 7/3/1962. [Atlanta, Ga.] (PHWc) 2 pp. MCMLK-RWWL: 6.2.0.5040. 620703–003. |
| 7/3/1962 | Cullen, George (National Press Club). Letter to Martin Luther King, Jr. 7/3/1962. Washington, D.C. (TLS) 1 p. MLKP-MBU. 620703–011. |
| **7/5/1962** | **King, Martin Luther, Jr. Draft, Address at the fifty-third annual convention of the NAACP. 7/5/1962. [*Atlanta, Ga.*] (ADf) 25 pp. MCMLK-RWWL: 2.3.0.70. 620705–004.** |
| 7/5/1962 | NAACP. Program, "N.A.A.C.P. Fight for Freedom Fund and Awards Dinner." 7/5/1962. Atlanta, Ga. (TD) 7 pp. MLKJP-GAMK: Box 23. 620705–010. |
| 7/5/1962 | King, C.B. (Chevene Bowers). Letter to Martin Luther King, Jr. 7/5/1962. Albany, Ga. (TLS) 1 p. MLKJP-GAMK: Box 14. 620705–011. |
| 7/5/1962 | King, Martin Luther, Jr. Press interview on hotel and restaurant desegregation. [7/5/1962]. Atlanta, Ga. (THD) 2 pp. MLKJP-GAMK. 620705–014. |
| 7/6/1962 | Fey, Harold Edward (Christian Century Press). Letter to Martin Luther King, Jr. 7/6/1962. Chicago, Ill. (TALS) 1 p. MLKJP-GAMK: Box 6. 620706–000. |
| 7/6/1962 | Young, Andrew (SCLC). Form letter to Friends. 7/6/1962. Atlanta, Ga. (TLc) 1 p. SCLCR-GAMK: Box 50. 620706–003. |
| 7/7/1962 | King, Martin Luther, Jr. "People in Action: The Wind of Change." *New York Amsterdam News*, 7 July 1962. (PD) 2 pp. 620707–001. |

7/9/1962    Kaplan, Kivie. Form letter to Martin Luther King, Jr. 7/9/1962. (TL) 2 pp. (Contains enclosure 620723–019, pp. 546–547, in this volume.) MLKJP-GAMK: Box 13. 620709–003.

7/9/1962    Farmer, James (CORE). Letter to Martin Luther King, Jr. 7/9/1962. (TLc) 1 p. CORER-WHi: Reel 5. 620709–012.

7/10/1962    Porter, W. Hubert (American Baptist Convention). Letter to Martin Luther King, Jr. 7/10/1962. Valley Forge, Pa. (TLS) 1 p. MLKJP-GAMK: Box 2. 620710–003.

7/10/1962    King, Martin Luther, Jr. Letter to Morris H. Rubin. 7/10/1962. Atlanta, Ga. (TLS) 1 p. PP-WHi: Box 19. 620710–005.

7/10/1962    [*McDonald, Dora E.*] Letter to Martin Luther King, Jr. 7/10/1962. (TLf) 2 pp. MLKJP-GAMK: Box 15. 620710–006.

7/10/1962    Marshall, Burke (U.S. Dept. of Justice). Letter to Martin Luther King, Jr. 7/10/1962. Washington, D.C. (TLS) 1 p. MLKJP-GAMK: Box 24. 620710–013.

7/10/1962    SCLC. Press release, "Dr. King in Albany for sentencing." [*7/10/1962*]. Atlanta, Ga. (TD) 1 p. SAVFC-WHi. 620710–014.

7/10/1962    Walker, Wyatt Tee (SCLC). Form Telegram to Friends. 7/10/1962. (PWSr) 2 pp. SCLCR-GAMK: Box 3. 620710–015.

7/10/1962    Film footage, Martin Luther King, Jr. and Ralph Abernathy enter Albany jail. [*7/10/1962*]. Albany, Ga. (F) 1.9 min. (1 videocassette.) WSB-TV-GU. 620710–019.

7/10/1962    SCLC. Press release, "Joint statement of Drs. Martin Luther King, Jr., and Ralph D. Abernathy, president and treasurer of SCLC respectively." [*7/10/1962*]. Atlanta, Ga. (TD) 1 p. MLKJP-GAMK: Box 2. 620710–020.

7/10/1962    Walker, Wyatt Tee. Draft, Telegram to Robert F. Kennedy. [*7/10/1962*]. (TWd) 1 p. MLKJP-GAMK: Box 2. 620710–022.

**7/10/1962– 7/11/1962**    **King, Martin Luther, Jr. Albany Jail Diary from 10 July–11 July 1962. [*Albany, Ga.*] (AD) 7 pp. MCMLK-RWWL: 2.6.0.90. 620711–002.**

7/11/1962    Golden, Harry. Telegram to S. Ernest (Samuel Ernest) Vandiver. 7/11/1962. (PAWSr) 1 p. JFKWHCNF-MBJFK: Box 1478. 620711–003.

7/11/1962    SCLC. Press release, "King and Abernathy choose jail." 7/11/1962. Atlanta, Ga. (TD) 3 pp. SCLCR-GAMK: Box 120. 620711–008.

7/12/1962    King, Martin Luther, Jr. Statement on SCLC's commitment to Albany. 7/12/1962. Albany, Ga. (TTa) 1 p. MLKJP-GAMK. 620712–000.

7/12/1962    Gandhi Society for Human Rights, Inc. Press release regarding the arrest of Martin Luther King, Jr. and Ralph Abernathy. 7/12/1962. (TD) 1 p. MLKJP-GAMK: Vault. 620712–001.

**7/12/1962**    **Associated Press. Photo of Martin Luther King, Jr. addressing Mt. Zion Baptist Church. [*7/12/1962*.] [*Albany, Ga.*] (Ph) 1 p. NNAPWW. 620712–004.**

7/12/1962    Bell, Colin W. (American Friends Service Committee). Letter to Martin Luther King, Jr. 7/12/1962. Philadelphia, Pa. (TLS) 1 p. (Enclosed in 620713–002.) MLKJP-GAMK: Box 2. 620712–005.

7/12/1962    King, Martin Luther, Jr. (SCLC). Form letter to Pastor. 7/12/1962. Albany, Ga. (TLS) 1 p. SCLCR-GAMK: Box 51. 620712–010.

7/12/1962    SCLC. Press release, "Governor Rockefeller declares Hall of Fame dinner red-letter day." 7/12/1962. Atlanta, Ga. (TD) 1 p. SCLCR-GAMK: Box 52. 620712–018.

7/12/1962    King, Martin Luther, Jr. (SCLC). Form letter to Friend of Freedom. 7/12/1962. [*Albany, Ga.*] (TLc) 1 p. SCLCR-GAMK: Box 116. 620712–019.

7/12/1962    King, Martin Luther, Jr. Press conference following release from Albany Jail. [*7/12/1962*]. [*Albany, Ga.*] (F) 1.5 min. (1 videocassette.) CBSNA-NNCBS. 620712–021.

7/12/1962    King, Martin Luther, Jr., Ralph Abernathy, and William G. Anderson. Press conference on release from jail in Albany, Ga. [*7/12/1962*]. [*Albany, Ga.*] (F) 8.3 min. (1 DVD.) WSB-TV-GU. 620712–022.

**7/12/1962**    **Associated Press. Photo of Martin Luther King, Jr., and Ralph Abernathy talking to reporters after their release from jail. [*7/12/1962*]. [*Albany, Ga.*] (Ph) 1 p. NNAPWW. 620712–028.**

**7/12/1962**    **Photo of Martin Luther King, Jr., Ralph Abernathy and William G. Anderson. [*7/12/1962*]. [*Albany, Ga.*] (Ph) 1 p. WAC. 620712–030.**

7/13/1962    Bell, Colin W. (American Friends Service Committee). Letter to Martin Luther King, Jr. 7/13/1962. Philadelphia, Pa. (THLS) 1 p. (Contains enclosure 620712–005.) MLKJP-GAMK: Box 2. 620713–002.

7/14/1962    King, Martin Luther, Jr. Statement on remaining in Albany. 7/14/1962. Albany, Ga. (TTa) 1 p. MLKJP-GAMK. 620714–000.

7/14/1962    King, Martin Luther, Jr. "People in Action: A Message From Jail." *New York Amsterdam News*, 14 July 1962. (PD) 2 pp. 620714–002.

| | | |
|---|---|---|
| **7/20/1962** | | **Associated Press. Photo of Martin Luther King, Jr., William G. Anderson, and Coretta Scott King at an Albany mass meeting at Third Kiokee Baptist Church. 7/20/1962. Albany, Ga. (Ph) 1 p. NNAPWW. 620720–017.** |

7/20/1962     King, Martin Luther, Jr. Interview upon arrival at airport in Albany, Ga. [*7/20/1962*]. [*Albany, Ga.*] (F) 3.2 min. (1 videocassette.) CBSNA-NNCBS. 620720–018.

7/21/1962     King, Martin Luther, Jr. Press conference on the court injunction in Albany, Ga. [*7/21/1962*]. Albany, Ga. (F) 4.7 min. (1 DVD.) WALB-TV-GU. 620721–015.

**7/21/1962**     **Uhrbrock, Donald. Photo of Martin Luther King, Jr., Ralph Abernathy, and William G. Anderson talking with reporters. 7/21/1962. Albany, Ga. (Ph) 1 p. GI-NNTI. 620721–021.**

7/22/1962     King, Martin Luther, Jr. (SCLC), and William G. Anderson (Albany Movement). Joint statement of Martin Luther King, Jr. and William G. Anderson. 7/22/1962. [*Albany, Ga.*] (TD) 1 p. MCMLK-RWWL: 6.1.0.100. 620722–000.

7/22/1962     Pritchett, Laurie, J. Ed. Friend, and Bill Manley (Albany Police Dept.). Statement of police officers concerning the demonstrations on 22 July. [*7/22/1962*]. Albany, Ga. (TDf) 2 pp. AMR-GAMK: Box 1. 620722–002.

7/22/1962     Committee for Justice to Hospital Workers. Announcement, "Hear Martin Luther King." [*7/22/1962*]. New York, N.Y. (PD) 1 p. CORER-WHi: Reel 2. 620722–004.

7/23/1962     Albany Movement. Memo to Robert F. Kennedy. 7/23/1962. [*Albany, Ga.*] (TL) 1 p. MLKJP-GAMK. 620723–004.

7/23/1962     Gay, Benjamin (Albany Movement). Memo to Laurie Pritchett. [*7/23/1962*]. (TL) 1 p. MLKJP-GAMK. 620723–005.

7/23/1962     Cole, Betty (*Meet the Press*). Letter to Martin Luther King, Jr. 7/23/1962. New York, N.Y. (TLS) 1 p. MLKP-MBU. 620723–007.

7/23/1962     King, Marion. Statement on beating at Mitchell County Jail. 7/23/1962. (TD) 2 pp. SKP-WHi: Box 1. 620723–008.

7/23/1962     Special Agent in Charge, Atlanta, Ga. (U.S. FBI). Telegram to J. Edgar Hoover. 7/23/1962. Atlanta, Ga. (PHW) 1 p. FBIDG-NN-Sc: Bureau File 157-6-2-453. 620723–011.

**7/24/1962**     **United Press International. Photo of Martin Luther King, Jr., Constance Baker Motley, and William M. (William Moses) Kunstler leaving the federal courthouse. 7/24/1962. Atlanta, Ga. (Ph) 1 p. UPIR-NNBETT. 620724–001.**

7/24/1962     King, Martin Luther, Jr. Signed statement to U.S. FBI. 7/24/1962. Atlanta, Ga. (THD) 2 pp. FBIDG-NN-Sc: Bureau File 157-6-2-504. 620724–019.

7/24/1962     [*Marshall, Burke*]. "Memorandum for the Attorney General—Monday Report." 7/24/1962. (TDf) 2 pp. BMPP-MBJFK. 620724–020.

7/24/1962     Pritchett, Laurie, J. Ed. Friend, and Bill Manley (Albany Police Dept.). Statement from police officers concerning activities of the Albany Movement on 24 July. [*7/24/1962*]. Albany, Ga. (TD) 3 pp. AMR-GAMK: Box 1. 620724–026.

7/24/1962     City of Albany, Georgia, et al., Defendant. "Petition to enjoin defendants from interfering with plaintiffs marching, demonstrating, etc.," *Anderson, et al. v. City of Albany, Georgia.* 7/24/1962. Albany, Ga. (PTFm) 1 p. USDCAlB-GEpNASR. 620724–030.

**7/24/1962**     **Associated Press. Photo of Martin Luther King, Jr. addressing Albany Movement mass meeting at Mt. Zion Baptist Church. [*7/24/1962*]. [*Albany, Ga.*] (Ph) 1 p. NNAPWW. 620724–032.**

7/25/1962     King, Martin Luther, Jr., and William G. Anderson. Statement on violence in Albany, Ga. and declaration of day of penance. 7/25/1962. [*Albany, Ga.*] (TADd) 1 p. MCMLK-RWWL: 6.1.0.120. 620725–001.

**7/25/1962**     **United Press International. Photo of Martin Luther King, Jr., Ralph Abernathy, and others at an Albany, Georgia pool hall. 7/25/1962. Albany, Ga. (Ph) 1 p. UPIR-NNBETT. 620725–003.**

**7/25/1962**     **Associated Press. Photo of Martin Luther King, Jr. and Wyatt Tee Walker giving a press conference. 7/25/1962. Albany, Ga. (Ph) 1 p. NNAPWW. 620725–005.**

7/25/1962     King, Martin Luther, Jr. Press conference about violence in Albany, Ga. [*7/25/1962*]. [*Albany, Ga.*] (F) 1.3 min. (1 DVD.) WSB-TV-GU. 620725–011.

7/25/1962     Pritchett, Laurie, J. Ed. Friend, and Bill Manley (Albany Police Dept.). Statement of police officers concerning activities of Martin Luther King Jr. [*7/25/1962*]. Albany, Ga. (TD) 2 pp. AMR-GAMK: Box 1. 620725–025.

**7/25/1962**     **[*Cochran, Ben*]. Photo of Martin Luther King, Jr., Ralph Abernathy, Bernard Scott Lee, Charles Sherrod, and Charles Jones in Albany, Ga. on the "Day of Penance." [*7/25/1962*]. [*Albany, Ga.*] (Ph) 1 p. AEJ. 620725–032.**

| | |
|---|---|
| 7/25/1962 | King, Martin Luther, Jr. Statement on violence in Albany. [7/25/1962]. Albany, Ga. (TTa) 1 p. MLKJP-GAMK. 620725–033. |
| 7/26/1962 | Marshall, Burke (U.S. Dept. of Justice). Letter to Martin Luther King, Jr. 7/26/1962. Washington, D.C. (TLS) 1 p. MLKJP-GAMK: Box 24. 620726–001. |
| **7/27/1962** | **United Press International. Photo of Martin Luther King, Jr., Ralph Abernathy, and William G. Anderson being escorted to jail by Laurie Pritchett. 7/27/1962. Albany, Ga. (Ph) 1 p. UPIR-NNBETT. 620727–004.** |
| **7/27/1962** | **King, Martin Luther, Jr. Diary from Albany jail. 7/27/1962. [*Albany, Ga.*] (AHD) 6 pp. MLKP-MBU. 620727–005.** |
| 7/27/1962 | Walker, Wyatt Tee (SCLC). Form letter to Friend of Freedom. 7/27/1962. Atlanta, Ga. (TLS) 2 pp. MLKJP-GAMK: Box 1. 620727–008. |
| 7/27/1962 | Abernathy, Ralph, and Martin Luther King, Jr. Prayer vigil and arrests at Albany City Hall. [7/27/1962]. Albany, Ga. (F) 4.0 min. (1 DVD.) WALB-TV-GU. 620727–015. |
| 7/27/1962 | Abernathy, Ralph, Martin Luther King, Jr., and Albany Movement. Press release, "Why our prayer vigil." [7/27/1962]. Albany, Ga. (TDf) 2 pp. MLKJP-GAMK: Box 2. 620727–025. |
| 7/27/1962 | SCLC. Press release, Martin Luther King, Jr., Ralph Abernathy, and Albany Movement officials arrested in pray-in. [7/27/1962]. Atlanta, Ga. (TD) 1 p. MLKJP-GAMK: Box 63. 620727–027. |
| 7/28/1962 | Walker, Wyatt Tee (SCLC). Form telegram to Supporters. 7/28/1962. Atlanta, Ga. (PWSr) 2 pp. APRC-DLC. 620728–000. |
| **7/27/1962–7/28/1962** | **King, Martin Luther, Jr. Notes on leaving Albany. [7/27/1962–7/28/1962]. [*Albany, Ga.*] (AHD) 1 p. DJG-GEU-S: Box 1.1. 620728–001.** |
| 7/28/1962 | CORE. Minutes, "Steering committee of the National Action Council." 7/28/1962. New York, N.Y. (TD) 3 pp. CORER-WHi. 620728–002. |
| 7/28/1962 | Hoover, J. Edgar (U.S. FBI). Memo to Robert F. Kennedy regarding the racial situation in Albany, Ga. 7/28/1962. (THL) 2 pp. FBIDG-NN-Sc: Bureau File 157–5–2–513. 620728–004. |
| 7/28/1962 | Martin Luther King and others speak at mass meeting. [7/28/1962]. Macon, Ga. (At) 64.6 min. (1 sound cassette: analog.) HETC-GU. 620728–013. |
| 7/29/1962 | Walker, Wyatt Tee (SCLC). Telegram to Edmund G. (Edmund Gerald) Brown. [7/29/1962]. Atlanta, Ga. (PWSr) 1 p. SCLCR-GAMK. 620729–000. |
| 7/29/1962 | Anderson, William G. (Albany Movement). Interview on *Meet the Press*. 7/29/1962. New York, N.Y. (At) 25.6 min. (1 sound cassette: analog.) MLKEC. 620729–001. |
| 7/29/1962 | Farmer, James (CORE). Telegram to John F. (John Fitzgerald) Kennedy. 7/29/1962. (PWSr) 1 p. JFKWHCSF-MBJFK: Reel 5. 620729–010. |
| 7/30/1962 | Western Christian Leadership Conference. Press release, Western Christian Leadership Conference calls for nation-wide public prayer demonstration. 7/30/1962. Los Angeles, Calif. (TD) 2 pp. SCLCR-GAMK: Box 51. 620730–007. |
| 7/30/1962 | Bell, Roy C. (SCLC). Telegram to Robert F. Kennedy, and John F. (John Fitzgerald) Kennedy. 7/30/1962. Atlanta, Ga. (PWc) 2 pp. SCLCR-GAMK: Box 34. 620730–008. |
| 7/30/1962 | Dempsey, John (Connecticut. Office of the Governor). Telegram to S. Ernest (Samuel Ernest) Vandiver. 7/30/1962. (TWc) 1 p. MLKJP-GAMK: Box 1. 620730–009. |
| 7/30/1962 | Dempsey, John (Connecticut. Office of the Governor). Telegram to John F. (John Fitzgerald) Kennedy. 7/30/1962. (TWc) 1 p. MLKJP-GAMK: Box 1. 620730–010. |
| 7/30/1962 | Farmer, James (CORE). Telegram to John F. (John Fitzgerald) Kennedy. 7/30/1962. New York, N.Y. (PWSr) 2 pp. JFKWHCSF-MBJFK: Reel 5. 620730–012. |
| 7/30/1962 | Wilkins, Roy (NAACP). Telegram to John F. (John Fitzgerald) Kennedy. 7/30/1962. New York, N.Y. (PWSr) 2 pp. JFKWHCSF-MBJFK: Reel 5. 620730–013. |
| 7/30/1962 | Randolph, A. Philip (Asa Philip) (Brotherhood of Sleeping Car Porters and Maids). Telegram to John F. (John Fitzgerald) Kennedy. 7/30/1962. (PWSr) 2 pp. JFKWHCSF-MBJFK: Reel 5. 620730–014. |
| 7/30/1962 | Seay, S. S. (Solomon Snowden) (MIA). Telegram to Robert F. Kennedy. 7/30/1962. (TWc) 1 p. MLKJP-GAMK. 620730–018. |
| 7/30/1962 | Sanders, Carl. Press conference on the events in Albany, Ga. [7/30/1962]. Albany, Ga. (F) 3.4 min. (1 DVD.) WALB-TV-GU. 620730–028. |
| 7/31/1962 | King, Martin Luther, Jr. (SCLC). Telegram to Roy Wilkins. 7/31/1962. Albany, Ga. (PHWSr) 1 p. NAACPP-DLC: Group III-A213. 620731–001. |

| | | |
|---|---|---|
| 7/31/1962 | Nix, Robert N.C. (U.S. Congress. House of Representatives). Letter to Wyatt Tee Walker. 7/31/1962. Washington, D.C. (TLS) 1 p. (Contains enclosure 620731–013.) SCLCR-GAMK: Box 34. 620731–012. |
| 7/31/1962 | Nix, Robert N.C. (U.S. Congress. House of Representatives). Telegram to S. Ernest (Samuel Ernest) Vandiver. [7/31/1962]. [*Washington, D.C.*] (PWSr) 1 p. (Enclosed in 620731–012.) SCLCR-GAMK: Box 34. 620731–013. |
| 7/31/1962 | Walker, Wyatt Tee (SCLC). Form letter to Board Member and Affiliate Head. 7/31/1962. Atlanta, Ga. (TL) 1 p. SCLCR-GAMK: Box 120. 620731–023. |
| 8/1962 | King, Martin Luther, Jr. Address intended for the national convention of the United Electrical Radio and Machine Workers of America. [8/1962]. Long Beach, Calif. (TD) 6 pp. MLKJP-GAMK. 620800–001. |
| 8/1962 | King, Martin Luther, Jr. (SCLC). Form letter to SCLC supporters. [8/1962]. Atlanta, Ga. (THLc) 1 p. MLKJP-GAMK: Box 2. 620800–002. |
| 7/1962–8/1962 | "Why Jail?" [7/1962–8/1962]. (TD) 3 pp. MLKJP-GAMK: Box 2. 620800–028. |
| 8/1/1962 | King, Martin Luther, Jr. Statement on stand of John F. (John Fitzgerald) Kennedy on negotiations in Albany, Ga. 8/1/1962. Albany, Ga. (TD) 2 pp. MCMLK-RWWL: 6.1.0.140. 620801–001. |
| 8/1/1962 | West, Irene. Letter to Martin Luther King, Jr., and Ralph Abernathy. 8/1/1962. Montgomery, Ala. (ALS) 3 pp. MLKJP-GAMK: Box 1. 620801–003. |
| 8/1/1962 | SCLC. Press release, "Nation-wide prayer vigils support Albany." 8/1/1962. Atlanta, Ga. (TD) 2 pp. SCLCR-GAMK: Box 34. 620801–009. |
| 8/1/1962 | Bluestone, Irving (International Union, United Automobile Workers of America). Telegram to Wyatt Tee Walker. 8/1/1962. Detroit, Mich. (PWSr) 1 p. SCLCR-GAMK: Box 34. 620801–010. |
| 8/1/1962 | "Gandhi Society Explained." *Christian Century* 79, (1 August 1962): 929–930. (PD) 2 pp. 620801–013. |
| 8/2/1962 | Smith, Kelly Miller (First Baptist Church). Letter to Martin Luther King, Jr. 8/2/1962. Nashville, Tenn. (TLS) 1 p. MLKJP-GAMK: Box 16. 620802–003. |
| 8/2/1962 | Ryan, William F. (U.S. Congress. House of Representatives). Letter to Martin Luther King, Jr. 8/2/1962. Washington, D.C. (THLS) 1 p. MLKJP-GAMK: Box 24. 620802–004. |
| 8/2/1962 | Anderson, William G. (Albany Movement). Telegram to John F. (John Fitzgerald) Kennedy. [8/2/1962]. (TWc) 1 p. MLKJP-GAMK: Box 2. 620802–008. |
| 8/2/1962 | Walker, Wyatt Tee (SCLC). Letter to Lee C. White. 8/2/1962. Atlanta, Ga. (TLS) 1 p. (Contains enclosure 620717–003.) JFKWHCSF-MBJFK. 620802–009. |
| 8/2/1962 | U.S. FBI. Memo, "Racial situation, Albany, Ga." 8/2/1962. Atlanta, Ga. (THL) 1 p. FBIDG-NN-Sc: Bureau File 157–6–2–597. 620802–013. |
| 8/2/1962 | Powell, Adam Clayton (U.S. Congress. House of Representatives). Telegram to John F. (John Fitzgerald) Kennedy. [8/2/1962]. Washington, D.C. (PWSr) 3 pp. JFKWHCSF-MBJFK. 620802–028. |
| 8/3/1962 | Williams, Samuel W. (Friendship Baptist Church). Letter to Martin Luther King, Jr. 8/3/1962. Atlanta, Ga. (TLS) 1 p. SCLCR-GAMK: Box 1. 620803–003. |
| 8/4/1962 | King, Martin Luther, Jr. "People in Action: Hall of Famer." *New York Amsterdam News*, 4 August 1962, pp. 11, 38. (PD) 2 pp. 620804–000. |
| 8/5/1962 | King, Martin Luther, Jr. "The Case Against 'Tokenism.'" *New York Times Magazine*, 5 August 1962, p. 11, 49–50. (PD) 3 pp. 620805–001. |
| 12/1961–<br>8/6/1962 | [*Zinn, Howard*]. Notes for SNCC: The New Abolitionists. [12/1961–8/6/1962]. (AD) 7 pp. HZP-WHi: Box 1. 620806–005. |
| 8/7/1962 | Fey, Harold Edward (*Christian Century*). Letter to Martin Luther King, Jr. 8/7/1962. Chicago, Ill. (TLS) 1 p. MLKJP-GAMK: Box 6. 620807–002. |
| 8/7/1962 | Hunter, Lillie Mae (SCLC). Letter to Martin Luther King, Jr. 8/7/1962. Atlanta, Ga. (TLS) 1 p. MLKJP-GAMK: Box 34. 620807–006. |
| 8/7/1962 | Jackson, Jesse. Letter to Martin Luther King, Jr. 8/7/1962. New York, N.Y. (TALS) 1 p. CSKC. 620807–013. |
| 8/8/1962 | Hoover, Carole F. Letter to Martin Luther King, Jr. 8/8/1962. Chattanooga, Tenn. (TLS) 1 p. MLKJP-GAMK: Box 34. 620808–004. |
| 8/9/1962 | King, Martin Luther, Jr. (SCLC). Form letter to Friend of Freedom. 8/9/1962. Albany, Ga. (TLS) 1 p. SAVFC-WHi. 620809–006. |
| 8/10/1962 | Brown, Theodore E. Telegram to Martin Luther King, Jr. 8/10/1962. New York, N.Y. (PWSr) 1 p. MLKJP-GAMK: Box 1. 620810–002. |
| 8/10/1962 | U.S. FBI. Memo, "Racial situation, Albany, Ga." 8/10/1962. Atlanta, Ga. (THL) 1 p. FBIDG-NN-Sc: Bureau File 157–6–2–644. 620810–009. |

| | |
|---|---|
| 8/10/1962 | **Photo of Slater King, Charles Sherrod, Norma L. Anderson, Lois Marian Steele, William G. Anderson, Martin Luther King, Jr., Coretta Scott King, and Ralph Abernathy. [*8/10/1962*]. [*Albany, Ga.*] (Ph) 1 p. WAC. 620810–033.** |
| 8/2/1962–<br>8/11/1962 | SCLC. "Statement of income and disbursement for August 2–11, 1962." 8/2/1962–8/11/1962. Atlanta, Ga. (TDc) 1 p. MLKJP-GAMK: Box 32. 620811–003. |
| 8/13/1962 | Kunstler, William M. (William Moses). Letter to Martin Luther King, Jr., and Coretta Scott King. 8/13/1962. New York, N.Y. (TLS) 1 p. MLKJP-GAMK: Box 14. 620813–004. |
| 8/13/1962 | King, Martin Luther, Jr. "Why Non-Violence Will Win In Albany." *Chicago Daily Defender*, 13 August 1962, pp. 1, 3. (PD) 2 pp. 620813–011. |
| 8/14/1962 | Davis, Leon J. (Retail, Wholesale, and Department Store Union. Local 1199 Drug and Hospital Employees Union). Letter to Martin Luther King, Jr. 8/14/1962. New York, N.Y. (THLS) 1 p. MLKJP-GAMK: Box 14. 620814–003. |
| 8/14/1962 | King, Martin Luther, Jr. "New Negro Battling For Rights In Albany." *Chicago Daily Defender*, 14 August 1962, pp. 1, 10, 12. (PD) 3 pp. 620814–012. |
| 8/15/1962 | King, Martin Luther, Jr. "Statement to prayer rally at wrecked church." 8/15/1962. Albany, Ga. (THTa) 1 p. MLKJP-GAMK. 620815–001. |
| 8/15/1962 | King, Martin Luther, Jr. Statement on church bombing. 8/15/1962. Leesburg, Ga. (TTa) 1 p. MLKJP-GAMK. 620815–002. |
| 8/15/1962 | Albany Movement. Press release, Voter registration program established. 8/15/1962. Albany, Ga. (TD) 1 p. ASRC-RWWL: Reel 177. 620815–017. |
| 8/15/1962 | SCLC. Press release, "Albany Movement begins vote drive to upset commissioners." 8/15/1962. Atlanta, Ga. (TD) 2 pp. SCLCR-GAMK: Box 120. 620815–021. |
| 8/15/1962 | SCLC. Press release, "SCLC pledges special fund to rebuild dynamited church." 8/15/1962. Atlanta, Ga. (TD) 2 pp. SCLCR-GAMK: Box 120. 620815–022. |
| 8/15/1962 | [*SCLC*]. Press release on voter registration. [*8/15/1962*]. [*Albany, Ga.*] (THD) 1 p. DJG-GEU-S: Box 1.4. 620815–027. |
| 8/15/1962 | King, Martin Luther, Jr. "U.S. Help Needed in Rights Fight." *Chicago Daily Defender*, 15 August 1962, p. 9 (PD) 1 p. 620815–030. |
| 8/15/1962 | **Photo of Wyatt Tee Walker, Bernard Scott Lee, Martin Luther King, Jr., Ralph Abernathy, Andrew Young, and James L. (James Luther) Bevel at the ruins of Shady Grove Baptist Church. [*8/15/1962*]. [*Leesburg, Ga.*] (Ph) 1 p. WGAC-GAMK: Box 1. 620815–032.** |
| 8/15/1962 | King, Martin Luther, Jr. Statement on the church bombing. [*8/15/1962*]. Leesburg, Ga. (TTa) 1 p. MLKJP-GAMK. 620815–033. |
| 8/18/1962 | King, Martin Luther, Jr. "People in Action: Why It's Albany." *New York Amsterdam News*, 18 August 1962, pp. 1, 11. (PD) 2 pp. 620818–000. |
| 8/18/1962 | [*SCLC*]. Press release on voter registration. 8/18/1962. Albany, Ga. (THD) 1 p. ASRC-RWWL: Reel 177. 620818–003. |
| 8/20/1962 | King, Martin Luther, Jr. Albany, Ga.: Tensions of the South. [*8/20/1962*]. [*Atlanta, Ga.*] (TAD) 12 pp. MLKJP-GAMK: Box 2. 620820–003. |
| 8/20/1962 | King, Martin Luther, Jr. (SCLC). Form letter. 8/20/1962. Atlanta, Ga. (TLc) 1 p. MLKJP-GAMK: Box 63. 620820–013. |
| 8/21/1962 | [*Jones, Clarence B.*] Letter to Martin Luther King, Jr. 8/21/1962. (ALS) 1 p. MLKJP-GAMK. 620821–008. |
| 8/22/1962 | King, Martin Luther, Jr. Letter to Nelson A. (Nelson Aldrich) Rockefeller. 8/22/1962. [*Atlanta, Ga.*] (TLc) 1 p. MCMLK-RWWL: 1.1.0.39800. 620822–001. |
| 8/22/1962 | King, Martin Luther, Jr. Letter to John Lamula. 8/22/1962. [*Atlanta, Ga.*] (TLc) 1 p. MLKJP-GAMK: Box 14. 620822–008. |
| 8/22/1962 | King, Martin Luther, Jr. Letter to O. Clay Maxwell. 8/22/1962. [*Atlanta, Ga.*] (TLc) 1 p. MLKJP-GAMK: Box 15. 620822–009. |
| 8/22/1962 | King, Martin Luther, Jr. (SCLC). Form letter to Friend of Freedom. 8/22/1962. Atlanta, Ga. (TLS) 1 p. SCLCR-GAMK: Box 34. 620822–011. |
| 8/22/1962 | King, Martin Luther, Jr. Letter to S.S. (Solomon Snowden) Seay. 8/22/1962. [*Atlanta, Ga.*] (TLc) 1 p. MLKP-MBU. 620822–015. |
| 8/22/1962 | SCLC. Press release, "SCLC sets annual meet in Birmingham." 8/22/1962. Atlanta, Ga. (TD) 2 pp. BWOF-AB: Box 26. 620822–018. |
| 8/23/1962 | King, Martin Luther, Jr. (SCLC). Letter to Myles Horton. 8/23/1962. Atlanta, Ga. (TLS) 1 p. HRECR-WHi. 620823–001. |
| 8/23/1962 | King, Martin Luther, Jr. Letter to Aaron L. Boykin. 8/23/1962. [*Atlanta, Ga.*] (THLc) 2 pp. MLKJP-GAMK: Box 67. 620823–004. |
| 8/23/1962 | King, Martin Luther, Jr. Letter to John Oliver Nelson. 8/23/1962. [*Atlanta, Ga.*] (TLc) 1 p. MLKJP-GAMK: Box 67. 620823–005. |

8/23/1962 Troutman, Robert B. (Robert Battey). "'Plans for progress' report." 8/23/1962. (TD) 12 pp. MLKJP-GAMK: Box 23. 620823–013.

8/24/1962 Horton, Myles. Letter to Martin Luther King, Jr. 8/24/1962. (TLc) 1 p. HRECR-WHi. 620824–000.

8/24/1962 Horton, Myles (Highlander Research and Education Center). Letter to Martin Luther King, Jr. 8/24/1962. Knoxville, Tenn. (THLS) 1 p. MLKJP-GAMK: Box 12. 620824–002.

8/24/1962 King, Martin Luther, Jr., and Wyatt Tee Walker (SCLC). Form letter to Initiator. 8/24/1962. Atlanta, Ga. (TLS) 1 p. SCLCR-GAMK: Box 116. 620824–014.

8/27/1962 Landesberg, Kieve. Letter to Martin Luther King, Jr. 8/27/1962. Atlanta, Ga. (TLc) 1 p. MLKJP-GAMK: Box 3. 620827–001.

8/27/1962 King, Martin Luther, Jr. Statement to the press concerning the Albany Movement. [8/27/1962]. (F) 1.1 min. (1 videocassette.) NBCNA-NNNBC. 620827–010.

**8/27/1962 Associated Press. Photo of Martin Luther King, Jr. welcoming Northern religious leaders to an Albany Movement mass meeting at Mt. Zion Baptist Church. [8/27/1962]. Albany, Ga. (Ph) 1 p. NNAPWW. 620827–012.**

8/28/1962 King, Martin Luther, Jr. Press statement concerning the arrest of ministers in Albany, Ga. [8/28/1962]. Albany, Ga. (F) 1.1 min (1 videocassette.) NBCNA-NNNBC. 620828–000.

8/28/1962 Walker, Wyatt Tee. Letter to Sandy F. Ray. 8/28/1962. [Atlanta, Ga.] (TLc) 1 p. MLKJP-GAMK: Box 31. 620828–005.

8/28/1962 Pritchett, Laurie. Statement on arrest of clergy in Albany, Ga. [8/28/1962]. Albany, Ga. (F) 3.2 min. (1 DVD.) WALB-TV-GU. 620828–010.

8/29/1962 Dodd, Thomas J. (Thomas Joseph) (U.S. Congress. Senate). Letter to Stephen A. Roos. 8/29/1962. Washington, D.C. (TLc) 1 p. (Enclosed in 620831–005.) MLKJP-GAMK: Box 1. 620829–001.

8/29/1962 Dodd, Thomas J. (Thomas Joseph) (U.S. Congress. Senate). Letter to Robert F. Kennedy. [8/29/1962]. Washington, D.C. (TLc) 1 p. (Enclosed in 620831–005.) MLKJP-GAMK: Box 1. 620829–002.

8/29/1962 SCLC. Press release, "Seventy-five religious leaders jailed in Albany." 8/29/1962. Atlanta, Ga. (TD) 2 pp. SCLCR-GAMK: Box 120. 620829–007.

8/29/1962 King, Martin Luther, Jr., and Wyatt Tee Walker (SCLC). Letter to Everett McKinley Dirksen. 8/29/1962. Albany, Ga. (PWSr) 1 p. EMDC-IPekDC. 620829–015.

8/29/1962 SCLC. Press release, Statement of Martin Luther King, Jr. on race for governorship of Georgia. 8/29/1962. Atlanta, Ga. (TD) 1 p. SCLCR-GAMK: Box 120. 620829–020.

8/30/1962 King, Martin Luther, Jr. (SCLC). Form letter to Pastor and Friend of Freedom. 8/30/1962. Albany, Ga. (TLc) 1 p. SCLCR-GAMK: Box 129. 620830–009.

8/30/1962 SCLC. Press release, "Albany Movement leader picked for SCLC award." 8/30/1962. Atlanta, Ga. (TD) 2 pp. BWOF-AB: Box 26. 620830–010.

8/31/1962 King, Martin Luther, Jr. Letter to Edward Hall Gardner. 8/31/1962. [Atlanta, Ga.] (TLc) 1 p. MLKJP-GAMK: Box 1. 620831–002.

8/31/1962 Keating, Kenneth B. (Kenneth Barnard), Jacob K. (Jacob Koppel) Javits, Hugh Scott, Paul H. (Paul Howard) Douglas, Philip A. (Philip Aloysius) Hart, Joseph S. Clark, William Proxmire, Thomas H. Kuchel, Clifford P. (Clifford Philip) Case, and Hubert H. (Hubert Horatio) Humphrey (U.S. Congress. Senate). Telegram to Martin Luther King, Jr. 8/31/1962. Washington, D.C. (PWSr) 4 pp. MLKJP-GAMK: Box 1. 620831–004.

8/31/1962 Dodd, Thomas J. (Thomas Joseph) (U.S. Congress. Senate). Letter to Martin Luther King, Jr. 8/31/1962. Washington, D.C. (TLS) 1 p. (Contains enclosures 620829–001 & 620829–002.) MLKJP-GAMK: Box 1. 620831–005.

9/1962 SCLC. Newsletter 1, no. 7. 9/1962. Atlanta, Ga. (PD) 4 pp. CSKC. 620900–003.

10/1961–9/1962 Walker, Wyatt Tee (SCLC). "Report of the director." 10/1961–9/1962. Atlanta, Ga. (TD) 13 pp. MLKJP-GAMK: Box 36. 620900–007.

9/2/1962 Kennedy, Robert F. (U.S. Dept. of Justice). Telegram to Martin Luther King, Jr. 9/2/1962. Washington, D.C. (PWSr) 2 pp. MLKJP-GAMK: Box 2. 620902–001.

9/4/1962 King, Martin Luther, Jr. Letter to W.E. Shortridge. 9/4/1962. [Atlanta, Ga.] (TLc) 1 p. MLKJP-GAMK: Box 1. 620904–001.

9/5/1962 King, Martin Luther, Jr. Letter to Melvin Arnold. 9/5/1962. [Atlanta, Ga.] (TLc) 2 pp. MCMLK-RWWL: 2.1.1.10. 620905–004.

9/6/1962 King, Martin Luther, Jr. Letter to Benjamin Elijah Mays. 9/6/1962. Atlanta, Ga. (TLc) 2 pp. MLKJP-GAMK: Box 15. 620906–008.

| | |
|---|---|
| 9/11/1962 | Tanenbaum, Marc H. (American Jewish Committee). Letter to Martin Luther King, Jr. 9/11/1962. New York, N.Y. (TLS) 2 pp. SCLCR-GAMK: Box 6. 620911–005. |
| 9/13/1962 | Albany Movement. Press release, "Albany Movement leader blasts National Baptist prexy on movement." [9/13/1962]. Albany, Ga. (TLc) 1 p. MLKJP-GAMK: Box 2. 620913–016. |
| 9/25/1962 | Robinson, Jackie. Freedom Dinner Address at the Sixth Annual Convention of the SCLC. 9/25/1962. Birmingham, Ala. (THD) 9 pp. MCMLK-RWWL: 6.1.0.4240. 620925–000. |
| 7/30/1962–9/26/1962 | Transcript of Trial Testimony, *Kelly v. Page*, 335 F.2d 114 (5th Cir. 1964). 7/30/1962–9/26/1962. (THD) 1,711 pp. USDCAlb-GEpNASR: Record Group 21. 620926–010. |
| 9/27/1962 | Bland, J.F. (U.S. FBI). Memo to W.C. Sullivan. 9/27/1962. (THLI) 3 pp. FBIDG-NN-Sc: Bureau File 100–106670. 620927–008. |
| 9/25/1962–9/28/1962 | SCLC. Program, "Annual Meeting of SCLC." 9/25/1962–9/28/1962. Birmingham, Ala. (PD) 16 pp. MLKJP-GAMK: Box 31. 620928–002. |
| 9/28/1962 | O'Dell, Jack H. (SCLC). "Report on voter registration work, February 15–September 1 1962." 9/28/1962. Atlanta, Ga. (TD) 13 pp. MLKJP-GAMK: Box 35. 620928–010. |
| 10/5/1962 | King, Martin Luther, Jr. (SCLC). Telegram to L. Francis Griffin. 10/5/1962. Atlanta, Ga. (PHWc) 1 p. MLKJP-GAMK: Box 7. 621005–008. |
| 10/5/1962 | King, Martin Luther, Jr. (SCLC). Letter to J. Irwin Miller. 10/5/1962. [Atlanta, Ga.] (TLc) 1 p. MLKP-MBU. 621005–009. |
| 10/10/1962 | King, Martin Luther, Jr. Form letter to Stanley Terry. 10/10/1962. [Atlanta, Ga.] (TLc) 2 pp. MLKJP-GAMK: Box 2. 621010–002. |
| 11/1962 | Houser, George M. (American Committee on Africa). Form letter to Friend. [11/1962]. New York, N.Y. (TLS) 1 p. (Contains enclosures 621100–004 & 621100–005.) MLKJP-GAMK: Box 2. 621100–001. |
| 11/1962 | American Committee on Africa. "Suggestions for Specific Action in Various Local Communities." [11/1962]. New York, N.Y. (PD) 4 pp. (Enclosed in 621100–001.) MLKJP-GAMK: Box 34. 621100–004. |
| 11/1962 | American Committee on Africa. Appeal for action against apartheid. [11/1962]. New York, N.Y. (PD) 6 pp. (Enclosed in 621100–001.) MLKJP-GAMK: Box 34. 621100–005. |
| 11/1/1962 | Jones, Clarence B. Letter to Martin Luther King, Jr. 11/1/1962. (TLSr) 2 pp. MLKP-MBU. 621101–009. |
| 12/1962 | SCLC. *Newsletter* 1, no. 8. 12/1962. Atlanta, Ga. (PHD) 4 pp. (Marginal comment by King.) TASC-MsToT. 621200–015. |
| 12/1962 | American Committee on Africa. "A brief review of action taken on and around Human Rights day, December 10, in connection with the Appeal for Action Against Apartheid campaign." [12/1962]. New York, N.Y. (TD) 4 pp. ACOA-ARC: Reel 3. 621200–027. |
| 12/22/1962 | King, Martin Luther, Jr. "People in Action: JFK's Executive Order." *New York Amsterdam News*, 22 December 1962, p. 13. (PD) 1 p. 621222–000. |
| 12/26/1962 | King, Slater. Letter to John F. (John Fitzgerald) Kennedy. 12/26/1962. (TLc) 2 pp. SKP-WHi: Box 1. 621226–003. |
| 1/1/1962–12/27/1962 | King, Martin Luther, Jr. *National Diary 1961–1962.* 1/1/1961–12/27/1962. [Atlanta, Ga.] (AD) 200 pp. MLKP-MBU. 621227–002. |
| 1/1963 | Southern Regional Council. Special report, "Plans for Progress: Atlanta survey." 1/1963. Atlanta, Ga. (TD) 17 pp. SRCC-AB: Reel 139. 630100–052. |
| 1/17/1963 | King, Martin Luther, Jr. (SCLC). "A Challenge to the Churches and Synagogues," Address delivered at the National Conference on Religion and Race. [1/17/1963]. [Chicago, Ill.] (At) 45.7 min. (1 compact disc.) NCCIJR-WMM. 630117–042. |
| 1/14/1963–1/17/1963 | National Conference on Religion and Race. Program, National Conference on Religion and Race. [1/14/1963–1/17/1963]. Chicago, Ill. (PD) 2 pp. SCLCR-GAMK: Box 35. 630117–052. |
| 11/12/1961–2/18/1963 | McDonald, Dora E. Phone Message Log. 11/12/1961–2/18/1963. (PHFm) 107 pp. MLKP-MBU. 630218–017. |
| 3/27/1963 | King, Martin Luther, Jr. Telegram to Robert F. Kennedy. [3/27/1963]. [Atlanta, Ga.] (PHWcSr) 2 pp. MLKJP-GAMK: Box 24. 630327–021. |
| 5/24/1963 | Baptist Press (Southern Baptist Convention). "Detroit Convention Condemns Race Bias." 5/24/1963. Nashville, Tenn. (PD) 4 pp. SBHLA. 630524–028. |
| 6/4/1963 | Taylor, Hobart (U.S. Equal Employment Opportunity Commission). Telegram to Martin Luther King, Jr. 6/4/1963. Washington, D.C. (PWSr) 1 p. SCLCR-GAMK: Box 34. 630604–001. |

Calendar   6/4/1963     King, Martin Luther, Jr. (SCLC). Telegram to Lyndon B. (Lyndon Baines) Johnson, Hobart Taylor, and Frank W. McCulloch. 6/4/1963. Atlanta, Ga. (TWc) 1 p. SCLCR-GAMK: Box 34. 630604–051.

9/1963     Young, Andrew (SCLC). Memo to Wiley A. Branton. [9/1963]. (TD) 4 pp. MLKJP-GAMK: Box 25. 630900–093.

3/9/1964     King, Martin Luther, Jr. Interview by Berl I. Bernhard. 3/9/1964. Atlanta, Ga. (TTa) 27 pp. JFKOH-MBJFK. 640309–001.

5/6/1964     Weaver, Robert Clifton. Oral history interview with Daniel P. Moynihan. 5/6/1964. [*Washington, D.C.*] (THDf) 32 pp. JFKOH-MBJFK. 640506–026.

5/29/1964     Marshall, Burke (U.S. Dept. of Justice). Oral history interview with Louis F. (Louis Falk) Oberdorfer. 5/29/1964. Washington, D.C. (TTaS) 30 pp. JFKOH-MBJFK: BM-01. 640529–022.

7/16/1964     King, Martin Luther, Jr. (SCLC). Press release, Statement on nomination of Barry M. (Barry Morris) Goldwater. 7/16/1964. Atlanta, Ga. (TD) 1 p. MLKJP-GAMK: Box 20. 640716–000.

8/3/1964     Southern Regional Council. Press release, Results of Voter Education Project programs. 8/3/1964. Atlanta, Ga. (TD) 4 pp. MLKJP-GAMK: Box 22. 640803–008.

12/4/1964     Marshall, Burke, and Robert F. Kennedy. Interview by Anthony Lewis. 12/4/1964. New York, N.Y. (TTa) 165 pp. JFKOH-MBJFK. 641204–003.

1/1965     King, Martin Luther, Jr. Interview by Alex Haley. *Playboy* 12 (January 1965): 65–68, 70–74, 76–78. (PD) 12 pp. 650100–001.

8/29/1967     King, Lonnie C. (Atlanta Committee on Appeal for Human Rights). Interview by John H. Britton. 8/29/1967. Washington, D.C. (THTa) 62 pp. RBOH-DHU-MS. 670829–001.

2/8/1968     Alston, Harry L. (Fund for Democracy). Memo to G.R. Hathaway. 2/8/1968. (THL) 1 p. UPWP-WHi: Box 404. 680208–002.

6/17/1969     Rustin, Bayard. Interview by T.H. Baker. 6/17/1969. (TTaS) 21 pp. LBJOH-TxAuLBJ. 690617–000.

12/24/1974–     Seigenthaler, John. Oral history interview with William Finger and Jim Tramel.
12/26/1974     12/24/1974–12/26/1974. (TTa) 64 pp. SOHP-NcU. 741226–000.

4/23/1976     Pritchett, Laurie. Interview by James Reston. 4/23/1976. South Mount, N.C. (TTa) 28 pp. SOHP-NcU. 760423–000.

11/18/1983     Farmer, James. Oral history interview by Taylor Branch. 11/18/1983. (At) 226.0 min. (MP3.) TBC-NcU. 831118–000.

6/1/1993     McCall, Duke. Letter to Henlee H. Barnette. 6/1/1993. (TLd) 1 p. HHBP-NcWsW. 930601–001.

3/31/1995     Orear, Leslie F. Interview by Cyril Robinson. 3/31/1995. (At) 94.5 min. (MP3.) CRLHRC-ICarbS. 950331–000.

Boldfaced page numbers in entries indicate that the material can be found in documents authored by Martin Luther King, Jr. Italicized page numbers in entries indicate the location of the main biographical entry for an individual, beginning with the volume number if other than the present volume.

704

| | |
|---:|:---|
| Text: | 10/12 Baskerville |
| Display: | New Baskerville |
| Index: | Connie Binder |
| Compositor: | BookMatters, Berkeley, CA |
| Printer and binder: | Maple Press |

12/6/2014